Uniform Numbers of the NFL

Uniform Numbers of the NFL

All-Time Rosters,
Facts and Figures

JOHN MAXYMUK

McFarland & Company, Inc., Publishers
Jefferson, North Carolina, and London

LIBRARY OF CONGRESS CATALOGUING-IN-PUBLICATION DATA

Maxymuk, John.
Uniform numbers of the NFL : all-time rosters, facts,
and figures / John Maxymuk.
p.   cm.
Includes index.

ISBN 0-7864-2057-X (soft cover : 50# alkaline paper)

1. National Football League — Miscellanea.
2. Football teams— United States— Miscellanea.
3. Football uniforms— Numbers— Miscellanea.   I. Title.
GV955.5N35M39   2005   796.332'64 — dc22   2005001719

British Library cataloguing data are available

Cover photograph ©2005 Comstock

Manufactured in the United States of America

*McFarland & Company, Inc., Publishers
Box 611, Jefferson, North Carolina 28640
www.mcfarlandpub.com*

For the 3 that I number the most important:
Suzanne, Juliane and Katie

ACKNOWLEDGMENTS

Special thanks to Chad Reese and the staff at the Pro Football Hall of Fame archives for accommodating me in my research in my trips to Canton and for answering several thorny e-mail queries with pleasant equanimity. George Rugg, the Curator of Special Collections at the University of Notre Dame's Hesburgh Library, was very responsive to my e-mail questions also. Jim Kennedy and Billy McClurg from the PortsmouthSpartans.org web site were very generous with their time and game programs. My Rutgers colleagues continue to show uncommon forbearance toward my research; special thanks goes to my very imaginative boss, Gary Golden. Thanks also to Mary Anne Nesbitt for borrowing countless reels of microfilm from far-flung institutions. Staff at the New York Public Library and Princeton University's Firestone Library as well as the University of Houston and Houston Public Library were helpful, too. My wife, Suzanne, and daughters Juliane and Katie deserve recognition for their understanding on the lengthy demands on my time in researching and writing this book (and all previous ones).

CONTENTS

INTRODUCTION

When New Orleans Saints All Pro linebacker Pat Swilling signed with the Detroit Lions as a free agent in 1993, there was one hangup, his uniform number. Swilling had always worn 56 in New Orleans, but in Detroit 56 belonged to Joe Schmidt, in whose name it had been retired. The Lions contacted Schmidt, and he gladly consented to let Swilling wear 56. At the Silverdome ceremony when Schmidt presented 56 to Swilling, he said, "I understand how a number is important to some people, and I'm happy to do this if it's part of making Pat feel more comfortable here. When you go out on the field that number becomes a part of you. It's an emotional and spiritual part of a player."

Uniform numbers conjure vivid memories in sports, and, in football where faces are hidden under helmets, players almost become their number. Number 19 is John Unitas, 4 is Brett Favre, 22 is Emmitt Smith, and 32 is Jim Brown. Players and fans both develop strong attachments to particular numbers and superstitions about others. Stories abound concerning players in all sports making deals with new teammates to secure their favorite number. Rob Burnett reportedly paid Adewale Ogunleye enough money to make a down payment on a house so that he could wear 90 in Miami; Jim Burt gave Rollin Putzier three cases of beer to wear 64 in San Francisco; Lonnie Marts simply gave 56 to Hardy Nickerson with no strings attached when Nickerson joined Jacksonville; when Washington safety Ifeanyi Ohalete, who had refused to give up 26 to Chad Morton in 2003, turned down Clinton Portis in 2004, Portis challenged him to a boxing match for the number. Fans spend a great deal of money purchasing the jerseys of their favorite players. Manufacturers not only make money meeting that demand, but have found a new market by producing retro jerseys of former players in the original styles. These are sported by both fans and players paying homage to the "old school" look.

Popular broadcaster John Madden took on the unusual duty of assigning uniform numbers to his players when he coached the Oakland Raiders in the 1970s because, "I've always felt that you can put a number on a person that tells about that person. Certain numbers have certain characteristics." In his book *One Size Doesn't Fit All*, Madden explains some of those characteristics and even fits them to nonathletes. The number 32, for example, "is a skills number, but it also fits people with some hardness." Thus, it fits O.J. Simpson and Raider safety Jack Tatum, but according to Madden, it also fits actress Elizabeth Taylor and boxer Muhammad Ali. Other numbers with characteristics he specifies include 12, "a leader with charisma"; 16, "a number with a certain softness about it"; 18, "a little classier, someone who's not out in front all the time"; and 22, "always a speed number." Some numbers, he insists, carry a physical image. The number 8 and 9 "are angular … you have to be really tall," so for 88 he sees a lanky guy like Pat Summerall. By contrast, Madden's tight end Dave Casper was "not quite tall enough to be an 89, but [was] a perfect 87." On the other hand, for short people, "2 is a good number."

One caveat with this view is that it depends on the time frame. Today, a player wearing 98 or 99 is likely either to be a husky defensive lineman or a rugged linebacker; in the 1930s and 1940s he very well could have been a shifty halfback like Tom Harmon or Marshall Goldberg. A hefty tackle in the 1930s might have worn 2, but today that number would only be worn by a kicker or quarterback. The NFL itself legislated this turn of events in 1952 by outlining what numbers could be worn by which positions. For some teams, that entailed wholesale changes to the game program. The Cleveland Browns had several star players switch numbers in 1952. Actually they were shifting from the old All America Conference numbering scheme to one newly instituted by the NFL. Tackle Lou Groza went from 46 to 76 while fullback Marion Motley went from 76 to 36. Browns Hall of Fame quarterback Otto Graham wore 60 from 1946 to 1951 and 14 from 1952 to 1955. His jersey is on display at the Pro Football Hall of Fame in Canton, Ohio, and you can see that instead of issuing him a new jersey, the team simply tore off the 60 and sewed a 14 on to his faded jersey with the outline of the original number still visible. There was no money to waste in those days. Over the years, those league numbering guidelines have been revised slightly and expanded over the full 0 to 99 spectrum as roster sizes increased.

My own interest in this topic arose from my research on my favorite team, the Green Bay Packers. That initial research I developed into a book I wrote called *Packers by the Numbers* (Prairie Oak Press, 2003) that provides a history of the team and its players through the uniform numbers that they wore. The success of that project led naturally to this one, where I have compiled uniform numbers for all 32 current NFL franchises.

Team web sites and media guides often present a cumulative list of uniform numbers worn by their players. For those teams, that served as my starting point, but several others had to be built entirely from scratch. Even if there was an existing list, it had to be fact-checked and corrected. These lists were not always up-to-date, did not include all the information fields I wanted to include, and featured mistakes of all kinds. Players were missing, their playing years were inaccurate, they had their names misspelled, and were listed as having worn numbers that they didn't. The ultimate source for uniform numbers is the game program, and I have looked at over 1,000 of them, but that is still a fraction of the 10,000-plus game programs these teams would have generated. Many other sources were used for identification, verification and corrections, including team media guides, annual *Sporting News Pro Football Guides,* contemporary newspaper and periodical sources, Internet resources, and even team pictures. The official NFL encyclopedia, *Total Football,* was used as the last word on correct names and years of play. I have tried to limit the listings to those who actually appeared in a game, not just on an active roster.

The main problems that had to be addressed fell into three categories: (1) a conflict between two players wearing the same number in the same year, (2) a potential conflict with one player being listed as wearing more than one number in the same year, and (3) a gap when no number is recorded for a player in a particular year or range of years. The first two types of problems sometimes were truly conflicts that had to be fixed and other times reflected two players who each played less than a full year or a player actually wearing multiple numbers in the same season. As to the third type of problem, of 30,880 possible player-team combinations, I was unable to find a number for only 141. That success rate of 99.54 percent is purer than Ivory Snow soap. Of the missing 141, the overwhelming majority are from pre–World War II players and from players who played three or fewer games with that team.

Players for whom I was unable to find any number or for whom I was unable to confirm their wearing of a particular additional number are listed separately at the end of each team entry and are included in the index. Two other player categories are included in the index: players from NFL teams that went out of business since 1933, the year league began to come into its own as a modern sports league, and players from defunct All America Conference teams, many of whom played for NFL teams before or after that league folded. Thus, there are 32,424 index entries, and 196 feature a question mark rather than a uniform number (99.4 percent).

Of course my listings are not perfect, but they are my best effort to be complete and accurate. For one thing, even game programs are sometimes wrong and include errors or omissions. Second, if a player wore more than one number in a year, I may not have caught the second number since I have not viewed every game program for every game for every team. Finally, despite thorough fact-checking and proofreading, typographical errors are probably inevitable in a project of this size as well. For any of those I apologize in advance.

Part One is the main text of this reference book. It presents entry by entry all of the NFL teams. Included in each entry are a number of categories of information:

The Franchise: A summation of the team covering the ownership, leading players and coaches and major events in team history. The city's relationship with pro football is also noted.

Origin of Name: How the team was given its nickname.

Record By Decade: Regular season and playoff won/lost records and championship seasons. Plus the number of winning and losing seasons. Information for all teams is compiled and sorted in Appendix B.

Time Till First Championship: Years from the team's inception to its first championship.

Time Since Last Championship: Years since the team last won the title.

Coaches: Regular season and postseason records for all of the team's coaches with championships won in parentheses. Coaches with over 100 regular season wins are listed in Appendix B.

Retired Numbers: Numbers officially set aside by the team in honor of a particular player. They are compiled and listed by number in Appendix B.

Other Numbers worn by these players: ...if they wore multiple numbers.

Those who wore Retired Numbers after the Honored player: Self-explanatory.

Numbers that should be retired: In my opinion, which is prejudiced toward Hall of Fame players who were dominant at their positions and leaders on the field.

Owned numbers: Number worn by only one player in team history and then retired. These are compiled and listed by number in Appendix B.

Numbers worn by Hall of Famers: Hall of Famers who spent any portion of their career with the team. These players are in **bold** type in the entries.

Star power: A lesser light gives up his number to an incoming star player.

Star eclipsed: Star is denied a number because someone else already has it.

Numbers with most great players: In my judgment.

Worst represented numbers: In my judgment.

Number worn by the most players: Self-explanatory. The most popular numbers leaguewide are included in Appendix B. The highest figure for any team is noted in Appendix B.

Player who wore the most numbers: Self-explanatory. Those who wore at least five numbers for one team are compiled in Appendix B, as are those who wore the most numbers for more than one team.

Longest tenure wearing a number: Player who wore a number for the longest time for the team. Those who wore a number for at least 15 years for a team are listed in Appendix B, as are those who wore the same number for the most different teams.

Number worn by first-ever draft pick: Self-explanatory.

Biggest draft busts: Draft busts are generally from the first 10 to 15 selections in the first round.

Number worn by first expansion draft pick: Category only appears for the 10 expansion franchises, and not all expansion drafts were conducted in easily numerated rounds. Also included is mention of the expansion draft pick who lasted the longest with the club.

Number worn by oldest player: Self-explanatory. All players older than 40 are listed.

Cameos: Notable veteran players who spent only one year with this team.

Ones who got away: Notable players who spent only a year or two with the team before becoming a star elsewhere.

Least popular numbers: Numbers worn by the fewest players. The least popular numbers leaguewide are included in Appendix B. All players who wore 0 or 00 also are listed in Appendix B.

Last number to be originated: Last number to be worn for the first time.

Longest dormant number: Number with the longest time between players wearing it. Retired numbers are excluded from this category. Longest dormancy period is listed in Appendix B.

Triskaidekaphobia Notes: Players who wore 13. Sometimes bad luck players who wore other numbers are noted here.

Shared numbers: Number worn by two stars of nearly equal value, especially when they play the same position.

Continuity: Number passed seamlessly from one star to another, preferably at the same position.

Discontinuity: Number made famous by one player that is worn next by a player of decidedly less ability.

Family connections: Two or more brothers and father/son combinations who played for this team.

Quarterback numbers over 19: Category is limited largely to teams that began before 1960 since quarterback numbers were stipulated in 1952 to be below 20. These are compiled and listed by number in Appendix B.

Number of first black player: Category limited to teams that began before 1962 when the last all-white team, the Redskins, finally added black players to their roster. Appendix B lists all 1920s and 1930s black players who played on current teams and those who broke the color barrier in 1946.

Numbers of future NFL head coaches: Numbers worn by NFL head coaches when they were players.

Numbers of future NFL referees: Numbers worn by NFL referees when they were players.

Players who played other sports: These sports include Major League Baseball, the National Basketball Association and its precursors, Olympic track and field, boxing, and wrestling of all types.

Players more famous after football: Actors, politicians, businessmen and so on.

First player to wear a number in the 70s: Category limited to teams that began before 1960. The earliest instance is listed in Appendix B.

First player to wear a number in the 80s: Category limited to teams that began before 1960. The earliest instance is listed in Appendix B.

First player to wear a number in the 90s: Category limited to teams that began before 1995. The earliest instance is listed in Appendix B.

Number with most points scored: Best combined point total for all players who wore the number for this team.

Number with most yards rushing: Best combined yardage total for all players who wore the number for this team.

Number with most receptions: Best combined reception total for all players who wore the number for this team.

Number with most touchdown passes: Best combined touchdown pass total for all players who wore the number for this team.

Number with most interceptions: Best combined interception total for all players who wore the number for this team.

Oddity: The strange but true category.

Team All-Time Numerical Roster: Players are listed in chronological order for each number. Those with an "r" following the year 1987 were replacement players during the players' strike. The player's position is noted as well. Pro Bowl players and pre–1950 All-Pros for each number are in *italics*; Hall of Famers are in **bold** type.

Part Two of this book is a master list of individuals of all teams, giving their team(s) (3-letter abbreviations) and number(s).

Finally, in addition to Appendix B noted, there are three other appendices. Appendix A lists the best players throughout the league to have worn each number. Appendix C lists the numbers worn by players on NFL teams that have ceased to exist since the league instituted significant rules and alignment changes in 1933 that ushered in the beginnings of stability and growth. Appendix D lists the numbers worn by players on the All America Conference teams that went out of business. AAC numbers for the Browns and 49ers are included in their Part One entries.

PART ONE

Team by Team Full Entries

ARIZONA CARDINALS

The franchise: The Cardinals franchise is the oldest in professional football and, historically, the worst run. Local businessman Chris O'Brien formed the Morgan Athletic Club in 1898 and ran the team as an independent team for most of the early years of the 20th century. As charter members of the American Professional Football Association that would later become the NFL, the Chicago Cardinals beat off a challenge to the Windy City territory by the Chicago Tigers in 1920 only to see George Halas move his Decatur Staleys into town the next year. At the time, the Cardinals had the best player in town, Hall of Famer Paddy Driscoll, who made them a competitive team and led them to a disputed NFL Championship in 1925. The Pottsville Maroons claimed they were the true 1925 champs by virtue of beating the Cardinals in their only meeting late in the season, which gave the Maroons a better record. However, the Maroons were suspended by the league for playing in an unsanctioned game against a Notre Dame all-star team that year, while the Cardinals scheduled two more games at the last minute and won them both to give them the best overall record.

Financial problems forced O'Brien to sell Driscoll to the crosstown Bears in 1926 and then sell the team to Dr. David Jones in 1929. Jones held the team for only four years before selling them to Charles Bidwill, a Bears executive and also—a bad omen—a Bears fan. The team's fortunes did not improve and culminated in a stretch from 1943 to 1945 in which the Cards went 1–29. At the close of World War II, the owner spent a great deal of money to field the "Million Dollar Backfield" of Charley Trippi, Elmer Angsman, Paul Christman, and Pat Harder and a talented supporting cast. In the wake of the deaths of player Jeff Burkett and Charles Bidwill, the Cardinals won the 1947 championship and, mourning the death of another player, Stan Mauldin, played in the 1948 title game. With Bidwill's wife, Violet, in charge, the team immediately followed their brief success with the worst full decade by any team in NFL history, finishing 33–84–3 for a .288 winning percentage in the 1950s.

The Cardinals moved to St. Louis in 1960, and Bidwill's sons Charles Jr. and William assumed control of the team in 1962. Bill bought out Charley in the early 1970s. On the field, the team was a sometime contender in the 1960s and 1970s. However, their last season of double-digit wins was 1976, and they have only had three winning records in the ensuing 27 years, which featured another move west to Arizona in 1988. After 70 years of Bidwill family ownership, the Cardinals continue to go through players and coaches quickly and be unable to fill their stadium.

Origin of name: The origin of the Cardinals name is something of a metaphor for the franchise itself. In 1901, owner Chris O'Brien purchased some used jerseys from

Record by Decade						
	Regular Season			Postseason		
	Won	Lost	Tied	Won	Lost	Championships
1920s	56	42	9	0	0	1925
1930s	35	67	9	0	0	
1940s	41	65	4	1	1	1947
1950s	33	84	3	0	0	
1960s	66	64	8	0	0	
1970s	69	71	4	0	2	
1980s	62	88	2	0	1	
1990s	58	102	0	1	1	
2000s	19	45	0	0	0	
All-Time	439	628	39	2	5	2

Winning seasons: 21. Losing seasons: 59. .500 seasons: 4.

the University of Chicago. The once-maroon jerseys had badly faded, but O'Brien tried to put a positive spin on the situation by calling them "Cardinal red." The independent team that had been known first as the Morgan Athletic Club and then the Chicago Normals became the Racine Street Cardinals and would later join the American Professional Football Association as the Chicago Cardinals. The cities have changed, but "Cardinals" has stayed constant — old wine in new bottles.

Time till first championship: Five years, 1925.

Time since last championship: 56 years since 1947.

Retired numbers: Of the four Cardinal numbers retired, only one is for a Hall of Fame player — 8, safety Larry Wilson. 99 is retired for All-Pro defensive back Marshall Gold-

Coaches			
	Years	*Record*	*Playoffs*
Paddy Driscoll	1920–2	17–8–4	0–0
Arnold Horween	1923–4	13–8–1	0–0
Norman Barry (1)	1925–6	16–8–2	0–0
Guy Chamberlin	1927	3–7–1	0–0
Fred Gillies	1928	1–5	0–0
Dewey Scanlon	1929	6–6–1	0–0
Ernie Nevers	1930–1	10–9–2	0–0
Leroy Andrews	1931	0–1	0–0
Jack Chevigny	1932	2–6–2	0–0
Paul Schissler	1933–4	6–15–1	0–0
Milan Creighton	1935–8	16–26–4	0–0
Ernie Nevers	1939	1–10	0–0
Jimmy Conzelman	1940–2	8–22–3	0–0
Phil Handler	1943	0–10	0–0
Phil Handler/Walt Kiesling	1944	0–10	0–0
Phil Handler	1945	1–9	0–0
Jimmy Conzelman (1)	1946–8	26–9	1–1
Phil Handler/Buddy Parker	1949	2–4	0–0
Buddy Parker	1949	4–1–1	0–0
Curly Lambeau	1950–1	8–15	0–0
Phil Handler/Cecil Isbell	1951	0–1	0–0
Joe Kuharich	1952	4–8	0–0
Joe Stydahar	1953–4	3–20–1	0–0
Ray Richards	1955–7	14–21–1	0–0
Pop Ivy	1958–61	14–32–2	0–0
Chuck Drulis/Ray Prochaska/Ray Wilsey	1961	2–0	0–0
Wally Lemm	1962–5	27–26–3	0–0
Charley Winner	1966–70	35–30–5	0–0
Bob Holloway	1971–2	8–18–2	0–0
Don Coryell	1973–7	42–27–1	0–2
Bud Wilkinson	1978–9	9–20	0–0
Larry Wilson	1979	2–1	0–0
Jim Hanifan	1980–5	39–49–1	0–1
Gene Stallings	1986–9	23–34–1	0–0
Hank Kuhlman	1989	0–5	0–0
Joe Bugel	1990–3	20–44	0–0
Buddy Ryan	1994–5	12–20	0–0
Vince Tobin	1996–2000	28–43–0	1–1
Dave McGinnis	2000–3	17–40	0–0

(Championships in parentheses)

berg. The other three commemorate tragedies: tackle Stan Mauldin, 77, died of a heart attack just after the 1948 season opener, tight end J.V. Cain, 88, died of a heart attack on his 28th birthday during training camp in 1979, Pat Tillman, 40, in the Afghan War.

Other numbers worn by these players: Goldberg also wore 42 and 89.

Those who wore retired numbers after the honored player: Bob "Bomber" Nussbaumer wore 99 in 1949–50.

Numbers that should be retired: Hall of Famer Paddy Driscoll, 1, was very possibly the finest player in the league at its outset; Ernie Nevers, 4/11/44, is a charter member of the Hall of Fame; Hall of Famer Charley Trippi, 2/62, was the best player and leader for the Cardinals best team in the late 1940s.

Owned numbers: None.

Numbers worn by Hall of Famers: Guy Chamberlin 13; Dan Dierdorf 72; Paddy Driscoll 1; Walt Kiesling 16/18/49; Dick Night Train Lane 81; Don Maynard 13; Ollie Matson 33; Ernie Nevers 4/11/44; Jackie Smith 81; Jim Thorpe (unknown); Charley Trippi 2/61/62; and Larry Wilson 8.

Star power: Seth Joyner took 59 from Ed Cunningham; Night Train Lane took 81 from Pat Summerall; Emmitt Smith took 22 from Duane Starks.

Star eclipsed: Wilber Marshall wore 55 because Eric Hill wore 58. Simeon Rice wore 79 till Chris Maumalanga, 97, left.

Numbers with most great players: 21 was worn by All Pro safety Jerry Stovall and runner Terry Metcalf as well as Terry's son Eric Metcalf and defensive back Dan Sandifer; 44 has been worn by Hall of Famer Ernie Nevers, star quarterback Paul Christman, star runner John David Crow, and star receiver John Gilliam; 81 was worn by Hall of Famers Night Train Lane and Jackie Smith as well as star receiver Roy Green and kicker Pat Summerall.

Worst represented numbers: 5, 6 and 9 have each been worn by a mix of 9 linemen, receivers, quarterbacks and kickers of no consequence; 26 has been worn by 27 nobodies.

Number worn by the most players: 21 has been worn by 31 players.

Player who wore the most numbers: Three players have worn five numbers— tackle Fred Gillies wore 5/9/10/11/66; guard Phil Handler wore 7/11/32/33/46; tackle Fred "Duke" Slater wore 7/14/16/47/91.

Longest tenure wearing a number: Quarterback Jim Hart wore 17 for 18 years from 1966 to 1983. Placekicker Jim Bakken wore 25 for 17 years from 1962 to 1978. Hall of Fame tight end Jackie Smith wore 81 for 15 years from 1963 to 1977.

Number worn by first ever draft pick: Jim Lawrence, the first round pick in 1936, wore 8, 11, and 30.

Biggest draft busts: Pass rusher Andre Wadsworth, 90, was the third selection in the 1998 draft and was out of football in three years. Runner Thomas Jones, 26, was the tenth selection in 2000 and departed three years later at 3.5 yards per carry. Receiver Clyde Duncan, 86, was the 11th selection in 1984 but only caught four passes in two years. Runner Larry Stegent, 35, the eighth selection in 1970, caught one pass and compiled 0 yards rushing. Finally, kicker Steve Little, 12, was the 15th selection in 1978, but succeeded on only 80 percent of his point after attempts and less than 50 percent of his field goal attempts.

Number worn by oldest player: Jim Thorpe played in one game with the Cardinals when he was 40, but his number that day is unknown. Longtime star quarterback Jim Hart, 17, finished with the Cardinals at age 39.

Cameos: Hall of Famers— Guy Chamberlin 13, Don Maynard 13; All Pros and other notables— Hardy Brown 37, Ward Cuff 14, Boomer Esiason 7, Carl Hairston 98; Don Joyce 11, Dave Kreig 17, Dexter Manley 92, Jim McMahon 9, Ken Willard 20.

Ones who got away: Tom Day 61 and Ron McDole 66 made up half of the Bills excellent front four in the mid 1960s. Gary Knafelc 83 was a solid receiver for the Packers, and Ahmad Rashad 28 was a star pass catcher in Minnesota.

Least popular numbers: 0 has never been worn. 99 has only been worn three times.

Last number to be originated: 94 was first worn by Jeff Faulkner in 1991.

Longest dormant number: 1 was dormant for the longest period in team history, 73 years, from Bill Stein in 1928 to Cedrick Oglesby in 2001. The oldest retired number is 77, which has not been worn since 1948. The number dormant for the longest time currently is 2, which has not been worn since 1994.

Triskaidekaphobia notes: The Cardinals are one of two teams (including the Bears) that have had two Hall of Fame players who wore 13. Guy Chamberlin and Don Maynard, along with three others, wore it for the Cards.

Shared numbers: Johnny Roland and Garrison Hearst were two star runners who wore 23; All Pros cornerback Pat Fischer and fullback Larry Centers both wore 37; two Hall of Famers, Night Trane Lane and Jackie Smith, both wore 81.

Continuity: Tackle Tootie Robbins was followed in 63 by defensive end Michael Bankston.

Discontinuity: Terry Metcalf was followed in 21 by wide receiver Dave Stief; Garrison Hearst was followed in 23 by cornerback Ronnie Bradford; Hall of Famer Ernie Nevers was followed in 44 by guard Al Graham; Hall of Famer Dan Dierdorf was followed in 72 by defensive tackle Dan Ralph; great receiver Mel Gray was followed in 85 by Danny Pittman.

Family Connections

Brothers

Arnie Horween	B	1921–4	?
Ralph Horween	B	1921–3	?
Buster Ramsey	G	1946–51	20
Knox Ramsey	G	1950–1	70
Bill Rooney	C	1929	11
Cobb Rooney	E	1929–30	34
Niko Noga	LB	1984–8	49/57
Pete Noga	LB	1987r	57

Father and son

Terry Metcalf	RB	1973–7	21
Eric Metcalf	KR	1998	21

Quarterback numbers over 19: 21/22/24 Jim Hardy 1949–51; 22/78/98 Ray Mallouf

1941, 1946–8; 35/40 Walt Masters 1943–4; 44 Paul Christman 1946–9; 49 Charles Eikenberg 1948; 55 Vince Oliver 1945; 66 Lloyd Cheatham 1942.

Number of first black player: Tackle Fred "Duke" Slater wore 7, 14, 16, 47, and 91 from 1926 to 1931. Other early black pioneers were guard Hal Bradley who wore 30 in 1928 and back Joe Lillard who wore 19 in 1932–3. When the color line was removed after World War II, the first blacks to play for the Cardinals came in 1952 — runner Ollie Matson, 33, runner Wally Triplett, 40, and end Cliff Anderson, 84 .

Numbers of future NFL head coaches: Norm Barry 4; Johnny Bryan 6; Guy Chamberlin 13; Milan Creighton 24/25; Jap Douds 47; Bob Dove 42; Paddy Driscoll 1; Hal Erickson 3; Fred Gillies 5/9/10/11/66; Phil Handler 7/11/32/33/46; Arnie Horween unknown; Pop Ivy 7/42/51; Joe Kuharich 17/88; Walt Kiesling 16/18/49; Ted Marchibroda 7; Ernie Nevers 4/11/44; Buddy Parker 15; Jack Patera 61; Buster Ramsey 20; Len Sachs 7/22; Red Strader 7; Jim Thorpe unknown; Larry Wilson 8; and Sam Wyche 15.

Numbers of future NFL referees: Paddy Driscoll 1 and Pat Harder 34.

Players who played other sports: Baseball — Garland Buckeye 10/14; Paddy Driscoll 1; Paul Florence unknown; Walt Masters 35/40; Howie Maple 35; Johnny Mohardt 2/15; Ernie Nevers 4/11/44; Evar Swanson 12; and Jim Thorpe unknown. Basketball — Dick Evans 28/35; Ike Mahoney 4; Joel Mason 17; Ray Ramsey 87; Len Sachs 7/22; Bob Shaw 60; and Clint Wager 69. Wrestling — Bob Duncum 69.

Players more famous after football: Pat Tillman, 40, quit football to join the Army after 9/11 and was killed in Afghanistan in 2004. Fred "Duke" Slater 7/14/16/47/91 later became a Superior Court Judge in Cook County, Illinois. Bobby Moore, 28, had his best years on the field with Minnesota as Ahmad Rashad and became more famous as a broadcaster after he retired. Dan Dierdorf, 72, and Pat Summerall, 81/85, also became more famous as broadcasters. Dave Meggysey, 60, was a linebacker in the 1960s who fashioned himself as something of an intellectual, wrote a scathing attack on pro football called *Out of Their League,* and ended up as an official with the NFL Players' Association.

First player to wear a number in the 70s: In 1940 Ed Beinor wore 73, Rupert Pate wore 74 and John Hall wore 77.

First player to wear a number in the 80s: In 1939 Keith Birlem wore 81 and Jon Bilbo wore 85.

First player to wear a number in the 90s: Gerry Lunz wore 91 in 1925.

Number with most points scored: 25 with 1,486 points scored by Jim Bakken (1,380), Roy Green (42), Charles Belden (30), Jerry Norton (12), Eric Blount (6), Fred McAfee (6), Bill Moore (6), Beryl Clark (3) and Mike Koken (1).

Number with most yards rushing: 32 with 14,730 yards rushing by Otiss Anderson (7,999), Michael Pittman (1,945), George Grosvenor (1,304), Doug Russell (1,048), LeShon Johnson (715), Jerry Latin (496), Walt Holmer (470), Tony Jordan (371), Hub Hinchman (171), Bill Daddio (108), Terrence Flagler (92), and Leo Hayden (11).

Number with most receptions: 81 with 1,714 passes caught by Roy Green (522), Jackie Smith (480), Frank Sanders (418), Randall Hill (174), Anquan Boldin (101), Night Train Lane (8), Mark Bell (8), Keith Birlem (2) and Jack Elwell (1).

Number with most touchdown passes: 17 with 275 touchdowns tossed by Jim Hart (209), Chris Chandler (19), Dave Kreig (16), Mack Reynolds (15), Jim Root (11), Dave Brown (4), and Ogden Compton (1).

Number with most interceptions: 22 with

57 passes picked off by Roger Wehrli (40), Adrian Wilson (6), Tom Knight (3), Fred Gehrke (3), Duane Starks (2), Dave Duerson (1), Ray Mallouf (1), Charley Jackson (1).

Oddity: The Cardinals were the opposite of most teams by first having players wear numbers in the 90s in the 1920s, then the 80s were first worn in the 1930s, and finally the 70s were not initiated until the 1940s. Also the number 77 was only worn in the 1940s.

Team All-Time Numerical Roster

Those with an "r" following the year 1987 were replacement players during the players' strike. Pro Bowl and pre–1950 All

Players with an Unconfirmed Number			
34	Howard Tipton	(B)	1933–7
12	Doug Russell	(B)	1934–9
48	Len Dugan	(C)	1937–9
40	Ev Fisher	(B)	1938–9
46	Lou Marotti	(G)	1943–5
9	Ralph Foster	(T)	1945–6
77	Ralph Foster	(T)	1945–6
68	*Bill Svoboda*	(LB)	1950–3

Players Whose Number Is Unknown		
Charles Knight	(C)	1920–21
Joe Carey	(G)	1920
Bill Clark	(G)	1920
Paul Florence	(E)	1920
Ralph Horween	(B)	1921–23
Arnold Horween	(B)	1921–24
Pete Steger	(B)	1921
Fred DeStefano	(B)	1924–25
Paul McNulty	(E)	1924–25
Charles Clark	(G)	1924
George Hartong	(G)	1924
Bill McElwain	(B)	1924
Bill Ryan	(T)	1924
Jim Woodruff	(E)	1926
Jay Berquist	(G)	1927
Aubrey Goodman	(T)	1927
Verne Mullen	(E)	1927
Jim Thorpe	(B)	1928
Homer Bliss	(G)	1928
Les Caywood	(G)	1931
Tom Cobb	(T)	1931
Latham Flanagan	(E)	1931
Forest Peters	(B)	1932
Ed Risk	(B)	1932
Carmen Scardine	(B)	1932
Ken Wendt	(G)	1932
Charles Bennett	(B)	1933
Paul Engebretsen	(G)	1933
Ed Brett	(E)	1936
Marv Ellstrom	(B)	1936
Charles McBride	(B)	1936
Hal Carlson	(G)	1937
Bill Muellner	(E)	1937
Ray Burnett	(B)	1938

Pro players for each number are in *italics*; Hall of Famers are in **bold** type.

1 **Paddy Driscoll** (B) 1920–5, Bill Stein (C) 1927–8, Cedrick Oglesby (K) 2001, Neil Rackers (K) 2003.

2 John Mohardt (B) 1922, *Clyde Zoia* (G) 1923, Joe Dunn (B) 1925–6, Ben Jones (B) 1927–8, **Charley Trippi** (B) 1952–5, Will Furrer (QB) 1993, Todd Peterson (K) 1994.

3 John Scanlon (B) 1921, Andy King (B) 1923–4, *Hal Erickson* (B) 1925–8, Ed Butts (B) 1929, Jim Lange (E) 1929, John Klumb (E) 1940, George Izo (QB) 1960, Ralph Guglielmi (QB) 1961, Billy Gambrell (WR) 1963–7, Timm Rosenbach (QB) 1989–92, Kevin Butler (K) 1996–7.

4 Norm Barry (B) 1921, *Ed Anderson* (B) 1923, Jim Tays (B) 1925, Ike Mahoney (B) 1925–8, 1931, **Ernie Nevers** (B) 1929, Bob McGee (T) 1938, Joe Reed (B) 1939, Chuck Levy (KR) 1994–5.

5 Paul LaRosa (E) 1920–1, *Fred Gillies* (T) 1922, *Bob Koehler* (G) 1923, *John Hurlburt* (G) 1924–5, Ray Risvold (B) 1927–8, *Jake Williams* (T) 1929, Gary Hogeboom (QB) 1989, Greg Davis (K) 1991–6, Tywan Mitchell (WR) 1999–2001.

6 Bernie Hallstrom (B) 1920–1, Jon Bryan (B) 1922, John Crangle (B) 1923, Rod Lamb (B) 1926–7, 1933, Ed Illman (B) 1928, Don Hill (B) 1929, Keith Ranspot (E) 1940, Dick Wedel (G) 1948, Joe Nedney (K) 1997–9, Tim Duncan (K) 2003.

7 Dick Egan (E) 1920–1, 1923, Len Sachs (E) 1922, 1925, Tom Hogan (T) 1926, Red Strader (B) 1927, Hugh Grant (B) 1928, *Fred Slater* (T) 1929, *Phil Handler* (G) 1930, *Bill Dewell* (E) 1940, Pop Ivy (E) 1940, Ray Johnson (B) 1940, Ross Nagel (T) 1942, John Hall (B) 1943, *Elmer Angsman* (B) 1946–52, Ray Nagel (B) 1953, Elmer Arterburn (B) 1954, Dave Leggett (B) 1955, Ted Marchibroda (QB) 1957, Robert Towns (DB) 1960, Craig Kupp (QB) 1991, Steve Beuerlein (QB) 1993–4, Boomer Esiason (QB) 1996, Bill Gramatica (K) 2001–3.

8 *Clyde Zoia* (G) 1920–2, Byron McMahon (G) 1923, Jim Lawrence (B) 1937–9, Frank Tripucka (QB) 1950–2, Lamar McHan (QB) 1954–8, **Larry Wilson** (S) 1960–72.

9 Dick Egan (E) 1922, Tom Bucklin (B) 1927, *Fred Gillies* (T) 1928, Russ Method (B) 1929, Jerry Cowhig (B) 1950, Don Panciera (QB) 1952, Jim McMahon (QB) 1994, Cory Sauter (QB) 1998, Sean Keenan (QB) 2000.

10 *Fred Gillies* (T) 1920–1, Nick McInerney (C) 1922, 1925–7, Garland Buckeye (T) 1923–4, John Vesser (E) 1927, *Ralph Claypool* (C) 1928, Ev Fisher (B) 1938–9, Lou Zontini (B) 1940–1, Pete Beathard (QB) 1970–1, Bill Donckers (QB) 1976–7, Larry Swider (P) 1980, Jess Atkinson (K) 1985, Sammy Garza (QB) 1987r, Stan Gelbaugh (QB) 1991, *Jeff Feagles* (P) 1994–7, John Lee (K) 1996, *Scott Player* (P) 1998–2003.

11 Nick McInerney (C) 1920–1, Elmer Runquist (T) 1922, *Fred Gillies* (T) 1923–5, *Chet Widerquist* (T) 1926, 1928, *Ray Weller* (T) 1927, Gene Francis (B) 1926, Bill Rooney (C) 1929, **Ernie Nevers** (B) 1930, *Tim Moynihan* (C) 1933, *Phil Handler* (G) 1934–6, Jim Lawrence (B) 1937, Sam Agee (B) 1938–9, Falt Elkins (B) 1939, *Gaynell Tinsley* (E) 1940, *Vince Banonis* (C) 1942, Cal Purdin (B) 1943, *Chet Bulger* (T) 1946–9, John Hock (T) 1950, Don Joyce (T) 1951, Buddy Humphrey (QB) 1963–5, Dennis Shaw (QB) 1974–5, Neil O'Donoghue (K) 1980–5, Novo Bojovic (K) 1985, Eric Schubert (K) 1986, Greg Horne (P) 1987–8, Jay Schroeder (QB) 1994, Kent Graham (QB) 1996–7, Sherdrick Bonner (QB) 1999, Bryan Gillmore (WR) 2000, Kevin Kaspar (WR) 2002, Jeff Blake (QB) 2003.

12 John Leonard (T) 1922, Nick McInerney (C) 1923–7, Evar Swanson (E) 1925–7, Joe Davidson (G) 1928, *Charles Kassel* (E) 1929–31, Charles Braidwood (E) 1932, Dave Nisbet (E) 1933, Otto Vokaty (B) 1933, Earl Pardoner (B) 1934–5, Charles Vaughn (B) 1936, Pete Tyler (B) 1937–8, Frank Zelencik (T) 1939, Bill Murphy (G) 1940, Steve Romanik (G) 1953–4, John Roach (QB) 1956, 1959–60, Paul Larson (QB) 1957, *Charley Johnson* (QB) 1961–9, Gary Keithley (QB) 1973–5, Duane Carrell (P) 1977, Steve Little (P/K) 1978–80, Kyle Mackey (QB) 1984, Scott Brunner (QB) 1985, Gregg Tipton (QB) 1987, Chad Carpenter (WR) 1997–9, Chad Stanley (P) 2001, Josh McCown (QB) 2002–3.

13 **Guy Chamberlin** (C) 1927, Earl Crowder (B) 1939, **Don Maynard** (WR) 1973, Jim Gallery (K) 1987, Chris Jacke (K) 1998–9.

14 Garland Buckeye (T) 1920–2, John Marquardt (E) 1921, Art Folz (B) 1923, *Bob Koehler* (G) 1924–6, *Fred Slater* (T) 1926–7, 1930, Ray Marelli (G) 1928, Ed Cherry (B) 1938–9, Lloyd Madden (B) 1940, Ward Cuff (B) 1946, Sam Etcheverry (QB) 1961–2, Terry Nofsinger (QB) 1965–6, Hal Roberts (P) 1974, Mike Loyd (QB) 1979–80, Rick McIvor (QB) 1984–5, Greg Cater (P) 1986–7, Mark Royals (P) 1987r, Kevin Williams (WR) 1997, Kevin Drake (WR) 1998, Chris Griesen (QB) 1999–2001.

15 Harry Curran (B) 1920–1, John Mohardt (B) 1923, *Herb Blumer* (E) 1925–6, 1930, Bill Springsteen (E) 1927, Harry Curzon (B) 1928, Buddy Parker (B) 1937–43, Les Bruckner (B) 1945, *Paul Christman* (QB) 1945, *Bob Zimny* (T) 1946–9, Jerry Houghton (T) 1951, Gary Cuozzo (QB) 1972, Sam Wyche (QB) 1976, Steve Pisarkiewicz (QB) 1977–9, *Neil Lomax* (QB) 1981–9, Stony Case (QB) 1995–8, Cary Blanchard (K) 2000–1, Preston Parsons (QB) 2002.

16 Charles Knight (C) 1920–1, *Ed Anderson* (B) 1922, *Willis Brennan* (T) 1923–7, *Fred Slater* (T) 1928, **Walt Kiesling** (G) 1929, Mickey Erickson (C) 1930–1, Joe Reed (B) 1937, Henry Adams (C) 1939, Dick Plasman (E) 1946–7, King Hill (QB) 1960–4, Tim Van Galder (QB) 1972–4, Rusty Lisch (QB) 1980–4, Kent Austin (QB) 1986, *Rich Camarillo* (P) 1989–93, Mike Buck (QB) 1995, Jake Plummer (QB) 1997–2002.

17 Frank Rydzewski (T) 1921, Ralph Montgomery (T) 1923, Art Folz (B) 1924–5, *Ray Weller* (T) 1926, Austin Waldron (G) 1927, Ed Butts (B) 1929, Fred Larson (C) 1929, *Herb Blumer* (E) 1930, 1933, Clare Randolph (C) 1930, Earl Nolan (T) 1937–8, Joel Mason (E) 1939, Herm Schneidman (B) 1940, Elmer Merkovsky (T) 1944, *Joe Kuharich* (G) 1945, Freeman Rexer (E) 1945, Bob Hanlon (B) 1948, Lin Lauro (B) 1951, Jim Root (QB) 1953, 1956, Ogden Compton (QB) 1955, Mack Reynolds (QB) 1958–9, *Jim Hart* (QB) 1966–83, Evan Arapostathis (P/K) 1986, Al Del Greco (K) 1987–90, Jason Staurovsky (K) 1987r, Chris Chandler (QB) 1991–3, Chris Swartz (QB) 1994, Dave Krieg (QB) 1995, Dave Brown (QB) 1998–2001.

18 *Bob Koehler* (G) 1920–1, *Willis Brennan* (T) 1922, Roger Kiley (E) 1923, *Walt Ellis* (T) 1926–7, Bill Springsteen (E) 1928, Lou Larson (B) 1929, **Walt Kiesling** (G) 1930, Bernie Holm (B) 1932, Elmer Schwartz (B) 1932, Hal Moe (B) 1933, *Bernie Hughes* (C) 1934–6, Ham Harmon (C) 1937, Al Babartsky (T) 1938, Lee Mulleneaux (C) 1938, Charles Gainor (E) 1939, Don Currivan (E) 1943, George Petrovich (T) 1949–50, *Fred Wallner* (G) 1951, Sergio Albert (K) 1974, Mark Manges (QB) 1978, *Carl Birdsong* (P) 1981–5, Cliff Stoudt (QB) 1986–8, John Jackson (WR) 1990, Kevin Knox (WR) 1994, Andy McCullough (WR) 1998–9, Jake Soliday (WR) 2002.

19 *Willis Brennan* (T) 1920–1, *Bob Koehler* (G) 1922, John Leonard (T) 1923, Lyons Killiher (G) 1928, Jim Murphy (B) 1928, John Underwood (G) 1929, *Jake Williams* (T) 1930–1, Joe Lillard (B) 1932–3, Pete Mehringer (T) 1935–6, Bill May (B) 1937–8, Joe Reed (B) 1939, *Ed Rucinski* (E) 1945–6, Charles Smith (B) 1947, Phil Spiller (DB) 1967, Mike Woods (P/K) 1978–9, Shawn Halloran (QB) 1987r, Tom Tupa (QB/P) 1988–91, Tony Sacca (QB) 1992–3, MarTay Jenkins (WR) 1999, Nathan Poole (WR) 2001–2.

20 Leon Chappell (G) 1920–1, *Herb Blumer* (E) 1927–9, George Kenneally (G) 1930, Howard Auer (T) 1933, Bob Neuman (E) 1934–6, Jim Coffee (B) 1937–8, Hal Robl (B) 1945, Joe Vodicka (B) 1945, *Garrard Ramsey* (G) 1946–51, Bill Cross (B) 1951–3, Les Goble (B) 1954–5, Woodley Lewis (B) 1956–9, Ken Hall (RB) 1959, 1961, Monk Bailey (DB) 1964–5, Mike Barnes (DB) 1967–8, Miller Farr (DB) 1970–2, Clancy Oliver (DB) 1973, Ken Willard (RB) 1974, Mike Sensibaugh (S) 1976–7, Gordon Bell (RB) 1978–9, Travis Curtis (S) 1987–8, Dwayne Anderson (DB) 1987r, Mike Barber (WR) 1989, *Johnny Bailey* (RB) 1992–3, Andre

Waters (S) 1994, Ron Moore (RB) 1997, Damian Anderson (RB) 2002–3.

21 Wilfred Smith (E) 1923–5, Ed Greene (E) 1926, Francis Moran (B) 1927, Don Yesley (E) 1927–8, Pat Dowling (E) 1929, Jess Tinsley (T) 1930, Les Malloy (B) 1931–3, Roy Horstmann (B) 1934, Hal Pangle (B) 1935–8, Al Johnson (B) 1939–41, Frank Bohlman (G) 1942, Marshall Robnett (G) 1943–4, Hal Blackwell (B) 1945, *Jim Hardy* (QB) 1949, Laverne Whitman (B) 1951–3, Dan Sandifer (DB) 1953, Jim Sears (DB) 1954, 1957–8, Ellsworth Kingery (B) 1954, Tom Keane (B) 1955, Norm Beal (DB) 1962, *Jerry Stovall* (DB) 1963–71, *Terry Metcalf* (RB) 1973–7, Dave Stief (WR) 1978–82, Mark Jackson (CB) 1987, Tracey Eaton (S) 1990, Dexter Davis (DB) 1992–3, James Williams (CB) 1994, Cedric Davis (DB) 1995, Kevin Minniefield (DB) 1997, Eric Metcalf (KR) 1998, Clarence Williams (RB) 1999–2000, Renaldo Hill (CB) 2002–3.

22 Len Sachs (E) 1920–1, 1923, *Ed Anderson* (B) 1924–5, Gene Rose (DB) 1929, *Lou Gordon* (T) 1930–5, *Conway Baker* (T) 1936–43, 1945, Ray Mallouf (QB) 1946–8, Fred Gehrke (B) 1950, *Jim Hardy* (QB) 1951, Don Paul (DB) 1952–3, Alex Burl (B) 1956, Charley Jackson (B) 1958, Prentice Gautt (RB) 1961–7, *Roger Wehrli* (DB) 1969–82, Bill Kay (DB) 1984, Terrence Anthony (DB) 1987r, Dave Duerson (DB) 1991–3, Mark Higgs (RB) 1994–5, Tom Knight (CB) 1997–2000, Adrian Wilson (DB) 2001, Duane Starks (CB) 2002, Emmitt Smith (RB) 2003.

23 Bill Whalen (T) 1920–4, Pete Mehringer (T) 1934, *Tony Blazine* (T) 1935–40, John Clement (B) 1941, John Butler (B) 1944, *Ed Rucinski* (E) 1945, Cliff Speegle (C) 1945, Charles Granger (G/T) 1961, Bob Paremore (RB) 1963–4, Johnny Roland (RB) 1966–72, Ken Stone (DB) 1977–80, Benny Perrin (S) 1982–5, Dennis Thurman (DB) 1986, Ed Scott (S) 1987r, Marcus Turner (DB) 1989–91, Garrison Hearst (RB) 1993–5, Ronnie Bradford (CB) 1996, Dell McGee (CB) 1998, Coby Rhinehart (DB) 1999–2003.

24 Dan O'Connor (G) 1920–4, Roy Baker (B) 1929–30, Milan Creighton (E) 1931–5, Clarence Kellogg (B) 1936, John Reynolds (C) 1937, Al Babartsky (T) 1938, Frank Patrick (B) 1938–9, John Kuzman (T) 1941, Carl Olson (T) 1942, John McCarthy (B) 1944, Paul Collins (B) 1945, Al Hust (E) 1946, John Cochran (B) 1947–9, *Jim Hardy* (QB) 1950, Emil Sitko (B) 1951–2, Jim Psaltis (B) 1953, 1955, Al Brosky (B) 1954, Jim Carr (B) 1955, 1957, Bob Watkins (B) 1958, Bill Stacy (DB) 1959–63, Terry Brown (DB) 1969–70, Wayne Morris (RB) 1976–83, Ron Wolfley (RB) 1985–91, Herschel Currie (DB) 1994, Patrick Hunter (CB) 1995, Dell McGee (CB) 1996–7, Mario Bates (RB) 1998–9, Tom Knight (CB) 2001, Adrian Wilson (DB) 2002–3.

25 Charles Belden (B) 1930, Bill Moore (B) 1932, Mike Koken (B) 1933, Frank Greene (B) 1934, Joe Krejci (E) 1934, Gwyn Dowell (B) 1935–6, Milan Creighton (E) 1936–7, Jon Bilbo (T) 1938, Jim Neil (B) 1939, Beryl Clark (B) 1940, Jim Higgins (G) 1941, Bill Murphy (G) 1941, Bob Eckl (T) 1945, Dick Nolan (DB) 1958, *Jerry Norton* (DB) 1959–61, *Jim Bakken* (K) 1962–78, *Roy Green* (DB/WR) 1979–81, Ken Sims (CB) 1987r, Roland Mitchell (CB) 1988–9, Andy Schillinger (WR) 1988, Stanley Blair (CB) 1990, Eric Blount (RB) 1992–3, Fred McAfee (RB) 1994, Carlos Brooks (DB) 1995, Corey Chavous (DB) 1998– 2001, Jason Goss (CB) 2003.

26 George Bogue (B) 1930, John Vesser (E) 1930, Larry Steinbach (T) 1931–3, Homer Ledbetter (B) 1932–3, Dave Cook (B) 1934–6, Milford Miller (G) 1936–7, Phil Dougherty (C) 1938, Ray Apolskis (T) 1941–2, George Smith (B) 1943, Frank Balasz (B) 1945, Jimmy Heidel (DB) 1966, Chuck Latourette (DB/P) 1967–8, 1970–1, Dwayne Crump (DB) 1973–6, Rondy Colbert (DB) 1977, Thomas Lott (RB) 1979, Mike Fisher (WR) 1981, George Schmitt (S) 1983, Lester Lyles (S) 1988, Michael Downs (S) 1989, Chris Oldham (DB) 1991–2, Amod Field (WR) 1991, Mitchell Price (DB) 1992, Chuck Cecil (S) 1993, Ben Smith (DB) 1995–6, Tony Jones (DB) 1995, J.B. Brown (DB) 1998, Thomas Jones (RB) 2000–2, Emmanuel McDaniel (CB) 2003.

27 Charles Diehl (G) 1930–1, Glen Martin (B) 1932, Howard Tipton (B) 1933–7, Len Dugan (C) 1939, Joe Lokanc (G) 1941, Roy Shivers (RB) 1966–72, Eddie Moss (RB) 1973–6, Carl Allen (DB) 1977–82, Greggory Johnson (S) 1987, Tony Mayes (S) 1987r, Jay Taylor (CB) 1989–92, Chris Oldham (DB) 1993–4, Tito Paul (DB) 1995–7, Tony Jones (DB) 1995, Ty Howard (CB) 1997–8.

28 Max Flenniken (B) 1930, Jesse Shaw (G) 1931, John Vesser (E) 1931, Frank Toscani (B) 1932, Porter Lainhart (B) 1933, Dick Nesbitt (B) 1933, Homer Griffith (B) 1934, Gil Berry (B) 1935, *Ross Carter* (G) 1936–9, Dick Evans (E) 1941, Ben Ciccone (C) 1942, Walt Rankin (B) 1943–4, Ernie Bonelli (B) 1945, Ray Ogden (WR) 1965–6, Charlie Pittman (RB) 1970, Ahmad Rashad (WR) 1972–3, Scott Stringer (DB) 1974, Robert Giblin (DB) 1977, Ted Farmer (RB) 1978, Tony Jeffery (RB) 1988, Steve Lofton (DB) 1993, Tommy Bennett (S) 1996–2000.

29 Mickey MacDonnell (B) 1925–30, Earl Britton (B) 1929, Dex Shelley (B) 1932, Don Cosner (B) 1939, Bob Wood (T) 1940, John Martin (B) 1941–4, Ted Doyle (E) 1944, Joe Carter (E) 1945, Brady Keys (DB) 1966, Gerard Williams (CB) 1980, Liffort Hobley (DB) 1985, Scott Holman (WR) 1986, Johnny Holloway (DB) 1987, Lorenzo Lynch (DB) 1990–5, Ty Howard (CB)

1997–8, Adrian Murrell (RB) 1998–9, Quentin Harris (DB) 2002–3.

30 *Ralph Claypool* (C) 1925–6, Ed Allen (E) 1928, Hal Bradley (G) 1928, Bill Boyd (B) 1930–1, Bill Simas (B) 1932–3, Bernie Finn (B) 1932, Cliff Hansen (B) 1933, Hub Hinchman (B) 1934, Ken Peterson (B) 1935, Jim Lawrence (B) 1936, John Morrow (G) 1937–8, Reg Monahan (G) 1939, Andy Chisick (C) 1940–1, Charlie Bryant (RB) 1966–7, Paul White (RB) 1970–1, Ara Person (TE) 1972, Gary Hammond (WR) 1973–6, Bill Bradley (DB) 1977, Willie Shelby (RB) 1978, Stump Mitchell (RB) 1981–9, David Little (TE) 1990, Ron Moore (RB) 1993–4, Lance Brown (DB) 1995–6, Leeland McElroy (RB) 1996–7.

31 Arnie Hummel (B) 1927, Paul Fitzgibbon (B) 1928, Jess Tinsley (T) 1929, 1931–3, Fred Failing (G) 1930, Charles Weaver (G) 1930, *Harry Field* (T) 1934–6, *Gaynell Tinsley* (E) 1938, 1940, Gordon Wilson (C) 1942–3, 1945, Ralph Fife (G) 1945, Jimmy Johnston (B) 1946, Jerry Davis (B) 1948–51, *Bill Svoboda* (LB) 1952–3, Malcom Hammack (RB) 1955, 1957–66, John Symank (DB) 1963, Jerry Daanen (WR) 1969–70, Chuck Beatty (DB) 1972, Don Shy (RB) 1973, Josh Ashton (RB) 1975, Earl Ferrell (RB) 1982–9, Richard Fain (DB) 1991, Odie Harris (DB) 1992–4, Ryan Terry (RB) 1995–6, Rod Brown (FB) 1997–8, Marcel Shipp (RB) 2001–3.

32 *Phil Handler* (G) 1930, Charles Weaver (G) 1930, Walt Holmer (B) 1931–2, Hub Hinchman (B) 1933, Doug Russell (B) 1934, Versil Deskin (E) 1935, Jim Mooney (T) 1935, *George Grosvenor* (B) 1936–7, Bill Daddio (E) 1941–2, *Vince Banonis* (C) 1942, 1946–50, Leo Hayden (RB) 1972–3, Reggie Harrison (RB) 1974, Jerry Latin (RB) 1975–8, *Ottis Anderson* (RB) 1979–86, Tony Jordan (RB) 1988–9, Terrence Flagler (RB) 1990–1, Frank Harvey (FB) 1994, Barry Word (RB) 1994, LeShon Johnson (RB) 1995–7, Michael Pittman (RB) 1998–2001.

33 Earl Evans (T) 1925, *Phil Handler* (G) 1930, Joe Pappio (B) 1930, Doug Russell (B) 1935–9, Homer Griffith (B) 1934, John Karwales (E) 1947, Hugh McCullough (B) 1940–1, John Knolla (B) 1942, 1945, Lloyd Cheatham (QB) 1942, Ron Cahill (B) 1943, Bernie Semes (B) 1944, Al Lindow (B) 1945, Ventan Yablonski (B) 1948–51, **Ollie Matson** (RB) 1952–8, Fred Glick (DB) 1959–60, Monte Lee (LB) 1961, Roland Jackson (FB) 1962, Willis Crenshaw (RB) 1964–9, Larry Willingham (DB) 1971–2, 1976, Willie Belton (RB) 1973–4, Tim Gray (DB) 1975, Steve Okoniewski (LB) 1976, Lawrence Barnes (RB) 1978, Theotis Brown (RB) 1979–81, Quentin Walker (RB) 1984–5, Derrick McAdoo (RB) 1987–8, John Burch (RB) 1989, Ivory Lee Brown (RB) 1991–2, Kevin Bouie (RB) 1997, Josh Scobey (RB) 2003.

34 Cobb Rooney (E) 1929–30, Willis Glasgow

(B) 1931, *Pat Harder* (B) 1946–50, *Bill Koman* (LB) 1959–67, Larry Hickman (FB) 1959, Rocky Rosema (LB) 1968–71, Don Heater (RB) 1972, Steve Jones (RB) 1974–8, Monty Hunter (DB) 1983, Tony Mumford (RB) 1985, Jessie Clark (RB) 1988–9, Anthony Thompson (RB) 1990–2, Terry Hoage (S) 1994–6, Joel Mackovicka (FB) 1999–2002, Dexter Jackson (S) 2003.

35 Howard Maple (B) 1930, George Duggins (E) 1934, Mike Kochel (G) 1939, Glynn Rogers (G) 1939, Arthur White (G) 1940–1, Dick Evans (E) 1942, Walt Masters (QB) 1944, Jeff Burkett (E) 1947, Joe Childress (RB) 1960, 1962–5, Larry Stegent (RB) 1971, *Jim Otis* (RB) 1973–8, Jeff Griffin (CB) 1981–5, Robert Mimbs (RB) 1988, Dennis Smith (TE) 1990, *Aeneas Williams* (CB) 1991–2000.

36 John Vesser (E) 1930–1, Loran Ribble (G) 1933, Dwight Sloan (QB) 1938, Joe Bukant (B) 1942–3, Walt Szot (T) 1946–8, Ralph Pasquariello (B) 1951–2, *Johnny Olszewski* (FB) 1953–7, Frank Mestnik (FB) 1960–1, Bill Thornton (RB) 1963–5, 1967, *MacArthur Lane* (RB) 1968–71, Jim Butler (RB) 1972, Ken Reaves (S) 1974–7, Steve Okoniewski (LB) 1976, Rod Phillips (RB) 1979–80, Perry Harrington (RB) 1984–5, *Vai Sikahema* (KR) 1986–90, Ryan Christopher (FB) 1996, David Barrett (CB) 2000–3.

37 Gene Rose (DB) 1930, Steve Lach (B) 1942, Vaughan Stewart (C) 1943, Vic Schwall (B) 1947, Clarence Self (DB) 1949, Don Paul (DB) 1950–1, Joe Geri (B) 1952, Jack Spinks (G) 1953, Emmett King (B) 1954, Hardy Brown (LB) 1956, Dean Philpott (B) 1958, *Pat Fischer* (CB) 1961–7, Mike Wilson (DB) 1969, Jeff Allen (DB) 1971, Tom Woodeshick (RB) 1972, Marv Owens (WR) 1973, Ken Greene (DB) 1978–82, Larry Cowan (RB) 1987, Don Goodman (RB) 1987r, Ricky Moore (FB) 1988, Kevin Guidry (CB) 1989, *Larry Centers* (RB) 1990–8.

38 Gene Rose (DB) 1931–2, Bill Crass (B) 1937, Elwyn Dunstan (T) 1938–9, Andy Sabados (G) 1939–40, Fred Shook (C) 1941, Bill Triplett (RB) 1962–3, 1965–6, Leon Burns (RB) 1972, Hurles Scales (DB) 1974, Lee Nelson (S) 1976–86, Mark Mathis (DB) 1987r, Mike Zordich (S) 1989–93, Kenny Harris (DB) 1997.

39 Charles Belden (B) 1931, John Perko (G) 1944, Al Drulis (B) 1945–6, Bill DeCorrevont (B) 1947–8, Tony Curcillo (B) 1953, Cid Edwards (RB) 1968–71, Will Harrell (RB) 1978–84, Broderick Sargent (RB) 1986–7, *Johnny Johnson* (RB) 1990–2, Brian Henesey (RB) 1994, C.J. Richardson (DB) 1995, Dennis McKinley (FB) 1999–2002.

40 *Tim Moynihan* (C) 1932, Tom Yarr (C) 1933, *Bill Smith* (E) 1934–9, Walt Masters (QB) 1943, John Popovich (B) 1944, Bob Norman (C) 1945, Walt Rankin (B) 1945, Paul Sarringhaus (B) 1946, Bill Gay (B) 1951, Wally Triplett (B) 1952–3,

Bill Bredde (B) 1954, Lindon Crow (DB) 1955–7, *Bobby Joe Conrad* (WR) 1960–8, Eric Washington (DB) 1972–3, Doug Greene (DB) 1978, Randy Love (RB) 1979–85, Don Goodman (RB) 1987r, Michael Adams (CB) 1989, *Robert Massey* (DB) 1991–3, Derrick Moore (RB) 1996–7, Pat Tillman (S) 1998–2001.

41 George Rogge (E) 1931–3, *Phil Sarboe* (B) 1934–6, Tom Murphy (B) 1934, Paul Shenefelt (T) 1934, Ernie Wheeler (B) 1939, 1942, Jim Thomas (G) 1939–40, *Bill Dewell* (E) 1941, 1945–9, Vernon Ghersanich (G) 1943, Tony Bova (E) 1944, *Fran Polsfoot* (E) 1950–2, Willie Carter (B) 1953, *Jimmy Hill* (DB) 1960–4, Jerry Daanen (WR) 1968, Nate Wright (DB) 1969–70, Ted Provost (DB) 1971, Clarence Duren (S) 1973–6, Vance Bedford (CB) 1982, Carl Carter (CB) 1986–9, Justin Lucas (DB) 1999–2003.

42 *Jake Williams* (T) 1932–3, Bill Wilson (E) 1935–7, *Marshall Goldberg* (B) 1939–40, 1942, Pop Ivy (E) 1940, Gil Duggan (T) 1945, Walt Rankin (B) 1946–7, *Bob Dove* (E) 1948–53, Abe Woodson (DB) 1965–6, Lonnie Sanders (DB) 1968–9, Norm Thompson (DB) 1971, Bob Wicks (WR) 1972, Chuck Detwiler (S) 1973, Herb Williams (DB) 1981–82, Bobby Johnson (DB) 1985–6, John Preston (S) 1987, Steve Lofton (DB) 1991–2, John Booty (DB) 1993, Kwamie Lassiter (DB) 1995–2002, James Hodgins (FB) 2003.

43 *Charles Kassel* (E) 1932–3, George Duggins (E) 1934, Al Nichelini (B) 1935–6, *Gaynell Tinsley* (E) 1937–8, Ray Busler (T) 1940–1, Marshall Robnett (G) 1945, Bill Montgomery (B) 1946, Mac Sauls (DB) 1968–9, Tony Plummer (DB) 1970, Norm Thompson (DB) 1972–6, Steve Carpenter (DB) 1981, Martin Bayless (DB) 1984, Lonnie Young (S) 1985–90, Stevie Anderson (WR) 1995, Matt Darby (S) 1996–7.

44 Ernie Nevers (B) 1931, Al Graham (G) 1932–3, Bill Volck (G) 1934–9, Hal Bradley (E) 1938–9, Frank Balasz (B) 1941, *Paul Christman* (QB) 1946–9, Mike Swistowicz (B) 1950, Joe Gasparella (B) 1951, John Karras (B) 1952, Paul Barry (B) 1954, Dave Mann (B) 1955–7, *John David Crow* (RB) 1958–64, John Gilliam (WR) 1969–71, Donny Anderson (RB) 1972–4, *Rolly Woolsey* (DB) 1978, Tim Collier (CB) 1980–1, Wayne Smith (CB) 1982–6, Michael Brim (CB) 1988, Tony Baker (RB) 1989, Terry Samuels (TE) 1995, D.J. Johnson (DB) 1996, J.J. McCleskey (DB) 1996–2000, Michael Stone (CB) 2001–2.

45 *Frank McNally* (C) 1931–4, Homer Hanson (G) 1935–6, Versil Deskin (E) 1936–9, Wilson Schwenk (B) 1942, Clarence Booth (T) 1943, Walt Kichefski (E) 1944, *Chet Bulger* (T) 1945, John Durko (E) 1945, Larry Fuller (B) 1945, Mitch Ucovich (T) 1945, Joe Driskill (DB) 1960–1, Carl Silvestri (DB) 1965, Bobby Williams (DB) 1966–7, George Hoey (DB) 1971, Jim Tolbert (S) 1973–5,

Perry Smith (DB) 1977–9, Leonard Smith (DB) 1983–8, Lydell Carr (FB) 1989, Mel Aldridge (S) 1995, Cedric Smith (FB) 1996–8, Renaldo Hill (CB) 2001.

46 *Phil Handler* (G) 1931–4, *Mike Mikulak* (B) 1934, Bert Pearson (C) 1935–6, Len Dugan (C) 1937–8, Al Babartsky (T) 1939, 1941–2, Lou Marotti (G) 1943, Bob Eckl (T) 1945, Frank Seno (B) 1946, Tom Longo (DB) 1971, Maurice Spencer (DB) 1974, Jeff Severson (CB) 1976–7, Jeff Lee (WR) 1980, Charles Johnson (DB) 1981, Don Bessillieu (S) 1982, Vic Heflin (DB) 1983, *Tim McDonald* (S) 1987–92, Charles Wright (CB) 1987, Brent Alexander (DB) 1994–7, Paris Johnson (DB) 1999.

47 Murrell Hogue (T) 1929, *Fred Slater* (T) 1931, Forrest Douds (T) 1932, Jim Bausch (B) 1933, Dick Nesbitt (B) 1933, *Bree Cuppoletti* (G) 1934–8, Joe Parker (E) 1946, Eli Popa (B) 1952, Al Campana (B) 1953, George Kinek (B) 1954, Bob Gordon (B) 1958, Bobby Lee (E) 1968, Steve Conley (LB) 1972, Cedric Mack (DB) 1983–90, Jordan Younger (DB) 2000, Don Morgan (DB) 2002.

48 Irv Hill (B) 1931–2, Gil Bergerson (T) 1933, *Mike Mikulak* (B) 1935–6, Bob Hoel (G) 1937–8, *Ki Aldrich* (C) 1939–40, 1943, Bob Morrow (G) 1941–3, Eberle Schultz (G) 1944, Jim Poole (E) 1945, Jim Strausbaugh (B) 1946, Robert Akins (DB) 1968–9, Craig Baynham (RB) 1972, Steve Henry (DB) 1979–80, Don Schwartz (DB) 1981, Lionel Washington (DB) 1983–6, Reggie Phillips (CB) 1988, Dexter Davis (DB) 1991, Oscar McBride (TE) 1996, Jarius Hayes (TE) 1998, Nathan Hodel (TE) 2001–3.

49 **Walt Kiesling** (G) 1931–3, Ted Isaacson (T) 1934–5, Jack Robinson (T) 1936–7, Frank Huffman (G) 1939–41, Bob Thurbon (B) 1944, Bill Reynolds (B) 1945, Bob Maddock (G) 1946, Charles Eikenberg (QB) 1948, Roy Barni (B) 1952–3, Frank Bernardi (B) 1955–7, Julian Spence (B) 1956, Jim Wagstaff (B) 1959, Willie West (DB) 1960–1, Jim Burson (DB) 1963–7, Dale Hackbart (DB) 1971–2, Niko Noga (LB) 1984, Greg Lasker (S) 1988, Chad Fann (TE) 1993, Lawrence Hart (TE) 2001.

50 Al Wukits (C) 1944, Bill Campbell (G) 1945, Leo Cantor (B) 1945, Walt Watt (B) 1945, Chet Maeda (B) 1946, Joe Coomer (T) 1947–9, John Jennings (T) 1950–1, *John Simmons* (C) 1951–6, Earl Putman (C) 1957, Don Gillis (C) 1958–61, Garland Boyette (LB) 1962–3, Mike Alford (C) 1965, Wayne Mulligan (C) 1969–73, Greg Hartle (LB) 1974–6, Al Beauchamp (LB) 1976, Kurt Allerman (LB) 1977–9, Jeff McIntyre (LB) 1980, Doak Field (LB) 1981, Craig Puki (LB) 1982, Bob Harris (LB) 1983–5, Freddie Nunn (DE) 1986, Ilia Jarostchuk (LB) 1987–9, Tony Buford (LB) 1987r, Jeroy Robinson (LB) 1990, David Merritt (LB) 1993–5, Tony McCombs (LB) 1997–8, Jason Starkey (C) 2000–3.

51 Marty Christenson (B) 1940, Pop Ivy (E) 1941–2, 1945–7, *Ed Rucinski* (E) 1943, Bernard Mertes (B) 1945, Frank Liebel (E) 1948, *Tom Wham* (E) 1949–51, *Leo Sanford* (C) 1952–7, Doug Eggers (LB) 1958, Ted Bates (LB) 1961–2, Dick Kasperek (C) 1966–8, Dave Olerich (LB) 1969–70, Don Parish (LB) 1972, Tom Brahaney (C) 1973–81, Kurt Allerman (LB) 1982–4, Rob Monaco (C) 1985, Mike Ruether (C) 1986–7, Gene Chilton (C) 1987, Keith Radecic (C) 1987r, Ricky Hunley (LB) 1988, Ron Burton (LB) 1989, Bill Lewis (C) 1990–2, Simon Shanks (LB) 1995, Lyron Cobbins (LB) 1997, Johnny Rutledge (LB) 1999–2001, Greg Jones (LB) 2002, James Darling (LB) 2003.

52 Marion Rushing (LB) 1959, 1962–5, Dave O'Brien (G) 1966–7, Rick Ogle (LB) 1971, Jack LeVeck (LB) 1973–4, Mike McDonald (LB) 1976, Mike McGraw (LB) 1976, Randy Gill (LB) 1978, Sean Clancy (LB) 1979–80, Charles Baker (LB) 1980–7, Jimmie Carter (LB) 1987r, Randy Kirk (LB) 1989, Chris Washington (LB) 1990, Jessie Small (LB) 1992, Willie Wright (TE) 1992, Wesley Leasy (LB) 1995–6, Mike Caldwell (LB) 1997, Zack Walz (LB) 1998–2001, Levar Fisher (LB) 2002–3.

53 George Faust (B) 1939, George Magulick (B) 1944, Bill Campbell (G) 1946–8, Jim Cain (E) 1949, Tony Klimek (E) 1951, Keever Jankovich (E) 1953, Jerry Tubbs (LB) 1957–8, Ernest Fritsch (C) 1960, Dave Simmons (LB) 1965–6, Jamie Rivers (LB) 1968–73, Steve Neils (LB) 1974–80, Craig Shaffer (LB) 1982–4, Wayne Davis (LB) 1987–8, Garth Jax (LB) 1989–95, Mark Maddox (LB) 1998–2000, Michael Young (LB) 2001–3.

54 Al Coppage (E) 1940–2, Don Currivan (E) 1943, Don Pierce (C) 1943, Frank Seno (B) 1945, Ted Wheeler (G) 1967–8, *Tom Banks* (C) 1971–80, *E.J. Junior* (LB) 1981–8, Reggie McKenzie (LB) 1989, David Braxton (LB) 1990–3, Darryl Hardy (LB) 1994–5, Aaron Graham (C) 1996–9, Sekou Sanyika (LB) 2000–1, Gerald Hayes (LB) 2003.

55 John Robbins (B) 1938–9, Vince Oliver (QB) 1945, Jake Colhouer (G) 1946–8, Bill Campbell (G) 1949, Ed Bagdon (G) 1950–1, Stan West (G) 1956–7, Jim Taylor (LB) 1957–8, Charles Ellzey (C) 1960–1, Bob Griffin (C/G) 1961, *Irv Goode* (G/C) 1962–71, Dave Bradley (G) 1972, Warren Koegel (G) 1973, Ray White (LB) 1975–6, Eric Williams (LB) 1977–82, Bill Whitaker (DB) 1983–4, Billy Davis (DB) 1984, Danny Spradlin (LB) 1985, Anthony Bell (LB) 1986–90, Jock Jones (LB) 1991–3, Wilbur Marshall (LB) 1994, Devon McDonald (LB) 1996, Patrick Sapp (LB) 1998–9, Ray Thompson (LB) 2000–3.

56 Coley McDonough (B) 1939, 1944, John Klumb (E) 1939, Rex Williams (C) 1940, Chip Healy (LB) 1969–70, Mike McGill (LB) 1971–2, Cal Withrow (LB) 1974, Tim Kearney (LB) 1976–81, Carlos Scott (C) 1983–5, Rick DiBernardo (LB) 1986, Ken Harvey (LB) 1988–93, Terry Irving (LB) 1994–8, Melvin Bradley (LB) 1999, LeVar Woods (LB) 2001–3.

57 Bill Davis (T) 1940–1, Ralph Fife (G) 1942, Bill Blackburn (C) 1946–50, *Jerry Groom* (C) 1951–5, Carl Brettschneider (LB) 1956–9, Mike Strofolino (LB) 1966–8, Don Parish (LB) 1970–1, Mark Arneson (LB) 1972–80, John Gillen (LB) 1981–2, Jim Eliopulos (LB) 1983, Chet Parlavecchio (LB) 1983, Niko Noga (LB) 1984–8, Peter Noga (LB) 1987r, Randy Kirk (LB) 1989, 1994–5, Kani Kauahi (C) 1989–91, 1993, Ronald McKinnon (LB) 1996–2003.

58 Mario Tonelli (B) 1940, Terry Miller (LB) 1971–4, Tim Black (LB) 1977, John Barefield (LB) 1978–80, Thomas Seabron (LB) 1980, Dave Ahrens (LB) 1981–4, Freddie Nunn (DE) 1985, Gene Chilton (C) 1986–7, Terrence Mack (LB) 1987, Eric Hill (LB) 1989–97, James Folston (LB) 1999–2001, Johnny Rutledge (LB) 2002.

59 Ernie Clark (LB) 1968, Jeff Lyman (LB) 1972, Pete Barnes (LB) 1973–5, Carl Gersbach (LB) 1976, Marv Kellum (LB) 1977, Curtis Townsend (LB) 1978, Calvin Favron (LB) 1979–82, Paul Davis (LB) 1983, Thomas Howard (LB) 1984–5, Phil Forney (LB) 1987r, Tyrone Jones (LB) 1988, David Bavaro (LB) 1990, Ed Cunningham (C) 1992–3, *Seth Joyner* (LB) 1994–6, Rob Fredrickson (LB) 1999–2002.

60 Jim German (B) 1940, Bob Kellogg (B) 1940, Gil Duggan (T) 1944, Ralph Foster (T) 1945, *Bob Shaw* (E) 1950, Gordon Polofsky (G) 1952–4, Harry Thompson (G) 1955, Dave Meggyesy (LB) 1963–9, Jim Hargrove (LB) 1971–2, *Conrad Dobler* (G) 1972, Roger Finnie (T) 1973–8, Barney Cotton (G) 1980–2, Al Baker (DE) 1983–6, Steve Alvord (DT) 1987–8, Willie Williams (T) 1990, Anthony Redmon (G) 1994–7, Thomas Burke (DE) 1999, Mike Gruttadauria (C) 2000–2.

61 **Charley Trippi** (B) 1947, Bob Ravensburg (E) 1948–9, Tony Klimek (E) 1952, Dave Suminski (G) 1953, Fred Wallner (G) 1954–5, Jack Patera (LB) 1958–9, Tom Day (G) 1960, *Bob DeMarco* (C) 1961–9, Henry Allison (T) 1975–7, Dan Audick (G) 1977, 1983, Chuck Brown (C/G) 1979–80, Chris Garlich (LB) 1979, Ron Coder (G) 1980–1, Lance Smith (G) 1985–93, Eric Floyd (G) 1995, Ryan Leahy (OL) 1997, Tony McCoy (DT) 2000, Jarvis Borum (T) 2001.

62 Libero Bertagnolli (G) 1942, Freeman Rexer (E) 1943, Lee Stokes (C) 1943, **Charley Trippi** (B) 1947–51, John Dittrich (G) 1956, *Dale Meinert* (LB) 1958–67, Martin Imhof (DE) 1972, Steve Wright (T) 1972, Dave Butz (DT) 1973–4, Keith Wortman (G) 1976–81, Dale Markham (T) 1981, Rick Kehr (G) 1982, Ramsey Dardar (DT) 1983–4, Ray Brown (T) 1986–8, Mike Zandofsky (G) 1989, Mike Brennan (G) 1991, Ben Coleman (T/G) 1993–5, Mike Devlin (C) 1996–9, Michael Cook (T) 2001.

63 John Shirk (E) 1940, Walt Rankin (B) 1941, Freeman Rexer (E) 1943, *Bob Zimny* (T) 1945, Bill Conoly (G) 1946, Dale Memmelaar (G) 1959, Fate Echols (T) 1962–3, Herschel Turner (G/T) 1964–5, Clyde Williams (T) 1967–71, Steve George (DT) 1974, John Zook (DE) 1976–9, Kirby Criswell (DE) 1980–1, Tootie Robbins (T) 1982–91, Michael Bankston (DL) 1992–7, Antonio Fleming (G) 1998, Frank Garcia (C) 2003.

64 Ray Ebli (E) 1942, Floyd Rhea (G) 1943, Lou Marotti (G) 1944–5, Ralph Foster (T) 1946, Dick Loepfe (T) 1948–9, Lloyd McDermott (T) 1950–1, Jim Lipinski (T) 1950, Mike Sikora (G) 1952, Gerry Watford (E) 1953–4, Larry Hartshorn (G) 1955, Doug Hogland (G) 1956–8, *Ken Gray* (G) 1958–69, *Bob Young* (G) 1972–9, Randy Clark (C) 1980–6, Todd Peat (G) 1987–9, Joe Bock (C) 1987r, Rick Cunningham (T) 1992–4, Jamie Dukes (C) 1995, James Dexter (T) 1996–9, Norberto Davidds-Garrido (T) 2000, Steve Grace (OL) 2002.

65 Jon Bilbo (T) 1939, Ed Hussman (G) 1953, John Hatley (G) 1954–5, Art Hauser (G) 1959, Michael Rabold (G) 1960, Thomas Redmond (DE) 1961–5, Ed Marcontell (G) 1967, Chuck Hutchison (G) 1970–2, Bob Crum (DE) 1974, Brad Oates (T) 1976–7, 1979–80, Tom Mullen (G) 1978, Jonathan Brooks (LB) 1980, David Galloway (DT) 1982–9, Ernest Dye (G) 1993–6, Anthony Clement (T) 1998–2003.

66 *Fred Gillies* (T) 1926–7, Clem Neacy (E) 1928, Milt Popovich (B) 1938–41, *John Grigas* (B) 1943–4, Libero Bertagnolli (G) 1945, Steve Enich (G) 1945, John Doolan (B) 1947–8, Jerry Hennessey (E) 1950–1, Ed Lipostad (G) 1952, Ed Hussman (G) 1955–9, Thomas Redmond (DE) 1960, Ron McDole (DE) 1961, John Houser (G/T) 1963, Rick Sortun (G) 1964–9, Mike LaHood (G) 1970, *Conrad Dobler* (G) 1972–7, George Collins (C) 1978–82, Doug Dawson (G) 1984–6, Tom Welter (G/T) 1987r, Jim Wahler (DT) 1989–92, Cecil Gray (G/T) 1995, Eric Jonassen (G) 1996–7, Ethan Brooks (T) 2000, Pete Kendall (G) 2001–3.

67 Joe Alton (T) 1942, 1944, Clarence Esser (E) 1947, Corwin Clatt (B) 1948–9, *Bill Svoboda* (LB) 1950–1, Bob Konovsky (G) 1956–8, *Larry Stallings* (LB) 1963–76, Bill Acker (DT) 1980–1, *Luis Sharpe* (T) 1982–94, Ron Pasquale (G) 1987r, Duval Love (G) 1995–6, Chris Dishman (G) 1997–2003.

68 Avery Monfort (B) 1941, Bob Maddock (G) 1942, Plato Andros (G) 1947–50, *Fred Wallner* (G) 1952, Nick Chickillo (G) 1953, Bill Lange (G) 1954–5, John Jennings (T) 1957, Michael McGee (G) 1960–2, Ed McQuarters (DT) 1965, Frank Roy (G) 1966, Mike Siwek (DT) 1970, Paul Dickson (DT) 1971, Mike Taylor (T) 1973, Terry Stieve (G) 1978–84, Mike Morris (G) 1987–8, Charles

Vatterott (T) 1987r, Joe Wolf (T/G) 1989–97, Yusuf Scott (G) 1999–2001, Tony Wragge (OL) 2002.

69 Gil Duggan (T) 1942, Clint Wager (E) 1943, 1945, Ray Apolskis (T) 1945, Tom Bienermann (E) 1951, Bobby Duncum (T) 1968, Andy Dorris (DE) 1973, Greg Kindle (T) 1974–5, Rush Brown (DT) 1980–3, Colin Scotts (DT) 1987–8, Victor Burnett (DE) 1987r, Vernice Smith (G/T) 1989–92, Mark Vander Poel (T) 1994, Eric Floyd (G) 1995, Allen DeGraffenreid (OL) 1997–8.

70 *Chet Bulger* (T) 1942–3, Tom Kearns (T) 1946, Sam Goldman (E) 1948, Knox Ramsey (G) 1950–1, John Jennings (T) 1952–6, Charley Toogood (G) 1957, Jim McCusker (T) 1958, Don Owens (DT) 1960–3, Rolf Krueger (DE) 1969–71, John Hoffman (DE) 1972, Leo Brooks (DE) 1973–6, Keith Simons (DT) 1978–9, Mark Goodspeed (T) 1980, Art Plunkett (T) 1981–4, Derek Kennard (G) 1986–89, Victor Perry (T) 1987r, Rob Baxley (T) 1992–3, Brian Bollinger (G) 1994, Lance Scott (C) 1995–6, Thomas Guynes (T) 1998, L.J. Shelton (T) 1999–2003.

71 Don Joyce (T) 1952–3, Tom Dahms (T) 1956, Bob Cross (T) 1958–9, Dale Memmelaar (G) 1960–1, *Bob Reynolds* (T) 1963–71, 1973, John Richardson (DT) 1972–3, Marvin Upshaw (DT) 1976, Joe Bostic (T) 1979–89, Mark Tucker (C) 1993–4, Larry Tharpe (T) 1995, Thomas Guynes (T) 1997, Lester Holmes (G) 1998–2000, Andy Bowers (DE) 2001, Teag Whiting (G) 2002.

72 *Bill Fischer* (T) 1949–53, Chuck Ulrich (T) 1954–8, Frank Fuller (DT) 1959–62, *Sam Silas* (DT) 1963–7, **Dan Dierdorf** (T) 1971–83, Dan Ralph (DT) 1984–6, Rod Saddler (DT) 1987–91, Anthony Burke (DT) 1987r, Chuckie Johnson (DT) 1993, Brandon Moore (T) 1995, Jerome Daniels (G) 1997–9, Jabari Issa (DE) 2000–1, Nate Dwyer (DL) 2002, Kenny King (DE) 2003.

73 Ed Beinor (E) 1940–1, Fred Vanzo (B) 1941, Champ Seibold (T) 1942, Gil Duggan (T) 1943, *Chet Bulger* (T) 1944–5, Ham Nichols (G) 1947–9, *Leo Sanford* (C) 1951, Mike Mergen (T) 1952, Tom Higgins (T) 1953, Ledio Fanucci (T) 1954, Dave Lunceford (T) 1957, Ed Culpepper (G) 1958–60, *Ernie McMillan* (T) 1961–74, Mike Dawson (DT) 1976–82, Mark Duda (DT) 1983–7, Scott Dill (T) 1988–9, Derek Kennard (G) 1990, Mark May (G/T) 1992–3, Sebastian Barrie (DT) 1994, Matt Joyce (OL) 1996–2000, Gary Hadd (DT) 1999, Raleigh Roundtree (G) 2002.

74 Rupert Pate (G) 1940, Len Teeuws (T) 1954–7, *Ken Panfil* (T) 1960–2, Ken Kortas (DT) 1964, Fred Heron (DT) 1966–72, Council Rudolph (DE) 1973–5, Walt Patulski (DE) 1977, Oudious Lee (DT) 1980, Ken Times (DT) 1981, Randy Holloway (DE) 1984, Scott Bergold (DT) 1985–6, Elston Ridgle (DE) 1990, Scott Evans (DL) 1991, Danny Villa (OL) 1992, Rob Selby (G) 1995–7,

Mike Moten (DT) 1998–9, John Fina (T) 2002, Reggie Wells (T) 2003.

75 Art Albrecht (T) 1943, *Ed Rucinski* (E) 1944, Vic Obeck (G) 1945, Ray Apolskis (T) 1946–50, Lynn Lynch (G) 1951, Dick Fugler (T) 1954, Tony Pasquesi (T) 1955–7, Ed Cook (G/T) 1960–5, Bob Rowe (DT) 1967–75, Bob Rozier (DE) 1979, Curtis Greer (DE) 1980–8, Shawn Knight (DT) 1989, Mike Graybill (T) 1990, Mike Jones (DE) 1991–3, Ernest Dye (G) 1994, Bernard Dafney (G) 1995, *Lomas Brown* (T) 1996–8, Darwin Walker (DT) 2000, Leonard Davis (G) 2001–3.

76 Lloyd Arms (G) 1946–8, Volney Peters (T) 1952–3, Bob Morgan (T) 1954, Burt Delevan (T) 1955–6, Harry Jagielski (T) 1956, Tom Finnin (T) 1957, Charles Lewis (T) 1959, George Hultz (DT) 1962, John McDowell (T) 1966, Vernon Emerson (T) 1969–71, Scott Palmer (DT) 1972, Ron Davis (DE) 1973, Charlie Davis (DT) 1975–9, Stafford Mays (DE) 1980–6, Mark Garalczyk (DT) 1987–8, Mark Traynowicz (G) 1988–9, Mark McDonald (G/C) 1988, Craig Patterson (DL) 1991, Rich Braham (G/T) 1994, Jerry Drake (DT) 1995–2000, Cameron Spikes (G) 2003.

77 John Hall (B) 1940–1, Milt Popovich (B) 1942, Lou Marotti (G) 1943, *Stan Mauldin* (T) 1946–8.

78 Ray Mallouf (QB) 1941, George Gilchrist (T) 1953, Wayne Bock (T) 1957, Luke Owens (DT) 1958–65, Ron Yankowski (DE) 1971–80, Elois Grooms (DE) 1982–5, Van Hughes (DT) 1986, Freddie Nunn (DE) 1987–93, Ron Bohm (DT) 1987r, Chadrick Brown (DE) 1993–5, Joe Staysniak (G) 1996, Brent Burnstein (DT) 1997, Carl Simpson (DE) 1998, Mao Tosi (DT) 2000–1.

79 Gerald Perry (K) 1960–2, *Charles Walker* (DL) 1964–72, Bonnie Sloan (DT) 1973, Bob Bell (DE) 1974–8, Jim Ramey (DE) 1979, Bruce Radford (DE) 1981, Bruce Thornton (DE) 1982, Gary Dulin (DE) 1986–7, Bob Clasby (DE) 1986–90, Keith Rucker (DT) 1992–3, Ed Cunningham (C) 1994–5, *Simeon Rice* (DE) 1996, Jon Clark (T) 1998–2000, Mario Fatafehi (DT) 2001, Calvin Pace (DE) 2003.

80 *Mal Kutner* (E) 1946–50, Don Stonesifer (E) 1951–6, John Tracey (LB) 1959–60, Ed Henke (DE) 1961–3, Dave Williams (WR) 1967–71, Jim McFarland (E) 1972–4, Jeff West (P) 1975, Eason Ramsen (TE) 1978, Tommy Southard (WR) 1978, Bill Murrell (TE) 1979, Chris Combs (TE) 1980–1, Doug Marsh (TE) 1982–4, Robert Awalt (TE) 1987–9, Bob Keseday (TE) 1987r, John Jackson (WR) 1991–2, Willie Wright (TE) 1992, Bryan Reeves (W) 1994–5, Pat Carter (TE) 1996–7, Terry Hardy (TE) 1998–2001, Mike Banks (TE) 2002, Jason McAddley (WR) 2003.

81 Keith Birlem (B) 1939, Joe Parker (E) 1947, Keever Jankovich (E) 1953, George Schmidt (E) 1953, Pat Summerall (K/E) 1953, **Night Train**

Lane (DB) 1954–9, Ted Bates (LB) 1959–60, Steve Meilinger (E) 1961, Jack Elwell (E) 1962, **Jackie Smith** (TE) 1963–77, Mark Bell (WR) 1981, *Roy Green* (DB/WR) 1982–90, Randal Hill (WR) 1991–4, Anthony Edwards (WR) 1991, Frank Sanders (WR) 1995–2002, *Anquan Boldin* (WR) 2003.

82 Leo Cantor (B) 1945, Caleb Martin (T) 1947, John Badaczewski (G) 1948, Marv Jacobs (T) 1948, John Goldsberry (T) 1949–50, Lou Ferry (T) 1951, Tom Bienermann (E) 1952–6, Mike Melinkovich (DE) 1965–6, Joe Schmiesing (DE) 1968–71, Martin Imhof (DE) 1972, Earl Thomas (WR) 1974–5, Bob Pollard (DE) 1978–81, Ricky Thompson (WR) 1982, Steve Bird (WR) 1983–4, Doug Marsh (TE) 1985–6, Ron Brown (WR) 1987, Greg Baty (TE) 1988, Phil McConkey (WR) 1989, Darryl Usher (WR) 1989, Butch Rolle (TE) 1992–3, Kevin Knox (WR) 1994, Patrick Robinson (WR) 1994, Stevie Anderson (WR) 1996, Ronnie Anderson (WR) 1998, Mac Cody (WR) 1999–2000, MarTay Jenkins (WR) 2000–2, Kevin Kaspar (WR) 2003.

83 Ray Pelfrey (E) 1952, Gary Knafelc (E) 1954, Max Boydston (E) 1955–8, Chuck Logan (E) 1965, 1967–8, Jim McFarland (E) 1970–1, *Pat Tilley* (WR) 1976–86, Don Holmes (WR) 1986–90, Ron Brown (WR) 1987, Anthony Edwards (WR) 1991–8, Derek Brown (TE) 1999–2000, Jason McAddley (WR) 2002, Bryant Johnson (WR) 2003.

84 Cliff Anderson (E) 1952–3, *Gern Nagler* (E) 1955–8, *Leo Sugar* (E) 1960, *Joe Robb* (DE) 1961–7, Walker Gillette (WR) 1972–3, Ike Harris (WR) 1975–7, Mike Schumann (WR) 1982–3, John Goode (TE) 1984, *J.T. Smith* (WR) 1985–90, Jay Novacek (TE) 1985, Clarence Collins (WR) 1987r, Tony Lomack (WR) 1991, Gary Clark (WR) 1993–4, Marcus Dowdell (WR) 1995–6, Chris Gedney (TE) 1997–8, 2000, Jay Tant (TE) 2000, Arnold Jackson (WR) 2001–2, Mike Banks (TE) 2003.

85 Jon Bilbo (T) 1939, Ralph Thomas (E) 1952, Pat Summerall (K/E) 1953–7, Perry Richards (E) 1959–60, Taz Anderson (E) 1961–4, *Mel Gray* (WR) 1971–82, Danny Pittman (WR) 1983–4, Jamie Williams (TE) 1983, Jay Novacek (TE) 1985–9, Tim Jorden (TE) 1990–91, Derek Ware (TE) 1992–4, *Rob Moore* (WR) 1995–2001, Freddie Jones (TE) 2003.

86 *Gern Nagler* (E) 1953, John Crittendon (E) 1954, Hugh McInnis (E) 1960–2, *Don Brumm* (DE) 1963–9, 1972, Mel Baker (WR) 1976, Jim Childs (WR) 1978–80, Ralph Clayton (WR) 1981, John Floyd (WR) 1981, Ken Thompson (WR) 1982–3, Clyde Duncan (WR) 1984–5, Chas Fox (WR) 1986, Adrian McBride (WR) 1987, Ernie Jones (WR) 1988–92, Chad Fann (TE) 1993–5, Trey Junkin (TE) 1996–2001, Kevin Jordan (WR) 1996, Bryan Gillmore (WR) 2000–3.

87 Babe Dimancheff (B) 1947–50, Ray Ramsey (B) 1950–3, Jim Ladd (E) 1954, Dick Brubaker (E)

1955, 1957, Charley Anderson (E) 1956, Maury Schleicher (LB) 1959, Chuck Bryant (E) 1962, Jerry Hillebrand (LB) 1967, Cal Snowden (DE) 1969–70, Jeff Staggs (LB) 1972–3, Terry Joyce (P) 1976–7, Al Chandler (TE) 1978–9, Jim Thaxton (TE) 1978, Richard Osborne (TE) 1979, Doug Marsh (TE) 1980–1, Eddie McGill (TE) 1982–4, Earnest Gray (WR) 1985, Troy Johnson (WR) 1986–7, Ricky Proehl (WR) 1990–4, Oscar McBride (TE) 1995, Johnny McWilliams (TE) 1996–9, Jay Tant (TE) 2000, Steve Bush (TE) 2001–3.

88 *Joe Kuharich* (G) 1940–1, Andy Puplis (B) 1943, George Sutch (B) 1946, Jeff Burkett (E) 1947, Floyd Sagely (E) 1957, *Sonny Randle* (WR) 1959–66, Fred Hyatt (WR) 1968–72, J.V. Cain (TE) 1974–7.

89 *Marshall Goldberg* (B) 1941, Jeff Burkett (E) 1947, Vic Schwall (B) 1948–50, Frank McPhee (E) 1955, Chuck Weber (LB) 1956–8, Dave Long (DE) 1966–8, Robert Brown (TE) 1969–70, Tom Beckman (DE) 1972, Warren Anderson (WR) 1978, Gary Parris (TE) 1979–80, Greg LaFleur (TE) 1981–5, Cap Boso (TE) 1986, William Harris (TE) 1987, Mark Walczak (TE) 1988, Walter Reeves (TE) 1989–93, Pat Beach (TE) 1993, Terry Samuels (TE) 1994, Wendall Gaines (TE/DT) 1995, Fred Brock (WR) 1996–8, Jarius Hayes (TE) 1996, *David Boston* (WR) 1999–2002, Larry Foster (WR) 2003, Nathan Poole (WR) 2003.

90 Robert Stallings (TE) 1986, Karl Wilson (DE) 1989, Eldonta Osborne (LB) 1990, Tyronne Stowe (LB) 1992–3, Keith McCants (DE) 1994–5, Mark Campbell (DT) 1997, Andre Wadsworth (DE) 1998–2000, Jarrett Procell (DE) 2001.

91 Gerry Lunz (G) 1925–6, *Fred Slater* (T) 1928, George Schmidt (E) 1953, Ron Monaco (LB) 1986, Tyronne Stowe (LB) 1991, Wendall Gaines (TE/DT) 1995, Rashod Swinger (DT) 1997–2000, Wendell Bryant (DL) 2002–3.

92 Richard Tardits (LB) 1989, Dexter Manley (DE) 1990, Brett Wallerstedt (LB) 1993, Eric England (DE) 1994–6, Jomo Cousins (DE) 1998, Angel Rubio (DT) 1999, Barron Tanner (DT) 2000–3.

93 Freddie Gilbert (DE) 1989, Sidney Coleman (LB) 1991, Reuben Davis (DE) 1992–3, Karl Dunbar (DE) 1994–5, Mark Smith (DT) 1997–2000, Kyle Vanden Bosch (DE) 2001–2.

94 Jeff Faulkner (DE) 1991–2, Bernard Wilson (DT) 1994–8, Corey Sears (DT) 1999–2000, Marcus Bell (DT) 2001–3.

95 Victor Burnett (DE) 1987r, Bob Buczkowski (DT) 1989, Dick Chapura (DT) 1990, Jamir Miller (LB) 1994–8, Thomas Burke (DE) 2000–2002, Derrick Ransom (NT) 2003.

96 Sean McNanie (DE) 1988, Chris Williams (DL) 1991, Clyde Simmons (DE) 1994–5, Brad Ottis (DT) 1996–2000, Dennis Johnson (DL) 2002–3.

97 Ray Busler (T) 1945, Chris Spachman (DE) 1988, Steve Hyche (LB) 1991–3, Bryan Hooks (DT) 1994, Chris Maumalanga (DT) 1995–6, *Simeon Rice* (DE) 1997–2000, Fred Wakefield (DE) 2001–3.

98 Ray Mallouf (QB) 1941, Carl Hairston (DT) 1990, *Eric Swann* (DT) 1991–9, Russell Davis (DT) 2000–3.

99 Mario Tonelli (B) 1940, *Marshall Goldberg* (B) 1946–8, Bob Nussbaumer (DB) 1949–50.

ATLANTA FALCONS

The franchise: In 1965 it appeared that the AFL was very close to adding Atlanta as a franchise city either with an expansion team or by the transfer of the troubled Denver Broncos team. Quickly, NFL Commissioner Pete Rozelle rounded up a local entrepreneur, insurance man H. Rankin Smith, to step in and claim the territory for the NFL as its 15th franchise and thwart the rival league. Although Atlanta stands as one of the top 10 television markets in the U.S., the team has met with only sporadic success with no championships, only one Super Bowl and seven playoff appearances, and a winning percentage (.398) second only to Tampa for ineptitude among established teams. This is a team that traded Brett Favre for a draft pick. This is a team that has never had a winning record for any decade. This is a team that hired Marion Campbell twice as its head coach, letting him go 17–51 over parts of six seasons. Only one non-interim coach, Leeman Bennett, has managed to leave Atlanta with a winning record and that was 20 years ago. Before Dan Reeves took the "Dirty Birds" to the Super Bowl following the 1998 season, Bennett's late–'70s playoff squads that relied on the relentless "Grits Blitz" defense and the passing of Steve Bartkowski and running of William Andrews on offense were the highpoint for the franchise. Therefore, the potential of Michael Vick is to be more than a great player, but to be a whole new face for this sorry Southern franchise that was purchased by Home Depot scion Arthur Blank in 2002.

Origin of name: After being awarded the NFL franchise in June 1965, owner Rankin Smith instituted a contest for fans to name the team. "Falcons" was entered by a number of people and was justified by the reasoning offered by a local school teacher Julia Elliott that "The Falcon is proud and dignified with great courage and fight. It never drops its prey. It's deadly and has a great sporting tradition."

Time till first championship: 38 years and counting.

Time since last championship: Never won one.

Retired numbers: The Falcons have retired four numbers which seems like a lot for a team with as thin a history as Atlanta has had. Steve Bartkowski, 10, was a good quarterback and William Andrews, 31, was a very good runner, but neither deserves their number retired. Jeff Van Note, 57, played for Atlanta for 18 years as a reliable center so maybe he deserves some sort of longevity

Record by Decade						
	Regular Season			Postseason		
	Won	Lost	Tied	Won	Lost	Championships
1960s	12	43	1	0	0	
1970s	60	81	3	1	1	
1980s	57	94	1	0	2	
1990s	72	88	0	3	3	
2000s	25	38	1	1	1	
All-Time	226	344	6	5	7	0

Winning seasons: 9. Losing seasons: 27. .500 seasons: 2.

Coaches

	Years	Record	Playoffs
Norb Hecker	1966–8	4–26–1	0–0
Norm Van Brocklin	1968–74	37–49–3	0–0
Marion Campbell	1974–6	6–19	0–0
Pat Peppler	1976	3–6	0–0
Leeman Bennett	1977–82	46–41	1–3
Dan Henning	1983–6	22–41–1	0–0
Marion Campbell	1987–9	11–32–0	0–0
Jim Hanifan	1989	0–4	0–0
Jerry Glanville	1990–3	27–37–0	1–1
June Jones	1994–6	19–29–0	0–1
Dan Reeves	1997–2003	49–59–1	3–2
Wade Phillips	2003	2–1	0–0

prize. Tommy Nobis, 60, is the only one of the four who really should have been so honored. He was the first draft pick of this expansion team and was an All Pro who very well may have gone to the Hall of Fame had it not been for bad knees and the fact that the team went 50–100–4 in his 11 years as a pro.

Other numbers worn by these players: None.

Those who wore retired numbers after the honored player: 10 was worn by quarterback Scott Campbell the year after Bartkowski left. 57 was worn again eight years after Van Note retired by linebacker Clay Matthews.

Numbers that should be retired: If he stays healthy, Michael Vick should finish off 7 for the Falcons. Long-time tackle Mike Kenn's 78 seems to be unofficially semi-retired since it has not been worn in 10 years.

Numbers worn by Hall of Famers: Eric Dickerson 29; Tommy McDonald 8.

Star power: Warrick Dunn took 28 from Corey Hall; Clay Mathews wore 57 despite the fact that it had been retired for Jeff Van Note.

Star eclipsed: Tommy McDonald wore 8 because Alex Hawkins wore 25. Michael Haynes wore 82 because Terance Mathis wore 81.

Numbers with most great players: 21 has been worn by runner Lynn Cain, All Pro cornerback Deion Sanders and star returners Eric Metcalf and Darrien Gordon.

Worst represented number: 14 has been worn by eight quarterbacks who never amounted to anything for anybody.

Number worn by the most players: 51 has been worn by 19 different players.

Player who wore the most numbers: Several have worn two numbers, but no one has worn more than that.

Longest tenure wearing a number: The aforementioned Jeff Van Note wore 57 for 18 years. Tackle Mike Kenn wore 78 for 17 years.

Number worn by first ever draft pick: 60 by Tommy Nobis, 1966.

Biggest draft busts: The Falcons have had several draft busts including runner Joe Profit, 23, who was selected seventh in 1971 and gained 197 yards in three years and defensive back Bruce Pickens, 39, who was selected third in 1991 and picked off two passes in three years. The biggest bust, though, would be pass rusher Aundray Bruce, 93, who was the first pick in the 1988 draft, but would only start 41 games over his 11 year career, the first four of which were spent in Atlanta.

Number worn by first player: Bob Paremore and Gary Barnes were the first players signed by the Falcons as free agents on September 9, 1965. Barnes made the team and wore 80. Of the players chosen from the expansion draft, only Junior Coffey (34) was still with the team four years later in 1969.

Number worn by oldest player: Steve Deberg wore 17 as a 44 year old in 1998. Jeff Van Note and Clay Matthews played at 40 in 1986 and 1996 respectively, both while wearing 57.

Cameos: Hall of Famers—Tommy McDonald 8 and Eric Dickerson 29; All Pros and other notables—Steve Deberg 17; Wade Wilson 18; Larry Morris 33; and 77 Bruce Bosley.

One who got away: Brett Favre 4.

Least popular numbers: 2 has only been worn by returner Clarence Verdin for two years and 60 was only worn by Tommy Nobis before it was retired.

Last number to be originated: 97 was first worn by Jumpy Geathers in 1993.

Longest dormant number: 8 has not been worn since 1986.

Triskaidekaphobia notes: 13 has been worn by four quarterback nonentities and one decent punter (Chris Mohr).

Shared numbers: 12 was represented by two good quarterbacks, Chris Miller and Chris Chandler; 34 has been worn by two decent runners (Junior Coffey and Craig Heyward) and one star cornerback (Ray Buchanan); 50 was worn by linebackers Greg Brezina and Buddy Curry; 81 has been worn by three star receivers (Billy Johnson, Michael Haynes, and Terance Mathis); 87 has been worn by defensive end Claude Humphrey and receiver Bert Emanuel.

Continuity: Tough runner Iron Head Heyward was replaced in 34 by tough cornerback Ray Buchanan; White Shoes Johnson was replaced in 81 by receiver Michael Haynes who in turn was replaced by all-time leading Falcon receiver Terance Mathis.

Discontinuity: Steve Bartkowski, the team's best quarterback, was followed in 10 by journeyman Scott Campbell.

Family connections: None

Numbers of future NFL head coaches: Herman Edwards 46; June Jones 11.

Players who played other sports: Baseball—Deion Sanders 21 and Brian Jordan 40. Wrestling—Bill Goldberg 71.

Players more famous after football: Author (and broadcaster) Tim Green, 99.

First player to wear a number in the '90s: Linebacker Johnnie Taylor wore 96 in 1984.

Number with most points scored: 5 with 924 points scored by: Morten Andersen (620), Greg Davis (236), Harmon Wages (60) and Brad Daluiso (8).

Number with most yards rushing: 42 with 6,631 yards gained by Gerald Riggs.

Number with most receptions: 81 with 1,146 passes caught by Terance Mathis (573), Michael Haynes (266), Billy Johnson (166), Peerless Price (64), Wes Chesson (40), Trevor Gaylor (25), Dennis Pearson (5), Gerald Tinker (4), Ralph Smith (2), and Bob Adams (1).

Number with most touchdown passes: 12 with 174 touchdowns tossed by Chris Miller (87) and Chris Chandler (87).

Number with most interceptions: 34 with 71 passes picked off by Ray Brown (31), Ray Buchanan (30), Robert Moore (8), and Blane Gaison (2).

Oddity: The Falcons have employed a lot of players with feminine names. Excluding common dual sex names like Chris, Terry, Pat and Lee, female-sounding Falcons include—6 Ali Haji-Sheikh, 11 Kim McQuilken, 14 June Jones, 15 Gail Cogdill, 21 Lynn Cain, 31 Molly McGee, 32 Tracey Eaton, 33 Ashley Ambrose, 51 Karon Riley, 77 Rosie Manning, 82 Stacey Bailey, and 83 Aubrey Matthews. The coach could either be the already-noted June Jones or perennially-unsuccessful Marion Campbell.

Players Whose Number Is Unknown		
Kent Lawrence	(TE)	1970
Garth Ten Napel	(LB)	1978
Tony Zackery	(DB)	1989

Team All-Time Numerical Roster

Those with an "r" following the year 1987 were replacement players during the players' strike. Pro Bowl players for each number are in *Italics*; Hall of Famers are in **Bold** type.

1 Fred Steinfort (K) 1977–8, Ralph Giacommaro (P) 1983–8, Jeff George (QB) 1994–95.

2 Clarence Verdin (KR) 1994.

3 *Bob Etter* (K) 1968–9, David Smigelesky (P) 1982, Rick Donnelly (P) 1985–8, John Starnes (P) 1987r, *Bobby Hebert* (QB) 1993–6, Scott Bentley (K) 1997.

4 Tim Mazzetti (K) 1978–80, Brett Favre (QB)

1991, Scott Tyner (P) 1994, Dan Stryzinski (P) 1995–2000, Jay Feely (K) 2001–3.

5 Harmon Wages (RB) 1968–71, 1973, Greg Davis (K) 1987–90, Brad Daluiso (K) 1991, Harold Alexander (P) 1993–4, *Morten Andersen* (K) 1995–2000.

6 *John James* (P) 1972–81, Ali Haji-Sheikh (K) 1986, Louis Berry (P) 1987r, Paul McFadden (K) 1989.

7 Wade Trayman (K) 1966–7, Pat Sullivan (QB) 1972–5, Hugh Millen (QB) 1988–90, Perry Klein (QB) 1994–5, Browning Nagle (QB) 1996, Tony Graziani (QB) 1999, *Michael Vick* (QB) 2001–3.

8 **Tommy McDonald** (WR) 1967, Kenny Vinyard (K) 1970, Bob Holly (QB) 1984–5, Steve Dils (QB) 1986.

9 Larry Fortner (QB) 1980, *Norm Johnson* (K) 1991–4.

10 Dennis Claridge (QB) 1966, Leo Hart (QB) 1971, *Steve Bartkowski* (QB) 1975–85, Scott Campbell (QB) 1986–90.

11 Randy Johnson (QB) 1966–70, Dick Shiner (QB) 1971–3, Kim McQuilken (QB) 1974–7, Kerwin Bell (QB) 1988, Billy Joe Tolliver (QB) 1996–7, Doug Johnson (QB) 2000–3.

12 *Nick Mike-Mayer* (K) 1973–7, George Roberts (P) 1982, *Chris Miller* (QB) 1987–92, *Chris Chandler* (QB) 1997–2001.

13 Billy Joe Tolliver (QB) 1991, 1993, Browning Nagle (QB) 1995, Tony Graziani (QB) 1997–8, Danny Kanell (QB) 1999–2000, Chris Mohr (P) 2001–3.

14 Steve Sloan (QB) 1966–7, Terry Nofsinger (QB) 1967, June Jones (QB) 1977–9, Jeff Komlo (QB) 1982, Turk Schonert (QB) 1986, Erik Kramer (QB) 1987r, Bob Gagliano (QB) 1993, Wally Richardson (QB) 1999.

15 Gail Cogdill (WR) 1969–70, Mike Moroski (QB) 1979–84, Jim Miller (QB) 1997, Eugene Baker (WR) 1999, Kurt Kittner (QB) 2002–3.

16 Scott Hunter (QB) 1976–8, Reggie Smith (WR) 1980–1, David Archer (QB) 1984–7.

17 *Bob Berry* (QB) 1968–72, Scott Fulhage (P) 1989–92, Steve DeBerg (QB) 1998.

18 Bruce Lemmerman (QB) 1968–9, Mike Luckhurst (K) 1981–7, Wade Wilson (QB) 1992.

19 Mike Brunson (WR/RB) 1970, Bob Lee (QB) 1973–4, Corey Dixon (WR) 1994, Shawn Mills (WR) 2001–2.

20 Bob Riggle (S) 1966–7, Tom McCauley (S/WR) 1969–71, Vince Kendrick (RB) 1974–5, Earl Jones (DB) 1980–3, Wendell Cason (CB) 1986–7, Struggy Smith (DB) 1987r, Evan Cooper (DB) 1988, Brad Edwards (S) 1994, Michael Booker (CB) 1997–9, Ron Rivers (RB) 2000, Rodney Thomas (RB) 2001, Allen Rossum (KR) 2002–3.

21 Tom Moore (RB) 1967, Lynn Cain (RB)

1979–84, Jimmy Turner (CB) 1986–7, Charles Huff (DB) 1987r, *Deion Sanders* (CB) 1989–93, Eric Metcalf (KR) 1995–6, Elijah Williams (CB) 1998–2000, Darrien Gordon (KR) 2001, Juran Bolden (DB) 2002–3.

22 Lee Calland (CB) 1966–8, John Mallory (S) 1969, *Rolland Lawrence* (DB) 1973–80, Richard Williams (RB) 1983, Sean Thomas (DB) 1985, Dennis Woodberry (CB) 1986, Brenard Wilson (S) 1987, Charles Dimry (DB) 1988–90, Tim McKyer (CB) 1991–2, Alton Montgomery (S) 1993–5, Lenny McGill (CB) 1997, Gerald McBurrows (S) 1999–2003.

23 Jeff Stanciel (RB) 1969, Joe Profit (RB) 1971–3, *Bobby Butler* (CB) 1981–92, Gary Moss (DB) 1987r, Ronnie Bradford (CB) 1997–2001, Kevin Mathis (CB) 2002–3.

24 Jimmy Sidle (RB/TE) 1966, Floyd Hudlow (DB) 1967, Nate Wright (S) 1969, Haskel Stanback (RB) 1974–9, David Toloumu (RB) 1982, Joe Washington (RB) 1985, Larry Emery (RB) 1987, Shelley Poole (RB) 1987r, Mike Pringle (RB) 1990, Brian Mitchell (CB) 1992–3, Terry Taylor (CB) 1995, Patrick Bates (S) 1996, Byron Hanspard (RB) 1997–9, Terry Cousin (CB) 2000, Fred Weary (CB) 2002, Brian Scott (CB) 2003.

25 Alex Hawkins (WR) 1966–7, Mike Fitzgerald (WR) 1967, Rick Eber (RB) 1968, Art Malone (RB) 1970–4, Larry Crowe (DB) 1975, Ray Strong (RB) 1978–82, *Scott Case* (DB) 1984–94, Leon Thomasson (DB) 1987r, Devin Bush (S) 1996–8, Marty Carter (S) 2000, Elijah Williams (CB) 2001, Derek Ross (CB) 2003.

26 Billy Lothridge (P/S) 1966–71, Mike Esposito (RB) 1976–9, James Britt (DB) 1983–7, Jerome Norris (DB) 1987r, Louis Riddick (S) 1992, Anthony Phillips (CB) 1994–6, Darren Anderson (CB) 1998, Keith Thibodeaux (CB) 1999, Winslow Oliver (RB) 2000.

27 Red Mack (WR) 1966, Nick Rassas (S) 1966–8, Tom Hayes (CB) 1971–5, Tom Pridemore (S) 1978–85, Calvin Loveall (CB) 1988, Vinnie Clark (CB) 1993, Brad Edwards (S) 1995–6, Omar Brown (S) 1998–9, Cory Hall (S) 2003.

28 Ray Ogden (TE) 1967–8, Mike Freeman (DB) 1969–70, Willie Belton (RB) 1971–2, Frank Reed (DB) 1976–80, Bret Clark (S) 1986–8, Undra Johnson (RB) 1989, Pat Chaffey (RB) 1991, Tony Smith (RB) 1992–3, Ron Davis (DB) 1995, Lenny McGill (DB) 1996, Harold Green (DB) 1997–8, Ken Oxendine (RB) 1999, Corey Hall (S) 2001–2, Warrick Dunn (RB) 2002–3.

29 Ron Rector (RB) 1966–7, Clarence Ellis (CB) 1972–4, Ron Mabra (DB) 1975–6, Sylvester Stamps (RB) 1986–8, Joe Fishback (S) 1992, **Eric Dickerson** (RB) 1993, Louis Riddick (S) 1996, Randy Fuller (CB) 1998, Keion Carpenter (S) 2002–3.

30 Ernie Wheelwright (FB) 1966–7, Doug

Goodwin (RB) 1968, Larry Shears (CB) 1971, Joe Washington (RB) 1973, Oscar Reed (RB) 1975, Ernie Jackson (CB) 1978, Scott Woerner (DB) 1981, Steve Haworth (DB) 1983–4, David Croudip (DB) 1985–8, Lydell Jones (DB) 1987r, Mike Rozier (RB) 1990–1, Terry Ray (S) 1992, Lemuel Stinson (S) 1993, Derrick Gardner (CB) 1999, Henry Jones (S) 2002, Woody Dantzler (S) 2003.

31 Charlie Scales (RB) 1966, Dwight Lee (RB) 1968, Willie Germany (S) 1972, Molly McGee (RB) 1974, *William Andrews* (RB) 1979–83, 1986.

32 Rudy Johnson (RB) 1966, Preston Ridlehuber (RB) 1966, Charles Bryant (RB) 1969, Grady Cavness (CB) 1970, Ray Easterling (S) 1972–9, Tim Tyrrell (RB) 1984–6, Norm Granger (RB) 1987r, Tracey Eaton (S) 1991–3, *Jamal Anderson* (RB) 1994–2001, Tod McBride (CB) 2003.

33 Larry Morris (LB) 1966, Jim Mankins (RB) 1967, Jim Butler (RB) 1968–71, Henry Matthews (RB) 1973, Ricky Patton (RB) 1978, Anthony Anderson (RB) 1980, Bo Robinson (RB) 1981–3, Tiger Greene (S) 1985, Leander Knight (CB) 1988, Gene Lang (RB) 1988–9, Erric Pegram (RB) 1993–4, Richard Huntley (RB) 1996, Ken Oxendine (RB) 1998, Winslow Oliver (RB) 1999, Ashley Ambrose (CB) 2000–2, Justin Griffith (RB) 2003.

34 Junior Coffey (RB) 1966–7, Ray Brown (S) 1971–8, Blane Gaison (S) 1981–4, Robert Moore (S) 1986–8, Mike Lush (DB) 1987r, Steve Broussard (RB) 1990–2, David Mims (WR) 1993, *Craig Heyward* (RB) 1994–6, *Ray Buchanan* (CB) 1997–2003.

35 Bill Harris (RB) 1968, Tony Plummer (S) 1971–3, Reggie Pleasant (DB) 1985, Keith Williams (RB) 1986, Mike Pritchard (WR) 1991–3, William White (S) 1997–8, Johndale Carty (S) 1999–2002.

36 *Ken Reaves* (DB) 1966–73, Rudy Holmes (DB) 1974, Bob Glazebrook (DB) 1978–83, Danny Wagoner (DB) 1985, Greg Paterra (FB) 1989, Eric Bergeson (DB) 1990, Brian Mitchell (CB) 1991, Kevin Ross (RB) 1994–5, Travis Jervey (RB) 2001–3.

37 Perry Lee Dunn (RB) 1966–8, Bill Bell (K) 1971–2, Kenny Johnson (DB) 1980–6, *Elbert Shelley* (S) 1987–96, Leander Knight (DB) 1987r, Darrick Vaughn (DB) 2000–2, Tyrone Williams (CB) 2003.

38 Joe Auer (RB) 1968, Rick Byas (DB) 1974–80, Keith Jones (RB) 1989–90, 1992, Rich Miano (S) 1995, Nate Odomes (CB) 1996, George Layne (FB) 2002–3.

39 Billy Ray Pritchett (RB) 1976–7, James Mayberry (RB) 1979–81, Cliff Austin (RB) 1984–6, Major Everett (RB) 1987, Roland Mitchell (CB) 1990, Bruce Pickens (DB) 1991–2, Eric Jack (CB) 1994, Siddeeq Shabazz (S) 2003.

40 Ron Smith (CB/WR) 1966–7, Paul Gibson (RB) 1969–70, Ron Lamb (RB) 1972, Bob Jones (DB) 1975–6, George Franklin (RB) 1978, Eddie Meyers (RB) 1982, Brian Jordan (DB) 1989–91, Anthony Wallace (RB) 1993, Jeff Paulk (FB) 1999.

41 Brendon McCarthy (RB) 1968, Al Dodd (WR) 1973–4, Sonny Collins (RB) 1976, Secedrick McIntyre (RB) 1977, Virgil Seay (WR) 1984, Tony Baker (RB) 1986, Tim Gordon (S) 1987–90, Erric Pegram (RB) 1991–2, Brett Maxie (S) 1994, *Eugene Robinson* (S) 1998–9, George Layne (FB) 2001–2.

42 Phil Spiller (S) 1968, Jim Weatherford (S) 1969, Mack Herron (RB) 1975, John Gilliam (WR) 1976, *Gerald Riggs* (RB) 1982–8, Michael Williams (RB) 1987r, Jeff Donaldson (S) 1991–3, Devin Bush (S) 1995, Sean Boyd (S) 1996.

43 Jerry Richardson (DB) 1966–7, Mike Freeman (DB) 1968, Monte Ledbetter (WR) 1969, Dave Hampton (RB) 1972–5, Tom Tutson (DB) 1983, Tracy Johnson (RB) 1990–1, Juran Bolden (DB) 1996–7, Maurice Smith (RB) 2000–2, Travaris Robinson (S) 2003.

44 Bill Wolski (RB) 1966, Jerry Simmons (WR) 1967–9, Eddie Ray (RB) 1972–4, Bubba Bean (RB) 1976–80, Rodney Tate (RB) 1984, *John Settle* (RB) 1987–90, Steve Broussard (RB) 1993, D.J. Johnson (C) 1994–5, Bob Christian (FB) 1997–2002.

45 Carl Silvestri (DB) 1966, Dave Dunaway (WR) 1968, John Wright (WR) 1968, Gary McDermott (RB) 1969, Sonny Campbell (RB) 1970–1, Tom Moriarty (S) 1977–9, Ken Wisenhunt (TE) 1985–8, Darryl Oliver (RB) 1987r, Darnell Walker (CB) 1993–6, Gary Downs (RB) 1997–2000, T.J. Duckett (RB) 2002–3.

46 Larry Suchi (CB) 1968, Ray Jarvis (WR) 1971–2, Monroe Eley (RB) 1975–8, Reggie Brown (RB) 1982, Herm Edwards (CB) 1986, Geno Zimmerlink (TE) 1987r, Charles Washington (S) 1992–4.

47 Rudy Redmond (CB) 1969–71, Brad Davis (RB) 1975, Mike Spivey (CB) 1982, Rick Badanjek (RB) 1987–8, John Kamana (TE/LB) 1987r, Roger Harper (S) 1993–5, Chris Bayne (S) 1997–8, Chris Hudson (S) 2001, Kevin McCadam (S) 2002–3.

48 Angelo Coia (WR) 1966, Tom Bleick (S) 1967, Ollie Cordill (WR) 1968, Woody Thompson (RB) 1975–7, Gerald Small (CB) 1984, Ray Phillips (LB) 1986, Kenny Flowers (RB) 1987, Joe McIntosh (RB) 1987r, Darryl Ford (LB) 1993, Marcus Wimberly (S) 1997, Derek Rackley (TE) 2000–3.

49 Glenn Glass (WR) 1966, Floyd Hudlow (DB) 1968, Jimmy Burson (DB) 1968, Al Lavan (S) 1969–70, Al Matthews (TE) 1983–5, James Primus (RB) 1988–9, Brian Saxton (TE) 1997, Dallas Neil (TE/P) 2000–2.

50 Jerry Jones (DT) 1966, *Greg Brezina* (LB) 1968–9, 1971–9, Buddy Curry (LB) 1980–7, Ron George (LB) 1993–6, Ed Sutter (LB) 1997, Lamont

Green (LB) 1999, Corey Atkins (LB) 2000, Artie Ulmer (LB) 2001–3.

51 Bob Whitlow (C) 1966, Andy Bowling (LB) 1967, Ted Cottrell (LB) 1969–70, Duane Benson (LB) 1972–3, Dick Palmer (LB) 1974, Jim Cope (LB) 1976, Andy Spiva (LB) 1977, Brian Cabral (LB) 1979, Jim Laughlin (LB) 1980–2, 1987, Rich Dixon (LB) 1983, Jeff Jackson (LB) 1984–5, Reggie Wilkes (LB) 1986–7, Herb Spencer (LB) 1987r, Marcus Cotton (LB) 1988–90, Wes Pritchett (LB) 1991, Howard Dinkins (LB) 1993, Jim Ritcher (G) 1994–5, David Brandon (LB) 1996–7, Jeff Kelly (LB) 1999–2002, Karon Riley (LB) 2002–3.

52 Marion Rushing (LB) 1966–8, Ron Acks (LB) 1968–71, Ken Mitchell (LB) 1973–4, Dewey McClain (LB) 1976–80, Lyman White (LB) 1981–2, John Harper (LB) 1983, Rydell Malancon (LB) 1984, Rich Kraynak (LB) 1987, Art Price (LB) 1987r, Vinson Smith (LB) 1988, Ken Tippins (LB) 1990–5, Craig Sauer (LB) 1996–9, Matt Stewart (LB) 2001–3.

53 Frank Marchlewski (C) 1966–8, Phil Sobocinski (C) 1968, John Matlock (C) 1970–1, Paul Ryczek (C) 1974–9, Chuck Correal (C) 1980, Neal Musser (LB) 1981–83, Thomas Benson (LB) 1984–5, Doug Barnett (C) 1987, Jim Hendley (C) 1987r, Galand Thaxton (LB) 1989, Dwayne Gordon (LB) 1993–4, Jamal Fountaine (LB) 1997, Mark Simoneau (LB) 2000–2, Keith Newman (LB) 2003.

54 Bob Sanders (LB) 1967, Grady Allen (LB) 1969–72, Fulton Kuykendall (LB) 1975–84, Joel Williams (LB) 1986–9, Eric Wiegand (C) 1987r, Robert Lyles (LB) 1990–1, Jesse Solomon (LB) 1992–3, Ruffin Hamilton (LB) 1997–9, Chris Draft (LB) 2000–3.

55 Ralph Heck (LB) 1966–8, Roy Schmidt (G/T) 1969, Jim Miller (G) 1971–2, Ralph Ortega (LB) 1975–8, Tony Daykin (LB) 1979–81, Dave Levenick (LB) 1983–4, Wayne Radloff (C) 1986–8, Mike Ruether (C) 1990–3, Nate Miller (OL) 1995–7, Whit Marshall (LB) 1999, Antony Jordan (LB) 2000, John Thierry (DE) 2002, Twan Russell (LB) 2003.

56 Joe Cerne (C) 1968, Dennis Havig (G) 1972–5, Guy Roberts (LB) 1976, Ron McCartney (LB) 1977–9, Al Richardson (LB) 1980–5, Joe Costello (LB) 1986–8, Darion Conner (LB) 1990–3, *Chris Doleman* (DE) 1994–5, Scott Fields (LB) 1996, *Keith Brooking* (LB) 1998–2003.

57 Bill Jobko (LB) 1966, Dick Absher (LB) 1967–8, *Jeff Van Note* (C) 1969–86, Clay Matthews (LB) 1994–6.

58 Don Hansen (LB) 1969–75, Jim Weatherley (C) 1976, Rick Kay (LB) 1977, Steve Stewart (LB) 1978, Joel Williams (LB) 1979–82, David Frye (LB) 1983–5, Ken Bowen (LB) 1987r, *Jessie Tuggle* (LB) 1987–2000.

59 Jim Ferguson (C) 1969, Jim Waskiewicz (C)

1969, Dean Halverson (LB) 1970, Rudy Kuechenberg (LB) 1971, Noel Jenke (LB) 1972, Lonnie Warwick (LB) 1973–4, Carl Russ (LB) 1975, Robert Pennywell (LB) 1977–80, Paul Davis (LB) 1981–2, John Rade (LB) 1983–91, Paul Gray (LB) 1987r, Lorenzo Styles (LB) 1995–6, Ben Talley (LB) 1998, John Holecek (LB) 2002, Sam Rogers (LB) 2003.

60 *Tommy Nobis* (LB) 1966–76.

61 Bill Sandeman (T) 1967–73, John Brooks (LB) 1980, Chuck Correal (C) 1980, Chuck Herman (G) 1980, John Scully (C) 1981–8, 1990, Robbie Tobeck (C) 1993–9, Anthony Redmon (G) 2000, Ellis Johnson (DT) 2002–3.

62 Gary Roberts (G) 1970, John Bramlett (LB) 1971, Brent Adams (T) 1975–8, Robert Jackson (LB) 1982, Brett Miller (T) 1983–8, Greg Quick (T) 1987r, Keith Alex (G) 1993, Dave Richards (G) 1994–5, Todd McClure (C) 1999–2003.

63 Jim Wilson (C) 1967, Dick Enderle (G) 1969–71, Nick Bebout (T) 1973–5, Greg Kindle (G) 1976, Mike Zele (DT) 1979–83, Jeff Kiewel (G) 1985–7, Evan Pilgrim (G/C) 1999–2000, Roberto Garza (G/C) 2001–3.

64 Tom Harmon (G) 1967, Randy Winkler (G) 1968, Andy Mauer (G) 1970–3, Royce Smith (G) 1974–6, Pat Howell (G) 1979–83, Joe Pellegrini (C) 1984–6, Jamie Dukes (G) 1987–93, Jeff Pahukoa (G/T) 1995–6, Bob Hallen (G) 1998–2001, Martin Bibla (G) 2002–3.

65 Lou Kirouac (G/K) 1966–7, Jake Kupp (G) 1967, Steve Duich (G) 1968, Bob Breitenstein (G/T) 1969–70, Lynn Gotshalk (T) 1972–6, Don Smith (DE) 1979–84, Lawrence Pillers (DT) 1985, Guy Bingham (C/G) 1989–91, Roman Fortin (C) 1993–7, Greg Bishop (G) 1999, Kynan Forney (G) 2001–3.

66 Jim Simon (G/T) 1966–8, John Small (DT) 1970–2, Ted Fritsch (C) 1973–5, Warren Bryant (T) 1978–83, Chuck Thomas (G) 1985, Billy Hinson (G) 1986, Randy Clark (C/T) 1987r, Tommy Robison (G) 1989, Joe Sims (T) 1991, Lincoln Kennedy (T) 1993–4, Michael Thompson (T) 2000–2.

67 Dan Grimm (G) 1966–8, Malcolm Snider (G/T) 1969–71, Walt Brett (G) 1976, Eric Sanders (T) 1981–6, Mark Mraz (DE) 1987, Paul Oswald (G) 1988, Malcolm Taylor (DE) 1989, Moe Gardner (NT) 1991–6, Adam Schreiber (C/G) 1997–8, Wes Shivers (T) 2000, Mike Malano (G) 2002, Michael Moore (G) 2003.

68 Bobby Richards (DE) 1966–7, Dave Hettema (T) 1970, Frank Gallagher (G) 1973, Larry Bailey (DT) 1974, Larron Jackson (G) 1975–7, *R.C. Thielemann* (G) 1977–84, Dennis Harrison (DE) 1986–7, Lawrence Jackson (G) 1987r, John Hunter (T) 1990, Mel Agee (DL) 1992–5, Calvin Collins (C/G) 1997–2000.

69 Mike Lewis (DT) 1971–9, Dan Benish (DT)

1983–6, Houston Hoover (T) 1988–92, Thomas Williams (DE) 1994, Gene Williams (G/T) 1995–9.

70 Rich Marshall (DT) 1966, Bob Hughes (DE) 1967, 1969, Jim Norton (DT) 1967–8, Kenny Vineyard (K) 1970, Dave Scott (T) 1976–82, Ron Lee (OL) 1983, Mike Chapman (G) 1984, Willard Goff (DT) 1985, Tony Bowick (NT) 1989, Reggie Redding (T) 1991, *Bob Whitfield* (T) 1992–2003.

71 Joe Szczecko (DT) 1966–8, *John Zook* (DE) 1969–75, Steve George (DT) 1976, Marv Montgomery (T) 1978, Mike Perko (DT) 1982, Dan Dufour (C/G) 1983–4, Glen Howe (T) 1985–6, Mark Studaway (DE) 1987r, Mitchell Young (DE) 1987r, *Chris Hinton* (T) 1990, Bill Goldberg (DT) 1992–4, Scott Adams (G/T) 1997, Travis Claridge (G/T) 2000–3.

72 Don Talbert (T) 1966–8, Greg Lens (DT) 1970–1, Jim Bailey (DT) 1976–8, Matthew Teague (DE) 1981, Andrew Provence (DT) 1983–7, Buddy Moor (DE) 1987r, Leonard Wingate (DT) 1987r, Ben Thomas (DE) 1989, Oliver Barnett (DT) 1990–2, Mike Zandofsky (G) 1994–6.

73 Errol Linden (T) 1966–8, David Cahill (DT) 1969, Phil McKinnely (T) 1976–80, Mike Simeta (DT) 1983, Gary Burley (DT) 1984, Leonard Mitchell (T) 1987, Doug Mackie (T) 1987r, Mitch Willis (DT) 1988, John Washington (DE) 1992, Ernie Logan (DE) 1993, Dunstan Anderson (DL) 1994, Ethan Brooks (DT/OL) 1996, Dave Kadela (T) 2001–2, Dwayne Morgan (T) 2003.

74 Karl Rubke (DT) 1966–7, Art Strahan (DT) 1968, Bill Sabatino (DT) 1969, Jim Sullivan (DE) 1970, Mike Tilleman (DT) 1973–6, Wilson Faumuina (DT) 1977–81, Mike Pitts (DE) 1983–6, Don Robinson (T) 1987r, Dan Clayton (T/G) 1988–9, Tory Epps (NT) 1990–3, Jeff Zgonina (DT) 1996, Ephraim Salaam (T) 1998–2001, Todd Weiner (T) 2002–3.

75 Ed Cook (G) 1966–67, *George Kunz* (T) 1969–74, Jeff Merrow (DE) 1975–83, Roy Harris (DT) 1984–5, Tony Casillas (DT) 1986–90, Dwight Bingham (DE) 1987r, *Chris Hinton* (T) 1991–3, Irv Eatman (T) 1994, Lincoln Kennedy (G/T) 1995, Shane Dronett (DT) 1997–2002.

76 Guy Reese (DT) 1966, Jim Garcia (DL) 1968, Mike Gann (DE) 1985–93, Dwaine Morris (NT/DT) 1987r, Antone Davis (T) 1997, Jose Portilla (T) 1998–9, Chris Banks (G) 2000, Kevin Shaffer (T) 2002–3.

77 Chuck Sieminski (DT) 1966–7, Bruce Bosley (C) 1969, Rosie Manning (T) 1972–5, Ron East (DT) 1976, Edgar Fields (DT) 1977–80, Doug Rodgers (DE) 1982, Rick Bryan (DT) 1984–92, Matt Willig (T) 1997, Pellom McDaniels (DE) 1999–2000.

78 Rich Koeper (T) 1966, Jerry Shay (DT) 1968–9, Greg Marx (DT) 1973, Roy Hilton (DE) 1975, Bill Windauer (DT) 1976, *Mike Kenn* (T) 1978–94.

79 Carlton Dabney (DT) 1968, Cleo Walker (LB) 1971, Chuck Walker (DT) 1972–5, Jeff Yeates (DT) 1976–84, *Bill Fralic* (G/T) 1985–91, Dave Widell (G) 1998, Henry Taylor (DT) 2000, Ronald Flemons (DE) 2001–2.

80 Gary Barnes (WR) 1966–7, Bob Long (WR) 1968, Bob Jones (WR) 1969, Todd Snyder (WR) 1970–2, Louis Neal (WR) 1973–4, Karl Farmer (WR) 1976–7, *Junior Miller* (TE) 1980–3, Mike Landrum (TE) 1984, Ron Heller (TE) 1989, *Andre Rison* (WR) 1990–4, Tyrone Brown (WR) 1995–6, Tony Martin (WR) 1998, Chris Calloway (WR) 1999, Eugene Baker (WR) 2000, Bobby Collins (TE) 2002, Willie Jackson (WR) 2002, Terrence Edwards (WR) 2003.

81 Bo Wood (DE) 1967, Ralph Smith (TE) 1969, Wes Chesson (WR) 1971–3, Gerald Tinker (WR) 1974–5, Bob Adams (TE) 1976, Dennis Pearson (WR) 1978–9, *Billy Johnson* (WR) 1982–7, James Shibest (WR) 1987r, Michael Haynes (WR) 1988–93, *Terance Mathis* (WR) 1994–2001, Trevor Gaylor (WR) 2002, Peerless Price (WR) 2003.

82 Bob Sherlag (WR) 1966, Bob Lee (WR) 1969, Ken Burrow (WR) 1971–5, Billy Ryckman (WR) 1977–9, Stacey Bailey (WR) 1982–90, Jason Phillips (WR) 1991–3, Leonard Harris (WR) 1994, Michael Haynes (WR) 1997, Ronnie Harris (WR) 1998–9, Mareno Philyaw (WR) 2000–1, Darrin Chiaverini (WR) 2002, LaTarence Dunbar (WR) 2003.

83 Tom Hutchinson (WR) 1966, Larry Mialik (TE) 1972–74, James Wright (TE) 1978–9, Floyd Hodge (WR) 1982–4, Aubrey Matthews (WR) 1986–8, Brad Beckman (TE) 1989, Tony Jones (WR) 1992, Ricky Sanders (WR) 1994–5, Ed West (TE) 1997, Tim Dwight (WR) 1998–2000, *Alge Crumpler* (TE) 2001–3.

84 Vern Burke (WR) 1966, Mike Donohoe (TE) 1968, 1970–1, Thomas Geredine (WR) 1973–4, *Alfred Jenkins* (WR) 1975–83, Sylvester Stamps (WR) 1984–5, Joey Jones (WR) 1986, Milton Barney (WR) 1987r, James Milling (WR) 1988, 1990, Darryl Spencer (WR) 1994, Freddie Scott (WR) 1996, Mercury Hayes (WR) 1997, Rod Monroe (TE) 1998–9, Shawn Jefferson (WR) 2000–2.

85 Billy Martin (TE) 1966–7, Paul Flatley (WR) 1968–9, Ray Poage (TE) 1971, Alfred Jackson (WR) 1978–84, Anthony Allen (WR) 1985–6, Kwante Hampton (WR) 1987r, Lew Barnes (WR) 1988, Shawn Collins (WR) 1989–90, Drew Hill (WR) 1992–3, David Mims (WR) 1994, Roell Preston (KR) 1995–6, Brian Kozlowski (TE) 1997–2003.

86 Tommy Tolleson (WR) 1966, *Jim Mitchell* (TE) 1969–79, Mike Smith (WR) 1980, Ben Young (TE) 1983, Perry Tuttle (WR) 1984, Floyd Dixon (WR) 1986–91, Steve Griffin (WR) 1987r, Mitch Lyons (TE) 1993–6, Ed Smith (TE) 1997–8, Bryan Still (WR) 1999, Brian Finneran (WR) 2000–3.

87 Taz Anderson (TE) 1966–7, *Claude Humphrey* (DE) 1968–74, 1976–8, Russ Mikeska (TE) 1979–83, Cliff Benson (TE) 1984–5, Ron Middleton (TE) 1986–7, John Evans (TE) 1987r, Danzell Lee (TE) 1988–9, Gary Wilkins (TE) 1989–90, James Milling (WR) 1992, Bert Emanuel (WR) 1994–7, Jammi German (WR) 1998–2000, Jimmy Farris (WR) 2003.

88 Sam Williams (DE) 1966–7, Glen Condren (DT) 1969–72, Henry Childs (TE) 1974, Greg McCrary (TE) 1975–7, Lewis Gilbert (TE) 1978–9, Clay Brown (TE) 1982, Keith Krepfle (TE) 1982, Arthur Cox (TE) 1983–7, Sylvester Byrd (TE) 1987r, Alex Higdon (TE) 1988, Troy Sadowski (TE) 1990, Harper LeBel (TE) 1992–6, O.J. Santiago (TE) 1997–9, Quentin McCord (WR) 2001–2.

89 Rich Cash (DE) 1968, Randy Marshall (DE) 1970–1, Wallace Francis (WR) 1975–81, Willie Curran (WR) 1982–4, Charlie Brown (WR) 1985–7, Leon Gonzalez (WR) 1987r, Jessie Hester (WR) 1988–9, George Thomas (WR) 1990–1, J.J. Birden (WR) 1995–6, Todd Kinchen (WR) 1997–8, Reggie Kelly (TE) 1999–2002, Sean Brewer (TE) 2003.

90 Chuck Smith (DE) 1992–9, Ron Moore (DT) 2001–2, Will Overstreet (LB) 2003.

91 Aaron Brown (LB) 1986–7, John Burrough (DT) 1995–8, Ben Huff (DT) 1999, Brady Smith (DE) 2000–3.

92 Ronnie Washington (LB) 1985, Lenny Taylor (WR) 1987r, George Yarno (C/G) 1988–9, Lester Archambeau (DE) 1993–9, Terrence Robinson (LB) 2003.

93 Aundray Bruce (LB) 1988–91, Dan Owens (DT) 1996–7, Shawn Swayda (DE) 1998–2001, Sam Rogers (LB) 2002.

94 Charles Martin (DT) 1988, Henri Crockett (LB) 1997–2001.

95 Michael Reid (LB) 1987–92, Pierce Holt (DE) 1993–5, Esera Tuaolo (DT) 1998, Ed Jasper (DT) 1999–2003.

96 Johnnie Taylor (LB) 1984–6, Dan Sharp (TE) 1987, James Hall (LB) 1987r, Gary Wilkins (TE) 1988–9, Reggie Camp (DE) 1988, Todd Kelly (DE) 1996, Anthony Pleasant (DE) 1997, Antonio Edwards (DE) 1998.

97 Jumpy Geathers (DT) 1993–5, Cornelius Bennett (LB) 1996–8, Patrick Kerney (DE/LB) 1999–2003.

98 Greg Brown (DE) 1987–8, Travis Hall (DT) 1995–2003.

99 Tim Green (DE) 1986–93, Darryl Talley (LB) 1995, Nathan Davis (DT) 1997, Chuck Wiley (DE) 2000–1, Demetrin Veal (DE) 2003.

BALTIMORE RAVENS

The franchise: The official NFL story is that the Ravens franchise began new in 1996 and returned football to the city of Baltimore after an 11 year absence, sort of a corporate immaculate conception. Actually, the Ravens are the original Cleveland Browns who deserted Cleveland after 50 years of vigorous fan support because the team could not extort a new stadium out of the city. The situation was so ugly that in the aftermath Cleveland got the NFL to promise that the city could reinstate the franchise as an expansion team once their new stadium was constructed. Original Ravens owner Art Modell, who since has sold the team to Steve Biscotti, still does not return to Cleveland because he is so reviled there.

Meanwhile, the Ravens took all the Browns players to Baltimore and hired popular former Baltimore Colts coach Ted Marchibroda to try to build a winner. The City of Baltimore has its own troubled history with pro football, and that is recounted in the Colts chapter. After three years Marchibroda was replaced by the hottest assistant coach in 1999, Brian Billick of the Vikings. Billick has proven to be a good choice, winning a Super Bowl in his second season with one of the most devastating defenses in league history. In another sign of professional football today, that team was decimated by salary cap problems within a year and missed the playoffs in 2002. Quickly rebuilt with youth, however, the Ravens won their first division title in 2003.

Origin of name: The naming of the Baltimore Ravens is one more example of the corporate nature of the NFL. The team couldn't simply hold a naming contest. Instead, NFL Properties developed a list of 100 possibilities that the club narrowed to 17. Then Baltimore-area focus groups reduced those 17 to six. Then, step four, a telephone survey produced three finalists: Ravens, Marauders and Americans. Finally, in step five, a phone-in poll, 21,000 of 33,000 respondents selected Ravens. Ultimately, it was a pretty smart choice since American literary giant and one-time Baltimore resident Edgar Allan Poe's most famous poem is "The Raven."

Record by Decade

	Regular Season			Postseason		
	Won	Lost	Tied	Won	Lost	Championships
1990s	24	39	1	0	0	
2000s	39	25	0	5	2	2000
All-Time	63	64	1	5	2	1

Winning seasons: 3. Losing seasons: 4. .500 seasons: 1.

Time till first championship: Five years.
Time since last championship: Three Years.

Coaches

	Years	Record	Playoffs
Ted Marchibroda	1996–8	16–31–1	0–0
Brian Billick (1)	1999–03	47–33	5–2

(Championships in parentheses)

Retired numbers: None.
Numbers that should be retired: When Ray Lewis retires, 52 will belong to him.
Owned numbers: It is doubtful that anyone will ever wear 52 after Ray Lewis retires.
Numbers worn by Hall of Famers: None.
Star power: Shannon Sharpe took 82 from Frank Wainwright.
Star eclipsed: Orlando Brown wore 78 because Ethan Brooks wore 77.
Number worn by the most players: 85 has been worn by six players.
Player who wore the most numbers: No one has worn more than two, several have worn two.
Longest tenure wearing a number: Eight years (1996–03) for 3 players, Matt Stover, 52, Ray Lewis, and 75, Jonathan Ogden.

Number worn by first ever draft pick: 75 by Jonathan Ogden, picked number one in 1996.
Biggest draft busts: Travis Taylor, 89, was selected 10th in 2000 but has averaged only 44 catches a year with 15 total touchdowns.
Number worn by oldest player: 38 year old Randall Cunningham wore 1 in 2001.
Cameos: All Pros and other notables—Jeff Blake 18; Ben Coates 81; Randall Cunningham 1; Elvis Grbac 18; Carnell Lake 37.
One who got away: Priest Holmes, 33, has been an All Pro touchdown-making machine in Kansas City.
Least popular numbers: Five numbers have yet to be worn —13, 17, 40, 46, and 68.
Last number to be originated: In 2002, 2, 6, 25, 26 and 47 were all worn for the first time.
Longest dormant number: The five unworn numbers above.
Triskaidekaphobia notes: 13 has not yet been worn. Perhaps it could be retired for the ghost of Edgar Allan Poe.
Shared numbers: 33 was worn by three runners who had their greatest success elsewhere — Priest Holmes, Leroy Hoard and Bam Morris.
Continuity: Powerful, but troubled runner Bam Morris was replaced in 33 by multidimensional runner Priest Holmes.
Discontinuity: Jamie Sharper was followed in 55 by fellow linebacker Bernardo Harris who was a former teammate of Jamie's brother Darren on Green Bay.
Family connections: None.
Players who played other sports: None.
Players more famous outside of sports: Ray Lewis gained a great deal of notoriety by being arrested on murder charges although he was exonerated. The Ravens have also employed a non-singing Michael Jackson and a non-revolutionary Sam Adams.

Number with most points scored: 3 with 889 points scored by Matt Stover.

Number with most yards rushing: 31 with 4,757 yards gained by Jamal Lewis.

Number with most receptions: 87 with 293 passes caught by Quadry Ismail (191), Floyd Turner (70) and Marcus Robinson (32).

Number with most touchdown passes: 12 with 76 touchdowns tossed by Vinny Testaverde (51) and Tony Banks (25).

Number with most interceptions: 22 with 20 passes picked off by Duane Starks and 26 with 20 picks by Rod Woodson.

Oddity: When the old Browns moved to Baltimore, two players switched numbers on their new jerseys— Derrick Alexander wore 85 for the Browns and 82 for the Ravens, while James Jones wore 96 for the Browns and 97 for the Ravens.

Team All-Time Numerical Roster

Pro Bowl players for each number are in *Italics*; Hall of Famers are in **Bold** type.

1 Randall Cunningham (QB) 2001.
2 Anthony Wright (QB) 2002–3.
3 *Matt Stover* (K) 1996–2003.
4 Jim Harbaugh (QB) 1998.
5 Kyle Richardson (P) 1998–2001.
6 J.R. Jenkins (K) 2002.
7 Chris Redman (QB) 2000–3.
8 Trent Dilfer (QB) 2000, Kyle Boller (QB) 2003.
9 Greg Montgomery (P) 1996–7, Wade Richey (K) 2003.
10 Eric Zeier (QB) 1996–8, Stony Case (QB) 1999.
11 Marcus Nash (WR) 1999.
12 *Vinny Testaverde* (QB) 1996–7, Tony Banks (QB) 1999–2000, Danny Kight (K) 2001.
13 none.
14 Wally Richardson (QB) 1998.
15 Dave Zastudil (P) 2002–3.
16 Milton Wynn (WR) 2002.
17 none.
18 Elvis Grbac (QB) 2001, Jeff Blake (QB) 2002.
19 Scott Mitchell (QB) 1999.
20 Kim Herring (S) 1997–2000, *Ed Reed* (S) 2002–3.
21 Earnest Byner (RB) 1996–7, *Chris McAlister* (CB) 1999–2003.
22 Dorian Brew (DB) 1996–7, Duane Starks

(CB) 1998–2001, Robert Tate (CB) 2002, Tom Knight (CB) 2003.
23 Randy Baldwin (RB) 1996, Earnest Hunter (RB) 1996, Kenyon Cotton (FB) 1997–8, Moe Williams (RB) 2001, Dameon Hunter (RB) 2002.
24 Donny Brady (DB) 1996–8, Alvin Porter (DB) 2001–2.
25 DeRon Jenkins (DB) 1996–9, Ray Perryman (DB) 2002.
26 Priest Holmes (RB) 1997, *Rod Woodson* (DB) 1998–2001, Corey Fuller (CB) 2003
27 Stevon Moore (S) 1996–9, Gerome Sapp (S) 2003.
28 Gary Baxter (DB) 2001–3.
29 *Eric Turner* (DB) 1996, Lamar Lyons (DB) 1997, Charlie Evans (FB) 1999–2000, Terry Allen (RB) 2001, Chester Taylor (RB) 2003.
30 Eugene Daniel (CB) 1997, Obafemi Ayandadejo (FB) 1999–2001.
31 Rondell Jones (S) 1997, *Jamal Lewis* (RB) 2000–3.
32 Errict Rhett (RB) 1998–9, Sam Gash (FB) 2000–2, Musa Smith (RB) 2003.
33 Leroy Hoard (RB) 1996, Bam Morris (RB) 1996–7, Priest Holmes (RB) 1997–2000, Reggie Wadell (DB) 2001, Harold Morrow (RB) 2003.
34 Jay Graham (RB) 1997–9, Ovie Mughelli (RB) 2003.
35 Carwell Gardner (FB) 1996, Robert Bailey (DB) 2000, Clarence Love (DB) 2000.
36 Isaac Booth (DB) 1996, Corey Dowden (DB) 1996, John Williams (CB) 1997–8.
37 *Bennie Thompson* (DB) 1996–9, Carnell Lake (S) 2001.
38 Antonio Langham (DB) 1996–7, James Trapp (DB) 1999–2002, Raymond Walls (CB) 2003.
39 Alan Ricard (RB) 2001–3.
40 none.
41 Ralph Staten (S) 1997–8.
42 Roosevelt Potts (FB) 1998, Anthony Mitchell (DB) 2001–2.
43 Vashone Adams (S) 1996, Anthony Poindexter (S) 2000.
44 Tony Vinson (RB) 1997, 1999, Jason Brookins (RB) 2001.
45 Corey Harris (S) 1998–2001, Lamont Brightful (DB) 2002–3.
46 none.
47 Will Demps (S) 2002–3.
48 Frank Hartley (TE) 1996.
49 Ryan Collins (TE) 1999, Chad Williams (DB) 2002–3.
50 Keith Goganious (LB) 1996, Brad Jackson (LB) 1998–2001.
51 Mike Croel (LB) 1996, Cornell Brown (LB) 1997–2002.
52 *Ray Lewis* (LB) 1996–2003.
53 Dexter Daniels (LB) 1996, Tyrell Peters (LB) 1997–9, T.J. Slaughter (LB) 2003.

54 Ed Sutter (LB) 1996, Tyrus McCloud (LB) 1997–8, Shannon Taylor (LB) 2001–2.

55 Sedric Clark (LB) 1996, Jamie Sharper (LB) 1997–2001, Bernardo Harris (LB) 2002, Terrell Suggs (LB) 2003.

56 Mike Caldwell (LB) 1996, Jerry Olsavsky (LB) 1998, Anthony Davis (LB) 2000, Edgerton Hartwell (LB) 2001–3.

57 Jerrol Williams (LB) 1996, Jeff Kopp (LB) 1998, O.J. Brigance (LB) 2000, Bart Scott (LB) 2002–3.

58 *Peter Boulware* (LB) 1997–2003.

59 Craig Powell (LB) 1996, Joe Maese (C) 2001–3.

60 Jeff Mitchell (C) 1998–2000.

61 Steve Everitt (C) 1996, Everett Lindsay (OL) 1999, Casey Rabach (C/G) 2002–3.

62 Leo Goeas (OL) 1997, Mike Flynn (C) 1999–2003.

63 Wally Williams (OL) 1996–8, Mike Collins (OL) 2002.

64 Sale Isaia (G) 1996, Edwin Mulitalo (G) 1999–2003.

65 Ben Cavil (OL) 1997–8, Jason Thomas (OL) 2002–3.

66 Tony Jones (T) 1996, John Hudson (C) 2000, Bennie Anderson (OL) 2001, 2003

67 Quentin Neujahr (C) 1996–7, Adam Hernandez (OL) 1998.

68 none

69 Jeff Blackshear (G) 1996–9, Aubrayo Franklin (DT) 2003.

70 Herman Arvie (OL) 1996, Mike Flynn (OL) 1998, Harry Swayne (OL) 1999–2000, Dale Hellestrae (C) 2001, David Nugent (DL) 2002.

71 Spencer Folau (OL) 1997–2000.

72 Bernard Dafney (OL) 1997, Sammy Williams (OL) 2000–1, Damion Cook (OL) 2002–3.

73 Tim Goad (DT) 1996, Kelly Gregg (DT) 2001–2.

74 James Atkins (OL) 1997–9, Orlando Bobo (OL) 2000–1.

75 *Jonathan Ogden* (T) 1996–2003.

76 Carl Powell (DE) 2000, Erik Williams (T) 2001, Jarret Johnson (DE) 2003.

77 Orlando Brown (T) 1996–8, Kipp Vickers (OL) 2000–1, Ethan Brooks (T) 2002–3.

78 Dan Footman (DL) 1996, Orlando Brown (T) 2003.

79 Larry Webster (DT) 1997–01.

80 Calvin Williams (WR) 1996, Ryan Yarborough (WR) 1997–8, Lovett Purnell (TE) 1999, Brandon Stokely (WR) 1999–2002.

81 Michael Jackson (WR) 1996–8, Aaron Pierce (TE) 1999, Ben Coates (TE) 2000, Randy Himes (WR) 2002, Frank Sanders (WR) 2003.

82 Derrick Alexander (WR) 1996–7, Harper LeBel (TE) 1998, Frank Wainwright (TE) 1999, *Shannon Sharpe* (TE) 2000–1, Terry Jones (TE) 2003.

83 James Roe (WR) 1996–8, Patrick Johnson (WR) 1999–2001, Ron Johnson (WR) 2002–3.

84 *Jermaine Lewis* (KR) 1996–2001, Javin Hunter (WR) 2002.

85 Ray Ethridge (WR) 1996–7, Patrick Johnson (WR) 1998, Greg DeLong (TE) 1999, John Jones (TE) 2000, Jonathan Burrough (TE) 2001, Dedric Ward (WR) 2003.

86 Billy Davis (WR) 1999–2000, *Todd Heap* (TE) 2001–3.

87 Floyd Turner (WR) 1996, 1998, Nate Singleton (WR) 1997, Qadry Ismail (WR) 1999–2001, Jeff Ogden (WR) 2002, Marcus Robinson (WR) 2003.

88 Brian Kinchen (TE) 1996–8, Justin Armour (WR) 1999, Frank Wainwright (TE) 2000, John Jones (TE) 2001–3.

89 Harold Bishop (TE) 1996, Al Ofodile (TE) 1997–9, Travis Taylor (WR) 2000–3.

90 Rob Burnett (DE) 1996–2001, Cornell Brown (LB) 2003.

91 Elliott Fortune (DL) 1996, Lionel Dalton (DT) 1998–2001, Riddick Parker (DL) 2002–3.

92 Leland Taylor (DL) 1997, Martin Chase (DT) 1999, Ma'ake Kemoeatu (DL) 2002–3.

93 Keith Washington (DE) 1997–2000.

94 Mike Frederick (DL) 1996–8, Marques Douglas (DL) 1999, 2001–3.

95 Rick Lyle (DL) 1996, Chris Ward (DL) 1997, Paul Frase (DE) 1998, *Sam Adams* (DT) 2000–1, Howard Green (DL) 2002.

96 Fernando Smith (DE) 1999, *Adalius Thomas* (DE) 2000–3.

97 James Jones (DL) 1996–8, Kelly Gregg (DT) 2003.

98 Anthony Pleasant (DE) 1996, Tony Siragusa (DT) 1997–2001, Anthony Weaver (DE) 2002–3.

99 *Mike McCrary* (DE) 1997–2002.

BUFFALO BILLS

The franchise: Buffalo has had charter franchises in three professional football leagues and has a lengthy history of supporting those teams. The Buffalo All-Americans were a charter member of the NFL (or American Professional Football Association as it was called in 1920). An initial success on the field, the team was derailed when several key players were suspended for simultaneously playing semi-pro football. Under different owners and names (All-Americans was followed by Bisons, Rangers and then Bisons again), the franchise lasted until the end of the 1920s. Buffalo was represented in the 1930s and early 1940s by franchises in two unsuccessful American Football Leagues, and then the Buffalo Bills became a charter member of the All-America Football Conference in 1946. Four years later when the AAFC merged with the NFL, only three teams were taken in: the two best teams, Cleveland and San Francisco, and, oddly, the last place Baltimore Colts. Buffalo fans immediately started a drive to get the Bills accepted into the NFL, raising $200,000 and selling 15,000 season tickets in a month, but were rebuffed by the established league.

Finally ten years later in 1959, today's Buffalo Bills were born as the seventh charter member of the newly formed American Football League. Ralph Wilson, a Detroit insurance man and minority stockholder in the Detroit Lions, originally sought to field a team in Miami, but met with resistance there so he turned his sights northward to upstate New York. In the intervening 44 years, the Bills have had four periods of success on the field intermixed with some fairly bad stretches. The first period began when Lou Saban became coach in 1962 and built the best team in the AFL as a mirror image of Vince Lombardi's Green Bay Packers—a ball control offense and punishing defense. That team won AFL championship in 1964 and 1965, but lost the 1966 title game (and the chance to go to the first Super Bowl) to the Chiefs.

By then, Saban was gone and the team collapsed.

Saban returned in 1972 to rescue the floundering career of O.J. Simpson and the second period of success featured O.J. running behind a skilled offensive line known as the "Electric Company" because they turned on the juice. The team made the playoffs once, Saban left again and the team declined again. Two years later in 1978, new coach "Ground Chuck" Knox rebuilt the Bills again with defense and the rushing offense of Joe Cribbs. Twice the Bills made the playoffs under Knox before sinking in the standings.

In 1986, Marv Levy was brought in and he led the Bills to their greatest success over the next decade, highlighted by an unprecedented four consecutive trips to the Super Bowl. Unfortunately for Bills fans, those were four consecutive losses. The toughness of Bills fans is reflected in the dark 1998 independent film "Buffalo 66" that touches tangentially but significantly on the frustrating history of the team. From "The Rockpile" of crumbling War Memorial Stadium to the chilling wind known as "The Hawk" at Rich Stadium, Ralph Wilson made the Bills a part of Buffalo—so much so that city fathers renamed the Bills' home Ralph Wilson Stadium in 1998. Now under a new coaching regime, the rebuilding continues and the championship dream remains.

Origin of name: The Bills were named in honor of their predecessors in the AAFC. That team was originally called the Bisons like the former NFL team and the existing minor league baseball and hockey teams. To differentiate themselves, the team held a contest in 1946 to come up with a new name and received over 4,500 entries. While several of them suggested Bills, James Dyson was chosen as the winner for comparing the team to frontier trailblazer Buffalo Bill Cody. Ralph Wilson decided to carry on that tradition in 1960.

Time till first championship: Five years

Record by Decade

	Regular Season			Postseason		
	Won	Lost	Tied	Won	Lost	Championships
1960s	65	69	6	2	2	1964, 1965 (AFL)
1970s	51	91	2	0	1	
1980s	69	83	0	2	4	
1990s	103	57	0	10	8	
2000s	25	39	8	0	0	
All-Time	313	339	8	14	15	2 (AFL)

Winning seasons: 20. Losing seasons: 21. .500 seasons: 2.

Coaches

	Years	Record	Playoffs
Buster Ramsey	1960–1	11–16–1	0–0
Lou Saban	1962–5	36–17–3	2–1
Joel Collier	1966–8	13–16–1	0–1
Harvey Johnson	1968	1–10–1	0–1
John Rauch	1969–70	7–20–1	0–0
Harvey Johnson	1971	1–13	0–0
Lou Saban	1972–6	32–28–1	0–1
Jim Ringo	1976–7	3–20	0–0
Chuck Knox	1978–82	38–36	0–2
Kay Stephenson	1983–5	10–26	0–0
Hank Bullough	1985–6	4–17	0–0
Marv Levy	1986–1997	132–104	11–8
Wade Phillips	1998–2000	29–19	0–2
Gregg Williams	2001–3	17–31	0–0

to AFL Championship; no NFL Championships in 38 years of Super Bowls.

Time since last championship: 38 years since last AFL Championship.

Retired numbers: 12 for Hall of Fame quarterback Jim Kelly, the leader of the K-Gun offense that went to four straight Super Bowls in the 1990s.

Other numbers worn by these players: None.

Those who wore retired numbers after the honored player: None.

Numbers that should be retired: 78 defensive end Bruce Smith, future Hall of Famer and all-time sack leader who spent 15 years in Buffalo.

Owned numbers: None.

Numbers worn by Hall of Famers: Joe DeLamielleure 68; Jim Kelly 12; James Lofton 80/86; Billy Shaw 66; and O.J. Simpson 32/36.

Star power: Takeo Spikes took 51 from Da-Shon Polk.

Star eclipsed: James Lofton wore 86 till Flip Johnson, 80, left. O.J. Simpson wore 36 till Gary McDermott, 32, left. Cornelius Bennett wore 55 till Scott Radecic, 97, left. Stew Barber wore 64 till Don Chelf, 77, left.

Numbers with most great players: For 23 out of 24 seasons from 1973 through 1996, 12 was worn by the two best quarterbacks in team history, Joe Ferguson and Jim Kelly; Daryle Lamonica also wore 12. 78 was worn by future Hall of Famer Bruce Smith and All Pro defensive linemen Jim Dunaway and Tom Day. 80 was worn by Hall of Famer James Lofton, All Pro Eric Moulds, and stars Jerry Butler and Bill Brooks. 20 has been worn by Pro Bowl runners Joe Cribbs and Travis Henry as well as star defensive backs Robert James and Henry Jones.

Worst represented numbers: Is it worse to be worn by six bad quarterbacks and one weak kicker over 11 seasons (17) or by only one bad quarterback and one bad receiver over two seasons (19)?

Number worn by the most players: 75 and 85 have been worn by 21 different Bills.

Player who wore the most numbers: Defensive end/guard Tom Day wore five numbers—60/64/78/88/89.

Longest tenure wearing a number: Bruce Smith wore 78 for 15 years from 1985 through 1999.

Number worn by first ever draft pick: Quarterback Richie Lucas was the first pick in 1960 and wore 11.

Biggest draft busts: Tight end Tony

Hunter, 49/87/90, was something of a bust, selected 12th in 1983 and gone in two years.

Number worn by oldest player: Bruce Smith, 78, James Lofton, 80, and Jim Kelly, 12, all were playing at age 36.

Cameos: All Pros and other notables— Dan Abramowicz 46; Vince Ferragamo 5; Billy Joe 33; Lawrence McCutcheon 30; Lemar Parrish 24; Art Powell 84; and Mike Pruitt 33/41.

Ones who got away: Daryle Lamonica 12; Tom Keating 74; and Bill Miller 81— all of whom would star for the Raiders.

Least popular numbers: 0 has never been worn. 2 has been worn by kicker Steve Christie and 44 has only been worn by two players.

Last number to be originated: 2 was first worn by Christie in 1992.

Longest dormant number: 2 was dormant for 32 years until 1992. Currently, 32 has been dormant for 26 years. Since it was O.J. Simpson's number, it is not so much dormant as it is radioactive.

Triskaidekaphobia notes: 13 has only been worn by three forgettables— quarterback Sam Wyche, replacement player Brian McClure, and kicker Chuck Nelson.

Shared numbers: 34 was worn by the first great running back in the AFL, Cookie Gilchrist and by the all-purpose running back star Thurman Thomas; 67 was worn by two stalwart offensive linemen who each played for the Bills for 11 years, guard Reggie McKenzie and center Kent Hull.

Continuity: Solid guard from Michigan Joe O'Donnell was replaced in 67 by solid guard from Michigan Reggie McKenzie.

Discontinuity: The best fullback in the league, Cookie Gilchrist, was followed in 34 by Don Stone; Hall of Fame guard Joe DeLamielleure was followed in 68 by two part-time nose tackles (Jerry Boyarsky and Mark Catano); a defensive end who would spend 18 years in the NFL, Ron McDole, was followed in 72 by a tackle who spent two games in the league, Bob Hews.

Quarterback numbers over 19: 21 Tom Flores; 40 Ed Rutkowski.

Number of first black player: In the Bills' first year they employed five blacks— end

Family Connections			
Brothers			
Charlie King	DB	1966–7	43/47
Tony King	DB	1967	46

Monte Crocket 80, receiver Elbert "Golden Wheels" Dubenion 44, halfback Wilmer Fowler 23, defensive end Leroy Moore 87, and defensive tackle Jim Sorey 79.

Numbers of future NFL head coaches: Tom Flores 16/21; Jim Haslett 55; Marty Schottenheimer 56/57; Kay Stephenson 18.

Numbers of future NFL referees: None.

Players who played other sports: None.

Players more famous after football: Guard Bob Kalsu, 61, was one of two NFL players killed in the Vietnam War. Quarterback Jack Kemp, 15, was a long-time Congressman from Buffalo and was the Republican candidate for Vice President in 1996. Ahmad Rashad, 27, is a sports broadcaster. O.J. Simpson, 32/36, became a broadcaster, actor and defendant in the biggest murder trial of the last century.

First player to wear a number in the 90s: Defensive end Ken Johnson wore 91 in 1979.

Number with most points scored: 2 with 1,011 points scored by Steve Christie.

Number with most yards rushing: 34 with 18,538 yards gained by Thurman Thomas (11,938), Cookie Gilchrist (3,056), Jim Braxton (2,842), Booker Moore (420), Allen Smith (148), Gary Wilkins (74), Don Stone (61), and Gene Donaldson (-1).

Number with most receptions: 80 with 1,243 passes caught by Eric Moulds (506), Jerry Butler (278), Bill Brooks (155), James Lofton (151), Charley Ferguson (46), Monte Crocket (35), Flip Johnson (34), John Holland (22), Jan White (13), Danny Fulton (2), and Ray Jarvis (1).

Number with most touchdown passes: 12 with 441 touchdowns tossed by Jim Kelly (237), Joe Ferguson (181), Daryle Lamonica (16), James Harris (5), and Al Dorow (2).

Number with most interceptions: 24 with 58 passes picked off by Booker Edgerson (23), Kurt Schulz (21), Doug Jones (5), Billy Kinard (4), Ernie Kellerman (2) and Lemar

Parrish (1) and 26 with 56 passes picked off by Charles Romes (28), George Saimes (22), Antoine Winfield (5), Terrence McGee (2) and Chris Hale (1).

Oddity: Three of the stalwarts from the Bills championship offenses of the 1960s all had their numbers lay unused for over 20 years until they were returned to circulation — Jack Kemp's 15 was unworn from 1970 through 1994, Elbert Dubenion's 44 was unworn from 1969 through 1994, and Billy Shaw's 66 was unworn from 1970 through 1991.

Players Whose Number Is Unknown

Jeff Lyman	(LB)	1972

Team All-Time Numerical Roster

Those with an "r" following the year 1987 were replacement players during the players' strike. Pro Bowl players for each number are in *Italics*; Hall of Famers are in **Bold** type.

1 Benny Ricardo (K) 1976, Efren Herrera (K) 1982, Mike Hollis (K) 2002.

2 Steve Christie (K) 1992–2000.

3 Pete Gogolak (K) 1964–5, Ben Russell (QB) 1968, John Leypoldt (K) 1971–6, Todd Schlopy (K) 1987r.

4 Rusty Jackson (P) 1978–9, John Kidd (P) 1984–9.

5 Booth Lusteg (K) 1966, George Jakowenko (K) 1976, Carson Long (K) 1977, Nick Mike-Mayer (K) 1979–82, Fred Steinfort (K) 1983, Vince Ferragamo (QB) 1985, Rick Partridge (P) 1987r, Kerry Brady (K) 1989, Brad Daluiso (K) 1991, Cole Ford (K) 1998, Travis Brown (QB) 2001, 2003.

6 Dave Chapple (P) 1971, Tom Dempsey (K) 1978–9, John Nies (P/K) 1990.

7 *Mike Mercer* (K) 1967–8, Ben Russell (QB) 1968, Grant Guthrie (K) 1970–1, Mike Clark (K) 1972, Marv Bateman (K) 1974–7, Greg Cater (P) 1980–3, Bruce Mathison (QB) 1985, Gale Gilbert (QB) 1989–93, *Doug Flutie* (QB) 1998–2000.

8 Neil O'Donoghue (K) 1977, Stan Gelbaugh (QB) 1986–9, Billy Joe Hobert (QB) 1997, Brian Moorman (P) 2003.

9 Bill Munson (QB) 1978–9, David Martin (CB) 1987r, Chris Mohr (P) 1991–2000, Jake Arians (K) 2001, Rian Lindell (K) 2003.

10 Dan Darragh (QB) 1968–70, Spike Jones (P) 1971, Leo Hart (QB) 1972–3, David Mays (QB) 1978, David Humm (QB) 1980, Matt Kofler (QB) 1982–4, Mark Miller (QB) 1987r, Rick Tuten (P) 1990, Alex Van Pelt (QB) 1995–2003.

11 Richie Lucas (QB/HB) 1960–1, Spike Jones (P) 1972–4, Fred Besana (QB) 1977, Dan Manucci (QB) 1979–80, 1987, Joe Dufek (QB) 1983, *Scott Norwood* (K) 1985–91, Rob Johnson (QB) 1998–2001, *Drew Bledsoe* (QB) 2002–3.

12 Al Dorow (QB) 1962, Manch Wheeler (QB) 1962, Daryle Lamonica (QB) 1963–6, James Harris (QB) 1969–71, Joe Ferguson (QB) 1973–84, **Jim Kelly** (QB) 1986–96.

13 Sam Wyche (QB) 1976, Chuck Nelson (K) 1984, Brian McClure (QB) 1987r.

14 Tom O'Connell (QB) 1960–1, M.C. Reynolds (QB) 1961, Tom Sherman (QB) 1969, Sam Wyche (QB) 1976, Ken Johnson (QB) 1977, Frank Reich (QB) 1985–94.

15 *Jack Kemp* (QB) 1962–9, Todd Collins (QB) 1995–7.

16 Tom Flores (QB) 1967, Dennis Shaw (QB) 1970–3, Scott Hunter (QB) 1974, Russell Copeland (WR) 1993.

17 Bob Brodhead (QB) 1960, Warren Rabb (QB) 1961–2, Mike Taliaferro (QB) 1972, Gary Marangi (QB) 1974–6, Matt Robinson (QB) 1981–2, Willie Totten (QB) 1987r, Shayne Graham (K) 2001.

18 John Green (QB) 1960–1, Kay Stephenson (QB) 1968, Tom Sherman (QB) 1969, Joe Danelo (K) 1983–4.

19 Duke Fergerson (WR) 1980, Joe Dufek (QB) 1984.

20 *Bill Atkins* (DB) 1960–1, 1963, Tom Minter (HB) 1962, Hank Rivera (DB) 1963, Bobby Smith (HB) 1964–5, *Keith Lincoln* (HB) 1967–8, *Robert James* (CB) 1969–74, *Joe Cribbs* (RB) 1980–3, 1985, John Armstrong (DB/KR) 1987, Sherman Cocroft (DB) 1988, Mickey Sutton (DB/PR) 1989, Richard Carey (DB) 1990, *Henry Jones* (S) 1991–2000, *Travis Henry* (RB) 2001–3.

21 *Bobby Burnett* (HB) 1966–7, Tom Flores (QB) 1968–9, Jerome Lawson (CB) 1968, Jackie Allen (DB) 1970–1, John Saunders (S) 1972, Larry Carwell (S) 1973, Gary Hayman (RB) 1974–5, Van Green (DB) 1976, Marvin Switzer (DB) 1978, Doug Greene (DB) 1979–80, Rufus Bess (CB) 1980–1, Arthur Whittington (RB) 1982, Mike Kennedy (S) 1983, Don Wilson (S) 1984–5, Wayne Davis (CB) 1987–9, Gerald Bess (CB) 1987r, Brian Taylor (DB) 1991, Nate Turner (RB) 1993–4, Manny Martin (DB) 1996–9, Chris Watson (CB) 2000–2.

22 Jim Wagstaff (DB) 1960–1, Wayne Crow (HB) 1962–3, Charley Warner (DB) 1964–6, Max Anderson (RB) 1968–70, Bill Cahill (S) 1973–4, Steve Freeman (DB) 1975–86, Erroll Tucker

(DB/KR) 1988–9, John Hagy (DB) 1990, Jeff Burris (DB) 1994–7, Daryl Porter (CB) 1998–2000, Nate Clements (CB) 2001–3.

23 Willmer Fowler (HB) 1960–1, Bill Shockley (HB) 1961, Carl Taseff (DB) 1962, Gene Sykes (DB) 1963–5, Bobby Ply (DB) 1967, Charley Brown (S) 1968, Ken Stone (S) 1973, Steve Schnarr (RB) 1975, Clifford Brooks (DB) 1976, Steve Powell (RB) 1978–9, Van Williams (RB) 1983–4, Jim Perryman (S) 1985, Kevin Williams (CB) 1986, Gerald Bess (CB) 1987r, Kerry Parker (CB) 1987r, Kenneth Davis (RB) 1989–94, Matt Stevens (DB) 1996, Antowain Smith (RB) 1997–2000, Pierson Prioleau (S) 2001–3.

24 Bill Kinard (DB) 1960, Booker Edgerson (CB) 1962–9, Bob Gladieux (RB) 1970, Ernie Kellerman (S) 1973, Ken Stone (S) 1973, Ed Jenkins (RB) 1974, Al Randolph (S) 1974, Doug Jones (DB) 1975–8, Lemar Parrish (CB) 1982, Gary Thompson (CB) 1983–4, Jim Perryman (S) 1985, Johnny Shepherd (RB) 1987r, Kurt Schulz (S) 1992–8, Raion Hill (DB) 2000–1, Billy Jenkins (S) 2002, Terrence McGee (CB) 2003.

25 Bill Majors (DB) 1961, Vernon Valdez (DB) 1961, Jim Crotty (DB) 1962, John Yaccino (DB) 1962, Fred Brown (HB) 1963, Jessie Murdock (FB) 1963, Oliver Dobbins (DB) 1964, *Haven Moses* (WR) 1968–72, Roland Hooks (RB) 1976–82, Rod Hill (CB) 1984–6, Roland Mitchell (CB) 1987–8, Bill Callahan (S) 1987r, David Martin (CB) 1987r, Mickey Washington (CB) 1993–4, Donovan Greer (DB) 1998–9, Tony Driver (S) 2001–2.

26 Fred Ford (HB) 1960, Dewey Bohling (RB) 1961, Carey Henley (RB) 1962, *George Saimes* (S) 1963–9, Clyde Glosson (WR) 1970, Linzy Cole (WR) 1972, Donnie Walker (DB) 1973–4, Ed Jones (DB) 1975, Tim Anderson (DB) 1976, Charles Romes (DB) 1977–86, Ricky Porter (RB) 1987, Leonard Williams (RB) 1987r, Chris Hale (DB) 1989–92, Antoine Winfield (CB) 1999–2003.

27 Harold Lewis (HB) 1960, Joe Cannavino (DB) 1962, Willie Jones (HB) 1962, Glenn Bass (E) 1963, *Tom Janik* (S) 1965–8, Tommy Pharr (S) 1970, Ahmad Rashad (WR) 1974–5, Chris Williams (CB) 1982–3, Craig White (WR) 1984, Ron Pitts (DB) 1986–7, John Lewis (CB) 1987r, Clifford Hicks (DB) 1990–2, David Pool (DB) 1993, Ken Irvin (CB) 1995–2001, Coy Wire (S) 2002–3.

28 Richard Trapp (WR) 1968, Roy Reeves (WR) 1969, Ike Hill (CB) 1970–1, Dwight Harrison (DB) 1972–7, Rufus Bess (CB) 1980, Roland Solomon (CB) 1980, Judson Flint (S) 1983, *Greg Bell* (RB) 1984–7, Larry Kinnebrew (FB) 1989–90, Chris Oldham (CB) 1991, Thomas Smith (CB) 1993–9, Traveres Tillman (S) 2000–1, Kevin Thomas (CB) 2002–3.

29 Don Calhoun (RB) 1974–5, Mario Clark (DB) 1976–83, John Mistler (WR) 1984, Derrick Burroughs (DB) 1985–9, David Pool (DB) 1990,

James Williams (CB) 1991–3, Jason Bratton (RB) 1996, Keion Carpenter (S) 1999–2001, Jason Bostic (CB) 2002.

30 *Wray Carlton* (FB) 1960–7, Herb Paterra (LB) 1963, Wayne Patrick (RB) 1968–72, Bo Cornell (LB) 1973–7, Lawrence McCutcheon (RB) 1981, Brian Carpenter (CB) 1984, Marco Tongue (DB) 1984, Anthony Hutchison (RB) 1985, Kerry Porter (RB) 1987, Warren Loving (FB) 1987r, Don Smith (RB) 1990, Yonel Jourdain (RB) 1994–5, Ken Simonton (RB) 2003.

31 Preston Ridlehuber (RB) 1969, James Williams (CB) 1990, Ray Jackson (DB) 1996–8, Lennox Gordon (RB) 1999, Lance Brown (DB) 2001, Charlie Rogers (WR) 2002, Sammy Morris (RB) 2003.

32 Don Stone (FB) 1965, Jack Spikes (FB) 1966–7, Gary McDermott (RB) 1968, **O.J. Simpson** (RB) 1969–77.

33 Ted Wegert (HB) 1960, Art Baker (RB) 1961–2, Hezekiah Braxton (HB) 1963, Billy Joe (FB) 1965, Bill Bailey (FB) 1967, Ben Gregory (RB) 1968–9, Lloyd Pate (RB) 1970, Randy Jackson (RB) 1972, Vic Washington (RB) 1975–6, Andy Reid (RB) 1976, Ted McKnight (RB) 1982, Mike Pruitt (FB) 1985, Ronnie Harmon (RB) 1986–9, Eddie Fuller (RB) 1991–3, Tim Tindale (RB) 1995–7, *Sam Gash* (FB) 1998–9, 2003, Sammy Morris (RB) 2001–2.

34 *Cookie Gilchrist* (FB) 1962–4, Don Stone (FB) 1965, Allen Smith (HB) 1966–7, Gene Donaldson (FB) 1967, Bubba Thornton (WR) 1969, Jim Braxton (RB) 1971–8, Booker Moore (FB) 1982–5, Gary Wilkins (FB) 1986–7, *Thurman Thomas* (RB) 1988–99.

35 Carl Smith (FB) 1960, Doug Goodwin (FB) 1966, Charley Bivins (HB) 1967, Darnell Powell (RB) 1976, Mike Collier (RB) 1977–9, Allan Clark (RB) 1982, Carl Byrum (FB) 1986–8, John Lewis (CB) 1987r, Carwell Gardner (FB) 1990–95, Jonathan Linton (RB) 1998–2000, Joe Burns (RB) 2002–3.

36 Bob Cappadona (RB) 1968, **O.J. Simpson** (RB) 1969, Preston Ridlehuber (RB) 1969, Greg Jones (RB) 1970–1, Pete Van Valkenberg (RB) 1973, Jeff Kinney (RB) 1976, Mike Frankowiak (TE) 1977, Rodney Bellinger (CB) 1984–6, Steve Clark (FS) 1987r, Jerome Henderson (DB) 1993–4, Lawyer Milloy (S) 2003.

37 Ted Koy (LB/TE) 1972–4, Ike Thomas (DB) 1975, Clayton Heath (RB) 1976, *Nate Odomes* (CB) 1987–93, Sean Woodson (DB) 1997, *Larry Centers* (FB) 2001–2, Dainon Sidney (CB) 2003.

38 Larry Watkins (FB) 1973–4, Eddie Ray (RB) 1976, Jeff Nixon (DB) 1979–82, Gary Thompson (CB) 1983–4, Mark Kelso (S) 1986–93, Mike Dumas (S) 1994, Ray Hill (CB) 1998, Shawn Bryson (RB) 2000–2, Raion Hill (DB) 2001.

39 Wayne Mosley (RB) 1974, Dennis Johnson

(FB) 1978–9, Jamie Mueller (FB) 1987–90, Larry Friday (S) 1987r, Filmel Johnson (DB) 1995, Clarence Williams (FB) 1998.

40 Ed Rutkowski (QB/WR) 1963–8, Roland Moss (RB) 1970, *J.D. Hill* (WR) 1971–5, Terry Miller (RB) 1978–80, Robb Riddick (RB) 1981, 1983–4, 1986–8, Chip Nuzzo (S) 1987r, Eric Smedley (DB) 1996–8.

41 Darrell Harper (HB) 1960, Dewey Bohling (RB) 1961, Bill Enyart (RB) 1969–70, Alvin Wyatt (DB) 1970–3, Clint Haselrig (RB) 1974, Royce McKinney (DB) 1975, Eddie McMillan (CB) 1978, Phil Villapiano (LB) 1980–3, Speedy Neal (FB) 1984, Mike Pruitt (FB) 1985, Jamie Mueller (FB) 1987, Ira Albright (NT) 1987r, Greg Evans (S) 1995, Phil Crosby (FB) 2001–2.

42 Jack Johnson (HB) 1960–1, Don McDonald (DB) 1961, *Butch Byrd* (CB) 1964–70, Maurice Tyler (S) 1972–3, Neal Craig (S) 1974, Frank Oliver (DB) 1975, Eddie Ray (RB) 1976, Rod Kush (S) 1980–4, Ricky Moore (FB) 1986, Durwood Roquemore (S) 1987, Chris Green (S) 1995.

43 Joe Kulbacki (HB) 1960, Carl Charon (DB) 1962–3, Joe Auer (HB) 1964–5, Charley King (CB) 1966, Monte Ledbetter (WR) 1967–9, *Tony Greene* (DB) 1971–9, Dave Kilson (CB) 1983, Martin Bayless (S) 1984–6, Chip Nuzzo (S) 1987r, Bo Wright (RB) 1988, Kim Phillips (DB) 1990, Matt Darby (S) 1992–5, Izell Reese (S) 2003.

44 *Elbert Dubenion* (WR) 1960–8, Darick Holmes (RB) 1995–8.

45 Richie McCabe (DB) 1960–1, Roger Kochman (HB) 1963, Hagood Clarke (DB) 1964–8, Hilton Crawford (S) 1969, Glenn Alexander (WR) 1970, Rex Kern (S) 1974, Charley Ford (DB) 1975, Bill Simpson (FS) 1980–2, Len Walterscheid (S) 1983–4, Anthony Steels (KR/RB) 1985, Dwight Drane (S) 1986–91, Carey Bender (RB) 1996, Sammy Morris (RB) 2000.

46 Fred Brown (HB) 1961, Jim Crotty (DB) 1961, Ray Abruzzese (DB) 1962–4, Bo Roberson (E) 1965, Tony King (DB) 1967, Bruce Alford (K) 1968–9, Charley Mitchell (HB) 1968, Tim Beamer (S) 1971, Steve Jones (RB) 1973–4, Dan Abramowicz (WR) 1975, Keith Moody (KR/DB) 1976–9, Roland Solomon (CB) 1980, Julius Dawkins (WR) 1983, Joe Chetti (FB) 1987r, Leonard Smith (DB) 1988–91, Marlon Kerner (CB) 1995–8.

47 *Willie West* (DB) 1962–3, Willie Ross (FB) 1964, Charley King (CB) 1967, Pete Richardson (CB) 1969–71, Leon Garror (S) 1972–3, Clint Haselrig (RB) 1975, Roscoe Word (DB) 1976, Curtis Brown (RB) 1977–82, Bill Hurley (S) 1983, Lucious Smith (CB) 1984, Mike Panepinto (RB) 1987r, Kirby Jackson (DB) 1988–92, Ahmad Brooks (CB) 2002.

48 Pete Mills (E/DB) 1965–6, John Pitts (S) 1967–73, Roosevelt Leaks (RB) 1980–3, Lawrence Johnson (DB) 1984–87.

49 Floyd Hudlow (DB) 1965, Booth Lusteg (K) 1966, Larry Walton (WR) 1978, Tony Hunter (TE) 1983, Ulysses Norris (TE) 1984, Bruce King (FB) 1986–7, John Hagy (DB) 1988–9, Nate Turner (RB) 1993, Jay Riemersma (TE) 1997.

50 Al Bemiller (C) 1961–9, Dick Palmer (LB) 1972, Jim Cheyunski (LB) 1973–4, Mark Johnson (LB) 1975–6, Greg Collins (LB) 1977, Mike Humiston (LB) 1981, Trey Junkin (LB) 1983–4, Joe Azelby (LB) 1984, Larry Kubin (LB) 1985, Eric Wilson (LB) 1985, Ray Bentley (LB) 1986–91, Bob LeBlanc (LB) 1987r, Keith Goganious (LB) 1993–4, David White (LB) 1995, Dominique Stevenson (LB) 2002–3.

51 Dave Behrman (C) 1963, *John Tracey* (LB) 1964–7, Jack Frantz (C) 1968, Jerald Collins (LB) 1969–71, Bruce Jarvis (C) 1971–4, Dan Jilek (LB) 1976–9, *Jim Ritcher* (G) 1980–93, Kevin Lamar (G) 1987r, David White (LB) 1996, Joe Cummings (LB) 1998–9, DaShon Polk (LB) 2000–2, *Takeo Spikes* (LB) 2003.

52 Dan McGrew (C) 1960, Bill Laskey (LB) 1965, Edgar Chandler (LB) 1968–72, Merv Krakau (LB) 1973–8, Doug Becker (LB) 1978, Chris Keating (LB) 1979–84, Guy Frazier (LB) 1985–6, John Kaiser (LB) 1987, Scott Schankweiler (LB) 1987r, David Bavaro (LB) 1991, Richard Harvey (LB) 1992–3, John Holecek (LB) 1995–2000, DaShon Polk (LB) 2003.

53 Dennis Remmert (T) 1960, Walt Cudzik (C) 1964, Wayne Frazier (C) 1967, Dave Ogas (LB) 1969, Wayne Fowler (C) 1970, John Matlock (C) 1972, Mike Montler (C) 1973–6, Connie Zelencik (C) 1977, Will Grant (C) 1978–85, 1987, Tony Furjanic (LB) 1986–7, Tom Erlandson (LB) 1988, Marvcus Patton (LB) 1990–4, Keith Newman (LB) 1999–2002, Mario Haggan (LB) 2003.

54 Sam Palumbo (C) 1960, Joe Hergert (LB) 1960–1, Frank Jackunas (C) 1962, Tom Louderback (LB) 1962, *Harry Jacobs* (LB) 1963, Howard Kindig (C/DE) 1970–1, Tom Beard (C) 1972, Phil Croyle (LB) 1973, Rick Kingrea (LB) 1973, Tom Ruud (LB) 1975–7, Randy McClanahan (LB) 1978, Tom Higgins (LB) 1979, Eugene Marve (LB) 1982–7, Carlton Bailey (LB) 1988–92, Chris Spielman (LB) 1996–8, Corey Moore (LB) 2000, Jon Dorenbos (C) 2003.

55 Bernie Buzynski (LB) 1960, Marv Matuszak (LB) 1962–3, Paul Maguire (LB/P) 1964–70, Bill McKinley (LB) 1971, John Skorupan (LB) 1973–7, Tom Graham (LB) 1978, Jim Haslett (LB) 1979–85, *Cornelius Bennett* (LB) 1987–9, Mark Shupe (C) 1987r, Mark Maddox (LB) 1992–7, Wayne Simmons (LB) 1998, Jay Foreman (LB) 1999–2001, Eddie Robinson (LB) 2002, Angelo Crowell (LB) 2003.

56 *Archie Matsos* (LB) 1960–2, *Harry Jacobs* (LB) 1963, Marty Schottenheimer (LB) 1966–8, Al Andrews (LB) 1970–1, Ken Lee (LB) 1972,

Richard Lewis (LB) 1973–4, Bob Nelson (LB) 1975–7, Tom Ehlers (LB) 1978, Willie Parker (C) 1979, *Darryl Talley* (LB) 1983–94, *Sam Cowart* (LB) 1998–2001, Anthony Denman (LB) 2002.

57 Jack Laraway (LB) 1960, Ralph Felton (LB) 1961–2, Marty Schottenheimer (LB) 1965, Bob Schmidt (C) 1966–7, Frank Marchlewski (C) 1970, Dale Farley (LB) 1972–3, Fred Forsberg (LB) 1973, John McCrumbly (LB) 1975, Lucius Sanford (LB) 1978–86, Mark Pike (LB) 1987–8, Mike Jones (LB) 1987r, Craig Walls (LB) 1987r, Matt Monger (LB) 1989–90, Damien Covington (LB) 1995–7, Kenyatta Wright (LB) 2001, Josh Stamer (LB) 2003.

58 *Mike Stratton* (LB) 1962–72, Mario Celotto (LB) 1978, Randy McClanahan (LB) 1978, Isiah Robertson (LB) 1979–82, Mark Merrill (LB) 1983–4, Steve Potter (LB) 1984, Anthony Dickerson (LB) 1985, George Cumby (LB) 1986, *Shane Conlan* (LB) 1987–92, Marlo Perry (LB) 1994–9, Brandon Spoon (LB) 2001–2.

59 Bob Lettner (LB) 1961, Paul Guidry (LB) 1966–72, Doug Allen (LB) 1974–5, Shane Nelson (LB) 1977–82, Joey Lumpkin (LB) 1983, Stan David (LB) 1984, Steve Maidlow (LB) 1985, Mitch Frerotte (G) 1987, 1990–2, Don Graham (LB) 1988, Sam Rogers (LB) 1994–2000, London Fletcher (LB) 2002–3.

60 Phil Blazer (G) 1960, John Dittrich (G) 1961, Wayne Wolff (G) 1961, Tom Day (DE) 1962, Dave Behrman (C) 1964–5, Jim LeMoine (G) 1967, Angelo Loukas (G) 1969, Bill Adams (G) 1972–7, Joey Lumpkin (LB) 1982, Al Wenglikowski (LB) 1984, 1987r, Scott Watters (LB) 1987r, Tom Myslinski (G) 1993, Jerry Ostroski (G/T) 1994–2001.

61 Bob Kalsu (G) 1968, Julian Nunamaker (DE) 1969, Jim Reilly (G) 1970–1, Willie Parker (C) 1973–8, Tom Lynch (G) 1981–4, Leonard Burton (T) 1986–9, Dusty Zeigler (C) 1996–9, Mike Pucillo (G) 2002–3.

62 Ed Meyer (T) 1960, Dick Cunningham (T) 1967–9, Levert Carr (T) 1971, Dick Hart (G) 1972, Jeff Yeates (DT) 1974–6, Ervin Parker (LB) 1980–3, Mark Traynowicz (G) 1985–8, Joe Bock (C) 1987r, Kevin Lamar (G) 1987r, Mike Devlin (C) 1993–5.

63 George Flint (G) 1968, Bob Kruse (G) 1969, Dick Cunningham (T) 1970–2, Justin Cross (C) 1983–6, Adam Lingner (C) 1987, 1989–95, Rick Leo (G) 1987r, Bill Conaty (OL) 1997–2002.

64 *Stew Barber* (OT) 1961, Tom Day (DE) 1963, Chuck Leo (G) 1963, *Harry Jacobs* (LB) 1964–9, Mike McCaffrey (LB) 1970, Chuck Hurston (DE) 1971, Andy Selfridge (LB) 1972, Dave Costa (DT) 1974, Joe Silipo (C) 1987r, Brent Griffith (OL) 1990, Mike Brennan (OL) 1991, Tom Nutten (C) 1995, Michael Early (C) 2001, Ben Sobieski (T) 2003.

65 Waddey Harvey (DT) 1969–70, Mike Wil-

son (G) 1971, Remi Prudhomme (C) 1972, Nick Nighswander (C) 1974, Pat Toomay (DE) 1975, Bob Patton (C) 1976, Tim Vogler (OL) 1979–88, Ed Fulton (G) 1979, John Davis (T/G) 1991–4, Jon Carman (T) 2000–1, Ross Tucker (G) 2003.

66 **Billy Shaw** (G) 1961–9, Jerry Crafts (OL) 1992–4, Victor Allotey (G) 1998–2000, Lauvale Sape (DT) 2003.

67 Joe Schaffer (LB) 1960, *Joe O'Donnell* (G) 1964–71, Reggie McKenzie (G) 1972–82, Darryl Caldwell (OT) 1983, *Kent Hull* (C) 1986–96, Craig Heimburger (C/G) 2001.

68 Remi Prudhomme (C) 1966–7, Willie Young (T) 1971–2, **Joe DeLamielleure** (G) 1973–9, 1985, Jerry Boyarksy (NT) 1986, Mark Catano (NT) 1986, Tony Brown (OL) 1987r, Corbin Lacina (OL) 1994–7, Mike Williams (OT) 2002–3.

69 Jerome Gantt (T) 1970, Robert Penchion (G) 1972–3, Ken Jones (DE/OT) 1976–9, Conrad Dobler (G) 1980–1, Greg Christy (T) 1985, Scott Garnett (NT) 1987r, *Will Wolford* (OL) 1990–2, Marcus Spriggs (OL) 1997–2000, Mike Houghton (OL) 2002.

70 Ed Muelhaupt (G) 1960–1, *Tom Sestak* (DT) 1962–8, Bob Kampa (DT) 1973–4, Joe Devlin (T/G) 1976–82, 1984–9, John Fina (T) 1992–2001, Trey Teague (C) 2002–3.

71 Mack Yoho (DE) 1960–1, Wayne Desutter (T) 1966, Bob Tatarek (DT) 1968–72, Mike Kadish (DT) 1973–81, Dale Hellestrae (T) 1985–8, Sean Dowling (T) 1987r, Ed Philion (DT) 1994, Corey Hulsey (G) 2001.

72 Gerry Delucca (T) 1962, *Ron McDole* (DE) 1963–70, Bob Hews (T) 1971, Don Croft (DT) 1972–5, John Little (DT) 1977, Ken Jones (DE/OT) 1980–6, Don Sommer (T) 1987r, Art Still (DE) 1988–9, Corey Louchiey (OT) 1994–7, Joe Panos (G) 1998–2000, Kris Farris (T) 2001, Chidi Ahanotu (DE) 2002.

73 *Chuck McMurtry* (DT) 1960–1, George Flint (G) 1962–5, Dave Costa (DT) 1966, Howard Kindig (C/DE) 1967–9, Richard Cheek (G) 1970–1, Jeff Curchin (G) 1972, Earl Edwards (DE) 1973–5, Mekeli Ieremia (DE) 1978, Jon Borchardt (T) 1979–84, Ken Jones (DE/OT) 1985, *Will Wolford* (OL) 1986–9, Mike Lodish (NT) 1990–4, Karl Wilson (DE) 1995, Marcus Price (OT) 2002–3.

74 *Harold Olson* (T) 1960–2, Gerry Delucca (T) 1963, Tom Keating (DT) 1964–5, Ray Rissmiller (T) 1968, Chuck Devliegher (DT) 1969, Levert Carr (T) 1970, Donnie Green (T) 1971–6, Dee Hardison (DT) 1978–80, Don Smith (DE) 1985–6, Bruce Mesner (NT) 1987, Joe McGrail (NT) 1987r, Richard Tharpe (DE) 1987r, Glenn Parker (OL) 1990–6, Jamie Nails (OL) 1997–2000, Marques Sullivan (OT) 2001–3.

75 Tony Discenzo (T) 1960, Bob Sedlock (DT) 1960, *Ken Rice* (T) 1961, 1963, Nate Borden (E) 1962, Don Healy (T) 1962, Tom Saidock (DT)

1962, Dudley Meredith (DE) 1964–8, Mike Richey (T) 1969, Art Laster (T) 1970, Cal Snowden (DE) 1971, Frank Cornish (DT) 1972, Jeff Winans (DT) 1973–5, Jeff Lloyd (DT) 1976, Dennis Johnson (DT) 1978, Bill Acker (NT) 1983–4, Mike Hamby (DE) 1986, Erik Rosenmeier (C) 1987r, *Howard Ballard* (OL) 1988–93, Ed Philion (DT) 1995, Marcellus Wiley (DE) 1997–2000, Jonas Jennings (OT) 2001–3.

76 John Scott (T) 1960–1, Sid Youngelman (T) 1962–3, Henry Schmidt (DT) 1965, Gary Bugenhagen (T) 1967, Mike McBath (DE) 1968–72, Halvor Hagen (T) 1974–5, Bill Dunstan (DT) 1977, Craig Hertwig (T) 1978, *Fred Smerlas* (NT) 1979–89, Steve Hoyem (OT) 1994, Ethan Albright (C) 1996–2000.

77 Don Chelf (G) 1960–1, *Stew Barber* (OT) 1962–9, Jerry Patton (DT) 1972–3, Dave Means (DE) 1974, *Ben Williams* (DE) 1976–85, Tony Brown (OL) 1987r, Mike Estep (G) 1987r, Reggie Rogers (DE) 1991, Oliver Barnett (DE) 1993–4, Jim Jeffcoat (DE) 1995–7, Robert Hicks (T) 1998–2000, Kendrick Office (DE) 2001–2.

78 Gene Grabosky (T) 1960, Tom Day (DE) 1961, *Jim Dunaway* (DT) 1963–71, *Dave Foley* (T) 1972–7, Scott Hutchinson (DE) 1978–80, Justin Cross (C) 1982, *Bruce Smith* (DE) 1985–99.

79 Jim Sorey (DT) 1960–2, Dick Hudson (T) 1963–8, *Paul Costa* (TE/T) 1969–72, Steve Okoniewski (DT) 1973, Marty Smith (DT) 1976, Greg Morton (DE) 1977, Elbert Drungo (T) 1978, Dean Prater (DE) 1984–8, John Davis (T/G) 1989–90, Joe Staysniak (OL) 1991, *Ruben Brown* (G) 1995–2003.

80 Monte Crockett (E) 1960–2, Charley Ferguson (WR) 1963–9, Jim McFarland (TE) 1970, Jan White (TE) 1971–2, Ray Jarvis (WR) 1973, John Holland (WR) 1975–7, *Jerry Butler* (WR) 1979–86, Dan Fulton (WR) 1979, Flip Johnson (WR) 1988–9, **James Lofton** (WR) 1990–2, Bill Brooks (WR) 1993–5, *Eric Moulds* (WR) 1996–2003.

81 Tom Rychlec (E) 1960–2, Bill Miller (E) 1963, Bill Groman (E) 1964–5, Rich Zecher (DT) 1967, Bob Chandler (WR) 1971–9, Ron Jessie (WR) 1980–1, Perry Tuttle (WR) 1982–3, Mitchell Brookins (WR) 1984–5, Walter Broughton (WR) 1987–8, Brad Lamb (WR) 1992–3, Bucky Brooks (WR) 1994, Justin Armour (WR) 1995–6, Jerry Reese (WR) 1997, Peerless Price (WR) 1999–2002, Bobby Shaw (WR) 2003.

82 Mack Yoho (DE) 1962–3, *Paul Costa* (TE/T) 1965–8, Al Cowlings (DE) 1970–2, Brian McConnell (LB) 1973, John Kimbrough (WR) 1977, *Frank Lewis* (WR) 1978–83, Eric Richardson (WR) 1985–6, Sheldon Gaines (WR) 1987r, Don Beebe (WR) 1989–94, Damon Thomas (WR) 1995, Chris Brantley (WR) 1996, Mitchell Galloway (WR) 1997, Kevin Williams (WR) 1998–9,

Kwame Cavil (WR) 2000, Josh Reed (WR) 2002–3.

83 Harrison Rosdahl (DE) 1964, Bobby Crockett (WR) 1966–9, Clyde Glosson (WR) 1970, Bob Christiansen (DT) 1972, Sherman White (DE) 1976–83, Preston Dennard (WR) 1984, *Andre Reed* (WR) 1985–99, Dave Moore (TE) 2002–3.

84 Robert Barrett (E) 1960, Perry Richards (E) 1961, *Ernie Warlick* (E) 1962–5, Art Powell (E) 1967, Austin Denney (TE) 1970–1, Mike Frankowiak (TE) 1978, Dan Fulton (WR) 1979, Duke Fergerson (WR) 1980, Buster Barnett (TE) 1981–4, Don Kern (TE) 1986, Keith McKeller (TE) 1987–93, Veno Belk (TE) 1987r, Lonnie Johnson (TE) 1994–8, Bobby Collins (TE) 1999–2000, Reggie Germany (WR) 2001–2, Mark Campbell (TE) 2003.

85 Charles Rutkowski (E) 1960, Dan Chamberlain (E) 1960–1, *John Tracey* (LB) 1962–3, Glenn Bass (E) 1964–6, Bob Petrich (DE) 1967, Willie Grate (TE) 1969–70, Ted Koy (LB/TE) 1971, Walt Patulski (DE) 1972–5, Fred Coleman (TE) 1976, Tody Smith (DE) 1976, Phil Dokes (DE) 1977–8, Ron Howard (TE) 1979, Artie Owens (WR) 1980, Byron Franklin (WR) 1981, 1983–4, Chris Burkett (WR) 1985–9, Kris Haines (WR) 1987r, Al Edwards (WR) 1991–2, Russell Copeland (WR) 1993–6, Jay Riemersma (TE) 1998–2002, Clarence Coleman (WR) 2003.

86 *Marlin Briscoe* (WR) 1969–71, Dave Washington (LB) 1972–4, Emmett Edwards (WR) 1976, Mike Holmes (WR) 1976, Len Willis (WR) 1977–9, Reggie Craig (WR) 1977, Mark Brammer (TE) 1980–4, Jimmy Teal (WR) 1985–6, Trumaine Johnson (WR) 1987–8, Marc Brown (WR) 1987r, Sheldon Gaines (WR) 1987r, **James Lofton** (WR) 1989, Vernon Turner (WR) 1990, Mike Alexander (WR) 1991, Rob Awalt (TE) 1992–3, Damon Thomas (WR) 1994, Tony Cline (TE) 1996–7, Jeremy McDaniel (WR) 1999–2001, Antonio Brown (WR) 2003.

87 Leroy Moore (DE) 1960, 1962–3, *LaVerne Torczon* (DE) 1960–2, Billy Masters (TE) 1967–9, Louis Ross (DE) 1971–2, Paul Seymour (TE) 1973–7, Mike Levenseller (WR) 1978, Joe Shipp (TE) 1979, Steve Alvers (TE) 1981, Robert Holt (WR) 1982, Dave Young (TE) 1983, Tony Hunter (TE) 1984, Eason Ramson (TE) 1985, Butch Rolle (TE) 1986–91, Mark Walczak (TE) 1987r, Chris Walsh (WR) 1992–3, Vince Marrow (TE) 1994, Robert Coons (TE) 1995–7, Duane Young (TE) 1998, Dan O'Leary (TE) 2001–2, Andre Rone (WR) 2002.

88 Richard Brubaker (E) 1960, Al Hoisington (E) 1960, Glenn Bass (E) 1961–2, Tom Day (DE) 1964–6, Julian Nunamaker (DE) 1970–1, Steve Okoniewski (DT) 1972, Halvor Hagen (T) 1973, Reuben Gant (TE) 1974–80, Mike Mosley (WR)

1982–4, Pete Metzelaars (TE) 1985–94, Reggie Bynum (WR) 1987r, Tony Cline (TE) 1995, Quinn Early (WR) 1996–8, Sheldon Jackson (TE) 1999–2001, Cory Geason (TE) 2002, Ryan Neufield (TE) 2003.

89 Tom Day (DE) 1968, Wes Grant (DE) 1971, Wallace Francis (WR) 1973–4, Bob Gaddis (WR) 1976, Lou Piccone (WR) 1977–82, Julius Dawkins (WR) 1984, Ulysses Norris (TE) 1985, Walter Broughton (WR) 1986, *Steve Tasker* (WR/KR) 1986–97, Thad McFadden (WR) 1987r, Kamil Loud (WR) 1998–9, Avion Black (WR) 2000–1, Charles Johnson (WR) 2002, Sam Aiken (WR) 2003, Tony Hunter (TE) 1983.

90 Scott Hutchinson (DE) 1983, Arnold Campbell (DE) 1987r, Steve Maidlow (LB) 1987r, Tim Cofield (LB) 1989, Phil Hansen (DE) 1991–2001, Ryan Denney (DE) 2002, Chris Kelsay (DE) 2003.

91 Ken Johnson (DE) 1979–84, Jack Bravyak (DE) 1987r, Joe McGrail (NT) 1987r, Jeff Wright (NT) 1988–94, Shawn Price (DE) 1996–2001, Keith McKenzie (DE) 2003.

92 Will Cokely (LB) 1987r, Gary Baldinger (NT) 1990–2, John Parrella (DL) 1993, *Ted Washington* (NT) 1995–2000, Tyrone Robertson (DT) 2001–2, Ryan Denney (DE) 2003.

93 Scott Virkus (DE) 1983–4, Scott Hernandez (NT) 1987r, Odell Haggins (NT) 1991, Keith Willis (DE) 1992, Pat Williams (DT) 1997–2003.

94 Richard Tharpe (DE) 1987r, Billy Witt (DE) 1987r, Mark Pike (LB) 1989–98, Aaron Schobel (DE) 2001–3.

95 Dave Young (TE) 1983, Sean McNanie (DE) 1984–7, Keith Goganious (LB) 1992, *Bryce Paup* (LB) 1995–7, Bryce Fisher (DL) 2001, Sam Adams (DT) 2003.

96 Leon Seals (DE) 1987–91, Craig Walls (LB) 1987r, Monty Brown (LB) 1993–5, Dan Brandenburg (LB) 1997–9, Erik Flowers (DE) 2000–1, Grant Irons (DE) 2002, Jeff Posey (LB) 2003.

97 Darrell Irvin (DE) 1980–3, Scott Radecic (LB) 1987–9, *Cornelius Bennett* (LB) 1990–5, Leif Larson (DT) 2000–1, Justin Bannan (DT) 2002–3.

98 Ira Albright (NT) 1987r, Elston Ridgle (DE) 1989, Jeff Hunter (DE) 1990, Sean Moran (DE) 1996–7, Kenyatta Wright (LB) 2000, Ron Edwards (DT) 2001–3.

99 Mark Roopenian (NT) 1982–3, Hal Garner (LB) 1985–8, 1990–1, James Patton (DL) 1993–4, Gabe Northern (LB) 1996–9, Fred Jones (LB) 2000–1, Ula Tuitele (LB) 2002.

CAROLINA PANTHERS

The franchise: Panthers founder Jerry Richardson went from being a rookie receiver on the 1959 champion Baltimore Colts to a successful businessman who built a food services empire beginning with acquiring the first Hardee's franchise in 1961. In 1987, his growing company purchased the Denny's restaurant chain, and he began a quest for an NFL franchise in North Carolina. In 1993 as he got closer to that goal, problems arose from several discrimination lawsuits brought against Denny's by both individuals and groups. An agreement brokered by the NAACP for Denny's to hire more minorities and to buy more from minority-owned businesses helped settle the dispute, and the Carolina Panthers were awarded an NFL franchise on October 26, 1993.

In their first year of operation, 1995, the Panthers set a record for a first-year expansion team by winning seven games. They followed that up with a 12–4 record and an appearance in the NFC Conference Championship in 1996. Dom Capers won Coach of the Year honors for that accomplishment, but within two years the wheels came off, and Capers was fired. He was replaced by George Seifert, who had the best winning percentage of any coach in NFL history at the time. Seifert lost both that record and his job within three years and capped it off by losing his last 15 games in 2001. Former Giants defensive coordinator John Fox became the third Panthers coach in 2002 and has begun building a winning tradition based on defense and a ball-control offense, getting the Panthers to the Super Bowl in his second season.

Origin of name: Panthers was suggested by team owner Jerry Richardson's son Mark, who also recommended the team's colors of black, blue and silver.

Record by Decade					
	Regular Season			Postseason	
	Won	Lost	Tied	Won	Lost	Championships
1990s	38	42	0	1	1	
2000s	26	38	0	3	0	
All-Time	64	80	0	4	1	None
Winning seasons: 2. Losing seasons: 6. .500 seasons: 1.						

Time till first championship: Nine years and counting.

Time since last championship: Never won a title.

Coaches			
	Years	Record	Playoffs
Dom Capers	1995–8	30–34	1–1
George Seifert	1999–2001	16–32	0–0
John Fox	2002–3	18–14	3–0

Retired numbers: None.

Numbers that should be retired: None yet.

Owned numbers: Although the number is not retired, 51 has not been worn since Sam Mills retired in 1997; Mills was the first Panther inducted in the team's Hall of Honor and it may not be worn again.

Numbers worn by Hall of Famers: 92 Reggie White.

Star power: Tshimanga Biakabutuka took 21 from Rod Smith.

Star eclipsed: Jim Harbaugh wore 5 because John Kasay wore 4. Steve Bono wore 12 because Ken Walter wore 13.

Numbers with most great players: 91 was worn by two quality pass rushers — Kevin Greene and Chuck Smith.

Worst represented numbers: 74 has been worn by six forgettable linemen.

Number worn by the most players: 89 has been worn by eight players.

Player who wore the most numbers: Tight end Luther Broughton has worn 49, 84 and 88 with Carolina.

Longest tenure wearing a number: 4 has been worn by kicker John Kasay for nine years, 1995–2003.

Number worn by first ever draft pick: 12 quarterback Kerry Collins, the first pick in 1995.

Biggest draft busts: Quarterback Kerry Collins, 12, was the fifth selection in 1995 and did lead the team to the NFC title game in his second year, but off the field problems caused him to beg out of starting in his fourth and last season in Carolina. Receiver Rae Carruth, 86/89, was the 27th selection in 1997, but after 62 catches in four years was convicted of conspiracy in the drive-by murder of his pregnant girlfriend in a high-profile trial in 2001.

Number worn by first expansion draft pick: 31 by defensive back Rod Smith. Wide receiver Mark Carrier, 83, lasted longest of any expansion draft picks— four years from 1995 to 19988.

Number worn by oldest player: 39 year old Reggie White wore 92 in 2000.

Cameos: All Pros and other notables— Jim Harbaugh 5; Eugene Robinson 41; Chuck Smith 91; Reggie White 92; Greg Lloyd 95; and Eric Swann 98.

Least popular numbers: 0, 1, and 19 have not yet been worn.

Last number to be originated: In 2003, 48 was worn for the first time by star runner Stephen Davis and 17 was worn for the first time by quarterback Jake Delhomme.

Longest dormant number: See Least Popular Numbers.

Triskaidekaphobia notes: Only punter Ken Walter has worn 13 so far in Carolina.

Shared numbers: 91 was worn by both linebacker Kevin Greene and defensive end Chuck Smith.

Continuity: 82 went from Pro Bowl returner Michael Bates to Pro Bowl returner Eric Metcalf.

Discontinuity: After Reggie White retired for good, 92 was taken by defensive end Gillis Wilson.

Family connections: None.

Quarterback numbers over 19: None.

Numbers of future NFL head coaches: None.

Numbers of future NFL referees: None.

Players who played other sports: Wild man linebacker Kevin Greene, 91, did a little wrestling.

Players more famous after football: Safety Ryan Sutter, 36, was the contestant on the popular reality television show *The Bachelor*.

Number with most points scored: 4 with 759 points scored by John Kasay.

Number with most yards rushing: 21 with 2,530 yards rushing by Tshimanga Biakabutuka.

Number with most receptions: 87 with 485 passes caught by Muhsin Muhammad.

Number with most touchdown passes: 7 with 86 touchdowns tossed by Steve Beurelein.

Number with most interceptions: 25 with 26 passes picked off by Eric Davis (25) and Bubba McDowell (1).

Oddity: Panther owner Jerry Richardson is the first former NFL player to own a league team since George Halas and, in a way, Curly Lambeau. Richardson wore 87 as a receiver for the Colts from 1959 to 1960.

Team All-Time Numerical Roster

Pro Bowl players for each number are in *Italics*; Hall of Famers are in **Bold** type.

1 none.

2 Dameyune Craig (QB) 1998–2001.

3 Rohn Stark (P) 1996, Richie Cunningham (K) 1999–2000, Ryan Tolhurst (WR) 2002.

4 *John Kasay* (K) 1995–2003.

5 Jim Harbaugh (QB) 2001, Jon Hilbert (K) 2002.

6 Tommy Barnhardt (P) 1995, Joe Nedney (K) 2000.

7 *Steve Beuerlein* (QB) 1996–2000, Tim Hasselbeck (QB) 2002.

8 Jeff Lewis (QB) 1999–2000.

9 Shane Matthews (QB) 1997–8, Matt Lytle (QB) 2000–1, Rodney Peete (QB) 2002–3.

10 Jack Trudeau (QB) 1995, Kerry Hood (WR) 2000, *Todd Sauerbrun* (P) 2001–3.

11 Jay Barker (QB) 1996, Shayne Graham (K) 2002.

12 *Kerry Collins* (QB) 1995–8, Steve Bono (QB) 1999, Randy Fasani (QB) 2002.

13 Ken Walter (P) 1997–2000.

14 Frank Reich (QB) 1995.

15 Jim Turner (WR) 2001.

16 Chris Weinke (QB) 2001–2.

17 Jake Delhomme (QB) 2003.

18 Nathan Black (WR) 2002.

19 none.

20 Derrick Moore (RB) 1995, Winslow Oliver (RB) 1996–8, Natrone Means (RB) 2000, Perry Phenix (S) 2001, DeShaun Foster (RB) 2002–3.

21 Rod Smith (CB) 1995, Tshimanga Biakabutuka (RB) 1996–2001, Terry Cousin (CB) 2002–3.

22 Tim McKyer (CB) 1995, Marquette Smith (RB) 1996–7, Lenny McGill (CB) 1998, Dee Brown (RB) 2001–2.

23 Anthony Johnson (RB) 1995–9, Randy Baldwin (RB) 1995, Reggie Howard (CB) 2000–3.

24 Alan Haller (CB) 1995, Clifton Abraham (CB) 1997, *Michael Bates* (KR) 1999–2000, Ricky Manning (CB) 2003.

25 Bubba McDowell (S) 1995, *Eric Davis* (CB) 1996–2000, Emmanuel McDaniel (CB) 2002.

26 Dewell Brewer (RB) 1995, Emmanuel McDaniel (CB) 1996, Michael Swift (CB) 1998–9, Lamar Smith (RB) 2002.

27 Damon Pieri (S) 1995–7, Deon Grant (S) 2000–3.

28 Tony Smith (RB) 1995, Roderick Mullen (DB) 1999, Deveron Harper (CB) 2000–1, Terry Fair (CB) 2002, Colin Branch (S) 2003.

29 Steve Lofton (CB) 1995–6, 1998–9, Ray Green (S) 2000, Dante Wesley (CB) 2002–3.

30 Howard Griffith (FB) 1995–6, Mike Minter (S) 1997–2003.

31 Blair Thomas (RB) 1995, Rod Smith (CB) 1996–8, Tony Booth (DB) 1999–2000, William Hampton (CB) 2003.

32 Dino Philyaw (RB) 1995–6, Nate Turner (FB) 1995, Fred Lane (RB) 1997–9, Rod Smart (RB) 2002–3.

33 Butler By'not'e (CB) 1995, Leroy Hoard (RB) 1996, Doug Evans (CB) 1998–2001, Joe Montgomery (RB) 2002.

34 Vince Workman (RB) 1995, Mike Dulaney (FB) 1998, Richard Huntley (RB) 2001, Ryan Sutter (S) 1998.

35 Deke Cooper (S) 2002.

36 Tony Veland (S) 1998, Nick Goings (RB) 2001–2.

37 Chad Cota (S) 1995–7, Leonard Wheeler (CB) 1998–9, Jimmy Hitchcock (CB) 2000–1, Nick Goings (RB) 2003.

38 Tyrone Poole (CB) 1995–7, Mike Scurlock (S) 1999.

39 Brett Maxie (S) 1995–6, Damien Richardson (S) 1998–2002.

40 Pat Terrell (S) 1995–7, William Floyd (FB) 1998–2000, Jarrod Cooper (S) 2001–3.

41 Toi Cook (CB) 1996–7, Eugene Robinson (S) 2000.

42 Skip Hicks (RB) 2002, Travares Tillman (S) 2003.

43 Scott Greene (FB) 1996–7, Juran Bolden (CB) 1998.

44 Bob Christian (FB) 1995–6, Derwin Gray (S) 1998, Chris Hetherington (FB) 1999–2001.

45 Michael Reed (CB) 1995–6, Brad Hoover (RB) 2000–3.

46 Kantroy Barber (RB) 1997, Brent Alexander (S) 1998–9, Rashard Anderson (CB) 2000–2.

47 Mike Senters (CB) 1995, Marco Battaglia (TE) 2003.

48 *Stephen Davis* (RB) 2003.

49 Jason Gavadza (TE) 2000, Luther Broughton (TE) 2001, Shawn Draper (TE) 2002.

50 Jamal Fountaine (LB) 1995, Duane Bickett (LB) 1996, Kinnon Tatum (LB) 1997–8, Chris Slade (DE) 2001, Brad Jackson (LB) 2002, Vinny Ciurciu (LB) 2003.

51 *Sam Mills* (LB) 1995–7.

52 Matt Elliott (G) 1995–7, Jeff Brady (LB) 1998, Kory Minor (LB) 1999–2001, Brian Allen (LB) 2002–3.

53 Paul Butcher (LB) 1995, Myron Baker (LB) 1996–7, Jerry Jensen (LB) 1998, Hannibal Navies (LB) 1999–2002, Greg Favors (LB) 2003.

54 Carlton Bailey (LB) 1995–7, Donta' Jones (LB) 1999, Lee Woodall (LB) 2000, Nate Hemsley (LB) 2001, Will Witherspoon (LB) 2002–3.

55 Brett Faryniarz (LB) 1995, Percell Gaskins (LB) 1997, Steve Tovar (LB) 1999, Dan Morgan (LB) 2001–3.

56 Darion Conner (LB) 1995, Micheal Barrow (LB) 1997–9, Spencer Reid (LB) 1998, 2000, Jason Kyle (LB) 2001–3.

57 *Lamar Lathon* (LB) 1995–8, Lester Towns (LB) 2000–3.

58 Andre Royal (LB) 1995–7, Deon Humphrey (LB) 2000, Rob Holmberg (LB) 2001, Mark Fields (LB) 2002–3.

59 Travis Hill (LB) 1995, Ernest Jones (LB) 1998–9, Michael Hawkes (LB) 2000–1, Darren Hambrick (LB) 2001, Kory Minor (LB) 2002, Terrance Simmons (DT) 2002, Mike Caldwell (LB) 2003.

60 Andrew Peterson (G) 1995, Bucky Greeley (C) 1996–8, Clay Shiver (G) 1999, Jeff Mitchell (C) 2001–3.

61 Anthony Redmon (G) 1998–9.

62 Mark Dennis (T) 1995, T.J. Washington (OL) 2001, Tim Stuber (OL) 2002.

63 Mark Rodenhauser (C) 1995–7, Jamar Nesbit (G) 1999–2002.

64 Curtis Whitley (C) 1995–6, Corbin Lacina (G) 1998, James Dexter (OL) 2000, Larry Chester (DT) 2001.

65 Frank Garcia (C) 1995–2000, Kevin Donnalley (G) 2001–3.

66 Matt Campbell (G) 1995–2000, Louis Williams (C) 2001–2.

67 Brandon Hayes (G) 1995–6, Bryan Stoltenberg (C) 1998–2000.

68 Blake Brockermeyer (T) 1995, Mitch Marrow (DL) 1998.

69 Les Miller (DE) 1996–8, Jordan Gross (T) 2003.

70 Kevin Farkas (T) 1995, Todd Stewart (T) 1997, Chris Terry (T) 1999–2002.

71 Greg Kragen (NT) 1995–7, Rick Terry (DE) 1998–9, Al Lucas (DT) 2000–1, Fernando Smith (DE) 2002, Matt Willig (T) 2003.

72 Steve Scifres (OL) 1998, Danny Villa (C) 1998, Robert Daniel (DE) 1999–2000, Bruce Nelson (G) 2003.

73 Jamie Wilson (T) 1997–8, Nate Newton (G) 1999, Melvin Tuten (T) 2000–2.

74 Derrick Graham (T) 1995, Mark Dennis (T) 1996, Paul Janus (C) 1998, Antonio Dingle (DT) 1999, Dwayne Ledford (G) 2001, Derrick Fletcher (G) 2002.

75 Greg Skrepenak (G) 1996–7, Ricky Siglar (T) 1998, Clarence Jones (T) 1999–2000, Todd Steussie (T) 2001–3.

76 Jason Childs (T) 1995, Norberto Davidds-Garrido (T) 1996–9, Leander Jordan (G) 2000–1, Tutan Reyes (OL) 2002.

77 *Kris Jenkins* (DT) 2001–3.

78 Emerson Martin (G) 1995, Blake Brockermeyer (T) 1995–8, Jeno James (G) 2000–3.

79 Sean Love (G) 1995, Rob Bohlinger (T) 1998, Viliami Maumau (DT) 1999, Doug Brzezinski (G) 2003.

80 Dwight Stone (WR) 1995–8, Jim Turner (WR) 2000, Keith Heinrich (TE) 2002, Eugene Baker (WR) 2003.

81 Reggie Jones (WR) 1995, Raghib Ismail (WR) 1996–8, Donald Hayes (WR) 1999–2001, Anthony Bright (WR) 2002, Ricky Proehl (WR) 2003.

82 Don Beebe (WR) 1995, *Michael Bates* (KR) 1996–8, Eric Metcalf (WR) 1999, Isaac Byrd (WR) 2000–2, Mike Siedman (TE) 2003.

83 Mark Carrier (WR) 1995–8, Patrick Jeffers (WR) 1999–2001, Walter Young (WR) 2003.

84 Eric Guliford (WR) 1995, Paul Burke (TE) 1996, Luther Broughton (TE) 1997, Casey Crawford (TE) 2000–1, Jermaine Wiggins (TE) 2002–3.

85 Lawyer Tillman (TE) 1995, *Wesley Walls* (TE) 1996–2002, Kevin Dyson (WR) 2003.

86 Willie Green (WR) 1995–6, Rae Carruth (WR) 1997, Kris Mangum (TE) 1997–2003.

87 *Muhsin Muhammad* (WR) 1996–2003.

88 Pete Metzelaars (TE) 1995, Walter Rasby (TE) 1996–7, Luther Broughton (TE) 1998, Donald Hayes (WR) 1998, Brian Kinchen (TE) 1999–2000, Karl Hankton (WR) 2000–3.

89 Elbert Ellis (WR) 1995, Walter Rasby (TE) 1995, Syii Tucker (TE) 1996, Ernie Mills (WR) 1997, Rae Carruth (WR) 1998–9, Dialleo Burks (WR) 1999–2000, Iheanyi Uwaezuoke (WR) 2000, *Steve Smith* (WR) 2001–3.

90 Jeff Zgonina (NT) 1995, Tim Colston (NT) 1996, Tim Morabito (DT) 1997–2000, Jeff Posey (LB) 2001, Julius Peppers (DE) 2002–3.

91 Mike Teeter (NT) 1995, *Kevin Greene* (LB) 1996, 1998–9, Chuck Smith (DE) 2000, Cedric Killings (DT) 2001, Josh Taves (DE) 2002.

92 Shawn Price (DE) 1995, Tarek Saleh (LB) 1997–8, Israel Raybon (DE) 1997, *Reggie White* (DE) 2000, Gillis Wilson (DE) 2001, Mario Fatafehi (DT) 2002, Kavika Pittman (DE) 2003.

93 Mike Fox (DE) 1995–8, Mike Rucker (DE) 1999–2003.

94 Sean Gilbert (DT) 1998–2002, Kindal Moorehead (DT) 2003.

95 Mark Thomas (DE) 1995–6, Greg Lloyd (LB) 1998, Dean Wells (LB) 1999–2001.

96 Shawn King (DE) 1995–8, Antonio Edwards (DE) 1999, Jay Williams (DE) 2000–1, Al Wallace (DE) 2002–3.

97 Jeff Fields (DL) 1995, Tommy Jeter (DE) 1996, Renaldo Turnbull (LB) 1997, Jason Peter (DE) 1998–2001, Kemp Rasmussen (DE) 2002–3.

98 Gerald Williams (DE) 1995–7, Don Sasa (DE) 1998, Esera Tuaolo (DT) 1999, Eric Swann (DT) 2000, John Milem (DE) 2001, Shane Burton (DT) 2002–3.

99 Jeremy Nunley (DE) 1995, Ray Seals (DE) 1997, Chuck Wiley (DE) 1998–9, Alvin McKinley (DT) 2000, Brentson Buckner (DT) 2001–3.

CHICAGO BEARS

The franchise: Along with the Cardinals, the Bears are one of two charter members of the NFL still playing. They were formed as the Decatur Staleys in 1920 by George Halas and sponsored by the Staley Starch Company. The next year, Halas showed he was a forward thinker by moving his team from the college town of Decatur to the big city of Chicago. While the league was primarily founded in smaller towns throughout the Midwest, the only such town that still survives with a football team today is the Green Bay Packers, the Bears' long-time rival.

In their first year in Chicago, the Bears won the league title in 1921, and they would remain competitive throughout the 1920s. Their next big splash was in signing the most spectacular college player in the nation, Red Grange, in 1925 and supplementing the team's league schedule with a full schedule of barnstorming appearances that attracted then-record crowds for professional football. Halas was an intimidating, driven leader who had a clear eye for talent and a strong in-

novative streak. He championed the T formation in the early 1930s and continued to tinker with it until the Bears became an unstoppable force known as the "Monsters of the Midway" in the early 1940s with their split T, man-in-motion offense operated by Halas' hand-picked field general Sid Luckman. The Bears who had won two titles in the 1930s, took three of the first four championships in the 1940s and would win four titles in six years in that decade. Two times they finished a regular season undefeated — although they lost the title game in both those years.

Halas followed a pattern of coaching for about 10 years, retiring to recharge his batteries, and then returning a few years later for another decade-long stretch. With Halas coaching the team for 40 of its first 50 years, the Bears stayed a rough, mauling, successful squad for most of that time. They won their last title under Halas in 1963 led by assistant coach George Allen's aggressive defense. Once Halas retired from coaching for good in 1967, though, the team went into decline for the next 15 years until they were brought back to prominence by the combination of an accumulation of talent, the defensive scheme of coordinator Buddy Ryan, and the motivation of head coach Mike Ditka. The culmination of this volatile amalgamation was the magical 1985 season in which the Bears displayed one of the most devastating defenses in league history and lost only one game en route to a Super Bowl championship. That team continued to make the playoffs for several seasons before a general decline set in again in the 1990s from which the team has not emerged yet. Although Halas passed away in 1983, the team remains in his family. The Bears are second only to the Packers with nine league championships and lead everyone with 24 former Bears in the Hall of Fame.

Origin of name: The Bears were originally called the Decatur Staleys after the starch company in Decatur, Illinois, that sponsored them. George Halas obtained full ownership of the team in 1921 and moved them to Chicago. In perhaps the first naming rights deal in NFL history, Halas was paid $5,000 to continue to call the team the Staleys for one year. When the year was up in 1922, Halas renamed the team the Bears as sort of a one-upsmanship over the local major league baseball team, the Cubs. Bears, like football players, are bigger, stronger, and more fearsome than Cubs or baseball players.

Time till first championship: One year.

Time since last championship: 19 years.

Retired numbers: The Bears have retired more numbers than any other NFL team by far, 13 of them — 3 for Bronko Nagurski, 5 for George McAfee, 7 for George Halas, 28 for Willie Galimore, 34 for Walter Payton, 40 for Gale Sayers, 41 for Brian Piccolo, 42 for Sid Luckman, 51 for Dick Butkus, 56 for Bill Hewitt, 61 for Bill George, 66 for Bulldog Turner, and 77 for Red Grange. All but Galimore who died in an auto accident and Piccolo who died of cancer are in the Hall of Fame.

Other numbers worn by these players: Nagurski also wore 16 briefly; Bill George wore 72 as a rookie; George McAfee reportedly wore 35 at some point but I have not confirmed that.

Those who wore retired numbers after the honored player: After Nagurski, 3 was worn by backs Albert Johnson, Lewis Hamity, Jim Fordham, Dante Magnani, Eddie Allen and Wally Dreyer; after George McAfee, 5 was worn by backs Frank Maznicki and Billys Stone; after George Halas, 7 was worn by backs Joe Lintzenich, John Sisk, Pug Rentner, John Oelerich, and Bill Geyer, by ends Eggs Manske and Ed Sprinkle and by quarterbacks John Huarte and Bob Avelini; after Gale Sayers, 40 was worn by replacement player Steve Trimble; after Dick Butkus, 51 was worn by centers Dan Neal and Mark Rodenhauser and by linebackers Mel Rogers, Bruce Herron, Doug Becker, and Jim Morrisey; after Bill George, 61 was worn by guards Don Croftcheck and Glen Holloway; during Bulldog Turner's career, 66 was worn by guard Phil Martinovich and center John Schiechl; when Red Grange left the Bears in 1926, 77 was worn fellow Hall of Famer Link Lyman for one year.

Numbers that should be retired: With 13 numbers retired, how could they have missed one?

Record by Decade

	Regular Season			Postseason		
	Won	Lost	Tied	Won	Lost	Championships
1920s	84	31	19	0	0	1921
1930s	85	28	11	1	2	1932, 1933
1940s	81	26	3	5	1	1940, 1941, 1943, 1946
1950s	70	48	2	0	2	
1960s	67	65	6	1	0	1963
1970s	60	83	1	0	2	
1980s	92	60	0	5	4	1985
1990s	73	87	0	2	3	
2000s	29	35	0	0	1	
All-Time	641	463	42	14	15	9

Winning seasons: 52. Losing seasons 29. .500 seasons: 3.

Coaches			
	Years	*Record*	*Playoffs*
George Halas (1)	1920–9	84–31–19	0–0
Ralph Jones (1)	1930–2	24–10–7	0–0
George Halas (3)	1933–42	84–21–4	4–3
Hunk Anderson/Luke Johnsos (1)	1942–5	23–12–2	1–0
George Halas (1)	1946–55	75–42–2	1–1
Paddy Driscoll	1956–7	14–9–1	0–1
George Halas (1)	1958–67	75–53–6	1–0
Jim Dooley	1968–71	20–36–0	0–0
Abe Gibron	1972–4	11–30–1	0–0
Jack Pardee	1975–7	20–22–0	0–1
Neill Armstrong	1978–81	30–34–0	0–1
Mike Ditka (1)	1982–92	106–62–0	6–6
Dave Wannstedt	1993–8	40–56–0	0–1
Dick Jauron	1999–2003	35–45–0	0–1
(Championships in parentheses)			

Owned numbers: 42 was only worn by Hall of Fame quarterback Sid Luckman and 56 was only worn by Hall of Fame end Bill Hewitt.

Numbers worn by Hall of Famers: Doug Atkins 81, George Blanda 16/22, Dick Butkus 51, Guy Chamberlain 13/23, George Connor 71/81, Jimmy Conzleman 1/15, Mike Ditka 89, Paddy Driscoll 1/20, Dan Fortman 21, Bill George 61/72, Red Grange 77, George Halas 7, Dan Hampton 99, Ed Healey 16, Bill Hewitt 56, Stan Jones 78, Walt Kiesling 25, Bobby Layne 22, Sid Luckman 42, Link Lyman 11/12/77 and maybe 2 and 14, George McAfee 5 and maybe 35, George Musso 16, Bronko Nagurski 3/16, Alan Page 82, Walter Payton 34, Gale Sayers 40, Mike Singletary 50, Joe Stydahar 13/18, George Trafton 13, Bulldog Turner 66.

Star power: Gary Fencik took 45 from Craig Clemons.

Star eclipsed: Bob Jeter wore 29 because Cecil Turner wore 21. Jim Flanigan wore 68 till Tim Ryan, 99, left. Edgar Bennett wore 32 because 34 was retired for Walter Payton.

Numbers with most great players: 13 was worn by Hall of Famers George Trafton, Ed Healey, Guy Chamberlain and Joe Stydahar; 9 was worn by star quarterbacks Bill Wade and Jim McMahon as well as halfback Bill Osmanski; 35 was worn by star runners Rick Casares, Neal Anderson and Anthony Thomas.

Worst represented numbers: 19 has been worn by 21 unmemorable Bears across all position groups—ends, tackles, guards, centers, quarterbacks, halfbacks, fullbacks and a punter.

Number worn by the most players: 22 has been worn by 27 players.

Player who wore the most numbers: Link Lyman wore 11/12/77 and unconfirmed reports claim he wore 2 and 14 too. Others who wore three numbers include: Johnny Bryan 4/8/9, Craig Clemons 25/43/45, Dante Magnani 3/4/8, Gerald Weatherly 45/50/84, and Bill Wightkin 53/72/86.

Longest tenure wearing a number: Linebacker Doug Buffone wore 55 for 14 years from 1966 to 1979. Five Bears wore their number for 13 years.

Number worn by first ever draft pick: Joe Stydahar was the first pick in 1936 and wore 13 and 18.

Biggest draft busts: The biggest draft bust was probably runner Curtis Enis, 39/44, who was selected fifth in 1998 and who averaged only 3.3 yards per carry in his three year career with the average gain decreasing each year.

Number worn by oldest player: 39 year old Mike Horan wore 2 in 1998.

Cameos: Hall of Famers—Walt Kiesling 25; All-Pros and other notables—Tom Bettis 65; Lee Roy Caffey 60; Paul Engebretsen 21; John Gilliam 82; Craig Heyward 45; Dave

Kreig 17; Greg Landry 11; Paul Lipscomb 74; Ed Neal 58; Ricky Proehl 87.

Ones who got away: The biggest was Lions Hall of Famer Bobby Layne 22, a third string quarterback in 1948 who was traded because the Bears also had Sid Luckman who would soon retire and Johnny Lujack who would soon get injured. Others who became stars elsewhere include expansion team stars Bill Brown 38 of the Vikings and Chuck Howley 54 of the Vikings as well as AFL receivers Willard Dewveall 88 of the Oilers and Lionel Taylor 32 of the Broncos. In addition, runner J.D. Smith 39 would star with the 49ers and cornerback Jesse Whittenton 46 was an All Pro with Green Bay.

Least popular numbers: 0 has never been worn. 90 and 99 have been worn five times each.

Last number to be originated: 94 and 97 were both worn for the first time in 1987 by defensive tackles Dick Chapura and Sean Smith respectively.

Longest dormant number: 1 was dormant for 51 years from 1945 till 1996. Currently, 19 has not been worn since 1983.

Triskaidekaphobia notes: The early Bears did not shy away from 13; it was worn by four Hall of Famers in the 1920s, 1930s and 1940s — George Trafton, Ed Healey, Guy Chamberlain, and Joe Stydahar. After Stydahar, it was still worn by several others in the 1940s, but then was dormant for 48 years until the Rick Mirer disaster in 1997.

Shared numbers: 16 was worn by two Hall of Fame tackles Ed Healey and George Musso; 78 was worn by Hall of Famer Stan Jones and long-time offensive line anchor Keith Van Horne; 83 was worn by two talented receivers Bill McColl and Willie Gault.

Continuity: Star linebacker Doug Buffone was replaced in 55 by star linebacker Otis Wilson; Hall of Famer Red Grange was replaced in 77 by Hall of Famer Link Lyman.

Discontinuity: Hall of Famer Bronko Nagurski was followed in 3 by fullback Albert Johnson; Hall of Famer Joe Stydahar was followed in 13 by guard Monte Merkel; Hall

of Famer George Musso was followed in 16 by guard Rudy Mucha; Hall of Famer Paddy Driscoll was followed in 20 by center Jack Mintum; Hall of Famer Doug Atkins was followed in 81 by Marty Amsler (who would also take Hall of Famer Willie Davis' number in Green Bay); Hall of Famer Mike Ditka was followed in 89 by guard Terry Stoepel.

Family Connections

Brothers

Red Grange	B	1925, 1929–34	77
Garland Grange	E	1929–31	25
Ron Morris	WR	1987–91	84
Bam Morris	RB	1998	33
Bill Osmanski	B	1939–43, 1946–7	9
Joe Osmanski	B	1946–9	18
Joe Sternaman	B	1922–5, 1927–30	4
Ed Sternaman	B	1920–7	2/3

Father and sons

Rich Leuwenburg	T	1965	57
Jay Leuwenburg	G	1992–5	58
John Sisk	B	1932–6	7
John Sisk	B	1964	27
Rosey Taylor	S	1961–8	24
Brian Taylor	RB	1989	27

Quarterback numbers over 19: 22 Bobby Layne and George Blanda; 23 Joe Barnes; 27 Owen Goodnight; 30 Bob Dunlap; 32 Johnny Lujack; 33 Bernie Masterson and Johnny Long; 36 Tom Farris; 37 Young Bussey; 42 Sid Luckman; 57 Billy Patterson; and 80 Tom Heardon.

Number of first black player: In 1952 back Emerson Cole 31, tackle Herman Clark 74 and back Eddie Macon 25 broke the color line in Chicago. The following season Willie Thrower, 14, became the first black NFL quarterback.

Numbers of future NFL head coaches: Hunk Anderson 18/24; Tom Bettis 65; Johnny Bryan 4/8/9; Guy Chamberlain 13/23; Red Conkright 47; Jimmy Conzleman 1/15; Mike Ditka 89; Jim Dooley 43; Paddy Driscoll 1/20; Chuck Drulis 14/21; Jeff Fisher 24; Abe Gibron 65; George Halas 7; Mike Holovak 15; Ken Huffine 5; Herb Joesting 33; Luke Johnsos 24; Walt Kiesling 25; Ray

McLean 57; Keith Moleworth 4; Richie Petitbon 17; Hamp Pool 76; Ray Richards 44; Gene Ronzani 6; Ralph Scott 17; Bob Snyder 13/17; Joey Sternaman 4; Pete Stinchcomb 8; Joe Stydahar 13/18; Bulldog Turner 66; and George Wilson 30.

Numbers of future NFL referees: Merrill Douglas 36, Paddy Driscoll 1/20, and George McAfee 5.

Players who played other sports: Baseball — Charley Dressen 5; Paddy Driscoll 1/20; George Halas 7; Johnny Mohardt 26; and Ernie Vick 23/26. Basketball — Connie Mack Berry 23; Jim Conzleman 1/15; Cookie Cunningham 14; Jack Dugger 13; Bob MacLeod 5; Tillie Voss 27; Clint Wager 51; Laurie Walquist 5; and George Wilson 30. Wrestling — Kay Bell 26, Steve McMichael 76, Bronko Nagurski 3/16, William Perry 72, Joe Savoldi 54; . Track — Willie Gault 83.

Players more famous after football: Young Bussey, 37, died in World War II; Alan Page, 82, became a Minnesota State Supreme Court Judge; Darnell Autrey, 21, and Dick Butkus, 51, did some acting; Brian Piccolo, 41, had the end of his life immortalized in a TV movie, *Brian's Song*, that became a pop culture event.

First player to wear a number in the 70s: Red Grange wore 77 in 1925.

First player to wear a number in the 80s: Earl Britton wore 80 in 1925.

First player to wear a number in the 90s: Jim Daniell wore 99 in 1945.

Number with most points scored: 6 with 1,422 points scored by Kevin Butler (1,116), Bill Senn (155), Gene Ronzani (57), Don Kindt (44), John Siegal (42), and Hans Nielsen (8).

Number with most yards rushing: 34 with 18,932 yards rushing by Walter Payton (16,726), John Dottley (1,122), Joe Marconi (1,002), and Bill Tucker (82).

Number with most receptions: 89 with 927 passes caught by Mike Ditka (316), James Scott (177), Ryan Wetnight (174), Bob Wallace (109), John Hoffman (75), Ken Margerum (39), Dusty Lyman (26), Keith Ortego (23), Mitch Krenk (2), and James Coley (1).

Number with most touchdown passes: 9 with 175 touchdowns tossed by Bill Wade (68), Jim McMahon (67), Shane Matthews (19), Bob Williams (10), Ray Buivid (6), and Walt Holmer (5).

Number with most interceptions: 21 with 79 passes picked off by Donnell Woolford (36), Leslie Frazier (20), Dan Fortman (8), R.W. McQuarters (7), Chuck Drulis (4), Terry Cousin (3), George Figner (1).

Oddity: The Bears have had several kickers wear a number in the 80s. Placekickers Roger Leclerc and Mac Percival both wore 83 and John Aveni wore 89. Punter Bobby Joe Green wore 88 and punter Bob Parsons wore 86.

Also, Doug Plank, 46, had Buddy Ryan's famed 46 defense named after him.

Finally, two of the three sons who played for the Bears wore 27, John Sisk Jr. and Brian Taylor.

Players Whose Number Is Unknown		
Hub Shoemaker	(G)	1920
Richard Barker	(G)	1921
Charles Harley	(HB)	1921
Bourbon Bonderant	(T/E)	1922
Frank Rydzewski	(OL)	1923
Harry O'Connell	(T)	1924
Damon Wetzel	(FB/LB)	1935

Players with an Unconfirmed Number			
2/14	Link Lyman	(T)	1934
5	Bill Buckler	(G)	1926–8, 1931–3
23	Ernie Vick	(C)	1927–8
33	George McAfee	(HB)	1940–1, 1945–50

Team All-Time Numerical Roster

Those with an "r" following the year 1987 were replacement players during the players' strike. Pro Bowl and pre–1950 All Pro players for each number are in *Italics*; Hall of Famers are in **Bold** type.

1 Jake Lanum (QB) 1920–4, **Jim Conzleman** (B) 1920, Oscar Johnson (B) 1924, **Paddy Driscoll** (B) 1926–9, *Lee Artoe* (T) 1945, Jeff Jaeger (K) 1996–9.

2 *Ed Sternaman* (B) 1920–1, Joe LaFleur (FB) 1922–4, Ralph King (T) 1925, *Dick Nesbitt* (B) 1930–3, Bill Pollock (B) 1935–6, *Gary Famiglietti* (FB) 1938–45, Doug Flutie (QB) 1986, Will Furrer (QB) 1992, Mike Horan (P) 1998, Paul Edinger (K) 2000–3.

3 Robert Koehler (FB) 1920–1, *Ed Sternaman* (B) 1922–7, **Bronko Nagurski** (FB/T) 1930–7, 1943, Albert Johnson (FB) 1938, Lewis Hamity (B) 1941, Jim Fordham (FB) 1944–5, Dante Magnani (B) 1946, Eddie Allen (FB) 1947, Wally Dreyer (HB) 1949.

4 Pard Pearce (QB) 1920–1, *Joe Sternaman* (B) 1922–5, 1927–30, Johnny Bryan (B) 1926, *Keith Molesworth* (B) 1931–7, Reino Nori (B) 1938, *Harry Clark* (B) 1940–3, Tipp Mooney (B) 1944–5, Frank Maznicki (B) 1946, Nick Sacrinty (QB) 1947, Dante Magnani (B) 1949, John Roveto (K) 1982, Steve Fuller (QB) 1984–6, Jim Harbaugh (QB) 1987–93, Steve Walsh (QB) 1994–5, Moses Moreno (QB) 1998, Brad Maynard (P) 2001–3.

5 Charley Dressen (B) 1920, Ken Huffine (FB) 1921, Laurie Walquist (QB) 1922, 1924–31, Carl Hanke (G) 1922, George Bolan (FB) 1923–4, George Corbett (B) 1932–8, Robert MacLeod (B) 1939, Anton Stolfa (B) 1939, **George McAfee** (HB) 1940–1, 1945–50, Frank Maznicki (B) 1942, Billy Stone (HB) 1951.

6 Sid Gepford (B) 1920, Hec Garvey (E) 1922–3, Jim Kendricks (T) 1924, *Bill Senn* (B) 1926–31, Bernie Leahy (B) 1932, *Gene Ronzani* (B) 1933–8, 1944–5, John Siegal (E) 1939–43, *Don Kindt* (HB) 1947–56, Hans Nielsen (K) 1981, Kevin Butler (K) 1985–95.

7 **George Halas** (E) 1920–8, Joseph Lintzenich (FB) 1930–1, John Sisk (B) 1932–6, Ernest Rentner (B) 1937, Edgar Manske (E) 1938–40, John Oelerich (B) 1938, Bill Geyer (B) 1942, *Ed Sprinkle* (E) 1944–55, John Huarte (QB) 1972, Bob Avellini (QB) 1975–84.

8 Leo Johnson (B) 1920, *Pete Stinchcomb* (QB) 1921–2, Johnny Bryan (B) 1924–5, Roy White (FB) 1927–9, *Carl Brumbaugh* (QB) 1930–4, 1936–8, Al Moore (QB) 1932, George Grosvenor (B) 1935–6, Charles Heileman (E) 1939, *Hugh Gallarneau* (B) 1941–2, 1945–7, Dante Magnani (B) 1943, Bill Glenn (QB) 1944, James Canady (B) 1948–9, Vince Evans (QB) 1977–83, Maury Buford (P) 1985–6, 1989–91, Mike Hohensee (QB) 1987r, Carlos Huerta (K) 1996, Cade McNown (QB) 1999–2000, Rex Grossman (QB) 2003.

9 Roy White (FB) 1925, Cliff Lemon (T) 1926, Johnny Bryan (B) 1927, *Walt Holmer* (FB) 1929–30, Paul Franklin (E) 1931–3, Ray Buivid (B) 1937–8, John Bettridge (HB) 1937, *Bill Osmanski*

(B) 1939–43, 1946–7, Dick Flanagan (G) 1948–9, Bob Williams (QB) 1951–2, 1955, *Bill Wade* (QB) 1961–6, John Roveto (K) 1981, *Jim McMahon* (QB) 1982–8, Shane Matthews (QB) 1993–6, 1999–2001.

10 *Burt Ingwerson* (G) 1920–1, Pard Pearce (QB) 1922, Gus Fetz (FB) 1923, Oscar Johnson (FB) 1924, Milt Romney (QB) 1925–9, Leland Elnes (QB) 1929, Leo Jensvold (QB) 1931, *Jack Manders* (B/K) 1933–40, John Petty (FB) 1942, Noah Mullins (HB) 1946–9, Al Campana (B) 1950–1, Tom O'Connell (QB) 1953, Rudy Bukich (QB) 1963–8, Bobby Douglass (QB) 1969–76, Peter Tom Willis (QB) 1990–3, Mark Butterfield (QB) 1996, Jaret Holmes (K) 1999, Louie Aguiar (P) 2000, Henry Burris (QB) 2002, Kordell Stewart (QB) 2003.

11 Andy Feichtinger (E) 1920–1, Oscar Knopp (FB) 1923–8, Leland Elnes (QB) 1929, **Link Lyman** (T) 1930–1, Lennon Blackmon (HB) 1930, Harold Ely (G) 1932, Art Buss (T) 1934–5, John Doehring (FB) 1936–7, Joe Maniaci (B) 1938–41, Frank Morris (B) 1942, Bill Geyer (B) 1943, 1946, Russ Reader (B) 1947, Fred Evans (HB) 1948, Julie Rykovich (HB) 1949–51, Jim Haluska (HB) 1956, Jack Concannon (QB) 1967–71, Virgil Carter (QB) 1976, Greg Landry (QB) 1984, Kevin Brown (P) 1987r, Brian Gowins (K) 1999, Mark Hartsell (QB) 2000.

12 Jerry Jones (G) 1920, Lou Usher (T) 1921, 1923, **Link Lyman** (T) 1927–8, 1932–4, John Ryan (T) 1929, Frank Sullivan (C) 1935–9, Anton Stolfa (B) 1939, Harold Lahar (G) 1941, Jim Benton (E) 1943, Abe Croft (E) 1944–5, Walter Lamb (E) 1946, Steve Romanik (QB) 1950–3, Zeke Bratkowski (QB) 1954–9, Dick Norman (QB) 1961–2, Larry Rakestraw (QB) 1964–7, Rusty Lisch (QB) 1984, Steve Bradley (QB) 1987r, Erik Kramer (QB) 1994–6, Brent Bartholomew (P) 2000, Chris Chandler (QB) 2002–3.

13 **George Trafton** (C) 1920–1, 1923–32, **Guy Chamberlin** (E) 1921, **Ed Healey** (T) 1922, **Joe Stydahar** (T) 1936–42, 1946, Monte Merkel (G) 1943, Bob Snyder (QB) 1943, Jake Sweeney (T) 1944, Frank Ramsey (G) 1945, Thurman Garrett (C) 1947–8, Jake Dugger (E) 1949, Rick Mirer (QB) 1997.

14 Kyle MacWherter (FB) 1920, Tarzan Taylor (G) 1921, Fred Larson (C) 1922, Harold Cuningham (E) 1929, Frank Don Pauley (T) 1930, Lloyd Burdick (T) 1931–2, Fred Crawford (T) 1934–5, *Dick Plasman* (E) 1937–41, 1944, *Chuck Drulis* (G) 1942, *George Zorich* (G) 1944–5, *Ed Cifers* (E) 1947–8, Wayne Hansen (C) 1950–1, Willie Thrower (QB) 1953, Ken Gorgal (HB) 1955–6, Rudy Bukich (QB) 1958–9, 1962, Buddy Lee (QB) 1971, Ben Bennett (QB) 1988.

15 **Jim Conzelman** (B) 1920, Walter Veach (B) 1920, Harry Englund (E) 1921–2, Pat Flaherty (E) 1923, Verne Mullen (E) 1924–6, Bill Fleckenstein

(G) 1925–30, *Bill Buckler* (G) 1931–2, Ted Rosequist (T) 1934, Henry Hammond (E) 1937, Al Matuza (C) 1941–3, Forest Masterson (C) 1945, Mike Holovak (FB) 1947–8, Curley Morrison (HB) 1950–3, *Ed Brown* (QB) 1954–61, Virgil Carter (QB) 1968–9, Mirro Roder (K) 1973–4, Mike Phipps (QB) 1977–81, Dave Finzer (P) 1984, Bryan Wagner (P) 1987–8, Jim Miller (QB) 1999–2002.

16 Randolph Young (T) 1920, Russell Smith (T) 1921–2, 1925, **Ed Healey** (T) 1923–7, John Polisky (G) 1929, Harry Richman (G) 1929, **Bronko Nagurski** (FB/T) 1930, **George Musso** (T) 1933–44, Rudy Mucha (G) 1945–6, Milt Vucinich (G) 1945, Hank Norberg (E) 1948, Ed Cody (FB) 1949–51, **George Blanda** (QB/K) 1952–8, Kent Nix (QB) 1970–1, Bob Thomas (K) 1975–84, Tim Lashar (K) 1987, Todd Sauerbrun (P) 1995–9, Brooks Barnard (P) 2003.

17 Ross Petty (G) 1920, Ralph Scott (T) 1921–5, Fred Larson (C) 1922, 1929, *Bill Buckler* (G) 1926–8, Elmer Wynne (FB) 1928, Everett Nelson (T) 1929, Milt Frump (G) 1930, George Lyon (T) 1931, Jim Pederson (B) 1932, Joe Zeller (G) 1938, Bob Snyder (QB) 1939–41, *Pete Gudauskas* (G) 1943–4, *Richie Petitbon* (S) 1959–68, Cliff Hardy (CB) 1971, Ike Hill (WR) 1973–4, Tommy Barnhardt (P) 1987, Sean Payton (QB) 1987r, Quintin Smith (WR) 1990, Chris Gardocki (P) 1992–4, Dave Krieg (QB) 1996, Danny Wuerffel (QB) 2001, Corey Sauter (QB) 2002.

18 J.L. Shank (B) 1920, *Hunk Anderson* (G) 1922, Ed Anderson (E) 1923, *Don Murry* (T) 1924–31, Ed Michaels (G) 1936, Edgar Manske (E) 1937, Alec Shellogg (T) 1939, Adolph Kissell (FB) 1942, **Joe Stydahar** (T) 1945, Joe Osmanski (B) 1946–9, Fred Negus (C) 1950, Ron Knox (QB) 1957, Jerry Moore (S) 1971–2, Mike Tomczak (QB) 1985–90, Steve Stenstrom (QB) 1995–8, Chris Boniol (K) 1999.

19 Walter May (G) 1920, George Bolan (FB) 1921–2, *Frank Hanny* (E) 1923–7, Earl Evans (T) 1928–9, Lennon Blackmon (HB) 1930, Eugene Smith (G) 1930, Charles Tackwell (E) 1931–3, Latham Flanagan (E) 1931, Dick Stahlman (T) 1933, *Ed Kawal* (C) 1934–6, Lou Gordon (T) 1938, John Siegal (E) 1939, Phil Martinovich (G) 1940, Nick Kerasiotis (G) 1942, 1945, Bill Hempel (T) 1942, Dominic Sigillo (T) 1943–4, Don Perkins (FB) 1945–6, Peter Perez (G) 1945, Harper Davis (HB) 1950, Gary Huff (QB) 1973–6, Ray Stachowicz (P) 1983.

20 **Paddy Driscoll** (B) 1920, Jack Mintum (C) 1921–2, Ted Drews (E) 1928, *Zuck Carlson* (G) 1929–36, Fred Dreher (E) 1938, *Bob Nowaskey* (G) 1940–2, Fred Mundee (C) 1943–5, James Logan (G) 1943, *Jim Keane* (E) 1946–51, Ray Gene Smith (HB) 1954–7, Pete Johnson (B) 1959, Justin Rowland (HB) 1960, Bobby Jackson (HB) 1961, Joe

Taylor (DB) 1967–74, Mike Adamle (RB) 1975–6, Reuben Henderson (CB) 1981–2, Kevin Potter (S) 1983–4, Thomas Sanders (RB) 1985–9, *Mark Carrier* (S) 1990–6, Corey Dowden (CB) 1997, James Allen (RB) 1998–2001, Roosevelt Williams (DB) 2002.

21 *Hugh Blacklock* (T) 1920–5, Verne Mullen (E) 1925–6, Dick Sturtridge (B) 1928–9, Daniel McMullen (G) 1930–1, Paul Engebretsen (G) 1932, Wayland Becker (E) 1934, **Dan Fortmann** (G) 1936–43, *Chuck Drulis* (G) 1945–9, Bunny Figner (HB) 1953, Ron Drzewiecki (HB) 1955, Perry Jeter (RB) 1956–7, Jon Arnett (RB) 1964–6, *Cecil Turner* (KR) 1968–73, Dave Gagnon (RB) 1974, Nemiah Wilson (DB) 1975, Leslie Frazier (DB) 1981–5, *Donnell Woolford* (DB) 1989–96, Darnell Autry (RB) 1997, Terry Cousin (CB) 1998–9, R.W. McQuarters (CB) 2000–3.

22 Roy Adkins (G) 1920–1, *Jim McMillen* (G) 1924–9, Paul Schuette (G) 1930–2, *Bill Karr* (E) 1933–8, Saul Sherman (QB) 1939–40, *Norm Standlee* (FB) 1941, Lloyd Reese (FB) 1946, Ed Ecker (T) 1947, **Bobby Layne** (QB) 1948, **George Blanda** (QB/K) 1949–51, S.J. Whitman (HB) 1953–4, Jesse Castete (HB) 1956, Ron Drzewiecki (HB) 1957, Billy Martin (HB) 1962–4, Bill Martin (E) 1965, Charley Brown (DB) 1966–7, Ross Montgomery (FB) 1969–70, Cyril Pinder (RB) 1971, Clifton Taylor (RB) 1974, Johnny Musso (RB) 1975–7, Dave Williams (RB) 1979–81, *Dave Duerson* (DB) 1983–8, Johnny Bailey (WR) 1990–1, Robert Green (RB) 1993–6, Ronnie Harmon (RB) 1997, Shawn Woodson (S) 2000, Than Merrill (DB) 2001, Brock Williams (CB) 2003.

23 **Guy Chamberlin** (E) 1920–1, Ralph Maillard (T) 1929, Lyle Drury (E) 1930–1, Gilbert Bergerson (G) 1932–3, Vince Zizak (G) 1934, Verne Oech (G) 1936, Ernest Rentner (B) 1937, *Aldo Forte* (G) 1939–41, Connie Berry (E) 1942–6, *Washington Serini* (G) 1948–51, Jerry Shipkey (FB) 1953, Dave Whitsell (CB) 1961–6, Al Dodd (DB) 1967, Clarence Childs (DB) 1968, Dick Daniels (S) 1969–70, Lee Calland (CB) 1969, Joe Barnes (QB) 1974, Len Walterscheid (S) 1977–82, *Shaun Gayle* (DB) 1984–94, Marty Carter (DB) 1995–8, *Jerry Azumah* (DB) 1999–2003.

24 Lennie High (B) 1920, *Hunk Anderson* (G) 1923–5, Chuck Kassel (E) 1927, Reginald Russell (E) 1928, *Luke Johnsos* (E) 1929–36, *Frank Bausch* (C) 1937–40, Billy Hughes (C) 1941, *Fred Davis* (T) 1946–51, *Erich Barnes* (CB) 1958–60, *Roosevelt Taylor* (S) 1961–8, Don Shy (RB) 1970–2, Willie Roberts (CB) 1973, Virgil Livers (CB) 1975–9, Jeff Fisher (DB) 1981–4, Vestee Jackson (DB) 1986–9, Eric Jefferies (DB) 1987r, Richard Fain (CB) 1992, Kevin Minniefield (CB) 1993–6, Terry Cousin (CB) 1997, *Glyn Milburn* (KR) 1998–2001, Cameron Worrell (S) 2003.

25 Garland Grange (E) 1929–31, **Walt Kies-**

ling (G) 1934, Forrest McPherson (G) 1935, *Ray Nolting* (B) 1936–43, Jackie Hunt (B) 1945, Mike Jarmoluk (T) 1946–7, Ed Macon (HB) 1952–4, *J.C. Caroline* (HB) 1956–65, Linzy Cole (WR) 1970, Craig Clemons (S) 1972–4, Ron Shanklin (WR) 1975–6, Art Best (RB) 1977–8, Lonnie Perrin (RB) 1979, *Todd Bell* (S) 1981–6, Brad Muster (RB) 1988–92, Keshon Johnson (CB) 1993–4, Pat Eilers (S) 1995, Anthony Johnson (RB) 1995, Chris Martin (CB) 1996, Tom Carter (DB) 1997–9, Thomas Smith (CB) 2000, Autry Denson (RB) 2001, Bobby Gray (DB) 2002–3.

26 Jim Kendricks (T) 1924, John Mohardt (B) 1925, Ernie Vick (C) 1927–8, *Bert Pearson* (C) 1929–34, Milford Miller (T) 1935, Kay Bell (T) 1937, Charles Apolskis (E) 1938, Al Baisi (G) 1940–1, 1946, Al Hoptowit (T) 1942–5, Joe Abbey (E) 1948–9, *Richard Barwegan* (G) 1950–1, Charles Sumner (HB) 1955–8, Bennie McRae (CB) 1962–70, Carl Garrett (RB) 1973–4, Matt Suhey (FB) 1980–9, John Mangum (S) 1990–8, Jermaine Jones (CB) 1999, Todd McMillon (CB) 2000–3.

27 James Crawford (G) 1925, Tillie Voss (E) 1927–8, Harvey Long (T) 1929, John Polisky (G) 1929, *Ed Kawal* (C) 1931, John Doehring (FB) 1932–4, Al Culver (T) 1932, Milt Trost (T) 1935–9, Joe Mihal (T) 1940–1, Edgar Jones (B) 1945, Owen Goodnight (QB) 1946, John Sisk Jr. (B) 1964, Randy Montgomery (CB) 1974, Bob Grim (WR) 1975, Mike Richardson (CB) 1983–8, Brian Taylor (RB) 1989, Lewis Tillman (RB) 1994–5, Walt Harris (DB) 1996–2001, Rabih Abdullah (RB) 2002–3.

28 Ed Garvey (HB) 1925, Aldous Haddon (B) 1928, Larry Steinbach (G) 1930–1, Fritz Febel (G) 1935, Robert Allman (E) 1936, Gust Zarnas (G) 1938, Chet Chesney (C) 1939–40, Bob Steuber (B) 1942–3, Lloyd Lowe (HB) 1953–4, *Willie Galimore* (RB) 1957–63.

29 Bill McElwain (B) 1925, John Wallace (E) 1928, *Joe Kopcha* (G) 1929, 1932–3, Gus Mastogany (E) 1931, Russ Thompson (T) 1936–9, *Ed Kolman* (T) 1940–2, 1946–7, Doug McEnulty (FB) 1943–4, Glenn Burgeis (T) 1945, John Hoffman (E) 1949–50, *McNeil Moore* (HB) 1954–6, Glenn Shaw (HB) 1960, Ron Bull (RB) 1962–70, Bob Jeter (CB) 1971–2, Mike Morgan (RB) 1978, Vaughn Lusby (CB) 1980, Dennis Gentry (WR) 1982–92, Raymont Harris (RB) 1994–7, Frankie Smith (DB) 1998–2001, Adrian Peterson (RB) 2002–3.

30 Gerald Seibering (FB) 1932, Bob Dunlap (QB) 1935, *George Wilson* (E) 1937–46, Allen Smith (E) 1948, Herb Falkenberg (FB) 1952, Bobby Jack Floyd (HB) 1953, Chick Jagade (FB) 1954–5, Jimmy Gunn (LB) 1970–5, John Skibinski (RB) 1978–81, Jack Cameron (WR) 1984, George Duarte (DB) 1987r, George Streeter (DB) 1989, James Rouse (RB) 1990–1, Tony Carter (RB)

1994–7, Ricky Bell (DB) 1998, Mike Brown (S) 2000–3.

31 Dick Schweidler (B) 1938–9, 1946, Len Akin (G) 1942, Paul Podmajersky (G) 1944, Stuart Clarkson (G) 1946–50, Emerson Cole (FB) 1952, *Joe Fortunato* (LB) 1955–66, Ross Brupbacher (LB) 1970–3, Bill Knox (DB) 1974–6, Anthony Hutchison (RB) 1983–4, Thomas Sanders (RB) 1985, Ken Taylor (CB) 1985, Eric Jefferies (CB) 1987r, Bruce McCray (DB) 1987r, Greg Laskar (S) 1988, Mark Green (RB) 1989–92, Rashaan Salaam (RB) 1995–7, Daimon Shelton (FB) 2001–2.

32 Art Buck (B) 1941, Al Grygo (B) 1944–5, Allen Smith (E) 1947, *Johnny Lujack* (QB) 1948–51, Leon Campbell (HB) 1952–4, Lionel Taylor (WR) 1959, Ralph Kurek (FB) 1965–70, Charlie Ford (CB) 1971–3, Garland Rivers (DB) 1987, Chris Brewer (RB) 1987r, Lemuel Stinson (DB) 1988–92, Dwayne Joseph (CB) 1995–6, Ricky Bell (DB) 1997, Edgar Bennett (RB) 1998–9, Marlon Barnes (RB) 2000, Leon Johnson (RB) 2001–2.

33 *Herb Joesting* (FB) 1931–2, Denny Myers (T) 1931, *Bernie Masterson* (QB) 1934–40, Johnny Long (QB) 1944–5, Bill Johnson (G) 1947, Allen Lawler (HB) 1948, Bob Perina (HB) 1949–50, Whizzer White (B) 1951–2, Jerry Shipkey (FB) 1953, Larry Morris (LB) 1959–65, Mike Hull (FB) 1968–70, Jim Grabowski (FB) 1971, Gary Kosins (RB) 1972–4, Ted Vactor (CB) 1975, Jack Deloplaine (RB) 1979, Calvin Thomas (RB) 1982–7, Lars Tate (RB) 1990, Darren Lewis (RB) 1991–2, Merril Hoge (RB) 1994, Tyrone Hughes (KR) 1997, Bam Morris (RB) 1998, Larry Whigham (DB) 2001–2, Charles Tillman (CB) 2003.

34 Jack Torrance (T) 1939–40, John Fedorovich (T) 1941, 1946, *John Dottley* (FB) 1951–3, *Joe Marconi* (FB) 1962–6, Tim Casey (LB) 1969, Bill Tucker (RB) 1971, Norm Hodgins (S) 1974, **Walter Payton** (RB) 1975–87.

35 Dick Bassi (G) 1938–9, *Lee Artoe* (T) 1940–2, 1945, *Ray Nolting* (B) 1940, Bill Steinkemper (T) 1943, Fred Hartman (T) 1947, Paul Stenn (G) 1948–51, *Rick Casares* (RB) 1955–64, Jim Harrison (RB) 1971–4, Roland Harper (RB) 1975–82, *Neal Anderson* (RB) 1986–93, Mike Hintz (DB) 1987r, James Burton (CB) 1994–7, Anthony Thomas (RB) 2001–3.

36 Stuart Clarkson (G) 1942, Fred Mundee (C) 1943–5, Bill Steinkemper (T) 1943, John Morton (B) 1945, Tom Farris (QB) 1946–7, Bill De-Correvont (B) 1948–9, Merrill Douglas (FB) 1958–60, James Smith (HB) 1961, Ron Copeland (WR) 1969, Roger Lawson (RB) 1972–3, Perry Williams (RB) 1974, Tom Donchez (RB) 1975, Larry Schreiber (RB) 1976, Wentford Gaines (CB) 1978–80, Maurice Douglas (DB) 1986–8, Frank Harris (RB) 1987r, Markus Paul (S) 1989–93, Anthony Marshall (DB) 1994–7, Ray Austin (S) 1998–9, Stanley Pritchett (FB) 2001–3.

37 Edward Aspatore (T) 1934, Young Bussey (QB) 1940–1, Bob Masters (FB) 1943–4, Bernie Digris (T) 1943, James Logan (G) 1943, Bob Steuber (B) 1943, Edgar Jones (HB) 1945, Charles Mitchell (B) 1945, Broughton Williams (T) 1947, John O'Quinn (E) 1950–1, George Youngblood (S) 1969, Rich Coady (C/E) 1970, Conrad Graham (DB) 1973, Cid Edwards (RB) 1975, Willie McClendon (RB) 1979–82, Darryl Clark (RB) 1987r, Maurice Douglas (DB) 1989–94, Pat Eilers (S) 1995, Keshon Johnson (CB) 1995, Tony Parrish (S) 1998–2001, Damon Moore (S) 2002, Jason McKie (RB) 2003.

38 Sam Francis (FB) 1937–8, Charlie Apolskis (E) 1939, Bill Milner (G) 1947–9, Ed Bradley (G) 1950, Bill Brown (FB) 1961, Ray Ogden (TE) 1969–71, Dave Juenger (WR) 1973, Lakei Heimuli (RB) 1987r, John Hardy (DB) 1991, Tim Worley (RB) 1993–4, Mike Dulaney (RB) 1995–7, Robert Chancey (FB) 1998, Eric Joyce (CB) 2002.

39 George Gulyanics (HB) 1947–52, Pete Perini (FB) 1953–4, J.D. Smith (RB) 1956, Ralph Anderson (E) 1958, John Adams (B) 1959–62, Phil Clark (DB) 1970, Reggie Sanderson (RB) 1973, Robin Earl (RB/TE) 1977–9, Al Wolden (RB) 1987r, Jeremy Lincoln (CB) 1992–5, Curtis Enis (RB) 1998, Reggie Austin (DB) 2001–2, Travis Coleman (DB) 2002.

40 Frank Dempsey (G) 1950–1, Al Campana (HB) 1952–3, Stan Wallace (DB) 1954, 1956–8, Don Mullins (HB) 1961–2, **Gale Sayers** (RB) 1965–71, Steve Trimble (DB) 1987r.

41 John Schiechl (C) 1945–6, Jack Matheson (E) 1947, Alf Bauman (T) 1948–50, Babe Dimancheff (HB) 1952, Harland Carl (HB) 1956, Brian Piccolo (RB) 1966–9.

42 **Sid Luckman** (QB) 1939–50.

43 Jim Dooley (E) 1952–4, 1956–61, Larry Glueck (B) 1963–5, Bob Jones (E) 1967–8, George Farmer (WR) 1970–5, Earl Douthitt (S) 1975, Craig Clemons (S) 1976–7, Mike Ulmer (CB) 1980, Emery Moorehead (TE) 1981, Walt Williams (CB) 1982–3, Lorenzo Lynch (DB) 1987–90, Dennis Lundy (RB) 1995, Mike Green (S) 2000–3.

44 Paul Goebel (E) 1925, Earl Evans (T) 1926–7, Ray Richards (T) 1933, 1935–6, *Bob Margarita* (B) 1944–6, Frank Minini (B) 1947–8, Frank Szymanski (C) 1949, W.D. Garrett (T) 1950, Gary Lyle (CB) 1968–74, Terry Schmidt (S) 1976–84, Mike Stoops (DB) 1987r, Todd Krumm (S) 1988, Bob Christian (FB) 1992–4, Michael Hicks (RB) 1996–7, Curtis Enis (RB) 1998–2000, Brock Forsey (RB) 2003.

45 *Walt Stickel* (T) 1946–9, Gerald Weatherly (C) 1950, Billy Stone (HB) 1952–4, Bobby Watkins (RB) 1955–7, Rocky Ryan (E) 1958, Don Bishop (E) 1959, *Dick Gordon* (WR) 1965–71, Craig Clemons (S) 1975, *Gary Fencik* (S) 1976–87, Craig Heyward (RB) 1993, Tony Stargell (CB) 1997, Scott Dragos (FB/TE) 2000–1.

46 Al Babartsky (T) 1943–5, Chuck Hunsinger (HB) 1950–2, William Anderson (HB) 1953–4, Don Bingham (HB) 1956, Jesse Whittenton (CB) 1958, Angelo Coia (WR) 1960–3, Curtiss Gentry (DB) 1966–8, Craig Baynham (RB) 1970, Matt Maslowski (WR) 1972, Pete Van Valkenberg (RB) 1974, Doug Plank (S) 1975–82, Anthony Mosley (RB) 1987r, Mickey Pruitt (LB) 1988, John Ivlow (RB) 1993, Marlon Forbes (S) 1996–8.

47 Ted Rosequist (T) 1935–6, Bill Conkright (C) 1937–8, Rex Proctor (B) 1953, *Johnny Morris* (WR) 1958–67, John Davis (DB) 1970, Ken Grandberry (RB) 1974, Mike Spivey (CB) 1977–9, Jonathan Hoke (CB) 1980, Egypt Allen (DB) 1987, Anthony Blaylock (CB) 1993, Randy Hilliard (CB) 1998, Chris Hudson (S) 1999, Ray McElroy (S) 2000.

48 *Beattie Feathers* (RB) 1934–7, Bob Swisher (B) 1938–41, 1945, Charley O'Rourke (QB) 1942, Joe Vodicka (B) 1943–5, Howie Livingston (DB) 1953, Harry Hugasian (HB) 1955, Vic Zucco (HB) 1957–9, Tommy Neck (HB) 1962, Andy Livingston (FB) 1964–5, *Ron Smith* (S/WR) 1970–2, *Allen Ellis* (CB) 1973–9, Reggie Phillips (CB) 1985–7, Clifton Abraham (CB) 1996, Van Hiles (S) 1997, Gabriel Reid (TE) 2003.

49 James Lesane (HB) 1952–3, Henry Mosley (HB) 1955, Jack Johnson (B) 1957–9, Charles Bivins (HB) 1960–6, Major Hazelton (DB) 1968–9, Joe Moore (RB) 1971–2, Dave Becker (S) 1980, Donald Jordan (RB) 1984, David Tate (S) 1988–92, Tremayne Allen (TE) 1997, Ty Hallock (FB) 1998–9, Marq Cerqua (LB) 2002.

50 Gerald Weatherly (C) 1952, John Damore (C) 1957–8, *Mike Pyle* (C) 1961–9, Bob Hyland (C) 1970, Gene Hamlin (C) 1971, Waymond Bryant (LB) 1974–7, Chris Devlin (LB) 1978, Mark Merrill (LB) 1979, **Mike Singletary** (LB) 1981–92.

51 *Ken Kavanaugh* (E) 1940–1, 1945–50, Clinton Wager (E) 1942–3, Rudy Smeja (E) 1944–5, Wayne Hansen (C) 1952–9, **Dick Butkus** (LB) 1965–73, Dan Neal (C) 1975–6, Mel Rogers (LB) 1977, Bruce Herron (LB) 1978–82, Doug Becker (LB) 1978, Kelvin Atkins (LB) 1983, Jim Morrissey (LB) 1985–93, Mark Rodenhauser (C) 1987.

52 Rich Coady (C/E) 1971–4, John Babinecz (LB) 1975, Dan Neal (C) 1977–84, Cliff Thrift (LB) 1985, Larry Rubens (C) 1986, Mark Rodenhauser (C) 1987–8, Mickey Pruitt (LB) 1989–91, Robert Bass (LB) 1995, Darwin Ireland (LB) 1995, Bryan Cox (LB) 1996–7, Andre Collins (LB) 1998, Keith Burns (LB) 1999, Bobbie Howard (LB) 2001–3.

53 Pat Preston (G) 1946–9, Bill Wightkin (DE) 1950–1, Billy Autrey (C) 1953, Ken Kirk (C) 1960, James Purnell (LB) 1964–8, Dave Martin (LB) 1969, Larry Rowden (LB) 1971, Gail Clark (LB) 1973, Dan Peiffer (C) 1975–7, Tommy Hart (DE) 1978–9, Paul Tabor (C) 1980, Dan Rains

(LB) 1982–6, Brent Johnson (C) 1987r, Dante Jones (LB) 1988–94, Michael Lowery (LB) 1996–7, Lemanski Hall (LB) 1998, Warrick Holdman (LB) 1999–2003.

54 Joe Savoldi (FB) 1930, Jesse Hibbs (T) 1931, Dick Klawitter (C) 1956–7, Chuck Howley (LB) 1958–9, Roger LeClerc (K) 1960–1, Bill McKinney (LB) 1972, Adrian Young (LB) 1973, Larry Ely (LB) 1975, Tom Hicks (LB) 1976–80, Brian Cabral (LB) 1981–4, John Adickes (C) 1987–8, Doug Rothschild (LB) 1987r, LaSalle Harper (LB) 1989, Ron Cox (LB) 1990–5, 1997, Greg Briggs (LB) 1996, Ric McDonald (LB) 1998–9, *Brian Urlacher* (LB) 2000–3.

55 Bob Fenimore (HB) 1947, J.R. Boone (KR) 1948–50, Fred Venturelli (T) 1948, Robert Moser (C) 1951–3, *Larry Strickland* (C) 1954–9, Doug Buffone (LB) 1966–79, *Otis Wilson* (LB) 1980–7, John Roper (LB) 1989–92, Vinson Smith (LB) 1993–6, Sean Harris (LB) 1997, Greg Jones (LB) 2001, Mike Caldwell (LB) 2002, Lance Briggs (LB) 2003.

56 Bill Hewitt (E) 1932–6.

57 Billy Patterson (QB) 1939, *Ray McLean* (B) 1940–7, J.R. Boone (KR) 1951, Rich Leeuwenberg (T) 1965, Dan Pride (LB) 1968–9, Don Rives (LB) 1973–8, Lee Kunz (LB) 1979–81, Al Chesley (LB) 1982, Bruce Huther (LB) 1982, David Simmons (LB) 1983, Tom Thayer (G) 1985–92, Eldridge Milton (LB) 1987r, Sean Harris (LB) 1995–6, Anthony Peterson (LB) 1997, *Olin Kreutz* (C) 1998–2003.

58 Ed Neal (G) 1951, John Kreamcheck (T) 1953–5, Bob Konovsky (G) 1960, Franklin McRae (DT) 1967, Jim Ferguson (C/LB) 1969, Bob Pifferini (LB) 1972–5, Jerry Muckensturm (LB) 1976–82, *Wilber Marshall* (LB) 1984–8, Steve Hyche (LB) 1989, Michael Stonebreaker (LB) 1991, Jay Leeuwenburg (G) 1992–5, Chris Villarrial (G) 1996–2003.

59 Rudy Kuechenberg (LB) 1967–9, Carl Gersbach (LB) 1975, Gary Campbell (LB) 1977–83, Ron Rivera (LB) 1984–92, Joe Cain (LB) 1993–6, Daryl Carter (LB) 1997, Jim Schwantz (LB) 1998, Roosevelt Colvin (LB) 1999–2002, Joe Odom (LB) 2003.

60 Don Healy (G) 1958–9, Roger Davis (G) 1960–3, Brian Schweda (DE) 1966, Doug Kriewald (G) 1967–8, Lee Roy Caffey (LB) 1970, *Wally Chambers* (DT) 1973–7, Lynn Boden (G) 1979, Tom Andrews (C) 1984–5, Stan Thomas (T) 1991–2, Gene McGuire (C) 1993–4, Darwin Ireland (LB) 1994–5, Casey Wiegmann (C/G) 1997–2000, Terrance Metcalf (OL) 2002–3.

61 *Richard Barwegan* (G) 1952, **Bill George** (LB) 1953–65, Don Croftcheck (G) 1967, Glen Holloway (G) 1970–3.

62 Frank Dempsey (G) 1952–3, *Kline Gilbert* (T) 1954–7, Mike Reilly (LB) 1964–8, Glen Holloway (G) 1970–3, Tom Forrest (G) 1974, Dan Jiggetts (T) 1976–82, *Mark Bortz* (G) 1983–93, Chris Gray (G) 1997, Robert Newkirk (DT) 2000–1.

63 M.L. Brackett (T) 1956–7, Bob Wetoska (T) 1960–9, John Neidert (LB) 1970, Steve Kinney (T) 1973–4, Mark Nordquist (G/C) 1975–6, Fred Dean (G) 1977, Jon Morris (C) 1978, Tony Ardizzone (C) 1979, *Jay Hilgenberg* (C) 1981–91, Todd Burger (G) 1993–7, Corbin Lacina (G) 2003.

64 Ted Daffer (E) 1954, Mike Rabold (G) 1964–6, Ernie Janet (G) 1972–4, Larry Horton (DT) 1972, Ted Albrecht (T) 1977–81, John Roehlk (G) 1987, Dave Zawatson (T) 1989, Glenell Sanders (LB) 1990, Mirko Jurkovic (G) 1992, Andy Heck (T) 1994–8, Rex Tucker (OL) 1999–2002.

65 John Hatley (G) 1953, Herman Clark (G) 1954–6, Abe Gibron (G) 1958–9, Stan Fanning (T) 1960–2, Tom Bettis (LB) 1963, Randy Jackson (T) 1967–74, Noah Jackson (G) 1975–83, Eugene Rowell (DT) 1987r, Tony Woods (DT) 1989, Terry Price (DT) 1990, Jim Schwantz (LB) 1992, Tory Epps (DT) 1993–4, Evan Pilgrim (G) 1995–7, Pat Mannelly (T) 1998–2003.

66 Bulldog Turner (C) 1940–52, Phil Martinovich (G) 1940, John Schiechl (C) 1945.

67 Ed Bradley (G) 1952, Tom Roggeman (G) 1956–7, Ted Karras (G) 1960–4, George Seals (G) 1965–71, Bill Line (DT) 1972, Mike Hoban (G) 1974, Dan Hultz (DT) 1974, Phil McKinnely (T) 1982, Phil Norman (G) 1983–6, John Arp (T) 1987r, Jerry Fontenot (G) 1989–96, Greg Huntington (G) 1997–9, Bill Schultz (G) 1997, Josh Warner (C) 2003.

68 Gerald Stautberg (G) 1951, John Badaczewski (G) 1953, George Burman (T) 1964, Howard Mudd (G) 1969–70, Jim Osborne (DT) 1972–84, Paul Blair (T) 1986–7, Sean McInerney (DE) 1987r, Chris Dyko (T) 1989, Jim Flanigan (DT) 1994, Carl Reeves (DE) 1996–8.

69 Ralph Jecha (G) 1955, William Roehnelt (G) 1958–9, Ted Wheeler (G) 1970, Revie Sorey (G) 1975–82, Stuart Rindy (T) 1987r, Tom Myslinski (OL) 1993–4, Vernice Smith (G) 1993, Octus Polk (G) 1995–6, Mike Gandy (T) 2001–3.

70 Al Culver (T) 1932, Art Davis (T) 1954, Herman Lee (T) 1958–66, Bob Pickens (T) 1967–8, Ken Kortas (T) 1969, Jeff Churchin (T) 1970–1, Andy Rice (DT) 1972–3, Dennis Lick (T) 1976–81, Henry Waechter (DE) 1984–6, Jim Althoff (DT) 1987–8, Troy Auzenne (T) 1992–5, Ken Anderson (DT) 1999, Alfonso Boone (DL) 2001–3.

71 George Connor (T) 1952–5, Earl Leggett (DT) 1957–66, Rufus Mayes (T) 1969, Tony McGee (DE) 1971–3, Roger Stillwell (DL) 1975–7, Rocco Moore (G) 1980, Perry Hartnett (G) 1982–3, Jack Oliver (T) 1987r, Caesar Rentie (T) 1988, *James Williams* (T) 1991–2002.

72 Bill George (LB) 1952, Bill Wightkin (DE)

1954–7, Ed Nickla (G) 1959, Jim Cadile (G) 1962–72, Gary Hrivnak (DT) 1973–6, Brad Shearer (DT) 1978–80, Jerry Doerger (T) 1982, John Janata (T) 1983, Wiliam Perry (DT) 1985–93, Scott Adams (T) 1995, Jon Clark (T) 1996–7, Chris Maumalanga (DT) 1997, Carl Powell (DT) 2001, Ernest Grant (DL) 2002, Qasim Mitchell (G) 2003.

73 *Bill Bishop* (T) 1952–60, Steve Barnett (T) 1963, Frank Cornish (DT) 1966–9, Steve Wright (T) 1971, Rich Buzin (T) 1972, Mike Hartenstine (DE) 1975–86, John Wojciechowski (T) 1987–93, Marcus Keyes (DT) 1996, Kevin Dogins (G) 2001–2, Tron LaFavor (DT) 2003.

74 Herman Clark (G) 1952, *Kline Gilbert* (T) 1953, Paul Lipscomb (DT) 1954, Bob Kilcullen (T) 1957–65, Dan James (T) 1967, Wayne Mass (T) 1968–70, Bob Asher (T) 1972–5, Jerry Meyers (DL) 1976–9, Jeff Williams (G) 1982, *Jim Covert* (T) 1983–90, Garland Hawkins (DE) 1995, Jimmy Herndon (T) 1997–2001, Bernard Robertson (OL) 2002, Scott Sanderson (T) 2003.

75 *Fred Williams* (DT) 1952–62, Riley Mattson (T) 1965, Dave Hale (DE) 1969–71, Jeff Sevy (T/DE) 1975–8, Henry Waechter (DE) 1982–3, Stefan Humphries (G) 1984–6, Chuck Harris (T) 1987, John Shannon (DT) 1988–9, Ron Mattes (T) 1991, Todd Perry (G) 1993–2000.

76 *Charles Miller* (C) 1932–6, Les McDonald (E) 1937–9, Hampton Pool (E) 1940–3, Elmo Kelly (E) 1944, Bob Cross (T) 1952–3, Ed Meadows (E) 1954, John Mellekas (T) 1956, 1958–61, John Johnson (T) 1963–8, Bill Staley (DT) 1970–1, Dave Gallagher (DE) 1974, Ron Rydalch (DT) 1975–80, *Steve McMichael* (DT) 1981–93, Marcus Spears (T) 1995–6, Shawn Lee (DE) 1998, Brad Culpepper (DT) 2000, Bobby Setzer (DL) 2002.

77 **Red Grange** (B) 1925, 1929–34, **Link Lyman** (T) 1926.

78 Art Davis (T) 1953, **Stan Jones** (G/DT) 1954–65, Harry Gunner (DE) 1970, Bob Newton (G) 1971–5, John Ward (C/G) 1976, Keith Van Horne (T) 1981–92, Pat Riley (DT) 1995, Blake Brockermeyer (T) 1999–2001, Aaron Gibson (T) 2002–3.

79 Dick Klein (T) 1958–9, Art Anderson (T) 1961–2, Dick Evey (DE) 1964–8, John Hoffman (DE) 1971, Lionel Antoine (T) 1972–6, Emanuel Zanders (G) 1981, Kurt Becker (G) 1982–9, Louis Age (T) 1992, Marcus Spears (DE) 1994, Scotty Lewis (DT) 1995, Jerry Wisne (T) 1999–2000, Steve Edwards (T) 2002–3.

80 John Helwig (LB) 1953–6, Ralph Anderson (E) 1958, Ed Cooke (E) 1958, Bob Jencks (E) 1963–4, Jimmy Jones (E) 1965–7, Jon Kilgore (P) 1968, Jerry Simmons (WR) 1969, Craig Cotton (TE) 1973, Bo Rather (WR) 1974–8, Rickey Watts (WR) 1979–83, Tim Wrightman (TE) 1985–6, Gary Mullen (WR) 1987r, James Thornton (TE)

1988–92, Curtis Conway (WR) 1993–9, Dez White (WR) 2000–3.

81 **George Connor** (T) 1948–51, Larry Brink (E) 1954, **Doug Atkins** (DE) 1955–66, Marty Amsler (DE) 1967–8, Mike Reppond (WR) 1973, Clint Haslerig (WR) 1974, Gary Butler (TE) 1975, Bob Bruer (TE) 1976, Chuck Bradley (TE) 1977, Harry Washington (WR) 1979, Robin Earl (TE) 1980–2, Jay Saldi (TE) 1983–4, James Maness (WR) 1985, Lew Barnes (WR) 1986, Don Kindt (TE) 1987r, Anthony Morgan (WR) 1991–3, Fred Banks (WR) 1993, Jeff Graham (WR) 1994–5, Bobby Engram (WR) 1996–2000, Ahmad Merritt (WR) 2001–3.

82 Del Bjork (T) 1937–8, *Ray Bray* (G) 1939–42, 1946–51, Anthony Ippolito (G) 1943, Tom Roberts (G) 1944–5, *Jack Hoffman* (E) 1952, 1955–8, Dick Hensley (E) 1953, Maury Youmans (T) 1960–3, Rich Kreitling (TE) 1964, Emilo Vallez (TE) 1968–9, Earl Thomas (WR) 1971–3, Matt Maslowski (WR) 1972, Fred Pagac (TE) 1974, Royce Berry (DE) 1976, John Gilliam (WR) 1977, **Alan Page** (DT) 1978–81, Ken Margerum (WR) 1982–4, Brian Glasglow (TE) 1987r, Wendell Davis (WR) 1988–93, Nate Lewis (WR) 1994–5, John Jackson (WR) 1996, Fabien Bownes (WR) 1997–8, Eddie Kennison (WR) 2000, John Davis (TE) 2001–2, Robert Johnson (TE) 2003.

83 Bill McColl (TE) 1952–9, Roger LeClerc (K) 1962–6, Mac Percival (K) 1967–73, Charley Wade (WR) 1974, Randy Burks (WR) 1976, Steve Rivera (WR) 1977, Golden Richards (WR) 1978–9, Kris Haines (WR) 1979–81, Willie Gault (WR) 1983–7, Lawrence White (WR) 1987r, Eric Wright (WR) 1991–2, Terry Obee (WR) 1993, Michael Timpson (WR) 1995–6, Eric Smith (WR) 1997, Macey Brooks (WR) 1999–2000, David Terrell (WR) 2001–3.

84 Gerald Weatherly (C) 1951, John Farrington (E) 1960–3, Ron Smith (S/WR) 1965, Austin Denney (E) 1967–9, Jim Seymour (WR) 1970–2, Richard Harris (DE) 1974–5, Brian Baschnagel (WR) 1976–84, Ron Morris (WR) 1987–92, Sam Bowers (TE) 1987r, Chris Gedney (TE) 1993–5, Kerry Cash (TE) 1996, John Allred (TE) 1997–2000, Fred Baxter (TE) 2001–2, Bobby Wade (WR) 2003.

85 Bob Carey (E) 1958, Bill Martin (TE) 1964, Duane Allen (E) 1966–7, Willie Holman (DE) 1968–73, Wayne Wheeler (WR) 1974, Steve Schubert (WR) 1975–9, Bob Fisher (TE) 1980–1, Dennis McKinnon (WR) 1983–9, Todd Black (WR) 1987r, Keith Jennings (TE) 1991–7, Alonzo Mayes (TE) 1998–2000, Kaseem Sinceno (TE) 2000, John Gilmore (TE) 2002–3.

86 Brad Rowland (HB) 1951, Bill Wightkin (DE) 1952–3, Ed Meadows (E) 1956–7, Bob Jewett (E) 1958, Pete Manning (E) 1960–1, Gary Barnes (E) 1964, Lloyd Phillips (DE) 1967–9, Jim

Hester (TE) 1970, Bob Parsons (TE/P) 1972–83, Brad Anderson (WR) 1984–5, Clay Pickering (WR) 1986, Cap Boso (TE) 1987–91, Barry Wagner (WR) 1992, Willie Harris (WR) 1993, Marv Cook (TE) 1994, Chris Penn (WR) 1997–8, *Marty Booker* (WR) 1999–2003.

87 *Harlon Hill* (WR) 1954–61, Ed O'Bradovich (DE) 1962–71, Steve DeLong (DE) 1972, Tom Reynolds (WR) 1973, Billy Newsome (DE) 1977, Mike Cobb (TE) 1978–81, Emery Moorehead (TE) 1982–8, Tom Waddle (WR) 1989–94, Greg Primus (WR) 1994–5, Andre President (TE) 1995, Bobby Neely (TE) 1996, Ricky Proehl (WR) 1997, D'Wayne Bates (WR) 1999–2001, Jamin Elliott (WR) 2002, Justin Gage (WR) 2003.

88 *Gene Schroeder* (E) 1951–2, 1954–7, Willard Dewveall (E) 1959–60, *Bobby Joe Green* (P) 1962–73, Jim Kelly (TE) 1974, Greg Latta (TE) 1975–80, Brooks Wiliams (TE) 1981–2, Marcus Anderson (WR) 1981, Glen Kozlowski (WR) 1987–92, Ken Knapczyk (WR) 1987r, Danta Whitaker (TE) 1993, Fabien Bownes (WR) 1995, John Jackson (WR) 1996, Harper LeBel (TE) 1997, Marcus Robinson (WR) 1998–2002, Desmond Clark (TE) 2003.

89 Les Cowan (T) 1951, John Hoffman (E) 1952–5, John Aveni (K) 1959–60, **Mike Ditka** (TE) 1961–6, Terry Stoepel (G) 1967, Bob Wallace (E) 1968–72, Mel Tom (DE) 1973–5, James Scott (WR) 1976–82, Ken Margerum (WR) 1981, Mitch Krenk (TE) 1984, Keith Ortego (WR) 1985–7, Will Johnson (LB) 1987, Brent Novoselsky (TE) 1988, James Coley (TE) 1990, Ryan Wetnight (TE) 1993–9, Dustin Lyman (TE) 2000–3.

90 Henry Mosley (HB) 1955, Al Harris (DE) 1979–87, Alonzo Spellman (DE) 1992–7, Van Tuinei (DE) 1999–2001, Brian Knight (LB) 2003.

91 Pat Dunsmore (TE) 1983–4, Jay Norvell (LB) 1987r, Fred Washington (DT) 1990, Kelly Blackwell (TE) 1992, Myron Baker (LB) 1993–5, Rob Davis (DT) 1996, John Thierry (DE) 1997–8, Khari Samuel (LB) 1999–2000.

92 Rob Fada (G) 1983–4, Raymond Morris (LB) 1987r, Troy Johnson (LB) 1988–9, Barry Minter (LB) 1993–2000, Ted Washington (DT) 2001–2, Hunter Hillenmeyer (LB) 2003.

93 Oliver Williams (WR) 1983, Will Johnson (LB) 1987, Guy Teafatiller (DT) 1987r, Trace Armstrong (DE) 1989–94, Ervin Collier (DT) 1995, Paul Grasmanis (DT) 1996–8, Phillip Daniels (DE) 2000–3.

94 Dick Chapura (DT) 1987–9, Mike January (LB) 1987r, John Thierry (DE) 1994–6, Shane Burton (DT) 1999, Ty Hallock (FB) 2000, Keith Traylor (DT) 2001–3.

95 *Richard Dent* (DE) 1983–93, 1995, Pat Riley (DT) 1995, Dana Howard (LB) 1996, Mark Thomas (DE) 1997–8, Russell Davis (DE) 1999, Troy Wilson (DE) 2000, Karon Riley (DL) 2001, John Stamper (DL) 2002, Ian Scott (DT) 2003.

96 Andy Frederick (T) 1983–5, Keith Ortego (WR) 1987, Greg Fitzgerald (DE) 1987r, Tim Ryan (DT) 1990–2, Percy Snow (LB) 1993, Al Fontenot (DE) 1994–6, Tyrone Williams (DT) 1997, Chris Draft (LB) 1998, Clyde Simmons (DE) 1999–2000, Alex Brown (DE) 2003.

97 Sean Smith (DT) 1987–8, Bobby Bell (LB) 1987r, Chris Zorich (DT) 1991–7, Mike Wells (DT) 1998–2000, Christian Peter (DT) 2002, Michael Haynes (DE) 2003.

98 Tyrone Keys (DE) 1983–5, Jon Norris (DE) 1987, Brian Glasglow (WR) 1987r, Greg Clark (LB) 1988, Carl Simpson (DT) 1993–7, Bryan Robinson (DT) 1998–2003.

99 Jim Daniell (T) 1945, **Dan Hampton** (DT) 1979–90, Tim Ryan (DT) 1993–4, Jim Flanigan (DT) 1995–2000, Joe Tafoya (DL) 2001–3.

CINCINNATI BENGALS

The franchise: The Bengals are the second Ohio franchise to owe their existence and early success to Paul Brown. In 1962 Brown was forced out of Cleveland whose Browns are named in his honor by new owner Art Modell. Three years later, Brown met with Ohio Governor Jim Rhodes to explore the possibility of a getting a second professional football franchise in the state. By 1966, the Cincinnati City Council approved construction of multipurpose Riverfront Stadium, and in 1968 the Bengals began play as an AFL expansion team.

The Bengals proved that Paul Brown still had much to offer professional football by posting their first winning season and divisional championship in only their third year of operation, 1970, a year that also saw them move into their new stadium. Brown still had an eye for talent, and in particular uncovered a strong-armed rookie quarterback with seemingly limitless potential in Greg Cook. Unfortunately, Cook injured his shoulder and was not able to meet those expectations. In response, Brown's offensive coach Bill Walsh developed a short passing attack tailored to weak-armed backup Virgil Carter, and that offense became known as the West Coast Offense when Walsh took it to San Francisco years later. In the Bengals' first eight years under coach Paul Brown the team made the playoffs three times, and he faced a crucial decision in 1976 when he stepped down as coach: who would succeed him, offensive coach Walsh or defensive coach Bill Johnson. Brown made the wrong choice for the Bengals' long-term success by picking Johnson. Walsh left Cincinnati and eventually landed the 49er job three years later. The organization he built there would win five Super Bowls and attain a period of sustained excellence lasting 25 years. The Bengals remained a good team throughout the 1980s, first under quarterback Kenny Anderson and then under Boomer Esiason. They would make Super Bowl appearances following the 1981 and 1988 seasons, and both times they would meet Walsh's 49ers and lose a close game. The second time was especially painful for Cincinnati who was then coached by former Bengal quarterback and Walsh assistant Sam Wyche as they succumbed to a classic Joe Montana last-minute 90-yard touchdown drive.

When Paul Brown died in 1991, the franchise was seven games over .500 for its first 23 years. Since then, the team has been incompetently managed by Brown's son Mike. Understaffed in the front office and outmanned on the field, they are 82 games under .500,

going 55–137 from 1991 to 2002, a pathetic winning percentage of .286. Highly-acclaimed coach Marvin Lewis took over in 2003 in a positive move, and he is beginning to turn this sorry franchise around. In 2003, Cincinnati turned in their first .500 season in eight years.

Origin of name: Paul Brown named his new team in honor of the tradition of Cincinnati Bengals franchises in American Football Leagues. However, in a bit of foreshadowing, the Bengals of the second AFL finished 2–4–2 in 1937 and the Bengals of the third AFL finished 2–12–2 in 1940–1.

Time till first championship: 36 years and counting.

Time since last championship: Never won one.

Retired numbers: The only number retired by the Bengals is 54 worn by the team's first draft choice ever in 1968, Bob Johnson. He played center for them for 12 years.

Other numbers worn by these players: None.

Those who wore retired numbers after the honored player: None.

Record by Decade

| | Regular Season | | | Postseason | | |
	Won	Lost	Tied	Won	Lost	Championships
1960s	7	20	1	0	0	
1970s	74	70	0	0	3	
1980s	81	71	0	4	3	
1990s	52	108	0	1	1	
2000s	20	44	0	0	0	
All-Time	234	313	1	5	7	None

Winning seasons: 11. Losing Seasons: 21. .500 seasons: 4.

Coaches

	Years	Record	Playoffs
Paul Brown	1968–75	55–56–1	0–3
Bill Johnson	1976–8	18–15–0	0–0
Homer Rice	1978–9	8–19–0	0–0
Forrest Gregg	1980–3	32–25–0	2–2
Sam Wyche	1984–91	61–66–0	3–2
Dave Shula	1992–6	19–52–0	0–0
Bruce Coslet	1996–2000	21–39–0	0–0
Dick LeBeau	2000–2	12–33–0	0–0
Marvin Lewis	2003–	8–8–0	0–0

Numbers that should be retired: 78 for Anthony Munoz who went into the Hall of Fame in 1998 as perhaps the finest lineman of his generation.

Owned numbers: No one but Bob Johnson ever wore 54.

Numbers worn by Hall of Famers: Charley Joiner 18; Anthony Munoz 78.

Star power: None.

Star eclipsed: Reinard Wilson wore 57 till Andre Collins, 55, left; David Klingler wore 12 till Boomer Esiason, 7, left.

Numbers with most great players: 28 was worn by runners Corey Dillon, Harold Green and Larry Kinnebrew.

Worst represented numbers: 38 was worn by six forgettable running backs, none of whom lasted more than one season. 39 has not been worn by anyone for longer than one year although only three backs have worn it.

Number worn by the most players: 83 has been worn 16 times.

Player who wore the most numbers: Dave Rimington wore three: 50, 52, and 64.

Longest tenure wearing a number: Quarterback Ken Anderson wore 14 for 16 years from 1971 to 1986; cornerback Ken Riley wore 13 for 15 years from 1969 to 1983; linebacker Reggie Williams wore 57 for 14 years from 1976 to 1990.

Number worn by first ever draft pick: The Bengals first draft pick in 1968 was center Bob Johnson who wore 54.

Biggest draft busts: Plenty of draft flops: quarterback Jack Thompson, 12, selected third 1979, four years, 13 tds, 19 interceptions, under 50 percent completions; Receiver David Verser, 81, selected tenth 1981, four years, 23 catches; quarterback David Klingler, 7/15, selected sixth 1992, four years, 16 tds, 21 interceptions; defensive lineman Dan Wilkinson, 99, selected first 1994, four years and out; runner Ki-Jana Carter, 32, selected first 1995, four years, 747 yards, 3.5 average; quarterback Akili Smith, 11, selected second 1999, four years, five tds, 13 interceptions, under 50 percent completions.

Number worn by first expansion pick: Picks were not in order, but guard Pat Matson, 73, lasted the longest with the team from 1968 to 1974.

Number worn by oldest player: Ken Anderson, 14, and punter Lee Johnson, 11, both played until they were 37.

Cameos: All Pros and other notables— Ray Bentley 57; Frank Buncom 55; Garrison Hearst 20; Sherrill Headrick 69; Walter Johnson 78; Ernie Kellerman 24; Gary Reasons 52; Clyde Simmons 96.

Ones who got away: All Pro linebacker Bill Bergey, 66, was traded to the Eagles over a contract dispute. Tackle Stan Walters, 75, also departed to the Eagles. The Bengals got Hall of Famer Charlie Joiner, 18, from the Oilers, but let him go to the Chargers where he had his greatest years.

Least popular numbers: 0, 1 and 2 have never been worn. 3, 4, 5, 6, 7, 8, 13, 14, and 69 have all been worn only twice.

Last number to be originated: 8 was not worn until quarterback Jeff Blake took it in 1994.

Longest dormant number: 6 was dormant for 30 years from 1968 until 1998. Currently, 14 has been dormant since Ken Anderson retired in 1986.

Triskaidekaphobia notes: All pro cornerback Ken Riley wore 13 for 15 years and punter Dan Pope wore it for one season.

Shared numbers: 18 was worn by the Bengals first 1,000 yard runner, Paul Robinson, and by Hall of Fame receiver Charlie Joiner who were traded for each other in 1972.

Continuity: Paul Robinson was replaced in 18 by Charlie Joiner; safety Bobby Hunt was replaced in 20 by cornerback Lemar Parrish.

Discontinuity: Boomer Esiason was followed in 7 by David Klingler; linebacker Reggie Williams was followed in 57 by Bernard Clark; Max Montoya was followed in 65 by Mike Arthur.

Family Connections

Brothers

Ross Browner	DE	1978–86	79
Jim Browner	DB	1979–80	21
Archie Griffin	RB	1976–82	45
Ray Griffin	DB	1978–84	44

Quarterback numbers over 19: None.

Numbers of future NFL head coaches: Bruce Coslet 88; Dick Jauron 30; Sam Wyche 14.

Numbers of future NFL referees: None.

Players who played other sports: Track — Tommy Smith 24. Wrestling — Walter Johnson 78; Brian Pillman 58/97; Ron Pritchard 60; Clem Turner 43.

Players more famous after football: Defensive tackle Mike Reid, 74, became a Grammy Award winning musician. Reggie Williams, 57, served on the Cincinnati City Council. First round bust Peter Koch, 71, has acted in nearly 20 movies.

First player to wear a number in the 90s: Linebacker Brian Pillman wore 97 in 1984.

Number with most points scored: 3 with 889 points scored by Jim Breech (859) and Jon Kitna (30).

Number with most yards rushing: 28 with 14,425 yards gained by Corey Dillon (8,051), Harold Green (3,727), Larry Kinnebrew (2,582), and Cleo Montgomery (12).

Number with most receptions: 81 with 972 catches by Carl Pickens (461), Eddie Brown (363), Ron Dugans (89), Jim Corbett (25), David Verser (23), Patrick Robinson (8), Marquis Pleasant (2), Al Chandler (1).

Number with most touchdown passes: 14 with 209 by Ken Anderson (197) and Sam Wyche (12).

Number with most interceptions: 13 with 65 by Ken Riley.

Oddity: Wide receiver Monk Williams is the only player that Paul Brown ever coached professionally to wear a single digit number. He wore 6 for his two game tenure with the Bengals in 1968.

Team All-Time Numerical Roster

Those with an "r" following the year 1987 were replacement players during the players' strike. Pro Bowl players for each number are in *Italics*; Hall of Famers are in **Bold** type.

1 none.

2 none.

3 Jim Breech (K) 1984–92, Jon Kitna (QB) 2001–3.

4 Erik Wilhelm (QB) 1990–91, 1993–7, Scott Covington (QB) 1999–2001.

5 Jeff Hayes (P) 1986, Neil Rackers (K) 2000–2.

6 Monk Williams (WR) 1968, Brad Costello (P) 1998–9.

7 *Boomer Esiason* (QB) 1984–92, 1997, David Klingler (QB) 1993–5.

8 *Jeff Blake* (QB) 1994–9, Nick Harris (P) 2001–3.

9 Massimo Manca (K) 1987r, Doug Pelfrey (K) 1993–9, Carson Palmer (QB) 2003.

10 Eric Crabtree (WR) 1969–71, Chris Bahr (K) 1976–9, Jim Breech (K) 1980–3, Greg Horne (P) 1987, Todd Philcox (QB) 1990, Jay Schroeder (QB) 1993, John Walsh (QB) 1995, Paul Justin (QB) 1998, Will Brice (P) 1999, Travis Dorsch (P) 2002, Kyle Richardson (P) 2003.

11 Dale Livingston (P/K) 1968–9, Virgil Carter (QB) 1970–2, Wayne Clark (QB) 1974, John Reaves (QB) 1975–8, Sandro Vitiello (K) 1980, Mike Ford (QB) 1982, Jeff Christiansen (QB) 1983, Bryan Clark (QB) 1984, Doug Gaynor (QB) 1986, Dave Walter (QB) 1987, Lee Johnson (P) 1988–98, Akili Smith (QB) 1999–2002.

12 Greg Cook (QB) 1969, 1973, Jack Thompson (QB) 1979–82, Mike Norseth (QB) 1987–8, Erik Wilhelm (QB) 1989, Don Hollas (QB) 1991–2, 1994, Kerry Joseph (QB) 1996, Neil O'Donnell (QB) 1998, Gus Frerotte (QB) 2002.

13 Ken Riley (CB) 1969–83, Daniel Pope (P) 2000.

14 Sam Wyche (QB) 1968–70, *Ken Anderson* (QB) 1971–86.

15 John Stofa (QB) 1968–9, Dave Lewis (P/QB) 1970–3, Mike Wells (QB) 1977, Turk Schonert (QB) 1980–5, 1987–9, David Klingler (QB) 1992, Eric Kresser (QB) 1997–9.

16 Dewey Warren (QB) 1968, Horst Muhlmann (KR) 1969–74, Rob Hertel (QB) 1978, Ben Bennett (QB) 1987r.

17 Speedy Thomas (WR) 1969–72, Mike Ernst (QB) 1973–4, Scott Fulhage (P) 1987–8, Gunnard Twyner (WR) 1997, Shayne Graham (K) 2003.

18 *Paul Robinson* (RB) 1968–72, **Charlie Joiner** (WR) 1972–5, Adrian Breen (QB) 1987r, Jim Gallery (K) 1989, Thomas Bailey (WR) 1995.

19 Essex Johnson (RB) 1968–75, Ian Sunter (K) 1980, Jeff Hill (WR) 1994, Scott Mitchell (QB) 2000–1.

20 Bobby Hunt (S) 1968–9, *Lemar Parrish* (CB) 1970–7, Elvis Peacock (RB) 1981, Ray Horton (CB) 1983–8, Craig Taylor (RB) 1989–91, Garrison Hearst (RB) 1996, Thomas Randolph (CB) 1998, Ty Howard (CB) 1999, Mark Roman (CB) 2000–3.

21 Paul Dunn (RB) 1970, Melvin Morgan (CB) 1976–8, Jim Browner (S) 1979–80, Oliver Davis (S) 1981–2, *James Brooks* (RB) 1984–91,

Ryan Benjamin (RB) 1993, Eric Bieniemy (RB) 1995-8, Tom Carter (CB) 1999-2001, Rico Clark (CB) 1999, Jeff Burris (DB) 2002-3.

22 Ted Washington (RB) 1968, Ken Sawyer (S) 1974, Deacon Turner (RB) 1978-80, James Griffin (S) 1983-5, *Eric Thomas* (CB) 1987-92, Marcello Simmons (CB) 1993, Jimmy Spencer (CB) 1996-7, Rodney Heath (CB) 1999-2001.

23 Rod Sherman (WR) 1968, Al Coleman (S) 1969-71, Bernard Jackson (DB) 1972-6, Shafer Suggs (S) 1980, Rodney Tate (RB) 1982-3, Marc Logan (RB) 1987r, Frank Robinson (CB) 1992, Corey Sawyer (CB) 1994-8, Robert Bean (CB) 2001, Dennis Weathersby (CB) 2003.

24 Tommie Smith (WR) 1969, Ernie Kellerman (S) 1972, Marvin Cobb (S) 1975-9, Clarence Chapman (CB) 1980-1, Sean Thomas (CB) 1985, Lewis Billups (CB) 1986-91, Alan Grant (CB) 1993, Roger Jones (CB) 1994-6, Ric Mathias (CB) 1998, Sirr Parker (CB) 2000, Lamont Thompson (DB) 2002.

25 *Chip Myers* (WR) 1969-76, Tony Davis (RB) 1977-8, John Simmons (CB) 1981-6, Daryl Smith (CB) 1987r, 1988, Roderick Jones (CB) 1990-6, Charles Fisher (CB) 1999, Ligarius Jennings (CB) 2001.

26 Jack Gehrke (WR) 1969, Jim Harris (DB) 1971, Reece Morrison (RB) 1972-3, Charlie Davis (RB) 1974, Bobby Kemp (S) 1981-6, Leonard Bell (S) 1987, Bo Orlando (S) 1996-7, Cory Hall (S) 1999-2002, Tory James (CB) 2003.

27 Saint Saffold (WR) 1968, Ken Dyer (S) 1969-71, Al Randolph (CB) 1972, Ricky Davis (S) 1975, Bryan Hicks (S) 1980-3, Barney Bussey (S) 1986-92, Lance Gunn (S) 1993, Bracey Walker (S) 1994-6, Tito Paul (CB) 1997, Artrell Hawkins (CB) 1998-2003.

28 John Guillory (DB) 1969-70, Scott Burk (S) 1979, Cleo Montgomery (KR) 1980, Larry Kinnebrew (FB) 1983-7, *Harold Green* (RB) 1990-5, *Corey Dillon* (RB) 1997-2003.

29 Jim Johnson (DB) 1969, Sandy Durko (S) 1970-1, Lyle Blackwood (S) 1973-5, Vaughn Lusby (KR) 1979, Marc Logan (RB) 1987r, Rickey Dixon (DB) 1988-92, Louis Oliver (S) 1994, Jeff Cothran (FB) 1995-6, Kelvin Moore (S) 1998, Curtis Keaton (RB) 2000-1.

30 Jess Phillips (RB) 1968-72, Willie Shelby (KR) 1976-7, Dick Jauron (S) 1978-80, Bill Johnson (RB) 1985-7, Icky Woods (RB) 1988-91, R.J. Kors (S) 1993, Chris Shelling (S) 1995-6, Anthone Lott (CB) 1997, Nick Luchey [Williams] (FB) 1999-2002, Terrell Roberts (CB) 2003.

31 Fletcher Smith (DB) 1968-71, Jerry Anderson (S) 1977, Ralph Battle (DB) 1984, Lee Davis (CB) 1985, Gary Hunt (DB) 1987, Icky Woods (RB) 1988, Richard Fain (CB) 1991, Darryl Williams (S) 1992-5, 2000-1, Greg Myers (S) 1996-9, Jason Perry (S) 2002, Jeremi Johnson (RB) 2003.

32 Bob Jones (S) 1973-4, Scott Perry (CB) 1976-9, Stanley Wilson (RB) 1983-4, 1986, 1988, Nate Borders (S) 1987r, Mitchell Price (CB) 1990-3, Ron Carpenter (S) 1993, Ki-Jana Carter (RB) 1996-9, Rudi Johnson (RB) 2001-3.

33 Jim Williams (DB) 1969, Kenny Graham (S) 1970, Fred Willis (RB) 1971-2, Stan Fritts (RB) 1975-6, John Farley (RB) 1984, *David Fulcher* (S) 1986-92, Steve Broussard (RB) 1994, *Ashley Ambrose* (CB) 1996-8, JoJuan Armour (S/LB) 1999-2002, Kenny Watson (RB) 2003.

34 Ken Herock (TE) 1968, Neil Craig (S) 1971-3, Louis Breeden (CB) 1978-87, Ellis Dillahunt (S) 1988, Richard Carey (CB) 1989, Fernandus Vinson (S) 1991-4, *Tremain Mack* (DB) 1997-2000, Kevin Kaesviharn (CB) 2001-3.

35 Mike Haffner (WR) 1971, Boobie Clark (RB) 1973, Tony Davis (RB) 1976, Nathan Poole (RB) 1979-80, Jimmy Turner (CB) 1983-6, Chris Barber (S) 1987r, 1989, Antoine Bennett (CB) 1991-2, Sam Shade (S) 1995-8, Michael Basnight (RB) 1999.

36 Lenvil Elliott (RB) 1973-8, Jo-Jo Heath (KR) 1980, Jim Hargrove (RB) 1981, Stanford Jennings (FB) 1984-90, Ostell Miles (RB) 1992-3, James Joseph (RB) 1995, Brandon Bennett (RB) 1998, 2000-3.

37 Bill Scott (CB) 1968, *Tommy Casanova* (S) 1972-7, Robert Jackson (S) 1982-7, 1989, Leonard Wheeler (CB) 1992-3, 1995-6, Roosevelt Blackmon (CB) 1998-9, Reggie Myles (DB) 2002-3.

38 Estes Banks (RB) 1968, Steve Conley (RB) 1972, Champ Henson (RB) 1975, Mike Dingle (RB) 1991, Jason Burns (RB) 1995, Michael Basnight (RB) 1999.

39 Pat Franklin (RB) 1987r, Sheldon White (CB) 1993, Sedrick Shaw (RB) 1999.

40 Ron Lamb (RB) 1968-71, Pete Watson (RB) 1972, Charles Alexander (RB) 1979-85, David McCluskey (RB) 1987r, John Holifield (RB) 1989, Myron Bell (S) 1998-9.

41 White Graves (S) 1968, Terry Swanson (P) 1969, Dave Green (P/K) 1974-5, Sam Washington (CB) 1985, Solomon Wilcots (DB) 1987-90, Joe King (S) 1991, Forey Duckett (DB) 1994, Adrian Hardy (CB) 1995, Scottie Graham (RB) 1997, *Lorenzo Neal* (FB) 2001-2, Chris Edmonds (TE) 2003.

42 Warren McVea (WR) 1968, Boobie Clark (RB) 1974-8, Mike Fuller (S) 1981-2, Clay Pickering (WR) 1984-5, Rob Niehoff (S) 1987r, Eric Ball (FB) 1989-94, Lawrence Wright (S) 1997, 1999, Chris Carter (S) 2000-1, Lavar Glover (DB) 2002.

43 Curt Frazier (CB) 1968, Clem Turner (RB) 1969, Ed Williams (RB) 1974-5, Mark Johnson (S) 1987r, Mike Brim (CB) 1993-5, Kirk McMullen (TE) 2001.

44 Rex Keeling (P) 1968, Doug Dressler (RB)

1970–2, 1974, Ray Griffin (CB) 1978–84, Aaron Manning (CB) 1987r, Derrick Fenner (FB) 1992–4, Brian Milne (FB) 1996–9, Marquand Manuel (DB) 2002.

45 Tom Smiley (RB) 1968, Archie Griffin (RB) 1976–82, Greg Meehan (WR) 1987r, Carl Carter (CB) 1990, Wayne Haddix (CB) 1991, Adrian Hardy (CB) 1994, Ty Douthard (RB) 1997, Michael Blair (FB) 1998, Rogers Beckett (S) 2003.

46 Joe Wilson (RB) 1973, *Pete Johnson* (FB) 1977–83, Dan Rice (RB) 1987r, Jeff Cothran (FB) 1994, Clif Groce (FB) 1999–2000.

47 Charlie King (CB) 1968–9, Greg Bright (S) 1980–1, Scott Maidlow (LB) 1983–4, David Frisch (TE) 1993.

48 Phil Spiller (S) 1968, Andy Gibler (TE) 1983, Dave Romasko (TE) 1987r, John Garrett (WR) 1989, Craig Thompson (TE) 1992–3, Brad St. Louis (TE) 2000–1, 2003.

49 Guy Frazier (LB) 1981–2, 1984, Dana Wright (RB) 1987, Jeff Thomason (TE) 1992–3, Robert Bean (CB) 2000.

50 Bernard Erickson (LB) 1968, Tom DeLeone (G/C) 1972–3, Vic Koegel (LB) 1974, Glenn Cameron (LB) 1975–85, Dave Rimington (C) 1986–7, James Francis (LB) 1990–8, Ben Peterson (LB) 1999, Riall Johnson (LB) 2001–3.

51 Ken Avery (LB) 1969–74, Chris Devlin (LB) 1975–6, 1978, Tom Ruud (LB) 1978–9, Rick Razzano (LB) 1980–4, Tom Dinkel (LB) 1985, Leon White (LB) 1986–91, David Ward (LB) 1987, Steve Tovar (LB) 1993–4, Gerald Dixon (LB) 1996–7, Takeo Spikes (LB) 1998–2002, Kevin Hardy (LB) 2003.

52 Paul Elzey (LB) 1968, John Matlock (C) 1968, Tim Buchanan (LB) 1969, Doug Adams (LB) 1971–4, Brad Cousino (LB) 1975, Tom Dinkel (LB) 1978–83, Dave Rimington (C) 1984–5, Tom Flaherty (LB) 1987r, Craig Ogletree (LB) 1990, Gary Reasons (LB) 1992, Randy Neal (LB) 1995–6, James Logan (LB) 1995, Tim Terry (LB) 1997, Jimmy Sprotle (LB) 1998–9, Dwayne Levels (LB) 2003.

53 John Neidert (LB) 1968, Bill Peterson (LB) 1969–72, Bo Harris (LB) 1975–82, Leo Barker (LB) 1984–91, Santo Stephens (LB) 1994, Tom Tumulty (LB) 1996–8, Khalid Abdullah (LB) 2003.

54 *Bob Johnson* (C) 1968–79.

55 Frank Buncom (LB) 1968, *Jim LeClair* (LB) 1972–83, Ed Brady (LB) 1986–91, Lance Sellers (LB) 1987r, Randy Kirk (LB) 1992–3, John Johnson (LB) 1994, Andre Collins (LB) 1995–7, Reinard Wilson (LB) 1998–2002, Frank Chamberlin (LB) 2003.

56 Mike Hibler (LB) 1968, Tim Kearney (LB) 1972–4, Tom DePaso (LB) 1978, Ron Simpkins (LB) 1980, 1982–6, Toney Catchings (LB) 1987r, Ric McDonald (LB) 1992–7, Brian Simmons (LB) 1998–2003.

57 John Matlock (C) 1968, Ed Harmon (LB) 1969, Evan Jolitz (LB) 1974, Reggie Williams (LB) 1976–89, Bernard Clark (LB) 1990–1, Ray Bentley (LB) 1992, Kevin Jefferson (LB) 1994–5, Reinard Wilson (LB) 1997, Adrian Ross (LB) 1998–2003.

58 Al Beauchamp (LB) 1968–75, Blair Bush (C) 1978–82, Guy Frazier (LB) 1983, Brian Pillman (LB) 1984, Joe Kelly (LB) 1986–9, Sam Manos (C) 1987r, Alex Gordon (LB) 1991–3, David Braxton (LB) 1994, Steve Tovar (LB) 1995–7, Jay Leeuwenburg (G/C) 1999, Marc Megna (LB) 2000, Jevon Langford (DE) 2001.

59 Larry Ely (LB) 1970–1, Ray Phillips (LB) 1977–8, Ron Shumon (LB) 1978, Howie Kurnick (LB) 1979, Andrew Melontree (LB) 1980, Jeff Schuh (LB) 1981–5, Scott Schutt (LB) 1987r, Kevin Walker (LB) 1988–92, Karmeeleyah McGill (LB) 1993, Greg Truitt (LS) 1994–8, Armegis Spearman (LB) 2000, 2002.

60 Ron Pritchard (LB) 1972–7, Blake Moore (C) 1980–3, Sam Manos (C) 1987r, Dave Smith (T) 1988, Mike Brennan (T) 1990–1, Mike Withycombe (T) 1991–2, Chuck Bradley (T) 1993, Eric Moore (T) 1994, Rodrek Jones (T/G) 1996–2000.

61 Jerry Boyarsky (DT) 1982–5, Doug Aronson (G) 1987, Bill Poe (G) 1987r, Brian Townsend (LB) 1992, Tom Rayam (G) 1992–3, Melvin Tuten (T/TE) 1995–6, Tony Coats (G) 1999.

62 Dave Lapham (OL) 1974–83, Gary Smith (G) 1984, Ken Smith (G) 1987r, Jon Melander (G) 1992, Todd Kalis (G) 1995, Brock Gutierrez (C/G) 1996–2002.

63 Guy Dennis (G) 1969–72, Greg Fairchild (G) 1976–7, Mike White (DT) 1979–80, Ray Wagner (T) 1982, Joe Walter (T) 1985–93, 1995–7, Mike Goff (G/T) 1998–2003.

64 Pete Perreault (G) 1968, Justin Canale (G) 1969, John Shinners (G) 1973–7, Bill Glass (G) 1980, Dave Rimington (C) 1983, Bruce Kozerski (OL) 1984–95, Rod Payne (C) 1998.

65 Bill Kindricks (DT) 1968, Wayne McClure (LB) 1970, Maulty Moore (DT) 1975, *Max Montoya* (G/T) 1979–89, Mike Arthur (C) 1991–2, Darrick Brilz (C) 1994–8, John Jackson (T) 2000–1, Eric Steinbach (G) 2003.

66 Wayne McClure (LB) 1968, *Bill Bergey* (LB) 1969–73, Mark Donahue (G) 1978–9, Jim Hannula (T) 1983, Bob Riley (T) 1987r, Dan Jones (T) 1993–5, Ken Blackman (G) 1996–8, Thacher Szalay (OL) 2002.

67 Mike Wilson (T) 1969–70, Gary Burley (DE) 1976–83, David Douglas (T) 1986–8, Jeff Reinke (DE) 1987r, Daniel Stubbs (DE) 1991, Kimo Von Oelhoffen (DL) 1994–9.

68 Dave Middendorf (G) 1968–9, Steve Lawson (G) 1971–2, Bill Kollar (DT) 1974–6, Dave Pureifory (DT) 1978, Mike Obrovac (G/T) 1981–3, Tom Richey (G/T) 1987r, Paul Jetton (C/G) 1989–91, Donnell Johnson (T) 1993, Dave Cadigan

(G) 1994, Scott Shaw (C) 1998, Ron Smith (DL) 2002.

69 Sherrill Headrick (LB) 1968, *Tim Krumrie* (DT) 1983–94.

70 Andy Rice (DT) 1968–9, Ron Carpenter (DL) 1970–6, Barney Cotton (G) 1979, Bobby Whitten (T) 1981, Emanuel Weaver (NT) 1982, Jim Skow (DE) 1986–9, James Eaddy (DT) 1987r, Wade Russell (TE) 1987r, Rod Saddler (DE) 1991, Artie Smith (DE) 1994–6, Glen Steele (DL) 1998–2003.

71 Rufus Mayes (T) 1970–8, Rod Horn (DT) 1980–1, Pete Koch (DT) 1984, Mike Hammerstein (DL) 1986–7, 1989–90, John Fletcher (G) 1987r, Ralph Tamm (G) 1991, Garry Howe (DT) 1993, *Willie Anderson* (T) 1996–2003.

72 Howard Fest (G/T) 1968–75, Ron Hunt (T) 1976–8, Mack Mitchell (DE) 1979, Mike St. Clair (DE) 1980–2, Skip McClendon (DE) 1987–91, Keith Cupp (T) 1987r, Elston Ridgle (DE) 1992, Scott Brumfield (G) 1993–7, Matt O'Dwyer (G) 1999–2003.

73 Pat Matson (G) 1968–74, Earl Edwards (DL) 1977–88, Ken Moyer (G/T) 1989–91, 1993–4, Brian DeMarco (G) 1999, Richmond Webb (T) 2001–2.

74 Willie Lee Jones (DL) 1968, Ernie Park (G) 1969, *Mike Reid* (DT) 1970–4, Glenn Bujnoch (G) 1976–82, Brian Blados (G) 1984–91, Tom Scott (T) 1993, Mark Dennis (T) 1994, Rich Braham (G/C) 1994, 1996–2003.

75 Ernie Wright (T) 1968–71, Stan Walters (T) 1972–4, Al Krevis (T) 1975, Wilson Whitley (DT) 1977–82, Bruce Reimers (G/T) 1984–91, Jack Linn (G/T) 1993, Anthony Brown (T/G) 1995–8, Jamain Stephens (T/TE) 1999–2001, Scott Kooistra (T) 2003.

76 Jim Griffin (DE) 1968, Frank Cornish (DT) 1970, Vernon Holland (T) 1971–9, Glen Collins (DE) 1982–5, Jeff Smith (DE) 1987r, Kirk Scrafford (T) 1990–2, Trent Pollard (G/T) 1994–5, Mike Doughty (T) 2000, Levi Jones (T) 2002–3.

77 Bob Kelly (T) 1968, Frank Peters (T) 1969, Bob Maddox (DE) 1974, Mike Wilson (T) 1978–85, Mark Tigges (T) 1987r, Jim Rourke (OL) 1988, Scott Jones (T) 1989, 1991, Kevin Sargent (T/G) 1992–5, 1997–8, Victor Leyva (G) 2001.

78 Dan Archer (T) 1968, Willie Lee Jones (DL) 1970–1, Lee Thomas (DE) 1973, Bob Brown (DT) 1975–6, Walter Johnson (DT) 1977, Ted Vincent (DT) 1978, **Anthony Munoz** (T) 1980–92.

79 Steve Chomyszak (DL) 1968–73, *Coy Bacon* (DE) 1976–7, Ross Browner (DE) 1978–86, Bill Berthusen (DE) 1987r, Dana Wells (NT) 1989, Lamar Rogers (DE) 1991–2, Ramondo Stallings (DE) 1994–7, Scott Rehberg (G) 2000–3.

80 Ken Johnson (DE) 1971–7, *Cris Collinsworth* (WR) 1981–8, Tom Brown (WR) 1987r, Lynn James (WR) 1990–1, *Carl Pickens* (WR)

1992–3, David Dunn (WR) 1995–8, Willie Jackson (WR) 1998–9, Peter Warrick (WR) 2000–3.

81 Dennis Randall (DE) 1968, Nick Roman (DE) 1970–1, Al Chandler (TE) 1973–4, Jim Corbett (TE) 1977–80, David Verser (WR) 1981–4, *Eddie Brown* (WR) 1985–91, Marquis Pleasant (WR) 1987r, Patrick Robinson (WR) 1993, *Carl Pickens* (WR) 1994–9, Ron Dugans (WR) 2000–2.

82 Ed McCall (WR) 1968, Royce Berry (DE) 1969–74, Billy Brooks (WR) 1976–9, Alton Alexis (WR) 1980, *Rodney Holman* (TE) 1982–92, Wade Russell (TE) 1987r, Tony McGee (TE) 1993–2001, Reggie Kelly (TE) 2003.

83 Bill Staley (DT) 1968–9, Ed Marshall (WR) 1971, Sherman White (DE) 1972–5, Steve Holden (WR) 1977, Dennis Law (KR) 1978, Rick Walker (TE) 1979, M.L. Harris (TE) 1980–5, Dave Romasko (TE) 1987r, Kendal Smith (WR) 1989–90, Brian Brennan (WR) 1992, Reggie Thornton (WR) 1993, David Frisch (TE) 1994, Tydus Winans (WR) 1996, Gunnard Twyner (WR) 1997, Danny Farmer (WR) 2000–2, Kevin Walter (WR) 2003.

84 *Bob Trumpy* (TE) 1968–77, Don Bass (WR) 1978–81, Gary Williams (WR) 1984, *Dan Ross* (TE) 1985, Eric Kattus (TE) 1986–91, Reggie Sims (TE) 1987r, Rodney Tweet (WR) 1987r, Milt Stegall (WR) 1992–4, Jeff Hill (WR) 1995–6, Mike Jenkins (WR) 1997, Damon Gibson (WR) 1998, Craig Yeast (WR) 1999–2000, T.J. Houshmandzadeh (WR) 2001–3.

85 Dan Brabham (LB) 1968, Martin Baccaglio (DE) 1968–70, *Isaac Curtis* (WR) 1973–84, Tim McGee (WR) 1986–92, 1994, Greg Meehan (WR) 1987r, Allen DeGraffenreid (WR) 1993, James Hundon (WR) 1996–9, Lavell Boyd (WR) 2000, *Chad Johnson* (WR) 2001–3.

86 Andre White (TE) 1968, John McDaniel (WR) 1974–7, Steve Kreider (WR) 1979–86, Ken Brown (WR) 1987r, Carl Parker (WR) 1988–9, Mike Barber (WR) 1990–1, Wesley Carroll (WR) 1993, Darnay Scott (WR) 1994–9, 2001, Tony Stewart (TE) 2002–3.

87 Bill Peterson (LB) 1968, Mike Kelly (TE) 1970–2, *Pat McInally* (P) 1976–85, Jim Riggs (TE) 1987–92, Curtis Jeffries (TE) 1987r, Troy Sadowski (TE) 1994–6, Stepfret Williams (WR) 1998, Damon Griffin (WR) 1999–2000, Chris Edmonds (TE) 2002, Kelly Washington (WR) 2003.

88 Bruce Coslett (TE) 1969–76, Rick Walker (TE) 1977–9, Mike Levenseller (WR) 1979–80, Mike Martin (WR) 1983–9, Reggie Rembert (WR) 1991–3, Derek Ware (TE) 1995, Steve Bush (TE) 1997–2000, Sean Brewer (TE) 2002, Lawrence Hamilton (WR) 2003.

89 Harry Gunner (DE) 1968–9, Marty Amsler (DE) 1970, Drew Buie (WR) 1972, Tim George (WR) 1973, Jack Novak (TE) 1975, Mike Cobb (TE) 1977, *Dan Ross* (TE) 1979–83, Don Kern

(TE) 1984–5, Ira Hillary (WR) 1987–9, Shane Garrett (WR) 1991, Jeff Query (WR) 1992–5, Marco Battaglia (TE) 1996–2001, Matt Schobel (TE) 2002–3.

90 Emanuel King (LB) 1985–8, Eric Shaw (LB) 1992–4, Gerald Collins (LB) 1995, Tim Johnson (DT) 1996, Michael Bankston (DE) 1998–2000, Justin Smith (DE) 2001–3.

91 Carl Zander (LB) 1985–91, Brad Smith (LB) 1993, Brett Wallerstedt (LB) 1994–5, Billy Granville (LB) 1997–2000, Randy Chevrier (DT) 2001, Carl Powell (DE) 2003.

92 Tim Inglis (LB) 1987–8, John Copeland (DL) 1993–2000, Eric Ogboqu (DL) 2002, Duane Clemons (DE) 2003.

93 Kiki DeAyala (LB) 1986–7, Ty Parten (DE) 1993–5, Tim Morabito (DT) 1996, Mike Thompson (DT) 1998, Tom Barndt (DT) 2000, Mario Monds (DT) 2001.

94 Rich Romer (LB) 1988–9, Alfred Williams (LB) 1991–4, Jevon Langford (DE) 1996–2000, Tony Williams (DT) 2001–3.

95 Roosevelt Nix (DE) 1992–3, Keith Rucker (DT) 1994–5, Steve Foley (LB) 1998–2001.

96 Willie Fears (DE) 1987r, Curtis Maxey (DT) 1988, Natu Tuatagaloa (DE) 1989–91, Daniel Stubbs (DE) 1992–3, Kanavis McGhee (LB) 1994, Alfred Oglesby (DT) 1995, Kenny Davidson (DE) 1996, Brentson Buckner (DE) 1997, Clyde Simmons (DE) 1998, Vaughn Booker (DE) 2000–2.

97 Brian Pillman (LB) 1984, Mike Frier (DE) 1992–4, Andre Purvis (DL) 1997–9, Bernard Whittington (DE) 2001–2, John Thornton (DT) 2003.

98 David Grant (DT) 1988–91, Tony Savage (DE) 1992, George Hinkle (DE) 1993, Todd Kelly (DE) 1995–6, Canute Curtis (LB) 1997–2002.

99 Jason Buck (DE) 1987–90, Bob Riley (T) 1987r, Alonzo Mitz (DE) 1991–2, Donnell Johnson (T) 1993, Dan Wilkinson (DL) 1994–7, Oliver Gibson (DT) 1999–2003.

CLEVELAND BROWNS

The franchise: The Browns are the franchise with the gap in their history, a three year hole from when the existing team moved to Baltimore to become the Ravens in 1996 to when new ownership restored the franchise as an expansion team in 1999. Cleveland has a long history of fielding teams in the NFL. Starting with the charter member Cleveland Tigers in 1920, there were three separate Cleveland franchises in the first 12 years of the league. In 1937, the Cleveland Rams were initiated into the league; they won a championship in 1945 and immediately abandoned Cleveland and moved to Los Angeles the next season. Meanwhile, a new league, the All America Football Conference, was formed, and the Cleveland Browns became a charter member under owner Mickey McBride. Brilliant coach and general manager Paul Brown assembled a juggernaut of future Hall of Famers that won all four AAFC titles and lost only one game in the last two seasons. They were so dominant that they may have contributed to the AAFC's collapse. When the leagues merged, the Browns were one of three AAFC teams accepted into the NFL.

From their first NFL game against the Philadelphia Eagles who had appeared in three consecutive championship games and had won the last two, the Browns continued their dominance. They beat the Eagles 35–10 on opening day, went 11–1 for the season and defeated the Los Angeles Rams for the title in Cleveland. Coming back late to beat the first team to desert the city was an especially sweet irony. The Browns were led by Hall of Fame quarterback Otto Graham and went to the NFL title game their first six years in the league, winning three of them. Graham thus played in a league championship game all 10 of his years as a professional, a remarkable achievement. In the middle of that run, McBride sold the team to David R. Jones. After Graham retired for good, Brown came up with a new superstar a year later in Jim Brown, often called the greatest running back in NFL history. However, Paul Brown would only make it back to the title game in Jim Brown's rookie year of 1957. For the next five years, the team seemed to slowly descend into mediocrity, and this led to Paul Brown being fired in 1962 by owner Art Modell, who had bought the team just one year before. It was the first decisive move for which the city would learn to despise Modell. Under former Paul Brown assistant Blanton Collier, though, the team immediately improved, winning the NFL championship in Collier's second year and returning to the title game the year after that. Jim Brown then retired, but the Browns rolled on behind his replacement, Leroy Kelly, who would also end up in the Hall of Fame.

The 1970s saw a period of decline that began to change at the end of the decade with the Kardiac Kids who specialized in last minute victories orchestrated by quarterback Brian Sipe. The 1980s were a mostly positive decade under coach Marty Schottenheimer and quarterback Bernie Kosar, a Cleveland native. The team's one weakness was John Elway, who led his Denver Broncos over the Browns in three AFC Conference Championships in four years. Marty would continue to be bedeviled by Elway when he moved on to coach the Kansas City Chiefs and never did solve this problem. The 1990s, of course, brought ruin and abandonment again as Art Modell tried to extort a new stadium out of the city and then moved the team to Baltimore when that city gave him everything he wanted in 1996. Due to the ugly nature of the move, a deal was quickly worked out between the league and Cleveland that the Browns would be replaced and Modell would relinquish the name, the team's colors, and its history to the new owner of the restored franchise, who turned out to be Al Lerner. As an expansion team under their second coach, the Browns are still struggling to recapture the glory that was once Cleveland's.

Origin of name: When the new Cleveland franchise of the fledgling All America Football Conference held a poll to name the team, the top entry was Browns to honor their coach and general manager Paul Brown. Brown was a legendary figure in Ohio football, having been successful at Massillon High School and Ohio State University. Brown at first refused the accolade, and the team chose another entry, the Panthers. However, the rights to Cleveland Panthers were still held by the owner of the former American Football League team with that name. Brown relented and the Cleveland Browns were christened.

Record by Decade

| | Regular Season | | | Postseason | | |
	Won	Lost	Tied	Won	Lost	Championships
1940s	47	4	3	5	0	1946, 1947, 1948, 1949 (AAFC)
1950s	88	30	2	4	5	1950, 1954, 1955
1960s	92	41	5	3	4	1964
1970s	72	70	2	0	2	
1980s	83	68	1	3	7	
1990s	41	71	0	1	1	
2000s	24	40	0	0	1	
All-Time	400	320	10	11	20	4 +4 in the AAFC

Winning seasons: 32. Losing Seasons: 16. .500 seasons: 3.

Time till first championship: First year in AAFC and first year in the NFL.

Time since last championship: 40 years.

Retired numbers: The Browns have retired five numbers, three of which are easy picks—Otto Graham 14, Jim Brown 32, and Lou Groza 76. Graham actually wore 60 longer than he did 14, but 14 is a quarterback's number. The other two retired numbers were set aside in memoriam. 46 was retired for defensive back Don Fleming, a good player but no Hall of Famer, who died in a car accident in 1963. 45 was retired in the name of Heisman Trophy winner Ernie Davis who contracted leukemia in 1962 and died before he ever got a chance to play in the NFL.

Other numbers worn by these players: Quarterback Otto Graham wore 60 until new rules for numbers by position were instituted

Coaches			
	Years	*Record*	*Playoffs*
Paul Brown (3)	1950–62	111–44–5	4–5
Blanton Collier (1)	1963–70	76–34–2	3–4
Nick Skorich	1971–4	30–24–2	0–2
Forrest Gregg	1975–7	18–23–0	0–0
Dick Modzelewski	1977	0–1–0	0–0
Sam Rutigliano	1978–84	47–50–0	0–2
Marty Schottenheimer	1984–8	44–27–0	2–4
Bud Carson	1989–90	11–13–1	1–1
Jim Shofner	1990	1–6–0	0–0
Bill Belichick	1991–5	36–44–0	1–1
Chris Palmer	1999–2000	5–27–0	0–0
Butch Davis	2001–3	21–27–0	0–1

in 1952; tackle Lou Groza wore 46 until that time.

Those who wore retired numbers after the honored player: None.

Numbers that should be retired: In 1946 Hall of Famers Bill Willis 30/45/60 and Marion Motley 36/76 broke the color barrier. They deserve to be fully remembered.

Owned numbers: No one but Otto Graham has ever worn 14 for Cleveland; no one but Bernie Kosar has ever worn 19, but his number is dormant not retired.

Numbers worn by Hall of Famers: Doug Atkins 83; Jim Brown 32; Willie Davis 77/89; Len Dawson 18; Joe DeLamielleure 64; Len Ford 53/80; Frank Gatski 22/52; Otto Graham 14/60; Lou Groza 46/76; Henry Jordan 72; Leroy Kelly 44; Dante Lavelli 56/86; Mike McCormack 74; Tommy McDonald 29; Bobby Mitchell 49; Marion Motley 36/76; Ozzie Newsome 82; Chuck Noll 65; Paul Warfield 42; and Bill Willis 30/45/60.

Star power: Bill Howton took 86 from Paul Wiggins.

Star eclipsed: Earnest Byner wore 20/21 because Tommy Vardell wore 44. Len Dawson wore 18 till Milt Plum, 16, left; Dick Schafrath wore 80 till Willie Davis, 77, left.

Numbers with most great players: 44 was worn by Hall of Famer Leroy Kelly, star runner Earnest Byner, and three solid players and future coaches— Don Shula, Lou Rymkus, and Jim Shofner. 60 was worn by two Hall of Famers, Otto Graham and Bill Willis, and star guard John Wooten. 86 was worn

by Hall of Fame receiver Dante Lavelli as well as Bill Howton, Gary Collins, Dub Jones, Brian Brennan and Paul Wiggin.

Worst represented numbers: 11 was worn by seven forgettable quarterbacks; 25 was worn by 13 backs including the immensely disappointing Heisman trophy winner Charles White who was the team's number draft pick; and 47 was worn by nine backs of whom only two lasted longer than a season in Cleveland.

Number worn by the most players: 21 players have worn numbers 70 and 80.

Player who wore the most numbers: Seven Browns have worn three different numbers— Earnest Byner 20/21/44; Jamie Caleb 36/37/47; John Kissell 45/70/72; Warren Lahr 24/66/80; Lou Saban 20/66/72; Tommy Thompson 24/36/54; and Hall of Famer Bill Willis 30/45/60.

Longest tenure wearing a number: Linebacker Clay Mathews wore 57 for 16 years from 1978 through 1993. After Lou Groza switched from 46 in 1952, he wore 76 through 1967. However, he retired for one year in 1960 so he only spent 15 years in 76.

Number worn by first ever draft pick: The Browns first draft pick in 1950 was Ken Carpenter who wore 84. The first draft pick of the reconstituted Browns franchise in 1999 was Tim Couch, number 2.

Biggest draft busts: Draft flops include quarterback Bob Garrett who was selected first in 1954, was traded to Green Bay where he got into nine games, and was eventually traded back to Cleveland, but who never played a down for the Browns; Touchdown Tommy Vardell, 44, a fullback who was selected ninth in 1992 and who scored twice in Cleveland; and injury-prone linebacker Mike Junkin, 54, from Duke who was selected fifth in 1987. The biggest bust, though, was quarterback Mike Phipps, 15, who was selected third in 1970 and in seven years completed less than 50 percent of his passes and threw 40 tds and 81 interceptions.

Number worn by first expansion draft pick: When the Browns were reformed in 1999, Jim Pyne was their first pick in the expansion draft and wore 71. From that expansion draft, defensive back Ray Jackson, 31, lasted longer than any other selection — three years from 1999 to 2001.

Number worn by oldest player: Lou Groza was 43 years old and still wearing 76 in 1967.

Cameos: Hall of Famers— Tommy McDonald 29; All Pros and other notables— Mark Bavaro 48/83; James Brooks 28; Lomas Brown 75; Ken Ellis 48; Earl Holmes 50; Bill Howton 86; Rich "Tombstone" Jackson 87; John Jefferson 89; Homer Jones 85; Terry Kirby 42; Andre Rison 80; Brad Van Pelt 50.

Ones who got away: Packer Hall of Fame defensive linemen Willie Davis, 77/89, and Henry Jordan, 72, both started in Cleveland, as did Bear Hall of Fame defensive end Doug Atkins 83. The Browns also had Hall of Famer Len Dawson, 18, and released him. Giants star runner Ron Johnson, 30, first flopped in Cleveland. Lion linebacker Mike Lucci was originally a Brown, as were Viking defensive end Jim Marshall, 80, Cowboy end Frank Clarke, 82, and future Colt defensive backs Don Shula, 44/96, and Carl Taseff, 98.

Least popular numbers: 0 has never been worn and 6 has only been worn briefly by a replacement player. 19 was only worn by Bernie Kosar.

Last number to be originated: 4 was first worn by punter Max Runager in 1988.

Longest dormant number: 6 has not been worn for 17 years since 1987. 98 was dormant for 37 years from 1951 to 1987.

Triskaidekaphobia notes: 13 has been worn only by four quarterbacks in Cleveland, one star (Frank Ryan) and three forgetables (Don Horn, Jeff Francis, and Spergon Wynn).

Shared numbers: Hall of Famer Ozzie Newsom and All Pro Jim Houston both wore 82; star defensive backs Hanford Dixon and Eric Turner both wore 29.

Continuity: The 1952 rules change regarding uniform numbers led to two Browns' Hall of Famers passing their numbers on to two other Famers. Otto Graham was replaced in 60 by Bill Willis and Marion Motley was replaced in 76 by Lou Groza.

Discontinuity: Star receiver Ray Renfro was followed in 26 by defensive back Dave Raimey; cornerback Hanford Dixon was followed in 29 by flop runner Brent Fullwood; Hall of Famer Bill Willis was followed in 30 by runner Emerson Cole; shifty Greg Pruitt was followed in 34 by David Green; linebacker Galen Fiss was followed in 35 by Larry Conjar; Hall of Famer Lou Groza was followed in 46 by Ace Loomis; Hall of Famer Frank Gatski was followed in 52 by Joe Amstutz; Dick Schaffrath was followed in 77 by Fest Cotton.

Family Connections

Brothers

Lin Houston	G	1946–53	32/62
Jim Houston	LB	1960–72	82
Ed Modzelewski	FB	1955–9	36
Dick Modzelewski	DT	1964–6	74
Jerry Ball	DT	1993, 1999	93
Anthony Malbrough	DB	2000	26

Quarterback numbers over 19: 60 Otto Graham; 62 Cliff Lewis; 66 Ermal Allen.

Number of first black player: In the Browns first year, 1946, Bill Willis wore 30 and Marion Motley wore 76 to break the color barrier. In 1947, Horace Gillom, 59, joined the team.

Numbers of future NFL head coaches: Monte Clark 73; Bill Cowher 53; Abe Gibron 34/64; Otto Graham 14/60; Mike McCormack 74; Walt Michaels 34; Dick Modzelewski 74; Chuck Noll 65; Lou Rymkus 44; Lou Saban 20/66/72; John Sandusky 49/78; Jim Shofner 44; Don Shula 44/96; Mac Speedie 58/88; Paul Wiggin 84/86.

Numbers of future NFL referees: Gary Lane 15; George Young 82.

Players who played other sports: Basketball — Len Ford 53/80; Otto Graham 14/60; Wrestling — Walter Johnson 71.

Players more famous after football: Jim Brown, 32, made a career of acting and has done a great deal of work inner city gang members. He has had a number of run-ins with the law over his treatment of women as well. End Don Steinbrunner, 56/74, is one of two NFL players to die in Vietnam.

First player to wear a number in the 70s: Three players wore 70s in the Browns first year of 1946 — Gene Fekete, 70; Gaylon Smith, 74; Marion Motley, 76.

First player to wear a number in the 80s: Five players wore 80s in the Browns first year of 1946 — Al Akins, 80; Bill Lund, 82; Ray Terrell, 84; Don Greenwood, 85; Bob Steuber, 88.

First player to wear a number in the 90s: Three players wore 90s in the Browns first year of 1946 — Edgar Jones, 90; Tom Colella, 92; Fred Evans, 99.

Number with most points scored: 76 with 1,232 points scored in the NFL by Lou Groza (1,202) and Marion Motley (30).

Number with most yards rushing: 32 with 14,431 yards rushed by Jim Brown (12,312), Fred Morrison (1,398) and Harry Jagade (721).

Number with most receptions: 86 with 1,160 passes caught by Gary Collins (331), Brian Brennan (315), Dante Lavelli (164), Dennis Northcutt (157), Dub Jones (61), Gern Nagler (55), Bill Howton (39), Leslie Shepherd (23), Walter Reeves (6), Dan Fulton (3), and Patrick (3).

Number with most touchdown passes: 16 with 177 touchdowns tossed by Bill Nelson (71), Milt Plum (66), Paul McDonald (24), George Ratterman (15), and Will Cureton (1).

Number with most interceptions: 22 with 115 passes picked off by Clarence Scott (39), Ken Konz (30), Felix Wright (26), Bobby Franklin (13), Vince Newsome (4), Rex Bumgardner (2), and Michael Jameson (1).

Oddity: The only two players to wear a number under 15 for coach Paul Brown (1946–62) were John Borton, 10, and Otto Graham, 14. No Brown wore a single digit number till 1977 when Terry Luck wore 7 and Greg Coleman wore 9.

The Browns are the only team to retire a number for a player who never played in an NFL game — 45 for Ernie Davis.

Team All-Time Numerical Roster

Those with an "r" following the year 1987 were replacement players during the players' strike. Pro Bowl players for each number are in *Italics*; Hall of Famers are in **Bold** type.

1 Homer Jordan (QB) 1987r, Michael Jackson (WR) 1991–3.

2 Tony Deleone (P) 1987, Jerry Kauric (K) 1990, Tim Couch (QB) 1999–2003.

3 Mark Moseley (K) 1986, Brian Franco (K) 1987r, Goran Lingmerth (K) 1987r, Matt Stover (K) 1991–5.

4 Max Runager (P) 1988, Rico Smith (WR) 1992, Phil Dawson (K) 1999–2003.

5 *Webster Slaughter* (WR) 1986, George Winslow (P) 1987, Dale Waters (P) 1987r, Brett Conway (K) 2003.

6 Remi Watson (WR) 1987r.

7 Terry Luck (QB) 1977, Jeff Gossett (P) 1983, 1985–7, Tom Tupa (P) 1994–5.

8 Johnny Evans (QB/P) 1978–80, Jeff Jaeger (K) 1987, Brad Goebel (QB) 1992–4.

9 Greg Coleman (P) 1977, Matt Bahr (K) 1981–9.

10 John Borton (QB) 1957, Chris Gartner (K) 1974, Dave Mays (QB) 1976–7, Dave Jacobs (K) 1981, Tom Flick (QB) 1984, Mike Pagel (QB) 1986–90, Eric Zeier (QB) 1995, Kevin Thompson (QB) 2000, Kelly Holcomb (QB) 2001–3.

11 Jim Ninowski (QB) 1964–6, Don Gault (QB) 1970, Lee Johnson (P) 1987–8, Jeff Christensen (QB) 1987r, Brian Hansen (P) 1991–3, Mark Rypien (QB) 1994, Ty Detmer (QB) 1999.

12 Don Cockroft (K/P) 1968–80, Rick Trocano (QB) 1981–3, Karlton Watson (QB) 1987r, Don Strock (QB) 1988, Vinnie Testaverde (QB) 1993–5, Josh Booty (QB) 2002.

13 *Frank Ryan* (QB) 1962–8, Don Horn (QB) 1973, Jeff Francis (QB) 1990, Spergon Wynn (QB) 2000.

14 **Otto Graham** (QB) 1952–5.

15 Bert Rechichar (DB) 1952, Ken Gorgal (DB) 1953–4, Tommy O'Connell (QB) 1956–7, Jim Ninowski (QB) 1958–9, 1962–3, Gary Lane (QB) 1966–7, Mike Phipps (QB) 1970–6, Mark Miller (QB) 1978–9, Steve Cox (P/K) 1981–4, Bryan Wagner (P) 1989–90, Donny Brady (DB) 1995.

16 George Ratterman (QB) 1952–6, *Milt Plum* (QB) 1957–61, *Bill Nelsen* (QB) 1968–72, Will Cureton (QB) 1975, Paul McDonald (QB) 1980–5,

Selwyn Jones (DB) 1993–4, Kevin Thompson (QB) 2000.

17 Jerry Rhome (QB) 1969, *Brian Sipe* (QB) 1974–83, Todd Philcox (QB) 1991–3, Chris Gardocki (P) 1999–2003.

18 Babe Parilli (QB) 1956, Bob Freeman (DB) 1957–8, Bob Ptacek (QB) 1959, **Len Dawson** (QB) 1960–1, John Furman (QB) 1962, Dick Shiner (QB) 1967, Ben Hawkins (WR) 1974, Gary Danielson (QB) 1985, 1987–8, Vernon Joines (WR) 1989–90, Mike Tomczak (QB) 1992, Doug Pederson (QB) 2000, Tony Simmons (WR) 2001.

19 *Bernie Kosar* (QB) 1985–93.

20 Mike Scarry (C) 1946–7, Lou Saban (LB) 1948–9, Hal Herring (LB) 1950–1, *Ken Carpenter* (RB) 1952–3, *Don Paul* (DB) 1954–8, Ross Fichtner (DB) 1960–7, Fred Summers (DB) 1969–71, Jim Steinke (DB) 1973, Tony Peters (DB) 1975–8, Doug Dennison (RB) 1979, Judson Flint (DB) 1980–2, Don Rogers (DB) 1984–5, Joe Morris (RB) 1991, Alan Haller (RB) 1992, Earnest Byner (RB) 1994, Johnny Thomas (CB) 1995, Earl Little (S) 1999–2003.

21 Dean Brown (DB) 1969, Stan Brown (WR) 1971, Van Green (DB) 1973–6, Oliver Davis (DB) 1977–80, Mike Whitwell (WR/S) 1983, Corey Gilmore (RB) 1987r, *Eric Metcalf* (KR) 1989–94, Earnest Byner (RB) 1995, Marquis Smith (S/LB) 1999–2001, Lewis Sanders (DB) 2002–3.

22 **Frank Gatski** (C) 1946–51, Rex Bumgardner (RB) 1952, *Ken Konz* (DB) 1953–9, Rich Mostardo (DB) 1960, Tom Watkins (RB) 1961, Lowell Caylor (DB) 1964, Bobby Franklin (DB) 1966, Billy Devrow (DB) 1967, *Clarence Scott* (DB) 1971–83, Felix Wright (DB) 1985–90, Perry Kemp (WR) 1987r, Vince Newsome (DB) 1991–2, Ricky Powers (RB) 1995, Tim McTyer (DB) 1999, Todd Franz (DB) 2000, Michael Jameson (DB) 2002–3.

23 Larry Benz (DB) 1963–5, Clifford Brooks (DB) 1972–4, Bill Craven (DB) 1976, Larry Collins (RB) 1978, Mark Kafentzis (S) 1982, Mark Harper (CB) 1986–90, DeJuan Robinson (DB) 1987r, Randy Baldwin (RB) 1992–4, Earnest Hunter (RB) 1995, Marquez Pope (DB) 1999, Errict Rhett (RB) 2000, Devin Bush (DB) 2001–2, Ron Israel (DB) 2003.

24 Mel Maceau (C) 1946–8, Tommy Thompson (LB) 1949–51, Warren Lahr (DB) 1952–9, Bobby Franklin (DB) 1960–5, *Ernie Kellerman* (DB) 1966–71, Bobby Majors (DB) 1972, Pete Athas (DB) 1975, Terry Brown (DB) 1976, Randy Rich (DB) 1978–9, Autry Beamon (DB) 1980–1, Cleotha Montgomery (KR) 1981, Vagas Ferguson (RB) 1983, Greg Best (S) 1984, Ray Ellis (S) 1986–7, Anthony Blaylock (DB) 1988–91, Terry Taylor (CB) 1992–3, Corey Fuller (CB) 1999–2001, Robert Griffith (S) 2002–3.

25 Charles Leigh (RB) 1968–9, Frank Pitts (WR) 1971–3, Rolly Woolsey (DB) 1977, Pat Mo-

riarty (RB) 1979, Charles White (RB) 1980–2, 1984, Vincent Barnett (S) 1987r, Alfred Jackson (DB) 1991–2, Anthony Florence (DB) 1991, Dana Hall (S) 1995, Sedrick Shaw (RB) 1999, Lewis Sanders (DB) 2000, Corey Fuller (CB) 2002, Chris Crocker (S) 2003.

26 *Ray Renfro* (WR) 1952–63, Dave Raimey (DB) 1964, Reece Morrison (RB) 1968–72, Billy Lefear (WR) 1972–5, Tom Sullivan (RB) 1978, Dino Hall (KR) 1979–83, Greg Allen (RB) 1985, Arthur Williams (WR) 1987r, Keith Jones (RB) 1989, Raymond Clayborn (DB) 1990–1, Ron Wolfley (RB) 1992–3, Michael Davis (CB) 1995, Anthony Malbrough (DB) 2000, Dyshod Carter (DB) 2001.

27 Walter Roberts (WR/KR) 1964–6, Carl Ward (DB) 1967–8, Randy Minniear (RB) 1970, Rickey Stevenson (CB) 1970, *Thom Darden* (DB) 1972–4, 1976–81, Mike Whitwell (WR/S) 1982, Al Gross (S) 1983–7, Brian Dudley (S) 1987r, Derrick Douglas (RB) 1991, Stevon Moore (DB) 1992–5, Karim Abdul-Jabbar (RB) 1999, Lamar Chapman (DB) 2000–1, Roosevelt Williams (CB) 2003.

28 Dick Deschaine (P) 1958, Ben Davis (DB) 1967–8, 1970–3, Eddie Brown (DB) 1974–5, Ron Bolton (DB) 1976–82, Herman Fontenot (RB) 1985–8, Robert Goins (S) 1987r, Steve Pierce (WR) 1987r, Tyrone Shavers (WR) 1991, James Brooks (RB) 1992, Everson Walls (DB) 1992–3, Erik McMillan (DB) 1993, Don Griffin (DB) 1994–5, Rashidi Barnes (DB) 2000, Leigh Bodden (CB) 2003.

29 **Tommy McDonald** (WR) 1968, Walt Sumner (DB) 1969–74, *Hanford Dixon* (CB) 1981–9, Brent Fullwood (RB) 1990, *Eric Turner* (DB) 1991–5, Rashaan Salaam (RB) 1999, James Jackson (RB) 2001–3.

30 **Bill Willis** (G) 1946–51, Emerson Cole (RB) 1952, Sherman Howard (RB) 1953, Maurice Bassett (FB) 1954–6, Lew Carpenter (HB) 1957–8, *Bernie Parrish* (CB) 1959–66, Ron Johnson (RB) 1969, Ken Brown (RB) 1970–5, Cleo Miller (RB) 1976–82, Boyce Green (RB) 1983–5, Billy Robinson (DB) 1987r, Thane Gash (S) 1988–90, Jamel White (RB) 2000–3.

31 Charley Harraway (RB) 1966–8, Bob Hunt (RB) 1974, Cleo Miller (RB) 1975, *Frank Minnifield* (CB) 1984–92, James Black (RB) 1984, Stacey Hairston (DB) 1993–5, Raymond Jackson (DB) 1999–2001, William Green (RB) 2002–3.

32 Lin Houston (G) 1946–51, *Harry Jagade* (RB) 1952–3, *Fred Morrison* (RB) 1954–6, **Jim Brown** (RB) 1957–65.

33 Randy Schultz (RB) 1966, Nathaniel James (DB) 1968, Tom Schoen (DB) 1970, Bo Cornell (RB) 1971–2, Reggie Rucker (WR) 1975–81, Curtis Dickey (RB) 1985–6, Kirk Jones (RB) 1987, Mike Oliphant (RB) 1989, *Leroy Hoard* (RB) 1990–5, Daylon McCutcheon (CB) 1999–2003.

34 George Cheroke (G) 1946, Bob Gaudio (G) 1947, *Abe Gibron* (G) 1950–1, *Walt Michaels* (LB) 1952–61, Stan Sczurek (LB) 1963, Ken Webb (RB) 1963, Mike Howell (DB) 1965–72, *Greg Pruitt* (RB) 1973–81, David Green (RB) 1982, *Kevin Mack* (RB) 1985–93, Marcus Lee (RB) 1994, Lorenzo White (RB) 1995, Madre Hill (RB) 1999, Chris Floyd (FB) 2000, Ben Gay (RB) 2001, R.J. Bowers (RB) 2002–3.

35 Alex Agase (G) 1948–51, *Galen Fiss* (LB) 1956–66, Larry Conjar (RB) 1967, Bo Scott (RB) 1969–74, Brian Duncan (RB) 1976–7, Calvin Hill (RB) 1978–81, Stacey Driver (RB) 1987r, Enis Jackson (CB) 1987r, Will Hill (S) 1988, Barry Redden (RB) 1989–90.

36 Ed Ulinski (G) 1946–9, Tommy Thompson (LB) 1950, **Marion Motley** (FB) 1952–3, Ed Modzelewski (FB) 1955–9, Billy Kinard (DB) 1956, Jamie Caleb (RB) 1960, Charley Scales (RB) 1962–5, Nick Pietrosante (FB) 1966–7, Dick Davis (RB) 1969, Steve Engel (RB) 1970, Henry Hynoski (RB) 1975, Eddie Payton (KR) 1977, Bill Jackson (S) 1982, Stephen Braggs (DB) 1987–91, Vince Carreker (DB) 1987r, Fred Foggie (DB) 1992, Issac Booth (DB) 1994–5, Chris Akins (DB) 2001–2.

37 George Groves (G) 1946, Bob Kolesar (G) 1946, Jamie Caleb (RB) 1965, Hugh McKinnis (RB) 1973–5, Chris Rockins (S) 1984–7, Harlon Barnett (S) 1990–2, Bennie Thompson (DB) 1994–5, Anthony Henry (DB) 2001–3.

38 *Weldon Humble* (LB) 1947–50, Bob Gaudio (G) 1951, Maurice Bassett (FB) 1954, Sam Baker (P/K) 1960–1, Stan Sczurek (LB) 1963–5, Larry Poole (RB) 1975–7, Johnny Davis (RB) 1982–7, Alvin Horn (DB) 1987r, Larry Mason (RB) 1987r, George Swarn (RB) 1987r, Odie Harris (DB) 1991–2, Antonio Langham (CB) 1994–5, 1999, Earthwind Moreland (DB) 2001.

39 Alex Kapter (E) 1946–7, Billy Pritchett (RB) 1975, Major Everett (RB) 1986, 1987r, Stanley Carraway (WR) 1987r, Randy Hilliard (CB) 1990–3, Marlon Forbes (S) 1999, Michael Lehan (CB) 2003.

40 Jim Daniell (T) 1946, *Dub Jones* (HB) 1952–5, Preston Carpenter (E) 1956–9, Prentice Gautt (RB) 1960, Preston Powell (RB) 1961, Jim Shorter (DB) 1962–3, Howard Cassady (RB) 1962, *Erich Barnes* (CB) 1965–71, Preston Anderson (DB) 1974, Tom London (DB) 1978, Rod Perry (CB) 1983–4, Mike McCade (WR) 1987r, Kyle Kramer (S) 1989, Lynn James (WR) 1991, Tarek Saleh (LB/FB) 1999–00.

41 Ralph Smith (TE) 1965–8, Dave Jones (WR) 1969–71, Jerry Wilkinson (DB) 1980, Troy Wilson (CB) 1987r, Anthony Florence (DB) 1991, Tim Jacobs (CB) 1993–5, Travis Prentice (RB) 2000.

42 Chet Adams (T) 1946–8, Derrell Palmer (DT) 1949–51, *Tommy James* (DB) 1952–5, Lowe

Wren (DB) 1956–9, Bob Crespino (WR) 1961–3, **Paul Warfield** (WR) 1964–9, 1976–7, Gloster Richardson (WR) 1972–4, Neal Craig (DB) 1975, Dwight Walker (RB) 1982–4, Tim Manoa (FB) 1987–9, Calvin Pierce (FB) 1987r, Latin Berry (DB) 1991–2, Louis Riddick (DB) 1993–5, Terry Kirby (RB) 1999, Carl Fair (RB) 2001, Raymond Walls (DB) 2002.

43 Bob Smith (LB) 1955–6, Billy Kinard (DB) 1956, Volney Quinlan (RB) 1956, Ron Green (WR) 1967–8, Fair Hooker (WR) 1969–74, *Mike Pruitt* (RB) 1976–84, Tony Baker (RB) 1986, 1988, Stacy Williams (DB) 1987r, Joe King (DB) 1991, Del Speer (S) 1993–4, Vashone Adams (DB) 1995, George Jones (RB) 1999, Percy Ellsworth (DB) 2001–2, Kalvin Pearson (DB) 2002.

44 Lou Rymkus (T) 1946–51, Sherman Howard (RB) 1952, Don Phelps (RB) 1952, **Don Shula** (DB) 1952, John Petitbon (DB) 1955–6, Chet Hanulak (RB) 1957, Jim Shofner (DB) 1958–63, **Leroy Kelly** (RB) 1964–73, Earnest Byner (RB) 1984–8, Stefon Adams (DB) 1990, Lee Rouson (RB) 1991, Tommy Vardell (FB) 1992–5, Marc Edwards (FB) 1999–2000, Mike Sellers (RB) 2001, Lee Suggs (RB) 2003.

45 Ray Piskor (T) 1947, Ben Pucci (DT) 1948, **Bill Willis** (G) 1949, John Kissell (T) 1951, Bob Smith (LB) 1955, Leroy Bolden (RB) 1958–9.

46 **Lou Groza** (T/K) 1946–51, Ace Loomis (RB) 1952, Billy Reynolds (RB) 1953–4, 1957, Henry Ford (RB) 1955, Bob White (RB) 1955, Don Fleming (DB) 1960–2.

47 Jamie Caleb (RB) 1960, Ricky Jones (LB) 1977–9, Larry Braziel (CB) 1982–5, Mike Crawford (RB) 1987r, Keith Bostic (DB) 1990, Barry Wilburn (CB) 1992, Tim Jacobs (CB) 1993, Ryan McNeil (CB) 1999, Scott Frost (S) 2001.

48 Ernie Blandin (T) 1946–7, Forrest Grigg (T) 1948–51, Preston Carpenter (E) 1956, Milt Campbell (RB) 1957, Chet Hanulak (RB) 1957, *Ernie Green* (RB) 1962–8, Dave Sullivan (WR) 1973–4, John Pitts (DB) 1975, Ken Ellis (DB) 1977, Lawrence Johnson (DB) 1979–84, D.D. Hoggard (CB) 1985–7, George Landry (RB) 1987r, Brian Washington (S) 1988, Brian Kinchen (TE) 1991, Mark Bavaro (TE) 1992, Najee Mustafaa (CB) 1993, Frank Hartley (TE) 1994–5.

49 Len Simonetti (DT) 1946–8, Joe Spencer (T) 1949, John Sandusky (T) 1950–1, **Bobby Mitchell** (HB) 1958–61, Tom Wilson (RB) 1962, Walter Beach (DB) 1963–6, George Youngblood (DB) 1967, Alvin Mitchell (DB) 1968–9, Jim Hill (DB) 1975, Neal Craig (DB) 1976, Clinton Burrell (DB) 1979–84, Steve Lauter (S) 1987r, Robert Lyons (S) 1989, Bruce McGonnigal (TE) 1991, Clarence Williams (RB) 1993, Darnell Sanders (TE) 2002, Keith Heinrich (TE) 2003.

50 John Yonakor (DE) 1946–9, Jim Martin (DT) 1950, Bob Oristaglio (DE) 1951, Hal Herring (LB) 1952, Tom Catlin (LB) 1953–4, Sam Palumbo (LB) 1955, Vince Costello (LB) 1957–66, John Garlington (LB) 1968–77, Don Goode (LB) 1980–1, Tom Cousineau (LB) 1982–5, Brad Van Pelt (LB) 1986, Lucius Sanford (LB) 1987, Mike Teifke (C) 1987r, Van Waiters (LB) 1988–91, Frank Stams (LB) 1992–5, Michael Hamilton (LB) 2000, Barry Minter (LB) 2001, Earl Holmes (LB) 2002, Jeff Faine (C) 2003.

51 Dale Lindsey (LB) 1965–72, Leo Tierney (C) 1978, Eddie Johnson (LB) 1981–90, Gerald Dixon (LB) 1993–5, Lenoy Jones (LB) 1999, 2001–2, Ryan Taylor (LB) 2000, Chaun Thompson (LB) 2003.

52 George Young (DE) 1946–51, **Frank Gatski** (C) 1952–6, Joe Amstutz (C) 1957, Dave Lloyd (LB) 1959–61, Mike Lucci (LB) 1962–4, Billy Andrews (LB) 1967–74, Mel Long (LB) 1974, Dick Ambrose (LB) 1975–83, Nick Miller (LB) 1987, David Grayson (LB) 1987r, Ken Rose (LB) 1990, Richard Brown (LB) 1991–2, *Pepper Johnson* (LB) 1994–5, Brant Boyer (LB) 2001–3.

53 Alton Coppage (DE) 1946, Marshall Shurnas (E) 1947, Frank Kosikowski (E) 1948, Bill O'-Connor (DE) 1949, **Len Ford** (DE) 1950–1, Frank Morze (C) 1963, Bob Whitlow (C) 1968, Tom Beautler (LB) 1970, Mel Long (LB) 1972–4, Bill Cowher (LB) 1980–2, Stuart Anderson (LB) 1984, Jim Dumont (LB) 1984, Anthony Griggs (LB) 1986–8, Tom Polley (LB) 1987r, Cedric Figaro (LB) 1991–2, *Pepper Johnson* (LB) 1993–4, John Thierry (DE) 1999, Rahim Abdullah (LB) 2000, Mason Unck (LB) 2003.

54 John Rokisky (DE) 1946, Tommy Thompson (LB) 1952–3, *Tony Adamle* (LB) 1954, Sam Palumbo (LB) 1955–6, Pete Perini (RB) 1955, Tom Catlin (LB) 1957–8, Bob Denton (DT) 1960, Sam Tidmore (LB) 1962–3, *Fred Hoaglin* (C) 1966–72, *Tom DeLeone* (C) 1974–84, Mike Junkin (LB) 1987–8, Jerry Parker (LB) 1987r, Randy Kirk (LB) 1991, Chester Burnett (LB) 2000, Tarek Saleh (LB) 2001, Andra Davis (LB) 2002–3.

55 John Harrington (DE) 1946, John Demarie (G/T) 1967, Chuck Reynolds (C) 1969–70, Dave Graf (LB) 1975–9, John Mohring (LB) 1980, Curtis Weathers (TE/LB) 1982–5, Tim Crawford (LB) 1987r, Jock Jones (LB) 1990–1, Rahim Abdullah (LB) 1999, Marty Moore (LB) 2000, Anthony Denman (LB) 2001, Barry Gardner (LB) 2003.

56 **Dante Lavelli** (WR) 1946–51, Don Steinbrunner (DE) 1953, *Art Hunter* (C) 1957–9, *John Morrow* (C) 1960–6, Bob Matheson (LB) 1967–70, Jim Romaniszyn (LB) 1973–4, Jack LeVeck (LB) 1975, Robert L. Jackson (LB) 1978–81, *Chip Banks* (LB) 1982–6, David Grayson (LB) 1987–90, Dick Teets (LB) 1987r, Bobby Abrams (LB) 1992, Mike Caldwell (LB) 1993–5, Lenoy Jones (LB) 2000, Sherrod Coates (LB) 2003.

57 *Clay Matthews* (LB) 1978–93, Steven Nave (LB) 1987r, Jason Kyle (LB) 1999, Dwayne Rudd (LB) 2001–2.

58 *Mac Speedie* (E) 1946–51, Frank Morze (C) 1962, Rick Kingrea (LB) 1971–2, Mark Johnson (LB) 1977, Clifton Odom (LB) 1980, Bruce Huther (LB) 1981, Scott Nicolas (LB) 1982–6, Cliff Hannemann (LB) 1987r, Clifford Charlton (LB) 1988–9, Marcus Cotton (LB) 1990, David Brandon (LB) 1991–3, Carl Banks (LB) 1994–5, Wali Rainier (LB) 1999–2001, Ben Taylor (LB) 2002–3.

59 Alton Coppage (DE) 1946, *Horace Gillom* (P/E) 1947–51, Wayne Meylan (LB) 1968–9, Rudy Kuechenberg (LB) 1970, Charlie Hall (LB) 1971–80, Kevin Turner (LB) 1982, Dale Carver (LB) 1983, David Marshall (LB) 1984, *Mike Johnson* (LB) 1986–93, James Capers (LB) 1987r, Craig Powell (LB) 1995, Kendall Ogle (LB) 1999, Doug Colman (LB) 2000, Kevin Bentley (LB) 2002–3.

60 **Otto Graham** (QB) 1946–51, **Bill Willis** (G) 1952–3, Harold Bradley (G) 1954–6, *John Wooten* (G) 1959–67, Al Jenkins (G) 1969–70, Bob Babich (LB) 1973–8, Jeff Wiska (G) 1986, Al Baker (DE) 1987, 1989–90, Lance Zeno (C) 1992–3, Doug Dawson (G) 1994, Shaun O'Hara (G) 2000–3.

61 Dale Memmelaar (G) 1964, Joe Bob Isbell (G) 1966, Bob DeMarco (C) 1972–4, Al Dennis (G) 1976, Greg Fairchild (G) 1978, Mike Baab (C) 1982–7, 1990–1, Steve Everitt (C) 1993–5, Everett Lindsay (OL) 2000.

62 Cliff Lewis (QB) 1946–51, Lin Houston (G) 1952–3, Herschel Forester (G) 1954–7, Duane Putnam (G) 1961, Dale Memmelaar (G) 1964–5, Joe Taffoni (T) 1967–70, Chris Morris (T) 1972–3, Glen Holloway (G) 1974, Al Dennis (G) 1977, George Lilja (G/T) 1984–6, Mike Katolin (C) 1987r, Gene Williams (T/G) 1993–4, Eric Moore (OL) 1995, Bill Duff (DL) 1999, Paul Zukauskas (OL) 2001, Craig Osika (G) 2003.

63 Fred Robinson (G) 1957, Andy Cvercko (G) 1963, Mike Sikich (G) 1971, Joe Carollo (T) 1972–3, Barry Darrow (T) 1974–8, *Cody Risien* (T) 1979–83, 1985–9, Jay Hilgenberg (C) 1992, Wally Williams (C) 1994–5, Brad Bedell (OL) 2000–1.

64 Bud Schwenk (QB) 1946, George Terlep (QB) 1948, *Abe Gibron* (G) 1952–6, Don Goss (DT) 1956, *Jim Ray Smith* (G) 1957–62, Ted Connolly (G) 1963, Tom Goosby (LB) 1963, Jim Copeland (G) 1967–74, Joe Jones (DE) 1975–8, George Buehler (G) 1978–9, **Joe DeLamielleure** (G) 1980–4, Frank Winters (C) 1987–8, Blake Wingle (G) 1987r, Tom Baugh (C) 1989, Houston Hoover (G) 1993, Dave Wohlabaugh (C) 1999–2002, Ryan Pontbriand (C) 2003.

65 Joe Skibinski (G) 1952, **Chuck Noll** (G) 1953–9, Stan Sheriff (G) 1957, Ed Bettridge (LB) 1964, John Demarie (G/T) 1967–75, Henry Sheppard (G/T) 1976–81, Bob Gruber (T) 1986, John

Askin (G) 1987r, Ralph Tamm (G) 1990–1, Jim Bundren (C) 1999–2000, Richard Mercier (OL) 2001.

66 Lou Saban (LB) 1946, Ermal Allen (QB) 1947, Warren Lahr (DB) 1948, Gene Donaldson (G) 1953, *Gene Hickerson* (G) 1958–60, 1962–73, Mike Seifert (DE) 1974, Earl Edwards (DE) 1976–8, Ted Petersen (T) 1984, Dave Sparenberg (G) 1987r, Tony Jones (T) 1989–95, Paul Zukauskas (OL) 2002–3.

67 Sidney Williams (LB) 1964–6, Craig Wycinsky (G) 1972, Mike Morris (C) 1990, Chris Thome (OL) 1991–2, John Jurkovic (DT) 1999, Tre Johnson (G) 2001, Mel Fowler (OL) 2002–3.

68 Ed Sharkey (G) 1952, Larry Stephens (DT) 1960–1, Bob Pena (G) 1972, Robert E. Jackson (G) 1975–85, Barry Lee (C) 1987r, Darryl Haley (OL) 1987r, 1988, Ted Banker (G) 1989, Ed King (OL) 1991–3, Chris Ruhman (OL) 1999, Chad Beasley (OL) 2002–3.

69 John Macerelli (G) 1956, Jim Kanicki (DT) 1963–9, Pete Adams (G) 1974, 1976, Leo Biederman (T) 1978, Joel Patten (T) 1980, Dan Fike (G) 1985–92, Doug Dawson (G) 1994, Roger Chanoine (OL) 1999–2001.

70 Gene Fekete (RB) 1946, Spiro Dellerba (RB) 1947, Ollie Cline (RB) 1948, Ed Sustersic (RB) 1949, Emerson Cole (RB) 1950–1, John Kissell (T) 1952, *Don Colo* (T) 1953–8, Francis O'Brien (T) 1959, Jim Prestel (T) 1960, Errol Linden (T) 1961, John Brown (T) 1962–6, Joe Righetti (DT) 1969–70, Mack Mitchell (DE) 1975–8, Andy Frederick (T) 1982, Tom Hopkins (T) 1983, Larry Williams (G) 1986–8, Daryle Smith (T) 1989, John Rienstra (OL) 1991–2, Herman Avrie (OL) 1995, Alvin McKinley (DL) 2001–2, Enoch DeMar (T) 2003.

71 *Walter Johnson* (DT) 1965–76, Jesse Turnbow (DT) 1978, Matt Miller (T) 1980–2, Ralph Van Dyke (T) 1987r, Tom Gibson (DE) 1989–90, Mike Bedosky (OL) 1994, Jim Pyne (G) 1999–2000, Gaylon Hyder (OL) 2001.

72 Lou Saban (LB) 1947, *Harry Jagade* (RB) 1951, Derrell Palmer (DT) 1952–3, John Kissell (T) 1954–6, **Henry Jordan** (DT) 1957–8, Sid Youngelman (DT) 1959, Floyd Peters (DT) 1960–2, Mike Bundra (DT) 1964, *Jerry Sherk* (DT) 1970–81, Dave Puzzuoli (DT) 1983–7, Charles Buchanan (DE) 1988, Bob Dahl (OL) 1992–5, Steve Zahursky (OL) 1999, Roman Oben (T) 2000–1, Ryan Tucker (T) 2002–3.

73 Floyd Peters (DT) 1959, Monte Clark (T) 1963–9, *Doug Dieken* (T) 1971–84, Gregg Rakoczy (OL) 1987–90, Keith Bosley (T) 1987r, Herman Avrie (OL) 1993–4, Tim Goad (DT) 1995, Darius Holland (DL) 1999–2000, Derrick Ham (DL) 2001, Toby Myles (T) 2001, Joaquin Gonzalez (OL) 2002–3.

74 Gaylon Smith (RB) 1946, *Tony Adamle*

(LB) 1947–51, *Bob Gain* (DT) 1952, Don Steinbrunner (DE) 1953, **Mike McCormack** (T) 1954–62, *Dick Modzelewski* (DT) 1964–6, Bill Sabatino (DT) 1968, Mitch Johnson (T) 1971, Carl Barisich (DT) 1973–5, Mike St. Clair (DE) 1976–9, Paul Farren (T) 1983–91, Tony Williams (T) 1993, Larry Webster (DT) 1995, Orlando Bobo (G) 1999, James Brown (OL) 2000, Felipe Claybrooks (DL) 2001, Mark Smith (DL) 2001.

75 Roger Shoals (T) 1963–4, Jim McCusker (T) 1963, Bill Yanchar (DT) 1970, Wes Grant (DE) 1972, Allen Aldridge (DE) 1974, Stan Lewis (DE) 1975, Bob Lingenfelter (T) 1977, Mark Buben (DT) 1982, Bill Contz (T) 1983–6, Alex Carter (DE) 1987, Chris Pike (DL) 1989–90, Pio Sagapolutele (DL) 1991–5, Lomas Brown (T) 1999, Steve Zahursky (OL) 2000.

76 **Marion Motley** (FB) 1946–51, **Lou Groza** (T/K) 1952–9, 1961–7.

77 **Willie Davis** (T) 1958–9, Dick Schafrath (T) 1960–71, Fest Cotton (DT) 1972, Mark Ilgenfritz (DE) 1974, Ron East (DE) 1975, Matt Miller (T) 1979, 1982, Lyle Alzado (DE) 1979–81, Rickey Bolden (T) 1984–9, Ken Reeves (OL) 1990, Fred Childress (T) 1992, Orlando Brown (T) 1994–5, 1999, Ross Verba (T) 2001–2.

78 John Sandusky (T) 1952–5, *Art Hunter* (C) 1956, Willie McClung (DT) 1958–9, Gene Selawski (T) 1960, Ed Nutting (DT) 1961, Frank Parker (DT) 1962–4, 1966–7, Bob McKay (T) 1970–5, Mickey Sims (DT) 1977–9, Carl Hairston (DE) 1984–9, Rob Woods (OL) 1991, Dan Footman (DE) 1993–5, Tyrone Rogers (DL) 1999–2003.

79 Jerry Helluin (T) 1952–3, Don King (T) 1954, *Bob Gain* (DT) 1954–64, Jim Battle (DE) 1966, Bob Oliver (DE) 1969, George Wright (DT) 1972, Gerry Sullivan (T/C) 1974–81, *Bob Golic* (DT) 1982–8, Mike Rusinek (DT) 1987r, Mike Graybill (OL) 1989, Scott Rehberg (OL) 1999, Noel LaMontagne (OL) 2000, DeVone Claybrooks (DL) 2001, Barry Stokes (T) 2002–3.

80 Al Akins (RB) 1946, Bob Cowan (RB) 1947–8, Warren Lahr (DB) 1949–51, **Len Ford** (DE) 1952–7, *Dick Schafrath* (T) 1959, Jim Marshall (DE) 1960, *Bill Glass* (DE) 1962–8, Joe Jones (DE) 1970–1, 1973, 1978, Willie Miller (WR) 1975–6, Lawrence Williams (KR) 1977, Willis Adams (WR) 1979–85, Terry Greer (WR) 1986, Chris Kelley (TE) 1987r, Vernon Joines (WR) 1990, Lynn James (WR) 1991, Danny Peebles (WR) 1991, Shawn Collins (WR) 1992, Tom McLemore (TE) 1993–4, Andre Rison (WR) 1995, Ronnie Powell (WR) 1999, Aaron Shea (TE) 2000–3.

81 Leon Clarke (WR) 1960–2, Jim Garcia (DE) 1965, *Jack Gregory* (DE) 1967–71, 1979, Nick Roman (DE) 1972–4, Oscar Roan (TE) 1975–8, Harry Holt (TE) 1983–6, Derek Tennell (TE) 1987r, 1987–9, Scott Galbraith (TE) 1990–2, Michael Jackson (WR) 1994–5, Damon Dunn

(WR) 1999, David Dunn (WR) 1999, Damon Gibson (WR) 1999, Lenzie Jackson (WR) 2000, Quincy Morgan (WR) 2001–3.

82 Bill Lund (RB) 1946–7, *Tommy James* (DB) 1948–51, George Young (DE) 1952–3, Carlton Massey (DE) 1954–6, Frank Clarke (WR) 1957–9, *Jim Houston* (LB) 1960–72, Tim George (WR) 1974, **Ozzie Newsome** (TE) 1978–90, Irv Smith (TE) 1999, David Patten (WR) 2000, Rickey Dudley (TE) 2001, Steve Heiden (TE) 2002–3.

83 *Darrel Brewster* (WR) 1952, **Doug Atkins** (DE) 1953–4, Chuck Weber (LB) 1955–6, A.D. Williams (E) 1960, *Johnny Brewer* (TE/LB) 1961–7, Chip Glass (TE) 1969–73, Jubilee Dunbar (WR) 1974, Ricky Feacher (WR) 1976–84, Glenn Young (WR) 1984, 1987–8, Fred Banks (WR) 1985, Donnie Echols (TE) 1987r, Leo Lewis (PR) 1990, Eugene Rowell (WR) 1990, Arthur Cox (TE) 1991, Darryl Ingram (TE) 1991, Mark Bavaro (TE) 1992, Mark Carrier (WR) 1993–4, Michael Bates (WR) 1995, Mark Campbell (TE) 1999–2000, 2002, Chad Mustard (TE) 2003.

84 Ray Terrell (RB) 1946–7, *Ken Carpenter* (RB) 1950–1, *Horace Gillom* (P/E) 1952–6, *Jim Ray Smith* (G) 1956, Bill Quinlan (DE) 1957–8, Paul Wiggin (DE) 1959–67, Marvin Upshaw (DE) 1968–9, Bob Briggs (DE) 1971–3, Jim Thaxton (TE) 1974, Gary Parris (TE) 1975–8, McDonald Oden (TE) 1980–2, Duriel Harris (WR) 1984, Glenn Young (WR) 1984, *Webster Slaughter* (WR) 1986–91, Keith Tinsley (WR) 1987r, Rico Smith (WR) 1992–5, Darrin Chiaverini (WR) 1999–2000, Andre King (WR) 2001–3.

85 Don Greenwood (RB) 1946–7, Lewis Mayne (RB) 1947, Ara Parseghian (RB) 1948–9, Ken Gorgal (DB) 1950, Charley Ferguson (DE) 1961, Clifton McNeil (WR) 1964–7, Homer Jones (WR) 1970, Frank Pitts (WR) 1971, Paul Staroba (WR) 1972, Ken Smith (TE) 1973, Dave Logan (WR) 1976–83, Bruce Davis (WR) 1984, Clarence Weathers (WR) 1985–8, David Verser (WR) 1987r, Ray Williams (WR) 1987r, Lawyer Tillman (WR) 1989, 1992–3, Derrick Alexander (WR) 1994–5, Kevin Johnson (WR) 1999–2003.

86 *Dub Jones* (HB) 1948–51, **Dante Lavelli** (WR) 1952–6, Paul Wiggin (DE) 1957–8, Bill Howton (WR) 1959, Gern Nagler (WR) 1960–1, Gary Collins (WR/P) 1962–71, Gerald Irons (DE) 1976–9, Dan Fulton (WR) 1981–2, Brian Brennan (WR) 1984–91, Terry Bell (WR) 1987r, Patrick Rowe (WR) 1992–3, Patrick Newman (WR) 1994, Walter Reeves (TE) 1995, Leslie Shepherd (WR) 1999, Dennis Northcutt (WR) 2000–3.

87 Fred Murphy (WR) 1960, Tom Hutchinson (WR) 1963–5, Eppie Barney (WR) 1967–8, Rich Jackson (DE) 1972, Curtis Weathers (TE/LB) 1979–81, Tim Stracka (TE) 1983–4, Travis Tucker (TE) 1985–7, Ron Middleton (TE) 1989, Keenan McCardell (WR) 1992–5, Jamie Holland (WR)

1992, Zola Davis (WR) 1999, Damon Dunn (WR) 2000, Andre Davis (WR) 2002–3.

88 Bob Steuber (RB) 1946, *Mac Speedie* (E) 1952, *Darrel Brewster* (WR) 1953–8, Rich Kreitling (E) 1959–63, Ron Duncan (TE) 1967, Ron Snidow (DE) 1968–72, Steve Holden (WR) 1973–6, John Smith (WR) 1979, Rocky Belk (WR) 1983, Darryl Lewis (TE) 1984, Reggie Langhorne (WR) 1985–91, Harold Stanfield (TE) 1987r, Brian Kinchen (TE) 1991–5, Ryan Collins (TE) 1999, Ja-Juan Dawson (WR) 2000–1, Frisman Jackson (WR) 2002–3.

89 Willie Davis (T) 1958, *Milt Morin* (TE) 1966–75, Keith Wright (WR/KR) 1978–80, Bobby Jones (WR) 1983, Preston Brown (KR) 1984, John Jefferson (WR) 1985, *Gerald McNeil* (WR) 1986–9, Louis Watson (WR) 1987r, Mike Oliphant (RB) 1990–1, Pete Holohan (TE) 1992, Walter Reeves (TE) 1994–5, Harold Bishop (TE) 1995, Randy Palmer (TE) 1999, Bobby Brown (WR) 2000, Jammi German (WR) 2001, Jake Moreland (TE) 2001, Darnell Sanders (TE) 2003.

90 Edgar Jones (RB) 1946–9, Rex Bumgardner (RB) 1950–1, Reggie Craig (WR) 1977, Marshall Harris (DE) 1980–2, Ralph Malone (DE) 1986, *Rob Burnett* (DE) 1990–5, James Williams (LB) 1999, Keith McKenzie (DE) 2000–1, Mark Word (DL) 2002–3.

91 Henry Bradley (DT) 1979–82, Sam Clancy (DE) 1985–8, Darryl Sims (DE) 1987r, John Thornton (DL) 1991, Marcus Spriggs (DL) 1999–2000, Felipe Claybrooks (DE) 2003.

92 Tom Colella (P/DB) 1946–8, Les Horvath (RB) 1949, Dom Moselle (B) 1950, Rich Dimler (DT) 1979, Mike Robinson (DE) 1981–2, Dave Butler (LB) 1987r, *Michael Dean Perry* (DT) 1988–94, Roy Barker (DE) 1999, Courtney Brown (DE) 2000–3.

93 Ron Crews (DE) 1980, Scott Cooper (DE) 1987r, Mike Wise (DL) 1991, Jerry Ball (DT) 1993, 1999, Travis Hill (LB) 1994–5, Stalin Colinet (DE) 1999–2001, Mark Smith (DL) 2001, Cedrick Scott (DL) 2002, Michael Myers (NT) 2003.

94 Jim Dewar (RB) 1947, Dean Sensanbaugher (RB) 1948, Don Phelps (RB) 1950–1, Elvis Franks (DE) 1980–4, Rusty Guilbeau (LB) 1987, Robert Brannon (DE) 1987r, Bob Buczkowski (DL) 1990, Frank Conover (DL) 1991, Bill Johnson (DT) 1992–4, Mike Frederick (DE) 1995, Derrick Alexander (DL) 1999, Gerard Warren (DT) 2001–3.

95 Marlon Jones (DE) 1987–9, Calvin Wallace (DE) 1987r, Rick Lyle (DE) 1994, Jamir Miller (LB) 1999–2001, Antonio Garay (DE) 2003.

96 **Don Shula** (DB) 1951, Reggie Camp (DE) 1983–7, Andrew Stewart (DE) 1989, James Jones (DL) 1991–4, Mike Thompson (DT) 1999–2000, Greg Spires (DL) 2001, Kenard Lang (DE) 2002–3.

97 Tom Brown (DE) 1981–3, Mike Kovaleski (LB) 1987r, Robert Banks (DE) 1989–90, Ernie

Logan (DL) 1991–3, Ryan Kuehl (DL) 1999–2002, Alvin McKinley (DT) 2003.

98 Carl Taseff (DB) 1951, Aaron Moog (DE) 1987r, Anthony Pleasant (DE) 1990–5, Arnold Miller (DL) 1999–2000.

99 Fred Evans (RB) 1946, Bill Boedeker (RB)

1947–9, Keith Baldwin (DE) 1982–5, Darryl Sims (DE) 1987–8, Johnie Cooks (LB) 1991, Alvin Wright (NT) 1992, Rich McKenzie (DE) 1995, Hurvin McCormack (DL) 1999, Orpheus Roye (DT) 2000–3.

DALLAS COWBOYS

The franchise: Dallas' first attempt to support a professional football team was a miserable failure that lasted less than a full season in 1952. Attendance and the team's finances were so bad that the Dallas Texans' ownership was turned back to the league by midseason, and the team was forced to finish out the year based in Hershey, Pennsylvania. That team would surface the next season as the new Baltimore Colts franchise. Eight years later, though, the NFL awarded Clint Murchison an expansion franchise, largely in response to American Football League founder Lamar Hunt's AFL Dallas Texans team. Despite being less competitive on the field than Hunt's team, the Cowboys forced the new Texans to move Kansas City within three years.

Murchison's smartest move was to hire former Ram GM Tex Schramm to run the team in 1960. In turn, Schramm hired Tom Landry as coach and Gil Brandt as player personnel director. This trio performed brilliantly over the next 29 years and made the Cowboys one of the most successful franchises in the league. The first year was difficult with the Cowboys finishing 0–11–1, but Schramm and Brandt began acquiring talented players, often from unlikely places, while Landry proceeded to develop his own system and coach the players to perform according to his specifications. His complicated offense featured a great deal of shifting and misdirection, and the coach called all the plays like only Paul Brown did at the time. Taking Brown's messenger guards one step further, he even had his quarterbacks, Eddie Lebaron and Don Meredith, alternating plays

at one point. His Flex Defense took longer to perfect, but within a few years the Doomsday Defense of Bob Lilly, Lee Roy Jordan, Chuck Howley and Mel Renfro was respected throughout the league.

The Cowboys achieved their first winning season in 1966 when they lost to the Packers in the NFL Championship game. The next year they lost to the Packers again in the Ice Bowl. Then came two consecutive playoff losses to the Browns before reaching the Super Bowl V only to lose to the Colts on the last play of the game. Bob Lilly encapsulated the team's frustration by throwing his helmet 30 yards downfield as the Colts celebrated. Dallas increasingly was disparaged as a team of chokers that couldn't win the big one until finally beating the Dolphins in Super Bowl VI the next year. The Cowboys set a record in the 1970s by appearing in five Super Bowls in a single decade, and they won two of them. Four of those Super Bowl appearances were behind the leadership of Roger Staubach, the best comeback quarterback of his time. Staubach was able to utilize the special talents of such skilled players as Tony Dorsett, Drew Pearson and Tony Hill to consistently pull games out in thrilling fashion. NFL Films referred to Dallas as "America's Team" at that time, and the Cowboys embraced this unelected title. From 1966 to 1985, the Cowboys had 20 straight winning seasons and made the playoffs 18 times.

Bum Bright bought the team in 1984, just as it began to slip from good to mediocre on its way to rotten by the end of the decade. At that lowest point, Jerry Jones bought out

Bright in 1989 and brought in his old college teammate Jimmy Johnson to coach the team. The result was the Cowboys' renaissance in the 1990s. Jones fired the living legend trio of Schramm, Landry and Brandt, and Johnson cleaned house on the field building a champion behind the skill-position triumvirate of quarterback Troy Aikman, running back Emmitt Smith and receiver Michael Irvin, as well as the best offensive line in the NFL and a swift, swarming defense. Johnson's Cowboys won back-to-back Super Bowls in 1992 and 1993, but friction between the owner and coach led to Barry Switzer being named coach in 1994. The Cowboys appeared in 16 of the first 30 NFC Championship games, winning eight, and then winning five of those eight Super Bowls. The team won their fifth Super Bowl in 1995 with Switzer, but the decline in coaching, discipline and talent became evident on the field shortly after. Jones' attempt to handle personnel matters was not helped by his subsequent coaching choices of Chan Gailey and then Dave Campo. In 2003, Jones admitted his mistakes and hired the testy genius Bill Parcells as coach to restore the franchise once again to the forefront of the league, and they returned to the playoffs in his first season in Texas.

Origin of name: When majority owner Clint Murchison was first awarded the Dallas franchise he intended to call the team the Steers, but changed that to Rangers within weeks. However, to distinguish themselves from the minor league baseball team by the same name, Murchison changed the name again to Cowboys before they began playing.

Time till first championship: 12 years.

Time since last championship: 9 years.

Coaches			
	Years	*Record*	*Playoffs*
Tom Landry (2)	1960–88	250–162–6	20–16
Jimmy Johnson (2)	1989–93	44–36–0	7–1
Barry Switzer (1)	1994–7	40–24–0	5–2
Chan Gailey	1998–9	18–14–0	0–2
Dave Campo	2000–2	15–33–0	0–0
Bill Parcells	2003	11–5–0	0–1
(Championships in parentheses)			

Retired numbers: None. The Cowboys and the Raiders are the only teams more than 10 years old that have not retired any players' numbers.

Other numbers worn by these players: NA

Those who wore retired numbers after the honored player: NA

Numbers that should be retired: Hall of Famer Bob Lilly, 74, was the team's first draft choices and one of the greatest defensive tackles in NFL history. Hall of Famer Roger Staubach, 12, was the leader of four Super Bowl teams and two champions. Troy Aikman, 8, led the Cowboys to three Super Bowl titles. Emmitt Smith, 22, is the leading rusher in NFL history.

Owned numbers: No one but Bob Lilly has ever worn 74, but the number is not officially retired.

Numbers worn by Hall of Famers: Herb Adderley 26; Lance Alworth 19; Mike Ditka 89; Tony Dorsett 33; Forrest Gregg 79; Bob Lilly 74; Tommy McDonald 25; Mel Renfro 20; Jackie Smith 81; Roger Staubach 12; Randy White 54.

Star power: Chuck Howley took 54 from Mike Connelly.

Record by Decade						
	Regular Season			*Postseason*		
	Won	Lost	Tied	Won	Lost	*Championships*
1960s	67	65	6	1	4	
1970s	105	39	0	14	7	1971, 1977
1980s	79	73	0	5	5	
1990s	101	59	0	12	5	1992, 1993, 1995
2000s	26	38	0	0	1	
All-Time	378	274	6	32	22	5

Winning seasons: 28. Losing Seasons: 14. .500 seasons: 2.

Star eclipsed: Forrest Gregg wore 79 because Jethro Pugh wore 75; Bernie Kosar wore 18 because John Jett wore 19; Alvin Harper wore 82 because Ernie Mills wore 80. Nate Newton wore 67 till Jim Cooper, 61, left.

Numbers with most great players: 84 was worn by most notably by Jay Novacek, but also by fellow tight ends Doug Cosbie, Jean Fugett and Pettis Norman as well as wideout Joey Galloway. 26 was worn by versatile back Preston Pearson and receiver Buddy Dial in addition to defensive backs Herb Adderley, Michael Downs and Kevin Smith

Worst represented numbers: 29 has been worn by four forgettable runners and six weak defensive backs. 39 has been worn by five forgettable runners and a safety of no particular talent.

Number worn by the most players: 81 has been worn 19 times.

Player who wore the most numbers: Two Cowboys have worn three numbers—cornerback Alundis Brice 21/23/29 and wide receiver Cornell Burbage 15/82/89.

Longest tenure wearing a number: Three Cowboys have worn the star for 15 years—defensive end Ed "Too Tall" Jones wore 72 from 1974 to 1978, 1980–9; special teams ace Bill Bates wore 40 from 1983 to 1997; tackle Mark Tuinei wore 71 from 1983 to 1997.

Number worn by first ever draft pick: The Cowboys first participated in the NFL draft in their second year, 1961. That year they traded their first pick to the Redskins for veteran quarterback Eddie Lebaron, 14. Dallas then traded its first pick in 1962 for the Browns first pick in 1961 and picked Bob Lilly, 74.

Biggest draft busts: Defensive lineman Dan Noonan, 73, was selected 12th in 1987 and was a nonentity for six seasons.

Number worn by first expansion draft pick: The expansion draft was not performed by rounds. However, in 1960 the team did sign college players Don Meredith, 17, and Don Perkins, 43, to personal service contracts. Since these players were drafted by the Bears and Colts respectively, the Cowboys gave up a 1961 third rounder to Chicago and ninth rounder to Baltimore. Of the players

obtained in the expansion draft, both Jerry Tubbs, 50, and Frank Clarke, 82, played in Dallas from 1960 to 1967.

Number worn by oldest player: 43-year-old kicker Eddie Murray wore 3 in 1999. Among position players both Ed Jones, 72, and Wade Wilson, 18, played until they were 38.

Cameos: Hall of Famers— Tommy McDonald 25; Jackie Smith 81; All Pros and other notables— Lee Roy Caffey 60; Harold Carmichael 17; Bobby Joe Conrad 40; Gene Cronin 85; Duriel Harris 86; Don Heinrich 11; Bernie Kosar 18; Woodley Lewis 23; Ray Matthews 25; Dick Nolan 25; Jerry Norton 25; Rodney Peete 9; Duane Putnam 61; Sonny Randle 88; Darnay Scott 85; John Williams 38.

Ones who got away: Jaguars receiver Jimmy Smith, 82, and Giant and 49er guard Ron Stone, 65, have been the biggest stars. Also of note were Browns receiver Reggie Rucker, 88, Browns tackle Monte Clark, 73, and Vikings defensive tackle Paul Dickson, 71.

Least popular numbers: 0 and 49 have never been worn. 13 has been worn only once.

Last number to be originated: 69 was not worn until George Hegamin joined the team in 1994.

Longest dormant number: 13 has not been worn since 1968.

Triskaidekaphobia notes: 13 has only been worn by quarterback Jerry Rhome who was drafted by Dallas in 1965 along with fellow quarterbacks Craig Morton and Roger Staubach.

Shared numbers: Future Hall of Famer Emmitt Smith and All Pro Bob Hayes both wore 22. All Pro Chuck Howley and Hall of Famer Randy White both wore 54. All Pro guards Blaine Nye and Nate Newton both wore 61. All Pro linemen Ralph Neely and Larry Allen both wore 73

Continuity: Lance Rentzel was replaced in 19 by Hall of Famer Lance Alworth; All Pro linebacker Jerry Tubbs was replaced in 50 by D.D. Lewis.

Discontinuity: 13-year veteran linebacker Dave Edwards was followed in 52 by

Jim Eidson; 15-year veteran Too Tall Jones was followed in 72 by Louis Cheek; 11-year veteran defensive end Harvey Martin was followed in 79 by John Hunt; ten-year receiver Tony Hill was followed in 80 by Rod Barksdale. These four followers each lasted only one year in Dallas.

```
+-------------------------------------------+
|           Family Connections              |
| Father and son                            |
| Jake Kupp      G      1965–6      67       |
| Craig Kupp     QB     1991        9        |
+-------------------------------------------+
```

The Cowboys also featured some multisport father-son combos. Runner Calvin Hill, 35, may be more well known as basketball star Grant Hill's dad. Runner Tommie Agee, 34, and linebacker Ken Norton, 51, were the namesakes of a champion baseball player and a boxer respectively.

Quarterback numbers over 19: None.

Number of first black players: In 1960 receiver Woodley Lewis wore 23, defensive back Don Bishop wore 44, receiver Frank Clarke wore 82 and defensive end Nate Borden wore 87.

Numbers of future NFL head coaches: Monte Clark 73; Jack Del Rio 55; Mike Ditka 89; Forrest Gregg 79; Dick Nolan 25; Jack Patera 56; and Dan Reeves 30.

Numbers of future NFL referees: Merrill Douglass 34.

Players who played other sports: Baseball — Deion Sanders 21. Basketball — Ron Widby 10/12. Track — Bob Hayes 22. Boxing — Ed "Too Tall" Jones 72.

Players more famous after football: Receiver Pete Gent, 35, became a novelist most famous for the book and subsequent movie *North Dallas Forty*. Linebacker Tom Braatz, 51, later became GM of the Packers. Receiver Lance Rentzel, 19, and kicker Rafael Septien, 1, both achieved notoriety by being charged with indecent exposure to underage girls.

First player to wear a number in the 90s: In 1985 David Ponder wore 97 and Kevin Brooks wore 99.

Number with most points scored: 22 with 1,478 points scored by Emmitt Smith (986), Bob Hayes (456), Amos Bullocks (30), and Victor Scott (6).

Number with most yards rushing: 22 with 17,789 yards gained by Emmitt Smith (17,162), Amos Bullocks (537), Bob Hayes (68), and George Peoples (22).

Number with most receptions: 88 with 1,418 passes caught by Michael Irvin (750), Drew Pearson (489), Antonio Bryant (83), Jackie Harris (54), Ron Sellers (31), Reggie Rucker (10), and Sonny Randle (1).

Number with most touchdown passes: 17 with 175 touchdowns tossed by Don Meredith (135), Quincy Carter (29) and Jason Garrett (11).

Number with most interceptions: 20 with 72 passes picked off by Mel Renfro (52), Derek Ross (5), Bob Bercich (5), Ray Horton (5), and Philipi Sparks (5).

Oddity: The Cowboys have had a lot of placekickers and punters wearing high numbers, i.e., numbers 20 and above. Cowboy placekickers have worn 30, 31, 33, 36, 38, 61, 62, 83 and 88. Cowboy punters have worn 38, 61, 81, 86, and 88.

Team All-Time Numerical Roster

Those with an "r" following the year 1987 were replacement players during the players' strike. Pro Bowl players for each number are in *Italics*; Hall of Famers are in **Bold** type.

1 Efren Herrerra (K) 1974, 1976–7, *Rafael Septien* (K) 1978–86, Kerry Brady (K) 1987r, Ken Willis (K) 1990–1.

2 Lin Elliot (K) 1992–3, Anthony Wright (QB) 2000–2.

3 Jim Miller (P) 1983–4, Steve Walsh (QB) 1989–90, Eddie Murray (K) 1993, 1999, Richie Cunningham (K) 1997–99, Billy Cundiff (K) 2002–3.

4 Mike Saxon (P) 1985–92, Toby Gowin (P) 1997–9, 2003, Micah Knorr (P) 2000–2.

5 John Warren (P) 1983–4, Clint Stoerner (QB) 2000–1.

6 Luis Zendejas (K) 1987–9, Tim Seder (K) 2000–1.

7 Steve Beuerlein (QB) 1991–2, Hugh Millen (QB) 1993, Randall Cunningham (QB) 2000, Chad Hutchinson (QB) 2002–3.

8 Buzz Sawyer (P) 1987r, *Troy Aikman* (QB) 1989–2000.

9 Mitch Hoopes (P) 1975, Roger Ruzek (K) 1987–9, Craig Kupp (QB) 1991, Rodney Peete (QB) 1994, Dan Gonzalez (QB) 1998.

10 Ron Widby (P) 1969–71, Duane Carrell (P) 1974, Reggie Collier (QB) 1986, Jimmy Armstrong (DB) 1987r, Scott Secules (QB) 1988, Tommy Hodson (QB) 1994, Jon Baker (K) 1995.

11 Don Heinrich (QB) 1960, Buddy Humphrey (QB) 1961, Sonny Gibbs (QB) 1963, Danny Villanueva (P/K) 1965–7, *Danny White* (QB/P) 1976–88, Wade Wilson (QB) 1995–6, Mike Quinn (QB) 1998–9.

12 John Roach (QB) 1964, Ron Widby (P) 1968, **Roger Staubach** (QB) 1969–79.

13 Jerry Rhome (QB) 1965–8.

14 *Eddie LeBaron* (QB) 1960–3, Craig Morton (QB) 1965–74, Gary Hogeboom (QB) 1980–5, Paul McDonald (QB) 1986–7.

15 Toni Fritsch (K) 1971–3, 1975, Brad Wright (QB) 1982, Cornell Burbage (WR) 1987r, 1988, Babe Laufenberg (QB) 1989–90.

16 Steve Pelluer (QB) 1984–8, Damon Hodge (WR) 2000, Ryan Leaf (QB) 2001.

17 *Don Meredith* (QB) 1960–8, Mike Clark (K) 1973, Harold Carmichael (WR) 1984, Jason Garrett (QB) 1993–9, Quincy Carter (QB) 2001–3.

18 Billy Lothridge (P/QB) 1964, Glenn Carano (QB) 1977–83, Loren Snyder (QB) 1987r, Cliff Stoudt (QB) 1990–1, Bernie Kosar (QB) 1993, Chris Boniol (K) 1994–6, Wade Wilson (QB) 1997.

19 Lance Rentzel (WR) 1967–70, **Lance Alworth** (WR) 1971–2, Clint Longley (QB) 1974–5, Kevin Sweeney (QB) 1987r, 1988, John Jett (P) 1993–6, Quinton Spotwood (WR) 2000.

20 Bob Bercich (S) 1960–1, Jerry Overton (S) 1963, **Mel Renfro** (DB/RB) 1964–77, Ron Springs (RB) 1979–84, Bruce Livingston (DB) 1987r, Ray Horton (S) 1989–92, Sherman Williams (RB) 1995–9, Phillippi Sparks (CB) 2000, Derek Ross (CB) 2002, Richie Anderson (RB) 2003.

21 Glynn Gregory (WR/DB) 1961–2, Dick Daniels (S) 1967–8, Billy Parks (WR) 1972, Doug Dennison (RB) 1974–8, Carl Howard (CB) 1984, David Adams (RB) 1987r, Mark Higgs (RB) 1988, James Dixon (WR/RB) 1991, Alundis Brice (CB) 1995, *Deion Sanders* (DB) 1995–9, Lynn Scott (S) 2001–2, Derek Ross (CB) 2003.

22 Bill Butler (S) 1960, Amos Bullocks (RB) 1962–4, *Bob Hayes* (WR) 1965–74, Wade Manning (CB) 1979, George Peoples (RB) 1982, Victor Scott (DB) 1984–8, *Emmitt Smith* (RB) 1990–2002.

23 Woodley Lewis (WR) 1960, Dick Nolan (S) 1962, Mike Johnson (CB) 1966–9, Margene Adkins (WR) 1970–1, Mike Montgomery (RB/WR) 1972–3, James Jones (RB) 1980–2, 1984–5, Johnny Holloway (CB) 1986, Robert Williams (CB) 1987–93, Robert Bailey (CB) 1995, Alundis Brice (CB) 1996, Kevin Mathis (DB) 1997–9, Dwayne Goodrich (CB) 2000, 2002, Aveion Cason (RB) 2003.

24 Jim Mooty (CB) 1960, J.D. Smith (RB) 1965–6, Dennis Homan (WR) 1968–70, Alois Blackwell (RB) 1978–9, *Everson Walls* (CB) 1981–9, Larry Brown (CB) 1991–5, Omar Stoutmire (DB) 1997–8, Tony Dixon (S) 2001–3.

25 Ray Mathews (WR) 1960, Jerry Norton (S) 1962, **Tommy McDonald** (WR) 1964, Obert Logan (S) 1965–6, Les Shy (RB) 1967–9, Aaron Kyle (CB) 1976–9, Rod Hill (CB) 1982–3, Junior Tautalatasi (RB) 1989, Derrick Lassic (RB) 1993–4, Scott Case (S) 1995, Charlie Williams (DB) 1998–2000, Jemeel Powell (CB) 2003.

26 Buddy Dial (WR) 1964–6, **Herb Adderley** (CB) 1970–2, Preston Pearson (RB) 1975–80, Michael Downs (S) 1981–8, Paul Palmer (RB) 1989, Kevin Smith (CB) 1992–9, Pat Dennis (CB) 2001, Andrew Davison (CB) 2003, Jeff Sanchez (CB) 2003.

27 Mike Gaechter (S) 1962–9, Bill Thomas (RB) 1972, Ron Fellows (CB) 1981–6, Tommy Haynes (S) 1987r, Curvin Richards (RB) 1991–3, *Thomas Everett* (S) 1992–3, Greg Tremble (S) 1995, Singor Mobley (DB) 1997–9, Mario Edwards (CB) 2000–3.

28 Norm Granger (RB) 1984, Alvin Blount (RB) 1987r, Curtin Stewart (RB) 1989, *Darren Woodson* (DB) 1992–2003.

29 Robert Lavette (RB) 1985–7, Alex Green (CB) 1987r, Undra Johnson (RB) 1989, Kenneth Gant (CB) 1990–4, Alundis Brice (CB) 1996, Terry Billups (CB) 1998, Chris Akins (S) 1999, Greg Myers (S) 2000, Adrian Murrell (RB) 2003, Michael Bates (KR) 2003.

30 Mike Dowdle (RB/LB) 1960–2, Dick Van Raaphorst (K) 1964, Dan Reeves (RB) 1965–72, Charles Young (RB) 1974–6, Timmy Newsome (RB) 1980–8, Issiac Holt (CB) 1989–92, Darren Studstill (S) 1994, George Teague (DB) 1996, Kenny Wheaton (DB) 1997–9, Earl Riley (S) 2000.

31 Fred Cone (K) 1960, Amos Marsh (RB) 1961–4, Sim Stokes (WR) 1967, Otto Brown (DB) 1969, Gloster Richardson (WR) 1971, Benny Barnes (DB) 1972–82, Gary Allen (RB) 1983–4, Bill Hill (CB) 1987r, Billy Owens (DB) 1988, *Thomas Everett* (S) 1992–3, Brock Marion (S) 1993–7, George Teague (DB) 1998–2001, *Roy Williams* (S) 2002–3.

32 Tom Franckhauser (CB) 1960–1, *Walt Garrison* (RB) 1966–74, Dennis Thurman (DB) 1978–85, Tim Jackson (S) 1989, Alonzo Highsmith (RB) 1990–1, Blair Thomas (RB) 1994, Tyrone Hughes (PR) 1998, Michael Wiley (RB) 2000–2.

33 Gene Babb (LB/RB) 1960–1, Wendell Hayes (RB) 1963, Russell Wayt (LB) 1965, Duane Thomas (RB) 1970–1, Cyril Pinder (RB) 1973, Mac Percival (K) 1974, **Tony Dorsett** (RB) 1977–87, Eric Brown (DB) 1989, Timmy Smith (RB) 1990, Jason Bell (CB) 2001.

34 Fred Doelling (S) 1960, Merrill Douglas

(RB) 1961, *Cornell Green* (DB) 1962–74, Aaron Mitchell (CB) 1979–80, Monty Hunter (S) 1982, *Herschel Walker* (RB) 1986–89, 1996–7, Tommie Agee (FB) 1990–4, Larry Brown (CB) 1998, Tim Lester (FB) 1999, Jamar Martin (RB) 2003.

35 Walt Kowalczyk (RB) 1960, J.W. Lockett (RB) 1961–2, Pete Gent (WR/TE) 1964–8, *Calvin Hill* (RB) 1969–74, Scott Laidlaw (RB) 1975–9, Chuck McSwain (RB) 1983–4, Jimmy Armstrong (DB) 1987r, Kevin Scott (RB) 1989, Wendell Davis (DB) 1996–7, 1999, Robert Chancey (RB) 1999, Troy Hambrick (RB) 2000.

36 *Dick Bielski* (TE/K) 1960–1, Joe Williams (RB) 1971, Larry Brinson (RB) 1977–9, Vince Albritton (S/LB) 1984–91, Dominique Ross (RB) 1995–6, Tarik Smith (RB) 1998–9.

37 Perry Dunn (RB) 1964–5, Phil Clark (DB) 1967–9, Ike Thomas (CB) 1971, Dennis Morgan (RB) 1974, Jim Jensen (RB) 1976, Gerald White (FB) 1987r, James Washington (S) 1990–4, Lee Vaughn (DB) 1997.

38 Sam Baker (P/K) 1962–3, John Williams (FB) 1985, Ron Francis (CB) 1987–90, Chris Hall (S) 1993, David Lang (RB) 1995, Duane Hawthorne (CB) 1999–2002, Lynn Scott (S) 2003.

39 E.J. Jones (RB) 1987r, Broderick Sargent (FB) 1989, Robert Perryman (FB) 1990, Donald Smith (S) 1991, Derrick Gainer (RB) 1992–3, Ryan Neufeld (FB) 1999.

40 Jim Harris (S) 1961, Jim Stiger (RB) 1963–5, Bobby Conrad (WR) 1969, Les Strayhorn (RB) 1973–4, Eric Hurt (CB) 1980, *Bill Bates* (S) 1983–97, Sean Key (S) 2000.

41 Warren Livingston (CB) 1961–6, *Charlie Waters* (DB) 1970–8, 1980–1, Anthony Coleman (DB) 1987r, Charles Wright (DB) 1988, Dave Thomas (CB) 1993–4, John Reece (CB) 1997, Kareem Larrimore (CB) 2000–1, Terrence Newman (CB) 2003.

42 Don McIlhenny (RB) 1960–1, Jim Ridlon (S) 1963–4, A.D. Whitfield (RB) 1965, Claxton Welch (RB) 1969–71, Randy Hughes (S) 1975–80, Ricky Easmon (DB) 1985, Darryl Clack (RB) 1986–9, Stan Smagala (DB) 1990–1, Robert Wilson (FB) 1994, Charlie Williams (DB) 1995–7, Chris Warren (RB) 1998–9, Troy Hambrick (RB) 2001–3.

43 *Don Perkins* (RB) 1961–8, *Cliff Harris* (S) 1970–9, Elvis Patterson (CB) 1993, Greg Briggs (S) 1995, Izell Reese (DB) 1998–2001.

44 *Don Bishop* (CB) 1960–5, Robert Newhouse (FB) 1972–83, Cornell Gowdy (DB) 1986, Vince Courville (WR) 1987r, Michael Brooks (S) 1990, Lincoln Coleman (RB) 1993–4, Robert Thomas (FB) 1999–2002.

45 L.G. Dupre (RB) 1960–1, Dick Daniels (S) 1966, Richmond Flowers (S) 1969–71, Larry Robinson (RB) 1973, Rolly Woosley (DB) 1975, Steve Wilson (WR/CB) 1980–1, Manny Hendrix (CB) 1986–91, Nicky Sualua (RB) 1997–8.

46 Les Shy (RB) 1966, Craig Baynham (RB) 1967–9, Mark Washington (CB) 1970–8, Roland Solomon (S) 1980, Todd Fowler (FB) 1985–8, Ricky Blake (RB) 1991, Joe Fishback (S) 1993–4, James Whalen (TE) 2000, Eric Bickerstaff (RB) 2003.

47 Dick Moegle (S) 1961, Dextor Clinkscale (S) 1980, 1982–5, Chuck Scott (WR) 1987r, Clayton Holmes (CB) 1992–5, Ryan McNeil (DB) 2000, Pete Hunter (CB) 2002–3.

48 Alex Green (CB) 1987r, *Daryl Johnston* (RB) 1989–99

49 none.

50 *Jerry Tubbs* (LB) 1960–7, D.D. Lewis (LB) 1968, 1970–81, Jeff Rohrer (LB) 1982–7, Steve Hendrickson (LB) 1989, Dave Harper (LB) 1990, Bobby Abrams (LB) 1992–3, Darrick Brownlow (LB) 1994, Clay Shiver (C) 1996–8, Brandon Tolbert (LB) 1999–2000, Jamal Brooks (LB) 2001.

51 Tom Braatz (LB) 1960, Lynn Hoyem (C/G) 1962–3, *Dave Manders* (C) 1964–6, 1968–74, Anthony Dickerson (LB) 1980–4, Dale Jones (LB) 1987r, Russ Swan (LB) 1987r, *Ken Norton* (LB) 1988–93, Broderick Thomas (LB) 1996–8, Kevin Hardy (LB) 2002, Al Singleton (LB) 2003.

52 Wayne Hansen (LB) 1960, Dave Edwards (LB) 1963–75, Jim Eidson (G/C) 1976, Robert Shaw (C) 1979–81, Scott McLean (LB) 1983, Billy Cannon (LB) 1984, Jeff Hurd (LB) 1987, Chris Duliban (LB) 1987r, Sean Scott (LB) 1988, Mickey Pruitt (LB) 1991–2, *Jim Schwantz* (LB) 1994–6, *Dexter Coakley* (LB) 1997–2003.

53 Mike Connelly (C) 1961–7, Dave Simmons (LB) 1968, Fred Whittingham (LB) 1969, John Babinecz (LB) 1972–3, *Bob Breunig* (LB) 1975–84, Garth Jax (LB) 1986–8, Victor Simmons (LB) 1987r, Onzy Elam (LB) 1989, Randy Shannon (LB) 1990, *Ray Donaldson* (C) 1995–6, Brandon Tolbert (LB) 1998, *Mark Stepnoski* (G/C) 1999–2001, Keith Adams (LB) 2002.

54 Mike Connelly (C) 1960, *Chuck Howley* (LB) 1961–73, **Randy White** (DT) 1975–88, Jesse Solomon (LB) 1989–90, Anthony Fieldings (LB) 1995, Darryl Hardy (LB) 1995, Darren Hambrick (LB) 1998–2001, Keith O'Neil (LB) 2003.

55 *Lee Roy Jordan* (LB) 1963–76, Danny Spradlin (LB) 1981–2, Bruce Huther (LB) 1983, Steve DeOssie (LB) 1984–8, Harry Flaharty (LB) 1987r, Jack Del Rio (LB) 1989–91, Robert Jones (LB) 1992–5, Fred Strickland (LB) 1996–8, Lemanski Hall (LB) 1999, Markus Steele (LB) 2001–3.

56 Jack Patera (LB) 1960–1, Bob Long (LB) 1962, Harold Hays (LB) 1963–7, Tom Stincic (LB) 1969–71, Rodrigo Barnes (LB) 1973–4, *Thomas Henderson* (LB) 1975–9, Bill Roe (LB) 1980, Eugene Lockhart (LB) 1984–90, John Roper (LB) 1993, Reggie Barnes (LB) 1995, Randall Godfrey (LB) 1996–9, Orantes Grant (LB) 2000–1, Bradie James (LB) 2003.

57 Malcolm Walker (C) 1966–9, Mike Keller (LB) 1972, Louis Walker (LB) 1974, Kyle Davis (C) 1975, Bruce Huther (LB) 1977–80, Angelo King (LB) 1981–3, Jimmie Turner (LB) 1984, Ron Burton (LB) 1987–9, Russ Swan (LB) 1987r, Vinson Smith (LB) 1990–2, 1997, Alan Campos (LB) 1996, Myron Smith (LB) 1998, Quentin Coryatt (LB) 1999, Barron Wortham (LB) 2000, Louis Mackey (LB) 2002.

58 Calvin Peterson (LB) 1974–5, Mike Hegman (LB) 1976–88, Jeff Hurd (LB) 1987r, Steve Hendrickson (LB) 1989, Dixon Edwards (LB) 1991–5, Nate Hemsley (LB) 1997–9, Joe Bowden (LB) 2000, Jeff Grau (LS) 2002, Scott Shanle (LB) 2003.

59 Ken Hutcherson (LB) 1974, Warren Capone (LB) 1975, Guy Brown (LB) 1977–82, Mike Walter (LB) 1983, Jesse Penn (LB) 1985–7, Kirk Timmer (LB) 1987r, Garry Cobb (LB) 1988–9, Darrick Brownlow (LB) 1991, Darrin Smith (LB) 1993–6, Robert Thomas (LB) 1998, Dat Nguyen (LB) 1999–2003.

60 Buzz Guy (G) 1960, Joe Isbell (G) 1962–4, Jackie Burkett (LB) 1968–9, Steve Kiner (LB) 1970, Lee Roy Caffey (LB) 1971, Gene Killian (G) 1974, Tom Randall (G) 1978, Don Smerek (DL) 1981–7, Dean Hamel (DT) 1989–90, Tony Hill (DE) 1991, Derek Kennard (G/C) 1994–6, Chris Brymer (OL) 1999, John Nix (DT) 2001–2.

61 Duane Putnam (G) 1960, Allen Green (P/K) 1961, *Blaine Nye* (G) 1968–76, Jim Cooper (OL) 1977–86, *Nate Newton* (G) 1987–98, Kelvin Garmon (G) 1999–2002.

62 Don Healy (DT) 1960, Andy Cvercko (G) 1961–2, Lance Poimboeuf (K) 1963, Leon Donohue (G) 1965–7, John Fitzgerald (C) 1971–80, Brian Baldinger (OL) 1982–4, 1986–7, Mike Zentic (C) 1987r, Bob Brotzki (T) 1988, Paul Oswald (G) 1988, *Tony Tolbert* (DE) 1989, Dale Hellestrae (T) 1990, James Parrish (T) 1993–4, Tom Myslinski (G) 1999.

63 Mike Falls (G) 1960–1, Larry Cole (C) 1968–80, Glen Titensor (G) 1981–6, 1988, Jon Shields (OL) 1987r, Lester Brinkley (DL) 1990, John Gesek (G) 1991–3, Shane Hannah (G) 1995, John Flannery (G) 1996–7, Mike Kiselak (G) 1998–9, Aaron Gibson (T) 2002, Gennaro DiNapoli (C) 2003.

64 Bob Grottkau (G) 1961, Jim Smith (G/T) 1963–4, Mitch Johnson (G) 1965, Halvor Hagen (C/G) 1969–70, Tony Liscio (T) 1971, Jim Arneson (C/G) 1973–4, Tom Rafferty (G/C) 1976–89, George Lilja (C) 1987r, Jorge Diaz (G) 2000, Dan Collins (G) 2002, Daleroy Stewart (DT) 2003.

65 Ray Schoenke (T) 1963–4, John Wilbur (T) 1966–9, Dave Stalls (DE) 1977–9, Kurt Petersen (G) 1980–5, Gary Westberry (C) 1987, Bob White (OL) 1988–9, Tony Slaton (G) 1990, Ron Stone (T) 1993–5, Andre Gurode (C) 2002–3.

66 Ed Husmann (DT) 1960, *George Andrie* (DE) 1962–72, Burton Lawless (G) 1975–9, Norm Wells (G) 1980, Chris Schultz (T) 1983, 1985, Jesse Baker (DE) 1986, Kevin Gogan (T) 1987–93, Tony Hutson (G) 1997–9, Ben Fricke (G/C) 2001.

67 John Houser (C/G) 1960–1, Jake Kupp (G) 1964–5, Pat Toomay (DE) 1970–4, *Pat Donovan* (T) 1975–83, Broderick Thompson (G) 1985, *Nate Newton* (G) 1986, George Lilja (C) 1987, Joe Shearin (C) 1987, Gary Walker (OL) 1987r, Sean Smith (DT) 1989, John Gesek (G) 1990, Russell Maryland (DT) 1991–5, Everett McIver (G) 1998–9.

68 Guy Reese (DT) 1962–3, Jim Boeke (T) 1964–7, *Herb Scott* (G) 1975–84, Crawford Ker (G) 1985–90, Frank Cornish (C) 1992–4, Michael Batiste (DT/G) 1995, Oliver Ross (T) 1998, Matt Lehr (G/C) 2001–3.

69 George Hegamin (T) 1994, 1996–7, Ben Fricke (C) 1999–2000.

70 Bob McCreary (T) 1961, Dale Memmelear (G) 1962–3, Bill Sandeman (DT) 1966, *Rayfield Wright* (TE/T) 1969–79, Howard Richards (G/T) 1981–6, Bob White (OL) 1987, *Mark Stepnoski* (G/C) 1989–94, Dale Hellestrae (T) 1990–2000, Javiar Collins (DT) 2001–3.

71 Paul Dickson (T) 1960, Charlie Granger (T) 1961, Don Talbert (DE/OT) 1962, 1965, Willie Townes (DE) 1966–8, Rodney Wallace (G/T) 1971–3, Andy Frederick (T) 1977–81, *Mark Tuinei* (OT/DL) 1983–97, Mike Dwyer (DT) 1987r, Alcender Jackson (G) 2000–1, Tyson Walter (T) 2002–3.

72 Bill Herchman (DE) 1960–1, Tony Liscio (T) 1963–4, 1966–70, Don Talbert (DE/OT) 1971, *Ed Jones* (DE) 1974–8, 1980–9, Louis Cheek (OL) 1990, Ray Childress (DT) 1996.

73 Ray Fisher (T) 1960, Monte Clark (T) 1962, *Ralph Neely* (G/T) 1965–77, Steve Wright (T) 1981–2, Syd Kitson (G) 1984, Kurt Ploeger (DL) 1986, Danny Noonan (DL) 1987–92, Dave Burnette (T) 1987r, *Larry Allen* (G) 1994–2003.

74 Bob Lilly (DT) 1961–74.

75 Bob Fry (T) 1960–4, Jethro Pugh (DT) 1965–78, Phil Pozderac (T) 1982–7, Daryle Smith (T) 1988, Jon Carter (DT) 1989, Tony Casillas (DT) 1991–3, 1996, Brandon Noble (DT) 1999–2002, Ryan Young (T) 2003.

76 John Gonzaga (DE) 1960, Ed Nutting (OT) 1963, Bill Frank (T) 1964, John Diehl (DT) 1965, *John Niland* (G) 1966–74, Larry Bethea (DL) 1978–83, Dowe Aughtman (OL) 1984, Bob Otto (DL) 1986, Jeff Zimmerman (G) 1987–90, Alan Veingrad (OL) 1991–2, Jerry Reynolds (T) 1994, *Flozell Adams* (T) 1998–2003.

77 Byron Bradfute (T) 1960–1, Clyde Brock (DT) 1962–3, Jim Colvin (DT) 1964–6, Ron East (DT) 1967, Larry Stephens (DE) 1967, Bill Gregory (DL) 1971–7, Bruce Thornton (DL) 1979–81,

Jim Jeffcoat (DE) 1983–94, Steve Cisowski (T) 1987r, Steve Scifres (G) 1997, Nathan Davis (DT) 1998, Solomon Page (T) 1999–2002, Torrin Tucker (T) 2003.

78 Don Healy (DT) 1961, John Meyers (DT) 1962–3, Maury Youmans (DE) 1964–5, Bob Asher (T) 1970, Bruce Walton (G) 1973–5, Greg Schaum (DE) 1976, John Dutton (DL) 1979–86, Dave Widell (T) 1988–9, *Leon Lett* (DE) 1991–2000, Kurt Vollers (T) 2003.

79 Dick Klein (T) 1960, Ken Frost (DT) 1961–2, Larry Stephens (DE) 1963–6, Ron East (DT) 1967–70, **Forrest Gregg** (G/T) 1971, *Harvey Martin* (DE) 1973–83, John Hunt (G/T) 1984, Daryle Smith (T) 1987–8, Sal Cesario (G) 1987r, Willie Broughton (DT) 1989–90, *Erik Williams* (T) 1991–2000, Char-ron Dorsey (T) 2001.

80 Ola Murchison (WR) 1961, Gary Barnes (WR) 1963, *Lee Folkins* (TE) 1964, David Mc-Daniels (WR) 1968, *Tony Hill* (WR) 1977–86, Rod Barksdale (WR) 1987, Sebron Spivey (WR) 1987r, Everett Gay (WR) 1988, Bernard Ford (WR) 1989, Rod Harris (WR) 1990, Alvin Harper (WR) 1991–4, Oronde Gadsden (WR) 1995, Stepfret Williams (WR) 1996–7, Ernie Mills (WR) 1999, Reggie Swinton (WR) 2001–2, Tony McGee (TE) 2003.

81 Bill Howton (WR) 1960–3, Marv Bateman (P) 1972–4, Percy Howard (WR) 1975, **Jackie Smith** (TE) 1978, Robert Steele (WR) 1978, Steve Wilson (WR/CB) 1979, Kirk Phillips (WR) 1984, Karl Powe (WR) 1985–6, Kelvin Edwards (WR) 1987, Vince Courville (WR) 1987r, Scott Ankrom (WR) 1989, Alexander Wright (WR) 1990–2, Tim Daniel (WR) 1993, Edward Hervey (WR) 1995, Tyji Armstrong (TE) 1996, Scott Galbraith (TE) 1997, Pat Jeffers (WR) 1998, Raghib Ismail (WR) 1999–2002, James Whalen (TE) 2003.

82 Frank Clarke (TE/WR) 1960–7, Otto Stowe (WR) 1973, Beasley Reece (CB/WR) 1976, Robert Steele (WR) 1978, Cleo Simmons (TE) 1983, Mike Renfro (WR) 1984–7, Cornell Burbage (WR) 1989, Derrick Shepard (WR) 1991, Jimmy Smith (WR) 1992, Cory Fleming (WR) 1994–5, Johnny Mitchell (TE) 1996, Macey Brooks (WR) 1997, Jeff Ogden (WR) 1998, Chris Brazzell (WR) 1999, Alvin Harper (WR) 1999, James McKnight (WR) 2000, Tony McGee (TE) 2002, Jason Witten (TE) 2003.

83 *Jim Doran* (WR) 1960–1, *Lee Folkins* (TE) 1962–4, Harold Deters (K) 1967, Mike Clark (K) 1968–71, Golden Richards (WR) 1973–8, Doug Donley (WR) 1981–4, Leon Gonzalez (WR) 1985, Kelvin Martin (WR) 1987–92, 1996, Joey Mickey (TE) 1993, Willie Jackson (WR) 1994, Kendall Watkins (TE) 1995, Anthony Miller (WR) 1997, Hayward Clay (TE) 1998, Wane McGarity (WR) 1999–2001, James Whalen (TE) 2002, Terry Glenn (WR) 2003.

84 Gary Wisener (WR) 1960, Pettis Norman

(TE) 1962–70, Jean Fugett (TE) 1972–5, *Doug Cosbie* (TE) 1979–88, Rich Borreson (TE) 1987r, Keith Jennings (TE) 1989, *Jay Novacek* (TE) 1990–6, Mike Lucky (TE) 1999, Joey Galloway (WR) 2000–3.

85 Gene Cronin (LB) 1960, *Rayfield Wright* (TE/T) 1967–8, Tody Smith (DL) 1971–2, Fred Cornwell (TE) 1984–5, Thornton Chandler (TE) 1986, Steve Folsom (TE) 1987–90, Tim Hendrix (TE) 1987r, Dennis McKinnon (WR) 1990, Kevin Williams (WR) 1993–6, Ernie Mills (WR) 1998, Jeff Ogden (WR) 1999, Chris Brazzell (WR) 2000, Darrin Chiaverini (WR) 2001, Darnay Scott (WR) 2002, Jeff Robinson (TE) 2003.

86 Dave Sherer (P) 1960, Garry Porterfield (DE) 1965, Ralph Coleman (LB) 1972, Bill Houston (WR) 1974, Butch Johnson (WR) 1976–83, Duriel Harris (WR) 1984, Waddell Smith (WR) 1984, Kenny Duckett (WR) 1985, Mike Sherrard (WR) 1986, James Dixon (WR/RB) 1989–90, Tyrone Williams (WR) 1993, Eric Bjornson (TE) 1995–9, Mike Lucky (TE) 1999–2002, Dan Campbell (TE) 2003.

87 Nate Borden (DE) 1960–1, Andy Stynchula (DE) 1968, Billy Truax (TE) 1971–3, Ron Howard (TE) 1974–5, Jay Saldi (TE) 1976–82, Gordon Banks (WR) 1985–7, Kelvin Edwards (WR) 1988, Ray Alexander (WR) 1988–9, Derrick Shepard (WR) 1989–90, Alfredo Roberts (TE) 1991–2, Billy Davis (WR) 1995–8, Jason Tucker (WR) 1999–2000, Ken-Yon Rambo (WR) 2001–2, Zuriel Smith (WR) 2003.

88 Sonny Davis (LB) 1961, Colin Ridgeway (K/P) 1965, Sonny Randle (WR) 1968, Reggie Rucker (WR) 1970–1, Ron Sellers (WR) 1972, *Drew Pearson* (WR) 1973–83, *Michael Irvin* (WR) 1988–99, Jackie Harris (TE) 2000–1, Antonio Bryant (WR) 2002–3.

89 Fred Dugan (WR) 1960, Donnie Davis (WR) 1962, **Mike Ditka** (TE) 1969–72, *Billy DuPree* (TE) 1973–83, Brian Salonen (TE/LB) 1984–5, Thornton Chandler (TE) 1987–9, Cornell Burbage (WR) 1989, Rob Awalt (TE) 1990–1, Derek Tennell (TE) 1992, Kelly Blackwell (TE) 1993, Jim Price (TE) 1993, Scott Galbraith (TE) 1993–4, Derek Ware (TE) 1996, David LaFleur (TE) 1997–2000, Randall Williams (WR) 2003.

90 Willis Crockett (LB) 1990, Tony Hill (DE) 1992, Toddrick McIntosh (DT) 1994, Oscar Sturgis (DE) 1995, Alonzo Spellman (DE) 1999–2000, Byron Frisch (DE) 2001, Eric Ogbogu (DE) 2003.

91 Walter Johnson (DT) 1987, Mike Vanderbeek (LB/DE) 1993–4, Darren Benson (DT) 1995–8, Dimitrius Underwood (DE) 2000–1, Leonardo Carson (DT) 2003.

92 Ray Perkins (DE) 1987r, *Tony Tolbert* (DE) 1989–91, 1993–7, Demetric Evans (DE) 2001–2, Jermaine Brooks (DT) 2003.

93 Reggie Cooper (LB) 1991, Mike Ulafale

(DT) 1996, Artie Smith (DT) 1998, Peppi Zellner (DE) 1999–2002, Kenyon Coleman (DE) 2003.

94 Randy Watts (DE) 1987, Randy Shannon (LB) 1989–90, *Charles Haley* (DE) 1992–6, Michael Myers (DT) 1998–2003.

95 Mark Walen (DT) 1987–8, Chad Hennings (DT) 1992–2000, Randy Chevrier (DT) 2001, Colston Weatherington (DL) 2002.

96 Daniel Stubbs (DE) 1990–1, Shante Carver (DE) 1994–6, Antonio Anderson (DE) 1997–8, Ebenezer Ekuban (DE) 1999–2003.

97 David Ponder (DT) 1985, Kevin Lilly (DT) 1989, Jimmie Jones (DL) 1990–3, Kavika Pittman (DE) 1996–9, Aaron Fields (DE) 2000, *La'Roi Glover* (DT) 2002–3.

98 Ken Tippins (LB) 1989, Mitch Willis (DT) 1990, Godfrey Myles (LB) 1991–6, Shante Carver (DE) 1997, Greg Ellis (DE) 1998–2003.

99 Kevin Brooks (DT) 1985–8, David Howard (LB) 1989–90, Hurvin McCormack (DT) 1994–8, Nathan Davis (DE) 1999, Willie Blade (DT) 2003.

DENVER BRONCOS

The franchise: The Broncos were so underfinanced at their outset in 1960 that owner Bob Howsam supplied the team with used uniforms he purchased cheaply from the late and unlamented Copper Bowl. These seal brown and light gold colored uniforms featured the legendary vertically-striped socks that were a source of deep embarrassment for Bronco players in the first two seasons. In that second season, Howsam sold out to Calvin Kunz and Gerald Phipps in 1961. When Jack Faulkner took over as coach and general manager in 1962, he staged a public burning of the offending garments, and the team assumed a new color scheme of orange, blue and white. Despite winning the first AFL game in history by beating the Boston Patriots 13–10 on Friday September 9, 1960 and scoring the first touchdown in league history on a 59 yard pass play from Frank Tripucka to Al Carmichael, Denver was the worst of the eight original AFL franchises with a 39–97–4 record in the 1960s. In 1965 majority owner Kunz was on the brink of moving the team to Atlanta when the Phipps brothers stepped up and saved the franchise for Denver, buying both the team and Bears Stadium where they played. Three years later the city of Denver bought the stadium, renamed it Mile High, and began a series of expansions that would increase seating from 34,000 to 75,000 in ten years.

On the field the team was noted for its perpetual unsuccessful search for an ade-quate quarterback. Under Lou Saban in the late 1960s, they began to assemble the beginnings of a defense, and 1972 brought a new coach, Stanford's John Ralston, and a canny veteran quarterback, Charley Johnson. Under Ralston the Broncos achieved the franchise's first winning seasons in 1973, 1974 and 1976. Under his successor Red Miller in 1977, the team won its first divisional title, made its first trip to the playoffs, and went all the way to the Super Bowl where they were crushed by the Cowboys. 1977 also brought the elevation of Denver's Orange Crush defense to the top of the league and the arrival of talented but flawed quarterback Craig Morton.

The Broncos would not have a losing season under Miller, but new owner Edgar Kaiser brought in Dan Reeves to coach the team in 1981. John Elway would arrive two years later as the team's first great quarterback, and Pat Bowlen would buy the team the following year to provide it with solid ownership. With this triumvirate in place, Denver would beat Cleveland three times in the AFC Conference Championship game in the 1980s. The first Broncos-Browns contest is known for "The Drive" in which Elway led the Broncos on a 98 yard drive touchdown drive in the closing minutes to take the game to overtime where Denver would triumph; the second match is known for "The Fumble" when Browns runner Earnest Bynar fumbled at the goal line at the close of the game to seal another Bronco victory. All three Super Bowl trips ended in overwhelming and humiliating defeats, however.

Friction between quarterback and coach led to Reeves dismissal in 1992. He was succeeded first by his defensive coordinator Wade Phillips and then two years later by his former offensive coordinator Mike Shanahan who had gone on to greater fame with the 49ers. The team's uniforms changed radically to emphasize blue accented with orange trim. Meanwhile, Shanahan built a West Coast Offense with an unusually strong run game that culminated in Super Bowl triumphs after the 1997 and 1998 seasons. At which point Elway retired, and Shanahan seemed to lose a few genius points working with Brian Griese and Jake Plummer as quarterbacks.

Origin of name: Broncos was chosen in a contest in 1960. Although the team was playing at Bears Stadium, home of team owner Bob Howsam's minor league Denver Bears baseball team, there had been a previous minor league baseball team in Denver called the Broncos.

Time till first championship: 37 years.

Time since last championship: 6 years.

Retired numbers: Of the three numbers retired by Denver, one is a no-brainer, one can be rationalized, and one is utterly bizarre. 7 is retired for John Elway, probably one of the top five quarterbacks in NFL history. 44 is retired for All Pro runner Floyd Little who led the AFC in rushing twice and the NFL once while playing for only two winning teams in nine years. Little had his number retired from his high school, prep school and college as well. 18, though, is retired for the

team's first quarterback Frank Tripucka, and that is a weird choice. Former CFL star Tripucka completed 51 percent of his passes, threw 51 touchdowns versus 85 interceptions, and led the team to a 14–27–1 record in his three years as a starter.

Other numbers worn by these players: None.

Those who wore retired numbers after the honored player: None.

Numbers that should be retired: None. While the Broncos have had a number of exciting stars including Tombstone Jackson, Lyle Alzado, Randy Gradishar, Tom Jackson, and Karl Mecklenburg on defense and Rod Smith, Ed McCaffrey, Terrell Davis, and Shannon Sharpe on offense, only Sharpe is likely to make the Hall of Fame.

Owned numbers: Only Frank Tripucka ever wore 18.

Numbers worn by Hall of Famers: Willie Brown 24; Tony Dorsett 33; John Elway 7.

Record by Decade

| | Regular Season | | | Postseason | | |
	Won	Lost	Tied	Won	Lost	Championships
1960s	39	97	4	0	0	
1970s	75	64	5	2	3	
1980s	93	58	1	6	5	
1990s	94	66	0	8	3	1997, 1998
2000s	38	26	0	0	2	
All-Time	339	311	10	16	13	2

Winning seasons: 21. Losing Seasons: 17. .500 seasons: 6.

Coaches

	Years	Record	Playoffs
Frank Filchock	1960–1	7–20–1	0–0
Jack Faulkner	1962–4	9–22–1	0–0
Mac Speedie	1964–6	6–19–1	0–0
Ray Malavasi	1966	4–8–0	0–0
Lou Saban	1967–71	20–42–3	0–0
Jerry Smith	1971	2–3–0	0–0
John Ralston	1972–6	34–33–3	0–0
Red Miller	1977–80	40–22–0	2–3
Dan Reeves	1981–92	110–73–1	7–6
Wade Phillips	1993–4	16–16–0	0–1
Mike Shanahan (2)	1995–2003	91–53–0	7–3

(Championships in parentheses)

Star power: Steve Atwater took 27 from Kevin Clark; Shannon Sharpe took 84 from Chris Cole.

Star eclipsed: Randy Gradishar wore 52 till Ken Criter, 53, left; Shannon Sharpe wore 81 till Ricky Nattiel, 84, left.

Numbers with most great players: 87 has been worn by All Pro defensive end Tombstone Jackson and star receivers Lionel Taylor and Ed McCaffrey. 77 was worn by defensive end Lyle Alzado, linebacker Karl Mecklenburg, and tackle Tony Jones. 80 has been worn by receivers Rod Smith, Mark Jackson and Rick Upchurch.

Worst represented numbers: 4 has been worn by three punters, a kicker and a receiver, but only punter Micah Knorr has lasted more than one season in Denver.

Number worn by the most players: 82 and 85 each have been worn by 19 players.

Player who wore the most numbers: Guard Sam Brunelli wore three: 64, 68, and 72.

Longest tenure wearing a number: John Elway wore 7 for 16 years from 1983 to 1998. Tom Jackson wore 57 for 14 years from 1973 to 1986 and Dennis Smith wore 49 also for 14 years from 1981 to 1994.

Number worn by first ever draft pick: The Broncos had a lot of trouble signing top draft picks in the early years of the AFL. The first regular draft choice to sign with Denver was Dale Evans, 40, a fifth round selection in 1961. The first number one pick to sign was Miller Farr, 44, in the 1965 Redshirt draft. The first regular number one choice to sign was Floyd Little, 44, in 1967.

Biggest draft busts: Linebacker Mike Croel, 51, was selected fourth in 1991 and had a promising rookie year but faded fast after that. Tommy Maddox, 8, was selected 25th in 1992 and threw 6 tds and 9 interceptions in two years.

Number worn by oldest player: Craig Morton, 7, was 39 in 1982. John Elway, 7, Tobin Rote, 11, and Jim Turner, 15, all played at age 38 in 1998, 1966 and 1979 respectively.

Cameos: Hall of Famers— Tony Dorsett 33; All Pros and other notables— Flipper Anderson 83, George Atkinson 47, Hardy Brown 34/46, Terrell Buckley 27, Butch Byrd 24, Dale Carter 40, Seth Joyner 99, Roger

LeClerc 53, Leon Lett 94, Lawrence McCutcheon 33, Chris Miller 12, Tobin Rote 11, George Shaw 17, George Tarasovic 65, Gene Washington 84, Lee Woodall 54.

Ones who got away: Hall of Fame cornerback Willie Brown, 24, was traded to Oakland, as were fullback Hewritt Dixon, 30, and defensive end Ike Lassiter, 73. All Pro cornerback Miller Farr, 44, went to Houston. Quarterback Marlin Briscoe, 15, had success as a receiver for Buffalo and Miami. Tommy Maddox, 8, surfaced in Pittsburgh many years later.

Least popular numbers: 0 has been worn only by Johnny Olszewski; 5 has been worn only by Brad Daluiso; 9 has been worn only by David Treadwell.

Last number to be originated: 5 was not worn until 1992 by Brad Daluiso.

Longest dormant number: 0 has been dormant for 42 years since 1962.

Triskaidekaphobia notes: 13 has been worn by two disappointing quarterbacks, Steve Tensi and Don Horn, in addition to punter Jack Weil.

Shared numbers: 53 was worn by linebackers Randy Gradishar and Bill Romanowski. 23 was worn by safety Goose Gonsoulin and runner Sammy Winder.

Continuity: Craig Morton was replaced in 7 by John Elway; Glyn Milburn was replaced in 22 by fellow returner Vaughn Hebron; defensive tackle Paul Smith was replaced in 70 by tackle Dave Studdard; pass catcher Lionel Taylor was replaced in 87 by pass rusher Rich "Tombstone" Jackson.

Discontinuity: Tom Jackson was followed in 57 by Matt Smith; Rubin Carter was followed in 68 by Larry Lee; Rick Upchurch was followed in 80 by Ray Alexander; Shannon Sharpe was followed in 84 by Chris Cole before Sharpe returned in 2002.

Family Connections			
Brothers			
Eldon Danenhauer	T	1960–5	75
Bill Danenhauer	E	1960	76
Doug Widell	G	1989 92	67
Dave Widell	G	1990–4	79

Quarterback numbers over 19: 33 Hub Lindsey 1968.

Number of first black players: In their first year of 1960, the Broncos had eight black players: halfback Henry Bell 20; tackle Al Day 84; defensive end Chuck Gavin 61; end Jim Greer 85; halfback Gene Mingo 21; center Mike Nichols 51; guard Willie Smith 71; and end Lionel Taylor 87.

Numbers of future NFL head coaches: None.

Numbers of future NFL referees: None.

Players who played other sports: Baseball — Norm Bass 46. Basketball — Lonnie Wright 42. Wrestling — Darren Drozdov 97 and Wahoo McDaniel 54.

Players more famous after football: Guard Ernie Barnes, 62, has been a successful painter. Lineman Archie Harris, 78, won $125,000 as a contestant on the television show *Who Wants to Be a Millionaire*.

First player to wear a number in the 90s: Linebacker Ricky Hunley wore 98 in 1984.

Number with most points scored: 1 with 1,313 points scored by Jason Elam.

Number with most yards rushing: 30 with 10,791 yards gained by Terrell Davis (7,607), Jim Jensen (1,019), Cookie Gilchrist (954), Steve Sewell (917), Oliver Ross (150), Hewritt Dixon (130), and Clarence Walker (14).

Number with most receptions: 80 with 1,283 catches by Rod Smith (633), Mark Jackson (276), Rick Upchurch (267), Jerry Simmons (65), Jim Jones (13), Tony Kimbrough (10), Ray Alexander (8), Shane Swanson (6), Tom Buckman (4), and Tom Rychlec (1).

Number with most touchdown passes: 7 with 390 touchdowns tossed by John Elway (300), Craig Morton (74), and Mickey Slaughter (16).

Number with most interceptions: 23 with 54 by Goose Gonsoulin (43), Darrien Gordon (4), Gene Sykes (2), Drake Garrett (2), Steve Preece (1), Maurice Tyler (1), and Ron Bradford (1).

Oddity: Twelfth round draft pick Karl Mecklenburg wore 77 for 179 games over 12 years as a Bronco, but wore 97 on November 22, 1992 in a 24–0 loss to the Raiders that marked quarterback Tommy Maddox's first NFL start.

Players Whose Number Is Unknown		
Harold Smith	(T)	1960
Leo Reed	(T)	1961

Team All-Time Numerical Roster

Those with an "r" following the year 1987 were replacement players during the players' strike. Pro Bowl players for each number are in *Italics*; Hall of Famers are in **Bold** type.

0 Johnny Olszewski (RB) 1962.

1 Chris Norman (P) 1984–5, Daren Parker (P) 1992, *Jason Elam* (K) 1993–2003.

2 *Cookie Gilchrist* (FB) 1965, Bob Humphreys (K) 1967–8, Joe DiVito (QB) 1968, Alex Moore (RB) 1968, *Mike Horan* (P) 1986–92, Will Furrer (QB) 1994, Steve Lindsey (K) 2000.

3 Billy Joe (FB) 1963–4, Bobby Howfield (K) 1968–70, Rich Karlis (K) 1982–8, Scott Bentley (K) 1997, 2000.

4 Rick Duncan (K) 1967, Chris Norman (P) 1986, Robert Thompson (WR) 1987r, Ruben Rodriguez (P) 1992, Micah Knorr (P) 2002–3.

5 Brad Daluiso (K) 1992.

6 Ralph Giacommaro (P) 1987, Bubby Brister (QB) 1997–9, Joe Nedney (K) 2000.

7 Mickey Slaughter (QB) 1963–4, Craig Morton (QB) 1977–82, **John Elway** (QB) 1983–98.

8 Gary Kubiak (QB) 1983–91, Tommy Maddox (QB) 1992–3, Jeff Lewis (QB) 1996–7, Todd Husak (QB) 2001.

9 *David Treadwell* (K) 1989–92.

10 John McCrormick (QB) 1963, 1965–6, Jim Leclair (QB) 1967–8, Steve Ramsey (QB) 1971–6, Bucky Dilts (P) 1977–8, Mark Herrmann (QB) 1981–2.

11 Tobin Rote (QB) 1966, John McCormick (QB) 1968, Bobby Anderson (HB) 1970–3, *Luke Prestridge* (P) 1979–83, T.J. Rubley (QB) 1996, Jeff Brohm (QB) 1999, Steve Beuerlein (QB) 2002–3.

12 Gary Kroner (K) 1965–7, Al Pastrana (QB) 1969–70, Charlie Johnson (QB) 1972–5, Craig Penrose (QB) 1976–9, Ken Karcher (QB) 1987r, 1988, Shawn Moore (QB) 1992–3, Chris Miller (QB) 1999, Gus Frerotte (QB) 2000–1, Charlie Adams (WR) 2003.

13 Steve Tensi (QB) 1967–70, Don Horn (QB) 1971–2, Jack Weil (P) 1986, Danny Kanell (QB) 2003.

14 Skip Doyle (HB) 1960, Hunter Enis (QB) 1962, Mickey Slaughter (QB) 1965–6, Don Smith (G) 1967, Pete Liske (QB) 1969–70, John Hufnagel (QB) 1974, Norris Weese (QB) 1976–9, Scott

Stankavage (QB) 1984, 1986, Dean May (QB) 1987, Bill Musgrave (QB) 1995–6, *Brian Griese* (QB) 1998–2002.

15 Philip Nugent (HB) 1961, Jacky Lee (QB) 1964–5, Max Chobian (QB) 1966, Marlin Briscoe (QB) 1968, Jim Turner (K) 1971–9, Mike Clendenen (K) 1987.

16 George Herring (QB) 1960–1, Dick Wood (QB) 1962, Mike Ernst (QB) 1972, John Hufnagel (QB) 1975, Jeff Knapple (QB) 1980, Monte McGuire (QB) 1987r, Tom Rouen (P) 1993–2002, Jake Plummer (QB) 2003.

17 George Shaw (QB) 1962, Scotty Glacken (QB) 1966–7, Matt Robinson (QB) 1980, Steve DeBerg (QB) 1981–3, Hugh Millen (QB) 1994–5, Jarious Jackson (QB) 2000–3.

18 *Frank Tripucka* (QB) 1960–3.

19 Don Breaux (QB) 1963, Fred Steinfort (K) 1979–81.

20 Henry Bell (HB) 1960, Daniel Smith (HB) 1961, Jerry Traynham (HB) 1961, Tommy Minter (HB) 1962, Willie West (DB) 1964, Billy Ray Fletcher (E) 1966, Charles Greer (DB) 1968–74, *Louis Wright* (CB) 1975–86, Daryll Jones (DB) 1987r, Kevin Clark (DB) 1990–1, Greg Lewis (RB) 1992, Tory James (CB) 1996, 1998–9, Delvin Hughley (CB) 2001.

21 *Gene Mingo* (HB) 1960–4, Gerry Bussell (DB) 1965, Goldie Sellers (DB) 1966–7, Tommy Luke (DB) 1968, Jesse Stokes (DB) 1968, Bobby Burnett (RB) 1969, Randy Montgomery (CB) 1971–3, Randy Polti (DB) 1975–7, Myron Dupree (CB) 1983, Earl Johnson (DB) 1987r, Le-Lo Lang (CB) 1990–3, Randy Hilliard (CB) 1994–7, Darrien Gordon (CB) 1998, Chris Watson (CB) 1999, KaRon Coleman (RB) 2001–2, Scott Turner (CB) 2003.

22 Bob Stransky (HB) 1960, Buddy Allen (HB) 1961, David Ames (HB) 1961, Gerry Bussell (DB) 1965, Bobby Ply (DB) 1967, Fran Lynch (HB) 1967–76, Steve Haggerty (DB) 1975, Aaron Kyle (DB) 1980–2, Tony Lilly (S) 1984–7, Alton Montgomery (S) 1990–2, *Glyn Milburn* (RB) 1993–5, Vaughn Hebron (RB) 1996–8, Olandis Gary (RB) 1999–2002, Quentin Griffin (RB) 2003.

23 *Goose Gonsoulin* (DB) 1960–6, Gene Sykes (DB) 1967, Drake Garrett (DB) 1968, 1970, Dickie Post (RB) 1971, Steve Preece (S) 1972, Maurice Tyler (S) 1973–4, Larry Steele (P) 1974, Alfred Haywood (RB) 1975, George Hoey (DB) 1975, Billy Hardee (CB) 1976, Chris Pane (DB) 1976–9, *Sammy Winder* (RB) 1982–90, Ronnie Bradford (CB) 1993–5, Darrien Gordon (CB) 1997, Jason Moore (S) 1999, Willie Middlebrooks (CB) 2001–3.

24 Donald Allen (FB) 1960, **Willie Brown** (CB) 1963–6, Phil Brady (S) 1969, Booker Edgerson (CB) 1970, Butch Byrd (DB) 1971, *Otis Armstrong* (RB) 1973–80, Rick Parros (RB) 1981–4,

Tony Boddie (RB) 1986–7, Wymon Henderson (CB) 1989–91, Randy Fuller (CB) 1994, *Deltha O'Neal* (CB) 2000–3.

25 Errol Prisby (DB) 1967, Ted Alflen (RB) 1969, *Haven Moses* (W) 1972–81, Daniel Hunter (CB) 1985–6, Roger Jackson (DB) 1987r, Kip Corrington (S) 1989–90, Charles Swann (DB) 1994, Darrius Johnson (CB) 1996–9, Eric Davis (CB) 2001, Nick Ferguson (S) 2003.

26 Tommy Janik (DB) 1963–4, Don Coffey (E) 1963, Darrell Lester (FB) 1965–6, Frank Quayle (RB) 1969, George Saimes (S) 1970–2, Calvin Jones (CB) 1973–6, Larry Riley (DB) 1977, J.T. Thomas (DB) 1982, Chris Brewer (RB) 1984, Lyle Pickens (DB) 1987r, *Bobby Humphrey* (RB) 1989–91, Chris Hale (DB) 1993, Ben Smith (CB) 1994, Eric Thomas (CB) 1995, Tim McKyer (CB) 1997, Eric Brown (S) 1998–2001, *Clinton Portis* (RB) 2002–3.

27 Charlie Mitchell (HB) 1963–7, Tom Oberg (S) 1968–9, Maurice Harvey (DB) 1978, 1980, Kevin Clark (DB) 1987–8, *Steve Atwater* (S) 1989–98, Terrell Buckley (CB) 2000, Denard Walker (CB) 2001–2.

28 Bobby Gaiters (HB) 1963, Billy Atkins (DB) 1964, Abner Haynes (RB) 1965–6, Jack Lentz (S) 1967–8, Cornell Gordon (CB) 1970–2, Roger Jackson (DB) 1982–5, Jeremiah Castille (CB) 1987–8, Scott Caldwell (RB) 1987r, Elliot Smith (CB) 1990, *Gaston Green* (RB) 1991–2, Butler By'not'e (RB) 1994, Clifford Hicks (CB) 1995, Tito Paul (CB) 1998, Kenoy Kennedy (S) 2000–3.

29 Wendell Hayes (RB) 1965, Wandy Williams (RB) 1969–70, Bill West (CB) 1972, Bernard Jackson (DB) 1977–80, Wilbur Myers (S) 1983, Warren Marshall (RB) 1987, Darren Carrington (DB) 1989, Charles Dimry (RB) 1991–3, Aaron Craver (RB) 1995–6, Howard Griffith (FB) 1997–2001.

30 Clarence Walker (HB) 1963, Hewitt Dixon (FB) 1963–5, *Cookie Gilchrist* (FB) 1967, Oliver Ross (RB) 1973–5, Jim Jensen (RB) 1977, 1979–80, Steve Sewell (RB) 1985–92, *Terrell Davis* (RB) 1995–2001.

31 Bo Hickey (FB) 1967, Mike Franckowiak (RB) 1975–6, Zachary Dixon (RB) 1979, Mike Harden (CB) 1980–88, Kerry Porter (RB) 1990, Victor Jones (RB) 1992, Rondell Jones (S) 1993–6, Derek Loville (RB) 1997–9, Darryl Pounds (CB) 2000, Kelly Herndon (DB) 2002–3.

32 Mike Kellogg (FB) 1966–7, Garrett Ford (FB) 1968, Dick Davis (RB) 1970, Jon Keyworth (RB) 1974–80, Tony Reed (RB) 1981, Leonard Jones (DB) 1987, Joe Dudek (RB) 1987r, Calvin Thomas (RB) 1988, Melvin Bratton (RB) 1989–90, Sammie Smith (RB) 1992, Tony Veland (S) 1997, Billy Jenkins (S) 2000–1, Chris Young (S) 2003.

33 Pete Mangum (LB) 1960, Fred Bukaty (FB) 1961, Justin Rowland (HB) 1962, Wendell Hayes (RB) 1966–7, Hub Lindsey (QB) 1968, Willis

Crenshaw (FB) 1970, Joe Dawkins (RB) 1971–3, Jim Kiick (RB) 1976–7, Lonnie Perrin (RB) 1978, Lawrence McCutcheon (RB) 1980, Gene Lang (RB) 1984–7, **Tony Dorsett** (RB) 1988, Robert Perryman (FB) 1991–2, Rod Bernstine (RB) 1993–5, Dedrick Dodge (S) 1997, John Avery (RB) 1999, Jimmy Spencer (CB) 2000–3.

34 Hardy Brown (LB) 1960, *Don Stone* (FB) 1961–4, Gus Holloman (DB) 1968–9, Nathan Poole (RB) 1982–3, 1985, 1987r, *Tyrone Braxton* (DB) 1987–93, 1995–9, Raymond Harris (RB) 2000, Reuben Droughns (RB) 2002–3.

35 Dave Rolle (FB) 1960, Jim Sears (HB) 1961, Richard Dickinson (FB) 1962–3, James Wright (HB) 1964, Henry Jones (RB) 1969, Clem Turner (RB) 1970–2, Lonnie Perrin (RB) 1976–7, Larry Canada (FB) 1978–9, 1981, Ken Bell (RB) 1986–9, Blake Ezor (RB) 1990, John Granby (DB) 1992, Jason Suttle (CB) 1999–2000, Lenny Walls (DB) 2002–3.

36 Red Brodnax (FB) 1960, Jim Stinnette (FB) 1961–2, *Billy Thompson* (DB) 1969–81, Mark Haynes (CB) 1986–9, Frank Robinson (CB) 1992–3.

37 Bob Wade (CB) 1970, Steve Trimble (DB) 1981–3, Steve Fitzhugh (DB) 1987r, Kevin Guidry (CB) 1988, Anthony Lynn (RB) 1993, 1997–9, Tim Hauck (S) 1995–6, Tony Carter (FB) 2001, Tyrone Poole (DB) 2002, Cecil Sapp (RB) 2003.

38 Ben Norman (RB) 1980, Bruce Plummer (DB) 1987–8, 1990, Reggie Rivers (RB) 1991–6, Mike Anderson (RB) 2000–3.

39 Tommie Smiley (RB) 1969, Roland Solomon (CB) 1981, Jesse Myles (RB) 1983–4, Darryl Russell (DB) 1987r, Robert Delpino (RB) 1993, Ray Crockett (CB) 1994–2000.

40 Al Carmichael (HB) 1960–1, Ted Wegert (FB) 1960, Jay Evans (HB) 1961, Paul Carmichael (HB) 1965, Ron Lamb (FB) 1968, Brendon McCarthy (FB) 1968–9, Grady Cavness (CB) 1969, Jack Gehrke (WR) 1971, Randy Rich (DB) 1977, Charlie West (DB) 1978–9, Martin Rudolph (DB) 1987, Jeff Alexander (RB) 1989, 1992, Darryl Hall (S) 1993–4, Dale Carter (CB) 1999.

41 Bob McNamara (HB) 1960–1, Jerry Tarr (E) 1962, Eric Crabtree (WR) 1966–8, George Burrell (S) 1969, Leroy Mitchell (CB) 1971–3, Rob Lytle (RB) 1977–83, Greg Lewis (RB) 1991, Deon Strother (RB) 1994.

42 Al Romine (HB) 1960, Al Frazier (HB) 1961, Odell Barry (HB) 1964–5, Lonnie Wright (CB) 1966–7, Bill Van Heusen (WR) 1968–76, Charlie West (DB) 1978, Muhammad Oliver (CB) 1992, Leonard Russell (RB) 1994, *Detron Smith* (FB) 1996–2001, Sam Brandon (DB) 2002–3.

43 Frank Bernardi (DB) 1960, Charles Marshall (HB) 1962, John Nocera (LB) 1963, Bob Richardson (DB) 1966, Pete Jaquess (DB) 1967–70, Lonnie Hepburn (CB) 1974, Steve Foley (DB) 1976–86, Derrick Clark (RB) 1994, Izell Reese (S) 2002.

44 Miller Farr (DB) 1965, *Floyd Little* (RB) 1967–75.

45 John Sklopan (HB) 1963, Jim McMillin (DB) 1964–5, Lew Scott (DB) 1966, Tom Cassese (DB) 1967, Bill Laskey (LB) 1973–4, Jeff Severson (DB) 1975, Perry Smith (DB) 1980–1, Steve Wilson (CB) 1982–8, Richard Shelton (CB) 1989, Gary Downs (RB) 1995.

46 Hardy Brown (LB) 1960, *Bob Zeman* (DB) 1962–3, John Griffin (HB) 1964–6, Norm Bass (DB) 1964, Jim Summers (DB) 1967, Terry Erwin (HB) 1968, John Rowser (DB) 1974–6, Dave Preston (HB) 1978–83, Bobby Micho (RB) 1986, KaRon Coleman (RB) 2000.

47 John McGeever (DB) 1962–5, James Smith (S) 1969, Paul Martha (S) 1970, Tony Harris (WR) 1972, George Atkinson (DB) 1979, Gerald Wilhite (RB) 1982–8, David Pool (DB) 1993, Darius Clark (S) 2000–1, Ryan McNeil (CB) 2003.

48 *Nemiah Wilson* (DB) 1965–7, Herman Lewis (DE) 1968, John Pitts (S) 1973–5, Dale Hackbart (S) 1973, Earlie Thomas (DB) 1975, Randy Robbins (DB) 1984–91, Lionel Washington (CB) 1995–6, George Coghill (S) 1998–2001, Mike Leach (TE) 2002.

49 Glenn Glass (D) 1966, Neal Sweeney (WR) 1967, Alvin Mitchell (S/WR) 1970, *Dennis Smith* (S) 1981–94, Matt Dominguez (TE) 2001.

50 Pat Lamberti (E) 1961, Jerry Hopkins (LB) 1963–6, Carl Cunningham (LB) 1967–70, Olen Underwood (LB) 1971, Bobby Maples (C) 1972–8, Jim Ryan (LB) 1979–88, John Sullins (LB) 1992, Ray Jacobs (LB) 1994–5, Jon Hesse (LB) 1997, Artie Ulmer (LB) 1999, Ben Hamilton (C) 2001–3.

51 Mike Nichols (C) 1960–1, Leon Simmons (LB) 1963, *Jim Fraser* (LB) 1964, Eugene Jeter (LB) 1965–7, Henry Sorrell (LB) 1967, Dave Tobey (LB) 1968, Tim Casey (LB) 1969, Gordon Lambert (LB) 1969, Bill Butler (LB) 1970, Mike Simone (LB) 1972–4, *Bob Swenson* (LB) 1975–9, 1981–3, Marc Munford (LB) 1987–90, Mike Croel (LB) 1991–4, John Mobley (LB) 1996–2003.

52 Frank Kuchta (C) 1960, James Barton (C) 1961–2, Frank Jackunas (C) 1963, Ray Kubala (C) 1964–7, Fred Forsberg (LB) 1968, 1970–3, *Randy Gradishar* (LB) 1974–5, Mike Montler (C) 1977, Greg Bracelin (LB) 1980, Ken Woodard (LB) 1982–6, Dan MacDonald (LB) 1987r, Jeff Mills (LB) 1990–3, Richard Harvey (LB) 1994, Dave Garnett (LB) 1995, David Bowens (LB) 1999, *Ian Gold* (LB) 2000–3.

53 Bob Hudson (LB) 1960–1, Tom Erlandson (LB) 1962–5, Don Gulseth (LB) 1966, Roger LeClerc (C) 1967, Ken Criter (LB) 1971–4, *Randy Gradishar* (LB) 1976–83, Anthony Thompson (LB) 1990, Dante Jones (LB) 1995, *Bill Romanowski* (LB) 1996–2001, Johnny Rutledge (LB) 2003.

54 Wahoo McDaniel (LB) 1961–3, Larry Jordan (LB) 1964, Ed Cummings (LB) 1965, Ron Sbranti (LB) 1966, Chip Myrtle (LB) 1967–72, Ralph Cindrich (LB) 1974, Mike Lemon (LB) 1975, Richard Baska (LB) 1976–7, *Keith Bishop* (C) 1980, 1982–9, Keith Traylor (LB) 1991–2, Mitch Donahue (LB) 1993–4, Britt Hager (LB) 1995–6, Nate Wayne (LB) 1998–9, Lee Woodall (LB) 2001.

55 *Jim Fraser* (LB) 1962–3, Marv Matuszak (LB) 1964, Archie Matsos (LB) 1966, Pete Duranko (DE) 1967–70, 1972–4, Godwin Turk (LB) 1976–8, Ken Brown (C) 1979, Art Smith (LB) 1980, Rick Dennison (LB) 1982–90, Bryant Winn (LB) 1987r, John Kacherski (LB) 1992, Glenell Sanders (LB) 1994, Ken Brown (LB) 1995, Keith Burns (LB) 2000–3.

56 Jim Price (LB) 1964, *John Bramlett* (LB) 1965–6, Dave Behrman (C) 1967, Walter Highsmith (C) 1968, Jay Bachman (C) 1969–70, Dave Washington (LB) 1971, Don Parish (LB) 1972, Ray May (LB) 1973–5, Larry Evans (LB) 1976–82, Aaron Smith (LB) 1984, *Michael Brooks* (LB) 1987–92, Mike Knox (LB) 1987r, Keith Burns (LB) 1994–8, *Al Wilson* (LB) 1999–2003.

57 John Huard (LB) 1967–9, Bob Geddes (LB) 1972, *Tom Jackson* (LB) 1973–86, Matt Smith (LB) 1987r, Mike Ruether (C) 1988–9, Ty Allert (LB) 1990, Mark Murray (LB) 1991, Dave Wyman (LB) 1993, Allen Aldridge (LB) 1994–7, Jashon Sykes (LB) 2003.

58 Jack Work (LB) 1960, Frank Richter (LB) 1967–9, Bill McKoy (LB) 1970–2, Tom Graham (LB) 1973–4, Phil Olsen (C) 1975–6, Rob Nairne (LB) 1977–80, Steve Busick (LB) 1981–5, Tim Lucas (LB) 1987, Scott Curtis (LB) 1989–90, Elijah Alexander (LB) 1992–5, Steve Russ (LB) 1997, 1999–2000, Terry Pierce (LB) 2003.

59 *Larry Kaminski* (C) 1966–73, Joe Rizzo (LB) 1974–80, Mark Merrill (LB) 1981–2, Darren Comeaux (LB) 1982–6, Tim Lucas (LB) 1987–93, Kirk Dodge (LB) 1987r, Brett Wallerstedt (LB) 1994, Glenn Cadrez (LB) 1995–2000, Donnie Spragen (LB) 2002–3.

60 *Ken Adamson* (G) 1960–2, Charlie Parker (G) 1965, Bob Young (G) 1966–70, Ernie Park (G) 1966, Paul Howard (G) 1973–5, 1977–86, Gerald Perry (G) 1988–90, Nick Subis (G) 1991, Joe Burch (C) 1994, K.C. Jones (C) 1998–2000.

61 Charles Gavin (DE) 1960–3, Bill Keating (DT) 1966–7, Bob Vaughn (G) 1968, Tom Lyons (G) 1971–6, Arland Thompson (G) 1980, Andre Townsend (DE) 1984–90, Bob Meeks (G) 1992–4, Eric Floyd (G) 1995.

62 Buddy Alliston (LB) 1960, Jack Davis (T) 1960, Jerry Stalcup (LB) 1961–2, Jim Eifrid (LB) 1961, Ernie Barnes (G) 1963–4, Jerry Inman (DT) 1966–71, Brian Goodman (G) 1975, Tom Glassic (G) 1976–83, Mike Freeman (G) 1984, 1986–7, Jeff Davidson (G) 1990–2, Dan Neil (C/G) 1997–2003.

63 Dave Strickland (G) 1960, Buzz Guy (G) 1961, *Dave Costa* (DT) 1967–71, John Grant (DE) 1973–9, Laval Short (DT) 1980, Mark Cooper (G) 1983–7, Sean Farrell (G) 1990–1, David Diaz-Infante (G/C) 1996–8, 2001, Richard Mercier (G) 2000.

64 *Bud McFadin* (DT) 1960–3, John Hohman (G) 1965–6, Sam Brunelli (G) 1967, George Gaiser (T) 1968, Mike Schnitker (G) 1969–74, Harvey Goodman (G) 1976, Billy Bryan (C) 1977–88, Scott Beavers (G) 1990, Jon Melander (G/T) 1993–4, Ralph Tramm (G/C) 1995–6, Lennie Friedman (G) 2000–2.

65 Joe Young (E) 1960–1, John Denvir (G) 1962, Don Shackelford (G) 1964, George Tarasovic (DE) 1967, Jay Bachman (C) 1968, 1970–1, Walter Highsmith (C) 1969, Lloyd Voss (DT) 1972, LeFrancis Arnold (G/C) 1974, Glenn Hyde (G) 1976–81, Walt Bowyer (DE) 1983–4, 1987–8, Monte Smith (G) 1989, *Gary Zimmerman* (T) 1993–7, Cooper Carlisle (T) 2000–3.

66 John Cash (E) 1961–2, Larry Cox (DT) 1966–7, Bill Cottrell (G) 1972, Jim O'Mally (LB) 1973–5, Brison Manor (DE) 1977–84, Scott Garnett (NT) 1984, Jim Juriga (T) 1988–90, Chuck Johnson (T) 1992–3, *Tom Nalen* (C) 1994–2003.

67 John Hatley (T) 1960, Jack Simpson (LB) 1961, Robert McCullough (G) 1962–5, *George Goedeke* (G) 1967–72, Carl Schaukowitch (G) 1975, Steve Schindler (G) 1977–8, Keith Uecker (T) 1982–3, Glenn Hyde (G) 1985, Dean Miraldi (T) 1985, John Ayers (G) 1987, Doug Widell (G) 1989–92, Ken Lanier (T) 1994, Mark Campbell (DT) 1996.

68 Bill Roehnelt (LB) 1961–2, Tom Nomina (T) 1963–5, Sam Brunelli (G) 1966, Gary Crane (LB) 1969, Steve Alexakos (G) 1970, Larron Jackson (G) 1971–4, Rubin Carter (DT) 1975–86, Larry Lee (C) 1987, Ron McLean (DL) 1987r, Brad Henke (DE) 1989, Crawford Kerr (G) 1991, Russell Freeman (T) 1992–4, Reggie McElroy (T) 1995–6, Mario Fatafehi (DT) 2003.

69 Brison Manor (DE) 1984, Tony Colorito (NT) 1986, David Jones (OL) 1987, Darrell Hamilton (T) 1989–91, *Mark Schlereth* (G) 1995–2000, Michael Moore (G) 2001.

70 Donald King (E) 1960, Charlie Janerette (DT) 1964–5, *Paul Smith* (DT) 1968–78, Dave Studdard (T) 1979–88, Brian Sochia (DL) 1991–2, Jamie Brown (T) 1995–7, Trey Teague (T) 1998–2001.

71 Willie Smith (G) 1960, Art Hauser (T) 1961, Jim Perkins (T) 1962–4, Wallace Dickey (T) 1968–9, Claudie Minor (T) 1974–82, *Greg Kragen* (NT) 1985–93, Jack Peavey (OL) 1987r, Melvin Tuten (T) 1999–2000, Blake Brockermeyer (OL) 2002–3.

72 *Jerry Sturm* (C) 1961–6, Richard Tyson (G) 1967, Sam Brunelli (G) 1968–71, Bob Kampa (DT)

1974, Wayne Hammond (DT) 1976, Don Latimer (DT) 1978–83, Marsharne Graves (T) 1984, Keith Kartz (C) 1987–94, Ernest Jones (DE) 1996–7, Brandon Winey (T) 2001, George Foster (T) 2003.

73 Gordon Holz (DT) 1960, Robert Konovsky (E) 1961, Isaac Lassiter (DE) 1962–4, Pat Matson (G) 1966–7, Walter Barnes (DE) 1969–71, Mike Askea (T) 1973, Stan Rogers (T) 1975, Martin Imhof (DE) 1976, Henry Allison (T) 1977, Kelvin Clark (T) 1979–81, Shawn Hollingsworth (T) 1983, Simon Fletcher (LB) 1985–95, Kevin Belcher (T) 1987r, Scott Adams (T) 1997, Cyron Brown (DE) 1998–9.

74 Gordon Holz (DT) 1960–3, Frank Atkinson (DE) 1964, Lee Bernet (T) 1965–6, *Mike Current* (T) 1967–75, Scott Parish (T) 1976, Andy Maurer (T) 1977, Jerry Baker (T) 1983, Winford Hood (G) 1984–5, Dan Remsberg (T) 1986–7, Bill Lobenstein (DL) 1987r, Harvey Salem (T) 1991, Bill Schultz (T) 1995, Harry Swayne (T) 1997–8, Evan Pilgrim (OL) 1999, Ephraim Salaam (T) 2002–3.

75 *Eldon Danenhauer* (T) 1960–5, Rex Mirich (DE) 1967–9, Roger Shoals (T) 1971, Rick Sharp (T) 1972, Ed Smith (DE) 1973–5, Bill Bain (T) 1976, 1978, Kit Lathrop (DE) 1979, *Rulon Jones* (DE) 1980–8, Brian Habib (T) 1993–7, Monsanto Pope (DL) 2002–3.

76 William Danenhauer (E) 1960, William Yelverton (E) 1960, Jack Mattox (T) 1961, Harold Olson (T) 1963–4, Bob Breitenstein (T) 1965–7, Gordon Lambert (LB) 1968, Tom Domres (DT) 1971–2, Steve Coleman (DE) 1974, Tom Drougas (T) 1974, Randy Moore (DT) 1976, Tom Neville (T) 1978, Ken Lanier (T) 1981–92, Kirk Scrafford (T) 1993–4, Broderick Thompson (T) 1995–6.

77 Carl Larpenter (G) 1960–1, Jack Mattox (T) 1962, Anton Peters (T) 1963, Dick Guesman (T/K) 1964, Jim Thompson (DT) 1965, Larry Cox (DT) 1968, Alden Roche (DE) 1970, *Lyle Alzado* (DE) 1971–8, Greg Boyd (DE) 1980–2, *Karl Mecklenburg* (LB) 1983–94, *Tony Jones* (T) 1997–2000.

78 Leroy Moore (DE) 1964–5, Marvin Davis (DT) 1966, Tom Cichowski (T) 1967–8, Ken Criter (LB) 1969–70, Marv Montgomery (T) 1971–6, Jim White (DE) 1976, Bruce Radford (DE) 1979, Brian Clark (T) 1982, Rich Stachowski (DE) 1983, Winford Hood (G) 1986–8, Archie Harris (OL) 1987, Don Maggs (T) 1993–4, Larry Jackson (DE) 1995, Matt Lepsis (T) 1998–2003.

79 John Gonzaga (G) 1966, Carter Campbell (DE) 1971, Barney Chavous (DE) 1973–85, Stefan Humphries (G) 1987–8, Dave Widell (G) 1990–4, Jumpy Geathers (DT) 1996, Chris Banks (G) 1998–9, Steve Herndon (G) 2001–3.

80 Ron Nery (E) 1963, Tom Rychlec (E) 1963, Ed Cooke (DE) 1964–5, Dan LaRose (DE) 1966, Jimmy Jones (WR) 1968, Tom Buckman (TE) 1969, Jerry Simmons (WR) 1971–4, *Rick Upchurch* (WR) 1975–83, Ray Alexander (WR) 1984, Mark Jackson (WR) 1986–92, Shane Swanson (WR) 1987r, Tony Kimbrough (WR) 1993–4, *Rod Smith* (WR) 1995–2003.

81 Bill Jessup (E) 1960, Max Leetzow (DE) 1965–6, Billy Masters (TE) 1970–4, Bob Adams (TE) 1975, *Steve Watson* (WR) 1979–87, *Shannon Sharpe* (TE) 1990–1, Barry Rose (WR) 1993, Kitrick Taylor (WR) 1993, Mike Pritchard (WR) 1994–5, Todd Kinchen (WR) 1996, Patrick Jeffers (WR) 1997, Andre Cooper (WR) 1999–2000, Keith Poole (WR) 2001, Chris Cole (WR) 2003.

82 *Bob Scarpitto* (P/WR) 1962–7, Dave Pivec (TE) 1969, Dwight Harrison (WR) 1971–2, Otto Stowe (WR) 1974, Jack Dolbin (WR) 1975–9, Larry Brunson (WR) 1980, Orlando McDaniel (WR) 1982, Zach Thomas (WR) 1983–4, Vance Johnson (WR) 1985–93, 1995, Laron Brown (WR) 1987r, Tony Kimbrough (WR) 1993, Melvin Bonner (WR) 1994, Patrick Jeffers (WR) 1996, David Gamble (WR) 1997, Marcus Nash (WR) 1998–9, Billy Miller (WR) 1999–2000, Kevin Kasper (WR) 2001–2, Herb Haygood (WR) 2002, Adrian Madise (WR) 2003.

83 John Pyeatt (HB) 1960, Don Joyce (DE) 1962, Ray Jacobs (DT) 1963–6, Jim Whalen (TE) 1970–1, Wade Manning (WR) 1981–2, John Sawyer (TE) 1983–4, Sam Graddy (WR) 1987–8, Rick Massie (WR) 1987, Michael Young (WR) 1989–92, Melvin Bonner (WR) 1993, *Anthony Miller* (WR) 1994–6, Flipper Anderson (WR) 1997, Justin Armour (WR) 1998, Travis McGriff (WR) 1999–2001, Scottie Montgomery (WR) 2001–2, Mike Leach (TE) 2003.

84 Albert Day (T) 1960, Jack Hill (HB) 1961, Matt Snorton (TE) 1964, Jim Thibert (LB) 1965, Jason Franci (E) 1966, Lou Andrus (LB) 1967, Mike Haffner (E) 1968–70, Rod Sherman (WR) 1972, Gene Washington (WR) 1973, John Schulz (WR) 1976–7, Vince Kinney (WR) 1978–9, Clint Sampson (WR) 1983–6, Ricky Nattiel (WR) 1987–91, *Shannon Sharpe* (TE) 1992–9, 2002–3, Chris Cole (WR) 2000–1.

85 James Greer (E) 1960, Larry Jordan (LB) 1962, Tom Beer (TE) 1967–9, John Mosier (TE) 1971, Ron Egloff (TE) 1977–83, Don Summers (TE) 1984–5, Mike Barber (TE) 1985, Joey Hackett (TE) 1986, Rick Massie (WR) 1987–8, Chris Woods (WR) 1989, Tim Stallworth (WR) 1990, Derek Russell (WR) 1991–4, Jeff Wilner (TE) 1995, Willie Green (WR) 1997–8, Chris Doering (WR) 1999, Robert Brooks (WR) 2000, Eddie Kennison (WR) 2001, Phil McGeoghan (WR) 2001, Ashley Lelei (WR) 2002–3.

86 Don Carothers (E) 1960, Stan Fanning (DE) 1964, Bobby Moten (TE) 1968, Jerry Hendren (WR) 1970, Jim Krieg (WR) 1972, Marv Frazier (WR) 1973–5, John Schulz (WR) 1978, Emery Moorehead (WR) 1980, Dean Barnett (TE) 1983, Butch Johnson (WR) 1984–5, Mitch Andrews

(TE) 1987, Pat Kelly (TE) 1988, Chris Verhulst (TE) 1990, Barry Johnson (WR) 1991, Arthur Marshall (WR) 1992–3, Jeff Campbell (WR) 1994, Byron Chamberlain (TE) 1995–2000, Patrick Hape (TE) 2001–3.

87 *Lionel Taylor* (WR) 1960–6, *Rich Jackson* (DE) 1967–72, John Hoffman (DE) 1972, Boyd Brown (TE) 1974–6, Bob Moore (TE) 1978, Jim Wright (TE) 1980–5, Bill Larson (TE) 1980, Bobby Micho (RB) 1986–7, Jason Johnson (WR) 1988, Paul Green (TE) 1989, Pat Kelly (TE) 1989, Cedric Tillman (WR) 1992–4, *Ed McCaffrey* (WR) 1995–2003.

88 Pat Epperson (E) 1960, Eugene Prebola (E) 1961–3, *Al Denson* (WR) 1964–70, *Riley Odoms* (TE) 1972–83, Clarence Kay (TE) 1984–91, Russell Payne (TE) 1987r, Jerry Evans (TE) 1993–5, Mike Sherrard (WR) 1996, Sir Mawn Wilson (WR) 1997, Desmond Clark (TE) 1999–2001, Jeb Putzier (TE) 2002–3.

89 Ken Carpenter (E) 1960, Bill Groman (HB) 1963, Gary Henson (E) 1964, Max Wettstein (E) 1966, Andre White (TE) 1967, John Embree (WR) 1969–70, Gordon Bowdell (WR) 1971, Clay Brown (TE) 1983, Dave Logan (WR) 1984, Keli McGregor (TE) 1985, Orson Mobley (TE) 1986–90, Kerry Locklin (TE) 1987r, Reggie Johnson (TE) 1991–3, *Dwayne Carswell* (TE) 1994–2003.

90 Freddie Gilbert (DE) 1986–8, Ron Holmes (DE) 1989–92, Dan Williams (DE) 1993–6, *Neil Smith* (DE) 1997–9, Jerry Johnson (DT) 2000–1, Darius Holland (DT) 2003.

91 Jeff Tupper (DL) 1987, Warren Powers (DE) 1989–91, Willie Oshodin (DE) 1992–5, Troy Wilson (DE) 1995, *Alfred Williams* (DE) 1996–9, Chester McGlockton (DT) 2001–2.

92 Alphonso Carreker (DE) 1989, 1991, Ron Geater (DE) 1992, Dave Wyman (LB) 1994–5, Lester Archambeau (DE) 2000, Bertrand Berry (DE) 2001–3.

93 Ronnie Haliburton (LB) 1990–2, James Jones (DE) 1995, *Trevor Pryce* (DT) 1997–2003.

94 Jim Szymanski (DE) 1991–2, Jeff Robinson (DE) 1993–6, Keith Traylor (DT) 1997–2000, Leon Lett (DT) 2001, Lionel Dalton (DT) 2002.

95 Steve Bryan (DE) 1987–8, Tim Joiner (LB) 1987r, Jeroy Robinson (LB) 1990, Alphonso Taylor (DT) 1993, *Michael Dean Perry* (DT) 1995–7, Marvin Washington (DE) 1998, Paul Grasmanis (DT) 1999, Kavika Pittman (DE) 2000–2.

96 Jake McCullough (DE) 1989–90, Kenny Walker (DE) 1991–2, Harald Hasselbach (DE) 1994–2000, Dorsett Davis (DL) 2002–3.

97 Bruce Klosterman (LB) 1987–9, *Karl Mecklenburg* (LB) 1992, Darren Drozdov (DT) 1993–4, Mike Lodish (DE) 1995–2000, Keith Washington (DE) 2001–2.

98 Ricky Hunley (LB) 1984–7, Ted Washington (DT) 1994, Maa Tanuvasa (DL) 1995–2000, Reggie Hayward (DE) 2001–3.

99 Ray Woodard (DE) 1987, Shawn Knight (NT) 1988, David Galloway (DE) 1990, Shane Dronett (DT) 1992–5, David Richie (DT) 1997, Seth Joyner (LB) 1998, Montae Reagor (DE) 1999–2002, Daryl Gardener (DT) 2003.

DETROIT LIONS

The franchise: If the Lions had a spokesman from history, it would be former Nebraska senator Roman Hruska who defended a dubious Nixon Supreme Court nominee in 1969 with, "There are a lot of mediocre judges and lawyers. They are entitled to a little representation, aren't they, and a little chance?" The history of this once great franchise has come to epitomize mediocrity over time. The Lions have gone 47 years without a championship; only the awful Cardinals franchise has gone longer (57 years) without a title, and they at least had the decency to move a couple of times to break the monotony. Detroit has been without a winner longer than any other NFL city, and in that long period the Lions have won only one playoff game out of 10. Even in the 1990s when the Lions made the playoffs six times, the attained a losing record overall due to the other four dreadful seasons in the decade. Bad teams and good teams, but no great teams; it wasn't always so.

Three Detroit NFL franchises had failed in the 1920s, but when Detroit radio executive George Richards bought the financially-struggling Portsmouth Spartans in 1934 success would come quickly. The Spartans were an excellent team with a great defense who were led by coach Potsy Clark and star players Dutch Clark, Ace Gutowsky, Glenn Press-nell and Ox Emerson. In 1935, these Lions won the title by beating the Giants in the championship game with the last touchdown being scored by Buddy Parker, who would later become the best coach in Detroit history. The Lions remained a contender throughout the decade, but Richards sold the team in 1940 to department store owner Fred Mandel. He met with little success on the field or at the box office and sold the team to a syndicate headed by Lyle Fife and Edwin Anderson in 1947. Those two battled for control of the club until Fife finally sold out to William Clay Ford in 1961. Ford would acquire full ownership in 1964. Under Anderson's hand, though, the team began to accumulate talent in the late 1940s so that when Buddy Parker was named coach in 1951 they were ready to take off. Anderson had made the most important trade in team history in 1950 when he dealt talented receiver Bob Mann to the New York Bulldogs for quarterback Bobby Layne. Behind Layne and his high school buddy Doak Walker in addition to a defense first led by 300 pound middle guard Les Bingaman and then by middle linebacker Joe Schmidt, the hell-bent-for-leather Lions became the team of the decade in the 1950s. They won titles in 1952, 1953 and 1957 — all over the Cleveland Browns.

By 1957, low-key George Wilson had taken over for the high-strung Parker who quit in training camp. Under Wilson, Detroit was a consistent contender, but the team of the '50s could not beat out the team of the '60s, the Packers. The two rivals did wage some fierce battles for control of the Western Conference in the early 1960s though, especially on the traditional Thanksgiving match that had started in 1945 with the Packers becoming the regular opponent in 1951. Green Bay begged out of the annual turkey shoot after 1963, but the Detroit Thanksgiving game has continued to the present day.

In the many years since, the Lions have featured some great players like Lem Barney, Billy Sims, Herman Moore and Barry Sanders, but no great teams. More specifically, they have not had a great quarterback since Layne was traded away in 1958. Most of that time they played their games in the Silverdome an enormous, but lifeless place where no coach who lasted at least one full season ever finished with a winning record. In 2002, the Lions moved back to Detroit to the new outdoor Ford Field, and in 2003 they hired proven winner and Michigan-native Steve Mariucci to lead them out of morass.

Origin of name: In keeping with the jungle cat theme of the Detroit Tigers baseball team, new owner George Richards renamed the Portsmouth Spartans the Lions when he moved them to Detroit in 1934.

Record by Decade						
	Regular Season			Postseason		
	Won	Lost	Tied	Won	Lost	Championships
1930s	73	39	9	1	0	1935
1940s	35	71	4	0	0	
1950s	68	48	4	5	1	1952, 1953, 1957
1960s	66	61	11	0	0	
1970s	66	75	3	0	1	
1980s	61	90	1	0	2	
1990s	79	81	0	1	6	
2000s	15	45	0	0	0	
All-Time	467	510	32	7	10	

Winning seasons: 32. Losing Seasons: 36. .500 seasons: 6.

Time till first championship: Six years.
Time since last championship: 47 years.
Retired numbers: Detroit has retired four numbers for Hall of Famers known for their leadership on championship teams: Dutch Clark 7; Bobby Layne 22; Doak Walker 37; and Joe Schmidt 56. The Lions also retired 85 in memory of Chuck Hughes who died from a heart attack in a game against the Bears in 1971 and 20 for Barry Sanders, Billy Sims and Lem Barney.

Other numbers worn by these players: Dutch Clark also wore 12 and 19.

Coaches

	Years	Record	Playoffs
Hal Griffen	1930	5–6–3	0–0
Potsy Clark (1)	1931–6, 1940	53–25–7	1–0
Dutch Clark	1937–8	14–8–0	0–0
Gus Henderson	1939	6–5–0	0–0
Bill Edwards	1941–2	4–9–1	0–0
John Karcis	1942	0–8–0	0–0
Gus Dorais	1943–7	20–31–2	0–0
Bo McMillin	1948–50	12–24–0	0–0
Buddy Parker (2)	1951–6	47–23–2	3–1
George Wilson (1)	1957–64	53–45–6	2–0
Harry Gilmer	1965–6	10–16–2	0–0
Joe Schmidt	1967–72	43–34–7	0–1
Don McCafferty	1973	6–7–1	0–0
Rick Forzano	1974–6	15–17–0	0–0
Tommy Hudspeth	1976–7	11–13–0	0–0
Monte Clark	1978–84	43–61–1	0–2
Darryl Rogers	1985–8	18–40–0	0–0
Wayne Fontes	1988–96	66–67–0	0–0
Bobby Ross	1997–2000	27–30–0	0–0
Gary Moeller	2000	4–3	0–0
Marty Mornhinweg	2001–2	5–27–0	0–0
Steve Mariucci	2003	5–11–0	0–0

(Championships in parentheses)

Those who wore retired numbers after the honored player: When the Lions signed All Pro linebacker Pat Swilling in 1993 he asked to wear 56 as he had in New Orleans. While it had not been officially retired at that point, no one had worn 56 in Detroit since Joe Schmidt. Schmidt gave his blessing, Swilling wore 56 for two years, but the number is retired now.

Numbers that should be retired: None.

Owned numbers: None.

Numbers worn by Hall of Famers: Lem Barney 20; Jack Christiansen 19/24; Dutch Clark 7/12/19; Lou Creekmur 76; Bill Dudley 35/44; Frank Gatski 52; John Henry Johnson 35; Night Train Lane 81; Yale Lary 28; Bobby Layne 22; Ollie Matson 30; Hugh McElhenny 39; Joe Schmidt 56; Doak Walker 37; Whizzer White 24/44; Alex Wojciechowicz 30/50.

Star power: Pat Swilling wore 56 despite it being retired for Joe Schmidt.

Star eclipsed: Ollie Matson wore 30 because Nick Pietrosante wore 33. Dutch Clark wore 12/19 till Ox Emerson, 7, left; Desmond Howard wore 18 till Iheanyi Uwaezuoke, 80, left; Ron Kramer wore 83 till Sam Williams, 88, left.

Numbers with most great players: 20 has been worn by Hall of Famers Lem Barney and Barry Sanders, All Pro runner Billy Sims, and 1930s stars back Glenn Pressnell and lineman Ox Emerson. 24 has been worn by Famers Whizzer White and Jack Christiansen, All Pro cornerback Dick LeBeau, and star runners Mel Farr and Dexter Bussey. 44 has been worn by Famers Whizzer White and Bill Dudley, as well as Dick LeBeau (again) and Dick Doll.

Worst represented numbers: 31 has been worn by 20 runners, defensive backs, and ends without distinction.

Number worn by the most players: 81 has been worn by 34 Lions

Player who wore the most numbers: Six Lions have worn four different numbers: back Gene Alford 25/37/54/59; tackle George Christensen 14/25/27/47; fullback Father Lumpkin 2/4/24/57; tackle Buster Mitchell 11/13/24/42; back Glenn Presnell 3/18/20/60; and lineman Clare Randolph 4/5/7/43.

Longest tenure wearing a number: Wayne Walker wore 55 for 15 years from 1958 to 1972.

Number worn by first ever draft pick: Guard Sid Wagner was picked number one in 1936 and wore 15.

Biggest draft busts: The two biggest draft busts were both quarterbacks. Chuck Long, 16, was selected 12th in 1986 and threw 19 tds and 28 interceptions in four years, while Andre Ware, 11, was selected seventh in 1990 and threw five tds and eight interceptions in four years.

Number worn by oldest player: Guard Ray Brown turned 41 wearing 61 in 2003.

Cameos: Hall of Famers — Frank Gatski

52; Ollie Matson 30; Hugh McElhenny 39. All Pros and other notables—John Baker 78; Ken Ellis 20; Miller Farr 27; Harlon Hill 82; Marv Hubbard 44; LeRoy Irvin 47; Dave Kreig 17; Dante Magnani 16; Wilbert Montgomery 28; Bill Quinlan 83; Brendan Stai 66; Henry Taylor 98; Gene Washington 18.

Ones who got away: Dave Whitsell 23, Mike Bass 26, and Jim Kearney 46 starred at defensive back for the Bears, Redskins and Chiefs respectively; linebackers Dave Lloyd 52 and Dennis Gaubatz 53 starred for the Eagles and Colts respectively; defensive end Bill Glass 53 starred in Cleveland; tackle Grady Alderman and linebacker Wally Hilgenberg both wore 67 for the Lions but starred for the Vikings; Pat Summerall 84 made his name for the Giants.

Least popular numbers: 0 has only been worn once; 7 has been worn twice and 69 has been worn four times.

Last number to be originated: 91 was first worn by Mark Duckens in 1990.

Longest dormant number: 13 has not been worn since 1947, 57 years.

Triskaidekaphobia notes: 13 has been worn by five linemen and one back, all over 50 years ago.

Shared numbers: 75 was worn by two tough linemen, John Gordy and Lomas Brown. 76 was worn by Hall of Fame tackle Lou Creekmur and All Pro defensive tackle Roger Brown. Long-time defensive linemen Darris McCord and Doug English both wore 78.

Continuity: Jack Christiansen was replaced in 24 by Dick LeBeau; Mel Farr was replaced in 24 by Dexter Bussey; Lou Creekmur was replaced in 76 by Roger Brown.

Discontinuity: Championship quarterback Tobin Rote was followed in 18 by Warren Rabb; Hall of Famer Alex Wojciechowicz was followed in 30 by back Steve Belichick (father of the Patriots coach); receiver Gail Cogdill was replaced in 89 by receiver John Wright.

Quarterback numbers over 19: 22 Bobby Layne and Clyde LeForce; 28 Frank Tripucka; 37 Cotton Price; 24/46 Fred Enke.

Number of first black players: Receiver

Family Connections

Brothers

Mel Farr	RB	1967–73	24
Miller Farr	DB	1973	27
Jim Jones	B	1946	42
Ralph Jones	E	1946	31
Alex Karras	DT	1958–70	71
Ted Karras	G	1965	65
Darnell Walker	CB	2000	41
Marquis Walker	CB	2000	38

Fathers and sons

Mel Farr	RB	1967–73	24
Mike Farr	WR	1990–2	81
Bob Kowalkowski	G	1966–76	66
Scott Kowalkowski	LB	1994–2001	52

Bob Mann, 87, and back Mel Groomes, 17, both broke in with the Lions in 1948.

Numbers of future NFL head coaches: Jack Christiansen 19/24; Dutch Clark 7/12/19; Jap Douds 12; Bob Dove 42/78; Harry Gilmer 12; Hal Griffen 26/85; Dick Jauron 26; Dick LeBeau 24/44; Buddy Parker 4; Ray Richards 25; Joe Schmidt 56; Dick Stanfel 63; Sam Wyche 17.

Numbers of future NFL referees: Pat Harder 34; Elvin Hutchison 21; Mule Wilson 8/56.

Players who played other sports: Baseball—Matt Kinzer 1; Bert Kuczynski 20. Basketball—Lou Barle 25; Connie Berry 83; Ted Cook 20; Jack Dugger 50/74; Vern Huffman 6; John Wiethe 48/68/78. Wrestling—Alex Karras 71.

Players more famous after football: Maurice Britt, 80, won the Medal of Honor in World War II. Five Lions lost their lives in that war—Charlie Behan 85; Chuck Braidwood 20; Alex Ketzko 64; Leo Kizzire 23; Chet Wetterlund 40. Earl Maves, 12, was killed in the Korean War. Actors include Alex Karras, 71, Pat Studstill, 25, from "The Dukes of Hazard," and Bill Radovich, 28/66, who sued the NFL over blacklisting, settled for $42,500, and appeared in several movies in the 1950s.

First player to wear a number in the 70s: In 1930 Red Joseph wore 70, Lou Jennings wore 71, Chuck Braidwood wore 72, and Emil Mayer wore 73.

First player to wear a number in the 80s: In 1930 Hal Griffen and Buck Weaver wore 85 and Sod Ryan wore 83.

First player to wear a number in the 90s: In 1984, linebackers Angelo King and Kirk Dodge wore 92 and 93 respectively.

Number with most points scored: 3 with 1,326 points scored by Eddie Murray (1,113), Glenn Pressnell (99), Lloyd Cardwell (72), and Billy Gambrell (42).

Number with most yards rushing: 20 with 20,714 yards gained by Barry Sanders (15,269), Billy Sims (5,106), Glenn Pressnell (232), Jim McDonald (80), Dick Weber (10), Dick Compton (8), Byron Eby (7), Bert Kuczynski (4), and Clyde Scott (-2).

Number with most receptions: 84 with 1,257 passes caught by Herman Moore (670), Dave Middleton (153), Richard Johnson (134), Dorne Dibble (90), Bill Schroeder (72), Rob Rubick (44), Dave Diehl (32), Jesse Thompson (29), Dick Booth (10), Paul Szakash (9), Bob Cifers (4), and Barney Hafen (1).

Number with most touchdown passes: 19 with 155 touchdowns tossed by Scott Mitchell (79), Bill Munson (56), Mark Komlo (12), and Tom Dublinski (8).

Number with most interceptions: 28 with 108 passes picked off by Yale Lary (50), James Hunter (27), Mike Weger (17), Ron Rice (12), Don Panciera (1), and Herb Welch (1).

Oddity: Five Lion players have also coached the team — Hal Griffen 26/85, Dutch Clark 7/12/19, Buddy Parker 4, Harry Gilmer 12, and Joe Schmidt 56. Only the Bears with seven and the Cardinals with six have had more present or former players coach the team.

Team All-Time Numerical Roster

Those with an "r" following the year 1987 were replacement players during the players' strike. Pro Bowl and pre–1950 All Pro players for each number are in *Italics*; Hall of Famers are in **Bold** type.

0 Johnny Olszewski (FB) 1961.

1 *Ernie Caddel* (B) 1934–8, Jim Hardy (QB) 1952, Garo Yepremian (K) 1966–7, Benny Ricardo (K) 1976, 1978–9, *Tom Skladany* (P) 1980–2, Matt

Players Whose Number Is Unknown		
Walt Ambrose	(G)	1930
Koester Christensen	(E)	1930
Lee Fenner	(E)	1930
Al Graham	(G)	1930
Aaron Grant	(C)	1930
Frosty Peters	(B)	1930
Ron Shearer	(T)	1930
George Hastings	(T)	1930–1
Biff Lee	(G)	1931
Dutch Miller	(C)	1931
Chief McLain	(B)	1931
Deck Shelley	(B)	1931
Dale Waters	(T/E/G)	1931
Ben Boswell	(T)	1933
Gil LeFebvre	(B)	1935
Bill O'Neill	(B)	1935
Charlie Payne	(B)	1937
Les McDonald	(E)	1940
Tony Arena	(C)	1942
Keith Ranspot	(E)	1942
Tony Zuzzio	(G)	1942
Sam Busich	(E)	1943
Robert Derleth	(T)	1947
Bill Hillman	(B)	1947
Tommy James	(B)	1947
Floyd Rhea	(G)	1947
Hal Prescott	(E)	1949
Rick Duncan	(P/K)	1969
Alan Pringle	(K)	1975
Edgar Fields	(DE)	1981
Eric Williams	(DB)	1987
Paul Kiser	(G)	1987r
Mike Williams	(WR)	1989

Kinzer (P) 1987r, Rich Karlis (K) 1990, Don Majkowski (QB) 1995–6.

2 *Father Lumpkin* (B) 1931–2, Frank Christensen (B) 1934–7, Rip Ryan (B) 1938, Hal Brill (B) 1939, Leo Araguz (P) 2001, Nick Harris (P) 2003.

3 *Glenn Presnell* (B) 1934–6, *Lloyd Cardwell* (B) 1937–40, Billy Gambrell (WR) 1968, *Eddie Murray* (K) 1980–91, Mark Royals (P) 1995–6, Joey Harrington (QB) 2002–3.

4 Louie Long (E) 1931, *Clare Randolph* (C) 1932, *Father Lumpkin* (B) 1934, Buddy Parker (B) 1935–6, Ray Reckmack (B) 1937, Dick Nardi (B) 1938, Darrell Tully (B) 1939, *Jason Hanson* (K) 1992–2003.

5 *Clare Randolph* (C) 1931, *Ace Gutowsky* (B) 1932, 1934–8, Howie Weiss (B) 1939–40, Aveion Cason (RB) 2001.

6 John Cavosie (B) 1931–2, Curly Hinchman (B) 1934, Bill McWilliams (B) 1934, Steve Banas

(B) 1935, Tony Kaska (B) 1935, Al Richins (B) 1935, Ike Peterson (B) 1936, Vern Huffman (B) 1937–8, Rip Ryan (HB) 1939–40, Damon Tassos (G) 1945–6, Roy Zimmerman (B) 1947, John James (P) 1982, *Jim Arnold* (P) 1986–93.

7 *Ox Emerson* (G/C) 1931–2, **Dutch Clark** (B) 1934–8.

8 *Harry Ebding* (E) 1931, Mule Wilson (B) 1932, Bob Rowe (B) 1934, Pug Vaughan (B) 1935, *Bill McKalip* (E/B) 1936, Paul Szakash (B) 1938–9, Sam Tsoutsouvas (C) 1940, Vernon Turner (RB) 1993, 1995, Mike McMahon (QB) 2001–3.

9 Les Peterson (E/T) 1931, John Wager (C/G/T) 1932, *Bill Shepherd* (B) 1935–40, Paco Craig (WR) 1988, Rodney Peete (QB) 1989–93, Greg Montgomery (P) 1994.

10 *Bill McKalip* (E) 1931–2, 1934, *Ed Klewicki* (E/B) 1935–8, Gordon Gore (HB) 1939, *Bill Fisk* (E) 1940, *Lloyd Cardwell* (B) 1941–3, John Greene (E) 1944–7, Sonny Gibbs (QB) 1964, Jack Concannon (QB) 1975, Ian Sunter (K) 1976, Steve Mike-Mayer (K) 1977, Wilbur Summers (P) 1977, Scott Hunter (QB) 1979, Brendon Folmer (QB) 1987r, Kez McCorvey (WR) 1995–6, Charlie Batch (QB) 1998–2001.

11 Danny McMullen (G) 1932, *Buster Mitchell* (E/T) 1932, *Harry Ebding* (E) 1934–7, Monk Moscrip (E) 1938–9, Dick Booth (B) 1941, Emil Banjevic (B) 1942, Art Van Tone (B) 1943–5, Ed Frutig (E) 1945–6, Clyde LeForce (QB) 1947, Max Baumgartner (E) 1948, Jim Gillette (B) 1948, Clarence Self (DB) 1950–1, *Greg Landry* (QB) 1968–78, Mike Black (P) 1983–7, Andre Ware (QB) 1990–3, David Kircus (WR) 2003.

12 *Jap Douds* (T/G) 1930–1, **Dutch Clark** (B) 1932, John Schneller (E) 1934–6, *Chuck Hanneman* (E) 1937–40, Ned Mathews (B) 1941–2, Dick Mesak (T) 1945, Dick Stovall (C) 1947, Earl Maves (B) 1948, Jim Hill (B) 1951, Harry Gilmer (QB) 1955–6, Errol Mann (K) 1969–76, Larry Swider (P) 1979, Bob Thomas (K) 1982, Joe Ferguson (QB) 1985–6, Rusty Hilger (QB) 1988, Erik Kramer (QB) 1991–3, Matt Blundin (QB) 1997, Gus Frerotte (QB) 1999, Jacquez Green (WR) 2002.

13 *Buster Mitchell* (E/T) 1934–5, Del Ritchhart (C) 1936–7, Butch Morse (E) 1938, Johnny Wiatrak (C) 1939, Clem Crabtree (T/G) 1940, Joe Watt (B) 1947.

14 Dave Ribble (G/T) 1932, *George Christensen* (T/G) 1934–6,1938, Bill Feldhaus (G/T) 1937, Ray George (T) 1939, John Noppenberg (B) 1941, Johnny Hall (B) 1942, Joe Watt (B) 1948, *Bob Hoernschemeyer* (B) 1950–5, Earl Morrall (QB) 1958–64, Karl Sweetan (QB) 1966–7, Greg Barton (QB) 1969, Joe Reed (QB) 1975–9, Mike Machurek (QB) 1984, John Misko (P) 1987r, Bob Gagliano (QB) 1989–90, Frank Reich (QB) 1997–8, Ty Detmer (QB) 2001, 2003.

15 Fred Roberts (G) 1931–2, Am Rascher (T/G) 1932, Sid Wagner (G) 1936–8, Ralph Isselhardt (G) 1937, Tony Tonelli (C) 1939, Cal Thomas (G) 1940, Lou Tomasetti (B) 1941, Joe Margucci (B) 1948, Jerry Reichow (E/QB) 1956, 1959, Jim Ninowski (QB) 1960–1, George Izo (QB) 1965, Jerry DePoyster (P) 1968, *Tom Skladany* (P) 1978–9, Russell Erxleben (P) 1987, Kevin Hickman (TE) 1995, Corey Thomas (WR) 1998, Stoney Case (QB) 2000.

16 *Maury Bodenger* (G) 1931–2, *Jack Johnson* (T) 1934–40, Jim Hunnicutt (G) 1948, *Camp Wilson* (B) 1949, Dante Magnani (B) 1950, Pete D'Alonzo (B) 1951, Milt Plum (QB) 1962–7, Gary Danielson (QB) 1976–8, 1980–4, Chuck Long (QB) 1986–9, James Williams (WR) 2003.

17 John Wager (C/G) 1931, Ray Davis (OL) 1932–3, *Clare Randolph* (C) 1934–6, Dixie Stokes (C) 1937–9, Mike Corgan (B) 1943, Tony Aiello (B) 1944, *Chuck DeShane* (B) 1945–7, Mel Groomes (B) 1948–9, Gerry Krall (B) 1950, Bill Cappleman (QB) 1973, Sam Wyche (QB) 1974, Mitch Hoopes (P) 1977, Jerry Golsteyn (QB) 1979, Eric Hipple (QB) 1980–6, 1988–9, Dave Krieg (QB) 1994, John Kidd (P) 1998, Larry Foster (WR) 2000.

18 *Glenn Presnell* (B) 1931, Bob Emerick (T/G) 1934, Elmer Ward (C) 1935, Joe Kopcha (G/T) 1936, Hal Cooper (G) 1937, Bill Rogers (T) 1938–40, Andy Dudish (C) 1948, Paul Sarringhaus (B) 1948, Wally Triplett (B) 1949–50, Tobin Rote (QB) 1957–9, Warren Rabb (QB) 1960, Tom Myers (QB) 1965–6, Herman Weaver (P) 1970–6, Gene Washington (WR) 1979, John Witkowski (QB) 1984, 1988, Todd Hons (QB) 1987r, John Jett (P) 1997–8, *Desmond Howard* (WR) 1999, Eddie Drummond (WR) 2002–3.

19 **Dutch Clark** (B) 1931, *Maury Bodenger* (G) 1934, Regis Monahan (G/T) 1935–8, Chuck Maggioli (B) 1949, **Jack Christiansen** (S) 1951, Tom Dublinski (QB) 1952–4, Bill Munson (QB) 1968–75, Jeff Komlo (QB) 1979–81, Mike Prindle (K) 1987r, Scott Mitchell (QB) 1994–8, John Jett (P) 1999–2003.

20 Byron Eby (B) 1930, Stud Stennett (B) 1931, *Glenn Presnell* (B) 1932, *Ox Emerson* (G/C) 1934–7, Jim McDonald (B) 1938–9, Bert Kuczynski (E) 1943, Sonny Liles (G) 1944–5, Bob Sneddon (B) 1945, Dick Weber (B) 1945, Lloyd Wickett (T) 1946, Ted Cook (E) 1947, Clyde Scott (B) 1952, *Bill Stits* (DB) 1954–6, Jim Steffen (DB) 1959–61, Dick Compton (WR) 1962–4, **Lem Barney** (CB) 1967–77, Ken Ellis (DB) 1979, *Billy Sims* (RB) 1980–4, *Barry Sanders* (RB) 1989–98.

21 *Chuck Bennett* (B) 1930–1, Sam Knox (G/T) 1934–6, Tom Fena (G) 1937, Maury Patt (E) 1938, Elvin Hutchison (B) 1939, Jack Morlock (B) 1940, *Frankie Sinkwich* (B) 1943–4, Ted Cremer (E) 1946–7, Carl Karilivacz (DB) 1953–7, Bruce Maher (DB) 1960–7, Al Clark (DB) 1971, Jim Thrower

(DB) 1973–4, Walt Williams (DB) 1977–80, Demetrious Johnson (DB) 1983–6, Butch Woolfolk (RB) 1987, Bob McDonough (DB) 1987r, Terry Taylor (CB) 1989–91, Harry Colon (S) 1992–4, Allen Williams (RB) 1995, Jerris McPhail (RB) 1998, Greg Hill (RB) 1999, Reuben Droughns (RB) 2001, Artose Pinner (RB) 2003.

22 *Bill Glassgow* (B) 1930, Elmer Schwartz (B) 1931, Danny McMullen (G) 1932, Tom Hupke (G/T) 1934–7, *Fred Vanzo* (B) 1938–41, Paul Szakash (B) 1942, Robert Nelson (C) 1945, Clyde LeForce (QB) 1948–9, **Bobby Layne** (QB) 1950–8.

23 Cy Kahl (B) 1930–1, Tony Holm (B) 1931, Russ Lay (G) 1934, Jim Steen (T) 1935–6, Lee Kizzire (FB) 1937, Les Graham (G) 1938, Paul Moore (FB) 1940–1, Murray Evans (B) 1942–3, Jug Girard (DB/HB) 1952–6, Dave Whitsell (DB) 1958–60, Tom Watkins (RB) 1962–5, 1967, Phil Odle (WR) 1968–70, Paul Gipson (RB) 1971, Levi Johnson (DB) 1973–7, Ray Oldham (DB) 1980–2, Maurice Harvey (DB) 1983, 1987r, Arnold Brown (DB) 1985, *Mel Gray* (WR) 1989–94, Terry Fair (CB) 1998–2001, Rafael Cooper (RB) 2002, Otis Smith (CB) 2003.

24 *Father Lumpkin* (B) 1930, *Buster Mitchell* (E/T) 1931, Roy Gagnon (G) 1935, Bob Reynolds (T) 1937–8, **Whizzer White** (RB) 1940, Fred Enke (QB) 1948–9, 1951, **Jack Christiansen** (S) 1951–8, *Dick LeBeau* (DB) 1959–60, Bruce McLenna (HB) 1966, *Mel Farr* (RB) 1967–73, Dexter Bussey (RB) 1974–84, Mike Whited (T) 1980, Alvin Moore (RB) 1985–6, Jason Phillips (WR) 1989–90, Melvin Jenkins (CB) 1991–3, Milton Mack (CB) 1994, Richard Woodley (CB) 1996, Kevin Abrams (CB) 1997–9, Todd Lyght (CB) 2001–2, Shawn Bryson (RB) 2003.

25 Chief McLain (B) 1930–1, Gene Alford (B) 1931–2, Ray Richards (G) 1934, Red Stacy (T/G) 1935–7, *George Christensen* (T/G) 1937, Lou Barle (B) 1938, Johnny Hackenbruck (T) 1940, Bill Callihan (B) 1941–5, Aldo Forte (G) 1946, *Jim David* (DB) 1952–9, *Pat Studstill* (WR/P) 1961–7, Earl McCullough (WR) 1968–73, Horace King (RB) 1975–83, Oscar Smith (RB) 1986, Karl Bernard (RB) 1987, Anthony Fields (DB) 1987r, Paul Palmer (RB) 1989, Sheldon White (CB) 1990–2, Greg Jeffries (CB) 1993–8, Tyree Talton (DB) 1999, Jeremy Lincoln (CB) 2000, Lamont Warren (RB) 2001–2, Corey Harris (CB) 2002–3.

26 Tiny Lewis (B) 1930, Hal Griffen (C/T) 1932, Doug Nott (B) 1935, Bill Feldhaus (G/T) 1938–40, Gene Gedman (HB) 1953, 1956–8, Mike Bass (DB) 1967, *Dick Jauron* (DB) 1973–7, Tony Leonard (DB) 1978–9, Hector Gray (DB) 1981–3, William Frizzell (S) 1984–5, Carl Painter (RB) 1988–9, Eric Lynch (RB) 1992–6, Brock Olivo (FB) 1998–2001, Eric Davis (DB) 2002, Rod Babers (DB) 2003.

27 Ray Novotny (B) 1930, *George Christensen* (T/G) 1931–2, Chuck Bernard (C) 1934, Butch Morse (E) 1935–7, 1940 Tony Matisi (T) 1938, Bobby Thompson (DB) 1964–8, Charlie Potts (DB) 1972, Miller Farr (DB) 1973, Reggie Pierson (DB) 1976, Maurice Tyler (DB) 1976, Luther Bradley (DB) 1978–81, Bobby Watkins (DB) 1982–8, Darren Carrington (S) 1990, Junior Robinson (CB) 1992, Jocelyn Borgella (CB) 1994, 1996, Mark Carrier (S) 1997–9, Jimmy Wyrick (CB) 2001–3.

28 Vin Schleusner (T) 1931, *Bill Radovich* (G) 1938–40, Larry Ellis (B) 1948, Frank Tripucka (QB) 1949, Don Panciera (B) 1950, **Yale Lary** (DB/P) 1952–3, 1956–64, Dave Middleton (E) 1955, Mike Weger (DB) 1967–73, 1975, James Hunter (DB) 1976–82, Wilbert Montgomery (RB) 1985, Chris Sheffield (DB) 1987, Lou Brock (DB) 1988, Jerry Woods (DB) 1989, Herb Welch (DB) 1990–1, Ron Rice (S) 1996–2001, Bracey Walker (S) 2002–3.

29 Jack Mackenroth (C) 1938, Jim Austin (E) 1939, Elmer Madarik (B) 1945, Vince Mazza (E) 1946, Ben Davis (DB) 1974–6, Mike Burns (DB) 1978, Bruce McNorton (DB) 1982–90, Sean Vanhorse (CB) 1995, Harry Colon (S) 1997, Kywin Supernaw (S) 1998–2000, Chris Cash (CB) 2002.

30 John Schneller (E) 1933, *Wilbur White* (B) 1936, **Alex Wojciechowicz** (C) 1938–40, Steve Belichick (B) 1941, Gene Spangler (B) 1946, Elmer Madarik (B) 1948, Ken Roskie (B) 1948, Tom Tracy (RB) 1956–7, **Ollie Matson** (RB) 1963, Pat Batten (FB) 1964, Larry Watkins (RB) 1969, Jim Hooks (RB) 1973–6, Nat Terry (DB) 1978, Ray Williams (RB) 1980, James Jones (RB) 1983–8, Nick Kowgios (RB) 1987r, Cedric Jackson (RB) 1991, Cory Schlesinger (FB) 1995–2003.

31 Bob Armstrong (T/G) 1931–2, Harry Hopp (B) 1941, Frank Grigonis (B) 1942, Ralph Jones (E) 1946, Ralph Heywood (E) 1947, Amos Marsh (RB) 1965–7, Leon Jenkins (DB) 1972, Jimmie Jones (RB) 1974, Randy Rich (DB) 1977, Tony Sumler (DB) 1978, Ken Callicutt (RB) 1978–82, Ken Jenkins (RB) 1983–4, Devon Mitchell (DB) 1986, 1988, Cleve Wester (RB) 1987r, Derrick Moore (RB) 1993–4, Corey Raymond (CB) 1995–7, Andre Dixon (CB) 1999, J.B. Brown (CB) 1999–2000, Mario Bates (RB) 2000, Aveion Cason (RB) 2002, Avon Cobourne (RB) 2003.

32 Dave Diehl (E) 1939–40, Lloyd Parsons (B) 1941, John Polanski (B) 1942, Bob Brumley (B) 1945, Lew Carpenter (RB/E) 1953, Joe Don Looney (FB) 1965–6, Lenny Dunlap (DB) 1975, Rick Kane (RB) 1977–83, 1985, Garry James (RB) 1986–7, Jessie Clark (RB) 1988, Bruce Alexander (CB) 1989–91, Willie Clay (S) 1992–5, Bryant Westbrook (CB) 1997–2001, Richard Huntley (RB) 2002, *Dre Bly* (CB) 2003.

33 *Harry Ebding* (E) 1932–3, Harry Smith (T) 1940, Harry Seltzer (B) 1942, Jim Thomason (B)

1945, Walt Vezmar (T) 1946–7, Steve Sucic (B) 1947–8, John Panelli (B) 1949–50, Ollie Cline (B) 1950–3, Bill Bowman (FB) 1954, 1956, *Nick Pietrosante* (FB) 1959–65, Bobby Thompson (RB) 1975–6, Bruce Rhodes (DB) 1978, William Graham (DB) 1982–7, Dexter Clark (DB) 1987r, Garry James (RB) 1988, Don Overton (RB) 1991–2, Tim McKyer (CB) 1993, Glyn Milburn (WR) 1996–7, Sedrick Irvin (RB) 1999–2000, Olandis Gary (RB) 2003.

34 Phil Martinovich (G/K) 1939, Bill Callihan (B) 1940, Elmer Hackney (B) 1942–6, George Hekkers (T) 1947, *Pat Harder* (B) 1951–3, Lew Carpenter (RB/E) 1954–5, Ken Webb (RB) 1958–62, Nick Ryder (FB) 1963–4, Jim Todd (HB) 1966, Mickey Zofko (RB) 1971–4, Eddie Payton (RB) 1977, Prentice McCray (DB) 1980, Dan Wagoner (DB) 1982–4, A.J. Jones (RB) 1985, James Griffin (DB) 1986–9, Creig Federico (DB) 1987r, James Wilder (RB) 1990, Ed Tillison (RB) 1992, Ron Rivers (RB) 1995–9, James Stewart (RB) 2000–2.

35 Bill Moore (E) 1939, Stillman Rouse (E) 1940, **Bill Dudley** (RB) 1947, 1949, *Camp Wilson* (B) 1948, George Karstens (C) 1949, Art Murakowski (LB) 1951, **John Henry Johnson** (FB) 1957–9, Tom Nowatzke (FB) 1965–9, Leon Crosswhite (RB) 1973–4, Jimmy Allen (DB) 1980–1, Alvin Hall (DB) 1981–5, 1987r, William White (S) 1988–93, Robert Bailey (CB) 1998–9, 2001, Jimmy Wyrick (CB) 2000, Andre Goodman (CB) 2002–3.

36 Dwight Sloan (B) 1939–40, Joe Bumgardner (HB) 1948, John Hollar (B) 1949, Bill Schroll (B) 1950, Bob L. Smith (B) 1953–4, *Steve Owens* (RB) 1970–4, Bo Robinson (RB) 1979–80, Mike Meade (RB) 1984–5, Herman Hunter (RB) 1986, *Bennie Blades* (S) 1988–96, Travis Reece (FB) 1998–9, Stephen Trejo (FB) 2001–3.

37 Gene Alford (B) 1933, Johnny Pingel (B) 1939, Cotton Price (QB) 1940, **Doak Walker** (RB/K) 1950–5.

38 *Maury Bodenger* (G) 1933, Tony Furst (T) 1940, Milt Piepul (B) 1941, Jim Mello (B) 1949, Bill Triplett (RB) 1968–72, Lawrence Gaines (RB) 1976, 1978–9, Vince Thompson (RB) 1981, 1983, Scott Williams (RB) 1986–8, Kevin Scott (CB) 1991–3, Ryan Stewart (S) 1996, Daryl Porter (CB) 1997, Marquis Walker (CB) 2000, Marty Carter (S) 2001, Jacoby Shepherd (CB) 2003.

39 Ramey Hunter (E) 1933, Bob DeFruiter (B) 1947, Pete D'Alonzo (B) 1952, **Hugh McElhenny** (HB) 1964, Bill Frohbose (DB) 1974, Leonard Thompson (WR/HB) 1975–86, Ray Crockett (CB) 1989–93, Van Malone (S) 1994–7, Lamar Campbell (S) 1998–2002, Doug Evans (CB) 2003.

40 Bull Wesley (C/G) 1930, Bob Winslow (E) 1940, Chet Wetterlund (B) 1942, Roy Stuart (T) 1943, Vince Mazza (E) 1945, Elmer Madarik (B) 1946–7, Charley Sarratt (B) 1948, *J. Bob Smith* (HB) 1949–54, Hopalong Cassady (HB) 1956–61,

1963, Willie Walker (WR) 1966, Nick Eddy (RB) 1968–70, 1972, Doug Wyatt (DB) 1974, Charlie West (DB) 1974–7, Jimmy Allen (DB) 1978–9, Billy Cesare (DB) 1982, Gardner Williams (DB) 1984, Duane Galloway (DB) 1985–7, Butch Woolfolk (RB) 1988, Reggie Barrett (WR) 1991–2, Robert Massey (CB) 1994–5, Dwayne Harper (CB) 1999, Chidi Iwuoma (CB) 2001, Alex Molden (CB) 2003, Paul Smith (FB) 2003.

41 Richard Brown (C) 1930, Harry Thayer (G/T) 1933, Terry Barr (WR) 1957–65, J.D. Hill (WR) 1976, James Caver (DB) 1983, Ricky Smith (DB) 1987, Darnell Walker (CB) 2000, Donovan Greer (CB) 2002, Leonard Myers (CB) 2003.

42 *Buster Mitchell* (E/T) 1933, Ray Hamilton (E) 1939, Tony Calvelli (C/G) 1940, Cotton Price (B) 1941, Mickey Sanzotta (B) 1942, Ned Mathews (B) 1943, Jackie Lowther (B) 1944, Andy Farkas (B) 1945, Jim Jones (B) 1946, Bob Ivory (G) 1947, Bill Ward (G) 1947, George Grimes (B) 1948, Lindy Pearson (B) 1950–2, Bob Dove (E/G) 1953, Don McIlhenny (RB) 1956, Marv Brown (RB) 1957, Altie Taylor (RB) 1969–75, Reggie Pinkney (DB) 1977–8, Nate Allen (DB) 1979, Robert Woods (WR) 1979, John Bostic (DB) 1985–7, Clarence Chapman (DB) 1985, Gary Ellerson (RB) 1987, Randall Morris (RB) 1988, Mike Brim (CB) 1989, Chris Oldham (CB) 1990, D.J. Dozier (RB) 1991, Ryan Stewart (S) 1997–2000, Tommy Bennett (S) 2001, Terrence Holt (S) 2003.

43 *Clare Randolph* (C) 1933, Harry Speelman (G) 1940, Dick Kercher (HB) 1954, Gary Lowe (DB) 1957–64, Jimmy Hill (DB) 1965, Bobby Smith (DB) 1965–6, Dave Kopay (RB) 1968, Andy Bolton (RB) 1976–8, Don Patterson (DB) 1979, Al Latimer (DB) 1982–4, Donnie Elder (CB) 1986, Ivan Hicks (DB) 1987r, Jerry Holmes (DB) 1988–9, Gary Anderson (RB) 1993.

44 John Wager (C/G) 1933, Steve Maronic (T) 1940, **Whizzer White** (B) 1941, Harry Hopp (B) 1942–3, Dave Ryan (B) 1945–7, Ben Chase (G) 1947, **Bill Dudley** (RB) 1948, *Don Doll* (DB) 1949–51, Lee Riley (DB) 1955, *Dick LeBeau* (DB) 1961–72, George Farmer (WR) 1975, Bob Picard (WR) 1976, Marv Hubbard (RB) 1977, Ernie Jackson (DB) 1979, Dave Parkin (DB) 1979, Wayne Smith (DB) 1980–2, Dave D'Addido (RB) 1984, Ivory Sully (DB) 1987, Tony Dollinger (RB) 1987r, John Miller (DB) 1989–90, Brad Ford (CB) 1996, Tommy Vardell (FB) 1997–8, Corwin Brown (S) 1999–2000, Julius Curry (DB) 2003.

45 *Ox Emerson* (G/C) 1933, Bob Keene (C) 1943–5, Ted Grefe (E) 1945, Larry Sartori (G) 1945, Pete Kmetovic (B) 1947, Byron Bailey (B) 1952, Dan Lewis (RB) 1958–64, Bobby Felts (RB) 1965–7, Bobby Williams (DB) 1969–71, Al Randolph (DB) 1972, Jim O'Brien (WR/K) 1973, Ray Jarvis (WR) 1974–8, Jeff Delaney (DB) 1981, Raphel Cherry (DB) 1987–8, Eric Truvillion

(WR) 1987r, Ed Smith (TE) 1999, Kurt Schulz (S) 2000–1, Brian Walker (S) 2002–3.

46 Jim Bowdoin (G) 1933, Billy Jefferson (B) 1941, Tom Colella (B) 1942–3, Harry Bolton (T) 1944, Joe Manzo (T) 1945, Leon Fichman (T) 1946–7, Reed Nilson (C) 1947, Bob Smith (HB) 1949, Fred Enke (QB) 1950–1, Larry Ferguson (RB) 1963, Jim Kearney (DB) 1965–6, Jim Welch (DB) 1968, Bruce Maxwell (RB) 1970, Rudy Redmond (DB) 1972, Doug Wyatt (DB) 1973, Carl Capria (DB) 1974, Doug Jones (DB) 1979, Jimmy Stewart (DB) 1979, Rick Porter (RB) 1982, Stan Edwards (RB) 1987r, Derek Tennell (TE) 1991, John Waerig (TE) 2001.

47 John Burleson (T/G) 1933, *George Christensen* (T/G) 1933, *Jim Martin* (LB/K) 1956–61, Wayne Rasmussen (DB) 1964–72, John Arnold (WR) 1979–80, Rod Hill (DB) 1986, Steve Hirsch (DB) 1987r, LeRoy Irvin (DB) 1990, Ryan McNeil (CB) 1993–7, Ray McElroy (CB) 2001.

48 *George Christensen* (T/G) 1933, *Socko Wiethe* (G) 1940, Chuck Fenenbock (B) 1943, 1945, Ken Reese (B) 1947, Jim Hill (B) 1952, Dom Fucci (DB) 1955, Dick Woit (DB) 1955, Tom Vaughn (DB) 1965–71, Willie Germany (DB) 1973, Eddie Lewis (DB) 1979–80, Robbie Martin (WR) 1981, Thomas Beer (LB) 1994–5, Steve Brooks (TE) 1996.

49 Earl Elser (T) 1933, Johnnie Robinson (DB) 1966, Larry Walton (WR) 1969–74, 1976, Tony Paige (FB) 1987–9, Ty Hallock (TE) 1993–4, Eric Stocz (TE) 1996–7, Matt Murphy (TE) 2002.

50 Fred Roberts (G) 1930, John Cavosie (B) 1933, **Alex Wojciechowicz** (C) 1941–6, Jack Dugger (E) 1947, Keith Flowers (C) 1952, *Charlie Ane* (C/T) 1953–9, Bob Scholtz (C/T) 1960–4, Mike Alford (C) 1966, *Paul Naumoff* (LB) 1970–8, Eddie Cole (LB) 1979–80, Terry Tautolo (LB) 1981–2, 1984, August Curly (LB) 1983–6, Danny Lockett (LB) 1987–8, Ernie Adams (LB) 1987r, Toby Caston (LB) 1989–93, Michael Brooks (LB) 1996, Ben Hanks (LB) 1997, Chris Claiborne (LB) 1999–2002, Earl Holmes (LB) 2003.

51 Ernie Meyer (G) 1930, Gene Smith (G) 1930, *Ernie Caddel* (B) 1933, Robert Nelson (C) 1941, Sloko Gill (G) 1942, Rex Williams (C) 1945, Les Lear (B) 1947, Joe Watson (C) 1950, Vince Banonis (C) 1951–3, Bob Whitlow (C) 1961–5, Lou Slaby (LB) 1966, Bill Swain (LB) 1968–9, Ken Lee (LB) 1971, Adrian Young (LB) 1972, Larry Ball (LB) 1975, James Harrell (LB) 1979–83, 1985–6, David Jones (C/G) 1984–5, Shelton Robinson (LB) 1986–8, Niko Noga (LB) 1989–91, Antonio London (LB) 1993, Broderick Thomas (LB) 1994, Thomas Beer (LB) 1996, Greg Engel (C) 1999, Dominic Raiola (C) 2001–3.

52 Ebby DeWeese (G) 1930, Red Davis (B) 1933, Dunc Obee (C) 1941, John Schiechl (C) 1942, Gerry Conlee (C) 1943, Freeman Rexer (E)

1944, George Sirochman (G) 1944, Dom Sigillo (T) 1945, Ed Stacco (T) 1947, Andy Miketa (C) 1954–5, **Frank Gatski** (C) 1957, Dave Lloyd (LB) 1962, Monte Lee (LB) 1963–4, Bill Cody (LB) 1966, Bill Cottrell (T/G) 1967–70, Jim Laslavic (LB) 1973–7, Dave Washington (LB) 1978–9, Stan White (LB) 1980–2, Steve Mott (C) 1983–8, Mark Brown (LB) 1990–1, John Derby (LB) 1992, Scott Kowalkowski (LB) 1994–2001, James Davis (LB) 2003.

53 Bill Fleckenstein (OL) 1930, Carroll Ringwalt (C/G) 1930, Howard Duncan (C) 1948, Bob Pifferini (C) 1949, Jack Simmons (C) 1949–50, *Lavern Torgeson* (LB) 1951–4, Bill Glass (DE) 1958–61, Dennis Gaubatz (LB) 1963–4, *Mike Lucci* (LB) 1965–73, Willie Brock (C) 1978, John Sokolosky (C) 1978, Jon Brooks (LB) 1979, Garry Cobb (LB) 1980–4, *Kevin Glover* (C) 1985–97, Tony Office (LB) 1987r, Rob Fredrickson (LB) 1998, Andre Collins (LB) 1999.

54 Gene Alford (B) 1933, Ted Topor (LB) 1955, Max Messner (LB) 1960–3, *Ed Flanagan* (C) 1965–74, Mike McGraw (LB) 1977, Larry Tearry (C) 1978–9, Roosevelt Barnes (LB) 1982–5, James Johnson (LB) 1986, Tom Boyd (LB) 1987, *Chris Spielman* (LB) 1988–95, Matt Russell (LB) 1997, Barrett Green (LB) 2000–3.

55 *Ace Gutowsky* (B) 1933, Ray Clemons (G) 1939, Ivan Schottel (B) 1946, Cecil Souders (E) 1947, Roger Harding (C) 1948, Bap Manzini (C) 1948, Jack Lininger (C) 1951, *Wayne Walker* (LB) 1958–72, Ed O'Neil (LB) 1974–9, Tom Turnure (C/G) 1980–3, *Michael Cofer* (LB) 1985–92, Antonio London (LB) 1994–7, Allen Aldridge (LB) 1998–2001, Donte' Curry (LB) 2002–3.

56 Mule Wilson (B) 1933, **Joe Schmidt** (LB) 1953–65, *Pat Swilling* (LB) 1993–4.

57 *Father Lumpkin* (B) 1933, Glen Morris (E) 1940, Merv Pregulman (G) 1948, Jack Lininger (C) 1950, Leon Cunningham (LB) 1955, Bo Lusk (C) 1956, Roger Zatkoff (LB) 1957–8, Carl Brettschneider (LB) 1960–3, Ron Goovert (LB) 1967, Terry Miller (LB) 1970, Jim Teal (LB) 1973, Garth Ten Napel (LB) 1976–7, Dan Dickel (LB) 1978, Ken Fantetti (LB) 1979–85, Vernon Maxwell (LB) 1986–7, Dave Ahrens (LB) 1988, Victor Jones (LB) 1989–94, *Stephen Boyd* (LB) 1995–2001, Josh Thornhill (LB) 2002, Jody Littleton (LB) 2003.

58 Walt Yowarsky (DE) 1955, *Paul Naumoff* (LB) 1967–9, Bill Saul (LB) 1970, Gene Hamlin (C) 1972, Rick Ogle (LB) 1972, Mike Hennigan (LB) 1973–5, Tony Daykin (LB) 1977–8, Dennis Franks (C) 1979, Derrel Luce (LB) 1980, Steve Doig (LB) 1982–4, Carl Carr (LB) 1987r, George Jamison (LB) 1988–93, 1997–8, Clint Kriewaldt (LB) 1999–2002, Wali Rainier (LB) 2003.

59 Gene Alford (B) 1933, Ernie Clark (LB) 1963–7, Charlie Weaver (LB) 1971–81, Jimmy Williams (LB) 1982–90, Anthony Bell (LB) 1991,

Tracy Scroggins (LB) 1992–3, Mike Johnson (LB) 1994–5, Reggie Brown (LB) 1996–7, Kevin O'Neill (LB) 1998–2000, Khari Samuel (LB) 2001, Jeff Gooch (LB) 2002–3.

60 Dud Harris (T) 1930, *Glenn Presnell* (B) 1933, Larry Sartori (G) 1942, Joe D'Orazio (T) 1944, *Chuck DeShane* (B) 1948–9, Joe Soboleski (T) 1950, Bruce Womack (G) 1951, Dick Flanagan (LB) 1952, Jim Salsbury (G/T) 1955–6, Karl Koepfer (G) 1958, Bob Grottkau (G) 1959–60, Doug Van Horn (G/T) 1966, Guy Dennis (G/C) 1973–5, R.W. Hicks (C) 1975, Gary Anderson (G) 1977–8, *Al Baker* (DE) 1978–82, Tom Turnure (C/G) 1985–6, Reggie Rogers (DE) 1987–8, Chuck Steele (C) 1987r, Mike Utley (G/T) 1990–1, Paul Spicer (DE) 1999.

61 Vin Schleusner (T) 1930, *Augie Lio* (G) 1941–2, Wayne Clark (E) 1944, *Jim Martin* (LB/K) 1955, Bob Whitlow (C) 1962, Lucien Reeberg (T) 1963, Chuck Sieminski (DT) 1968, Fred Rothwell (C) 1974, Homer Elias (G/T) 1978–84, Willie Parker (C/G) 1980, Ray Snell (G/T) 1985, Scott Barrows (G/C) 1986–8, Trevor Matich (C) 1989, Jim Pyne (C) 1998, Ray Brown (T/G) 2002–3.

62 Duke Hanny (E/T) 1930, Spider Johnson (T) 1930, Jack Mattiford (G) 1941, Sonny Liles (G) 1943, Ed Eiden (B) 1944, Bill Rogers (T) 1944, Cotton Price (B) 1945, Mickey Sanzotta (B) 1946, Bill O'Brien (B) 1947, Elmer Jones (G) 1948, *Jim Martin* (LB/K) 1951–4, George Atkins (G) 1955, Ted Karras (G) 1965, Ed Mooney (LB) 1968–71, Lynn Boden (G/T) 1975–8, Don Morrison (T/C) 1979, John Mohring (LB) 1980, Curtis Green (DE) 1981–9, Dennis McKnight (C/G) 1990, Blake Miller (C) 1992, Tony Semple (G) 1995–2002.

63 Babe Lyon (T/G) 1930, Bill Miklich (B) 1948, Mario DeMarco (G) 1949, Bob Momsen (G) 1951, *Dick Stanfel* (G) 1952–5, Chuck Walton (G) 1967–74, Jon Morris (C) 1975–7, Donnie Hickman (G) 1978, Mike Montler (C/T) 1978, Garry Cobb (LB) 1979, Alva Liles (NT) 1980, Mike McCoy (DT) 1980, Dave Simmons (LB) 1980, Martin Moss (DE) 1982–5, Steve Kenney (G/T) 1986, Dennis McKnight (C/G) 1992, Mark Rodenhauser (C) 1993–4, James Hall (DE) 2000.

64 Steve Maronic (T) 1939, Alex Ketzko (T) 1943, Buzz Trebotich (B) 1944–5, Howie Brown (G) 1948–50, Dan Rogas (G) 1951, Doug Hogland (G/T) 1958, Mike Rabold (G) 1959, John Lomakoski (T) 1962, Gordon Jolley (T/G) 1972–5, Mel Mitchell (G/C) 1977, Dan Gray (DT) 1978, John Mendenhall (DE) 1980, Larry Lee (G/C) 1981–5, Eric Sanders (T/G) 1986–92, Joe Felton (G) 1987r, Jeff Hartings (G) 1996–2000, Tyrone Hopson (G) 2002.

65 Tony Calvelli (C) 1939, *Stan Batinski* (G) 1941, 1943–7, *Les Bingaman* (DG) 1948–54, Roger LaLonde (DT) 1964, Dave Thompson (C/T) 1971–3, Ken Long (G) 1976, Amos Fowler (C/G) 1978–

84, Mark Stevenson (G/C) 1985, Patrick Cain (C/G) 1987r, Eric Andolsek (G) 1988–91, Kerlin Blaise (G) 1999–2002.

66 Elmer Schaake (B) 1933, *Bill Radovich* (G) 1941, Bill Kennedy (E) 1942, Tony Rubino (G) 1943, 1946, Lake Roberson (E) 1945, *Camp Wilson* (B) 1946–7, Dick Stovall (C) 1948, *Harley Sewell* (G) 1953–62, Jim Simon (G/T) 1964–5, Bob Kowalkowski (G) 1966–76, Karl Chandler (C/G) 1978–9, Tommie Ginn (G/C) 1980–1, Burton Lawless (G) 1980, *Michael Cofer* (LB) 1983–4, Leon Evans (DE) 1985–6, Shawn Bouwens (G) 1991–4, Hessley Hempstead (G) 1995–7, Brenden Stai (G) 2001.

67 Merv Pregulman (G) 1947, Bill Ward (G) 1948–9, Barry French (G) 1951, Stan Campbell (G) 1952, 1955–8, Grady Alderman (T/G) 1960, Dick Mills (G) 1961–2, Wally Hilgenberg (LB) 1964–6, Rocky Rasley (G) 1969–70, 1972–3, Daryl White (G) 1974, Donnie Green (T) 1978, Wally Pesuit (G/C) 1979–80, Rod Walters (G/T) 1980, Don Greco (G) 1982–5, Greg Orton (G) 1987r, Ken Dallafior (G/C) 1989–92, Dave Richards (G) 1993, Doug Widell (G) 1994–5, Travis Kirschke (DT) 1997, 1999–2002.

68 *Socko Wiethe* (G) 1941–2, Lyle Rockenbach (G) 1943, Tom Kennedy (T) 1944, Larry Knorr (C) 1945, Tony Rubino (G) 1946, Gene Cronin (DE) 1956, Frank Gallagher (G) 1967–72, Mark Markovich (C/G) 1976–7, Steve Baack (DT) 1984–7, Jerry Quaerna (T) 1987r, Leonard Burton (C) 1992, Antwan Lake (DT) 2002.

69 Charles Benson (DE) 1987r, Mike Utley (G/T) 1989, Roman Fortin (C) 1991, Mike Hinnant (TE) 1992.

70 Red Joseph (E) 1930, John Tripson (T) 1941, George Hekkers (T) 1948–9, Gus Cifelli (T) 1950–2, Ray Krouse (DT) 1956–7, Willie McClung (T) 1960–1, Daryl Sanders (T) 1963–6, Denis Moore (DT) 1967–9, Larry Woods (DT) 1971–2, Billy Howard (DT) 1974–6, Bill Fifer (T) 1978, *Keith Dorney* (T/G) 1979–80, 1982–7, Chris Gambol (T/G) 1989, Dan Owens (DE) 1990, Jeff Jones (T) 1995–6, Andre Johnson (T) 1998, Josh Lovelady (G) 2002–3.

71 Lou Jennings (C/E) 1930, Ted Pavelec (G) 1941–3, Ed Opalewski (T) 1943–4, Michael Kostiuk (T) 1945, *Russ Thomas* (T) 1946–9, Chet Bulger (T/G) 1950, *Alex Karras* (DT) 1958–62, 1964–70, Bob Tatarek (DT) 1972, Craig Hertwig (T) 1975–7, Dave Gallagher (DE) 1978–9, Tom Tuinei (DT) 1980, *Keith Dorney* (T/G) 1981, Steve Furness (DE) 1981, Rich Strenger (T) 1983–7, Chris Geile (G) 1987r, Gary Hadd (DT) 1988, Larry Tharpe (T) 1992–3, 1997–8, Zefross Moss (T) 1995–6, Aaron Gibson (T) 2000–1.

72 Chuck Braidwood (E) 1930, Clem Crabtree (T) 1941, Hank Goodman (T) 1942, Floyd Jaszewski (T) 1950–1, Gil Mains (DT) 1954–61, Floyd Peters (DT) 1963, J.D. Smith (G) 1964, 1966, Dan Goich (DT) 1969–70, Ernie Price (DE) 1973–8, Bill Cooke (DT) 1978, Cleveland Elam (DT) 1979, Vern Holland (T) 1980, Chris Dieterich (T/G) 1980–6, Jim Warne (T) 1987r, Curt Singer (T) 1988, Jack Linn (G/T) 1992–3, Ray Roberts (T) 1996–2000, Dan Wilkinson (DT) 2003.

73 Emil Mayer (E/T) 1930, Tony Furst (T) 1941, 1944, George Speth (T) 1942, *Augie Lio* (G) 1943, *Bill Radovich* (G) 1945, Jim Montgomery (T) 1946, Elmer Jones (G) 1947, Jack Simmons (C) 1949, *Thurman McGraw* (T) 1950–4, Ken Russell (T) 1957–9, Ollie Spencer (T/G) 1959–61, Paul Ward (DT) 1962, Roger Shoals (T) 1965–70, Bob Bell (DT) 1971–3, Russ Bolinger (G/T) 1976–82, Mike Dawson (DT) 1983, Donald Laster (T) 1983, Harvey Salem (T) 1986–90, Jeff Kacmarek (NT) 1987r, David Lutz (G/T) 1993–5, Juan Roque (T) 1997, Darius Holland (DT) 1998, Stockar McDougle (T) 2000–3.

74 Jack Dugger (E) 1948, Lloyd McDermott (T) 1950, Dick Flanagan (LB) 1950–1, Bob Miller (T) 1952–8, Jim Weatherall (DT) 1959–60, Paul Ward (DT) 1961, Mike Bundra (DT) 1962–3, Larry Hand (DE) 1965–77, Brad Oates (T/G) 1978, Joe Ehrmann (DT) 1981–2, Mike Fanning (DT) 1983, Joe Milinichik (G) 1987–9, Mike Compton (C/G) 1993, Chris Harrison (G) 1996, Juan Roque (T) 1999, James Atkins (G) 2000.

75 Cal Thomas (G) 1939, *Emil Uremovich* (T) 1941–2, Al Kaporch (T) 1944–5, Bob Wiese (B) 1947–8, John Prchlik (T) 1949–53, Ollie Spencer (T/G) 1956, *John Gordy* (G) 1957, 1959–67, Jim Yarbrough (T) 1969–77, Dave Pureifory (DT) 1978–82, *Lomas Brown* (T) 1985–95, Tony Ramirez (T) 1997–9, Matt Joyce (G) 2001–3.

76 Andy Logan (T) 1941, Tom Chantiles (T) 1942, Al Kaporch (T) 1943, Bill DeCorrevont (B) 1946, Paul Briggs (T) 1948, Mike Roussos (T) 1949, John Treadaway (T) 1949, **Lou Creekmur** (T/G) 1950–9, *Roger Brown* (DT) 1960–6, *Rocky Freitas* (T) 1968–77, Karl Baldischwiler (T) 1978–82, Eric Williams (DT) 1984–9, Scott Conover (T) 1991–6, Barrett Brooks (T) 1999–2000, Jeff Backus (T) 2001–3.

77 Luke Lindon (T) 1944–5, Garvin Mugg (T) 1945, John Sanchez (T) 1947, Dale Hanson (T) 1948, Ben Paolucci (DT) 1959, Dan LaRose (DE) 1961–3, Randy Winkler (T/G) 1967, Dick Evey (DT/DE) 1971, John Gordon (DT) 1972, Mike Haggerty (T) 1973, John Woodcock (DT) 1976–8, 1980, Curley Culp (DT) 1980–1, Keith Ferguson (DE) 1985–90, Rick Johnson (T) 1987r, Mike Compton (C/G) 1994–2000, Anthony Herron (DE) 2001, Kerlin Blaise (T) 2003.

78 *Socko Wiethe* (G) 1939, Alex Schibanoff (T) 1942, Ernie Rosteck (C) 1943–4, Frank Kring (B) 1945, Kelley Mote (E) 1947, Ollie Spencer (OL) 1953, Bob Dove (E/G) 1954, *Darris McCord* (DE)

1955–67, John Baker (DE) 1968, *Doug English* (DT) 1975–85, Cory Redding (DE) 2003.

79 Stan Anderson (E) 1941, Alex Schibanoff (T) 1941, Gerry Perry (DT) 1954–9, John Gonzaga (T/G) 1961–5, Charlie Bradshaw (T) 1967–8, Ray Parson (T) 1971, Don Croft (DT) 1976, Dave Simonson (T) 1977, *Bill Gay* (DE) 1979–87, Darryl Milburn (DE) 1991, Bill Fralic (G) 1993, Eric Beverly (C/T) 1998–2003.

80 Maurice Britt (E) 1941, *Bill Fisk* (E) 1942–3, Walt Jurkiewicz (C) 1946, Ralph Heywood (E) 1948, *Cloyce Box* (E) 1949–50, 1952–4, Jerry Reichow (E/QB) 1957, *Jim Gibbons* (TE) 1958–68, Dave Haverdick (DT) 1970, Herb Orvis (DE/DT) 1972–7, Ulysses Norris (TE) 1979–83, Carl Bland (WR) 1984–8, Darrell Grymes (WR) 1987r, John Ford (WR) 1989, Brett Perriman (WR) 1991–6, Tommie Boyd (WR) 1997–8, Iheanyi Uwaezuoke (WR) 1999, *Desmond Howard* (WR) 2000–2, Charles Rogers (WR) 2003.

81 *Bill Fisk* (E) 1941, Joe Stringfellow (E) 1942, Bob Layden (E) 1943, Dale Hansen (T) 1944–5, Joe Krol (B) 1945, *Emil Uremovich* (T) 1945–6, Joe Margucci (B) 1947, John Greene (E) 1948–50, Rex Grossman (B) 1950, Dan Sandifer (DB) 1950, Bill Swiacki (E) 1951–2, Tom Rychlec (E) 1958, **Night Train Lane** (CB) 1960–5, Bill Malinchak (WR) 1966–9, Charlie Brown (WR) 1970, John Hilton (TE) 1972–3, Thomas Blair (TE) 1974, John McMakin (TE) 1975, *David Hill* (TE) 1976–82, Reese McCall (TE) 1983–5, Jimmie Giles (TE) 1986–7, Mark Lewis (TE) 1987–8, Mark Witte (TE) 1987r, Stephen Starring (WR) 1988, Stacey Mobley (WR) 1989, Mike Farr (WR) 1990–2, Marty Thompson (TE) 1993, Anthony Carter (WR) 1994–5, Pete Chryplewicz (TE) 1997–9, Kevin Hickman (TE) 1998, Alfred Pupunu (TE) 2000, Larry Foster (WR) 2001, Az-Zahir Hakim (WR) 2002–3.

82 John Jett (E) 1941, Perry Scott (E) 1942, Jack Matheson (E) 1943–6, Mitch Olenski (T) 1947, Cecil Souders (E) 1948–9, Leon Hart (E/FB) 1950–7, Harlon Hill (E) 1962, Al Greer (E) 1963, Jerry Rush (DT) 1965–71, Ken Sanders (DE) 1972–9, Pete Mandley (WR) 1984–8, Mark Wheeler (TE) 1987r, Robert Clark (WR) 1989–91, Thomas McLemore (TE) 1992, Rodney Holman (TE) 1993–5, Derek Price (TE) 1996, Kevin Hickman (TE) 1997, Germane Crowell (WR) 1998–2002, Casey Fitzsimmons (TE) 2003.

83 Sod Ryan (T) 1930, Connie Mack Berry (E) 1939, *Riley Matheson* (G) 1943, Paul Blessing (E) 1944, Frank Szymanski (C) 1945–7, Kelley Mote (E) 1949, Jim Doran (E) 1951–9, Jim Simon (G/T) 1963, Bill Quinlan (DE) 1964, Ron Kramer (TE) 1965, Jerry Mazzanti (DE) 1966, Mike Melinkovich (DE) 1967, Greg Kent (T) 1968, Jim Mitchell (DE/DT) 1970–7, *Bill Gay* (DE) 1978, Robbie Martin (WR) 1981–4, James McDonald (TE) 1985, Gary Lee (WR) 1987–8, Melvin Hoover (WR)

1987r, Troy Johnson (WR) 1989, Aubrey Matthews (WR) 1990–6, Kez McCorvey (WR) 1997, Brian Stablein (WR) 1998–2000, Bert Emanuel (WR) 2001, Pete Mitchell (TE) 2001, John Owens (TE) 2002–3.

84 Paul Szakash (B) 1941, Dave Diehl (E) 1944–5, Dick Booth (B) 1945, Arch Milano (E) 1945, Bob Cifers (B) 1946, Barney Hafen (E) 1949–50, Dorne Dibble (E) 1951, 1954–5, Pat Summerall (E/K) 1952, Gil Mains (DT) 1953, Hal Turner (WR) 1954, Dave Middleton (E) 1956–60, Leo Sugar (DE) 1962, Hugh McInnis (TE) 1964, Joe Robb (DE) 1968–71, Joe Schmiesing (DT) 1972, John Small (DT) 1973–4, Jesse Thompson (WR) 1978, 1980, Rob Rubick (TE) 1982–8, Jerry Diorio (TE) 1987r, Richard Johnson (WR) 1989–90, *Herman Moore* (WR) 1991–2001, Bill Schroeder (WR) 2002–3.

85 Hal Griffen (C/T) 1930, Buck Weaver (G) 1930, Chuck Behan (E) 1942, Fred Dawley (B) 1944, Joel McCoy (B) 1946, Ted Cremer (E) 1948, Abe Addams (E) 1949, Sam Goldman (E) 1949, Ed Berrang (E) 1951, Sonny Gandee (E) 1952–6, Gene Cronin (DE) 1957–9, Sam Williams (DE) 1960–1, Larry Vargo (DB) 1962–3, Lew Kamanu (DE) 1967–8, Jery Zawadzkas (TE) 1967, Chuck Hughes (WR) 1970–1.

86 Owen Thuerk (E) 1941, Gran Harrison (E) 1942, Ben Hightower (E) 1943, *Bob Westfall* (B) 1944–7, Al Russas (T) 1949, Blaine Earon (E) 1952–3, Bob Long (LB) 1955–9, Tom Hall (WR) 1962–3, John McCambridge (DE) 1967, Al Barnes (WR) 1972–3, Bob Pickard (WR) 1974, Marlin Briscoe (WR) 1975, Jon Staggers (WR) 1975, J.D. Hill (WR) 1976–7, Willie McGee (WR) 1978, Mike Friede (WR) 1980, Mark Nichols (WR) 1981–5, 1987, Danny Bradley (RB) 1987r, Willie Green (WR) 1991–3, Troy Stradford (WR) 1992, *David Sloan* (TE) 1995–2001, Mikhael Ricks (TE) 2002–3.

87 Bob Mann (E) 1948–9, Kelley Mote (E) 1948, Dorne Dibble (E) 1953–4, 1956–7, Perry Richards (E) 1958, Glenn Davis (WR) 1960–1, Warren Wells (WR) 1964, John Henderson (WR) 1965–7, Craig Cotton (TE) 1969–72, Bill Larson (TE) 1977, Freddie Scott (WR) 1978–83, David Lewis (TE) 1984–6, Vyto Kab (TE) 1987, Derrick Ramsey (TE) 1987, Gilvanni Johnson (WR) 1987r, Pat Carter (TE) 1988, Walter Stanley (WR) 1989, Jeff Campbell (WR) 1990–3, Johnnie Morton (WR) 1994–2001, Larry Foster (WR) 2002, Shawn Jefferson (WR) 2003.

88 *Chuck Hanneman* (E) 1941, Larry Knorr (C) 1942, Jim Callahan (B) 1946, Ivan Schottel (B) 1948, Ollie Poole (E) 1949, Jim Cain (E) 1950, 1953–5, Steve Junker (E) 1957, 1959–60, Gene

Cook (E) 1959, Sam Williams (DE) 1962–65, Ron Kramer (TE) 1966–7, *Charlie Sanders* (TE) 1968–77, Scotty Anderson (WR) 2001–3.

89 Dick Rifenberg (E) 1950, Walt Jenkins (DE) 1955, *Gail Cogdill* (WR) 1960–8, John Wright (WR) 1969, Ron Jessie (WR) 1971–4, Dennis Franklin (WR) 1975–6, Luther Blue (WR) 1977–9, Tracy Porter (WR) 1981–2, Jeff Chadwick (WR) 1983–9, Keith McDonald (WR) 1989, Terry Greer (WR) 1990, Dave Little (TE) 1991, Eugene Riley (TE) 1991, Jimmie Johnson (TE) 1992–3, Ron Hall (TE) 1994–5, Pete Metzelaars (TE) 1996–7, Walter Rasby (TE) 1998–2000, Brad Banta (TE) 2001, 2003.

90 Robert Thompson (LB) 1987r, Keith Karpinski (LB) 1989, Dan Owens (DE) 1991–5, 1998–9, Keith Washington (DE) 1996, Alonzo Spellman (DE) 2001.

91 Mark Duckens (DE) 1990, *Robert Porcher* (DE) 1992–2003.

92 Angelo King (LB) 1984–6, 1987r, Marc Spindler (DE) 1990–2, 1997–8, Mack Travis (DT) 1993, Shane Dronett (DE) 1996, Mike Pringley (DE) 1999, Shaun Rogers (DT) 2001–3.

93 Kirk Dodge (LB) 1984, *Jerry Ball* (DT) 1987–92, Tim Ross (LB) 1987r, Marc Spindler (DE) 1993–4, Kerwin Waldroup (DE) 1996–8, Kelvin Pritchett (DT) 1999–2003.

94 Mark Hicks (LB) 1987r, Thomas Strauthers (DE) 1988, Byron Darby (DE/NT) 1989, Jackie Cline (DE) 1990, Kelvin Pritchett (DT) 1991–4, *Luther Elliss* (DE) 1995–2003.

95 Kurt Allerman (LB) 1985, George Jamison (LB) 1987, Steve Boadway (LB) 1987r, Mark Brown (LB) 1989, Troy Johnson (LB) 1992, Mike Wells (DE) 1994–7, Mike Chalenski (DT) 1998, Jared DeVries (DE) 1999–2003.

96 June James (LB) 1985, Paul Butcher (LB) 1986–8, Lawrence Pete (NT) 1989–93, Shane Bonham (DT) 1994–7, Henry Taylor (DT) 1998, James Hall (DE) 2001–3.

97 Dan Bunz (LB) 1985, Dan Saleaumua (DT) 1987–8, George McDuffie (DE) 1987r, Kevin Brooks (DE) 1989–90, Jeff Hunter (DE) 1990–2, Mike McDonald (LB) 1992, Darryl Ford (LB) 1992–3, Tracy Scroggins (LB) 1994–2001, Boss Bailey (LB) 2003.

98 Vernon Maxwell (LB) 1985, Dennis Gibson (LB) 1987–93, Jerome Davis (NT) 1987r, Henry Thomas (DT) 1995–6, Don Sasa (DT) 1998, Marvin Thomas (DE) 1998, James Jones (DT) 1999–2000, Kalimba Edwards (DE) 2002–3.

99 Bob Beemer (DE) 1987r, Stuart Tolle (NT) 1987r, James Cribbs (DE) 1989, Tracy Hayworth (LB) 1990–5, Pepper Johnson (LB) 1996, Richard Jordan (LB) 1997–9, Brian Williams (LB) 2001–2.

GREEN BAY PACKERS

The franchise: Beginning as a local independent team in 1919, the Green Bay Packers predated the American Professional Football Association that was formed in 1920 and was renamed the National Football League two years later. Initially, the Packers were corporately sponsored by the Acme Packing Company when they joined the fledgling league in 1921. The franchise was revoked by the league at the end of the year for rules violations, but was reinstated in Curly Lambeau's name for 1922. Undercapitalized, the club was sinking financially when *Green Bay Press Gazette* publisher Andrew Turnbull became involved late in the 1922 season. Under his ingenious and dedicated leadership, the team began a stock sale that ultimately would convert the team to a publicly-owned non-profit corporation. While there would be additional financial crises in the team's future that would lead to four future stock sales, the one-time town team has survived for over 80 years and is the last remaining link to the league's early days as a shifting conglomeration of squads representing Midwestern small towns. It continues to be the only publicly-owned franchise in major league sports. With that, it also has been one of the most successful teams on the field, boasting a league high 12 NFL titles that include three Super Bowl championships. The Packers are the only team to win three consecutive championships and they have done it twice, first under Curly Lambeau from 1929 to 1931 and then again under Vince Lombardi from 1965 to 1967.

Lambeau, who coached the team for its first 30 years, was noted as a devotee of passing in a grind-it-out era. His first three championships featured the league's best receiver and most colorful character, Johnny Blood; his final three championships featured the greatest receiver in league history before Jerry Rice, Don Hutson, who set several records that were not exceeded for 30–40 years. Once Hutson retired, Lambeau could not replace him, and the team faded. Curly was soon fired, but the team would not recover for another decade until Vince Lombardi arrived with his grind-it-out style that contrasted with the pass-happy late 1950s.

Lombardi's Packers would win five titles in seven years in the 1960s and featured an incredible 11 Hall of Famers, including Bart Starr at quarterback and Ray Nitschke at middle linebacker. They were a machine like no other in league history who culminated their run by winning three NFL titles in a row and the first two Super Bowls. Their excellence would stand in sharp contrast to the 25 years with only two playoff appearances that followed.

That changed when Ron Wolf was hired as general manager in 1991. He hired Mike Holmgren as coach, traded for Brett Favre as quarterback and signed Reggie White as a free agent. In the next decade, the Packers would reach the postseason eight times and the Super Bowl twice, winning the title in 1996. The team is now run by coach and GM Mike Sherman, a Holmgren protégé, and in the coming years will face a monumental challenge — replacing Favre, the greatest Packer in the team's long, rich history.

Origin of name: Predating their NFL membership, the Packers were named after the Indian Packing Company (later bought out by the Acme Packing Company) that employed team captain Curly Lambeau and paid for the first uniforms in 1919.

Time till first championship: 9 years (1929).

Time since last championship: 8 years (1996).

Retired numbers: 3 for Hall of Fame back Tony Canadeo; 14 for Hall of Fame end Don Hutson; 15 for Hall of Fame quarterback Bart Starr; 66 for Hall of Fame linebacker Ray Nitschke. The 92 "jersey" was retired for Reggie White.

Other numbers worn by these players: Starr also wore 16 in 1956 and Ray Nitschke wore 33 in 1958.

Record by Decade

	Regular Season			Postseason		
	Won	Lost	Tied	Won	Lost	Championships
1920s	61	25	13			1929
1930s	86	35	4	2	1	1930, 1931, 1936, 1939
1940s	62	44	4	1	1	1944
1950s	39	79	2			
1960s	96	37	5	9	1	1961, 1962, 1965, 1966, 1967
1970s	57	82	5	0	1	
1980s	65	84	3	1	1	
1990s	93	67		8	5	1996
2000s	43	21		2	3	
All-Time	602	472	36	23	13	12

Winning seasons: 50. Losing seasons: 26. .500 seasons: 7.

Those who wore retired numbers after the honored player: 3 was worn by back Roy McKay while Canadeo was serving in World War II in 1944–5 and by kicker Ben Agajanian in 1961 even after the number was officially retired; 66 was worn by linebacker Paul Rudzinski in 1978–9 and nose tackle Mike Lewis in 1980.

Numbers that should be retired: Curly Lambeau has the team's stadium named after him, but since he is the only Packer ever to wear number 1, it should be officially retired. No one will ever wear number 4 after Brett Favre retires.

Owned numbers: Curly Lambeau is the only player ever to wear 1, and it probably will remain so.

Numbers worn by Hall of Famers: Herb Adderley 26; Tony Canadeo 3; Willie Davis 87; Len Ford 83; Forrest Gregg 75; Ted Hendricks 56; Arnie Herber 12/16/17/26/38/41/45/68; Clarke Hinkle 27/30/33/39/41/45/48; Paul Hornung 5; Cal Hubbard 27/38/39/40/51; Don Hutson 14; Henry Jordan 74; Walt Kiesling 49/60; Curly Lambeau 1/14/20/42; James Lofton 80; Johnny Blood McNally 14/20/24/26/55; Mike Michalske 19/24/28/30/31/33/36/40/63; Ray Nitschke 33/66; Jim Ringo 51; Bart Starr 15/16; Jan Stenerud 10; Jim Taylor 31; Emlen Tunnell 45; Willie Wood 24.

Star power: Keith Jackson took 88 from Terry Mickens; Reggie White took 92 from John Jurkovic; Terry Glenn took 83 from David Martin. Ben Agajanian wore 3 despite it being retired for Tony Canadeo.

Star eclipsed: Ted Hendricks wore 56 because Clarence Williams wore 83; Des-

Coaches

	Years	Record	Playoffs
Curly Lambeau (6)	1921–49	209–104–21	3–2
Gene Ronzani	1950–3	14–31–1	
Hugh Devore/Scooter McLean	1953	0–2	
Lisle Blackbourn	1954–7	17–31	
Scooter McLean	1958	1–10–1	
Vince Lombardi (5)	1959–67	89–29–4	9–1
Phil Bengtson	1968–70	20–21–1	
Dan Devine	1971–4	25–27–4	0–1
Bart Starr	1975–83	52–76–3	1–1
Forrest Gregg	1984–7	25–37–1	
Lindy Infante	1988–91	24–40	
Mike Holmgren (1)	1992–8	75–37	8–5
Ray Rhodes	1999	8–8	
Mike Sherman	2000–3	43–21	2–3

(Championships in parentheses)

mond Howard wore 82 because Tyrone Davis wore 81. Jan Stenerud wore 10 because 3 was retired for Tony Canadeo. William Henderson wore 30 till Doug Evans, 33, left.

Numbers with most great players: 24 was worn by three Hall of Famers (Mike Michalske, Johnny Blood McNally and Willie Wood) as well as solid safety Johnnie Gray; 33 was worn by three Hall of Famers (Clarke Hinkle, Mike Michalske and Ray Nitschke) plus All Pro tackle Bill Kern and fullback William Henderson; 45 was worn by three Hall of Famers (Arnie Herber, Clarke Hinkle and Emlen Tunnell) plus All-Pros Verne Lewellen and Dick Wildung.

Worst represented number: The best player to wear 67 was washed-up defensive tackle Russell Maryland; 98 and 99 are best represented by mediocre defensive linemen Gabe Wilkins and Don Davey respectively.

Number worn by the most players: 23 has been worn by 35 players.

Player who wore the most numbers: Hall of Fame guard Mike Michalske wore nine different numbers—19/24/28/30/31/33/36/40/63. Hall of Fame tailback Arnie Herber wore eight different numbers—12/16/17/26/38/41/45/68. Hall of Fame fullback Clarke Hinkle wore seven different numbers—27/30/33/39/41/45/48. Six numbers were worn by Hank Bruder 5/13/18/27/47/55; Art Bultman 17/32/33/38/45/52; Red Dunn 7/11/15/16/17; Lon Evans 17/25/39/46/51/65; Herdis McCrary 19/28/29/38/43/53; Bob Monnett 3/5/12/18/50/66; and Claude Perry 24/26/27/32/37/50. Five numbers were worn by Frank Butler 26/35/48/59/60; Jug Earp 7/9/29/38/39; Milt Gantenbein 21/22/30/46/47; Cal Hubbard 27/38/39/40/51; Verne Lewellen 4/21/31/45/46; Johnny Blood McNally 14/20/24/26/55; Tom Nash 19/21/26/35/37; Al Rose 34/37/47/49/52; and Ade Schwammel 40/50/53/57/58.

Longest tenure wearing a number: Hall of Fame Bart Starr wore 15 for 16 years from 1956 to 1971.

Number worn by first ever draft pick: Guard Russ Letlow, the Packers first pick in 1936, wore 46 and 62.

Biggest draft busts: Quarterback Stan Heath, 39, was selected twice by Green Bay,

in 1948 and then as the second selection in 1949. He played one season in Green Bay, completing 24.5 percent of his passes and throwing 1 td against 14 interceptions. In 1959, the Packers took quarterback Randy Duncan as the first selection, but Duncan went to Canada instead before later surfacing briefly as a backup in the AFL. More recently, quarterback Rich Campbell, 19, was selected sixth in 1981 and completed 45 percent of his passes for three tds and nine interceptions in four years; tackle Tony Mandarich, 77, selected second in 1989 washed out of the league quickly; and Jamal Reynolds, 99, selected tenth in 2001 has been inactive more than he has been on the active roster.

Number worn by oldest player: 42 year old kicker Ben Agajanian wore 3 in 1961 even though it had already been retired ten years before. Other 40 year olds include kicker Jan Stenerud, 10, and quarterback Zeke Bratkowski, 12.

Cameos: Hall of Famers—Walt Kiesling 49/60; Ted Hendricks 56; Len Ford 83. All-Stars—Beattie Feathers 3; Vince Ferragamo 5; Dick Gordon 7/85; Ward Cuff 21; Paul Christman 28; Ray Bray 63; Ernie McMillan 70; Mark Clayton 83; Steve McMichael 90.

Ones who got away: Tim Brown 25; Walt Michaels 35; Art Hunter 70; Ben Davidson 72.

Least popular numbers: 0 has never been worn. 1 and 2 have only been by one player each.

Last number to be originated: 96 was first worn by replacement player Tony Leiker in 1987 and by defensive end Shawn Patterson in 1988.

Longest dormant number: Neither 1 nor 2 has been worn in 77 years since 1926.

Triskaidekaphobia notes: 13 has been worn by a number of talented players for Green Bay—early backs Marty Norton, Ed Kotal and Hank Bruder as well as skilled placekickers Chester Marcol and Chris Jacke.

Shared numbers: 13 was worn by two placekickers Chester Marcol and Chris Jacke; 14 was worn by the one-time leading receiver in league history (Johnny Blood) and by Don Hutson who demolished Blood's records; 22

was worn by the best end in the 1920s Lavvie Dilweg and by his All-Pro successor Milt Gantenbein; 30 was worn by Hall of Fame fullback Clarke Hinkle and Pro Bowl running back Ahman Green; 42 was worn by All Pro runner John Brockington and by All Pro safety Darren Sharper; 44 was worn by giant tackle Baby Ray, All Pro defensive back Bobby Dillon and running back Donny Anderson; 84 was worn by two All Pro receivers Carroll Dale and, years later, Sterling Sharpe; 86 was worn by three star receivers: Bill Howton in the 1950s, Boyd Dowler in the 1960s and Antonio Freeman in the 1990s; 89 was worn by All Pro linebacker Dave Robinson and Pro Bowl tight end Mark Chmura.

Continuity: Hall of Famer Curly Lambeau was replaced in 20 by Hall of Famer Johnny Blood; All Pro end Lavvie Dilweg was replaced in 22 by star end Milt Gantenbein; All Pro receiver Billy Howton was replaced in 86 by clutch flanker Boyd Dowler.

Discontinuity: All Pro Fred Carr was followed in 53 by fellow linebacker Francis Chesley; Hall of Famer Forrest Gregg was followed in 75 by kicker Lou Michaels; Hall of Famer James Lofton was followed in 80 by fellow receiver Frankie Neal; Hall of Famer Willie Davis was followed in 87 by fellow defensive end Marty Amsler.

Quarterback numbers over 19: 20, Joe Francis; 21, John Hadl; 27, Jack Jacobs; 28 Paul Christman, Bobby Thomason; 38 Tobin Rote; 39, Stan Heath; 76, Tom O'Malley.

Number of first black player: Former Lion Bob Mann first wore 31 in 1951 and then switched to 87 the next year. Tom Johnson was the first black to be drafted by the Packers, and he wore 72 in 1952. The team's first black quarterback Charley Brackins wore 15 in 1955. Other minorities include early Hispanic center Waldo Don Carlos who wore 24 and two gay players who came out after they retired, Dave Kopay (40) and Esera Tualo (98).

Family Connections

Brothers

Bud Svendsen	C	1937, 1939	7/53/66
George Svendsen	C	1935–7, 1940–1	43/66
Bob Kahler	B	1942–4	8
Royal Kahler	T	1942	72
Carl Mulleneaux	E	1938–41, 1945–6	19
Lee Mulleneaux	C	1938	18
Walt Michaels	LB	1951	35
Lou Michaels	K	1971	75
Dick Zoll	G	1939	57
Carl Zoll	G	1921–2	NA
Martin Zoll	G	1921	NA

Fathers and sons

Elijah Pitts	RB	1961–9, 1971	22
Ron Pitts	DB	1988–90	28
Jim Flanigan	LB	1967–70	55
Jim Flanigan Jr.	DT	2001	75

Grandfather and grandson

Lavvie Dilweg	E	1927–34	22/61
Anthony Dilweg	QB	1989–90	8

Numbers of future NFL head coaches: Norm Barry (NA), Tom Bettis 58/65, Hank Bullough 61/67, Jim Crowley unknown, Chuck Drulis 18, Forrest Gregg 75, Dutch Hendrian (NA), Cecil Isbell 17, Walt Kiesling 49/60, Curly Lambeau 1/14/20/42, Johnny Blood McNally 14/20/24/26/55, Walt Michaels 35, Elijah Pitts 22, Jim Ringo 51, Clive Rush 81, John Sandusky 77, Bart Starr 15/16.

Numbers of future NFL referees: Lon Evans 17/25/39/46/51/65, Verne Lewellen 4/21/31/45/46, Steve Pritko 23, Herman Rohrig 8/80, George Vergara 6, and Mule Wilson 17.

Players who played other sports: Baseball — Cliff Aberson 78, Larry Bettencourt 29/30/39, Tom Brown 40, Pid Purdy 5/7/18, Red Smith 7/15/19/28 and Cal Hubbard 27/38/29/40/51 who was an umpire. Basketball — Connie Berry 37, Ted Cook 48, Dick Evans 22/53, Len Ford 83, Ted Fritsch 64, Joel Mason 7, George Svendsen 43/66, Tillie Voss (NA), and Ron Widby 20. Wrestling — Hank Bruder 5/13/18/27/47/55, Buckets Goldenberg 21/43/44/51, Bill Kuusisto 45/52, Bill Lee 40, Steve McMichael 90, and even Reggie White 92.

Players more famous after football: Lavvie Dilweg, 22/61, U.S. congressman; Verne Lewellen, 4/21/31/45/46, local district attorney; Lon Evans, 17/25/39/46/51/65, sheriff of Dallas, Texas during the Kennedy assassination; Carlos Brown, 19, actor (as Alan Autry); Tim Brown, 25, actor; Ben Davidson, 72, actor; Ernie Smith, 45/61, actor; Dutch Hendrian, no number, actor; Russ Saunders, 18, model for Tommy Trojan statue on USC campus; Max McGee, 85, broadcaster and founder of Chi Chi's restaurant chain.

First player to wear a number in the 70s: In 1942 tackles Royal Kahler and Milburn "Tiny" Croft wore 72 and 75 respectively.

First player to wear a number in the 80s: End Ed Frutig wore 80 in 1945.

First player to wear a number in the 90s: Guard Leon Manley wore 90 in 1950.

Number with most points scored: 13 with 1,419 points scored by Chris Jacke (820), Chester Marcol (521), Hank Bruder (60), Ed Kotal (12) and Don Horn (6).

Number with most yards rushing: 31 with 13,625 yards rushed by Jim Taylor (8,207), Garry Ellis (3,826), Fred Cone (966), Perry Williams (329), Jim Culbreath (153), Allen Rice (100), Buford McGee (19), Bill Boedecker (16), Bob Mann (9).

Number with most receptions: 86 with 1,419 passes received by Boyd Dowler (448), Antonio Freeman (431), Bill Howton (303), Ed West (202), John Hilton (25), Don Summer (7), Mike Donohoe (2) and Pete Lammons (1).

Number with most touchdown passes: 4 with 346 touchdown passes thrown all by Brett Favre.

Number with most interceptions: 24 with 111 interceptions picked off by Willie Wood (48), Johnnie Gray (22) Joe Laws (18), Johnny Blood McNally (10), Antuan Edwards (7), Mossy Cade (5) and Van Jakes (1).

Oddity: The Packers are the only team whose stadium is named after a former NFL player, Curly Lambeau —1/14/20/42. Also, the famous statue of #88 catching a pass that stood in front of the Packer Hall of Fame building for close to 30 years is a number that has been worn by 11 tight ends and nine wide receivers, including three All-Pros.

The Packers did not start using numbers until 1925. These players never had a number:

Nate Abrams	(E)	1921
Norm Barry	(B)	1921
Walt Buland	(T/G)	1924
Joe Carey	(G/T)	1921
James Cook	(G)	1921
Frank Coughlin	(T)	1921
Tommy Cronin	(B)	1922
Paul Davis	(G/E)	1922
Wilfred Duford	(E/B)	1924
Bill DuMoe	(E)	1921
Pat Dunningan	(T/G)	1922
Gus Gardella	(FB)	1922
Buck Gavin	(B)	1923
Eddie Glick	(B)	1922
Jack Gray	(E)	1923
Hal Hansen	(B/E)	1923
Dave Hayes	(E)	1921–2
Norb Hayes	(E/B)	1923
Les Hearden	(B)	1924
Dutch Hendrian	(B)	1924
Lynn Howard	(E/B)	1921–2
Emmett Keefe	(G)	1921
Fee Klaus	(C	1921
Adolph Kliebhan	(B)	1921
Wally Ladrow	(B)	1921
Dutch Lauer	(B)	1922
Wes Leaper	(E)	1923
Dewey Lyle	(G/T)	1922
Grover Malone	(B)	1921
Herman Martell	(E)	1921
Ray McLean	(B)	1921
Stan Mills	(B/E)	1922–3
Jab Murray	(T/E)	1921–4
Romanus Nadolney	(G/T)	1922
Walter Niemann	(C	1922–4
Rip Owens	(G)	1922
Sammy Powers	(G/T)	1921
Pete Regnier	(B)	1922
Art Schmaehl	(B)	1921
Joe Secord	(C	1922
Rex Smith	(E)	1922
Warren Smith	(G)	1921
Claude Taugher	(B)	1922
Eddie Usher	(B)	1922, 1924
Walter Voss	(E/T)	1924
Buff Wagner	(B)	1921
Lyle Wheeler	(E)	1921–3
Milt Wilson	(G)	1921
Carl Zoll	(G)	1922
Martin Zoll	(G)	1921

```
┌─────────────────────────────────────────┐
│          Players Whose Number            │
│              Is Unknown                   │
│                                           │
│  Adolph Bieberstein      (G)     1926    │
│  Jim Crowley             (B)     1925    │
└─────────────────────────────────────────┘
```

Team All-Time Numerical Roster

Those with an "r" following the year 1987 were replacement players during the players' strike. Pro Bowl and pre–1950 All Pro players for each number are in *Italics*; Hall of Famers are in **Bold** type.

1 **Curly Lambeau** (B) 1925–26.

2 Charles Mathys (B) 1925–6.

3 Hector Cyre (T) 1926, Bob Monnett (B) 1935, Paul Miller (B) 1936–8, Beattie Feathers (B) 1940, **Tony Canadeo** (B) 1941–4, 1946–52, Roy McKay (B) 1944–5, Ben Agajanian (K) 1961.

4 *Verne Lewellen* (B) 1925–6, Herm Schneidman (B) 1935–7, Chuck Fusina (QB) 1986, Dale Dawson (K) 1988, Mike Norseth (QB) 1990, *Brett Favre* (QB) 1992–2003.

5 Dick O'Donnell (E) 1925–6, Pid Purdy (B) 1927, Roy Baker (B) 1928, Bob Monnett (B) 1936–7, Hank Bruder (B) 1938–9, *Ray Riddick* (E) 1940–2, **Paul Hornung** (HB) 1957–66, Vince Ferragamo (QB) 1986, *Don Majkowski* (QB) 1987, Willie Gilius (QB) 1987r, Curtis Burrow (K) 1988.

6 George Vergara (E) 1925, Dick Flaherty (E) 1926, Mal Bross (B) 1927.

7 *Jug Earp* (C) 1925–26, Pid Purdy (B) 1927, Red Smith (G) 1927, *Red Dunn* (B) 1930, Earl Svendsen (C) 1937, Ed Jankowski (B) 1938–41, Joel Mason (E) 1942–5, *Walt Schlinkman* (FB) 1946–49, Ace Loomis (B) 1951, Dick Gordon (WR) 1973, *Don Majkowski* (QB) 1988–92, Sean Landeta (P) 1998, Chris Hanson (P) 1999, Danny Wuerffel (QB) 2000.

8 Walt Lejeune (T) 1925–6, Andy Uram (B) 1938, Herm Rohrig (B) 1941, Bob Kahler (B) 1942–4, Russ Mosley (B) 1945–6, Bob Forte (B) 1946–50, 1952–3, Ray Pelfrey (E) 1951–2, Max Zendejas (K) 1987–8, Anthony Dilweg (QB) 1989–90, Mark Brunell (QB) 1993–4, Ryan Longwell (K) 1997–2003.

9 Whitey Woodin (G) 1925–6, *Jug Earp* (C) 1928, Fritz Borak (E) 1938, Dean Dorsey (K) 1988, Bryan Wagner (P) 1992–3, Jim McMahon (QB) 1995–6, Dirk Borgognone (K) 1995, Josh Bidwell (P) 2000–3.

10 Cub Buck (T) 1925, Tiny Cahoon (T) 1926, *Ed Kotal* (B) 1927–29, Dave Zuidmulder (B) 1930, Roger Grove (B) 1934, Perry Moss (QB) 1948, Babe Parilli (QB) 1957–8, John Roach (QB) 1961–3, Dennis Claridge (QB) 1965, Billy Stevens (QB)

1968–9, Frank Patrick (QB) 1970–2, Jack Concannon (QB) 1974, Lynn Dickey (QB) 1976–7, 1979, **Jan Stenerud** (K) 1980–83, Bill Troup (QB) 1980, Al Del Greco (K) 1984–7, Blair Kiel (QB) 1990–1, Louis Aguiar (P) 1999.

11 Wes Carlson (G) 1926, Walter McGaw (G) 1926, *Red Dunn* (B) 1927–8, Elbert Bloodgood (B) 1930, Roger Grove (B) 1931–5, Bernie Scherer (E) 1937, Leo Katalinas (T) 1938, Rick Norton (QB) 1970, Dave Beverly (P) 1975–81, Steve Broussard (P) 1975, Eddie Garcia (K) 1983–4, Joe Prokop (P) 1985, Alan Risher (QB) 1987r, Ty Detmer (QB) 1993–4, Matt Hasselbeck (QB) 1999–2000.

12 *George Abramson* (G) 1925, Rudy Rosatti (T) 1926, Tom Hearden (B) 1927–8, Roy Baker (B) 1928, Dave Zuidmulder (B) 1929, **Arnie Herber** (B) 1930, Frank Baker (E) 1931, Bob Monnett (B) 1935–6, Zeke Bratkowski (QB) 1963–8, 1971, Jim Del Gaizo (QB) 1973, John Hadl (QB) 1974, Don Milan (QB) 1975, Brian Dowling (QB) 1977, Lynn Dickey (QB) 1980–85, T.J. Rubley (QB) 1995, Craig Nall (QB) 2002.

13 Marty Norton (B) 1925, *Ed Kotal* (B) 1926, Hank Bruder (B) 1931–3, Don Horn (QB) 1967–70, *Chester Marcol* (K) 1972–80, Bucky Scribner (P) 1983–4, Bill Renner (P) 1986–7, Chris Jacke (K) 1989–96, Steve Bono (K) 1997.

14 Moose Gardner (G) 1925–6, **Curly Lambeau** (B) 1927, Slick Lollar (FB) 1928, Don Hill (B) 1929, Merle Zuver (C) 1930, Paul Fitzgibbon (B) 1931–2, **Johnny Blood** (B) 1933, **Don Hutson** (E) 1935–45.

15 Myrt Basing (B) 1925–6, Rex Enright (FB) 1927, Paul Minick (G) 1928, Red Smith (G) 1929, *Red Dunn* (B) 1931, Dexter Shelley (B) 1932, Paul Young (C) 1933, Swede Johnston (FB) 1935–8, Lou Brock (B) 1940, Del Lyman (T) 1941, Hal Hhite (E) 1942, Ray Frankowski (G) 1945, Earl Bennett (G) 1946, Damon Tassos (G) 1947–9, Dick Afflis (G) 1951, Babe Parilli (QB) 1952–3, Bob Garrett (QB) 1954, Charley Brackins (QB) 1955, Paul Held (QB) 1955, **Bart Starr** (QB) 1956–71.

16 Jack Harris (B) 1925–6, Gil Skeate (FB) 1927, *Red Dunn* (B) 1929, Don Hill (B) 1929, Bill Davenport (HB) 1931, *Joe Zeller* (G) 1932, **Arnie Herber** (B) 1933, Bernie Scherer (E) 1937, John Biolo (G) 1939, Lou Brock (B) 1941–5, Charles Mitchell (B) 1946, Jim Gillette (B) 1947, Bob Cifers (B) 1949, *Ab Wimberly* (E) 1950–1, Wally Dreyer (B) 1950, Babe Parilli (QB) 1953, **Bart Starr** (QB) 1956, Lamar McHan (QB) 1960, Claudis James (WR) 1967, Scott Hunter (QB) 1971–3, Randy Johnson (QB) 1976, Tom Birney (K) 1980, Ray Stachowicz (P) 1981–2, Randy Wright (QB) 1984–8, Paul McJulien (P) 1991–2, Russell Copeland (WR) 1998, Craig Nall (QB) 2003.

17 Fred Larson (C) 1925, *Carl Lidberg* (FB)

1926, Boob Darling (C) 1927–8, Roy Baker (B) 1929, *Red Dunn* (B) 1930, Faye Wilson (B) 1931, *Lon Evans* (G) 1933, Art Bultman (C) 1934, *George Sauer* (B) 1937, *Cecil Isbell* (B) 1938–42, Ray Wheba (E) 1944, Mike Bucchianeri (G) 1945, Merv Pregulman (G) 1946, Ed Cody (B) 1947–8, Carl Schuette (C/DB) 1950–1, Lamar McHan (QB) 1959–60, Travis Williams (KR) 1967, Jerry Tagge (QB) 1972–4, David Whitehurst (QB) 1977–83, Don Bracken (QB) 1985–90, Don King (DB) 1987r, Craig Hentrich (P) 1994–7.

18 Elmer Wilkens (E) 1925, Pid Purdy (B) 1926, Bob Rose (C) 1926, George Tuttle (E) 1927, Billy Young (G) 1929, Paul Fitzgibbon (B) 1930, Russ Saunders (FB) 1931, Bob Monnett (B) 1933, Hank Bruder (B) 1936–8, Lee Mulleneaux (C) 1938, Leo Disend (T) 1940, Bob Shiry (T) 1940, Fred Vant Hull (G) 1942, Tony Falkenstein (FB) 1943, Bob Kercher (DE) 1944, Alex Urban (E) 1944, Ken Keuper (B) 1945–7, Ted Cremer (E) 1948, Lou Ferry (T) 1949, Chuck Drulis (G) 1950, Charley Robinson (G) 1951, *Tobin Rote* (QB) 1952–6, John Roach (QB) 1961, Ken Duncan (P) 1971, Randy Walker (P) 1974, Joe Danelo (K) 1975, Randy Vataha (WR) 1977, Jim Zorn (QB) 1985, Joe Shield (QB) 1986, Chuck Washington (DB) 1987r, Mike Tomczak (QB) 1991, Doug Pederson (QB) 1996–8, 2001–3.

19 Jack McAuliffe (HB) 1926, Frank Mayer (G) 1927, Red Smith (G) 1927, Jim Bowdoin (G) 1928, *Tom Nash* (E) 1929, Frank Hanney (T) 1930, Hurdis McCrary (FB) 1931, **Mike Michalske** (G) 1932, Norm Mott (B) 1932, Al Norgard (E) 1934, **Arnie Herber** (B) 1937, *Carl Mulleneaux* (E) 1938–41, 1945–6, Art Albrecht (T) 1942, Mike Bucchianeri (G) 1944–5, *Ray Riddick* (E) 1946, Bob McDougal (B) 1947, Ralph Olsen (E) 1949, Al Baldwin (E) 1950, Dan Orlich (E) 1951, Carlos Brown (QB) 1975–6, Bobby Douglass (QB) 1978, Tom Birney (K) 1979–80, Steve Pisarkiewicz (QB) 1980, Rich Campbell (QB) 1981–4, Bill Schroeder (WR) 1994.

20 Rex Enright (FB) 1926, Dick O'Donnell (E) 1927–8, **Curly Lambeau** (B) 1929–30, **Johnny Blood** (B) 1931–2, Norm Greeney (G) 1933, Charley Caspar (B) 1934, Dan Sandifer (DB) 1952, Byron Bailey (HB) 1953, Don Miller (B) 1954, Billy Bookout (DB) 1955–6, John Petitbon (DB) 1957, Joe Francis (QB) 1958–9, Ron Widby (P) 1972–3, Walter Tullis (WR) 1978, Wylie Turner (DB) 1979–80, Del Williams (RB) 1981, Chet Winters (RB) 1983, Maurice Turner (RB) 1985, Ed Berry (DB) 1986, Kelly Cook (RB) 1987, James Hargrove (RB) 1987r, Michael McGruder (CB) 1989, Kevin Williams (RB) 1993, Allen Rossum (KR) 2000–1, Marques Anderson (S) 2002–3.

21 *Verne Lewellen* (B) 1927, Roy Baker (B) 1928, *Tom Nash* (E) 1928, Jack Evans (B) 1929, Ken Haycraft (E) 1930, *Milt Gantenbein* (E) 1931–2, *Charles Goldenberg* (G/B) 1933, Herb Banet (B)

1937, *Pete Tinsley* (G) 1938–45, Al Sparlis (G) 1946, Ward Cuff (B) 1947, Ed Smith (B) 1948–9, Ray DiPierro (G) 1950–1, *Bob Jeter* (DB) 1963–70, Charlie Hall (DB) 1971–4, John Hadl (QB) 1975, Steve Wagner (DB) 1976–9, Mike Jolly (S) 1980, 1982–3, Ray Crouse (RB) 1984, *Brent Fullwood* (RB) 1987–90, Joe Fuller (CB) 1991, Carl Carter (CB) 1992, Forey Duckett (CB) 1994, Craig Newsome (CB) 1995–8, Gary Berry (S) 2000, Bhawoh Jue (DB) 2001–3.

22 *Lavvie Dilweg* (E) 1927–34, *Milt Gantenbein* (E) 1935–40, Ernie Pannell (T) 1941–2, 1945, *Ray Riddick* (E) 1942, Dick Evans (E) 1943, Dick Bilda (B) 1944, Roy McKay (B) 1946–7, Jay Rhodemyre (C) 1948–9, *Billy Grimes* (HB) 1950–2, J.R. Boone (B) 1953, Johnny Papit (HB) 1953, Bill Roberts (HB) 1956, Jim Shanley (HB) 1958, Bill Butler (B) 1959, Elijah Pitts (HB) 1961–9, 1971, Jon Staggers (WR) 1972–4, Mark Lee (CB) 1980–90, Lewis Billups (CB) 1992, Lenny McGill (CB) 1994–5, Bucky Brooks (CB) 1996–7, Darick Holmes (RB) 1998, Demond Parker (RB) 1999–2000, Keith Thibodeaux (CB) 2001, Eric Metcalf (KR) 2002, Nick Luchey (FB) 2003.

23 Whitey Woodin (G) 1927–31, Paul Minick (G) 1929, Jess Quatse (T) 1933, Ben Smith (E) 1933, Earl Witte (B) 1934, Harry Mattos (B) 1936, Av Daniell (T) 1937, Alex Urban (E) 1941, Earl Ohlgren (DE) 1942, Bob Kercher (DE) 1943, Jim Lankas (FB) 1943, Don Perkins (FB) 1944, Clyde Goodnight (E) 1945–9, Steve Pritko (E) 1949–50, Val Jansante (E) 1951, Bob Nussbaumer (B) 1951, Dan Sandifer (B) 1953, Al Romine (HB) 1955, 1958, Jim Capuzzi (B) 1955, Glenn Young (DB) 1956, Paul Winslow (HB) 1960, Jerry Norton (DB) 1963–4, Travis Williams (KR) 1967–70, Bob Hudson (RB) 1972, Charlie Leigh (RB) 1974, Terry Randolph (DB) 1977, Maurice Harvey (S) 1981–3, Chuck Clanton (DB) 1985, Tiger Greene (S) 1986–90, Dave McCloughan (CB) 1992, Sammy Walker (CB) 1993, Matthew Dorsett (CB) 1995, Roosevelt Blackmon (CB) 1998, Billy Jenkins (S) 2001, Darrien Gordon (KR) 2002.

24 Bruce Jones (G) 1927–8, **Johnny Blood** (B) 1929–30, Waldo Don Carlos (C) 1931, Claude Perry (T) 1932, Al Sarafiny (C) 1933, **Mike Michalske** (G) 1934, Bob O'Connor (T) 1935, Joe Laws (B) 1937–45, Floyd Reid (HB) 1952–6, **Willie Wood** (S) 1960–71, Ron McBride (RB) 1973, Johnnie Gray (S) 1975–83, Mossy Cade (CB) 1985–6, Van Jakes (CB) 1989, Tim Hauck (S) 1991–4, Aaron Hayden (RB) 1997, Antuan Edwards (DB) 1999–2003.

25 Rudy Rosatti (T) 1927, Harold Griffin (C) 1928, Paul Minick (G) 1929, Whitey Woodin (G) 1929, Wuert Englemann (B) 1931–3, *Lon Evans* (G) 1934, *George Sauer* (B) 1935–6, Ed Jankowski (B) 1937, Al Zupek (E) 1946, Pat West (B) 1948, Alex Wizbicki (B) 1950, Harper Davis (B) 1951,

Jack Losch (HB) 1956, Billy Kinard (B) 1957–8, Tim Brown (HB) 1959, Bill Butler (B) 1959, *Tom Moore* (HB) 1960–5, Dave Hampton (RB) 1969–71, Les Goodman (RB) 1973–4, Harlan Huckleby (RB) 1980–5, Lee Weigel (RB) 1987r, Patrick Collins (RB) 1988, Vinnie Clark (CB) 1991–2, Muhammad Oliver (CB) 1993, *Dorsey Levens* (RB) 1995–2001, James Whitley (CB) 2003.

26 Claude Perry (T) 1927–30, *Tom Nash* (E) 1929, **Arnie Herber** (B) 1931, Clyde Van Sickle (C) 1933, Frank Butler (C) 1934, **Johnny Blood** (B) 1935, Lyle Sturgeon (T) 1937, Bob Forte (B) 1946, Bill Kelley (E) 1949, Lindell Pearson (HB) 1952, Ray Pelfrey (E) 1952, Gib Dawson (HB) 1953, Jim Capuzzi (B) 1956, Ken Gorgal (DB) 1956, **Herb Adderley** (CB) 1961–9, Ward Walsh (RB) 1972, Eric Torkelson (RB) 1974–9, 1981, Tim Lewis (CB) 1983–6, Craig Jay (TE) 1987r, *Chuck Cecil* (S) 1988–92, Darrell Thompson (RB) 1994, Mark Collins (CB) 1997, Erwin Swiney (CB) 2002–3.

27 Myrt Basing (B) 1927, *Bo Molenda* (B) 1929–30, Claude Perry (T) 1931, **Clarke Hinkle** (FB) 1932, **Cal Hubbard** (T) 1933, Hank Bruder (B) 1935–6, Lou Midler (DE) 1940, Don Miller (B) 1942, Keith Ranspot (E) 1942, *Chet Adams* (T) 1943, Solon Barnett (T) 1945, Chuck Tollefson (G) 1946, Jack Jacobs (QB) 1947–9, Larry Coutre (HB) 1950, 1953, Veryl Switzer (B) 1954–5, Johnny Symank (DB) 1957–62, Red Mack (WR) 1966, Claudis James (WR) 1967–8, Al Randolph (DB) 1971, Hise Austin (CB) 1973, Cliff Taylor (RB) 1976, Gary Hayes (DB) 1984–6, Tony Elliot (DB) 1987r, Herman Fontenot (RB) 1989–90, Terrell Buckley (CB) 1992–4, Calvin Jones (RB) 1996, Michael Blair (RB) 1998, Tod McBride (DB) 1999–2002, Michael Hawthorne (S) 2003.

28 Red Smith (G) 1927, Hurdis McCrary (FB) 1929–30, Mike Michalske (G) 1931, Joe Kurth (T) 1933, George Maddox (T) 1935, Ed Smith (B) 1937, Paul Christman (QB) 1950, Bobby Thomason (QB) 1951, Clarence Self (B) 1952, 1954–5, John Rowser (DB) 1967, Leon Harden (S) 1970, *Willie Buchanan* (CB) 1972–8, Mike McLeod (DB) 1984–5, Elbert Watts (DB) 1986, Ron Pitts (CB) 1988–90, Roderick Mullen (DB) 1995–7, Basil Mitchell (RB) 1999–2000, Matt Bowen (S) 2001–2.

29 *Jug Earp* (C) 1927–8, Boob Darling (C) 1929–31, Hurdis McCrary (FB) 1929, Les Peterson (E) 1932, Larry Bettencourt (C) 1933, Joe Laws (B) 1935–6, Darrell Lester (C) 1937–8, *Charley Brock* (C) 1939–47, Bobby Wood (T) 1940, Howie Williams (DB) 1962–3, Dave Dunaway (WR) 1968, Al Matthews (DB) 1970–5, Mike C. McCoy (DB) 1976–83, Ken Stills (S) 1985–9, Jerry Woods (S) 1990, Marcus Wilson (RB) 1992–5, Raymont Harris (RB) 1998, Herbert Goodman (RB) 2000–1, Curtis Fuller (S) 2003.

30 Tiny Cahoon (T) 1927–8, Dick O'Donnell (E) 1929–30, *Bo Molenda* (FB) 1931–2, **Mike**

Michalske (G) 1932, **Clarke Hinkle** (FB) 1933, 1935, 1937–41, Larry Bettencourt (C) 1933, *Milt Gantenbein* (E) 1933, *Nate Barragar* (C) 1934, Chuck Mercein (FB) 1967–9, Larry Krause (RB) 1970–1, 1973–4, Ricky Patton (RB) 1979, Bill Whitaker (DB) 1981–2, Paul Ott Carruth (RB) 1986–8, Jim Bob Morris (DB) 1987r, Chuck Webb (RB) 1991, Corey Harris (DB/WR) 1993–4, William Henderson (FB) 1995–7, *Ahman Green* (RB) 2000–3.

31 Verne Lewellen (B) 1929–30, *Nate Barragar* (C) 1931, 1935, Ray Jenison (T) 1931, Clyde Van Sickle (C) 1932, **Mike Michalske** (G) 1933, Joe Kurth (T) 1934, Harold Prescott (E) 1946, Roger Harding (C) 1949, Bob Mann (E) 1950–1, Bill Boedeker (B) 1950, Fred Cone (FB) 1952–7, **Jim Taylor** (FB) 1958–66, Perry Williams (RB) 1969–73, Jim Culbreath (FB) 1977–9, Gerry Ellis (FB) 1980–6, Tony Hunter (RB) 1987r, Allen Rice (RB) 1991, Buford McGee (FB) 1992, George Teague (S) 1993–5, Rod Smith (CB) 1998, Fred Vinson (CB) 1999, Chris Akins (S) 2000–1, Al Harris (CB) 2003.

32 Jim Bowdoin (G) 1929–30, *Red Dunn* (B) 1929, Rudy Comstock (G) 1931–3, Art Bultman (C) 1934, Claude Perry (T) 1935, Wayland Becker (E) 1936–8, John Biolo (G) 1939, Booth Lusteg (K) 1969, Don Highsmith (RB) 1973, Ken Starch (RB) 1976, Steve Atkins (RB) 1979–81, John Simmons (DB) 1986, Dave Brown (CB) 1987–9, Don King (DB) 1987r, Steve Avery (FB) 1991, John Stephens (RB) 1993, Reggie Cobb (RB) 1994, *Travis Jervey* (RB) 1995–8, Rondell Mealey (RB) 2001–2, Bryant Westbrook (CB) 2002.

33 *Bill Kern* (T) 1929, Wuert Englemann (B) 1930, Ken Radick (E) 1931, **Clarke Hinkle** (FB) 1932, Art Bultman (C) 1933, **Mike Michalske** (G) 1935, Cal Clemens (B) 1936, Ray Peterson (B) 1937, Dick Weisgerber (B) 1938–40, 1942, Mike Bucchianeri (G) 1941, Glen Sorenson (G) 1943–5, Les Gatewood (C) 1946–7, Lloyd Baxter (C) 1948, Buddy Burris (G) 1949–51, Bobby Floyd (FB) 1952, Bob Clemens (FB) 1955, Frank Purnell (FB) 1957, **Ray Nitschke** (LB) 1958, Lew Carpenter (B) 1959–63, Jim Grabowski (FB) 1966–70, Barty Smith (RB) 1974–80, Jim Jensen (RB) 1981–2, Jessie Clark (FB) 1983–7, John Sterling (RB) 1987r, Keith Woodside (RB) 1988–91, Doug Evans (CB) 1993–7, William Henderson (FB) 1998–2003.

34 *Carl Lidberg* (FB) 1929, Elmer Sleight (G) 1930, Jim Bowdoin (G) 1931, *Dick Stahlman* (T) 1932, Al Rose (E) 1933, Tiny Engebretsen (G) 1935–41, Ken Roskie (B) 1948, Joe Spencer (T) 1950–1, *Don Chandler* (K) 1965–7, *Terdell Middleton* (RB) 1977–81, Allan Clark (RB) 1982, Lou Rash (DB) 1987r, Larry Mason (RB) 1988, Edgar Bennett (RB) 1992–6, Mike McKenzie (CB) 1999–2003.

35 *Roger Ashmore* (T) 1929, Ken Radick (E)

1930, *Tom Nash* (E) 1931-2, Dominic Vairo (E) 1935, Frank Butler (C) 1938, Frank Balasz (B) 1939-41, Bob Flowers (C/LB) 1942-49, Glenn Johnson (T) 1949, *Clayton Tonnemaker* (LB) 1950, Walt Michaels (G) 1951, Bob Clemens (FB) 1955, Frank Mestnik (FB) 1963, Allen Jacobs (HB) 1965, Dave Conway (K) 1971, Del Rodgers (RB) 1982, 1984, Kevin Wilhite (RB) 1987r, Michael Haddix (FB) 1989-90, Ray Wilson (S) 1994, Jay Graham (RB) 2002.

36 Mike Michalske (G) 1929-30, *Dick Stahlman* (T) 1931, Jess Quatse (T) 1933, Bob Tenner (E) 1935, Bernie Scherer (E) 1938, Frank Steen (E) 1939, Hal Van Every (B) 1940-1, Earl Bennett (G) 1946, Jug Girard (B) 1948-51, Ben Wilson (FB) 1967, Mike Carter (WR) 1970, Macarthur Lane (RB) 1972-4, Howard Sampson (DB) 1978-9, Kenneth Davis (RB) 1986-8, *Leroy Butler* (DB) 1990-2001.

37 Claude Perry (T) 1929, 1933, *Tom Nash* (E) 1930, Elmer Sleight (G) 1931, Al Rose (E) 1932, Swede Johnston (FB) 1934, Champ Seibold (T) 1935-6, Francis Schammel (G) 1937, Tom Jones (G) 1938, Jack Brennan (G) 1939, Connie Berry (E) 1940, Lee McLaughlin (G) 1941, Bill Reichardt (FB) 1952, *Howie Ferguson* (FB) 1953-8, Larry Hickman (FB) 1960, Tommy Joe Crutcher (LB) 1964, Phil Vandersea (LB) 1966, Dale Livingston (K) 1970, Ike Thomas (DB) 1972-3, Terry Wells (RB) 1975, Tim Moresco (DB) 1977, Mark Murphy (S) 1980-85, 1987-91, KeShon Johnson (DB) 1994, Tyrone Williams (CB) 1996-2002.

38 *Jug Earp* (C) 1929, *Carl Lidberg* (FB) 1930, **Cal Hubbard** (T) 1931, Art Bultman (C) 1933, Hurdis McCrary (FB) 1933, Joe Laws (B) 1934, **Arnie Herber** (B) 1935-40, Chuck Sample (B) 1942, 1945, *Nolan Luhn* (E) 1945-9, *Tobin Rote* (QB) 1950-51, Mike Mercer (K) 1968-9, Tim Webster (K) 1971, Hurles Scales (DB) 1975, Estes Hood (DB) 1978-84, John Sullivan (DB) 1986, Norm Jefferson (DB) 1987-8, Chuck Washington (DB) 1987r, Adrian White (S) 1992, Bruce Pickens (CB) 1993, Brian Saterfield (FB) 1996, Blaine McElmurry (S) 1997-8, Matt Snider (FB) 1999.

39 Cal Hubbard (T) 1929, *Jug Earp* (C) 1930-2, Larry Bettencourt (C) 1933, **Clarke Hinkle** (FB) 1933, Tony Paulekas (C) 1936, *Lon Evans* (G) 1937, Stan Heath (QB) 1949, *John Martinkovic* (DE) 1951, Errol Mann (K) 1968, Jim Hill (DB) 1972-4, Sammy Johnson (RB) 1979, Mike Meade (FB) 1982-3, Ronnie Burgess (DB) 1985, Kenneth Johnson (DB) 1987, Freddie Parker (RB) 1987r, Darrell Thompson (RB) 1990-3, Mike Prior (S) 1994-8, Tony Carter (FB) 2002.

40 Tiny Cahoon (T) 1929, **Cal Hubbard** (T) 1930, 1932, **Mike Michalske** (G) 1935, Bernie Scherer (E) 1936, Bill Lee (T) 1937-42, 1946, *Ade Schwammel* (T) 1943, Aldo Forte (G) 1947, Roger Eason (G) 1949, Carlton Elliot (E) 1951, Ben

Aldridge (B) 1953, Joe Johnson (HB) 1954-8, Dale Hackbart (DB) 1960-61, Earl Gros (FB) 1962-3, Tom Brown (S) 1964-8, Dave Kopay (RB) 1972, Pete Van Valkenberg (RB) 1974, Will Harrell (RB) 1975-7, Eddie Lee Ivery (RB) 1979-86, David King (DB) 1987r, Johnnie Jackson (S) 1992, Chris Hayes (S) 1996, Pat Terrell (S) 1998, Jason Moore (S) 2000, Tony Fisher (RB) 2002-3.

41 Harry O'Boyle (B) 1928, Dave Zuidmulder (B) 1931, **Arnie Herber** (B) 1932-3, Joe Laws (B) 1934, **Clarke Hinkle** (FB) 1936, Champ Seibold (T) 1937-8, Paul Kell (T) 1939-40, Ralph Earhart (B) 1948-9, Marvin Johnson (DB) 1952-3, Bill Robinson (HB) 1952, Lou Mihajlovich (DE) 1954, Doyle Nix (DB) 1955, Bobby Freeman (DB) 1959, Junior Coffey (RB) 1965, Paul Gibson (WR) 1972, Jim Burrow (DB) 1976, Dave Osborn (RB) 1976, Tom Flynn (S) 1984-6, Kenneth Johnson (DB) 1987, Chuck Compton (DB) 1987r, Eugene Robinson (S) 1996-97, Torrance Marshall (LB) 2002.

42 Curly Lambeau (B) 1928, Harry O'Boyle (B) 1932, Bob Monnett (B) 1934, Dustin McDonald (G) 1935, Roy Schoeman (C) 1938, Andy Uram (B) 1939-43, Paul Duhart (B) 1944, Bruce Smith (B) 1945-8, Kenneth Kranz (B) 1949, Al Cannava (B) 1950, Wally Dreyer (B) 1950, Al Carmichael (HB) 1953-4, Don McIlhenny (HB) 1957-9, *John Brockington* (FB) 1971-7, Walt Landers (FB) 1978-9, Gary Ellerson (FB) 1985-6, Walter Dean (FB) 1991, Harry Sydney (FB) 1992, Leshon Johnson (RB) 1994-5, Corey Dowden (CB) 1996, *Darren Sharper* (S) 1997-2003.

43 Dutch Webber (E) 1928, Hurdis McCrary (FB) 1932, Les Peterson (E) 1934, *George Svendsen* (C) 1935-7, *Charles Goldenberg* (G) 1938-45, Don Wells (E) 1946-9, Jack Kirby (B) 1949, *Ab Wimberly* (E) 1950, Ace Loomis (B) 1952, Don Barton (B) 1953, J.R. Boone (B) 1953, Doug Hart (DB) 1964-71, Dave Mason (DB) 1974, Aundra Thompson (WR) 1977-8, Henry Monroe (DB) 1979, Daryll Jones (DB) 1984-5, Larry Morris (RB) 1987r, Randy Kinder (CB) 1997, Scott McGarrahan (S) 1998-2000, Moe Smith (RB) 2002.

44 Larry Marks (B) 1928, Marger Apsit (B) 1932, Charley Caspar (B) 1934, *Charles Goldenberg* (G) 1935-7, *Baby Ray* (T) 1938-48, Clarence McGeary (DT) 1950, Dave Stephenson (G) 1951, *Bobby Dillon* (DB) 1952-9, *Donny Anderson* (RB) 1966-71, Bob Kroll (S) 1972-3, Charlie Hall (CB) 1975-6, Vickey Anderson (FB) 1980, Dwayne O'Steen (CB) 1983-4, Chris Mandeville (DB) 1987, Von Mansfield (DB) 1987r, Jerry Holmes (CB) 1990-1, Dexter McNabb (FB) 1993, Chris Darkins (RB) 1996-7, Matt Snider (FB) 2000, Najeh Davenport (RB) 2002-3.

45 *Verne Lewellen* (B) 1928, Art Bultman (C) 1932-3, **Arnie Herber** (B) 1934, **Clarke Hinkle** (FB) 1934, *Ernie Smith* (T) 1935-7, 1939, Bill Kuusisto (G) 1941-5, *Dick Wildung* (T) 1946-51,

Doyle Nix (DB) 1955, *Emlen Tunnell* (S) 1959–61, Dave Hathcock (DB) 1966, John Rowser (DB) 1967–69, Ervin Hunt (DB) 1970, Perry Smith (DB) 1973–6, Lavale Thomas (RB) 1987–8, Vai Sikahema (KR) 1991, Dexter McNabb (FB) 1992–3, Mike Prior (S) 1993, Keith Crawford (CB/WR) 1995, 1999, Kerry Cooks (S) 1998, Derek Combs (CB) 2003.

46 *Roger Ashmore* (T) 1928, *Verne Lewellen* (B) 1931–2, *Milt Gantenbein* (E) 1933–4, *Lon Evans* (G) 1935, *Russ Letlow* (G) 1936–42, 1946, Sherwood Fries (G) 1943, Chuck Tollefson (G) 1944–5, Ray Clemens (G) 1947, Larry Olsonoski (C) 1949, Hamilton Nichols (G) 1951, Hank Gremminger (DB) 1956–65, Leland Glass (WR) 1972–3, Steve Luke (DB) 1975–80, Anthony Harrison (DB) 1987r, Gary Richard (DB) 1988, Vince Workman (RB) 1989–92, Michael Robinson (CB) 1996, Juran Bolden (CB) 1998, Rodney Artmore (S) 1999.

47 *Milt Gantenbein* (E) 1933, Hank Bruder (B) 1934, Al Rose (E) 1935–6, Lou Gordon (T) 1937, Paul Berezney (T) 1942–4, Paul Lipscomb (T) 1945–9, Len Szafaryn (T) 1950, *John Martinkovic* (DE) 1951, Dom Moselle (B) 1952, Val Joe Walker (DB) 1953–6, *Jesse Whittenton* (CB) 1958–64, Gordon Rule (DB) 1968–9, Dave Davis (WR) 1971–2, David Petway (S) 1981, Jim Bob Morris (DB) 1987, Roland Mitchell (DB) 1991–4, Scott Galbraith (TE) 1998, Tyrone Bell (CB) 1999.

48 **Clarke Hinkle** (FB) 1934, Frank Butler (C) 1935–6, Ookie Miller (C) 1938, Harry Jacunski (E) 1939–44, Don Perkins (FB) 1945, Bob Nussbaumer (DB) 1946, Ted Cook (E) 1948–9, Ace Loomis (B) 1953, Jim Psaltis (DB) 1954, Al Carmichael (HB) 1955–8, Dick Pesonen (DB) 1960, *Ken Ellis* (CB) 1970–75, Nate Simpson (RB) 1977–9, Lee Morris (WR) 1987r, *Dorsey Levens* (RB) 1994, Mike Bartrum (TE) 1995, Jim Kitts (FB) 1998.

49 Paul Fitzgibbon (B) 1932, Al Rose (E) 1934, **Walt Kiesling** (G) 1935–6, John Howell (B) 1938, Dan Orlich (E) 1949–51, Bob Wicks (WR) 1974, Ed West (TE) 1984, David Greenwood (S) 1986, Mickey Sutton (CB) 1989, Jeff Wilner (TE) 1995, Kevin Smith (FB) 1996, Lamont Hall (TE) 1999, Todd Franz (S) 2002.

50 Claude Perry (T) 1934, *Ade Schwammel* (T) 1935–6, Bob Monnett (B) 1938, Clarence Thompson (B) 1939, Bill Johnson (DE) 1941, Ken Roskie (B) 1948, Jay Rhodemyre (C) 1952, Bill Curry (C) 1965–6, Bob Hyland (C) 1967–9, Jim Carter (LB) 1970–8, Rich Wingo (LB) 1979, 1981–4, Johnny Holland (LB) 1987–93, Vince Rafferty (C) 1987r, Mike Arthur (C) 1995–6, Anthony Davis (LB) 1999, K.D. Williams (LB) 2000–2001, Hannibal Navies (LB) 2003.

51 *Charles Goldenberg* (G/B) 1934, **Cal Hubbard** (T) 1935, *Lon Evans* (G) 1936, Herm Schneid-

man (B) 1938–9, Jim Lawrence (B) 1939, Ed Frutig (E) 1941, 1945, John Stonebreaker (E) 1942, Irv Comp (B) 1943–9, Len Szafaryn (T) 1950, Hal Faverty (C) 1951, **Jim Ringo** (C) 1953–63, Bill Hayhoe (T) 1969, Larry Hefner (LB) 1972–5, Jim Gueno (LB) 1976–80, Guy Prather (LB) 1981–5, Clayton Weishuhn (LB) 1987, Ron Monaco (LB) 1987r, Ron Simpkins (LB) 1988, Blair Bush (C) 1989–91, Jeff Brady (LB) 1992, Jim Morrissey (LB) 1993, Mark Williams (LB) 1994, Brian Williams (LB) 1995–2000, Torrance Marshall (LB) 2001–3.

52 Al Rose (E) 1932, Art Bultman (C) 1934, Tiny Engebretsen (G) 1936, Larry Buhler (B) 1939–41, Ken Snelling (B) 1945, Bill Kuusisto (G) 1946, Bob Skoglund (DE) 1947, Cleo Walker (C/LB) 1970, Wimpy Winther (C) 1971, John Schmitt (C) 1974, Gary Weaver (LB) 1975–9, George Cumby (LB) 1980–5, Mike Weddington (LB) 1986–90, James Melka (LB) 1987r, *Frank Winters* (C) 1992–2002.

53 Hurdis McCrary (FB) 1933, *Ade Schwammel* (T) 1934, Lou Gordon (T) 1936, Earl Svendsen (C) 1939, Dick Evans (E) 1940, Bob Ingalls (C/LB) 1942, Don Perkins (FB) 1943, Dave Stephenson (G) 1953–55, Sam Palumbo (LB) 1955, George Timberlake (LB) 1955, Ken Iman (C) 1960–63, *Fred Carr* (LB) 1968–77, Francis Chesley (LB) 1978, Mike Douglass (LB) 1979–85, Bobby Leopold (LB) 1986, Miles Turpin (LB) 1986a, Aric Anderson (LB) 1987r, John Corker (LB) 1988, George Koonce (LB) 1992–9, Mike Morton (LB) 2000, Andre O'Neal (LB) 2001, Paris Lenon (LB) 2002–3.

54 Al Culver (T) 1932, Carl Jorgenson (T) 1934, Swede Johnston (FB) 1936, *Larry Craig* (E/B) 1939–49, George Schmidt (C) 1952, Malcolm Walker (C) 1970, Wimpy Winther (C) 1971, *Larry McCarren* (C) 1973–84, Jeff Schuh (LB) 1986, Scott Stephen (LB) 1987–91, Greg Jensen (G) 1987r, Rydell Malancon (LB) 1987r, Keo Coleman (LB) 1993, Bernardo Harris (LB) 1995, Ron Cox (LB) 1996, Seth Joyner (LB) 1997, Jude Waddy (LB) 1998–99, Nate Wayne (LB) 2000–2.

55 Herb Franta (T) 1930, Hank Bruder (B) 1933, Bob Jones (G) 1934, **Johnny Blood** (B) 1936, Allen Moore (E) 1939, Bob Adkins (B) 1940–1, Ed Ecker (T) 1950–1, Jim Flanigan (LB) 1967–70, Noel Jenke (LB) 1973–4, Tom Hull (LB) 1975, Bob Hyland (C) 1976, Jim Cheyunski (LB) 1977, Mike Hunt (LB) 1978–80, Randy Scott (LB) 1981–6, Kenneth Jordan (LB) 1987r, Reggie Burnette (LB) 1991, Greg Clark (LB) 1991, Brett Collins (LB) 1992–3, Joe Mott (LB) 1993, Fred Strickland (LB) 1994–5, Bernardo Harris (LB) 1996–2001, Marcus Wilkins (LB) 2002–3.

56 Oran Pape (B) 1930, *Nate Barragar* (C) 1932, Harry Wunsch (G) 1934, Tom Greenfield (C/LB) 1939–41, Tommy Joe Crutcher (LB) 1965–7, 1971–2, Tom MacLeod (LB) 1973, **Ted Hen-**

dricks (LB) 1974, Tom Perko (LB) 1976, Blaine Smith (LB) 1977, Rick Nuzum (C) 1978, Ed O'Neil (LB) 1980, Cliff Lewis (LB) 1981–4, Burnell Dent (LB) 1986–92, John Pointer (LB) 1987r, James Willis (LB) 1993–4, Lamont Hollinquest (LB) 1996–8, Kivuusama Mays (LB) 1999, Eugene Mc-Caslin (LB) 2000, Rob Holmberg (LB) 2001, Hardy Nickerson (LB) 2002, Nick Barnett (LB) 2003.

57 Clyde Van Sickle (C) 1932, Champ Seibold (T) 1934, 1939–40, *Ade Schwammel* (T) 1936, Dick Zoll (G) 1939, Ray Wehba (E) 1944, Ken Bowman (C) 1964–73, Ron Acks (LB) 1974–6, Derrel Gofourth (G) 1977–82, Mike Curcio (LB) 1983, Chet Parlavecchio (LB) 1983, Rich Moran (G) 1985–93, Putt Choate (LB) 1987r, Joe Kelly (LB) 1995, Jim Nelson (LB) 1998–9, Antonio London (LB) 1998, Chris Gizzi (LB) 2000–1, T.J. Slaughter (LB) 2003.

58 Joe Kurth (T) 1934, Champ Seibold (T) 1936, Warren Kilbourn (T) 1939, *Baby Ray* (T) 1940, Joe Carter (E) 1942, Don Perkins (FB) 1943, *Ade Schwammel* (T) 1944, *Ed Neal* (DT) 1945–51, *Clayton Tonnemaker* (LB) 1953–4, Tom Bettis (LB) 1955, Larry Lauer (C) 1956–7, *Dan Currie* (LB) 1958–64, Francis Winkler (DE) 1968–9, Cal Withrow (C) 1972–3, Mark Cooney (LB) 1974, Bob McCaffrey (C) 1975, Don Hansen (LB) 1976–7, Bob Lally (LB) 1976, Danny Johnson (LB) 1978, Paul Rudzinski (LB) 1979, Steve Stewart (LB) 1979, Bruce Beekley (LB) 1980, Larry Rubens (C) 1982–3, Mark Cannon (C) 1984–9, Mark D'Onofrio (LB) 1992, Ruffin Hamilton (LB) 1994, *Mike Flanagan* (C) 1998–2003.

59 Frank Butler (C) 1936, Jim Lawrence (B) 1939, Rudy Kuechenberg (LB) 1970, Tom Toner (LB) 1973, 1975–7, John Anderson (LB) 1979–89, Kurt Larson (LB) 1991, Wayne Simmons (LB) 1993–7, Na'il Diggs (LB) 2000–3.

60 Frank Butler (C) 1934, **Walt Kiesling** (G) 1936, Charles Schultz (T) 1939–41, Ed Blaine (G) 1962, *Lee Roy Caffey* (LB) 1964–9, Steve Knutson (T) 1976–7, John Anderson (LB) 1978, Kurt Allerman (LB) 1980–1, Jim Laslavic (LB) 1982, Blake Moore (C) 1984–5, Greg Jensen (G) 1987r, Rydell Malancon (LB) 1987r, Dave Croston (T) 1988, Bobby Houston (LB) 1990, Lance Zeno (C) 1993, Gene McGuire (C) 1996, Rob Davis (C) 1997–2003.

61 *Lavvie Dilweg* (E) 1934, *Ernie Smith* (T) 1936, Steve Ruzich (G) 1952–4, Jack Spinks (G) 1955–6, Jerry Smith (G) 1956, Hank Bullough (G) 1958, Nelson Toburen (LB) 1961–2, Gene Breen (LB) 1964, Dave Bradley (G) 1969–71, Bruce Van Dyke (G) 1975–6, Herb McMath (DT) 1977, Dave Simmons (LB) 1979, Charley Ane (C) 1981, Dave Dreschler (G) 1983–4, Blake Wingle (G) 1985, Jerry Boyarsky (NT) 1986–9, John McGarry (G) 1987r, Tom Neville (T) 1992, Scott Curry (T) 1999.

62 Al Norgard (E) 1934, *Russ Letlow* (G) 1936, Francis Twedell (G) 1939, Dick Afflis (G) 1952, Buddy Brown (G) 1953–6, Norm Amundsen (G) 1957, Andy Cvercko (G) 1960, Lionel Aldridge (DE) 1963, Bill Lueck (G) 1968–74, Pat Matson (G) 1975, Dennis Havig (G) 1977, Joe McLaughlin (LB) 1979, Buddy Aydelette (G) 1980, Mark Merrill (LB) 1982, Jim Laughlin (LB) 1983, Rubin Mendoza (G) 1986, Jim Meyer (T) 1987r, Kani Kauahi (C) 1988, Matt Brock (DE) 1989–93, Guy McIntyre (G) 1994, *Marco Rivera* (G) 1997–2003.

63 **Mike Michalske** (G) 1934, Gus Zarnas (G) 1939–40, Ben Starret (B) 1942–5, Urban Odson (T) 1946–9, Don Stansauk (T) 1950–1, Ray Bray (G) 1952, Al Barry (G) 1954, Joe Skibinski (G) 1955–6, Marv Matuszak (LB) 1958, *Fuzzy Thurston* (G) 1959–67, Randy Winkler (G) 1971, Ernie Janet (G) 1975, Terry Jones (NT) 1978–84, Perry Hartnett (G) 1987r, James Campen (C) 1989–93, Adam Timmerman (G) 1994–8, Jamie Dukes (C) 1994, Raleigh McKenzie (G) 1999–2000, Bill Ferrario (G) 2002.

64 *Nate Barragar* (C) 1934, Howard Johnson (G) 1940–1, *Ted Fritsch* (FB) 1942–50, Ernie Danjean (LB) 1957, *Jerry Kramer* (G) 1958–68, Kevin Hunt (T) 1972, Syd Kitson (G) 1980–4, Steve Collier (T) 1987, Vince Villanucci (NT) 1987r, John Jurkovic (NT) 1993–5, Bruce Wilkerson (T) 1996–7, Alcender Jackson (G) 2002.

65 *Lon Evans* (G) 1934, Gene Wilson (E) 1947–8, Rip Collins (HB) 1951, Chuck Boerio (LB) 1952, Tom Bettis (LB) 1956–61, Ed Holler (LB) 1963, Keith Wortman (G) 1972–5, Mike Douglass (LB) 1978, Mike Wellman (C) 1979–80, Brian Cabral (LB) 1980, Ron Hallstrom (G) 1982–92, Lindsay Knapp (G) 1996, Mark Tauscher (T) 2000–3.

66 Bob Monnett (B) 1934, Earl Svendsen (C) 1939, *George Svendsen* (C) 1940–1, Ralph Davis (G) 1947–8, Don Stansauk (T) 1950, Fred Cone (FB) 1951, *Deral Teteak* (LB) 1952–6, Al Barry (G) 1957, **Ray Nitschke** (LB) 1959–72, Paul Rudzinski (LB) 1978–9, Mike Lewis (NT) 1980.

67 Dick Logan (T) 1952–3, Hank Bullough (G) 1955, Jim Salsbury (G) 1957–8, Andy Cvercko (G) 1960, Dan Grimm (G) 1963–5, Leo Carroll (DE) 1968, Malcolm Snider (T/G) 1972–4, Dick Enderle (G) 1976, Bob Kowalkowski (G) 1977, Karl Swanke (T) 1980–86, Travis Simpson (C) 1987r, Billy Ard (G) 1989–91, Sebastian Barrie (DE) 1992, Paul Hutchins (T) 1993–4, Jeff Dellenbach (C) 1996–8, Russell Maryland (DT) 2000, Grey Ruegamer (G) 2003.

68 **Arnie Herber** (B) 1934, George Seeman (E) 1940, George Paskvan (B) 1941, Len Szafaryn (T) 1953–6, John Dittrich (G) 1959, *Gale Gillingham* (G) 1966–74, 1976, Greg Koch (T) 1977–85, Ed Konopasek (T) 1987r, Blaise Winter (DE) 1988–90, Reggie Singletary (T) 1991, Joe Sims (T)

1992–5, Gary Brown (G) 1994–6, Mike Wahle (G) 2000–3.

69 Tiny Engebretsen (G) 1934, Dave Stephenson (G) 1952, *Bill Forester* (LB) 1953–59, Nelson Toburen (LB) 1961, Bill Bain (T) 1975, Leotis Harris (G) 1978–83, Bill Cherry (C) 1986–7, Bob Gruber (T) 1987r, Jeff Blackshear (G) 2002.

70 Steve Dowden (T) 1952, *Dick Wildung* (T) 1953, Art Hunter (C) 1954, Don King (DT) 1956, Rich Marshall (DT) 1965, Leon Crenshaw (DT) 1968, Rich Moore (DT) 1969–70, Lee Nystrom (T) 1974, Ernie McMillan (T) 1975, Bob Barber (DE) 1976–9, Paul Rudzinski (LB) 1980, Ron Sams (G) 1983, Keith Uecker (G) 1984–5, 1987–88, 1990–1, Steve Collier (T) 1987r, David Grant (DE) 1993, Charles Hope (G) 1994, Joe Andruzzi (G) 1998–9.

71 Bill Lucky (DT) 1955, Tom Finnin (DT) 1957, *Bill Forester* (LB) 1960–63, Lloyd Voss (DT) 1964–5, Francis Peay (T) 1968–72, Kent Branstetter (T) 1973, Mike Basinger (DE) 1974, Mike Fanucci (DE) 1974, Mel Jackson (G) 1976–80, Arland Thompson (G) 1981, Boyd Jones (T) 1984, Mark Shumate (NT) 1985, Kurt Ploeger (DE) 1986, Jeff Drost (DT) 1987r, Scott Jones (T) 1991, Cecil Gray (T) 1992, Gilbert Brown (DT) 1993, Gary Brown (G) 1994–5, Santana Dotson (DT) 1996–2001, Kevin Barry (T) 2002–3.

72 Royal Kahler (T) 1942, Forrest McPherson (T) 1943–5, Solon Barnett (T) 1945–6, Jim Kekeris (T) 1948, Tom Johnson (DT) 1952, Dick Afflis (G) 1953, Jerry Helluin (DT) 1954–7, J.D. Kimmel (DT) 1958, John Miller (T) 1960, Ben Davidson (DE) 1961, Steve Wright (T) 1964–7, Dick Himes (T) 1968–77, Kit Lathrop (DT) 1979–80, Brad Oates (T) 1981, Greg Boyd (DE) 1983, Tom Neville (T) 1986–8, Todd Auer (LB) 1987r, Warren Bone (DE) 1987r, Mark Hall (LB) 1989–90, Steve Gabbard (T) 1991, Harvey Salem (T) 1992, Earl Dotson (T) 1993–2002.

73 Wash Serini (G) 1952, Gus Cifelli (T) 1953, Ken Beck (DT) 1959–60, Ron Gassert (DT) 1962, John McDowell (G) 1964, Jim Weatherwax (DT) 1966–7, 1969, Kevin Hardy (DT) 1970, Vernon Vanoy (DT) 1972, Carleton Oats (DT) 1973, Steve Okoniewski (DT) 1974–5, Gerald Skinner (T) 1978, Earl Edwards (DT) 1979, Byron Braggs (DE) 1981–3, Alan Veingrad (T) 1986–90, David Caldwell (NT) 1987r, Tootie Robbins (T) 1992–3, Aaron Taylor (G) 1995–7, Keith McKenzie (DE) 2002.

74 Larry Olsonoski (G) 1948, Rebel Steiner (E) 1950–1, *Roger Zatkoff* (LB) 1953–6, Carl Vereen (T) 1957, **Henry Jordan** (DT) 1959–69, Donnell Smith (DE) 1971, Cal Withrow (C) 1971, Aaron Brown (DE) 1973–4, Dave Roller (DT) 1975–8, Ken Brown (C) 1980, Tim Huffman (G) 1981–5, Steve Collier (T) 1987r, Darryl Haley (T) 1988, Lester Archambeau (DE) 1990–2, Doug

Widell (G) 1992, Antonio Dingle (DT) 1999, Aaron Kampman (DE) 2002–3.

75 Milburn Croft (T) 1942–7, Howard Ruetz (DT) 1951–3, Dick Afflis (G) 1954, **Forrest Gregg** (T) 1956, 1958–70, Lou Michaels (K) 1971, Dave Pureifory (DT) 1972–77, Carl Barzilauskas (DT) 1978–9, Rich Turner (NT) 1981–3, Ken Ruettgers (T) 1985–96, Craig Heimburger (G) 1999, Jim Flanigan (DT) 2001, Jared Tomich (DE) 2002, Grady Jackson (DT) 2003.

76 Bernie Crimmins (G/B) 1945, Tom Miller (E) 1946, John Kovatch (E) 1947, Tom O'Malley (QB) 1950, Bob Dees (T) 1952, *Bob Skoronski* (T) 1956, 1959–69, Mike McCoy (DT) 1970–6, Tim Stokes (T) 1978–82, Alphonso Carreker (DE) 1984–8, Mike Ariey (T) 1989, David Viaene (T) 1992, Harry Galbreath (G) 1993–5, Matt Willig (T) 1998, Chad Clifton (T) 2000–3.

77 Les Gatewood (C) 1946, Chuck Tollefson (G) 1947, Bob Summerhays (B) 1949–51, *Dave Hanner* (DT) 1952–4, John Sandusky (T) 1956, Ollie Spencer (T) 1957–8, Ron Kostelnik (DT) 1961–8, Bill Hayhoe (T) 1969–73, Mike Butler (DE) 1977–82, 1985, Charlie Getty (T) 1983, Bill Neill (NT) 1984, Greg Feasel (T) 1986, Tommy Robison (G) 1987, Sylvester McGrew (DE) 1987r, Tony Mandarich (T) 1989–91, Keith Millard (DE) 1992, Bill Maas (NT) 1993, John Michels (T) 1996–7, Barrett Brooks (T) 2002, Jerry Wisne (T) 2002.

78 Cliff Aberson (B) 1946, Tom Dahms (T) 1955, Norm Masters (T) 1957–64, *Bob Brown* (DT) 1966–73, Carl Wafer (DT) 1974, Bill Cooke (DE) 1975, *Ezra Johnson* (DE) 1977–8, Casey Merrill (DE) 1979–83, Gary Hoffman (T) 1984, Jim Hobbins (G) 1987r, Louis Cheek (T) 1991, Ross Verba (T) 1997–2000, Terdell Sands (DT) 2003.

79 Bob Adkins (B) 1945, Alex Urban (E) 1945, Evan Vogds (G) 1948–9, Dick Moje (E) 1951, Joe Spencer (T) 1951, *Dave Hanner* (DT) 1955–64, Jim Delisle (DT) 1971, Harry Schuh (T) 1974, Mark Koncar (T) 1976–7, 1979–81, Angelo Fields (T) 1982, Ron Spears (DE) 1983, Donnie Humphrey (DE) 1984–6, Ross Browner (DE) 1987, Mike Estep (G) 1987r, Bob Nelson (NT) 1988–90, Tunch Ilkin (T) 1993, Barry Stokes (T) 2000–1, Marcus Spriggs (T) 2003.

80 Ed Frutig (E) 1945, Herm Rohrig (B) 1946–7, Fred Provo (B) 1948, Floyd Reid (HB) 1950–1, Carlton Elliott (E) 1952–4, Dick Deschaine (P) 1955–7, Steve Meilinger (E) 1958–60, Gary Barnes (E) 1962, Bob Long (WR) 1964–7, Bucky Pope (WR) 1968, Jack Clancy (WR) 1970, Barry Smith (WR) 1973–5, Don Zimmerman (WR) 1976, **James Lofton** (WR) 1978–86, Frankie Neal (WR) 1987, Clint Didier (TE) 1988–9, Jackie Harris (TE) 1990–3, Charles Jordan (WR) 1994, Derrick Mayes (WR) 1996–8, *Donald Driver* (WR) 1999–2003.

81 Ed Berrang (E) 1952, Jim Keane (E) 1952, Clive Rush (E) 1953, Gene Knutson (DE) 1954, 1956, Pat O'Donahue (DE) 1955, Carlton Massey (DE) 1957–8, A.D. Williams (E) 1959, Lee Folkins (TE) 1961, Marv Fleming (TE) 1963–9, Rich McGeorge (TE) 1970–8, Gary Lewis (TE) 1981–4, Dan Ross (TE) 1986, Lee Morris (WR) 1987, Craig Jay (TE) 1987r, Perry Kemp (WR) 1988–91, Shawn Collins (WR) 1992, Corey Harris (WR/DB) 1992, Anthony Morgan (WR) 1993–5, Desmond Howard (KR) 1996, Tyrone Davis (TE) 1997–2002, Chris Jackson (WR) 2003.

82 Ed Bell (G) 1947–9, Jack Cloud (FB) 1950–1, Jim Temp (DE) 1957–60, Jan Barrett (TE) 1963, Lionel Aldridge (DE) 1964–71, Gerald Tinker (WR) 1975, Keith Hartwig (WR) 1977, *Paul Coffman* (TE) 1978–85, Mike Moffitt (WR) 1986, Keith Paskett (WR) 1987, Derrick Harden (WR) 1987r, Scott Bolton (WR) 1988, Erik Affholter (WR) 1991, Sanjay Beach (WR) 1992, Reggie Johnson (TE) 1994, Mark Ingram (WR) 1995, Don Beebe (WR) 1996–7, Brian Manning (WR) 1998, Desmond Howard (KR) 1999, Charles Jordan (WR) 1999, Charles Lee (WR) 2000–2, Wesley Walls (TE) 2003.

83 *John Martinkovic* (DE) 1952–6, **Len Ford** (DE) 1958, Bill Quinlan (DE) 1959–62, Urban Henry (DT) 1963, Allen Brown (TE) 1966–7, Phil Vandersea (LB) 1968–9, Clarence Williams (DE) 1970–3, 1975–7, John Thompson (TE) 1979–80, *John Jefferson* (WR) 1981–4, Patrick Scott (WR) 1987–8, Carl Bland (WR) 1989–90, Mark Clayton (WR) 1993, Jeff Wilner (TE) 1994–5, Jeff Thomason (TE) 1995–9, Ryan Wetnight (TE) 2000, David Martin (TE) 2001, Terry Glenn (WR) 2002, Antonio Chatman (WR) 2003.

84 Don Wells (E) 1946, Gary Knafelc (E) 1954–62, *Carroll Dale* (WR) 1965–72, *Steve Odom* (KR) 1974–9, Fred Nixon (WR) 1980–1, Lenny Taylor (WR) 1984, Nolan Franz (WR) 1986, Wes Smith (WR) 1987r, *Sterling Sharpe* (WR) 1988–94, Anthony Morgan (WR) 1996, Andre Rison (WR) 1996, Bill Schroeder (WR) 1997–2001, Javon Walker (WR) 2002–3.

85 Don Deeks (T) 1948, Joe Ethridge (T) 1949, Jay Rhodemyre (C) 1951, *Ab Wimberly* (E) 1952, *Max McGee* (E) 1954, 1957–67, Jim Jennings (E) 1955, Al Romine (HB) 1955, Emery Barnes (DE) 1956, John Spilis (WR) 1969–71, Dick Gordon (WR) 1973, Paul Staroba (WR) 1973, Ken Payne (WR) 1974–7, Elmo Boyd (WR) 1978, Bobby Kimball (WR) 1979–80, Phillip Epps (WR) 1982–8, Lee Morris (WR) 1987r, Jeff Query (WR) 1989–91, Kitrick Taylor (WR) 1992, Ron Lewis (WR) 1993–4, Terry Mickens (WR) 1995–7, Corey Bradford (WR) 1998–2001, Karsten Bailey (WR) 2002–3.

86 Charles Schroll (G) 1951, *Bill Howton* (E) 1952–8, *Boyd Dowler* (WR) 1959–69, John Hilton

(TE) 1970, Pete Lammons (TE) 1972, Mike Donohoe (TE) 1973–4, Kent Gaydos (WR) 1975, Jessie Green (WR) 1976, Ed West (TE) 1984–94, Don Summers (TE) 1987r, *Antonio Freeman* (WR) 1995–2001, 2003, Chris Jackson (WR) 2002, J.J. Moses (KR) 2002.

87 Bob Mann (E) 1952–4, Nate Borden (DE) 1955–59, **Willie Davis** (DE) 1960–9, Marty Amsler (DE) 1970, Alden Roche (DE) 1971–6, Walter Tullis (WR) 1979, Bill Larson (TE) 1980, John Thompson (TE) 1981–2, Walter Stanley (WR) 1985–8, Cornelius Redick (WR) 1987r, Clarence Weathers (WR) 1990–1, Robert Brooks (WR) 1992–8, Bobby Collins (TE) 2001, David Martin (TE) 2002–3.

88 Rip Collins (HB) 1951, George Hays (DE) 1953, Gene White (DB) 1954, *Ron Kramer* (TE) 1957, 1959–64, Bill Anderson (TE) 1965–6, Dick Capp (TE) 1967, Ron Jones (TE) 1969, Len Garrett (TE) 1971–3, Bert Askson (TE) 1975–7, Ron Cassidy (WR) 1979–81, 1983–4, Preston Dennard (WR) 1985, Phil McConkey (WR) 1986, Aubrey Matthews (WR) 1988–9, Albert Bell (WR) 1988, Charles Wilson (WR) 1990–1, Darryl Ingram (TE) 1992–3, Terry Mickens (WR) 1994, *Keith Jackson* (TE) 1995–6, *Roell Preston* (KR) 1997–8, Reggie Johnson (TE) 1997, Jahine Arnold (WR) 1999, Lamont Hall (TE) 1999, *Bubba Franks* (TE) 2000–3.

89 *Dave Robinson* (LB) 1963–72, Charley Wade (WR) 1975, Ollie Smith (WR) 1976–7, Willie Taylor (WR) 1978, Aundra Thompson (WR) 1979–81, Henry Childs (TE) 1984, Mark Lewis (TE) 1985–7, Joey Hackett (TE) 1987–8, Kevin Fitzgerald (TE) 1987r, John Spagnola (TE) 1989, William Harris (TE) 1990, *Mark Chmura* (TE) 1993–9, Robert Ferguson (WR) 2001–3.

90 Leon Manley (G) 1950–1, *Ezra Johnson* (DE) 1979–87, Nate Hill (DE) 1988, Tony Bennett (LB) 1990–3, Steve McMichael (DT) 1994, Darius Holland (DE) 1995–7, Vonnie Holliday (DE) 1998–2002, Chukie Nwokorie (DE) 2003.

91 Daryle Skaugstad (NT) 1983, Brian Noble (LB) 1985–93, Shannon Clavelle (DE) 1995–7, Jonathan Brown (DE) 1998, John Thierry (DE) 2000–1, Joe Johnson (DE) 2002–3.

92 Rich Dimler (DT) 1980, Matt Koart (DE) 1986, Ben Thomas (DE) 1986, Steve Collier (T) 1987r, John Jurkovic (NT) 1991–2, *Reggie White* (DE) 1993–8.

93 Dom Moselle (B) 1951, Robert Brown (DE) 1982–92, Calvin Wallace (DE) 1987r, Gilbert Brown (DT) 1993–9, 2001–3.

94 Charles Martin (DE) 1984–7, David Logan (NT) 1987, Stan Matalele (NT) 1987r, Matt Brock (DE) 1994, Bob Kuberski (DT) 1995–8, Roy Barker (DE) 1999, *Kabeer Gbaja-Biamila* (DE) 2000–3.

95 Tony Degrate (DE) 1985, Carl Sullivan (DE) 1987r, *Bryce Paup* (LB) 1990–4, Keith

McKenzie (DE/LB) 1996–9, Steve Warren (DT) 2000, Rod Walker (DT) 2001–3.

96 Tony Leiker (DE) 1987r, Shawn Patterson (DE) 1988–91, 1993, Sean Jones (DE) 1994–6, Gerald Williams (DE) 1997, Vaughn Booker (DE) 1998–9, David Bowens (DE) 2000, Steve Warren (DT) 2002, Larry Smith (DT) 2003.

97 *Tim Harris* (LB) 1986–90, John Miller (LB) 1987r, Danny Noonan (NT) 1992, Mike Merriweather (LB) 1993, Keith Traylor (LB) 1993, Matt Labounty (DE) 1995, Paul Frase (DE) 1997, Cletidus Hunt (DT) 1999–2003.

98 Tony DeLuca (NT) 1984, Brent Moore (DE) 1987, Todd Auer (LB) 1987r, Esera Tuaolo (NT) 1991–2, Alfred Oglesby (NT) 1992, Gabe Wilkins (DE) 1994–7, Billy Lyon (DT) 1998–2002, Kenny Peterson (DT) 2003.

99 Charles Johnson (DT) 1979–80, 1983, John Dorsey (LB) 1984–8, Don Davey (DE) 1991–4, Jermaine Smith (DT) 1997, 1999, Austin Robbins (DT) 2000, Jamal Reynolds (DE) 2001–3.

HOUSTON TEXANS

The franchise: The relationship among the Houston Oilers, their fans and the city took a nosedive in the mid–1990s when the team deemed its housing, the Astrodome, substandard and demanded the city supply an upgrade. When the demand went unmet, the Oilers took off for Tennessee, but not without first spending an ugly, lame-duck 1996 season in Houston.

Spurned, Houston developed plans for a new stadium with a retractable roof and soon the competition for a planned NFL expansion franchise was between Los Angeles, which expressed little interest in building a new stadium, and Houston. With Houston's stadium moving forward, the NFL awarded their 32nd franchise to Houston businessman Bob McNair on October 6, 1999. McNair had owned an energy company that he sold in 1999 to Enron. McNair hired former Redskins general manager Charlie Casserly as his GM in 2000 and former Carolina Panthers coach Dom Capers as head coach in 2001, and the Texans took the field in state-of-the-art Reliant Stadium on September 8, 2002, beating the cross-state Dallas Cowboys 19–10 in their first game.

Origin of name: As a sign of the marketing-savvy times, the Texans name was chosen after months of research and focus groups conducted by the Houston franchise and NFL Properties. Five original finalists— Apollos, Bobcats, Stallions, Texans, and Wildcatters— were first narrowed to three and then to the winner.

Time till first championship: Two years and counting

Time since last championship: Never won.

Retired numbers: None.

Numbers that should be retired: None.

Record by Decade

| | Regular Season | | | Postseason | | |
	Won	Lost	Tied	Won	Lost	Championships
2000s	9	23	0	0	0	
All-Time	9	23	0	0	0	0

Winning seasons: 0. Losing Seasons: 2. .500 seasons: 0.

Coaches

	Years	Record	Playoffs
Dom Capers	2002–3	9-23-0	0-0

Numbers worn by Hall of Famers: None.

Star power: None.

Star eclipsed: None.

Number worn by the most players: 87 has been worn three times.

Player who wore the most numbers: No one has worn more than one yet.

Number worn by first ever draft pick: David Carr the first pick in 2002 wears 8.

Number worn by first expansion draft pick: Tony Boselli wore 71.

Number worn by oldest player: Aaron Glenn, 31, Charlie Clemons, 50, and Zach Wiegert, 72, all reached 31 years of age in 2003.

Least popular numbers: 0, 1, 2, 5, 6, 9, 10, 13, 14, 15, 16, 17, 19, 27, 39, 46, 49, 60, 63, 73 and 93 have all yet to be worn.

Triskaidekaphobia notes: 13 has not been worn yet.

Number with most points scored: 3 with 152 points scored by Kris Brown.

Number with most yards rushing: 37 with 1,031 yards gained by Domanick Davis.

Number with most receptions: 82 with 91 passes caught by Billy Miller.

Number with most touchdown passes: 8 with 17 touchdowns tossed by David Carr.

Number with most interceptions: 42 with 8 passes picked off by Marcus Coleman.

Oddity: The 80s were the first number group to all be worn; single digit and numbers in the teens are the least used.

Team All-Time Numerical Roster

Pro Bowl players for each number are in *Italics*; Hall of Famers are in **Bold** type.

1 none.
2 none.
3 Kris Brown (K) 2002–3.
4 Dave Ragone (QB) 2003.
5 none.
6 none.
7 Chad Stanley (P) 2002–3.
8 David Carr (QB) 2002–3.
9 none.
10 none.
11 Mike Quinn (QB) 2002.
12 Tony Banks (QB) 2002–3.
13 none.
14 none.
15 none.
16 none.
17 none.
18 Dwaune Jones (WR) 2002.
19 none.
20 James Allen (RB) 2002.
21 Darrick Vaughn (CB) 2003.
22 Curry Burns (S) 2003.
23 Kevin Williams (S) 2002.
24 Eric Brown (S) 2002–3.
25 Tony Hollings (RB) 2003.
26 Matt Stevens (S) 2002–3.
27 none.
28 Pat Dennis (CB) 2002.
29 Marlon McCree (S) 2003.
30 Jason Simmons (CB) 2002–3.
31 *Aaron Glenn* (CB) 2002–3.
32 Jonathan Wells (RB) 2002–3.
33 Jason Bell (CB) 2002–3.
34 Stacey Mack (RB) 2003.
35 Leomont Evans (S) 2002.
36 Chris Carter (S) 2002, Kyries Hebert (S) 2002.
37 Domanick Davis (RB) 2003.
38 DeMarcus Faggins (CB) 2002–3.
39 none.
40 Ed Stansbury (FB) 2002.
41 Ramon Walker (S) 2002–3.
42 Marcus Coleman (CB) 2002–3.
43 Kenny Wright (CB) 2002–3.
44 Moran Norris (FB) 2002–3.
45 Greg Comella (FB) 2003.
46 none.
47 Jarrod Baxter (FB) 2002.
48 Bryan Pittman (C) 2003.
49 none.
50 Charlie Clemons (LB) 2003.
51 Jimmy McClain (LB) 2002–3.
52 Kailee Wong (LB) 2002–3.
53 Shantee Orr (LB) 2003.
54 Troy Evans (LB) 2002–3.
55 Jamie Sharper (LB) 2002–3.
56 Jay Foreman (LB) 2002–3.
57 Erik Flowers (LB) 2002, Jason Lamar (LB) 2002.
58 Steve Foley (LB) 2003.
59 Keith Mitchell (LB) 2002, Travis Carroll (LB) 2003.
60 none.
61 Fred Weary (G) 2002–3.
62 Chris Lorenti (C) 2002.
63 none.
64 Mike Newell (C) 2002.
65 Ryan Schau (G) 2002.
66 Charron Dorsey (T) 2002.
67 Milford Brown (G) 2002–3.
68 Greg Randall (T) 2003.
69 Chester Pitts (G) 2002–3.
70 Demingo Graham (G) 2002, Barry Hall (T) 2002.

71 Tony Boselli (T) 2002.
73 none.
72 Zach Wiegert (T) 2003.
74 Ryan Young (T) 2002.
75 Jimmy Herndon (T) 2002.
76 Steve McKinney (C) 2002–3.
77 Tarlos Thomas (T) 2002, Todd Washington (C) 2003.
78 Cameron Spikes (G/T) 2002, Seth Wand (OT) 2003.
79 Chad Overhauser (G) 2002, Jeremy Slechta (DT) 2003.
80 Sean McDermott (TE) 2002, Andre Johnson (WR) 2003.
81 Atnaf Harris (WR) 2002, Matt Murphy (TE) 2003.
82 Billy Miller (TE) 2002–3.
83 Frank Murphy (WR) 2002, Rod Rutledge (TE) 2002.
84 J.J. Moses (WR) 2003.

85 Corey Bradford (WR) 2002–3.
86 Jabar Gaffney (WR) 2002–3.
87 JaJuan Dawson (WR) 2002, Trevor Insley (WR) 2002, Derick Armstrong (WR) 2003.
88 Avion Black (WR) 2002, Rashod Kent (TE) 2003.
89 Jabari Holloway (TE) 2002–3.
90 Howard Green (DT) 2002, Terrance Martin (DE) 2003.
91 Seth Payne (DT) 2002–3.
92 Corey Sears (DE) 2002–3.
93 none.
94 Charles Hill (DT) 2002, Junior Ionae (DT) 2003.
95 Jerry DeLoach (DT) 2002–3.
96 *Gary Walker* (DT) 2002–3.
97 Shawn Worthen (DT) 2002.
98 Jeff Posey (LB) 2002, Antwan Peek (LB) 2003.
99 Steve Martin (DT) 2003.

INDIANAPOLIS COLTS

The franchise: Although the Colts began as a new NFL franchise in Baltimore in 1953, the team had antecedents running on two tracks that would eventually converge. On track one were the All America Football Conference's Baltimore Colts that, despite finishing 1–11–1 in 1949, were one of three AAFC teams merged into the NFL when the upstart league folded. The 1950 Colts continued their sad tradition and finished 1–11 before folding at the end of the year despite a surprising amount of fan support.

On the second track, theatrical agent Ted Collins was awarded an NFL franchise for the Boston Yanks in 1944 and that team ran through the 1948 season. At that point, Collins had the league cancel that franchise for tax reasons and he acquired a new New York Bulldog franchise for the 1949 season. When the All America Football Conference folded and was partially merged into the NFL in 1950, the Bulldogs acquired the players from the AAFC New York Yankees and then changed their name from Bulldogs to Yanks for 1950 and 1951. By this time, Collins had had enough and sold the franchise back to

the league which then created a new Dallas Texans franchise, selling the Yanks' players and equipment to the new Dallas ownership. The Texans would go 1–11 and were such a monumental flop at the box office that they were turned back to the league in midseason and were operated as a road team out of Hershey, Pennsylvania for the rest of 1952.

Confronted with the disaster in Dallas and with a group of Baltimore Colts fans threatening a lawsuit regarding the loss of their team two years before, NFL Commissioner Bert Bell made the best of a bad situation and awarded a new franchise to Baltimore, using the existing Texan players and equipment, and persuaded a former player of his from the University of Pennsylvania, Carroll Rosenblum, to buy the franchise. Out of this messy birth process, the Colts became a steady and successful franchise under Rosenblum and fostered a close and affectionate bond between the city and its team that was possibly best expressed in the cult movie *Diner*.

Rosenblum hired Paul Brown assistant Weeb Ewbank to coach the team in 1954, and

Ewbank embarked on an openly expressed five year plan to turn the Colts into champions that came to full fruition in 1958. Ewbank employed Hall of Famers Gino Marchetti and Art Donovan that he inherited and acquired others through the draft (Raymond Berry, Lenny Moore, and Jim Parker) and as free agents (John Unitas) to create a powerhouse. Unitas, perhaps the greatest quarterback in league history, was the biggest key, and throughout his 17 years in Baltimore the Colts were among the top teams in the NFL, winning titles under Ewbank in 1958 and 1959 and under Don McCafferty in 1970, as well as losing two championship games under Don Shula.

They also participated in two of the most famous and most important games in league history. The first being the 1958 championship game against the Giants that the Colts won in the first sudden death overtime game in history after Unitas had tied the game with an 86 yard two minute drill in the fourth quarter. With all this excitement caught on television, this game ushered in a tremendous growth spurt for the league in the 1960s. The second big game was Super Bowl III where the 18-point favorite Colts lost to Weeb Ewbank's Jets led by Joe Namath that solidified the fans' view of the AFL, the merger, and the Super Bowl.

The golden era for the team came to a close in 1972 when Rosenblum traded franchises with Robert Irsay who had just purchased the Los Angeles Rams. Irsay hired Joe Thomas as general manager, and he dismantled the aging Colts—even sending the incomparable Unitas to San Diego. Within three years, though, the Colts were transformed into three-time division winners under coach Ted Marchibroda and new quarterback Bert Jones. That team was never able to win a playoff game, however, and faded quickly. Unhappy with the stadium sit-

uation in 1984, Irsay had moving vans back up to Memorial Stadium in the dead of the night and snuck out of town to Indianapolis where a new domed home awaited them. The Colts would only experience five winning seasons in the next 15 years, and in no season won more than nine games. Their ineptitude finally paid off in 1998 when they selected Peyton Manning with the number one selection in that year's draft. With Manning, Edgerin James and Marvin Harrison, the Colts began a new winning tradition in Indianapolis although the postseason continues to prove frustrating.

Origin of name: When Baltimore got its second chance at an NFL franchise in 1953, the team was named after the 1950 Baltimore Colts franchise. That team began in the AAFC and was named from a fan contest. The region is known for horse breeding and racing, in particular the Preakness which is part of horse racing's triple crown.

Record by Decade

	Regular Season			Postseason		
	Won	Lost	Tied	Won	Lost	Championships
1950s	41	42	1	2	0	1958, 1959
1960s	92	42	4	2	3	
1970s	73	70	1	4	4	1970
1980s	54	97	1	0	1	
1990s	66	94	0	2	3	
2000s	38	26	0	2	3	
All-Time	364	371	7	12	14	3

Winning seasons: 24. Losing Seasons: 23. .500 seasons: 4.

Time till first championship: Six years.
Time since last championship: 34 years.
Retired numbers: The Colts have retired seven numbers, six of them of Hall of Fame players from the great championship squads of the late 1950s—Johnny Unitas 19; Lenny Moore 24; Art Donovan 70; Jim Parker 77; Raymond Berry 82; and Gino Marchetti 89. The seventh retired number is 22 for Buddy Young, the team's first black player and a very popular team leader.

Other numbers worn by these players: Gino Marchetti also wore 75 for one season.

Coaches

	Years	Record	Playoffs
Keith Molesworth	1953	3–9–0	0–0
Weeb Ewbank (2)	1954–62	59–52–1	2–0
Don Shula	1963–9	71–23–4	2–3
Don McCafferty (1)	1970–2	22–10–1	4–1
John Sandusky	1972	4–5–0	0–0
Howard Schnellenberger	1973–4	4–13–0	0–0
Joe Thomas	1974	2–9–0	0–0
Ted Marchibroda	1975–9	41–33–0	0–3
Mike McCormack	1980–1	9–23–0	0–0
Frank Kush	1982–4	11–28–1	0–0
Hal Hunter	1984	0–1–0	0–0
Rod Dowhower	1985–6	5–24–0	0–0
Ron Meyer	1986–91	36–35–0	0–1
Rick Venturi	1991	1–10–0	0–0
Ted Marchibroda	1992–5	30–34–0	2–1
Lindy Infante	1996–7	12–20–0	0–1
Jim Mora	1998–2001	32–32–0	0–2
Tony Dungy	2002–3	22–10–0	2–2

(Championships in parentheses)

Those who wore retired numbers after the honored player: None.

Numbers that should be retired: None now, but Peyton Manning and Marvin Harrison may change that in time.

Owned numbers: Buddy Young, 22, and Art Donovan, 70.

Numbers worn by Hall of Famers: Raymond Berry 82; Eric Dickerson 29; Art Donovan 70; Ted Hendricks 83; John Mackey 88; Gino Marchetti 75/89; Lenny Moore 24; Jim Parker 77; Joe Perry 34; Don Shula 25; Johnny Unitas 19.

Star power: R.C. Owens took 27 from Tom Matte; Marshall Faulk took 28 from Ed Toner.

Star eclipsed: Tim Brown wore 2 because 22 was retired for Buddy Young. Jim Harbaugh wore 12 till Dean Biasucci, 4, left; Mike Vanderjagt wore 12 till Kelly Holcomb, 13, left.

Numbers with most great players: 20 has been worn by star defensive backs Milt Davis and Jerry Logan as well as talented runners Joe Washington, Albert Bentley and George Taliaferro. 53 has been worn by tough linebackers Dennis Gaubatz and Stan White as well as All Pro center Ray Donaldson. 83 has been worn by Hall of Fame linebacker Ted Hendricks, star defensive linemen Don Joyce and Billy Ray Smith, and by receiver Clarence Verdin.

Worst represented numbers: 58 has been worn by 11 unremarkable linebackers and two forgettable offensive linemen.

Number worn by the most players: 87 has been worn by 23 Colts.

Player who wore the most numbers: Three numbers have been worn by Monte Brethauer 80/86/88; Cotton Davidson 18/19/21; Don Thorp 62/78/96; and Jim Winkler 76/79/84.

Longest tenure wearing a number: John Unitas wore 19 for 17 years from 1956 to 1972.

Number worn by first ever draft pick: Billy Vessels, the number one pick in 1953, played three years in Canada before joining the Colts as number 21 in 1956. The number one pick in 1954, Cotton Davidson, wore 19 as a rookie.

Biggest draft busts: Draft flops include Art Schlichter, 10, a quarterback with a gambling problem who was selected fourth in 1982 and who completed 45 percent of his passes over three years; defensive back Leonard Coleman, 31, who was selected eighth in 1984 and who had four interceptions in three years; quarterback Jeff George, 11, who was selected first in 1990 but proved to be a coach-killer and was gone in four years; defensive tackle Steve Emtman, 79, who was selected first in 1992, but whose injuries limited him to 18 games in three years; and linebacker Trev Alberts, 51, who was selected fifth in 1994, but who only played in 29 games in three years.

Numbers worn by those who played for both NFL Baltimore Colt franchises: Sisto Averno, 32 in 1950 and 60 from 1953 to 1954; Dick Barwegen, 31 in 1950 and 61 from 1953 to 1954; Art Donovan, 49/70 in 1950 and 70 from 1953 to 1961; Art Spinney, 53 in 1950 and 63 from 1956 to 1960.

Number worn by oldest player: Joe Ferguson wore 12 as a 40 year old in 1990.

Cameos: All Pros and other notables— Ed Brown 14; Tim Brown 2; Gail Cogdill 80; Joe Cribbs 30; Richard Dent 96; Joe Ferguson 12; Dwight Hicks 29; Fred Hoaglin 54; Roy Jefferson 87; Joe Klecko 73; Ron Kostelnik 65; Ray Krouse 78; Jim Martin 47; Carl Mauck 65; Stanley Morgan 86; R.C. Owens 27; Dave Rowe 74; Mark Rypien 16; Torrance Small 87; Don Strock 12.

Ones who got away: Weeb Ewbank took several young Colts with him to the Jets, including—tackle Sherman Plunkett 79, fullback Mark Smolinski 32, and receiver Bake Turner 30. Fuzzy Thurston, 64, would become an All Pro guard with the Packers. Linebacker Bill Koman, 65, started for the Cardinals for several seasons. Runner/receiver Preston Pearson, 26, would star with the Steelers and Cowboys. Problem-child Andre Rison, 87, would catch many passes for many teams for many years. Chris Chandler, 17, would prove to be a solid quarterback for numerous teams whenever he could stay healthy.

Least popular numbers: 0 has never been worn. 1, 6, 22, and 70 have been worn only once each.

Last number to be originated: 6 was worn for the first (and only) time by replacement kicker Steve Jordan in 1987.

Longest dormant number: 1 has been dormant since 1982.

Triskaidekaphobia notes: 13 has been worn by two backup quarterbacks, Sean Salisbury and Kelly Holcomb, and by kicker Mike Vanderjagt.

Shared numbers: 28 was worn by deep threat receiver Jimmy Orr and future Hall of Fame runner Marshall Faulk. 32 has been worn by All Pro Linebacker Mike Curtis and All Pro runner Edgerin James. 88 has been worn by Hall of Fame tight end John Mackey and future Hall of Fame receiver Marvin Harrison.

Continuity: Linebacker Stan White was replaced in 53 by center Ray Donaldson; defensive tackle Fred Miller was replaced in 76 by fellow tackle Joe Ehrman.

Discontinuity: Jimmy Orr was followed in 28 by fellow receiver Cotton Speyrer; Marshall Faulk was followed in 28 by defensive back Tito Wooten; Ted Hendricks was followed in 83 by tight end Ron Mayo; John Mackey was followed in 88 by fellow tight end John Mosier.

Family Connections

Brothers

Brian Baldinger	OL	1988–91	62
Gary Baldinger	DL	1990–2	94

Fathers and sons

Don Shula	DB	1953–6	25
David Shula	WR	1981	85
Fred Scott	WR	1974–7	86
Freddie Scott	WR	1998	15

Quarterback numbers over 19: 21 Cotton Davidson.

Number of first black player: In 1953, backs Buddy Young, 22, and George Taliaferro, 20, both continued with the franchise. Both had played previously on the New York Yankee and Dallas Texan teams that preceded the Colts.

Numbers of future NFL head coaches: Raymond Berry 82; Jack Patera 61; Ray Perkins 27; Don Shula 25.

Numbers of future NFL referees: None, *Players who played other sports*: None.

Players more famous after football: Dean Biasucci, 4/5, Tim Brown, 2, and Bubba Smith, 78, have all done some movie acting. Gino Marchetti, 75/89, and Alan Ameche, 35, joined together to start the very successful fast food franchise Gino's in the 1950s. Jerry Richardson, 87, got rich from Hardee's and Denny's franchises and founded the Carolina Panthers. Art Schlichter, 10, became notorious for his gambling problem.

First player to wear a number in the 90s: Defensive tackle Jim Krahl wore 90 in 1979.

Number with most points scored: 88 with 872 points scored by Marvin Harrison (508), John Mackey (228), Kerry Cash (42), Bernard Henry (36), Stanley Morgan (30), and Floyd Turner (28).

Number with most yards rushing: 32 with 11,518 yards gained by Edgerin James (6,162), Randy McMillan (3,876), Ken Clark (510), Zack Crockett (469), Mark Smolinski (363), Joe Don Looney (127) and Nate Craddock (1).

Number with most receptions: 88 with 1,309 passes caught by Marvin Harrison (759), John Mackey (320), Kerry Cash (103), Bernard Henry (51), Floyd Turner (35), Stanley Morgan (23), Bob Mrosko (8), John Brandes (5), RickyThompson (2), Robbie Martin (1), and John Mosier (1).

Number with most touchdown passes: 19 with 288 touchdowns tossed by John Unitas (287) and Jack Del Belo (1).

Number with most interceptions: 20 with 84 passes picked off by Jerry Logan (34), Milt Davis (27), Jeff Burris (10), Jackie Wallace (9), Bob Harrison (3), and Mike Doss (1).

Oddity: No numbers below 15 were worn before 1968.

These Colts wore these numbers as New York Yanks (1950–1) or Dallas Texans (1952):

	As Colt	1950	1951	1952
Tom Keane	21			21
Zollie Toth	36		86	33/36
Gino Marchetti	75/89			75/84
Ken Jackson	74			74
Joe Campanella	73			73
Sisto Averno	60		44	60
Art Donovan	70		39	70
Dan Edwards	82	4	4	82
George Taliaferro	20	20	20	20
Buddy Young	22	76	76	22
Brad Ecklund	50	22	22	50
Barney Poole	83	84	84	68/62

Team All-Time Numerical Roster

Those with an "r" following the year 1987 were replacement players during the players' strike. Pro Bowl players for each number are in *Italics*; Hall of Famers are in **Bold** type.

1 Dan Miller (K) 1982

2 Tim Brown (RB) 1968, Boris Shlapak (K) 1972, Toni Linhart (K) 1974–9, Raul Allegre (K) 1983–5, Gino Torretta (QB) 1997.

3 *Rohn Stark* (P) 1982–94, Mike Cofer (K) 1995.

4 Mike Bragg (P) 1980, *Dean Biasucci* (K) 1986–94, *Jim Harbaugh* (QB) 1995–7, Steve Walsh (QB) 1999.

5 Steve Mike–Mayer (K) 1979–80, Blair Kiel (QB) 1986–7, *Dean Biasucci* (K) 1984, Craig Colquitt (P) 1987r.

6 Steve Jordan (K) 1987r.

7 *Bert Jones* (QB) 1973–81, Gary Hogeboom (QB) 1986–8, Rusty Hilger (QB) 1990, Tom Tupa (QB) 1992, Don Majkowski (QB) 1993–4, Craig Erickson (QB) 1995, Danny Kight (K) 1999–2000, Brock Huard (QB) 2002–3.

8 Mark Reed (QB) 1983, Sean Salisbury (QB) 1987, Roderick Robinson (QB) 2001.

9 Mike Garrett (P) 1981, Mark Herrmann (QB) 1983–4, 1990–2, Kerry Brady (K) 1988.

10 George Hunt (K) 1973, Bucky Dilts (P) 1979, Art Schlichter (QB) 1982, 1984–5, David Humm (QB) 1982, Jack Trudeau (QB) 1986–93, Wendell Davis (WR) 1995, Mark Stock (WR) 1996, Kaipo McGuire (WR) 1998, Doug Brien (K) 2001, Terrence Wilkins (WR) 2003.

11 Jack Mildren (S) 1972–3, Greg Landry (QB) 1979–81, David Humm (QB) 1981, Ed Luther (QB) 1986, Bob Gagliano (QB) 1988, Jeff George (QB) 1990–3, Paul Justin (QB) 1995–7, Kaipo McGuire (WR) 1997, Mike Quinn (QB) 1998.

12 Bill Troup (QB) 1974, 1976–8, Jerry Golsteyn (QB) 1979, Jim Bob Taylor (QB) 1983, Matt Kofler (QB) 1985, Ricky Turner (QB) 1988, Don Strock (QB) 1989, Joe Ferguson (QB) 1990, Rusty Hilger (QB) 1991, Kerwin Bell (QB) 1996–7, *Jim Harbaugh* (QB) 1994, *Mike Vanderjagt* (K) 1998–2000, Desmond Kitchings (WR) 2001.

13 Sean Salisbury (QB) 1987, Kelly Holcomb (QB) 1996–2000, *Mike Vanderjagt* (K) 2001–3.

14 George Shaw (QB) 1955–8, Lamar McHan (QB) 1961, Ed Brown (QB) 1965, Marty Domres (QB) 1972–5, Jay Venuto (QB) 1981, Terry Nugent (QB) 1987, Jess Atkinson (K) 1988, Tom Ramsey (QB) 1989, *Cary Blanchard* (K) 1995–7, Billy Joe Hobert (QB) 2000.

15 Gary Cuozzo (QB) 1963–6, *Earl Morrall* (QB) 1968–71, Mike Kirkland (QB) 1976–8, Jerry Golsteyn (QB) 1979, Chris Doering (WR) 1996–7, Mark Stock (WR) 1996, Freddie Scott (WR) 1998, Isaac Jones (WR) 1999–2000, Tony Simmons (WR) 2001.

16 Jim Ward (QB) 1967–9, Mike Wood (K) 1981–2, Bobby Olive (WR) 1995, Chad Plummer

(WR) 1999, Joey Kent (WR) 2000, Mark Rypien (QB) 2001, Cory Sauter (QB) 2003.

17 Fred Enke (QB) 1953–4, Ray Brown (DB) 1958–60, Lamar McHan (QB) 1962–3, Sam Havrilak (B) 1969–73, Chris Chandler (QB) 1988–9, *Chris Gardocki* (P) 1995–8, Hunter Smith (P) 1999–2003.

18 Dick Flowers (B) 1953, Gary Kerkorian (QB) 1954–6, Cotton Davidson (QB) 1957, Dick Horn (B) 1958, Mike Pagel (QB) 1982–5, Wayne Johnson (QB) 1989, Eugene Benhart (QB) 1990, Browning Nagle (QB) 1994, Ben Bronson (WR) 1995, Bobby Olive (WR) 1996, Nate Jacquet (WR) 1997, *Peyton Manning* (QB) 1998–2003.

19 Jack Del Bello (B) 1953, Cotton Davidson (QB) 1954, **John Unitas** (QB) 1956–72.

20 *George Taliaferro* (QB) 1953–4, Dean Renfro (B) 1955, Jim Harness (B) 1956, John Hermann (B) 1956, Milt Davis (DB) 1957–60, Bob Harrison (B) 1961, *Jerry Logan* (S) 1963–72, Jackie Wallace (S) 1975–6, *Joe Washington* (RB) 1978–80, Ricky Porter (RB) 1983, Albert Bentley (RB) 1985–91, Leon Neal (RB) 1996–7, Jeff Burris (DB) 1998–2001, Joe Walker (DB) 2002, Mike Doss (S) 2003.

21 *Tom Keane* (DB) 1953–4, Walter Bryan (B) 1955, Billy Vessels (RB) 1956, Cotton Davidson (QB) 1957, Dick Nyers (B) 1957, Art DeCarlo (E) 1958–60, *Rick Volk* (S) 1967–75, Kevin Williams (WR) 1981, Aundra Thompson (WR) 1983, George Radachowsky (DB) 1984–5, John Holt (CB) 1986–8, Brian Lattimore (RB) 1991, Will White (DB) 1993, Lamont Warren (RB) 1994–8, Paul Miranda (DB) 1999, Mustafah Muhammad (DB) 2000, Thomas Smith (DB) 2001, Walt Harris (CB) 2002–3.

22 *Buddy Young* (B) 1953–5.

23 Carl Taseff (DB) 1953–61, Art DeCarlo (E) 1957, Jack Maitland (RB) 1970, Don McCauley (RB) 1971–81, Alvin Moore (RB) 1983–4, Ken Daniel (S) 1986–7, Bruce Plummer (DB) 1989, Anthony Johnson (RB) 1990–3, Leonard Humphries (DB) 1994, Dedric Mathis (DB) 1996–7, Keith Elias (RB) 1998–9, James Mungo (RB) 2002–3.

24 Larry Coutre (B) 1953, Dick Young (B) 1955, **Lenny Moore** (HB) 1956–67.

25 **Don Shula** (DB) 1953–6, Bob White (B) 1955, Jack Call (B) 1957–8, Alex Hawkins (B) 1959–65, 1967–8, Tom Bleick (B) 1966, Tom Curtis (DB) 1970–1, Ray Oldham (S) 1973–7, Nesby Glasgow (DB) 1979–87, Cornell Holloway (DB) 1990–2, Ronald Humphrey (RB) 1994–5, Robert Blackman (DB) 1997–8, Nick Harper (DB) 2001–3.

26 Ed Mioduszewski (B) 1953, Royce Womble (RB) 1954–7, *Lenny Lyles* (DB) 1958, Mike Sommer (RB) 1959–61, Wendell Harris (DB) 1962–5, Preston Pearson (RB) 1967–9, *Lydell Mitchell* (RB)

1972–7, Kim Anderson (DB) 1980–4, Pat Ballage (S) 1986, Craig Swoope (DB) 1987–8, Alan Grant (DB) 1990–1, Dewell Brewer (RB) 1994, Carlton Gray (DB) 1997, Tony Blevins (DB) 1999–2000, Rodregis Brooks (DB) 2001, David Gibson (DB) 2002.

27 Henry Moore (B) 1957, *Tom Matte* (RB) 1961, R.C. Owens (WR) 1962, Ray Perkins (WR) 1967–71, Hubert Ginn (RB) 1973, Howard Stevens (RB) 1975–7, Curtis Dickey (RB) 1980–2, Darryl Hemphill (S) 1982, Preston Davis (CB) 1984–6, Terry Wright (DB) 1987, Keith Taylor (DB) 1988–91, Clif Grace (RB) 1995, Arnold Mickens (RB) 1996, Rico Clark (DB) 1997–8, Thomas Randolph (DB) 1999, David Macklin (DB) 2000–3.

28 *Jimmy Orr* (WR) 1961–70, Cotton Speyrer (WR) 1972–4, Perry Griggs (KR) 1977, Howard Satterwhite (WR) 1977, Dwight Harrison (DB) 1978–9, Cleveland Franklin (RB) 1981–2, Bo Metcalf (DB) 1984, Mike Lush (DB) 1986, Lee Davis (DB) 1987r, Chuckie Miller (DB) 1988, Ed Toner (RB) 1992–3, *Marshall Faulk* (RB) 1994–8, Tito Wooten (DB) 1999, Payton Williams (DB) 2000, Idrees Bashir (DB) 2001–3.

29 Don Alley (WR) 1967, Brian Herosian (S) 1973, Marshall Johnson (WR) 1975–6, Ben Garry (RB) 1979–80, Mark Kafentzis (S) 1983–4, Dwight Hicks (S) 1986, **Eric Dickerson** (RB) 1987–91, Jitter Fields (DB) 1987, Jason Belser (DB) 1992–2000, Joseph Jefferson (DB) 2002.

30 Bake Turner (WR) 1962, Alvin Haymond (DB) 1964–7, Ron Gardin (DB) 1970–1, Willie Franklin (WR) 1972, Doug Nettles (CB) 1974–9, Larry Anderson (DB) 1982–4, Hubert Oliver (FB) 1986, Melvin Carver (RB) 1987, Joe Cribbs (RB) 1988, Derwin Gray (DB) 1993–7, Lennox Gordon (RB) 2000, Shyrone Stith (RB) 2001–2, Donald Strickland (CB) 2003.

31 Buck McPhail (RB) 1953, Jimmy Lesane (B) 1954, Chuck McMillan (B) 1954, Harry Hugasian (B) 1955, Burrell Shields (B) 1955, Dick Young (B) 1956, Billy Pricer (RB) 1957–60, Dick Bielski (E) 1962–3, Steve Stonebreaker (LB) 1964–6, Perry Lee Dunn (RB) 1969, Nelson Munsey (CB) 1972–7, Zachary Dixon (RB) 1980–2, Robbie Martin (WR) 1985, Leonard Coleman (DB) 1986–7, Michael Ball (DB) 1988–93, Derrick Frazier (DB) 1996, Mustafah Muhammad (DB) 1999, Clifton Crosby (DB) 2001–3.

32 Mark Smolinski (FB) 1961–2, Nate Craddock (RB) 1963, Joe Don Looney (RB) 1964, *Mike Curtis* (LB) 1965–75, Randy McMillan (RB) 1981–6, Ken Clark (RB) 1990–2, Robert O'Neal (DB) 1993–4, Zack Crockett (RB) 1995–8, *Edgerin James* (RB) 1999–2003.

33 Tony Lorick (FB) 1964–7, Ed Hinton (WR) 1969–72, Randy Hall (CB) 1974, 1976, Curtis Dickey (RB) 1983–5, Bryant Jones (DB) 1987r, Ashley Ambrose (CB) 1992–5, Clif Grace (RB)

1996–7, Craig Heyward (FB) 1998, Karim-Abdul Jabbar (RB) 2000, Dominic Rhodes (RB) 2001, 2003.

34 Joe Perry (RB) 1961–2, Bob Baldwin (B) 1966–7, Terry Cole (RB) 1968–9, Tom Nowatzke (RB) 1970–2, Ron Lee (RB) 1976–8, Jeff Delaney (S) 1982–3, George Wonsley (RB) 1984–8, Bruce Perkins (RB) 1991, Ray Buchanan (CB) 1993–6, Monty Montgomery (DB) 1997–9, Jason Doering (DB) 2001–3.

35 *Alan Ameche* (FB) 1955–60, J.W. Lockett (B) 1963, Ted Davis (LB) 1964–6, James Duncan (DB) 1969–71, Glenn Doughty (WR) 1972–9, Dwayne O'Steen (DB) 1982, Tate Randle (CB) 1983– 6, Rodney Culver (RB) 1992–3, Conrad Clarks (DB) 1995, Steven Hall (DB) 1996, Roosevelt Potts (RB) 1997, Ricky Williams (RB) 2002–3.

36 Zollie Toth (RB) 1953–4, Bill Pellington (LB) 1955–64, Barry Brown (E) 1966–7, *Norm Bulaich* (RB) 1970–2, John Andrews (TE) 1973, Don Hardeman (RB) 1978–9, Don Anderson (DB) 1985, Chris McLemore (RB) 1987, John Baylor (DB) 1989–93, Damon Watts (DB) 1994–7, Jim Finn (RB) 2000–2, Tom Lopienski (RB) 2003.

37 Ocie Austin (DB) 1968–9, Joe Orduna (RB) 1974, Reggie Pinkney (DB) 1979–81, Anthony Young (DB) 1985, Chris Goode (DB) 1987–93, Chuck Banks (RB) 1987r, Abu Wilson (RB) 1998, Chad Cota (S) 1999–2001, Eric Vance (DB) 2002.

38 John Huzvar (RB) 1953–4, Bill Olds (RB) 1973–5, Johnnie Wright (RB) 1982, Eugene Daniel (CB) 1984–96, Tyrone Poole (DB) 1998–2000.

39 Hubert Ginn (RB) 1973, Marvin Sims (RB) 1980–1, Newton Williams (RB) 1983, Victor Jackson (DB) 1986, Mike Prior (S) 1987–92, John Covington (DB) 1994, Richard Jones (DB) 1996, Emmanuel McDaniel (DB) 1997–8, Paul Shields (RB) 1999–2000, Anthony Floyd (CB) 2003.

40 Tom Kalmanir (B) 1953, Bob Leberman (B) 1954, Jesse Thomas (B) 1955–7, *Bob Boyd* (CB) 1960–8, Jack Maitland (RB) 1970, *Bruce Laird* (DB) 1972–81, Vaughn Williams (DB) 1984, John Williams (RB) 1987, Pat Ballage (S) 1987r, Terry Wright (DB) 1988, Ray McElroy (DB) 1995–8, Eric Smedley (DB) 1999, Autry Denson (RB) 2002, Brian Leigeb (DB) 2002.

41 Ernie Blandin (T) 1953, Jim Harness (B) 1956, Jack Simpson (B) 1958–60, Avatus Stone (B) 1958, *Tom Matte* (RB) 1962–72, John Simmons (CB) 1987, Cory Bird (DB) 2001–3.

42 Tommy James (DB) 1956, George Harold (B) 1966–7, Tom Maxwell (B) 1969–70, Charlie Pittman (RB) 1971, Lloyd Mumphord (CB) 1975–8, Derrick Hatchett (CB) 1980–3, Keith Lee (DB) 1985, Willie Tullis (CB) 1987–8, Gordon Brown (RB) 1987r, Dave McCloughan (DB) 1991, Roosevelt Potts (RB) 1993–6, Ric Mathias (DB) 1998, Raymond Walls (DB) 2001, Detron Smith (RB) 2002–3.

43 Harold Lewis (B) 1959, Ed Kovac (B) 1960, *Lenny Lyles* (DB) 1961–9, Lonnie Hepburn (DB) 1971–2, Tim Rudnick (DB) 1974, Norm Thompson (DB) 1977–9, Frank Middleton (RB) 1984, Jim Perryman (DB) 1987, Anthony Parker (DB) 1989, Vance Joseph (DB) 1996, Scott Greene (RB) 1998–9, Kevin McDougal (RB) 2000–1, Brian Allen (RB) 2003.

44 *Bert Rechichar* (DB/K) 1953–9, John Sample (CB) 1960, Gerald Allen (B) 1966, Roland Moss (FB) 1969, Rex Kern (DB) 1971–3, Lyle Blackwood (S) 1977–80, Steve Henry (DB) 1981, Sid Justin (CB) 1982, Kendall Williams (CB) 1983, Owen Gill (RB) 1985–6, Tim Manoa (RB) 1991, Maurice Carthon (FB) 1992, Warren Williams (RB) 1993, Ed Toner (RB) 1994, Chris Hetherington (RB) 1996–8, Darick Holmes (RB) 1999, Wes Ours (FB) 2001, Dallas Clark (TE) 2003.

45 L.G. Dupre (RB) 1955–9, Jerry Hill (FB) 1961, 1963–70, Mike Siani (WR) 1978–80, James Burroughs (CB) 1982–4, Tommy Sims (S) 1986, Craig Curry (DB) 1987r, Ivy Joe Hunter (RB) 1989–90, Tony Stargell (DB) 1992–3, Tim Hauck (S) 1998.

46 Jim Welch (DB) 1960–7, Len Dunlap (DB) 1971, Bryant Slater (DB) 1976, Spencer Thomas (DB) 1976, Marco Tongue (CB) 1983, Charles Washington (DB) 1989, George Streeter (DB) 1990, Vince Workman (RB) 1995–6, Kantroy Barber (RB) 1998.

47 John Sample (CB) 1958–9, Gary Glick (B) 1961, Jim Martin (K) 1963, Bob Felts (B) 1965, Charlie Stukes (DB) 1967–72, Tim Baylor (DB) 1976–8, Larry Braziel (DB) 1979–81, Leonard Coleman (DB) 1985, Dextor Clinkscale (S) 1986, Freddie Robinson (DB) 1987–8, Billy Austin (DB) 1998–2000, Jermaine Hampton (DB) 2001.

48 Bob Clemens (B) 1962, Larry Conjar (B) 1969–70, Don Nottingham (RB) 1971–3, Roosevelt Leaks (RB) 1975–9, Mark Bell (DE) 1983, Donnie Dee (TE) 1988–9, Justin Snow (TE) 2001–3.

49 David Lee (P) 1966–78, Cliff Odom (LB) 1982–4, Mike McCloskey (HB) 1987, James Pruitt (WR) 1988, David Tate (DB) 1994–7, Joe Dean Davenport (TE) 2001.

50 Brad Ecklund (C) 1953, Buzz Nutter (C) 1954–60, 1965, Bill Saul (LB) 1962–3, *Bill Curry* (C) 1967–72, Dan Neal (C) 1973–4, Forrest Blue (C) 1975–8, Joe Federspiel (LB) 1981, Joe Harris (LB) 1982, Grant Feasel (C) 1983–4, *Duane Bickett* (LB) 1985–93, Elijah Alexander (LB) 1996–8, Larry Moore (OL) 1999–2001, David Thornton (LB) 2002–3.

51 Dave Yohn (C) 1962, Mike Strofolino (LB) 1965, Bob Grant (LB) 1968–70, Bill Laskey (LB) 1971–2, Tony Bertuca (LB) 1974, Mike Varty (LB) 1975, Calvin O'Neal (LB) 1978, Mike Ozdowski (DE) 1979, Ricky Jones (LB) 1980–3, Kevin Hancock (LB) 1987, Bob Ontko (LB) 1987r, Chip

Banks (LB) 1989–92, Eric Naposki (LB) 1989, Trev Alberts (LB) 1994–6, Scott Vonder Ahe (LB) 1997, Ratcliff Thomas (LB) 1998, Jeff Brady (LB) 1999, Mike Morton (LB) 2001.

52 George Radosevich (C) 1954, *Dick Szymanski* (C/LB) 1955, 1957–68, Robbie Nichols (LB) 1970–1, Randy Edmunds (LB) 1972, Mike Kaczmarek (LB) 1973, Tom MacLeod (LB) 1974–8, Lee Gross (C) 1979, Ed Smith (LB) 1980–1, Greg Bracelin (LB) 1982–4, Ricky Chatman (LB) 1987r, Dan Murray (LB) 1989, Scott Radecic (LB) 1990–2, Brian Ratigan (LB) 1994, Steve Morrison (LB) 1997–8, Mike Peterson (LB) 1999–2002, Keyon Whiteside (LB) 2003.

53 Butch Maples (C) 1963, Dennis Gaubatz (LB) 1965–9, Tom Beutler (LB) 1971, Stan White (LB) 1973–9, *Ray Donaldson* (C) 1980–92, Paul Butcher (LB) 1993–4, Sammie Burroughs (LB) 1996–7, Michael Barber (LB) 1998–9, Marcus Washington (LB) 2000–3.

54 Butch Riley (LB) 1969, Tom Goode (C) 1970, Stan White (LB) 1972, Fred Hoaglin (C) 1973, Sanders Shiver (LB) 1976–83, Bill Benjamin (LB) 1987, Jeff Herrod (LB) 1988–96, 1998, Phillip Armour (C) 2000, Donnell Thompson (LB) 2001–2.

55 Leo Sanford (C) 1958, Jack Burkett (LB) 1961–6, Ron Porter (LB) 1967–9, John Campbell (LB) 1969, Dan Dickel (LB) 1974–7, Stu O'Dell (LB) 1978, Barry Krauss (LB) 1979–88, Quentin Coryatt (LB) 1992–7, Ratcliff Thomas (LB) 1999–2000, Sean Harris (LB) 2001.

56 Ray May (LB) 1970–2, Danny Rhodes (LB) 1974, Ed Simonini (LB) 1976–81, Vernon Maxwell (LB) 1983–4, LaMonte Hunley (LB) 1985–6, Ed Grimsley (LB) 1987, Fredd Young (LB) 1988–90, Brian Jones (LB) 1991, Tony Bennett (LB) 1994–7, Andre Royal (LB) 1998, Spencer Reid (LB) 1999, Dwight Hollier (LB) 2000, Ryan Phillips (L) 2001, Tupe Peko (OL) 2002–3.

57 Ken Mendenhall (C) 1971–80, Dallas Hickman (LB) 1981, Mike Humiston (LB) 1982, 1984, Dave Ahrens (LB) 1985–7, Brian Bulluck (LB) 1987r, Ronnie Washington (LB) 1989, Pat Snyder (OL) 1991, Devon McDonald (LB) 1993–5, Phil Yeboah-Kodie (LB) 1996, Bertrand Berry (LB) 1997–9, Jim Nelson (LB) 2003.

58 Ed Mooney (LB) 1972–3, Derrel Luce (LB) 1975–8, Steve Heimkreiter (LB) 1980, Steve Hathaway (LB) 1984, Glen Redd (LB) 1986, June James (LB) 1987, Orlando Lowry (LB) 1988–9, Matt Vanderbeek (LB) 1990–2, Mark Cannon (C) 1991, Cedric Figaro (LB) 1991, Glenell Sanders (LB) 1995, Jay Leeuwenburg (G) 1996–8, Gary Brackett (LB) 2003.

59 Stan Cherry (LB) 1973, Jim Cheyunski (LB) 1975–6, Mike Woods (LB) 1979–81, Orlando Lowry (LB) 1985–7, Brad Saar (LB) 1987r, Kurt Larson (LB) 1989–90, Matt Jaworski (LB) 1991,

Stephen Grant (LB) 1992–7, Steven Conley (LB) 1998, Rob Holmberg (LB) 1998, Jason Johnson (C) 1999, Cato June (LB) 2003.

60 Sisto Averno (G) 1953–4, Gene Pepper (G) 1954, Jim Raiff (G) 1954, George Preas (T) 1955–65, George Wright (DT) 1970, Dave Simonson (T) 1974, Ron Baker (G) 1978–9, Dave Simmons (LB) 1982, Gary Padjen (LB) 1983–4, Mark Boggs (T) 1987, Dan McQuaid (OL) 1988, Jason Johnson (C) 1997–8.

61 *Dick Barwegen* (G) 1953–4, Jack Patera (LB) 1955–7, Zeke Smith (LB) 1960, Wiley Feagin (G) 1961–2, Lou Kirouac (T) 1964, Cornelius Johnson (G) 1968–72, Robert Pratt (G) 1974–81, Don Bailey (C) 1984–5, Marsharne Graves (T) 1987r, Tony McCoy (NT) 1997–9, Rob Murphy (OL) 2002.

62 Alex Agase (G) 1953, Palmer Pyle (G) 1960–3, Glenn Ressler (G) 1965–74, Ken Huff (G) 1975–82, George Achica (NT) 1985, Don Thorp (NT) 1987, Jeff Criswell (G) 1987r, Brian Baldinger (T) 1988–91, Ellis Johnson (DT) 1995–2001.

63 *Art Spinney* (G) 1956–60, Norman Davis (G) 1967, *Mike Barnes* (DE) 1973–81, Nat Hudson (G) 1982, Mark Kirchner (T) 1984, 1986, Steve Knight (OL) 1987, Brian Blados (OL) 1991, Kirk Lowdermilk (C) 1993–6, Jeff Saturday (C) 1999–2003.

64 Ed Sharkey (G) 1953, Fred Thurston (G) 1958, Marv Matuszak (LB) 1959–61, Bill Kirchiro (G) 1962, Sid Williams (LB) 1968, John Shinners (G) 1972, David Taylor (T) 1973–9, Ben Utt (G) 1982–9, Darin Shoulders (T) 1991, Trevor Matich (OL) 1992–3, Garin Patrick (OL) 1995, Doug Widell (G) 1996–7, Larry Chester (DL) 1998–2000, Rick DeMulling (G) 2001–3.

65 Bill Pellington (LB) 1953–4, Bill Koman (LB) 1956, Steve Myhra (LB/K) 1957–61, Ron Kostelnik (DT) 1969, Carl Mauck (LB) 1969, Bill Windauer (DT) 1973–4, Dave Pear (DT) 1975, Jimmy Moore (G) 1981, Glenn Hyde (T) 1982, Ellis Gardner (OL) 1984, Joel Patten (T) 1987–8, Jim Merritts (DL) 1987r, Joey Banes (OL) 1990, Frank Giannetti (DL) 1991, Eric Mahlum (G) 1994–6, Brandon Miller (DT) 2000.

66 Bill Lange (G) 1953, Ernie Cheatham (T) 1954, Charles Robinson (G) 1954, Don Shinnick (LB) 1957–68, Elmer Collett (G) 1973–7, Greg Marshall (DT) 1978, Chris Foote (C) 1980–1, *Ron Solt* (G) 1984–8, 1992, Chris Conlin (OL) 1990–1, Steve Hardin (OL) 1996, Eugene Chung (OL) 1997.

67 Doug Eggers (LB) 1954–7, Jim Colvin (T) 1960–1, Monte Lee (C) 1965, Dale Memmelaar (G) 1966–7, Dan Grimm (G) 1969, Lynn Larson (T) 1971–2, Bob Van Duyne (G) 1974–80, Arland Thomas (G) 1982, Roger Caron (T) 1985, Ron Plantz (OL) 1987, Stan Eisenhooth (OL) 1989, Jack Linn (T) 1991, *Will Wolford* (T) 1993–5, Jason

Mathews (T) 1996–7, Tom Myslinski (OL) 1998, Hans Olsen (DT) 2001.

68 Alex Sandusky (G) 1954–66, Dennis Nelson (T) 1970–4, Jeff Hart (T) 1979–83, Willie Broughton (NT) 1985–6, Milt Carthens (T) 1987r, Pat Tomberlin (T) 1989–90, Tom Ricketts (G) 1992, John Ray (OL) 1993, Casey Wiegmann (OL) 1996, Josh Mallard (DL) 2002.

69 Wade Griffith (T) 1977–81, Leo Wisniewski (NT) 1982–4, Randy Dixon (T) 1987–95, Sid Abramowitz (OL) 1987r, Ben Gilbert (G) 2000–1, Pete Pierson (OL) 2002, Jim Newton (T) 2003.

70 **Art Donovan** (DT) 1953–61.

71 Dan Sullivan (G/T) 1962–72, Glenn Robinson (DE) 1975, Mike Ozdowski (DE) 1978–81, Henry Waechter (DE) 1983–4, Ted Petersen (T) 1984, Kevin Call (T) 1985–93, Kipp Vickers (OL) 1995–7, Jon Blackmon (OL) 1998, Jamie Wilson (OL) 1999, Ryan Diem (G) 2001–3.

72 Jack Little (T) 1953–4, George Radosevich (C) 1955–6, Luke Owens (T) 1957, Joe Lewis (T) 1961, *Bob Vogel* (T) 1963–72, Fred Cook (DE) 1974–80, Mike Fultz (DT) 1981, Steve Durham (DE) 1982, Karl Baldischwiler (T) 1983, 1985–6, Kevin Call (T) 1984, Byron Darby (NT) 1987–8, Pat Cunningham (OL) 1990, Mark Vander Poel (T) 1992, Garry Howe (DT) 1994, Derek West (T) 1995–7, Larry Moore (OL) 1998, Shane Bonham (DT) 1999, Tom Ridder (T) 2000–1, Brandon Hicks (DT) 2003.

73 Joe Campanella (T) 1957–8, Lebron Shields (G) 1960, Tom Gilburg (T/P) 1961–5, Sam Ball (T) 1966–70, Rusty Ganas (DT) 1971, Richard Amman (DE) 1972–3, Ed George (T) 1975, Ron Fernandes (DE) 1976–9, Cleveland Crosby (DE) 1982, Steve Wright (T) 1983–4, Steve Knight (OL) 1987, Joe Klecko (DT) 1988, Zefross Moss (T) 1989–94, Adam Meadows (T) 1997–2003.

74 Ken Jackson (G) 1953–7, Billy Ray Smith (DT) 1963–70, George Wright (DT) 1971, Tom Drougas (T) 1972–3, Steve Williams (DT) 1974, Ken Novak (DT) 1976–7, David Rowe (DT) 1978, Sid Abramowitz (OL) 1983, Bob Brotzki (T) 1986–8, Roger Caron (T) 1986, Chris Gambol (T) 1988, William Schultz (OL) 1990–2, Jason Mathews (T) 1994–5, Waverly Jackson (OL) 1998–2002, Steve Sciullo (G) 2003.

75 **Gino Marchetti** (DE) 1953, Jim Colvin (T) 1962–3, Guy Reese (T) 1964–5, John Williams (G) 1968–71, Chuck Hinton (DT) 1972, Joe Schmiesing (DL) 1973, *George Kunz* (T) 1975–7, 1980, Terry Crouch (G) 1982, *Chris Hinton* (G/T) 1983–7, Irv Pankey (T) 1991–2, Mark Vander Poel (T) 1991, Ron Mattes (T) 1992, Cecil Gray (DL) 1993–4, Shawn Harper (T) 1995, Troy Auzenne (TE) 1996, Mark Thomas (DL) 1998–9, Larry Triplett (DT) 2002–3.

76 Jim Winkler (T) 1953, *Don Joyce* (DE) 1954, *Gene Lipscomb* (DT) 1956–60, Gerald Peterson (T) 1956, *Fred Miller* (DT) 1963–72, Joe Ehrmann (DT) 1973–80, Tom Tabor (DT) 1982, Jim Mills (T) 1983–4, Jerome Sally (NT) 1987, Marcus Jackson (DL) 1987r, Sam Clancy (DL) 1989–93, Steve McKinney (G) 1998–2001, Makoa Freitas (G) 2003.

77 Tom Finnin (DT) 1953–6, **Jim Parker** (T/G) 1957–67.

78 Dick Chorovich (T) 1955–6, Ray Krouse (DE) 1958, John Diehl (T) 1961–4, *Bubba Smith* (DE) 1967–71, *John Dutton* (DE) 1974–8, Tim Foley (T) 1981, Greg Murtha (T) 1982, Steve Parker (DE) 1983–4, Jon Hand (DE) 1986–94, Don Thorp (NT) 1988, Tarik Glenn (G) 1997–2003.

79 Jim Winkler (T) 1953, Bob Myers (T) 1955, Tom Feamster (T) 1956, Sherman Plunkett (T) 1958–60, Lou Michaels (DE/K) 1964–9, Greg Johnson (DT) 1977, Don Morrison (T) 1978, Greg Fields (DE) 1979–80, Randy Van Divier (T) 1981, John Sinnot (T) 1982, Lindsey Mason (T) 1983, Andy Ekern (T) 1984, Harvey Armstrong (NT) 1986–90, Shawn Heffern (OL) 1987, William Paris (T) 1991, Steve Emtman (DT) 1992, Joe Staysniak (T) 1993–5, Tony Mandarich (T) 1996–8, Bernard Holsey (DL) 2000, Raheem Brock (DL) 2002–3.

80 Jack Bighead (E) 1954, Monte Brethauer (E) 1955, Dick Nyers (B) 1956, *Andy Nelson* (DB) 1957–63, Gail Cogdill (WR) 1968, Jim O'Brien (K/WR) 1970–2, Ollie Smith (WR) 1973–4, Marshall Johnson (WR) 1977–8, Ray Butler (WR) 1980–5, Ricky Nichols (WR) 1985, Bill Brooks (WR) 1986–92, Steve Bryant (WR) 1987r, Aaron Cox (WR) 1993, Aaron Bailey (WR) 1994–8, Terrence Wilkins (WR) 1999–2001, Joe Dean Davenport (TE) 2002–3.

81 *Art Spinney* (G) 1953–5, Bernie Flowers (E) 1956, *Ordell Braase* (DE) 1957–68, Billy Newsome (DE) 1970–2, *Roger Carr* (WR) 1974–81, Pat Beach (TE) 1982–3, 1985–91, Dave Young (TE) 1984, Joe Jones (TE) 1987r, Charles Arbuckle (TE) 1992–5, Carlos Etheredge (TE) 1994, Marcus Pollard (TE) 1995–2003, Thomas McLemore (TE) 1995.

82 Dan Edwards (E) 1953–4, **Raymond Berry** (WR) 1955–67.

83 Barney Poole (E) 1953, Bob Langas (E) 1954, *Don Joyce* (DE) 1955–60, Billy Ray Smith (DT) 1961, Don Thompson (DE) 1962–3, Andy Stynchula (T) 1966–7, **Ted Hendricks** (LB) 1969–73, Ron Mayo (TE) 1974, Mack Alston (TE) 1977–80, Tim Sherwin (TE) 1981–7, Keli McGregor (TE) 1985, Greg LaFleur (TE) 1986, Mark Walczak (TE) 1987, Greg Hawthorne (TE) 1987r, *Clarence Verdin* (WR) 1988–93, Bradford Banta (TE) 1994–9, Josh Keur (TE) 2000, Trevor Insley (WR) 2001, Qadry Ismail (WR) 2002, Brandon Stokeley (WR) 2003.

84 Elmer Wingate (E) 1953, Jim Winkler (T) 1953, *Jim Mutscheller* (TE) 1954–61, Neal Petties (E) 1964–6, Tom Mitchell (TE) 1968–73, Tim

Berra (WR) 1974, Randy Burke (WR) 1978–81, Holden Smith (WR) 1982, Victor Oatis (WR) 1983, Mark Boyer (TE) 1985–9, Mark Walczak (TE) 1987, Kelley Johnson (WR) 1987r, Jessie Hester (WR) 1990–3, Shannon Baker (WR) 1993–4, Mark Jackson (WR) 1994, Willie Anderson (WR) 1995, Scott Slutzker (TE) 1996–7, E.G. Green (WR) 1998–2000, Drew Haddad (WR) 2001–2, Brad Pyatt (WR) 2003.

85 Mel Embree (E) 1953, Ed Cooke (E) 1959, Dee Mackey (E) 1961–2, Roy Hilton (DE) 1965–73, Jimmie Kennedy (TE) 1975–7, Ron LaPointe (TE) 1980, Bob Raba (TE) 1980, David Shula (WR) 1981, Matt Bouza (WR) 1982–9, Tim Kearse (WR) 1987, Clarence Weathers (WR) 1989, Stacey Simmons (WR) 1990, Darvell Huffman (WR) 1991, Reggie Langhorne (WR) 1992–3, Floyd Turner (WR) 1994, *Ken Dilger* (TE) 1995–2001, Mike Roberg (TE) 2002, Jermaine Wiggins (TE) 2002, Aaron Moorehead (WR) 2003.

86 Monte Brethauer (E) 1953, Dave Sherer (E) 1959, Butch Wilson (E) 1963–7, Freddie Scott (WR) 1974–7, Reese McCall (TE) 1978–82, Phil Smith (WR) 1983–4, Dave Young (TE) 1983, Oliver Williams (WR) 1985–6, Walter Murray (WR) 1986–7, Roy Banks (WR) 1987–8, James Pruitt (WR) 1989, Stanley Morgan (WR) 1990, Sammy Martin (WR) 1991, Reggie Thornton (WR) 1991, Eddie Miller (WR) 1992–3, Brian Stablein (WR) 1994–7, Jerome Pathon (WR) 1998–2001, Troy Walters (WR) 2002–3.

87 Lloyd Colteryahn (E) 1954–6, Jerry Richardson (E) 1959–60, Aubrey Linne (E) 1961, *Willie Richardson* (WR) 1963–9, 1971, Roy Jefferson (WR) 1970, Raymond Chester (TE) 1973–7, Brian DeRoo (WR) 1979–81, Elmer Bailey (WR) 1982, Matt Bouza (WR) 1982, Tracy Porter (WR) 1983–4, Wayne Capers (WR) 1985–6, James Harbour (WR) 1986, Mark Bellini (WR) 1987–8, James Noble (WR) 1987, Titus Dixon (WR) 1989, Andre Rison (WR) 1989, Eugene Riley (TE) 1990, James Coley (TE) 1991, Sean Dawkins (WR) 1993–7, Torrance Small (WR) 1998, Lake Dawson (WR) 1999, Chad Plummer (WR) 2000, Reggie Wayne (WR) 2001–3.

88 Monte Brethauer (E) 1954, Ken Gregory (E) 1961, **John Mackey** (TE) 1963–71, John Mosier (TE) 1972, John Andrews (TE) 1974, Ricky Thompson (WR) 1976–7, Herb Orvis (DT) 1979–81, Bernard Henry (WR) 1982–5, Robbie Martin (WR) 1986, John Brandes (TE) 1987–9, Keith Lester (TE) 1987, Stanley Morgan (WR) 1990, Kerry Cash (TE) 1991–4, Bob Mrosko (TE) 1991, Floyd Turner (WR) 1995, *Marvin Harrison* (WR) 1996–2003.

89 Elmer Wingate (E) 1953, **Gino Marchetti** (DE) 1954–64, 1966.

90 Jim Krahl (DT) 1979–80, Hosea Taylor (DE) 1981, 1983, Gary Padjen (LB) 1982, Mark Bell (DE) 1984, John Haines (DL) 1986, Roger Remo (LB) 1987r, Ezra Johnson (DE) 1988–9, Sean McNanie (DL) 1990, Mel Agee (DE) 1991–2, Steve Emtman (DT) 1993–4, Steve Martin (DT) 1996–8, Mark Thomas (DL) 2000–1, Montae Reagor (DT) 2003.

91 Anthony Green (DT) 1981, Byron Smith (DE) 1984–5, Shane Curry (DL) 1991, Antony Jordan (LB) 1998, Chukie Nwokorie (DE) 1999–2002.

92 Mike Fultz (DT) 1981, Daryl Wilkerson (DE) 1981, James Hunter (NT) 1982, Brad White (DT) 1984–5, Jeff Leiding (LB) 1986–7, Tony Walker (LB) 1990–2, Thomas Sims (DL) 1993, Steve Morrison (LB) 1995–6, Carl Powell (DL) 1997, Chad Bratzke (DE) 1999–2003.

93 Harry Stanback (DE) 1982, Cliff Odom (LB) 1985–9, Ralph Jarvis (DL) 1990, Freddie Joe Nunn (DE) 1994–6, Jason Chorak (LB) 1998, Lionel Barnes (DE) 2000–1, *Dwight Freeney* (DE) 2002–3.

94 Fletcher Jenkins (DE) 1982, Scott Virkus (DE) 1984–5, Scott Kellar (NT) 1986–7, Gary Baldinger (DL) 1990, Jeff Faulkner (DL) 1990, Tony McCoy (NT) 1992–6, Rob Morris (LB) 2000–3.

95 Ernie Barnes (NT) 1983, Chris Scott (DE) 1984–5, Bob Hamm (DE) 1987, Mitchell Benson (DL) 1989–90, Travis Davis (NT) 1991, Skip McClendon (DL) 1992–3, Bernard Whittington (DE) 1994–2000, Mike Wells (DT) 2001, David Pugh (DL) 2002–3.

96 Dave Simmons (LB) 1982, Blaise Winter (DE) 1984, Bill Elko (NT) 1987r, Don Thorp (NT) 1988, Quintus McDonald (LB) 1989–91, Willis Peguese (DE) 1992–3, Trevor Wilmot (LB) 1995, Richard Dent (DE) 1996, Van Tuinei (DL) 1998, Shawn King (DE) 1999, Josh Williams (DT) 2000–3.

97 Quinton Ballard (NT) 1983, Frank Mattiace (DL) 1987r, O'Brien Alston (LB) 1988–9, Scott Radecic (LB) 1993–5, Kendel Shello (DL) 1996–8, Cornelius Bennett (LB) 1999–2000, Christian Peter (DT) 2001.

98 Johnie Cooks (LB) 1982–8, Tony Siragusa (DT) 1990–6, Dan Footman (DE) 1997–8, Sam Sword (LB) 2000–2, James Cannida (DL) 2002, Robert Mathis (DE) 2003.

99 Donnell Thompson (DE) 1981–91, Michael Brandon (DE) 1993, Al Noga (DE) 1994, Lance Teichelman (DL) 1994, Mike Pelton (DL) 1995, Al Fontenot (DE) 1997–8, Brad Scioli (DE) 1999–2003.

JACKSONVILLE JAGUARS

The franchise: Although Jacksonville began as an underdog in the expansion franchise derby, the solid partnership forged between the city and the ownership group led by Wayne Weaver won the day in 1993 when Weaver was awarded the NFL's 30th franchise for the city. The Jaguars began operations in 1995 under Bill Parcells–protégé and strict disciplinarian Tom Coughlin. Blessed from the beginning, the Jaguars selected solid tackle Tony Boselli with their first draft pick, traded for skilled, mobile, young quarterback Mark Brunell, and signed talented, unknown receivers Jimmy Smith and (later) Keenan McCardell as free agents. In 1995, Jacksonville won more games, four, than any previous expansion team — although the Carolina Panthers won seven that year setting a record. In their second year, the Jaguars reached the AFC Championship game, losing to Parcells' Patriots on the road. Jacksonville would win division titles in years four and five and would return to the AFC title game in 1999, losing to the Titans this time. Salary cap woes, age, and injuries began to catch up to the team in the new millennium, and Coughlin was fired after the 2002 season. New coach Jack Del Rio drafted a new quarterback of the future, Byron Leftwich, to start the rebuilding process.

Origin of name: The Jaguars held a naming contest. Finalists included Sharks, Stingrays, Panthers, and Jaguars. Jaguars was selected on December 6, 1991, two years before Jacksonville was actually awarded an NFL franchise.

Time till first championship: Nine years and counting.

Time since last championship: Never won.

Retired numbers: None.

Other numbers worn by these players: NA.

Those who wore retired numbers after the honored player: NA.

Numbers that should be retired: None.

Owned numbers: None

Numbers worn by Hall of Famers: None.

Star power: Bryce Paup took 95 from Jose White; Hardy Nickerson took 56 from Lonnie Marts.

Star eclipsed: Deon Figures wore 27 because Aaron Beasley wore 21.

Numbers with most great players: 20 has been worn by runner Natroné Means and safety Donovan Darius.

Worst represented numbers: No one of consequence has worn 5, 9, 10 or 23.

Number worn by the most players: 54 has been worn by seven Jaguars.

Player who wore the most numbers: Ty Hallock has worn 49, 54 and 88.

Longest tenure wearing a number: Mark Brunell, 8, and Jimmy Smith, 82, have each played for the Jaguars for all nine years.

Number worn by first ever draft pick: Tony Boselli was drafted number one in 1995 and wore 71.

Biggest draft busts: Receiver R. Jay Soward, 81, was selected 29th in 2000 and caught 14 balls in 13 career games.

Record by Decade

	Regular Season			Postseason		
	Won	Lost	Tied	Won	Lost	Championships
1990s	49	31	0	4	4	
2000s	24	40	0	0	0	
All-Time	73	71	0	4	4	

Winning seasons: 4. Losing Seasons: 5. .500 seasons: 0.

Coaches

	Years	Record	Playoffs
Tom Coughlin	1995–2002	68–60–0	4–4
Jack Del Rio	2003	5–11–0	0–0

Number worn by first expansion draft pick: Quarterback Steve Beurlein was the first pick in the expansion draft and wore number 7. Linebacker Brant Boyer lasted the longest time of any of the expansion draft selections—six years from 1995 to 2000.

Number worn by oldest player: 36 year old linebacker Hardy Nickerson wore 56 in 2001.

Cameos: All Pros and other notables— Steve Beurlein 7; Ernest Givins 84; Desmond Howard 81; Andre Rison 81; Bruce Wilkerson 68.

Ones who got away: Rob Johnson and Jay Fiedler, two backup quarterbacks who both wore 11, have both started in other cities although not with a great deal of success.

Least popular numbers: 0, 13, 14, 15, 19, 46, 47, and 60 have not yet been worn in Jacksonville.

Last number to be originated: 18 was worn for the first time in 2003 by Troy Edwards.

Longest dormant number: 48 has not been worn in seven years since 1996.

Triskaidekaphobia notes: 13 has not been worn yet.

Shared numbers: 20 was worn by fullback Natrone Means and Donovan Darius, two hard-hitters.

Continuity: Natrone Means was replaced in 20 by Donovan Darius; defensive end Joel Smeenge was replaced in 94 by massive defensive tackle Marcus Stroud.

Discontinuity: Linebacker Kevin Hardy was followed in 51 by linebacker Akin Ayodele; tackle Leon Searcy was followed in 72 by tackle Steve Zahursky.

Family connections: None.

Quarterback numbers over 19: None.

Numbers of future NFL head coaches: None.

Numbers of future NFL referees: None.

Players who played other sports: None.

Players more famous after football: None.

Number with most points scored: 1 with 764 points scored by Mike Hollis.

Number with most yards rushing: 28 with 6,356 yards gained by Fred Taylor.

Number with most receptions: 82 with 718 passes caught by Jimmy Smith.

Number with most touchdown passes: 8 with 144 touchdowns tossed by Mark Brunell.

Number with most interceptions: 21 with 15 passes picked off by Aaron Beasley.

Oddity: Steve Beurlein, the first expansion pick in 1995, inaugurated the number 7 for both the Jaguars and for their fellow 1995 expansion franchise the Panthers.

Team All-Time Numerical Roster

Pro Bowl players for each number are in *Italics*; Hall of Famers are in **Bold** type.

1 *Mike Hollis* (K) 1995–2001.

2 Steve Lindsey (K) 1999–2000, *Chris Hanson* (P) 2001–3.

3 Jaret Holmes (K) 2001, Tim Seder (K) 2002, Mark Royals (P) 2003.

4 Bryan Barker (P) 1995–2000.

5 Todd Philcox (QB) 1996, Jim Tarle (K) 2000-1, Danny Boyd (K) 2002, Hayden Epstein (K) 2002, Seth Marler (K) 2003.

6 none.

7 Steve Beuerlein (QB) 1995, Will Furrer (QB) 1998, Richie Cunningham (K) 2002, Byron Leftwich (QB) 2003.

8 *Mark Brunell* (QB) 1995–2003.

9 Brad Goebel (QB) 1995, David Garrard (QB) 2002–3.

10 Jamie Martin (QB) 1998, 2000, Roderick Robinson (QB) 2001, Kent Graham (QB) 2002.

11 Rob Johnson (QB) 1995–7, Jay Fiedler (QB) 1999.

12 Jim Miller (QB) 1997, Jonathan Quinn (QB) 1998–2000

13 none.

14 none.

15 none.

16 Steve Matthews (QB) 1997.

17 Phil Stambaugh (QB) 2001, Jimmy Redmond (WR) 2003.

18 Troy Edwards (WR) 2003.

19 none.

20 Chris Hudson (S) 1995, Natrone Means (RB) 1996–7, Donovan Darius (S) 1998–2003.

21 Deral Boykin (S) 1995, Tommy Johnson (CB) 1995, Aaron Beasley (CB) 1996–2001, Steve Smith (CB) 2002.

22 Bucky Brooks (CB) 1996–7, Tavian Banks (RB) 1998–9, Frank Moreau (RB) 2001, Reggie White (RB) 2001, Robert Bean (CB) 2002, La-Brandon Toefield (RB) 2003.

23 Randy Jordan (RB) 1995–7, Cordell Taylor (CB) 1998, Corey Chamblin (CB) 1999, Anthony

Johnson (RB) 2000, Ike Charlton (DB) 2002, Ray Perryman (S) 2003.

24 Harry Colon (S) 1995, Rashid Gayle (CB) 1996, Chris Howard (RB) 1998–2000, Craig Miller (S) 2000, Delvin Brown (S) 2001, Kiwaukee Thomas (CB) 2003.

25 Mickey Washington (CB) 1995–6, Curtis Anderson (CB) 1997, Fernando Bryant (CB) 1999–2003.

26 Rogerick Green (CB) 1995, Kevin Devine (CB) 1997–8, Rayna Stewart (S) 1999–2000, Ainsley Battles (S) 2001–1, Blue Adams (CB) 2003.

27 Vinnie Clark (CB) 1995–6, Deon Figures (CB) 1997–8, Shad Criss (CB) 2000, Earthwind Moreland (CB) 2001, Damen Wheeler (CB) 2001, Rasheen Mathis (S) 2003.

28 Monty Grow (S) 1995, Dana Hall (S) 1996–7, Fred Taylor (RB) 1998–2003.

29 Darren Carrington (S) 1995, Rickey Parker (CB) 1997, Tawambi Settles (S) 1998, Jason Craft (CB) 1999–2003.

30 Darren Studstill (S) 1995–6, Michael Swift (CB) 2000.

31 Daimon Shelton (FB) 1997–2000, Patrick Washington (FB) 2001–1, Chris Brown (DB) 2003.

32 Vaughn Dunbar (RB) 1995, Mike Logan (S) 1997–2000, Marlon McCree (S) 2001–3.

33 James Stewart (RB) 1995–9, Shyrone Stith (RB) 2000, James Trapp (S) 2003.

34 Reggie Cobb (RB) 1995, Roger Graham (RB) 1996, Zack Crockett (FB) 1998, Stacy Mack (RB) 1999–2002, David Allen (RB) 2003.

35 Le'Shai Maston (FB) 1995–6, Elvis Joseph (RB) 2001–1, Deke Cooper (S) 2003.

36 Ryan Christopherson (FB) 1995–6, Ron Janes (FB) 1998, Renard Cox (DB) 2001.

37 Chris Hudson (S) 1996–8, *Carnell Lake* (S) 1999–2000.

38 Mike Dumas (S) 1995, Blaine McElmurry (S) 1998–9, Dan Alexander (RB) 2002.

39 Chris Parker (RB) 1997.

40 Gordon Laro (TE) 1995, Robert Massey (CB) 1996.

41 Dave Thomas (CB) 1995–9, Kiwaukee Thomas (CB) 2000–1, Nick Sorensen (S) 2003.

42 Ricky Bell (CB) 1996, Chad Dukes (RB) 2000, James Boyd (S) 2001–1, Anthony Mitchell (S) 2003.

43 George Jones (RB) 1998, Jermaine Williams (FB) 2000.

44 Bryan Dickerson (FB) 1995, Marc Edwards (FB) 2003.

45 Travis Davis (S) 1995–8, JoJuan Armour (S) 1999, Erik Olson (S) 2000, Chris Fuamatu-Ma'afala (RB) 2003.

46 none.

47 none.

48 Chris Griffin (FB/TE) 1996.

49 Ty Hallock (FB/TE) 1997.

50 Tom Myslinski (G) 1995, Eddie Robinson (LB) 1996–7, Eric Storz (LB) 1998–2000, Joe Wesley (LB) 2001, Tony Gilbert (LB) 2003.

51 Mark Williams (LB) 1995, *Kevin Hardy* (LB) 1996–2001, Akin Ayodele (LB) 2002–3.

52 Brant Boyer (LB) 1995–2000, Eric Westmoreland (LB) 2001–3.

53 Santo Stephens (LB) 1995, Nate Dingle (LB) 1996, Eddie Mason (LB) 1998, T.J. Slaughter (LB) 2000–3.

54 Keith Goganious (LB) 1995, Ty Hallock (FB/TE) 1996, James Hamilton (LB) 1997–8, Chester Burnett (LB) 1999, Troy Pelshak (LB) 2000, Donny Green (LB) 2001, Mike Peterson (LB) 2003.

55 Tom McManus (LB) 1995–9, Danny Clark (LB) 2000–3.

56 Jeff Lageman (DE) 1995–8, Lonnie Marts (LB) 1999, Hardy Nickerson (LB) 2000-1, Bobby Brooks (LB) 2002, Shannon Taylor (LB) 2003, Deon Humphrey (LB) 2003.

57 Jeff Kopp (LB) 1996–8, Reggie Lowe (LB) 1998, Corey Terry (LB) 1999, Joseph Tuipala (LB) 2001-1.

58 Bryan Schwartz (LB) 1995–9, Lonnie Marts (LB) 2000, Jeff Posey (LB) 2001, Hugh Douglas (DE) 2003.

59 Reggie Clark (LB) 1995–6, Edward Thomas (LB) 2000-1, Keith Mitchell (LB) 2003.

60 none.

61 Emarlos Leroy (DT) 1999.

62 Ben Coleman (G) 1995–9.

63 Frank Cornish (CB) 1995, Michael Cheever (CB) 1996–8, Brad Meester (G) 2000–3.

64 John Jurkovic (DT) 1996–8, Aaron Koch (G/T) 2000-1, Jamar Nesbit (G) 2003.

65 Bronzell Miller (DE) 1995, Quentin Neu jahr (C) 1998–2000, Chris Naeole (G) 2003.

66 Shawn Bouwens (G) 1995, Greg Huntington (G/C) 1996–7, John Wade (C) 1998–2002.

67 Jeff Novak (G/T) 1995–8, Steve Ingram (G/T) 1999, Gannon Shepherd (T) 2000-1, Daryl Terrell (T/G) 2002, Vince Manuwai (G) 2003.

68 Bruce Wilkerson (T) 1995, Mark Nori (G) 1997–8, Brenden Stai (T) 2000.

69 Eugene Chung (G) 1995, Mark Baniewicz (T) 2000-1, Roger Chanoine (OL) 2002.

70 Patrick Venzke (T) 2001.

71 *Tony Boselli* (T) 1995–2001.

72 *Leon Searcy* (T) 1996–2000, Steve Zahursky (T) 2001, Mike Pearson (T) 2003.

73 Brian DeMarco (T) 1995–8, Jeff Smith (C) 2000-1.

74 Jimmy Herndon (T) 1996, Lamanzar Williams (DE) 1998, Chris White (DE) 1999, Maurice Williams (T) 2001–3.

75 Eric Curry (DE) 1998–9, Michael Mason (DE) 2000.

76 Rich Tylski (G) 1996–9, Dwayne Ledford (G) 2000, Leander Jordan (T) 2003.

77 Andre Davis (DT) 1996, Zach Wiegert (G/T) 1999–2002.

78 Greg Huntington (G/C) 1995, Todd Fordham (G/T) 1997–2002.

79 Dave Widell (C) 1995–7, Anthony Cesario (G) 1999, Reggie Nelson (T) 2000, Drew Inzer (G/C) 2002.

80 Willie Jackson (WR) 1995–7, Kyle Brady (TE) 1999–2003.

81 Desmond Howard (KR) 1995, Andre Rison (WR) 1996, Will Moore (WR) 1997–8, R.Jay Soward (WR) 2000-1, Bobby Shaw (WR) 2002, Matthew Hatchette (WR) 2003.

82 *Jimmy Smith* (WR) 1995–2003.

83 Pete Mitchell (TE) 1995–8, 2002, Lenzie Jackson (WR) 1999, Greg DeLong (TE) 2000, Ryan Neufeld (TE) 2000, Joe Zelenka (TE) 2001, Kevin Johnson (WR) 2003.

84 Ernest Givins (WR) 1995, Reggie Barlow (WR) 1996–2000, Sean Dawkins (WR) 2001, Patrick Johnson (WR) 2002, Jermaine Lewis (KR) 2003.

85 Rich Griffith (TE) 1995–2000, Damon Gibson (WR) 2001-1, Kevin Lockett (WR) 2002, Cortez Hankton (WR) 2003, Derek Brown (TE) 1995–7.

86 Alvis Whitted (WR) 1998–2001, Micah Ross (WR) 2001-1, Troy Edwards (WR) 2003.

87 Cedric Tillman (WR) 1995, *Keenan McCardell* (WR) 1996–2001, Jimmy Redmond (WR) 2002, George Wrighster (TE) 2003.

88 Craig Keith (TE) 1995, Kendrick Bullard (WR) 1996, Ty Hallock (FB/TE) 1996, Damon Jones (TE) 1997–2001, Joe Zelenka (TE) 2002–3.

89 Curtis Marsh (WR) 1995–6, Troy Sadowski (TE) 1998, Emanuel Smith (WR) 2000, Ryan Prince (TE) 2001, Chris Luzar (TE) 2002–3.

90 James Williams (LB) 1995, *Tony Brackens* (DE) 1996–2003.

91 Paul Frase (DE) 1995–6, Seth Payne (DT) 1997–2001, Marco Coleman (DE) 2002.

92 Don Davey (DE) 1995–8, James Roberson (DE) 1999, Rob Meier (DE) 2000–3.

93 Ernie Logan (DE) 1995–6, Esera Tuaolo (DT) 1997, Jose White (DE) 1998, Kevin Landolt (DT) 1999, Emarlos Leroy (DT) 2000.

94 Kelvin Pritchett (DT) 1995–8, Larry Smith (DT) 1999–2002, Lionel Barnes (DE) 2003.

95 Mike Thompson (DT) 1995, Jose White (DT) 1997, Bryce Paup (LB) 1998–9, Paul Spicer (DE) 2000–3.

96 Bernard Carter (LB) 1995, Ashley Sheppard (LB) 1995, Clyde Simmons (DE) 1996–7, Fernando Smith (DE) 1998, *Gary Walker* (DT) 1999–2001, Chris Combs (DE) 2002, Matt Leonard (DT) 2003.

97 Ray Hall (DT) 1995, Juan Hammonds (DE) 1996, Renaldo Wynn (DT) 1997–2001, Clenton Ballard (DT) 2002.

98 Corey Mayfield (DT) 1995, Jabbar Threats (DE) 1997–8, Regan Upshaw (DE) 1999, David Richie (DE) 2000, John Henderson (DT) 2002–3.

99 Joel Smeenge (DE) 1995–2000, *Marcus Stroud* (DT) 2001-3.

KANSAS CITY CHIEFS

The franchise: When the NFL rebuffed multimillionaire businessman Lamar Hunt's interest in an expansion team for Dallas and the Bidwill family turned away his bid to buy the Chicago Cardinals in 1959, no one could imagine the far-reaching consequences. On the flight home from Chicago, Hunt thought of all the other cities that had made bids to move the Cardinals and realized that it might be an opportune time to start a new league. Hunt contacted Bud Adams in Houston and others in Denver and Minnesota and began planning. Those plans developed quickly and in 1960 the American Football League began play in eight cities.

Hunt's Dallas Texans were going head-to-head against the NFL expansion Dallas Cowboys while sharing the Cotton Bowl with them. The Texans had the better team, but the Cowboys had the attraction of quality NFL opponents. Hunt hired Purdue assistant Hank Stram to coach his team, and Stram produced consistent contenders for a dozen years, particularly once he signed his college quarterback Len Dawson who had washed out of the NFL. Dawson led the Texans to the AFL title in 1962, his first season in the league. That title game was the longest game in pro football history at the time and was decided by Tommy Brooker's field goal at

2:54 of the second overtime period. The only NFL game to last longer was the 1971 playoff matchup between the Chiefs and Dolphins, that Miami won with a field goal halfway through the second overtime period.

Tired of the battle for his home town, Hunt started checking out other cities and was considering moving the team to New Orleans when Kansas City stepped in with a forceful and successful pitch for the league champions to move west. Kansas City had not held a professional football franchise since the 1924 Kansas City Blues and the 1925–6 Kansas City Cowboys of the NFL. In the AFL, the Chiefs were a league power, the only three-time champions in the league's 10-year history — winning all three title games on the road. The Chiefs also appeared in the first Super Bowl which was appropriate because Hunt was instrumental in engineering the merger of the leagues and even named the championship game after his daughter's super ball. Although the Chiefs lost to Green Bay, they did field a defense led by Hall of Famers Bobby Bell and Buck Buchanan and All Pros Johnny Robinson, Jerry Mays and Bobby Hunt as well as an wide-open offense featuring a large, powerful line and the Len Dawson to Otis Taylor passing combo.

When the Chiefs returned to the Super Bowl three years later, Kansas City had filled their holes and greatly improved their depth. In Super Bowl IV against the favored Minnesota Vikings, the Chiefs proved that the Jets upset win in Super Bowl III was no fluke. The leagues were on equal footing. Stram called his motion offense that relied on a moving pocket the "offense of the future," and his defense was rock solid, but they never made it back to the Super Bowl. From that high point, the team began to slip. After the 1971 double overtime loss to the Dolphins, Kansas City would not return to the postseason again until 1986. When Marty Schottenheimer took over as coach in 1989, he fully restored Chiefs football, making the playoffs seven times in ten years, but he could not reach the Super Bowl either. Dick Vermeil, who has taken two other teams to the Super Bowl, made that his challenge when he took over in 2001.

Origin of name: The Dallas Texans moved to Kansas City largely because of the aggressive efforts of the KC mayor at the time, H. Roe "Chief" Bartle. The mayor's nickname influenced Hunt's renaming of his team.

Time till first championship: 10 years.
Time since last championship: 35 years.

Record by Decade

	Regular Season			Postseason		
	Won	Lost	Tied	Won	Lost	Championships
1960s	87	48	5	5	2	1969 (1962 AFL Champions)
1970s	60	79	5	0	1	
1980s	66	84	2	0	1	
1990s	102	58	0	3	7	
2000s	34	30	0	0	1	
All-Time	349	299	12	8	12	1

Winning seasons: 24. Losing Seasons: 16. .500 seasons: 4.

Coaches

	Years	Record	Playoffs
Hank Stram (1)	1960–74	124–76–10	5–3
Paul Wiggin	1975–7	11–24–0	0–0
Tom Bettis	1977	1–6–0	0–0
Marv Levy	1978–82	31–42–0	0–0
John Mackovic	1983–6	30–34–0	0–1
Frank Gansz	1987–8	8–22–1	0–0
Marty Schottenheimer	1989–98	101–58–1	3–7
Gunther Cunningham	1999–2000	16–16–0	0–0
Dick Vermeil	2001–3	27–21–0	0–1

(Championships in parentheses)

Retired numbers: The Chiefs have retired eight numbers. Five were retired for Hall of Famers: Jan Stenerud 3; Len Dawson 16; Willie Lanier 63; Bobby Bell 78; and Buck Buchanan 86. They also retired 28 for Abner Haynes who was the first star on the team. In addition, they retired 33 for Stone Johnson and 36 for Mack Lee Hill, both of whom died while playing for the team. Johnson actually never played for Kansas City in a league game since he died during the exhibition season of his rookie year.

Other numbers worn by these players: None.

Those who wore retired numbers after the honored player: Willie Lanier's 63 was later worn by linebacker John Olenchalk and defensive tackle Bill Maas. Bobby Bell's 78 was later worn by defensive tackle Willie Lee. Buck Buchanan's 86 was later worn by tight end Tony Samuels and wide receivers Gerald Butler, J.T. Smith, Emile Harry and Eric Brown.

Numbers that should be retired: If Derrick Thomas, 58, makes the Hall of Fame, a case could be made for him.

Owned numbers: No one but Len Dawson ever wore 16, and only Abner Haynes ever wore 28.

Numbers worn by Hall of Famers: Marcus Allen 32; Bobby Bell 78; Buck Buchanan 86; Len Dawson 16; Willie Lanier 63; Joe Montana 19; Jan Stenerud 3; Mike Webster 53.

Star power: Marcus Allen took 32 from Doug Terry.

Star eclipsed: Pete Beathard wore 11 because Mike Livingston wore 10; Paul Lowe wore 26 because Bert Coan wore 23; John Brockington wore 43 because Macarthur Lane wore 42; Mike Webster wore 53 because Angelo Snipes wore 52. Joe Montana wore 19 because 16 was retired for Len Dawson.

Numbers with most great players: 88 has been worn such outstanding receivers as Tony Gonzalez, Chris Burford and Carlos Carson; likewise 89 has been worn by receivers Otis Taylor, Henry Marshall, and Andre Rison.

Worst represented numbers: 43 has been worn several backs of no great measure.

Number worn by the most players: 80 has been worn 20 times.

Player who wore the most numbers: Safety Doug Terry wore 24, 25 and 32.

Longest tenure wearing a number: Punter Jerrel Wilson wore 44 for 15 years from 1963 to 1977.

Number worn by first ever draft pick: Don Meredith was the regional first pick of the Dallas Texans in 1960, but he signed with the crosstown Cowboys. The Texans' first pick in 1961 was another local college star, E.J. Holub who wore 55 in Dallas and Kansas City.

Biggest draft busts: The biggest draft flop for the Chiefs was Todd Blackledge, 14, one of the vaunted quarterback class of 1983. Todd lasted five years, throwing 26 tds and 33 interceptions while completing less than 50 percent of his passes.

Number worn by oldest player: Warren Moon wore 1 as a 44 year old in 2000; Morten Andersen wore 8 as a 43 year old in 2003; Len Dawson wore 16 as a 40 year old in 1975.

Cameos: All Pros and other notables— John Brockington 43; Billy Cannon 80; Cris Dishman 26; Tom Flores 12; Ron Jaworski 7; Bam Morris 39; Brett Perriman 85; Michael Dean Perry 95; Webster Slaughter 85/88.

Ones who got away: Rich Gannon, 12, has at long last starred for the Raiders; Clem Daniels 36 was a great runner in Oakland; Sonny Bishop 66 was a fine guard for the Oilers; Frank Winters 65 clicked as Brett Favre's center in Green Bay; John Matuszak 79 fit in on the Raiders' defensive lineman; Joe Horn 84 has been a star deep threat in New Orleans.

Least popular numbers: 0 has never been worn. 16 and 28 were both retired after having been only worn by one player. 3, 19, and 37 all have been worn by only two players.

Last number to be originated: In 1986 linebacker Aaron Pearson wore 96 and defensive end Leonard Griffin wore 98, both for the first time.

Longest dormant number: 37 has been dormant since 1982. 19 was dormant for 32 years from 1961 until 1993.

Triskaidekaphobia notes: 13 has been worn by a punter and three quarterbacks, most notably by Steve Bono.

Shared numbers: 58 was worn by hardy center Jack Rudnay and All Pro linebacker Derrick Thomas; 61 was worn by stumpy defensive tackle Curly Culp and solid center Tim Grunhard.

Continuity: Veteran signal caller Steve Deberg was replaced in 17 by veteran signal caller Dave Kreig; safety Lloyd Burruss was replaced in 34 by cornerback Dale Carter; receiver Derrick Alexander was replaced in 82 by game-breaking returner Dante Hall.

Discontinuity: Runner Mike Garrett was followed in 21 by receiver Dennis Homan; Jack Rudnay was followed in 58 by linebacker Steve Potter; 12-year starting tackle Dave Hill was followed in 73 by Gery Palmer; Stephone Paige was followed in 83 by fellow receiver Michael Smith; Fred Arbanas was followed in 84 by fellow tight end Bruce Bergey; defensive end Neil Smith was followed in 90 by linebacker Terry Wooden.

Quarterback numbers over 19: None

Number of first black player: In 1960, defensive back Dave Webster 21, runners Abner Haynes 28 and Clem Daniels 36, and defensive tackle Walt Napier 76.

Numbers of future NFL head coaches: Tom Flores 12 and Jack Del Rio 50.

Numbers of future NFL referees: None.

Players who played other sports: Track star Jimmy Hines wore 81 as a wide receiver.

Players more famous after football: Fred "Hammer" Williamson, 24, was a successful actor in action films. Center Mike Oriard, 50, has made an unusual transition from football to literature professor and has published several scholarly works.

First player to wear a number in the 90s: Defensive tackle Ernie Ladd wore 99 in 1967.

Number with most points scored: 8 with 1,583 points scored by Nick Lowery (1,466) and Morten Andersen (117).

Number with most yards rushing: 32 with 9,043 yards gained by Marcus Allen (3,698), Curtis McClinton (3,124), Tony Reed (1,382), Bo Dickinson (406), Larry Moriarty (284), Ethan Horton (146), and Tommie Agee (3).

Number with most receptions: 88 with 1,421 passes caught by Tony Gonzalez (468), Chris Burford (391), Carlos Carson (351), J.J. Birden (183), Webster Slaughter (34), Walter White (23), and Victor Bailey (1).

Number with most touchdown passes: 16 with 237 touchdowns tossed by Len Dawson.

Number with most interceptions: 20 with 110 passes picked off by Deron Cherry (50), Bobby Hunt (37), Mike Sensibaugh (20), and Goldie Sellers (3).

Oddity: The Chiefs have had four active players die tragically. Stone Johnson, 33, died when he broke his neck during an exhibition game in his rookie year of 1963. Mack Lee Hill, 36, died during a knee operation at the end of the 1965 season. Joe Delaney, 37, jumped into a lake to save a drowning child in 1983. Delaney could not swim himself and drowned, but managed to save the child. Derrick Thomas, 58, died in an offseason car accident in 2000.

Family Connections

Brothers

Dave Lindstrom	DE	1978–85	71
Chris Lindstrom	DE	1987	60
Rich Baldinger	T	1983–92	77
Gary Baldinger	DL	1986–8	91
Jewerl Thomas	CB	1983	31
Ken Thomas	RB	1983	35

Fathers and Sons

Ed Budde	G	1963–76	71
Brad Budde	G	1980–6	66/71
Caesar Belser	DB	1968–71	24
Jason Belser	DB	2001	29

Team All-Time Numerical Roster

Those with an "r" following the year 1987 were replacement players during the players' strike. Pro Bowl players for each number are in *Italics*; Hall of Famers are in **Bold** type.

1 Durwood Pennington (K) 1962, Noland Smith (KR) 1967–70, Mike Adamle (RB) 1971–2, *Bob Grupp* (P) 1979–81, Matt Stevens (QB) 1987r, Warren Moon (QB) 1999–2000.

2 Tom Clements (QB) 1980, Kelly Goodburn (P) 1987–90, Eddie Murray (K) 1992, Lin Elliott (K) 1994–5, Todd Peterson (K) 2000–1.

3 Ben Agajanian (K) 1961, **Jan Stenerud** (K) 1967–79.

4 Steve Fuller (QB) 1979–82, James Hamrick (K) 1987r, Bryan Barker (P) 1990–3, Dan Stryzinski (P) 2001–2.

5 Jim McCann (P) 1975, Case deBruijn (P) 1982, Lewis Colbert (P) 1986–7, Louie Aguiar (P) 1994–8, Todd Sauerbrun (P) 2000.

6 Warren McVea (RB) 1969–73, Mark Vitali (QB) 1977, Jim Arnold (P) 1983–5.

7 John Huarte (QB) 1969–71, Mike Nott (QB) 1976, Zenon Andrusyshyn (P) 1978, Jeff Gossett (P) 1981–2, Ron Jaworski (QB) 1989, Ted White (QB) 1999, Joe Germaine (QB) 2001, Michael Husted (K) 2002.

8 *Nick Lowery* (K) 1980–93, Billy Joe Tolliver (QB) 1997, Morten Andersen (K) 2002–3.

9 Dean Carlson (QB) 1972–4, *Bill Kenney* (QB) 1979–88, Reggie Jones (WR) 1997, Scott Bentley (K) 1999, Jason Baker (P) 2003.

10 James Saxton (RB) 1962, Pete Beathard (QB) 1964–7, Mike Livingston (QB) 1968–79, Frank Seurer (QB) 1986–7, Mike Elkins (QB) 1989–90, Kent Sullivan (P) 1992, Alex Van Pelt (QB) 1993, Pete Stoyanovich (K) 1996–2000, *Trent Green* (QB) 2001–3.

11 Pete Beathard (QB) 1973, Tony Adams (QB) 1975–8, Bob Gagliano (QB) 1981–3, Sandy Osiecki (QB) 1984, Doug Hudson (QB) 1987, Steve Pelluer (QB) 1989–91, *Elvis Grbac* (QB) 1997–8, Reggie Jones (WR) 2001.

12 Eddie Wilson (QB/P) 1962–4, Jim Hill (DB) 1966, Tom Flores (QB) 1969, Dave Jaynes (QB) 1974, Dennis Shaw (QB) 1978, Alex Espinoza (QB) 1987r, Rich Gannon (QB) 1995–8, Jon Baker (K) 1999, Joe Perez (WR) 2000, Jonathan Quinn (QB) 2002.

13 Wayne Clark (QB) 1975, Mark Vlasic (QB) 1991–2, *Steve Bono* (QB) 1995–6, Daniel Pope (P) 1999.

14 Hunter Enis (QB) 1960, Tom Greene (QB) 1961, Bobby Ply (DB) 1962–7, Ed Podolak (RB) 1969–77, Todd Blackledge (QB) 1983–7, Danny McManus (QB) 1988, Matt Blundin (QB) 1992–5.

15 Randy Duncan (QB) 1961, Mike Mercer (K) 1966, Sam Longmire (DB) 1967–8, Jacky Lee (QB) 1967–9, Kerry Reardon (CB) 1971–6, David Whitehurst (QB) 1984, Steve Matthews (QB) 1994–6, Todd Collins (QB) 1998–2003.

16 **Len Dawson** (QB) 1962–75.

17 Fletcher Smith (DB) 1966–7, Jack Gehrke (WR) 1968, Elmo Wright (WR) 1971–4, Steve Deberg (QB) 1988–91, Dave Krieg (QB) 1992–3, Pat Barnes (QB) 1997.

18 Don Flynn (DB) 1960–1, *Emmitt Thomas* (CB) 1966–78, Sean LaChapelle (WR) 1996, *Elvis Grbac* (QB) 1999–2000.

19 *Cotton Davidson* (QB/P) 1960–1, **Joe Montana** (QB) 1993–4.

20 *Bobby Hunt* (S) 1962–7, Goldie Sellers (DB) 1968–9, Mike Sensibaugh (S) 1971–5, Horace Perkins (CB) 1979, *Deron Cherry* (S) 1981–91, *Dante Hall* (KR) 2000–1.

21 *David Webster* (DB) 1960–1, *Mike Garrett* (RB) 1966–70, Dennis Homan (WR) 1971–2, Hise Austin (CB) 1975, Tommy Reamon (RB) 1976, Arnold Morgado (RB) 1977–80, Clark Gaines (RB) 1981–2, Kerry Parker (CB) 1984, Odis McKinney (S) 1985, Ralph Stockemer (RB) 1987r, James Saxon (RB) 1988–91, Tahuan Lewis (CB) 1992, Garry Lewis (CB) 1993, John Stephens (RB) 1993, Jon Vaughn (RB) 1994, Martin Bayless (S) 1995–6, *Jerome Woods* (S) 1997–2001, 2003.

22 John Bookman (DB) 1960, Willie Mitchell (DB) 1964–71, Larry Marshall (DB) 1972–3, 1978, Donnie Joe Morris (RB) 1974, Glynn Harrison (RB) 1976, Ted McKnight (RB) 1977–81, Van Jakes (DB) 1983–4, Sherman Cocroft (S) 1985–7, John Hagy (S) 1991, Harvey Williams (RB) 1992–3, Monty Grow (S) 1994, Perry Carter (CB) 1995, Rashaan Shehee (RB) 1998–9, Dexter McCleon (CB) 2003.

23 Jim Swink (HB) 1960, Bert Coan (RB) 1963–8, David Hadley (CB) 1970–2, Leroy Keyes (RB) 1973, Earl Gant (RB) 1979–80, Lucious Smith (CB) 1983, Greg Hill (CB) 1984–8, Kevin Wyatt (CB) 1987r, Barry Word (RB) 1990–2, Ron Dickerson (WR) 1993–4, Clyde Johnson (CB) 1997, Carlton Gray (CB) 1999–2000, Derrick Blaylock (RB) 2001–3.

24 Fred Williamson (CB) 1965–7, Caeser Belser (DB) 1968–71, Willie Ellison (RB) 1973–4, Gary Green (CB) 1977–83, Jayice Pearson (CB) 1986–92, Erik McMillan (S) 1993, Doug Terry (S) 1994–5, Jason Kaiser (CB) 1998, William Bartee (CB) 2000–3.

25 Doyle Nix (DB) 1961, Charley Warner (DB) 1963–4, Frank Pitts (WR) 1965–71, Ricky Wesson (CB) 1977, Jack Epps (S) 1987r, David Hollis (DB) 1988, Danny Copeland (S) 1989–90, Troy Stradford (RB) 1991, Doug Terry (S) 1992–3, Mark Collins (DB) 1994–6, Reggie Tongue (S) 1997–9, Greg Wesley (S) 2000–1, 2003.

26 *Frank Jackson* (WR) 1961–5, Paul Lowe (RB) 1968–9, Lewis Porter (E) 1970, Robert West (WR) 1972–3, *Gary Barbaro* (S) 1976–82, Skip Lane (DB) 1984, Paul Palmer (RB) 1987–8, Cornelius Dozier (S) 1987r, Muhammad Oliver (CB) 1993, Tim Watson (S) 1993–5, Vashone Adams (S) 1998, Cris Dishman (CB) 1999, Taje Allen (CB) 2001–2, Julian Battle (CB) 2003.

27 Dan Kratzer (WR) 1973, Woody Green (RB) 1974–6, Ray Milo (S) 1978, Donovan Rose (CB) 1980, Theotis Brown (RB) 1983–4, Blane Smith (S) 1987, Kevin Porter (S) 1988–92, Jay Taylor (CB) 1993–4, Greg Hill (RB) 1995–7, Bracey Walker (S) 1998–2001, Jarmar Julien (RB) 2002.

28 *Abner Haynes* (RB) 1960–5.

29 Clyde Powers (S) 1978, *Albert Lewis* (CB) 1983–93, Greg Hill (RB) 1994, Brian Washington (S) 1995, Mark McMillian (CB) 1997–8, Robert Williams (CB) 1999, Jason Belser (S) 2001–2.

30 Jack Spikes (RB) 1960–4, Gloster Richardson (WR) 1967–70, Cleophus Miller (RB) 1974–5, Curtis Bledsoe (RB) 1981–2, Mark Robinson (S) 1984–7, Paul Ott Carruth (RB) 1989, Martin Bayless (S) 1992–3, Donnell Bennett (RB) 1994–2000, Lyle West (DB) 2002–3.

31 Jeff Kinney (RB) 1972–6, Jerry Reese (S) 1979–80, Jewerl Thomas (RB) 1983, *Kevin Ross* (CB) 1984–93, 1997, Leroy Thompson (RB) 1995, *Jerome Woods* (CB) 1996, *Priest Holmes* (RB) 2001–3.

32 Bo Dickinson (RB) 1960–1, Jack Johnson (DB) 1961, *Curtis McClinton* (RB) 1962–9, Doug Jones (DB) 1973–4, Tony Reed (RB) 1977–80, Ethan Horton (RB) 1985, Larry Moriarty (RB) 1986–8, Tommie Agee (RB) 1989, Doug Terry (S) 1992, **Marcus Allen** (RB) 1993–7.

33 Curley Johnson (HB) 1960, Bill Pricer (RB) 1961.

34 Eddie Payton (KR) 1978, Wilbert Haslip (RB) 1979, *Lloyd Burruss* (S) 1981–91, *Dale Carter* (CB) 1992–8, Mike Cloud (RB) 1999–2002, Larry Johnson (RB) 2003.

35 Smokey Stover (LB) 1960–6, Jim Otis (RB) 1971–2, Horace Belton (RB) 1978–81, Ken Thomas (RB) 1983, *Christian Okoye* (RB) 1987–92, William White (S) 1994–6, Melvin Johnson (S) 1998, Larry Atkins (S) 1999–2000.

36 Clem Daniels (RB) 1960, *Mack Lee Hill* (RB) 1964–5.

37 Tim Collier (CB) 1976–9, *Joe Delaney* (RB) 1981–2.

38 Solomon Brannan (DB) 1965–6, Wendell Hayes (RB) 1968–74, Ricky Odom (S) 1978, Gerald Jackson (S) 1979, Durwood Roquemore (CB) 1982–3, Michael Gunter (RB) 1984, Carlton Thomas (CB) 1987, Calvin Loveall (CB) 1988, *Kimble Anders* (FB) 1991–2000, Clint Finley (S) 2002–3.

39 Mark Bailey (RB) 1977–8, Del Thompson (RB) 1982, Stephen Griffin (RB) 1987, Eric Everett (CB) 1991, Bruce Pickens (CB) 1993, Bam Morris (RB) 1999, Ray Crockett (CB) 2001–2.

40 Charlie Jackson (DT) 1960, *Jim Marsalis* (CB) 1969–75, Lawrence Williams (KR) 1976, Ricky Davis (S) 1977, Ken Lacy (RB) 1984–5, 1987r, Boyce Green (RB) 1986, Billy Bell (CB) 1991, Cedric Mack (CB) 1992, Robert Williams (CB) 1993, Bracey Walker (S) 1994, *James Hasty* (CB) 1995–2000, Corey Harris (CB) 2001–2.

41 Bruce Jankowski (WR) 1971–2, Doug Dressler (RB) 1975, Herb Christopher (S) 1979–82, Garcia Lane (CB) 1985, 1987r, James Evans (RB) 1987, Woodie Pippins (RB) 1987r, Keyvan Jenkins (RB) 1988, Kenny Hill (S) 1989, Anthony Parker (CB) 1991, David Whitmore (S) 1993–4, Reggie Tongue (S) 1996, Keith Crawford (S) 1998, Pat Dennis (CB) 2000–1.

42 *Johnny Robinson* (S) 1960–71, MacArthur Lane (RB) 1975–8, M.L. Carter (CB) 1979–81, Tim Washington (CB) 1982, Lawrence Ricks (RB) 1983–4, Jeff Smith (RB) 1985–6, Jeff Donaldson (S) 1990, Charles Mincy (S) 1991–4, Darrell Malone (CB) 1992, Shaunard Harts (S) 2001–3.

43 Bill Thomas (RB) 1974, John Brockington (RB) 1977, Billy Jackson (RB) 1981–4, Mike Pruitt (RB) 1985–6, Robert Parker (RB) 1987, Bill Jones (RB) 1990–2, Juran Bolden (CB) 1999, Jermaine Williams (FB) 2001, Omar Easy (RB) 2002–3.

44 Jimmy Harris (DB) 1960, Ed Kelley (DB) 1961, *Jerrel Wilson* (P) 1963–77, Eric Harris (CB) 1980–2, Herman Heard (RB) 1984–9, Harvey Williams (RB) 1991, Darren Anderson (CB) 1994–7, Eric Warfield (CB) 1998–2003.

45 *Dave Grayson* (DB) 1961–4, Gene Thomas (FB) 1966–7, *Robert Holmes* (RB) 1968–71, Morris LaGrand (RB) 1975, Pat McNeil (RB) 1976–7, Ken Talton (RB) 1980, Trent Bryant (CB) 1982–3, 1987r, Sidney Johnson (CB) 1988, James Saxon (RB) 1988, Stan Petry (CB) 1989–91, Ernie Thompson (RB) 1993, Jimmie Johnson (TE) 1994, Tony Stargell (CB) 1996, Bucky Brooks (CB) 1997–8, Billy Baber (TE) 2001–3.

46 Carroll Zaruba (DB) 1960, Noland Smith (KR) 1967, Jim Kearney (DB) 1967–75, Tim Gray (S) 1976–8, Paul Dombroski (S) 1980–1, Bruce King (RB) 1985–6, Michael Clemons (RB) 1987, Jitter Fields (KR) 1987, Charles Washington (DB) 1990–1, Bennie Thompson (S) 1992–3, Victor Jones (RB) 1994, Robert Williams (CB) 1998, Frank Moreau (RB) 2000.

47 Willie Osley (DB) 1974, Don Martin (CB) 1975, Chris Golub (S) 1977, Chris Smith (RB) 1987r, Todd Scott (S) 1997.

48 *Duane Wood* (DB) 1960–4, Nate Allen (CB) 1971–4, Steve Taylor (S) 1976, Ted Burgmeier (S) 1978, James Hadnot (RB) 1980–3, E.J. Jones (RB) 1985, Jeff Colter (DB) 1987r, Kenny Gamble (RB) 1988–90, Todd McNair (RB) 1989–93, 1996, Tommie Stowers (RB) 1994, Brian Washington (S) 1995, Ted Popson (TE) 1997–8.

49 Charlie Thomas (KR) 1975, Teddy Nelson (CB) 1987r, Matt Gay (S) 1994, *Tony Richardson* (FB) 1995–2001, 2003.

50 Jim Barton (C) 1960, Mike Oriard (C) 1970–3, Bob Thornbladh (LB) 1974, Tim Kearney (LB) 1975, Clarence Sanders (LB) 1978, Cal Peterson (LB) 1979–81, Calvin Daniels (LB) 1982–5, Jack Del Rio (LB) 1987–8, Rob McGovern (LB) 1989–90, Erick Anderson (LB) 1992–3, Anthony Davis (LB) 1994–8, Larry Atkins (LB) 2001–2, Kawika Mitchell (LB) 2003.

51 *Jim Fraser* (LB) 1965, *Jim Lynch* (LB) 1967–77, Charles Jackson (LB) 1978–84, Rick Donnalley (C) 1986–7, Adam Linger (C) 1988, Lonnie Marts (LB) 1991–3, Greg Manusky (LB) 1994–9, Lew Bush (LB) 2000, Glenn Cadrez (LB) 2001, Scott Fujita (LB) 2002–3.

52 Bud Abell (LB) 1966–8, Tom Humphrey (C) 1974, Orrin Olsen (C/G) 1976, Thomas Howard (LB) 1977–83, Ken Jolly (LB) 1984–5, Glenn Hyde (C) 1987, Angelo Snipes (LB) 1987–9, Tracy Rogers (LB) 1990–6, Andre O'Neal (LB) 2000–1, Quinton Caver (LB) 2002.

53 Ken Avery (LB) 1975, Billy Andrews (LB) 1976–7, Whitney Paul (DE/LB) 1980–81, 1986, Bob Rush (C) 1983–5, Todd Howard (LB) 1987–8, Gary Moten (LB) 1987r, **Mike Webster** (C) 1989–90, Santo Stephens (LB) 1993, Rick Hamilton (DE) 1994–5, Marvcus Patton (LB) 1999–2002, Fred Jones (LB) 2003.

54 Ted Greene (LB) 1960–2, Mike Hudock (C) 1967, Clyde Walker (LB) 1970–4, 1976, Frank Manumaleuga (LB) 1979–81, James Walker (LB) 1983, Tim Cofield (LB) 1986–8, Walker Ashley (LB) 1989, Tracy Simien (LB) 1991–7, Greg Favors (LB) 1998, Brian Waters (C) 2000–3.

55 Tom Dimmick (C) 1960, *E.J. Holub* (C/LB) 1961–70, Keith Best (LB) 1972, Bill Peterson (LB) 1975, Dave Rozumek (LB) 1976–9, Dave Klug (LB) 1981–3, Louis Cooper (LB) 1985–90, Ervin Randle (LB) 1991–2, Frank Stams (LB) 1995, Tony Dumas (LB) 1996–7, Ron George (LB) 1998–2000, *Gary Stills* (LB) 2001–3.

56 Walt Corey (LB) 1960–6, Tom Graham (LB) 1974, Charlie Ane (C) 1975–80, Phil Cancik (LB) 1981, Louis Haynes (LB) 1982–3, *Dino Hackett* (LB) 1986–92, Arnold Ale (LB) 1994, Wayne Simmons (LB) 1997–8, Ernest Dixon (LB) 1998, *Gary Stills* (LB) 1999–2000, Lew Bush (LB) 2001–2, Monty Beisel (LB) 2003.

57 Al Palewicz (LB) 1973–5, Jimbo Elrod (LB) 1976–8, Jerry Blanton (LB) 1979–85, James Harrell (LB) 1987, Bruce Holmes (LB) 1987r, Chris Martin (LB) 1988–92, George Jamison (LB) 1994–6, Bobby Houston (LB) 1997, Jerrott Willard (LB) 1998, Mike Maslowski (LB) 1999–2003.

58 Andrew Rice (DT) 1966–7, Dave Martin (LB) 1968, *Jack Rudnay* (C) 1970–82, Steve Potter (LB) 1983, Tom Baugh (C) 1986–8, Arland Thompson (G) 1987r, *Derrick Thomas* (LB) 1989–99.

59 Ray Burks (LB) 1977, Gary Spani (LB) 1978–86, Andy Hawkins (LB) 1988, Stacy Harvey (LB) 1989, Percy Snow (LB) 1990–2, Jamie Fields (LB) 1993–5, Donnie Edwards (LB) 1996–2001, Glenn Cadrez (LB) 2002, Shawn Barber (LB) 2003.

60 Al Reynolds (G) 1960–7, George Daney (G) 1968–74, Matt Herkenhoff (T) 1976–85, Byron Ingram (G) 1987–8, Chris Lindstrom (DE) 1987r, Mike Baab (C) 1992, Donald Willis (G) 2000–3.

61 Bob Hudson (LB) 1960, John Cadwell (G) 1961, Dennis Biodrowski (G) 1963–7, *Curley Culp*

(DT) 1968–74, Cliff Fazier (DT) 1977, Don Parrish (NT) 1978–82, John Zamberlin (LB) 1983–4, Mark Adickes (G) 1986–9, *Tim Grunhard* (C) 1990–2000, Montique Sharpe (DT) 2003.

62 Sid Fournet (G) 1960–1, Bob Liggett (DT) 1970, Bill Story (G) 1975, Darius Helton (G) 1977, Kelly Kirchbaum (LB) 1980, Todd Thomas (C) 1981, Adam Linger (C) 1983–6, Jim Pietrzak (C) 1987r, Ron McLean (NT) 1988, Gene Chilton (G/C) 1989, Glenn Parker (G/T) 1997–9, Casey Wiegmann (C) 2001–3.

63 *Marvin Terrell* (G) 1960–3, **Willie Lanier** (LB) 1967–77, John Olenchalk (C/LB) 1981–2, *Bill Maas* (DL) 1984–92.

64 *Bill Krisher* (G) 1960–1, Curt Merz (G/DE) 1962–8, Randy Beisler (G) 1975, Whitney Paul (DE/LB) 1976–9, Bill Acker (DL) 1982, Les Studdard (C) 1982, Mark Kirchner (T/G) 1983, Bob Olderman (G) 1985, James Harvey (G) 1987r, 1988, Gerry Feehery (C) 1988, Tom Ricketts (G) 1993, Ralph Tamm (G) 1997–9, Thomas Washington (DT) 2000.

65 *Jon Gilliam* (C) 1961–7, Remi Prudhomme (G) 1968–9, Tom Condon (G) 1974–84, Rob Fada (G) 1985, Kevin Adkins (C) 1987, Curt DiGiacomo (G) 1988, Frank Winters (G/C) 1990–1, Kani Kauahi (C) 1992, Lindsay Knapp (G/T) 1993–4, Jeff Smith (C/G) 1996–9.

66 Dick Frey (DE) 1960, Sonny Bishop (G) 1962, Wayne Frazier (C) 1966–7, Bob Stein (LB) 1969–72, Rocky Rasley (G) 1975, Tom Wickert (G) 1977, Brad Budde (G) 1980–5, Dan Doubiago (T) 1987r, Ricky Siglar (T) 1993–6, Victor Riley (T) 1998–2001, Tony Newson (LB) 2002, Jimmy Wilkerson (DE) 2003.

67 Carl Larpenter (G) 1962, George Seals (DT) 1972–3, Mike Wilson (G) 1975, *Art Still* (DE) 1978–87, James Black (DE) 1987, Mike Stensrud (DL) 1988, Patrick Swoops (NT) 1991, Bryan Proby (DT) 1995, Mark Word (DE) 1999, Jason Andersen (G/C) 2002.

68 R.B. Nunnery (DT) 1960, Wayne Walker (K) 1967, Roger Bernhardt (G) 1975, Scott Auer (G/T) 1984–5, Michael Morris (C) 1989, Joe Staysniak (G) 1992, *Will Shields* (G) 1993–2003.

69 *Sherrill Headrick* (LB) 1960–7, Fred DeBernardi (DE) 1974, Al Steinfeld (C) 1982, Greg Meisner (DE) 1989–90, Jeff Criswell (T) 1995–8, Jeff Blackshear (G) 2000, Victory Allotey (OL) 2001–2.

70 Jack Stone (T) 1960, Curt Farrier (DT) 1963–5, Bobby Kelly (T) 1967, Sid Smith (T) 1970–2, Dave Smith (WR) 1973, Jim Nicholson (T) 1974–9, Jim Rourke (G) 1980–4, 1986, Billy Shields (T) 1985, Kit Lathrop (DE) 1986, Ray Woodard (DE) 1987, Mark Nelson (T) 1987r, Jerome Sally (NT) 1988, Mark Cannon (C) 1989, Reggie McElroy (T) 1993, Steve Wallace (T) 1997, Marcus Spears (T) 1997–2003.

71 Ray Collins (DT) 1960–1, *Ed Budde* (G) 1963–76, Dave Lindstrom (DE) 1978–85, Brad Budde (G) 1986, Lee Getz (G) 1987r, Don Thorp (DE) 1988, Tom Dohring (T) 1992, Greg Kragen (DT) 1994, Tom Barndt (DT/G) 1996–9, Norris McCleary (DT) 2000, Eddie Freeman (DL) 2002–3.

72 *Paul Rochester* (DT) 1960–3, John Maczuzak (DT) 1964, Tony DiMidio (T) 1966–7, Wayne Walton (G/T) 1973–4, Keith Simons (DT) 1976–7, Brad Oates (T) 1980–1, Franky Smith (T) 1980, David Lutz (G/T) 1983–92, Danny Villa (G) 1993–6, Nate Parks (T) 1997, Ricky Siglar (T) 1998, Sammy Williams (T) 1999, Darnell Alford (T) 2000–2.

73 Dave Hill (T) 1963–74, Gery Palmer (G) 1975, James Wolf (DT) 1976, Bob Simmons (G) 1977–83, Mike Dawson (NT) 1984, Brian Jozwiak (G) 1986–8, Michael Harris (C/G) 1989, Joe Valerio (T) 1991–5, Pete Swanson (G/T) 1998, Willie Jones (T) 2000–2.

74 *Jerry Cornelison* (T) 1960–5, Gene Trosch (DE) 1967–9, Pat Holmes (DE) 1973, Tom Keating (DT) 1974–5, Lawrence Estes (DE) 1975–6, Jeff Lloyd (NT) 1978, Dino Mangiero (NT) 1980–3, Pete Koch (DE) 1985–7, Bill Acker (DL) 1987r, Derrick Graham (T) 1990–4, Trezelle Jenkins (T) 1995–7, Steve Wallace (T) 1997.

75 Rufus Granderson (T) 1960, *Jerry Mays* (DE) 1961–70, Francis Peay (T) 1973–4, Bob Maddox (DE) 1975–6, Louis Ross (DE) 1975, Sylvester Hicks (DE) 1978–81, Ellis Gardner (T) 1983, Irv Eatman (T) 1986–90, Joe Phillips (DT) 1992–7, Chester McGlockton (DT) 1998–2000, Norris McCleary (DT) 2001.

76 Walter Napier (DT) 1960–1, Hatch Rosdahl (DE) 1964–5, Mo Moorman (G) 1968–72, Tom Drougas (T) 1974, Rod Walters (G) 1976, 1978–80, Roger Taylor (T) 1981, *John Alt* (T) 1984–96, John Tait (T) 1999–2003.

77 *Jim Tyrer* (T) 1961–73, Charlie Getty (T) 1974–82, Rich Baldinger (T) 1983–92, Steve Rogers (T) 1987r, Pellom McDaniels (DE) 1993–8, *William Roaf* (T) 2002–3.

78 **Bobby Bell** (LB) 1963–74, Willie Lee (DT) 1976–7.

79 Charlie Diamond (T) 1960–3, Al Dotson (DT) 1965, Larry Gagner (G) 1972, John Matuszak (DT) 1974–5, Larry Brown (T) 1978–9, Jerry Meyers (DE) 1980, Dean Prater (DE) 1982–3, Doug Hoppock (T) 1987r, Dave Szott (G) 1990–2000, Eric Downing (DT) 2001–2.

80 Tony Romeo (E) 1961, *Reg Carolan* (E) 1964–8, Billy Cannon (TE) 1970, Andy Hamilton (WR) 1973–4, Reggie Craig (WR) 1975–6, Lawrence Williams (KR) 1977, Larry Dorsey (WR) 1978, Mike Williams (TE) 1979–81, Johnny Dirden (KR) 1979, Bubba Garcia (WR) 1980, James Murphy (WR) 1981, George Shorthose (WR)

1985, Mark Keel (TE) 1987, Stein Koss (TE) 1987r, Lew Barnes (WR) 1989, Clarence Weathers (WR) 1989, Fred Jones (WR) 1990–3, Lake Dawson (WR) 1994–7, Willy Tate (TE) 1998, Larry Parker (WR) 1999–2001, Johnnie Morton (WR) 2002–3.

81 Max Boydston (E) 1960–1, *Tommy Brooker* (E/K) 1962–6, Mickey McCarthy (TE) 1969, Jimmy Hines (WR) 1970, Marvin Upshaw (DE) 1970–5, Walter White (TE) 1975, Tony Samuels (TE) 1977–80, Willie Scott (TE) 1981–5, Darrell Colbert (WR) 1987–8, Rod Jones (TE) 1987r, 1988, Robb Thomas (WR) 1989–91, Tony Hargain (WR) 1992, Hassan Jones (WR) 1993, Chris Penn (WR) 1994–6, Kevin Lockett (WR) 1997–2000, Marvin Minnis (WR) 2001–2.

82 Charley Barnes (E) 1961, Bill Miller (E) 1962, Ed Lothamer (DT) 1964–9, 1971–2, Gary Butler (TE) 1973, Bill Keelar (WR) 1978, Anthony Hancock (WR) 1982–6, Kitrick Taylor (WR) 1988, Danta Whitaker (TE) 1990, Tim Barnett (WR) 1991–3, Derrick Walker (TE) 1994–7, Derrick Alexander (WR) 1998–2001, *Dante Hall* (WR) 2002–3.

83 Morris Stroud (TE) 1969–74, Willie Frazier (TE) 1971–2, Larry Brunson (WR) 1974–7, Jerrold McRae (WR) 1978, Steve Gaunty (WR) 1979, Marvin Harvey (TE) 1981, Robert Blakely (WR) 1982, Stephone Paige (WR) 1983–91, John Trahan (WR) 1987r, Michael Smith (WR) 1992, Danan Hughes (WR) 1993–8, Lonnie Johnson (TE) 1999, Kendall Gammon (TE) 2000–3.

84 *Fred Arbanas* (TE) 1962–70, Bruce Bergey (TE) 1971, Bob Briggs (DE) 1974, Billy Masters (TE) 1975–6, Charlie Wade (WR) 1977, Al Dixon (TE) 1979–82, Dave Little (TE) 1984, Mike Holston (WR) 1985, Paul Coffman (TE) 1986–7, Richard Estell (WR) 1987r, Naz Worthen (WR) 1989–90, Willie Davis (WR) 1991–5, Joe Horn (WR) 1996–9, Sylvester Morris (WR) 2000–1, LaShaun Ward (WR) 2003.

85 Ed Benet (E) 1960, Bill Hull (DE) 1962, Dick Johnson (E) 1963, Chuck Hurston (DE) 1965–70, Barry Pearson (WR) 1974–6, Ed Beckman (TE) 1977–84, Jonathon Hayes (TE) 1985–93, Kenny Nash (WR) 1987, Eric Martin (WR) 1994, Michael Young (WR) 1994, Webster Slaughter (WR) 1995, Victor Bailey (WR) 1996, Reggie Johnson (TE) 1996, Brett Perriman (WR) 1997, Alfred Pupunu (TE) 1997, Brian Roche (TE) 1998, Mitch Jacoby (TE) 1999, Mikhael Ricks (WR) 2000–1, Marc Boerigter (WR) 2002–3.

86 Paul Miller (DE) 1960–1, Dick Davis (DE) 1962, **Buck Buchanan** (DT) 1963–75, Gerald Butler (WR) 1977, *J.T. Smith* (WR) 1978–84, Emile Harry (WR) 1986, 1988–92, Eric Brown (WR) 1987.

87 *Mel Branch* (E) 1960–1, Aaron Brown (DE) 1966–72, John Lohmeyer (DE) 1973, 1975–7, John Strada (TE) 1974, Stan Rome (WR) 1979–82, Ron

Wetzel (TE) 1983, Walt Arnold (TE) 1984–7, Dave Montagne (WR) 1987, Alfredo Roberts (TE) 1988–90, Troy Sadowski (TE) 1991, Mike Dyal (TE) 1992–3, Mike Bartrum (TE) 1993, Tracy Greene (TE) 1994, Tamarick Vanover (WR) 1995–9, Troy Drayton (TE) 2000, Chris Thomas (WR) 2001, Eddie Kennison (WR) 2001–3.

88 *Chris Burford* (E) 1960–7, Walter White (TE) 1976–9, *Carlos Carson* (WR) 1980–9, Riley Walton (TE) 1987r, J.J. Birden (WR) 1990–4, Webster Slaughter (WR) 1995, Victor Bailey (WR) 1996, *Tony Gonzalez* (TE) 1997–2003.

89 Bob Bryant (E) 1960, Luther Jeralds (DE) 1961, *Otis Taylor* (WR) 1965–75, Henry Marshall (WR) 1976–87, Eric Hodges (WR) 1987r, Pete Mandley (WR) 1989–90, Pete Holohan (TE) 1991, Keith Cash (TE) 1992–6, *Andre Rison* (WR) 1997–9, Jason Dunn (TE) 2001–3.

90 Curtis Anderson (DE) 1979, Bob Hamm (DE) 1985, *Neil Smith* (DE) 1988–96, Terry Wooden (LB) 1997, Ronnie Dixon (DT) 1998, Steve Martin (DT) 2000, Tyrone Williams (DL) 2001, Ryan Sims (DT) 2003.

91 Ken Kremer (NT) 1979–84, Gary Baldinger (DE) 1986–8, Lloyd Mumphrey (DE) 1987r, Ty Parten (DT) 1997, Leslie O'Neal (DE) 1998–9, Terdell Sands (DT) 2001, R-Kal Truluck (DL) 2002–3.

92 Ray Yakavonis (NT) 1983, Hal Stephens (DE) 1985, Bob Harris (LB) 1987r, Jerry McCabe (LB) 1988, Darren Mickell (DE) 1992–5, Dan Williams (DE) 1997, 1999–2001, Eric Downing (DT) 2003.

93 Eric Holle (DE) 1984–7, Dee Hardison (NT) 1988, Chris Dressel (TE) 1989, Mike Junkin (LB) 1989, John Browning (DL) 1996–2003.

94 Ken McAlister (LB) 1984–7, Gary Spann (LB) 1987r, Troy Stedman (LB) 1988, Mike Evans (DE) 1992, Keith Traylor (DT) 1995–6, Kerry Hicks (DL) 1996–7, Nate Hobgood-Chittick (DL) 2001–2.

95 Frank Case (DE) 1981, Jeff Paine (LB) 1984–5, Randy Fazier (LB) 1987r, Bruce Clark (DE) 1989, Tom Sims (NT) 1991–2, 1996, Jerrol Williams (LB) 1994, Michael Dean Perry (DT) 1997, Sean Manuel (TE) 1998, Derrick Ransom (DT) 1998–2002.

96 Aaron Pearson (LB) 1986–8, Fred Jones (LB) 1987r, Tim Newton (DT) 1993–4, Keith Rucker (DT) 1997, Tyrone Williams (Dl) 2000, Monty Beisel (LB) 2001–2.

97 Scott Radecic (LB) 1984–6, Tony Holloway (LB) 1987r, Ken Johnson (DE) 1987r, *Dan Saleaumua* (DT) 1989–96, Ty Parten (DT) 1997–2000, Rich Owens (DE) 2001–2.

98 Leonard Griffin (DE) 1986–93, John Walker (DT) 1987r, Rob Waldrop (DT) 1994, Eric Hicks (DE) 1998–2003.

99 Ernie Ladd (DT) 1967–8, Wilbur Young (DE) 1971–7, Mike Bell (DE) 1979–85, 1987–91, Vaughn Booker (DE) 1994–7, Darius Holland (DT) 1998, Duane Clemons (DE) 2000–2, Vonnie Holliday (DE) 2003.

MIAMI DOLPHINS

The franchise: Miami's debut in Pro Football was inauspicious. In 1946, the Miami Seahawks were a charter member of the All America Football Conference and lost the very first AAFC game 44–14 to the Cleveland Browns. After finishing the season 3–11 and drawing just 7,000 fans per game, Seahawks owner Harvey Hester sold the team back to the league which moved it to Baltimore. Twenty years later, American Football League commissioner Joe Foss asked his friend Joe Robbie if he was interested in starting an AFL expansion team, and Robbie suggested he'd be interested in Philadelphia. Not wanting to compete with the established NFL Eagles, Foss countered with Miami, and the Dolphins were conceived.

Robbie hired former Bear end and Lions coach George Wilson who had won championships in both places to lead his team. The high point in his tenure came quickly when Joe Auer returned the opening kickoff 95 yards for a touchdown in the Dolphins first game, although they eventually lost that game to the Raiders 23–14. After four years, Wilson was fired with a 15–39–2 record — a fairly normal record for an expansion team.

What new coach Don Shula did, though, was extraordinary. Shula supplemented the modicum of existing talent —

Bob Griese, Larry Csonka, Jim Kiick and Mercury Morris—with three new offensive linemen and several new defensive starters on a "No Name" defense. Then, general manager Joe Thomas, who had traded for Nick Buoniconti in 1969, obtained Paul Warfield in 1970. The new Dolphins went 10–4 and made the playoffs for the first time in 1970. The next year they reached the Super Bowl, and the following two seasons they won the championship. The 1972 season the Dolphins finished a perfect 17–0, the only undefeated season in NFL history. Injuries and defections to the new World Football League caused the Dolphin dynasty to slip a notch in the mid– 1970s as the Steelers surged forward as the team of the decade.

The Dolphins made the playoffs 16 times in Shula's 26 years at the helm and returned to the Super Bowl twice. In 1982 mediocre quarterback David Woodley and the "Killer B's" on defense lost to the Redskins and in 1984 future Hall of Famer Dan Marino's passes came up short against the more complete 49er team. Shula's early champions were known for their ball control offense and fast and light defense. Shula's later teams with Marino featured a down-the-field passing offense. If the coach had been able to supplement that with a consistent running attack and a tough defense, Marino may have brought the Dolphins back to the Super Bowl again.

In 1994, Blockbuster Video magnate Wayne Huizenga purchased the Dolphins from the Robbie family. Two seasons later, he replaced Shula with Jimmy Johnson who had previously replaced 29-year coaching legend Tom Landry in Dallas. Johnson built a fast, active defense, but also failed to support the aging Marino with a run-ning game. In the last game as a Dolphin for both Marino and Johnson, Miami lost to Jacksonville Jaguars 62–7 in the playoffs. It was the worst postseason beating since the 1940 Bears, featuring George Wilson at end, mauled the Redskins 73–0. Johnson's long-time lieutenant Dave Wannstedt was named coach and finally built a running game in Miami, but the Dolphins have yet to perform well after the weather turns cold.

Origin of name: Dolphins was a popular entry in a fan contest to name the team, and owner Joe Robbie liked it because dolphins are known for their intelligence and speed.

Time till first championship: Seven years.

Time since last championship: 31 years.

Retired numbers: Miami has retired the numbers of its two great quarterbacks— Bob Griese 12 and Dan Marino 13 — as well as Hall of Fame fullback Larry Csonka 39.

Other numbers worn by these players: None.

Those who wore retired numbers after the honored player: None.

Numbers that should be retired: Hall of Fame linebacker Nick Buoniconti, 85, was

Record by Decade

| | Regular Season | | | Postseason | | |
	Won	Lost	Tied	Won	Lost	Championships
1960s	15	39	2	0	0	
1970s	104	39	1	8	5	1972, 1973
1980s	94	57	1	6	5	
1990s	95	65	0	5	7	
2000s	41	23	0	1	2	
All-Time	349	223	4	20	19	2

Winning seasons: 27. Losing Seasons: 6. .500 seasons: 5.

Coaches

	Years	Record	Playoffs
George Wilson	1966–9	15–39–2	0–0
Don Shula (2)	1970–95	257–133–2	17–14
Jimmy Johnson	1996–9	36–28–0	2–3
Dave Wannstedt	2000–3	41–23–0	1–2

(Championships in parentheses)

the leader of the "No Name" defense that won back-to-back Super Bowls.

Owned numbers: 12 has only been worn by Bob Griese, and only Larry Csonka has worn 39.

Numbers worn by Hall of Famers: Nick Buoniconti 85; Larry Csonka 39; Bob Griese 12; Jim Langer 62; Larry Little 66; Dwight Stephenson 57; and Paul Warfield 42.

Star power: Ricky Williams took 34 from Travis Minor.

Star eclipsed: Ron Jaworski wore 17 because Fuad Reveiz wore 7; Cris Carter wore 88 because James McKnight wore 80.

Numbers with most great players: Several numbers have been worn by two outstanding Dolphins (see Shared Numbers). 25 has been worn by a number of fine defensive backs, Dick Westmoreland, Tim Foley, and Louis Oliver. 61 has been worn by center Bob DeMarco, guard Roy Foster and center Tim Ruddy.

Worst represented numbers: 52 has been worn by a center and 17 linebackers, none of whom have lasted more than three years in Miami. 71 has been worn by 13 anonymous linemen. 87 has been worn by 14 forgettable receivers.

Number worn by the most players: 82 has been worn 19 times.

Player who wore the most numbers: Several players have worn three numbers— Aaron Craver 32/34/44; Kirby Dar Dar 15/80/87; Hubert Ginn 28/32/33; Nate Jacquet 19/83/88; and James Pruitt 81/82/87.

Longest tenure wearing a number: Quarterback Dan Marino wore 13 for 17 years from 1983 to 1999. Guard Bob Kuechenberg wore 67 for 15 years from 1970 to 1984.

Number worn by first ever draft pick: Jim Grabowski and Rick Norton were picked at the top of the AFL's 1966 draft. Grabowski signed with Green Bay, but Norton would wear 11 in his short Dolphin career.

Biggest draft busts: Biggest draft busts include quarterback Rick Norton, 11, who was selected first in 1966 and who completed 41 percent of his passes and threw 6 tds against 30 interceptions in four years; runner Sammie Smith, 33, who was selected ninth in 1989 and who averaged 3.5 yards

over three years; and receiver Yatil Green, 87, who was selected 15th in 1997 and who had 18 catches in eight games.

Number worn by first expansion draft pick: The expansion draft was not conducted in rounds. The expansion pick who lasted longest with the Dolphins was tackle Norm Evans who wore 73 for ten years from 1966 to 1975.

Number worn by oldest player: Earl Morrall wore 15 as a 42 year old in 1976.

Cameos: All Pros and other notables— Jim Braxton 34; Preston Carpenter 36; Rick Casares 35; Neal Colzie 20; Joe Cribbs 20; Jim Dunaway 78; Ken Ellis 48; Bert Emanuel 87; Earl Faison 84; Tony Franklin 1; Cookie Gilchrist 2; Mike Golic 96; Eric Green 86; Abner Haynes 28;Bobby Humphrey 44; Quadry Ismail 86; Billy Joe 33; Pete Johnson 46; Dave Kocourek 83; Willie Richardson 87; Henry Taylor 98; Thurman Thomas 34.

Ones who got away: Center Carl Mauck, 60, made his mark with the Oilers. Freddie Solomon, 86, starred as a receiver for Bill Walsh's 49ers. Norman Hand, 98, has been an effective defensive tackle for the Chargers and Saints.

Least popular numbers: 0 has never been worn. 8 has been worn only once. 2, 9, 13, and 95 all have been worn just twice.

Last number to be originated: 8 was first worn by punter Klaus Wilmsmeyer in 1998.

Longest dormant number: 16 has been dormant since 1983.

Triskaidekaphobia notes: No bad luck here. 13 has been worn by All Pro and Super Bowl MVP safety Jake Scott and Dan Marino.

Shared numbers: 13 was worn by All Pro safety Jake Scott and Dan Marino; shifty runner Mercury Morris and Tony Nathan wore 22; cover corners Troy Vincent and Patrick Surtain wore 23; tackle Norm Evans and "Killer B" Bob Baumhower wore 73; "No Name" Manny Fernandez and "Killer B" Doug Betters wore 75; quick defensive end Vern Den Herder and "Marks Brother" Mark Clayton wore 83; Hall of Fame Linebacker Nick Buoniconti and "Marks Brother" Mark Duper wore 85.

Continuity: Cornerback Dick Westmoreland was replaced in 25 by safety Tim Foley; Irving Fryar was replaced in 80 by fellow deep threat Fred Barnett; wideout O.J. McDuffie was replaced in 81 by tight end Randy McMichael.

Discontinuity: Troy Vincent was followed in 23 by fellow corner Robert Bailey; Marv Fleming was followed in 80 by fellow tight end Jim McFarland; Hall of Famer Nick Buoniconti was followed in 85 by receiver Terry Anderson; Keith Jackson was followed in 88 by fellow tight end Joe Planansky; receiver Nat Moore was followed in 89 by tight end David Lewis.

Family Connections

Brothers

Glenn Blackwood	S	1979–87	47
Lyle Blackwood	S	1982–6	42

Fathers and Sons

Bob Griese	QB	1967–80	12
Brian Griese	QB	2003	14
Rudy Barber	LB	1968	72
Kantroy Barber	RB	1999	48

Quarterback numbers over 19: None.

Numbers of future NFL head coaches: Terry Robiskie 38.

Numbers of future NFL referees: None.

Players who played other sports: Wrestling — Wahoo McDaniel 54 and Bob Bruggers 54/56. Track — Jimmy Hines 99.

Players more famous after football: Dick Anderson, 40, later served in the Florida State Legislature.

First player to wear a number in the 90s: Tight end Bill Cronin wore 90 in 1966.

Number with most points scored: 10 with 1,574 points scored by Olindo Mare (786), Pete Stoyanovich (774), Don Strock (12) and George Wilson Jr. (2).

Number with most yards rushing: 22 with 7,456 yards gained by Mercury Morris (3,877), Tony Nathan (3,543) and Jimmy Saxon (36).

Number with most receptions: 89 with 842 passes caught by Nat Moore (510), Karl Noonan (136), Tony Martin (109), Ed Perry (39), Randall Hill (33), Leland Douglas (9), and David Lewis (6).

Number with most touchdown passes: 13 with 420 touchdowns tossed by Dan Marino.

Number with most interceptions: 25 with 59 passes picked off by Louis Oliver (24), Tim Foley (19), Dick Westmoreland (15) and Greg Jeffries (1).

Oddity: Don Shula got his start as the Detroit Lions defensive coach under head coach George Wilson. Wilson was the first Dolphins coach and was replaced by Shula after four years. Both Wilson and Shula had sons who played briefly in the NFL. George Wilson Jr. quarterbacked the Dolphins under his father in 1966; David Shula played for his father's old team, the Colts. Both of Shula's sons, David and Mike, coached under him in Miami. David, who later coached the Bengals and lost to the Dolphins in the first head-to-head father-son coaching match in NFL history, is now out of coaching. Mike is the Dolphins quarterback coach under Dave Wannstedt.

Also, versatile linebacker Bob Matheson had the "53 Defense" of the 1971–2 Dolphins named after his number. The 53 was an early version of the 3–4 alignment in which Matheson would sometimes line up as a down lineman and other times as a stand up linebacker.

Team All-Time Numerical Roster

Those with an "r" following the year 1987 were replacement players during the players' strike. Pro Bowl players for each number are in *Italics*; Hall of Famers are in **Bold** type.

1 *Garo Yepremian* (K) 1970–8, Tony Franklin (K) 1988, Willie Beecher (K) 1988, Matt Turk (P) 2000–1, 2003.

2 Cookie Gilchrist (FB) 1966, Willie Beecher (K) 1987r.

3 Tom Orosz (P) 1981–2, Van Tiffin (K) 1987, Stacy Gore (P) 1987r, Mark Royals (P) 2002–3.

4 George Roberts (P) 1978–80, *Reggie Roby* (P) 1983–92, Tom Hutton (P) 1999.

5 Booth Lusteg (K) 1967, John Stofa (QB) 1969–70, Uwe Von Schamann (K) 1979–84, Jeff Hayes (P) 1987, Kyle Richardson (P) 1997.

6 Jim Arnold (P) 1994, Joe Nedney (K) 1996–7,

Brent Bartholomew (P) 1999, Ray Lucas (QB) 2001–2.

7 Billy Lothridge (P) 1972, Guy Benjamin (QB) 1978–9, Fuad Reveiz (K) 1985–8, Charlie Baumann (K) 1991, Joe Prokop (P) 1992, Dale Hatcher (P) 1993, Craig Erickson (QB) 1996–8.

8 Klaus Wilmsmeyer (P) 1998.

9 Scott Secules (QB) 1989–92, Jay Fiedler (QB) 2000–3.

10 George Wilson (QB) 1966, George Mira (QB) 1971, Don Strock (QB) 1974–87, Pete Stoyanovich (K) 1989–95, *Olindo Mare* (K) 1997–2003.

11 Rick Norton (QB) 1966–9, Jim Del Gaizo (QB) 1972, 1975, Jim Jensen (QB/RB) 1981–92, Dan McGwire (QB) 1995, Damon Huard (QB) 1997–2000.

12 **Bob Griese** (QB) 1967–80.

13 *Jake Scott* (S) 1970–5, *Dan Marino* (QB) 1983–99.

14 Scott Stankavage (QB) 1987r, Doug Pederson (QB) 1993, Scott Zolak (QB) 1999, Brian Griese (QB) 2003.

15 John Stofa (QB) 1966–7, Kim Hammond (QB) 1968, Karl Kremser (K) 1969–70, Charles Leigh (RB) 1971, Earl Morrall (QB) 1972–6, Kyle Mackey (QB) 1987r, Kirby Dar Dar (WR) 1995.

16 Archie Roberts (QB) 1967, Tom Boutwell (QB) 1969, David Woodley (QB) 1980–3.

17 Mike Michel (P/K) 1977, Ron Jaworski (QB) 1987–8, Steve DeBerg (QB) 1993, John Kidd (P) 1994–7, Todd Doxzon (QB/WR) 1998.

18 Dick Wood (QB) 1966, Cliff Stoudt (QB) 1989, Sage Rosenfels (QB) 2002–3.

19 Reyna Thompson (CB) 1986, Scott Mitchell (QB) 1990–3, Bernie Kosar (QB) 1994–6, Nate Jacquet (WR) 1998.

20 Larry Seiple (P/TE) 1967–77, Neal Colzie (DB) 1979, David Overstreet (RB) 1983, Ricky Isom (FB) 1987r, Joe Cribbs (RB) 1988, Marc Logan (FB) 1989–91, Muhammad Oliver (CB) 1994, Ray Nealy (RB) 1997, John Avery (RB) 1998–9, Ben Kelly (DB) 2000–1, Arturo Freeman (S) 2003.

21 Gene Mingo (K) 1966–7, *Jim Kiick* (RB) 1968–74, Rick Volk (DB) 1977–8, Tate Randle (S) 1987r, Mark Higgs (RB) 1990–4, Lawrence Phillips (RB) 1997, Rayna Stewart (S) 1998, Autry Denson (RB) 1999–2000, Terry Cousin (DB) 2001, Jamar Fletcher (CB) 2002–3.

22 *Willie West* (S) 1966–8, *Mercury Morris* (RB) 1969–75, Tony Nathan (RB) 1979–87, Kerry Goode (RB) 1989, Tim McKyer (CB) 1990, James Saxon (RB) 1992–4, Shawn Wooden (S) 1996–9, 2001–3, Terrance Shaw (CB) 2000.

23 Wes Matthews (WR) 1966, Charles Leigh (RB) 1973–4, Joe Carter (RB) 1984–6, Troy Stradford (RB) 1987–90, Demetrious Johnson (DB) 1987r, Troy Vincent (CB) 1992–5, Robert Bailey

(CB) 1996, George Teague (S) 1997, *Patrick Surtain* (CB) 1998–2003.

24 Billy Hunter (RB) 1966, Jack Clancy (WR) 1967–9, *Del Williams* (RB) 1978–80, Reyna Thompson (CB) 1986–8, Floyd Raglin (CB) 1987r, Rodney Thomas (CB) 1989–90, Vestee Jackson (DB) 1991–3, Pat Johnson (S) 1995, Jerry Wilson (CB) 1996–2000, Jamar Fletcher (CB) 2001, Omar Lowe (DB) 2002, Sammy Knight (S) 2003.

25 *Dick Westmoreland* (CB) 1966–9, *Tim Foley* (S) 1970–80, Mike Smith (CB) 1985–7, Louis Oliver (S) 1989–93, 1995–6, Corey Harris (DB) 1997, Greg Jeffries (DB) 1999–2000, Paul Miranda (DB) 2002, Jimmy Wyrick (CB) 2003.

26 Frank Jackson (WR) 1966–7, Lloyd Mumphord (CB) 1969–74, Duriel Harris (WR) 1976, Donovan Rose (S) 1986–7, Jarvis Williams (S) 1988–93, Bracey Walker (S) 1997, Lamar Smith (RB) 2000–1.

27 Gary Tucker (RB) 1968, Gary Davis (RB) 1976–9, Lorenzo Hampton (RB) 1985–9, Stevon Moore (S) 1990, David Pool (CB) 1994, Terrell Buckley (CB) 1995–9, 2003, Arturo Freeman (S) 2000–2.

28 George Chesser (RB) 1966, Abner Haynes (RB) 1967, Gene Milton (WR) 1968–9, Ed Jenkins (RB) 1972, Hubert Ginn (RB) 1975, Don McNeal (CB) 1980–9, Michael McGruder (CB) 1990–1, Frankie Smith (CB) 1993, Gene Atkins (S) 1994–6, Ray Hill (CB) 1998–2000, Travis Minor (RB) 2002–3.

29 Jack Harper (RB) 1967–8, Garry Grady (S) 1969, Tom Smith (RB) 1973, John Swain (CB) 1985, Liffort Hobley (S) 1987–93, Frankie Smith (CB) 1994–5, *Sam Madison* (CB) 1997–2003.

30 Sam Price (RB) 1966–8, Bryant Salter (DB) 1976, Ron Davenport (FB) 1985–9, Bernie Parmalee (RB) 1992–8, Obafemi Ayanbadejo (RB) 2003.

31 George Chesser (RB) 1967, Barry Pryor (RB) 1969–70, Terry Cole (RB) 1971, Norm Bulaich (RB) 1975–9, Rick Moser (RB) 1980, Eddie Hill (RB) 1981–4, Sean Hill (DB) 1994–6, *Brock Marion* (S) 1998–2003.

32 Joe Auer (RB) 1966–7, Hubert Ginn (RB) 1970–3, Benny Malone (RB) 1974–8, Tom Vigorito (RB/WR) 1981–5, Donald Brown (CB) 1986, Pete Roth (FB) 1987r, Garrett Limbrick (FB) 1990, Bruce Alexander (CB) 1992–3, Aaron Craver (RB) 1994, Cleveland Gary (RB) 1994, Jerris McPhail (RB) 1996–7, J.J. Johnson (RB) 1999–2001.

33 Billy Joe (FB) 1966, Hubert Ginn (RB) 1974, Stan Winfrey (RB) 1975–7, Billy Cesare (S) 1980, Bo Matthews (FB) 1981, Rich Diana (RB) 1982, Craig Ellis (RB) 1986, Ronald Scott (RB) 1987r, Sammie Smith (RB) 1989–91, Karim Abdul-Jabbar (RB) 1996–9, Deon Dyer (RB) 2000–2.

34 Ron Sellers (WR) 1973, Jim Braxton (RB)

1978, Woody Bennett (RB) 1980–8, Don Tester-man (FB) 1980, Nuu Faaola (FB) 1989, Tony Collins (RB) 1990, Aaron Craver (RB) 1991–3, Tyrone Braxton (S) 1994, Tim Jacobs (CB) 1996–7, Ron Moore (RB) 1998, Cecil Collins (RB) 1999, Thurman Thomas (RB) 2000, Travis Minor (RB) 2001, *Ricky Williams* (RB) 2002–3.

35 Rick Casares (RB) 1966, Stan Mitchell (RB) 1966–70, Clayton Heath (RB) 1976, Nick Giaquinto (RB) 1980–1, John Tagliaferri (RB) 1987r, Kerry Glenn (CB) 1990–2, Michael Stewart (S) 1994–6, Irving Spikes (RB) 1997, Ben Kelly (DB) 2000.

36 Preston Carpenter (TE) 1966, Charles Leigh (RB) 1972, Don Nottingham (FB) 1973–7, Steve Howell (FB) 1979–81, Tom Brown (FB) 1987–9, Stephen Braggs (DB) 1992–3, Stanley Pritchett (FB) 1996–9.

37 Charley Wade (WR) 1973, Mike Kozlowski (S) 1979–80, *Andra Franklin* (RB) 1981–4, J.B. Brown (CB) 1989–96, Zebbie Lethridge (CB) 2001, Lloyd Harrison (CB) 2002.

38 Leroy Harris (RB) 1977–8, Bob Torrey (FB) 1979, Terry Robiskie (FB) 1980–1, Ron Landry (FB) 1984, Clarence Bailey (FB) 1987r, Bruce Plummer (CB) 1988, Willard Reaves (RB) 1989, Calvin Jackson (DB) 1994–9, Kevin Williams (S) 2000.

39 **Larry Csonka** (FB) 1968–74, 1979.

40 Bo Roberson (WR) 1966, *Dick Anderson* (S) 1968–77, Mike Kozlowski (S) 1981–6, John Swain (CB) 1987r, Irving Spikes (RB) 1994–6, Ray Green (DB) 2001–2.

41 Willie Pearson (CB) 1969, Jerris White (CB) 1974–6, Norris Thomas (CB) 1977–9, Fulton Walker (CB) 1981–4, Mark Konecny (RB) 1987r, African Grant (S) 1990, *Keith Byars* (FB) 1993–6, Scott McGarrahan (S) 2001–2.

42 Bill Darnell (WR) 1968–9, **Paul Warfield** (WR) 1970–4, Vern Roberson (S) 1977, Lyle Blackwood (S) 1981–6, Robert Sowell (CB) 1987r, Ernest Gibson (CB) 1989, Chris Green (DB) 1991–4, Terry Kirby (RB) 1995, Roosevelt Potts (FB) 1997, Trent Gamble (DB) 2001–3.

43 Bob Neff (S) 1966–8, Mike Holmes (WR) 1976, Jeff Allen (CB) 1980, Ricky Ray (CB) 1981, Larry Cowan (RB) 1982, Bud Brown (S) 1984–8, Terry Kirby (RB) 1993–4.

44 Pete Jaquess (S) 1966–7, Dick Washington (CB) 1968, Dean Brown (S) 1970, Mike Howell (S) 1972, Barry Hill (S) 1975–6, Charles Cornelius (CB) 1977–8, Doug Beaudoin (S) 1980, Paul Lankford (CB) 1982–91, Bobby Humphrey (RB) 1992, Aaron Craver (RB) 1994, Rob Konrad (FB) 1999–2003.

45 Mack Lamb (CB) 1967–8, Curtis Johnson (CB) 1970–8, Ed Taylor (CB) 1979–82, Robert Sowell (CB) 1983–5, Trell Hooper (CB) 1987r, Rodney Thomas (CB) 1988, Bobby Harden (S) 1990–3, Brian Walker (DB) 1997–8, 2000–1.

46 Hal Wantland (S) 1966, Don Bessillieu (S) 1979–81, Pete Johnson (FB) 1984, Mark Irvin (S) 1987r, Dave Moore (TE) 1992.

47 John McGeever (S) 1966, Tom Beier (S) 1967, 1969, Ted Bachman (CB) 1976, Glenn Blackwood (S) 1979–87, Stefon Adams (S) 1990, Darrell Malone (CB) 1992–4, Robert Edwards (RB) 2002, Jeff Grau (C) 2003.

48 Bob Petrella (S) 1966–71, Henry Stuckey (CB) 1972–4, Ken Ellis (CB) 1976, Wade Bosarge (S) 1977, Gerald Small (CB) 1978–83, Mike Iaquaniello (S) 1991, Jim Kitts (FB) 1997–8, Kantroy Barber (FB) 1999, Brody Heffner-Liddiard (TE) 2000.

49 *Jimmy Warren* (CB) 1966–9, Ray Jones (CB) 1971, Charlie Babb (S) 1972–9, William Judson (CB) 1982–9, Marvell Burgess (S) 1987r, Tony Paige (RB) 1990–2, Robert Wilson (FB) 1994–6, Dewayne Dotson (LB/FB) 1997.

50 Frank Emanuel (LB) 1968–9, Dick Palmer (LB) 1970, Bruce Elia (LB) 1975, Larry Gordon (LB) 1976–82, Jackie Shipp (LB) 1984–8, Greg Storr (LB) 1987r, Dave Ahrens (LB) 1989, Louis Cooper (LB) 1991, Dwight Hollier (LB) 1992–9, Michael Hamilton (LB) 2000, Brendon Ayanbadejo (LB) 2003.

51 Jerry Hopkins (LB) 1967, Ed Weisacosky (LB) 1968–70, Larry Ball (LB) 1972–4, Rodrigo Barnes (LB) 1975, Andy Selfridge (LB) 1976, Rusty Chambers (LB) 1976–80, Mark Brown (LB) 1983–8, Greg Clark (LB) 1989, *Bryan Cox* (LB) 1991–5, Anthony Harris (LB) 1996–9, Tommy Hendricks (LB) 2000–3.

52 Mike Hudock (C) 1966, Jimmy Keyes (LB/K) 1968–9, Mike Dennery (LB) 1976, Larry Ball (LB) 1977–8, Mel Land (LB) 1979, Steve Shull (LB) 1980–2, Terry Tautolo (LB) 1983, Emmitt Tilley (LB) 1983, Sanders Shiver (LB) 1984, Robin Sendlein (LB) 1985, Scott Nicolas (LB) 1987, Dennis Fowlkes (LB) 1987r, Mike Reichenbach (LB) 1990–1, Roosevelt Collins (LB) 1992, Brant Boyer (LB) 1994, Jeff Kopp (LB) 1995, Robert Jones (LB) 1998–2000, Morlon Greenwood (LB) 2001–3.

53 *Tom Erlandson* (LB) 1966–7, Norm McBride (DE) 1969–70, Bob Matheson (LB) 1971–9, Rodell Thomas (LB) 1981, Ron Hester (LB) 1982, Jay Brophy (LB) 1984–6, David Frye (LB) 1986–9, Jack Squirek (LB) 1986, Ned Bolcar (LB) 1991–2, Aubrey Beavers (LB) 1994–5, *Larry Izzo* (LB) 1996–2000.

54 Wahoo McDaniel (LB) 1966–8, Bob Bruggers (LB) 1968, Dave McCullers (LB) 1969, Ted Davis (LB) 1970, Howard Kindig (G/C) 1972–3, Ralph Ortega (LB) 1979–80, Steve Potter (LB) 1981–2, Rodell Thomas (LB) 1983–4, Alex Moyer (LB) 1985–6, Johnny Taylor (LB) 1986, Larry Kolic (LB) 1987–8, Steve Lubischer (LB) 1987r, E.J. Junior (LB) 1989–91, Chuck Bullough (LB) 1993–4, *Zach Thomas* (LB) 1996–2003.

55 Jack Rudolph (LB) 1966, Randall Edmunds (LB) 1968–9, Irv Goode (C) 1973–4, Earnie Rhone (LB) 1975–84, Hugh Green (LB) 1985–91, Chris Singleton (LB) 1993–6, David Merritt (LB) 1993, Ronnie Ward (LB) 1997, Justin Seaverns (LB) 2002, Junior Seau (LB) 2003.

56 Bob Bruggers (LB) 1966–7, Jesse Powell (LB) 1969–73, Steve Towle (LB) 1975–80, Charles Bowser (LB) 1982–5, *John Offerdahl* (LB) 1986–93, Mike Crawford (LB) 1997–8, Twan Russell (LB) 2000–2.

57 *John Bramlett* (LB) 1967–8, Mike Kolen (LB) 1970–5, 1977, Sean Clancy (LB) 1978, **Dwight Stephenson** (C) 1980–7, Scott Nicolas (LB) 1987r, Tom Thayer (G/C) 1993, Dion Foxx (LB) 1994–5, O.J. Brigance (LB) 1997–9, Corey Moore (LB) 2001, Corey Jenkins (LB) 2003.

58 *Tom Goode* (C) 1966–9, Dale Farley (LB) 1971, Al Jenkins (T) 1972, Bruce Bannon (LB) 1973–4, *Kim Bokamper* (LB) 1977–85, Rick Graf (LB) 1987, Tony Furjanic (LB) 1988, Chris Gaines (LB) 1988, Ilia Jarostchuk (LB) 1988, Barry Krause (LB) 1989, Mark Sander (LB) 1992, Jesse Solomon (LB) 1994, Antonio Armstrong (LB) 1995, O.J. Brigance (LB) 1996, Scott Galyon (LB) 2000–2.

59 Jack Thornton (LB) 1966, Doug Swift (LB) 1970–5, Guy Roberts (LB) 1977, Steve Shull (LB) 1980, Bob Brudzinski (LB) 1981–9, John Grimsley (LB) 1991–3, Dewayne Dotson (LB/RB) 1994–5, Derrick Rodgers (LB) 1997–2002.

60 Carl Mauck (C) 1970, Tom Wickert (T) 1974, Don Reese (LB) 1976, Melvin Mitchell (G) 1977–8, Jeff Toews (G) 1979–85, Duke Schamel (LB) 1987r, Greg Clark (LB) 1989, Bert Weidner (G/C) 1990–5, John Bock (G) 1996–2000, Spencer Folau (T) 2001, Greg Jerman (T) 2002–3.

61 Ernie Park (G) 1966, Fred Woodson (G) 1967–9, Bob DeMarco (C) 1970–1, Cleveland Green (T) 1979, Thom Dornbrook (G) 1980, *Roy Foster* (G) 1982–90, Greg Cleveland (T) 1987r, Gene Williams (G) 1991–2, *Tim Ruddy* (C) 1994–2003.

62 **Jim Langer** (C) 1970–9, Harry Galbreath (G) 1988–92, Chris Gray (G) 1993–6.

63 Billy Neighbors (G) 1966–9, Mark Dennard (C) 1979–83, Larry Lee (G/C) 1985, Greg Ours (C) 1987r, Jeff Uhlenhake (C) 1989–93, Cal Dixon (C) 1996, Mark Dixon (G) 1998–2003.

64 *Ed Newman* (G) 1973–84, Houston Hoover (G) 1994, Larry Chester (DT) 2002–3.

65 Jim Higgins (G) 1966, Jack Pyburn (T) 1967–8, Maulty Moore (DT) 1972–4, Wally Pesuit (T) 1977–8, Jeff Dellenbach (C/T) 1985–94, Bill Beales (T) 1987r, Kevin Donnalley (G) 1998–2000, Troy Andrew (OL) 2001–2.

66 **Larry Little** (G) 1969–80, Larry Lee (G/C) 1986, Jim Gilmore (G) 1987r, Everett McIver (G) 1996–7, Kevin Gogan (G) 1999, Heath Irwin (G) 2000–1, Jamie Nails (G) 2002–3.

67 *Bob Kuechenberg* (G) 1970–84, Chris Ward (T) 1986, Chris Conlin (G/C) 1987, Guy Goar (C) 1987r, Pat Swoopes (DE) 1991, Jeff Novak (T) 1994, Barry Stokes (T) 1998.

68 Melvin Mitchell (G) 1976, Eric Laakso (T) 1978–84, Greg Koch (T) 1986–7, Louis Oubre (G) 1987r, Andrew Greene (G) 1995, Mike Sheldon (T) 1997–9, Seth McKinney (OL) 2002–3.

69 Mike Lambrecht (DT) 1987–9, *Keith Sims* (G) 1990–7.

70 Jim Riley (DE) 1967–71, Larry Woods (DT) 1973, Tom Funchess (T) 1974, John Andrews (DE) 1975–6, Bob Simpson (DE) 1978, Bill Barnett (DT) 1980–5, *Brian Sochia* (DT) 1986–91, Eric Moore (T) 1995, Mike Chalenski (DE) 1997, Harry Swayne (T) 2001.

71 Jack Pyburn (T) 1966, Charlie Fowler (G) 1967–8, John Boynton (T) 1969, Frank Cornish (DT) 1970–1, Darryl Carlton (T) 1975–6, Mike Current (T) 1977–9, Burton Lawless (DT) 1981, Mike Charles (DT) 1983–6, Bob Gruber (T) 1987, Scott Kehoe (T) 1987r, Ethan Albright (T) 1995, Dunstan Anderson (DE) 1997, Todd Wade (T) 2000–3.

72 Whit Canale (DE) 1966, Bill Keating (DT) 1967, Rudy Barber (LB) 1968, Bob Heinz (DT) 1969–77, Mike Fultz (DT) 1981, Richard Bishop (DE) 1982, Ronnie Lee (T/TE) 1984–9, Steve Jacobson (DE) 1987r, Tom McHale (G) 1995, Barron Tanner (DT) 1997–8.

73 *Norm Evans* (T) 1966–75, *Bob Baumhower* (DT) 1977–86, Greg Johnson (G) 1988, Ron Heller (T) 1993–5, Dario Romero (DL) 2002, Billy Yates (G) 2003.

74 John Richardson (DT) 1967–71, Randy Crowder (DT) 1974–6, Steve Young (T) 1977, Cleveland Green (T) 1980–6, Mark Dennis (T) 1987–93, Jeff Wiska (G) 1987r, Ed Hawthorne (NT) 1995, Brent Smith (OL) 1997–2002, Wade Smith (T) 2003.

75 Ken Rice (G) 1966–7, Manny Fernandez (DT) 1968–75, Rick Dvorak (DE) 1977, *Doug Betters* (DE) 1978–87, Jeff Faulkner (DE) 1990, Dave Zawatson (T) 1991, Shane Burton (DE) 1996–8, Damian Gregory (DT) 2000, Todd Perry (G) 2001–3.

76 Tom Nomina (DT) 1966–8, Jeff Richardson (T) 1969, Willie Young (T) 1973, Don Reese (DT) 1974–5, John Alexander (DE) 1977–8, Rod Walters (G) 1980, Mike Fultz (DT) 1981, Steve Clark (G) 1982–5, Tom Toth (G) 1986–9, Tim Irwin (T) 1994, James Brown (T) 1996–9, Marcus Spriggs (OL) 2001–2.

77 Rich Zecher (DT) 1966–7, Doug Crusan (T) 1968–74, *A.J. Duhe* (DE) 1977–84, Stanley Scott (DE) 1987r, Louis Cheek (T) 1988–9, Karl Wilson (DE) 1990, Jeff Buckey (G/T) 1996–8.

78 Maxie Williams (T) 1966–70, Wayne Mass (T) 1971, Jim Dunaway (DT) 1972, Tom Drougas

(T) 1975–6, Carl Barisich (DT) 1977–80, Ken Poole (DT) 1981–2, Charles Benson (DE) 1983–4, Jerome Foster (DT) 1986, Doug Marrone (G/C) 1987, Derek Wimberly (DE) 1987r, Alvin Powell (G) 1989, *Richmond Webb* (T) 1990–2000.

79 Al Dotson (DT) 1966, Claude Brownlee (DE) 1967, Mike Current (T) 1967, Jim Urbanek (DT) 1968, *Wayne Moore* (T) 1970–8, Jon Giesler (T) 1979–88, Ike Readon (DT) 1987r, Donnie Gardner (DE) 1991, Larry Webster (DT) 1992–4, Billy Milner (T) 1995–6, Kenny Mixon (DE) 1998–2001.

80 *Ed Cooke* (DE) 1966–7, Bob Joswick (DE) 1968–9, Marv Fleming (TE) 1970–4, Jim McFarland (TE) 1975, Loaird McCreary (TE) 1976–8, Joe Rose (TE) 1980–5, Lawrence Sampleton (TE) 1987r, *Ferrell Edmunds* (TE) 1988–92, *Irving Fryar* (WR) 1993–5, Fred Barnett (WR) 1996–7, Brett Perriman (WR) 1997, Kirby Dar Dar (WR) 1998, Iheanyi Uwaezuoke (WR) 1998, Tony Martin (WR) 1999–2000, James McKnight (WR) 2001–3.

81 Howard Twilley (WR) 1966–76, Ike Hill (WR) 1976, Jimmy Cefalo (WR) 1978–84, Scott Schwedes (WR) 1987–90, Mike Caterbone (WR) 1987r, Randal Hill (WR) 1991, James Pruitt (WR) 1991, Robert Clark (WR) 1992, O.J. McDuffie (WR) 1993–2001, Randy McMichael (TE) 2002–3.

82 Doug Moreau (TE) 1966–9, Otto Stowe (WR) 1971–2, Bo Rather (RB) 1973, Mel Baker (WR) 1974, Cotton Speyrer (WR) 1975, Morris Owens (WR) 1975–6, Duriel Harris (WR) 1977–83, 1985, Fernanza Burgess (WR) 1984, James Pruitt (WR) 1986–8, Todd Feldman (WR) 1987r, Andre Brown (WR) 1989–90, Scott Miller (WR) 1991–2, Mark Ingram (WR) 1993–4, Frank Wainwright (TE) 1995–8, Kevin McKenzie (WR) 1999, Roell Preston (WR) 1999, Larry Shannon (WR) 1999, Jed Weaver (TE) 2000–2, Kendall Newson (WR) 2003.

83 Dave Kocourek (TE) 1966, Jim Cox (TE) 1968, Vern Den Herder (DE) 1972–82, *Mark Clayton* (WR) 1983–92, Dameon Reilly (WR) 1987r, Scott Miller (WR) 1993–6, Brian Manning (WR) 1997, Nate Jacquet (WR) 1998, Hendrick Lusk (TE) 1998, Hunter Goodwin (TE) 1999–2001, Robert Baker (WR) 2002, Albert Johnson (WR) 2002, Sam Simmons (WR) 2003.

84 Earl Faison (DE) 1966, Ray Jacobs (DT) 1967–8, *Bill Stanfill* (DE) 1969–76, Bruce Hardy (TE) 1978–89, Willie Smith (TE) 1987r, Greg Baty (TE) 1990–4, Gary Clark (WR) 1995, Brett Carolan (TE) 1996, Troy Drayton (TE) 1996–9, Leslie Shepherd (WR) 2000, Chris Chambers (WR) 2001–3.

85 John Holmes (DE) 1966, **Nick Buoniconti** (LB) 1969–76, Terry Anderson (WR) 1977–8, Bo Rather (RB) 1978, Jeff Groth (WR) 1979, *Mark Duper* (WR) 1982–92, Eddie Chavis (WR) 1987r, Ronnie Williams (TE) 1993–5, Lamar Thomas

(WR) 1996–2000, Desmond Clark (TE) 2002, Donald Lee (TE) 2003.

86 Mel Branch (DE) 1966–8, Vern Den Herder (DE) 1971, Marlin Briscoe (WR) 1972–4, Freddie Solomon (WR) 1975–7, Ronnie Lee (T/TE) 1979–82, John Chesley (TE) 1984, Fred Banks (WR) 1987–93, George Farmer (WR) 1987r, Dennis McKinnon (WR) 1990, Eric Green (TE) 1995, Brett Carolan (TE) 1996, Qadry Ismail (WR) 1997, Oronde Gadsden (WR) 1998–2003.

87 John Roderick (WR) 1966–7, Jim Mertens (TE) 1969, Willie Richardson (WR) 1970, Andre Tillman (TE) 1975–8, Dan Johnson (TE) 1983–7, David Lewis (TE) 1987r, Rich Siler (TE) 1987r, James Pruitt (WR) 1990, Mike Williams (WR) 1991–5, Charles Henry (TE) 1991, Kirby Dar Dar (WR) 1996, Yatil Green (WR) 1997–9, Bert Emanuel (WR) 2000, Dedrick Ward (WR) 2001–2.

88 LaVerne Torczon (DE) 1966, Jim Mandich (TE) 1970–7, Elmer Bailey (WR) 1980–1, Vince Heflin (WR) 1982–5, Joel Williams (TE) 1987, Brian Kinchen (TE) 1988–90, Arthur Cox (TE) 1991, *Keith Jackson* (TE) 1992–4, Joe Planansky (TE) 1995, Charles Jordan (WR) 1996–8, Nate Jacquet (WR) 1998–9, Jeff Ogden (WR) 2000–1, Cris Carter (WR) 2002, Derrius Thompson (WR) 2003.

89 *Karl Noonan* (WR) 1966–71, *Nat Moore* (WR) 1974–86, David Lewis (TE) 1987, Leland Douglas (WR) 1987r, Tony Martin (WR) 1990–3, Randal Hill (WR) 1995–6, Ed Perry (TE) 1997–2002.

90 Bill Cronin (TE) 1966, Andy Hendel (LB) 1986, Eric Kumerow (DE) 1988–90, Marco Coleman (DE) 1992–5, *Adewale Ogunleye* (DE) 2000–1, Rob Burnett (DE) 2002–3.

91 Ed Judie (LB) 1984, Mack Moore (DE) 1985–6, Fred Robinson (LB) 1986, Victor Morris (LB) 1987r, *Jeff Cross* (DE) 1988–95, Lorenzo Bromell (DE) 1998–2001, Jay Williams (DL) 2002–3.

92 Laz Chavez (LB) 1987r, Nate Hill (DE) 1988, David Griggs (LB) 1989–93, Daryl Gardener (DT) 1996–2001, Jeff Zgonina (DT) 2003.

93 Charles Bennett (DE) 1987r, Cliff Odom (LB) 1990–3, William Gaines (DT) 1994, Trace Armstrong (DE) 1995–2000, *Adewale Ogunleye* (DE) 2002–3.

94 Larry Kolic (LB) 1986, Tim Pidgeon (LB) 1987r, Greg Mark (LB) 1990, Craig Veasey (DT) 1993–4, Steve Emtman (DT) 1995–6, Jermaine Haley (DT) 2000–2, Dario Romero (DT) 2003.

95 T.J. Turner (DE) 1986–92, Tim Bowens (DT) 1994–2001, 2003.

96 David Marshall (LB) 1987, Alfred Oglesby (DE) 1990–2, Mike Golic (DT) 1993, Daniel Stubbs (DE) 1996–8, Rich Owens (DE) 1999–2000, David Bowens (DE) 2001–3.

97 John Bosa (DE) 1987–9, Jeff Hunter (DE)

1992–3, Tyoka Jackson (DE) 1994, Aaron Jones (DE) 1996, Ernest Grant (DT) 2000–1.

98 Jackie Cline (DT) 1987–9, Shawn Lee (NT) 1990–1, Norman Hand (DT) 1996, Antoine Simpson (DT) 1999, Damian Gregory (DT) 2001, Henry Taylor (DT) 2001.

99 Jimmy Hines (WR) 1969, George Little (DE) 1985–7, Rick Graf (LB) 1988–90, Chuck Klingbeil (NT) 1991–5, *Jason Taylor* (DE) 1997–2003.

MINNESOTA VIKINGS

The franchise: Professional football in Minnesota extends back to the 1920s with the Minneapolis Marines (1921–4), Duluth Kelleys (1923–5), Duluth Eskimos (1926–7), and Minneapolis Red Jackets (1929–30). The most successful of these squads were the Eskimos who boasted three future Hall of Famers: Ernie Nevers, Johnny Blood McNally, and Walt Kiesling, the latter two being Minnesota natives. A push to bring pro football back to Minnesota began in the late 1950s. At first spurned by the NFL, an ownership group of five (Max Winter, Bill Boyer, Ole Haugsrud who was the treasurer for the old Duluth Eskimos, Bernie Ridder, and H.P. Skoglund) accepted an invitation from the fledgling American Football League in 1959 to join the new circuit. This spurred league representative George Halas to offer an NFL expansion franchise to the Minnesota group which then withdrew from the still-organizing AFL.

With former Rams executive Bert Rose hired as general manager and Joe Thomas as chief scout and Norm Van Brocklin as coach, the team was set to begin play in open-air Metropolitan Stadium in 1961. Although the Vikings traded a number one draft pick to obtain veteran quarterback George Shaw, he was beaten out for the starting job by rookie Fran Tarkenton, and Tarkenton led the Vikings to a stunning 37–13 upset of the Bears in the franchise's first game. Tarkenton, of course, is remembered for his scrambling ability and that echoed the nature of the new team, scrambling to cover up too many holes any way they could. Rose resigned in 1964 and was replaced by future

Hall of Fame executive Jim Finks. Minnesota posted its first winning record that year.

Van Brocklin quit after the 1966 season and was replaced by stoic Bud Grant from the Canadian league. A disgruntled Tarkenton was traded to New York, and CFL quarterback Joe Kapp was brought in to replace him. Finks continued to build the fierce Purple People Eater defense that was led by a light and fast front four of Jim Marshall, Carl Eller, Alan Page and either Paul Dickson or Gary Larsen along with ball-hawking safety Paul Krause playing centerfield. Grant's second season would begin a string of 11 division titles in 13 years, including four losing trips to the Super Bowl. The first Super Bowl team was heavily favored over the Chiefs, but were overpowered by Kansas City. That would continue to be the pattern in their other trips as well. Tarkenton was brought back in 1972 and he led an offense that was spearheaded by versatile back Chuck Foreman. Each time they would reach the Super Bowl for the 1973, 1974 and 1976 seasons, they would be overrun by, in turn, the Dolphins, Steelers, and Raiders.

Finks left after the 1974 season in a dispute over the location of the planned future stadium, and his spot was taken by Mike Lynn who would run the team until 1991. After that fourth Super Bowl run, the team declined into mediocrity in the later days of Grant's tenure. In 1982, they moved indoors into the Metrodome and the character of the team changed. Former assistant to both Vince Lombardi and Bud Grant, Jerry Burns took over as coach in 1986, and the retooled team was building towards another Super

Bowl when Lynn swung the largest trade in NFL history in 1989, obtaining Herschel Walker from the Cowboys for several players and high draft choices with which Jimmy Johnson was able to build a Super Bowl dynasty in Texas. Meanwhile, Walker never fit in Minnesota, and the result was disastrous for the Vikings. Roger Headrick took over as leader of the ownership group and the team itself in 1991.

Dennis Green was hired as coach in 1992 to straighten out a chaotic situation and quickly achieved consistent success on the field as well as constant controversy off it. He even managed to survive a power struggle with the ownership group when they sold out to new owner Red McCombs in 1998. Green changed quarterbacks almost every year, using Rich Gannon, Sean Salisbury, Jim McMahon, Warren Moon, Brad Johnson, Randall Cunningham, Jeff George, and Daunte Culpepper to reach the playoffs in eight of his ten years as coach. He would never win more than one postseason game in any year, though, even with the talented receiving tandem of Cris Carter and Randy Moss, and lost two NFC title games in which the Vikings were favored. He was replaced at the end of 2001 by his former player and assistant Mike Tice.

Origin of name: The team's first general manager Bert Rose named the team in recognition of the high percentage of people of Nordic descent living in the Minnesota area and because Vikings were aggressive adventurers with a strong will to win.

Time till first championship: 43 years and counting.

Time since last championship: Never won one.

Retired numbers: The Vikings have retired

five numbers, but only two for Hall of Famers—Fran Tarkenton 10 and Alan Page 88. Longtime defensive end Jim Marshall, 70, holds the NFL record for consecutive games played with 282. He is best remembered for a 1964 gaffe when he recovered a 49er fumble and ran 66 yards with it the wrong way for a safety, although the Vikings ultimately won the game. Six-time Pro Bowl center Mick Tingelhoff, 53, played in 240 consecutive games for the Vikings. Korey Stringer, 77, was a Pro Bowl tackle who died in training camp.

Other numbers worn by these players: None.

Those who wore retired numbers after the honored player: Fran Tarkenton's 10 was worn by King Hill when Fran was with the Giants. Alan Page's 88 was worn by Mardye McDole, Don Hasselbeck, Bill Waddy, Buster Rhymes, and Marc May. Mick Tingelhoff's 53 was worn by Henry Johnson, Tim Meamber, Jeff Scuh, Sam Anno, Steve Ache, David Braxton, Richard Newbill, Ivan Caesar, Fred Strickland, Tuineau Alipate, Artie Ulmer, and Kivuusama Mays.

Numbers that should be retired: Hall of

Record by Decade						
	Regular Season			*Postseason*		
	Won	Lost	Tied	Won	Lost	Championships
1960s	52	67	7	2	2	
1970s	99	43	2	7	8	
1980s	77	75	0	4	5	
1990s	95	65	0	3	7	
2000s	31	33	0	1	1	
All-Time	354	283	9	17	23	

Winning seasons: 25. Losing Seasons: 14. .500 seasons: 5.

Coaches			
	Years	*Record*	*Playoffs*
Norm Van Brocklin	1961–6	29–51–4	0–0
Bud Grant	1967–83	151–87–5	10–12
Les Steckel	1984	3–13–0	0–0
Bud Grant	1985	7–9–0	0–0
Jerry Burns	1986–91	52–43–0	3–3
Dennis Green	1992–2001	97–62–0	4–8
Mike Tice	2001–3	15–18–0	0–0

Fame safety Paul Krause, 22, is the all-time NFL interception leader.

Owned numbers: No one but Jim Marshall ever wore 70.

Numbers worn by Hall of Famers: Dave Casper 44; Carl Eller 81; Paul Krause 22; Jim Langer 58; Hugh McElhenny 39; Alan Page 88; Jan Stenerud 3; Fran Tarkenton 10; Ron Yary 73.

Star power: Dale Carter took 21 from Moe Williams; Chris Doleman took 56 from Chris Martin.

Star eclipsed: Archie Manning wore 4 because Greg Coleman wore 8; Dave Casper wore 45 because Leo Lewis wore 87; Sam McCullum wore 84 because Terry LeCount wore 80. Robert Smith wore 20 till Audray McMillan, 26, left.

Numbers with most great players: 20 has been worn by Pro Bowl runners Tommy Mason, Darrin Nelson, and Robert Smith as well as All Pro cornerback Bobby Bryant. 58 has been worn by star linebackers Rip Hawkins, Wally Hilgenberg, and Ed McDaniel as well as Hall of Fame center Jim Langer. 81 has been worn by Hall of Fame defensive end Carl Eller in addition to tight end Joe Senser and wideout Anthony Carter.

Worst represented numbers: 35 has been worn by six forgettable runners, three anonymous safeties and a wide receiver of no reputation.

Number worn by the most players: 89 has been worn 23 times.

Player who wore the most numbers: Chris Martin is listed as having worn 56, 57, 94, and 98. Andrew Jordan wore three numbers, 83/85/89.

Longest tenure wearing a number: Jim Marshall wore 70 for 19 years from 1961 to 1979. Mick Tingelhoff wore 53 for 17 years from 1962 to 1978. Roy Winston wore 60 for 15 years from 1962 to 1976. Fred Cox wore 14 for 15 years from 1963 to 1977. Carl Eller wore 81 for 15 years from 1964 to 1978.

Number worn by first ever draft pick: Tommy Mason was the first pick in 1961 and wore 20.

Biggest Busts: D.J. Dozier, 42, was the fourteenth selection in the 1987 draft and had a high of 257 rushing yards in his four year career. Dimitrius Underwood was a first round pick in 1999, but never actually made it on to the field.

Number worn by first expansion draft pick: The draft was not conducted in rounds. The expansion draft pick who lasted longest was Pro Bowl tackle Grady Alderman who spent 14 years in Minnesota from 1961 to 1974.

Number worn by oldest player: Gary Anderson wore 1 as a 43 year old in 2002. Jan Stenerud wore 3 as a 41 year old in 1985. Jim Marshall wore 70 as a 41 year old in 1979.

Cameos: All Pros and other notables— Al Baker 60/77; Gary Ballman 85; Preston Carpenter 40; Paul Coffman 89; Carroll Dale 84; Ted Dean 24; Cris Dishman 25; Don Hasselbeck 88; Harold Jackson 89; Dick James 47; Don Joyce 83; Brady Keys 43; Cliff Livingston 55; Marlin McKeever 86; Jim McMahon 9; Dave Middleton 84; Bryce Paup 95; Karl Rubke 54; Bob Schnelker 80; George Shaw 14; Norm Snead 16; Darryl Talley 55; Broderick Thomas 51; John Vella 71; Tom Wilson 24.

Ones who got away: The Vikings have done well in recognizing young talent. One who did elude them is Jay Fiedler, 11, who has been a starting quarterback with Miami.

Least popular numbers: 0 has never been worn. 2 and 16 have only been worn twice.

Last number to be originated: 2 was first worn in 1989 by kicker Teddy Garcia.

Longest dormant number: 15 has not been worn for 30 years since 1974.

Triskaidekaphobia notes: 13 has been worn briefly by three quarterbacks and two punters.

Shared numbers: 57 was worn by linebackers Mike Merriweather and Dwayne Rudd; 59 was worn by linebackers Lonnie Warwick and Matt Blair; 62 was worn by guard Ed White and center Jeff Christy; 64 was worn by guards Milt Sunde and Randall McDaniel; 76 was worn by defensive tackle Paul Dickson and tackle Tim Irwin for over a decade a piece; 83 was worn by tight ends Stu Voigt and Steve Jordan.

Continuity: Runner Tommy Mason was replaced in 20 by cornerback Bobby Bryant;

Gary Larsen was replaced in 77 by fellow defensive lineman Mark Mullaney.

Discontinuity: Robert Griffith was followed in 24 by fellow defensive back Willie Offord; Bob Grim was followed in 27 by fellow receiver Calvin Demery; Jeff Siemon was followed in 50 by fellow linebacker Dennis Fowlkes; Henry Thomas was followed in 97 by fellow defensive tackle Jose White.

Family Connections			
Brothers			
Jake Reed	WR	1991–9, 2001	86
Dale Carter	DB	2001	21
Eric Moss	G	1997–9	79
Randy Moss	WR	1998–2003	84

Quarterback numbers over 19: None.

Number of first black player: In their first year, 1961, the Vikings employed runners Jamie Caleb, 23, and Mel Triplett, 33, end A.D. Williams, 82, and defensive end Jim Marshall, 70.

Numbers of future NFL head coaches: Jack Del Rio 55; Mike Mularkey 86; and Mike Tice 83/87.

Numbers of future NFL referees: None.

Players who played other sports: Baseball — D.J. Dozier 42.

Players more famous after football: Ed Marinaro, 49, is an actor most famous for the television show *Hill Street Blues*. Alan Page, 88, is a Justice on the Minnesota Supreme Court.

First player to wear a number in the 90s: Defensive tackle Ron Yakavonis wore 91 in 1980.

Number with most points scored: 14 with 1,381 points scored by Fred Cox (1,365) and Brad Johnson (16).

Number with most yards rushing: 26 with 8,427 yards gained by Robert Smith (6,419) and Clinton Jones (2,008).

Number with most receptions: 80 with 1,248 passes caught by Cris Carter (1,004), John Henderson (81), Terry LeCount (79), Jim Gustafson (38), Sam McCullum (33), Bob Schnelker (6), Jim Boylan (6), and Harry Washington (1).

Number with most touchdown passes: 10 with 239 touchdowns tossed by Fran Tarkenton.

Number with most interceptions: 22 with 69 passes picked off by Paul Krause (53), Bill Butler (7), Jeff Jordan (4), Felix Wright (3), Ken Irvin (1), and Tyrone Carter (1).

Oddity: The Vikings have had at least 15 players who played with Minnesota, went to another team and then returned for a second term as a Viking. Six year gap — Sam McCullum, 80/84, 1974–5, 1982–3. Five year gap — Fran Tarkenton, 10, 1961–66, 1972–8; Bob Berry, 17, 1965–7, 1973–5; Chris Doleman, 56, 1985–93, 1999. Four year gap — Bob Grim, 26/27, 1967–71, 1976–7; Roy Barker, 92, 1992–5, 2000. Three year gap — Hunter Goodwin, 87, 1996–8, 2002–3. Two year gap — Bob Lee, 19, 1969–72, 1975–8; Everett Lindsay, 61/62, 1993–8, 2001–3; Martin Harrison, 91, 1995–6, 1999; Fernando Smith, 95, 1994–7, 2000. One year gap — John Turner, 27, 1978–83, 1985; Jake Reed, 86, 1991–9, 2001; Stalin Colinet, 93/99, 1997–9, 2001; Andrew Jordan, 83/85/89, 1994–7, 1999–2001.

Team All-Time Numerical Roster

Those with an "r" following the year 1987 were replacement players during the players' strike. Pro Bowl players for each number are in *Italics*; Hall of Famers are in **Bold** type.

1 Benny Ricardo (K) 1983, Chuck Nelson (K) 1986–88, *Warren Moon* (QB) 1994–6, *Gary Anderson* (K) 1998–2002, Jose Cortez (K) 2003.

2 Teddy Garcia (K) 1989, Leo Araguz (P) 2003.

3 **Jan Stenerud** (K) 1984–5, Rich Karlis (K) 1989, Eddie Murray (K) 1997, Jeff George (QB) 1999, Spergon Wynn (QB) 2001.

4 Archie Manning (QB) 1983–4, Dale Dawson (K) 1987r, Donald Igwebuike (K) 1990, Mike Saxon (P) 1994–5, Doug Brien (K) 2002, Eddie Johnson (P) 2003.

5 Mike Wood (P) 1978, Larry Miller (QB) 1987r, Chad May (QB) 1995, Greg Davis (K) 1997, Kyle Richardson (P) 2002.

6 Jim Gallery (K) 1990, Jay Walker (QB) 1996–7, Bubby Brister (QB) 2000, Hayden Epstein (K) 2002.

7 Rick Danmeier (K) 1977–82, Tony Adams

(QB) 1987r, *Fuad Reveiz* (K) 1990–5, *Randall Cunningham* (QB) 1997–9.

8 Greg Coleman (P) 1978–87, Todd Bouman (QB) 1997–2002, Aaron Elling (K) 2003.

9 *Tommy Kramer* (QB) 1977–89, Jim McMahon (QB) 1993, Scott Sisson (K) 1996.

10 Fran Tarkenton (QB) 1961–6, 1972–8, King Hill (QB) 1968.

11 *Joe Kapp* (QB) 1967–9, Mike Eischied (P) 1972–4, John Reaves (QB) 1979, *Wade Wilson* (QB) 1981–91, Jay Fiedler (QB) 1998, *Daunte Culpepper* (QB) 1999–2003.

12 Tom McNeill (P) 1970, Neil Clabo (P) 1975–7, Steve Dils (QB) 1979–84, Keith Bishop (QB) 1987, Sean Salisbury (QB) 1992–4, *Daunte Culpepper* (QB) 1999, Lee Johnson (P) 2001, Shaun Hill (QB) 2002, Gus Frerotte (QB) 2003.

13 Mike Livingston (QB) 1980, Steve Bono (QB) 1985–6, Bucky Scribner (P) 1987–9, Dave Bruno (P) 1987r, Gino Torretta (QB) 1993.

14 George Shaw (QB) 1961, *Fred Cox* (K) 1963–77, Gilbert Renfroe (QB) 1990, Brad Johnson (QB) 1994–8.

15 John McCormick (QB/P) 1962, Ron Vander Kelen (QB) 1963–7, Gary Cuozzo (QB) 1968–71, Mike Wells (QB) 1973–4.

16 Norm Snead (QB) 1971, Rich Gannon (QB) 1987–92, Kelly Campbell (WR) 2003.

17 Charlie Britt (S) 1964, Bob Berry (QB) 1965–7, 1973–6, Bill Cappleman (QB) 1970, *Mitch Berger* (P) 1996–2001.

18 Mike Mercer (K) 1961–2, Harry Newsome (P) 1990–3, Tony Bland (WR) 1996.

19 Lance Rentzel (WR) 1965–6, Bob Lee (QB/P) 1969–72, 1975–8, Matthew Hatchette (WR) 1997, Yo Murphy (WR) 1999.

20 *Tommy Mason* (RB) 1961–6, *Bobby Bryant* (CB) 1967–80, Darrin Nelson (RB) 1982–9, 1991–2, *Robert Smith* (RB) 1993, Dewayne Washington (CB) 1994–7, Kenny Wright (CB) 1999–2001, Moe Williams (RB) 2002–3.

21 Chuck Lamson (S) 1962–3, Tom Michel (RB) 1964, Jim Lindsey (RB) 1966–72, Joe Blahak (CB) 1974–5, 1977, Rufus Bess (CB) 1982–7, Terry Allen (RB) 1991–2, 1994, Charles Mincy (S) 1995, Moe Williams (RB) 1996–2000, Dale Carter (CB) 2001, Henry Jones (S) 2001, *Corey Chavous* (S) 2002–3.

22 Dick Pesonen (CB) 1961, Billy Butler (S/RB) 1962–4, Jeff Jordan (S) 1965–7, **Paul Krause** (S) 1968–79, Jarvis Redwine (RB) 1981–3, Steve Freeman (S) 1987, Ken Johnson (S) 1989–90, Felix Wright (S) 1991–2, David Palmer (RB) 1994–2000, Tyrone Carter (S) 2001–2, Ken Irvin (CB) 2003.

23 Jamie Caleb (RB) 1961, Lee Calland (CB) 1963–5, Jeff Williams (RB) 1966, Jeff Wright (S) 1971–7, Ted Brown (RB) 1979–86, Terry Love (S) 1987r, Mike Mayes (CB) 1991, Barry Word (RB) 1993, Shelly Hammonds (CB) 1995, Tomur Barnes

(CB) 1996, Steven Hall (S) 1996, Torrian Gray (S) 1997–8, *Michael Bennett* (RB) 2001–3.

24 Rich Mostardo (S) 1961, Tom Wilson (RB) 1963, Ted Dean (S) 1964, Phil King (RB) 1965–6, Terry Brown (S) 1972–5, Larry Brune (S) 1980, Bryan Howard (S) 1982, Maurice Turner (RB) 1984–5, Wymon Henderson (CB) 1987–8, Pat Eilers (S) 1990–1, David Wilson (S) 1992, Jayice Pearson (S) 1993, *Robert Griffith* (S) 1994–2001, Willie Offord (DB) 2002–3.

25 Dean Derby (DB) 1961–2, Terry Dillon (CB) 1963, Larry Vargo (S) 1964–5, John Charles (S) 1970, Jackie Wallace (CB) 1973–4, Nate Allen (DB) 1976–9, Kurt Knoff (S) 1979–82, Marcellus Greene (CB) 1984, Daryl Smith (CB) 1989, Alonzo Hampton (CB) 1990, Vencie Glenn (S) 1992–4, Alfred Jackson (CB) 1995–6, Tony Darden (CB) 1998, Cris Dishman (CB) 2000, Eric Kelly (CB) 2001–3.

26 Charley Sumner (CB) 1961–2, Terry Kosens (S) 1963, Clinton Jones (RB) 1967–72, *Bob Grim* (WR) 1976–7, Marvin Cobb (S) 1980, David Evans (CB) 1986–7, *Audray McMillian* (CB) 1989–93, *Robert Smith* (RB) 1994–2000, Ronnie Bradford (S) 2002, Denard Walker (CB) 2003.

27 Bob Reed (RB) 1962–3, *Bob Grim* (WR) 1967–71, Calvin Demery (WR) 1972, Autry Beamon (S) 1975–6, John Turner (S) 1978–83, 1985, 1987r, Mike Lush (S) 1986, Brett Wilson (RB) 1987, Brad Edwards (S) 1988–9, Ken Stills (S) 1990, Anthony Parker (CB) 1992–4, Corey Fuller (CB) 1995–8, Kevin Devine (CB) 1999, Keith Thibodeaux (CB) 1999–2001, Brian Russell (DB) 2002–3.

28 Dick Haley (WR) 1961, Tom Hall (WR) 1964–6, Earl Denny (RB) 1967–8, Ted Provost (CB) 1970, *Ahmad Rashad* (WR) 1976–82, Ted Rosnagle (S) 1985–7, Izel Jenkins (CB) 1993, James Stewart (RB) 1995, Anthony Phillips (CB) 1998, Robert Tate (WR/CB) 1999–2001, Larry Ned (RB) 2003.

29 *Karl Kassulke* (DB) 1963–72, Randy Poltl (S) 1974, Phil Wise (S) 1977–9, John Swain (CB) 1981–4, Jamie Fitzgerald (CB) 1987r, Darrell Fullington (S) 1988–90, Charles Evans (RB) 1993–8, Chris Rogers (CB) 1999, Wasswa Serwanga (CB) 2000–1, Brian Williams (CB) 2002–3.

30 *Bill Brown* (RB) 1962–1974, Issiac Holt (CB) 1985–9, Cedric Smith (RB) 1990, Keith Henderson (RB) 1992, Bobby Phillips (RB) 1995, Antonio Banks (CB) 1998–2000, Travis Prentice (RB) 2001.

31 Clancy Osborne (LB) 1961–2, Darrell Lester (RB) 1964, Willie Spencer (RB) 1976, Nelson Munsey (CB) 1978, Eddie Payton (RB) 1980–2, Dan Wagoner (S) 1984, Rick Fenney (RB) 1987–91, Eric Everett (CB) 1992, Scottie Graham (RB) 1993–6, Duane Butler (S) 1997–8, Don Morgan (S) 1999–2001, Jason Perry (DB) 2002, Rushen Jones (RB) 2003.

32 Ray Hayes (RB) 1961, Bill McWatters (RB) 1964, Oscar Reed (RB) 1968–74, Jimmy Edwards (RB) 1979, Tony Galbreath (RB) 1981–3, David Nelson (RB) 1984, Tony Truelove (RB) 1987, Steve Harris (RB) 1987r, Darryl Harris (RB) 1988, Rick Bayless (RB) 1989, Tripp Welborne (S) 1992, Shawn Jones (S) 1993, Amp Lee (RB) 1994–6, Robert Green (RB) 1997, Anthony Bass (DB) 1998–9, Onterrio Smith (RB) 2003.

33 Mel Triplett (RB) 1961–2, Bill Barnes (RB) 1965–6, Pete Tatman (RB) 1967, Brent McClanahan (RB) 1973–80, Rick Bell (RB) 1983, Jeff Womack (RB) 1987r, Jessie Clark (RB) 1989–90, Roger Craig (RB) 1992–3, Harold Morrow (RB) 1996–2002, John Avery (RB) 2003.

34 Jim Young (RB) 1965–6, Al Randolph (CB) 1973, Rickey Young (RB) 1978–83, Tim Starks (CB) 1987r, Herschel Walker (RB) 1989–91, Brian Davis (CB) 1994, Ramos McDonald (CB) 1998–9, Doug Chapman (RB) 2000–3.

35 Doug Mayberry (RB) 1961–2, Bob Ferguson (RB) 1963, Bill Harris (RB) 1969–70, Robert Miller (RB) 1975–80, Kyle Morrell (S) 1985–6, Mark Slaton (S) 1987r, Andre Thomas (RB) 1987r, Ronnie West (WR) 1992, Chris Johnson (S) 1996, James Lynch (RB) 2003.

36 Jim Christopherson (K/LB) 1962, John Kirby (LB) 1964–8, Carl Winfrey (LB) 1971, Manfred Moore (RB) 1977, Sam Harrell (RB) 1980–2, 1987r, Allen Rice (RB) 1984–90, Ron Carpenter (S) 1993, Malik Boyd (CB) 1994.

37 Mike Fitzgerald (CB) 1966–7, Al Coleman (CB) 1967, Willie Teal (CB) 1980–6, Phil Frye (RB) 1987r, Randy Baldwin (RB) 1991, Lamar McGriggs (S) 1993–4, Donald Frank (CB) 1995, Sean Vanhorse (CB) 1996, Leonard Wheeler (CB) 1997, Jimmy Hitchcock (CB) 1998–9, Tyrone Carter (S) 2000, Ron Israel (CB) 2003.

38 Bob Tucker (TE) 1977–80, Fletcher Louallen (S) 1987r, *Todd Scott* (S) 1991–4, Rhett Nelson (DB) 2003.

39 **Hugh McElhenny** (RB) 1961–2, Bobby Walden (P) 1964–7, Mark Kellar (RB) 1976–8, *Carl Lee* (CB) 1983–93.

40 Jack Morris (CB) 1961, Tom Frankhauser (S) 1962–3, Preston Carpenter (TE) 1966, Charlie West (S) 1968–73, Windlan Hall (S) 1976–7, Doug Paschal (RB) 1980–1, Wayne Smith (CB) 1987, Anthony Prior (CB) 1996–7, Jim Kleinsasser (FB) 1999–2003.

41 Gene Johnson (S) 1961, *Dave Osborn* (RB) 1965–75, Neal Guggemos (DB) 1986–7, Solomon Wilcots (S) 1991.

42 *John Gilliam* (WR) 1972–75, D.J. Dozier (RB) 1987–91, Harlon Barnett (S) 1995–6, Orlando Thomas (S) 1997–2001, Jack Brewer (DB) 2002–3.

43 Will Sherman (DB) 1961, Gary Hill (S) 1965, Brady Keys (CB) 1967, Nate Wright (CB) 1971–80, Jeff Colter (CB) 1984, Jim Smith (RB) 1987r, Orlando Thomas (S) 1995–6, Greg Briggs (S) 1997, Brody Heffner-Liddiard (LS) 2001–3.

44 Billy Gault (CB) 1961, Leo Hayden (RB) 1971, *Chuck Foreman* (RB) 1973–9, Walt Williams (CB) 1981–2, **Dave Casper** (TE) 1983, John Harris (S) 1985–6, Keith Kidd (WR) 1987r, Michael Brim (CB) 1989–90, Leroy Hoard (RB) 1996–9, Matt Snider (FB) 2001, James Wofford (RB) 2002.

45 Ed Sharockman (CB) 1962–72, Pete Athas (CB) 1975, Tom Hannon (S) 1977–84, Wayne Wilson (RB) 1986, Leonard Moore (RB) 1987r, John Henry Mills (FB) 1999, Charles Stackhouse (FB) 2003

46 Earsell Mackbee (CB) 1965–9, Alfred Anderson (RB) 1984–91, Derek Tennell (TE) 1992–3, John Gerak (TE/G) 1994–6.

47 Justin Rowland (CB) 1961, George Rose (CB) 1964–6, Dick James (RB) 1965, Ron Groce (RB) 1976, Tim Baylor (S) 1979–80, *Joey Browner* (S) 1983–91, Rod Smith (CB) 1996, Charles Emmanuel (S) 1997, Richard Angulo (TE) 2003.

48 Larry Marshall (S) 1974, Sammy Johnson (RB) 1976–8, Najee Mustafaa (CB) 1987–92, Todd Harrison (TE) 1993, Matt Cercone (FB) 2000.

49 Dale Hackbart (S) 1966–70, Ed Marinaro (RB) 1972–5, Keith Nord (S) 1979–85, Adam Walker (RB) 1987r, Travis Curtis (S) 1989, Obafemi Ayanbadejo (FB) 1998–9.

50 Dick Grecni (LB) 1961, Jim Hargrove (LB) 1967–70, *Jeff Siemon* (LB) 1972–82, Dennis Fowlkes (LB) 1983–5, Ray Berry (LB) 1987–92, Randy Scott (LB) 1987r, Bobby Abrams (LB) 1993–4, Jeff Brady (LB) 1995–7, Antico Dalton (LB) 1999, Patrick Chukwurah (LB) 2001–2.

51 Dave Tobey (LB) 1966, Hap Farber (LB) 1970, Godfrey Zaunbrecher (C) 1971–3, Jim Hough (G) 1978–86, Pete Najarian (LB) 1987, David Howard (LB) 1988–9, Carlos Jenkins (LB) 1991–4, Broderick Thomas (LB) 1995, Ben Hanks (LB) 1996, Rob Holmberg (LB) 1999, Mitch Palmer (LS) 2000, Lance Johnstone (DE) 2001–3.

52 Bill Lapham (C) 1961, Bill Swain (LB) 1964, Noel Jenke (LB) 1971, Ron Porter (LB) 1973, Bob Stein (LB) 1975, Joe Harris (LB) 1979, Dennis Johnson (LB) 1980–5, Randy Rasmussen (G) 1987–9, Jim Dick (LB) 1987r, William Kirksey (LB) 1990, David Bavaro (LB) 1992, Richard Brown (LB) 1994–6, Kailee Wong (LB) 1998–2001, Henri Crockett (LB) 2002–3.

53 *Mick Tingelhoff* (C) 1962–78, Henry Johnson (LB) 1980–3, Tim Meamber (LB) 1985, Jeff Schuh (LB) 1986, Sam Anno (LB) 1987–8, Steve Ache (LB) 1987r, David Braxton (LB) 1989–90, Richard Newbill (LB) 1990, Ivan Caesar (LB) 1991, Fred Strickland (LB) 1993, Tuineau Alipate (LB) 1995, Artie Ulmer (LB) 1997, Kivuusama Mays (LB) 1998–9.

54 Karl Rubke (LB) 1961, Bob Schmitz (LB) 1966, Paul Faust (LB) 1967, Fred McNeill (LB) 1974–85, Jesse Solomon (LB) 1986–89, Van Waiters (LB) 1992, Bruce Holmes (LB) 1993, David Garnett (LB) 1993–4, 1996, Greg Briggs (S) 1997, Antonio Wilson (LB) 2000–1, Greg Biekert (LB) 2002–3.

55 Cliff Livingston (LB) 1962, John Campbell (LB) 1963–4, Don Hansen (LB) 1966–7, Mike McGill (LB) 1968–70, Amos Martin (LB) 1972–6, *Scott Studwell* (LB) 1977–90, *Jack Del Rio* (LB) 1992–5, Darryl Talley (LB) 1996, Ron George (LB) 1997, Bobby Houston (LB) 1998, Corey Miller (LB) 1999, Lemanski Hall (LB) 2000–2, Chris Claiborne (LB) 2003.

56 Mike Reilly (LB) 1969, Wayne Meylan (LB) 1970, Carl Gersbach (LB) 1971–2, Scott Anderson (C) 1974, 1976, David Huffman (G/T) 1979–83, Bill Dugan (G) 1984, Chris Martin (LB) 1984, *Chris Doleman* (DE) 1985–93, 1999, Pete Bercich (LB) 1995–8, 2000, Jim Nelson (LB) 2001–2, E.J. Henderson (LB) 2003.

57 Bill Jobko (LB) 1963–65, Doug Dumler (C) 1976–7, Derrel Luce (LB) 1979–80, Robin Sendlein (LB) 1981–4, Chris Martin (LB) 1985–8, Mike Merriweather (LB) 1989–92, William Sims (LB) 1994, Dwayne Rudd (LB) 1997–2000, Raonall Smith (LB) 2002–3.

58 *Rip Hawkins* (LB) 1961–5, Wally Hilgenberg (LB) 1968–79, **Jim Langer** (C) 1980–1, Walker Lee Ashley (LB) 1983–8, 1990, Jimmy Williams (LB) 1990–1, *Ed McDaniel* (LB) 1992–2001, Nick Rogers (LB) 2002–3.

59 Jim Leo (DE) 1961–2, Lonnie Warwick (LB) 1965–72, *Matt Blair* (LB) 1974–85, Pete Najarian (LB) 1987, Fabray Collins (LB) 1987r, Mark Dusbabek (LB) 1989–92, Ashley Sheppard (LB) 1993–5, Dixon Edwards (LB) 1996–8, Corey Miller (LB) 1999, Craig Sauer (LB) 2000, Fearon Wright (LB) 2001, Antonio Wilson (LB) 2002, Michael Nattiel (LB) 2003.

60 Roy Winston (LB) 1962–76, Matt Hernandez (T) 1984, Ron Selesky (C) 1987r, Al Baker (DE) 1988, Dan McQuaid (T) 1988, Mark Rodenhauser (C) 1989, Adam Schreiber (C) 1990–3, Reggie McElroy (T) 1994, Cory Withrow (C) 1999–2003.

61 Larry Bowie (G) 1962–8, Wes Hamilton (G) 1976–85, Mike Turner (T) 1987, Don Bramlett (DT) 1987r, Everett Lindsay (G/T) 1993–5, 1997–8, Lewis Kelly (T) 2001–3.

62 Bob Denton (DE) 1961–4, *Ed White* (G) 1969–77, Brent Boyd (G) 1980–6, Chris Foote (C) 1987–91, Brad White (DT) 1987r, *Jeff Christy* (C) 1993–9, Everett Lindsay (G/T) 2001–3.

63 Jim Battle (G) 1963, Jim Vellone (G) 1966–70, Nick Bebout (T) 1980, Robert Cobb (DE) 1984, Kirk Lowdermilk (C) 1985–92, Mark Hanson (G) 1987r, Kurt Ploeger (DT) 1987r, Frank

Cornish (C) 1994, Keith Alex (G) 1995, Isaac Davis (G) 1998, Corbin Lacina (G) 1999–2002.

64 Mike Rabold (G) 1961–2, *Milt Sunde* (G) 1964–74, Grant Feasel (T) 1984–6, Ted Million (G) 1987r, *Randall McDaniel* (G) 1988–99.

65 Gerry Huth (G) 1961–3, Steve Lawson (G) 1973–5, Neil Elshire (DE) 1981, Charlie Johnson (NT) 1982–4, *Gary Zimmerman* (T) 1986–92, Mike Ruether (C) 1994, Calvin Collins (G) 2001.

66 Ken Peterson (C) 1961, Ken Byers (G) 1964–6, John Pentecost (G) 1967, Bookie Bolin (G) 1968–9, Frank Gallagher (G) 1973, Andy Maurer (G) 1974–5, Terry Tausch (G) 1982–8, John Gerak (TE/G) 1993–4.

67 *Grady Alderman* (T) 1961–74, Dennis Swilley (C) 1977–83, 1985–7, Mike Teeter (DT) 1991, Rick Cunningham (T) 1995, Jay Humphrey (T) 1999.

68 Pete Perreault (G) 1971, Roy Schmidt (G) 1971, Charles Goodrum (G) 1972–78, Mel Mitchell (G) 1980, Curtis Rouse (G) 1982–6, Greg Koch (G) 1987, Kevin Webster (C) 1987r, John Adickes (C) 1989, Paul Blair (T) 1990, Mike Morris (C) 1991–9.

69 Palmer Pyle (G) 1964, Arnie Simkus (DT) 1967, Doug Sutherland (DT) 1971–81, Hasson Arbubakrr (DE) 1984, Ruben Vaughan (DT) 1984, Wayne Jones (T) 1987, Frank Ori (G) 1987r, Todd Kalis (G) 1988–93, Ariel Solomon (G) 1996, LeShun Daniels (G) 1997.

70 *Jim Marshall* (DE) 1961–79.

71 Ed Culpepper (DT) 1961, Doug Davis (T) 1966–72, David Boone (DE) 1974, Steve Niehaus (DT) 1979, John Vella (T) 1980, Bill Stephanos (T) 1982, Mark MacDonald (G) 1985–8, Derek Burton (T) 1987r, Ken Clarke (DT) 1989–91, Bernard Dafney (G) 1992–3, David Dixon (G) 1994–2003.

72 Frank Youso (T) 1961–2, John Ward (G/T) 1970–5, James White (DT) 1976–83, Ron Sams (C) 1984, David Huffman (G/T) 1985–90, Scott Adams (OL) 1991–3, Jason Fisk (DT) 1995–8, Adam Haayer (OL) 2002.

73 Bill Bishop (DT) 1961, Errol Linden (T) 1962–5, Jerry Shay (DT) 1966–7, **Ron Yary** (T) 1968–81, Neil Elshire (DE) 1982–6, Stafford Mays (DT) 1987–8, Joe Stepanek (DT) 1987r, Craig Wolfley (G) 1990–1, Rory Graves (T) 1993, *Todd Steussie* (T) 1994–2000.

74 Dave O'Brien (G) 1963–4, Mike Tilleman (DT) 1966, Steve Smith (DE) 1968–70, Bart Buetow (T) 1976–7, Frank Myers (T) 1978–80, Mike McCurry (G) 1987r, Brian Habib (G) 1989–92, Orlando Bobo (G) 1997–8, Brad Badger (G) 2000–1, Bryant McKinnie (T) 2002–3.

75 Pat Russ (DT) 1963, Mike Bundra (DT) 1964, Howard Simpson (T) 1964, Bob Breitenstein (T) 1967, Bob Lurtsema (DE) 1972–6, Randy Holloway (DE) 1978–84, *Keith Millard* (DT) 1985–91, Bernard Dafney (G) 1994, Chris Hinton (T) 1995,

James Manley (DT) 1996–7, *Matt Birk* (C) 1998, Joe Phillips (DT) 1999, Mike Rosenthal (T) 2003.

76 Paul Dickson (DT) 1961–70, Joe Jackson (DT) 1977, Bob Lingenfelter (T) 1978, Dave Roller (DT) 1979–80, Tim Irwin (T) 1981–93, Scott Dill (T) 1996–7, Chris Liwienski (T) 1998–2003.

77 Lebron Shields (DE) 1961, *Gary Larsen* (DT) 1965–74, Mark Mullaney (DE) 1975–87, Al Baker (DE) 1988, Brad Culpepper (DT) 1992–93, *Korey Stringer* (T) 1995–2000.

78 Steve Riley (T) 1974–84, Mike Hartenstine (DT) 1987, John Scardina (T) 1987r, Barry Bennett (DE) 1988, William Gay (DE) 1988, Chris Hinton (T) 1994, Bob Sapp (G) 1997–8, *Matt Birk* (C) 1999–2003.

79 Jim Prestel (DT) 1961–5, Chuck Arrobio (T) 1966, Jerry Patton (DT) 1971, Lyman Smith (DT) 1978, Doug Martin (DE) 1980–9, Roosevelt Nix (DT) 1994, Eric Moss (OL) 1997, Kenny Mixon (DE) 2002–3.

80 Bob Schnelker (TE) 1961, Jim Boylan (WR) 1963, John Henderson (WR) 1968–72, Sam Mc-Cullum (WR) 1974–5, Leonard Willis (WR) 1976, Harry Washington (WR) 1978, Terry LeCount (WR) 1979–83, 1987r, Bill Waddy (WR) 1984, Jim Gustafson (WR) 1986–9, Larry Brown (WR) 1987r, *Cris Carter* (WR) 1990–2001.

81 Leon Clarke (WR) 1963, *Carl Eller* (DE) 1964–78, *Joe Senser* (TE) 1979–84, *Anthony Carter* (WR) 1985–93, Rickey Parks (WR) 1987r, Chris Walsh (WR) 1994–2002, Nate Burleson (WR) 2003.

82 A.D. Williams (WR) 1961, Steve Stonebreaker (LB) 1962–3, Jim Phillips (WR) 1965–7, Bob Goodridge (WR) 1968, Jim Lash (WR) 1973–6, Robert Steele (WR) 1979, Bob Bruer (TE) 1980–3, Carl Hilton (TE) 1986–9, Ron Daugherty (WR) 1987r, Darrin Whitaker (TE) 1992, Qadry Ismail (WR) 1993–6, Andrew Glover (TE) 1997–9, Troy Walters (WR) 2000–1, Derrick Alexander (WR) 2002, Keenan Howry (WR) 2003.

83 Don Joyce (DE) 1961, Don Hultz (DE) 1963, John Powers (TE) 1966, Stu Voigt (TE) 1970–80, *Steve Jordan* (TE) 1982–94, Andrew Jordan (TE) 1994, Mike Tice (TE) 1995, David Frisch (TE) 1996, Robert Tate (WR/CB) 1997–8, Nate Jacquet (WR) 2000–1, Hunter Goodwin (TE) 2002–3.

84 Dave Middleton (WR) 1961, Oscar Donahue (WR) 1962, *Gene Washington* (WR) 1967–72, Carroll Dale (WR) 1973, Steve Craig (TE) 1974–8, Sam McCullum (WR) 1982–3, Dwight Collins (WR) 1984, Jay Carroll (TE) 1985, Hassan Jones (WR) 1986–92, James Brim (WR) 1987, Eric Guliford (WR) 1993–4, Tony Bland (WR) 1996–7, *Randy Moss* (WR) 1998–2003.

85 Tom Adams (WR) 1962, *Paul Flatley* (WR) 1963–7, John Hilton (TE) 1970, Gary Ballman (TE) 1973, John Holland (WR) 1974, *Sammy*

White (WR) 1976–86, Steve Finch (WR) 1987r, Ryan Bethea (WR) 1988, Brent Novoselsky (TE) 1989–94, Greg DeLong (TE) 1995–8, Andrew Jordan (TE) 1999–2001, Jim Kleinsasser (FB) 1999, D'wayne Bates (WR) 2002–3.

86 Ray Poage (TE) 1963, Hal Bedsole (TE) 1964–6, Marlin McKeever (TE) 1967, Tom Hall (WR) 1968–9, Al Denson (WR) 1971, Rhett Dawson (WR) 1973, Mike Mularkey (TE) 1983–8, Clifton Eley (TE) 1987r, Willie Gillespie (WR) 1987r, Darryl Ingram (TE) 1989, Pat Newman (WR) 1990, Jake Reed (WR) 1991–9, 2001, John Davis (TE) 2000, Nick Davis (WR) 2002.

87 Gordon Smith (TE) 1961–5, John Beasley (TE) 1967–73, Clint Haslerig (WR) 1975, Kevin Miller (WR) 1978–80, Leo Lewis (WR) 1981–91, Mike Tice (TE) 1992–3, Adrian Cooper (TE) 1994–5, Hunter Goodwin (TE) 1996–8, Carlester Crumpler (TE) 1999, Johnny McWilliams (TE) 2000, *Byron Chamberlain* (TE) 2001–2, Sean Berton (TE) 2003.

88 Fred Murphy (TE) 1961, Charley Ferguson (WR) 1962, Bob Lacey (WR) 1964, **Alan Page** (DT) 1967–78, Mardye McDole (WR) 1981–3, Don Hasselbeck (TE) 1984, Buster Rhymes (WR) 1985–7, Marc May (TE) 1987r.

89 *Jerry Reichow* (WR) 1961–4, Billy Martin (TE) 1968, Kent Kramer (TE) 1969–70, Robert Brown (TE) 1971, Doug Kingsriter (TE) 1973–5, Doug Cunningham (WR) 1979, Ken Sanders (DE) 1980–1, Harold Jackson (WR) 1982, Mike Anthony Jones (WR) 1983–5, Greg Richardson (WR) 1987–8, Ed Schenk (TE) 1987r, Paul Coffman (TE) 1988, Jarrod Delaney (WR) 1989, Ira Hillary (WR) 1990, Mike Jones (TE) 1990–1, Terry Obee (WR) 1991, Joe Johnson (WR) 1992, Olanda Truitt (WR) 1993, Ray Rowe (TE) 1994, Andrew Jordan (TE) 1995–7, Matthew Hatchette (WR) 1998–2000, Cedric James (WR) 2002, Kenny Clark (WR) 2003.

90 John Haines (DT) 1984, Fred Molden (DT) 1987r, John Galvin (LB) 1989, Robert Harris (DE) 1992–4, Derrick Alexander (DE,) 1995–8, Gabe Northern (DE) 2000.

91 Ray Yakavonis (DT) 1980–3, Greg Smith (DT) 1984, Joe Phillips (DT) 1986, Dan Coleman (DE) 1987, Brian Habib (G) 1988, Willie Fears (DT) 1990, Greg Manusky (LB) 1991–3, Martin Harrison (DE) 1994–6, 1999, John Burrough (DE) 1999–2000, Willie Howard (DT) 2001, Lorenzo Bromell (DL) 2002.

92 Leroy Howell (DT) 1986, Kelly Quinn (LB) 1987r, David Westbrooks (DE) 1990, Roy Barker (DT) 1992–5, 2000, Duane Clemons (DE) 1996–9, Winfield Garnett (DT) 2001.

93 Jimmy Walker (DT) 1987, *John Randle* (DT) 1990–2000, Stalin Colinet (DE) 2001, Darius Holland (DL) 2002, Kevin Williams (DE) 2003.

94 Chris Martin (LB) 1984, Paul Sverchek (DT) 1984, Tim Bryant (LB) 1987r, Thomas Strauthers (DE) 1989–91, John Thornton (DT) 1993, Robert Goff (DT) 1996, Tony Williams (DT) 1997–2000, Pete Monty (LB) 2001, Chuck Wiley (DL) 2002–3.

95 Mark Stewart (LB) 1983–4, Gerald Robinson (DE) 1986–7, Mac Stephens (LB) 1991, Esera Tuaolo (DT) 1992, Fernando Smith (DE) 1994–7, 2000, Bryce Paup (DE) 2000, Shawn Worthen (DT) 2001, Cedric Killings (DT) 2003.

96 Tim Newton (DT) 1985–9, Skip McClendon (DE) 1992, Keith Washington (DE) 1995, Jerry Ball (DT) 1997–9, Michael Boireau (DE) 2000, Andre O'Neal (LB) 2001, Billy Lyon (DE) 2003.

97 *Henry Thomas* (DT) 1987–94, Tony Norman (DE) 1987r, Jose White (DT) 1995, Talance Sawyer (DE) 1999–2003.

98 Phil Micech (DE) 1987r, George Hinkle (DT) 1992, Esera Tuaolo (DT) 1993–6, Ben Williams (DE) 1998, Fred Robbins (DT) 2000–3.

99 David Howard (LB) 1985–7, Al Noga (DE) 1988–92, James Harris (DE) 1993–5, Stalin Colinet (DE) 1997–9, Chris Hovan (DT) 2001–3.

NEW ENGLAND PATRIOTS

The franchise: Professional football took a long time to become established in Boston, longer than any comparable 20th century city. Boston's first brush came in 1929 when the Pottsville Maroons moved to the Hub City and became the Boston Bulldogs. The franchise disappeared after one year. In 1932, George Marshall bought into the NFL by founding the Boston Braves, who would be renamed the Redskins after one season. Despite building a division winner by their fifth year, the Redskins were not supported by Boston, and Marshall moved the 1936 title game from Boston to New York and then took the franchise to Washington in 1937. Theatrical promoter Ted Collins tried next with the Boston Yanks who lasted from 1944 to 1948 before moving to New York to become the New York Bulldogs and then Yanks. Finally, with the startup of the American Football League in 1960, football returned to New England for good when local sports promoter Billy Sullivan received one of the league's charter franchises. The good news was that Sullivan was a positive force for football in Boston. The bad news was that he was perennially underfinanced and could not find a permanent home for his team within the city. From 1960 to 1970, the Patriots played in four stadiums, all primarily used by another team. The solution would not arrive until 1971 in Foxboro, Massachusetts, with a stadium built on the cheap for $2 million that somehow lasted for 30 years. The team was renamed the New England Patriots at that time.

Meanwhile the team on the field had its ups and downs. Mike Holovak was named the team's first general manager and Lou Saban its first coach. The Patriots lost the first game in AFL history 13–10 to the Broncos. Saban did not work out in Boston and was replaced in 1961 by Holovak who spent a mostly successful eight years as Patriots coach. The team was powered by quarterback Babe Parilli and receiver/kicker Gino Cappelletti on offense complementing a blitzing defense with a sturdy front four of Bob Dee, Larry Eisenhauer, Houston Antwine and Jim Hunt backed by undersized middle linebacker Nick Buoniconti. After two 9–4–1 seasons, Boston tied with Buffalo for the Eastern Division title in 1963 and beat the Bills 26–8 in a snowy playoff game in upstate New York. The next week the Patriots were crushed 51–10 by the Chargers in the AFL championship.

Despite having the best runner in the AFL in Jim Nance, the team started to slip and Holovak was fired in 1968. Several weak seasons followed until Chuck Fairbanks was brought in as coach from the University of Oklahoma in 1973. Slowly, Fairbanks built a winner behind the passing of Steve Grogan, who supplanted Jim Plunkett at quarterback, and the power of fullback Sam "Bam" Cunningham running behind the finest guard of the time, John Hannah. On defense, the Patriots were an early proponent of the 3–4 alignment that took hold in the 1970s. In 1976 New England went 11–3 and returned to the playoffs for the first time in 13 years. Two years later, the team was rocked in the preseason when star receiver Daryl Stingley was permanently paralyzed after being hit by Raider Jack Tatum. The Patriots rallied that year to win their first division title in 15 years. However, Fairbanks shocked everyone by announcing before the season finale that he was returning to the college ranks at the University of Colorado in 1979. Sullivan threw him out for that game, but brought him back to coach the playoffs when a demoralized Patriot team lost 23–3 to Miami.

New England would not return to the playoffs until 1982 and would not win another postseason game until 1985 when coach Raymond Berry guided the Cinderella Patriots to three wins as a wildcard team before they were overwhelmed by the Chicago Bears 46–10 in Super Bowl XX. Three years later, the Sullivan family sold the team to Victor Kiam, and Berry was fired a year after that. In the four years that Kiam owned the team, the Patriots went 8–50 under three coaches, and New England was sold to James Orthwein in 1992. Orthwein would only own the team for two years, but he had the good judgment to hire Bill Parcells as coach in 1993. Parcells drafted Drew Bledsoe with the first choice in the 1993 draft and constructed a solid foundation in New England that would last for a decade. He did not get along with new owner Robert Kraft, however, and uttered the famous coach's line regarding player personnel, "If they want you to cook the meal, they should at least let you buy the groceries."

Parcells took the Patriots to the Super Bowl in his fourth year where they lost decisively to the Packers 35–21. Then, for the second time in franchise history, a successful team was abandoned by its coach when Parcells did not accompany his team back to New England, but quit instead. After much wrangling, he would end up coaching the Jets. Pete Carroll was hired to replace Parcells and was fired in three years. At this point, Parcells was stepping down from the Jets and handing the job to his longtime lieutenant Bill Bellichick. Surprisingly, Bellichick refused the Jets job only to turn up weeks later as the new coach in New England. In his second season there, Bellichick and unsung new quarterback Tom Brady led the Patriots to a magical Super Bowl XXXVI last-second upset of the vaunted Rams. At long last, the Patriots were the champions. Two years later they won Super Bowl XXXVIII with another last-second field goal by clutch kicker Adam Vinatieri.

Origin of name: A newspaper contest was held to name the team and Patriots was chosen to reflect Boston's place in American history from the start. Needless to say, red white and blue were chosen as team colors.

Record by Decade

	Regular Season			Postseason		
	Won	Lost	Tied	Won	Lost	Championships
1960s	63	68	9	1	1	
1970s	66	78	0	0	2	
1980s	78	74	0	3	3	
1990s	68	92	0	3	4	
2000s	39	25	0	6	0	2001, 2003
All-Time	314	337	9	13	10	2

Winning seasons: 22. Losing Seasons: 19. .500 seasons: 3.

Time till first championship: 42 years.
Time since last championship: none.
Retired numbers: The Patriots have retired a lot of numbers for a team with such middling success. Fully deserving of the honor were Hall of Famers John Hannah, 73, and Mike Haynes, 40, both dominant throughout their careers. The other five players range from good to very good, but none were great. Three stars from the 1960s have

Coaches

	Years	Record	Playoffs
Lou Saban	1960–1	7–12–0	0–0
Mike Holovak	1961–8	52–46–9	1–1
Clive Rush	1969–70	5–16–0	0–0
John Mazur	1970–2	10–25–0	0–0
Chuck Fairbanks	1973–8	46–39–0	0–2
Hank Bullough/Ron Erhardt	1978	0–1–0	0–0
Ron Erhardt	1979–81	21–27–0	0–0
Ron Meyer	1982–4	18–15–0	0–1
Raymond Berry	1984–9	48–39–0	3–2
Rod Rust	1990	1–15–0	0–0
Dick MacPherson	1991–2	8–24–0	0–0
Bill Parcells	1993–6	32–32–0	2–2
Pete Carroll	1997–9	27–21–0	1–2
Bill Belichick (2)	2000–3	39–25–0	6–0

(Championships in parentheses)

seen their numbers retired: receiver/kicker Gino Cappelletti 20, defensive tackle "Earthquake" Jim Hunt 79, and defensive end Bob Dee 89. Two leaders from the 1970s also had their numbers retired: solid quarterback Steve Grogan 14 and Pro Bowl linebacker Steve Nelson 57.

Other numbers worn by these players: None.

Those who wore retired numbers after the honored player: Oddly, this only happened to the two most deserving players. Mike Haynes's 40 was later worn by Elgin Davis, Tim Hauck, Harry Colon, Scott Lockwood, and Carlos Yancy. John Hannah's 73 was later worn by Brandon Gorin.

Numbers that should be retired: There are too many already.

Owned numbers: No one but Gino Cappelletti ever wore 20; no one but Bob Dee ever wore 89.

Numbers worn by Hall of Famers: Nick Buoniconti 85; John Hannah 73; and Mike Haynes 40.

Star power: Larry Garron took 40 from Chuck Shonta.

Star eclipsed: Larry Centers wore 31 because Rodney Harrison wore 37; Todd Collins wore 59 because Tedy Bruschi wore 54; J.J. Stokes wore 85 because Deion Branch wore 83.

Numbers with most great players: 53 has been worn by three Pro Bowlers—linebackers Tom Addison and Chris Slade in addition to special teams star Larry Izzo. 54 has been worn by three pretty solid linebackers—Steve Zabel, Todd Collins and Tedy Bruschi.

Worst represented numbers: 49 has been worn by two wideouts, two linebackers, two tight ends, and a safety; none of them lasted more than two years.

Number worn by the most players: 51 has been worn 18 times.

Player who wore the most numbers: Although several players have worn two numbers, none has worn more than two.

Longest tenure wearing a number: Quarterback Steve Grogan wore 14 for 16 consecutive years from 1975 to 1990; defensive end Julius Adams wore 85 for 16 years all together from 1971 to 1985 and in 1987.

Number worn by first ever draft pick: Ron Burton was the regional first pick in 1960 and wore 22.

Biggest draft busts: The biggest busts were receiver Hart Lee Dykes, 88, the 16th selection in 1989 who caught 83 passes in three years and runner Reggie Dupard, 21, the 26th selection in 1986 who averaged 3.1 yards per carry in his three years in New England.

Number worn by oldest player: Punter Lee Johnson wore 10 as a 40 year old in 2001.

Cameos: All Pros and other notables—Terry Allen 22; Bill Bain 62; Marlin Briscoe 86; Marion Butts 44; Bryan Cox 51; Jeff Dellenbach 66; Chuck Foreman 22; Raymont Harris 29; Gary Jeter 99; Charles Johnson 81; Joe Kapp 11; Antonio Langham 38; Nick Lowery 7; Zeke Mowatt 81; Bob Scarpitto 46; Torrance Small 84; Walter Stanley 81; Pat Studstill 2; Bake Turner 40; Mark Washington 21; Jerrell Wilson 4.

Ones who got away: Receiver Reggie

Rucker, 33, caught a lot of passes in Cleveland. Harry Jacobs, 83, moved on to become the middle linebacker on the Bills 1960s championship defense. Defensive end Greg Spires, 94, became a starter on the Tampa Bay Bucs Super Bowl champs.

Least popular numbers: 0 has never been worn; 69 has been worn only once; 9, 16, and 18 have only been worn twice each.

Last number to be originated: 69 was first worn in 1992 by Eugene Chung.

Longest dormant number: 1 has not been worn since 1987.

Triskaidekaphobia notes: 13 has been worn by on runner, one receiver, on quarterback, and one punter. The punter, Ken Walter, was the best of them.

Shared numbers: 56 was worn by star center Jon Morris and blitzing linebacker Andre Tippett. 65 has been worn by defensive tackle standout Houston Antwine and center Damien Woody. 80 has been worn by two Pro Bowl receivers, Irving Fryar and Troy Brown. 85 was worn by Hall of Fame linebacker Nick Buoniconti and the Patriot with the longest career in New England, defensive end Julius Adams.

Continuity: John Smith was replaced in 1 by fellow kicker Tony Franklin; Chris Slade was replaced in 53 by Larry Izzo; Irving Fryar was replaced in 80 by Troy Brown; Henry Thomas was replaced in 95 by Roman Phifer.

Discontinuity: Babe Parilli left to back up Joe Namath in New York and was followed in 15 by Namath wannabe Jim "King" Corcoran; runner Jim Nance was followed in 35 by Henry Matthews; Houston Antwine was followed in 65 by Conway Hayman; Charlie Long was followed in 76 by Rex Mirich; Stanley Morgan was followed in 86 by Greg McMurtry; Ben Coates was followed in 87 by Dane Looker. Finally, defensive end Julius Adams retired and was followed in 85 by Greg Baty for a season. Adams returned for a season and then was replaced in 85 by Steve Johnson.

Quarterback numbers over 19: None.

Number of first black player: In their first year of 1960: runner Ron Burton 22; defensive back Walter Beach 26; defensive back Clyde Washington 31; runner Larry Garron

Family Connections

Brothers

John Canale	DL	1968	67
Justin Canale	G	1965–8	63
Chuck McSwain	RB	1987	32
Rod McSwain	DB	1984–90	23
Clarence Weathers	WR	1983–4	82
Robert Weathers	FB	1982–4	24

40; tackle George McGee 75; and defensive tackle Jim Hunt 79.

Numbers of future NFL head coaches: Fred Bruney 33; Ed Khayat 73; and Marty Schottenheimer 54.

Numbers of future NFL referees: None.

Players who played other sports: Baseball — Tom Yewcik 14. Wrestling — Russ Francis 81.

Players more famous after football: Pat Studstill, 2, acted on the "Dukes of Hazard."

First player to wear a number in the 90s: George Webster wore 90 in 1974.

Number with most points scored: 4 with 1,169 points scored by Adam Vinatieri (917) and Jason Staurovsky (252).

Number with most yards rushing: 32 with 10,908 yards gained by Antowain Smith (2,781), Craig James (2,469), Leonard Russell (2,437), Andy Johnson (2,017), Billy Lott (573), J.D. Garrett (434), Odell Larson (107), Blair Thomas (67), and Chuck McSwain (23).

Number with most receptions: 80 with 962 passes caught by Troy Brown (458), Irving Fryar (363), Don Hasselbeck (100), Bob Adams (27), Larry Linne (11), Steve Hawkins (2), and Brooks Williams (1).

Number with most touchdown passes: 11 with 265 touchdowns tossed by Drew Bledsoe (166), Tony Eason (60), Butch Songin (36), and Joe Kapp (3).

Number with most interceptions: 42 with 50 passes picked off by Ronnie Lippett (24), Don Webb (16), Harlon Bennett (4), Chris Carter (3), Chuck Solitis (2), and Ron Shegog (1).

Oddity: The Patriots have employed 10 quarterbacks named Tom. Tom Dimitroff 15, Tom Greene 14, Tom Yewcik 14, Tom Sherman 14, Tom Flick 10, Tom Owen 17, Tom

Ramsey 12, Tommy Hodson 13, and Tom Tupa 19 all preceded two-time Super Bowl winner Tom Brady 12.

```
┌──────────────────────────────────────┐
│         Player Whose Number           │
│            Is Unknown                 │
│  Willis Perkins        (G)      1961  │
└──────────────────────────────────────┘
```

Team All-Time Numerical Roster

Those with an "r" following the year 1987 were replacement players during the players' strike. Pro Bowl players for each number are in *Italics*; Hall of Famers are in **Bold** type.

1 *John Smith* (K) 1974–83, *Tony Franklin* (K) 1984–7, Eric Schubert (K) 1987.

2 Pat Studstill (P) 1972, Jeff White (K/P) 1973, Mike Patrick (P) 1975–8, Joaquin Zendejas (K) 1983, Doug Flutie (QB) 1987–9.

3 Bruce Barnes (P) 1973–4, *Rich Camarillo* (P) 1981–7, Matt Bahr (K) 1993–5.

4 Jerrel Wilson (P) 1978, Jason Staurovsky (K) 1988–91, Mike Saxon (P) 1993, *Adam Vinatieri* (K) 1996–2003.

5 Fred Steinfort (K) 1983, Greg Davis (K) 1989, Pat O'Neill (P) 1994–5.

6 Mike Hubach (P) 1980–1, Don Miller (K) 1982, Alan Herline (P) 1987r, Jeff Feagles (P) 1988–9, Rohan Davey (QB) 2002–3.

7 John Huarte (QB) 1966–7, Charlie Gogolak (K) 1970–2, Nick Lowery (K) 1978, Ken Hartley (P) 1981, Rex Robinson (K) 1982, Teddy Garcia (K) 1988, Hugh Millen (QB) 1991–2, Michael Bishop (QB) 1999–2000.

8 Bill Bell (K) 1973, Eddie Hare (P) 1979, Charlie Baumann (K) 1991–2, Brooks Barnard (P) 2003.

9 Bryan Wagner (P) 1991, 1995, Scott Sisson (K) 1993.

10 Harvey White (QB) 1960, Eric Crabtree (WR) 1971, Dave Chapple (P) 1974, Tom Flick (QB) 1982, Bob Bleier (QB) 1987r, Brian Hansen (P) 1990, Scott Secules (QB) 1993, Lee Johnson (P) 1999–2001.

11 Butch Songin (QB) 1960–1, Joe Kapp (QB) 1970, Dick Shiner (QB) 1973–4, Tony Eason (QB) 1983–9, Shawn McCarthy (P) 1991–2, *Drew Bledsoe* (QB) 1993–2001.

12 Don Allard (QB) 1962, Ed Wilson (QB) 1965, Mike Walker (K) 1972, Matt Cavanaugh (QB) 1978–82, Tom Ramsey (QB) 1985–8, *Tom Brady* (QB) 2000–3.

13 R.C. Gamble (RB) 1968–9, Alfred Sykes (WR) 1971, Tommy Hodson (QB) 1990–2, Ken Walter (P) 2001–3.

14 Tom Greene (QB) 1960, Tom Yewcik (P/QB) 1961–6, Tom Sherman (QB) 1968–9, Brian Dowling (QB) 1972–3, Steve Grogan (QB) 1975–90.

15 Tom Dimitroff (QB) 1960, *Babe Parilli* (QB) 1961–7, Jim Corcoran (QB) 1968, Kim Hammond (QB) 1969–70, Neil Graff (QB) 1974–5, Todd Whitten (QB) 1987r, Marc Wilson (QB) 1989–90, Ray Lucas (WR) 1996.

16 Jim Plunkett (QB) 1971–5, Scott Zolak (QB) 1992–8.

17 *Mike Taliaferro* (QB) 1968–71, Elmo Wright (WR) 1975, Tom Owen (QB) 1976–81, Luke Prestridge (P) 1984, Jeff Carlson (QB) 1992, Tony Gaiter (WR) 1997, Henry Ellard (WR) 1998, John Friesz (QB) 1999–2000, Dedric Ward (WR) 2003.

18 Randy Vataha (WR) 1971–6, Anthony Ladd (WR) 1998, David Givens (WR) 2002.

19 Don Trull (QB) 1967, Mike Kerrigan (QB) 1983–4, Tom Tupa (P) 1996–7, Damon Huard (QB) 2001–3.

20 *Gino Cappelletti* (WR/K) 1960–70.

21 Bob Suci (DB) 1963, Jay Cunningham (DB) 1965–7, Tom Janik (DB/P) 1969–71, Tom Reynolds (WR) 1972, Allen Carter (RB) 1975–6, Joe Blahak (CB) 1976, Sidney Brown (CB) 1978, Mark Washington (CB) 1979, Reggie Dupard (RB) 1986–9, Erroll Tucker (DB) 1989, Reyna Thompson (CB) 1993, Ricky Reynolds (CB) 1994–6, Steve Israel (CB) 1997–9, J.R. Redmond (RB) 2000–2, Mike Cloud (RB) 2003.

22 Ron Burton (RB) 1960–5, Gene Thomas (RB) 1968, Sid Blanks (RB) 1969–70, Phil Clark (DB) 1971, Sandy Durko (S) 1973–4, Dick Conn (S) 1975–9, Chuck Foreman (RB) 1980, Keith Lee (DB) 1981–4, Eugene Profit (DB) 1986–8, Eric Coleman (DB) 1989, Rod Smith (DB) 1992–4, *Dave Meggett* (RB) 1995–7, Terry Allen (RB) 1999, Terrance Shaw (CB) 2001, Terrell Buckley (CB) 2002, Asante Samuel (CB) 2003.

23 Dick Christy (RB) 1960, Ray Ratkowski (RB) 1961, Ron Hall (DB) 1961–7, Daryl Johnson (DB) 1968–71, George Hoey (DB) 1972–3, Joe Wilson (RB) 1974, Horace Ivory (RB) 1977–81, Kevin Donnalley (DB) 1981, Rod McSwain (CB) 1984–90, Terry Ray (S) 1993–6, Sedrick Shaw (RB) 1997–8, Terry Billups (CB) 1999, Antwan Harris (CB) 2000–3.

24 Walt Livingston (RB) 1960, Joe Johnson (E) 1960–1, Mel West (RB) 1961, *Dick Felt* (DB) 1962–6, Bobby Leo (WR) 1967–8, Bob Gladieux (RB) 1969–72, Bob McCall (RB) 1973, Bob Howard (CB) 1975–7, Robert Weathers (RB) 1982–6, Bruce Hansen (RB) 1987, Jamie Morris (RB) 1990, Jon Vaughn (RB) 1991–2, *Ty Law* (CB) 1995–2003.

25 Ross O'Hanley (DB) 1960–5, John Charles (DB) 1967–9, Rickie Harris (DB) 1971–2, John Sanders (S) 1974–6, Rick Sanford (S) 1979–84, Vencie Glenn (DB) 1986, Tony Zackery (S) 1990–1, Darren Anderson (CB) 1992, *Larry Whigham* (S) 1994–2000, Hakim Akbar (S) 2001, Leonard Myers (CB) 2001–2.

26 Walter Beach (DB) 1960, Clarence Scott (DB) 1969–72, *Raymond Clayborn* (CB) 1977–89, David Key (S) 1991, David Wilson (DB) 1992, Corey Croom (RB) 1993–5, Jerome Henderson (CB) 1996, Chris Canty (CB) 1997–8, Matt Stevens (S) 2000–1, Eugene Wilson (CB) 2003.

27 Joe Bellino (RB) 1965–7, Willie Porter (DB) 1968, Randy Beverly (DB) 1970–1, Ron Bolton (DB) 1972–5, Doug Beaudoin (S) 1976–9, Ricky Smith (DB) 1982–4, Greg Hawthorne (RB) 1984–6, Michael LeBlanc (RB) 1987, Junior Robinson (CB) 1990, David Pool (CB) 1991–2, Darryl Wren (CB) 1993–4, Scooter McGruder (CB) 1996–7, Lamont Warren (RB) 1999, Terrell Buckley (CB) 2001, Victor Green (S) 2002.

28 Dave Cloutier (DB) 1964, Art McMahon (DB) 1968–72, Dave Mason (S) 1973, Bill Currier (DB) 1980, Jim Bowman (S) 1985–9, David Hendley (DB) 1987r, Dion Lambert (DB) 1992–3, *Curtis Martin* (RB) 1995–7.

29 Aaron Marsh (WR) 1968–9, Honor Jackson (DB) 1972–3, Greg Boyd (S) 1973, Durwood Keeton (S) 1975, Willie Germany (S) 1976, Harold Jackson (WR) 1978–81, 1987, Jamie Lawson (RB) 1990, Don Overton (RB) 1990, Darrell Fullington (S) 1991, Myron Guyton (S) 1994–5, Derrick Cullors (RB) 1997–9, Raymont Harris (RB) 2000, Chris Hayes (DB) 2002, Aric Morris (S) 2003.

30 Jim Crawford (RB) 1960–4, Tom Hennessey (DB) 1965–6, *Carl Garrett* (RB) 1969–72, Ed Jenkins (RB) 1974, *Mosi Tatupu* (RB) 1978–90, Frank Bianchini (RB) 1987r, Corwin Brown (S) 1993–5, Tony Carter (FB) 1998–2000, Je'Rod Cherry (S) 2001–3.

31 Clyde Washington (DB) 1960–1, Harry Crump (RB) 1963, Vic Purvis (WR) 1966–7, Bill Murphy (WR) 1968, Josh Ashton (RB) 1972–4, Leon McQuay (RB) 1975, *Fred Marion* (S) 1982–91, Jon Sawyer (CB) 1987r, Jimmy Hitchcock (CB) 1995–7, Kato Serwanga (CB) 1998–2000, Ben Kelly (CB) 2001–2, Larry Centers (FB) 2003.

32 Al Miller (RB) 1960, Billy Lott (RB) 1961–3, J.D. Garrett (RB) 1964–7, Odell Lawson (RB) 1970–1, Andy Johnson (RB) 1974–6, 1978–81, *Craig James* (RB) 1984–8, Chuck McSwain (RB) 1987r, Leonard Russell (RB) 1991–3, Blair Thomas (RB) 1994, Willie Clay (S) 1996–8, Antowain Smith (RB) 2001–3.

33 *Fred Bruney* (DB) 1960–2, Bob Cappadona (RB) 1966–7, Bill Rademacher (WR) 1969–70, Reggie Rucker (WR) 1971–4, Bob Anderson (RB) 1975, *Tony Collins* (RB) 1981–7, Patrick Egu (RB)

1989, George Adams (RB) 1990–1, Sam Gash (FB) 1992–7, Kevin Faulk (RB) 1999–2003.

34 Joe Biscaha (E) 1960, Jake Crouthamel (RB) 1960, William Larson (RB) 1960, *Chuck Shonta* (DB) 1960–7, Bobby Towns (DB) 1961, *Ron Sellers* (WR) 1969–71, Prentice McCray (S) 1974–80, Mark Van Eeghen (RB) 1982–3, Robert Perryman (RB) 1987–9, Carl Woods (RB) 1987r, Kevin Turner (FB) 1992–4, Rupert Grant (FB) 1995, Tebucky Jones (CB) 1998–2002, Chris Akins (S) 2003.

35 *Jim Nance* (RB) 1965–71, Henry Matthews (RB) 1972, Jess Phillips (RB) 1976–7, Allan Clark (RB) 1979–80, George Peoples (RB) 1983, Burnie Legette (RB) 1993–4, Mario Grier (RB) 1996–7, Jerry Ellison (RB) 1999, Patrick Pass (RB) 2000–3.

36 Tom Neumann (RB) 1963, Terry Swanson (P) 1967–8, Ken Herock (LB) 1969, Eddie Ray (RB) 1970, John Tarver (RB) 1972–4, Howard Feggins (CB) 1989, Brian Hutson (S) 1990, Jerome Henderson (CB) 1991–3, Leroy Thompson (RB) 1994, *Lawyer Milloy* (S) 1996–2002.

37 Bill Bailey (RB) 1969, Ron Gardin (WR) 1971, Willie Osley (CB) 1974, James McAlister (RB) 1978, Ricky Atkinson (DB) 1987r, Maurice Hurst (CB) 1989–95, Chris Floyd (FB) 1998–2000, Rodney Harrison (S) 2003.

38 Al Snyder (WR) 1964, Ellis Johnson (RB) 1965–6, Donald Martin (CB) 1973, Noe Gonzalez (RB) 1974, Ike Forte (RB) 1976–8, Roland James (S) 1980–90, Perry Williams (CB) 1987r, Adrian White (S) 1993, David Green (RB) 1995, Steve Lofton (CB) 1997, Antonio Langham (CB) 2000, Tyrone Poole (CB) 2003.

39 Perry Pruett (DB) 1971, *Sam Cunningham* (RB) 1973–9, 1981–2, Marvin Allen (RB) 1988–91, Rico Clark (CB) 1999, Shawn Mayer (DB) 2003.

40 *Chuck Shonta* (DB) 1960, *Larry Garron* (RB) 1960–8, Bake Turner (WR) 1970, Jack Maitland (RB) 1971–2, Dave McCurry (S) 1974, **Mike Haynes** (CB) 1976–82, Elgin Davis (RB) 1987–8, Tim Hauck (S) 1990, Harry Colon (S) 1991, Scott Lockwood (RB) 1992–3, Carlos Yancy (CB) 1995.

41 Billy Wells (RB) 1960, Walter Beach (DB) 1961, Claude King (RB) 1962, *Leroy Mitchell* (DB) 1967–8, Larry Carwell (DB) 1969–72, Ken Pope (CB) 1974, Bo Robinson (RB) 1984, Darryl Holmes (S) 1987–9, Tim Gordon (S) 1991–2, Eddie Cade (S) 1995, Keith Byars (FB) 1996–7, Tony George (S) 1999–2000.

42 Bob Solitis (DB) 1960–1, *Don Webb* (DB) 1962–71, Mack Herron (RB) 1973–5, Ronnie Lippett (DB) 1983–8, 1990–1, Ron Shegog (S) 1987r, Harlon Barnett (S) 1993–4, Chris Carter (S) 1997–9.

43 Irvin Mallory (DB) 1971, Claxton Welch (RB) 1973, Vagas Ferguson (RB) 1980–2, Ernest Gibson (CB) 1984–8, Duffy Cobbs (DB) 1987r, Rodney Rice (DB) 1989, Vernon Lewis (CB) 1993–6.

44 Gerhardt Schwedes (RB) 1960–1, White Graves (DB) 1965–7, John Outlaw (DB) 1969–72, Doug Dressler (RB) 1975, Don Calhoun (RB) 1975–81, Larry Cowan (LB) 1982, Jon Williams (RB) 1984, Todd Frain (TE) 1987r, *John Stephens* (RB) 1988–92, Marion Butts (RB) 1994, Harold Shaw (FB) 1998–2000, Marc Edwards (FB) 2001–2, Fred McCrary (FB) 2003.

45 Jerry Green (RB) 1960, Tom Stephens (DB) 1960–4, Ray Ilg (LB) 1967–8, Dan Kecman (LB) 1970, Jack Mildren (S) 1974, Greg Taylor (RB) 1982, Joe Peterson (CB) 1987r, Ivy Joe Hunter (RB) 1991, Otis Smith (CB) 1996, 2000–2, Dana Cottrell (LB) 1998.

46 Al Romine (DB) 1961, Bob Scarpitto (P/WR) 1968, Paul Gipson (RB) 1973, Marv Cook (TE) 1989–90, Mickey Washington (CB) 1990–1, Jeff Paulk (FB) 2000, Brian Kinchen (TE) 2003.

47 Billy Johnson (DB) 1966–9, Jim Massey (CB) 1974–5, Darrell Wilson (DB) 1981, Paul Dombroski (DB) 1981–4, Pat Coleman (WR) 1990, Roger Brown (S) 1992, Robert Edwards (RB) 1998–2000.

48 *Don Webb* (DB) 1961, Preston Johnson (RB) 1968, *Tim Fox* (S) 1976–81, Darryal Wilson (WR) 1983, Clay Pickering (WR) 1987, Dennis Gadbois (WR) 1987r, 1988, Glenn Antrum (WR) 1989, Randy Robbins (S) 1992, Lovett Purnell (TE) 1996, Tully Banta-Cain (LB) 2003.

49 Tom Richardson (WR) 1969–70, Dick Blanchard (LB) 1972, Ralph Anderson (S) 1973, Brian Williams (TE) 1982, Eric Naposki (LB) 1988–9, Kitrick Taylor (WR) 1989, Sean McDermott (TE) 2003.

50 Bob Yates (OL) 1960–5, Joe Avezzano (C) 1966, Jim Cheyunski (LB) 1968–72, Edgar Chandler (LB) 1973, Sam Hunt (LB) 1974–9, Lawrence McGrew (LB) 1980–9, Ilia Jarostchuk (LB) 1990, Steve DeOssie (LB) 1994, Bobby Abrams (LB) 1995, Rob Holmberg (LB) 2000, Mike Vrabel (LB) 2001–3.

51 Frank Robotti (LB) 1961, Don McKinnon (LB) 1963–4, Jim Fraser (LB) 1966, Mike Ballou (LB) 1970, Randy Edmunds (LB) 1971, Ron Acks (LB) 1972–3, Kent Carter (LB) 1974, Maury Damkroger (LB) 1974, Donnie Thomas (LB) 1976, Bob Golic (LB) 1979–81, Brian Ingram (LB) 1982–5, Bruce Scholtz (LB) 1989, Eugene Lockhart (LB) 1991–2, David White (LB) 1993, Bernard Russ (LB) 1997–9, Olrick Johnson (LB) 2000, Bryan Cox (LB) 2001, Don Davis (LB) 2003.

52 Phil Bennett (LB) 1960, Ed Meixler (LB) 1965, Ed Phillpott (LB) 1967–71, Roin Kadziel (LB) 1972, Steve King (LB) 1973–81, *Johnny Rembert* (LB) 1983–92, Jerry McCabe (LB) 1987r, David Bavaro (LB) 1993–4, Ted Johnson (LB) 1995–2003.

53 *Tom Addison* (LB) 1960–7, Fred Whittingham (LB) 1970, Dennis Coleman (LB) 1971, John

Tanner (LB) 1973–4, Jim Romaniszyn (LB) 1976, Merv Krakau (LB) 1978, Bill Matthews (LB) 1979–81, Clayton Weishuhn (LB) 1982–4, 1986, Thomas Benson (LB) 1988, George Wonsley (RB) 1989, Richard Tardits (LB) 1990–2, *Chris Slade* (LB) 1993–2000, *Larry Izzo* (LB) 2001–3.

54 Bill Brown (LB) 1960, Walt Cudzik (C) 1961–3, Mike Dukes (LB) 1964–5, Ed Koontz (LB) 1968, Marty Schottenheimer (LB) 1969–70, Kenny Price (LB) 1971, Gail Clark (LB) 1974, Steve Zabel (LB) 1975–8, John Zamberlin (LB) 1979–82, John Gillen (LB) 1983, Ed Williams (LB) 1984–7, 1990, Greg Moore (LB) 1987r, Todd Collins (LB) 1992–4, Alcides Catanho (LB) 1995, Tedy Bruschi (LB) 1996–2003.

55 Lonnie Farmer (LB) 1964–6, J.R. Williamson (LB/C) 1968–70, Ralph Cindrich (LB) 1972, Will Foster (LB) 1973–4, Kevin Reilly (LB) 1975, Ray Costict (LB) 1977–9, Don Blackmon (LB) 1981–7, Joe McHale (LB) 1987r, Chris Singleton (LB) 1990–3, *Willie McGinest* (LB) 1994–2003.

56 Walt Cudzik (C) 1960, *Jon Morris* (C) 1964–74, Rod Shoate (LB) 1975–81, *Andre Tippett* (LB) 1982–8, 1990–3.

57 John Bramlett (LB) 1969–70, Steve Kiner (LB) 1971, 1973, *Steve Nelson* (LB) 1974–87.

58 Doug Satcher (LB) 1966–8, Doug Dumler (C) 1973–5, Pete Brock (C) 1976–87, Terrence Cooks (LB) 1989, Richard Harvey (LB) 1990, Rob McGovern (LB) 1992, Marty Moore (LB) 1994–9, 2001, Maugaula Tuitele (LB) 2000–2, Matt Chatham (LB) 2000–3.

59 Brian Stenger (LB) 1973, Bob Geddes (LB) 1973–5, Rodrigo Barnes (LB) 1974–5, Pete Barnes (LB) 1976–7, Mike Hawkins (LB) 1978–81, Tim Golden (LB) 1982–4, Steve Doig (LB) 1986–7, Randy Sealby (LB) 1987r, Vincent Brown (LB) 1988–95, Todd Collins (LB) 1996–8, Andy Katzenmoyer (LB) 1999–2001, Rosevelt Colvin (LB) 2003.

60 Robert Lee (G) 1960, Rommie Loudd (LB) 1961–2, *Len St. Jean* (G) 1964–73, Dave Tipton (DT) 1975–6, Bob Hyland (C) 1977, Garin Veris (DE) 1985–8, Marion Hobby (DE) 1990–2, Sean Holcomb (LB) 1995, Scott Rehberg (T) 1997–8, Garrett Johnson (NT) 2000, Wilbert Brown (G) 2003.

61 Leroy Moore (DE) 1961–2, Bill Hudson (DT) 1965, Sam Adams (G) 1972–80, Ron Wooten (G) 1982–8, Greg Robinson (T) 1987r, Fred Childress (G) 1991, Bob Kratch (G) 1994–6, Damon Denson (G) 1997–9.

62 Abe Cohen (G) 1960, Dick Klein (T) 1961–2, John Cagle (DT/LB) 1969, Halvor Hagen (G/DE) 1971–2, Kevin Hunt (T) 1973, Steve Corbett (G) 1975, Dwight Wheeler (T) 1978–83, Bill Bain (T) 1986, Sean Farrell (G) 1987–90, Dave Richards (OL) 1996.

63 *Charlie Leo* (G) 1960–2, Justin Canale (G)

1965–8, Rick Cash (DT) 1972–3, Shelby Jordan (T) 1975, Fred Sturt (G) 1976–8, Ernie Holmes (DT) 1978, Mark Buben (DL) 1979, 1981, Tom Condon (G) 1985, George Colton (T) 1987, Gerry Feehery (G) 1989, Gene Chilton (CB) 1990–2, Todd Jones (OL) 1993, Sylvester Stanley (NT) 1994, Heath Irwin (G) 1996–9, Joe Andruzzi (G) 2000–3.

64 Tony Sardisco (G) 1960–2, Jim Boudreaux (DE) 1966–8, Mike Montler (T) 1969–72, Allen Gallaher (T) 1974, Martin Imhof (DE) 1975, Richard Bishop (NT) 1976–81, Trevor Matich (C) 1985–8, Darren Twombly (C) 1987, Jon Melander (G) 1991, Dave Wohlabaugh (C) 1995–8, Derrick Fletcher (OL) 1999, Greg Randall (T) 2000–2.

65 Jack Davis (G) 1960, *Houston Antwine* (DT) 1961–71, Conway Hayman (G) 1972, Donnell Smith (DE) 1973–4, Greg Boyd (DE) 1977–8, Steve Clark (DE) 1981, Doug Rogers (DE) 1984, Mike Ruth (NT) 1986–7, Tom Porell (NT) 1987r, Edmund Nelson (DE) 1988, Elbert Crawford (OL) 1990–1, Mike Arthur (C) 1993–4, *Damien Woody* (C) 1999–2003.

66 Paul Feldhausen (T) 1968, Barry Brown (LB) 1969, Angelo Loukas (G) 1970, Ed Weisacosky (LB) 1971–2, Nate Dorsey (DE) 1973, Bob McKay (T) 1976–8, John Lee (DE) 1981, Paul Fairchild (G) 1984–90, Jeff Dellenbach (C) 1995, Ed Ellis (T) 1997, 1999, Lonnie Paxton (C) 2000–3.

67 Art Hauser (DT) 1960, Paul Lindquist (DT) 1961, Dave Watson (G) 1963–4, Whit Canale (DE) 1968, Gary Bugenhagen (T/G) 1969–70, Bill Lenkaitis (C) 1971–81, Steve Moore (T) 1983–7, David Douglas (G) 1989–90, Mike Gisler (G) 1993–7, Jason Andersen (C) 1998–2000, Grey Ruegamer (C/G) 2000–2, Dan Koppen (C) 2003.

68 Karl Singer (T) 1966–8, Bill DuLac (G) 1974–5, Terry Falcon (G) 1978–9, Darryl Haley (G) 1982–4, 1986, Mike Baab (C) 1988–9, Damian Johnson (G) 1990, Calvin Stephens (G) 1992, Max Lane (T) 1994–2000, Tom Ashworth (OL) 2002–3.

69 Eugene Chung (OL) 1992–4.

70 Hal Smith (DT) 1960, Milt Graham (T) 1961–3, Mel Witt (DT) 1967–8, Dennis Wirgowski (DE) 1970–2, *Leon Gray* (T) 1973–8, Doug McDougald (DE) 1980, Luther Henson (NT) 1982–4, Scott Virkus (DE) 1984, Art Plunkett (T) 1985, 1987, David Viaene (T) 1989–90, Reggie Redding (OL) 1992, Brandon Moore (T) 1993–5, Adrian Klemm (G/T) 2000–3.

71 *Don Oakes* (T) 1963–8, Mel Witt (DT) 1969–70, Art May (DE) 1971, Ray Hamilton (DE) 1973–81, Benton Reed (DE) 1987r, Fred DeRiggi (DT) 1990, Gregg Rakoczy (OL) 1991–2, Todd Rucci (G) 1993–9, Matt Light (T) 2001–2, Russ Hochstein (OL) 2002–3.

72 Albert Crow (DT) 1960, Bill Striegal (LB) 1960, *Larry Eisenhauer* (DE) 1961–9, Mel Lunsford (DE) 1973–80, Jerry Patton (DE) 1975, Lester Williams (NT) 1982–5, Todd Sandham (G) 1987r, Tim Goad (NT) 1988–94, Devin Wyman (DT) 1996–8, Sale Isaia (G) 2000, Matt Light (T) 2003.

73 Harry Jagielski (DT) 1960–1, *Billy Neighbors* (G) 1962–5, Ed Khayat (DT) 1966, Tom Funchess (T) 1968–70, Bill Atessis (DE) 1971, **John Hannah** (G) 1973–85, Danny Villa (T) 1987–91, Brandon Gorin (T) 2002.

74 Gerry Delucca (T) 1960–3, Bob Schmidt (T) 1964, John Mangum (DT) 1966–7, Ezell Jones (T) 1969–70, Bob Reynolds (T) 1972–3, Craig Hanneman (DE) 1974–5, Shelby Jordan (T) 1977–82, Dave Browning (DE) 1983, Bill Turner (DE) 1987r, Chris Gambol (OL) 1990, Rich Baldinger (OL) 1993, Doug Skene (G) 1994, Chris Sullivan (DE) 1996–9, 2001–2, Kenyatta Jones (T) 2001–2.

75 George McGee (T) 1960, John Simerson (T) 1961, Jesse Richardson (DT) 1962–4, George Pyne (T) 1965, Ed Toner (DT) 1967–70, Mike Haggerty (T/DE) 1971, Wayne Mass (T) 1972, Arthur Moore (DT) 1973–7, Bob Cryder (G) 1978–83, Guy Morris (C) 1984–7, Larry Williams (G) 1992, Bill Lewis (C) 1993, Pio Sagapolutele (DT) 1996, Danny Villa (T) 1997, Leonta Rheams (DL) 1998.

76 Tony Discenzo (T) 1960, *Charlie Long* (G) 1961–9, Rex Mirich (DT) 1970, Dave Rowe (DT) 1971–3, Pete Cusick (NT) 1975, Greg Schaum (DE) 1978, *Brian Holloway* (T) 1981–6, Tom Rehder (T) 1988–9, Stan Clayton (T) 1990, Fred Smerlas (NT) 1991–2, John Washington (DT) 1993, William Roberts (G) 1995–6, Grant Williams (T) 2000–1, Brandon Gorin (T) 2003.

77 Bob Cross (T) 1960, Bill Danenhauer (DE) 1960, *Tommy Neville* (T) 1965–77, Garry Puetz (G) 1979–81, Kenneth Sims (DE) 1982–9, Pat Harlow (T) 1991–5, Zefross Moss (T) 1997–9, Mike Compton (C/G) 2001–3.

78 Dennis Byrd (DT) 1968, Willie Banks (G) 1973, Tony McGee (DE) 1974–81, Ron Spears (DE) 1982–3, Marshall Harris (DE) 1983, Art Kuehn (C) 1983, *Bruce Armstrong* (T) 1987–2000, Eric Stokes (C/G) 1987r.

79 Al Richardson (DE) 1960, *Jim Hunt* (DT) 1960–71.

80 Jack Rudolph (LB) 1960–5, Karl Henke (T) 1969, Bob Adams (TE) 1973–4, Don Hasselbeck (TE) 1977–83, Brooks Williams (TE) 1983, *Irving Fryar* (WR) 1984–92, Larry Linne (WR) 1987r, *Troy Brown* (WR) 1993–2003, Steve Hawkins (WR) 1994.

81 *Jim Colclough* (WR) 1960–8, Charley Frazier (WR) 1969–70, Joe Sweet (WR) 1974, *Russ Francis* (TE) 1975–80, 1987–8, Preston Brown (WR) 1981–2, Stephen Starring (WR) 1983–7, Brian Carey (WR) 1987r, Zeke Mowatt (TE) 1990, Rob Carpenter (WR) 1991, Walter Stanley (WR) 1992, Ray Crittenden (WR) 1993–4, Hason Graham (WR) 1995–6, Tony Simmons (WR) 1998–2000, Charles Johnson (WR) 2001, Donald Hayes (WR) 2002, Bethel Johnson (WR) 2003.

82 Jim Whalen (TE) 1965–9, Tom Beer (TE) 1970–2, Eddie Hinton (WR) 1974, Steve Burks (WR) 1975–7, Al Chandler (TE) 1978–9, Ken Toler (WR) 1981–2, Clarence Weathers (WR) 1983–4, Derwin Wiliams (WR) 1985–7, Sammy Martin (WR) 1988–91, Gene Taylor (WR) 1991, Vincent Brisby (WR) 1993–9, Chris Calloway (WR) 2000, Curtis Jackson (WR) 2000–1, Daniel Graham (TE) 2002–3.

83 Harry Jacobs (LB) 1960–2, Bill Dawson (E) 1965, Tom Fussell (DE) 1967, Melvin Baker (WR) 1975, Ricky Feacher (WR) 1976, Don Westbrook (WR) 1977–81, Cedric Jones (WR) 1982–90, Wayne Coffey (WR) 1987r, Michael Timpson (WR) 1989–94, Will Moore (WR) 1995, Dietrich Jells (WR) 1996–7, Rod Rutledge (TE) 1998–2001, Deion Branch (WR) 2002–3.

84 Art Graham (WR) 1963–8, Gayle Knief (WR) 1970, Hubie Bryant (WR) 1971–2, Darryl Stingley (WR) 1973–7, Ronnie Harris (WR) 1993–4, Shawn Jefferson (WR) 1996–9, Shockmain Davis (WR) 2000, Torrance Small (WR) 2001, Fred Coleman (WR) 2001–2, Fred Baxter (TE) 2003.

85 Jack Atchason (E) 1960, Don McComb (DE) 1960, **Nick Buoniconti** (LB) 1962–68, *Julius Adams* (DE) 1971–85, 1987, Greg Baty (TE) 1986, Steve Johnson (TE) 1988, Eric Sievers (TE) 1989–90, *Marv Cook* (TE) 1990–93, John Burke (TE) 1994–6, Lovett Purnell (TE) 1997–8, Sean Morey (WR) 1999, Jermaine Wiggins (TE) 2001, J.J. Stokes (WR) 2003.

86 Oscar Lofton (E) 1960, Bill Kimber (E) 1961, Tony Romeo (TE) 1962–7, Barry Brown (LB) 1970, Roland Moss (TE) 1971, Bob Windsor (TE) 1972–5, *Stanley Morgan* (WR) 1977–89, Greg McMurtry (WR) 1990–3, Kevin Lee (WR) 1994–5, Mike Bartrum (TE) 1996–9, Eric Bjornson (TE) 2000, Chris Eitzmann (TE) 2000, David Patten (WR) 2001–3.

87 Mike Long (E) 1960, Bob Nichols (TE) 1967–8, Ray Jacobs (DT) 1969, Ike Lassiter (DE) 1970–1, Jim White (DE) 1972, Steve Schubert (WR) 1974, Al Chandler (TE) 1976–7, Ray Jarvis (WR) 1979, Preston Brown (WR) 1980, Lin Dawson (TE) 1981–90, Arnold Franklin (TE) 1987r, *Ben Coates* (TE) 1991–9, Dane Looker (WR) 2000, Bert Emanuel (WR) 2001, Cam Cleeland (TE) 2002, David Givens (WR) 2003.

88 Ron Berger (DE) 1969–72, John Mosier (TE) 1973, Al Marshall (WR) 1974, Marlin Briscoe (WR) 1976, Carlos Pennywell (WR) 1978–81, Morris Bradshaw (WR) 1982, Derrick Ramsey (TE) 1983–5, Willie Scott (TE) 1986–8, Hart Lee Dykes (WR) 1989–90, Richard Griffith (TE) 1993, David Frisch (TE) 1995, Andre President (TE) 1995, *Terry Glenn* (WR) 1996–2001, Christian Fauria (TE) 2002–3.

89 *Bob Dee* (DE) 1960–7.

90 George Webster (LB) 1974–6, Toby Williams (DE) 1983–8, Murray Wichard (DE) 1987r, Peter Shorts (DE) 1989, Garin Veris (DE) 1990–1, Reggie White (DT) 1995, Chad Eaton (DT) 1996–2000, Steve Martin (DL) 2002, Dan Klecko (DT) 2003.

91 Rogers Alexander (LB) 1987, Orlando Lowry (LB) 1989, Chris Gannon (DE) 1990–3, Bruce Walker (DT) 1994–5, Jeff Kopp (LB) 1999, Bobby Hamilton (DE) 2000–3.

92 Emanuel McNeil (NT) 1989, Ray Agnew (DE) 1990–4, Ferric Collons (DE) 1995–9, David Nugent (DE) 2000–2, Ted Washington (DT) 2003.

93 Tim Jordan (LB) 1987–9, Rico Corsetti (LB) 1987r, Mike Pitts (DE) 1993–4, Monty Brown (LB) 1996, Shawn Stuckey (LB) 1998, Bob Kuberski (DT) 1999, Antico Dalton (LB) 2000, *Richard Seymour* (DE) 2001–3.

94 Mel Black (LB) 1986–7r, David Ward (LB) 1989, Tim Roberts (DE) 1995, Walter Scott (DL) 1996, Greg Spires (DE) 1998–2000, Jace Sayler (DL) 2001, Ty Warren (DT) 2003.

95 Ed Reynolds (LB) 1983–91, Frank Sacco (LB) 1987r, Dwayne Sabb (LB) 1992–6, Henry Thomas (DT) 1997–2000, Roman Phifer (LB) 2001–3.

96 Brent Williams (DE) 1986–93, Dino Mangiero (NT) 1987r, Mike Jones (DE) 1994–7, Marc Megna (LB) 1999–2000, Rick Lyle (DE) 2002–3.

97 Milford Hodge (DE) 1986–9, John Guzik (NT) 1987r, Sean Smith (DE) 1990–1, Aaron Jones (DE) 1993–5, Mark Wheeler (DT) 1996–8, Reggie Grimes (DE) 2000, Riddick Parker (DT) 2001, Jarvis Green (DL) 2002–3.

98 Dennis Owens (NT) 1982–6, Tim Edwards (DE) 1992, Mario Johnson (DL) 1993, Troy Barnett (DE) 1994–5, Brandon Mitchell (DE) 1997–2001, Anthony Pleasant (DE) 2001–3.

99 Ben Thomas (DE) 1985, Steve Wilburn (DE) 1987r, Gary Jeter (DE) 1989, David Howard (LB) 1991–2, Jason Carthen (LB) 1993–4, Steve DeOssie (LB) 1995, Vernon Crawford (LB) 1997–9, Kole Ayi (LB) 2001, T.J. Turner (LB) 2001, Bernard Holsey (DL) 2002.

NEW ORLEANS SAINTS

The franchise: In 1963, Lamar Hunt was interested in moving his AFL champion Dallas Texans to New Orleans but could not get permission to play in Tulane Stadium, so they went to Kansas City to become the Chiefs instead. Three years later, the NFL awarded its 16th franchise to a New Orleans syndicate headed by 28-year-old businessman John Mecom. Looking to the champion Packers for inspiration, he hired former Lombardi assistant Tom Fears as coach, signed Packer fullback Jim Taylor as a free agent and drafted Packer halfback Paul Hornung in the expansion draft. Hornung immediately retired and Taylor should have as the Saints' high point in the 1967 season came when John Gilliam returned the opening kickoff in their first game 94 yards for a touchdown. Of course, the Saints would lose that game to the Rams.

In the next decade, Saints highlights consisted of stump-footed kicker Tom Dempsey kicking an NFL record 63 yard field goal to beat the Lions in 1970 and the heroic struggles of talented quarterback Archie Manning, who endured a steady pounding game after game. New Orleans would not gain its first .500 season until year 13 in 1979. Their first winning season would not come until 1987, two years after Mecom sold out to local car dealer Tom Benson. Benson made the shrewd move of hiring Jim Finks, who had built Super Bowl teams in Minnesota and Chicago as general manager. Finks hired tough Jim Mora as his coach, and the Saints had a run of seven non-losing seasons in a row led by their skilled linebacker quartet of Sam Mills, Ricky Jackson, Pat Swilling and Vaughn Johnson. Under Mora, the Saints made their first trip to the playoffs in 1987 and won their first division title in 1991.

Unfortunately, Jim Mora also is the only coach with over 100 wins in the NFL who never won a playoff game — that streak would continue later when he coached the Colts led by Archie Manning's son Peyton. Perhaps New Orleans hoodoo is to blame. Proven winners Hank Stram, Dick Nolan and Bum Phillips all came to the Crescent City and failed. When Mora quit, Mike Ditka was hired the next year and flopped spectacularly — even trading his whole 1999 draft for one player, Ricky Williams, who did not quite pan out. After Ditka, the combination of new general manager Randy Mueller and new coach Jim Haslett righted the ship in 2000 behind new quarterback Aaron Brooks. In that year the Saints won their first playoff game in history. However, Haslett's four seasons have been plagued persistently by letdowns and late season collapses. The Saints have had the fewest winning seasons of any franchise existing before 1995; their one playoff victory is also the lowest of those 28 oldest teams. The Saints, it seems, never have had their mojo working.

Origin of name: It was no accident that the NFL franchise was awarded to New Orleans on November 1, 1966, All Saints Day, since the city is commonly equated with the traditional song "When the Saints Go Marching In." A "name that team" contest was held and Saints was chosen.

Time till first championship: 37 years and counting.

Record by Decade

	Regular Season			Postseason		
	Won	Lost	Tied	Won	Lost	Championships
1960s	12	29	1	0	0	
1970s	42	98	4	0	0	
1980s	67	85	0	0	1	
1990s	71	89	0	0	3	
2000s	34	30	0	1	1	
All-Time	226	331	5	1	5	0

Winning seasons: 7. Losing Seasons: 25. .500 seasons: 5.

Time since last championship: Never won one.

Coaches			
	Years	*Record*	*Playoffs*
Tom Fears	1967–70	13–34–2	0–0
J.D. Roberts	1970–2	7–25–3	0–0
John North	1973–5	11–23–0	0–0
Ernie Hefferle	1975	1–7–0	0–0
Hank Stram	1976–7	7–21–0	0–0
Dick Nolan	1978–80	15–29–0	0–0
Dick Stanfel	1980	1–3–0	0–0
Bum Phillips	1981–5	27–42–0	0–0
Wade Phillips	1985	1–3–0	0–0
Jim Mora	1986–96	93–74–0	0–4
Rick Venturi	1996	1–7–0	0–0
Mike Ditka	1997–9	15–33–0	0–0
Jim Haslett	2000–3	34–30–0	1–1

Retired numbers: 8 was retired for Archie Manning whose hard luck it was to be forced to squander his quarterbacking skills on a series of terrible teams.

Other numbers worn by these players: None.

Those who wore retired numbers after the honored player: None.

Numbers that should be retired: None.

Owned numbers: No one but Archie Manning ever wore 8.

Numbers worn by Hall of Famers: Doug Atkins 81; Earl Campbell 35; and Jim Taylor 31.

Star power: Eric Allen took 21 from Derek Brown.

Star eclipsed: Craig Heyward wore 45 till Barry Word, 34, left.

Numbers with most great players: 85 has been worn by several good tight ends— Henry Childs, Hoby Brenner, Wesley Walls and Cam Cleeland. 97 has been worn by some outstanding pass rushers— Jumpy Geathers, Renaldo Turnbull and La'Roi Glover.

Worst represented numbers: 14 has been worn by six quarterback failures and draft flop kicker Russell Erxleben. 47 has been worn seven defensive backs, six runners and one tight end, none of whom lasted more than a couple of years in New Orleans.

Number worn by the most players: 86 has been worn 26 times.

Player who wore the most numbers: Kendall Gammon wore four numbers: 46, 60, 62 and 86.

Longest tenure wearing a number: In keeping with the New Orleans bizarre mix of luck, seven Saints have played for the team for 13 years: Kicker Morten Andersen, 7, from 1982 to 1994; linebacker Ricky Jackson, 57, from 1981 to 1993; tackle Stan Brock, 67, from 1980 to 1992; defensive end Frank Warren, 73, from 1981 to 1989 and 1991 to 1994; nose tackle Derland Moore, 74, from 1973 to 1985; tight end Hoby Brenner, 85, from 1981 to 1993; and defensive lineman Jim Wilks, 94, from 1981 to 1993. The careers of all seven overlapped in the early 1980s, and four of the players began in 1981.

Number worn by first ever draft pick: The Saints traded the first pick in the 1967 draft (Bubba Smith) for Gary Cuozzo and the last pick in the first round with which they picked forgettable linebacker Les Kelley who would wear 30.

Biggest draft busts: Draft busts have been in strong supply. Linebacker Les Kelley, 30, was selected 26th in 1967 and appeared in 30 games in three years, while guard John Shinners, 67, was selected 17th in 1969 and appeared in 25 games in three years. Kicker Russell Erxleben, 14, was selected 11th in 1979 and scored 19 points for the Saints. In 1982, the Saints were to have two first round picks. They used one on quarterback Dave Wilson, 18, in the 1981 supplemental draft and used the 13th selection in 1982 to pick receiver Lindsay Scott, 80, who caught 69 passes for one touchdown in four years while Wilson threw 36 tds and 53 interceptions in seven seasons. Finally, the Saints traded their whole draft in 1999 plus their first and second round picks in 2000 to grab runner Ricky Williams, 34, fifth. After 3,000 yards, 20 fumbles, and much controversy, Ricky was sent packing in 2002.

Number worn by first expansion draft pick: The expansion draft was not conducted in rounds. Guard Jake Kupp, 50, lasted the longest—nine years from 1967 to 1975. Billy Kilmer, 17, was the best player the Saints picked.

Number worn by oldest player: Doug Atkins wore 81 as a 39 year old in 1969.

Cameos: Hall of Famers— Jim Taylor 31. All Pros and other notables— Terry Allen 20; Cary Blanchard 10; Dwaine Board 76; Dale Carter 21; Rich Caster 86; Gary Cuozzo 15; Sean Dawkins 86; Ross Fichtner 28; Toni Fritsch 15; Hoyle Granger 40; Earl Gros 40; Alvin Harper 80; Tommy Hart 53; Quadry Ismail 82; Harry Jacobs 52; Haywood Jeffries 80; Jim Kearney 46; Eddie Kennison 82; Tommy Kramer 9; Carl Lee 39; Mark Lee 32; Louis Lipps 86; Jim Marsalis 40; Earl McCullough 80; Darren Perry 39; Elijah Pitts 22; Nate Ramsey 21; Ken Reaves 21; Walt Roberts 27; Joe Scarpati 20; Monty Stickles 87; Skip Vanderbundt 52.

Ones who got away: The Carolina Panthers picked up a Pro Bowl tight end in the expansion draft in Wesley Walls 85. The Saints picked up quarterback Kerry Collins, 13, on waivers from Carolina, but he moved on to the Giants before gaining success. The Panthers signed quarterback Jake Delhomme, 9/12, in 2003 and he took them to the Super Bowl. The high flying Chargers of the early 1980s were led by former Saints Chuck Muncie, 42, and Wes Chandler 89. Chad Morton, 30, has been an exciting returner for the Jets and Redskins.

Least popular numbers: 6, 8, and 31 have each only been worn once.

Last number to be originated: 2 was first worn in 1995 by Chip Lohmiller.

Longest dormant number: 0 has been dormant since 1970. 31 was dormant from 1968 to 2001.

Triskaidekaphobia notes: 13 has featured three quarterback flops.

Shared numbers: All-time Saints receiver Eric Martin and Pro Bowl returner Michael Lewis both wore 84; receivers Wes Chandler and Quinn Early both wore 89; Jim Wilks and Joe Johnson played defensive end for the Saints for a combined 21 years.

Continuity: Henry Childs was replaced in 85 by fellow tight end Hoby Brenner. Defensive end Jim Wilks was replaced in 94 by Joe Johnson. Pro Bowl rusher Renaldo Turnbull was replaced in 97 by Pro Bowl defensive tackle La'Roi Glover.

Discontinuity: Pro Bowl linebacker Sam

Mills was followed in 51 by Ron Childs; Pro Bowl receiver Eric Martin was followed in 84 by Steve Rhem.

Family Connections			
Brothers			
John Fourcade	QB	1987–90	11
Keith Fourcade	LB	1987	53
Jay Hilgenberg	C	1993	62
Joel Hilgenberg	C	1984–93	61
Jake Reed	WR	2000, 2002	86
Dale Carter	DB	2002–3	21
Fathers and Sons			
Earl Leggett	DT	1967–8	72
Brad Leggett	C	1991	62
Steve Stonebreaker	LB	1967–8	37
Mike Stonebreaker	LB	1994	52

Quarterback numbers over 19: None.

Numbers of future NFL head coaches: Jack Del Rio 50.

Numbers of future NFL referees: None.

Players who played other sports: None.

Players more famous after football: None.

First player to wear a number in the 90s: Defensive end Steve Parker wore 96 in 1980.

Number with most points scored: 7 with 1,335 points scored by Morten Andersen (1,318), Toni Linhart (11), and Danny Wuerffel (6).

Number with most yards rushing: 34 with 10,545 yards gained by Ricky Wiliams (3,129), Tony Galbreath (2,865), Craig Heyward (1,458), Ray Zellars (1,351), Jess Phillips (1,219), Tony Lorick (355), Barry Word (133), and Jeff Roddenberger (35).

Number with most receptions: 85 with 791 passes caught by Hoby Brenner (265), Henry Childs (207), Wesley Walls (95), Cam Cleeland (93), Ray Poage (58), John Beasley (36), Ernie Conwell (26), Paul Green (7), Curt Thomas (1), and Nicky Savoie (1).

Number with most touchdown passes: 8 with 115 touchdowns tossed by Archie Manning.

Number with most interceptions: 29 with 53 passes picked off by Sammy Knight (28), Gene Howard (5), Mo Spencer (5), Keith Taylor (4), Vencie Glenn (4), Reggie Sutton

(3), Mark McMillan (2), Vinnie Clark (1), and Rodney Lewis (1).

Oddity: As befitting their Cajun region, the Saints have had at least 25 players with French-sounding first or last names: Bobby Hebert 3; Jake Delhomme 9/12; John Fourcade 11; D'Artagnan Martin 22; Darrell Toussaint 32; Earl Gros 40; Hoyle Granger 40; Toussaint Tyler 42; Garland Jean Batiste 43; Tyrone Legette 43; Elbert Kimbrough 45; Hokie Gajan 46; Keith Fourcade 53; Tom Roussel 54; Brad Leggett 62; Jerry Fontenot 62; Remi Prudhomme 65; Petey Perot 71; Spencer Folau 71; Earl Leggett 72; Jubilee Dunbar 86; Andre Hastings 88; Jonathan Dumbauld 95; Marquess Douglas 95.

Team All-Time Numerical Roster

Those with an "r" following the year 1987 were replacement players during the players' strike. Pro Bowl players for each number are in *Italics*; Hall of Famers are in **Bold** type.

0 Obert Logan (S) 1967.
00 Ken Burrough (WR) 1970.
1 Garo Yepremian (K) 1979, Benny Ricardo (K) 1980-1.
2 Chip Lohmiller (K) 1995, Aaron Brooks (QB) 2000-3.
3 Skip Butler (K) 1971, John Leypoldt (K) 1978, Bobby Hebert (QB) 1985-9, 1991-2, Mark Royals (P) 1997-8, John Carney (K) 2001-3.
4 Mike Cofer (K) 1987r, Steve Walsh (QB) 1990-3, Klaus Wilmsmeyer (P) 1995-6, Toby Gowin (P) 2000-2, Todd Bouman (QB) 2003.
5 Florian Kempf (K) 1987r, Heath Shuler (QB) 1997-8.
6 Tommy Barnhardt (P) 1989-94, 1999.
7 Toni Linhart (K) 1972, Guy Benjamin (QB) 1980, Morten Andersen (K) 1982-94, Danny Wuerffel (QB) 1997-9.
8 *Archie Manning* (QB) 1971-5, 1977-82.
9 Happy Feller (K) 1972-3, George Winslow (P) 1989, Tommy Kramer (QB) 1990, Jake Delhomme (QB) 1998-2000.
10 Charlie Durkee (K) 1967, Julian Fagan (P) 1970-2, Steve O'Neal (P) 1973, Bobby Douglass (QB) 1976-7, Tom Jurich (K) 1978, Steve Mike-Mayer (K) 1978, Brian Hansen (P) 1984-8, Tommy Barnhardt (P) 1987, Cary Blanchard (K) 1992, Doug Brien (K) 1995-2000.
11 Ronnie South (QB) 1968, Jim Ninowski (QB) 1969, Bivian Lee (CB) 1971-5, Ed Burns (QB) 1978-80, Richard Todd (QB) 1984, John Fourcade (QB) 1987-90, Billy Joe Tolliver (QB) 1998-2000.
12 Tom McNeill (P) 1967-9, Bobby Scott (QB) 1973-82, Babe Laufenberg (QB) 1986, Kevin Ingram (QB) 1987, Billy Joe Hobert (QB) 1997-9, Jake Delhomme (QB) 2001-2.
13 Larry Cipa (QB) 1974-5, Doug Nussmeier (QB) 1994-7, Kerry Collins (QB) 1998.
14 Karl Sweetan (QB) 1968, Edd Hargett (QB) 1969-72, Russell Erxleben (K-P) 1979-83, Richard Todd (QB) 1985, Tim Riordan (QB) 1987r, Tom Hodson (QB) 1995-6, J.T. Sullivan (QB) 2002.
15 Gary Cuozzo (QB) 1967, Karl Sweetan (QB) 1968, Charlie Durkee (K) 1968, 1971-2, Bob Davis (QB) 1973, Donnie Gibbs (P) 1974, Rich Szaro (K) 1975-8, Toni Fritsch (K) 1982.
16 Bo Burris (S) 1967-9, Steve Ramsey (QB) 1970, Tom Blanchard (P) 1974-8, Ken Stabler (QB) 1982-4, Mike Buck (QB) 1990-3.
17 Billy Kilmer (QB) 1967-70, Speedy Thomas (WR) 1973-4, Rick Partridge (P) 1979, Jim Everett (QB) 1994-6, Mitch Berger (P) 2003.
18 Hugo Hollas (S) 1970-2, Dave Wilson (QB) 1981,1983-9, Wade Wilson (QB) 1993-4, Terry Guess (WR) 1996, Jeff Blake (QB) 2000-1.
19 Gary Wood (QB) 1967, Tom Dempsey (K) 1969-70, Bill McClard (K) 1973-5, Guido Merkens (QB/WR/DB) 1980-5, Brett Bech (WR) 1997, Alonzo Johnson (WR) 1998, Charlie Jones (WR) 2000.
20 George Youngblood (S) 1967-8, Delles Howell (CB) 1970-2, Eric Felton (CB) 1978-80, Russell Gary (S) 1981-6, John Sutton (CB) 1987r, Othello Henderson (S) 1993-4, Derek Brown (RB) 1995-6, Earl Little (DB) 1999, Terry Allen (RB) 2000, Jay Bellamy (S) 2001-3.
21 John Douglas (CB) 1967-8, Carl Ward (S) 1969, Joe Scarpati (DB) 1970, Reynaud Moore (CB) 1971, Nate Ramsey (CB) 1973, Greg Boyd (S) 1974, Ken Reaves (CB) 1974, David Gray (DB) 1979, John Krimm (S) 1982, Earl Johnson (CB) 1985, *Dalton Hilliard* (RB) 1987-93, Derek Brown (RB) 1994, *Eric Allen* (CB) 1995-7, Earl Little (DB) 1998, Robert Williams (CB) 1999, Steve Israel (DB) 2000-1, Dale Carter (CB) 2002-3.
22 Charlie Brown (RB) 1967-8, Gary Lewis (RB) 1970, Elijah Pitts (RB) 1970, D'Artagnan Martin (CB) 1971, Howard Stevens (RB) 1973-4, Benny Johnson (CB) 1976, Ricky Ray (CB) 1979-80, Tyrone Anthony (RB) 1984-5, Van Jakes (CB) 1986-8, Derrick Taylor (S) 1987r, Michael Mayes (CB) 1989, Gill Fenerty (RB) 1990-1, Brad Muster (FB) 1993, Lorenzo Neal (FB) 1994-6, Tyronne Drakeford (CB) 1998-9, Fred Thomas (CB) 2000-3.
23 *Dave Whitsell* (CB) 1967-9, Doug Wyatt (S) 1970-2, Joe Profit (RB) 1973, Charlie Thomas (KR) 1975, Craig Cassady (DB) 1977, James Mar-

shall (DB) 1980, Buford Jordan (FB) 1986–92, Lorenzo Neal (FB) 1993, Ricky Whittle (RB) 1996, Chris Hewitt (S) 1997–9, Kevin Mathis (CB) 2000–1, Victor Green (S) 2003.

24 Elijah Nevett (CB) 1967–70, Joe Williams (RB) 1972, Johnny Fuller (S) 1973–5, Clarence Chapman (CB) 1976–80, Marvin Lewis (RB) 1982, Terry Hoage (DB) 1984–5, Milton Mack (CB) 1987–91, Scott Woerner (DB) 1987r, Derek Brown (RB) 1993, Mario Bates (RB) 1994–7, Rob Kelly (DB) 1998, Fred Weary (CB) 1999–2001.

25 Jerry Simmons (WR) 1967, Al Dodd (WR) 1969–71, Jerry Moore (S) 1973–4, Leon McQuay (RB) 1976, Wade Bosarge (DB) 1977, Johnnie Poe (CB) 1981–7, *Fred McAfee* (RB) 1991–3, 2000–3, Brad Muster (FB) 1994, Alex Molden (CB) 1996–2000.

26 Jimmy Heidel (S) 1967, Joe Don Looney (RB) 1969, Richard Harvey Sr. (DB) 1971, Margene Adkins (WR) 1972, Steve Rogers (RB) 1975, Jimmy Stewart (S) 1977, Jitter Fields (KR) 1984, Willie Tullis (CB) 1985–6, Stacey Dawsey (WR) 1987r, Vince Buck (DB) 1990–5, Mickey Washington (CB) 1997, Lamar Smith (RB) 1999, *Deuce McAllister* (RB) 2001–3.

27 Walt Roberts (WR) 1967, Bobby Thompson (S) 1969, Rod McNeill (RB) 1974–5, Ray Brown (S) 1978–80, Greg Stemrick (CB) 1983, Antonio Gibson (S) 1986–9, 1992, Reginald Jones (CB) 1991–4, Selwyn Jones (CB) 1994, Vashone Adams (S) 1997, Ken Irvin (DB) 2002, James Fenderson (RB) 2003.

28 Ross Fichtner (S) 1968, Don Shy (RB) 1969, James Ford (RB) 1971–2, Alvin Maxson (RB) 1974–6, Bill Hurley (DB) 1982–3, Greg Harding (DB) 1984, Gene Atkins (S) 1987–93, Derrick Hoskins (S) 1996, Troy Davis (RB) 1997–9, Chris Oldham (DB) 2000–1, Curtis Keaton (RB) 2002, Deveron Harper (CB) 2003.

29 Ray Ogden (WR) 1967, Gene Howard (CB) 1968–70, Billie Hayes (CB) 1972, Maurice Spencer (CB) 1974–6, 1978, Rodney Lewis (CB) 1982–4, Reggie Sutton (CB) 1987–8, Undra Johnson (RB) 1989, Vencie Glenn (S) 1991, Keith Taylor (S) 1992–3, Vinnie Clark (CB) 1994, Mark McMillian (CB) 1996, *Sammy Knight* (S) 1997–2002, Keyuo Craver (CB) 2003.

30 Les Kelley (LB) 1967–9, Bob Shaw (WR) 1970, Bill Harris (RB) 1971, Ernie Jackson (CB) 1972–7, Wayne Wilson (FB) 1979–86, Vincent Alexander (FB) 1987r, Cedric Smith (FB) 1991, Anthony Newman (S) 1995–7, Je'Rod Cherry (DB) 1998–9, Chad Morton (RB) 2000.

31 **Jim Taylor** (RB) 1967, Richard Newsome (DB) 2001.

32 Tom Barrington (RB) 1967–70, Lincoln Minor (RB) 1973, Jim DeRatt (DB) 1975, Kim Jones (FB) 1976–9, Scott Stauch (RB) 1981, Vernon Perry (S) 1983, Darrell Toussaint (DB) 1987r, Paul Frazier (RB) 1989, Mark Lee (CB) 1991, Vaughn Dunbar (RB) 1992, 1994–5, Earnest Hunter (RB) 1996, Aaron Craver (RB) 1998–9, Jerald Moore (RB) 2000, Ki-Jana Carter (RB) 2003.

33 Randy Schultz (RB) 1967–8, Steve Preece (DB) 1969, Mike Strachan (RB) 1975–80, Kevin Gray (DB) 1982, Junior Thurman (DB) 1987r, Ernest Spears (S) 1990, *Tyrone Hughes* (CB) 1993–6, Rob Kelly (DB) 1997, Wilmont Perry (RB) 1998–9, Moran Norris (RB) 2001, Ashley Ambrose (CB) 2003.

34 Tony Lorick (RB) 1968–9, Carlos Bell (TE) 1971, Jess Phillips (RB) 1973–4, Tony Galbreath (RB) 1976–80, Bobby Johnson (DB) 1983–4, 1986, Barry Word (RB) 1987–8, Jeff Rodenberger (FB) 1987r, Craig Heyward (FB) 1989–92, Ray Zellars (FB) 1995–8, Ricky Williams (RB) 1999–2001, Tebucky Jones (S) 2003.

35 Ted Davis (LB) 1967–9, Jim Otis (RB) 1970, Bob Gresham (RB) 1971–2, Henry Matthews (RB) 1973, Jim Van Wagner (FB) 1978, **Earl Campbell** (RB) 1984–5, Bobby Morse (FB) 1989–91, Shane Pahukoa (S) 1995, Chris Canty (DB) 2000, Fakhir Brown (CB) 2002–3.

36 Don McCall (RB) 1967–8, 1970, Dick Davis (RB) 1970, Vic Nyval (RB) 1970, Don Burchfield (TE) 1971, Bob Brown (TE) 1972–3, Andrew Jones (RB) 1975–6, Greg Boykin (RB) 1977, *Rueben Mayes* (RB) 1986–8, 1990, Stanford Jennings (RB) 1991, Derrick Ned (FB) 1993–5, Lamar Smith (RB) 1998, 2003, Corey Harris (CB) 1999, Michael Hawthorne (DB) 2000–2.

37 Steve Stonebreaker (LB) 1967–8, *Tommy Myers* (S) 1972–81, Mel Gray (RB) 1986–8, *Bennie Thompson* (S) 1989–91, Jimmy Spencer (CB) 1992–5, Je'Rod Cherry (DB) 1996–7, Chad Cota (S) 1998, Dino Philyaw (RB) 1999, Steve Gleason (DD) 2000–3.

38 Phil Vandersea (LB) 1967, *Tony Baker* (RB) 1968–71, Bill Butler (RB) 1972–4, *George Rogers* (HB) 1981–4, Calvin Nicholson (CB) 1989, 1991, Donovan Greer (CB) 1997.

39 Ernie Wheelwright (RB) 1967–70, Odell Lawson (RB) 1973–4, Morris LaGrand (RB) 1975, Brett Maxie (S) 1985–93, Carl Lee (DB) 1994, John Covington (S) 1995, Darren Perry (DB) 2000.

40 Earl Gros (RB) 1970, Hoyle Granger (RB) 1971, Terry Schmidt (CB) 1974–5, Jim Marsalis (S) 1977, Greg Knafelc (TE) 1983, *Dalton Hilliard* (RB) 1986, Michael Adams (DB) 1987–8, Robert Massey (CB) 1989–90, Wes Bender (FB) 1997, Marvin Powell (FB) 1999, Brian Milne (RB) 2000, Mel Mitchell (DB) 2002.

41 John Gilliam (WR) 1967, 1977, Bob Newland (WR) 1971–4, Jimmy Rogers (RB) 1980–4, Toi Cook (CB) 1987–93, William Strong (CB) 1995–6.

42 John Gilliam (WR) 1968, Claxton Welch (RB) 1970, Jim Strong (RB) 1971–2, Joel Parker

(WR) 1974–5, *Chuck Muncie* (RB) 1976–80, Toussaint Tyler (RB) 1981–2, Dana McLemore (DB) 1986, Ray Wilson (S) 1994, Fred Weary (CB) 1998, Willie Clay (S) 1999.

43 Dicky Lyons (S) 1970, Dave Kopay (RB) 1971, Larry Collins (RB) 1980, Bobby Fowler (FB) 1984–5, Jean Batiste Garland (FB) 1987, Kim Phillips (CB) 1989, Tyrone Legette (CB) 1992–5, Ashley Ambrose (CB) 1999, Keyuo Craver (DB) 2002.

44 George Rose (CB) 1967, Ollie Cordill (P) 1969, Mike Fink (CB) 1973, Chris Farasopoulos (S) 1974, Chuck Crist (S) 1975–7, *Dave Waymer* (DB) 1980–9, J.J. McCleskey (S) 1995–6, Fred McCrary (FB) 1997, Rob Kelly (DB) 1999–2000, Terrelle Smith (FB) 2000–3.

45 Jimmy Jordan (RB) 1967, Elbert Kimbrough (S) 1968, Arthur Green (RB) 1972, Pete Athas (S) 1976, Jack Holmes (RB) 1978–82, Tim Wilson (FB) 1983–4, John Williams (FB) 1986, Nate Johnson (RB) 1987r, Craig Heyward (FB) 1988, Stan Petry (CB) 1991, Israel Byrd (CB) 1993–5.

46 Dan Abramowicz (WR) 1967–73, Jim Kearney (S) 1976, Hokie Gajan (FB) 1982–5, Sean Lumpkin (S) 1992–6, Kendall Gammon (C) 1998.

47 Bruce Cortez (CB) 1967, Marv Woodson (S) 1969, Bill Dusenberry (RB) 1970, Virgil Robinson (RB) 1971–2, Jack DeGrenier (RB) 1974, Mike Spivey (CB) 1980–1, Cliff Austin (RB) 1983, David Rackley (DB) 1985, Dwight Beverly (RB) 1987r, Cedric Mack (CB) 1992–3, Travis Davis (S) 1995, Greg Jackson (S) 1996, Josh Wilcox (TE) 1998–9, Kevin Houser (RB) 2000–3.

48 *Andy Livingston* (RB) 1969–70, Don Schwartz (S) 1978–80, Jeff Groth (WR) 1981, James Fenderson (RB) 2002, David Sloan (TE) 2003.

49 Major Hazelton (DB) 1970, Bob Wicks (WR) 1974, Ralph McGill (S) 1978–9, Artie Owens (WR) 1980, Frank Wattelet (S) 1981–7, Tommie Stowers (TE) 1992–3.

50 *Jake Kupp* (G) 1967–75, Ken Bordelon (LB) 1976–7, 1979–82, Jack Del Rio (LB) 1985–6, Philip James (C) 1987r, John Johnson (LB) 1995, Ink Aleaga (LB) 1997, Kevin Mitchell (LB) 1999, Corey Terry (LB) 2000, James Allen (LB) 2002–3.

51 Jim Fraser (P) 1968, Bill Saul (LB) 1969, John Didion (LB-C) 1971–4, Rusty Chambers (LB) 1975–6, Sylvester Croom (C) 1975, Warren Capone (LB) 1976, Ron Crosby (LB) 1978, Stan Holloway (LB) 1980, Whitney Paul (LB) 1982–5, *Sam Mills* (LB) 1986–94, Larry McCoy (LB) 1987r, Ron Childs (LB) 1995, Derrick Barnes (LB) 1997, Phil Clarke (LB) 1999–2001, Bryan Cox (LB) 2002.

52 Frank Emanuel (LB) 1970, Harry Jacobs (LB) 1970, John Huard (LB) 1971, Dick Palmer (LB) 1972–3, Mike Lemon (LB) 1975, Skip Vanderbundt (LB) 1978, Jim Kovach (LB) 1979–85, Brian Forde (LB) 1988–91, Mike Stonebreaker (LB) 1994, Richard Harvey Jr. (LB) 1995–7, Vin-

son Smith (LB) 1998–9, Sedrick Hodge (LB) 2001–3.

53 Dave Simmons (LB) 1967, Dick Absher (LB) 1969–71, Billy Hobbs (LB) 1972, Rick Kingrea (LB) 1973–7, Tommy Hart (DE) 1980, Scott Pelluer (LB) 1981–5, 1987, *Vaughan Johnson* (LB) 1986–93, Keith Fourcade (LB) 1987r, Don Davis (LB) 1996–8, Donta Jones (LB) 2000, Roger Knight (LB) 2002–3.

54 Joe Wendryhoski (C) 1967–8, Tom Roussel (LB) 1971–2, Dale Lindsey (LB) 1973, Rick Middleton (LB) 1974–5, Pat Hughes (LB) 1977–9, Paul Ryczek (C) 1981, Ed Simonini (LB) 1982, Alvin Toles (LB) 1985–8, Bill Roe (LB) 1987r, Winfred Tubbs (LB) 1994–7, Ink Aleaga (LB) 1998–9, Darrin Smith (LB) 2000–3.

55 Jackie Burkett (LB) 1967–70, Jim Flanigan (LB) 1971, Tom Stincic (LB) 1972, Bob Creech (LB) 1973, Don Coleman (LB) 1974–5, Floyd Rice (LB) 1978, Dave Washington (LB) 1980, Rob Nairne (LB) 1981–3, Joe Kohlbrand (LB) 1985–9, Joe DeForest (LB) 1987r, Scott Ross (LB) 1991, Reggie Freeman (LB) 1993, Mark Fields (LB) 1995–2000, Deshone Myles (LB) 2001, Travis Carroll (LB) 2002–3.

56 Jim Ferguson (LB) 1968, Hap Farber (LB) 1970, Willie Hall (LB) 1972–3, Lee Gross (C) 1975–7, Rusty Rebowe (LB) 1978, Reggie Mathis (LB) 1979–80, Dennis Winston (LB) 1982–5, *Pat Swilling* (LB) 1986–92, Ron Weissenhofer (LB) 1987r, Ernest Dixon (LB) 1994–7, Chris Bordano (LB) 1998–9, Charlie Clemons (LB) 2000–2, Orlando Ruff (LB) 2003.

57 Mike Morgan (LB) 1969–70, Jim Merlo (LB) 1973–4, 1976–9, Larry Coombs (C) 1980, *Rickey Jackson* (LB) 1981–93, Curtis Holden (LB) 2001.

58 Eli Strand (G) 1967, Joe Federspiel (LB) 1972–80, Glen Redd (LB) 1981, 1983–6, Scott Leach (LB) 1987r, Darion Conner (LB) 1994, Brian Jones (LB) 1995–6, 1998, Joe Tuipala (LB) 1999, Brian Williams (LB) 2001, Junior Johnson (LB) 2002, Willie Grant (LB) 2003.

59 Fred Whittingham (LB) 1967–8, Wayne Colman (LB) 1969–74, 1976, Chuck Evans (LB) 1980–1, Chris Martin (LB) 1983, James Campen (C/G) 1987–8, Rufus Porter (LB) 1995–6, *Keith Mitchell* (LB) 1997–2001, J.J. Jones (LB) 2002, Derrick Rodgers (LB) 2003.

60 Brian Schweda (DE) 1967–8, Doug Sutherland (G) 1970, Carl Cunningham (LB) 1971, Greg Westbrooks (LB) 1975–7, Don Reese (DE) 1978–80, Steve Korte (C) 1983–90, Derek Kennard (G) 1991–3, Craig Novitsky (C/T) 1994–6, Kendall Gammon (C) 1997, Robert Hunt (G) 1999.

61 Del Williams (G) 1967–73, Mike Watson (T) 1977, Sam Adams (G) 1981, *Joel Hilgenberg* (C/G) 1984–93, Greg Loberg (G/T) 1987r, Ed King (G) 1995–7, Montrae Holland (G) 2003.

62 Ross Gwinn (G) 1968, John Hill (C) 1975–84, Brad Leggett (C) 1990–1, Jay Hilgenberg (C) 1993, Jeff Uhlenhake (C) 1994–5, Kendall Gammon (C) 1996, Jerry Fontenot (C) 1997–2003.

63 Roy Schmidt (G) 1967–8, Norman Davis (G) 1969, Steve Baumgartner (DE) 1973–7, Barry Bennett (DE) 1978–81, Roger Finnie (T) 1979, *Brad Edelman* (G) 1982–9, Karl Dunbar (DE) 1993, Donald Willis (G) 1995–7, Wally Williams (G) 1999–2002.

64 Ray Hester (LB) 1971–3, Andy Maurer (G) 1974, Dave Lafary (T) 1977–85, Ted Elliott (NT) 1987r, Scott Adams (G) 1994, Robert Newkirk (DE) 1999, Kendyl Jacox (G) 2002–3.

65 Tom Carr (DE) 1968, Remi Prudhomme (G/C) 1971–72, Dave Thompson (T) 1974–5, Robert Woods (T) 1977–80, Bob Young (G) 1981, David Carter (C) 1984–5, Adam Schreiber (G) 1985, Steve Trapilo (G) 1987–90, 1992, Willie Williams (T) 1994, Chris Naeole (G) 1997–2001, *LeCharles Bentley* (G) 2002–3.

66 Bill Cody (LB) 1967–70, Royce Smith (G) 1972–3, Rocky Rasley (G) 1974, Tom Wickert (G) 1975–6, David Knowles (T) 1977, Conrad Dobler (G) 1978–9, Louis Oubre (G) 1982–4, Chuck Commiskey (G) 1986–8, Larry Williams (G) 1991, Mike Verstegen (G) 1995–7, Victor Riley (OL) 2002.

67 George Harvey (G) 1967, John Shinners (G) 1969–71, Bob Kuziel (C) 1972, Phil LaPorta (T) 1974–5, John Watson (T) 1977–9, Stan Brock (T) 1980–92, Andy McCollum (G) 1994–8, Bubba Miller (C) 2002.

68 Wimpy Winther (C) 1972, Terry Stieve (G) 1976–7, Richard Neal (DE) 1978, Fred Sturt (G) 1978–81, Pat Saindon (G) 1986, Walter Housman (T/G) 1987r, Paul Jetton (G) 1992–3, Alan Kline (T) 1994–5, Kyle Turley (G/T) 1998–2002, Victor Riley (T) 2003.

69 Oakley Dalton (DT) 1977, Bill Fifer (G) 1978, Nat Hudson (G) 1981, Ralph Williams (G) 1985–6, Pat Swoopes (NT) 1987, 1989, Les Miller (NT) 1991–4, Tom Ackerman (C/G) 1996–2001.

70 Errol Linden (T) 1969–70, Sam Holden (T) 1971, Craig Robinson (T) 1972–3, Dave Hubbard (T) 1977, Mark Meseroll (T) 1978, Jim Rourke (T) 1985, Bill Contz (T) 1986–8, Kevin Haverdink (T) 1989–90, Chris Port (G/T) 1991–5, Uhuru Hamiter (DL) 1998, Marcus Price (OL) 2000–1.

71 Dick Anderson (T) 1967, Dave McCormick (T) 1968, Willie Townes (DE) 1970, Faddie Tillman (DT) 1972, Paul Fersen (T) 1973–4, Kurt Schumacher (G) 1975–7, James Taylor (T) 1978–81, Petey Perot (G) 1985, Casey Merrill (DT) 1986, Ken Kaplan (T) 1987, Richard Cooper (T) 1990–5, Fred Stokes (DE) 1996, Ricky Siglar (T) 1997–8, Spencer Folau (T) 2002–3.

72 Earl Leggett (DT) 1967–8, Don Talbert (T) 1969–70, Joe Owens (DE) 1971–5, Jeff Hart (T) 1976, Mike Fultz (DT) 1977–80, Leon Gray (T)

1982–3, Chris Ward (T) 1984, Jim Dombrowski (G/T) 1986–96, Trezelle Jenkins (T) 1997, Wayne Gandy (T) 2003.

73 Jerry Sturm (T/C) 1967–70, Bill Sandeman (T) 1967, John Mooring (T) 1974, Jeff Winans (DT) 1976, Joe Campbell (DE) 1977–80, Frank Warren (DE) 1981–9, 1991–4, Isaac Davis (G) 1997.

74 Mike Tilleman (DT) 1967–70, Doug Mooers (DE) 1971–2, Derland Moore (NT) 1973–85, William Leach (G/T) 1987r, Ted Gregory (NT) 1988, Kevin Haverdink (T) 1991, Cecil Gray (T) 1993, Herman Carroll (DE) 1994, Clarence Jones (T) 1996–8, Steve Scifres (T) 1999, Scott Sanderson (T) 2001–2, Dave McCormick (T) 1967.

75 Mike Rengel (DT) 1969, Mike Richey (T) 1970, Mike Crangle (DE) 1972, Elex Price (DT) 1973–80, *Bruce Clark* (DE) 1982–8, Doug Marrone (G) 1989, Baron Rollins (G) 1994, Emile Palmer (DT) 1996, Julian Pittman (DT) 1998.

76 Dave Rowe (DT) 1967–70, Don Morrison (T) 1971–7, Kevin Hunt (T) 1978, Jim Pietrzak (C) 1979–84, Dwaine Board (DE) 1988, Gene McGuire (C) 1992, Rickie Shaw (T) 1993, Jeff Davidson (T) 1994, Keno Hills (G/T) 1996–9, Tutan Reyes (T) 2000–1.

77 Ray Rissmiller (T) 1967, Jim Boeke (T) 1968, Mike Taylor (T) 1969–70, Dan Goich (DT) 1971, Carl Johnson (G) 1972–3, Chris Morris (T) 1975, Marv Montgomery (T) 1976–7, Gary Anderson (G) 1978, Jerry Boyarsky (NT) 1981, Daren Gilbert (T) 1985–8, *William Roaf* (T) 1993–2001.

78 Jerry Jones (T) 1967–9, Glen Ray Hines (T) 1971–2, Billy Newsome (DE) 1973–4, Elois Grooms (DE) 1975–81, Kelvin Clark (G) 1982–5, Shawn Knight (DE) 1987, Jeff Walker (G) 1988–9, Mike Keim (T) 1991, Tom Backes (G) 1993, Tom Roth (C/G) 1994, Daryl Terrell (T) 1999–2001, Jon Stinchcomb (T) 2003.

79 Lou Cordileone (DT) 1967–8, Clovis Swinney (DT) 1970, Emanuel Zanders (G) 1974–80, Chuck Slaughter (T) 1982, Henry Thomas (G) 1987r, Glenn Derby (T) 1989–90, Tory Epps (DT) 1995, Troy Wilson (DE) 1998, Mike Halapin (G) 1999.

80 Jim Garcia (DE) 1967, Mike Walker (DE) 1971, Doug Winslow (WR) 1973, Sam Havrilak (WR) 1974, Earl McCullough (WR) 1974, Larry Burton (WR) 1975–7, Gordon Banks (WR) 1980–1, Lindsay Scott (WR) 1982–5, Malcolm Barnwell (WR) 1985, Mike Miller (WR) 1985, Herbert Harris (WR) 1986–7, Stacey Dawsey (WR) 1987r, Brett Perriman (WR) 1988–90, Wesley Carroll (WR) 1991–2, Marcus Dowdell (WR) 1993, Tyrone Johnson (WR) 1994, Tony Johnson (TE) 1996, 1998, Haywood Jeffires (WR) 1996, Daryl Hobbs (WR) 1997, P.J. Franklin (WR) 1999, Robert Wilson (WR) 2000–1, Jerome Pathon (WR) 2002–3.

81 Doug Atkins (DE) 1967–9, Jesse Anderson

(TE) 1993, Michael Haynes (WR) 1994–6, Randal Hill (WR) 1997, Scott Slutzker (TE) 1998, Lawrence Dawsey (WR) 1999, Lamont Hall (TE) 2000–1, Zachary Hilton (TE) 2003.

82 Johnny Brewer (LB) 1968–70, Bob Pollard (DE) 1971–7, Ike Harris (WR) 1978–81, John Tice (TE) 1983–92, Darren Gottschalk (TE) 1987r, Ken O'Neal (TE) 1987r, Irv Smith (TE) 1993–7, Qadry Ismail (WR) 1998, Eddie Kennison (WR) 1999, Boo Williams (TE) 2001–3.

83 Vern Burke (TE) 1967, Dave Parks (TE) 1968–72, Len Garrett (TE) 1973–5, Andy Hamilton (WR) 1975, Tinker Owens (WR) 1976, 1978–80, Kenny Duckett (WR) 1983–4, Carl Roaches (KR) 1985, Kelvin Edwards (WR) 1986, Cliff Benson (TE) 1987, Dwight Walker (WR) 1987r, Greg Scales (TE) 1988–91, Torrance Small (WR) 1992–6, Keith Poole (WR) 1997–2000, Albert Connell (WR) 2001, Donte Stallworth (WR) 2002–3.

84 Jim Hester (TE) 1967–9, Lawrence Estes (DE) 1970–1, Preston Riley (WR) 1973, Paul Seal (TE) 1974–6, Rich Mauti (WR) 1977–80, 1982–3, Junior Miller (TE) 1984, *Eric Martin* (WR) 1985–93, Steve Rhem (WR) 1994–5, Eric Guliford (WR) 1997–8, Scott Slutzker (TE) 1999, *Michael Lewis* (KR) 2001–3.

85 Ray Poage (TE) 1967–70, Cephus Weatherspoon (WR) 1972, John Beasley (TE) 1973–4, *Henry Childs* (TE) 1974–80, *Hoby Brenner* (TE) 1981–93, Curtland Thomas (WR) 1987r, Wesley Walls (TE) 1994–5, Paul Green (TE) 1996, Nicky Savoie (TE) 1997, Cameron Cleeland (TE) 1998–2001, Ernie Conwell (TE) 2003.

86 Tom Hall (WR) 1967, Dan Colchico (DE) 1969, Creston Whitaker (WR) 1972, Jubilee Dunbar (WR) 1973, Dave Davis (WR) 1974, Richard Williams (WR) 1974, Melvin Baker (WR) 1975, James Thaxton (TE) 1976–7, Tom Donovan (WR) 1980, Rich Caster (TE) 1981, Rich Martini (WR) 1981, Jeff Groth (WR) 1982–5, Mike Jones (WR) 1986–7, Victor Harrison (WR) 1987r, Cliff Benson (TE) 1988, Rod Harris (WR) 1989, Gerald Alphin (WR) 1990–1, Patrick Newman (WR) 1991–4, Marcus Dowdell (WR) 1992, Louis Lipps (WR) 1992, J.J. McCleskey (S) 1994, Kirk Botkin (TE) 1994–5, Tony Johnson (TE) 1996–7, Gunnard Twyner (WR) 1997, Sean Dawkins (WR) 1998, Kendall Gammon (TE) 1999, Jake Reed (WR) 2000, 2002, Onome Ojo (WR) 2001, Walter Rasby (TE) 2003.

87 Monty Stickles (TE) 1968, Richard Neal (DE) 1969–72, Mike Kelly (TE) 1973, Don Herrmann (WR) 1975–7, Larry Hardy (TE) 1978–85, Lonzell Hill (WR) 1987–90, Malcolm Scott (TE) 1987r, Frank Wainwright (TE) 1991–3, Lee DeRamus (WR) 1995–6, John Farquhar (TE) 1997–8, *Joe Horn* (WR) 2000–3.

88 Ben Hart (S) 1967, Dave Szymakowski

(WR) 1968, Andy Dorris (DE) 1973–6, Fred Hyatt (WR) 1973, Joel Parker (WR) 1977, Brooks Williams (TE) 1978–81, Don Bass (TE) 1982, Eugene Goodlow (WR) 1983–6, Mike Waters (TE) 1987, Mark Pattison (WR) 1987–8, Floyd Turner (WR) 1989–93, Derrell Mitchell (WR) 1994, Hendrick Lusk (TE) 1996, Andre Hastings (WR) 1997–9, Willie Jackson (WR) 2000–1, David Sloan (TE) 2002, Talman Gardner (WR) 2003.

89 Kent Kramer (TE) 1967, Dave Long (DE) 1969–72, Bert Askson (TE) 1973, Gil Chapman (WR) 1975, Len Willis (WR) 1977, *Wes Chandler* (WR) 1978–81, Aundra Thompson (WR) 1981–2, Tyrone Young (WR) 1983–4, Robert Clark (WR) 1987–8, Joe Thomas (WR) 1987r, Mike Jones (WR) 1989, Derrick Shepard (WR) 1989, Quinn Early (WR) 1991–5, Mercury Hayes (WR) 1996–7, Brett Bech (WR) 1998–9, Dave Stachelski (TE) 2000–1, Wane McGarity (WR) 2001, Derrick Lewis (WR) 2002–3.

90 Walter Johnson (LB) 1989, James Williams (LB) 1990–4, Israel Stanley (DE) 1995, Jared Tomich (DE) 1997–2000, Kenny Smith (DL) 2001–3.

91 Monte Bennett (DT) 1981, Ken Marchiol (LB) 1987r, Robert Goff (NT) 1990–5, Brady Smith (DE) 1996–9, Grady Jackson (DT) 2002–3.

92 James Haynes (LB) 1984–9, DeMond Winston (LB) 1990, 1992–4, Toddrick McIntosh (DE) 1995, Darren Mickell (DE) 1996–7, Ernest Jones (DE) 1998, Troy Wilson (DE) 1999, Martin Chase (DE) 2000–2, Henry Ford (DT) 2003.

93 Gary Lewis (NT) 1983, Kevin Young (DE) 1987r, *Wayne Martin* (DE/DT) 1989–99, Darren Howard (DE) 2000–3.

94 Jim Wilks (DE/NT) 1981–93, *Joe Johnson* (DE) 1994–2001, Charles Grant (DL) 2002–3.

95 Jonathan Dumbauld (DE) 1986, 1988, Robert Brannon (DE) 1987r, Travis Davis (NT) 1990, Ronnie Dixon (NT) 1993, Ernest Jones (DE) 1995, Austin Robbins (DT) 1996–9, Marques Douglas (DE) 2000, Howard Green (DE) 2003.

96 Steve Parker (DE) 1980, Don Thorp (NT) 1984, Sheldon Andrus (NT) 1986–7, Michael Simmons (DE) 1989–90, Jeff Faulkner (DE) 1993, Mark Gunn (DE) 1994, Dameian Jeffries (DE) 1995, Uhuru Hamiter (DL) 1999, Melvin Williams (DE) 2003.

97 James Geathers (DE) 1984–9, *Renaldo Turnbull* (DE/LB) 1990–6, *La'Roi Glover* (DT) 1997–2001, Jonathan Sullivan (DT) 2003.

98 Reggie Lewis (DE) 1982–4, Milford Hodge (DE) 1986, Jim Hanna (NT) 1994, Ron Warner (LB) 1998, Willie Whitehead (LB) 1999–2003.

99 Tony Elliott (NT) 1982–8, Joel Smeenge (DE/LB) 1990–4, Willie Broughton (DT) 1995–6, Pio Sagapolutele (DT) 1997, Darren Mickell (DE) 1999, Norman Hand (DT) 2000–2, Kendrick Allen (DT) 2003.

NEW YORK GIANTS

The franchise: Harvard's drop kicking star Charlie Brickley formed the NFL's original New York Giants in 1921, but they went 0–2 and folded in the same season. Five years later legal bookmaker Tim Mara brought the NFL into New York permanently by buying the football rights to the nation's largest city for $500 in 1925. Mara poured money into the club in the first year and was looking at a major loss until he scheduled a postseason exhibition game against the Chicago Bears featuring newly-signed sensation Red Grange. Grange drew a crowd of 70,000 and put the Giants in the black. The next year, Grange formed his own American Football League and placed himself on the AFL's New York Yankees. The AFL only lasted a year, but the Yankees were brought into the NFL where they competed against the Giants for two more years before that franchise folded.

On the field, the Giants were a success from the start, posting winning seasons in 1925 and 1926 before winning the NFL championship in 1927. Two years later, New York obtained Benny Friedman, the best passer in football, and won 13 games in both 1929 and 1930, but finished second to Green Bay each year. A new era began in 1931 with the hiring of tackle Steve Owen as head coach; he would remain in that position for 23 years. Owen specialized in defensive alignments and eventually devised the Umbrella Defense that would evolve into the modern 4–3 defense. He also was noted for such offensive innovations as the A Formation and the swing T. Owen fashioned a perennial contender that was led by rock-solid center Mel Hein for 15 years and that played in eight championship games in his first 16 years, winning two. The Giants lost the first NFL title game in 1933 to the Bears on a tricky hook-and-lateral on the game's final play; they got their revenge on the Bears the following year by winning the first "Sneaker Game" on an icy, slick field. Also in 1934, Tim Mara began transferring ownership and control of the team to his two sons

Jack and Wellington. The early Giants featured a host of talented backs including Ken Strong, Tuffy Leemans, Hank Soar and Ward Cuff as well as top ends like Red Badgro, Jim Lee Howell and Jim Poole. The 1946 title game made news when it was learned that back Merle Hapes and quarterback Frank Filchock were approached by gamblers and failed to report the contact to the league. Hapes was suspended immediately and Filchock was suspended right after the championship loss to another superior Bear team.

From that point on, Owen was only able to manage one more playoff appearance in his final seven seasons as coach. These were tough years for the Giants since they were faced also with competition from the AAFC's New York Yankees and the NFL's New York Bulldogs (a shift of the Boston Yanks franchise). Once the AAFC went out of business, the Yankees and Bulldogs merged as the New York Yanks for 1950 and 1951 before they too failed. The two positive additions to the Giants in that time were its first black player, Hall of Famer Emlen Tunnell—"Mr. Offense on Defense," and astute defensive back Tom Landry. When Jim Lee Howell was named coach in 1954, he lost no time delegating defensive authority to Landry and hiring Vince Lombardi to handle the offense. No team has ever had two more high-powered assistants.

The 1950s Giants were guided by quarterback Charlie Conerly and halfback Frank Gifford on offense, but the real strength of the team was its defense. Soon, the fans would join in with chants of "DEFENSE" to stir the team on. That defense was led by a great front four featuring Andy Robustelli and free-floating, rough-and-dirty middle linebacker named Sam Huff. Everything came together in 1956 when the Giants, again wearing sneakers, demolished the Bears 47–7 in the title game. They returned to the championship game in both 1958 and 1959, but lost twice to the Colts, with the 1958 sudden death overtime game being the harbinger of the NFL's rapid growth via television in the coming decade. Another loss in 1959 was the death of founder Tim Mara at the age of 72.

At the start of the new decade, Howell quit and with Lombardi and Landry already gone to Green Bay and Dallas, assistant Allie Sherman was hired as head man. Trades for quarterback Y.A. Tittle and receiver Del Shofner opened up the passing game, and the Giants played for three straight championships from 1961 to 1963, but lost every one. As the Giants' stars aged, Sherman traded them away, but did not replace them with players of equal value, so the bottom fell out in 1964. Wellington's brother Jack died in 1965, and Jack's son Tim took control of 50 percent of the team. During the next 20 years under five coaches, New York would have only three winning seasons and would move into the Meadowlands of North Jersey.

George Young was brought in as general manager in 1979 by the feuding Maras, Wellington and his nephew Tim. Four years later, Young hired Bill Parcells as coach, and the 1980s Giants were a combination of a grind-it-out offense directed by efficient quarterback Phil Simms and a blitzing, disruptive defense led by seminal linebacker Lawrence Taylor. The Giants' smash-mouth approach delivered wins in Super Bowl XXI (39–20 over the Broncos) and XXV (20–19 over the Bills). In 1991, Parcells retired for the first time and Tim Mara sold his half interest in the Giants to Bob Tisch. In 1997 Jim Fassell became coach, and he got the Giants back to Super Bowl XXXV in 2000

when they lost badly to the Ravens. However, they have remained a competitive club year after year. Both Tim Mara the elder and his son Wellington are in the Pro Football Hall of Fame.

Origin of name: As was a common custom of the time, the football Giants were named after the Major League baseball team in town, the team whose stadium they used.

Time till first championship: Three years.

Time since last championship: 14 years and counting.

Retired numbers: The Giants have a rich

Record by Decade

	Regular Season			Postseason		
	Won	Lost	Tied	Won	Lost	Championships
1920s	44	17	5	0	0	1927
1930s	80	39	8	2	3	1934, 1938
1940s	55	47	8	0	4	
1950s	76	41	3	2	3	1956
1960s	69	63	6	0	3	
1970s	50	93	1	0	0	
1980s	81	70	1	6	4	1986
1990s	83	76	1	4	2	1990
2000s	33	31	0	2	2	
All-Time	571	477	33	16	21	6

Winning seasons: 44. Losing Seasons: 28. .500 seasons: 7.

Coaches

	Years	Record	Playoffs
Robert Folwell	1925	8–4–0	0–0
Joe Alexander	1926	8–4–1	0–0
Earl Potteiger (1)	1927–8	15–8–3	0–0
LeRoy Andrews	1929–30	24–5–1	0–0
Benny Friedman/Steve Owen	1930	2–0–0	0–0
Steve Owen (2)	1931–53	151–100–17	2–8
Jim Lee Howell (1)	1954–60	53–27–4	2–2
Allie Sherman	1961–8	57–51–4	0–3
Alex Webster	1969–73	29–40–1	0–0
Bill Arnsparger	1974–6	7–28–0	0–0
John McVay	1976–8	14–23–0	0–0
Ray Perkins	1979–82	23–34–0	1–1
Bill Parcells (2)	1983–90	77–49–1	8–3
Ray Handley	1991–2	14–18–0	0–0
Dan Reeves	1993–6	31–33–0	1–1
Jim Fassell	1997–03	58–53–1	2–3

(Championships in parentheses)

history, and only the Bears have retired more uniform numbers in the NFL. Many of these are questionable, though. There is no argument about Hall of Famers Mel Hein 7, Frank Gifford 16, or Lawrence Taylor 56. However, other Hall of Famers have weaker cases. Ray Flaherty, 1, was a talented end for the Giants, but is in Canton primarily as a Redskins coach; Y.A. Tittle, 14, was very productive in New York, but spent only four years as a Giant; Tuffy Leemans, 4, and Ken Strong, 50, were both great backs in the 1930s and 1940s, but both don't deserve their uniforms retired. Of the non–Hall of Famers, quarterbacks Phil Simms, 11, and Charlie Conerly, 42, both may have made the Hall if they had had better receivers, and both were champions who deserve to have their numbers honored. Al Blozis, 32, had his number retired in memory of his making the ultimate sacrifice in World War II. Joe Morrison, 40, was a fine and versatile player for many years, but retiring his number is inexplicable.

Other numbers worn by these players: Ken Strong also wore 30; Ray Flaherty also wore 6, 8 and 44.

Those who wore retired numbers after the honored player: Ray Flaherty's 1 was worn later by Frank Cope. Tuffy Leemans' 4 was worn later by Leland Shaffer, Frank Reagan, and Joe Prokop. Frank Gifford's 16 was worn later by Milt Plum and Norm Snead. Ken Strong's 50 was worn later by Ed Widseth, Kay Bell, Bull Karcis, Rolland Caranci, and Bobby Abrams.

Numbers that should be retired: A better case can be made for dominant Hall of Famers tackle Rosey Brown, 79, safety Emlen Tunnell, 45, and even linebacker Sam Huff, 70, than for Flaherty, Leemans, Tittle, Blozis, and Morrison.

Owned numbers: None.

Numbers worn by Hall of Famers: Red Badgro 17; Roosevelt Brown 79; Larry Csonka 39; Ray Flaherty 1/6/8/44; Frank Gifford 16; Joe Guyon 11; Mel Hein 7; Pete Henry 55; Arnie Herber 20; Cal Hubbard 41/60; Sam Huff 70; Tuffy Leemans 4; Don Maynard 13; Hugh McElhenny 39; Steve Owen 6/12/36/44/50/55; Andy Robustelli 81; Ken Strong 30/50; Fran Tarkenton 10; Lawrence Taylor 56; Jim Thorpe 21; Y.A. Tittle 14; Emlen Tunnell 45; and Arnie Weinmeister 73.

Star power: Larry Csonka took 39 from Clyde Powers; Lawrence Taylor took 56 from Jim Clack.

Star eclipsed: Matt Hazeltine wore 64 because Ralph Heck wore 55. Amani Toomer wore 89 till Thomas Lewis, 81, left.

Numbers with most great players: All five players who wore 1 made All Pro. 20 has been worn by Hall of Famer Arnie Herber, and Pro Bowl safety Jim Patton and runner Joe Morris. 60 has been worn by Hall of Famer Cal Hubbard and five other star linemen — Monk Edwards, Len Younce, Jon Baker, Bill Austin and Brad Benson. 70 has been worn by Hall of Famer Sam Huff and solid defensive linemen Ray Krouse, Gary Jeter and Leonard Marshall. 75 has been worn by star defensive linemen Jim Katcavage, George Martin and Keith Hamilton. 81 has been worn by Hall of Famer Andy Robustelli as well as ends Jim Lee Howell, Bill Swiacki, and Jack Gregory in addition to receiver Amani Toomer.

Worst represented numbers: 46 has only been worn four times by three defensive backs and a wide receiver for a total of seven seasons. 19 has been worn by seven ineffectual linemen, backs and kickers.

Number worn by the most players: 33 has been worn 29 times.

Player who wore the most numbers: Tackle and coach Steve Owen wore six numbers: 6/12/36/44/50/55.

Longest tenure wearing a number: Center Mel Hein wore 7 for 15 years from 1931 to 1945. Quarterback Phil Simms wore 11 over a 15 year period from 1979 to 1993, but missed all of 1982 due to injury.

Number worn by first ever draft pick: Tackle Art Lewis was the first round pick in 1936 and wore 23.

Biggest draft busts: The Giants have had their share of draft busts, particularly at running back: Rocky Thompson, 22, was selected 18th in 1971 and ran for 217 yards with a 3.2 average in three years; Butch Woolfolk, 25, also was selected 18th in 1982 and ran for 1,388 yards with a 3.5 average and 14 fumbles over three years; George Adams, 33, was selected 19th in 1985 and ran for 722 yards with a 3.3 average over four years; Jarrod Bunch, 33, was selected 27th in 1991 and ran for 629 yards in three years; Ron Dayne, 27, was selected 11th in 2000 and ran for 1,888 yards with a 3.5 average over three years.

Number worn by oldest player: Four Giants have played at age 41: Ken Strong wore 50 in 1947; Morten Andersen wore 8 and Trey Junkin wore 48 in 2002; Sean Landetta wore 5 in 2003. Charlie Conerly wore 42 as a 40 year old in 1961.

Cameos: Hall of Famers— Joe Guyon 11; Pete Henry 55; Hugh McElhenny 39; Jim Thorpe 21. All Pros and other notables— Morten Andersen 8; Gary Ballman 82; Todd Christensen 41; Dave Duerson 26; Frank Filchock 40; Matt Hazeltine 64; Curley Johnson 75; Roland Lakes 76; John Martinkovic 83; Bennie McRae 26; Herman Moore 82; Andy Nelson 26; Steve Odom 84; R.C. Owens 37; Bosh Pritchard 35; Johnny Roland 23; Sam Silas 72; Rick Volk 23; Herschel Walker 34; Gene Washington 84; Stan West 62.

Ones who got away: Receiver Don Maynard, 13, became a Hall of Famer for the crosstown Jets. Guard Bob Mischak, 62, also starred with the Jets. Runner Tyrone Wheatley, 28, has been more successful in Oakland than in New York. Flashy runner Frenchy Fuqua, 29, had success in Pittsburgh. Hall of Famer Cal Hubbard, 41/60, wanted out of the big city and went to Green Bay. Center Frank Winters, 69, also moved to Green Bay to star. Reggie Rucker was a solid receiver in Cleveland. Defensive end Fred Dryer, 89, switched coasts to star with the Rams.

Least popular numbers: 92 has only been worn twice. 32, 91, 97 and 98 have all only been worn three times.

Last number to be originated: 98 was first worn by linebacker Johnnie Cooks in 1988.

Longest dormant number: 0 has not been worn since 1945.

Triskaidekaphobia notes: 13 was worn by four players in the 1930s and 1940s, but since has only been worn by Hall of Famer who got away Don Maynard, longtime punter Dave Jennings and backup quarterback Danny Kanell.

Shared numbers: 14 was worn by fullback Ward Cuff and quarterback Y.A. Tittle. 45 was worn by Hall of Fame safety Emlen Tunnell and speedy receiver Homer Jones. Two tough defensive backs wore 49, Tom Landry and Erich Barnes. Two rugged linebackers wore 52, John Cannady and Pepper Johnson. Two longtime veterans wore 53, 14-year center Greg Larson and 13-year linebacker Harry Carson. 76 was worn by two giant Giants, defensive tackle Rosey Grier and tackle Jumbo Elliott. Two Pro Bowl receivers wore 85, Bob Schnelker and Del Shofner.

Continuity: All League quarterback Benny Friedman was replaced in 1 by Hall of Fame end Ray Flaherty; All Pro guard Len Younce was replaced in 32 by tackle Al Blozis; Pro Bowl guard Jon Baker was replaced in 60 by Pro Bowl guard Bill Austin; Tex Coulter was replaced in 79 by Hall of Fame tackle Rosey Brown; Pro Bowl tight end Bob Schnelker was replaced in 85 by Pro Bowl wide receiver Del Shofner.

Discontinuity: Safety Jimmy Patton was followed in 20 by defensive back Don Sutherin; Alex Webster was followed in 29 by fellow runner Chuck Mercein; Hall of Fame tackle Cal Hubbard was followed in 41 by lineman Saul Mielziner; 14-year defensive end George Martin was followed in 75 by 1-year defensive end Mark Duckens; defensive tackle star Dick Modzelewski was followed in 77 by tackles John Contoulis and Frank Lasky; Pro Bowl tight end Aaron Thomas was followed in 88 by receiver Coleman Zeno.

Quarterback numbers over 19: 20 Arnie Herber, Travis Tidwell, and Bill Mackrides; 22 Ed Danowski, Ray Mallouf; 40 Frank Filchock; 41 Emery Nix, Paul Governali; 42 Charlie Conerly; 44 Emery Nix; 47 Fred Benners.

Number of first black player: Emlen Tunnell wore 45 in 1948.

Numbers of future NFL head coaches: Joe Alexander 10/20/25; Bill Austin 60/75; Frank Filchock 40; Ray Flaherty 1/6/8/44; Benny Friedman 1; Hinkey Haines 1, 2; Mel Hein 7; Dutch Hendrian 6; Pete Henry 55; Jim Lee Howell 21/81; Ed Hughes 48; Tut Imlay 4;

Family Connections

Brothers

Steve Owen	T	1926–31, 1933	6/12/36/44/50/55
Bill Owen	T	1929–36	36
Howie Livingston	DB	1944–7	10/24
Cliff Livingston	LB	1954–61	89
Jim Poole	E	1945–6	23/80
Ray Poole	E	1947–52	82
Barney Poole	E	1954	78
Mel Triplett	FB	1955–60	33
Bill Triplett	FB	1967	38

Fathers and sons

Willie Young	T	1966–75	69
Rodney Young	S	1995–8	47

John Karcis 11/50; Jim Kendricks 26; Walt Koppisch 0; Rich Kotite 86/87; Tom Landry 49; Art Lewis 23; Don McCafferty 87; Dick Modzelewski 77; Al Nesser 7/40; Dick Nolan 25; Steve Owen 6/12/36/44/50/55; Mike Palm 9; Earl Potteiger 3/4/9; Ray Rhodes 22/82; Harland Svare 84; Jim Thorpe 21; Joe Walton 80; Alex Webster 29; Doug Wycoff 8.

Numbers of future NFL referees: Joe Alexander 10/20/25; Hinkey Haines 1, 2; Gary Lane 15; Lou Palazzi 57; Steve Pritko 11; Mule Wilson 6/16.

Players who played other sports: Baseball — Red Badgro 17; Bruce Caldwell 48; Chuck Corgan 10; Ox Eckhardt 0; Steve Filopowicz 8/23; Hinkey Haines 1, 2; Red Smith 5; Jim Thorpe 21; Hoge Workman 14; Joe Zapustas 14; plus umpires Cal Hubbard 41/60, Hank Soar 15, and Frank Umont 69. Basketball — Neil Adams 30; Otto Schnellenberger 83; Tillie Voss 11. Wrestling — Steve Owen 6/12/36/44/50/55; Sam Stein 23; Lawrence Taylor 56; Tarzan White 12/66; Doug Wycoff 8.

Players more famous after football: Tackle Al Blozis, 32, and end Jack Lummus, 29, both died in World War II. Jarrod Bunch, 33, has acted in movies; Fred Dryer, 89, played *Hunter* on television; Conrad Goode, 62, acted in movies and television.

First player to wear a number in the 70s: Back Andy Marefos wore 70 in 1941.

First player to wear a number in the 80s: In 1946, the ends wore the following numbers — Jim Poole 80, Jim Lee Howell 81, John Weiss 83, Jack Mead 85, Don McCafferty 87 and Frank Liebel 88.

First player to wear a number in the 90s: Tackle Vic Carroll wore 90 in 1946.

Number with most points scored: 3 with 1,302 points scored by Pete Gogolak (646), Brad Daluiso (526), Eric Schubert (56), Bjorn Nittmo (39), Ken Willis (13), George Benyola (12), and Joe Cooper (10).

Number with most yards rushing: 27 with 10,327 yards gained by Rodney Hampton (6,897), Ron Dayne (1,888), Steve Thurlow (657), Larry Heater (373), Randy Minniear (277), Willie Spencer (245), and Bob Grim (-10).

Number with most receptions: 88 with 1,020 passes caught by Ike Hilliard (319), Aaron Thomas (247), Mike Sherrard (121), Bobby Johnson (112), Bob McChesney (54), Mike Fried (39), Frank Liebel (36), Floyd Eddings (28), Joe Johnson (19), Lawrence Dawsey (18), Edwin Lovelady (10), Don Clune (5), Coleman Zeno (5), Dick Wilkins (4), and Joey Smith (3).

Number with most touchdown passes: 11 with 261 touchdowns tossed by Phil Simms (199), Earl Morrall (32), Don Heinrich (13), Randy Johnson (13), Lee Grosscup (2) and Tony Sarausky (2).

Number with most interceptions: 45 with 89 passes picked off by Emlen Tunnell (74), Pete Athas (13), and Alan Caldwell (2).

Oddity: Numbers 0–10 all experienced long periods of dormancy as they changed from being worn by backs, ends, and linemen to being worn only by kickers, punters and quarterbacks. 0 dormant since 1945; 1 retired and not worn since 1947; 2 dormant from 1945 to 1985; 3 dormant from 1945 to 1961; 4 dormant from 1947 to 1991; 5 dormant from 1946 to 1984; 6 dormant from 1946 to 1982; 7 retired and not worn since 1945; 8 dormant from 1958 to 1987; 9 dormant from 1946 to 1974; and 10 dormant from 1948 to 1963.

Players Whose Number Is Unknown

Bill Kenyon	(B)	1925
Red Smith	(G)	1928
Marion Broadstone	(T/G)	1931
Cowboy Hill	(B)	1925
Les Caywood	(G/T)	1927
John Holman	(T)	1928
Mack Flenniken	(B)	1931
Harvey Sark	(G)	1931
Ray Schwab	(FB/E)	1931
Carl Tomasello	(E)	1940
Bob Morrow	(B)	1945
John Hall	(E)	1955
Bob Lacey	(WR)	1965
Skip Butler	(K)	1971
Jim Miller	(P)	1987r

Team All-Time Numerical Roster

Those with an "r" following the year 1987 were replacement players during the players' strike. Pro Bowl and pre–1950 All Pro players for each number are in *Italics*; Hall of Famers are in **Bold** type.

0 Phil White (B) 1925, 1927, Walt Koppisch (B) 1926, Ox Eckhardt (B) 1928, Danny McMullen (G) 1929, Ted Bucklin (FB) 1931, Lee Mulleneaux (C) 1932, Reb Russell (B) 1933, Wee Willie Smith (FB) 1934, Lou Eaton (T) 1945.

1 *Hinkey Haines* (B) 1925, *Jack McBride* (B) 1926–8, *Benny Friedman* (B) 1929–31, **Ray Flaherty** (E) 1932–5, *Frank Cope* (T) 1946–7.

2 *Heinie Benkert* (B) 1925, *Hinkey Haines* (B) 1926–8, Orian Rice (B) 1929, Mickey Murtagh (C) 1930–2, Jim Zyntell (G) 1933, *Johnny Dell Isola* (G) 1934–40, Len Eshmont (B) 1941, Len Calligaro (B) 1944, Raul Allegre (K) 1986–91, Mike Horan (P) 1993–6, Jose Cortez (K) 1999, Jaret Holmes (P/K) 2000, Rodney Williams (P) 2001.

3 Al Bedner (G/T) 1925, Glenn Killinger (B) 1926, Earl Potteiger (B) 1926, *Len Grant* (T) 1930–7, Bill Petrilas (E) 1944, Ralph Guglielmi (QB) 1962–3, Pete Gogolak (K) 1966–74, Eric Schubert (K) 1985, Joe Cooper (K) 1986, George Benyola (K) 1987r, Bjorn Nittmo (K) 1989, Ken Willis (K) 1992, Brad Daluiso (K) 1993–2000, Jesse Palmer (QB) 2002–3.

4 Tommy Myers (B) 1925, Earl Potteiger (B) 1925, Paul Hogan (B) 1926, Tut Imlay (B) 1927, Al Bloodgood (B) 1928, Len Sedbrook (B) 1929, *Les Caywood* (G/T) 1930–2, Stu Clancy (B) 1932–5, **Tuffy Leemans** (FB) 1936–43, Leland Shaffer (QB) 1945, Frank Reagan (B) 1946, Joe Prokop (P) 1992.

5 Matt Brennan (B) 1925, Jack Hagerty (B)

1926–9, Dosey Howard (G/T) 1930, Red Smith (G) 1931, Otto Vokaty (B) 1932, Les Borden (E) 1935, Buster Mitchell (E) 1935, Len Dugan (C) 1936, *Kayo Lunday* (C) 1937–41, Dave Brown (B) 1943, George Franck (B) 1945, Ed Shedlosky (B) 1945, Marion Pugh (QB) 1945–6, *Sean Landeta* (P) 1985–93, Kerry Collins (QB) 1999–2003.

6 Dutch Hendrian (B) 1925, Cowboy Hill (B) 1926, Mule Wilson (B) 1927–9, Saul Mielziner (C/T/G/) 1930, **Ray Flaherty** (E) 1931, **Steve Owen** (T) 1933, Al Owen (B) 1939–40, Jack Hinkle (B) 1940, Howie Yeager (B) 1941, Elmer Barber (C) 1945, *Ali Haji-Sheikh* (K) 1983–5, Dana Moore (P) 1987r, Paul McFadden (K) 1988, Matt Cavanaugh (QB) 1991.

7 *Lynn Bomar* (E) 1925–6, Al Nesser (E) 1926, *Tony Plansky* (B) 1928, *Joe Westoupal* (C) 1929–30, **Mel Hein** (C) 1931–45.

8 Tom Moran (B) 1925, Tex Grigg (B) 1926, Doug Wycoff (B) 1927, 1931, **Ray Flaherty** (E) 1928, *Tony Plansky* (B) 1929, Tiny Feather (B) 1932–3, Bob Bellinger (G) 1934–5, Walt Nielson (B) 1940, Frank Reagan (B) 1941, Al Owen (B) 1942, *Bill Paschal* (B) 1943–5, Steve Filopowicz (B) 1945, Ben Agajanian (K) 1949, 1954–7, Bud Sherrod (E) 1952, Mike Busch (QB) 1987, Maury Buford (P) 1988, Ruben Rodriguez (P) 1992, Morten Andersen (K) 2001, Matt Bryant (K) 2002–3.

9 Jim Frugone (B) 1925, Mike Palm (B) 1925–6, Kid Hill (T) 1926, Earl Potteiger (B) 1927–8, Glenn Campbell (E) 1929, *Rudy Comstock* (G/T) 1930, George Munday (T/G) 1931–2, John Cannella (G/C) 1933–4, Jess Quatse (T) 1935, Jack Haden (T) 1936–8, Eddie Miller (QB) 1939–40, Bob Garner (B) 1945, George Hunt (K) 1975, Joe Pisarcik (QB) 1977–9, Bob Thomas (K) 1986, Jim Crocicchia (QB) 1987r, Matt Bahr (K) 1990–2, Brad Maynard (P) 1997–2000, Owen Pochman (K) 2001, Brett Conway (K) 2003.

10 Ed McGinley (T) 1925, Swede Nordstrom (G/T) 1925, *Doc Alexander* (OL) 1926, Chuck Corgan (B) 1927, Hal Hilpert (E/B) 1930, Corrie Artman (T) 1931, *Potsy Jones* (G) 1932–6, Mickey Kobrosky (QB) 1937, Len Barnum (B) 1938–40, Lou DeFilippo (G) 1945, Howie Livingston (B) 1946–7, Henry Schichtle (QB) 1964, **Fran Tarkenton** (QB) 1967–71, *Brad Van Pelt* (LB) 1973–83, Beau Almodobar (WR) 1987r, Kent Graham (QB) 1992–4, 1998–9, Tom Rouen (P) 2002, Jeff Feagles (P) 2003.

11 Tillie Voss (E/T) 1926, **Joe Guyon** (B) 1927, Neely Allison (E) 1928, Dosey Howard (G/T) 1929, *Butch Gibson* (G/T) 1930–4, Tony Sarausky (B) 1935–7, Bull Karcis (B) 1938–9, Chet Gladchuk (C/T) 1941, Emmett Barrett (C) 1942, Steve Pritko (E) 1943, John Weiss (E) 1944–5, John Doolan (B) 1946, Bob Morris (HB) 1947, Don Heinrich (QB) 1954–9, Lee Grosscup (QB) 1960–1, Earl Morrall (QB) 1965–7, Randy Johnson

(QB) 1971–3, *Phil Simms* (QB) 1979–81, 1983–93.

12 Babe Parnell (T/G) 1925, **Steve Owen** (T) 1930, Chris Cagle (B) 1930–2, *Harry Newman* (B) 1933–5, Bob Dunlap (QB) 1936, Jim Neill (B) 1937, Kay Eakin (B) 1940–1, Leo Cantor (B) 1942, Walt Dubzinski (G) 1943, Tarzan White (G) 1945, Dave Brown (B) 1946–7, Bob Greenhalgh (B) 1949, Randy Clay (B) 1950, 1953, John Amberg (B) 1951–2, Bobby Clatterbuck (QB) 1954–7, Pete Hall (E) 1961, Jim Del Gaizo (QB) 1974, Jerry Golsteyn (QB) 1977–8, Scott Brunner (QB) 1980–3, Jess Atkinson (K) 1985, Mark Jackson (WR) 1993, Tommy Maddox (QB) 1995, Matt Allen (P) 2002.

13 Jack Hagerty (B) 1930, 1932, *Dutch Kitzmiller* (FB) 1931, *Kink Richards* (B) 1933–9, George Franck (B) 1941, **Don Maynard** (WR) 1958, *Dave Jennings* (P) 1974–84, Danny Kanell (QB) 1996–8.

14 Swede Nordstrom (G/T) 1925, Tommy Tomlin (G/T) 1925, Len Sedbrook (B) 1930–1, Hoge Workman (B) 1932, Tony Rovinski (E) 1933, Joe Zapustas (E) 1933, John Norby (B) 1934, *Tod Goodwin* (E) 1935–6, *Ward Cuff* (FB) 1937–45, **Y.A. Tittle** (QB) 1961–4.

15 Larry Walbridge (C) 1925, Mickey Murtagh (C) 1926–8, Cliff Marker (B) 1927, Lyle Munn (E) 1929, Glenn Campbell (E) 1930–3, Walt Singer (E) 1935–6, Hank Soar (B) 1937–44, 1946, Win Pedersen (T) 1945, George Shaw (QB) 1959–60, Glynn Griffing (QB) 1963, Gary Lane (QB) 1968, Tom Blanchard (P) 1971–3, Jim McCann (P) 1973, Craig Morton (QB) 1974–6, Randy Dean (QB) 1977–9, Jeff Hostetler (QB) 1985–6, 1988–92, Keith Crawford (CB) 1993, Tony Simmons (WR) 2002.

16 *Jack McBride* (B) 1925, Art Stevenson (C) 1926, Dutch Webber (B) 1926, Mule Wilson (B) 1930, Tilly Manton (B) 1936–8, Jim Little (T) 1945, John Atwood (B) 1948, Jim Ostendarp (B) 1950–1, **Frank Gifford** (HB) 1952–60, 1962–4, Milt Plum (QB) 1969, *Norm Snead* (QB) 1972–4, 1976.

17 Owens Reynolds (E/B) 1925, Art Harms (T) 1926, Paul Jappe (E) 1927, Max Reed (C) 1928, Bull Wesley (C/G) 1928, Cliff Ashburn (G) 1929, **Red Badgro** (E) 1930–5, Buster Mitchell (E) 1936, Red Corzine (FB) 1937, Johnny Gildea (B) 1938, John McLaughry (FB) 1940, Clint McClain (FB) 1941, Bob Trocolor (B) 1942–3, Carl Grate (C) 1945–6, George Cheverko (B) 1947–8, Arnold Galifa (QB) 1953, Tom Dublinski (QB) 1958, Dick Shiner (QB) 1970, Jeff Rutledge (QB) 1983–9, Dave Brown (QB) 1992–7, Jason Garrett (QB) 2000–1.

18 Bob Nash (T/E) 1925, Bill Rooney (B) 1925, Dale Burnett (B) 1930–9, Frank Martin (B) 1945, Bill Petrilas (E) 1945, Bob Timberlake (K) 1965, Tom Kennedy (QB) 1966, Clifton McNeil (WR) 1970–1, Eldridge Small (DB) 1972–4, Joe Danelo

(K) 1976–82, Reggie McGowan (WR) 1987r, David Treadwell (K) 1993–4, Mike Cherry (QB) 1997–8.

19 Ewell Phillips (G) 1936, Red Wolfe (FB) 1938, John Doolan (B) 1945, Gary Wood (QB) 1964–6, 1968–9, Carl Summerall (QB) 1974–5, Mack Cummings (WR) 1987r, Cary Blanchard (K) 1999.

20 *Doc Alexander* (OL) 1925, Tiny Feather (B) 1930–1, Shipwreck Kelly (B) 1932, *Jack McBride* (B) 1932–4, Harry Stafford (B) 1934, Leland Shaffer (QB) 1935–43, **Arnie Herber** (TB) 1944–5, Ken Keuper (LB) 1948, Noah Mullins (B) 1949, Travis Tidwell (QB) 1950–1, George Thomas (B) 1952, Bill Mackrides (QB) 1953, Herb Johnson (B) 1954, *Jimmy Patton* (DB) 1955–66, Scott Eaton (DB) 1967–71, Honor Jackson (DB) 1973, Jim Stienke (DB) 1974–7, Gary Woolford (DB) 1980, *Joe Morris* (RB) 1982–8, Keith Elias (RB) 1994–6, Sam Garnes (S) 1997–2001, Sean Bennett (RB) 2002, Jim Finn (RB) 2003.

21 **Jim Thorpe** (B) 1925, Babe Scheuer (T) 1934, Ike Frankian (E) 1934–5, *Jim Lee Howell* (E) 1937–42, Roy Clay (B) 1944, Joe Sulaitis (B) 1948–53, Ed Crawford (DB) 1957, Carl Karilivacz (DB) 1958, Lee Riley (DB) 1960, Allan Webb (DB) 1961–5, Bruce Maher (DB) 1968–9, Otto Brown (DB) 1970–3, Bill Bryant (DB) 1976–8, Don Patterson (DB) 1980, Louie Jackson (RB) 1981, Ted Watts (DB) 1985, Harvey Clayton (DB) 1987, Boris Byrd (DB) 1987r, *Reyna Thompson* (CB) 1989–92, Troy Kyles (WR) 1990, Willie Beamon (CB) 1997–2003, Tiki Barber (RB) 1997–2003.

22 Paul Jappe (E) 1925, *Hap Moran* (B) 1930–3, *Ed Danowski* (QB) 1934–9, 1941, Grenny Lansdell (B) 1940, *Frank Liebel* (E) 1942–5, Cecil Hare (B) 1946, Duke Iverson (B) 1947, Ray Mallouf (QB) 1949, Harmon Rowe (B) 1950–2, Buford Long (B) 1953–5, Henry Moore (DB) 1956, Johnny Bookman (DB) 1957, Billy Lott (FB) 1958, *Dick Lynch* (DB) 1959–66, Bobby Post (DB) 1967, Ronnie Blye (RB) 1968, Rocky Thompson (RB) 1971–3, Honor Jackson (DB) 1974, Ray Rhodes (DB) 1977–9, Eric Felton (DB) 1980, Doug Nettles (DB) 1980, Brian Carpenter (DB) 1982, Lee Rouson (RB) 1985–90, Phillippi Sparks (CB) 1992–9, Ralph Brown (DB) 2000–3.

23 *Art Carney* (G) 1925, Ossie Wiberg (B) 1930, Sammy Stein (E) 1931, Dick Powell (E) 1932, Bo Molenda (FB) 1932–5, Art Lewis (T/G) 1936, *Jim Poole* (E) 1937–41, 1945, Steve Filopowicz (B) 1946, Paul Dudley (HB) 1962, Louis Guy (DB) 1963, *Ernie Koy* (RB) 1965–70, Johnny Roland (RB) 1973, Rick Volk (DB) 1976, Odis McKinney (DB) 1978–9, Tony Blount (DB) 1980, Perry Williams (CB) 1984–93, Thomas Randolph (CB) 1994–7, Carlton Gray (CB) 1998, LeShon Johnson (RB) 1999, Omar Stoutmire (S) 2000–3.

24 *Century Milstead* (T) 1925, Red Howard

(G) 1927, Winnie Anderson (E) 1936, Will Walls (E) 1937–9, 1941–3, Charles Barnard (E) 1938, Bolo Perdue (E) 1940, Howie Livingston (B) 1944–5, Sonny Grandelius (B) 1953, Wayne Berry (B) 1954, Phil King (RB) 1958–63, *Tucker Frederickson* (RB) 1965–71, Chuck Crist (DB) 1972–4, Terry Jackson (DB) 1978–83, Kenny Daniel (DB) 1984, Ottis Anderson (RB) 1986–92, Izel Jenkins (CB) 1993, Maurice Douglass (S) 1995–6, Bashir Levingston (DB) 1999–2000, Will Peterson (CB) 2001–3.

25 *Joe Williams* (G) 1925–6, *Doc Alexander* (OL) 1927, *Century Milstead* (T) 1927, Paul Jappe (E) 1928, Snitz Snyder (B) 1929, Max Krause (B) 1933–6, Johnny Mackorell (B) 1935, Dom Principe (B) 1941–2, Carl Kinscherf (B) 1943–4, Pete Gorgone (B) 1946, Dick Nolan (DB) 1954–7, 1959–61, Dick Pesonen (DB) 1962–4, Larry Vargo (DB) 1966, Les Shy (RB) 1970, Leon McQuay (RB) 1974, Gordon Bell (RB) 1976–7, Maurice Tyler (DB) 1978, Ray Oldham (DB) 1979, Alvin Garrett (RB) 1980, Butch Woolfolk (RB) 1982–4, Mark Collins (DB) 1986–93, Vencie Glenn (S) 1995, Ramos McDonald (CB) 2000, Will Allen (CB) 2001–3.

26 Jim Kendrick (B) 1927, Gene Rose (E) 1936, Dom Principe (B) 1940, Victor Carroll (T) 1943–6, Don Sutherin (DB) 1959, Ed Sutton (RB) 1960, Sam Horner (HB) 1962, Andy Nelson (DB) 1964, Wendell Harris (DB) 1966–7, Kenny Parker (DB) 1970, Bennie McRae (DB) 1971, Joe Dawkins (RB) 1974–5, Rondy Colbert (DB) 1976, Bud Hebert (DB) 1980, Rob Carpenter (RB) 1981–5, Earl Beecham (RB) 1987r, Dave Duerson (S) 1990, Roger Brown (S) 1990–1, Jarvis Williams (S) 1994, Kory Blackwell (CB) 1998, Emmanuel McDaniel (CB) 1999–2001, Kato Serwanga (DB) 2002–3.

27 *Bill Morgan* (T) 1933–6, Jiggs Kline (E) 1939–40, Eulis Keahey (G) 1942, Hal Springer (E) 1945, Herb Rich (DB) 1954–6, Steve Thurlow (RB) 1964–6, Steve Bowman (HB) 1966, Mike Fitzgerald (DB) 1967, Randy Minniear (RB) 1967–9, Bob Grim (WR) 1972–4, Charlie Ford (DB) 1975, Willie Spencer (RB) 1977–8, Larry Heater (RB) 1980, 1982–3, Herb Welch (DB) 1985–7, *Rodney Hampton* (RB) 1990–7, Ron Dayne (RB) 2000–2.

28 Nello Falaschi (FB) 1938–41, Don Lieberum (B) 1942, Verlin Adams (T) 1943–5, Larrye Weaver (B) 1955, Joel Wells (HB) 1961, Henry Carr (DB) 1965–7, Bobby Duhon (RB) 1968, 1970–2, Robert Giblin (DB) 1975, Beasley Reece (DB) 1977–83, Tom Flynn (DB) 1986–8, Robert Porter (DB) 1987r, Everson Walls (CB) 1990–2, Tyrone Wheatley (RB) 1995–8, Curtis Buckley (S) 1998, Reggie Stephens (CB) 1999–2000, DeWayne Patmon (S) 2001–2.

29 *Art Carney* (G) 1926, Babe Parnell (T/G) 1927–8, *Century Milstead* (T) 1928, *Les Caywood* (G/T) 1929, Dick Stahlman (E) 1930, Milt Rehn-

quist (C) 1931, Tex Irvin (T/G) 1932–5, Gaines Davis (G) 1936, Chuck Gelatka (E) 1937–40, Jack Lummus (E) 1941, Ed Hienstra (C) 1942, Bill Piccolo (C) 1943–5, *Alex Webster* (HB) 1955–64, Chuck Mercein (RB) 1965–7, John Fuqua (RB) 1969, Vince Clements (RB) 1972–3, Ed Jenkins (RB) 1974, Marsh White (RB) 1975–6, Clyde Powers (DB) 1976–7, Eddie Hicks (RB) 1979–80, Jim Culbreath (RB) 1980, Bill Currier (DB) 1981–5, Jamie Covington (RB) 1987r, Myron Guyton (S) 1989–93, Tito Wooten (S) 1994–8, Tre Thomas (S) 1999, Damon Washington (RB) 2000–2, Ray Green (CB) 2003.

30 Al Bedner (G/T) 1926, Babe Lyon (T/G) 1929, **Ken Strong** (FB/K) 1939, Marion Pugh (QB) 1941, O'Neal Adams (E) 1942–5, Larry Visnic (G) 1945, Harry Wynne (E) 1945, Merle Hapes (B) 1946, Joe Scott (B) 1948–53, Bill Svoboda (LB) 1954–8, Jim Leo (LB) 1960, Dick Lasse (LB) 1962, Ernie Wheelwright (RB) 1964–5, Allen Jacobs (FB) 1966–7, *Ron Johnson* (RB) 1970–5, Jimmy Gunn (LB) 1975, Harold Hart (RB) 1977, Leon Perry (RB) 1980–2, Tony Galbreath (RB) 1984–7, *Dave Meggett* (RB) 1989–94, Charles Way (FB) 1995–9, Brian Mitchell (KR) 2003.

31 Bob Tarrant (E) 1936, Larry Johnson (C) 1936–9, Max Harrison (E) 1940, Ed Lechner (T) 1942, Larry Visnic (G) 1943–4, Bill Miklich (B) 1947, Joyce Pipkin (E) 1948, *Eddie Price* (RB) 1950–5, George Scott (RB) 1959, Bill Winter (LB) 1962–4, Charlie Evans (RB) 1971–3, Ernie Jones (DB) 1977–9, Cliff Chatman (RB) 1982, Frank Cephous (RB) 1984, Jason Sehorn (CB) 1994–7, 1999–2002, Ike Charlton (CB) 2003.

32 Tommy Tomlin (G/T) 1926, *Len Younce* (G) 1941, *Al Blozis* (T) 1942–4.

33 Dick Stahlman (E) 1927, Rosey Rosatti (T) 1928, Tiny Feather (B) 1929, Dick Marsh (G) 1933, Ollie Satenstein (G) 1933, Knuckles Boyle (T) 1934, Red Corzine (B) 1935–6, *John Mellus* (T) 1938–41, Red Seick (C) 1942, Jim Sivell (G) 1944–5, Frank Williams (B) 1948, Mel Triplett (FB) 1955–60, Al Gursky (LB) 1963, Smith Reed (HB) 1965–6, Pep Menefee (WR) 1966, Joe Green (DB) 1970–1, Steve Crosby (RB) 1974–6, Bob Hammond (RB) 1976–9, Roscoe Word (DB) 1976, Jerome King (DB) 1980, LeCharls McDaniel (DB) 1983, George Adams (RB) 1985, 1987–9, Jarrod Bunch (FB) 1991–3, Tim Watson (S) 1995, Robert Walker (RB) 1996, Erric Pegram (RB) 1997, Gary Brown (RB) 1998–9, Joe Montgomery (RB) 1999–2000, Delvin Joyce (RB) 2002–3.

34 John Alexander (T/E) 1926, Stan Galazin (C) 1937–9, John Lascari (E) 1942, Sal Marone (G) 1943, Joe Lindahl G) 1945, Jules Siegle (B) 1948, Bus Mertes (B) 1949, Bob Jackson (B) 1950–1, Butch Avinger (B) 1953, Pat Knight (B) 1954–5, Don Chandler (K) 1956–64, Junior Coffey (RB) 1969, 1971, Jack Rizzo (RB) 1973, Mickey

Zofko (RB) 1974, Larry Mallory (DB) 1976–8, Zachary Dixon (RB) 1979, Tony Green (RB) 1979, Nate Rivers (RB) 1980, Elvis Patterson (S) 1984–7, Lewis Tillman (RB) 1989–93, Herschel Walker (RB) 1995, Brandon Sanders (S) 1997–9, Greg Comella (FB) 1998–2001, Reggie Stephens (CB) 2002.

35 Riley Biggs (C) 1927, Ken Moore (G) 1940, *Choo-Choo Roberts* (RB) 1947–50, Bosh Pritchard (B) 1951, Pat Knight (B) 1952, Merwin Hodel (B) 1953, Bobby Epps (FB) 1954–5, 1957, Bob Gaiters (HB) 1961, Rondy Colbert (DB) 1975, Scott Laidlaw (RB) 1980, Ike Forte (RB) 1981, Billy Campfield (RB) 1983, Van Williams (RB) 1987r, Andre Weathers (DB) 1999–2000, Clarence LeBlanc (S) 2003.

36 **Steve Owen** (T) 1926, Paul Schuette (G) 1928, *Bill Owen* (T) 1929–36, Pete Cole (G/T) 1937, *Frank Cope* (T) 1938–45, Bill Johnson (P) 1970, Larry Watkins (RB) 1975–7, Alvin Maxson (RB) 1978, *Mark Haynes* (DB) 1980–5, Adrian White (S) 1987–9, 1991, Robert DiRico (RB) 1987r, Shaun Williams (S) 1998–2003.

37 Ray Hanken (E) 1937–8, Joe Sulaitis (B) 1943–5, George Franck (B) 1946–7, Larry Hayes (LB) 1961, Charlie Killett (HB) 1963, R.C. Owens (WR) 1964, Bobby Brooks (DB) 1974–6, Don Harris (DB) 1980, Larry Flowers (DB) 1981–5, Wayne Haddix (CB) 1987–8, Pat Morrison (DB) 1987r, Steve Rehage (DB) 1987r, Jesse Campbell (S) 1992–6, Eric Lane (RB) 1997, Lyle West (DB) 1999–2000, Johnnie Harris (DB) 2002–3.

38 Mike Klotovich (B) 1945, *Bill Paschal* (B) 1946–7, Don Menasco (B) 1952–3, Stan Sczurek (LB) 1966, Bill Triplett (RB) 1967, Bob Tucker (TE) 1970–7, Billy Taylor (RB) 1978–81, John Tuggle (RB) 1983, Doug Smith (DB) 1987r, Greg Cox (DB) 1989, Lamar McGriggs (S) 1991–2.

39 *Doug Oldershaw* (G) 1939–41, John Chickerneo (B) 1942, Tom Roberts (T) 1943, Herb Kane (T) 1944–5, Phil Ragazzo (T) 1945, Jerry Niles (B) 1947, Skippy Minisi (B) 1948, *Tex Coulter* (T) 1951, **Hugh McElhenny** (HB) 1963, Clyde Powers (DB) 1974–5, **Larry Csonka** (RB) 1976–8, Dan Doornink (RB) 1978, Bob Torrey (RB) 1979, Art Best (RB) 1980, Mike Mayock (DB) 1982–3, Tyrone Davis (DB) 1985, Kaulana Park (RB) 1987r, Sheldon White (CB) 1988–9, Corey Raymond (CB) 1992–4, Jeremy Lincoln (CB) 1998–9, Ryan Clark (S) 2002–3.

40 Al Nesser (E) 1927–8, *Frank Filchock* (QB) 1946, Art Faircloth (B) 1947–8, Jack Salscheider (B) 1949, Gene Filipski (HB) 1956–7, Joe Morrison (HB/WR/DB) 1959–72.

41 Babe Parnell (T/G) 1926, **Cal Hubbard** (T/E) 1927–8, Saul Mielziner (C/T/G) 1929, Wen Goldsmith (C) 1940, Emery Nix (QB) 1946, Paul Governali (QB) 1947–8, Ben Agajanian (K) 1949, Forrest Griffith (B) 1950–1, *Lindon Crow* (DB)

1958–60, Gene Johnson (DB) 1961, Bob Anderson (HB) 1963, *Willie Williams* (DB) 1965, 1967–73, Dan Lewis (RB) 1966, Todd Christensen (TE) 1979, Bo Matthews (RB) 1980–1, Fred DiRenzo (RB) 1987r, Neal Guggemos (DB) 1988, David Whitmore (S) 1990, A.J. Greene (DB) 1991, John Booty (S) 1994, Conrad Hamilton (S) 1996–9, Dave Thomas (CB) 2000–1, Darnell Dinkins (S) 2002, Frank Walker (CB) 2003.

42 *Orville Tuttle* (G) 1937, 1939–41, Bill Hutchinson (B) 1942, Hubert Barker (B) 1942–5, Jim Blumenstock (B) 1947, *Charlie Conerly* (QB) 1948–61.

43 *Orville Tuttle* (G) 1938, Junie Hovius (B) 1945, *Carl Lockhart* (DB) 1965–75, *Terry Kinard* (DB) 1983–9, Percy Ellsworth (S) 1996–9.

44 Riley Biggs (C) 1926, **Steve Owen** (T) 1927, Bug Hartzog (OL) 1928, **Ray Flaherty** (E) 1929, Ox Parry (T) 1937–9, Ed McGee (T) 1940, Ben Sohn (G) 1941, Merle Hapes (B) 1942, Emery Nix (QB) 1943, Keith Beebe (B) 1944, Frank Reagan (B) 1947–9, *Kyle Rote* (E) 1951–61, Tom Longo (DB) 1969–70, Richmond Flowers (DB) 1971–3, Doug Kotar (RB) 1974–9, 1981, Pete Shaw (DB) 1982–4, Maurice Carthon (RB) 1985–91, Kenyon Rasheed (FB) 1993–4, Robert Massey (CB) 1997, Sean Bennett (RB) 1999, Dan O'Leary (TE) 2002, Tony McGee (TE) 2003.

45 **Emlen Tunnell** (DB) 1948–58, *Homer Jones* (WR) 1964–9, Pete Athas (DB) 1971–4, Alan Caldwell (DB) 1979, Mike Hogan (RB) 1980, Leon Bright (RB) 1981–3, Jim Yarbrough (DB) 1987r, Gary Downs (RB) 1994, 1996, Craig Walendy (RB) 2000, Charles Stackhouse (FB) 2002.

46 Phil Harris (DB) 1966, Dave Hathcock (DB) 1967, Walt Love (WR) 1973, Mike Dennis (DB) 1980–3.

47 Fred Benners (QB) 1952, Leo Miles (B) 1953, Dick James (RB) 1964, Joe Koontz (WR) 1968, Ron Lumpkin (DB) 1973, Steve Henry (DB) 1980, Greg Lasker (DB) 1986–8, Don Brown (DB) 1987, Greg Jackson (S) 1989–93, Rodney Young (S) 1995–7.

48 Bruce Caldwell (B) 1928, *Hap Moran* (B) 1928–9, Joe Heap (B) 1955, Ed Hughes (DB) 1956–8, Bill Stits (DB) 1959–61, Johnny Counts (HB) 1962–3, Eddie Dove (DB) 1963, Clarence Childs (DB) 1964–7, Al Brenner (DB) 1969–70, Henry Stuckey (DB) 1975–6, Ken Johnson (RB) 1979, Kenny Hill (DB) 1984–8, Trey Junkin (C) 2002.

49 Dick Horne (E) 1941, Don Vosberg (E) 1941, Harold Hall (C) 1942, Frank Damiani (T) 1944, Ray Coates (B) 1948–9, **Tom Landry** (DB) 1950–5, *Erich Barnes* (DB) 1961–4, Jim Holifield (DB) 1968–9, Joe Orduna (RB) 1972–3, Jimmy Norris (DB) 1987r, David Tate (S) 1993.

50 **Steve Owen** (T) 1928, Mickey Murtagh (C) 1929, **Ken Strong** (FB/K) 1933–5, 1944–7, *Ed Wid-*

seth (T) 1937–40, Kay Bell (T) 1942, Bull Karcis (B) 1943, Roland Caranci (T) 1944, Bobby Abrams (LB) 1990–2.

51 Chet Gladchuk (C) 1946–7, Dick Woodard (C) 1950–1, 1953, Pete Mangum (LB) 1954, Lou Slaby (LB) 1964–5, Ed Weisacosky (LB) 1967, John Douglas (LB) 1970–3, Frank Marion (LB) 1977–83, Robbie Jones (LB) 1984–7, Ricky Shaw (LB) 1988–9, Andre Powell (LB) 1993–4, Mike Croel (LB) 1995, Pete Monty (LB) 1997–2000, Jack Golden (LB) 2001, Wesly Mallard (LB) 2002–3.

52 Vince Dennery (E) 1941, Harry Buffington (G) 1942, *John Cannady* (LB) 1947–54, Bob Schmidt (T) 1959–60, Bill Swain (LB) 1965, 1967, John Kirby (LB) 1969–70, John Hill (C/T) 1972–4, Ralph Hill (C) 1976–7, Leo Tierney (C) 1978, Joe McLaughlin (LB) 1980–4, Steve Tobin (C) 1980, *Pepper Johnson* (LB) 1986–92, Scott Galyon (LB) 1996–7, Dusty Zeigler (C/G) 2000–2.

53 Johnny Rapacz (C) 1950–4, *Greg Larson* (C) 1961–73, *Harry Carson* (LB) 1976–88, Brandon Short (LB) 2000–3.

54 Max Messner (LB) 1964, Ken Avery (LB) 1967–8, Gene Ceppetelli (C) 1969, Bill Singletary (LB) 1974, Dan Lloyd (LB) 1976–9, Andy Headen (LB) 1983–8, LaSalle Harper (LB) 1989, Dwayne Jiles (LB) 1989, Carlton Bailey (LB) 1993–4, Ben Talley (LB) 1995, Nick Greisen (LB) 2002–3.

55 **Pete Henry** (T) 1927, Hec Garvey (G/T) 1927–8, **Steve Owen** (T) 1929, 1931, Jim Bowdoin (G) 1932, Maury Dubofsky (G) 1932, Hank Reese (C/G) 1933–4, Bernie Kaplan (G) 1935–6, Jerry Dennerlein (T) 1937, Pete Cole (G/T) 1938–40, Lou DeFilippo (G) 1941, 1946–7, Chuck Avedisian (G) 1942–4, Army Tomaini (T) 1945, Carl Fennema (C) 1948–9, *Ray Wietecha* (C) 1953–62, Bob Scholtz (C/T) 1965–6, Ralph Heck (LB) 1969–71, Brian Kelley (LB) 1973–83, Gary Reasons (LB) 1984–92, Marcus Buckley (LB) 1993–9, Dhani Jones (LB) 2001–3.

56 Olen Underwood (LB) 1965, Chuck Hinton (C) 1967, Tommy Crutcher (LB) 1968–9, Pat Hughes (LB) 1970–6, Jim Clack (C/G) 1978–80, **Lawrence Taylor** (LB) 1981–93.

57 Lou Palazzi (C) 1946–7, Jeff Smith (LB) 1966, Vince Costello (LB) 1967–8, Ray Hickl (LB) 1969–70, Andy Selfridge (LB) 1974–5, 1977, Brad Cousino (LB) 1976, John Skorupan (LB) 1978–80, Byron Hunt (LB) 1981–8, Larry McGrew (LB) 1990, Corey Miller (LB) 1991–7, O.J. Childress (LB) 1999, Clayton White (LB) 2001, Carson Dach (C) 2003.

58 Walt Yowarsky (DE) 1955–7, Mike Ciccolella (LB) 1966–8, Jim Files (LB) 1970–3, John Tate (LB) 1976, Keith Eck (C/G) 1979, Mike Whittington (LB) 1980–3, Jim Clack (C/G) 1981, *Carl Banks* (LB) 1984–92, Pete Shufelt (LB) 1994, Doug Colman (LB) 1996–8, Scott Galyon (LB) 1998–9, Michael Barrow (LB) 2000–3.

59 Joe Wellborn (C) 1966, Chuck Hinton (C) 1968–9, Len Johnson (G) 1970, Bob Schmit (LB) 1975–6, Randy Coffield (LB) 1978–9, Ralph Perretta (C/G) 1980, Kelly Saalfeld (C) 1980, Whip Walton (LB) 1980, Ed McGlasson (C) 1981, Rich Umphrey (C/G) 1982–4, Brian Johnston (C) 1986–7, Gregg Swartwoudt (T) 1987r, Brian Williams (C/G) 1989–96, 1999, Kevin Lewis (LB) 2000–2.

60 **Cal Hubbard** (T) 1936, *Monk Edwards* (G) 1940–2, *Len Younce* (G) 1943–4, 1946–8, Tom Kearns (T) 1945, *Jon Baker* (G) 1950–2, *Bill Austin* (G) 1953–7, Buzz Guy (G/T) 1958–9, Bill Crawford (G) 1960, Ken Byers (G) 1962–4, Jim Carroll (LB) 1965–6, Willie Banks (G) 1970, Steve Alexakos (G) 1971, *Brad Benson* (T) 1978–87, Eric Moore (G) 1988–93.

61 *Orville Tuttle* (G) 1946, Ed Royston (G) 1948–9, Bill Milner (G) 1950, Ray Beck (DT) 1955–7, Zeke Smith (LB) 1961, Ed Adamchik (C) 1965, Charlie Harper (T/G) 1966–72, Karl Chandler (C/G) 1974–7, Phil Cancik (LB) 1980, Ernie Hughes (C/G) 1981–3, Chris Godfrey (G/T) 1984–7, Dan Morgan (G) 1987r, Bob Kratch (G) 1989–93, Lance Smith (G) 1994–6.

62 George Tobin (G) 1947, Carl Butkus (T) 1949, Earl Murray (G) 1951, Stan West (G) 1955, Jack Spinks (G) 1956–7, Bob Mischak (G) 1958, *Darrell Dess* (G/T) 1959–64, 1966–9, Dick Enderle (G) 1972–5, Ron Mikolajczyk (T/G) 1976–9, Ben Apuna (LB) 1980, Terry Falcon (G/T) 1980, Conrad Goode (T) 1984–5, Scott Davis (G) 1993–4, Glenn Parker (G/T) 2000–1, Wayne Lucier (C) 2003.

63 Mike Garzoni (G) 1948, Jake Colhouer (G) 1949, Bookie Bolin (G) 1962–7, Doug Van Horn (G/T) 1968–79, Bruce Kimball (G) 1982, Paul Davis (LB) 1983, Al Steinfeld (C) 1983, Karl Nelson (T) 1984–8, Scott Peters (C) 2003.

64 Mickey Walker (G) 1963–5, Andy Gross (G) 1967–8, Matt Hazeltine (LB) 1970, John Mendenhall (DT) 1972–9, *Jim Burt* (NT) 1981–8, Tom Rehder (T/G) 1990.

65 *Kayo Lunday* (C) 1946–7, Bill Miklich (B) 1948, Fritz Barzilauskas (G) 1951, Ray Beck (DT) 1952, Chet Lagod (G) 1953, John Bauer (G) 1954, Russ Carroccio (G) 1954–5, Jerry Huth (G) 1956, Mickey Walker (G) 1961–2, Bob Taylor (DE) 1963–4, Pete Case (G) 1965–70, Mark Ellison (G) 1972–3, Bill Ellenbogan (G/T) 1976–7, Dan Fowler (G) 1979, John Tautolo (G) 1982–3, *Bart Oates* (C) 1985–93, Jerry Kimmel (LB) 1987r, *Ron Stone* (T/G) 1996–2001, Tam Hopkins (G) 2002.

66 Tarzan White (G) 1937–9, Jerry Dennerlein (T) 1940, Win Pedersen (T) 1941, Jiggs Kline (E) 1942, *Monk Edwards* (G) 1946, Paul Hachten (G) 1947, John Mastrangelo (G) 1950, Hal Mitchell (T) 1952, *Jack Stroud* (G/T) 1953–64, Roger Davis (G/T) 1966, Henry Davis (LB)

1968–9, Rick Dvorak (DE) 1974–7, Kevin Turner (LB) 1980, Chris Foote (C/G) 1982–3, *William Roberts* (T) 1984, 1986–94, Jerry Reynolds (T/G) 1996–8, Jason Whittle (T) 1998–2002, David Diehl (G) 2003.

67 Bob Dobelstein (G) 1946–8, Duke Maronic (G) 1951, George Kennard G() 1952–5, Ron Hornsby (LB) 1971–4, Dave Simonson (T) 1975, Billy Ard (G) 1981–8, Adam Schreiber (C/G) 1994–6, Bryan Stoltenberg (C) 1997, Lonnie Palelei (G) 1998, Chris Bober (T) 2001–3.

68 Al Barry (G) 1958–9, Dave O'Brien (DT) 1965, Dan Goich (DT) 1972–3, J.T. Turner (G) 1977–83, Damian Johnson (T/G) 1986–9, Bill Dugan (G/T) 1987r, Lorenzo Freeman (NT) 1991, Clarence Jones (T) 1991–3, Omar Smith (G) 2002–3.

69 Gil Duggan (T) 1940, Tony Blazine (T) 1941, Paul Stenn (T) 1942, Frank Umont (T) 1944–5, Willie Young (T) 1966–75, Roy Simmons (G) 1979–81, David Jordan (G) 1984–5, Mike Black (T) 1987r, Joe Fields (C/G) 1988, Frank Winters (C) 1989, Greg Meisner (NT) 1991, Derek Engler (C) 1997–2000, Rich Seubert (T) 2001–3.

70 Andy Marefos (B) 1941–2, Lou Eaton (T) 1945, Sam Fox (E) 1945, Joe Byler (T) 1946, Gordon Paschka (G) 1947, John Treadaway (T) 1948, John Sanchez (T) 1950, Ray Krouse (DT) 1951–5, **Sam Huff** (LB) 1956–63, John McDowell (T/G) 1965, Glen Condren (DT) 1965, 1967, Jim Garcia (DE) 1966, Bill Matan (DE) 1966, Bob Hyland (C/G) 1971–5, Gary Jeter (DE) 1977–82, *Leonard Marshall* (DT) 1983–92, Lance Scott (C) 1998, Toby Myles (T) 1999, Lance Legree (DT) 2001–3.

71 Phil Ragazzo (T) 1946–7, Ernie Williamson (T) 1948, Ralph Hutchinson (T) 1949, Robert Patton (T) 1952, Ray Collins (T) 1954, M.L. Brackett (DE) 1958, Ellison Kelly (G) 1959, Lou Kirouac (G/T) 1963, Frank Lasky (T) 1965, Bob Lurtsema (DT) 1967–71, Dave Tipton (DE) 1971–3, Gary Pettigrew (DT) 1974, Dave Gallagher (DE) 1975–6, Gordon Gravelle (T) 1977–9, Myron Lapka (NT) 1980, Casey Merrill (DE) 1983–5, Anthony Howard (NT) 1987r, Robb White (DE) 1988–9, John Washington (DE) 1989–91, Stacey Dillard (DT) 1992–5.

72 Larry Beil (T) 1948, Ed Kolman (T) 1949, Dick Yelvington (T) 1952–7, Frank Youso (T) 1958–60, Chuck Janerette (DT) 1961–2, Andy Stynchula (DE) 1964–5, Jim Prestel (DT) 1966, Jim Colvin (DT) 1967, Sam Silas (DT) 1968, Frank Parker (DT) 1969, John Baker (DE) 1970, Joe Taffoni (T/G) 1972–3, George Hasenohrl (DT) 1974, Carl Wafer (DE) 1974, Bill Windauer (DT) 1975, Gordon King (T/G) 1978–83, 1985, Doug Riesenberg (T) 1987–95, Kelvin Davis (G) 1987r, Dan DeRose (LB) 1987r, Roman Oben (T) 1996–9, Osi Umenyiora (DE) 2003.

73 Arnie Weinmeister (T) 1950–3, Rex Bogan (T) 1955, Proverb Jacobs (T) 1960, Reed Bohovich (G/T) 1962, Roger Anderson (DT) 1964–5, 1967–8, Frank Molden (DT) 1969, Jim Kanicki (DT) 1970–1, Tom Mullen (G/T) 1974–7, Jeff Weston (T) 1979–82, Kevin Belcher (G) 1983–4, John Washington (DE) 1986–8, 1992, Scott Urch (T) 1987r, Rob Zatechka (G) 1995–7, Jeff Roehl (T) 2003.

74 *Don Ettinger* (G) 1948–50, Billy Shipp (T) 1954, Art Hauser (T/G) 1959, Lou Cordileone (DT) 1960, Jim Moran (DT) 1964, 1966–7, Mike Bundra (DT) 1965, Roger Davis (G/T) 1965, Tim McCann (DT) 1969, Dennis Crane (DT) 1970, Dave Roller (DT) 1971, Vern Vanoy (DT) 1971, Bart Buetow (T) 1973, John Hicks (G) 1974–7, Jim Krahl (DT) 1978, Tom Neville (T) 1979, Chris Linnin (DE) 1980, Tim Stokes (T) 1981, Rich Baldinger (T/G) 1982–3, Charles Cook (DE) 1983, *Erik Howard* (DT) 1986–94, Russell Mitchell (C) 1987r, Scott Gragg (T) 1995–9, Chris Ziemann (T) 2000, Ian Allen (T) 2002–3.

75 Bill Schuler (T) 1948, *Bill Austin* (G) 1949–50, Bill Albright (G) 1951–4, *Jim Katcavage* (DE) 1956–68, Curley Johnson (P) 1969, John Johnson (DT) 1969, Jim Norton (DT) 1970, Jerry Shay (DT) 1970–1, Larry Jacobson (DT) 1972–4, George Martin (DE) 1975–88, Mark Duckens (DE) 1989, Keith Hamilton (DT) 1992–2003.

76 Bill Schuler (T) 1947, Bill Erickson (G) 1948, *Jon Baker* (G) 1949, John Sanchez (T) 1949, Bob Peviani (G) 1953, *Rosey Grier* (DT) 1955–62, *John LoVetere* (DT) 1963–5, Don Davis (DT) 1966, Joe Szczecko (DT) 1969, Roland Lakes (DT) 1971, Jim Pietrzak (C) 1974–5, 1977–9, Mike Gibbons (T) 1976, Calvin Miller (NT) 1979, Curtis McGriff (DE) 1980–5, Frank Sutton (T) 1987r, *Jumbo Elliott* (T) 1988–95, Lomas Brown (T) 2000–1, Jeff Hatch (T) 2003.

77 *Jim White* (T) 1946–51, Herb Hannah (T) 1951, Dick Modzelewski (DT) 1956–63, John Contoulis (DT) 1964, Frank Lasky (T) 1964, Rosey Davis (DE) 1965–7, Rich Buzin (T) 1968–70, Dick Hanson (T) 1971, Rich Glover (DT) 1973, Troy Archer (DT) 1976–8, Vern Holland (T) 1980, Bill Neill (NT) 1981–3, Eric Dorsey (DE) 1986–92, Dennis Borcky (NT) 1987r, Chad Bratzke (DE) 1994–8, Luke Petitgout (G) 1999–2003.

78 *Al DeRogatis* (DE) 1949–52, Everett Douglass (T) 1953, Barney Poole (E) 1954, Don Boll (T/G) 1960, Lane Howell (T) 1963–4, Roger LaLonde (DT) 1965, Francis Peay (T) 1966–7, Steve Wright (T) 1968–9, Wayne Walton (T/G) 1971, Roy Hilton (DE) 1974, Gus Coppens (T) 1979, George Small (NT) 1980, Carl Barisich (DT) 1981, Jerome Sally (NT) 1982–6, Kevin Meuth (T) 1987r, Greg Bishop (T) 1993–9, Mike Rosenthal (G/T) 1999–2002.

79 *Tex Coulter* (T) 1946–9, 1952, George Roman (T) 1950, **Rosey Brown** (T) 1953–65,

Bruce Anderson (DE) 1967–9, Carter Campbell (LB) 1972–3, Al Simpson (T/G) 1975–6, Mike Gibbons (T) 1977, Mike McCoy (DT) 1979–80, Dale Markham (T) 1980, Dee Hardison (DE) 1982–5, Bill Berthusen (NT) 1987, George Thornton (DT) 1993, Bernard Holsey (DT) 1996–9, Jeremiah Parker (DE) 2000, Bob Jones (DE) 2002.

80 *Jim Poole* (E) 1946, Gregg Browning (E) 1947, Kelley Mote (E) 1950–2, Ray Pelfrey (B) 1953, Ken MacAfee (E) 1954–8, Joe Biscaha (E) 1959, Joe Walton (TE) 1961–3, Henry Reed (LB) 1971–4, John Strada (TE) 1974, Emery Moorehead (TE) 1977–9, Phil Tabor (DE) 1979–82, Malcolm Scott (TE) 1983, Phil McConkey (WR) 1984–8, Bob Mrosko (TE) 1990, Chris Calloway (WR) 1992–8, Brian Alford (WR) 1999, *Jeremy Shockey* (TE) 2002–3.

81 *Jim Lee Howell* (E) 1946–7, *Bill Swiacki* (E) 1948–50, Bill Stribling (E) 1951–3, **Andy Robustelli** (DE) 1956–64, Freeman White (TE) 1966–9, *Jack Gregory* (DE) 1972–8, Cleveland Jackson (TE) 1979, Tom Mullady (WR) 1979–84, Stacy Robinson (WR) 1985–90, Torin Smith (DE) 1987r, Ed McCaffrey (WR) 1991–3, Thomas Lewis (WR) 1994–7, Amani Toomer (WR) 1998–2003.

82 Ray Poole (E) 1947–52, Cliff Anderson (E) 1953, Hank Burnine (E) 1956, Tom Scott (LB) 1959–64, McKinley Boston (DE) 1968–9, Gary Ballman (WR) 1973, Ray Rhodes (WR) 1974–6, Ernest Pough (WR) 1978, Danny Pittman (WR) 1980–3, Vyto Kab (TE) 1985, Mark Ingram (WR) 1987–92, Joe Taibi (DE) 1987r, John Brandes (TE) 1992, Omar Douglas (WR) 1994–6, Thabiti Davis (WR) 2000–1, Herman Moore (WR) 2002, Vishante Shiancoe (TE) 2003.

83 John Weiss (E) 1946–7, Bruce Gherke (E) 1948, *Otto Schnellbacher* (B) 1950–1, John Martinkovic (DE) 1957, Jon Jelacic (DE/G) 1958, Bob Simms (LB) 1960–2, Tom Costello (LB) 1964–5, Glen Condren (DT) 1966, Randy Staten (DE) 1967, Barry Brown (DE) 1968, Dave Dunaway (WR) 1969, Reggie Rucker (WR) 1971, Tom Gatewood (TE) 1972–3, Chip Glass (TE) 1974, Boyd Brown (TE) 1977, Earnest Gray (WR) 1979–84, Vince Warren (WR) 1986, Odessa Turner (WR) 1987–91, Charles Coleman (TE) 1987r, Arthur Marshall (WR) 1994–6, Brian Saxton (TE) 1996, David Patten (WR) 1997–8, Pete Mitchell (TE) 1999–2000, Marcellus Rivers (TE) 2001–3.

84 Harland Svare (LB) 1955–60, Les Murdock (K) 1967, Rich Houston (WR) 1969–73, Walker Gillette (WR) 1974–6, Al Dixon (TE) 1977–9, Steve Odom (WR) 1979, Gene Washington (WR) 1979, Nate Johnson (WR) 1980, Alvin Garrett (RB) 1981, Zeke Mowatt (TE) 1983–4, 1986–9, 1991, Warren Seitz (TE/WR) 1987r, Aaron Pierce (TE) 1992–7, Joe Jurevicius (WR) 1998–2001, Brian Alford (WR) 1998, Tim Carter (WR) 2002–3.

85 Jack Mead (E) 1946–7, Dick Hensley (E) 1949, Ellery Williams (E) 1950, *Bob Schnelker* (E) 1954–60, *Del Shofner* (WR) 1961–7, Don Herrmann (WR) 1969–74, Jim Robinson (WR) 1976–9, John Mistler (WR) 1981–4, Don Hasselbeck (TE) 1985, Stephen Baker (WR) 1987–92, Jeff Smith (TE) 1987r, Keith Crawford (WR) 1993, Brian Kozlowski (TE) 1994–6, Alfred Pupunu (TE) 1998, David Patten (WR) 1999, Mark Thomas (TE) 1999, Jonathan Carter (WR) 2001–2, Derek Dorris (WR) 2002, David Tyree (WR) 2003.

86 Paul Walker (E) 1948–9, George Kershaw (E) 1949, Jim Duncan (E) 1951–3, Bill Kimber (E) 1959–60, Rich Kotite (TE) 1967, Butch Wilson (TE) 1968–9, Danny Buggs (WR) 1975, Johhny Perkins (WR) 1977–83, Lionel Manuel (WR) 1984–90, Derek Brown (TE) 1992–4, Moses Regular (TE) 1996, Kevin Alexander (WR) 1996–7, Ron Dixon (WR) 2000–2.

87 Don McCafferty (E) 1946, Dick Duden (E) 1949, Clete Fischer (B) 1949, Jim Duncan (E) 1950, Lee Skladany (E) 1950, Bob Wilkinson (E) 1951–2, Bob Topp (E) 1954, Jerry Hillebrand (LB) 1963–6, Rich Kotite (TE) 1969, 1971–2, Gary Shirk (TE) 1976–82, Byron Williams (WR) 1983–5, Solomon Miller (WR) 1986, Lewis Bennett (WR) 1987r, Howard Cross (TE) 1989–2001, Daryl Jones (WR) 2002, Willie Ponder (WR) 2003.

88 *Frank Liebel* (E) 1946–7, Joe Johnson (B) 1948, Bob McChesney (E) 1950–2, Dick Wilkins (E) 1954, Pat Summerall (DE/K) 1958–61, *Aaron Thomas* (TE) 1962–70, Coleman Zeno (WR) 1971, Don Clune (WR) 1974–5, Danny Buggs (WR) 1976, Roger Wallace (WR) 1976, Dwight Scales (WR) 1979, Mike Friede (WR) 1980–1, Floyd Eddings (WR) 1982–3, Bobby Johnson (WR) 1984–6, Edwin Lovelady (WR) 1987r, Brad Beckman (TE) 1988, Tim Sherwin (TE) 1988, Joey Smith (WR) 1991–2, Mike Sherrard (WR) 1993–5, Lawrence Dawsey (WR) 1996, Ike Hilliard (WR) 1997–2003.

89 Frank LoVuolo (E) 1949, Bob Hudson (E) 1951–2, Cliff Livingston (LB) 1954–61, Jim Collier (TE) 1962, Bob Crespino (TE) 1964–8, Fred Dryer (DE) 1969–71, Jim Obradovich (TE) 1975, Ed Marshall (WR) 1976–7, James Thompson (WR) 1978, Loaird McCreary (TE) 1979, Dennis Johnson (RB) 1980, Dave Young (TE) 1981, Mike Miller (WR) 1983, *Mark Bavaro* (TE) 1985–90, Mark Jackson (WR) 1993–4, Derek Allen (C) 1995, Gary Harrell (WR) 1995, Amani Toomer (WR) 1996–7, Andy Haase (TE) 1998, Dan Campbell (TE) 1999–2002, Darnell Dinkins (TE) 2003.

90 Victor Carroll (T) 1946–7, Chris Jones (C) 1987r, Corey Widmer (LB) 1992–9, Jack Golden (LB) 2000, Kenny Holmes (DE) 2001–3.

91 Charlie Burgess (LB) 1987r, Coleman Rudolph (DE) 1994–6, Ryan Phillips (LB) 1997–2000.

92 Jeff Tootle (LB) 1987r, *Michael Strahan* (DE) 1993–2003.

93 Brian Sisley (DE) 1987r, Mike Fox (DE) 1990–4, Ray Agnew (DT) 1995–7, Ryan Hale (DT) 1999–2000, Quincy Monk (LB) 2002–3.

94 Curtis Garrett (DE) 1987r, Michael Brooks (LB) 1993–5, Cedric Jones (DE) 1996–2000, Dwight Johnson (DE) 2002, William Joseph (DT) 2003.

95 Chris Davis (LB) 1987r, Kent Wells (DT) 1990, Ed Reynolds (LB) 1992, Mark Flythe (DE) 1993, Antonio Edwards (DE) 1997, Frank Ferrara (DE) 2001–3.

96 Frank Nicholson (LB) 1987r, Kanavis Mc-Ghee (LB) 1991–3, Jamal Duff (DE) 1995, George Williams (DE) 1998–2000, Cedric Scott (DE) 2001.

97 Warren Thompson (LB) 1987r, Robert Harris (DE) 1995–9, Cornelius Griffin (DT) 2000–3.

98 Johnie Cooks (LB) 1988–90, *Jessie Armstead* (LB) 1993–2001, Matt Mitrione (DT) 2002.

99 Kervin Wyatt (LB) 1980, Reggie Carr (DE) 1987r, Steve DeOssie (LB) 1989–93, Chris Maumalanga (DT) 1994, Christian Peter (DT) 1997–2000, Ross Kolodziej (DT) 2001–2, Byron Frisch (DE) 2002, Keith Washington (DE) 2003.

NEW YORK JETS

The franchise: Although the Jets won what was probably the most important game in AFL and even NFL history, Super Bowl III, they hold the worst overall record of any of the eight original American Football League teams. They were born as the New York Titans in 1960 when well-known broadcaster Harry Wismer bought a charter membership into the "Foolish Club" of original AFL owners. A fly-by-night operation from the start, the blue-and-gold clad Titans played in the smelly, decrepit Polo Grounds that the baseball Giants had abandoned three years before, and they drew an average crowd of about 15,000 per game for their first two seasons. Wismer ran the team from his cramped hotel suite; that's where you could go to buy tickets, and that's where he introduced football legend Sammy Baugh as the team's first coach.

Those first two squads scored a lot of points through the air with their two star receivers Don Maynard and Art Powell, but a weak defense led to back-to-back 7–7 seasons. Wismer brought in another Hall of Famer, Bulldog Turner, as coach in 1962, but the team declined on the field and financially. They dropped to an average of 5,000 fans per game, players' checks began to bounce, and the team finished 5–9. Wismer was bankrupt and forced to sell the team. A five-man syndicate led by theatrical agent Sonny Werblin purchased the club in 1963. Werblin changed the team's name to Jets, their colors to Kelly-green-and-white, and hired former Colts coach Weeb Ewbank to build a winner in New York. Werblin understood the value of star power and that football was entertainment. Not averse to spending money, in 1965 he not only signed rookie quarterback Joe Namath to a record $427,000 contract, but signed Heisman Trophy winning quarterback John Huarte for $200,000 as well.

Ewbank, as he had done in Baltimore, brought about slow but steady progress on the field. After five years Werblin sold out to the other four owners (Phil Iselin, Don Lillis, Townsend Martin and Leon Hess with Iselin in charge) in 1968 just as the Jets were about to make football history. In Ewbank's sixth season, the Jets won their first Eastern Division title and went to the Super Bowl where they were 18-point underdogs to the Colts. Exacting revenge for Ewbank and establishing the AFL as the NFL's equal, the Jets upset the Colts 16–7 by playing a ball control game on offense and forcing five Colt turnovers. 1968 was also notable for the "Heidi" game in which NBC cut coverage of the conclusion of an exciting Jets-Raiders game to go to its regularly scheduled "Heidi" special. The outraged and vociferous public response was clear indication of just how important football had become in American life.

Things started turning sour almost immediately for the Jets after the Super Bowl. Namath retired briefly the following June over his ownership of the bar Bachelors III, a supposed gamblers' hangout. While that was worked out and the Jets repeated as Eastern Division champs in 1969, they lost to the Chiefs 13–6 in the playoffs. They would not win another division title for 29 years. They wouldn't even have another winning season until 1981. Namath's career was shortened and diminished by injuries as were those of other offensive stars Matt Snell and Emerson Boozer. Over the years, the Jets would have some notable performers like runners John Riggins and Freeman McNeil, receivers Wesley Walker, Al Toon and Keyshawn Johnson, and the forceful front four known as the "Sack Exchange" and featuring Joe Klecko and Mark Gastineau, but never a great team.

Off the field, Iselin died in 1968, and Leon Hess assumed control of the franchise eventually buying out all other owners by 1983. Finally to stem a quarter century of losing, Hess hired Bill Parcells as coach in 1997, and the "Tuna" began to turn the team around. When Parcells retired three years later, he was the first Jets coach in history to leave the team with a winning record. Under him and his successors, the Jets turned in five winning records in six seasons led by the running of Curtis Martin. Hess passed away in 1999, and Robert Wood Johnson, Jr. bought the team from the Hess estate.

Origin of name: The team was originally known as the Titans, larger and more powerful than the Giants across the river. When Sonny Werblin bought the team in 1963, he renamed them the Jets, accenting modern technology. It also rhymed with Mets, the

Record by Decade

| | Regular Season | | | Postseason | | |
	Won	Lost	Tied	Won	Lost	Championships
1960s	69	65	6	2	1	1968
1970s	53	91	0	0	0	
1980s	73	77	2	3	4	
1990s	65	95	0	1	2	
2000s	34	30	0	1	2	
All-Time	294	358	8	7	9	1

Winning seasons: 13. Losing Seasons: 21. .500 seasons: 10.

Coaches

	Years	Record	Playoffs
Sammy Baugh	1960–1	14–14–0	0–0
Bulldog Turner	1962	5–9–0	0–0
Weeb Ewbank	1963–73	71–77–6	2–1
Charley Winner	1974–5	9–14–0	0–0
Ken Shipp	1975	1–4–0	0–0
Lou Holtz	1976	3–10–0	0–0
Mike Holovak	1976	0–1–0	0–0
Walt Michaels	1977–82	39–47–1	2–2
Joe Walton	1983–9	53–57–1	1–2
Bruce Coslet	1990–3	26–38–0	0–1
Pete Carroll	1994	6–10–0	0–0
Rich Kotite	1995–6	4–28–0	0–0
Bill Parcells	1997–9	29–19–0	1–1
Al Groh	2000	9–7–0	0–0
Herman Edwards	2001–3	25–23–0	1–2

baseball team with whom they would share Shea Stadium for two decades.

Time till first championship: Nine years.

Time since last championship: 36 years.

Retired numbers: The Jets have retired the numbers of their Hall of Fame long distance, pitch-and-catch team of quarterback Joe Namath, 12, and receiver Don Maynard, 13. Defensive tackle Joe Klecko's 73 is also retired.

Other numbers worn by these players: None.

Those who wore retired numbers after the honored player: Punter Dave Jennings wore 13 in 1985–6.

Numbers that should be retired: None.

Owned numbers: None.

Numbers worn by Hall of Famers: Ronnie Lott 42; Don Maynard 13; Joe Namath 12; and John Riggins 44.

Star power: Freeman McNeil took 24 from Kenny Lewis.

Star eclipsed: Mike Merriweather wore 58 because Mo Lewis wore 57. Kyle Brady wore 81 till Curtis Caesar, 88, left.

Numbers with most great players: 56 has been worn by linebackers Lance Mehl and Roman Phifer as well as defensive end Jeff Lageman.

Worst represented numbers: 17 has been worn by six undistinguished quarterbacks and a punter; 89 has been worn by 15 undistinguished receivers.

Number worn by the most players: 86 has been worn 20 times.

Player who wore the most numbers: Three players have worn three numbers—receiver Nick Bruckner 22/83/86, runner Kenny Lewis 20/22/24, and center John Schmitt 52/56/70.

Longest tenure wearing a number: Kicker Pat Leahy wore 5 for 17 years from 1975 to 1991. Guard Randy Rasmussen wore 66 for 15 years from 1967 to 1981.

Number worn by first ever draft pick: The 1960 draft was not conducted by rounds. From that draft, three draftees played for the Titans in 1960 — linebacker Larry Grantham, 60; halfback Blanche Martin, 36; and end David Ross, 80. The first 1st round pick signed by the Jets was runner Matt Snell, 41, in 1964.

Biggest draft busts: The biggest bust was speedy receiver Lam Jones, 80, selected second in 1980 who caught 138 balls in five years. Another disappointment was runner Blair Thomas, 32, selected second in 1990 who gained 2,009 yards in four years.

Number worn by oldest player: Kickers Pat Leahy, 5, and Nick Lowery, 8, were both 40 when they last played in New York in 1991 and 1996 respectively.

Cameos: All Pros and other notables—Steve Atwater 27; Keith Byars 41; Quinn Early 88; Harry Galbreath 64; Eric Green 86; Mark Malone 16; Ed Marinaro 49; Leonard Marshall 70; Dave Meggett 22; Art Monk 81; Jim Nance 35; Frank Reich 7; Webster Slaughter 87; Bob Talamini 61; Pat Terrell 27.

Ones who got away: Receiver Laveranues Coles, 87, is doing quite well with the Redskins.

Least popular numbers: 0 has never been worn. 9, 13, and 97 have all been worn only twice.

Last number to be originated: 9 was first worn by Jeff Blake in 1992.

Longest dormant number: Currently, 15 and 46 both have been dormant since 1989. 2 was dormant for 26 years from 1965 to 1990.

Triskaidekaphobia notes: 13 was worn by Hall of Famer Don Maynard and punter Dave Jennings, two former Giants. Jennings had worn 13 after Maynard for the Giants as well.

Shared numbers: 67 was worn by two All Pro guards, Bob Mischak and Dave Herman. 79 was worn by two massive tackles, Sherman Plunkett and Marvin Powell. 80 has been worn by a quick defensive tackle, John Elliott, and a clever receiver, Wayne Chrebet. 83 was worn by two Pro Bowl receivers, George Sauer and Jerome Barkum.

Continuity: Ken O'Brien was replaced in 7 by Boomer Esiason; Victor Green was replaced in 21 by fellow cornerback Aaron Beasley; Bobby Jackson was replaced in 40 by fellow cornerback James Hasty; Mike Hudock was replaced in 52 by fellow center John Schmitt; Gerry Philbin was replaced in 81 by fellow defensive end Richard Neal; Wesley Walker was replaced in 85 by fellow Pro Bowl receiver Rob Moore.

Discontinuity: Veteran runner Johnny Hector was followed in 34 by Kenyon Rasheed; ball-hawking safety Dainard Paulson was followed in 40 by Henry King; Pro Bowl linebacker Lance Mehl was followed in 56 by Don Graham; Pro Bowl guard Bob Mischak was followed in 67 by Jim Price; Pro Bowl receiver Art Powell was followed in 84 by Ken Gregory.

Quarterback numbers over 19: 27 Don Allard; 30 Dean Look; 46 Bob Scrabis.

Number of first black player: In 1960, halfback Bill Shockley 29, end Art Powell 84, and guards Howard Glenn 66 and Ernie Barnes 73. Glenn died tragically of a broken neck suffered in midseason.

Numbers of future NFL head coaches:

Family Connections

Brothers

Larry Woods	DT	1971–2	70
Robert Woods	T	1973–7	72

Father and son

Dee Mackey	TE	1963–6	89
Kyle Mackey	QB	1989	15

Wayne Fontes 26; Jim Haslett 51; Walt Michaels 34.

Numbers of future NFL referees: Pete Liske 18; Dean Look 30.

Players who played other sports: Baseball — Dean Look 30. Boxing — Mark Gastineau 99. Wrestling — Wahoo McDaniel 54.

Players more famous after football: Joe Namath, 12, has acted in movies and on television; Ed Marinaro, 49, starred on *Hill Street Blues* on television; Keith Neubert, 86, acted on television. Ernie Barnes, 73, is a painter.

First player to wear a number in the 90s: Linebacker Steve Reese wore 94 in 1974.

Number with most points scored: 5 with 1,470 points scored by Pat Leahy.

Number with most yards rushing: 24 with 8,236 yards gained by Freeman McNeil (8,074), Leon Burton (119), and Jim Tiller (43).

Number with most receptions: 88 with 1,003 passes caught by Al Toon (517), Rich Caster (245), Anthony Becht (120), Kyle Brady (67), Thurlow Cooper (36), Stevie Anderrson (9), Quinn Early (6), and Tony Sweet (3).

Number with most touchdown passes: 12 with 225 touchdowns tossed by Joe Namath (170), Al Dorow (45), and Johnny Green (10).

Number with most interceptions: 40 with 76 passes picked off by Dainard Paulson (29), James Hasty (24), Bobby Jackson (21), Mike Battle (1) and Marc Hogan (1).

Oddity: The Titans and early Jets employed several former players from nearby NFL teams. Seven came from the Giants — John Bookman 29, Lee Grosscup 17, Proverb Jacobs 75, Chuck Janerette 72, Don Maynard 13, Bob Mischak 67 and Lee Riley 22. 14 were former Philadelphia Eagles — Ed Bell 25, Bob Butler 63, Ed Cooke 82, Frank D'Agostino 61, Al Dorow 12, Roy Hord 63, Proverb Jacobs 75, Jim McCusker 70, Joe Pagliei 40, Art Powell 84, Lee Riley 22, Tom Saidock 75, Ted Wegert 20 and Sid Youngelman 77. 13 players who had been affiliated with the Baltimore Colts became Jets, most of them after Weeb Ewbank was hired as coach — Ed Cooke 82, Ken Gregory 84, Winston Hill 75, Dick Jamieson 15, Curley Johnson 20/33, Ed Kovac 35, Dee Mackey 89, Sherman Plunkett 79, Bert Rechichar 44, John Sample 24, Mark Smolinski 30, Bake Turner 29 and Dave Yohn 57.

Players Whose Number Is Unknown

Bill Robinson	(HB)	1960
Bob Fowler	(FB)	1962
Steve Rogers	(RB)	1976
Jim Rosecrans	(LB)	1976
Rich Szaro	(K)	1979
Reggie Smith	(WR)	1987
Maurice Turner	(RB)	1987
Sanjay Beach	(WR)	1989

Team All-Time Numerical Roster

Those with an "r" following the year 1987 were replacement players during the players' strike. Pro Bowl players for each number are in *Italics*; Hall of Famers are in **Bold** type.

1 Mike Adamle (RB) 1973–4, Dave Jacobs (K) 1979, Brett Conway (K) 2000, Matt Turk (P) 2002.

2 Bill Atkins (DB) 1962–3, Ed Chlebek (QB) 1963, Vince Turner (DB) 1964, Toni Linhart (K) 1979, Raul Allegre (K) 1991, Jason Staurovsky (K) 1992.

3 Bobby Howfield (K) 1971–3, Duane Carrell (P) 1976–7, Rick Mirer (QB) 1999.

4 Pat Ryan (QB) 1978–80, Dave Jennings (P) 1987, Louie Aguiar (P/K) 1991–3, Glenn Foley (QB) 1995–8, Dan Stryzinski (P) 2003.

5 Booth Lusteg (K) 1967, Pat Leahy (K) 1975–91, Don Silvestri (K) 1995–6.

6 Bill Demory (QB) 1973, Joe Prokop (P) 1988–90, Bubby Brister (QB) 1995, Ray Lucas (QB) 1998–2000, Doug Brien (K) 2003.

7 Sherman Lewis (DB) 1966–7, Ed Bell (WR)

1970–5, *Ken O'Brien* (QB) 1984–92, *Boomer Esiason* (QB) 1993–5, Frank Reich (QB) 1996, Chuck Clements (QB) 1997, *Tom Tupa* (P/QB) 1999–2001, Marquel Blackwell (QB) 2003.

8 Greg Gantt (P) 1974–5, Tom Flick (QB) 1987, Browning Nagle (QB) 1991–3, Nick Lowery (K) 1994–6, Todd Husak (QB) 2002.

9 Jeff Blake (QB) 1992–3, John Hall (K) 1997–2002.

10 Bobby Renn (DB) 1961, Julian Fagan (P) 1973, Marty Domres (QB) 1977, Pat Ryan (QB) 1981–9, Cary Blanchard (K) 1992–3, Jack Trudeau (QB) 1994, Chad Pennington (QB) 2000–3.

11 Butch Songin (QB) 1962, Jim Turner (K/QB) 1964–70, John Jones (QB) 1975, Steve Joachim (QB) 1976, Craig Penrose (QB) 1980, Pat Ragusa (K) 1987r, Tony Eason (QB) 1989–90, Brian Hansen (P) 1994–8, Tory Woodbury (QB) 2001.

12 *Al Dorow* (QB) 1960–1, Harold Stephens (QB) 1962, John Green (QB) 1962–3, **Joe Namath** (QB) 1965–76.

13 **Don Maynard** (WR) 1960–72, Dave Jennings (P) 1985–6.

14 Richard Todd (QB) 1976–83, 1986, Tom O'Connor (P) 1987r, Glenn Foley (QB) 1994, Neil O'Donnell (QB) 1996–7.

15 Dick Jamieson (QB) 1960–1, Don Flynn (HB) 1961, Babe Parilli (QB) 1968–9, Bob Davis (QB) 1970–2, Chuck Ramsey (P) 1977–84, Kyle Mackey (QB) 1989.

16 *Ken O'Brien* (QB) 1983, Walter Briggs (QB) 1987r, Mark Malone (QB) 1989, *Vinny Testaverde* (QB) 1998–2003.

17 Lee Grosscup (QB) 1962, Galen Hall (QB) 1963, Mike Taliaferro (QB) 1964–7, Matt Robinson (QB) 1977–9, Bob Avellini (QB) 1984, David Norris (QB) 1987r, John Kidd (P) 1998.

18 Pete Liske (QB) 1964, Al Woodall (QB) 1969–74, Ray Lucas (QB) 1997.

19 Bill Wood (DB) 1963, Dick Wood (QB) 1963–4, Chris Farasopoulos (S) 1971–3, Pat Kelly (TE) 1990, *Keyshawn Johnson* (WR) 1996–9.

20 Don Herndon (DB) 1960, Ted Wegert (HB) 1960, Lowe Wren (DB) 1961, Curley Johnson (P) 1961–2, Bob Schweikert (WR) 1965–7, Steve O'Neal (P) 1969–72, Delles Howell (CB) 1973–5, Darnell Powell (RB) 1978, Kenny Lewis (RB) 1981, Davlin Mullen (CB) 1983–6, Leander Knight (CB) 1989, Dennis Price (DB) 1991–2, *Richie Anderson* (RB) 1993–2002, Michael Bates (KR) 2003.

21 Steve Tannen (DB) 1970–4, Clark Gaines (RB) 1976–80, Kirk Springs (DB) 1982–5, Sid Lewis (CB) 1987, Treg Songy (DB) 1987r, Don Odegard (CB) 1990–1, Sheldon Canley (RB) 1992, Victor Green (CB) 1993–2001, Aaron Beasley (CB) 2002–3.

22 Americo Sapienza (HB) 1960, Lee Riley (DB) 1961–2, Willie West (DB) 1964–5, Jim Hudson (S) 1966–70, Vern Studdard (WR) 1971, Burgess Owens (S) 1973–9, Kenny Lewis (RB) 1983, Mike Dennis (CB) 1984, Nick Bruckner (WR) 1985, Sean Dykes (CB) 1987, *Erik McMillan* (S) 1988–92, Eric Thomas (CB) 1993–4, Carl Greenwood (CB) 1995–6, Dave Meggett (RB) 1998, Damien Robinson (S) 2001–2, Tyrone Carter (S) 2003.

23 *Dick Felt* (DB) 1960–1, Mark Johnston (DB) 1964, Bill Rademacher (DB) 1967–8, Jerry Davis (DB) 1975, Shafer Suggs (DB) 1976–80, Mike Harmon (WR) 1983, Dennis Bligen (RB) 1984–7, Mike Mayes (CB) 1990, Marcus Turner (DB) 1992–5, Eric Zomalt (S) 1996, Kevin Williams (S) 1998–2000, Jamie Henderson (CB) 2001–3.

24 Leon Burton (HB) 1960, Jim Tiller (HB) 1962, John Sample (CB) 1966–8, Artimus Parker (S) 1977, Kenny Lewis (RB) 1980, *Freeman McNeil* (RB) 1981–92, Ray Mickens (CB) 1996–2003.

25 Ed Bell (DB) 1960, Dave Ames (HB) 1961, Mel West (HB) 1961–3, Marshall Starks (DB) 1963–4, Ray Abruzzese (DB) 1965–6, Bob Prout (S) 1975, Scott Dierking (RB) 1977–83, Cedric Minter (RB) 1984–5, George Radachowsky (S) 1987–9, R.J. Kors (S) 1991–2, Clifford Hicks (CB) 1993–4, Gary Jones (S) 1995–6, Robert Farmer (RB) 1999, Nick Ferguson (S) 2000–2, Derek Pagel (S) 2003.

26 Dewey Bohling (HB) 1960–1, Wayne Fontes (DB) 1962, Tony Stricker (DB) 1963, Bill Pashe (DB) 1964, Dave West (DB) 1964, Jim Richards (S) 1968–9, Margene Adkins (WR) 1973, Carl Garrett (RB) 1975, Donald Dykes (CB) 1979–81, Lester Lyles (S) 1985–7, Ken Johnson (S) 1990, Damon Pieri (S) 1993, Ron Carpenter (S) 1995–6, Jerome Henderson (DB) 1997–8, Omar Stoutmire (S) 1999, Chad Morton (KR) 2001–2, Omare Lowe (CB) 2003.

27 Don Allard (QB) 1961, Jim Apple (HB) 1961, Phil Wise (S) 1971–6, Ron Mabra (CB) 1977, Jesse Johnson (DB) 1980–3, Russell Carter (DB) 1984–7, Kevin Porter (S) 1992, Pat Terrell (S) 1994, Lou D'Agostino (RB) 1996, Jerald Sowell (FB) 1997, Steve Atwater (S) 1999, Tony Scott (CB) 2000–1.

28 Chuck Dupre (DB) 1960, Jerry Robinson (WR) 1965, Jim Gray (DB) 1966, Pat Gucciardo (DB) 1966, Abner Haynes (RB) 1967, Cecil Leonard (DB) 1969–70, Darrol Ray (S) 1980–4, Carl Howard (CB) 1985–90, Pat Chaffey (RB) 1992–3, Reggie Cobb (RB) 1996, Raymond Austin (DB) 1997, *Curtis Martin* (RB) 1998–2003.

29 Bill Shockley (HB) 1960–2, John Bookman (DB) 1961, Bake Turner (WR) 1963–9, Rocky Turner (WR) 1972–3, Carl Capria (S) 1975, Donnie Walker (S) 1975, Johnny Lynn (DB) 1979–86, Joe Burke (RB) 1987r, A.B. Brown (RB) 1989–92, Adrian Murrell (RB) 1993–7, Donnie Abraham (CB) 2002–3.

30 Gerhard Schwedes (FB) 1960, Dean Look (QB) 1962, Mark Smolinski (FB) 1963–8, George Nock (RB) 1969, Chuck Mercein (RB) 1970, Dennis Cambal (TE) 1973, Charlie White (RB) 1977, Rocky Klever (RB) 1982–3, Nuu Faaola (FB) 1986–8, Brad Baxter (RB) 1989–95, Chris Hayes (S) 1997–2001.

31 *Bill Mathis* (RB) 1960–9, Marion Barber (RB) 1982–8, Lonnie Young (S) 1991–3, *Aaron Glenn* (CB) 1994–2001, Ray Green (CB) 2003.

32 Charlie Browning (HB) 1965, *Emerson Boozer* (RB) 1966–75, Blair Thomas (RB) 1990–3, Anthony Johnson (RB) 1994, Sherriden May (FB) 1995–6, Leon Johnson (RB) 1997–8, 2000, Jacoby Shepherd (CB) 2003.

33 Pete Hart (FB) 1960, Paul Hynes (DB) 1961–2, Curley Johnson (P) 1963–9, W.K. Hicks (S) 1970–2, Bob Burns (RB) 1974, Kevin Long (RB) 1977–81, John Chirico (RB) 1987r, Terry Williams (CB) 1988–9, Ron Moore (RB) 1995–6, Jerald Sowell (FB) 1998–2003.

34 Walt Michaels (LB) 1963, Lee White (RB) 1968–70, Larry Riley (CB) 1978, Johnny Hector (RB) 1983–92, Kenyon Rasheed (RB) 1995, Bernie Parmalee (RB) 1999–2000, LaMont Jordan (RB) 2001–3.

35 Roger Donnahoo (DB) 1960, Bob Brooks (HB) 1961, Ed Kovac (HB) 1962, Billy Joe (FB) 1967–8, Dennis Onkontz (LB) 1970, Jim Nance (RB) 1973, Steve Davis (RB) 1975–6, Mike Augustyniak (FB) 1981–3, Kerry Glenn (CB) 1985–9, Tim Newman (RB) 1987r, Scottie Graham (RB) 1992, Dexter Carter (RB) 1995, Del Lee (CB) 1999, B.J. Askew (RB) 2003.

36 Blanche Martin (HB) 1960, Steve Harkey (RB) 1971–2, Bob Gresham (RB) 1975–6, Rich Miano (S) 1985–9, Joe Fishback (DB) 1992, Buddy Crutchfield (CB) 1999.

37 Allen Smith (HB) 1966, George Nock (RB) 1970–1, Marv Owens (WR) 1974, Billy Hardee (CB) 1977, Tim Moresco (S) 1978–80, Skip Lane (CB) 1984, Donnie Elder (CB) 1985, Jo Jo Heath (DB) 1987r, Anthony Prior (CB) 1993–5, Jake Moreland (RB) 2000, David Young (S) 2003.

38 Ed Taylor (CB) 1975–9, Billy Taylor (RB) 1981, George Floyd (DB) 1982–4, Larry Flowers (S) 1985, Mike Zordich (S) 1987–8, Todd Scott (S) 1995, Kwame Ellis (CB) 1996, Jon McGraw (DB) 2002–3.

39 Fred Julian (DB) 1960–1, Harry Howard (S) 1976, Maurice Tyler (CB) 1977, Saladin Martin (DB) 1980, Harry Hamilton (S) 1984–7, Johnny Johnson (RB) 1993–4, Andrew Davison (DB) 2002.

40 Joe Paglei (FB) 1960, *Dainard Paulson* (DB) 1961–6, Henry King (DB) 1967, Mike Battle (DB) 1969–70, Hank Bjorklund (RB) 1972–4, Bobby Jackson (CB) 1978–85, Marc Hogan (DB) 1987r, James Hasty (CB) 1988–94.

41 Charlie Flowers (RB) 1962, *Matt Snell* (FB) 1964–72, Tuineau Alipate (LB) 1994, Keith Byars (FB) 1998, Leonard Myers (CB) 2003.

42 Clyde Washington (DB) 1963–5, Randy Beverly (CB) 1967–9, Cliff McClain (RB) 1970–3, Bruce Harper (RB) 1977–84, John Booty (DB) 1988–90, **Ronnie Lott** (S) 1993–4, Marcus Coleman (CB) 1996–2001, Sam Garnes (S) 2002–3.

43 John Dockery (CB) 1968–71, Clarence Jackson (RB) 1974–6, Roger Vick (FB) 1987–9, Mike Brim (CB) 1991–2, Vance Joseph (CB) 1995.

44 Bert Rechichar (FB) 1961, Jim Hudson (S) 1965, **John Riggins** (FB) 1971–5, Tom Newton (RB) 1977–82, Trent Collins (DB) 1987r, Lonnie Young (S) 1995–6, Corwin Brown (CB) 1997–8.

45 Corky Tharp (DB) 1960, *Dick Christy* (HB) 1961–3, Kern Carson (HB) 1965, Cosmo Iacavazzi (FB) 1965, Earl Christy (DB) 1966–8, Earlie Thomas (CB) 1970–4, Louie Giammona (RB) 1976, Kirk Springs (DB) 1981, Dwayne Crutchfield (FB) 1982–3, Eddie Hunter (RB) 1987r, Tony Stargell (CB) 1990–1, Otis Smith (CB) 1995–8.

46 Bob Scrabis (QB) 1960–2, Bill Baird (DB) 1963–9, Rich Sowells (CB) 1971–6, Woody Bennett (RB) 1979–80, Fernanza Burgess (S) 1984, Michael Harper (WR) 1986, Derrick Foster (RB) 1987r, Michael Mitchell (CB) 1989.

47 Solomon Brannan (DB) 1967, Mike D'Amato (DB) 1968, Roscoe Word (CB) 1974–6, Tommy Marvaso (DB) 1976–7, Jim Earley (FB) 1978, Jerry Holmes (CB) 1980–3, 1986–7, Clifford Hicks (CB) 1993–4, Scott Frost (S) 1998–2000.

48 Cornell Gordon (CB) 1965–9, Gus Hollomon (S) 1970–2, Cliff Brooks (S) 1976, Ken Schroy (S) 1977–84, Bobby Humphrey (CB) 1986–9, Brian Washington (S) 1990–4.

49 George Hoey (DB) 1975, Ed Marinaro (RB) 1976, Steve Carpenter (S) 1980, Tony Paige (FB) 1984–6, Larry Robinson (DB) 1987r, Travis Curtis (S) 1990, Eric Kattus (TE) 1992, Troy Johnson (LB) 1994, Casey Dailey (LB) 1998.

50 James Furey (DB) 1961, Carl McAdams (DT/LB) 1967–9, Michael Taylor (LB) 1972–3, Wayne Mulligan (C) 1974–5, Mike Mock (LB) 1978, John Sullivan (LB) 1979–80, Bob Crable (LB) 1982–7, Tim Cofield (LB) 1989, Glenn Cadrez (LB) 1992–5, Rob Holmberg (LB) 1998, Kelvin Moses (LB) 2001–2, Mark Brown (LB) 2003.

51 Ralph Baker (LB) 1964–74, Greg Buttle (LB) 1976–84, Rogers Alexander (LB) 1986, Jim Haslett (LB) 1987r, John Galvin (LB) 1988, Joe Mott (LB) 1989–90, Don Jones (LB) 1992–3, Matt Finkes (LB) 1997, Bryan Cox (LB) 1998–2000, James Darling (LB) 2001–2, Quincy Stewart (LB) 2003.

52 Mike Hudock (C) 1960–5, John Schmitt (C) 1966–73, Steve Reese (LB) 1974–5, Mike Hennigan (LB) 1976–8, Al Washington (LB) 1981, Jim

Eliopulos (LB) 1983–5, Onzy Elam (LB) 1987–8, Adam Bob (LB) 1989, John Galvin (LB) 1990–1, Cal Dixon (C) 1992–5, Pepper Johnson (LB) 1997–8, Kenyatta Wright (LB) 2003.

53 Bill Zapalac (DE) 1971–3, Warren Koegel (C) 1974, Richard Lewis (LB) 1974, Ken Bernich (LB) 1975, Carl Russ (LB) 1976, Al Palewicz (LB) 1977, Mike McKibben (LB) 1979–80, Jim Sweeney (OL) 1984–94, Chad Cascadden (LB) 1995–8, Courtney Ledyard (LB) 2000, Khary Campbell (LB) 2002–3.

54 Wahoo McDaniel (LB) 1964–5, Jim Waskiewicz (LB) 1966–7, Jamie Rivers (LB) 1974–5, Steve Poole (LB) 1976, Stan Blinka (LB) 1979–83, Troy Benson (LB) 1986–9, Marvin Jones (LB) 1993–6, Dwayne Gordon (LB) 1997–2000, Victor Hobson (LB) 2003.

55 Robert Marquess (C) 1960, Pasquale Lamberti (HB) 1961, Alex Kroll (C) 1962, Mike Dukes (LB) 1965, Jim Carroll (LB) 1969, John Ebersole (LB) 1970–7, Ron Crosby (LB) 1979–83, Charles Jackson (LB) 1985–6, Alex Gordon (LB) 1987–9, Mike Witteck (LB) 1987r, Bobby Houston (LB) 1991–6, Marvin Jones (LB) 1997–2003.

56 Roger Ellis (C) 1960–2, Ted Bates (LB) 1963, John Schmitt (C) 1964, Paul Crane (LB) 1966–72, Godwin Turk (LB) 1974–5, Larry Keller (LB) 1976–8, *Lance Mehl* (LB) 1980–7, Don Graham (LB) 1988, Jeff Lageman (DE) 1989–94, Rick Hamilton (LB) 1996, Roman Phifer (LB) 1999–2000, Jason Glenn (LB) 2001–2, Sam Cowart (LB) 2002–3.

57 Hubert Bobo (LB) 1961–2, Dave Yohn (LB) 1963, John Matlock (C) 1967, John Little (DL) 1970–4, Richard Lewis (LB) 1975, Jim Jerome (LB) 1977, Blake Whitlach (LB) 1978, John Woodring (LB) 1981–5, Kevin MacArthur (LB) 1986–9, Mac Stephens (LB) 1990, *Mo Lewis* (LB) 1991–2003.

58 Bill Ferguson (LB) 1973–4, Richard Wood (LB) 1975, Mark Merrill (LB) 1978–9, Marty Wetzel (LB) 1981, Bobby Bell (LB) 1984, Matt Monger (LB) 1985–7, Lynwood Alford (LB) 1987r, Joe Kelly (LB) 1990–2, Mike Merriweather (LB) 1993, Wilber Marshall (LB) 1995, Aubrey Beavers (LB) 1996, James Farrior (LB) 1997–2001, Jason Glenn (LB) 2003.

59 Rob Spicer (LB) 1973, Howard Kindig (C) 1974, Bob Martin (LB) 1976–9, George Lilja (T) 1983, Kyle Clifton (LB) 1984–96.

60 *Larry Grantham* (LB) 1960–72, Dan Alexander (G) 1977–89, Dennis O'Sullivan (OL) 2002.

61 Frank D'Agostino (G) 1960, Leon Dombrowski (G) 1960, Dan Callahan (G) 1960–1, Dan Ficca (G) 1963–6, Bob Talamini (G) 1968, Roger Finnie (T) 1969–72, John Roman (T) 1976–82, Greg Lilja (T) 1984, Greg Gunter (C) 1985, Jeff Criswell (T) 1988–90, Terrance Wisdom (G) 1995.

62 Bob O'Neill (G) 1961, Sid Fournet (G) 1962–3, Ed Cummings (LB) 1964, *Al Atkinson*

(LB) 1966–74, Joe Pellegrini (C/G) 1982–3, Bill Bain (T) 1986, Eric Coss (C) 1987r, Roger Duffy (C/G) 1990–7, Todd Burger (G) 1998.

63 Bob Butler (G) 1963, Roy Hord (G) 1963, Bob Rowley (LB) 1964, Jim O'Mahoney (LB) 1965–6, John Neidert (LB) 1969, Roy Kirksey (G) 1971–2, Travis Roach (G) 1974, John Hennessey (DE) 1977–9, Ted Banker (G/T) 1984–8, Dave Zawatson (G/T) 1990, Carlton Haselrig (G) 1995, Lamont Burns (G/C) 1997, J.P. Machado (G/C) 1999–2002, Dewayne Robertson (DT) 2003.

64 Tom Budrewicz (G) 1961, Ed Walsh (T) 1961, Jerry Fields (LB) 1961–2, Pete Perreault (T/G) 1963–67, 1969–70, Chuck Hinton (DT) 1971, Gregg Robinson (DL) 1978, Guy Bingham (OL) 1980–8, Martin Cornelson (C) 1987r, Trevor Matich (OL) 1990–1, Harry Galbreath (G) 1996, J.R. Conrad (OL) 1997.

65 Sam DeLuca (G) 1964–6, Jimmie Jones (DE) 1969–70, *Joe Fields* (C) 1975–87, John Hudson (C) 1996–9, Brandon Moore (G) 2003.

66 Howard Glenn (G) 1960, Randy Rasmussen (G) 1967–81, Billy Shields (T) 1985, Vince Jasper (G) 1987r, Dave Cadigan (G/T) 1988–93, Donald Evans (DT) 1994–5, Lonnie Palelei (G/T) 1997.

67 *Bob Mischak* (G) 1960–2, Jim Price (LB) 1963, *Dave Herman* (G) 1964–73, Darrell Austin (G/C) 1975–8, Ed McGlasson (C) 1979, Anthony Corvino (G/T) 1987r, Dwayne White (G) 1990–4, Everett McIver (T) 1995, Mike Gisler (C/G) 1998–9, Kareem McKenzie (T) 2001–3.

68 John McMullan (G) 1960–1, Mike Stromberg (LB) 1968, Gordon Wright (G) 1969, Roger Bernhardt (G) 1974, Tank Marshall (DT) 1977, Eric Cunningham (G) 1979–80, Reggie McElroy (T) 1983–9, David Ware (T/G) 1993, John Bock (C) 1995, *Kevin Mawae* (C) 1998–2003.

69 Sid Abramowitz (T) 1985, Tom Humphrey (G/T) 1987r, Jeff Criswell (T) 1991–4, Harry Boatswain (G/T) 1996, Jason Fabini (T) 1998–2003.

70 Gene Cockrell (T) 1960–2, Jim McCusker (T) 1964, John Schmitt (C) 1965, Karl Henke (DE) 1968, Dave Foley (T) 1969–71, Larry Woods (DT) 1974–5, Stan Waldemore (OL) 1978–84, Ken Jones (T) 1987, Tony Garbarczyk (DE) 1987r, Jeff Oliver (G) 1989, Leonard Marshall (DT) 1993, Matt O'Dwyer (G) 1995–8.

71 Paul Seiler (T/C) 1967, Sam Walton (T) 1968–9, John Mooring (G) 1971–3, Al Krevis (T) 1976, Jeff Bleamer (T) 1977, Joe Moreino (DE) 1978, Lim Luscinski (T) 1982, Mark Shumate (DE) 1985, Jim Stuckey (DE) 1986, Pete McCartney (T) 1987r, Bill Pickel (DT) 1991–4, Mike Chalenski (DL) 1996, Kerry Jenkins (G/T) 1997–2001, Chris Smith (OL) 2002.

72 Dick Guesman (DT/K) 1960–1, Charlie Janerette (DT) 1963, Paul Rochester (DT) 1965–9,

Scott Palmer (DT) 1971, Robert Woods (T) 1973–6, Al Burton (DE) 1977, Chris Ward (T) 1978–83, Gordon King (T) 1986–7, Brett Miller (T) 1990–2, Karl Wilson (DE) 1993, Dave Alexander (C) 1996, Jason Ferguson (DT) 1997–2003.

73 Larry Baker (T) 1960, Ernie Barnes (T) 1960, Joe Katcik (T) 1960, Moses Gray (T) 1961–2, George Strugar (DT) 1962–3, Paul Rochester (DT) 1964, Nick DeFelice (T) 1965, Mitch Dudek (G) 1966, Dennis Randall (DT) 1967, Ray Hayes (DT) 1968, *Joe Klecko* (DL) 1977–87, David Williams (T) 1996.

74 Nick Mumley (DE) 1960–2, Gordy Holz (DT) 1964, Henry Schmidt (DT) 1966, Jeff Richardson (G) 1967–8, Joe Schmiesing (DT) 1974, Abdul Salaam (DT) 1976–83, Ron Faurot (DE/LB) 1984–5, Elvis Franks (DE) 1986, Derland Moore (DT) 1986, Don Smith (DT) 1987, Mark Garalczyk (DE) 1988, Curt Singer (T) 1989, Everett McIver (T) 1994, Erik Howard (DT) 1995–6, Ryan Young (T) 1999–2001, Brent Smith (G) 2003.

75 Tom Saidock (T) 1960–1, Proverb Jacobs (T) 1961–2, John Kennerson (G) 1962, *Winston Hill* (T) 1963–76, Tony Chickillo (DL) 1987r, Adam Schreiber (C) 1988–9, Irv Eatman (T) 1991–2, Carl Hansen (DT) 1998, Ian Rafferty (T) 1999, Larry Webster (DT) 2002, Chester McGlockton (DT) 2003.

76 Sid Youngelman (DE) 1960–1, Bob Watters (DE) 1962, Arnie Simkus (DT) 1965, Bob Svihus (T) 1971–2, Jim Bailey (DT) 1975, Lawrence Pillers (DE) 1976–80, Ben Rudolph (DT) 1981–6, John Thomas (T) 1987r, Mike Withycombe (T) 1988–9, James Brown (T) 1993–5, Jumbo Elliott (T) 1996–2000, 2002.

77 Joe Ryan (E) 1960, Dick Guesman (DT/K) 1962–3, Bert Wilder (DT) 1964, Tom Bayless (G) 1970, Carl Barzilauskas (DT) 1974–7, Joe Pellegrini (DT) 1978–9, Kenny Neil (DE) 1981–3, Ron Sams (C/G) 1986, Gerald Nichols (DT) 1987–90, Matt Willig (T) 1992–5, Jay Hagood (T) 1997, Randy Thomas (G) 1999–2002, J.P. Machado (C) 2003.

78 Jack Klotz (T) 1960–3, Jim Harris (DT) 1965–7, Garry Puetz (G/T) 1973–8, Barry Bennett (DL) 1982–7, Scott Jones (T) 1990, Mario Johnson (DT) 1992, Lou Benfatti (DT) 1994–6, Terry Day (DE) 1997, Jonathan Goodwin (OL) 2002–3.

79 Bob Reifsnyder (DE) 1960–1, Francis Morelli (T) 1962, *Sherman Plunkett* (T) 1963–7, Paul Seiler (T/C) 1969, Clovis Swiney (DT) 1971, Gordie Brown (T) 1974–5, Marvin Powell (T) 1977–85, Mike Haight (G/T) 1986–91, Chris Brown (T) 1987r, Melvin Hayes (T) 1995, David Loverne (G) 1999–2001, Dave Szott (G) 2002–3.

80 Dave Ross (E) 1960–1, Perry Richards (WR) 1962, Jim Evans (WR) 1964, Bob Werl (DE) 1966, *John Elliott* (DT) 1967–73, Howard Satterwhite (WR) 1976, Shelton Diggs (WR) 1977,

Kevin Bell (WR) 1978, Roger Farmer (WR) 1979, Lam Jones (WR) 1980–5, Scott Holman (WR) 1987r, K.D. Dunn (TE) 1988, Greg Werner (TE) 1989, Mark Boyer (TE) 1990–2, James Thornton (TE) 1993–4, Wayne Chrebet (WR) 1995–2003.

81 *Gerry Philbin* (DE) 1964–72, Richard Neal (DL) 1973–7, Derrick Gaffney (WR) 1978–83, Billy Griggs (TE) 1985–8, Derrick Gaffney (WR) 1987r, Terance Mathis (WR) 1990–3, Art Monk (WR) 1994, Kyle Brady (TE) 1995, Jeff Graham (WR) 1996–7, Bradford Banta (TE) 2000, Matthew Hatchette (WR) 2001, Chris Baker (TE) 2002, Curtis Conway (WR) 2003.

82 Ken Campbell (E) 1960, Ed Cooke (DE) 1960–2, Bert Wilder (DT) 1965–7, Gary Arthur (TE) 1970–1, David Knight (WR) 1973–7, *Mickey Shuler* (TE) 1978–89, Jamie Kurisko (TE) 1987r, Pat Kelly (TE) 1991, Rob Carpenter (WR) 1992–4, Blake Spence (TE) 1998–9, Vincent Brisby (WR) 2000, Kevin Swayne (WR) 2001–3.

83 *George Sauer* (WR) 1965–70, *Jerome Barkum* (WR) 1972–83, Nick Bruckner (WR) 1984, Jo Jo Townsell (WR) 1985–90, Johnny Mitchell (TE) 1992, Troy Sadowski (TE) 1993, Tyrone Davis (TE) 1995–6, Dwight Stone (WR) 1999–2000, Santana Moss (WR) 2001–3.

84 Art Powell (WR) 1960–2, Ken Gregory (WR) 1963, Sammy Weir (WR) 1966, Mark Lomas (DL) 1970–4, Clint Haslerig (WR) 1976, Paul Darby (WR) 1979–80, Bobby Humphrey (WR) 1983–5, Michael Harper (WR) 1986–8, Chris Dressel (TE) 1989–91, Troy Sadowski (TE) 1992, Fred Baxter (TE) 1993–2000, Craig Yeast (WR) 2001, Jonathan Carter (WR) 2002–3.

85 Gene Heeter (TE) 1963–5, Steve Thompson (DT) 1969–70, Ed Galigher (DL) 1972–6, *Wesley Walker* (WR) 1977–89, *Rob Moore* (WR) 1990–4, Jeff Sydner (WR) 1995, Henry Bailey (WR) 1996, John Burke (TE) 1997, Jermaine Wiggins (TE) 2000, James Dearth (TE) 2001–3.

86 Karl Kalimer (TE) 1962, Bob Watters (DE) 1963–4, *Verlon Biggs* (DE) 1965–70, Joe Jackson (DE) 1972–3, Willie Brister (TE) 1974–5, Richard Osborne (TE) 1976, Bob Raba (TE) 1977–9, Steve Stephens (TE) 1981, Steve Alvers (TE/C) 1982, Nick Bruckner (WR) 1983, Glenn Dennison (TE) 1984–5, Tracy Martin (WR) 1987, Stan Hunter (WR) 1987r, Keith Neubert (TE) 1988–9, Ken Whisenhunt (TE) 1991–2, Johnny Mitchell (TE) 1993–5, Alex Van Dyke (WR) 1996–8, Eric Green (TE) 1999, Windrell Hayes (WR) 2000, Chris Baker (WR) 2003.

87 Laverne Torczon (DE) 1962–5, *Pete Lammons* (TE) 1966–71, Steve Thompson (DT) 1972–3, Billy Newsome (DE) 1975–6, Bruce Stephens (WR) 1978, Kurt Sohn (WR) 1981–8, Eric Riley (TE) 1987r, Chris Burkett (WR) 1989–93, Ryan Yarborough (WR) 1994–5, Webster Slaughter

(WR) 1996, Laveranues Coles (WR) 2000–2, Lawrence Hamilton (WR) 2003.

88 Thurlow Cooper (TE) 1960–2, Bob McAdams (DE) 1963–4, Bill Yearby (DT) 1966, *Richard Caster* (TE/WR) 1970–7, Mark Iwanowski (TE) 1978, Tom Coombs (TE) 1982, Chy Davidson (WR) 1984, *Al Toon* (WR) 1985–92, Tony Sweet (TE) 1987r, Stevie Anderson (WR) 1994, Curtis Ceasar (WR) 1995, Kyle Brady (TE) 1996–8, Quinn Early (WR) 1999, Anthony Becht (TE) 2000–3.

89 Dee Mackey (TE) 1963–5, Wayne Stewart (TE) 1969–72, Lou Piccone (WR) 1974–6, Bobby Jones (WR) 1978–82, Preston Brown (WR) 1983, Rocky Klever (RB) 1984–7, Titus Dixon (WR) 1989, Phillip Epps (WR) 1989, Dale Dawkins (WR) 1990–3, Orlando Parker (WR) 1994, Charles Wilson (WR) 1995, Dedric Ward (WR) 1997–2000, Tory Woodbury (WR) 2002, Albert Johnson (WR) 2003, Kevin Lockett (WR) 2003.

90 Chris Godfrey (DT) 1980, Jay Brophy (LB) 1987r, Robin Cole (LB) 1988, Dennis Byrd (DL) 1989–92.

91 Don Buckey (WR) 1976, Ladell Wills (LB) 1987r, Paul Frase (DL) 1988–94, Brent Williams (DE) 1996, Jason Wiltz (DT) 1999–2000, Steve Martin (DT) 2001, Josh Evans (DT) 2002–3.

92 Wesley Roberts (DE) 1980, Ken Rose (LB) 1987–9, Emanuel McNeil (DT) 1990, Coleman Rudolph (DL) 1993, Tony Casillas (DT) 1994–5, Bobby Hamilton (DE) 1996–9, *Shaun Ellis* (DE) 2000–3.

93 Marty Lyons (DL) 1979–89, Marc Spindler (DT) 1995–6, Ernie Logan (NT) 1998–2000, James Reed (DT) 2001–3.

94 Steve Reese (LB) 1974, Ralph DeLoach (DE) 1981, Rusty Guilbeau (LB) 1982–5, Scott Mesereau (DL) 1987–93, Matt Brock (DT) 1995–6, *John Abraham* (DE) 2000–3.

95 Tom Baldwin (DT) 1984–8, Troy Johnson (LB) 1990–1, Huey Richardson (DE) 1992, Alfred Oglesby (DT) 1994, Rick Lyle (DE) 1997–2001, Steve White (DE) 2002, Matt Walters (DE) 2003.

96 Henry Walls (LB) 1987r, Steve Hammond (LB) 1988, Ron Stallworth (DE) 1989–90, Mark Gunn (DE) 1991–4, Jeff Faulkner (DT) 1996, Tom Barndt (DT) 2001.

97 Marvin Washington (DE) 1989–96, Dorian Boose (DE) 1998–2000.

98 Jerome Foster (DE) 1986–7, Darrell Davis (DE) 1990, Kurt Barber (LB) 1992–5, Mark Gunn (DE) 1996, Ronnie Dixon (DT) 1997, Anthony Pleasant (DE) 1998–9, Shane Burton (DL) 2000–1, Alan Harper (DL) 2002.

99 *Mark Gastineau* (DE) 1979–88, Keo Coleman (LB) 1992, Steve DeOssie (LB) 1993, Hugh Douglas (DE) 1995–7, Eric Ogbogu (DE) 1998–2001, Bryan Thomas (DL) 2002–3.

Oakland Raiders

The franchise: When the American Football League was formed in the summer of 1959, Oakland was not in the plans. However, the owners of the Minneapolis franchise pulled out in January 1960 to accept an expansion franchise offered by the NFL, so the AFL had to move fast. Barron Hilton of the Los Angeles Chargers wanted a second West Coast team, and the final charter AFL franchise was awarded to an eight-man Oakland partnership headed by Chet Soda. After one disastrous season, Soda and four other partners sold out to the three remaining partners Wayne Valley, Ed McGah and Robert Osborne. This group was further stabilized by a sizeable loan from Bills owner Ralph Wilson.

For its first two seasons, the Raiders played their home games in San Francisco before Oakland built them a glorified high school stadium known as Frank Youell Field in 1962. On the field, the Raiders followed a 6–8 initial season with 2–12 and 1–13 records that included a 19 game losing streak. Realizing that something major had to change if the franchise were to survive, the Raiders hired Al Davis, an assistant to Chargers coach Sid Gillman, as coach and general manger in 1963. Progress was instantaneous; the Raiders went 10–4 that year, a nine game improvement. Davis changed everything, even the uniforms went from black-and-gold to the now-familiar silver-and-black. More importantly, he traded for star receiver Art Powell to help establish the vertical passing attack that would signify the team's offense from that point on. Furthermore, Davis' intimidating, belligerent attitude was transfused permanently to his team, still among the most penalized teams in the league.

After three years, Davis hired John Rauch as coach and left Oakland to become Commissioner of the AFL in April 1966. He hit the ground running, starting an aggressive practice of NFL player raids leaguewide. Meanwhile, unknown to Davis, Lamar Hunt of the Chiefs and Tex Schramm of the Cowboys were secretly hammering out a deal for a merger of the two leagues. In June, Davis returned to the Raiders and was made Managing General Partner, part of the ownership group. Rauch would go 33–8–1 with a trip to Super Bowl II, but was replaced by John Madden in 1969. Madden attained a magnificent 103–32–7 record over 10 years, a .750 wining percentage, and won the Raiders first Super Bowl trophy in 1976 by beating the Vikings. Madden was replaced by Tom Flores who would win two Super Bowls in 1980 and 1983 during his nine years as coach.

During those two decades, there was remarkable continuity on the field. "Mad Bomber" Daryle Lamonica was followed at quarterback by Ken Stabler who was followed by Jim Plunkett. Receivers Fred Biletnikoff and Cliff Branch both served the team for 14 years. Hard-running fullback Marv Hubbard was replaced by hard-running fullback Mark Van Eeghen who was replaced by Hall of Famer Marcus Allen. The progression of All Pro tight ends went from Billy Cannon to Raymond Chester to Dave Casper to Todd Christensen. The fast and powerful offensive line featured three Hall of Famers who lasted at least 15 years each in Jim Otto, Gene Upshaw and Art Shell. On the defensive side, the team was known for such robust linemen as Ben Davidson, Otis Sistrunk, Lyle Alzado and Howie Long, such smart linebackers as Phil Villapiano, Ted Hendricks and Matt Millen, and physical, bump-and-run

corners like Willie Brown, Lester Hayes and Mike Haynes.

In 1982, the litigious Davis won an antitrust suit against the NFL that allowed him to abandon the Oakland Coliseum against league wishes for more lucrative promises in Los Angeles. Thirteen years later, Davis would move the Raiders back to Oakland in 1995 lured by promised luxury box revenue that he would sue the city of Oakland over when it failed to materialize. He has also sued the Ravens, over their uniform design, and the IRS; the Raiders regularly lead the league in legal expenses. On the field, though, the team declined into mediocrity as Davis seemed to have lost his touch in the late 1980s and throughout the 1990s. In 1998, he hired Jon Gruden as coach, and Gruden began to change things—even the vertical passing attack was scrapped for a version of the popular West Coast Offense. Gruden rebuilt the Raiders into a league power, but after four years Davis traded Gruden to Tampa for draft picks. Gruden's protege Bill Callahan was named as his successor and got the Raiders to Super Bowl XXXVII where they were creamed by Gruden's Bucs. The 2003 season was a disaster, and Callahan was axed. It is unclear what the future holds for the "Pride and Poise Boys" whose cultivated outsider personality in the image of their owner often seems to be a case of style over content anymore.

Origin of name: At first, one of the partners wanted to call the team the Senors, but that was vetoed and replaced with Raiders.
Time till first championship: 17 years.
Time since last championship: 21 years.

Record by Decade

	Regular Season			Postseason		
	Won	Lost	Tied	Won	Lost	Championships
1960s	77	58	5	3	3	
1970s	100	38	6	8	6	1976
1980s	89	63	0	8	3	1980, 1983
1990s	82	78	0	2	3	
2000s	37	27	0	4	3	
All-Time	385	264	11	25	18	3

Winning seasons: 28. Losing Seasons: 11. .500 seasons: 5.

Coaches

	Years	Record	Playoffs
Eddie Erdelatz	1960–1	6–10–0	0–0
Marty Feldman	1961–2	2–15–0	0–0
Red Conkright	1962	1–8–0	0–0
Al Davis	1963–5	23–16–3	0–0
John Rauch	1966–8	33–8–1	2–2
John Madden	1969–78	103–32–7	9–7
Tom Flores	1979–87	83–53–0	8–3
Mike Shanahan	1988–9	8–12–0	0–0
Art Shell	1989–94	54–38–0	2–3
Mike White	1995–6	15–17–0	0–0
Joe Bugel	1997	4–12–0	0–0
Jon Gruden	1998–2001	38–26–0	2–2
Bill Callahan	2002–3	15–17–0	2–1

Retired numbers: The Raiders, like the Cowboys, have a policy against retiring numbers.

Other numbers worn by these players: NA

Those who wore retired numbers after the honored player: NA

Numbers that should be retired: Three Hall of Fame linemen (Jim Otto 00, Gene Upshaw 63, and Art Shell 78), two receivers (Fred Biletnikoff 25 and, once he retires, Tim Brown 81), and Hall of Fame cornerback Willie Brown 24.

Owned numbers: None.

Numbers worn by Hall of Famers: Marcus Allen 32; Fred Biletnikoff 14/25; George Blanda 16; Willie Brown 24; Dave Casper 87; Eric Dickerson 29; Mike Haynes 22; Ted Hendricks 83; James Lofton 80; Howie Long 75; Ronnie Lott 42; Ron Mix 77; Jim Otto 00/50; Art Shell 78; Gene Upshaw 63.

Star power: Rod Woodson took 26 from Derrick Gibson; Bill Romanowski took 53 from Travian Smith.

Star eclipsed: Ron Mix wore 77 because Tom Keating wore 74; Raymond Chester wore 88 because Dave Casper wore 87. Fred Biletnikoff wore 14 till Claude Gibson, 25, left; Albert Lewis wore 24 till Patrick Bates, 29, left; Jack Tatum wore 31 till Don Highsmith, 32, left; Eric Turner wore 42 till Albert Lewis, 29, left.

Numbers with most great players: 24 has been worn by Hall of Fame cornerback Willie

Brown and Pro Bowl corners Fred Williamson, Albert Lewis and Charles Woodson. 65 has been worn by three very good guards in Wayne Hawkins, Mickey Marvin, and Max Montoya. 80 has been worn by three great receivers who had their greatest days elsewhere — James Lofton, Jerry Rice and Andre Rison.

Worst represented numbers: 4 is the number for bad kickers and punters; 17 is a number for bad quarterbacks; 38 is for bad runners and defensive backs; 61 is for bad linemen.

Number worn by the most players: 74 and 77 have been worn 17 times each.

Player who wore the most numbers: Runner Bo Dickinson, 23/30/33, and receiver Herman Urenda, 39/83/89 both wore three numbers.

Longest tenure wearing a number: Tim Brown has worn 81 for 16 years from 1988 to 2003. Gene Upshaw wore 63 for 16 years from 1967 to 1982. Art Shell wore 78 for 15 years from 1968 to 1982.

Number worn by first ever draft pick: The 1960 draft was not conducted in rounds, and three draft choices made the Raiders that year — Jim Otto 50/00, defensive end Carmen Cavalli 85 and guard Don Deskin 79. The first 1st round draft pick to sign with the Raiders was Harry Schuh 71/79 in 1965.

Biggest draft busts: The biggest draft bust was USC quarterback Todd Marinovich, 12, selected 24th in 1991 who threw eight tds and nine interceptions in two years.

Number worn by oldest player: George Blanda was 48 when he wore 16 in 1975. Other 40 year olds include: Jerry Rice, 80, who was 41 in 2003; Vince Evans, 11, who was 40 in 1995; and Wade Wilson, 16, who was 40 in 1999.

Cameos: All Pros and other notables — Sam Adams 95; Ben Agajanian 3; Roger Craig 22; David Fulcher 45; Don Heinrich 11; Babe Parilli 10; Dan Pastorini 7; Rodney Peete 16; Tom Rathman 44; Andre Rison 80; Karl Rubke 54; Ollie Spencer 63/67; Dave Waymer 44; Otis Wilson 50.

Ones who got away: Jim Breech, 5, had

success kicking for Cincinnati; Rich Jackson, 32, was known as "Tombstone" for the Broncos; Sonny Bishop, 66, played guard for the Oilers; Jim Lachey, 74, anchored the Redskins line; La'Roi Glover, 92, has been a star defensive lineman in New Orleans and Dallas; Sean Jones, 99, attained most of his 100+ sacks for the Oilers and Packers.

Least popular numbers: 00, 1 and 2 have all only been worn once.

Last number to be originated: 1 was worn first by defensive back Ronald Curry in 2002.

Longest dormant number: 00 has not been worn since 1974.

Triskaidekaphobia notes: Receiver Rod Sherman and forgettable quarterbacks Larry Lawrence and Jay Schroeder wore 13 for the Raiders.

Shared numbers: 12 has been worn by Super Bowl quarterbacks Ken Stabler and Rich Gannon. 16 was worn by "old pro" quarterbacks George Blanda and Jim Plunkett. 32 was worn by hard-hitting safety Jack Tatum and Hall of Fame runner Marcus Allen. 55 was worn by Pro Bowl middle linebackers Dan Conners and Matt Millen. 63 has been worn by Hall of Fame guard Gene Upshaw and Pro Bowl center Barrett Robbins. 83 was worn by flaky defenders Ben Davidson and Ted Hendricks. 87 was worn by star tight ends Dave Casper and Raymond Chester.

Continuity: Receiver Bo Roberson was replaced in 40 by runner Pete Banaszak.

Discontinuity: Cornerback Lionel Washington was followed in 48 by Najee Mustafaa; defensive tackle Otis Sistrunk was followed in 60 by Alva Liles; Art Powell was followed in 84 by Ken Herock.

Quarterback numbers over 19: None.

Number of first black player: In 1960, defensive back John Harris 29, runner James Smith 38, receiver Charley Hardy 82, and linebacker Riley Morris 92.

Numbers of future NFL head coaches: Tom Flores 15; Terry Robiskie 35; Art Shell 78.

Numbers of future NFL referees: None.

Players who played other sports: Base-

Family Connections			
Brothers			
Charlie Powell	E	1960–1	87
Art Powell	WR	1963–6	84
Cleo Montgomery	WR	1981–5	28
Tyrone Montgomery	RB	1993–4	21
Fathers and sons			
Marv Marinovich	LB	1965	68
Todd Marinovich	QB	1991–2	12
Charley Smith	RB	1968–74	23
Kevin Smith	TE	1992–4	39/83

ball — Bo Jackson 34. Boxing — Charlie Powell 87. Wrestling — Don Manoukian 67 and Otis Sistrunk 60. Track — Willie Gault 83.

Players more famous after football: Fred Williamson, 24, Ben Davidson, 83, Jarrod Bunch, 45, and Howie Long, 75, have all done some acting. Rodney Peete, 16, is married to an actress (Holly Peete Robinson.)

First player to wear a number in the 90s: Linebacker Riley Morris wore 92 in 1960.

Number with most points scored: 10 with 1,046 points scored by Chris Bahr (817), Mike Mercer (217), Babe Parilli (6) and Eldridge Dickey (6).

Number with most yards rushing: 32 with 9,619 yards gained by Marcus Allen (8,545), Zack Crockett (629), Don Highsmith (320), Glenn Shaw (72) and Bob Jackson (53).

Number with most receptions: 81 with 1,376 passes caught by Tim Brown (1,070), Warren Wells (156), Morris Bradshaw (90), Al Goldstein (27), Dick Dorsey (21), Andy Parker (6), Greg Lathan (5) and Pervis Atkins (1).

Number with most touchdown passes: 12 with 297 touchdowns tossed by Ken Stabler (150), Rich Gannon (111), Billy Joe Hobert (10), Donald Hollas (10), Todd Marinovich (8), Rusty Hilger (4), Nick Pappas (2) and Chon Gallegos (2).

Number with most interceptions: 24 with 80 passes picked off by Willie Brown (39), Fred Williamson (25), Charles Woodson (15) and Larry Brown (1).

Oddity: Jim Otto was the first and only AFL player to wear 00.

Players Whose Number Is Unknown

Bill Striegel	(LB)	1960
Jesse Murdock	(HB)	1963
Mark Johnston	(DB)	1964

Team All-Time Numerical Roster

Those with an "r" following the year 1987 were replacement players during the players' strike. Pro Bowl players for each number are in *Italics*; Hall of Famers are in **Bold** type.

00 **Jim Otto** (C) 1961–74.

1 Ronald Curry (DB) 2002.

2 Leo Araguz (P) 1996–9.

3 Ben Agajanian (K) 1962, *Daryle Lamonica* (QB) 1967–74, Vince Gamache (K) 1987r, Jeff George (QB) 1997–8, Rick Mirer (QB) 2002–3.

4 Jerry Depoyster (P) 1971–2, Fred Steinfort (K) 1976, David Hardy (K) 1987r, Pat Barnes (QB) 1998.

5 Jim Breech (K) 1976–9, Stan Talley (P) 1987, Cole Ford (K) 1995–7, Michael Husted (K) 1999, Brett Conway (K) 2000.

6 George Jakowenko (K) 1974, Marc Wilson (QB) 1980–7, *Jeff Gossett* (P) 1988–90, 1996, Joe Nedney (K) 1999.

7 Dan Pastorini (QB) 1980, Steve Beuerlein (QB) 1988–90, *Jeff Gossett* (P) 1991–5, David Klingler (QB) 1996–7, Rob Johnson (QB) 2003.

8 *Ray Guy* (P) 1973–86, Jeff Graham (WR) 1995, Marques Tuiasosopo (QB) 2001–3.

9 Billy Joe Hobert (QB) 1993–4, *Shane Lechler* (P) 2000–3.

10 Babe Parilli (QB) 1960, Mike Mercer (K/P) 1963–5, Eldridge Dickey (WR) 1968, 1971, Chris Bahr (K) 1980–8, Jay Schroeder (QB) 1992, Alfred Montez (QB) 1996, Scott Dreisbach (QB) 1999–2000, Kevin Stemke (P) 2002.

11 Don Heinrich (QB) 1962, Mike Eischeid (P) 1966–71, David Humm (QB) 1975–9, 1983–4, Vince Evans (QB) 1987–95, Sebastian Janikowski (K) 2000–3.

12 Paul Larson (QB) 1960, Nick Papas (QB) 1961, Chon Gallegos (QB) 1962, Charley Green (QB) 1966, *Ken Stabler* (QB) 1970–9, Rusty Hilger (QB) 1985–7, Todd Marinovich (QB) 1991–2, Billy Joe Hobert (QB) 1995–6, Donald Hollas (QB) 1997–8, *Rich Gannon* (QB) 1999–2003.

13 Rod Sherman (WR) 1969–71, Larry Lawrence (QB) 1974–5, Jay Schroeder (QB) 1988–91.

14 Hunter Enis (QB) 1962, **Fred Biletnikoff** (WR) 1965, Errol Mann (K) 1976–8, Jerry Golsteyn (QB) 1984, Bobby Hoying (QB) 1999–2001.

15 *Tom Flores* (QB) 1960–1, 1963–6, Mike Rae (QB) 1976–8, Tim Ware (WR) 1989, *Jeff Hostetler* (QB) 1993–6.

16 **George Blanda** (K/QB) 1967–75, Jim Plunkett (QB) 1978–86, Rich Camarillo (P) 1996, Wade Wilson (QB) 1998–9, Rodney Peete (QB) 2001.

17 M.C. Reynolds (QB) 1961, Kyle Grossart (QB) 1980, Scott Wolff (QB) 1987r, Olanda Truitt (WR) 1996, Tee Martin (QB) 2003.

18 Dick Wood (QB) 1965, Russ Jensen (QB) 1985, *Jeff Jaeger* (K) 1989–95.

19 *Cotton Davidson* (QB) 1962–9, David Williams (WR) 1987, Siddeeq Shabazz (S) 2003.

20 Charles Fuller (WR) 1961–2, Willie Simpson (RB) 1962, Warren Powers (DB) 1963–8, Jackie Allen (DB) 1969, Jimmy Warren (DB) 1970–4, Neal Colzie (DB) 1975–8, I.M. Hipp (RB) 1980, Ted Watts (DB) 1981–4, Chris McLemore (RB) 1987–8, Chetti Carr (WR) 1987r, Willie Teal (DB) 1987r, Dennis Price (DB) 1988–9, Tahaun Lewis (DB) 1991, Derrick Hoskins (DB) 1992–5, Perry Carter (DB) 1996–7, Tory James (DB) 2000–2, Justin Fargas (RB) 2003.

21 George Fleming (CB) 1961, Dick Dorsey (WR) 1962, Harold Lewis (DB) 1962, Gene Mingo (K/RB) 1964–5, Rodger Bird (S) 1967–71, *Cliff Branch* (WR) 1972–85, Ron Fellows (DB) 1987–8, Rick Calhoun (RB) 1987r, Garry Lewis (DB) 1990–1, Tyrone Montgomery (RB) 1993–4, Darren Carrington (DB) 1996, Eric Allen (CB) 1998–2001, Nnamdi Asomugha (CB) 2003.

22 Wayne Crow (B) 1960–1, Mel Montalbo (DB) 1962, Louie Guy (DB) 1964, Larry Todd (RB) 1965–70, Jimmy Warren (DB) 1977, Arthur Whittington (RB) 1978–81, **Mike Haynes** (CB) 1983–9, Roger Craig (RB) 1991, Harvey Williams (RB) 1994–8, Terrance Shaw (CB) 2002–3.

23 Jack Larshied (RB) 1960–1, Hank Rivera (DB) 1962, Bo Dickinson (RB) 1964, Rod Sherman (WR) 1967, Charlie Smith (RB) 1968–74, Harold Hart (RB) 1978, Odis McKinney (DB) 1980–6, *Ethan Horton* (RB/TE) 1987, Derrick Crudup (S) 1989, 1991, Lionel Washington (CB) 1997, Darrien Gordon (DB/PR) 1999–2000, Marquez Pope (CB) 2001, Madre Hill (RB) 2002.

24 Bob Keyes (RB) 1960, *Fred Williamson* (CB) 1961–4, **Willie Brown** (CB) 1967–78, Lance Harkey (DB) 1987r, Ron Brown (WR) 1990, Patrick Bates (DB) 1993, Albert Lewis (CB) 1994, Larry Brown (CB) 1996–7, *Charles Woodson* (CB) 1998–2003.

25 Tony Teresa (RB) 1960, Vernon Valdez (DB) 1962, Claude Gibson (CB) 1963–5, **Fred Biletnikoff** (WR) 1966–78, Ricky Williams (DB) 1985, 1987r, Rob Harrison (RB) 1987r, Dan Land (DB) 1989–97, Irvin Phillips (DB) 1993, Anthony Prior (DB) 1998, Charlie Garner (RB) 2001–3.

26 Nyle McFarlane (HB) 1960, Nemiah Wilson (DB) 1968–70, Skip Thomas (DB) 1972–8, Clarence Hawkins (RB) 1979, Keith Moody (DB) 1980, *Vann McElroy* (DB) 1982–7, Napoleon Kaufman (RB) 1995–2000, Derrick Gibson (S) 2001, *Rod Woodson* (S) 2002–3.

27 Joe Cannavino (DB) 1960–1, George Boynton (DB) 1962, Rich Mostardo (DB) 1962, Joe Krakoski (DB) 1963–6, Glen Ellison (RB) 1971, Ron Smith (DB/WR) 1974, Randy Rich (DB) 1978, Frank Hawkins (RB) 1981–7, Derrick Gainer (RB) 1992, James Trapp (DB) 1993, Calvin Jones (RB) 1994, Calvin Branch (S) 1997–2000, Ronney Jenkins (RB) 2003, J.R. Redmond (RB) 2003.

28 Ed Macon (B) 1960, Bob Garner (DB) 1961–2, Clarence Davis (RB) 1971–8, Dwight Harrison (DB) 1980, Cleo Montgomery (WR) 1981–5, Greg Bell (RB) 1990, Greg Robinson (RB) 1993–4, Randy Jordan (RB) 1993, 1998–2002.

29 John Harris (DB) 1960–1, Eugene White (HB) 1962, Mike Sommer (B) 1963, Howie Williams (DB) 1964–9, Bob Prout (DB) 1974, Hubie Ginn (RB) 1976–8, Jimmy Smith (RB) 1984, Tony Tillmon (DB) 1987r, Russell Carter (DB) 1988–9, **Eric Dickerson** (RB) 1992, Patrick Bates (DB) 1994, Albert Lewis (DB) 1995–8, Eric Turner (DB) 1999.

30 Bo Dickinson (RB) 1964, Roger Hagberg (RB) 1965–9, *Mark Van Eeghen* (RB) 1974–81, Stacey Toran (DB) 1984–8.

31 Billy Lott (RB) 1960, *Jack Tatum* (S) 1971–2, Carl Garrett (RB) 1976–7, Derrick Jensen (RB/TE) 1979–86, Vance Mueller (RB) 1986–8, Kerry Porter (RB) 1989, Rickey Dixon (DB) 1993, Joe King (DB) 1995, Chad Levitt (RB) 1997, Ray Perryman (S) 2001, Phillip Buchanon (CB) 2002–3.

32 Jim Jones (LB) 1961, Charles Rieves (LB) 1962, Glenn Shaw (FB) 1963–4, Bobby Jackson (RB) 1964, Richard Jackson (LB) 1966, Don Highsmith (RB) 1970–2, *Jack Tatum* (S) 1973–9, **Marcus Allen** (RB) 1982–92, Zack Crockett (RB) 1999–2003.

33 Doug Mayberry (FB) 1963, Bo Dickinson (RB) 1964, *Billy Cannon* (TE) 1964–9, Louis Carter (RB) 1975, Rick Jennings (WR) 1976–7, *Kenny King* (RB) 1980–5, Demise Williams (DB) 1987, Eddie Anderson (DB) 1987–97, Craig Ellis (RB) 1987r, Bucky Brooks (CB) 1998, Anthony Dorsett (DB) 2000–3.

34 *Gus Otto* (LB) 1965–72, Harold Hart (R) 1974–5, Terry Kunz (RB) 1976–7, Booker Russell (RB) 1978–9, *Greg Pruitt* (RB) 1982–4, Napoleon McCallum (RB) 1986, 1990–4, *Bo Jackson* (RB) 1987–90, Derrick Fenner (RB) 1996–7, Jermaine Williams (RB) 1998–9, 2001, Darrien Gordon (DB/PR) 2002.

35 Walt Kowalczyk (RB) 1961, Tom Morrow (DB/P) 1962–4, *Hewritt Dixon* (FB) 1966–70, Jess Philips (RB) 1975, Terry Robiskie (RB) 1977–9,

Dwayne O'Steen (DB) 1980–1, Steve Smith (FB) 1987–93, Joe Aska (RB) 1995–7.

36 *Clem Daniels* (RB) 1961–7, Lloyd Edwards (TE) 1969, Bob Hudson (RB) 1973–4, Manfred Moore (RB) 1976, Mike Davis (DB) 1978–85, Greg Hill (DB) 1987, *Terry McDaniel* (DB) 1988–97, Derrick Gibson (S) 2002–3.

37 *Alan Miller* (FB) 1961–3, 1965, Preston Ridlehuber (RB) 1968, Jacque MacKinnon (TE) 1970, Mike Reinfeldt (DB) 1976, *Lester Hayes* (CB) 1977–86, Doug Lloyd (RB) 1991, James Trapp (DB) 1994–8, Johnnie Harris (DB) 2001, Carey Scott (CB) 2003.

38 James Smith (RB) 1960, Estes Banks (RB) 1967, Ted Koy (TE) 1970, Rufus Bess (DB) 1979, Chester Willis (RB) 1981–4, Rod Hill (DB) 1987, Nick Bell (RB) 1991–3, Marquis Walker (CB) 1998–9, Clarence Love (CB) 2002–3.

39 Willie Simpson (RB) 1962, Herman Urenda (WR) 1963, Pervis Atkins (WR) 1965–6, *Marv Hubbard* (RB) 1969, Willie Hall (LB) 1975–8, Steve Strachan (RB) 1985–9, Kevin Smith (TE) 1992–3, Bruce Pickens (DB) 1995, Brandon Jennings (DB) 2001–2.

40 *Bo Roberson* (WR) 1962–5, Pete Banaszak (RB) 1966–78, Rick Berns (RB) 1982–3, Zeph Lee (RB) 1987–9, Marcus Wilson (RB) 1991, Cary Brabham (DB) 1994, Jon Ritchie (FB) 1998–2002.

41 Hank Rivera (DB) 1962, John Roderick (WR) 1968, Alvin Wyatt (DB) 1970, *Phil Villapiano* (LB) 1971–9, Ted Watts (DB) 1981–4, Fulton Walker (DB) 1985–6, Ron Foster (DB) 1987r, David Greenwood (DB) 1988, Bobby Joe Edmonds (WR) 1989, Louis Riddick (DB) 1998, Eric Johnson (DB) 2001–3.

42 Dobie Craig (WR) 1962–3, Bill Laskey (LB) 1966–70, Tom Maxwell (DB) 1971–3, Steve Jackson (DB) 1977, Monte Jackson (DB) 1978–82, Vance Mueller (RB) 1989–90, **Ronnie Lott** (DB) 1991–2, Eric Ball (RB) 1995, Eric Turner (DB) 1997–8, Marcus Ray (DB) 1999, Terry Kirby (RB) 2000–2.

43 Bob Coolbaugh (WR) 1961, *George Atkinson* (DB) 1968–77, Ira Matthews (RB/WR) 1979–81, Joe McCall (RB) 1984, Sam Seale (CB) 1984–7, Elvis Patterson (DB) 1990–3, Nick Bell (RB) 1993, Lorenzo Lynch (DB) 1996–7, Derek Combs (CB) 2002.

44 Bob Dougherty (LB) 1960–3, Fred Gillett (TE) 1964, *Marv Hubbard* (RB) 1970–5, Burgess Owens (DB) 1980–2, Stefon Adams (DB) 1986–9, Dave Waymer (DB) 1992, Tom Rathman (FB) 1994, Calvin Jones (RB) 1995, Lamar Lyons (DB) 1996, Chris Hetherington (RB) 2003.

45 Jim McMillin (DB) 1963–4, *David Grayson* (DB) 1965–70, Greg Slough (LB) 1972, Henry Williams (DB) 1979, Mike Spivey (DB) 1980, James Davis (DB) 1982–7, Mike Harden (DB)

1989–90, David Fulcher (LB) 1993, Jarrod Bunch (FB) 1994, Tim Hall (RB) 1996–7.

46 L.C. Joyner (DB) 1960, Billy Reynolds (QB) 1960, *Dave Costa* (DT) 1963–5, Bill Enyart (LB) 1971, Warren Bankston (RB/TE) 1973–8, *Todd Christensen* (TE) 1979–88, Torin Dorn (DB) 1990–3, Carl Kidd (DB) 1995–6.

47 Alex Bravo (DB) 1960–1, *Kent McCloughan* (CB) 1965–70, Jeff Queen (RB/TE) 1973, Charles Phillips (DB) 1975–80, Don Bessillieu (DB) 1983, 1985, Jim Browne (RB) 1987r, Donald Frank (DB) 1994, Tyrone Wheatley (RB) 1999–2003.

48 Charles Rieves (LB) 1963, Bill Budness (LB) 1964–70, Nemiah Wilson (DB) 1971–4, Kenny Hill (DB) 1981–3, Lionel Washington (DB) 1987–94, Najee Mustafaa (CB) 1995, Jerone Davison (RB) 1996–7.

49 Jack Simpson (LB) 1962–3, Dick Hermann (LB) 1965, Willie Williams (DB) 1966, Carl Weathers (LB) 1970, Mike Siani (WR) 1972–7, Billy Taylor (RB) 1982, Earl Cooper (TE) 1986, Victor Jackson (DB) 1987r, Wes Bender (RB) 1994, Marquez Pope (CB) 2000.

50 **Jim Otto** (C) 1960–1, Jack Simpson (LB) 1964, Duane Benson (LB) 1967–71, *Dave Dalby* (C) 1972–85, Darryl Byrd (LB) 1987r, Norwood Vann (LB) 1988, Otis Wilson (LB) 1989, Riki Ellison (LB) 1990–2, Mike Morton (LB) 1995–8, Eric Barton (LB) 1999–2003.

51 Carl Weathers (LB) 1971, Joe Carroll (LB) 1972–3, Rodrigo Barnes (LB) 1976, Bob Nelson (LB) 1980–5, Bill Lewis (C/G) 1986–9, Keith Browner (LB) 1987r, Aaron Wallace (LB) 1990–5, Lance Johnstone (DE) 1996–2000, Tim Johnson (LB) 2002–3.

52 Larry Barnes (FB/DE) 1960, J.R. Williamson (LB/C) 1964–7, Jerry Hopkins (LB) 1968, Gary Weaver (LB) 1973, Floyd Rice (LB) 1976–7, Greg Westbrooks (LB) 1978–81, Mario Celotto (LB) 1980–1, Jim Romano (C) 1982–4, Mark Merrill (LB) 1984, Trey Junkin (TE) 1985, Linden King (LB) 1986–9, Mike Jones (LB) 1991–6, 2002, Shay Muirbrook (LB) 1997, Richard Harvey (LB) 1998–9.

53 Al Bansavage (LB) 1961, *Dan Birdwell* (DT) 1962–9, *Rod Martin* (LB) 1977–88, Mike Noble (LB) 1987r, Rob Fredrickson (LB) 1994–7, Travian Smith (LB) 1998–2001, Bill Romanowski (LB) 2002–3.

54 Karl Rubke (DT) 1968, Terry Mendenhall (LB) 1971–2, Mike Dennery (LB) 1974–5, Rik Bonness (LB) 1976, Robert Watts (LB) 1978, Greg Bracelin (LB) 1981, Calvin Peterson (LB) 1982, Darryl Byrd (LB) 1983–4, Reggie McKenzie (LB) 1985–8, Paul Dufault (C) 1987r, Tom Benson (LB) 1989–91, Greg Biekert (LB) 1993–2001, Sam Williams (DE) 2003.

55 Riley Morris (LB) 1960–1, *Dan Conners* (LB) 1966–74, *Matt Millen* (LB) 1980–8, Alex Gordon (LB) 1990, James Folston (LB) 1994–7, Bobby Brooks (LB) 2000–1, Shurron Pierson (DE) 2003.

56 *Archie Matsos* (LB) 1963–5, Ralph Oliver (LB) 1968–9, Warren Koegel (C) 1971, Jeff Barnes (LB) 1977–87, Milt McColl (LB) 1988, Aundray Bruce (LB) 1992–4, Pat Swilling (LB) 1995–6, 1998, John Henry Mills (TE) 1997, Sam Sword (LB) 1999, Travian Smith (LB) 2002–3.

57 Greg Blankenship (LB) 1976, Randy McClanahan (LB) 1977, 1980–2, John Huddleston (LB) 1978–9, Mike Hawkins (LB) 1982, Tony Caldwell (LB) 1983–5, Jerry Robinson (LB) 1985–91, Joe Kelly (LB) 1993, Rob Holmberg (LB) 1994–7, Terry Wooden (LB) 1998, Roderick Coleman (DT) 1999–2003.

58 Ray Schmautz (LB) 1966, Greg Slough (LB) 1971, Monte Johnson (LB) 1973–80, Jack Squirek (LB) 1982–5, Rick Ackerman (DT) 1987, Jim Ellis (LB) 1987r, Jackie Shipp (LB) 1989, A.J. Jimerson (LB) 1990–1, Keith Franklin (LB) 1995, Ernest Dixon (LB) 1998, Elijah Alexander (LB) 2000–1, Napoleon Harris (LB) 2002–3.

59 Stanley Adams (LB) 1984, Jamie Kimmel (LB) 1986–8, Ron Burton (LB) 1990, Anthony Bell (LB) 1992, Matt Dyson (DT/LB) 1995, Paul Butcher (LB) 1996, Aaron Wallace (LB) 1997, K.D. Williams (LB) 1999, William Thomas (LB) 2000–1.

60 Tom Louderback (LB) 1960–1, *Dan Conners* (LB) 1964–5, *Otis Sistrunk* (DT) 1972–9, Alva Liles (DT) 1980, Curt Marsh (G) 1981–6, Rory Graves (T) 1988–91.

61 Herb Roedal (G) 1961, Dave Ogas (LB) 1968, Herb McMath (DT) 1976, Dave Stalls (DL) 1983, 1985, John Tautolo (T) 1987r, Mike Freeman (G) 1988, Roy Hart (DT) 1991.

62 Bob Kruse (G) 1963–6, Reggie Kinlaw (DT) 1979–84, Shawn Regent (C) 1987r, Adam Treu (OL) 1997–2003.

63 Willie Smith (G/T) 1961, Ollie Spencer (OL) 1963, **Gene Upshaw** (G) 1967–82, John Gesek (G) 1987–9, David Pyles (T) 1987r, *Barret Robbins* (C) 1995–2003.

64 Ron Sabal (T/G) 1960–1, George Buehler (G) 1967–78, Shelby Jordan (T) 1983, Andy Dickerson (G) 1987, Dean Miraldi (G/T) 1987, Ron Brown (LB) 1988, Todd Peat (G) 1991–3, Robert Jenkins (T) 1994–6, Gennaro DiNapoli (G) 1998–9.

65 *Wayne Hawkins* (G) 1960–70, Paul Seiler (T/C) 1971–3, Mickey Marvin (G) 1977–87, *Max Montoya* (G) 1990–4, Barry Sims (G) 1999–2003.

66 Ramon Armstrong (T) 1960, Sonny Bishop (G) 1963, Steve Sylvester (T) 1975–83, Warren Bryant (T) 1984, Steve Wright (T) 1987–93, *Kevin Gogan* (G) 1994–6, Curtis Whitley (C) 1997, Langston Walker (T) 2002–3.

67 Don Manoukian (G) 1960, Stan Campbell (G) 1962, Ollie Spencer (OL) 1963, Bob Mischak

(G) 1964–5, Harold Rice (DE) 1971, Pat Toomay (DE) 1977–9, Dwight Wheeler (OL) 1984, 1987–8, Barry Black (G) 1987, Dan Turk (C) 1989–96, Russell Maryland (DT) 1997–9.

68 John Dittrich (G) 1960, Marv Marinovich (G) 1965, Palmer Pyle (G) 1966, Joe Bell (DE) 1979, Johnny Robinson (DL) 1981–3, Bruce Wilkerson (T) 1987–94, 1998, Rick Cuningham (T) 1996–7, Aaron Graham (C) 2001.

69 Dan Ficca (G) 1962, John Zogg (G) 1987r.

70 Harry Jagielski (DT) 1961, Pete Nicklas (T) 1962, Dick Klein (T) 1963–4, James Harvey (G) 1966–71, *Henry Lawrence* (T) 1974–86, Scott Davis (DE) 1988–91, 1994, Russell Freeman (T) 1995, Toby Myles (T) 2001, Brad Badger (G) 2002–3.

71 Cliff Roberts (DT) 1961, Joe Novsek (DE) 1962, *Harry Schuh* (T) 1965, Richard Tyson (G) 1966, Al Dotson (DT) 1968–70, Kelvin Korver (DT) 1973–7, Lindsey Mason (T) 1978–81, Bill Pickel (DL) 1983–90, Joel Patten (T) 1991, Gerald Perry (T) 1993–5, Lester Holmes (G) 1997, Nate Parks (G/T) 1999–2001, Corey Hulsey (G) 2003.

72 Dalton Truax (DT) 1960, Hal Smith (DT) 1961, Jim Norris (DT) 1962, John Matuszak (DT) 1976–82, *Don Mosebar* (C) 1983–94, *Lincoln Kennedy* (T) 1996–2003, Tim Kohn (G) 1997.

73 Billy Ray Locklin (G) 1960, Jim Brewington (T) 1961, Chuck McMurtry (DT) 1962–3, John Diehl (DT) 1965, Greg Kent (T) 1966, Richard Sligh (DT) 1967, Tom Gipson (DT) 1971, Dave Browning (DE) 1978–82, Charley Hannah (G) 1983–8, James Fitzpatrick (G/T) 1990–1, Charles McRae (T/G) 1996, Darryl Ashmore (G/T) 1998–2000, Frank Middleton (G) 2001–3.

74 Paul Oglesby (T) 1960, Jim Norris (DT) 1963, Doug Brown (DT) 1964, Rich Zecher (T) 1965, *Tom Keating* (DT) 1966–72, Dave Rowe (DT) 1975–8, Dave Pear (DT) 1979–80, Archie Reese (DT) 1982–3, Dave Stalls (DL) 1983, Shelby Jordan (T) 1984–6, Mike Rodriguez (DT) 1987, Jim Lachey (T) 1988, Pete Koch (DE) 1989, Todd Peat (G) 1990, Nolan Harrison (DL) 1991–6, Derrick Graham (G) 1998, Matt Stinchcomb (DL) 1999–2003.

75 Hansen Churchwell (DT) 1960, Jack Stone (T) 1961–2, Ken Rice (T) 1964–5, David Daniels (DT) 1966, John Vella (T) 1972–9, **Howie Long** (DL) 1981–93, Pat Harlow (T) 1996, Chris Cooper (DE) 2001–3.

76 Gary Finneran (DT) 1961, Charles Brown (T) 1962, Bob Svihus (T) 1965–70, **Bob Brown** (T) 1971–3, Mike McCoy (DT) 1977–8, Ed Muransky (T) 1982–4, Greg Boyd (DE) 1984, Kevin Belcher (T) 1985, Brian Holloway (G/T) 1987–8, *Steve Wisniewski* (G) 1989–2001.

77 Joe Barbee (DT) 1960, George Shirkey (DT) 1962, Proverb Jacobs (T) 1963–4, *Issac Lassiter* (DE) 1965–9, **Ron Mix** (T) 1971, Bubba Smith (DT) 1973–4, Charles Philyaw (DE) 1976–9, Joe Campbell (DE) 1980–1, Lyle Alzado (DE) 1982–5, Chris Riehm (G) 1986–8, Ted Chapman (DE) 1987r, Reggie McElroy (T) 1991–2, Rich Stephens (G) 1993, 1995, Pat Harlow (T) 1997, Toby Myles (T) 2000, Darryl Ashmore (G/T) 2001, Joe Wong (T) 2003.

78 John Warzeka (DT) 1960, Bob Voight (DE) 1961, Frank Youso (T) 1963–5, Rex Mirich (T) 1966, Dan Archer (T) 1967, **Art Shell** (T) 1968–82, John Clay (T) 1987, Tim Rother (T) 1989–90, Greg Skrepenak (T) 1992–5, Scott Whittaker (DL) 1997, Chad Slaughter (T) 2002–3.

79 Don Deskins (G) 1960, Volney Peters (DT) 1961, Orville Trask (T) 1962, *Harry Schuh* (T) 1966–70, Dan Medlin (G) 1974–6, 1979, Bruce Davis (T) 1979–87, Brian Belway (DE) 1987r, Bob Golic (DT) 1989–92, Ken Lanier (T) 1993, Jeff Kysar (T) 1995–6, Mo Collins (G/T) 1998–2003.

80 George Fields (DT) 1960–1, Dalva Allen (DE) 1962–4, Greg Kent (T) 1966, Art Thoms (T) 1969–76, Joe Stewart (WR) 1978–9, Malcolm Barnwell (WR) 1981–4, **James Lofton** (WR) 1987–8, Mike Alexander (WR) 1989–90, Daryl Hobbs (WR) 1993–6, Desmond Howard (KR) 1997–8, Horace Copeland (WR) 1999, Andre Rison (WR) 2000, *Jerry Rice* (WR) 2001–3.

81 Alan Goldstein (WR) 1960, Dick Dorsey (WR) 1962, Clancy Osborne (LB) 1963–4, Pervis Atkins (WR) 1965, *Warren Wells* (WR) 1967–70, Morris Bradshaw (WR) 1974–81, Andy Parker (TE) 1984–8, Greg Lathan (WR) 1987r, *Tim Brown* (WR) 1988–2003.

82 Charles Hardy (WR) 1960–2, Jan Barrett (TE) 1963–4, Tom Mitchell (TE) 1966, John Eason (TE) 1968, Horace Jones (DE) 1971–5, Larry Brunson (WR) 1978–9, Calvin Muhammad (WR) 1982–3, Ron Wheeler (OL) 1987, Jamie Holland (WR) 1990–1, David Jones (TE) 1992, James Jett (WR) 1993–2002, Teyo Johnson (TE) 2003.

83 Doug Asad (TE) 1960–1, Herman Urenda (WR) 1963, *Ben Davidson* (DE) 1964–71, **Ted Hendricks** (LB) 1975–83, Tim Moffett (WR) 1985–6, Carl Aikens (WR) 1987r, Willie Gault (WR) 1988–93, Kevin Smith (TE) 1994, Rickey Dudley (TE) 1996–2000, Marcus Knight (WR) 2001–2, O.J. Santiago (TE) 2003.

84 Al Hoisington (WR) 1960, Max Boydston (E) 1962, *Art Powell* (WR) 1963–6, Ken Herock (TE) 1967, Tony Cline (DE) 1970–5, Derrick Ramsey (TE) 1978–83, Jessie Hester (WR) 1985–7, Mario Perry (TE) 1987r, Mike Dyal (TE) 1989–90, John Duff (TE) 1993–4, Kenny Shedd (WR) 1996–9, Jerry Porter (WR) 2001–3.

85 Carmen Cavalli (DE) 1960, Carleton Oats (DT) 1965–72, Frank Pitts (WR) 1974, Bob Chandler (WR) 1980–1, Dokie Williams (WR) 1983–7, Sam Graddy (WR) 1990–2, Charles Jordan (WR) 1993, Marcus Hinton (TE) 1995–6, Terry Mickens

(WR) 1998–2000, Marcus Williams (WR) 2002, Doug Gabriel (WR) 2003.

86 Gerald Burch (WR/P) 1961, Ken Herock (TE) 1963–5, Bill Fairband (LB) 1967–8, Gerald Irons (LB) 1970–5, Cedrick Hardman (DE) 1980–1, Jim Smith (WR) 1985, Mervyn Fernandez (WR) 1987–92, Raghib Ismail (WR) 1993–5, Derek Brown (TE) 1998, Derrick Walker (TE) 1999, Jerry Porter (WR) 2000, Roland Williams (TE) 2001–2, John Stone (WR) 2003.

87 Charlie Powell (DE) 1960–1, Bob Mischak (T) 1963, Rex Mirich (T) 1964–5, *Raymond Chester* (TE) 1970–2, **Dave Casper** (TE) 1974–80, 1984, Don Hasselbeck (TE) 1983, Trey Junkin (TE) 1986–9, 1996, Wade Lockett (WR) 1987r, Andrew Glover (TE) 1991–6, Jeremy Brigham (TE) 1998–2001, Alvis Whitted (WR) 2002–3.

88 Jon Jelacic (DE) 1961–4, Dave Kocourek (TE) 1967–8, Bob Moore (TE) 1971–5, *Raymond Chester* (TE) 1978–81, Rod Barksdale (WR) 1986, Chris Woods (WR) 1987–8, *Ethan Horton* (TE) 1989–93, Jamie Williams (TE) 1994, Kerry Cash (TE) 1995, Olanda Truitt (WR) 1996–7, David Dunn (WR) 2000–1, Doug Jolley (TE) 2002–3.

89 Gene Prebola (TE) 1960, Herman Urenda (WR) 1963, Bill Miller (WR) 1964, 1966–8, Drew Buie (WR) 1967–71, Steve Sweeney (WR) 1973, Ted Kwalick (TE) 1975–7, Rich Martini (WR) 1979–80, Mark Pattison (WR) 1986, David Williams (WR) 1987, Alexander Wright (WR) 1992–4, Bob Rosensteil (TE) 1997, Mondriel Fulcher (TE) 2000–1, Ronald Curry (WR) 2003.

90 Willie Jones (DE) 1979–82, Larry McCoy (LB) 1984, Mike Wise (DE) 1986–90, Darryl Goodlow (LB) 1987r, Grady Jackson (DT) 1997–2001, Kenyon Coleman (DE) 2002, Sean Gilbert (DT) 2003.

91 Brad Van Pelt (LB) 1984–5, Leonard Jackson (LB) 1987r, Ronnie Washington (LB) 1987r, *Chester McGlockton* (DT) 1992–7, Regan Upshaw (DE) 2000–2, Tyler Brayton (DE) 2003.

92 Riley Morris (LB) 1962, Dan McMillen (DE) 1987r, Emanuel King (LB) 1989, Ferric Collons (DT) 1993, La'Roi Glover (DT) 1996, Vince Amey (DT) 1998, Junior Ioane (DT) 2000–2, Terdell Sands (DT) 2003.

93 *Greg Townsend* (DE) 1983–93, 1997, Jerry Ball (DT) 1994–6, Trace Armstrong (DE) 2001–3.

94 Elvis Franks (DE) 1985–6, Rick Goltz (DE) 1987r, Joe Costello (LB) 1989, Anthony Smith (DE) 1991–7, Tony Bryant (DE) 1999–2002, Dana Stubblefield (DT) 2003.

95 Bob Buczkowski (DE) 1987, Joe Cormier (LB) 1987r, Mike Charles (DT) 1990, Austin Robbins (DT) 1994–5, 2000, DeLawrence Grant (DE) 2001, Sam Adams (DT) 2002, Lorenzo Bromell (DE) 2003.

96 Ron Brown (LB) 1987, Malcolm Taylor (DT) 1987–8, Alberto White (DE) 1994, *Darrell Russell* (DT) 1997–2001.

97 Rick Ackerman (DT) 1984, Phil Grimes (DE) 1987, Mark Mraz (DE) 1989, Willie Broughton (DT) 1992–4, Russell Maryland (DT) 1996, John Parrella (DT) 2002–3.

98 Mitch Willis (DT) 1985–7, Darryl Goodlow (LB) 1987r, Kevin Johnson (DT) 1997, Chuck Osborne (DT) 1998–9, Akbar Gbaja-Biamila (DE) 2003.

99 Ruben Vaughan (DL) 1982, Sean Jones (DE) 1984–7, Ricky Hunley (LB) 1989–90, Winston Moss (LB) 1991–4, Aundray Bruce (LB) 1995–7, Josh Taves (DE) 2000–1, DeLawrence Grant (DE) 2002–3, Grant Irons (DE) 2003.

PHILADELPHIA EAGLES

The franchise: The first NFL franchise in Philadelphia was the Frankford Yellow Jackets who won almost 70 percent of their games in the 1920s and were league champions in 1926. By 1931, though, the team went belly-up in the Great Depression. Two years later, former University of Pennsylvania player and coach Bert Bell joined forces with Lud Wray and others and purchased a new franchise for the City of Brotherly Love. Wray became the first coach, but the team

only won 9 games in its first three years. Bell bought out Wray and made himself coach; the Eagles "responded" with 10 wins in the next five years. In 1941, Pittsburgh owner Art Rooney sold the Steelers to Alexis Thompson and bought half the Eagles from his friend Bell. Within months, the two ownership parties exchanged franchises so that Thompson owned the Eagles and hired Greasy Neale as his coach. Steeler co-owner Bell meanwhile became NFL Commissioner five years later and moved the league offices to his Philadelphia hometown. He would die there of a heart attack while watching the Steelers play the Eagles at the University of Pennsylvania's Franklin Field in 1959.

Neale took over a horrible franchise and posted a winning season in his third year, 1943, when they merged with the Steelers for one year during World War II to form the Steagles. Neale followed that season by driving the Eagles to three consecutive second place finishes and then three straight Eastern Division crowns during the rest of the 1940s, winning titles in 1948 and 1949. Those Eagles were led by the running of Steve Van Buren and the ferocious line play of Al Wistert, Alex Wojciechowicz, Chuck Bednarik, Vic Sears and Bucko Kilroy. Thompson sold the team in 1949 to a 100-man syndicate headed by James Clark and Frank McNamee.

The Eagles were the class of the league at the time, and when the NFL merged with the All America Football Conference in 1950, the first regular season game of the season pitted the two league champions— Eagles vs. Browns. When the Browns triumphed 35–10, it signaled that there was a new sheriff in town. The Eagles were still noted as a rough-and-tumble team throughout the 1950s, but only fashioned four winning seasons for the decade. By 1958, they had sunk to last place and tried to hire Giants assistant coach Vince Lombardi. When that failed, they hired former 49er head coach Buck Shaw and traded for quarterback Norm Van Brocklin. In 1960, Van Brocklin and Bednarik led the team to an upset victory over Lombardi's Green Bay Packers in the NFL title game; it would be the only playoff game Lombardi would ever lose.

Shaw and Van Brocklin immediately retired. Van Brocklin expected to be named coach, but the Eagles promoted assistant Nick Skorich instead, and the Dutchman went on to coach Minnesota. Sonny Jurgensen replaced Van Brocklin at quarterback and led the team to 10 wins in 1961, but injuries and age led to the deterioration of the team over the next two seasons. Construction wunderkind Jerry Wolman purchased the team in 1963 and rashly gave Joe Kuharich a 15-year contract as coach the next sea-

son. Kuharich believed in having no stars on his team and had failed before in Washington and at Notre Dame. Within five years, Franklin Field was featuring "Joe Must Go" banners, while Santa Claus himself felt the wrath of Eagle fans in 1968 when he was pelted with snowballs.

In 1969, Wolman got into financial trouble and had to sell the team to trucking executive Leonard Tose. Coaches came and went, but the losing continued. Finally in 1976, Tose hired UCLA's Dick Vermeil as his coach, and despite having few draft picks to work with, Vermeil had a winning team in his third year and a Super Bowl team in his fifth. That Super Bowl team in 1980 was led by the offensive trio of quarterback Ron Jaworski, runner Wilbert Montgomery and receiver Harold Carmichael and a very strong group of linebackers on defense, including Bill Bergey. Vermeil burned out on coaching and quit while Tose's finances declined. Norman Braman bought the team in 1985 and hired Bears defensive coach and self-proclaimed genius Buddy Ryan in 1986. Ryan built a talented and undisciplined squad led by Reggie White on defense and Randall Cunningham on offense that could not win a playoff game. Ryan was replaced after five years by his assistant Rich Kotite who drove the team into the ground in four years. Braman sold out for a large profit in 1995 to Jeffrey Lurie. Lurie's second coach, Andy Reid, has proven to be a winner, developing a young star quarterback in Donovan McNabb and getting the Eagles to three consecutive NFC championships although they have yet to win one.

Origin of name: The Eagles were born as a franchise amidst the Great Depression in 1933, the same year as new President Franklin Roosevelt's New Deal for the nation. Bert Bell took the symbol of Roosevelt's National Recovery Administration, the Eagle, as the name of his new franchise.

Time till first championship: 16 years.

Time since last championship: 44 years.

Retired numbers: The Eagles have retired the numbers of two Hall of Famers who each played on two of the team's three championships— Steve Van Buren 15 and Chuck

Record by Decade

| | Regular Season | | | Postseason | | |
	Won	Lost	Tied	Won	Lost	Championships
1930s	18	55	3	0	0	
1940s	58	47	5	3	1	1948, 1949
1950s	51	64	5	0	0	
1960s	57	76	5	1	0	1960
1970s	56	84	4	1	2	
1980s	76	74	2	2	4	
1990s	80	79	1	2	4	
2000s	46	18	0	5	4	
All-Time	442	497	25	14	15	3

Winning seasons: 29. Losing Seasons: 29. .500 seasons: 3.

Coaches

	Years	Record	Playoffs
Lud Wray	1933–5	9–21–1	0–0
Bert Bell	1936–40	10–44–2	0–0
Greasy Neale (2)	1941–50	63–45–5	3–1
Bo McMillin	1951	2–0–0	0–0
Wayne Millner	1951	2–8–0	0–0
Jim Trimble	1952–5	25–20–3	0–0
Hugh Devore	1956–7	7–16–1	0–0
Buck Shaw (1)	1958–60	19–16–1	1–0
Nick Skorich	1961–3	15–24–3	0–0
Joe Kuharich	1964–8	28–41–1	0–0
Jerry Williams	1969–71	7–22–2	0–0
Ed Khayat	1971–2	8–15–2	0–0
Mike McCormack	1973–5	16–25–1	0–0
Dick Vermeil	1976–82	54–47–0	3–4
Marion Campbell	1983–5	17–29–1	0–0
Fred Bruney	1985	1–0–0	0–0
Buddy Ryan	1986–90	43–35–1	0–3
Rich Kotite	1991–4	36–28–0	1–1
Ray Rhodes	1995–8	29–34–1	1–2
Andy Reid	1999–2003	51–29–0	5–4

(Championships in parentheses)

Bednarik 60. They also retired 70 for Al Wistert a perennial All Pro who probably deserves to be in Canton. Tom Brooksheir, 40, and Pete Retzlaff, 44, were two All Pros who became local broadcasters and institutions, especially Brooky. Jerome Brown, 99, was a strong, popular defensive tackle who died young.

Other numbers worn by these players: Tom Brooksheir also wore 45 and Pete Retzlaff also wore 25.

Those who wore retired numbers after the honored player: 70 was later worn by linemen Don Owens and Jim Skaggs.

Numbers that should be retired: Reggie White, 92, was perhaps the best defensive end in history. The Packers have already retired his jersey in Green Bay.

Owned numbers: None.

Numbers worn by Hall of Famers: Chuck Bednarik 60; Bob Brown 76; Mike Ditka 89/98; Bill Hewitt 56/82; Sonny Jurgensen 9; James Lofton 80; Ollie Matson 33; Tommy McDonald 25; Pete Pihos 35; Jim Ringo 54; Norm Van Brocklin 11; Steve Van Buren 15; Alex Wojciechowicz 53.

Star power: Tommy McDonald took 25 from Pete Retzlaff; Bill Bergey took 66 from Roy Kirksey.

Star eclipsed: Jim Ringo wore 54 because Jim Schrader wore 51. Roman Gabriel wore 5 till Ben Hawkins, 18, left; Keith Byars wore 42 till Earnest Jackson, 41, left; Mike Ditka wore 98 till Mike Morgan, 89, left, Reggie White wore 91 till Smiley Creswell, 92, left.

Numbers with most great players: 21 has been worn outstanding defensive backs Eric Allen, Bobby Taylor, Joe Scarpati and Gummy Carr. 72 has been worn by tough linemen Jesse Richardson, Floyd Peters, David Alexander and Tra Thomas. 76 has been worn Pro Bowl tackles, Bucko Kilroy, J.D. Smith, Bob Brown and Jerry Sisemore and guard John Welbourn. 78 has been worn by more tough linemen, Mike Jarmoluk, Marion Campbell, Carl Hairston, and Hollis Thomas.

Worst represented numbers: 57 has been worn by nine linebackers and a defensive tackle while 67 has been worn 14 times by linemen, and none of the 24 players lasted very long for good reason.

Number worn by the most players: 80 has been worn 32 times.

Player who wore the most numbers: Four numbers have been worn by Joe Pilconis 2/18/24/28 and Luther Broughton 49/84/86/88.

Longest tenure wearing a number: Chuck Bednarik wore 60 for 14 years from 1949 to 1962.

Number worn by first ever draft pick: Jay Berwanger was the first draft pick of any NFL team in 1936, but never played pro football. The first draft pick to play for the Eagles was Fran Murray, 11, who was picked in the second round in 1937. The first first round pick to play for the Eagles was quarterback Davey O'Brien, 5/8, in 1939.

Biggest draft busts: The draft has frequently been disappointing in Philadelphia starting from the first draft when Heisman Trophy winner Jay Berwanger decided against pro football. In 1969, the Eagles lost out on the O.J. Simpson sweepstakes and ended up with the third pick, Leroy Keyes, 20, who turned out to be a jack of all trades but master of none. In the last 20 years, many high picks have been wasted on flop linemen — Kevin Allen, 72, selected ninth in 1985; Antone Davis, 77/78, selected eighth in 1991; Bernard Williams, 74, selected 14th in 1994; Mike Mamula, 59, selected seventh in 1995; and Jon Harris, 90, selected 26th in 1997.

Number worn by oldest player: Lee Johnson wore 6 as a 41 year old in 2002. Sean Landetta wore 7 as a 40 year old in 2001. Both were punters.

Cameos: Hall of Famers— James Lofton 80; All Pros and other notables— Houston Antwine 75; Matt Bahr 11; Todd Bell 49; Blaine Bishop 24; Carlos Carson 87; Don Chuy 66; Richard Dent 95; Antonio Freeman 86; Kurt Gouveia 54; Mel Gray 28; Dave Hampton 34; Tim Harris 97; Vaughn Johnson 52; Amp Lee 28; Dorsey Levens 25; Marlin McKeever 85; Keith Millard 77; Art Monk 85; Eddie Murray 3; Ken O'Brien 7; Gerry Philbin 77; Mark Rypien 11; Rod Smart 24; Freddie Solomon 17; Leo Sugar 84; Carl Taseff 23.

Ones who got away: Mark Mosely, 3, kicked a lot of field goals for the Redskins and Sonny Jurgensen, 9, threw a lot of touchdowns for them. Lee Roy Caffey, 34, was a star linebacker for the Packers in the 1960s. Bruce Van Dyke, 66, and Ray Mansfield, 77, were star linemen for Pittsburgh. Chris Carter, 80, caught a ton of touchdowns in Minnesota. Bob Schnelker, 85, was a skilled receiver for the Giants. Art Powell, 87, was All Pro in the AFL. Ben Agajanian, 89, became a reliable kicker for the Giants.

Least popular numbers: 0 has never been worn. 92 has only been worn twice.

Last number to be originated: In 1985, 90 (Aaron Brown), 91 (Reggie White and Tim Golden) and 92 (Smiley Creswell and Reggie White) were all worn for the first time.

Longest dormant number: 13 has not been worn since 1978. 2 was dormant for 43 years from 1935 through 1977.

Triskaidekaphobia notes: 13 has been worn by three backs, two ends and a punter, all unremarkable.

Shared numbers: 11 was worn by the Eagles' two championship quarterbacks, Tommy Thompson and Norm Van Brocklin. Hard-hitting safeties Andre Waters and Brian Dawkins wore 20. Small, but versatile runners Tim Brown and Duce Staley have worn 22. 52 was worn by Pro Bowl linebackers Wayne Robinson and Dave Lloyd. 55 was worn by two more Pro Bowl linebackers, Maxie Baughan and Frank Lemaster. 56 was worn by Hall of Fame end Bill Hewitt and Pro Bowl linebacker Jerry Robinson.

Continuity: Bobby Thomason was replaced in 11 by fellow quarterback Norm Van Brocklin; receiver Ben Hawkins was replaced in 18 by Roman Gabriel; Eric Allen was replaced in 21 by fellow Pro Bowl cornerback Bobby Taylor; Willie Thomas was replaced in 51 by fellow linebacker Carlos Emmons; Hall of Fame center Alex Wojciechowicz was replaced in 53 by Pro Bowl center Ken Farragut; J.D. Smith was replaced in 76 by fellow Pro Bowl tackle Bob Brown; Mike Jarmoluk was replaced in 78 by fellow Pro Bowl tackle Marion Campbell.

Discontinuity: Pro Bowl cornerback Irv Cross was followed in 27 by Trent Jackson;

Hall of Fame center Jim Ringo was followed in 54 by Gene Cepetelli; Pro Bowl receiver Mike Quick was followed in 82 by Mickey Shuler; Pro Bowl end Bobby Walston was followed in 83 by defensive end Bill Quinlan; Pro Bowl receiver Fred Barnett was followed in 86 by Dialleo Burks; Pro Bowl defensive end Clyde Simmons was followed in 96 by Mike Flores.

Family Connections

Brothers

Steve Van Buren	RB	1944–51	15
Ebert Van Buren	LB	1951–3	17/31
Ty Detmer	QB	1996–7	14
Koy Detmer	QB	1998–2003	10

Quarterback numbers over 19: 39 Bill Mackrides.

Number of first black player: In 1952 backs Don Stephens, 20, and Ralph Goldston 22.

Numbers of future NFL head coaches: Neill Armstrong 80; Marion Campbell 78; Algy Clark 28; Bill Cowher 57; Mike Ditka 98/89; Herm Edwards 46; Abe Gibron 64; Bud Grant 86; Ed Khayat 73; Jim Leonard 19; John Rauch 11; Jim Ringo 54; Allie Sherman 10; Norm Van Brocklin 11; and Jerry Williams 49.

Numbers of future NFL referees: Adrian Burk 10, Merrill Douglass 33, Pete Liske 14, John Don Looney 30; and Joe Muha 36.

Players who played other sports: Baseball — Jim Castiglia 31; Walt Masters 53; Bert Kuczynski 80; as well as coach Greasy Neale. Basketball — Bud Grant 86. Wrestling — Joe Carollo 76 and Don Chuy 66.

Players more famous after football: Nick Basca, 47, and Len Supulski, 80, died in World War II. Irv Kupcinet, 31/37, was a longtime newspaper columnist in Chicago. Walter Barnes, 74, appeared in over 50 movies. Tim Rossovich, 82, has been an actor and stunt man. Matt Battaglia, 52, has appeared in action movies. Darnell Autry, 24/26, has tried acting. Rodney Peete, 9, is married to actress Holly Robinson.

First player to wear a number in the 70s: Lester McDonald wore 76 in 1940.

First player to wear a number in the 80s: In 1941, the numbers 80 (Granville Harrison, Kirk Hershey), 81 (Dick Humbert), 82 (Robert Krueger), 83 (Jack Ferrante), 84 (Larry Cabrelli), 85 (John Shonk), and 89 (Henry Piro) were all broken in when the Eagles experimented with a new numbering scheme. The basics of the scheme (10s for quarterbacks, 20s for halfbacks, 30s for fullbacks, 40s for tailbacks, 50s for centers, 60s for guards, 70s for tackles, and 80s for ends) were adopted a dozen years later in 1952 by the NFL.

First player to wear a number in the 90s: Mike Ditka reversed his familiar 89 to wear 98 in 1967.

Number with most points scored: 83 with 1,049 points scored by Bobby Walston (881), Jeff Thomason (42), Tony Woodruff (30), Jimmy Giles (24), Rodney Parker (12), Pat Beach (12), Michael Young (12), Michael Timpson (12), Dietrich Jells (12), Kevin Bowman (6), and Ed West (6).

Number with most yards rushing: 22 with 10,541 yards gained by Duce Staley (4,807), Tim Brown (3,703), Cyril Pinder (1,083), Ed Storm (445), Ralph Goldston (203), Mark Higgs (184), Jacque Robinson (114), and Vai Sikahema (2).

Number with most receptions: 86 with 787 passes caught by Fred Barnett (308), Charlie Young (197), Fred Hill (85), Greg Garrity (59), Bud Grant (56), Antonio Freeman (46), Russell Copeland (18), Mike Siano (9), Al Dixon (4), Brian Finneran (2), Harold Prescott (1), Lewis Gilbert (1), and Van Dyke (1).

Number with most touchdown passes: 7 with 228 touchdowns tossed by Ron Jaworski (175), Roy Zimmerman (30), Bobby Hoying (11), John Reaves (7), Ken O'Brien (4), and John Huarte (1).

Number with most interceptions: 21 with 102 passes picked off by Eric Allen (34), Joe Scarpatti (24), Bobby Taylor (19), Jim Carr (13), John Sciarra (4), Evan Cooper (4), Ray Jones (2), Chuck Cherundolo (1), and Al Clark (1).

Oddity: Five of the top 12 Eagle reception leaders wore unusual numbers for receivers. Their top three are Harold Carmichael 17, Pete Retzlaff 44, and Pete Pihos 35. Ninth is Hall of Famer Tommy McDonald 25 and 12th is Ben Hawkins 18. Carmichael, Retzlaff and Pihos all caught more passes than any other end in the league at their numbers.

Player Whose Number Is Unconfirmed

| 5 | *Davey O'Brien* | (QB) | 1939–40 |

Players Whose Number Is Unknown

| Herald Frahm | (B) | 1935 |
| William Holcomb | (T) | 1937 |

Team All-Time Numerical Roster

Those with an "r" following the year 1987 were replacement players during the players' strike. Pro Bowl and pre–1950 All Pro players for each number are in *Italics*; Hall of Famers are in **Bold** type.

1 Happy Feller (K) 1971, Nick Mike-Mayer (K) 1977–8, Tony Franklin (K) 1979–83, Gary Anderson (K) 1995–6.

2 Joe Pilconis (E) 1934, Mike Michel (P/K) 1978, Mike Horan (P) 1984–5, Dean Dorsey (K) 1988, Steve DeLine (K) 1989, *David Akers* (K) 1999–2003.

3 Roger Kirkman (B) 1934–5, Jack Concannon (QB) 1964–6, Mark Moseley (K) 1970, Eddie Murray (K) 1994.

4 Benjy Dial (B) 1967, Max Runager (P) 1979–83, 1989, David Jacobs (K) 1987r, Dale Dawson (K) 1988, Bryan Barker (P) 1994, Tom Hutton (P) 1995–8.

5 Joe Kresky (G) 1934–5, *Roman Gabriel* (QB) 1973, Tom Skladany (P) 1983, Dean May (QB) 1984, Mark Royals (P) 1987r, Jeff Feagles (P) 1990–3, *Donovan McNabb* (QB) 1999–2003.

6 Jim MacMurdo (T) 1934–6, Gary Adams (DB) 1969, John Reaves (QB) 1972, Spike Jones (P) 1975–7, Dan Pastorini (QB) 1982–3, Matt Cavanaugh (QB) 1986–9, Bubby Brister (QB) 1993–4, Lee Johnson (P) 2002.

7 *Roy Zimmerman* (B) 1943–6, John Huarte (QB) 1968, Jim Ward (QB) 1971, John Reaves (QB) 1972–4, *Ron Jaworski* (QB) 1977–86, Roger Ruzek (K) 1989–93, Ken O'Brien (QB) 1993, Bobby Hoying (QB) 1996–8, Sean Landeta (P) 1999–2002, Jason Baker (P) 2002.

8 Charles Hajek (C) 1934, *Davey O'Brien* (QB) 1939–40, Al Coleman (DB) 1972, Paul McFadden (K) 1984–7, Luis Zendejas (K) 1988–9, Brad Goebel (QB) 1991, Preston Jones (QB) 1993, Dirk Johnson (P) 2003.

9 James Zyntell (G) 1934, **Sonny Jurgensen** (QB) 1957–63, Jim Nettles (DB) 1965–8, Billy Walik (WR) 1970–2, Joe Pisarcik (QB) 1980–4, Don McPherson (QB) 1988–90, Jim McMahon (QB) 1990–2, Rodney Peete (QB) 1995–8, Norm Johnson (K) 1999.

10 Marv Ellstrom (B) 1934, George Kavel (B) 1934, Isadore Weinstock (B) 1935, Don Jackson (B) 1936, Maurice Harper (C) 1937–40, *Tommy Thompson* (QB) 1941–2, Al Sherman (QB) 1943–7, Frank Tripucka (QB) 1949, *Adrian Burk* (QB) 1951–6, Al Dorow (QB) 1957, King Hill (QB) 1961–8, George Mira (QB) 1969, *Mike Boryla* (QB) 1974–6, Ove Johansson (K) 1977, John Walton (QB) 1978–9, John Teltschik (P) 1986–90, Pat Ryan (QB) 1991, Koy Detmer (QB) 1997–2003.

11 Lee Woodruff (B) 1933, Joe Knapper (B) 1934, Ed Manske (E) 1936, John Ferko (G) 1937, Bernie Lee (B) 1938, Francis Murray (B) 1939–40, Lou Ghecas (B) 1941, Richard Erdlitz (B) 1942, *Tommy Thompson* (QB) 1945–50, John Rauch (QB) 1951, *Bobby Thomason* (QB) 1952–7, **Norm Van Brocklin** (QB) 1958–60, Rick Arrington (QB) 1970–3, John Walton (QB) 1976–7, Jeff Christensen (QB) 1984–5, Kyle Mackey (QB) 1986, Scott Tinsley (QB) 1987r, Casey Weldon (QB) 1992, Matt Bahr (K) 1993, Jay Fiedler (QB) 1994–5, Mark Rypien (QB) 1996, Ron Powlus (QB) 2000, Tim Hasselbeck (QB) 2002.

12 John Roberts (B) 1933–4, Ed Matesic (B) 1934–5, Art Buss (T) 1936–7, Herschel Ramsey (E) 1938–40, Kent Lawrence (WR) 1969, Tom McNeill (P) 1973, Bill Troup (QB) 1975, Bob Holly (QB) 1984, *Randall Cunningham* (QB) 1985–95.

13 George Kenneally (E) 1933–5, Dave Smukler (B) 1936–9, Leonard Barnum (B) 1940–2, Chuck Hughes (WR) 1967–9, Rick Engles (P) 1978.

14 *Swede Hanson* (B) 1933–6, Rudy Gollomb (G) 1936, Elwood Dow (B) 1938–40, Bob Gambold (B) 1953, Pete Liske (QB) 1971–2, Marty Horn (QB) 1987r, Rick Tuten (P) 1989, Jeff Wilkins (K) 1994, Ty Detmer (QB) 1996–7, Doug Pederson (QB) 1999, A.J. Feeley (QB) 2001–2.

15 Laf Russell (B) 1933, Dick Lackman (B) 1933, Osborne Willson (G) 1934–5, Stumpy Thomason (B) 1936, William Hughes (C) 1937, Clem Woltman (T) 1938–40, Lou Tomasetti (B) 1940–1, Ted Laux (B) 1942–3, **Steve Van Buren** (RB) 1944–51.

16 Sylvester Davis (B) 1933, Henry O'Boyle (B) 1933, James Zyntell (G) 1935, John Kusko (B) 1937–8, Elmer Kolberg (B) 1940, *Norm Snead* (QB) 1964–70, Vern Davis (DB) 1971, Horst

Muhlmann (K) 1975–7, Rob Hertel (QB) 1980, Jeff Kemp (QB) 1991, Gari Scott (WR) 2000.

17 *Joe Carter* (E) 1935–40, James Russell (T) 1937, Ebert Van Buren (B) 1951, Fred Enke (B) 1952, Jerry Reichow (E) 1960, Ralph Guglielmi (QB) 1963, Taft Reed (B) 1967, *Harold Carmichael* (WR) 1971–83, Mitch Berger (P) 1994, Freddie Solomon (WR) 1995, Lonny Calicchio (K) 1997.

18 Porter Lainhart (B) 1933, Nick Prisco (B) 1933, Albert Weiner (B) 1934, Joe Pilconis (E) 1936–7, Herbert Roton (E) 1937, Rankin Britt (E) 1939, Ray Hamilton (E) 1940, Ben Hawkins (WR) 1966–73, *Roman Gabriel* (QB) 1974–7, Dave Archer (QB) 1991–2, Chris Boniol (K) 1997–8.

19 Roger Kirkman (B) 1933, Jim Leonard (B) 1934–7, Herman Bassman (B) 1936, Tom Burnette (B) 1938, John Ferko (G) 1938, George Somers (T) 1939–40, Harold Pegg (C) 1940, Dan Berry (B) 1967, Tom Dempsey (K) 1971–4, Guido Merkens (QB) 1987r, Troy Smith (WR) 1999, Sean Morey (WR) 2001.

20 John Lipski (C) 1933–4, Howard Bailey (T) 1935, Clyde Williams (T) 1935, Pete Stevens (C) 1936, Henry Reese (C/LB) 1937–9, Jim MacMurdo (T) 1937, Elmer Hackney (B) 1940–1, Don Stevens (B) 1952, 1954, Ed Bawel (B) 1955–6, Jim Harris (B) 1957, Frank Budd (E) 1962, Leroy Keyes (DB) 1969–72, John Outlaw (DB) 1973–8, Leroy Harris (FB) 1979–82, Andre Waters (S/LB) 1984–93, Vaughn Hebron (RB) 1994–5, *Brian Dawkins* (S) 1996–2003.

21 James Zyntell (G) 1933, Paul Cuba (T) 1934–5, John Kusko (B) 1936, Herschel Stockton (G) 1937–8, Allison White (T) 1939, Chuck Cherundolo (C) 1940, William Boedeker (B) 1950, Al Pollard (B) 1951–3, Jim Carr (S) 1959–63, Joe Scarpati (S) 1964–9, 1971, Ray Jones (DB) 1970, Jackie Allen (DB) 1972, Woo Chosson (WR) 1973–4, Al Clark (CB) 1976, John Sciarra (DB) 1978–83, Evan Cooper (DB) 1984–7, *Eric Allen* (CB) 1988–94, *Bobby Taylor* (CB) 1995–2003.

22 Henry Obst (G) 1933, Edward Storm (B) 1934–5, James Russell (T) 1936, Elmer Kolberg (B) 1939, Don Jones (B) 1940, Ralph Goldston (B) 1952, 1954–5, Lee Riley (DB) 1956, 1958–9, *Tim Brown* (RB) 1960–7, Cyril Pinder (RB) 1968–70, Larry Marshall (KR) 1974–7, Brenard Wilson (S) 1979–86, Robert Lavette (RB) 1987, Jacque Robinson (FB) 1987r, Mark Higgs (RB) 1989, Vai Sikahema (KR) 1992–3, Marvin Goodwin (S) 1994, James Saxon (FB) 1995, James Fuller (S) 1996, Duce Staley (RB) 1997–2003.

23 Paul Cuba (T) 1933, Vince Zizak (T) 1934–7, Phil Poth (G) 1934, Harry Shaub (G) 1935, Bill Wilson (E) 1938, Zed Coston (C) 1939, Raymond George (T) 1940, William Roffler (B) 1954, Ken Keller (B) 1956–7, Carl Taseff (DB) 1961, Mike McClellan (B) 1962–3, Claude Crabb (DB) 1964–5, Willie Brown (WR) 1966, Harry Jones (RB)

1967–72, Roger Williams (DB) 1973, Clifford Brooks (DB) 1975–6, Bob Howard (CB) 1978–9, Cedric Brown (CB) 1987, Willie Turral (RB) 1987r, Heath Sherman (RB) 1989–93, Derrick Frazier (CB) 1994–5, *Troy Vincent* (CB) 1996–2003.

24 Howard Auer (T) 1933, Joe Carpe (T) 1933, Dick Lackman (B) 1933–5, Joe Knapper (B) 1934, Herman Bassman (B) 1936, Joe Pilconis (E) 1937, Allen Keen (B) 1937–8, Bill Schneller (B) 1940, Dom Moselle (B) 1954, George Taliaferro (B) 1955, Don Schaefer (B) 1956, Nate Ramsey (DB) 1963–72, Artimus Parker (DB) 1974–6, Henry Monroe (CB) 1979, Zac Henderson (S) 1980, Ray Ellis (S) 1981–5, Russell Gary (DB) 1986, Alan Reid (RB) 1987, Reggie Brown (RB) 1987r, Alan Dial (DB) 1989, Corey Barlow (CB) 1992–4, Tim McTyer (CB) 1997–8, Darnell Autry (RB) 2000, Rod Smart (RB) 2001, Blaine Bishop (S) 2002, Sheldon Brown (CB) 2003.

25 Osborne Willson (G) 1933, Leonard Gudd (E) 1934, Henry Reese (C/LB) 1935–6, Emmet Kriel (G) 1939, Russ Thompson (T) 1940, Hugh McCullough (B) 1943, Toy Ledbetter (B) 1950, 1953–5, *Pete Retzlaff* (TE) 1956, **Tommy McDonald** (WR) 1957–63, Bill Mack (WR) 1964, Bob Shann (B) 1965, 1967, Larry Conjar (FB) 1968, Tom Sullivan (RB) 1972–7, Bill Bryant (CB) 1978, Zach Dixon (RB) 1980, Dennis DeVaughn (DB) 1982–3, Anthony Toney (FB) 1986–90, Tom Gerhart (DB) 1992, Charlie Garner (RB) 1994, Greg Tremble (DB) 1995, Deral Boykin (S) 1996, Willie Clay (CB) 1997, Allen Rossum (KR) 1998–9, Je'Rod Cherry (S) 2000, Monty Montgomery (CB) 2001, Dorsey Levens (RB) 2002.

26 Joe Kresky (G) 1933, Dan Barnhardt (B) 1934, Jack Norby (B) 1934, Forrest McPherson (T) 1935–6, Winford Baze (B) 1937, Herschel Giddens (T) 1938, Lester McDonald (E) 1940, Dave DiFilippo (G) 1941, Clarence Peaks (FB) 1957–63, Al Nelson (DB) 1965–73, Art Malone (RB) 1975–6, John Sanders (DB) 1977–9, Michael Haddix (FB) 1983–8, Ben Smith (DB) 1990–3, Al Jackson (CB) 1994, Jerome Henderson (CB) 1995, Darnell Autry (RB) 1998, Lito Sheppard (CB) 2002–3.

27 Robert Gonya (T) 1933–4, Milton Leathers (G) 1933, Jack Dempsey (T) 1934, 1937, Burle Robinson (E) 1935, George Rado (E) 1937–8, Milt Trost (T) 1940, Sam Bartholomew (B) 1941, Bob Davis (B) 1942, John Butler (B) 1943, 1945, Ted Laux (B) 1944, Pete Kmetovic (B) 1946, Tom Johnson (B) 1948, Clyde Scott (B) 1949–52, Neil Ferris (B) 1952, Hal Giancanelli (B) 1953–6, Billy Wells (B) 1958, Gene Johnson (B) 1959–60, *Irv Cross* (DB) 1961–5, 1969, Trent Jackson (WR) 1966, Po James (RB) 1972–4, Richard Blackmore (CB) 1979–82, Topper Clemons (RB) 1987r, Siran Stacy (RB) 1992, Eric Zomalt (S) 1994–6, James Bostic (RB) 1998–9, Julian Jones (S) 2001.

28 Richard Thornton (B) 1933, Myers Clark

(B) 1934, Guy Turnbow (T) 1934, Max Padlow (E) 1935, Harry Kopenberg (T) 1936, Joe Pilconis (E) 1937, Ray Keeling (T) 1938–9, Bob Jackson (B) 1960, Don Jonas (B) 1962, Paul Dudley (B) 1963, Jim Gray (B) 1967, *Bill Bradley* (S) 1969–76, Lou Rash (CB) 1984, Greg Harding (DB) 1987r, Don Griffin (CB) 1996, Mel Gray (KR) 1997, Clarence Love (CB) 1998, Amp Lee (RB) 2000, Correll Buckhalter (RB) 2001, 2003.

29 Richard Fenci (E) 1933, Ray Smith (C) 1933, Stephen Banas (B) 1935, Glenn Campbell (E) 1935, Stumpy Thomason (B) 1935, Herman Bassman (B) 1936, Joe Pivarnick (G) 1936, Charles Knox (T) 1937, William Hughes (C) 1938–40, John Nocera (LB) 1959–62, Israel Lang (FB) 1964–8, *Harold Jackson* (WR) 1969–72, Mark Burke (DB) 1976, Al Latimer (CB) 1979, Jo Jo Heath (DB) 1981, Elbert Foules (CB) 1983–7, Mark McMillian (CB) 1992–5, Adam Walker (FB) 1996, Corey Walker (RB) 1998, Darrel Crutchfield (CB) 2001, Roderick Hood (CB) 2003.

30 Art Koeninger (C) 1933, Barnes Milon (G) 1934, Henry Benson (G) 1935, Bob Masters (B) 1937–8, *Don Looney* (E) 1940, Mort Landsberg (B) 1941, Bosh Pritchard (B) 1942, 1946–51, John Binotto (B) 1942, Richard Erdlitz (B) 1945, Milton Smith (E) 1945, Theron Sapp (B) 1959–63, Alvin Haymond (DB) 1968, Jim Raye (DB) 1969, Joe Lavender (CB) 1973–5, Ron Lou (C) 1975, Cleveland Franklin (RB) 1977–8, Mike Hogan (FB) 1980, Don Calhoun (RB) 1982, Chris Johnson (DB) 1987r, Otis Smith (CB) 1991–4, Charlie Garner (RB) 1995–8, Brian Mitchell (KR) 2000–2.

31 *Joe Carter* (E) 1933–4, Tom Graham (G) 1935, Irv Kupcinet (B) 1935, William Brian (T) 1935–6, Emmett Mortell (B) 1937–9, Jerry Ginney (G) 1940, *Phil Ragazzo* (T) 1940, Jim Castiglia (B) 1941, 1945–6, Ted Williams (B) 1942, Bob Masters (B) 1943, Art Macioszczyk (B) 1944, 1947, Dan Sandifer (DB) 1950–1, Ebert Van Buren (B) 1952–3, Ron Goodwin (E) 1963, Tom Bailey (B) 1971–4, *Wilbert Montgomery* (RB) 1977–84, Troy West (S) 1987r, Tyrone Jones (DB) 1989, Brian O'Neal (FB) 1994, Derrick Witherspoon (RB) 1995–7, Al Harris (CB) 1998–2002, Daryon Brutley (CB) 2003.

32 Fred Felber (E) 1933, Everitt Rowan (E) 1933, Glenn Frey (B) 1936–7, Hugh Wolfe (B) 1940, Irving Hall (B) 1942, Charley Gauer (E) 1943–4, Toimi Jarvi (B) 1944, John Rogalla (B) 1945, Jack Myers (B) 1948–50, Neil Worden (RB) 1954, 1957, Joe Pagliei (B) 1959, Roger Gill (B) 1964–5, Rick Duncan (K) 1968, Jackie Smith (DB) 1971, Charles Ford (DB) 1974, Herb Lusk (RB) 1976–8, Earl Carr (RB) 1979, Jim Culbreath (FB) 1980, Booker Russell (FB) 1981, Michael Williams (RB) 1983–4, Michael Ulmer (DB) 1987r, Walter Abercrombie (RB) 1988, James Joseph (RB) 1991–4, *Ricky Watters* (RB) 1995–7, Jason Bostic (CB) 1999–2000, Michael Lewis (S) 2002–3.

33 Guy Turnbow (T) 1933, Ray Spillers (T) 1937, Taldon Manton (B) 1940, Jack Banta (B) 1941, 1944–5, Bob Masters (B) 1942, Steve Sader (B) 1943, *Russ Craft* (B) 1946–53, Roy Barni (B) 1954–5, Willie Berzinski (B) 1956, *Billy Ray Barnes* (RB) 1957–61, Merrill Douglas (B) 1962, **Ollie Matson** (RB) 1964–6, Ron Blye (RB) 1969, Steve Preece (DB) 1970–2, Randy Jackson (RB) 1974, Po James (RB) 1975, Louie Giammona (RB) 1978–82, William Frizzell (S) 1986–90, 1992–3, Mike Waters (FB) 1986, Kevin Bouie (RB) 1996, Tim Watson (S) 1997, Aaron Hayden (RB) 1998, Eric Bieniemy (RB) 1999, Thomas Hamner (RB) 2000, Terrence Carroll (S) 2001, Clinton Hart (S) 2003.

34 Roy Lechthaler (G) 1933, Laurence Steinbach (T) 1933, Mike Sebastian (B) 1935, Jay Arnold (B) 1937–40, Lee Roy Caffey (LB) 1963, Earl Gros (FB) 1964–6, Larry Watkins (B) 1970–2, Dave Hampton (RB) 1976, James Betterson (RB) 1977–8, Hubie Oliver (FB) 1981–5, Terry Hoage (S) 1986–90, Herschel Walker (RB) 1992–4, Kevin Turner (FB) 1995–9, Jamie Reader (FB) 2001, Reno Mahe (RB) 2003.

35 Charles Leyendecker (T) 1933, Rich Smith (C) 1933, Forrest McPherson (T) 1937, Drew Ellis (T) 1938–40, *Dick Bassi* (G) 1940, **Pete Pihos** (E) 1947–55, *Ted Dean* (RB) 1960–3, Ray Poage (E) 1964–5, Adrian Young (LB) 1968–72, Mike Hogan (FB) 1976–8, Perry Harrington (RB) 1980–3, Mike Kullman (S) 1987r, Mark Konecny (RB) 1988, Kevin Bouie (RB) 1995, Deauntae Brown (CB) 1997, Anthony Marshall (S) 1998, Edwin Watson (RB) 1999, Chris Warren (RB) 2000.

36 Ed Manske (E) 1935, Carl Kane (B) 1936, Herbert Roton (E) 1937, Joe Bukant (B) 1938–40, Terry Fox (B) 1941, 1945, John Stackpool (B) 1942, Dean Steward (B) 1943, *Joe Muha* (B) 1946–50, Jerry Cowhig (B) 1951, John Brewer (B) 1952–3, Dick Bielski (B) 1955–9, Tom McNeill (P) 1971–2, Norm Bulaich (RB) 1973–4, Herman Hunter (RB) 1985, Bobby Morse (RB) 1987, Robert Drummond (RB) 1989–91, Mike Zordich (S) 1994–8, Stanley Pritchett (FB) 2000, Brian Westbrook (RB) 2002–3.

37 Irv Kupcinet (B) 1935, Robert Rowe (B) 1935, Winford Baze (B) 1937, John Cole (B) 1938, 1940, Bree Cuppoletti (G) 1939, Fred Gloden (B) 1941, *Ernie Steele* (B) 1942–8, *Tom Woodeshick* (RB) 1963–71, Merritt Kersey (P) 1974–5, Tommy Campbell (DB) 1976, Billy Campfield (RB) 1978–82, Taivale Tautalatasi (RB) 1986–8, Sammy Lilly (DB) 1989–90, Sean Woodson (S) 1998.

38 Bill Fiedler (G) 1938, Jake Schuehle (B) 1939, John Huzvar (B) 1952, Rob Goode (B) 1955, *Sam Baker* (K) 1964–9, Tony Baker (B) 1971–2, George Amundson (RB) 1975, Bill Olds (RB) 1976, Larry Barnes (FB) 1978–9, Steve Atkins (FB) 1981, Mickey Fitzgerald (FB) 1981, Jairo Penaranda (RB) 1985, Russell Gary (DB) 1986, Rich Miano (DB) 1991-4, Dexter McNabb (FB) 1995, Charles Dimry (DB) 1997, Cecil Martin (FB) 1999-2002.

39 Henry Benson (G) 1935, Bob Pylman (T) 1938-9, Foster Watkins (B) 1940, Bill Mackrides (QB) 1947-51, Pete Emelianchik (E) 1967, Kermit Alexander (DB) 1972-3, Bill Olds (RB) 1976, Bob Torrey (FB) 1980, Major Everett (FB) 1983-5, Victor Bellamy (CB) 1987r, Tony Brooks (RB) 1992-3, Corey Walker (RB) 1997, Michael Reed (FB) 1998, Sheldon Brown (DB) 2002.

40 Charles Newton (B) 1939-40, Wesley McAfee (B) 1941, Sonny Karnofsky (B) 1945, Elliott Ormsbe (B) 1946, Leslie Palmer (B) 1948, Frank Reagan (B) 1949-51, Don Johnson (B) 1953-5, *Tom Brookshier* (CB) 1956-61.

41 Ted Schmitt (C) 1938-40, Foster Watkins (B) 1941, Gil Steinke (B) 1945-8, Busit Warren (B) 1945, Frank Ziegler (B) 1949-53, *Jerry Norton* (DB) 1954-8, Bob Freeman (DB) 1960-1, Howard Cassady (B) 1962, Harry Wilson (B) 1967-70, Richard Harvey (DB) 1970, *Randy Logan* (S) 1973-83, Earnest Jackson (RB) 1985-6, Keith Byars (RB) 1987-92, Alvin Ross (FB) 1987r, Fred McCrary (FB) 1995, Johnny Thomas (CB) 1996, William Hampton (CB) 2001.

42 Carl Jorgenson (T) 1935, George Mulligan (E) 1936, *Swede Hanson* (B) 1936-7, Raymond George (T) 1940, Bob Hudson (B) 1954-5, 1957-8, Bob Harrison (LB) 1962-3, Aaron Martin (DB) 1966-7, Dennis Morgan (KR) 1975, Steve Wagner (S) 1980, Calvin Murray (HB) 1981-2, Keith Byars (RB) 1986, Angelo James (CB) 1987r, Eric Everett (CB) 1988-9, John Booty (DB) 1991-2, Mike Reid (S) 1993-4, David Whitmore (S) 1995, Dialleo Burks (WR) 1996, Rashard Cook (S) 1999-2002.

43 *Jack Hinkle* (B) 1941-7, William Jefferson (B) 1942, James Lankas (B) 1942, Jim Parmer (B) 1948-56, Robert Smith (B) 1956, Walt Kowalczyk (B) 1958-9, Ralph Heck (LB) 1963-5, Al Davis (B) 1971-2, James McAlister (RB) 1975-6, *Roynell Young* (CB) 1980-8, Roger Vick (RB) 1990, Erik McMillan (S) 1993, Randy Kinder (CB) 1997, Damon Moore (S) 1999-2001.

44 Franklin Emmons (B) 1940, Albert Johnson (B) 1942, Ben Kish (B) 1943-9, *Norm Willey* (DE) 1950-1, Bob Stringer (B) 1952-3, Harry Dowda (B) 1954-5, *Pete Retzlaff* (TE) 1957-66.

45 Thomas Bushby (B) 1935, Leo Raskowski (T) 1935, Art Buss (T) 1937, Dick Riffle (B) 1938-40, Noble Doss (B) 1947-8, Joe Sutton (B) 1950-2, *Tom Brookshier* (CB) 1953, Rocky Ryan (E) 1956-8, Paige Cothren (B) 1959, Don Burroughs (DB) 1960-4, Ron Medved (DB) 1966-70, Pat Gibbs (DB) 1972, Marion Reeves (DB) 1974, Von Mansfield (DB) 1982, Charles Crawford (RB) 1986-7, Jeff Griffin (CB) 1987r, Thomas Sanders (RB) 1990-1, Vaughn Hebron (RB) 1993, Barry

Wilburn (S) 1995-6, Matt Stevens (S) 1997-8, Tim Hauck (S) 1999-2001.

46 Don Miller (B) 1954, Ted Wegert (B) 1955-6, Brad Myers (B) 1958, Glen Amerson (B) 1961, Lee Bouggess (RB) 1970-3, Herman Edwards (CB) 1977-85, Chris Gerhard (S) 1987r, Izel Jenkins (CB) 1988-92, Markus Thomas (RB) 1993, Fredric Ford (CB) 1997, Quintin Mikell (S) 2003.

47 Nick Basca (B) 1941, John Mallory (B) 1968, Ed Hayes (DB) 1970, Ron Bull (RB) 1971, Larry Crowe (RB) 1972, Charlie Williams (CB) 1978, Andre Hardy (RB) 1984, Greg Jackson (S) 1994-5, Charles Emanuel (S) 1997.

48 *Eberle Schultz* (G) 1940, Ben Scotti (B) 1962-3, Jay Johnson (LB) 1969, Greg Oliver (RB) 1973-4, Martin Mitchell (DB) 1977, *Wes Hopkins* (S) 1983-93, Steve Hendrickson (LB) 1995, Andre President (TE) 1997, Jon Ritchie (FB) 2003.

49 Dan DeSantis (B) 1941, Robert Thurbon (B) 1943, Mel Bleeker (B) 1944-6, Pat McHugh (B) 1947-51, Jerry Williams (B) 1953-4, Glenn Glass (B) 1964-5, Wayne Colman (DB) 1968-9, Jim Thrower (DB) 1970-2, John Tarver (RB) 1975, Eric Johnson (DB) 1977-8, Tom Caterbone (CB) 1987r, Todd Bell (LB) 1989, Luther Broughton (TE) 1997, Andrew Jordan (TE) 1998.

50 Alabama Pitts (B) 1935, Don Jackson (B) 1936, Robert Bjorklund (C) 1941, Ken Hayden (C) 1942, Al Wukits (C) 1943, Baptiste Manzini (C) 1944-5, Bob Kelley (C) 1955-6, Darrel Aschbacher (G) 1959, Dave Recher (C) 1966-8, Ron Porter (LB) 1969-72, Guy Morriss (C) 1974-83, Garry Cobb (LB) 1985-7, Dave Rimington (C) 1988-9, Ephesians Bartley (LB) 1992, James Willis (LB) 1995-8, Alonzo Ephraim (C) 2003.

51 Lyle Graham (C) 1941, Al Milling (G) 1942, Robert Wear (C) 1942, Enio Conti (G) 1944-5, Ray Graves (C) 1946, Boyd Williams (C) 1947, Frank Szymanski (C) 1948, Chuck Weber (LB) 1959-61, Jim Schrader (C) 1962-4, Dave Recher (C) 1965, Dwight Kelley (LB) 1966-72, Dick Cunningham (LB) 1973, Ron Lou (C) 1975, Reggie Wilkes (LB) 1978-85, Chuck Gorecki (LB) 1987r, Ricky Shaw (LB) 1989-90, *William Thomas* (LB) 1991-9, Carlos Emmons (LB) 2000-3.

52 Ray Graves (C) 1942-3, Vic Lindskog (C) 1944-51, *Wayne Robinson* (LB) 1952-6, *Dave Lloyd* (LB) 1963-70, Kevin Reilly (LB) 1973-4, Ray Phillips (LB) 1978-81, Rich Kraynak (LB) 1983-6, Matt Battaglia (LB) 1987r, Todd Bell (LB) 1988, Jessie Small (LB) 1989-91, Louis Cooper (LB) 1993, Vaughan Johnson (LB) 1994, Sylvester Wright (LB) 1995-6, DeShawn Fogle (LB) 1997, Jon Haskins (LB) 1998, Barry Gardner (LB) 1999-2002.

53 Walt Masters (B) 1936, **Alex Wojciechowicz** (C) 1946-50, *Ken Farragut* (C) 1951-4, Bob Pellegrini (LB) 1956, 1958-61, John Simerson (C) 1957, Bob Butler (G) 1962, Harold Wells (LB)

1965–8, Fred Whittingham (LB) 1971, Dick Absher (LB) 1972, Dennis Franks (C) 1976–8, Jody Schulz (LB) 1983–4, Dwayne Jiles (LB) 1985–9, Fred Smalls (LB) 1987r, Maurice Henry (LB) 1990, John Roper (LB) 1993, Bill Romanowski (LB) 1994–5, N.D. Kalu (DE) 1997, *Hugh Douglas* (DE) 1998–2002, Mark Simoneau (LB) 2003.

54 Gerry Huth (G) 1959, Bill Lapham (C) 1960, **Jim Ringo** (C) 1964–7, Gene Ceppetelli (C) 1968–9, Calvin Hunt (C) 1970, Chuck Allen (LB) 1972, Tom Roussel (LB) 1973, Jim Opperman (LB) 1975, Drew Mahalic (LB) 1976–8, Zack Valentine (LB) 1982–3, Jon Kimmel (LB) 1985, Alonzo Johnson (LB) 1986–7, Kelly Kirchbaum (LB) 1987r, Britt Hager (LB) 1989–94, Kurt Gouveia (LB) 1995, Terry Crews (LB) 1996, DeShawn Fogle (LB) 1997, Jeff Herrod (LB) 1997, *Jeremiah Trotter* (LB) 1998–2001, Nate Wayne (LB) 2003.

55 Frank Bausch (C) 1941, Basilio Marchi (C) 1942, *Maxie Baughan* (LB) 1960–5, Fred Brown (LB) 1967–8, Jerry Sturm (C) 1972, *Frank Lemaster* (LB) 1974–83, Mike Reichenbach (LB) 1984–9, Ken Rose (LB) 1990–4, Nate Dingle (LB) 1995, Ray Farmer (LB) 1996–8, Quinton Caver (LB) 2001, Tyreo Harrison (LB) 2003.

56 **Bill Hewitt** (E) 1936–9, Fred Whittingham (LB) 1966, Bill Hobbs (LB) 1969–71, Bill Overmeyer (LB) 1972, Dean Halverson (LB) 1973–6, *Jerry Robinson* (LB) 1979–84, Byron Evans (LB) 1987–94, David Brown (LB) 1987r, Joe Kelly (LB) 1996, Darrin Smith (LB) 1997, Mike Caldwell (LB) 1998–2001, Shawn Barber (LB) 2002, Derrick Burgess (DE) 2003.

57 Ernie Calloway (DT) 1969, James Reed (LB) 1977, Mike Osborn (LB) 1978, Mike Curcio (LB) 1981–2, Bill Cowher (LB) 1983–4, Tom Polley (LB) 1985, Scott Kowalkowski (LB) 1991–3, Marc Woodard (LB) 1994–6, James Darling (LB) 1997–2000, Keith Adams (LB) 2002–3.

58 Dave Cahill (DT) 1966, Mel Tom (DE) 1967–70, Bob Creech (LB) 1971–2, Steve Colavito (LB) 1975, Terry Tautolo (LB) 1976–9, Anthony Griggs (LB) 1982–5, Byron Lee (LB) 1986–7, Ty Allert (LB) 1987–9, Derrick Oden (LB) 1993–5, Whit Marshall (LB) 1996, Ike Reese (LB) 1998–2003.

59 Joseph Wendlick (B) 1940, Mike Evans (C) 1968–73, Tom Ehlers (LB) 1975–7, Al Chesley (LB) 1979–82, Joel Williams (LB) 1983–5, *Seth Joyner* (LB) 1986–93, Carlos Bradley (LB) 1987r, Mike Mamula (DE) 1995–2000, Derrick Burgess (DE) 2001–2, Tyreo Harrison (LB) 2002, Justin Ena (LB) 2003.

60 *Bob Suffridge* (G) 1941, Alvin Thacker (B) 1942, Ed Michaels (G) 1943–6, Don Weedon (G) 1947, **Chuck Bednarik** (C/LB) 1949–62.

61 Tony Cemore (G) 1941, Joseph Frank (T) 1943, Gordon Paschka (G) 1943, Duke Maronic (G) 1944–50, John Michels (G) 1953, Tom Loud-

erback (LB) 1958–9, Howard Keys (T/C) 1960–4, Arunas Vasys (LB) 1966–8, Tony Guillory (LB) 1969, Bill Dunstan (DT) 1973–6, Mark Slater (C) 1979–83, Ben Tamburello (C/G) 1987–90, Matt Long (C) 1987r, Eric Floyd (G) 1992–3, Theo Adams (G) 1995, Steve Everitt (C) 1997–9, Giradie Mercer (DT) 2000.

62 Elwood Gerber (G) 1941–2, Mike Mandarino (G) 1944–5, *Augie Lio* (G) 1946, Don Talcott (T) 1947, Bill Horrell (G) 1952, Knox Ramsey (G) 1952, John Wittenborn (G) 1960–2, Jerry Mazzanti (E) 1963, Mike Dirks (G) 1968–71, Guy Morriss (C) 1973, Bill Lueck (G) 1975, Johnny Jackson (DE) 1977, Pete Perot (G) 1979–84, Nick Haden (G) 1986, Dennis McKnight (G) 1991, Brian Baldinger (G) 1992–3, Guy McIntyre (G) 1995–6, Ian Beckles (G) 1997–8, Dwight Johnson (DE) 2000, Scott Peters (OL) 2002.

63 Ralph Fritz (G) 1941, Rupert Pate (G) 1942, *Bruno Banducci* (G) 1944–5, Albert Baisi (G) 1947, Leo Skladany (E) 1949, *Norm Willey* (DE) 1952, Ken Huxhold (G) 1954–8, Tom Catlin (LB) 1959, Mike Woulfe (LB) 1962, Lynn Hoyem (G) 1964–7, Tom Luken (G) 1972–8, Ron Baker (G) 1980–8, Daryle Smith (T) 1991–2, Joe Panos (G) 1994, Raleigh McKenzie (C) 1995–6, David Diaz-Infante (G) 1999, Hank Fraley (C) 2000–3.

64 Robert McDonough (G) 1942–6, Mario Giannelli (G) 1948–51, George Savitsky (T) 1949, Menil Mavraides (G) 1954, Russ Carroccio (G) 1955, Abe Gibron (G) 1956–7, Bob Gaona (T) 1957, Galen Laack (G) 1958, John Simerson (C) 1958, Roy Hord (G) 1962, Ed Blaine (G) 1963–6, Dean Wink (DT) 1967–8, Randy Beisler (DE) 1968, Norm Davis (G) 1970, Joe Jones (DE) 1974–5, Ernie Janet (T) 1975, Ed George (T) 1976–8, Garry Puetz (T) 1979, Dean Miraldi (T) 1982–4, Mike Perrino (T) 1987r, Joe Rudolph (G) 1995, Sean Love (G) 1997.

65 *Cliff Patton* (G) 1946–50, Dan Rogas (G) 1952, *Jess Richardson* (DT) 1953, Tom Dimmick (T) 1956, Menil Mavraides (G) 1957, Hal Bradley (G) 1958, Gerry Huth (G) 1960, Jim Beaver (G) 1962, John Mellekas (T) 1963, Bill Stetz (G) 1967, Henry Allison (G) 1971–2, Roy Kirksey (G) 1974, Roosevelt Manning (DT) 1975, *Charlie Johnson* (DT) 1977–81, Mark Dennard (C) 1984–5, Bob Landsee (G/C) 1986–7, Gary Bolden (DT) 1987r, Ron Solt (G) 1988–91, Ron Hallstrom (G) 1993, Moe Elewonibi (T) 1995, Bubba Miller (C/G) 1996–2001.

66 John Wyhonic (G) 1946–7, Baptiste Manzini (C) 1948, Ed Sharkey (T) 1954–5, Frank D'Agostino (G) 1956, Ed Meadows (E) 1958, Joe Robb (DE) 1959–60, Will Renfro (E) 1961, Bill Byrne (G) 1963, Bruce Van Dyke (G) 1966, Gordon Wright (G) 1967, Don Chuy (G) 1969, Bill Cody (LB) 1972, Roy Kirksey (G) 1973, *Bill Bergey* (LB) 1974–80, Ken Reeves (T) 1985–9, John Hudson (G) 1991–5, Mike Zandofsky (G) 1997, Jerry Crafts (T/G) 1998, Jeff Dellenbach (G/C) 1999, Bobbie Williams (G) 2000, 2003.

67 Enio Conti (G) 1941–3, John Sanders (G) 1945, John Magee (G) 1948–55, Proverb Jacobs (T) 1958, Stan Campbell (G) 1959–61, Pete Case (G) 1962–4, Erwin Will (DT) 1965, Vern Winfield (G) 1972–3, Herb Dobbins (T) 1974, Jeff Bleamer (T) 1975–6, Lem Burnham (DE) 1977–80, Gerry Feehery (C/G) 1983–7, Steve Gabbard (T) 1989, Ryan Schau (G/T) 1999–2001.

68 Ray Romero (G) 1951, Maurice Nipp (G) 1952–3, 1956, Dick Murley (T) 1956, Bill Koman (LB) 1957–8, Bill Striegel (G) 1959, Bobby Richards (DE) 1962–5, Mark Nordquist (G) 1968–74, Blenda Gay (DE) 1975–6, *Dennis Harrison* (DE) 1978–84, Reggie Singletary (DT/G) 1987–90, Pete Walters (G) 1987r, Tom McHale (G/T) 1993–4, Frank Cornish (C) 1995, Morris Unutoa (C) 1996–8.

69 Dave DiFilippo (G) 1941, Joe Tyrell (G) 1952, Carl Gersbach (LB) 1970, Rich Glover (DT) 1975, Woody Peoples (G) 1978–80, Dwaine Morris (DT) 1985, Jeff Tupper (DE) 1986, Jim Angelo (G) 1987r, Bruce Collie (G) 1990–1, Burt Grossman (DE) 1994, Harry Boatswain (G/T) 1995, 1997, George Hegamin (G/T) 1998, *John Runyan* (T) 2000–3.

70 Joseph Frank (T) 1941, Leo Brennan (T) 1942, *Al Wistert* (T) 1943–51, Don Owens (T) 1958–60, Jim Skaggs (G) 1963–72.

71 Cecil Sturgeon (T) 1941, Frank Hrabetin (T) 1942, *Eberle Schultz* (G) 1943, Edmund Eiden (B) 1944, George Fritts (T) 1945, Otis Douglas (T) 1946–9, Tom Higgins (T) 1954–5, Jim Ricca (T) 1955–6, Don King (T) 1956, John Wilcox (T) 1960, Joe Lewis (T) 1962, Dick Hart (G) 1967–71, William Wynn (DE) 1973–6, Ken Clarke (DT) 1978–87, Cecil Gray (G/DT) 1990–1, Mike Chalenski (DL) 1993–5, *Jermane Mayberry* (G/T) 1996–2003.

72 Hodges West (T) 1941, Leon Cook (T) 1942, Stephen Levanities (T) 1942, Ted Doyle (T) 1943, Bob Friedman (G) 1944, Marshall Shires (T) 1945, Thomas Campion (T) 1947, Roger Harding (C) 1947, Dick Steere (T) 1951, George Mrkonic (T) 1953, *Jess Richardson* (DT) 1954–61, Frank Fuller (T) 1963, *Floyd Peters* (DT) 1964–9, Wade Key (G/T) 1970–80, Jim Fritzsche (T/G) 1983, Dave Pacella (G/C) 1984, Kevin Allen (T) 1985, David Alexander (C) 1987–94, Jeff Wenzel (T) 1987r, Joe Panos (G) 1995–7, *Tra Thomas* (T) 1998–2003.

73 Ed Kasky (T) 1942, Rocco Canale (G) 1943–5, Henry Gude (G) 1946, Alfred Bauman (T) 1947, Fred Hartman (T) 1948, Roscoe Hansen (T) 1951, *Lum Snyder* (T) 1952–5, Sid Youngelman (T) 1956–8, Ed Khayat (DT) 1958–61, 1964–5, Jim Norton (T) 1968, Richard Stevens (T) 1970–4, Pete Lazetich (DT) 1976–7, Steve Kenney (G)

1980–5, Paul Ryczek (C) 1987r, Ron Heller (T) 1988–92, Lester Holmes (G) 1993–6, Jerry Crafts (T/G) 1997, Steve Martin (DT) 1998, Oliver Ross (T) 1999, Jim Pyne (C/G) 2001.

74 *Walter Barnes* (G) 1948–51, Frank Wydo (T) 1957, Len Szafaryn (T) 1958, Gerry Delucca (T) 1959, Riley Gunnels (T) 1960–4, Frank Molden (T) 1968, Steve Smith (T) 1972–4, John Niland (G) 1975–6, Donnie Green (T) 1977, Leonard Mitchell (T) 1984–6, Mike Pitts (DL) 1987–92, Tim Mooney (DE) 1987r, Gerald Nichols (DT) 1993, Bernard Williams (T) 1994, Ed Jasper (DT) 1997–8, Doug Brzezinski (G) 1999–2002.

75 Bill Halverson (T) 1942, *Bob Suffridge* (G) 1945, George Savitsky (T) 1948–9, Walt Stickel (T) 1950–1, Frank Wydo (T) 1952–6, Tom Saidock (T) 1957, Jim McCusker (T) 1959–62, John Meyers (T) 1964–7, Tuufuli Upersa (G) 1971, Houston Antwine (DT) 1972, Dennis Wirgowski (DE) 1973, Willie Cullars (DE) 1974, *Stan Walters* (T) 1975–83, Jim Gilmore (T) 1986, Scott Leggett (G) 1987r, Louis Cheek (T) 1990, Daryle Smith (T) 1990, Rob Selby (G) 1991–4, Troy Drake (T) 1995–7, John Michels (T) 1999.

76 Lester McDonald (E) 1940, John Eibner (T) 1941–2, *Bucko Kilroy* (T) 1943–55, Len Szafaryn (T) 1957, Volney Peters (T) 1958, *J.D. Smith* (T) 1959–63, **Bob Brown** (T) 1964–8, Joe Carollo (T) 1969–70, *Jerry Sisemore* (T) 1973–84, Adam Schreiber (C/G) 1986–8, Broderick Thompson (T) 1993–4, Barrett Brooks (T) 1995–8, John Welbourn (G/T) 1999–2003.

77 *Phil Ragazzo* (T) 1941, Bennie Kaplan (G) 1942, Tex Williams (G) 1942, Carl Fagioli (G) 1944, John Eibner (T) 1946, Jim Kekeris (T) 1947, Gus Cifelli (T) 1954, *Jim Weatherall* (T) 1955–7, Don Oakes (T) 1961–2, John Kapele (T) 1962, Ray Mansfield (C) 1963, Ray Rissmiller (T) 1966, Ernie Calloway (DT) 1970–2, Gerry Philbin (DE) 1973, Jerry Patton (DT) 1974, Don Ratliff (DE) 1975, Dennis Nelson (T) 1976–7, Rufus Mayes (T) 1979, Tom Jelesky (T) 1985, Michael Black (T/G) 1986, Donald Evans (DE) 1988, Antone Davis (T) 1991, Keith Millard (DT) 1993, Howard Smothers (G) 1995, Richard Cooper (T) 1996–8, Lonnie Palelei (T/G) 1999, Artis Hicks (T) 2002–3.

78 *Mike Jarmoluk* (T) 1949–55, *Marion Campbell* (DT) 1956–61, John Baker (DE) 1962, Dave Graham (T) 1963–9, Steve Smith (T) 1971, Wayne Mass (T) 1972, Jim Cagle (DT) 1974, Carl Hairston (DE) 1976–83, Matt Darwin (C) 1986–90, Mike Nease (C/T) 1987r, Antone Davis (T) 1991–5, Hollis Thomas (DT) 1996–2003.

79 *Vic Sears* (T) 1941–53, *Buck Lansford* (T) 1955–7, *Lum Snyder* (T) 1958, Gene Gossage (E) 1960–2, Lane Howell (T) 1965–9, Mitch Sutton (DT) 1974–5, Manny Sistrunk (DT) 1976–9, Frank Giddens (T) 1981–2, Rusty Russell (T) 1984,

Joe Conwell (T) 1986–7, Mike Schad (G) 1989–93, Mike Finn (T) 1994, Greg Jackson (DE) 1995–2000, Jeremy Slechta (DT) 2002.

80 Granville Harrison (E) 1941, Kirk Hershey (E) 1941, Leonard Supulski (E) 1942, Fred Meyer (E) 1943, Bert Kuczynski (E) 1946, Neill Armstrong (E) 1947–51, Bill Stribling (E) 1955–7, Gene Mitcham (E) 1958, Ken MacAfee (E) 1959, John Tracey (DE) 1961, Ken Gregory (E) 1962, Gary Henson (E) 1963, Randy Beisler (DE) 1966–8, Don Brumm (DE) 1970–1, Clark Hoss (TE) 1972, Don Zimmerman (WR) 1973–6, Art Thoms (DE) 1977, Luther Blue (WR) 1980, Alvin Hooks (WR) 1981, Byron Williams (WR) 1983, Joe Hayes (WR) 1984, Keith Baker (WR) 1985, Bobby Duckworth (WR) 1986, Cris Carter (WR) 1987–9, Rod Harris (WR) 1990–1, Marvin Hargrove (WR) 1990, Reggie Lawrence (WR) 1993, **James Lofton** (WR) 1993, Reggie Johnson (TE) 1995, *Irving Fryar* (WR) 1996–8, Torrance Small (WR) 1999–2000, James Thrash (WR) 2001–3.

81 *Dick Humbert* (E) 1941, 1945–9, Robert Priestly (E) 1942, Ray Reutt (E) 1943, Walt Nowak (E) 1944, John Yovicsin (E) 1944, Don McDonald (E) 1944–6, John O'Quinn (E) 1951, Ed Bawel (B) 1952, Willie Irvin (B) 1953, Eddie Bell (DB) 1955–8, Ron Goodwin (E) 1963–8, Jim Whalen (TE) 1971, Larry Estes (DE) 1972, Stan Davis (B) 1973, Oren Middlebrook (WR) 1978, Scott Fitzkee (WR) 1979–80, Ron Smith (WR) 1981–3, Kenny Jackson (WR) 1984–5, Otis Grant (WR) 1987r, Shawn Beals (WR) 1988, Henry Williams (WR) 1989, Mike Bellamy (WR) 1990, Roy Green (WR) 1991–2, Paul Richardson (WR) 1993, Rob Carpenter (WR) 1995, Mark Seay (WR) 1996–7, Jeff Graham (WR) 1998, Charles Johnson (WR) 1999–2000, Tony Stewart (TE) 2001, Billy McMullen (WR) 2003.

82 Robert Krieger (E) 1941, William Combs (E) 1942, **Bill Hewitt** (E) 1943, Milton Smith (E) 1945, Rudy Smeja (E) 1946, Danny DiRenzo (P) 1948, Joe Restic (E) 1952, *Tom Scott* (DE) 1953–8, George Tarasovic (DE) 1963–5, *Tim Rossovich* (LB) 1968–71, Bob Picard (WR) 1973–6, Ken Payne (WR) 1978, Jerrold McRae (WR) 1979, *Mike Quick* (WR) 1982–90, Mickey Shuler (TE) 1991, Victor Bailey (WR) 1993–4, Chris Jones (WR) 1995–7, Karl Hankton (WR) 1998, Dameane Douglas (WR) 1999–2002, L.J. Smith (TE) 2003.

83 *Jack Ferrante* (E) 1941, Jack Smith (E) 1942, John Smith (T) 1945, *Bobby Walston* (E/K) 1951–62, Bill Quinlan (DE) 1963, Don Hultz (DT) 1964–73, Vince Papale (WR) 1976–8, Rodney Parker (WR) 1980–1, Tony Woodruff (WR) 1982–4, Phil Smith (WR) 1986, Jimmie Giles (TE) 1987–9, Kevin Bowman (WR) 1987r, Kenny Jackson (WR) 1990–1, Pat Beach (TE) 1992, Michael Young (WR) 1993, Ed West (TE) 1995–6, Michael Timpson (WR) 1997, Dietrich Jells (WR) 1998–9,

Troy Smith (WR) 1999, Jeff Thomason (TE) 2000–2, Greg Lewis (WR) 2003.

84 Larry Cabrelli (E) 1941–7, Leslie Palmer (B) 1948, Hank Burnine (E) 1956–7, Leo Sugar (DE) 1961, Mike Clark (K/E) 1963, Don Thompson (E) 1964, Jim Kelly (E) 1965–7, Richard Harris (DE) 1971–3, Keith Krepfle (TE) 1975–81, Vyto Kab (TE) 1982–5, Kenny Jackson (WR) 1986–8, Mike McCloskey (TE) 1987, Anthony Edwards (WR) 1989–90, Floyd Dixon (WR) 1992, Mark Bavaro (TE) 1993–4, Kelvin Martin (WR) 1995, Freddie Solomon (WR) 1996–8, Jamie Asher (TE) 1999, Luther Broughton (TE) 2000, Freddie Mitchell (WR) 2001–3.

85 John Shonk (E) 1941, Tony Bova (E) 1943, Bob Friedlund (E) 1944, Charley Gauer (E) 1945, Jay MacDowell (E) 1946, Billy Hix (E) 1950, Bob Schnelker (E) 1953, Ralph Smith (E) 1962–4, Gary Ballman (TE) 1967–72, Marlin McKeever (LB) 1973, Charles Smith (WR) 1974–81, Mel Hoover (WR) 1982–4, Ron Johnson (WR) 1985–9, Jesse Bendross (WR) 1987r, Mickey Shuler (TE) 1990, Jeff Sydner (WR) 1992–4, Art Monk (WR) 1995, Mark Ingram (WR) 1996, Antwuan Wyatt (WR) 1997, Chris Fontenot (TE) 1998, Na Brown (WR) 1999–2001, Freddie Milons (WR) 2002, Sean Morey (WR) 2003.

86 Harold Prescott (E) 1947–9, Bob McChesney (E) 1950, Bud Grant (E) 1951–2, *Norm Willey* (DE) 1953–7, Ed Cooke (E) 1958, Dick Stafford (E) 1962–3, Fred Hill (E) 1965–71, *Charles Young* (TE) 1973–6, Richard Osborne (TE) 1977–8, Ken Dunek (TE) 1980, Lewis Gilbert (TE) 1980, Steve Folsom (TE) 1981, Al Dixon (TE) 1983, Gregg Garrity (WR) 1984–9, Mike Siano (WR) 1987r, *Fred Barnett* (WR) 1990–5, Dialleo Burks (WR) 1996, Justin Armour (WR) 1997, Luther Broughton (TE) 1997, Russell Copeland (WR) 1998, Alex Van Dyke (WR) 1999–2000, Brian Finneran (WR) 1999, Gari Scott (WR) 2000, Antonio Freeman (WR) 2002, Kori Dickerson (TE) 2003.

87 *Jack Ferrante* (E) 1944–50, Andy Nacelli (E) 1958, Art Powell (WR) 1959, Dick Lucas (E) 1960–3, Bill Cronin (E) 1965, Dave Lince (E) 1966–7, Fred Brown (LB) 1969, Kent Kramer (TE) 1971–4, Claude Humphrey (DE) 1979–81, Lawrence Sampleton (TE) 1982–4, John Goode (TE) 1985, Eric Bailey (TE) 1987r, Ron Fazio (TE) 1987r, Carlos Carson (WR) 1989, Harper LeBel (TE) 1990, Maurice Johnson (TE) 1991–4, Frank Wainwright (TE) 1995, Jason Dunn (TE) 1996–8, Jed Weaver (TE) 1999, Todd Pinkston (WR) 2000–3.

88 John Durko (E) 1944, Herschel Ramsey (E) 1945, Jay MacDowell (E) 1947–51, John Zilly (E) 1952, Bob Hudson (B) 1953, Jerry Wilson (E) 1959–60, Gary Pettigrew (DT) 1966–74, Richard Osborne (TE) 1976, Bill Larson (TE) 1978, John Spagnola (TE) 1979–87, *Keith Jackson* (TE)

1988–91, Jimmie Johnson (TE) 1995–8, Kevin McKenzie (WR) 1998, Luther Broughton (TE) 1999, Mike Bartrum (TE) 2000–3.

89 Henry Piro (E) 1941, Fred Meyer (E) 1942, Tom Miller (E) 1943–4, Ben Agajanian (G) 1945, Robert Krieger (E) 1946, *John Green* (E) 1947–51, Bob Oristaglio (E) 1952, Don Luft (E) 1954, John Bredice (E) 1956, Mike Morgan (LB) 1964–7, **Mike Ditka** (E) 1968, Steve Zabel (LB) 1970–4, *Wally Henry* (WR) 1977–82, Glen Young (WR) 1983, Dave Little (TE) 1985–9, Jay Repko (TE) 1987r, Calvin Williams (WR) 1990–6, Dialleo Burks (WR) 1996, *Chad Lewis* (TE) 1997–2003, Kaseem Sinceno (TE) 1998, Ron Leshinski (TE) 1999, Ed Smith (TE) 1999, Justin Swift (TE) 1999.

90 Aaron Brown (LB) 1985, Mike Golic (DT) 1987–92, Randall Mitchell (NT) 1987r, William Perry (DT) 1993–4, Ronnie Dixon (DT) 1995–6, Jon Harris (DE) 1997–8, Ben Williams (DT) 1999, *Corey Simon* (DT) 2000–3.

91 Tim Golden (LB) 1985, *Reggie White* (DE) 1985, Ray Conlin (DT) 1987r, George Cumby (LB) 1987r, Scott Curtis (LB) 1988, Greg Mark (DE) 1990, Andy Harmon (DT) 1991–7, Steve Martin (DT) 1999, Uhuru Hamiter (DE) 2000–1, Sam Rayburn (DT) 2003.

92 Smiley Creswell (DE) 1985, *Reggie White* (DE) 1985–92.

93 Tom Strauthers (DE) 1983–6, John Dumbauld (DE) 1987–8, Ray Phillips (DE) 1987r, David Bailey (DE) 1990, Greg Townsend (DE) 1994, Dan Stubbs (DE) 1995, Darion Conner (DE) 1996–7, Pernell Davis (DT) 1999–2000, Levon Kirkland (LB) 2002.

94 Byron Darby (DE/TE) 1983–6, Dan McMillen (DE) 1987r, Steve Kaufusi (DE) 1989–90, Leonard Renfro (DT) 1993–4, Kevin Johnson (DT) 1995–6, Bill Johnson (DT) 1998–9, Kelly Gregg (DT) 1999–2000, N.D. Kalu (DE) 2001–3.

95 John Bunting (LB) 1972–82, Jody Schulz (LB) 1985–7, Doug Bartlett (DT) 1988, Al Harris (LB) 1989–90, Mike Flores (DT) 1991–3, *William Fuller* (DE) 1994–6, Richard Dent (DE) 1997, Henry Slay (DT) 1998, Tyrone Williams (DE) 1999–2000, Justin Ena (LB) 2002, Jerome McDougle (DE) 2003.

96 John Sodaski (LB) 1972–3, Harvey Armstrong (DT) 1982–4, *Clyde Simmons* (DE) 1986–93, Marvin Ayers (DE) 1987r, Mike Flores (DT) 1994, Mark Gunn (DL) 1995–6, Keith Rucker (DT) 1996, Al Wallace (DE/LB) 1997–9, Paul Grasmanis (DT) 2000–3.

97 Thomas Brown (DE) 1980, Reggie Singletary (DT/G) 1986, John Kliagel (DE) 1987–8, Jim Auer (DE) 1987r, Dick Chapura (DT) 1990, Leon Seals (DT) 1992, Tim Harris (DE) 1993, Rhett Hall (DT) 1995–8, Mark Wheeler (DT) 1999, Darwin Walker (DT) 2000–3.

98 Mike Ditka (E) 1967, Greg Brown (DE) 1981–6, Elois Grooms (DE) 1987r, Tommy Jeter (DT) 1992–5, Michael Samson (DT) 1996, Jimmie Jones (DL) 1997, Brandon Whiting (DL) 1998–2003.

99 Mel Tom (DE) 1971–3, Leonard Mitchell (DL) 1981–3, Joe Drake (DT) 1985, *Jerome Brown* (DT) 1987–91, Skip Hamilton (DT) 1987r, Greg Liter (DE) 1987r.

PITTSBURGH STEELERS

The franchise: The legend holds that Art Rooney purchased the new Pittsburgh franchise for $2,500 from $250,000 in winnings from a couple of days at the race track in New York State in 1933. More recent research, however, pinpoints Rooney's big score at the track as occurring in 1937 four years after he established the team. Nonetheless, the contrast with contemporary strictures regarding the NFL and gambling is interesting. Today, the team is still run by the Rooney family as it has been for 70 years with one exception. After the 1940 season, Rooney sold the team to Alexis Thompson and bought half of the Philadelphia Eagles owned by his friend Bert Bell. Before the start of the 1941 season though, Rooney and Bell traded franchises with Thompson so that Rooney was back in his native Pittsburgh although technically with the former Eagles franchise. Bell remained a co-owner until he became NFL Commissioner in 1946. The Steeler and Eagle franchises merged for the 1943 wartime season as the Steagles, and the following year the Steelers merged with the Chicago Cardinals (an 0–10 team known derisively as the Carpets). Generous, sweet-tempered Hall of Famer Art Rooney is a revered figure in

NFL history, but the team has fared much better under his son, Dan, who took over in the late 1960s and is also in the Hall of Fame.

Under the elder Rooney, the Steelers did not gain their first winning season until their 10th season in 1942 when they went 6–4. In 1947 they went 8–4 to tie for the Eastern Conference crown but lost in a playoff to Philadelphia. Pittsburgh always has been a blue collar team for a blue collar town. They were the last NFL team to switch from the single wing to the T formation and were always noted for their tough defense even throughout the mediocre 1950s. In 1957, former coach of the champion Lions, Buddy Parker took over the Steelers and soon brought Bobby Layne with him. While that familiar partnership made Pittsburgh competitive, they would ultimately do no better than a 9–5 second place finish in Layne's final year of 1962.

When Dan Rooney brought in Chuck Noll as coach in 1969, the team had not had a winning record in six years. Over the next half dozen seasons, the Steelers drafted incredibly well, picking 20 starters including nine Hall of Famers. Four Hall of Famers were drafted in 1974 alone (Lynn Swann, John Stallworth, Jack Lambert, and Mike Webster). By 1972, Pittsburgh won its first division title and first playoff game (via Franco Harris' "Immaculate Reception"). Led by quarterback Terry Bradshaw and Mean Joe Greene's Steel Curtain Defense, the Steelers were the Team of the 1970s. They won four Super Bowls in that decade with one of the greatest defenses in NFL history. 1976, a year they did not win it all, may have been the most remarkable season. They started off 1–4 and then won their last nine games, even though Bradshaw was injured, by giving up only 28 points and tossing five shutouts. When Harris and Rocky Bleier got hurt in the

playoffs, though, it was too much adversity to overcome.

That team aged, of course, and the Hall of Fame greats were replaced by very good players who were able to keep the team a perennial contender, but they have not been able to win another title. In 1991, Noll stepped down after 23 years and Bill Cowher replaced him. In a dozen years under Cowher, the Steelers have won seven division titles and been to one Super Bowl. His teams have generally carried on the Steeler tradition of a bruising running attack and a rugged defense. While they have not reached the heights of the 1970s again, the continuity of winning over 35 years with only two coaches has been remarkable.

Origin of name: Pittsburgh was originally known as the Pirates after the major league baseball team. They became the Steelers in 1940 in a contest suspiciously won by the wife of the team's ticket manager.

Record by Decade

	Regular Season			Postseason		
	Won	Lost	Tied	Won	Lost	Championships
1930s	22	55	3	0	0	
1940s	40	64	6	0	1	
1950s	54	63	3	0	0	
1960s	46	85	7	0	0	
1970s	99	44	1	14	4	1974, 1975, 1978, 1979
1980s	77	75	0	2	4	
1990s	93	67	0	5	6	
2000s	38	25	1	2	2	
All-Time	469	478	21	23	17	4

Winning seasons: 31. Losing seasons: 34. .500 seasons: 6.

Time till first championship: 41 years.
Time since last championship: 25 years.
Retired numbers: 70 for Ernie Stautner 1951–63.

Other numbers worn by these players: Stautner also wore 89 in 1951.

Those who wore retired numbers after the honored player: None.

Numbers that should be retired: The Steelers have six numbers that have long been inactive and were worn by Hall of Famers from their 1970s dynasty — Terry Bradshaw's 12, Franco Harris' 32, Mike Web-

Coaches

	Years	Record	Playoffs
Jap Douds	1933	3-6-2	
Luby DiMelio	1934	2-10	
Joe Bach	1935-6, 1952-3	21-27	
Johnny Blood McNally	1937-9	6-19	
Walt Kiesling	1939-44, 1954-6	30-55-5	
Buff Donelli	1941	0-5	
Bert Bell	1941	0-2	
Jim Leonard	1945	2-8	
Jock Sutherland	1946-7	13-9-1	0-1
John Michelosen	1948-51	20-26-2	
Buddy Parker	1957-64	51-47-6	
Mike Nixon	1965	2-12	
Bill Austin	1966-8	11-28-3	
Chuck Noll (4)	1969-91	193-148-1	16-8
Bill Cowher	1992-2003	115-76-1	7-8

(Championships in parentheses)

ster's 52, Jack Lambert's 58, Jack Ham's 59 and Joe Greene's 75.

Owned numbers: None although the aforementioned Ernie Stautner's 70 was worn otherwise only by Al Wistert of the Steagles in 1943.

Numbers worn by Hall of Famers: Mel Blount 47; Terry Bradshaw 12; Len Dawson 16; Bill Dudley 3/35; Joe Greene 72/75; Jack Ham 59; Franco Harris 32; Bill Hewitt 82 (Steagles); John Henry Johnson 35; Walt Kiesling 35; Jack Lambert 58; Bobby Layne 22; Johnny Blood McNally 15/35; Marion Motley 36/37; John Stallworth 82, Ernie Stautner 70/89; Lynn Swann 88; Mike Webster 52; Byron "Whizzer" White 10.

Star power: Bobby Layne took 22 from Richie McCabe; John Henry Johnson took 35 from Rudy Hayes.

Star eclipsed: Rocky Bleir wore 26 because Paul Martha wore 20. Joe Greene wore 72 till Ken Kortas, 75, left.

Numbers with most great players: 35 was worn by five Hall of Famers (Blood, Hubbard, Kiesling, Dudley and Johnson) although only Johnson and Dudley played significant seasons with Pittsburgh.

Worst represented number: The best players who have worn 11 and 18 are backup-level quarterbacks Kent Graham and Mike Tomczak. 11 was worn by 15 players while 18 was worn by 17 men.

Number worn by the most players: 23 players have worn 85 and 88.

Player who wore the most numbers: Defensive end George Tarasovic worked his way through the 50s wearing 50, 52, 53, 56 as well as wearing 63 and 82 in his lengthy stay in Pittsburgh from 1952 to 1953 and, after military service, from 1956 to 1963.

Longest tenure wearing a number: Mike Webster wore 52 for 16 years.

Number worn by first ever draft pick: 1936 first round pick Bill Shakespeare of Notre Dame never played for the Steelers. Fifth round pick Wayne Sandefur wore 10. The first round pick in 1937 Mike Basrak wore 11.

Biggest draft busts: Fullback Dick Leftridge, 31, was the Steelers first round pick in 1966, but only got into four games and gained 17 yards. Runner Tim Worley, 38, was selected seventh in 1989 and gained only 1,300 yards with 16 fumbles in four years.

Number worn by oldest player: 70 by Ernie Stautner and 9 by Norm Johnson both when they were 38.

Cameos. Hall of Famers— Bill Hewitt 82 (Steagles); Marion Motley 36/37. All-Pros and other notables— Paul Younger 35; Tom Bettis 65; Bucko Kilroy 76 (Steagles); Tom Keating 74; Harlon Hill 87.

Ones who got away: Len Dawson 16 had a Hall of Fame career in Kansas City. Jack Kemp 7/18 and Earl Morrall 10 quarterbacked teams to championships. Dave Brown 36 was an All Pro cornerback for Seattle.

Least popular numbers: 00 was worn only by Johnny Clement. 8 has been worn only three times.

Last number to be originated: 95 was first worn by defensive lineman Xavier Warren and 97 was first worn by linebacker Joe Williams, both in 1987.

Longest dormant number: Before

Tommy Maddox slipped on number 8 in 2001, it had not been worn in 61 years. 00 has not been worn in 55 years.

Triskaidekaphobia notes: 13 was worn by five Steelers in the 1930s, but only by quarterback Bill Mackrides in 1954 since then.

Shared numbers: Star receivers Ray Mathews and Ron Shanklin both wore 25. 33 was worn by running backs Frenchy Fuqua, Merrill Hoge and Bam Morris. 60 has been worn by two defensive linemen of note, Dale Dodrill and Ben McGee, as has 78 by Dwight White and John Baker.

Continuity: Merrill Hoge was replaced in 33 by Bam Morris; the "Old Ranger," center Ray Mansfield, was replaced in 56 by linebacker Robin Cole.

Discontinuity: Lynn Swann was followed in 88 by tight end Craig Dunaway.

Family Connections			
Brothers			
Ed Modzelewski	FB	1952	39
Dick Modzelewski	DT	1955	79
Silas Titus	E	1945	49
George Titus	C	1946	43

Quarterback numbers over 19: 21, John Vaughn 1934; 22, Bobby Layne 1957–62; 23, John Gildea 1936; 23, Joe Gasparella 1951; 24, John Turley 1936; 25, Coley McDonough 1940; 29, Stu Smith 1937; 30, Truett Smith 1951; 33, John Gildea 1935–7 ; 48, Joe Gasparella 1948, 1951; 49, Chuck Ortman 1951; 66, Gerald Leahy 1957; 67, Truett Smith 1952; 77, Paul Davis 1948.

Number of first black player: Tackle Ray Kemp played for the Steelers in 1933 and wore 45. Guard Jack Spinks wore 37 in 1952 as the first black Steeler after the color ban was lifted after World War II.

Numbers of future NFL head coaches: Tom Bettis 65, Fred Bruney 22/41, Al Donelli 16/33, Tony Dungy 21, Frank Filchock 55, Red Hickey 39, Frank Ivy 22, John Karcis 30/64, Walt Kiesling 35, Rich Kotite 88, Ted Marchibroda 17/18, Johnny Blood McNally 15/35, Bill McPeak 37/84, Ron Meyer 11, Dick Modzelewski 79, Mike Mularkey 84, Mike

Nixon 12, Allie Sherman 10, Nick Skorich 12.

Numbers of future NFL referees: John Don Looney 30 and Frankie Sinkovitz 57.

Players who played other sports: Baseball — Rex Johnston 28, Andy Tomasic 3/4, Jim Levey 12/13, and Walt Masters 40. Basketball — Clint Wager 69. Wrestling — Hank Bruder 5, Kevin Greene 91, Ernie "Fats" Holmes 63.

Players more famous after football: Byron "Whizzer" White, 10, Supreme Court Justice; Jack Kemp, 7/18, Congressman; Fred Williamson, 46, actor; Mike Henry, 37/68, actor (Tarzan).

First player to wear a number in the 70s: End Tom Brown 76 in 1942.

First player to wear a number in the 80s: Ends Larry Cabrelli 84, Tony Bova 85, and Tom Miller 89 — all in 1943 with the Steagles.

First player to wear a number in the 90s: End John Stock 93 and tackle Dick Murley 94 — both in 1956.

Number with most points scored: 1 with 1,453 points scored by Gary Anderson (1,343), David Trout (74), Warren Heller (24), and Merlyn Condit (12).

Number with most yards rushing: 32 with 12,147 yards rushed by Franco Harris (11,950), Joe Womack (128) and Charley Gauer (69).

Number with most receptions: 82 with 1,134 passes received by John Stallworth (537), Yancey Thigpen (222), John Hilton (108), Bobby Shaw (92), Antwaan Randle El (84), Derek Hill (53), Henry Minarik (35), Bill Long (2) and Chuck Logan (1).

Number with most touchdown passes: 12 with 218 touchdowns thrown by Terry Bradshaw (212), Bill Patterson (3), Jack Scarbath (2) and Dick Riffle (1).

Number with most interceptions: 47 with 81 interceptions picked off by Mel Blount (57), Marv Woodson (18) and Dick Moegle (6).

Oddity: The Steelers have had two Hall of Fame halfbacks who led the league in rushing as rookies, left football the next season, and then led the league in rushing again after returning to the game. Whizzer White,

10, left the NFL to study in England; four years later Bill Dudley, 3/35, left for World War II. Both also played for Detroit. Also, number 7 has only been worn by quarterbacks.

Players Whose Number Is Unknown		
Glenn Campbell	(E)	1935
Joe Kresky	(G)	1935
Bill Harris	(E)	1937
Joe Matesic	(T)	1954
Bill Priatko	(LB)	1957
Ed Adamchik	(T)	1967
Ben Lawrence	(G)	1987r

Team All-Time Numerical Roster

Those with an "r" following the year 1987 were replacement players during the players' strike. Pro Bowl and pre–1950 All Pro players for each number are in *Italics*; Hall of Famers are in **Bold** type.

00 *Johnny Clement* (B) 1946–8.

1 Warren Heller (B) 1936, Merlyn Condit (B) 1940, Dave Trout (K) 1981, *Gary Anderson* (K) 1982–94, Anthony Wright (QB) 1999.

2 Sigurd Sandberg (T) 1935, Bill Lajousky (G) 1936, Jon Staggers (WR) 1970–2, Matt George (K) 1998, Todd Peterson (K) 2002.

3 Maurice Bray (T) 1935, Thomas Thompson (QB) 1940, **Bill Dudley** (B) 1942, Andy Tomasic (B) 1942, Mark Royals (P) 1992–4, Rohn Stark (P) 1995, Kris Brown (K) 1999–2001, Jeff Reed (K) 2002–3.

4 Mel Pittman (C) 1935, Frank Bykowski (G) 1940, Andy Tomasic (B) 1942, Dan Stryzinski (P) 1990–1, Josh Miller (P) 1996–2003.

5 Gene Augustferner (B) 1935, *George Rado* (G) 1936, Henry Bruder (B) 1940, Les Dodson (B) 1941, John Binotto (B) 1942, Terry Hanratty (QB) 1969–76, Craig Colquitt (P) 1978–81, 1983–4, David Trout (K) 1987r.

6 Thomas Cosgrove (B) 1935, Chester Johnson (FB) 1940, Jim Elliott (K) 1967, Bubby Brister (QB) 1986–92.

7 *Leroy Zimmerman* (QB) 1943, *James Finks* (QB) 1951–2, 1954–5, Jack Kemp (QB) 1957, Reggie Collier (QB) 1987r, Pete Gonzalez (QB) 1998–9.

8 Everett Fisher (B) 1940, Elmer Kolberg (E) 1941, Tommy Maddox (QB) 2001–3.

9 George Kiick (B) 1940, John Foruria (B)

1967–8, Matt Bahr (K) 1979–80, Norm Johnson (K) 1995–8.

10 Marv Ellstrom (B) 1935, Damon Wetzel (B) 1935, Wayne Sandefur (B) 1936–7, Dom Cara (E) 1937, **Byron "Whizzer" White** (B) 1938, Dick Nardi (B) 1939, Boyd Brumbaugh (B) 1940, Russell Cotton (B) 1942, Allie Sherman (QB) 1943, Al Postus (B) 1945, *Earl Morrall* (QB) 1957–8, Rudy Bukich (QB) 1960–1, Ron Smith (QB) 1966, Kent Nix (QB) 1967–9, *Roy Gerela* (K) 1971–8, Scott Campbell (QB) 1984–6, John Bruno (P) 1987r, *Kordell Stewart* (QB) 1995–2002.

11 Maurice Bray (T) 1935–6, *Mike Basrak* (C) 1937, Ted Grabinski (C) 1939, John Schmidt (C) 1940, John Yurchey (B) 1940, Curtis Sandig (B) 1942, John Petrella (B) 1945, Norm Mosley (B) 1948, Howard Hartley (B) 1949–51, Ron Meyer (QB) 1965, Rich Badar (QB) 1967, Gene Mingo (K) 1969, Rick Strom (QB) 1989–93, Mike Quinn (QB) 1997, Kent Graham (QB) 2000.

12 Alex Rado (B) 1934, Mike Nixon (B) 1935, Henry Weisenbaugh (B) 1935, Jim Levey (B) 1935–6, Bill Davidson (B) 1937, William Patterson (QB) 1940, *Art Jones* (B) 1941, Dick Riffle (B) 1942, Morgan Tiller (E) 1945, Nick Skorich (G) 1948, Vic Eaton (QB) 1955, Jack Scarbath (QB) 1956–7, Terry Nofsinger (QB) 1963–4, **Terry Bradshaw** (QB) 1970–83.

13 Jim Levey (B) 1934, Norm Mott (B) 1934, *George Rado* (G) 1935, 1937, Lee Mulleneaux (C) 1936, Carroll Raborn (C) 1937, Bill Mackrides (QB) 1954.

14 Angelo Brovelli (QB) 1934, *John Gildea* (QB) 1935, Henry Hayduk (G) 1935, George Kakasic (G) 1936–9, Joseph Maras (C) 1940, George Nicksich (G) 1950, *Lynn Chandnois* (HB) 1951, Ed Kissell (B) 1952, Vic Eaton (QB) 1955, Bill Nelsen (QB) 1963–7, Bill Shockley (K) 1968, Alan Watson (K) 1970, Todd Blackledge (QB) 1988–9, *Neil O'Donnell* (QB) 1990–5, Shane Edge (P) 1996, Tom Rouen (P) 2002.

15 Warren Heller (B) 1935, Vic Vidoni (E) 1936, **John Blood McNally** (B) 1937, Ernie Wheeler (B) 1939, Ben Starret (B) 1941, Vernon Martin (B) 1942, Ted Laux (B) 1943, Busit Warren (B) 1945, Ed Brown (QB) 1962–4, George Izo (QB) 1965, Mike Kruczek (QB) 1976–9, Steve Bono (QB) 1987–8, Bobby Shaw (WR) 1998.

16 Clarence Janecek (G) 1933, Ben Ciccone (C) 1935, Carroll Raborn (C) 1936–7, John Lee (B) 1939, Allan Donelli (B) 1942, Bill Dutton (B) 1946, Gonzalo Morales (B) 1947–8, **Len Dawson** (QB) 1957–9, Tommy Wade (QB) 1964–5, Ken Hebert (E/K) 1968, Bob Leahy (QB) 1971, Neil Graff (QB) 1976–7, Mark Malone (QB) 1980–7, Jim Miller (QB) 1994–6, Charlie Batch (QB) 2002–3.

17 *Armand Niccolai* (T/K) 1935–7, 1940, John Patrick (B) 1941, Joe Hoague (B) 1942, Joe Glamp

(B) 1947–9, Gary Kerkorian (QB) 1952, Ted Marchibroda (QB) 1953, Paul Held (QB) 1954, Dick Shiner (QB) 1968–9, Joe Gilliam (QB) 1972–5, Rick Engles (P) 1977, John Goodson (P) 1982, Curtis Marsh (WR) 1997, Tee Martin (QB) 2000–1.

18 Lee Mulleneaux (C) 1935, *George Rado* (G) 1935, Loran Ribble (G) 1935, Frank Billock (G) 1937, Max Fiske (B) 1937, *Byron Gentry* (G) 1937–9, Frank Sullivan (C) 1940, Maurice Harper (C) 1941, Leon Pense (QB) 1945, Chuck Ortmann (QB) 1952, Pat Brady (B) 1954, Ted Marchibroda (QB) 1955–6, Jack Kemp (QB) 1957–8, Terry Nofsinger (QB) 1961–2, Cliff Stoudt (QB) 1977–83, Harry Newsome (P) 1985–9, Darrick Owens (WR) 1992, Mike Tomczak (QB) 1993–9.

19 Cvonimir Kvaternik (G) 1934, Pete Rajkovich (B) 1934, John Roberts (B) 1934, Vic Vidoni (E) 1935–6, Max Fiske (B) 1937, Edgar Cherry (B) 1939, Frank Souchak (E) 1939, George Somers (T) 1942, David Woodley (QB) 1984–5, Andre Coleman (WR) 1997.

20 Wilbur Sortet (E) 1934–7, 1940, Elmer Hackney (B) 1941, George Sirochman (G) 1942, Walt Gorinski (B) 1946, Howard Hartley (B) 1952, Eugene Cichowski (B) 1957, Dick Christy (B) 1958, Jack Call (B) 1959, Don Sutherin (B) 1959–60, Jack Morris (B) 1960, Bill Butler (DB) 1961, Jack Stanton (B) 1961, Paul Martha (DB) 1964–9, Rocky Bleier (RB) 1971–80, Ernest French (S) 1982, Dwight Stone (WR) 1987–94, Erric Pegram (RB) 1995–6, Dewayne Washington (CB) 1998–2003.

21 John Vaughan (QB) 1934, Charles Casper (QB) 1935, Paul McDonough (E) 1938, Lou Tomasetti (B) 1940, *Chuck Cherundolo* (C) 1941–2, 1945–8, Marshall Robnett (C) 1944, Lou Levanti (G) 1951, Jim Bradshaw (B) 1964, Jim Shorter (DB) 1969, Gene Mingo (K) 1970, Glenn Scolnick (WR) 1973, Tony Dungy (DB) 1977–8, Eric Williams (S) 1983–6, Greg Lee (DB) 1988, Richard Bell (RB) 1990, Alan Haller (CB) 1992–3, Deon Figures (CB) 1993–6, Donnell Woolford (CB) 1997, Bo Orlando (S) 1998, Amos Zereoue (RB) 1999–2003.

22 Ted Dailey (E) 1933, Silvio Zaninelli (B) 1935–7, Karl McDade (C) 1938, Frank Ivy (E) 1940, John Klumb (E) 1940, Ralph Wenzel (E) 1942, Conway Baker (T) 1944, Jerry Nuzum (B) 1948–9, 1951–2, Fred Bruney (B) 1957, Richie McCabe (B) 1958, **Bobby Layne** (QB) 1958–62, Dick Conn (DB) 1974, Ernie Pough (WR) 1976, Rick Woods (DB) 1982–5, Larry Griffin (DB) 1987–93, John L. Williams (RB) 1994–5, Hank Poteat (CB) 2000–2, Dee Brown (RB) 2003.

23 Bill Moore (B) 1933, Joe Skladany (E) 1934, Mike Sebastian (B) 1935, *John Gildea* (QB) 1936, Ed Farrell (B) 1938, Lou Tsoutsouvas (C) 1938, Lou Midler (G) 1939, Rocco Pirro (G) 1940, *Armand Niccolai* (T/K) 1942, John Butler (B)

1943–4, Sam Gray (E) 1946–7, Joe Gasparella (QB) 1951, Red Mack (WR) 1961–3, Jim Butler (HB) 1965–7, Bob Campbell (HB) 1969, *Mike Wagner* (S) 1971–80, Fred Bohannon (DB) 1982, Chris Brown (DB) 1983–5, Spark Clark (RB) 1987r, Tim Tyrrell (RB) 1989, Sammy Walker (CB) 1991–2, Anthony Daigle (RB) 1994–5, Jason Simmons (CB) 1998–2001.

24 Sam Cooper (T) 1933, John Turley (QB) 1935–6, Ed Brett (E) 1937, Bernard Scherer (E) 1939, Joe Coomer (T) 1941, John McCarthy (B) 1944, Claude Hipps (B) 1952, Russ Craft (B) 1954, Richie McCabe (B) 1955, 1958, Henry Ford (B) 1956, Dick Hughes (B) 1957, Billy Wells (B) 1957, Bob Luna (B) 1959, John Sample (CB) 1961–2, Jim Bradshaw (B) 1964–5, Jon Henderson (B) 1968–9, Kenny Graham (DB) 1970, *J.T. Thomas* (CB) 1973–81, Rich Erenberg (RB) 1984–6, Rodney Carter (RB) 1988–9, Richard Shelton (CB) 1991–3, Tim McKyer (CB) 1994, Chris Oldham (CB) 1995–9, Nakia Codie (S) 2000, Ike Taylor (CB) 2003.

25 John Burleson (G) 1933, Gil Robinson (E) 1933, Ben Smith (E) 1934, Bill Snyder (G) 1935, Vince Sites (E) 1936–7, Tom Burnette (B) 1938, Vince Farrar (B) 1938, Hugh McCullough (B) 1939, 1943, Coley McDonough (QB) 1940, John Naiota (B) 1942, Ed Stofko (B) 1945, Cullen Rogers (B) 1946, Al Drulis (B) 1947, Frank Minini (B) 1949, *Jack Butler* (DB) 1951, Dick Hendley (QB) 1951, *Ray Mathews* (E) 1952, 1954–9, Dick Hensley (E) 1952, Roy Curry (B) 1963, Jerry Simmons (WR) 1965–6, Don Shy (B) 1967–9, *Ron Shanklin* (WR) 1970–4, Ray Oldham (DB) 1978, Marvin Cobb (DB) 1980, Greg Best (S) 1983, Anthony Tuggle (DB) 1985–7, David Arnold (CB) 1989, Gary Jones (S) 1990–1, 1993–4, Fred McAfee (RB) 1995–8.

26 Paul Engebretsen (G) 1933, Tom Whelan (B) 1933, *John Oehler* (C) 1934, Henry Weinberg (G) 1934, John Doehring [B] 1935, Joe Wiehl (T) 1935, Ed Skoronski (E) 1935–6, Bill Holcomb (T) 1937, Ralph Fife (C) 1946, Art DeCarlo (B) 1953, Dewey McConnell (E) 1954, Lou Baldacci (B) 1956, Gary Glick (B) 1957–9, Ron Hall (B) 1959, Joe Scudero (B) 1960, *Brady Keys* (CB) 1961–7, Rocky Bleier (RB) 1968, John Sodaski (DB) 1969, Preston Pearson (RB) 1970–4, Scoop Gillespie (RB) 1984, John Swain (CB) 1985–6, *Rod Woodson* (CB) 1987–96, Deshea Townsend (CB) 1998–2003.

27 Jim Clark (B) 1933–4, George Kavel (B) 1934, Charles Casper (QB) 1935, Ed McDonald (B) 1936, Clarence Thompson (B) 1937–8, Joe Williams (B) 1939, Dick Riffle (B) 1942, John Butler (B) 1943, John Patrick (B) 1945–6, Robert Sullivan (B) 1947, George Papach (B) 1948–9, 1951, *Fran Rogel* (FB) 1951, Jim Brandt (B) 1952–4, Tad Weed (K) 1955, Lou Baldacci (B) 1956, Gary Glick

(B) 1956, *Dean Derby* (B) 1957–61, Dick Haley (DB) 1961–4, Red Mack (WR) 1965, Clarence Oliver (DB) 1969–70, *Glen Edwards* (DB) 1971–7, Greg Hawthorne (RB) 1979–83, Thomas Everett (S) 1988–91, Willie Williams (CB) 1993–6, J.B. Brown (DB) 1997, Travis Davis (S) 1999, Brent Alexander (S) 2000–3.

28 Nick DeCarbo (G) 1933, John Dempsey (T) 1934, Sigurd Sandberg (T) 1935–7, Ted Doyle (T) 1940–2, Walt Rankin (B) 1944, Robert Davis (E) 1946–50, Tony Momsen (C) 1951, Pat Brady (B) 1952, Ed Kissell (B) 1954, Leon Campbell (B) 1955, Dick Hughes (B) 1957, Don Bishop (B) 1959, Rex Johnston (B) 1960, Henry Clement (E) 1961, *Clendon Thomas* (DB) 1962–8, Ocie Austin (DB) 1970–1, Alvin Maxson (RB) 1977–8, Robert Williams (S) 1984, Lupe Sanchez (CB) 1986–8, Albert Bentley (RB) 1992, Alvoid Mays (CB) 1995, John Jenkins (S) 1998, Ainsley Battles (S) 2000, Chris Hope (S) 2002–3.

29 Angelo Brovelli (QB) 1933, Ben Smith (E) 1935, Stu Smith (QB) 1937, John Nosich (T) 1938, Jack Robinson (T) 1938, Jim Rorison (T) 1938, Don Campbell (T) 1940, Joe Lamas (G) 1942, John Martin (B) 1944, Jules Koshlap (B) 1945, Bob Hohn (B) 1965–9, Fred Barry (DB) 1970, John Dockery (DB) 1972–3, Brent Sexton (DB) 1977, Ron Johnson (CB) 1977–84, Cornell Gowdy (CB) 1987–8, *Barry Foster* (RB) 1990–4, Randy Fuller (DB) 1995–7, Lance Brown (CB) 1998–9, Chidi Iwuoma (CB) 2002–3.

30 Paul Moss (E) 1933, Norm Greeney (G) 1934, Stan Olejniczak (T) 1935, Winfield Croft (G) 1936, *John Karcis* (B) 1936, Joe Cardwell (T) 1937, Clarence Tommerson (B) 1938–9, Wayland Becker (E) 1939, Stan Pavkov (G) 1940, George Gonda (B) 1942, Don Looney (E) 1942, Bill Garnaas (B) 1948, Vince Ragunas (B) 1949, Truett Smith (QB) 1951, *Tom Tracy* (HB) 1958–63, Bob Harrison (LB) 1964, Bill Asbury (FB) 1966–9, Terry Cole (B) 1970, Larry Anderson (DB) 1978–81, Frank Pollard (RB) 1983–8, Albert Bentley (RB) 1992, Victor Jones (FB) 1993, Chad Scott (CB) 1997–2003.

31 Jim Letsinger (G) 1933, Tony Bova (E) 1942, Bob Masters (B) 1943, Walt Slater (B) 1947, Larry Krutko (HB) 1958, Ed Holler (LB) 1964, Dick Leftridge (B) 1966, Carl Crennel (LB) 1970, Al Young (WR) 1972, *Donnie Shell* (S) 1974–87, Mike Logan (S) 2001–3.

32 Montgomery Lantz (C) 1933, Henry Marker (B) 1934, Dick Dolly (E) 1941, Tom Brown (E) 1942, Charles Gauer (E) 1943, Toimi Jarvi (B) 1945, Willie Simpson (B) 1961, Joe Womack (B) 1962–3, Hubie Bryant (WR) 1970, **Franco Harris** (RB) 1972–83.

33 *John Oehler* (C) 1933–4, Silvio Zaninelli (B) 1934, Joe Malkovich (C) 1935, *John Gildea* (QB) 1935–7, Tom Hanson (B) 1938, George

Piatukis (E) 1940, Allan Donelli (B) 1941, Joe Lamas (G) 1942, Stephen Sader (B) 1943, Bernard Semes (B) 1944, Russ Lowther (B) 1945, Charles Seabright (QB) 1948–9, *Jerry Shipkey* (B) 1951–2, *Fran Rogel* (FB) 1954–7, Dick Young (B) 1958, Theron Sapp (B) 1963–5, John Fuqua (RB) 1970–6, Anthony Anderson (RB) 1979, Harvey Clayton (CB) 1983–6, Merril Hoge (RB) 1987–93, Bam Morris (RB) 1994–5, Richard Huntley (RB) 1998–2000, R.J. Bowers (RB) 2001, Russell Stuvaints (DB) 2003.

34 Larry Critchfield (G) 1933, Warren Heller (B) 1934, Jay Arnold (QB) 1941, Hubbard Law (C) 1942, *Fran Rogel* (FB) 1952, Ed Fullerton (B) 1953, Paul Cameron (B) 1954, Lem Harkey (B) 1955, Leo Elter (B) 1958–9, Charles Scales (B) 1960–1, Bob Simms (E) 1962, Bob Soleau (LB) 1964, *Andy Russell* (LB) 1966–76, Walter Abercrombie (RB) 1982–7, Leroy Thompson (RB) 1991–3, Tim Lester (FB) 1995–8, Verron Haynes (FB) 2002–3.

35 **John Blood McNally** (B) 1934, **Cal Hubbard** (T) 1936, Ed Karpowich (T) 1936, **Walt Kiesling** (G) 1937, Karl Schuelke (B) 1939, Dick Bassi (G) 1941, **Bill Dudley** (B) 1942, 1945–6, John Schiechl (C) 1942, Al Olszewski (E) 1945, Gene Hubka (B) 1947, Joe Geri (B) 1949–51, Tom Calvin (B) 1952, 1954–5, Charles Shepard (B) 1956, Dick Young (B) 1957, Paul Younger (FB) 1958, Rudy Hayes (LB) 1959, **John Henry Johnson** (FB) 1960–5, Booth Lusteg (K) 1968, Tom Watkins (RB) 1968, Steve Davis (RB) 1972–4, Jack Deloplaine (RB) 1976–9, Delton Hall (CB) 1987–91, Ray Williams (CB) 1987r, Fred McAfee (RB) 1994, Carlos King (FB) 1998, Dan Kreider (FB) 2000–3.

36 Bernard Holm (B) 1933, Basilio Marchi (C) 1934, Sylvester Saumer (B) 1934, Ed Karpowich (T) 1936–9, John Woudenberg (T) 1940, 1942, Denn Steward (B) 1943, Marion Motley (FB) 1955, Rudy Hayes (LB) 1960, 1962, Wilbert Scott (LB) 1961, *Andy Russell* (LB) 1963, Clarence Peaks (FB) 1964–5, Charlie Bivins (B) 1967, Don McCall (RB) 1969, Jim Brumfield (RB) 1971, Carl Winfrey (LB) 1972, Dave Brown (CB) 1975, Wentford Gaines (DB) 1976, Guy Ruff (LB) 1982, Todd Spencer (RB) 1984–5, David Hughes (RB) 1986, Fred Foggie (CB) 1994, *Jerome Bettis* (RB) 1996–2003.

37 Mose Kelsch (B) 1934, Clure Mosher (C) 1942, *Ernest Steele* (B) 1943, John Itzel (B) 1945, Steve Lach (B) 1946–7, *Bill McPeak* (E) 1949, Joe Hollingsworth (B) 1951, Henry Minarik (E) 1951, Jack Spinks (B) 1952, Burrell Shields (B) 1954, **Marion Motley** (FB) 1955, Mike Henry (LB) 1960–1, Ken Kirk (LB) 1962, Bob Smith (B) 1966, Bob Morgan (B) 1967, Charles Beatty (DB) 1969–70, 1972, Laverne Smith (RB) 1977, Frank Wilson (TE) 1982, Donnie Elder (CB) 1986, Kelvin Middleton (S) 1987r, *Carnell Lake* (DB) 1989–98.

38 Walt Holmer (B) 1933, George Shaffer (B)

1933, Don Williams (G) 1941, Frank Pastin (G) 1942, Joe Repko (T) 1946–7, Mike Lind (FB) 1965–6, Earl Gros (FB) 1967–9, Ed Bradley (LB) 1972–5, Sidney Thornton (RB) 1977–81, Elton Veals (RB) 1984, Rock Richmond (DB) 1987r, Tim Worley (FB) 1989–91, 1993, Jon Witman (FB) 1996–2001.

39 Elmer Schwartz (B) 1933, *Armand Niccolai* (T/K) 1934, Max Fiske (B) 1936, John Perko (G) 1937, 1940, Len Dugan (C) 1939, Howard Hickey (E) 1941, Ed Modzelewski (FB) 1952, Leo Elter (B) 1954, Sid Watson (B) 1955–7, Larry Krutko (HB) 1958–61, *Bobby Walden* (P) 1968–77, Sidney Thornton (RB) 1978, Rick Moser (RB) 1979–82, Darren Perry (S) 1992–8, Erik Totten (S) 2002.

40 Rudy Tesser (E) 1933–4, Al Arndt (G) 1935, Hayden Mayhew (G) 1937, Vince Farrar (B) 1939, Carl Nery (G) 1940, Mike Rodak (B) 1942, John Popovich (B) 1944–5, Walt Masters (B) 1944, Mel O'Delli (B) 1945, Earl Klapstein (T) 1946, Bill Hornick (T) 1947, *George Hughes* (G) 1950–1, Russ Craft (B) 1954, *Preston Carpenter* (E) 1960–3, Randy Reutershan (DB) 1978, Anthony Corley (CB) 1984, Dan Reeder (RB) 1986–7, Eric Wilkerson (RB) 1989, Richard Shelton (CB) 1990, Myron Bell (S) 1994–7, 2001.

41 Martin Kottler (B) 1933, Tony Bova (E) 1942, *Johnny Lattner* (B) 1954, Dick Doyle (B) 1955, Fred Bruney (B) 1956, Lowell Perry (B) 1956, Earl Girard (B) 1957–8, Dennis Meyer (DB) 1972–3, Nat Terry (CB) 1978, Tom Moriarty (S) 1980, Sam Washington (CB) 1982–5, Chris Sheffield (CB) 1986–7, Kevin Smith (S) 1991, Solomon Wilcots (S) 1992, Lee Flowers (S) 1995–2002.

42 Jim Tanguay (B) 1933, Bernard Lee (B) 1938, Samuel Boyd (E) 1940, Walter Kichefski (E) 1942, Paul Duhart (B) 1945, Paul White (B) 1947, Ray Evans (B) 1948, Joe Hollingsworth (B) 1949–51, Pat Brady (B) 1952, Jim Hill (DB) 1955, Dick Alban (B) 1956–9, Lowe Wren (DB) 1960, *Dick Hoak* (HB) 1961–70, Anthony Washington (CB) 1981–2, Dave Edwards (RB) 1985–7, Warren Williams (RB) 1988–92, Randy Cuthbert (RB) 1993, Myron Bell (S) 2000.

43 Leo Raskowski (T) 1933, Don Rhodes (T) 1933, *Jack Hinkle* (B) 1943, Ben Agajanian (K) 1945, George Titus (C) 1946, Jim Hill (DB) 1955, William Bowman (FB) 1957, Tom Barnett (B) 1959–60, Glenn Glass (B) 1963, Erwin Williams (WR) 1969, Frank Lewis (WR) 1971–7, Tim Harris (RB) 1983, *Earnest Jackson* (RB) 1987–8, Ray Wallace (RB) 1989, Shawn Vincent (CB) 1991, Steve Avery (FB) 1994–5, George Jones (RB) 1997, Troy Polamalu (S) 2003.

44 Corwan Artman (T) 1933, Forrest Douds (T) 1933–4, Art Strutt (B) 1935–6, Bill Breedon (B) 1937, Stu Smith (QB) 1938, Earl Bartlett (B) 1939, Ernie Wheeler (B) 1939, Carl Littlefield (B) 1941, John Sanders (G) 1942, Ben Kish (B) 1943, *Art Jones* (B) 1945, Tony Compagno (B) 1948,

Tom McWilliams (B) 1950, *Ray Mathews* (E) 1951, Dick Hensley (E) 1952, Earl Girard (B) 1957, Art Davis (B) 1958, Bert Rechichar (DB) 1960, Bill Daniels (DB) 1961–6, Bob Wade (DB) 1968, Lee Calland (DB) 1969–72, Mike Collier (RB) 1975–6, Frank Pollard (RB) 1980–2, Henry Odom (RB) 1983, Rodney Carter (RB) 1987, D.J. Johnson (CB) 1989–93, Terry Richardson (RB) 1996.

45 Frank Hood (B) 1933, Ray Kemp (T) 1933, Norm Greeney (G) 1934–5, Lou Lassahn (E) 1938, Walter Kichefski (E) 1940, 1942, Clarence Booth (B) 1944, Art Brandau (C) 1946, Bob Cifers (B) 1947–8, Bob Hanlon (B) 1949, Paul Cameron (B) 1954, Art Davis (B) 1956, Dick Compton (E) 1967–8, Jim Allen (DB) 1974–7, Russell Davis (RB) 1980–3, Chuck Sanders (B) 1986–7, Tracy Simien (LB) 1989, Chris Fuamatu-Ma'afala (RB) 1998–2002.

46 Royal Kahler (T) 1941, Art Albrecht (C/T) 1942, Joe Pierre (E) 1945, Ed Ryan (E) 1948, *Bill Walsh* (C) 1949–51, Billy Reynolds (B) 1958, Fred Williamson (CB) 1960, Bob Coronado (E) 1961, Bob Ferguson (RB) 1962–3, Phil King (HB) 1964, Frank Lambert (P) 1965–6, Chet Anderson (E) 1967, Warren Bankston (TE) 1969–73, Reggie Harrison (RB) 1974–7, Eddie Miles (LB) 1990, Troy Sadowski (TE) 1997–8.

47 Ed Westfall (B) 1933, Bob Hoel (G) 1935, Ed Matesic (B) 1936, Izzy Weinstock (B) 1937, Jesse Tatum (E) 1938, Ralph Calcagni (T) 1947, Dick Moegle (B) 1960, Jackie Simpson (B) 1961–2, *Marv Woodson* (DB) 1964–9, **Mel Blount** (CB) 1970–83, Steve Morse (RB) 1985, Bruce Jones (S) 1987r, Cameron Riley (DB) 1987r, Scott Shields (S) 1999–2000.

48 Jesse Quatse (T) 1934, *Eberle Schultz* (G) 1942, Sid Tinsley (B) 1945, Art McCaffray (T) 1946, Joe Gasparella (QB) 1948, 1951, *Gary Ballman* (B/E) 1962, John Rowser (DB) 1970–3, *David Little* (LB) 1981, Tony Cline (TE) 1999, Matt Cushing (TE) 2000–3.

49 John Oelerich (B) 1938, Bob Thurbon (B) 1943, Silas Titus (E) 1945, *Jerry Shipkey* (B) 1948–9, Charles Ortman (QB) 1951, *Lynn Chandnois* (HB) 1952, 1954–6, William Bowman (FB) 1957, Ronnie Hall (B) 1959, Bob Sherman (B) 1964–5, Amos Bullocks (RB) 1966, Lou Harris (B) 1968–9, John Sodaski (DB) 1970, Ralph Anderson (DB) 1971–2, Dwayne Woodruff (CB) 1979–90.

50 Sam Francis (B) 1939, John Noppenburg (B) 1940, Harold Hinte (E) 1942, Al Wukits (C) 1943, George Tarasovic (E) 1952, Stan Sheriff (LB) 1954, *John Reger* (LB) 1955–63, Bill Saul (LB) 1964, 1966–8, Jim Clack (C) 1969–77, Tom Graves (C) 1979, *David Little* (LB) 1980–92, Darryl Knox (LB) 1987r, Reggie Barnes (LB) 1993, Earl Holmes (LB) 1996–2001, Larry Foote (LB) 2002–3.

51 Allen Nichols (B) 1945, Roy Kurrasch (E) 1948, *Buzz Nutter* (C) 1961–4, Ken Henson (C)

1965, Jim Powell (E) 1966, Bob Maples (C) 1971, Loren Toews (LB) 1973–83, Dan Turk (C) 1985–6, Paul Oswald (C) 1987, John Lott (C) 1987r, Chuck Lanza (C) 1988–9, Ed Robinson (LB) 1994, Carlos Emmons (LB) 1996–9, Mike Jones (LB) 2001, James Farrior (LB) 2002–3.

52 Ray Graves (C) 1943, George Tarasovic (E) 1957–8, Mike Connelly (C) 1963, Gene Breen (LB) 1965, Sidney Williams (LB) 1969, **Mike Webster** (C) 1974–88.

53 Byron Haines (B) 1937, Edgar Manske (E) 1938, Ted Grabinski (C) 1940, George Magulick (B) 1944, George Tarasovic (E) 1956, Ken Kirk (LB) 1962, John Campbell (LB) 1965–9, *Henry Davis* (LB) 1970–3, Greg Blankenship (G) 1976, Ray Pinney (OL) 1976, Dennis Winston (LB) 1977–81, Bryan Hinkle (LB) 1982–93, Steven Conley (LB) 1996–8, Clark Haggans (LB) 2000–3.

54 *Val Jansante* (E) 1946–51, Max Messner (LB) 1964–5, Doug Fisher (LB) 1969–70, Marv Kellum (LB) 1974–6, Dave LaCrosse (LB) 1977, Zack Valentine (LB) 1979–81, Craig Bingham (LB) 1982–4, 1987r, Fred Small (LB) 1985, Hardy Nickerson (LB) 1987–92, Donta Jones (LB) 1995–8, Mike Schneck (C) 1999–2003.

55 Frank Filchock (QB) 1938, Randall Bond (QB) 1939, John Sanders (G) 1940–1, *Milt Simington* (B) 1942, Carl Buda (G) 1945, *Charles Mehelich* (E) 1946–51, Tony Momsen (C) 1951, Lou Tepe (C) 1955, John Cenci (C) 1956, Dan James (T) 1960, Pat Killorin (C) 1966, Jon Kolb (T) 1969–81, Rick Donnalley (G) 1982–3, Dennis Winston (LB) 1985–6, Ken Woodard (LB) 1987r, Darin Jordan (LB) 1988, Jerry Olsavsky (LB) 1990–7, *Joey Porter* (LB) 1999–2003.

56 Joe Coomer (T) 1946, Bob Balog (C) 1949–51, *Bill Walsh* (C) 1951–2, 1954, Marv Matuszak (LB) 1953, Fred Broussard (C) 1955, George Tarasovic (E) 1956, Bob Rowley (LB) 1963, Ray Mansfield (C) 1968–76, *Robin Cole* (LB) 1977–87, Tyronne Stowe (LB) 1987, Rob McGovern (LB) 1991, Rico Mack (LB) 1993–4, Mike Vrabel (LB) 1998–2000, Chukky Okobi (C) 2001–3.

57 John Petchel (QB) 1945, Frank Sinkovitz (C) 1947–52, Dick Flanagan (G) 1954–5, Jim Taylor (LB) 1956, Ed Beatty (C) 1957–61, Art Hunter (C) 1965, Sam Davis (G) 1967–79, *Mike Merriweather* (LB) 1982–7, Jerrol Williams (LB) 1990–2, Reggie Clark (LB) 1994, Eric Ravotti (LB) 1994–6, John Fiala (LB) 1998–2002, Clint Kriewaldt (LB) 2003.

58 Roger Pillath (T) 1960, Ed Pine (LB) 1965, Chuck Allen (LB) 1970–1, **Jack Lambert** (LB) 1974–84.

59 Joe Wendlick (E) 1941, Vernon Foltz (C) 1945, Lou Levanti (G) 1951–2, Ray May (LB) 1967–9, **Jack Ham** (LB) 1971–82, Todd Seabaugh (LB) 1984.

60 Ed Michaels (G) 1943, Gil Duggan (T) 1944, Carmine DePascal (E) 1945, Frank Kimble (E) 1945, Leo Nobile (G) 1948–9, *Dale Dodrill* (G) 1951–2, 1954–9, *Ben McGee* (DE) 1964–72, Brad Cousino (LB) 1977, Randy Rasmussen (G) 1986, Brian Blankenship (G) 1987–91, Kendall Gammon (OL) 1992–5, Mark Rodenhauser (C) 1998, Anthony Brown (T) 1999.

61 Gordon Paschka (G) 1943, Henry DePaul (G) 1945, Lou Tepe (C) 1953–5, Marv Matuszak (LB) 1955, Marv McFadden (G) 1956, Ted Karras (T) 1958–9, Riley Gunnels (T) 1965, Fran Mallick (T) 1965, Eli Strand (G) 1966, Jerry Mazzanti (E) 1967, Brian Stenger (LB) 1969–73, Tyrone McGriff (G) 1980–2, Blake Wingle (G) 1983–5, Charlie Dickey (G) 1987r, Dean Caliguire (G) 1991, Tim Simpson (G) 1994, Tom Myslinski (OL) 2000.

62 John Kondria (T) 1945, Steve Suhey (G) 1948–9, Dick Tomlinson (G) 1951–2, Pete Ladygo (G) 1954, Art Michalik (G) 1955–6, *Mike Sandusky* (G) 1957–65, Ralph Wenzel (G) 1966–70, Jim Wolf (DE) 1974–5, *Tunch Ilkin* (T) 1980–92, Todd Kalis (G) 1994, Tom Myslinski (OL) 1996–7, Roger Duffy (C) 1998–2001, Jeff Smith (C) 2002.

63 Don Currivan (E) 1944, *Darrell Hogan* (G) 1949, 1951–2, George Tarasovic (E) 1956, Bob Dougherty (LB) 1958, Art Anderson (T) 1963, Rod Breedlove (LB) 1965–7, Ernie Holmes (DT) 1972–7, Thom Dornbrook (G) 1979, Pete Rostosky (T) 1984–6, Robert Washington (T) 1987r, *Dermontti Dawson* (C) 1988–2000.

64 *John Karcis* (B) 1936–7, John Tosi (B) 1939, Clark Goff (T) 1940, Lou Marotti (G) 1944, Felix Bucek (G) 1946, Bryant Meeks (C) 1947–8, Rudy Andabaker (G) 1952–4, Marv Matuszak (LB) 1956, Bill Michael (G) 1957, Bill Krisher (G) 1958–9, John Kapele (T) 1960–2, Chuck Hinton (T) 1964–71, Steve Furness (DT) 1972–80, Edmund Nelson (DL) 1982–7, Alan Huff (NT) 1987r, Jerry Reese (DE) 1988, Kenny Davidson (DE) 1990–3, Jeff Hartings (C) 2001–3.

65 Garth Chamberlain (G) 1945, John Mastrangelo (G) 1948, Walter Szot (T) 1949, Louis Allen (T) 1951, *George Hughes* (G) 1952–4, Ralph Jecha (G) 1956, Bob O'Neil (G) 1957, *John Nisby* (G) 1957–61, Tom Bettis (LB) 1962, Bob Nicholas (T) 1965, Lloyd Voss (DT) 1966–71, Tom Beasley (DL) 1978–83, Ray Pinney (OL) 1985–7, Jim Boyle (T) 1987r, John Jackson (T) 1988–97, *Alan Faneca* (G) 1998–9, Rich Tylski (G) 2000–1.

66 John Grigas (B) 1944, Don Samuel (B) 1949, 1951, Pete Ladygo (G) 1952, John Schweder (G) 1954–5, Marv Matuszak (LB) 1956, Gerald Leahy (QB) 1957, Aubrey Rozzell (LB) 1957, Ray Campbell (LB) 1958–60, *Myron Pottios* (LB) 1961–3, 1965, *Bruce Van Dyke* (G) 1967–73, Ted Petersen (T) 1977–83, Mark Behning (T) 1986, Donald Evans (DE) 1990–3, Lonnie Palelei (G) 1994, Tom Newberry (G) 1995, Jim Sweeney (C/G) 1996–9, *Alan Faneca* (G) 2000–3.

67 Enio Conti (G) 1943, Truett Smith (QB) 1952, Nick Feher (G) 1955, *John Nisby* (G) 1957, Bob Schmitz (LB) 1961–4, 1966, Dick Capp (TE) 1968, Clarence Washington (DT) 1969–70, Craig Hanneman (DE) 1972–3, Gary Dunn (DT) 1976, 1978–87, Mike Hinnant (TE) 1989, *Duval Love* (G) 1992–4, Jamain Stephens (T) 1996–8, Shar Pourdanesh (T) 1999, Kimo Von Oelhoffen (DT) 2000–3.

68 Ed McNamara (T) 1945, John Schweder (G) 1951–2, Ed Beatty (C) 1957, Bob Dougherty (LB) 1958, Mike Henry (LB) 1959, Ron Stehower (B) 1960–4, Mike Magac (G) 1965–6, *L.C. Greenwood* (DE) 1969–81, Lorenzo Freeman (DT) 1987–90, Jeff Lucas (T) 1987, Mike Withycombe (C) 1991, Lonnie Palelei (G) 1993, Brenden Stai (G) 1995–9, Shar Pourdanesh (T) 2000, Keydrick Vincent (G) 2001–3.

69 Clint Wager (E) 1944, Tom Alberghini (G) 1945, Jerry Hillebrand (LB) 1968–70, Fred Anderson (DE) 1978, Gabe Rivera (DT) 1983, David Opfar (DL) 1987, Ben Thomas (DL) 1988, Ariel Solomon (G) 1991–5.

70 *Al Wistert* (T) 1943, **Ernie Stautner** (DT) 1951–63.

71 *Eberle Schultz* (G) 1943, Dick Dolly (E) 1945, Joe Lewis (T) 1958–60, Ken Longenecker (T) 1961, *Charles Bradshaw* (T) 1961–6, Dick Arndt (DT) 1967–70, Gordon Gravelle (T) 1972–6, Emil Boures (C/G) 1983–4, Ted Petersen (T) 1987r, Tom Ricketts (T) 1989–91, Dan Fike (OL) 1993, Orpheus Roye (DE) 1996–9, Larry Tharpe (T) 2000, Todd Fordham (T) 2003.

72 Ted Doyle (T) 1943, *Red Moore* (G) 1947–9, *Dale Dodrill* (G) 1951, Paul Lea (G) 1951, Earl Murray (G) 1952, Alex Smail (LB) 1952, Bob Gaona (T) 1953–6, Sid Fournet (G) 1957, Herman Lee (T) 1957, Darrell Dess (G) 1958, John Simerson (T) 1958, Byron Beams (T) 1959–60, Dick Klein (T) 1961, Ray Lemek (G) 1962–5, Fran O'Brien (T) 1966–8, **Joe Greene** (DT) 1969, Gerry Mullins (T) 1971–9, Ray Snell (T) 1984–5, Buddy Aydelette (G) 1987, Leon Searcy (T) 1992–5, Bernard Dafney (OL) 1996, Wayne Gandy (T) 1999–2002.

73 Rocco Canale (G) 1943, Chester Bulger (T) 1944, Max Kielbasa (B) 1946, Bill Cregar (G) 1948, *Darrell Hogan* (G) 1951, Louis Allen (T) 1951–2, Ray Fisher (T) 1959, Will Renfro (G) 1960, John Baker (DE) 1962, Frank Atkinson (T) 1963, Ray Mansfield (C) 1964–7, Ernie Ruple (T) 1968–9, Rick Sharp (T) 1970–1, Rick Druschel (G/T) 1974–5, Craig Wolfley (G/T) 1980–9, Justin Strzelczyk (T) 1990–9, Chris Combs (DE) 2000–1, Kendall Simmons (G) 2002–3.

74 Ernie Bonelli (B) 1946, Jim Reynolds (B) 1946, Pete Ladygo (G) 1952, *Frank Varrichione* (T) 1955–60, George Demko (T) 1961, Lou Cordileone (DT) 1962–3, John Kenerson (G) 1962, George

Strugar (DT) 1962, Urban Henry (DT) 1964, Riley Gunnels (T) 1965–6, John Brown (T) 1967–71, Tom Keating (DT) 1973, Dave Reavis (DT) 1974–5, Ray Pinney (OL) 1976–82, Mark Kirchner (T) 1983, Terry Long (G) 1984–91, Nolan Harrison (DE) 1997–9, Chris Sullivan (DE) 2000.

75 Ed Rucinski (E) 1944, Glen Stough (T) 1945, Jack Wiley (T) 1948–9, George Hays (E) 1951, John Schweder (G) 1951, Dick Fugler (T) 1952, Nick Bolkovac (T) 1954, *Joe Krupa* (T) 1956–64, Ken Kortas (DT) 1965–9, **Joe Greene** (DT) 1969–82.

76 Francis Maher (B) 1941, Frank Zopetti (B) 1941, Tom Brown (E) 1942, Bucko Kilroy (T) 1943, Pete Ladygo (G) 1952, 1954, Bill Hegarty (T) 1953, Bill McClung (T) 1955–7, Ken Longenecker (T) 1960, *Gene Lipscomb* (DT) 1961–2, Mike Haggerty (G) 1967, 1969–70, Bert Askson (DE) 1971, Glen Ray Hines (T) 1973, John Banaszak (DL) 1975–81, Glen Howe (T) 1985, Jerry Quick (T/G) 1987, Rollin Putzier (DT) 1988, Kevin Henry (DE) 1993–2000, Chris Hoke (DT) 2001–2.

77 Paul Davis (QB) 1947–8, Bob Gage (B) 1949–50, *Ray Mathews* (E) 1951, John Schweder (G) 1952, Tom Palmer (T) 1953–4, Gus Cifelli (T) 1954, Billy Ray Smith (DT) 1958–60, Dan James (T) 1961–6, Mike Taylor (T) 1968–9, Mel Holmes (T) 1971–3, Charlie Davis (DT) 1974–5, Steve Courson (G) 1978–83, Steve August (T) 1984, Jim Boyle (T) 1987–8, *Carlton Haselrig* (G) 1990–3, Will Wolford (G/T) 1996–8, Kris Farris (T) 1999, Marvel Smith (OL) 2000–3.

78 Joe Cibulas (T) 1945, Paul Stenn (T) 1947, Carl Samuelson (T) 1948–51, George Nicksich (G) 1950, Lou Ferry (T) 1952–5, Dave Liddick (T) 1957, John Baker (DE) 1963–7, Frank Parker (DT) 1968–9, *Dwight White* (DE) 1971–80, Mark Catano (DL) 1984–5, Tim Johnson (DL) 1987–9, Garry Howe (NT) 1992, Taase Faumui (DL) 1994–5, Chris Conrad (T) 1998–2000, Mathias Nkwenti (T) 2001–3.

79 *Vic Sears* (T) 1943, Art Brandau (C) 1945, Frank Wydo (T) 1947–51, Ernie Cheatham (T) 1954, Dick Modzelewski (DT) 1955, Dick Murley (T) 1956, John Simerson (T) 1958, Riley Gunnels (T) 1959, *Lou Michaels* (DE) 1961–3, Larry Gagner (G) 1966–9, Larry Brown (TE/T) 1977–84, John Rienstra (G) 1986–90, James Parrish (OL) 1995, Paul Wiggins (T) 1997, Oliver Ross (OL) 2000–3.

80 Fred Meyer (E) 1943, Len Frketich (T) 1945, George Hays (E) 1951, *Jack Butler* (DB) 1951–9, Wayne Capers (WR) 1983–4, Frank Pokorny (WR) 1985, Warren Seitz (TE) 1986, Theo Young (TE) 1987, Russell Hairston (WR) 1987r, Mark Stock (WR) 1989, Charles Davenport (WR) 1992–4, Johnnie Barnes (WR) 1995, Jahine Arnold (WR) 1996–8, Matt Cushing (TE) 1999, Plaxico Burress (WR) 2000–3.

81 Ray Reutt (E) 1943, Ross Sorce (T) 1945, *Elbie Nickel* (E) 1948–9, 1951–7, Paul Skansi (WR) 1983, Darrell Nelson (TE) 1984–5, Lyneal Alston (WR) 1987r, Mike Hinnant (TE) 1988, Jeff Graham (WR) 1991–3, Charles Johnson (WR) 1994–8, Troy Edwards (WR) 1999–2001, Marco Battaglia (TE) 2002, Dan O'Leary (TE) 2002.

82 Bill Hewitt (E) 1943, Joe Coomer (T) 1945, Bill Long (E) 1949–50, Henry Minarik (E) 1951, George Hays (E) 1952, Pat Brady (B) 1953, Ernie Cheatham (T) 1954, Joe Zombek (E) 1954, Ed Meadows (E) 1955, Bob Gunderman (B) 1957, Tom Miner (E) 1958, Chuck Logan (E) 1964, John Hilton (TE) 1965–9, Dennis Hughes (TE) 1970–1, Dave Williams (WR) 1973, **John Stallworth** (WR) 1974–87, Derek Hill (WR) 1989–90, *Yancey Thigpen* (WR) 1992–7, Henry Bailey (WR) 1998, Bobby Shaw (WR) 1999–2001, Antwaan Randle El (WR) 2002–3.

83 John Alderton (E) 1953, Dewey Brundage (E) 1954, Ed Bernet (E) 1955, 1958, Fred Glatz (E) 1956, *John Nisby* (G) 1957, *Buddy Dial* (WR) 1959, *Mike Clark* (K) 1964–7, Don Alley (WR) 1969, Barry Pearson (WR) 1972–3, Theo Bell (WR) 1976–80, Willie Sydnor (WR) 1982, *Louis Lipps* (WR) 1984–91, Melvin Anderson (WR) 1987r, Corey Holliday (WR) 1995–7, Andre Coleman (WR) 1998, David Dunn (WR) 1998, Malcolm Johnson (WR) 1999–2000, Lenzie Jackson (WR) 2001, Chris Doering (WR) 2003.

84 Larry Cabrelli (E) 1943, *Bill McPeak* (E) 1951–2, 1954–7, Gern Nagler (E) 1959, *Buddy Dial* (WR) 1960–3, Lee Folkins (TE) 1965, Tony Jeter (E) 1966–8, Dave Kalina (WR) 1970, Chuck Dicus (WR) 1973, Randy Grossman (TE) 1974–80, Chris Kolodziejski (TE) 1984, Danzell Lee (TE) 1987, Jeff Markland (TE) 1988, Mike Mularkey (TE) 1989–91, Tim Jorden (TE) 1992–3, Walter Rasby (TE) 1994, Tracey Greene (TE) 1995, Kirk Botkin (TE) 1996–7, Harold Bishop (TE) 1998, Jerame Tuman (TE) 1999–2003.

85 Tony Bova (E) 1943, *Val Jansante* (E) 1951, Dick Hensley (E) 1952, Joe Zombek (E) 1954–5, Joe O'Malley (E) 1955–6, Bill Michael (G) 1957, Don Bishop (B) 1958–9, Bob Schnelker (TE) 1962, *Gary Ballman* (B/E) 1963–6, Jerry Marion (B) 1967, Bob Adams (WR) 1969–71, Dave Davis (WR) 1973, Ernie Pough (WR) 1976–7, Calvin Sweeney (WR) 1980–7, Troy Johnson (WR) 1988, Terry O'Shea (TE) 1989–90, Russ Campbell (TE) 1992, Craig Keith (TE) 1993, Jonathan Hayes (TE) 1994–6, Mitch Lyons (TE) 1997–9, Cory Geason (TE) 2000–1, John Allred (TE) 2002, Jay Riemersma (TE) 2003.

86 Carl Samuelson (T) 1949, 1951, *Charles Mehelich* (E) 1951, Tom Jelley (E) 1951–2, Ed Meadows (E) 1955, Bob O'Neil (G) 1956–7, Perry Richards (E) 1957, Jon Evans (E) 1958, *Jimmie Orr* (WR) 1958–60, Len Burnett (DB) 1961, John Bur-

rell (E) 1962–4, J.R. Wilburn (WR) 1966–70, Glenn Scolnick (WR) 1973, Reggie Garrett (WR) 1974–5, Jim Smith (WR) 1977–82, Gregg Garrity (WR) 1983–4, Preston Gothard (TE) 1985–8, Ralph Britt (TE) 1987r, *Eric Green* (TE) 1990–4, John Farquhar (TE) 1996, Mike Adams (WR) 1997, *Hines Ward* (WR) 1998–2003.

87 *Jack McClairen* (E) 1955–60, Glenn Glass (B) 1962, Harlon Hill (E) 1962, Dan Larose (T) 1964, *Roy Jefferson* (WR) 1965–9, Larry Brown (TE/T) 1971–6, Jim Mandich (TE) 1978, Johnny Dirden (WR) 1981, John Rodgers (TE) 1982–3, Weegie Thompson (WR) 1984–9, Moses Ford (WR) 1987, Adrian Cooper (TE) 1991–3, Craig Keith (TE) 1994, Mark Bruener (TE) 1995–2003.

88 George Nicksich (G) 1951, George Sulima (E) 1952, 1954–6, John Stock (E) 1956, Tom Miner (E) 1958, Pete Brewster (E) 1959–60, Steve Meilinger (TE) 1961, Bob Schnelker (TE) 1961, John Powers (E) 1962–5, Steve Smith (E) 1966, Dick Kotite (TE) 1968, Dave Smith (WR) 1970–2, **Lynn Swann** (WR) 1974–82, Craig Dunaway (TE) 1983, John Rodgers (TE) 1984, Jessie Britt (WR) 1986, Joey Clinkscales (WR) 1987–8, Jason Johnson (WR) 1989, Chris Calloway (WR) 1990–1, Jesse Anderson (TE) 1992, Mark Didio (WR) 1992, Andre Hastings (WR) 1993–6, Courtney Hawkins (WR) 1997–2000, Terance Mathis (WR) 2002.

89 Tom Miller (E) 1943, Hubert Shurtz (T) 1948, Pete Barbolak (T) 1949, Walter Szot (T) 1950, **Ernie Stautner** (DT) 1951, Jack O'Brien (E) 1954–6, Perry Richards (E) 1957, Dick Lasse (LB) 1958–9, Bobby Joe Green (P) 1960–1, Jim Kelly (E) 1964, Marsh Cropper (E) 1967–9, John McMakin (TE) 1972–4, Bennie Cunningham (TE) 1976–85, Charles Lockett (WR) 1987–8, Lorenzo Davis (WR) 1990, Ernie Mills (WR) 1991–6, Will Blackwell (WR) 1997–2001, Lee Mays (WR) 2002–3.

90 Dick Lasse (LB) 1958, George Webster (LB) 1972–3, Bob Kohrs (LB) 1981–5, Larry Station (LB) 1986, Steve Apke (LB) 1987, Tyronne Stowe (LB) 1987–90, Huey Richardson (LB) 1991–2, Jeff Zgonina (DL) 1993–4, Bill Johnson (DT) 1995–6, Reggie Lowe (LB) 1999, Donnell Thompson (LB) 2000, Justin Kurpeikis (LB) 2001–2.

91 Gregg Carr (LB) 1985–8, Tommy Dawkins (DE) 1987, Jerrol Williams (LB) 1989, Craig Veasey (DL) 1991, *Kevin Greene* (LB) 1993–5, Israel Raybon (DE) 1996, Aaron Smith (DE) 1999–2003.

92 Fran Mattioli (G) 1946, Keith Gary (DE) 1983–8, Michael Minter (DT) 1987r, Jerry Olsavsky (LB) 1989, Elnardo Webster (LB) 1992, *Jason Gildon* (LB) 1994–2003.

93 John Stock (E) 1956, Keith Willis (DE) 1981–7, 1989–91, *Joel Steed* (NT) 1992–9, James Harrison (LB) 2002.

94 Dick Murley (T) 1956, Terry Echols (LB) 1984, Albert Williams (LB) 1987r, Jeff Brady (LB) 1991, Darryl Ford (LB) 1992, *Chad Brown* (LB) 1993–6, Jeremy Staat (DE) 1998–2000, Rodney Bailey (DE) 2001–3.

95 John Goodman (DL) 1981–5, Jackie Cline (DE) 1987, Bret Shugarts (DE) 1987r, Xavier Warren (DL) 1987r, *Greg Lloyd* (LB) 1988–97, Mike Jones (LB) 2002, Alonzo Jackson (LB) 2003.

96 Anthony Henton (LB) 1986, 1988, Jackie Cline (DE) 1987, Ricky Sutton (DL) 1993, Brentson Buckner (DE) 1994–6, Mike Vrabel (LB) 1997, Kendrick Clancy (DT) 2000–3.

97 Joe Williams (LB) 1987r, Aaron Jones (DE/LB) 1988–92, Ray Seals (DE) 1994–6, Rod Manuel (DE) 1997–8, Chad Kelsay (LB) 1999, *Kendrell Bell* (LB) 2002–3.

98 Gerald Williams (DE) 1986–94, Xavier Warren (DL) 1987r, Oliver Gibson (DT) 1995–8, Ernie Brown (DL) 1999, *Casey Hampton* (DT) 2001–3.

99 Darryl Sims (DE) 1985–6, Michael Minter (DT) 1987r, Avon Riley (LB) 1987r, A.J. Jenkins (LB) 1989–90, *Levon Kirkland* (LB) 1992–2000, Brett Keisel (DE) 2002.

St. Louis Rams

The franchise: The Rams have had a remarkable odyssey over two leagues and through four cities in their 68 year history. They began as the Cleveland Rams in the second American Football League in 1936. After one year, owner Homer Marshman was granted an NFL franchise which won only one of its first 14 games. The early years continued to be a struggle on the field and Marshman sold the team to 28-year-old Dan Reeves in 1941. From the beginning, Reeves envisioned moving the club to the west coast to play in the Los Angeles Coliseum; ironically, decades later that same Coliseum would drive both the Rams and Raiders out of Los Angeles due to its aging condition. In 1943, Reeves and many of his players were in the military, and he got league permission to disband for a year. Those Ram players not in the service were distributed throughout the league for one year. The Rams returned for another losing season in 1944, but their fortunes were about to change.

In 1945, behind rookie quarterback/kicker Bob Waterfield, who was married to silver screen bombshell Jane Russell, the Rams recorded their first winning season and won their first championship 15–14 over the Redskins with the decisive points coming when Sammy Baugh's pass from his own end zone hit the goal post for a safety. The champion Rams then did something unprecedented for a championship club — they moved. The Los Angeles territory was opened at last, but it would be a struggle for Reeves. The club slipped a bit on the field in 1946 and was competing with the new All America Conference Los Angeles Dons for the LA professional football fan. Both teams were also competing with the more popular USC and UCLA football teams as well and would bleed money for the next few years.

Reeves introduced many innovations — the first black NFL players since the color bar of the 1930s, the first scouting department, the first painted helmet design, and the first televised home games. On the field the team was led by a series of former Bears, Bob Snyder, then offensive genius Clark Shaughnessy, then Joe Stydahar, and then another brilliant offensive mind, Hampton Pool. Four times between 1949 and 1955 the Rams played in the NFL title game although they only won once. Their formidable offense featured Hall of Fame passers Waterfield and Norm Van Brocklin and receivers Tom Fears and Elroy Hirsch and a fleet of swift and powerful runners like Dan Towler and Paul Younger. They did not have a great defense, but could outscore most opponents. When offensive master Sid Gillman led the team to a division title in his 1955 rookie year, no one realized that the Rams would not seriously compete for the title for the next ten seasons.

After watching former players Waterfield and Svare fail as coaches, Reeves brought in another former Bear, George Allen, to turn things around. Allen did just that, importing several veteran players and building the Rams around a vaunted defense led by its Fearsome Foursome line of Deacon Jones, Merlin Olsen, Lamar Lundy and Rosey Grier followed by Roger Brown. Allen was unable to win in the playoffs, though, and was dispatched after five winning years. Reeves died in 1971, and Robert Irsay bought the team only to swap franchises with Colt owner Carroll Rosenbloom. Rosenbloom brought in Chuck Knox, who built a strong defense-oriented team that would go to the playoffs eight straight seasons but end each postseason with a loss. Knox was followed by Ray Malavasi and then John Robinson, and the Rams consistently fielded a winning team throughout the 1970s and 1980s. They only reached the Super Bowl once, though, in 1979, the year that Rosenbloom died and was supplanted by his widow Georgia Frontiere.

In the 1990s, however, the Rams kost at least nine games for the first nine years of the decade and moved to a new dome home in St. Louis in 1995. In Dick Vermeil's third season as coach in 1999 everything clicked at last. With a wide-open passing offense that hearkened back to the 1950s Ram teams, the Kurt Warner–led Rams swept to a Super Bowl championship. Vermeil quickly stepped aside and offensive coordinator Mike Martz assumed control. Under Martz, the offense has remained top-notch and the team has been successful, but has not won another title.

Origin of name: Original general manager Buzz Wetzel's favorite college football team was the Fordham Rams, prominent at the time for their "Seven Blocks of Granite."

Record by Decade

	Regular Season			Postseason		
	Won	Lost	Tied	Won	Lost	Championships
1930s	10	22	1	0	0	
1940s	50	45	5	1	1	1945
1950s	68	49	3	2	3	1951
1960s	63	68	7	0	2	
1970s	98	42	4	6	7	
1980s	86	66	0	4	7	
1990s	58	102	0	3	0	1999
2000s	43	21	0	2	3	
All-Time	476	415	20	18	23	3

Winning seasons: 35. Losing Seasons: 29. .500 seasons: 3.

Coaches

	Years	Record	Playoffs
Hugo Bezdek	1937–8	1–13–0	0–0
Art Lewis	1938	4–4–0	0–0
Dutch Clark	1939–42	16–26–2	0–0
Buff Donelli	1944	4–6–0	0–0
Adam Walsh (1)	1945–6	15–5–1	1–0
Bob Snyder	1947	6–6–0	0–0
Clark Shaughnessy	1948–9	14–8–3	0–1
Joe Stydahar (1)	1950–2	17–7–0	2–1
Hamp Pool	1952–4	23–10–2	0–1
Sid Gillman	1955–9	28–31–1	0–1
Bob Waterfield	1960–2	9–24–1	0–0
Harland Svare	1962–5	14–31–3	0–0
George Allen	1966–70	49–17–4	0–2
Tommy Prothro	1971–2	14–12–2	0–0
Chuck Knox	1973–7	54–15–1	3–5
Ray Malavasi	1978–82	40–33–0	3–3
John Robinson	1983–91	75–68–0	4–6
Chuck Knox	1992–4	15–33–0	0–0
Rich Brooks	1995–6	13–19–0	0–0
Dick Vermeil (1)	1997–9	22–26–0	3–0
Mike Martz	2000–3	43–21–0	2–3

(Championships in parentheses)

Time till first championship: Nine years.

Time since last championship: Five years.

Retired numbers: The Rams have only retired the numbers of two of their Hall of Famers— Bob Waterfield 7 and Merlin Olsen 74.

Other numbers worn by these players: None.

Those who wore retired numbers after the honored player: None.

Numbers that should be retired: Deacon Jones 75 and Norm Van Brocklin 11.

Owned numbers: None.

Numbers worn by Hall of Famers: Bob Brown 76; Eric Dickerson 29; Tom Fears 55/80; Bill George 61; Elroy Hirsch 40; Deacon Jones 75; Dick "Night Train" Lane 81; James Lofton 22; Tom Mack 65; Ollie Matson 33; Tommy McDonald 29; Joe Namath 12; Merlin Olsen 74; Andy Robustelli 84; Jackie Slater 78; Norm Van Brocklin 11/25; Bob Waterfield 7; Ron Yary 73; Jack Youngblood 85.

Star power: Tom Fears took 80 from Bob Boyd.

Star eclipsed: James Lofton wore 22 because Henry Ellard wore 80; Curt Warner wore 20 because Clifford Hicks wore 28. Lance Rentzel wore 13 till Jim Nettles, 19, left; Kurt Warner wore 10 till Steve Bono, 13, left; Harry Schuh wore 76 till Coy Bacon, 79, left; Tory Holt wore 88 till Az-Zahir Hakim, 81, left. Bert Jones wore 17 because 7 was retired for Bob Waterfield.

Numbers with most great players: 21 has been worn by defensive backs Ed Meador, Nolan Cromwell, and Dexter McCleon as well as quarterback John Hadl, tackle Tom Dahms and center Charles Cherundolo. 29 has been worn by Pro Bowlers Del Shofner and Harold Jackson as well as Hall of Famers Tommy McDonald and Eric Dickerson. 55 was worn by Hall of Famer Tom Fears as well as defensive end Lou Michaels, and linebackers Maxie Baughn and Carl Ekern. 58 was worn by three decade-long linebackers— Isiah Robertson, Mel Owens and Roman Phifer. 75 was worn by Hall of Famer Deacon Jones as well as star linemen John Williams, Irv Pankey and D'Marco Farr. 80 has been worn by defensive ends Billy Ray Smith and Gene Brito as well as receivers Isaac Bruce, Henry Ellard and Bucky Pope. 85 was worn by defensive line stalwarts Jack Youngblood, Lamar Lundy and Big Daddy Lipscomb.

Worst represented numbers: 68 has been worn by 12 linemen, none for more than a couple of years.

Number worn by the most players: 22 has been worn 25 times.

Player who wore the most numbers: Linebacker Dick Dougherty wore 50/54/67.

Longest tenure wearing a number: Jackie Slater wore 78 for 20 years from 1976 to 1995. Merlin Olsen wore 74 for 15 years from 1962 to 1976; Charlie Cowan wore 73 and Joe Scibelli wore 71 for 15 years from 1961 to 1975.

Number worn by first ever draft pick: Fullback Corby Davis was taken in the first round in 1938 and wore 3/32.

Biggest draft busts: Runner Lawrence Phillips, 21, was selected sixth in 1996 and averaged only 3.4 yards per carry in two seasons before he was bounced out of town as a headcase.

Number worn by oldest player: Jackie Slater wore 78 as a 41 year old in 1995. Sean Landetta wore 5 as a 41 year old punter in 2003, and Mike Horan wore 2 as a 40 year old punter in 1999.

Cameos: Hall of Famers— Bill George 61; James Lofton 22; Ron Yary 73; All Pros and other notables— Ben Agajanian 3; Steve Bartkowski 10; Pete Beathard 12; Lynn Cain 31; Chris Chandler 17; Bill Curry 55; Bob DeMarco 55; Herm Edwards 46; Ken Ellis 28; Steve Everitt 60; Trent Green 10; Hank Gremminger 46; Dennis Harrison 68; Winston Hill 73; Bert Jones 17; Ted Karras 67; Earl Leggett 72; Chris Miller 12; Tom Moore 25; Joe Namath 12; Dan Pastorini 10; Elijah Pitts 22; Milt Plum 16; Rafael Septien 1; Curt Warner 21; Travis Williams 25.

Ones who got away: Frank Ryan, 15, won a championship in Cleveland. Ron Jaworski, 16, took the Eagles to the Super Bowl. Jesse Whittenton, 44, and Carroll Dale, 84, excelled on the 1960s Packers. Diron Talbert, 71, was a steady force on the Redskin defensive line. Night Train Lane, 81, had a Hall of Fame career with the Cardinals and Lions. Gary Larsen, 83, was a member of the Vikings star front four. Andy Robustelli, 84, went to the Hall of Fame from the Giants. Big Daddy Lipscomb, 85, and Billy Ray Smith, 80, starred on the Colt defensive line.

Least popular numbers: 00 has been worn only once. 2 has been worn three times.

Last number to be originated: 92 was first worn by linebacker Richard Brown in 1987.

Longest dormant number: 00 has not been worn since 1947.

Triskaidekaphobia notes: Among the prominent Rams to wear 13 have been the first black NFL player once the color bar was lifted in 1946, Kenny Washington, and the first NFL player to come from a predominantly black college, Paul Younger who came from Grambling. Another All Pro from the early days was Riley Matheson. More recently Kurt Warner, Chris Miller and Lance Rentzel have all worn 13 as well as six others.

Shared numbers: 32 was worn by Pro Bowl runner Dan Towler and Pro Bowl linebacker Jack Pardee. 35 has been worn by Pro Bowlers runner Paul Younger and cornerback Aeneas Williams. 64 was worn by Pro Bowl linebackers Stan West and Hacksaw Reynolds. 84 was worn by Hall of Fame defensive end Andy Robustelli and Pro Bowl receiver Jack Snow.

Continuity: Pro Bowl guard Stan West was replaced in 11 by Hall of Famer Norm Van Brocklin; Ken Washington was replaced in 13 by Paul Younger; Dick Daugherty was replaced in 67 by Les Richter; Bob Boyd was replaced in 82 by Red Phillips.

Discontinuity: Ed Meador was followed in 21 by Gene Howard; Jim Benton was followed in 26 by Wilfred Thorpe; Jon Arnett was followed in 26 by Willie Brown; Dick Hoerner was followed in 31 by Jack Myers; Crazy Legs Hirsch was followed in 40 by Jack Morris; Will Sherman was followed in 43 by Ross Coyle; Fred Dryer was followed in 89 by Lewis Gilbert.

Quarterback numbers over 19: 21 Jim

Family Connections			
Brothers			
Bill Lazetich	DB	1939, 1942	24
Milan Lazetich	LB	1945–50	27
Walt West	FB	1944	21
Pat West	LB	1945–8	11/64
Merlin Olsen	DT	1962–76	74
Phil Olsen	DT	1971–4	72
Ernie Thompson	FB	1991	32
Anthony Thompson	RB	1992	32

Hardy; 25 Norm Van Brocklin; 35 John Karrs; 40 Earl Crowder; 43 Jack Jacobs; 50 John Petchel, Paul Richards; 58 Warren Plunkett; 65 Rob Thompson.

Number of first black player: Runner Kenny Washington 13 and end Woody Strode 39 broke the league-wide color bar in 1946.

Numbers of future NFL head coaches: Fred Bruney 38; Red Conkright 37; Herm Edwards 46; Tom Fears 55/80; Norb Hecker 88; Red Hickey 53; Mike Holovak 45; Ed Hughes 49; Art Lewis 11/23; Jack Pardee 32; Ritchie Petitbon 17; Ray Prochaska 8; Bob Snyder 1/4; Harland Svare 65/76; Ron Waller 27; Norm Van Brocklin 11/25; Bob Waterfield 7; Jerry Williams 22/33.

Numbers of future NFL referees: Steve Pritko 30.

Players who played other sports: Basketball — Lou Barle 8, Connie Berry 6, and Bob Shaw 32. Wrestling — Joe Carollo 63/70, Don Chuy 62, Kevin Greene 91, Butch Levy 76, and Woody Strode 39.

Players more famous after football: Marion "Suge" Knight, 79, is a notorious rap record producer who has served time. Fred Dryer, 89, had his own television show, *Hunter*. Pat Studstill was on *The Dukes of Hazard*. Joe Namath, 12, acted in movies. Fred Gehrke was a painter who first designed the horns on the Rams helmet.

First player to wear a number in the 70s: End George Patukas wore 70 in 1942.

First player to wear a number in the 80s: In 1947 guard Hal Dean wore 84 and tackle Ed Champagne wore 86.

First player to wear a number in the 90s: Runner Tom Harmon wore 98 in 1946.

Number with most points scored: 14 with

989 points scored by Jeff Wilkins (789), John Drake (134) and Wendell Tucker (66).

Number with most yards rushing: 30 with 8,242 yards gained by Lawrence McCutcheon (6,186), Barry Redden (1,490), Harold Green (527), Howard Griffith (30), and Ron Wolfey (9).

Number with most receptions: 80 with 1,737 passes caught by Isaac Bruce (688), Henry Ellard (593), Tom Fears (156), Bob Klein (128), Billy Waddy (120), Bucky Pope (34), and Bob Boyd (18).

Number with most touchdown passes: 11 with 284 touchdowns tossed by Jim Everett (142), Norm Van Brocklin (81), Pat Haden (52) and Mark Rypien (9).

Number with most interceptions: 21 with 112 interceptions by Eddie Meador (46), Nolan Cromwell (37), Dexter McCleon (20), and Gene Howard (9).

Oddity: Fullback Ernie Thompson wore 32 in 1991. He was replaced in that number by his brother Anthony, also a running back, in 1992. Both brothers only lasted a single season as Rams.

Players Whose Number Is Unknown

William O'Neill	(RB)	1937
Oliver Savatsky	(E)	1937
Edmund Skoronski	(C)	1937
Joe Williams	(B)	1937
Jack Boone	(B)	1942
Donald Johnson	(C)	1942
Darryl Hall	(CB)	1987r

Team All-Time Numerical Roster

Those with an "r" following the year 1987 were replacement players during the players' strike. Pro Bowl and pre–1950 All Pro players for each number are in *Italics*; Hall of Famers are in **Bold** type.

00 Steve Bagarus (RB) 1947.

1 Stanley Pincura (QB) 1937, Robert Snyder (RB) 1938, Thomas Hupke (G) 1939, Oliver Cordill (RB) 1940, Anthony Gallovich (B) 1941, Delbert Lyman (T) 1941, Rafael Septien (K) 1977, Mike Lansford (K) 1983–90.

2 Bud Cooper (RB) 1937, *John Drake* (RB) 1937, Mike Horan (P) 1997, 1999.

3 Wayne Gift (QB) 1937, Richard Davis (RB) 1939, 1941, Peter Gudauskas (G) 1940, William Rieth (C/G) 1944–5, Ben Agajanian (K) 1953, Frank Corral (K/P) 1978–81, Dale Hatcher (P) 1985–9, 1991, Rich Camarillo (P) 1988, Steve McLaughlin (K) 1995, Pete Stoyanovich (K) 2000.

4 Mike Sebastian (B) 1937, Robert Snyder (RB) 1937, Doug Russell (RB) 1939, Ralph Stevenson (G) 1940, George Morris (RB) 1941–2, Mike Lansford (K) 1982, Steve Fuller (QB) 1983, Dean Biasucci (K) 1995, John Baker (P) 2000-1, Scott Covington (QB) 2002.

5 Julius Alfonse (RB) 1937, Martin Slovak (RB) 1939–41, Dick Gordon (WR) 1972–3, Dieter Brock (QB) 1985, Sean Landeta (P) 1993–6, 2003, Jeff Hall (K) 2000.

6 Mark Barber (RB) 1937, John Benridge (B) 1937, Emmett Moan (RB) 1939, Michael Perrie (B) 1939, Connie Berry (B) 1940, John Nix (B) 1940, William Rieth (C/G) 1941–2, John Misko (P) 1982–4, Don Bracken (P) 1992–3, Carlos Huerta (K) 1996.

7 Edwin Goddard (RB) 1937, Harry Mattos (RB) 1937, Joel Hitt (E) 1939, Ken Heineman (B) 1940, **Bob Waterfield** (QB/K) 1945–52.

8 Carl Brumbaugh (QB) 1937, Louis Barle (OB) 1939, *Dante Magnani* (RB) 1940–2, Raymond Prochaska (E) 1941, Clyde Johnson (T) 1946–7, Jeff Rutledge (QB) 1979–81, Steve Dils (QB) 1984–7, Keith English (P) 1990, Tommy Maddox (QB) 1994, Chip Lohmiller (K) 1996, Joe Germaine (QB) 1999–2000.

9 Joe Keeble (RB) 1937, Gerald Dowd (C) 1939, *James Gillette* (RB) 1940, Michael Kinek (E) 1940, Francis Maher (B) 1941, Jerry Cowhig (RB) 1947–9, Paul Barry (RB) 1950–2, *Bill Wade* (QB) 1954–60, Ron Miller (QB) 1962, Rusty Jackson (P) 1976, Jeff Kemp (QB) 1981–5, Bernard Quarles (QB) 1987r, Mark Herrmann (QB) 1988–9, Barry Helton (P) 1991, Will Furrer (QB) 1997.

10 Bob Davis (RB) 1938, Gaylon Smith (RB) 1939–42, Stephen Nemeth (QB) 1945, Tom Keaner (DB) 1948–51, Don Klosterman (QB) 1952, Rudy Bukich (QB) 1953–6, Buddy Humphrey (QB) 1959–60, Billy Lothridge (P) 1965, Karl Sweetan (QB) 1969–70, Dave Chapple (P) 1972–4, Tom Dempsey (K) 1975–6, Dan Pastorini (QB) 1981, Steve Bartkowski (QB) 1986, Tony Zendejas (K) 1991–3, Jamie Martin (QB) 1996, Will Brice (P) 1997, *Kurt Warner* (QB) 1998, Trent Green (QB) 2000, *Marc Bulger* (QB) 2001–3.

11 Forest Underwood (T/G) 1937, Nelson Peterson (RB) 1938, Arthur Lewis (G) 1939, *Riley Matheson* (G/LB) 1939–40, 1944–7, *Stan West* (MG) 1950-1, **Norm Van Brocklin** (QB) 1952–7, Danny Villanueva (P/K) 1960–4, Mike Burke (P) 1974, *Pat Haden* (QB) 1976–81, *Jim Everett* (QB) 1986–93, Mark Rypien (QB) 1995, 1997, Rick Tuten (P) 1998–9.

12 Ray Johnson (HB) 1937–8, Victor Markov (T) 1938, John Wilson (B) 1939–42, Harvey Jones (RB) 1944–5, Les Horvath (RB) 1947–8, Zeke Bratkowski (QB) 1961–3, Pete Beathard (QB) 1972, *James Harris* (QB) 1973–6, **Joe Namath** (QB) 1977, Hugh Millen (QB) 1987, T.J. Rubley (QB) 1992–3, Chris Miller (QB) 1995, Tony Banks (QB) 1996–8, Jamie Martin (QB) 2001–2.

13 James Turner (C) 1937, Ted Livingston (T/G) 1938–40, *Riley Matheson* (G/LB) 1941–2, Ken Washington (RB/DB) 1946–8, *Paul Younger* (RB/LB) 1949–51, Jon Kilgore (P) 1965–7, Lance Rentzel (WR) 1971–2, Ken Clark (P) 1979, Chuck Nelson (K) 1983, Chris Miller (QB) 1995, Steve Bono (QB) 1998, *Kurt Warner* (QB) 1999–2003.

14 *John Drake* (RB) 1937–41, Ron Smith (QB) 1965, Wendell Tucker (WR) 1967–70, Mike Pagel (QB) 1991–3, *Jeff Wilkins* (K) 1997–2003.

15 Ralph Isselhardt (G) 1937, Stanley Pincura (QB) 1938, John Haman (C) 1940–1, Roger Harding (C) 1945–6, Frank Ryan (QB) 1958–61, Terry Baker (QB/RB) 1963–5, Vince Ferragamo (QB) 1977–80, 1982–4.

16 Paul Halleck (E) 1937, John Kovatch (E) 1938, Michael Kabealo (RB) 1944, Raymond Monaco (G) 1945, George Phillips (LB) 1945, Walter Zirinsky (RB) 1945, Bob Hoffman (RB) 1946–8, Milt Plum (QB) 1968, Ron Jaworski (OB) 1974–6, Chuck Long (QB) 1990, Paul McJulien (P) 1993, Dave Barr (QB) 1995, Donald Sellers (WR/QB) 1997–8, Paul Justin (QB) 1999.

17 Ted Rosequist (T) 1937, Gerald Conlee (C/G) 1938, *Charles Cherundolo* (C) 1937–9, Henry Rockwell (G/C) 1940–42, John Petchel (QB) 1944, Elvin Liles (G) 1945, George Sims (DB) 1949–50, Charlie Britt (DB) 1960–3, Dan McIlhany (DB) 1965, Richie Petitbon (DB) 1969–70, Jerry Rhome (QB) 1971, Duane Carrell (P) 1975, Bert Jones (QB) 1982, Chris Chandler (GB) 1994, Mitch Berger (P) 2002.

18 Ted Livingston (T/G) 1937, Carl Brazell (QB) 1938, Alexander Atty (G) 1939, *Fred Gehrke* (RB) 1940, 1945–9, Graham Armstrong (T) 1941, *Roman Gabriel* (QB) 1962–72, John Carney (K) 1990, Jimmy Raye Jr. (WR) 1991, Sean LaChapelle (WR) 1993, J.T. Thomas (WR) 1998.

19 Sam Busich (E) 1937, John Giannoni (E) 1938, Jack Robinson (T/G) 1938, Paul McDonough (E) 1939–41, Thomas Corbo (G) 1944, George Koch (RB) 1945, Bill Munson (QB) 1964–7, Jim Nettles (DB) 1969–72, Lance Rentzel (WR) 1974, Glen Walker (P) 1977, Bob Lee (QB) 1979–80, Billy Williams (WR) 1995–6.

20 Walter Uzdavinis (E) 1937, Richard Zoll (G) 1938, Moose Dunstan (T) 1939–41, Ralph Ruthstrom (RB) 1945–6, *Dick Huffman* (T) 1947–50, *Woodley Lewis* (DB/E) 1952–4, Hall Haynes (DB) 1955, Steve Heckard (E) 1965–6, Tommy Mason (RB) 1967–70, Steve Preece (S) 1973–6,

Jackie Wallace (DB) 1977–9, Johnnie Johnson (S) 1980–9, Darryl Henley (CB) 1989–94, Johnny Bailey (RB) 1995, Keith Crawford (DB/WR) 1996–7, Taje Allen (CB) 1997–2000, Kim Herring (S) 2001–2.

21 *Charles Cherundolo* (C) 1937–8, Bronco Smilanich (B) 1939, Gordon Wilson (T) 1941, Boyd Clay (T) 1942, Walter West (RB) 1944, James Warden (RB) 1945, Jim Hardy (QB) 1946–8, Art Statuto (C) 1950, Tom Dahms (T) 1951, *Skeets Quinlan* (RB) 1952–6, Alex Bravo (DB) 1957–8, *Ed Meador* (DB) 1959–70, Gene Howard (DB) 1971–2, *John Hadl* (QB) 1973–4, Tony Plummer (DB) 1974, *Nolan Cromwell* (S) 1977–87, Curt Warner (RB) 1990, Rodney Thomas (CB) 1991, Troy Stradford (RB) 1992, Deral Boykin (S) 1993, Johnny Bailey (RB) 1994, John Reece (CB) 1995, Lawrence Phillips (RB) 1996–7, Dexter McCleon (CB) 1998–2002, Kevin Garrett (CB) 2003.

22 Philip Bucklew (E) 1937–8, Thomas Hupke (G) 1938, William McRaven (FB) 1939, Kirk Hershey (E) 1941, David Bernard (B) 1942, 1944–5, *Fred Naumetz* (LB/C) 1946-1950, Jerry Williams (DB) 1951–2, Hall Haynes (DB) 1954, Ray Shiver (OB) 1956, *Dick Bass* (RB) 1960–9, Steve Heckard (E) 1965, Elijah Pitts (RB) 1970, John Cappelletti (RB) 1974–8, Lydell Mitchell (RB) 1980, Jairo Penaranda (RB) 1981, Vince Newsome (S) 1983–90, Marcus Dupree (RB) 1990-1, Emile Harry (WR) 1992, **James Lofton** (WR) 1993, Sam Seale (CB) 1993, Marquez Pope (S) 1994, Mike Scurlock (CB) 1995–6, Billy Jenkins Jr. (S) 1997–99, Jacoby Shepherd (DB) 2000-1, Travis Fisher (CB) 2002–3.

23 Robert Emerick (O/L) 1937, Arthur Lewis (G) 1938, Michael Rodak (RB/E) 1939–40, Jack Gregory (G) 1941, Louis Zontini (B) 1944, John Martin (C) 1947–9, Tom McCormick (RB) 1953–5, Jesse Castete (DB) 1956–7, Bobby Smith (DB) 1962–5, Mac Byrd (LB) 1965, Alvin Haymond (DB) 1969–71, Anthony Davis (RB) 1978, Ricky Odom (DB) 1979, Lucious Smith (CE) 1980–2, Henry Williams (DB) 1983, Michael Stewart (S) 1987–93, Clifford Hicks (CB) 1987, Gerald McBurrows (S) 1995–8, Devin Bush (S) 1999–2000, Jerametrius Butler (DB) 2002–3.

24 Forrest Burmeister (T-G) 1937–8, Jack May (C) 1938, *William Lazetich* (RB) 1939, 1942, James Goolsby (C) 1940, *Dante Magnani* (RB) 1941, 1947–8, *James Gillette* (RB) 1944–5, Tommy Kalmanir (RB) 1949–51, *Tom Wilson* (RB) 1958–61, Clarence Williams (DE) 1965–72, Willie McGee (WR) 1974–5, Eddie Hill (RB) 1979–80, A.J. Jones (RB) 1982–5, Buford McGee (RB) 1987–91, Wymon Henderson (CB) 1993–4, Dexter McCleon (CB) 1997, Ron Carpenter (S) 1998–9, Trung Canidate (RB) 2000–2, DeJuan Groce (CB) 2003.

25 Ookie Miller (C) 1937, John Stephens (E) 1938, Lewis Bostic (G) 1939, Glenn Olson (B) 1940, Charles Seabright (OB) 1941, Albert Gutknecht (G) 1944, Joseph Winkler (C) 1945, Joe Corn (RB) 1948, **Norm Van Brocklin** (QB) 1949–51, Don Burroughs (DB) 1955–9, Duane Allen (E) 1961–4, Tom Moore (RB) 1966, *Bernie Casey* (WR) 1967–8, Travis Williams (RB) 1971, Eddie Brown (S) 1978–9, Gordon Jones (WR) 1983, *Jerry Gray* (CB) 1985–91, Chris Crooms (S) 1992, Tyrone Montgomery (RB) 1995, Robert Holcombe (RB) 1998–2001, Rich Coady (S) 2003.

26 Richard Zoll (G) 1937, *Jim Benton* (E) 1938–40, Wilfred Thorpe (G) 1941–2, Albie Reisz (QB) 1944–6, John Ksionyak (QB) 1947, Bill Lange (G) 1951, Jon Arnett (RB) 1957–63, Willie Brown (E/RB) 1964–5, Jim Stiger (RB) 1966–7, Wendell Tyler (RB) 1977–82, Eric Harris (DB) 1983–5, Anthony Newman (S) 1988–94, June Henley (RB) 1998, Joffrey Reynolds (CB) 2003.

27 Ralph Miller (T) 1937, Raymond Hamilton (E) 1938, Rudolph Mucha (G) 1941–5, Milan Lazetich (G) 1945–50, Marvin Johnson (DB) 1951–2, *Ron Waller* (RB) 1955–8, Pervis Atkins (RB) 1961–3, Irv Cross (DB) 1966–8, David Ray (K/WR) 1969–74, *Pat Thomas* (CB) 1976–82, *Gary Green* (CB) 1984–5, Sammy Lilly (CB) 1991–2, Mitchell Price (CB) 1993, Anthony Parker (CB) 1995–6, Greg Hill (RB) 1998, Matt Bowen (S) 2000, James Whitley (S) 2002–3.

28 Edwin Goddard (RB) 1938, Ham Murphy (E) 1940, Michael Kostiuk (T) 1941, Brad Myers (RB) 1953–6, Pat Studstill (WR/P) 1968–71, *Monte Jackson* (CB) 1975–7, Ken Ellis (CB) 1979, Mike Williams (DB) 1983, David Croudip (CB) 1984, Clifford Hicks (CB) 1987–90, Robert Bailey (CB) 1991–4, Greg Robinson (RB) 1995–6, David Thompson (RB) 1997–8, *Marshall Faulk* (RB) 1999–2003.

29 Julius Alfonse (RB) 1938, Jack Dwyer (DB) 1952–4, *Del Shofner* (E) 1957–60, **Tommy McDonald** (WR) 1965–6, *Harold Jackson* (WR) 1968, 1973–7, Sid Justin (CB) 1979, **Eric Dickerson** (RB) 1983–7, Dexter Davis (CB) 1993–5.

30 Dale Prather (E) 1938, Barney McGarry (G) 1939–42, *Stephen Pritko* (DE) 1944–7, Bob Agler (RB) 1948–9, *Woodley Lewis* (DB/E) 1950-1, 1955, Bill Bowers (DB) 1954, Bruce Gossett (K) 1964–9, *Lawrence McCutcheon* (RB) 1972–9, Berry Redden (RB) 1982–6, Owen Gill (RB) 1987, Mosi Tatupu (FB) 1991, Howard Griffith (RB) 1993–4, Ron Wolfley (RB) 1995, Harold Green (RB) 1996, Shevin Smith (DB) 2000, Willie Gary (DB) 2001.

31 Charles Hanneman (E) 1941, Charles Riffle (G) 1944, Art Mergenthal (G) 1945–6, *Dick Hoerner* (RB) 1947–51, Jack Myers (RB/DB) 1952, Larry Morris (LB) 1955–6, Carl Karilivacz (DB) 1959–60, Larry Hayes (C) 1962–3, Jeff Jordan (RB) 1970, Lynn Cain (RB) 1985, Alonzo Williams (RB) 1987r, Alfred Jackson (CB) 1989–90, Steve Israel (CB) 1992–4, Brent Moss (RB) 1995, Marcus Holliday (RB) 1996, Amp Lee (RB) 1997–9, Adam Archuleta (S) 2001–3.

32 Richard Davis (RB) 1938, *Parker Hall* (FB) 1939–42, Graham Armstrong (T) 1945, Bob Shaw (E) 1945–6, 1949, *Dan Towler* (RB) 1950–5, *Jack Pardee* (LB) 1957–70, Cullen Bryant (RB) 1973–82, 1987r, Tim Tyrrell (RB) 1986–8, Ernie Thompson (FB) 1991, Anthony Thompson (RB) 1992, Toby Wright (S) 1994–8, Dre Bly (CB) 1999–2002, Fred Weary (CB) 2003.

33 Victor Spadaccini (QB) 1938–40, Milton Simington (T) 1941, Jack Banta (RB) 1946–8, Jerry Williams (DB) 1949–50, **Ollie Matson** (RB) 1959–62, *Willie Ellison* (RB) 1967–72, Rob Scribner (RB) 1973–6, Dwayne O'Steen (CB) 1978–9, Jewerl Thomas (RB) 1980–2, *Charles White* (RB) 1985–8, James Bostic (RB) 1994, Derrick Harris (RB) 1997–8, Justin Watson (RB) 1999–2001, Arlen Harris (RB) 2003.

34 Carl Littlefield (RB) 1938, *Chester Adams* (T) 1939–42, Thomas Colella (RB) 1944–5, Mel Bleaker (RB) 1947, Don Currivan (DE) 1948–9, Dave Stephenson (G) 1950, Joe Marconi (RB) 1956–61, Glenn Shaw (RB) 1962, *Les Josephson* (RB) 1964–7, 1969–74, Elvis Peacock (RB) 1979–80, Donald Evans (FB) 1987, Mel Farr Jr. (RB) 1989, Tim Lester (RB) 1992–4, Derrick Harris (RB) 1996, Craig Heyward (RB) 1997, Chad Dukes (RB) 2000, Lamar Gordon (RB) 2002–3.

35 Red Cheubro (G) 1938, Benjamin Friend (T) 1939, John Karrs (QB) 1944, Vic Vasicek (LB) 1950, Joe Reid (LB) 1951, *Paul Younger* (RB/LB) 1952–7, Clendon Thomas (RB) 1961, Henry Dyer (RB) 1966–8, Bob Thomas (RB) 1971–2, Tony Baker (RB) 1973–4, Jon Francis (RB) 1987, Keith Lyle (S) 1994–2000, *Aeneas Williams* (CB) 2001–3.

36 Phil Ragazzo (G) 1938–40, Frederick Shirey (T) 1940-1, Joe Gibson (E) 1944, Pat West (RB) 1945–8, Ralph Pasquariello (RB) 1950, Jack Halliday (DT) 1951, Paige Cothren (K) 1957–8, Frank Williams (RB) 1961, Ben Wilson (RB) 1963–5, Ken Geddes (B) 1971–5, Jerry Latin (RB) 1978, Kirby Jackson (CB) 1987, *Jerome Bettis* (RB) 1993–5.

37 William Krause (G) 1938, Richard Tuckey (RB) 1938, Red Conkright (G) 1939–42, 1944, *Tom Wilson* (RB) 1956–7, Jimmy Jones (RB) 1958, Art Perkins (RB) 1962–3, Vilnis Ezerins (RB) 1968, Bill Drake (DB) 1973–4, Ivory Sully (DE) 1979–84, Reggie Richardson (S) 1987r, James Washington (S) 1988–9, Pat Terrell (S) 1990–3, Mike Scurlock (CB) 1997–8, Jerametrius Butler (DB) 2001, Chad Cota (S) 2002.

38 Ralph Miller (T) 1938, Nathan Schenker (T) 1939, Len Janiak (FB) 1940–2, Floyd Konetsky (E) 1944–5, *Jim Winkler* (DT) 1951, Fred Bruney (DB) 1958, Larry Smith (RB) 1969–73, Rob Carpenter (RB) 1986, David Lang (RB) 1991–4, Marquis Walker (CB) 1996–7, Rich Coady (DB) 1999–2001, Shane Walton (S) 2003.

39 Charles Ream (T) 1938, Stanley Andersen

(T) 1940-1, *Michael Scarry* (C) 1944–5, Woody Strode (E) 1946, Israel Lang (RB) 1969, Kermit Alexander (DB) 1970-1, Rod Phillips (RB) 1975–8, Robert Alexander (RB) 1982–3, Robert Delpino (FB) 1988–92, Jeremy Lincoln (CB) 1996.

40 Earl Crowder (QB) 1940, Chester Pudloski (T) 1944, *Eberle Schultz* (T) 1945–7, **Elroy Hirsch** (E/RB) 1949–57, Jack Morris (DB) 1958–60.

41 Leslie Lear (G) 1944–6, *Glenn Davis* (RB) 1950-1, Jim Cason (DB) 1955–6, Lindon Crow (DB) 1961–4, Eddie McMillan (CB) 1973–5, Jeff Delaney (S) 1980, Mario Celotto (LB) 1981, Frank Wattelet (S) 1987–8, Ed Zemen (S) 1987r, *Todd Lyght* (CB) 1991–2000, Nick Sorensen (DB) 2002.

42 Jake Fawcett (T) 1944, 1946, *Gilbert Bouley* (T) 1945, Jack Zilly (TE/DE) 1947, Joe Repko (DT) 1948–9, Herb Rich (DE) 1951–3, Aaron Martin (DB) 1964–5, Ron Smith (DE) 1968–9, Dave Elmendorf (DB) 1971–79, Kirk Collins (CB) 1982–3, Greg Ball (RB) 1987–9, Chris Pacheco (NT) 1987r, Casey Tiumalu (RB) 1987r, Latin Berry (CB) 1990, Courtney Griffin (CB) 1992–3, Leonard Russell (RB) 1995, Herman O'Berry (CB) 1996, Joe Rowe (CE) 1997, James Hodgins (FB) 1999–2002, Jason Sehorn (S) 2003.

43 Boyd Clay (T) 1940–2, Jack Jacobs (QB) 1942, 1945, *Roger Eason* (G/T) 1945–8, *Will Sherman* (DB) 1954–60, Ross Coyle (DB) 1961, Jerry Richardson (DB) 1964–5, Mike Dennis (RB) 1968–9, Jim Jodat (RB) 1977–9, Mike Pleasant (CB) 1984, Greg Williamson (CB) 1987r, Cleveland Gary (RB) 1989–93.

44 Raymond Hamilton (E) 1944–7, Alan Sparkman (DT) 1948–9, Harry Thompson (G) 1950-1, Jesse Whittenton (DB) 1956–7, Jim Harris (DB) 1958, Don Ellersick (DR) 1960, Nat Whitmyer (DB) 1963, Chuck Lamson (DB) 1965–7, Nate Shaw (DB) 1969–70, Lee White (RB) 1971, Al Clark (CB) 1972–5, Larry Marshall (WR) 1978, Mike Guman (RB) 1980–8, Gaston Green (RB) 1988–90, Russell White (RB) 1993, Jerald Moore (RB) 1996–8, Chris Hetherington (FB) 2002, Joey Goodspeed (FB) 2003.

45 Roy Stuart (G) 1942, Delbert Lyman (T) 1944, Mike Holovak (RB) 1946, John Griffin (DB) 1963, Frank Budka (DB) 1964, George Youngblood (DB) 1966, *Jim Bertelsen* (RB) 1972–6, Jeff Severson (DB) 1979, Dwayne Crutchfield (RB) 1984, Darren Long (TE) 1986, Ernie Conwell (TE) 1996, Aaron Laing (TE) 1998, Jeff Robinson (TE) 2000-1, Chris Massey (C) 2002–3.

46 Herbert Godfrey (E) 1942, Tom Farmer (RB) 1946, Steve Sucic (RB) 1946, Frank Hubbell (DE/TE) 1947–9, Bob Holladay (RB) 1956, Clendon Thomas (DB) 1958–60, Alvin Hall (DB) 1961–3, Andy Von Sonn (LB) 1964, Hank Gremminger (DB) 1966, Wlllie Daniel (DB) 1967–9, Roger Williams (DB) 1971–2, John Kamana (RB) 1984, Herman Edwards (CB) 1986, Holbert Johnson (CB) 1987r, Torin Dorn (CB) 1995–6, Mitch Jacoby (TE) 1997.

47 Vernon Valdez (DB) 1960, Carver Shannon (DB/RB) 1962–4, Kelton Winston (DB) 1967–8, Charlie Stukes (CB) 1973–4, *LeRoy Irvin* (CB) 1980–9, Tony Hargain (WR) 1993, Marv Cook (TE) 1995, Ryan McNeil (CB) 1997–8, Spencer Nead (TE) 2003.

48 Rudolph Sikich (T) 1945, Bob Heckar (DB) 1952, Don Doll (DB) 1954, Cecil Taylor (RB) 1955–7, *Les Richter* (LB) 1961–2, Jim Stiger (RB) 1965, Matt Maslowski (WR) 1971, Bill Simpson (DB) 1974–8, Tim Fox (S) 1985–6, Craig Rutledge (S) 1987r, Bobby Humphrey (CB) 1990, Rickey Brady (TE) 1994, Richard Angulo (TE) 2003.

49 *Jim Benton* (E) 1942, 1944–7, Cart Mayes (RB) 1952, Ed Hughes (DB) 1954–5, Floyd Iglehart (DB) 1958, Claude Crabb (DB) 1966–8, John Love (WR) 1972, *Rod Perry* (CB) 1975–82, Mickey Sutton (CB) 1986–8, 1990, Chad Lewis (TE) 1998–9.

50 John Petchel (QB) 1942, Jack Wilson (RB) 1946–7, Bob DeFruiter (NT) 1948, Paul Richards (QB) 1948, *Leon McLaughlin* (C) 1951–5, *Dick Daugherty* (LB) 1956–8, Larry Stephens (DT) 1962, Ken Iman (C) 1965–74, Kevin McLain (LB) 1976–9, *Jim Collins* (LB) 1982–8, Frank Seams (LB) 1989–91, Scott Stephen (LB) 1992, Dana Howard (LB) 1995, Ryan Tucker (C/G) 1997–2001, Pisa Tinoisamoa (LB) 2003.

51 John Morrow (C) 1956, 1958–9, Bob Dougherty (LB) 1957, Lou Cordileone (LB) 1962, Ken Kirk (C) 1963, George Burman (C/G) 1967–70, Rick Nuzum (C) 1977, Joe Harris (LB) 1979–81, David Lewis (LB) 1983, Norwood Van (LB) 1984–7, Chris Matau (G) 1987r, Brett Faryniarz (LB) 1988–91, Blair Bush (C) 1992–4, Carlos Jenkins (LB) 1995–6, Lorenzo Styles (LB) 1997–2000, Brian Allen (LB) 2001, Courtland Bullard (LB) 2002–3.

52 Bill Swain (LB) 1963, John Pergine (LB) 1969–72, Rick Kay (LB) 1973, 1975–7, George Andrews (LB) 1979–85, Steve Busick (LB) 1986, Cliff Thrift (LB/E) 1986, Sam Anno (LB) 1987, Larry Kelm (LB) 1987–92, Kyle Whittingham (LB) 1987r, Joe Kelly (LB) 1994, Mike A. Jones (LB) 1997–2000, Tommy Polley (LB) 2001–3.

53 Red Hickey (E) 1941, 1945–8, Ben Hightower (E) 1942, Roy Huggins (FB) 1944, Mike Henry (LB) 1962–4, Gene Breen (LB) 1967–8, Jim Purcell (LB) 1969–72, *Jim Youngblood* (LB) 1973–84, Rick DiBernardo (LB) 1987r, Fred Strickland (LB) 1988–92, Chris Martin (LB) 1993–4, Cedric Figaro (LB) 1995–6, Nate Dingle (LB) 1997, Brett Wallerstedt (LB) 1997, Jon Hesse (LB) 1998, Mike Morton (LB) 1999, Keith Miller (LB) 2000, Hakim Akbar (LB) 2002, Justin Smith (LB) 2003.

54 Ray Yagiello (G) 1948–9, Bob Reinhard (T/DT) 1950, *Dick Daugherty* (LB) 1954–5, Joe

Wendryhoski (C) 1964-6, *Jack Reynolds* (LB) 1970-1, Geoff Reece (C) 1976, Bob Pifferini (LB) 1977, Dan Ryczek (C) 1978-9, Ed McGlasson (C) 1980, Howard Carson (LB) 1981-3, Brett Collins (LB) 1993, Percell Gaskins (LB) 1996, Tray Dumas (LB) 1997, Eric Hill (LB) 1998, Todd Collins (LB) 1999-2000, Kole Ayi (LB) 2002, Scott Shanle (LB) 2003.

55 Arthur Elston (LB) 1942, Robert Delauer (C) 1945-6, **Tom Fears** (E) 1948-51, Lou Michaels (DE) 1958-60, Fred Whittingham (LB) 1964, *Maxie Baughan* (LB) 1966-70, Bill Curry (C) 1974, Bob DeMarco (C) 1975, *Carl Ekern* (LB) 1976-88, Glenell Sanders (LB) 1991, Lean White (LB) 1992-3, Paschall Davis (LB) 1995-6, Robert Jones (LB) 1996-7, Phillip Ward (LB) 1998, Mark Fields (LB) 2001, Robert Thomas (LB) 2002-3.

56 Bosh Pritchard (RB) 1942, Jack Zilly (TE/DE) 1947, Bruce Smith (RB) 1948, Hugh Pitts (LB) 1956, Larry Morris (LB) 1957, Art Hunter (C) 1960-4, Frank Marchlewskl (C) 1965, 1968-9, Dean Halverson (LB) 1968, 1972, *Doug Smith* (C) 1978-91, Shane Conlan (LB) 1993-5, Mark Williams (LB) 1996, Charlie Clemons (LB) 1997-9, Jeremy Loyd (LB) 2003.

57 Jake Fawcett (T) 1942, *Don Paul* (LB) 1948-55, Bobby Cross (T) 1955, Bill Jobko (LB) 1958-62, Doug Woodlief (LB) 1965-9, Don Parish (LB) 1971, Jim Peterson (LB) 1974-5, Mel Rogers (LB) 1976, Greg Westbrooks (LB) 1979-80, Mike Reilly (LB) 1982, Jim Laughlin (LB) 1985-6, Cary Whittingham (LB) 1987r, Thomas Homco (LB) 1993-6, Britt Hager (LB) 1997, *Leonard Little* (LB) 1998-2000, O.J. Brigance (LB) 2001-2.

58 Warren Plunkett (QB) 1942, Bob Griffin (C) 1953-7, Dan Currie (LB) 1965-6, *Isiah Robertson* (LB) 1971-8, Mel Owens (LB) 1981-9, Roman Phifer (LB) 1991-8, Don Davis (LB) 2001-2.

59 Lawrence Brahm (G) 1942, Bob Brudzinski (LB) 1977-80, George Lilja (C) 1982, Mark Jerue (LB) 1983-9, Paul Butcher (LB) 1990-2, Henry Rolling (LB) 1993-4, Ashley Sheppard (LB) 1995, Muadianvita Kazadi (LB) 1997, London Fletcher (LB) 1998-2001, Jamie Duncan (LB) 2002-3.

60 Jack Elena (G) 1955-6, John Guzik (LB) 1959, Jerry Stalcup (LB) 1960, Marv Harris (LB) 1964, John Wilbur (G) 1970, *Dennis Harrah* (G) 1975-87, Mark Messner (LB) 1989, Fred Stokes (DE) 1993-5, Mike Gruttadauria (C) 1996-9, Steve Everitt (C) 2000, Rod Jones (OL) 2001.

61 *Duane Putnam* (G) 1952-9, 1962, Bruce Tarbox (G) 1961, Mike Strofolino (LB) 1965, **Bill George** (LB) 1966, *Rich Saul* (C) 1970-81, Tony Slaton (C) 1984-9, Bern Brostek (C) 1990-7, Tom Nutten (C/G) 1998-2002, David Loverne (G) 2003.

62 *Bud McFadin* (DT/T) 1952-6, John Houser (C/G) 1957-9, Willie Hector (T) 1961, Don Chuy (G) 1963-8, Jeff Williams (T) 1977, Bill Bain (G) 1979-85, Tom Taylor (G) 1987r, Vernice Smith (G) 1997, Adam Timmerman (G) 1999-2003.

63 Joe Gibson (E) 1942, *Larry Brink* (DE) 1948-52, John Hock (C) 1953, 1955-7, Buck Lansford (G) 1958-60, *Joe Carollo* (T) 1962-8, Greg Horton (G) 1976-8, 1980, Conrad Rucker (G/T) 1980, Mike McDonald (LB) 1983-4, 1986-91, Hank Goebel (T) 1987r, John Flannery (C) 1998, Heath Irwin (G) 2002.

64 *Stan West* (G) 1952-4, Roy Hord (C) 1960-2, Tim Powell (DE) 1965, Mike LaHood (G) 1969, 1971, *Jack Reynolds* (LB) 1972-80, Joe Shearin (G) 1983-4, Greg Sinnott (T) 1987r, Gerald Perry (T) 1991-2, Keith Loneker (G) 1993-5, Joe Valerie (G) 1996, Frank Garcia (G) 2001-2, Dave Wohlabaugh (C) 2003.

65 Joe Pasqua (T) 1942, 1946, Norman Olsen (T) 1944, Robert Delauer (C) 1945, Jim Mello (RB) 1948, Bob Thomason (QB) 1949, Don Simensen (T) 1951, Bill Lange (G) 1952, Harland Svare (LB) 1953, Art Hauser (DT) 1954-7, John Guzik (LB) 1960, **Tom Mack** (G) 1966-78, Richard Bishop (NT) 1983, Fred Stokes (DE) 1987-8, Jon Kirksey (G/DT) 1995-6, Ernest Dye (C) 1997, Andy King (G) 2003.

66 *Donald Greenwood* (RB) 1945, *Gilbert Bouley* (T) 1946-50, Harry Thompson (G) 1952-4, Harley Sewell (G) 1963, Myron Pottlos (LB) 1966-70, Bob Stein (LB) 1973-4, Bill Dunstan (DT) 1979, Eric Williams (LB) 1982-3, Booker Reece (DE) 1984-5, Tom Newberry (G) 1986-94, Corey Swinson (OL) 1995, John Gerak (G) 1997, Joe Phillips (DT) 1998, Brian Young (DT) 2000-3.

67 Manual Rapp (B) 1942, *Dick Daugherty* (LB) 1951-3, *Les Richter* (LB) 1954-60, Charlie Janerette (G) 1960, Urban Henry (DT) 1961, Roger Davis (G) 1964, Ted Karras (G) 1966, Bill Nelson (DT) 1971-5, Myron Lapka (DT) 1982-3, Duval Love (G) 1985-91, Dave Purling (DE) 1987r, Ronald Edwards (C) 1994, Dwayne White (G) 1995-6, Mike Verstegen (G) 1998, Andy McCollum (C/G) 1999-2003.

68 Jack Finlay (G) 1947-51, Sid Fournet (DT) 1955-6, Mike LaHood (G) 1971-2, Ed Fulton (G) 1978, Dennis Harrison (DE) 1985, Navy Tuiasosopo (C) 1987r, George Bethune (LB) 1989-90, Jim Skow (DB) 1992, Brad Fichtel (G) 1994, Jeremy McKinney (T) 1998, Pete Swanson (G) 2000, Kyle Turley (T) 2003.

69 Greg Meisner (DE) 1981-8, Jeff Pahukoa (G) 1991-3, Jesse James (C) 1995-6, Andy King (G) 2002.

70 George Platukas (E) 1942, Charlie Toogood (T) 1951-6, Gene Selawski (T) 1959, *Frank Varrichione* (T) 1961-5, Dave Cahill (OT) 1967, Mitch Johnson (T) 1969-70, *Joe Carollo* (T) 1971, Al Cowlings (DE) 1975, 1977, Jerry Wilkinson (DE) 1979, Charles DeJurnett (DT) 1982-6, Bill Hawkins (DT) 1989-92, Frank Boadreaux (DE) 1993,

Wayne Gandy (T) 1994–8, John St. Clair (T) 2001–3.

71 Tom Dahms (T) 1952–4, Frank Fuller (DT) 1955–8, Paul Dickson (T) 1959, *Joe Scibelli* (G) 1961–75, Reggie Doss (DE) 1978–87, Joe Milinichik (G) 1990–2, Chuck Belim (G) 1994–6, Fred Miller (T) 1996–9, Kaulana Noa (T) 2000–1.

72 Bob Collier (T) 1951, John Kenerson (T) 1960, Roger Pillath (T) 1965, Earl Leggett (DT) 1966, Diron Talbert (DT) 1967–70, Phil Olsen (DT/DE) 1971–4, *Kent Hill* (C) 1979–86, Robert Jenkins (T) 1987–93, Tom Cox (C) 1987r, Kevin Robbins (T) 1993, Clarence Jones (T) 1994–5, Andrew Kline (T) 2000, Chidi Ahanotu (DE) 2001.

73 Bobby Cross (T) 1954–5, Ken Panfil (T) 1956–8, *Charlie Cowan* (T) 1961–75, Winston Hill (T) 1977, Gordon Gravelle (T) 1979, Phil McKinnely (T) 1981, **Ron Yary** (T) 1982, Russ Bolinger (G) 1983–5, Kelly Thomas (T) 1987r, Zach Wiegert (G) 1995–8, Cameron Spikes (G) 1999–2001, Jimmy Kennedy (DT) 2003.

74 Len Teeuws (T) 1952–3, John Baker (DT) 1958–61, **Merlin Olsen** (DT) 1962–76.

75 Bob Fry (T) 1953–9, **David Jones** (DE) 1961–71, John Williams (T) 1972–9, Irv Pankey (T) 1980–90, Tom Gibson (DE) 1991, Irv Eatmen (T) 1993, Darryl Ashmore (T) 1994, D'Marco Farr (DT) 1994–2000.

76 Leonard Levy (T) 1945–6, Don Simensen (T) 1952, Harland Svare (LB) 1954, John LoVetere (DT) 1959–62, Roosevelt Grier (DT) 1963–6, **Bob Brown** (T) 1969–70, Harry Schuh (T) 1971–2, *Cody Jones* (DT) 1974–8, 1980–2, Gary Kowalski (T) 1983, Mike Schad (G/T) 1987–8, Joe Murray (G) 1987r, Robert Young (DE) 1991–5, *Orlando Pace* (T) 1997–2003.

77 Bob David (G) 1947–8, Vitamin Smith (RB) 1949–53, George Strugar (DT) 1957–61, Jim Wilson (T) 1968, Rich Buzin (T) 1971, *Doug France* (T) 1975–81, Gary Jeter (DE) 1983–8, Jeff Mickel (T) 1990, Karl Wilson (DE) 1991, Darryl Ashmore (T) 1993–6, Billy Milner (T) 1996, Ethan Brooks (T) 1997–8, Sean Moran (DT) 2000–1, Grant Williams (T) 2002–3.

78 *Jim Winkler* (DT) 1952, Gene Lipscomb (DT) 1954–5, Ray Wilkins (LB) 1958–9, Jim Boeke (T) 1960–3, Frank Molden (DT) 1965, *Roger Brown* (OT) 1967, 1969, Clark Miller (DE) 1970, Greg Wojcik (DT) 1971, Tim Stokes (T) 1974, **Jackie Slater** (T) 1976–95.

79 Bill Smyth (T/TE) 1947–50, Ken Casner (T) 1952, Frank Fuller (DT) 1953, Glenn Holtzman (T) 1955–7, Charlie Bradshaw (T) 1958–60, Stan Fanning (DE) 1963, Bruce Anderson (DE) 1966, *Coy Bacon* (OT) 1968–72, Harry Schuh (T) 1973, Mike Fanning (DT) 1975–82, Wally Kersten (T) 1982, Marion Knight (DE) 1987r, Kurt Becker (G) 1989, Mike Charles (DT) 1991, Leo Goeas (G)

1993–6, Bill Johnson (DT) 1997, Ryan Pickett (DT) 2001–3.

80 *Bob Boyd* (E) 1950–1, **Tom Fears** (E) 1952–6, Neil Ferris (DB) 1953, Billy Ray Smith (DE) 1957, Gene Brito (DE) 1959–60, Bucky Pope (WR) 1964, 1966–7, Bob Klein (TE) 1969–76, Billy Waddy (WR) 1977–81, *Henry Ellard* (WR) 1983–93, *Isaac Bruce* (WR) 1994–2003.

81 **Night Train Lane** (DB) 1952–3, *Paul Miller* (DE) 1954–7, Tom Franckhauser (DB) 1959, Carroll Dale (E) 1960–4, Fred Brown (LB) 1965, Gregg Schumacher (DE) 1967–8, *Ron Jessie* (WR) 1975–9, Victor Hicks (TE) 1980, Ron Battle (TE) 1981–2, David Hill (TE) 1983–7, Stacey Mobley (WR) 1987, Pete Holohan (TE) 1988–90, Ron Brown (WR) 1991, Hayward Clay (TE) 1996, Az-Zahir Hakim (WR) 1998–2001, *Tory Holt* (WR) 2002–3.

82 *Bob Boyd* (E) 1952–7, *Jim Phillips* (E) 1958–64, Dick Evey (DT) 1970, Joe Sweet (WR) 1972–3, Willie Miller (WR) 1978–82, Otis Grant (WR) 1983–4, Bobby Duckworth (WR) 1985–6, Bernard Henry (WR) 1987r, Eric Severs (TE) 1988, Tony Lomack (WR) 1990, Vernon Turner (WR) 1991–2, Jermaine Ross (WR) 1994–7, Malcolm Floyd (WR) 1997, Tony Horne (WR) 1998–2000, Aveion Cason (WR) 2001, Terrence Wilkins (WR) 2002, Mike Furrey (WR) 2003.

83 *Larry Brink* (DE) 1953, Duane Wardlow (DE) 1956, Tom Braatz (E) 1958, Elbert Kimbrough (DB) 1961, Gary Larsen (DT) 1964, Dave Pivec (TE) 1966–8, Charles Williams (WR) 1970, Terry Nelson (TE) 1973–80, Henry Childs (TE) 1981, Kerry Locklin (TE) 1982, James McDonald (TE) 1983–5, 1987, Mark Pattison (WR) 1986, Kevin House (WR) 1986–7, Willie Anderson (WR) 1988–94, Lovell Pinkney (TE) 1995, Donnell Baker (WR) 1996, Torrance Small (WR) 1997, Darius Blevins (WR) 2000, Yo Murphy (WR) 2001–2, Kevin Curtis (WR) 2003.

84 Hal Dean (G) 1947–9, **Andy Robustelli** (DE) 1951–5, *Leon Clarke* (E) 1956–9, Bob Long (LB) 1960–1, *Jack Snow* (WR) 1965–75, Ron Smith (WR) 1978–9, Walt Arnold (TE) 1980–1, George Farmer (WR) 1982–4, Chuck Scott (WR) 1986, Greg Baty (TE) 1987, Malcolm Moore (TE) 1987r, Aaron Cox (WR) 1988–92, Troy Drayton (TE) 1993–6, Ernie Conwell (TE) 1997–2002, Shaun McDonald (WR) 2003.

85 Gene Lipscomb (DT) 1953, *Lamar Lundy* (DE) 1957–69, **Jack Youngblood** (DE) 1971–84.

86 Ed Champagne (T) 1947–50, Jack Bighead (B) 1955, *Marlin McKeever* (LB/TE) 1961–6, 1971–2, Bob Long (WR) 1970, Rod Sherman (WR) 1973, Charlie Young (TE) 1977–9, Jeff Moore (WR) 1980–1, Mike Barber (TE) 1983–5, Damone Johnson (TE) 1986–92, Don Noble (TE) 1987r, Ernie Jones (WR) 1993, Jessie Hester (WR) 1994–5, Aaron Laing (TE) 1996–7, Roland Williams (TE)

1998–2000, Brandon Manumaleuna (TE) 2001–3, Troy Edwards (WR) 2002.

87 John Adams (TE) 1963, Billy Truax (TE) 1964–70, Dwight Scales (WR) 1976–8, Drew Hill (WR) 1979–84, Tony Hunter (TE) 1985–6, Jon Embree (TE) 1987–8, Joe Rose (TE) 1987r, Richard Ashe (TB) 1990, Jim Price (TE) 1991–2, 1995, Ron Middleton (TE) 1994, J.T. Thomas (WR) 1995–7, Ricky Proehl (WR) 1998–2002, Cam Cleeland (TE) 2003.

88 Norb Hecker (DB) 1951–53, Bob Carey (E) 1954, 1956, Sam Williams (DE) 1959, Karl Finch (E) 1962, Anthony Guillory (LB) 1965, 1967–8, Preston Dennard (WR) 1978–83, Chris Faulkner (TE) 1984, Michael Young (WR) 1985–8, Phil Smith (WR) 1987r, Pat Carter (TE) 1989–93, 1995, Sean LaChapelle (WR) 1993, Chris Brantley (WR) 1994, Eddie Kennison (WR) 1996–8, *Tory Holt* (WR) 1999–2001.

89 Bob Carey (E) 1952, Duane Wardlow (DE) 1954–5, Ron Miller (E) 1956, Glenn Holtzman (T) 1958, Cliff Livingston (LB) 1963–5, Rick Cash (DE) 1969–70, *Fred Dryer* (DE) 1972–81, Lewis Gilbert (TE) 1981, Mike Barber (TE) 1982, Jeff Simmons (WR) 1983, Ron Brown (WR) 1984–9, Samuel Johnson (WR) 1987r, Derrick Faison (WR) 1990, Jeff Chadwick (WR) 1992, Richard Buchanan (WR) 1993–4, Alexander Wright (WR) 1995–6, Tyji Armstrong (TE) 1998, Mitch Jacoby (TE) 1998, Chris Thomas (WR) 1999–2000, Dane Looker (WR) 2002–3.

90 *Larry Brooks* (DT) 1972–82, Ed Brady (LB) 1984, David Aupiu (LB) 1987r, *Sean Gilbert* (DT) 1992–5, Jeff Zgonina (DT) 1997, 1999–2002, Mike D. Jones (DE) 1998.

91 *Kevin Greene* (LB) 1985–92, Kyle Borland (LB) 1987r, Tony Weeds (DE) 1993, Leslie O'Neal (DE) 1996–7, Troy Pelshak (LB) 1999, *Leonard Little* (DE) 2001–3.

92 Richard Brown (LB) 1987, 1989, Jim Kalafat (LB) 1987r, Greg Clark (LB) 1990, David Rocker (DT) 1991–4, Bryan Robinson (DE) 1997, Lionel Barnes (DT) 1999–2000, Damione Lewis (DT) 2001–3.

93 Doug Reed (DE) 1984–90, Chris Pike (DT) 1991, Eric Hayes (DT) 1992, *Kevin Carter* (DE) 1995–2000.

94 Mike Wilcher (LB) 1983–90, Dan Clark (LB) 1987r, Terry Crews (LB) 1991, Ben Thomas (DT) 1991, Alberto White (DE) 1995–6, Jeff Robinson (DE) 1997–9, Gaylon Hyder (DT) 1999–2000, Bryce Fisher (DT) 2002–3.

95 Phil Murphy (DT) 1980-1, Dennis Edwards (DE) 1987r, Mike Piel (DT) 1989–92, Jeff Brady (LB) 1993, Brad Ottis (DE) 1995, Corey Sears (DE) 1998, John Burrough (DE) 2002.

96 Doug Barnes (DE) 1982–3, Neil Hope (LB) 1987r, Brian Smith (LB) 1989–90, Mark Boutte (OT) 1992–3, Jay Williams (DE) 1994–9, Erik Flowers (LB) 2003.

97 Bob Cobb (DE) 1981, Sean Smith (DT) 1989, Bruce Klosterman (LB) 1990, Gerald Robinson (DE) 1991–4, Chuck Osborne (DT) 1996, Tyoka Jackson (DL) 2001–3.

98 Tom Harmon (RB) 1946–7, Shawn Miller (NT) 1984–9, Warren Powers (DE) 1992, Jimmie Jones (DT) 1994–6, Chris Maumalanga (DT) 1997, Grant Wistrom (DE) 1998–2003.

99 Alvin Wright (NT) 1986–92, James Harris (DE) 1996, Ray Agnew (DT) 1998–2000.

SAN DIEGO CHARGERS

The franchise: In 1960 hotel tycoon Barron Hilton bought a charter membership in the "Foolish Club" of American Football League owners. His Chargers began as one of a long line of Los Angeles professional football franchises, and, as with those that both came before and followed, moved from the City of Angels due to weak fan support. Sid Gillman was the team's first coach and he quickly established an exciting team that won five of the first six Western Division titles, although they would win the AFL championship only once.

Gillman's Chargers personified the fast and aggressive offensive style of the AFL, and his downfield passing attack later became a model for the Raiders, Don Coryell's Chargers, Joe Gibbs' Redskins, and Mike Martz's Rams. Those early sixties Chargers teams featured quarterbacks Jack Kemp, Tobin Rote and John Hadl and Hall of Famers Lance Alworth and Ron Mix on offense, backed up by a defense led by a massive defensive linemen Ernie Ladd and Earl Faison. Gillman's wide-open approach led to one AFL title in 1963 when San Diego overwhelmed the Patriots in the championship game 51–10. However, they lost twice to the Oilers in 1960 and 1961 and twice to the rugged Bills in 1964 and 1965.

Gene Klein bought the team in 1966, but the Chargers lost their edge in the late 1960s, and Gillman retired for health reasons in 1971. Several losing seasons followed until former San Diego State University and St. Louis Cardinals coach Don Coryell was hired in 1978. Coryell brought back the deep-threat passing offense with Hall of Fame quarterback Dan Fouts throwing to Hall Famers Kellen Winslow and Charlie Joiner as well as Pro Bowlers John Jefferson and Wes Chandler. Twice in Coryell's tenure the Chargers reached the conference championship game, but their defense was never good enough for them to advance further. When that team began to fade, Klein sold the team to Alex Spanos in 1984.

Spanos eventually hired Bobby Beathard as general manager who hired Bobby Ross as coach in 1992. Together they built a different kind of Charger team, one whose strength was a defense led by linebacker Junior Seau and safety Rodney Harrison. In Ross' third year of 1994, San Diego reached the Super Bowl for the first time, but unfortunately ran into an awesome 49er team that took them apart in Super Bowl XXIX 49–26. From that point, the team went into a decline from which it has not yet emerged.

Origin of name: There are two stories offered for the origin of the name Chargers. One is that it was an entry in a naming con-

test submitted by a fan and selected by original owner Barron Hilton to tie in with his new Carte Blanche credit card. The second is that Hilton liked the "CHARGE" cheer heard at University of Southern California games in Los Angeles at the time.

Record by Decade

	Regular Season			Postseason		
	Won	Lost	Tied	Won	Lost	Championships
1960s	86	48	6	1	4	1963 AFL
1970s	58	81	5	0	1	
1980s	72	80	0	3	3	
1990s	74	86	0	3	3	
2000s	18	46	0	0	0	
All-Time	308	341	11	7	11	(1 AFL)

Winning seasons: 18. Losing Seasons: 20. .500 seasons: 6.

Coaches

	Years	Record	Playoffs
Sid Gillman	1960–9	82–47–6	1–4
Charlie Waller	1969–70	9–7–3	0–0
Sid Gillman(1 AFL)	1971	4–6–0	0–0
Harland Svare	1971–3	7–17–2	0–0
Ron Waller	1973	1–5–0	0–0
Tommy Prothro	1974–8	21–39–0	0–0
Don Coryell	1978–86	69–56–0	3–4
Al Saunders	1986–8	17–22–0	0–0
Dan Henning	1989–91	16–32–0	0–0
Bobby Ross	1992–6	47–33–0	3–3
Kevin Gilbride	1997–8	6–16–0	0–0
June Jones	1998	3–7–0	0–0
Mike Riley	1999–2001	14–34–0	0–0
Marty Schottenheimer	2002–3	12–20–0	0–0

(Championships in parentheses)

Time till first championship: AFL Championship in fourth year; 44 years and counting for NFL.

Time since last championship: Never won one.

Retired numbers: The Chargers have only retired 14 for record-setting Hall of Fame quarterback Dan Fouts.

Other numbers worn by these players: None.

Those who wore retired numbers after the honored player: None.

Numbers that should be retired: 19 for

Lance Alworth, the greatest deep threat of his time, who epitomized the offensive-minded AFL and 80 for Kellen Winslow the Hall of Fame tight end.

Owned numbers: None.

Numbers worn by Hall of Famers: Lance Alworth 19/24; Dan Fouts 14; Charlie Joiner 18; Deacon Jones 75; Larry Little 73; John Mackey 89; Ron Mix 74; John Unitas 19; and Kellen Winslow 80.

Star power: LaDainian Tomlinson took 21 from Scott Turner.

Star eclipsed: Louie Kelcher wore 64 till Dave Rowe, 74, left; Gary Johnson wore 72 till Coy Bacon, 79, left.

Numbers with most great players: 21 has been worn by Pro Bowl quarterback John Hadl, shifty returners Darrien Gordon and Eric Metcalf, and star runners James Brooks and LaDainian Tomlinson. 83 was worn by Pro Bowl tight ends Dave Kocourek and Willie Frazier as well as Pro Bowl wide receivers John Jefferson and Anthony Miller.

Worst represented numbers: 31 has been worn by five runners and five defensive backs without distinction.

Number worn by the most players: 84 has been worn 24 times.

Player who wore the most numbers: Several Chargers have worn two numbers, but no one has worn more than that.

Longest tenure wearing a number: Dan Fouts wore 14 for 15 years from 1973 to 1987.

Number worn by first ever draft pick: The 1960 draft was not conducted in rounds, and only three draftees played for the Chargers—Bob Zeman 34, Charlie Flowers 41 and Paul Maguire 84. The Chargers first round pick in 1961 was Earl Faison, 86.

Biggest draft busts: The biggest draft bust was quarterback Ryan Leaf, 16, selected second in 1998. He completed less than 50 percent of his passes, threw 13 TDs against 33 interceptions, and washed out of football within three years.

Number worn by oldest player: Ben Agajanian was 45 when he wore 3 in 1964. John Unitas was 40 when he wore 19 in 1973.

Cameos: Hall of Famers—John Mackey 89; Johnny Unitas 19; All Pros and other notables—Chris Bahr 3; Marlin Briscoe 86;

Billy Brooks 82; Bob Brown 78; Lee Roy Caffey 50; Roger Carr 81; Tom Day 88; Bobby Douglass 10; Roy Gerela 9; Dick Gordon 88; Erik Kramer 12; Jim McMahon 9; Mercury Morris 23; Bill Munson 19; Volney Peters 70; Webster Slaughter 84; Neil Smith 91; Ron Waller 27; Joe Washington 24.

Ones who got away: Larry Little 73 became a Hall of Fame guard in Miami. Miller Farr 20 was a Pro Bowl cornerback with the Oilers. Sherman Plunkett 70 was a massive tackle for the Jets. Yancy Thigpen 84 caught a lot of passes in Pittsburgh.

Least popular numbers: 0 has never been worn. 1, 2, and 14 have been worn twice.

Last number to be originated: 5 was first worn in 1989 by punter Lewis Colbert.

Longest dormant number: 18 has not been worn since 1986. 3 was dormant from 1965 until 1989.

Triskaidekaphobia notes: 13 has been worn by six lesser quarterbacks and a wide-out.

Shared numbers: 2 has been worn by two Pro Bowl punters, Darren Bennett and Ralf Mojsiejenko. 18 was worn by veteran quarterback Tobin Rote and Hall of Fame receiver Charlie Joiner. 19 was worn by Hall of Famers Lance Alworth and John Unitas. 55 was worn by Pro Bowl linebackers Frank Buncom and Junior Seau.

Continuity: Ray Wersching was replaced in 6 by fellow German kicker Rolf Benirschke; Keith Lincoln was replaced in 22 by fellow Pro Bowl runner Dickie Post; Emil Karas was replaced in 56 by fellow Pro Bowl defensive end Steve DeLong; Coy Bacon was replaced in 79 by fellow defensive line stalwart Gary Johnson; Dave Kocourek was replaced in 83 by fellow Pro Bowl tight end Willie Frazier.

Discontinuity: Marion Butts was followed in 35 by Rodney Culver; 14-year star guard Doug Wilkerson was followed in 63 by Jim Leonard; massive Pro Bowl defensive tackle Ernie Ladd was followed in 77 by Jim Griffin.

Quarterback numbers over 19: 21—John Hadl.

Number of first black player: In 1960, runner Paul Lowe 23, defensive back Char-

Family Connections			
Brothers			
Darren Flutie	WR	1986	86
Doug Flutie	QB	2001–3	7
Moses Moreno	QB	1999–2000	13
Zeke Moreno	LB	2001	57

lie McNeil 27, tackle Ernie Wright 75, and linebacker Rommie Loud 51.

Numbers of future NFL head coaches: Dan Henning 15; Kay Stephenson 18; Ron Waller 27.

Numbers of future NFL referees: Ron Botchan 54.

Players who played other sports: Wrestling — Ernie Ladd 99 and Bob Bruggers 56.

Players more famous after football: Jack Kemp, 15, was a long-time Congressman and one-time Vice Presidential candidate. Ernie Barnes, 61, became a painter. Tim Rossovich, 82, was an actor and stunt man. Rolf Benirschke, 6, hosted *Wheel of Fortune*.

First player to wear a number in the 90s: Defensive end Wilber Young wore 99 in 1978.

Number with most points scored: 3 with 1,255 points scored by John Carney (1,076), Ben Agajanian (99), and Chris Bahr (85).

Number with most yards rushing: 21 with 7,956 yards gained by LaDainian Tomlinson (4,564), James Brooks (1,471), John Hadl (1,013), Buford McGee (594), Glen Bonner (319), and Eric Metcalf (-5).

Number with most receptions: 83 with 1,0343 passes caught by Anthony Miller (374), Dave Kocourek (218), John Jefferson (199), Willie Frazier (137), Andre Coleman (40), Trumaine Johnson (34), Josh Norman (22), Steve Heiden (14), and Mike Carter (2).

Number with most touchdown passes: 14 with 247 touchdowns tossed by Dan Fouts (242) and Marty Domres (5).

Number with most interceptions: 29 with 55 passes picked off by Mike Williams (24), Terrence Shaw (19), Armon Hatcher (7), Doyle Nix (4), and Joe Fuller (1).

Oddity: Aside from Ben Agajanian's 3, all Charger placekickers until 1975 wore a back's numbers— George Blair and Dick Van

Raaphorst 39, Herb Travenio 35, and Dennis Partee 29.

Players Whose Number Is Unknown		
Harold Paul	(T)	1974
Rickey Hagood	(NT)	1984

Team All-Time Numerical Roster

Those with an "r" following the year 1987 were replacement players during the players' strike. Pro Bowl players for each number are in *Italics*; Hall of Famers are in **Bold** type.

1 Benny Ricardo (K) 1984, Kent Sullivan (P) 1993.

2 *Ralf Mojsiejenko* (P) 1985–8, *Darren Bennett* (P) 1995–2003.

3 Ben Agajanian (K) 1960, 1964, Chris Bahr (K) 1989, *John Carney* (K) 1990–2000.

4 George Roberts (P) 1981, Jeff Gaffney (K) 1987r, Jim Harbaugh (QB) 1999–2000, James Tuthill (K) 2002.

5 Lewis Colbert (P) 1989, Craig Whelihan (QB) 1997–8, Mike Scifres (P) 2003.

6 Ray Wersching (K) 1976, *Rolf Benirschke* (K) 1977–86, Steve DeLine (K) 1988, Nate Turner (WR) 2001.

7 Virgil Carter (QB) 1975, Eddie Bell (WR) 1976, Maury Buford (P) 1982–4, Rick Neuheisel (QB) 1987r, Fuad Reveiz (K) 1990, Greg Davis (K) 1997, Doug Flutie (QB) 2001–3.

8 Jeff West (P/TE) 1979, Joe Prokop (P) 1987, Hank Ilesic (P) 1989, Walter Stanley (WR) 1992, Sean Salisbury (QB) 1996, Steve Christie (K) 2001–3.

9 Roy Gerela (K) 1979, Mark Herrmann (QB) 1985–7, Jim McMahon (QB) 1989, Bryan Wagner (P) 1994, *Drew Brees* (QB) 2001–3.

10 Bill McClard (K) 1972, Bobby Douglass (QB) 1975, Mitch Hoopes (P) 1976, Cliff Olander (QB) 1977–9, Vince Abbott (K) 1987–8, Mike Kelley (QB) 1987r, John Kidd (P) 1990–4, Wade Richey (K) 2001–2, Dondre Gilliam (WR) 2003.

11 Ed Luther (QB) 1980–4, Billy Joe Tolliver (QB) 1989–90, Micah Ross (WR) 2003.

12 James Harris (QB) 1977–9, Bruce Mathison (QB) 1983–4, 1986, Tom Flick (QB) 1986, Babe Laufenberg (QB) 1988, Stan Humphries (QB) 1992–7, Erik Kramer (QB) 1999.

13 Steve Tensi (QB) 1965–6, Wayne Clark (QB) 1970, 1972–3, Don Horn (QB) 1974, Mark Vlasic (QB) 1987–8, 1990, Brian Brennan (WR)

1992, Gale Gilbert (QB) 1994–5, Moses Moreno (QB) 1999–2000.

14 Marty Domres (QB) 1969–71, **Dan Fouts** (QB) 1973–87.

15 *Jack Kemp* (QB) 1960–2, Don Breaux (QB) 1965, Dan Henning (QB) 1966, Jon Brittenum (QB) 1968, Pete Mikolajewski (QB) 1969, Mike Mercer (K) 1970, Ray Wersching (K) 1973–5, Toni Fritsch (K) 1976, David Archer (QB) 1989, Todd Philcox (QB) 1997.

16 Val Keckin (QB) 1962, Clint Longley (QB) 1976, Mike Wood (K) 1979–80, Bob Thomas (K) 1985, Mark Malone (QB) 1988, Bob Gagliano (QB) 1991–2, Ryan Leaf (QB) 1998, 2000.

17 Bob Laraba (QB) 1960, Hunter Enis (QB) 1961, Dick Wood (QB) 1962, Jesse Freitas (QB) 1974–5, Rick Partridge (P) 1980, John Friesz (QB) 1990–1, 1993, Charlie Jones (WR) 1996.

18 *Tobin Rote* (QB) 1963–4, Kay Stephenson (QB) 1967, **Charlie Joiner** (WR) 1976–86.

19 Bobby Clatterbuck (QB) 1960, **Lance Alworth** (WR) 1963–70, **Johnny Unitas** (QB) 1973, Neal Jeffrey (QB) 1976, Bill Munson (QB) 1977, Johnnie Barnes (WR) 1992.

20 Fred Ford (HB) 1960, Jesse Thomas (DB) 1960, Gerry McDougall (FB) 1962–4, Miller Farr (DB) 1965–6, Russ Smith (RB) 1967–70, Mike Garrett (RB) 1971–3, Johnny Rodgers (WR) 1977–8, Reuben Henderson (DB) 1983–4, Wayne Davis (DB) 1985–6, Barry Redden (RB) 1987–8, Darrin Nelson (RB) 1989–90, Chris Samuels (RB) 1991, *Natrone Means* (RB) 1993–5, 1998–9, Mike Dumas (S) 1997, Jerry Wilson (CB) 2002–3.

21 *John Hadl* (QB) 1962–72, Glen Bonner (RB) 1974–5, Clarence Duren (DB) 1977, James Brooks (RB) 1981–3, Buford McGee (RB) 1984–6, Phil McConkey (WR) 1989, Darrien Gordon (CB) 1993–4, 1996, *Eric Metcalf* (RB) 1997, Scott Turner (CB) 1998–2000, *LaDainian Tomlinson* (RB) 2001–3.

22 *Keith Lincoln* (FB) 1961–6, 1968, *Dickie Post* (RB) 1967–70, Tom Hayes (DB) 1976, Mike Thomas (RB) 1979–80, *Gill Byrd* (CB/S) 1983–92, Rodney Culver (RB) 1995, Freddie Bradley (RB) 1996, Dorian Brew (CB) 1997, Jimmy Spencer (CB) 1998–9, Tim Denton (DB) 2000, Lloyd Harrison (DB) 2001, Sammy Davis (CB) 2003.

23 *Paul Lowe* (RB) 1960–1, 1963–8, Mike Montgomery (RB/WR) 1971, Ray Jones (DB) 1972, George Hoey (DB) 1974, Mercury Morris (RB) 1976, Irvin Phillips (DB) 1981, Danny Walters (DB) 1983–7, Roy Bennett (DB) 1988–9, Anthony Shelton (S) 1990–1, Shaun Gayle (S) 1995, Gerome Williams (S) 1997–8, DeRon Jenkins (CB) 2000, Quentin Jammer (CB) 2002–3.

24 Luther Hayes (E) 1961, **Lance Alworth** (WR) 1962, Keith Kinderman (FB/DB) 1963–4, Jack Jacobson (DB) 1965, Bob Howard (DB) 1967–74, Joe Washington (RB) 1977, Miles McPherson

(DB) 1982–5, Ken Taylor (DB) 1986, Anthony Anderson (DB) 1987, Kevin Scott (RB) 1988, Lester Lyles (DB/LB) 1989–90, Stanley Richard (S) 1991–4, Aaron Hayden (RB) 1995–6, Erric Pegram (RB) 1997, Fakhir Brown (DB) 1999–2000, Glyn Milburn (WR) 2001, Jesse Chatman (RB) 2002–3.

25 Claude Gibson (DB) 1961–2, Dick Westmoreland (DB) 1963–5, Steve Newell (WR) 1967, Dick Speights (DB) 1968, Mike Garrett (RB) 1970, Jerry LeVias (WR) 1971–4, Maurice Tyler (DB) 1975, John Cappelletti (RB) 1980–3, Wayne Morris (RB) 1984, Vencie Glenn (S) 1986–90, Sean Vanhorse (CB) 1992–4, Paul Bradford (CB) 1997, Reggie Rusk (CB) 1999–2000, Alex Molden (CB) 2001–2.

26 Jimmy Sears (HB/DB) 1960, Bo Roberson (WR) 1961, Bert Coan (HB) 1962, Kern Carson (HB) 1965, *Brad Hubbert* (RB) 1967–70, Clint Jones (RB) 1973, Dave Atkins (RB) 1975, Lydell Mitchell (RB) 1978–9, Bernard Jackson (DB) 1980, Donald Dykes (DB) 1982, Lionel James (RB/WR) 1984–8, Darryl Usher (WR) 1989, Sammy Lilly (CB) 1990, Floyd Fields (S) 1991–3, Bo Orlando (S) 1995, Darryll Lewis (CB) 1999–2000.

27 Ron Waller (HB) 1960, *Charlie McNeil* (DB) 1960–4, *Gary Garrison* (WR) 1966–76, Glen Edwards (DB) 1978–81, Jeff Allen (DB) 1982, John Turner (DB) 1984, Ronnie O'Bard (DB) 1985, Daniel Hunter (DB) 1986–7, Victor Floyd (RB) 1989, Donald Frank (LB) 1990–3, Michael Swift (CB) 1997, Charles Dimry (CB) 1998–9, Tony Darden (CB) 2000, Tay Cody (CB) 2001–3.

28 Royce Womble (HB/WR) 1960, Mario Mendez (HB) 1964, Chuck Dicus (WR) 1971–2, Willie McGee (WR) 1973, Willie Buchanan (DB) 1979–82, Ken Greene (DB) 1983–4, David Croudip (DB) 1985, Jim Rockford (DB) 1985, Mike Hudson (DB) 1987, Ted Watts (DB) 1987, Elliot Smith (DB) 1989, Donnie Elder (CB) 1990–1, Dwayne Harper (CB) 1994–8, Ronney Jenkins (RB) 2000–2.

29 Doyle Nix (DB) 1960, Jerry Robinson (WR) 1962–4, Dennis Partee (K) 1968–75, Mike Williams (DB) 1975–82, John Hendy (DB) 1985, Charles Romes (DB) 1987, Joe Fuller (DB) 1990, Darren Carrington (S) 1991–4, Terrance Shaw (CB) 1995–9, Scott Turner (CB) 2001, Armon Hatcher (DB) 2000, Drayton Florence (CB) 2003.

30 Bob Horton (LB) 1964–5, Bryant Salter (DB) 1971–3, Sam Scarber (RB) 1975–6, Bruce Laird (DB) 1982–3, Scott Byers (DB) 1984, David King (DB) 1985, Kevin Wyatt (DB) 1986, Frank Middleton (RB) 1987r, Sam Seale (CB) 1988–91, Marquez Pope (CB) 1992–3, Robert Carswell (S) 2001–2, Andrew Pinnock (RB) 2003.

31 Ron Sayers (RB) 1969, Linden King (LB) 1978, Darrell Pattillo (DB) 1983, Bill Kay (DB) 1984, Anthony Corley (RB) 1985, Jeff Powell (RB) 1987r, Leonard Coleman (DB) 1988–9, Craig

McEwen (HB) 1989–91, Brian Davis (CB) 1993, Willie Clark (CB) 1994–6, 1998, Jason Perry (DB) 1999–2001.

32 Jim Allison (RB) 1965–8, Billy Parks (WR) 1971, Scott Perry (DB) 1980, Wyatt Henderson (DB) 1981, Jewerl Thomas (RB) 1984, Terry Lewis (DB) 1985, Donald Brown (DB) 1986, Todd Spencer (RB) 1987r, Michael Brooks (S) 1989–90, Eric Bieniemy (RB) 1991–4, Robert Chancey (FB) 1997, 2000, Kevin House (CB) 2002–3.

33 Blanche Martin (FB) 1960, Fred Gillett (HB/E) 1962, *Kenny Graham* (DB) 1964–9, Don Woods (RB) 1974–80, Lucious Smith (DB) 1984–5, David Martin (DB) 1986, John Sullivan (DB) 1986, Ken Zachary (RB) 1987r, Dana Brinson (WR) 1989, *Ronnie Harmon* (RB) 1990–5, Kevin Bouie (RB) 1996, Gary Brown (RB) 1997, Dedrick Dodge (S) 1998, Davis Sanchez (CB) 2001–2.

34 *Bob Zeman* (DB) 1960–1, 1965–6, Oscar Dragon (RB) 1972, Rickey Young (RB) 1975–7, LaRue Harrington (RB) 1980, Elvis Patterson (S) 1987–9, Steve Hendrickson (RB) 1990–4, Aaron Craver (RB) 1997, Tremayne Stephens (RB) 1998–9, Tony Okanlawon (CB) 2003.

35 Bob Garner (DB) 1960, Hez Braxton (FB) 1962, Herb Travenio (K) 1964–5, Chuck Detwiler (DB) 1970–2, Bob Thomas (RB) 1973–4, Tony Baker (RB) 1975, Larry Barnes (RB) 1977–8, Martin Sartin (RB) 1987r, *Marion Butts* (RB) 1989–93, Rodney Culver (RB) 1994, Carwell Gardner (FB) 1997, Jermaine Fazande (RB) 1999–2000, Keith Lyle (S) 2002, Leon Johnson (RB) 2003.

36 *Dick Harris* (DB) 1960–5, Frank Marsh (DB) 1967, Dick Farley (DB) 1968–9, Eddie Ray (RB/TE) 1971, Mike Davis (DB) 1987, Joe Mickles (RB) 1990, Delton Hall (S) 1992, Kevin Ross (CB) 1996, Lloyd Lee (S) 1998, Vernon Fox (S) 2002 3.

37 Howie Ferguson (FB) 1960, Gene Foster (RB) 1965–70, Cid Edwards (RB) 1972–4, Charlie Smith (RB) 1975, Hank Bauer (RB) 1977–82, Jeffery Dale (DB) 1985–6, 1988, Terry Orr (TE) 1990, Anthony Blaylock (CB) 1991–2, *Rodney Harrison* (S) 1994–2002.

38 *Jacque MacKinnon* (TE/RB) 1961–9, Gene Huey (DB) 1969, Roland Moss (TE) 1970, Leon Burns (RB) 1971, Lee White (RB) 1972, Robert Holmes (RB) 1973, Tommy Thompson (RB) 1974, Lou Brock (DB) 1987, Ed Berry (DB) 1987r, David Hendrix (S) 1995–7, Mike Dumas (S) 1997–2000.

39 *George Blair* (DB/K) 1961–4, *Dick Van Raaphorst* (K) 1966–7, Jim Hill (DB) 1969–71, Lenny Dunlap (DB) 1972–4, Keyvan Jenkins (RB) 1987r.

40 Bobby Jackson (FB) 1962–3, Joe Beauchamp (DB) 1966–75, Clarence Williams (RB) 1977–81, Jim Jodat (RB) 1982–3, *Gary Anderson* (RB) 1985–8, James Fuller (S) 1993, Mark Montreuil (CB) 1995–7, Derrick Harris (RB) 2001.

41 Charlie Flowers (FB) 1960–1, Nat Whitmyer (DB) 1966, Phil Tuckett (WR) 1968, Bo Matthews (RB) 1974–9, Booker Russell (RB) 1980, *Earnest Jackson* (RB) 1983–4, King Simmons (DB) 1987r, Terrell Fletcher (RB) 1995–2002, Lorenzo Neal (FB) 2003.

42 Lane Fenner (WR) 1968, Dave Smith (RB) 1970, Jesse Taylor (RB) 1972, Mike Fuller (DB) 1975–80, Ricky Bell (RB) 1982, Pete Johnson (RB) 1984, Curtis Adams (RB) 1985–8, Leonard Russell (RB) 1996, Greg Jackson (S) 1997–2000, Rogers Beckett (S) 2000–2, Kwamie Lassiter (S) 2003.

43 Bobby Bethune (DB) 1962, Gary Glick (DB/RB) 1963, Jim Tolbert (DB) 1966–71, 1976, Rickey Anderson (RB) 1978, Bob Gregor (DB) 1981–4, Tim Spencer (RB) 1985–90, Peter Tuipulotu (RB) 1992, Lonnie Young (S) 1994, Kenny Bynum (RB) 1997–2000.

44 Trusse Norris (E) 1960, John Travis (FB) 1966, Ollie Cordill (DB/P) 1967, Richard Trapp (WR) 1969, Chris Fletcher (DB) 1970–6, Pete Shaw (DB) 1977–81, Martin Bayless (S) 1987–91, Eric Castle (S) 1993–6, Fred McCrary (FB) 1999–2002.

45 Henry Wallace (DB) 1960, *Speedy Duncan* (DB) 1964–70, Reggie Berry (DB) 1972–4, Hal Stringert (DB) 1975–80, Doug Beaudion (DB) 1981, Henry Williams (DB) 1983, Mike Dennis (DB) 1984, Johnny Ray Smith (DB) 1984, Anthony Steels (RB) 1985, 1987, Joey Goodspeed (FB) 2002.

46 Bob Scarpitto (WR/P) 1961, John Sykes (WR) 1972, Danny Colbert (DB) 1974–6, *Chuck Muncie* (RB) 1980–4, Walter Harris (DB) 1987r, Joe Caravello (TE) 1989–90, Walter Reeves (TE) 1996.

47 Bud Whitehead (DB) 1961–8, Jeff Queen (RB/TE) 1969 71, Sam Williams (DB) 1974–5, Frank Duncan (DB) 1979–81, Sherman Smith (RB) 1983, Darrell Hopper (DB) 1987, Johnny Thomas (CB) 1989, Jerry Mays (RB) 1990, Cedric Mack (CB) 1991, A.J. Johnson (CB) 1995, Ron Middleton (TE) 1995, *Ryan McNeil* (CB) 2001–2.

48 Larry Rentz (DB) 1969, Ron Smith (DB/WR) 1973, Jerome Dove (DB) 1977–80, Allan Ellis (DB) 1981, Tim Fox (DB) 1982–4, Carl Brazley (DB) 1987r, Doug Miller (LB) 1993–4, Terrence Kiel (S) 2003.

49 Jimmy Warren (DB) 1964–5, Ken Dyer (DB/WR) 1968, Rick Eber (WR) 1969–70, Andre Young (DB) 1982–4.

50 Ben Donnell (DE) 1960, *Chuck Allen* (LB) 1961–9, Jack Protz (LB) 1970, Lee Roy Caffey (LB) 1972, Don Goode (LB) 1974–9, Carlos Bradley (LB) 1981–5, Gary Plummer (LB) 1986–93, Mike Humiston (LB) 1987, Dave Binn (C) 1994–2003.

51 Rommie Loudd (LB) 1960, Wayne Frazier (C/LB) 1962, Dick Degen (LB) 1965–6, Bill Lenkaitis (C/G) 1968–70, Pete Lazetich (LB)

1972–4, Billy Andrews (LB) 1975, Woodrow Lowe (LB) 1976–86, Cedric Figaro (LB) 1988–90, Terry Crews (LB) 1993, Joe Cummings (LB) 1996, Gerald Dixon (LB) 1998–2001, Ben Leber (LB) 2002–3.

52 Don Rogers (C) 1960–4, Paul Latzke (C) 1966–8, Ray White (LB) 1971–2, Jay Douglas (C) 1973–4, Bob Stein (LB) 1975, Ray Preston (LB) 1976–84, Mark Fellows (LB) 1985–6, Angelo Snipes (LB) 1986–7, Jeff Jackson (LB) 1987–8, Brian Ingram (LB) 1987r, James Johnson (LB) 1987r, Jeff Mills (LB) 1990, Sam Anno (LB) 1992–3, Dwayne Gordon (LB) 1995–6, James Burgess (LB) 1997–8, John Reeves (LB) 1999–2000, John Holecek (LB) 2001, Carlos Polk (LB) 2002–3.

53 Charlie Brueckman (LB) 1960, Bob Laraba (LB) 1961, Jim Campbell (LB) 1969, Dan Sartin (DT) 1969, Mel Rogers (LB) 1971, 1973–4, Chip Myrtle (LB) 1974, Drew Mahalic (LB) 1975, Ralph Perretta (C/G) 1976–80, Dave Lewis (LB) 1982, Mike Guendling (LB) 1985, Mike Douglass (LB) 1986, Chuck Faucette (LB) 1987–8, Stacey Price (LB) 1987r, Courtney Hall (C) 1989–96, Michael Hamilton (LB) 1997–9, Deon Humphrey (LB) 2000–1.

54 Ron Botchan (LB) 1960, Tom Good (LB) 1966, Ralph Wenzel (G) 1972, Carl Gersbach (LB) 1973–4, Ed Flanagan (C) 1975–6, Jim Laslavic (LB) 1978, 1980–1, Billy Ray Smith (LB) 1983–9, Kurt Gouveia (LB) 1996–8, Eric Hill (LB) 1999, Stephen Cooper (LB) 2003.

55 *Frank Buncom* (LB) 1962–7, Carl Mauck (C) 1971–4, Ken Hutcherson (LB) 1975, Bob Horn (LB) 1976–81, Derrie Nelson (LB) 1983–6, Steve Busick (LB) 1987, Jim Collins (LB) 1989, *Junior Seau* (LB) 1990–2002.

56 *Emil Karas* (LB/DE) 1960–4, 1966, *Steve DeLong* (DE/DT) 1965–6, Bob Bruggers (LB) 1968–71, Fred Forsberg (LB) 1974, Mark Markovich (C/G) 1975, Bob Rush (C/T) 1977–82, Larry Evans (LB) 1983, Vince Osby (LB) 1984–5, Ty Allert (LB) 1986–7, Chip Banks (LB) 1987, Galand Thaxton (LB) 1991, Patrick Sapp (LB) 1996–7, Steve Tovar (LB) 1998, Orlando Ruff (LB) 1999–2002, Matt Wilhelm (LB) 2003.

57 Al Bansavage (LB) 1960, Hubert Bobo (LB) 1960, George Belotti (C) 1961, Bobby Lane (LB) 1963–4, Mike London (LB) 1966, Bob Print (LB) 1967–8, Cal Withrow (C) 1970, Jack Porter (C) 1971, Floyd Rice (LB) 1973–5, Rick Middleton (LB) 1976–8, Linden King (LB) 1979–85, Thomas Benson (LB) 1986–7, Keith Browner (LB) 1988, Henry Rolling (LB) 1990–2, Jerrol Williams (LB) 1993, Dennis Gibson (LB) 1994–5, Arnold Ale (LB) 1996, Bobby Houston (LB) 1997, Marc Raab (C) 1998, Tracy Simien (LB) 1999, Zeke Moreno (LB) 2001–3.

58 Doug Cline (LB/FB) 1966, Tom Erlandson

(LB) 1968, Harris Jones (G) 1971, Mike Stratton (LB) 1973, Mike Lee (LB) 1974, Tom Graham (LB) 1975–7, Mark Slater (C) 1978, Carl McGee (LB) 1980, Dewey Selmon (LB/DT) 1982, Mike Green (LB) 1983–5, David Brandon (LB) 1987–9, 1995, David Grayson (LB) 1991, Kevin Murphy (LB) 1992, Lewis Bush (LB) 1993–9, Richard Harvey (LB) 2000.

59 Pete Barnes (LB) 1969–72, Charles Anthony (LB) 1974, Franklin Tate (LB) 1975, Cliff Thrift (LB) 1979–84, Craig Bingham (LB) 1985, Andy Hawkins (LB) 1986–7, Johnny Taylor (LB) 1987, Ken Woodard (LB) 1988–9, Greg Clark (LB) 1991, Glen Young (LB) 1995–6, Toran James (LB) 1997, Jon Haskins (LB) 1998, Steve Tovar (LB) 2000, Donnie Edwards (LB) 2002–3.

60 John Kompara (DT) 1960, Sam DeLuca (G/T) 1961, 1963, Jack Klotz (T) 1962, Ed Mitchell (G) 1965–7, Bob Babich (LB) 1970–2, Dan Audick (T/G) 1978–80, Don Reese (DE/DT) 1981, Dennis McKnight (C/G) 1982–8, Greg Engel (C) 1995–7, Wilbert Brown (G) 1999, Jason Ball (C) 2002–3.

61 Ernie Barnes (G/T) 1961–2, Ernie Park (T/G) 1963–5, John Milks (LB) 1966, Jim Fetherston (LB) 1968–9, Al Dennis (G) 1973, Blenda Gay (DE) 1974, Ralph Perretta (C/G) 1975, Jimmy Webb (DT/DE) 1981, Don Brown (T) 1983, Ken Dallafior (G/C) 1985–8, Eric Floyd (G) 1990–1, Michael Keathley (T) 2001–3.

62 Al Barry (G) 1960, John Farris (G) 1965, Bernie Erickson (LB) 1967–8, Ralph Wenzel (G) 1973, Don Macek (C/G) 1976–89, Ben Coleman (G/T) 2000, Bob Hallen (C/G) 2002–3.

63 *Doug Wilkerson* (G) 1971–84, Jim Leonard (C/G) 1985–6, Dwight Wheeler (C/T) 1987, David Diaz-Infante (G) 1987r, Frank Cornish (C/G) 1990–1, Raymond Smoot (G/T) 1993, Raleigh McKenzie (C/G) 1997–8, Kelvin Garmon (G) 2002–3.

64 Pat Shea (G) 1962–5, Jim Schmedding (G) 1968–70, Dave Costa (DT/DE) 1972–3, *Louie Kelcher* (DT) 1975, Charles Aiu (G) 1976–8, Chuck Loewen (T/G) 1980–2, 1984, Bill Searcey (G) 1985, Mark Rodenhauser (C) 1990–1, Curtis Whitley (C) 1992–4, Bryan Stoltenberg (C) 1996, Kendyl Jacox (C) 1998–2001.

65 Sam Gruneisen (C/G) 1962–72, Mark Markovich (C/G) 1974, Booker Brown (T/G) 1975, 1977, Jerry Doerger (C/T) 1985, John Stadnik (C) 1987r, Dave Richards (G) 1988–92, Troy Sienkiewicz (G) 1996–7, John Jackson (T) 1998–9.

66 Fred Cole (G) 1960, *Rick Redman* (LB) 1965–73, Billy Shields (T) 1975–83, Rich Umphrey (C/G) 1985, Dan Rosado (G/C) 1987–8, Richard Brown (LB) 1990, Jim Mills (T) 1996–7, Reggie Nelson (G/T) 1999, Kevin Gogan (G/T) 2000, Cory Raymer (C) 2002–3.

67 Charlie Kempinska (G) 1960, Archie Matsos (LB) 1966, *Ed White* (G) 1978–85, Greg Feasel

(T) 1987r, Leo Goeas (G/T) 1990–2, Stan Brock (T) 1993–5, Roman Fortin (C) 1998–2000, Kevin Breedlove (G) 2003.

68 Orlando Ferrante (G) 1960–1, Lloyd McCoy (G) 1964, Don Estes (G) 1966, Bob Briggs (DT/DE) 1968–70, Greg Wojcik (DT) 1972–3, 1975, Brian Vertefeuille (T) 1974, Leroy Jones (DE) 1976–83, Bill Elko (G/NT) 1984, Gary Kowalski (T/G) 1985–8, Joe Cocozzo (G) 1993–7, Elliot Silvers (T) 2001, Kris Dielman (DT) 2003.

69 Curtis Jones (LB) 1968, Ira Gordon (G/T) 1970–5, John Lee (DE) 1976–80, Derrell Gofourth (G/C) 1983–4, Les Miller (DE) 1987–90, 1994, Monte Bennett (LB) 1987r, Ben Bordelon (T) 1997, Ed Ellis (T) 2001–2.

70 Volney Peters (DT/T) 1960, Sherman Plunkett (T) 1961–2, Scott Appleton (DT) 1967–8, *Russ Washington* (T) 1970–82, James Fitzpatrick (G) 1986–9, Mike Zandofsky (C/G) 1990–3, Vaughn Parker (G/T) 1994–2003.

71 Dick Chorovich (T) 1960, Fred Moore (DT/DE) 1964–5, Harold Akin (T) 1967–8, Levert Carr (T/DT) 1969, Cal Snowden (DE) 1972–3, *Fred Dean* (DE) 1975–81, Mike Charles (NT/DT) 1987–9, Joe Milinichik (G) 1993–4, DeMingo Graham (G) 1999–2001, Toniu Fonoti (G) 2002.

72 Sam DeLuca (G/T) 1960, Gary Kirner (T/G) 1964–9, Joe Owens (DE) 1970, *Gary Johnson* (DT) 1975, Ron Singleton (T) 1976, Jeff Williams (G/T) 1981, Jeff Walker (T/G) 1986, Karl Wilson (DT/DE) 1987–8, Emil Slovacek (T) 1987r, Harry Swayne (T) 1991–6, Troy Sienkiewicz (G) 1998, Courtney Van Buren (T) 2003.

73 Larry Martin (DT) 1966, **Larry Little** (G/T) 1967–8, Lee Thomas (DE) 1971–2, Bon Boatright (DT) 1974, Charles DeJurnett (DB) 1976–80, Keith Guthrie (NT) 1984, Darrick Brilz (C) 1988, Tom Toth (G/T) 1990, Mark May (G) 1991–2, Mike Mooney (T) 1993, Isaac Davis (G) 1994–7, Aaron Taylor (G) 1998–9.

74 **Ron Mix** (T/G) 1960–9, Dave Rowe (DT) 1974–5, *Louie Kelcher* (DT) 1976–83, *Jim Lachey* (T) 1985–7, Chris Gambol (T/G) 1988, Brett Miller (T) 1989, Eric Jonassen (T) 1993–4, Raleigh Roundtree (T/G) 1998–2001, Jacques Cesaire (DT) 2003.

75 *Ernie Wright* (T) 1960–7, Gene Ferguson (T/DT) 1969–70, Gary Nowak (DT) 1971, **Deacon Jones** (DE) 1972–3, Dave Tipton (DE/DT) 1974–5, Raymond Baylor (DE) 1974, Andrew Gissinger (T) 1982–4, Curt DiGiacomo (G/C) 1986, Joe Phillips (DT) 1987–91, Tony Berti (T) 1995–7, *Marcellus Wiley* (DE) 2001–3.

76 Gary Finneran (DT) 1960, Henry Schmidt (DT/DE) 1961–4, Terry Owens (T) 1966–75, Keith Ferguson (DE) 1981–5, Broderick Thompson (T/G) 1987–92, Willard Goff (DT) 1987r, Van Tuinei (DE) 1997, Jamal Williams (DT) 1998–2003.

77 *Ernie Ladd* (DT) 1961–5, Jim Griffin (DE)

1966–7, Bob Wells (T) 1968–70, Ron East (DT/DE) 1971–3, John Teerlinck (DT) 1974–5, Buddy Hardaway (T) 1978, Sam Claphan (T/G) 1981–7, John Clay (T) 1988, Eric Moten (G/T) 1991–3, 1995–6, Damion McIntosh (T) 2000–3, Ed Ellis (T) 2003.

78 Gene Selawski (T/G) 1961, Dick Hudson (T/G) 1962, *Walt Sweeney* (G) 1963–73, Robert Brown (DT/DE) 1974, Chuck Ehin (NT/DE) 1983–7, Joel Patten (T) 1989–90, Dequincy Scott (DT) 2002–3.

79 *Bill Hudson* (DT) 1961–2, George Gross (DT) 1963–7, Andy Rice (DT) 1970–1, *Ernie Wright* (T) 1972, Coy Bacon (DE/DT) 1973–5, *Gary Johnson* (DT) 1976–84, Joey Howard (T) 1989, Tony Savage (DT) 1990, 1992, Marcus Price (T) 1997–8, Mike Pringley (DE) 2000–1, Sammy Williams (T) 2002, Solomon Page (G) 2003.

80 Ron Nery (DE) 1960–2, Houston Ridge (DE/DT) 1966–9, Kevin Hardy (DT) 1971–2, Gary Parris (TE) 1973–4, Jeff West (P/TE) 1976–8, **Kellen Winslow** (TE) 1979–87, Wayne Walker (WR) 1989, Shawn Jefferson (WR) 1991–5, Bryan Still (WR) 1996–9, Curtis Conway (WR) 2000–2, Stephen Alexander (TE) 2003.

81 Maury Schleicher (LB/DE) 1960–2, Sammie Taylor (WR) 1965, Dave Plump (DB) 1966, Jeff Staggs (LB/DE) 1967–71, 1974, John Andrews (LB) 1972, Ron Holliday (WR) 1973, Melvin Baker (WR) 1975, Scott Fitzkee (WR) 1981–2, Aundra Thompson (WR) 1981, Roger Carr (WR) 1983, Steve Bird (WR) 1984, Timmie Ware (WR) 1986–7, Calvin Muhammad (WR) 1987r, Anthony Jones (TE) 1988, Wilbur Strozier (TE) 1988, Mark Walczak (TE) 1989, 1991, Nate Lewis (WR) 1990–93, *Tony Martin* (WR) 1994–7, Jeff Graham (WR) 1999–2001, Stephen Alexander (TE) 2002, Kassim Osgood (WR) 2003.

82 Ralph Anderson (E) 1960, Bob Mitinger (LB) 1962–4, 1966, 1968, *Steve DeLong* (DE/DT) 1967–71, Tim Rossovich (LB/DE) 1972–3, Dave Grannel (TE) 1974, Pat Curran (TE/RB) 1975–8, Billy Brooks (WR) 1981, Bobby Duckworth (WR) 1982–4, Tag Rome (WR) 1987r, Mark Seay (WR) 1993–5, Charlie Jones (WR) 1996–9, Walter Reeves (TE) 1996, Trevor Gaylor (WR) 2000–1, Reche Caldwell (WR) 2002–3.

83 *Dave Kocourek* (TE) 1960–5, *Willie Frazier* (TE) 1966–70, Mike Carter (WR) 1972, Larry Mialik (TE) 1976, *John Jefferson* (WR) 1978–80, Bobby Micho (TE/FB) 1984, Trumaine Johnson (WR) 1985–6, Bruce Davis (WR) 1987, *Anthony Miller* (WR) 1988–93, Andre Coleman (WR) 1994–6, John Burke (TE) 1998, Steve Heiden (TE) 1999–2001, Josh Norman (TE) 2002–3.

84 Paul Maguire (LB/P) 1960–3, Johnny Baker (LB/DE) 1967, Marty Baccaglio (DE) 1968, Walker Gillette (WR) 1970–1, Dave Williams (WR) 1972–3, Bob Klein (TE) 1977–9, Ron Smith (WR)

1980–1, Hosea Fortune (WR) 1983, Ron Egloff (TE) 1984, Chris Faulkner (TE) 1985, Rod Bernstine (RB) 1987–92, Al Williams (WR) 1987r, Chris Gannon (DE) 1989, Walter Wilson (WR) 1990, Yancey Thigpen (WR) 1991, Robert Claiborne (WR) 1992, Mike Dyal (TE) 1993, Aaron Laing (TE) 1994, Omar Ellison (WR) 1995–6, Ray Crittenden (WR) 1997, Webster Slaughter (WR) 1998, Reggie Davis (TE) 1999–2000, Josh Whitman (TE) 2001, Justin Peelle (TE) 2002–3.

85 Paul Miller (DE) 1962, Bob Petrich (DE) 1963–6, *Russ Washington* (T) 1968–9, John Tanner (LB) 1971, Jim Beirne (WR/TE) 1973–4, Joe Sweet (WR) 1975, Artie Owens (WR) 1976–9, Eric Sievers (TE) 1981–8, Harry Holt (TE) 1987r, Andy Parker (TE) 1989, Kitrick Taylor (WR) 1990–1, Scott Schwedes (WR) 1990, Johnnie Barnes (WR) 1992–4, Latario Rachal (WR) 1997–8, Tony Gaiter (WR) 1998, Robert Reed (WR) 1999, Tim Dwight (WR) 2001–2, Antonio Gates (TE) 2003.

86 *Earl Faison* (DE) 1961–6, Ron Billingsley (DT/DE) 1967–70, Wes Grant (DE/DT) 1971, Jim Thaxton (TE/WR) 1973–4, Marlin Briscoe (WR) 1975, John Floyd (WR) 1979–80, Jesse Bendross (WR) 1984–5, Jamie Holland (WR) 1987–9, Tim Moffett (WR) 1987r, Darren Flutie (WR) 1988, Alfred Pupunu (TE) 1992–7, Mikhael Ricks (WR) 1998–2000, Pat Batteaux (WR) 2001, Dondre Gilliam (WR) 2002, Grant Mattos (WR) 2003.

87 Howard Clark (E) 1960–1, Howard Kindig (DE/T) 1965–7, Andre White (TE) 1968, Tom Williams (DT/DE) 1970–1, Lionel Aldridge (DE) 1972–3, Harrison Davis (WR) 1974, Larry Dorsey (WR) 1976–7, Larry Burton (WR) 1978–9, Dwight Scales (WR) 1981–3, Curtis Rouse (G/T) 1987, Kevin Ferguson (TE) 1987r, Quinn Early (WR) 1988–90, Duane Young (TE) 1991–5, Brian Roche (TE) 1996–7, Ryan Thelwell (WR) 1998, Chris Penn (WR) 1999, Reggie Jones (WR) 2000–1, Tamarick Vanover (WR) 2002, Tim Dwight (WR) 2003.

88 *Don Norton* (WR) 1960–6, Tom Day (DE) 1967, Pettis Norman (TE) 1971–3, Dick Gordon (WR) 1974, Chuck Bradley (TE) 1975–7, Craig Cotton (TE) 1975, Greg McCrary (TE) 1978–80, Pete Holohan (TE) 1981–7, Arthur Cox (TE) 1988–91, Deems May (TE) 1992–6, Freddie Jones (TE) 1997–2001, Eric Parker (WR) 2002–3.

89 Art Gob (DE) 1960, *Reg Carolan* (TE) 1962–3, Ron Carpenter (LB) 1964–5, Ron McCall (LB) 1967–8, Art Strozier (TE) 1970–1, **John**

Mackey (TE) 1972, Wayne Stewart (TE) 1974, Dwight McDonald (WR) 1975–8, *Wes Chandler* (WR) 1981–7, Anthony Allen (WR) 1989, Derrick Walker (TE) 1990–3, Shannon Mitchell (TE) 1994–7, Frank Hartley (TE) 1997–8, Wendell Davis (CB) 1998, Reggie Davis (TE) 1999, Alfred Pupunu (TE) 1999, Nate Jacquet (WR) 2000, David Boston (WR) 2003.

90 John Woodcock (DT) 1981–2, Bill Elko (G/NT) 1983, Fred Robinson (DE/LB) 1984–6, Mack Moore (DE) 1986, Reggie White (DT) 1992–4, Sebastian Barrie (DE) 1995, Marco Coleman (DE) 1996–8, Adrian Dingle (DT) 2000–3.

91 Rick Ackerman (DT) 1982–4, Tony Chickillo (NT/DE) 1984–5, Leslie O'Neal (DE) 1986, 1988–95, Neil Smith (DE) 2000, Shawn Price (DE) 2002, Omari Hand (DE) 2003.

92 Eric Williams (LB) 1984, Scott Garnett (NT/DE) 1985, Dee Hardison (DE/NT) 1986–7, Burt Grossman (DE) 1989–93, David Griggs (DE) 1994, Cedric Harden (DE) 1999, Darren Mickell (DE) 2000, Jason Fisk (DT) 2002–3.

93 Earl Wilson (DE) 1985–7, Duane Pettitt (DE) 1987r, Tyrone Keys (DE) 1988, George Thornton (DT) 1991–2, Reuben Davis (DT) 1994–6, Antoine Simpson (DT) 2000, Carlos Polk (LB) 2001, Otis Leverette (DE) 2003.

94 Randy Kirk (LB) 1987–8, 1991, Chris Mims (DE) 1992–6, 1998–9, Mike Mohring (DT) 1997, Shannon Taylor (LB) 2000, Maa Tanuvasa (DT) 2001.

95 Joseph Campbell (DE) 1988–9, Mitchell Benson (NT) 1991, Jeff Brady (LB) 1993, Vernon Edwards (DE) 1996, William Fuller (DE) 1997–8, Al Fontenot (DE) 1999–2001, Joe Salave'a (DT) 2003.

96 Lester Williams (NT/DE) 1986, Blaise Winter (DT) 1986–7, 1992–4, Keith Baldwin (DE) 1987–8, Don Sasa (DT) 1995–6, Norman Hand (DT) 1997–9, Leonardo Carson (DT) 2000–3.

97 Tony Simmons (DE) 1985, 1987, George Hinkle (DT) 1988–92, John Parrella (DT) 1994–2001.

98 Terry Unrein (NT/DE) 1986–7, Gerald Robinson (DE) 1989–90, Skip McClendon (DE) 1991, Jim Skow (DE) 1992, Shawn Lee (DT) 1992–7, Mike Mohring (DT) 1998–2001.

99 Wilbur Young (DE/DT) 1978–82, *Lee Williams* (DE/DT) 1984–90, Eugene Marve (LB) 1992, Raylee Johnson (DE) 1993–2003.

SAN FRANCISCO 49ERS

The franchise: The San Francisco 49ers are the oldest team founded on the West Coast. They were established as a charter member of the All America Football Conference in 1946 by owner Tony Morabito and were clearly the second best team in that league during its four years of existence. When the AAFC folded, the 49ers were one of three teams accepted into the NFL in 1950, but promptly fell on their faces by going 3–9 in that first NFL season despite the efforts of star quarterback Frankie Albert. The rest of the decade would see San Francisco and its "Million Dollar Backfield" of four Hall of Famers (Y.A. Tittle, Hugh McElhenny, Joe Perry and John Henry Johnson) annually contend for the Western title but always fall short.

Morabito would die in 1957, and control of the team would pass to his widow and then his brother Vic. When Vic Morabito died in 1964, the Morabito family retained ownership, but Lou Spadia ran the team. On the field, San Francisco was no better than mediocre throughout the 1960s. Former Cowboy assistant Dick Nolan was hired as coach in 1968 and led the team to three consecutive divisional titles from 1970 to 1972. His defense oriented approach relied on a fierce "Gold Rush" front four led by Cedrick Hardman and Tommy Hart while the John Brodie to Gene Washington aerial connection supplied the offense. However, each of those three seasons ended with a loss to Dallas in the postseason. Within a few years, Nolan was gone and the team was at the bottom of the standings, but that was about to change.

Eddie DeBartolo bought the team from the Morabito family in 1977 and hired Bill Walsh to run it in 1979. What followed has been 25 years of almost-unbroken excellence with Walsh involved in some capacity for most of that time. Walsh had a great gift at the NFL draft, and he built a powerhouse with some great picks—Joe Montana in 1979, Ronnie Lott, Eric Wright and Carlton Wil-liamson in 1981, Roger Craig in 1983, and Jerry Rice in 1985. The 49ers became the "Team of the Eighties" by winning 69 percent of their games and four Super Bowls during that decade—the last under Walsh's hand-picked successor, George Seifert. In the 1990s San Francisco switched from one Hall of Fame quarterback (Montana) to another, Steve Young, whom Walsh had picked up in a trade, and won 71 percent of its games in the that decade.

Seifert and Young delivered the team's fifth Super Bowl trophy in the middle of the 1990s, but it would be the team's last up to this point. Four times they would lose in the playoffs to Brett Favre's Packers. With all the success came impatience from the fans and the front office. Seifert was forced out in 1997 for Steve Mariucci, coincidentally the year that owner DeBartolo began to have legal problems that would eventually force him to sell to the club to his sister Denise York in 2000. Despite an impressive tenure that included quickly rebuilding an older, salary-cap ravaged team into a young and aggressive squad and replacing the Young to Rice connection with a Jeff Garcia to Terrell Owens link, Mariucci himself was fired after winning a division title in 2002. Dennis Erickson was brought in to inhabit the hot seat and got off to an inauspicious start in 2003.

Origin of name: The name was selected to emphasize the adventurous Gold Rush miners who came to the area in 1849.

Time till first championship: 32 years.

Time since last championship: 10 years.

Retired numbers: The 49ers have retired the numbers of several Hall of Famers—Joe Perry 34, Hugh McElhenny 39, Leo Nomellini 73, Jimmy Johnson 37, Joe Montana 16, and Ronnie Lott 42. They have also retired the numbers for three long-time sentimental favorites—John Brodie 12, Charlie Krueger 70, and Dwight Clark 87.

Other numbers worn by these players: Perry also wore 74, while Nomellini also wore 42.

Record by Decade

	Regular Season			Postseason		
	Won	Lost	Tied	Won	Lost	Championships
1940s AAFC	38	14	2	1	1	
1950s	63	54	3	0	1	
1960s	57	74	7	0	0	
1970s	60	82	2	2	3	
1980s	104	47	1	13	4	1981, 1984, 1988, 1989
1990s	113	47	0	9	7	1994
2000s	35	29	0	1	2	
NFL All-Time	432	333	13	25	17	5

Winning seasons: 33. Losing Seasons: 18. .500 seasons: 3.

Coaches

	Years	Record	Playoffs
Buck Shaw	1950–4	33–25–2	0–0
Red Strader	1955	4–8–0	0–0
Frankie Albert	1956–8	19–16–1	0–1
Red Hickey	1959–63	27–27–1	0–0
Jack Christiansen	1963–7	26–38–3	0–0
Dick Nolan	1968–75	54–53–5	2–3
Monte Clark	1976	8–6–0	0–0
Ken Meyer	1977	5–9–0	0–0
Pete McCulley	1978	1–8–0	0–0
Fred O'Connor	1978	1–6–0	0–0
Bill Walsh (3)	1979–88	92–59–1	10–4
George Seifert (2)	1989–96	98–30–0	10–5
Steve Mariucci	1997–2002	57–39–0	3–4
Dennis Erickson	2003	7–9–0	0–0

(Championships in parentheses)

Those who wore retired numbers after the honored player: 12 was later worn by Maury Duncan; 34 was later worn by Bill Cooper, Dick Witcher, and Clem Daniels; 39 was later worn by Kermit Alexander; and 73 was later worn by Dave McCormick and Lance Olssen.

Numbers that should be retired: Jerry Rice, 80, is the finest receiver in league history. Steve Young, 8, is one of the highest rated passers in NFL history.

Owned numbers: None, but only Steve Young has ever worn 8.

Numbers worn by Hall of Famers: Jimmy Johnson 37; John Henry Johnson 35; Ronnie Lott 42; Hugh McElhenny 39; Joe Montana 16; Leo Nomellini 73/42; Joe Perry 34/74; Bob St. Clair 79; O.J. Simpson 32; Y.A. Tittle 14/64; and Dave Wilcox 64.

Star power: Gary Plummer took 50 from Chris Dalman; Jim Burt took 64 from Rollin Putzier; Kevin Greene took 91 from Daryl Price; Richard Dent took 95 from Artie Smith.

Star eclipsed: Gary Johnson wore 97 because Harris Barton wore 79; Tim Harris wore 92 because Ted Washington wore 97.

Numbers with most great players: 40 has been worn by Pro Bowl runners Ken Willard and Wilbur Jackson as well as Pro Bowl defensive back Abe Woodson and fullbacks William Floyd and Fred Beasley. 53 has been worn by Pro Bowlers including end Alyn Beals, center Bill Johnson, defensive end Tommy Hart, and linebacker Bill Romanowski. 62 has been worn by Pro Bowl linemen Bob Toneff, Art Michalik, Randy Cross, Guy McIntyre, and Jeremy Newberry. 64 has been worn by Hall of Famers Y.A. Tittle and Dave Wilcox and Pro Bowl guards Visco Grgich and Ted Connolly. 79 has been worn by Hall of Famer Bob St. Clair, star tackles Harris Barton and Cas Bandaszek as well defensive end Jim Stuckey.

Worst represented numbers: 15 and 19 each have been worn by a small but ugly assortment of quarterbacks, punters, and receivers, none of whom lasted for more than a year or two.

Number worn by the most players: 32 and 50 have both been worn 22 times.

Player who wore the most numbers: Don Burke wore six numbers— 6/32/38/66/68/73.

Longest tenure wearing a number: John Brodie wore 12 for 17 years from 1957 to 1973. Jerry Rice wore 80 for 16 years from 1985 to 2000 and Jimmy Johnson wore 37 for 16 years from 1961 to 1976. Three players wore their number for 15 years— Charlie Krueger 70 from 1959 to 1973, Len Rohde 76 from 1960 to 1974, and Jessie Sapolu 61 from 1983 to 1997.

Number worn by first ever draft pick: Leo Nomellini was selected in the first round in 1950 and wore 42 and then 73.

Biggest draft busts: Quarterback Jim Druckenmiller, 14, was selected 26th in 1997 and completed 40 percent of his passes while throwing only one td pass. J.J. Stokes, 83, was selected 10th in 1995 and lasted eight years but caught only 327 passes for a 12.7 yard average.

Number worn by oldest player: Ray Brown was 39 when he wore 65 in 2001.

Cameos: All Pros and other notables— Gary Anderson 1; Matt Bahr 10; Wes Chandler 81; Clem Daniels 33/34; Richard Dent 95; Goose Gonsoulin 35; Jacob Green 76; Dennis Harrison 96; Bob Hayes 22; Thomas Henderson 50; Gary Knafelc 84; Mark Lee 27; Lenny Lyles 26; Matt Millen 54; Sonny Randle 83; Reggie Roby 4; Fred Smerlas 76.

Ones who got away: John Henry Johnson 35 was part of the 49ers' "Million Dollar Backfield," but had his best years in Pittsburgh. Jeff Wilkins 14 is the leading scorer in Rams history. Billy Kilmer 17 became a winning quarterback for New Orleans and Washington. Jerry Tubbs 50 was a Pro Bowl linebacker in Dallas. Ed McCaffrey 81 caught a lot of passes in Denver; Aaron Thomas 89 caught a lot of passes in New York; Wesley Walls 89 caught a lot of passes in New Orleans and Carolina. Ted Washington 97 has plugged the middle for Buffalo, Chicago and New England.

Least popular numbers: 0 has never been worn. 8 has been worn once, while 5 has been worn twice.

Last number to be originated: 2 was first worn by punter Ralf Mojsiejenko in 1991.

Longest dormant number: 9 has not been worn since 1990. 93 was dormant from 1952 until 1987.

Triskaidekaphobia notes: 13 was first worn by the great Frankie Albert and then by four other lesser quarterbacks and a wideout.

Shared numbers: 36 was worn by Pro Bowl kicker Tommy Davis and Pro Bowl safety Merton Hanks. 39 was worn by Hall of Famer Hugh McElhenny and Pro Bowl defensive back Kermit Alexander. 51 was worn by Pro Bowlers Randy Cross and Ken Norton. 94 was worn by Pro Bowl defensive linemen Charles Haley and Dana Stubblefield.

Continuity: Dwight Hicks was replaced in 22 by fellow defensive back Tim McKyer; Pro Bowl guard Visco Grgich was replaced in 34 by Hall of Famer Joe Perry; Pro Bowl defensive back Abe Woodson was replaced in 40 by Pro Bowler Ken Willard who in turn was replaced by runner Wilbur Jackson; Pro Bowl end Alyn Beals was replaced in 53 by Pro Bowl center Bill Johnson; Pro Bowl quarterback Frankie Albert was replaced in 63 by Pro Bowl guard Bruno Banducci; Ray Brown was replaced in 65 by fellow Pro Bowl guard Ron Stone; Pro Bowl pass rusher Fred Dean was replaced in 74 by Pro Bowl tackle Steve Wallace; Pro Bowl defensive end Cedrick Harman was replaced in 86 by star tight end Charlie Young.

Discontinuity: Del Williams was followed in 24 by Chuck Crist; Ricky Watters was followed in 32 by Ricky Ervins; John Henry Johnson was followed in 35 by Larry Barnes; Howard Mudd was followed in 68 by Kevin Hardy.

Quarterback numbers over 19: 62 Jesse Freitas; 63 Frankie Albert; 64 Y.A. Tittle, Parker Hall, Bev Wallace.

Number of first black player: Joe Perry in 1948 who wore 74 and later switched to 34.

Numbers of future NFL head coaches: Frankie Albert 63/13; Fred Bruney 45; Marion Campbell 76; Monte Clark 63; Tony Dungy 27; Bill Johnson 23/53; Ned Mathews 73/83; Ray Rhodes 26; and Steve Spurrier 11.

Numbers of future NFL referees: Royal Cathcart 94 and Jack Nix 58.

Players who played other sports: Baseball— Carroll Hardy 27, Deion Sanders 21,

Family Connections			
Brothers			
Sam Cathcart	DB	1949–52	28/83/86
Royal Cathcart	HB	1950	94
Charlie Krueger	DT	1959–73	70
Rolf Krueger	DL	1972–4	78
Keith Fahnhorst	T	1974–87	71/89
Jim Fahnhorst	LB	1984–90	55
Father and son			
Monte Clark	T	1959–61	63
Bryan Clark	QB	1982–4	15

and Wally Yonamine 94 (Japanese League). Wrestling — Leo Nomellini 42/73, Russ Francis 81, and Kevin Greene 91. Boxing — Charlie Powell 87. Track — Renaldo Nehemiah 83.

Players more famous after football: Bob St. Clair was the mayor of Daly City, CA. Fred Gehrke painted the horns on the Rams helmet.

First player to wear a number in the 80s: In 1946, Len Eshmont wore 81, Joe Vetrano wore 82 and Ken Casanega wore 83.

First player to wear a number in the 90s: In 1946, John Strzykalski wore 91, Joe Vetrano wore 92, Don Durdan wore 93 and Earl Parson wore 94.

Number with most points scored: 14 with 1,326 points scored by Ray Wersching (979), Jeff Wilkins (193), Y.A. Tittle (132), Dennis Patera (16), and Tom Owen (6).

Number with most yards rushing: 40 with 10,546 yards gained by Ken Willard (5,930), Wilbur Jackson (2,955), William Floyd (959), Fred Beasley (595), Vince Williams (68), and Abe Woodson (39).

Number with most receptions: 80 with 1,256 passes caught by Jerry Rice (1,206), Eason Ramsen (44), Terry LeCount (10), Steve Rivera (1), and Charles Smith (1).

Number with most touchdown passes: 16 with 277 touchdowns tossed by Joe Montana (244), Jim Plunkett (22), and Norm Snead (11).

Number with most interceptions: 42 with 71 passes picked off by Ronnie Lott (51), Lowell Wagner (12), Jim Ridlon (5), Ricky Odom (2), and Ernie Smith (1). And 22 with 71 passes picked off by Dwight Hicks (30),

Tim McKyer (16), Tyronne Drakeford (12), Joe Arenas (6), Pete Wisman (3), Eddie Lewis (3), and Todd Bowles (1).

Oddity: The 49ers used the strict AAFC numbering scheme until 1952 when they adopted the new NFL guidelines. In the AAFC scheme, centers wore 20s, guards wore 30s, tackles wore 40s, ends wore 50s, quarterbacks wore 60s, fullbacks wore 70s and halfbacks wore 80s and 90s. Numbers below 20 were not used.

Team All-Time Numerical Roster

Those with an "r" following the year 1987 were replacement players during the players' strike. Pro Bowl players for each number are in *Italics*; Hall of Famers are in **Bold** type.

1 Noland Smith (RB) 1969, Gary Anderson (K) 1997, Jason Baker (P) 2001–2.

2 Ralf Mojsiejenko (P) 1991, Eddie Howard (P) 1998, Todd Peterson (K) 2003.

3 Jim Miller (P) 1980–82, Tom Orosz (P) 1983, Tommy Thompson (P) 1995–97, Jeff Chandler (K) 2002–3.

4 Max Runager (P) 1984–88, Joe Prokop (P) 1991, Doug Brien (K) 1994–5, Reggie Roby (P) 1998, Chad Stanley (P) 1999, Billy Lafleur (P) 2002–3.

5 Jeff Brockhaus (K) 1987r, *Jeff Garcia* (QB) 1999–2003.

6 Don Burke (FB/G) 1950–1, Matt Cavanaugh (QB) 1983–5, Mike Cofer (K) 1988–93, Cary Conklin (QB) 1995, Jose Cortez (K) 2001–2.

7 Benjamin Guy (QB) 1981–3, Mark Stevens (QB) 1987r, Todd Santos (QB) 1988, Tony Zendejas (K) 1995, Wade Richey (K) 1998–9.

8 *Steve Young* (QB) 1987–99.

9 Jeff Kemp (QB) 1986, Jim Asmus (P) 1987r, Barry Helton (P) 1988–90.

10 George Mira (QB) 1964–8, Dennis Morrison (QB) 1974, Steve Mike-Meyer (K) 1975–6, Mike Connell (P) 1978, Matt Bahr (K) 1981, Ed Blount (QB) 1987r, Klaus Wilmsmeyer (P) 1992–4, Pat Barnes (QB) 1999.

11 Earl Morrall (QB) 1956, Bob Waters (QB) 1960–4, Steve Spurrier (QB) 1967–75, Dan Melville (P) 1979, Bob Gagliano (QB) 1986–7, Jeff Brohm (QB) 1995–97, Ty Detmer (QB) 1998, Brandon Doman (QB) 2002, Owen Pochman (K) 2003.

12 Hal Ledyard (QB) 1953, *John Brodie* (QB) 1957–73, Maury Duncan (P) 1979.

13 *Frank Albert* (QB) 1952, Joe Reed (QB) 1972, *Tom Wittum* (P) 1973–7, Steve Bono (QB) 1989–93, Gino Torretta (QB) 1995, Mike Caldwell (WR) 1996, Tim Rattay (QB) 2000–3.

14 Y.A. Tittle (QB) 1952–60, Sam Etcheverry (QB) 1963, Dennis Patera (K) 1968, Tom Owen (QB) 1974–5, Marty Domres (QB) 1976, Jim Plunkett (QB) 1976, Ray Wersching (K) 1977–87, Bill Musgrave (QB) 1991, 1993, Jeff Wilkins (K) 1995–6, Jim Druckenmiller (QB) 1997–8, Vinnie Sutherland (WR) 2001.

15 Jim Powers (HB) 1952–3, Lamar McHan (QB) 1963, Jon Kilgore (P) 1969, Jim McCann (P) 1971–2, Bryan Clark (QB) 1982–3, Mike Moroski (QB) 1986, John Paye (QB) 1988, Roell Preston (KR) 1999.

16 Andy Galiffa (QB) 1954, Norman Snead (QB) 1974–5, Jim Plunkett (QB) 1976–7, **Joe Montana** (QB) 1979–92.

17 Billy Kilmer (QB) 1961–6, Momcilo Gavric (K) 1969, John Isenbarger (RB) 1970–3, Joe Reed (QB) 1973–4, Steve DeBerg (QB) 1977–80, Tony Gladney (WR) 1987r, Mike Caldwell (WR) 1996, Kevin Lee (WR) 1996, Kevin Daft (QB) 2001.

18 Fred Gehrke (HB) 1950, *Gene Washington* (WR) 1969–77, Elvis Grbac (QB) 1993–6, Steve Stenstrom (QB) 1999, James Jordan (WR) 2002–3.

19 Joe Reed (QB) 1973–4, Scott Bull (QB) 1976–8, Gary Huff (QB) 1980, Tom Orosz (P) 1984, John Faylor (S) 1987r, Terrance Warren (WR) 1995, Mark Harris (WR) 1996, Giovanni Carmazzi (QB) 2000, Arland Bruce (WR) 2003.

20 Bill Stits (DB) 1957–8, Charley Britt (DB) 1964, George Donnelly (DB) 1965–7, Tony Harris (WR) 1971, Mike Holmes (DB) 1974–5, James Owens (WR) 1979, Terry Anderson (WR) 1980, Amos Lawrence (RB) 1981–2, Tory Nixon (CB) 1985–8, Sheldon Canley (RB) 1991–2, Derek Loville (RB) 1994–5, *Garrison Hearst* (RB) 1997–2003.

21 Art Elston (C) 1946, 1948, Tony Calvelli (C) 1947, Larry Jones (WR) 1978, Eric Wright (CB) 1981–90, Troy Kyles (WR) 1992, *Deion Sanders* (CB) 1994, Randy Baldwin (RB) 1995, R.W. McQuarters (CB) 1998–9.

22 Gerry Conlee (C) 1946–7, Joel Williams (C) 1948, Pete Wismann (C/LB) 1949–51, Joe Arenas (HB) 1952–7, Gary Lewis (FB) 1964–9, Vic Washington (RB) 1971–3, Bob Hayes (WR) 1975, Eddie Lewis (CB) 1976–9, *Dwight Hicks* (S) 1979–85, Tim McKyer (CB) 1986–9, Ray Brown (RB) 1987r, Todd Bowles (S) 1991, Amp Lee (RB) 1992–3, Tyrone Drakeford (DB) 1994–7, Tony Blevins (S) 1998, Terry Jackson (RB) 1999–2003.

23 Bill Remington (C) 1946, George Smith (C) 1947, *Bill Johnson* (C) 1948–51, Rex Berry (HB) 1952–6, Ray Norton (HB) 1960–1, Wayne Swin-

ford (DB) 1965–7, Johnny Fuller (S) 1970–2, Bruce Rhodes (DB) 1975, Bruce Threadgill (S) 1978, Herb Williams (CB) 1980, Tony Cherry (RB) 1986–7, Spencer Tillman (HB) 1989–91, Marquez Pope (CB) 1995–8, Pierson Prioleau (DB) 1999–2000, Jimmy Williams (DB) 2001–3.

24 Ed Forrest (C) 1946, John Schiechl (C) 1947, Tino Sabuco (C) 1949, Howie Livingston (HB) 1950, J.R. Boone (HB) 1952, Bill Tidwell (HB) 1954, *J.D Smith* (HB) 1956–64, Wayne Trimble (DB) 1967, Jimmy Thomas (RB) 1969–73, *Delvin Williams* (RB) 1974–7, Chuck Crist (DB) 1978, Eric Johnson (S) 1979, Rick Gervais (S) 1981–3, Derrick Harmon (RB) 1984–6, Harry Sydney (FB) 1987–91, *Eric Davis* (CB) 1990, Alan Grant (CB) 1992–3, Jamal Willis (RB) 1995, Monty Montgomery (CB) 1999–2000, George McCullough (DB) 2001, Mike Rumph (CB) 2002–3.

25 John Baldwin (C) 1947, George Smith (C) 1947, Tino Sabuco (C) 1949, Bob White (HB) 1952, Johnny Williams (HB) 1954, *Dave Baker* (HB) 1959–61, Roosevelt Taylor (S) 1969–73, Wonder Monds (S) 1978, Jeff Moore (RB) 1982–3, Doug DuBose (RB) 1987–8, Del Rodgers (RB) 1987, *Eric Davis* (CB) 1990–5, Brett Maxie (S) 1997, *Charlie Garner* (RB) 1999–2000, Jamal Robertson (RB) 2002–3.

26 Dick Handley (C) 1947, Tony Teresa (HB) 1958, Lenny Lyles (HB) 1959, Kay McFarland (HB) 1962–8, Tim Anderson (S) 1975, Stan Black (DB) 1977, Bob Jury (S) 1978, Ray Rhodes (CB) 1980, *Wendell Tyler* (RB) 1983–6, Darryl Pollard (CB) 1987–91, John Butler (S) 1987r, Michael McGruder (CB) 1992–3, Alan Grant (CB) 1992, Brian O'Neal (RB) 1995, Rod Woodson (CB) 1997, Anthony Parker (CB) 1999–2000, Rashad Holman (DB) 2001–3.

27 Bob Myers (FB) 1952, Ken Bahnsen (FB) 1953, Carroll Hardy (HB) 1955, Bob Holladay (HB) 1956, R.C. Owens (HB) 1957–61, Alvin Randolph (DB) 1966–70, Dennis Braggonier (DB) 1974, Nate Allen (CB) 1975, Tony Dungy (DB) 1979, *Carlton Williamson* (S) 1981–7, Mike Richardson (CB) 1989, Mark Lee (CB) 1991, Adam Walker (RB) 1992, Frankie Smith (CB) 1996–7, James Williams (CB) 1996, Craig Newsome (CB) 1999, Paul Smith (RB) 2000–2.

28 Sam Cathcart (HB) 1952, Howie Williams (HB) 1963, Ben Scotti (DB) 1964, Jim Strong (RB) 1970, David Watkins (RB) 1973, Mike Burns (DB) 1977, Charles Cornelius (DB) 1979–80, Lynn Thomas (DB) 1981–2, Tom Holmoe (S) 1983–5, Joe Cribbs (RB) 1986–7, Bruce Plummer (CB) 1990, Dana Hall (S) 1992–4, Curtis Buckley (S) 1996–8, John Keith (S) 2000, 2002–3.

29 Bill Atkins (HB) 1958–9, Dale Messer (HB) 1961–5, Bob Daugherty (HB) 1966–7, David Atkins (HB) 1975, John Bristor (S) 1979, Gerard Williams (DB) 1979–80, Saladin Martin (DB)

1981, Mario Clark (CB) 1984, Don Griffin (CB) 1986–93, Terry Greer (WR) 1987r, Anthony Lynn (RB) 1995–6, Frankie Smith (CB) 1997, Mark McMillian (CB) 1999, Ahmed Plummer (CB) 2000–3.

30 Bernie Casey (E) 1961–6, Johnny Fuller (S) 1969, Bruce Gossett (K) 1970–4, Dave Williams (RB) 1977, Tim Gray (DB) 1979, Bill Ring (RB) 1981–6, Jo Nathan (CB) 1987, Keith Henderson (FB) 1989–92, Mike Salmon (DB) 1996–7, *Lance Schulters* (S) 1998–2002.

31 Tony Calvelli (C) 1947, Don Clark (G) 1948–9, Charles Shaw (G) 1950, Joe Orduna (RB) 1971, Earl Carr (RB) 1978, Walt Easley (FB) 1981–2, Derrick Martin (LB) 1987r, Chet Brooks (DB) 1988–90, Thane Gash (S) 1992, Steve Israel (CB) 1995–6, Zack Bronson (S) 1997–2003.

32 *Garlin Gregory* (G) 1946–7, James Cox (G) 1948, Don Burke (FB/G) 1950, Bob Downs (G) 1951, *Norm Standlee* (FB) 1952, Frank Cassara (FB) 1954, Lem Harkey (HB) 1955, Gene Babb (FB) 1957–8, C.R. Roberts (FB) 1959–62, Lloyd Winston (FB) 1962–3, Rudy Johnson (HB) 1964–5, Mel Phillips (DB) 1966–76, **O.J. Simpson** (RB) 1978–9, Scott Perry (S) 1980, Ricky Patton (RB) 1981–2, Carl Monroe (RB/KR) 1983–4, Terrence Flagler (RB) 1987–9, *Ricky Watters* (RB) 1991–4, Ricky Ervins (RB) 1995, Chuck Levy (RB/KR) 1996–8, Travis Jervey (RB) 1999–2000, Kevan Barlow (RB) 2001–3.

33 *Bruno Banducci* (G) 1946–51, Hardy Brown (LB) 1952–6, Clancy Osborne (LB) 1959–60, Jim Vollenweider (FB) 1962–3, Clem Daniels (RB) 1968, Bill Wondolowski (WR) 1969, Randy Jackson (RB) 1973, John Saunders (DB) 1974–5, Greg Boykin (FB) 1978, Ricky Churchman (S) 1980–1, *Roger Craig* (RB) 1983–90, Derrick Dodge (S) 1994–6, Lawrence Phillips (RB) 1999, Jason Moore (S) 2000, 2002, Tony Parrish (S) 2002–3.

34 Ed Forrest (C) 1947, *Visco Grgich* (G) 1948–51, **Joe Perry** (FB) 1952–60, 1963, Bill Cooper (FB) 1961–2, Dick Witcher (E) 1966, Clem Daniels (RB) 1968.

35 Rupe Thornton (G) 1946, Dick Bassi (G) 1947, Bishop Strickland (FB) 1951, **John Henry Johnson** (HB) 1954–6, Larry Barnes (FB) 1957, J.W. Lockett (FB) 1961, Don McIlhenny (HB) 1961, Bob Gaiters (HB) 1962, Bill Cooper (FB) 1963–4, Goose Gonsoulin (DB) 1967, Larry Schreiber (RB) 1971–5, Elliott Walker (RB) 1978, Lenvil Elliott (RB) 1979–81, Del Rodgers (RB) 1987–8, Dexter Carter (RB) 1990–5, Ramos McDonald (CB) 1999, Dwaine Carpenter (S) 2003.

36 Dick Bassi (G) 1946, Art Elston (C) 1947, Paul Evansen (G) 1948, John Morton (LB) 1953, Bud Laughlin (FB) 1955, Paul Goad (FB) 1956, *Tommy Davis* (K) 1959–69, Paul Hofer (RB) 1976–81, Darryl Pollard (CB) 1987r, *Merton Hanks* (CB/S) 1991–8, Jason Webster (CB) 2000–3.

37 Chuck Pavlich (G) 1946, *Riley Matheson* (G/LB) 1948, Homer Hobbs (G) 1949–50, Nick Feher (G) 1951–4, **Jimmy Johnson** (HB) 1961–76.

38 *Visco Grgich* (G) 1947, Walt McCormick (C) 1948, Ray Evans (G) 1949–50, Don Burke (FB/G) 1951, Ben Aldridge (HB) 1952, Mike Lind (FB) 1963–4, Jim Jackson (HB) 1966–7, Mike Simpson (DB) 1970–2, Bob Ferrell (RB) 1976–80, Johnny Davis (FB) 1981, Blanchard Montgomery (LB) 1983, Greg Cox (S) 1988, 1990–1, Damien Russell (S) 1993, Darnell Walker (CB) 1997–9, Ronnie Heard (S) 2000–3.

39 Dave Sparks (G) 1951, **Hugh McElhenny** (HB) 1952–60, *Kermit Alexander* (DB) 1963–9.

40 John Carpenter (T) 1949, Harley Dow (G) 1950, George Maderas (HB) 1955–6, Bob Holladay (HB) 1957, Julian Spence (HB) 1957, *Abe Woodson* (DB) 1958–64, *Ken Willard* (FB) 1965–73, Wilbur Jackson (RB) 1974–9, Arrington Jones (FB) 1981, Vince Williams (FB) 1982–3, Mike Wells (TE) 1987r, Johnnie Jackson (S) 1989–92, William Floyd (FB) 1994–7, Fred Beasley (FB) 1998–2003.

41 *John Woudenberg* (T) 1946–9, Don Campora (T) 1950, Paul Hofer (RB) 1976, Mike Baldassin (LB) 1977–8, Carl Keever (LB) 1987r, Steve Bartolo (RB) 1988, David Whitmore (S) 1991–2, Terry Hoage (S) 1993, Toi Cook (DB) 1994, Terry Kirby (RB) 1996–8, Jason Isom (FB) 2003.

42 Bob Bryant (T) 1946–9, **Leo Nomellini** (T) 1950–1, Lowell Wagner (HB) 1952–3, 1955, Ernie Smith (HB) 1955–6, Jim Ridlon (HB) 1957–62, Don Libson (HB) 1963–4, Doug Cunningham (HB) 1967–73, Anthony Leonard (KR) 1976–8, Ricky Odom (DB) 1978, Ricky Patton (RB) 1980, **Ronnie Lott** (CB/S) 1981–90.

43 *Ray Collins* (T) 1950–1, *Jim Cason* (HB) 1952, 1954, Tom McCormick (HB) 1956, Jim Pace (HB) 1958, Dave Kopay (HB) 1964–7, Gene Moore (RB) 1969, Windlan Hall (S) 1972–5, Dana McLemore (KR) 1982–7, John Sullivan (S) 1987r, Dave Waymer (DB) 1990–1, Marc Logan (RB) 1992–4, Darryl Hall (S) 1995, Antonio Langham (CB) 1998, Wasswa Serwanga (CB) 1999, Jonas Lewis (RB) 2000–1, Duane Hawthorne (CB) 2002.

44 Pete Schabarum (HB) 1953–4, Joe Val (HB) 1957, *Eddie Dove* (HB) 1959–62, *John David Crow* (HB/TE) 1965–8, Bruce Taylor (CB) 1970–7, Charles Johnson (CB) 1979–80, Richard Blackmore (CB) 1983, Tom Rathman (FB) 1986–93, Tommy Vardell (FB) 1996, 1999, Marc Edwards (FB) 1997–8.

45 John Mellus (T) 1946, Odis Crowell (T) 1947, Fred Land (T/G) 1948, Chuck Quilter (T) 1949, *Al Carapella* (T) 1951, *John Strzykalski* (HB) 1952, Fred Bruney (HB) 1953, 1956, Elbert Kimbrough (DB) 1962–6, Bill Tucker (RB) 1967–70, Manfred Moore (RB) 1974–5, Mike Hogan (FB) 1979, Newton Williams (RB) 1982, Bobby Leopold (LB) 1983, Matt Courtney (S) 1987r, Kevin Lewis

(DB) 1990–2, Adrian Hardy (CB) 1993–4, Michael Williams (CB) 1995, Tyrone Legette (CB) 1998, Al Blades (DB) 2001, Tim Hauck (S) 2002.

46 John Kuzman (T) 1946, Rupe Thornton (G) 1947, Roman Bentz (T) 1948, Harold Puddy (T) 1948, Ray Evans (G) 1949, Clay Matthews (E) 1950, Hampton Tanner (T) 1951, Chip Myers (E) 1967, Danny Abramowicz (WR) 1973–4, Melvin Morgan (DB) 1979–80, Tim Washington (CB) 1982, Tom Holmoe (S) 1986–9, Del Rodgers (RB) 1987, *Tim McDonald* (S) 1993–9.

47 *Visco Grgich* (G) 1947, Bob Mike (T) 1948–9, *Ed Henke* (DE) 1951, *Dick Moegle* (HB) 1955, Hugo Hollas (DB) 1974, Kermit Johnson (RB) 1975–6, Al Matthews (S/CB) 1977, Jerry Aldridge (HB) 1980, Don Woods (RB) 1980, Tim Collier (CB) 1982–4, Chris Dressel (TE) 1987r, John Faylor (S) 1987r, Andre Hardy (FB) 1987r.

48 Alf Satterfield (T) 1947, Floyd Collier (T) 1948, Joe Morgan (T) 1949, Bill Mixon (HB) 1953–4, Ben Scotti (DB) 1964, John Woitt (DB) 1968–9, Sammy Johnson (RB) 1974–6, Phil Francis (RB) 1979–80, Ken McAlister (LB/S) 1983, Mike Varajon (FB) 1987r, Tim Jorden (TE) 1995.

49 Jim Monachino (HB) 1953, Bob Luna (HB) 1955, Dwight Lee (RB) 1968, Ralph McGill (CB) 1972–6, Van Roberson (DB) 1978, Earl Cooper (FB/TE) 1980–2, Jeff Fuller (S/LB) 1984–9, Adrian Cooper (TE) 1996, Aaron Walker (TE) 2003.

50 Leo Rucka (C) 1956, Stan Sheriff (LB) 1956–7, Jerry Tubbs (LB) 1958–9, Floyd Dean (LB) 1964, Ed Beard (LB) 1965–72, Caesar Belser (LB) 1974, *Dave Washington* (LB) 1975–7, Joe Harris (LB) 1978, Dave Morton (LB) 1979, Ron Shuman (LB) 1979, Thomas Henderson (LB) 1980, Terry Tautolo (LB) 1980–1, Jim Looney (LB) 1981, Ed Judie (LB) 1982–3, Riki Ellison (LB) 1983–9, LeRoy Etienne (LB) 1990, Reggie McKenzie (LB) 1992, Chris Dalman (G/C) 1993, Gary Plummer (LB) 1994–7, Anthony Peterson (LB) 1998–9, Artie Ulmer (LB) 2000, Derek Smith (LB) 2001–3.

51 Bob Titchenal (E) 1946, Dick Horne (E) 1947, *Gordy Soltau* (E) 1950–1, Carter Campbell (LB) 1970, Bruce Elia (LB) 1976, *Randy Cross* (G/C) 1977–88, *Ken Norton* (LB) 1994–2000, Saleem Rasheed (LB) 2002–3.

52 Hal Shoener (E) 1948–50, Billy Wilson (E) 1951, Pete Wismann (C) 1952, 1954, George Morris (C) 1956, Karl Rubke (C) 1957–60, 1962–5, Skip Vanderbundt (LB) 1968–77, Jeff McIntyre (LB) 1979, Bobby Leopold (LB) 1980–3, Blanchard Montgomery (LB) 1984, John Hill (C) 1985, George Cooper (LB) 1987, Larry Kelm (LB) 1993, Jamal Fountaine (DE) 1995, Jim Schwantz (LB) 1997, Randy Neal (LB) 1998, Joe Zelenka (LS) 1999, Brock Gutierrez (C) 2003.

53 *Alyn Beals* (E) 1946–51, *Bill Johnson* (C) 1952–6, Frank Morze (C) 1957–61, Mike Dowdle

(LB) 1963–5, *Tommy Hart* (DE) 1968–77, Dean Moore (LB) 1978, Thomas Seabron (LB) 1979–80, Milt McColl (LB) 1981–7, Bill Romanowski (LB) 1988–93, Anthony Peterson (LB) 1994–5, James Williams (LB) 1997–8, Jeff Ulbrich (LB) 2000–3.

54 Gail Bruce (E) 1948–51, Joe Manley (LB) 1953, Ed Beatty (C) 1955–6, *Marv Matuszak* (LB) 1957–8, Bob Harrison (LB) 1959–61, 1965–7, Ed Pine (LB) 1962–4, Harold Hays (LB) 1968–9, Marty Huff (LB) 1972, Tom Hull (LB) 1974, Bill Reid (C) 1975, Ed Bradley (LB) 1977–8, Bob Martin (LB) 1979, Craig Puki (LB) 1980–1, Ron Ferrari (LB) 1982, Ron Hadley (LB) 1987–8, Matt Millen (LB) 1989, Martin Harrison (LB) 1990, Mitch Donahue (LB) 1991–2, *Lee Woodall* (LB) 1994–9, Quincy Stewart (LB) 2001–2.

55 Hank Norberg (E) 1946–7, Paul Salata (E) 1949–50, Bill Jessup (E) 1951, *Matt Hazeltine* (LB) 1955–68, Greg Collins (LB) 1975, Bruce Elia (LB) 1977–8, Scott Hilton (LB) 1979–80, Bob Horn (LB) 1982–3, Jim Fahnhorst (LB) 1984–90, John Johnson (LB) 1991–3, Kevin Mitchell (LB) 1994–7, *Winfred Tubbs* (LB) 1998–2000, Jamie Winborn (LB) 2001–3.

56 Bill Fisk (E) 1946–7, Clarence Howell (E) 1948, Pete Brown (C) 1953–4, Joe Cerne (C) 1965–7, Bob Hoskins (DT) 1970–5, *Fred Quillan* (C) 1978–87, Darren Comeaux (LB) 1987, James Johnson (LB) 1987r, Steve Hendrickson (LB) 1989, Martin Harrison (LB) 1992–4, Jamal Fountaine (DE) 1995, *Chris Doleman* (DE) 1996–8, Joe Wesley (LB) 1999–2000, Terry Killens (LB) 2001, Brandon Moore (LB) 2002–3.

57 Ed Balatti (E) 1946–8, Paul Carr (LB) 1955–8, Dennit Morris (LB) 1958, Bill Lopasky (G) 1961, Floyd Dean (LB) 1964, Frank Nunley (LB) 1967–76, Dan Bunz (LB) 1978–84, Jim Kovach (LB) 1985, Tom Cousineau (LB) 1986–7, Kevin Dean (LB) 1987, Sam Kennedy (LB) 1988, Brett Faryniarz (LB) 1993, Rickey Jackson (DE/LB) 1994–5, Randy Kirk (LB/LS) 1996–8, Chris Draft (LB) 1999, Jason Kyle (LB) 2000, Cornelius Anthony (LB) 2002–3.

58 Nick Susoeff (E) 1946–9, Jack Nix (E) 1950, Walt Yowarsky (C) 1958, Jack Chapple (LB) 1965, Walter Johnson (DE) 1967, Jim Sniadecki (LB) 1969–73, Billy McKoy (LB) 1974, Howard Stidham (LB) 1977, Marc Nichols (LB) 1978, Gordy Ceresino (LB) 1979, *Keena Turner* (LB) 1980–90, Todd Kelly (DE) 1993–4, Randy Kirk (LB/LS) 1999, Frank Strong (LB) 2002.

59 Norm Maloney (E) 1948–9, Alex Loyd (E) 1950, Fritz Greenlee (LB) 1969, Willie Harper (LB) 1973–83, Gary Moten (LB) 1983, Fulton Kuykendall (LB) 1985, Darren Comeaux (LB) 1987, Tom Cousineau (LB) 1987, Keith Browner (LB) 1987r, Keith DeLong (LB) 1989–93, Israel Ifeanyi (DE) 1995, Steve Gordon (C) 1997, Reggie Givens (LB) 1998–9, Shane Elam (LB) 2001.

60 Roland Lakes (DT) 1961–70, Bill Sandifer (DT) 1974–6, Steve Knutson (G/T) 1978, Mike Calhoun (DT) 1980, Mel Land (DE) 1980, Kenny Times (DT) 1980, Jerry Wikinson (DE) 1980, John Choma (G/C) 1981–2, Blanchard Montgomery (LB) 1983, Vince Stroth (T) 1985, Chuck Thomas (C) 1987–92, Joe Rudolph (G) 1997, Ben Lynch (C) 1999–2002.

61 Charlie Hunt (LB) 1973, Andy Maurer (G) 1976, Dan Audick (T/G) 1981–2, *Jesse Sapolu* (C/G) 1983–97, Joe Drake (NT) 1987r.

62 Jesse Freitas (QB) 1946, Jim Powers (HB) 1950–1, *Bob Toneff* (T) 1952, *Art Michalik* (G) 1953–4, Mike Magac (G) 1960–4, Dave Hettema (T) 1967, *Randy Cross* (G/C) 1976, Walt Downing (C/G) 1978–83, *Guy McIntyre* (G) 1984–93, *Jeremy Newberry* (C) 1998–2003.

63 *Frank Albert* (QB) 1946–51, *Bruno Banducci* (G) 1952–4, Ed Sharkey (G) 1955–6, Monte Clark (T) 1959–61, Frank Morze (C) 1964, Jim Wilson (G) 1965–6, Don Parker (G) 1967, Edgar Hardy (G) 1973, Dick Enderle (G) 1976, Rocky Rasley (G) 1976, Terry Beeson (LB) 1982, Eric Scoggins (LB) 1982, Gary Moten (LB) 1983, Jim Leonard (CB) 1985, Tracy Franz (G) 1987r, Ricky Siglar (G/T) 1990, Derrick Deese (G) 1992–2003.

64 Parker Hall (QB) 1946, Bev Wallace (QB) 1947–9, **Y.A. Tittle** (QB) 1951, *Visco Grgich* (G) 1952, Doug Hogland (G) 1953–5, *Ted Connolly* (G) 1956–62, **Dave Wilcox** (LB) 1964–74, Dale Mitchell (LB) 1976, Kyle Davis (C) 1978, Ken Bungranda (T) 1980, Jack Reynolds (LB) 1981–4, Michael Durrette (G) 1986–7, Rollin Putizer (NT) 1989, Jim Burt (NT) 1989–91, Dean Caliguire (C) 1991, Ralph Tamm (G) 1992–4, Steve Gordon (C) 1998.

65 *Ted Connolly* (G) 1954, Eldred Kraemer (G) 1955, Tony Sardisco (G) 1956, Charlie Sieminski (T) 1963–5, Dave Hettema (T) 1967, Randy Beisler (G/T) 1969–74, Steve Lawson (G) 1976, Ernie Hughes (G) 1978–80, Lawrence Pillers (DE) 1980–4, Doug Rogers (DE) 1986, Jeff Bregel (G) 1987–9, Kevin Reach (G) 1987r, Harry Boatswain (T) 1992–4, *Ray Brown* (G) 1996–2001, *Ron Stone* (G) 2002–3.

66 Don Burke (FB/LB) 1952–4, John Wittenborn (G) 1958–60, Carlton Kammerer (LB) 1961–2, Roy Williams (T) 1963–4, *Elmer Collett* (G) 1967–72, Bob Penchion (T) 1974–5, Johnny Miller (G) 1977, Bob Nelson (LB) 1979, Ted Vincent (DT) 1979, Allan Kennedy (T) 1981–4, Mark Cochran (T) 1987r, Limbo Parks (G) 1987r, Terry Tausch (G) 1989, David Wilkins (LB) 1992, *Bart Oates* (C) 1994–5, *Kevin Gogan* (G) 1997–8, Tyrone Hopson (G) 1999–2000, Eric Heitmann (G) 2002–3.

67 Nick Feher (G) 1951–4, *Walter Rock* (T) 1963–7, John Watson (T) 1971–6, Ron Singleton (T) 1977–80, Jim Nicholson (T) 1981, Pete Kugler

(DT) 1982–3,1986–90, John Macauley (OL) 1984, Billy Shields (T) 1984, Roy Foster (G) 1991–3, Chris Dalman (G/C) 1994–2000, Dwayne Ledford (C) 2003.

68 Dave Sparks (G) 1951, Bob Momsen (G) 1952, Don Burke (FB/LB) 1953, Lou Palatella (G) 1955–8, John Sutro (T) 1962, *Howard Mudd* (G) 1964–9, Kevin Hardy (DT/G) 1970, John Ayers (G) 1977–86, Tim Long (C) 1987r, Dave Cullity (T) 1989, Rob Murphy (C) 2003.

69 Jerry Smith (G) 1952–3, Bob Hantla (G) 1954–5, *Woody Peoples* (G) 1968–77, Riki Ellison (LB) 1983, Bruce Collie (T/G) 1985–9, Tom Neville (G) 1991, Rod Milstead (G) 1994–7, Phil Ostrowski (G) 1998–2000, Kyle Kosier (T) 2003.

70 Tom Dahms (T) 1957, *Charles Krueger* (DT) 1959–73.

71 Zigmond Zamlynsky (HB) 1946, Ed Robnett (HB) 1947, Verl Lillywhite (HB) 1948–50, *Keith Fahnhorst* (T) 1974–87, Brian Bollinger (G) 1992–3, Charles Mann (DE) 1994, Daryl Price (DE) 1996, Albert Reese (DT) 1997, Chris Ruhman (T) 1998, Jeff Buckey (T) 1999, Cedric Killings (DT) 2000, Craig Osika (T) 2002.

72 *Norm Standlee* (FB) 1946–51, *Ray Collins* (T) 1952, Bill Herchman (T) 1956–9, Leon Donohue (T) 1962–4, Charlie Johnson (DT) 1966–7, Bill Belk (DE) 1968–74, *Cleveland Elam* (DT) 1975–8, Ruben Vaughan (DT) 1979, Ken Bungarada (T) 1980, Jeff Stover (DE) 1982–8, Limbo Parks (G) 1987r, Frank Pollack (T/G) 1990–1, Mark Thomas (DE) 1992–4, Oliver Barnett (DE) 1995, Dave Fiore (T/TE) 1996, Jamie Brown (T) 1998, Dan Goodspeed (T) 2001, Kyle Kosier (T) 2002, Chidi Ahanotu (DE) 2003.

73 Ned Mathews (HB) 1946, Dick Renfro (FB) 1946, Don Burke (FB/LB) 1950, Hardy Brown (LB) 1951, **Leo Nomellini** (T) 1952–63, Dave McCormick (T) 1966, Lance Olssen (T) 1968–9.

74 Ken Roskie (FB) 1946, Leonard Masini (FB) 1947–8, **Joe Perry** (FB) 1948–51, *Bob Toneff* (T) 1954–9, Henry Schmidt (T) 1959–60, Lou Cordileone (G) 1961, Clark Miller (DE) 1962–8, Earl Edwards (DT) 1969–72, Stan Hindman (DE) 1974, Jimmy Webb (DT) 1975–80, *Fred Dean* (DE) 1981–5, *Steve Wallace* (T) 1986–96, Dave Fiore (T) 1998–2002.

75 Bishop Strickland (FB) 1951, *Al Carapella* (T) 1953–5, *Ed Henke* (DE) 1956–60, John Mellekas (C) 1962, Clyde Brock (T) 1963, Jim Norton (T) 1965–6, *Forest Blue* (C) 1968–74, Ed Galigher (DT) 1977–9, Ted Vincent (DT) 1979–80, John Harty (DT) 1981–3, 1985–6, Kevin Fagan (DE) 1987–93, Frank Pollack (T/G) 1994–6, Matt Keneley (DT) 1999, Jim Flanigan (DT) 2002.

76 Don Campora (T) 1952, Marion Campbell (T) 1954–5, John Gonzaga (T) 1956, *Len Rohde* (T) 1960–74, Bill Cooke (DE) 1976, Willie McCray (DE) 1978, Dwaine Board (DE) 1979–88,

Mark Cochran (T) 1987r, Rollin Putzier (NT) 1989, Fred Smerlas (NT) 1990, Jacob Green (DE) 1992, John Childs (T) 1993, Kirk Scrafford (G/T) 1995–8, Dwayne Ledford (G/T) 1999–2000, Nate Hobgood-Chittick (DT) 2000.

77 Hampton Tanner (T) 1951, Hal Miller (T) 1953, Sid Youngelman (T) 1955, *Bruce Bosley* (C/G) 1956–68, Jean Barrett (T) 1973–80, Pete Kugler (DT) 1981, Bubba Paris (T) 1982–90, Greg Liter (DE) 1987r, James Parish (T) 1993, Karl Wilson (DL) 1993, Brian Bollinger (G) 1994, Oliver Barnett (DE) 1995, Tim Hanshaw (G) 1997–8, Matt Willig (T) 2000–2, Kwame Harris (T) 2003.

78 Bob Cross (T) 1956–7, *John Thomas* (G) 1958–67, Sam Silas (DE) 1969–70, Rolf Krueger (DT) 1972–4, Wayne Baker (DT) 1975, Archie Reese (DE) 1978–81, Lindsey Mason (T) 1982, John Choma (G/C) 1983, Daryle Skaugstad (DT) 1983, Manu Tuiasosopo (DT) 1984–6, Gary Hoffman (T) 1987r, *Pierce Holt* (DE) 1989–92, Michael Brandon (DE) 1995–6, Shane Bonham (DT) 1998–9, Scott Gragg (T) 2000–3.

79 **Bob St. Clair** (T) 1953–64, Casimir Bandaszek (T) 1967–77, Al Cowlings (DE) 1979, Jim Stuckey (DE) 1980–5, *Harris Barton* (T) 1987–98, Glen Collins (DE) 1987r, Dan Dercher (T) 1999–2000.

80 Jackson Brumfield (E) 1954, Charles Smith (E) 1956, *Jerry Mertens* (HB) 1958–65, Stan Hindman (DE) 1966–71,1973, Mike Bettiga (WR) 1973, Steve Rivera (WR) 1976, Terry LeCount (WR) 1978, Eason Ramson (TE) 1979–83, *Jerry Rice* (WR) 1985–2000.

81 Len Eshmont (HB) 1946–9, Dan Sandifer (DB) 1950, Verl Lillywhite (HB) 1951, *Dave Parks* (E) 1964–7, Leo Johnson (WR) 1969–70, Ed Beverly (WR) 1973, Willie McGee (E) 1976, Ken MacAfee (TE) 1978–9, Matt Bouza (WR) 1981, Russ Francis (TE) 1982–7, Wes Chandler (WR) 1988, Jamie Williams (TE) 1989–93, Ed McCaffrey (WR) 1994, Mike Caldwell (WR) 1995, *Terrell Owens* (WR) 1996–2003.

82 Pete Franceschi (HB) 1946, Joe Vetrano (HB) 1946–9, Emil Sitko (HB) 1950, Joe Arenas (HB) 1951, *Gordy Soltau* (E) 1952–8, Jerry Wilson (LB) 1960, Floyd Dean (LB) 1963, Bob Poole (TE) 1964–5, *Ted Kwalick* (TE) 1969–74, Len Garrett (TE) 1975, Tony Cline (DE) 1976, Lon Boyett (TE) 1978, Bob Bruer (TE) 1979–80, Lewis Gilbert (TE) 1980, Brian Peets (TE) 1981, *John Taylor* (WR) 1986–95, Terry Greer (WR) 1987r, Irv Smith (TE) 1998, Shonn Bell (TE) 1999, Kevin Williams (WR/KR) 2000, Eric Johnson (TE) 2001–2.

83 Ken Casanega (HB) 1946, 1948, Ned Mathews (HB) 1947, Sam Cathcart (HB) 1949–50, Rex Berry (HB) 1951, Pat O'Donahue (E) 1952, Clay Matthews (E) 1953–5, Gordon Kelly (LB) 1960–1, Sonny Randle (E) 1967, Terry Beasley (WR)

1972–3, Kenny Harrison (WR) 1976–8, Renaldo Nehemiah (WR) 1982–4, Carl Monroe (HB) 1985–7, Derrick Crawford (WR) 1986, Terry Greer (WR) 1988–9, Ronald Lewis (WR) 1990–2, Sanjay Beach (WR) 1993, J.J. Stokes (WR) 1995–2002, Arnaz Battle (WR) 2003.

84 Earle Parsons (HB) 1946–7, Parker Hall (QB) 1946, *Billy Wilson* (E) 1952–60, Gary Knafelc (E) 1963, Vern Burke (E) 1965, Dave Olerich (E) 1967–8,1972–3, Tom Mitchell (TE) 1974–7, Elmo Boyd (WR) 1978, Mike Schumann (WR) 1978–9, 1981, Darius Durham (WR) 1983, Al Dixon (TE) 1984, Ken Margerum (WR) 1986–7, Thomas Henley (WR) 1987, *Brent Jones* (TE) 1988–97, Tony Cline (TE) 1999, Terrence Dupree (TE) 2000, Cedrick Wilson (WR) 2001–3.

85 Eddie Carr (HB) 1947–9, Bob White (HB) 1951, Al Endriss (E) 1952, Bill Jessup (E) 1952, 1954–8, Monty Stickles (TE) 1960–7, *Clifton McNeil* (CB) 1968–9, Preston Riley (WR) 1970–2, Robert West (WR) 1974, Bill Larson (TE) 1975, Paul Seal (TE) 1977–9, Jimmy Robinson (WR) 1980, Michael Wilson (WR) 1981–90, Trot Kyles (WR) 1992, John Brandes (TE) 1993, Ted Popson (TE) 1994–5, Greg Clark (TE) 1997–2001, Mark Anelli (TE) 2002, Brandon Loyd (WR) 2003.

86 Sam Cathcart (HB) 1949–50, Jackson Brumfield (E) 1954, Tom Stolhandske (E) 1955, Clyde Conner (E) 1956–63, Dan Colchico (DE) 1960–4,1967, Steve Smith (TE) 1966–7, Kevin Hardy (DT/G) 1968–9, *Cedrick Hardman* (DE) 1970–9, Charlie Young (TE) 1980–2, John Frank (TE) 1984–8, Tony Gladney (WR) 1987r, Mike Barber (WR) 1989, Sanjay Beach (WR) 1991, Odessa Turner (WR) 1992–3, Brett Carolan (TE) 1994–5, Sean Manuel (TE) 1996, Chad Fann (WR) 1997–9, Brian Jennings (TE) 2000–3.

87 Charles Powell (E) 1952–3,1955–7, Fred Dugan (E) 1958–9, Dee Mackey (TE) 1960, Dan LaRose (DE) 1965, Tom Holzer (DE) 1967, Mike Raines (DT) 1974, Jim Lash (WR) 1976, Larry Jones (WR) 1978, Jack Steptoe (WR) 1978, *Dwight Clark* (WR) 1979–87.

88 Forrest Hall (HB) 1948, Don Garlin (HB) 1949–50, Pete Schabarum (HB) 1951, Gail Bruce (E) 1952, Harry Babcock (E) 1953–5, Clyde Conner (E) 1956–63, Dick Witcher (E) 1966–73, Terry Beasley (WR) 1974, Rick Jennings (WR) 1977, Freddie Solomon (WR) 1978–85, *Brent Jones* (TE) 1987, Calvin Nicholas (WR) 1988, Mike Sherrard (WR) 1989–92, Chris Dressel (TE) 1992, Nate Singleton (WR) 1993–5, Mark Harris (WR) 1997–9, Justin Swift (TE) 2000–2, Jed Weaver (TE) 2003.

89 *Ed Henke* (DE) 1952, Bob Van (E) 1953, Floyd Sagely (E) 1954, 1956, Ted Vaught (E) 1955, Aaron Thomas (E) 1961, Kent Kramer (TE) 1966, Bob Windsor (TE) 1967–71, *Keith Fahnhorst* (T) 1974, Jim Obradovich (TE) 1976, James Owens (WR) 1980, Earl Cooper (FB/TE) 1983–5, Ron

Heller (TE) 1987–8, Wesley Walls (TE) 1989–93, Chris Thomas (WR) 1995, Iheanyi Uwaezuoke (WR) 1996–8, Tai Streets (WR) 1999–2003.

90 Jim Krahl (DT) 1980, George Visger (DT) 1980, Mike Clark (DE) 1982, Todd Shell (LB) 1984–7, Mark Korff (LB) 1987r, Darin Jordan (LB) 1991–4, Junior Bryant (DE) 1995–2000, Bobby Setzer (DL) 2001, Jerome Davis (DL) 2002, Travis Kirschke (DT) 2003.

91 *John Strzykalski* (HB) 1946–51, Larry Roberts (DE) 1986–92, Rhett Hall (DT) 1994, Alfred Williams (DE) 1995, Daryl Price (DE) 1996–7, Kevin Greene (DE/LB) 1997, Chike Okeafor (DE) 1999–2002, Anthony Adams (DT) 2003.

92 Joe Vetrano (HB) 1946, Paul Crowe (HB) 1948, Lowell Wagner (HB) 1949–51, Scott Garnett (NT) 1985, Reno Patterson (DE) 1987r, Kevin Lilly (NT) 1988–9, Tim Harris (LB) 1991–2, 1994–95, Troy Wilson (LB/DE) 1993–4, Roy Barker (DE) 1996–8, Reggie McGrew (DT) 1999–2001, Devone Claybrooks (DT) 2003.

93 Don Durdan (HB) 1946, *Jim Cason* (HB) 1948–51, Clyde Glover (DE) 1987, Greg Joelson (DE) 1991, Garin Veris (DE) 1992, Matt LaBounty (DE) 1993, David Richie (DE) 1999, John Milem (DE) 2000, John Schlect (DL) 2001, Josh Shaw (DL) 2002.

94 Earle Parsons (HB) 1946, Wally Yonamine (HB) 1947, Bob Sullivan (HB) 1948, Royal Cathcart (HB) 1950, Howie Livingston (HB) 1950, Louie Kelcher (NT) 1984, *Charles Haley* (LB) 1988–91, 1999, *Dana Stubblefield* (DT) 1993–7, 2001–2, David Richie (DT) 1998, Anthony Pleasant (DE) 2000, Andrew Williams (DE) 2003.

95 *Michael Carter* (NT) 1984–92, Artie Smith (DL) 1993–4, Richard Dent (DE) 1994, Israel Ifeanyi (DE/ELE) 1996, Marvin Washington (DE) 1997, 1999, *Charles Haley* (DE) 1999, John Engelberger (DE) 2000–3.

96 Charles Elliott (RB) 1948, Dennis Harrison (DE) 1986, Elston Ridgle (DE) 1987r, Daniel Stubbs (DE) 1988–9, Dennis Brown (DE) 1990–6, Daryl Price (DE) 1997, Jeff Posey (DE) 1998–2002, Andre Carter (DE) 2001–3.

97 Gary Johnson (DT) 1984–5, Doug Mikolas (NT) 1987–8, Ted Washington (NT) 1991–3, *Bryant Young* (DT) 1994–2003.

98 Greg Boyd (DE) 1985, Jerry Keeble (LB) 1987r, *Pierce Holt* (DE) 1988, Antonio Goss (LB) 1989,1991–5, Gabe Wilkins (DE/DT) 1998–9, *Julian Peterson* (LB) 2000–3.

99 Jim Monachino (HB) 1951, Michael Walter (LB) 1984–93, Artie Smith (DT) 1994, Tim Harris (LB) 1994, 1995, David Benefield (LB) 1996, Brentson Buckner (DT) 1998–2000, Sean Moran (DL) 2002–3.

SEATTLE SEAHAWKS

The franchise: The Seattle franchise was awarded to Lloyd Nordstrom in 1974 and the Seahawks first took flight in 1976 as a companion expansion team to the Tampa Bay Buccaneers. While the Seahawks' won-lost percentage is nearly 100 points higher than the Bucs (.470 to .384), one can make an argument that the Bucs have been the more successful franchise — they've been to the playoffs eight times to the Hawks' six and have won a championship.

While they started out well under coach Jack Patera, posting winning records in their third and fourth seasons, Seattle has been a consistently mediocre team; the only full-season coach to leave Seattle with a winning record was Chuck Knox, who went 80–63 with four playoff berths from 1983 to 1991. Those years of Steve Largent, Curt Warner and Dave Kreig were the high point of the franchise. Midway through that time Ken Behring bought the team in 1988 and the coaches he hired, Tom Flores and Dennis Erickson, did not fare well with the Seahawks although they had been successful elsewhere.

In 1997, Microsoft billionaire Paul Allen bought the team and two years later hired Mike Holmgren from the Packers as Coach/GM. In his first four years, however, Holmgren managed the exact same record as his predecessor Erickson and was stripped of his GM duties. The Seahawks showed promise as an improving team in 2003 by making the playoffs, but looks can be deceiving in the rainy Northwest.

Origin of name: Seahawks was submitted by 151 entrants in a fan contest to name the new Seattle franchise, and the ownership group liked it the best of the 1,742 different names entered.

Record by Decade

	Regular Season			Postseason		
	Won	Lost	Tied	Won	Lost	Championships
1970s	25	35	0	0	0	
1980s	78	74	0	3	4	
1990s	70	90	0	0	1	
2000s	32	32	0	0	0	
All-Time	205	231	0	3	5	0

Winning seasons: 11. Losing Seasons: 13. .500 seasons: 4.

Time till first championship: 28 years and counting.

Time since last championship: Never won one.

Coaches

	Years	Record	Playoffs
Jack Patera	1976–82	35–59–0	0–0
Mike McCormack	1982	4–3–0	0–0
Chuck Knox	1983–91	80–63–0	3–4
Tom Flores	1992–4	14–34–0	0–0
Dennis Erickson	1995–8	31–33–0	0–0
Mike Holmgren	1999–2003	41–39–0	0–2

Retired numbers: The Seahawks were a bit overeager and rushed to retire number 12 in honor of their fans, the 12th man of their team, before they had any great former players to honor. Finally, when Steve Largent retired, so was his number 80, appropriately.

Other numbers worn by these players: None.

Those who wore retired numbers after the honored player: None.

Numbers that should be retired: None.

Owned numbers: Only Steve Largent ever wore 80. Although it was not retired in his honor, only backup quarterback Steve Adkins ever wore 12.

Numbers worn by Hall of Famers: Carl Eller 71; Franco Harris 34; Steve Largent 80.

Star power: Bennie Blades took 36 from Lamar Smith; Levon Kirkland took 99 from Matt LaBounty.

Star eclipsed: Franco Harris wore 34 because Cullen Bryant wore 32.

Numbers with most great players: 32 has been worn by runners John L. Williams and Ricky Watters as well as linebacker Mike Curtis.

Worst represented numbers: 6 has only been worn by two punters; 16 has only been worn by a backup quarterback and replacement cornerback.

Number worn by the most players: 88 has been worn 13 times.

Player who wore the most numbers: Defensive ends Matt Labounty 67/91/99 and Mike McCrary 75/92/99 both wore three numbers and so has tight end Itula Mili 49/88/89.

Longest tenure wearing a number: Steve Largent wore 80 for 14 years from 1976 to 1989.

Number worn by first ever draft pick: Defensive tackle Steve Niehaus was selected in the first round of the 1976 NFL draft and wore 71.

Biggest draft busts: Linebacker Brian Bosworth 55 was selected at the top of the 1987 supplemental draft and went on to play in only 24 of 48 games in the three years he spent in Seattle. Quarterback Rick Mirer 3, selected second in 1993, threw 41 tds and 57 interceptions in his four years as a Seahawk. Quarterback Dan McGwire 10, selected 16th in 1991, was the unsuccessful brother of baseball star Mark McGwire. Dan threw only 147 passes in his four years in Seattle.

Number worn by first expansion draft pick: The expansion draft was not conducted in rounds, but the best player and the player who had the longest tenure in Seattle was cornerback Dave Brown, who wore 22 from 1976 to 1986.

Number worn by oldest player: Warren Moon wore 1 as a 42 year old in 1998.

Cameos: Hall of Famers— Carl Eller 71;

Franco Harris 34; All Pros and other notables— Lyle Blackwood 28; Mike Curtis 32; Vernon Dean 31; Jeff George 3; Merton Hanks 36; Harold Jackson 29; Levon Kirkland 99; George Koonce 53; Ed Marinaro 49; Lawrence McCutcheon 30; Keith Millard 75; Bill Munson 19; Rohn Stark 3.

Ones who got away: Runner Ahman Green is second on the Packers all-time rushing leaders list. Kevin Mawae has been a very effective center for the Jets.

Least popular numbers: 0 has never been worn. 12 and 80 have been worn once.

Last number to be originated: Linebacker Donald Miller wore 99 for the first time in 1990.

Longest dormant number: 45 and 46 have both been unused since 1987.

Triskaidekaphobia notes: 13 has been worn by two replacement players and two unsuccessful quarterbacks.

Shared numbers: 32 was worn by two Pro Bowl runners, John L. Williams and Ricky Watters.

Continuity: Michael McCrary was replaced in 75 by Howard Ballard; Sean Dawkins was replaced in 81 by Koren Robinson.

Discontinuity: Kevin Mawae was followed in 52 by Jason McEndoo; Michael Jackson was followed in 55 by Brian Bosworth; Michael Sinclair was followed in 70 by Jerry Wunsch.

Family Connections			
Brothers			
John Eisenhooth	NT	1987	68
Stan Eisenhooth	C	1987–8	66
Brian Blades	WR	1988–98	89
Bennie Blades	DB	1997	36

Quarterback numbers over 19: None.

Numbers of future NFL head coaches: Mike Tice 86/87.

Numbers of future NFL referees: None.

Players who played other sports: None.

Players more famous after football: Steve Largent 80 served as a congressman from Oklahoma. Ed Marinaro 49 acted on *Hill*

Street Blues. Brian Bosworth 55 was a flop in action movies.

First player to wear a number in the 90s: Linebacker Charles McShane first wore 90 in 1977.

Number with most points scored: 9 with 1,080 points scored by Norm Johnson (810) and Rian Lindell (270).

Number with most yards rushing: 32 with 9,209 yards gained by John L. Williams (4,579), Ricky Watters (4,009), Jeff Moore (385), Cullen Bryant (145), Horace Ivory (89), Oscar Gray (4), and Kerry Carter (–2).

Number with most receptions: 80 with 819 passes caught by Steve Largent.

Number with most touchdown passes: 17 with 211 touchdowns tossed by Dave Kreig (195) and John Friesz (16).

Number with most interceptions: 22 with 54 passes picked off by Dave Brown (50), Nesby Glasgow (3), and Damien Robinson (1).

Oddity: The Seahawks are the only NFL team to retire a number for a non-football player, i.e., 12 for the 12th Man, the fans.

Players Whose Number Is Unknown		
Alvin Moore	(RB)	1987r
Howard Richards	(DL)	1987r

Team All-Time Numerical Roster

Those with an "r" following the year 1987 were replacement players during the players' strike. Pro Bowl players for each number are in *Italics*; Hall of Famers are in **Bold** type.

1 Efren Herrera (K) 1978–81, Scott Hagler (K) 1987r, *Warren Moon* (QB) 1997–8.

2 Wilson Alvarez (K) 1981, Vince Gamache (P) 1986, Todd Peterson (K) 1995–9.

3 John Leypoldt (K) 1976–8, Rick Donnelly (P) 1990–1, Brian Treggs (WR) 1992, Rick Mirer (QB) 1993–6, Rohn Stark (P) 1997, Kris Heppner (K) 2000, Jeff George (QB) 2002, Josh Brown (K) 2003.

4 Don Bitterlich (K) 1976, John Kasay (K) 1991–4, Trent Dilfer (QB) 2001–3.

5 Rick Engles (P) 1976–7, Jim Colquitt (P)

1985, Ruben Rodriguez (P) 1987–9, Alex Waits (P) 1991, Kyle Richardson (P) 1997, Travis Brown (QB) 2000.

6 Frank Garcia (P) 1981, Russell Griffith (P) 1987r.

7 Gale Gilbert (QB) 1985–6, Jon Kitna (QB) 1997–2000.

8 Jeff West (P) 1981–5, Stan Gelbaugh (QB) 1992, Matt Lytle (QB) 2000, *Matt Hasselbeck* (QB) 2001–3.

9 Norm Johnson (K) 1982–90, Rian Lindell (K) 2000–2.

10 Jim Zorn (QB) 1976–84, Barry Bowman (P) 1987r, Dan McGwire (QB) 1991–4, Jeff Feagles (P) 1998–2002.

11 Kelly Stouffer (QB) 1988–92, Andre Coleman (WR) 1997, Brock Huard (QB) 1999–2001.

12 Sam Adkins (QB) 1977–82.

13 Brant Bengen (WR) 1987r, Bruce Mathison (QB) 1987r, Gino Torretta (QB) 1996–7, Glenn Foley (QB) 1999.

14 Rick Tuten (P) 1991–7, Kevin Cook (WR) 2001.

15 Dave Finzer (P) 1985, Jeff Kemp (QB) 1987–91.

16 Steve Myer (QB) 1976–9, Charles Glaze (CB) 1987r, Tom Rouen (P) 2003.

17 *Dave Krieg* (QB) 1980–91, John Friesz (QB) 1995–8.

18 Herman Weaver (P) 1977–80, Stan Gelbaugh (QB) 1992–6, Daryl Hobbs (WR) 1997, Taco Wallace (WR) 2003.

19 Bill Munson (QB) 1976, James McKnight (WR) 1994, Fabien Bownes (WR) 1999–2000.

20 Steve Preece (S) 1977, Mike O'Brien (S) 1979, Terry Taylor (CB) 1984–8, Arnold Brown (CB) 1987r, Derek Loville (RB) 1991, James Jefferson (CB) 1992–3, Jay Bellamy (S) 1994–2000, Charlie Rogers (KR) 2001, Maurice Morris (RB) 2002–3.

21 Vic Minor (S) 1980–1, Paul Moyer (S) 1983–9, Chris White (S) 1987r, Rafael Robinson (S) 1992, T.J. Cunningham (S) 1996, Reggie Rusk (CB) 1997, Randy Fuller (CB) 1999, Cordell Taylor (CB) 1999, Ken Lucas (CB) 2001–3.

22 *Dave Brown* (CB) 1976–86, Anthony Blue (CB) 1987r, Nesby Glasgow (S) 1988–92, Jon Vaughn (RB) 1993–4, Beno Bryant (RB) 1994, Fred Thomas (CB) 1996–9, Paul Miranda (CB) 2000–1, Damien Robinson (S) 2003.

23 Patrick Hunter (CB) 1986–8, Thom Kaumeyer (S) 1989–90, Forey Duckett (S) 1994, Dexter Seigler (CB) 1996–7, Robert Williams (CB) 1999, Ike Charlton (CB) 2000–1, Marcus Trufant (CB) 2003.

24 Al Hunter (RB) 1977–80, Terry Jackson (CB) 1984–5, Melvin Jenkins (CB) 1987–90, Terry Taylor (CB) 1994, Selwyn Jones (CB) 1995–6, Shawn Springs (CB) 1997–2003.

25 Don Dufek (S) 1976–7, 1979–84, Rick Sanford (S) 1985, David Hollis (DB) 1987–9, Dallis Smith (S) 1987r, Robert Blackmon (S) 1990–6, Lamar Smith (RB) 1997, Mark Collins (S) 1998, Brian Walker (S) 1999, Reggie Tongue (S) 2000–3.

26 Kerry Justin (CB) 1978–83, 1986–7, Johnnie Johnson (S) 1989, James Jefferson (CB) 1989–91, Carlton Gray (CB) 1993–6, Tim Hauck (S) 1997, Chris Canty (CB) 1999–2000, Ken Hamlin (S) 2003.

27 Autry Beamon (S) 1977–9, Greggory Johnson (CB) 1981–3, 1986, James Williams (FB) 1987, Patrick Hunter (CB) 1989–94, Tony Covington (S) 1995, Willie Williams (CB) 1997–2003.

28 Lyle Blackwood (S) 1976, *Curt Warner* (RB) 1983–9, Del Speer (S) 1994, Dou Innocent (WR) 1996, Kerry Joseph (S) 1999–2001, Harold Blackmon (CB) 2001–2.

29 Al Matthews (S) 1976, Harold Jackson (WR) 1983, Rick Parros (FB) 1985, 1987r, Dwayne Harper (CB) 1988–93, Tony Brown (CB) 1994–5, C.J. Richardson (S) 1997, Curtis Fuller (S) 2001–2.

30 Oliver Ross (RB) 1976, Lawrence McCutcheon (RB) 1980, Theotis Brown (RB) 1981–3, *Bobby Joe Edmonds* (RB) 1986–8, Boyce Green (RB) 1987, James Jones (FB) 1989–92, Corey Harris (CB) 1995–6, Ahman Green (RB) 1998–9.

31 Tony Benjamin (FB) 1977–9, Zachary Dixon (RB) 1983–4, Fred Davis (CB) 1987r, Vernon Dean (S) 1988, Vann McElroy (S) 1990, Malcolm Frank (CB) 1992, Orlando Watters (CB) 1994, Steve Broussard (RB) 1995–8, Charlie Rogers (KR) 1999–2000, Marcus Robertson (S) 2001–2.

32 Mike Curtis (LB) 1976, Jeff Moore (RB) 1979–81, Horace Ivory (RB) 1981–2, Cullen Bryant (FB) 1983–4, *John L. Williams* (FB) 1986–93, Oscar Gray (FB) 1996–7, Ricky Watters (RB) 1998–2001, Kerry Carter (RB) 2003.

33 Andrew Bolton (RB) 1976, Dan Doornink (FB) 1979–85, Tommie Agee (FB) 1988, Elroy Harris (RB) 1989, Derek Loville (RB) 1990, Dedrick Dodge (S) 1991–2, 1994, *Darryl Williams* (S) 1996–9, Maurice Kelly (S) 2000–1, Doug Evans (CB) 2002–3.

34 Rufus Crawford (RB) 1978, Tony Green (KR) 1979, Jim Walsh (FB) 1980, Terry Miller (RB) 1981, **Franco Harris** (RB) 1984, Tony Burse (FB) 1987, Mike Hagen (FB) 1987r, Kevin Harmon (RB) 1988–9, Brian Davis (CB) 1991–2, Dion Lambert (S) 1994–5, Reggie Brown (FB) 1996–2000, Terreal Beirria (DB) 2002.

35 David Sims (FB) 1977–9, Mark Moore (S) 1987, Renard Young (CB) 1987r, Steve Smith (FB) 1994–5, Jay Graham (RB) 2001, Chris Davis (RB) 2003.

36 Ken Geddes (LB) 1976–8, Larry Brinson (RB) 1980, Michael Morton (RB) 1987r, David Daniels (WR) 1991, Brian Davis (CB) 1991, Rueben Mayes (RB) 1992–3, Lamar Smith (RB) 1994–6, Bennie Blades (S) 1997, Terry McDaniel (CB) 1998, Merton Hanks (S) 1999.

37 Hugh McKinnis (FB) 1976, Eric Lane (FB) 1981–7, Chad Stark (FB) 1987r, Rafael Robinson (S) 1993–5, Eric Stokes (S) 1997–8, *Shaun Alexander* (RB) 2000–3.

38 Ed Bradley (LB) 1976, Cornell Webster (CB) 1977–80, Ray Wilmer (S) 1984, Curtis Baham (CB) 1987r, Lou Brock (CB) 1988, Mack Strong (FB) 1994–2003.

39 Bill Olds (FB) 1976, Brian Allred (CB) 1993–4, Jeremy Lincoln (CB) 1997.

40 Walter Packer (CB) 1977, John Williams (FB) 1985, Kim Mack (S) 1987r, Ricky Thomas (S) 1987r, Kerry Joseph (S) 1998.

41 Eddie McMillan (CB) 1976–7, Will Lewis (CB) 1980–1, *Eugene Robinson* (S) 1985–95, Dustin Johnson (FB) 1999.

42 Don Testerman (FB) 1976–8, Keith Simpson (DB) 1980–5, *Chris Warren* (RB) 1990–7, Kris Richard (DB) 2002–3.

43 Jim Jodat (FB) 1980–1, Randall Morris (RB) 1984–8, Tracy Johnson (FB) 1992–5, Joey Eloms (CB) 1998–9.

44 Ralph Nelson (RB) 1976, John Harris (S) 1978–85, Derrick Fenner (RB) 1989–91, Dave McCloughan (CB) 1993–4, Brian Milne (FB) 1999, Heath Evans (FB) 2001–3.

45 Rolly Woolsey (CB) 1976, *Kenny Easley* (S) 1981–7.

46 Ted Bachman (CB) 1976, David Hughes (FB) 1981–5, Harvey Allen (S) 1987r.

47 Sherman Smith (RB) 1976–82, Andre Hardy (FB) 1985, Eddie Anderson (S) 1986, Mike Jones (TE) 1992.

48 Keith Simpson (DB) 1978–9, Ken McAlister (S) 1982–3, Gary Wimmer (LB) 1983, Carlester Crumpler (TE) 1994.

49 Ernie Jones (CB) 1976, Ed Marinaro (FB) 1977, Itula Mili (TE) 1998–9.

50 Greg Collins (LB) 1976, Amos Martin (LB) 1977, Larry Polowski (LB) 1979, Brian Flones (LB) 1981–2, Fredd Young (LB) 1984–7, Joe Terry (LB) 1987r, Vernon Maxwell (LB) 1989, Dave Ahrens (LB) 1990, Anthony Davis (LB) 1993, Duane Bickett (LB) 1994–5, DeShone Myles (LB) 1998–2000, Solomon Bates (LB) 2003.

51 John Yarno (C) 1977–82, Sam Merriman (LB) 1983–7, Dean Perryman (C) 1987, Ty Allert (LB) 1990, Marcus Cotton (LB) 1991, David Brandon (LB) 1993–4, Anthony Simmons (LB) 1998–2003.

52 Randy Coffield (LB) 1976, Joe Norman (LB) 1979–81, 1983, Will Grant (C) 1986, M. L. Johnson (LB) 1987–9, Rico Tipton (LB) 1987r, Ricky Andrews (LB) 1990, Richard Newbill (LB) 1990–2, Kevin Mawae (C/G) 1994–7, Jason McEndoo (C) 1998, Jean-Philippe Darche (C) 2000–3.

53 Fred Hoaglin (C) 1976, Mike Jones (LB) 1977, Keith Butler (LB) 1978–87, John McVeigh (LB) 1987r, Darren Comeaux (LB) 1988–91, Ray Donaldson (C) 1993–4, Jim Sweeney (C) 1995, Eric Unverzagt (LB) 1996–7, Kevin Glover (C) 1998–9, George Koonce (LB) 2000, Keith Miller (LB) 2002, Randall Godfrey (LB) 2003.

54 Art Kuehn (C/G) 1976–82, Eugene Williams (LB) 1982–3, Grant Feasel (C) 1987–93, Joe Jackson (LB) 1987r, Michael Barber (LB) 1995–7, D.D. Lewis (LB) 2002–3.

55 Geoff Reece (C) 1977, Michael Jackson (LB) 1979–86, Brian Bosworth (LB) 1987–9, Paul Lavine (LB) 1987r, Ned Bolcar (LB) 1990, Bob Spitulski (LB) 1993–4, Dino Hackett (LB) 1993, Winston Moss (LB) 1995–7, Hillary Butler (LB) 1998, Marcus Bell (LB) 2000–2.

56 Sammy Green (LB) 1976–9, Tim Walker (LB) 1980, Greg Gaines (LB) 1981, 1983–8, Julio Cortes (LB) 1987r, Joe Tofflemire (C) 1989–94, James Logan (LB) 1995–2000, Terry Killens (LB) 2002, Chike Okeafor (DE) 2003.

57 Peter Cronan (LB) 1977–9, 1981, Shelton Robinson (LB) 1982–5, Tony Woods (LB) 1987–92, Tony Caldwell (LB) 1987r, Ray Berry (LB) 1993, Jason Kyle (LB) 1995–8, Orlando Huff (LB) 2001–3.

58 Don Hansen (LB) 1976, Terry Beeson (LB) 1977–81, Bruce Scholtz (LB) 1982–8, Rob DeVita (LB) 1987r, Greg Clark (LB) 1992, Darryl Hardy (LB) 1997, Scott Fields (LB) 1999, Isaish Kacyvenski (LB) 2000–3.

59 Terry Rennaker (LB) 1980, Rodell Thomas (LB) 1981–2, Blair Bush (C) 1983–8, Fred Orns (LB) 1987r, Joe Cain (LB) 1989–92, 1997, Tyronne Stowe (LB) 1995, Darrin Smith (LB) 1998–9, Tim Terry (LB) 2000–2, Tracy White (LB) 2003.

60 Ron Coder (G) 1976–7, 1979, Kevin Turner (LB) 1981, Jerome Boyd (LB) 1983, John Kaiser (LB) 1984–6, Glenn Hyde (C) 1986, Doug Hire (C) 1987, Chris Godfrey (G) 1988, Greg Bloedorn (G) 1997–9, Joe Brown (DT) 2001.

61 Tom Lynch (G) 1977–80, Robert Pratt (G) 1982–5, Alonzo Mitz (DE) 1986–9, Jack Sims (G) 1987r, Michael Morris (LS) 1990, Theo Adams (TE) 1992, Mark Rodenhauser (C) 1999, Robbie Tobeck (C) 2000–3.

62 Dave Simonson (TE) 1976, Ernie Price (DE) 1978–9, Terry Dion (DE) 1980, Kani Kauahi (C) 1982–6, Sean Farrell (G) 1992, Chris Gray (G/C) 1998–2003.

63 Nick Bebout (T) 1976–9, Fredell Anderson (DE) 1980–2, Mark Hicks (LB) 1983, Reggie Kinlaw (NT) 1985–6, Roy Hart (NT) 1988–9, Ronnie Lee (T) 1990–2, Frank Beede (G) 1996–2000.

64 Gordon Jolley (G/T) 1976–7, Charlie Aiu (G) 1978, Ron Essink (T) 1980–5, Tom Andrews (C/G) 1987, Wes Dove (DE) 1987, Darrick Brilz (G/C) 1989–93.

65 John Demarie (G) 1976, Edwin Bailey (G/T) 1981–91.

66 Bill Sandifer (DT) 1977–8, Bill Dugan (G) 1981–3, Stan Eisenhooth (C) 1987–8, Andy Heck (T/G) 1989–93, Pete Kendall (G) 1996–2000.

67 Bob Penchion (G) 1976, Bill Cooke (DL) 1978–80, Reggie McKenzie (G) 1983–4, Matt Hanousek (T/G) 1987r, Ken Clarke (NT) 1988, Antonio Edwards (DE) 1993–4, Matt LaBounty (DE) 1996–7, Rich Owens (DE) 2002.

68 Dennis Boyd (DL) 1977–9, 1981–2, Randy Edwards (DE) 1984–7, John Eisenhooth (NT) 1987r, John Hunter (G) 1992, Brian Habib (G) 1998–9, Dennis Norman (T) 2002–3.

69 Andy Dorris (DE) 1977, Doug Sutherland (DT) 1981, Matt Hernandez (T) 1983, Sid Abramowitz (T) 1984, Garth Thomas (G) 1987r, Jeff Blackshear (G) 1993–5, Grant Williams (T) 1996, Floyd Wedderburn (T/G) 1999–2002.

70 Larry Woods (DT) 1976, Bob Lurtsema (DL) 1976–7, Dave Kraayeveld (DL) 1978, Jeff Sevy (G/T) 1979–80, Mike White (DT) 1981–2, Darrell Irvin (DE) 1983, Ron Mattes (T) 1986–90, *Michael Sinclair* (DE) 1991–2001, Jerry Wunsch (T) 2002–3.

71 Steve Niehaus (DL) 1976–8, Carl Eller (DE) 1979, Jack Campbell (T) 1982, Bryan Millard (G/T) 1984–91, *Walter Jones* (T) 1997–2003.

72 Al Cowlings (DE) 1976, Louis Bullard (T) 1978–80, *Joe Nash* (DT) 1982–96, Lester Williams (NT) 1987r, Andrew Greene (G) 1998, Chris Terry (T) 2002–3.

73 Norm Evans (T) 1976–8, Andre Hines (T) 1980, Dino Mangiero (NT) 1984, Curt Singer (T) 1986, 1990–1, Alvin Powell (G) 1987–8, Ron Scoggins (T) 1987r, Ray Roberts (T) 1992–5.

74 Carl Barisich (DE) 1976, Ron East (DT) 1977, Manu Tuiasosopo (DL) 1979–83, Mike Fanning (DE) 1984, Curt Singer (T) 1986, 1990–1, Don Fairbanks (DE) 1987r, Warren Wheat (G) 1989–91, James Atkins (T/G) 1994–7, Todd Weiner (T) 1998–2001, Matt Hill (OL) 2002–3.

75 Dave Tipton (DE) 1976, Alden Roche (DE) 1977–8, Robert Hardy (DT) 1979–82, Adam Schreiber (G) 1984, Mike Wilson (T) 1986–9, Van Hughes (T) 1987r, Keith Millard (DT) 1992, Michael McCrary (DE) 1993, Howard Ballard (T) 1994–8, Chris McIntosh (T) 2000.

76 Steve August (T) 1977–84, Jon Borchardt (G/T) 1985–7, Greg Ramsey (DE) 1987r, Bill Hitchcock (T/G) 1991–4, Riddick Parker (DT) 1997–8, *Steve Hutchinson* (G) 2001–3.

77 Richard Harris (DL) 1976–7, Bill Gregory (DL) 1978–80, Jeff Bryant (DL) 1982–93, Charles Wiley (DT) 1987r, Matt Joyce (G) 1995, Derrick Graham (G) 1996–7, Floyd Womack (T) 2001–3.

78 Bob Newton (G) 1976–81, David Graham (DL) 1982, 1987r, Bob Cryder (T) 1984–6, Tim Burnham (T) 1987r, Doug Hollie (DE) 1987r,

1988, Eric Hayes (DT) 1990–1, Mike Keim (T) 1992–5, Patrick Riley (DT) 1996, Antonio Cochran (DT) 2001–3.

79 Jim White (DE) 1976, Horace Jones (DE) 1977, *Jacob Green* (DE) 1980–91, Dale Dorning (DE) 1987r, Ed Cunningham (C) 1996, Grant Williams (T) 1997–9.

80 Steve Largent (WR) 1976–89.

81 John McMakin (TE) 1976, John Sawyer (TE) 1977–8, 1980–2, Daryl Turner (WR) 1984–7, Tommy Kane (WR) 1988–92, Donnie Dee (TE) 1989, Michael Bates (WR) 1993–4, Ronnie Harris (WR) 1994–8, Bobby Shaw (WR) 1998, Sean Dawkins (WR) 1999–2000, Koren Robinson (WR) 2001–3.

82 Fred Rayhle (TE) 1977, Mark Bell (TE) 1979–80, 1982, Paul Skansi (WR) 1984–91, Curt Pardridge (WR) 1987r, Ferrell Edmunds (TE) 1993–4, James McKnight (WR) 1995–8, Charles Jordan (WR) 1999, Darrell Jackson (WR) 2000–3.

83 Steve Raible (WR) 1976–81, Chris Castor (WR) 1983–4, Ray Butler (WR) 1985–8, Rod Jones (TE) 1989, Trey Junkin (TE) 1990–5, Ronnie Williams (TE) 1996, Tyree Davis (WR) 1997, Robert Wilson (WR) 1998–9, Karsten Bailey (WR) 1999–2000, Fabien Bownes (WR) 2001, Ryan Hannam (TE) 2002–3.

84 Sam McCullum (WR) 1976–81, Sam Clancy (DE) 1983, Dwight Scales (WR) 1984, Danny Greene (WR) 1985, Louis Clark (WR) 1987–92, Chris Corley (TE) 1987r, Kelvin Martin (WR) 1993–4, Joey Galloway (WR) 1995–9, Bobby Engram (WR) 2001–3.

85 Paul Johns (WR) 1981–4, Dan Ross (TE) 1985, Gordon Hudson (TE) 1986, Mark Keel (TE) 1987, Jimmy Teal (WR) 1987–8, Harper LeBel (TE) 1989, Ron Heller (TE) 1990, 1992, Doug Thomas (WR) 1991–3, Christian Fauria (TE) 1995, Mike Pritchard (WR) 1996–9, James Hill (TE) 2000, *Alex Bannister* (WR) 2001–3.

86 Jessie Green (WR) 1979–80, Mike Tice (TE) 1981–8, Donald Snell (WR) 1987r, Travis McNeal (TE) 1989–91, Robb Thomas (WR) 1992–5, Christian Fauria (TE) 1996–2001, Jerramy Stevens (TE) 2002–3.

87 Ron Howard (TE) 1976–8, Roger Carr (WR) 1982, Charlie Young (TE) 1983–5, Wilbur Strozier (TE) 1987, Kevin Juma (WR) 1987r, Robert Tyler (TE) 1989, Mike Tice (TE) 1990–1, Paul Green (TE) 1992–4, Carlester Crumpler (TE) 1994–8, Derrick Mayes (WR) 1999–2000, Kevin Kaspar (WR) 2002.

88 Don Clune (WR) 1976, Doug Long (WR) 1977–8, Brian Peets (TE) 1978–9, Pete Metzelaars (TE) 1982–4, Byron Franklin (WR) 1985–7, Russell Evans (WR) 1987r, John Spagnola (TE) 1988, Jeff Chadwick (WR) 1989–91, Willie Bouyer (WR) 1989, David Daniels (WR) 1991–2, Terrence Warren (WR) 1993–4, Ricky Proehl (WR) 1995–6,

Deems May (TE) 1997–9, James Williams (WR) 2000–2, Itula Mili (TE) 2003.

89 Alvis Darby (TE) 1976, Duke Fergerson (WR) 1977–9, Mark McGrath (WR) 1981, Byron Walker (WR) 1982–6, Jim Laughton (TE) 1986, Ken Sager (TE) 1987r, *Brian Blades* (WR) 1988–98, Itula Mili (TE) 2000–2.

90 Charles McShane (LB) 1977–9, Jethro Franklin (DE) 1989, Terry Wooden (LB) 1990–6, Mike Croel (DE) 1998, Antonio Cochran (DT) 1999–2000, Chad Eaton (DT) 2001–2.

91 John O'Callaghan (TE) 1987r, Darrin Miller (LB) 1988–9, Jim Skow (DE) 1991, Tyrone Rodgers (DT) 1992–4, Martin Harrison (DE) 1997, Matt LaBounty (DE) 2001, Anton Palepoi (DL) 2002–3.

92 David Wyman (LB) 1987–92, Mike Frier (DT) 1994, Michael McCrary (DE) 1994, Henry McMillan (DE) 1995–6, Lamar King (DE) 1999–2003.

93 E.J. Junior (LB) 1992–3, Brent Williams (DE) 1994–5, Phillip Daniels (DE) 1996–9, *John Randle* (DT) 2001–3.

94 Rod Stephens (LB) 1989–94, Antonio Edwards (DE) 1995–7, *Chad Brown* (LB) 1997–2003.

95 Roland Barbay (NT) 1987, Dean Wells (LB) 1993–8, James Willis (LB) 1999, John Hilliard (DE) 2000–2, Rashad Moore (DT) 2003.

96 Chuck Butler (LB) 1984, *Cortez Kennedy* (DT) 1990–1, 1994–2000, Natu Tuatagaloa (DE) 1992–3, Norman Hand (DT) 2003.

97 *Rufus Porter* (LB) 1988–94, Glenn Montgomery (DT) 1996, Dan Saleaumua (DT) 1997–8, Riddick Parker (DT) 1999–2000, Brandon Mitchell (DL) 2002–3.

98 Elston Ridgle (DE) 1989, Kevin Murphy (LB) 1993, Sam Adams (DT) 1994–9, Cedric Woodard (DT) 2000–3.

99 Donald Miller (LB) 1990, Bernard Clark (LB) 1991, *Cortez Kennedy* (DT) 1992–3, Michael McCrary (DE) 1995–6, Matt LaBounty (DE) 1998–2000, Levon Kirkland (LB) 2001, Rocky Bernard (DL) 2002–3.

TAMPA BAY BUCCANEERS

The franchise: The Bucs were laughing stocks of the league for much of their history. Formed as an expansion team awarded to tax lawyer Hugh Culverhouse in 1976, they would visit the postseason only three times in their first 21 seasons. Legendary University of Southern California coach John McKay was hired as their first head man, and watched his new pro team lose its first 26 games over two seasons. In his nine seasons as coach McKay did get the Bucs to the playoffs three times, but his overall record was 44–88–1. Of the team's first five coaches, only Sam Wyche won more (slightly) than one-third of his games. Just about the only bright spot in those two decades was the play of the team's first ever draft pick and only Hall of Famer, Lee Roy Selmon.

McKay got his whole family involved with the team. While his son Jay proved to be no great shakes as a receiver, his other son Rich was very good as general manager. The Glazer family bought the Bucs from Culver-house in 1995 and promoted Rich McKay to GM. McKay then hired Tony Dungy as head coach in 1996. Through astute coaching and player development, the Bucs became perennial contenders led by All Pros Warren Sapp and Derrick Brooks on defense and made the playoffs four times in Dungy's six seasons. Dungy could not get them over the hump in the postseason, though, and was fired. He left the team as the only former Bucs coach with a winning record.

To replace Dungy, the Bucs traded high draft picks to the Raiders for Jon Gruden. The payoff was immediate as Gruden's Bucs beat his former team in Super Bowl XXXVII. The Bucs had reached the top at long last.

Origin of name: The name was chosen by a team advisory board.

Time till first championship: 27 years.

Time since last championship: One year.

Retired numbers: Only one, Hall of Famer Lee Roy Selmon 63.

Record by Decade

| | Regular Season | | | Postseason | | |
	Won	Lost	Tied	Won	Lost	Championships
1970s	17	43	0	1	1	
1980s	45	106	1	0	2	
1990s	67	93	0	2	2	
2000s	38	26	0	3	2	2002
All-Time	167	268	1	6	7	1

Winning seasons: 8. Losing Seasons: 19. .500 seasons: 1.

Coaches

	Years	Record	Playoffs
John McKay	1976–84	44–88–1	1–3
Leeman Bennett	1985–6	4–28–0	0–0
Ray Perkins	1987–90	19–41–0	0–0
Richard Williamson	1990–1	4–15–0	0–0
Sam Wyche	1992–5	23–41–0	0–0
Tony Dungy	1996–2001	54–42–0	2–4
Jon Gruden (1)	2002–3	19–13–0	3–0

(Championships in parentheses)

Other numbers worn by these players: None.

Those who wore retired numbers after the honored player: None.

Numbers that should be retired: None, but Warren Sapp, 99, and Derrick Brooks, 55, may have that honor after they retire.

Owned numbers: 63 by Lee Roy Selmon.

Numbers worn by Hall of Famers: Lee Roy Selmon 63.

Star power: Warrick Dunn took 28 from Reggie Rusk; Brad Johnson took 14 from Joe Hamilton; Derrick Brooks took 55 from Lonnie Marts; Hardy Nickerson took 56 from Reggie Burnette.

Star eclipsed: Dewey Selmon wore 61 till Calvin Peterson, 58, left; Alvin Harper wore 82 till Lawrence Dawsey, 80, left.

Numbers with most great players: 32 has been worn by runners James Wilder, Erict Rhett and Michael Pittman. 88 has been worn by receivers Mark Carrier, Jimmy Giles and Horace Copeland.

Worst represented numbers: Sadly, there's quite a menu to choose from, but 84 and 80 have been worn 17 and 14 times respectively by a series of undistinguished receivers.

Number worn by the most players: 84 and 89 have been worn 17 times each.

Player who wore the most numbers: Terdell Middleton wore 39/43/44/45.

Longest tenure wearing a number: Paul Gruber wore 79 for 12 years from 1988 to 1999.

Number worn by first ever draft pick: Lee Roy Selmon, 63, was picked first in 1976.

Biggest draft busts: The biggest draft busts were Keith McCants 52, selected fourth in 1990, who lasted three years and Eric Curry 75, selected sixth in 1993, who lasted five years. Vinny Testaverde, 12, selected first in 1987 was a bust in Tampa, but has played well elsewhere.

Number worn by first expansion draft pick: The draft was not conducted in rounds. Dave Reavis, 75 lasted eight years from 1976 to 1983; Mark Cotney, 33, also played eight years for Tampa from 1976 to 1980 and 1982 to 1984.

Number worn by oldest player: Lomas Brown wore 75 as a 40 year old in 2003.

Cameos: All Pros and other notables— James Brooks 20; Joey Browner 47; Terry Hanratty 5; Andrew Jordan 48; E.J. Junior 50; Sean Landetta 7; Dexter Manley 92; Eddie Murray 3; Steve Spurrier 11; Pat Toomay 66; Jim Zorn 10.

Ones who got away: Steve Christie, 2, and John Carney, 3/4, had long kicking careers elsewhere. Steve Young, 8, will vault from San Francisco to the Hall of Fame. Vinny Testaverde, 12, and Chris Chandler, 17, had long quarterback careers elsewhere. Santana Dotson, 71 and Mike Prior, 24, both turned up on the Packers 1996 Super Bowl team.

Least popular numbers: 0 has never been worn and 18 has only been worn once.

Last number to be originated: 96 was worn by defensive tackle Tim Newton in 1990.

Longest dormant number: 18 has been dormant since 1976.

Triskaidekaphobia notes: Three poor quarterbacks and a punter have worn 13.

Shared numbers: 12 was worn by quarterbacks Doug Williams and Trent Dilfer.

Continuity: Joey Browner was replaced in 47 by fellow hard-hitting safety John Lynch.

Discontinuity: Steve Young was followed in 8 by kicker Greg Davis.

Family Connections

Brothers

Lee Roy Selmon	DE	1976–85	63
Dewey Selmon	LB	1976–80	61/58
Keith Browner	LB	1984–6	57
Joey Browner	S	1992	47
Eric Everett	DB	1990	42
Thomas Everett	DB	1994–5	22

Quarterback numbers over 19: None.

Numbers of future NFL head coaches: Steve Spurrier 11. Rick Neuheisel 7 is a prominent college coach.

Numbers of future NFL referees: None.

Players who played other sports: None.

Players more famous after football: Conrad Goode, 79, became an actor.

First player to wear a number in the 90s: Brad White wore 90 in 1981.

Number with most points scored: 7 with 544 points scored by Martin Gramatica (538) and Craig Erickson (6).

Number with most yards rushing: 32 with 11,249 yards gained by James Wilder (5,957), Erict Rhett (2,853), Michael Pittman (1,469), Louis Carter (913), Alonzo Highsmith (44), and Bruce Perkins (13).

Number with most receptions: 88 with 746 passes caught by Mark Carrier (321), Jimmy Giles (279), Horace Copeland (115), Rickey Dudley (23), Yo Murphy (4), and Barry Smith (4).

Number with most touchdown passes: 12 with 149 touchdowns tossed by Doug Williams (73), Trent Dilfer (70), and Joe Ferguson (6).

Number with most interceptions: 21 with 44 passes picked off by Donnie Abraham (31), John Holt (6), Milton Mack (4), and Vito McKeever (3).

Oddity: The Bucs have had more players wear number 1 (9) than any other team. They have also had two receivers who were the sons of NFL coaches — Jay McKay 89 and Mike Shula 11.

Players with an Unconfirmed Number

69	George Yarno	(G/C/T)	1979–87

Team All-Time Numerical Roster

Those with an "r" following the year 1987 were replacement players during the players' strike. Pro Bowl players for each number are in *Italics*; Hall of Famers are in **Bold** type.

1 Isaac Hagins (WR) 1976, Garo Yepremian (K) 1980–1, Michael Morton (RB) 1982–3, Donald Igwebuike (K) 1985–9, Van Tiffin (K) 1987r, Ken Willis (K) 1992, Reggie Roby (P) 1995, Marvin Marshall (WR) 1996, Joe Hamilton (QB) 2000.

2 Dave Warnke (K) 1983, Obed Ariri (K) 1984, Steve Christie (K) 1990–1.

3 Bill Capece (K) 1981–3, John Carney (K) 1989, Mark Royals (P) 1990–1, 1999–2001, Eddie Murray (K) 1992, Edell Shepherd (WR) 2003.

4 Dave Green (P) 1976–8, John Carney (K) 1988, Pat O'Hara (QB) 1991, Dan Stryzinski (P) 1992–4, Steve Walsh (QB) 1997–8, Doug Brien (K) 2001.

5 Terry Hanratty (QB) 1976, Mirro Roder (K) 1976, Brian Clark (K) 1982, Frank Garcia (P) 1983–7, Chris Mohr (P) 1989, Courtney Hawkins (WR) 1992, Michael Husted (K) 1993–8.

6 Neil O'Donoghue (K) 1978–9, Tommy Barnhardt (P) 1996–8.

7 Jeff Komlo (QB) 1983, Alan Risher (QB) 1985, Rick Neuheisel (QB) 1987, Mike Hold (QB) 1987r, John Reaves (QB) 1987r, Jeff Carlson (QB) 1990–1, Craig Erickson (QB) 1992–4, Sean Landeta (P) 1997, Martin Gramatica (K) 1999–2003.

8 Bob Hewko (QB) 1983, Steve Young (QB) 1985–6, Greg Davis (K) 1987.

9 Allan Leavitt (K) 1977, Larry Swider (P)

1981–2, Mike Pawlawski (QB) 1992, Tom Tupa (P) 2002–3.

10 Mike Boryla (QB) 1978, Mike Ford (QB) 1981–2, Jim Zorn (QB) 1987r, Shaun King (QB) 1999–2003.

11 Steve Spurrier (QB) 1976, Jerry Golsteyn (QB) 1982–3, Mike Shula (QB) 1987, Kerwin Bell (QB) 1989, Casey Weldon (QB) 1993–6, Rob Johnson (QB) 2002.

12 Doug Williams (QB) 1978–82, Joe Ferguson (QB) 1988–9, *Trent Dilfer* (QB) 1994–9.

13 Larry Lawrence (QB) 1976, Ray Criswell (P) 1987–8, Mark Vlasic (QB) 1993, Scott Milanovich (QB) 1996–9.

14 Randy Hedberg (QB) 1977, Chuck Fusina (QB) 1979–81, Jack Thompson (QB) 1983–4, Vinny Testaverde (QB) 1987–92, Joe Hamilton (QB) 2000, *Brad Johnson* (QB) 2001–3.

15 Mike Rae (QB) 1978–9, Jeff Quinn (QB) 1982, Todd Philcox (QB) 1995.

16 Tom Blanchard (P) 1979–81, Blair Kiel (QB) 1984.

17 Jeb Blount (QB) 1977, Steve DeBerg (QB) 1984–7, 1992–3, Chris Chandler (QB) 1990–1.

18 Parnell Dickinson (QB) 1976.

19 Essex Johnson (RB) 1976, Gary Huff (QB) 1977–8, Brice Hunter (WR) 1997, *Keyshawn Johnson* (WR) 2000–3.

20 Vince Kendrick (RB) 1976, Reggie Pierson (CB) 1976, Neal Colzie (S) 1980–3, Michael Morton (RB) 1984, Ron Springs (RB) 1985–6, Rick Woods (S) 1987, Odie Harris (S) 1988–90, Robert Wilson (FB) 1991, James Brooks (RB) 1992, Jerry Gray (S) 1993, *Ronde Barber* (CB) 1997–2003.

21 Joe Blahak (CB) 1976, Don Martin (DB) 1976, John Holt (CB) 1981–5, Vito McKeever (CB) 1986–7, Charles Wright (CB) 1988, Glenn Rogers (CB) 1991, Milton Mack (CB) 1992–3, Mike McGruder (CB) 1995, *Donnie Abraham* (CB) 1996–2001, Hank Poteat (CB) 2003, Scott Frost (S) 2003.

22 Rod McNeill (RB) 1976, Johnny Ray Smith (CB) 1982–3, Rod Jones (CB) 1986–9, Torin Clark (DB) 1987r, Alonzo Hampton (CB) 1991, Garry Lewis (CB) 1992, Thomas Everett (S) 1994–5, Charles Mincy (S) 1996–8, Aaron Stecker (RB) 2000–2, Thomas Jones (RB) 2003.

23 George Ragsdale (RB) 1977–9, Jeremiah Castille (CB) 1983–6, Don Anderson (CB) 1987, Tim King (DB) 1987r, Marty Carter (S) 1991–4, Tony Bouie (S) 1995–8, Jermaine Phillips (S) 2003.

24 Roscoe Word (CB) 1976, Jeff Delaney (S) 1981, Thomas Morris (CB) 1982–3, Maurice Harvey (CB) 1984, Mike Prior (S) 1985, Paul Tripoli (S) 1987, Dan Land (CB) 1987r, Sylvester Stamps (RB/KR) 1989, Roger Jones (CB) 1991–3, Jerry Wilson (CB) 1995, Damien Robinson (S) 1997–2000.

25 Curtis Jordan (S/CB) 1976–80, Scott Dierking (FB/RB) 1984, Carl Howard (CB) 1985, Bobby Howard (RB) 1986–8, Sherman Cocroft (S) 1989, Tony Covington (S) 1991–2, 1994, Melvin Johnson (S) 1995–7, Brian Kelly (CB) 1998–2003.

26 Charlie Davis (RB) 1976, James Owens (RB) 1981–4, Ricky Easmon (CB) 1985–6, John Harvey (RB) 1990, Rogerick Green (CB) 1992, 1994, Clifton Abraham (CB) 1995, Reggie Rusk (CB) 1996–7, Rabih Abdullah (RB) 1998–9, Dwight Smith (CB) 2001–3.

27 Ricky Davis (DB) 1976, Tony Davis (RB) 1979–81, Fred Acorn (CB) 1984, Kerry Goode (RB) 1988, Darrell Fullington (S) 1991–2, Barney Bussey (S/LB) 1993–5, Eric Austin (S) 1996, Anthony Parker (CB) 1997–8, Rabih Abdullah (RB) 2000–1, Aaron Stecker (RB) 2003.

28 Ken Stone (S) 1976, Anthony Davis (RB) 1977, Alvin Maxson (RB) 1978, Charlie White (RB) 1978, Gary Davis (RB) 1980–1, Melvin Carver (RB) 1982–5, Greg Allen (RB) 1986, Ray Isom (S) 1987–8, Selwyn Brown (S) 1988, Stanford Jennings (RB) 1992, Curtis Buckley (S) 1993–5, Reggie Rusk (CB) 1996, Warrick Dunn (RB) 1997–2001, Travaris Robinson (S) 2003.

29 Sandy LaBeaux (S) 1983, Leon Bright (RB/KR) 1984–5, Ricky Reynolds (CB) 1987–93, Lee Paige (DB) 1987r, Kenneth Gant (S) 1995–7, Shevin Smith (S) 1998, Roynell Whitaker (DB) 2003.

30 Jimmy Gunn (LB) 1976, Walter Packer (RB) 1977, David Barrett (RB) 1982, David Greenwood (S) 1985, Mark Robinson (S) 1988–90, Vernon Turner (RB/KR) 1994, Fred Lester (FB) 1995, Shevin Smith (S) 1999–2001, Darian Barnes (RB) 2002–3.

31 Jerry Anderson (S) 1978, Randy Clark (S) 1984, Craig Curry (S) 1984–6, Sonny Gordon (S) 1987, Ivory Curry (DB) 1987r, Rodney Rice (CB) 1990, Darryl Pollard (CB) 1992, Mazio Royster (RB) 1994, Floyd Young (CB) 1997–2000, Tim Wansley (DB) 2002–3.

32 Louis Carter (RB) 1976–8, *James Wilder* (RB) 1981–9, Bruce Perkins (RB) 1990, Alonzo Highsmith (FB) 1991–2, Errict Rhett (RB) 1994–7, Michael Pittman (RB) 2002–3.

33 Mark Cotney (S) 1976–80, 1982–4, Bobby Kemp (S) 1987, Derrick McAdoo (RB) 1988, Reggie Cobb (RB) 1990, William Frizzell (S) 1991, Chris Barber (CB) 1992, Mazio Royster (RB) 1992–3, Anthony McDowell (FB) 1994, Robert Staten (FB) 1996, Eric Vance (S) 1998–2001, Jermaine Phillips (DB) 2002.

34 Cedric Brown (S) 1976–84, Mack Boatner (RB) 1986, Adrian Wright (RB) 1987r, Lars Tate (RB) 1988–9, Reggie Cobb (RB) 1991–3, LeRoy Thompson (RB) 1996, Dexter Jackson (S) 1999–2002, David Gibson (S) 2003.

35 Jimmy DuBose (RB) 1976–8, Rick Moser

(RB) 1982, Pat Franklin (RB) 1986, Jeff Smith (RB) 1987–8, Martin Mayhew (CB) 1993–6, Fred McAfee (RB) 1999, Corey Ivy (CB) 2001–3.

36 Stan Winfrey (RB) 1977, Rick Berns (RB) 1979–80, Bobby Futrell (CB/S) 1986–90, Robert Hardy (RB) 1991, Markus Paul (S) 1993, Travis Stephens (RB) 2002.

37 Kevin Walker (CB) 1986–7, Eddie Hunter (RB) 1987, Charles Gladman (RB) 1987r, Derrick Douglas (RB) 1990, Chuck Weatherspoon (RB) 1991, Anthony McDowell (FB) 1992–3, Jerry Ellison (RB) 1995–8, Cecil Martin (FB) 2003.

38 Jack Wender (RB) 1977, Johnny Davis (FB) 1978–80, George Peoples (RB) 1984–5, Dennis Bligen (RB) 1986, James Evans (FB) 1987, Jamie Lawson (FB) 1989–90, Mike McGruder (CB) 1994, Todd Scott (S) 1995–6, John Howell (S) 2001–3.

39 Terdell Middleton (RB) 1982, Cliff Austin (RB) 1987, Greg Boone (RB) 1987r, Harry Hamilton (S) 1988–91, Charles Dimry (CB) 1994–6.

40 Mike Washington (CB) 1976–84, Adger Armstrong (FB) 1985, Donnie Elder (S/CB) 1988–9, Gary Anderson (RB) 1990–3, *Mike Alstott* (FB) 1996–2003.

41 Dave Farmer (FB) 1978, Norris Thomas (CB) 1980–4, Craig Swoope (S) 1986–7, Alvin Mitchell (FB) 1989, Joe King (S) 1992–3, Bobby Joe Edmonds (RB/KR) 1995, Reggie Brooks (RB) 1996, Lorenzo Neal (FB) 1998.

42 Frank Oliver (DB) 1976, Ricky Bell (RB) 1977–81, Steve Bartalo (RB) 1987, Eric Everett (CB/S) 1990.

43 Ed Williams (FB) 1976–7, Jerry Eckwood (RB) 1979–81, Terdell Middleton (RB) 1983, Beasley Reece (S) 1983–4, William Howard (FB) 1988–9, Rudy Harris (FB) 1993–4, Tracy Johnson (FB) 1996, Kevin McLeod (FB) 1999, Jameel Cook (FB) 2001–3.

44 Manfred Moore (RB) 1976, Billy Cesare (CB) 1978–9, 1981, Dwayne O'Steen (CB) 1982–3, Terdell Middleton (RB) 1983, Ivory Sully (S) 1985–6, Carl Carter (CB) 1991, Darren Anderson (CB) 1992–3, John Booty (S) 1995, Vinny Ciurciu (LB) 2003.

45 Jeris White (CB) 1977–9, Aaron Mitchell (CB) 1981, Terdell Middleton (RB) 1982, Miles Turpin (LB) 1987r, *Wayne Haddix* (CB/S) 1990–1, Vernon Turner (RB/KR) 1993, Tony Stargell (CB) 1994–5, Tyrone Legette (CB) 1996–7, Mike Solvold (OL) 2002.

46 Danny Reece (CB/S) 1976–80, Adger Armstrong (FB) 1983–4, Nathan Wonsley (RB) 1986, Vince Workman (RB) 1993–4, David Gibson (S) 2000–2.

47 Paul Dombroski (S) 1985, Harold Ricks (RB) 1987r, Don Smith (RB/WR) 1988–9, Joey Browner (S) 1992, *John Lynch* (S) 1993–2003.

48 Andrew Jordan (TE) 1997, Charles Kirby (FB) 2000.

49 Randy Gill (LB) 1978, Cedric Saunders (TE) 1995.

50 Tim Kearney (LB) 1976, Steve Wilson (C/T/G) 1978–85, Dan Turk (G/C) 1987–8, Sidney Coleman (LB) 1992, E.J. Junior (LB) 1992, Reggie Burnette (LB) 1993, Jeff Gooch (LB) 1996–2001.

51 Dan Ryczek (C) 1976–7, Dana Nafziger (LB/TE) 1978–9, 1981–2, Ed Judie (LB) 1983, Chris Washington (LB) 1984–8, Broderick Thomas (LB) 1989–93, Lonnie Marts (LB) 1995–6, Alshermond Singleton (LB) 1997–2002.

52 Steve Reese (LB) 1976, Paul Harris (LB) 1977–8, Scot Brantley (LB) 1980–7, Pat Teague (LB) 1987r, Victor Jones (LB) 1988, Keith McCants (DE/LB) 1990–2, Wardell Rouse (LB) 1995, Greg Bellisari (LB) 1997–8, Nate Webster (LB) 2000–3.

53 Larry Ball (LB) 1976, Rik Bonness (LB) 1977–9, *Hugh Green* (LB) 1981–5, Don Graham (LB) 1987, Fred McCallister (LB) 1987r, Sidney Coleman (LB) 1988–90, Ed Brady (LB) 1992–5, Shelton Quarles (LB) 1997–2003.

54 Richard Wood (LB) 1976–84, Ervin Randle (LB) 1985–90, Jesse Solomon (LB) 1991, Jimmy Williams (LB) 1992–3, Darnell Stephens (LB) 1995–6, Mitch Palmer (LB) 1998–2001.

55 Charles Hunt (LB) 1976, Jimmie Sims (LB) 1976, Aaron Brown (LB) 1978–80, Lemont Jeffers (LB) 1982, Danny Spradlin (LB) 1983–4, Dennis Johnson (LB) 1985, Charles Pitcock (C) 1987r, Henry Rolling (LB) 1988–9, Maurice Oliver (LB) 1991, Jesse Solomon (LB) 1991, Darrick Brownlow (LB) 1992–3, Lonnie Marts (LB) 1994, *Derrick Brooks* (LB) 1995–2003.

56 Bert Cooper (LB) 1976, Cecil Johnson (LB) 1977–85, Robert Thompson (LB) 1983, Jackie Walker (LB/TE) 1986–8, Sanker Montoute (LB) 1987r, Sam Anno (LB) 1989–91, Reggie Burnette (LB) 1992, *Hardy Nickerson* (LB) 1993–9, Ryan Nece (LB) 2002–3.

57 Jim Peterson (LB) 1976, *David Lewis* (LB) 1977–81, Jim Leonard (C/G) 1982–3, Keith Browner (LB) 1984–6, Winston Moss (LB) 1987–8, Pete Najarian (LB) 1989, Al Chamblee (DE) 1991–2, Jeff Brady (LB) 1994, LaCurtis Jones (LB) 1996, Dwayne Rudd (LB) 2003.

58 Calvin Peterson (LB) 1976, Dewey Selmon (DT/LB) 1977–80, Jeff Davis (LB) 1982–7, Pete Najarian (LB) 1988, Winston Moss (LB) 1989–90, Calvin Tiggle (LB) 1991, Mark Williams (LB) 1996, Don Davis (LB) 1998–2000, Marq Cerqua (LB) 2001, Jack Golden (LB) 2002–3.

59 Mike Lemon (LB) 1976–7, Earl Inmon (LB) 1978, Andy Hawkins (LB) 1980–3, Robert Thompson (LB) 1984, Larry Kubin (LB) 1985, Kevin Murphy (LB) 1986–91, Leon Pennington (LB) 1987r, Elijah Alexander (LB) 1992, Rufus Porter (LB) 1997, Jamie Duncan (LB) 1998–2001, Justin Smith (LB) 2002.

60 Wally Chambers (DE) 1978–9, Randy Grimes (G/C) 1983–90, 1992, Paul O'Connor (G) 1987r, Jim Pyne (G) 1994–7, Cosey Coleman (G) 2000–3.

61 Dewey Selmon (DT/LB) 1976, Greg Roberts (G) 1979–82, Don Bailey (C) 1983, Wally Kersten (T) 1985, David Jordan (G) 1987, Byron Ingram (T/G) 1989, *Tony Mayberry* (C) 1990–9, Cleveland Pinkney (DT) 2003.

62 Jeff Winans (T/G) 1977–8, Jim Leonard (C/G) 1980–1, Sean Farrell (G/T) 1982–6, Mike Simmonds (G) 1989, Ian Beckles (G) 1990–6, *Jeff Christy* (C) 2000–2.

63 **Lee Roy Selmon** (DE) 1976–84.

64 Glenn Robinson (DE) 1976–7, Greg Horton (G) 1978–9, Laval Short (DT) 1981, Quentin Lowry (LB) 1983, Joe Shearin (G/C) 1985, Greg Robinson (G) 1986, Don Pumphrey (G) 1987r, Kevin Thomas (C) 1988, Tim Ryan (G/C) 1991–3, Jorge Diaz (G) 1996–9, *Randall McDaniel* (G) 2000–1.

65 Maulty Moore (DT) 1976, Randy Johnson (C/G) 1977–8, Dave Stalls (DE) 1980–3, Noah Jackson (G) 1984, Don Fielder (DE) 1985, Dan Graham (C) 1989, Stephen Ingram (T/G) 1995, Kevin Dogins (C/G) 1996–2000, Russ Hochstein (G) 2001, Jason Whittle (G) 2003.

66 Pat Toomay (DE) 1976, Blanchard Carter (G) 1977, Booker Reese (DE) 1982–4, George Yarno (G/C/T) 1985–7, Dave Heffernan (G) 1987r, Willie Wyatt (DT) 1990, Rhett Hall (DT) 1991, Bruce Reimers (G) 1992–3, Ken Blackman (G) 1999–2001, Ryan Benjamin (G) 2002–3.

67 Tom Alward (G) 1976, Brett Moritz (G/C) 1978, Robert Cobb (DE) 1982, Karl Morgan (DT) 1984–6, Roy Harris (DE) 1987r, Mike Sullivan (C/G) 1992–5, Stephen Ingram (T/G) 1995, Kenyatta Walker (T) 2001–3.

68 Dan Medlin (G) 1977–8, George Yarno (G/C/T) 1979–83, Rick Mallory (G) 1985–8, Pat Tomberlin (G) 1993, Joel Crisman (G) 1996, Morris Unutoa (C/LS) 1999–2000, Shane Grice (G) 2001.

69 Larry Jameson (DT) 1976, Ed McAleney (DE) 1976, Darrell Austin (G/C/T) 1979–80, Hasson Arbubakrr (DE) 1983, John Bruhin (G) 1988–91, Brian Blados (G) 1992, Pete Pierson (T) 1994–2001.

70 Randy Young (T) 1976, Darryl Carlton (T) 1977–9, Mike Calhoun (DT/DE) 1980, Scott Hutchinson (DE) 1981, Kelly Thomas (T) 1983–4, Harry Swayne (DE/T) 1987–90, Calvin Turner (DE) 1987r, Charles McRae (G/T) 1991–5, Jason Odom (T) 1996–2000, Leon Hires (C) 2001.

71 Steve Young (T) 1976, Randy Crowder (DE/DT) 1978–80, Byron Braggs (DE) 1984, Chris Lindstrom (DE) 1985, Mark Studaway (DE) 1985, Bob Nelson (DT) 1986, Mark Cooper (T/G) 1987–9, Jim Huddleston (G) 1987r, Jim Skow (DE) 1990,

Santana Dotson (DT/DE) 1992–5, Scott Adams (G) 1996, Jerry Wunsch (T) 1997–2001, Kerry Jenkins (G) 2002–3.

72 Howard Fest (G-T) 1976–7, Greg Johnson (DE) 1977, Garry Puetz (G/T) 1978, Ray Snell (G) 1980–3, Steve Courson (G) 1984–5, Rob Taylor (T) 1986–93, John Hunt (T) 1987r, Chidi Ahanotu (DE/DT) 1994–2000, Roman Oben (T) 2002–3.

73 John Ward (G-C) 1976, Charley Hannah (DE) 1977–82, Ron Heller (T) 1984–7, Tom McHale (G/DE) 1987–92, Hoss Johnson (T) 1987r, Theo Adams (T) 1993, Brad Culpepper (DT) 1994–6, Regan Upshaw (DE) 1996, Frank Middleton (G) 1997–2000.

74 Mike Current (T) 1976, Rockne Freitas (T) 1978, Gene Sanders (DT/G/T) 1979–85, Marvin Powell (T) 1986–7, Paul Gruber (T) 1988–99, Cornell Green (T) 2002–3.

75 Dave Reavis (T) 1976–83, Phil Darns (DE) 1984, Brison Manor (DE) 1984, Chris Lindstrom (DE) 1985, Kevin Kellin (DE) 1986–8, Carl Bax (G) 1989–90, Reggie Rogers (DE) 1992, Eric Curry (DE) 1993–7, Todd Washington (C/G) 1998–2002, Lomas Brown (T) 2002.

76 *Dave Pear* (DT) 1976–8, David Logan (DT) 1979–86, Fred Norgren (DT) 1987r, Scott Dill (G/T) 1990–5, DeMarcus Curry (T) 2000–1, John Wade (C) 2003.

77 Everett Little (G/T) 1976, Bill Kollar (DE/DT) 1977–81, Glenn Bujnoch (G) 1983–4, J.D. Maarleveld (T) 1986–7, Rhondy Weston (DE) 1989, Gerald Nichols (DT) 1991, Mark Wheeler (DT) 1992–5, Brad Culpepper (DT) 1996–9.

78 Council Rudolph (DE) 1976–7, Kurt Schumacher (G) 1978, Bruce Radford (DE/DT) 1980, John Cannon (DE/DT) 1982–90, Walter Carter (DE) 1987r, Corey Mayfield (DT) 1992, Tim Irwin (T) 1994, Marcus Jones (DT) 1996–2001, Sean Mahan (G) 2003.

79 Steve Wilson (C/T/G) 1976–7, Reggie Lewis (DE) 1979–80, Joe Campbell (DE) 1981, Ken Kaplan (T) 1984–5, Conrad Goode (G) 1987, Reuben Davis (DE) 1988–92, Sean Love (G) 1993–4, Doug Riesenberg (T) 1996, George Hegamin (T) 1999–2000.

80 Jack Novak (TE) 1976–7, Larry Franklin (WR) 1978, Conrad Rucker (TE) 1980, Tony Samuels (TE) 1980, Gene Branton (TE/WR) 1983, 1985, K.D. Dunn (TE) 1985, David Williams (WR) 1986, Steve Holloway (TE) 1987, Frank Pillow (WR) 1988–90, Lawrence Dawsey (WR) 1991–5, Alvin Harper (WR) 1996, Jackie Harris (TE) 1997, John Davis (TE) 1998–9, Todd Yoder (TE) 2000–3.

81 Rick Jennings (WR) 1976, Isaac Hagins (WR) 1977–80, Andre Tyler (WR) 1982–3, Dwayne Dixon (WR) 1984, 1987r, Perry Tuttle (WR) 1984, Phil Freeman (WR) 1985–7, Stanley

Shakespeare (WR) 1987r, Stephen Starring (WR) 1988, Chris Ford (WR) 1990, Willie Culpepper (WR) 1992, Robert Claiborne (WR) 1993, Jackie Harris (TE) 1994–7, Jacquez Green (WR) 1998–2001, Charles Lee (WR) 2002, Roland Williams (TE) 2003.

82 Fred Pagac (TE/LB) 1976, Gary Butler (TE) 1977, Alvis Darby (TE) 1978, Mike Shumann (WR) 1980, Jerry Bell (TE) 1982–6, Ron Hall (TE) 1987–93, Jeff Modesitt (TE) 1987r, Willie Green (WR) 1994, Tyree Davis (WR) 1995, Alvin Harper (WR) 1995, Willy Tate (TE) 1996, Patrick Hape (TE) 1997–2000, Marquise Walker (WR) 2002, Charles Lee (WR) 2003.

83 Lee McGriff (WR) 1976, Dana Nafziger (LB/TE) 1977, Frank Grant (WR) 1978, Theo Bell (WR) 1981–5, Willie Gillespie (WR) 1986, Derek Holloway (WR) 1987, Solomon Miller (WR) 1987, Joey Clinkscales (WR) 1988, Danny Peebles (WR) 1989–90, Dave Moore (TE/FB) 1992–2001, Jeff Parker (WR) 1992, Joe Jurevicius (WR) 2002–3.

84 Freddie Douglas (WR) 1976, Lon Boyett (TE) 1977, Karl Farmer (WR) 1978, Mike Levenseller (WR) 1978, Gordon Jones (WR) 1979–82, Zach Thomas (WR) 1984, David Verser (WR) 1985, Leonard Harris (WR) 1986, Bruce Hill (WR) 1987–91, David Jackson (WR) 1987r, Mike Barber (WR) 1992, Charles Wilson (WR) 1992–4, Robb Thomas (WR) 1996–8, Darnell McDonald (WR) 1999, Blake Spence (TE) 2000, Sean McDermott (TE) 2001, Reggie Barlow (WR) 2002–3.

85 Morris Owens (WR) 1976–9, Mark Witte (TE) 1983–5, K.D. Dunn (TE) 1986, Gene Taylor (WR) 1987–8, Arthur Wells (TE) 1987r, Jeff Parks (TE) 1988, Jackie Walker (LB/TE) 1989, Terry Anthony (WR) 1990–1, Courtney Hawkins (WR) 1993–6, Reidel Anthony (WR) 1997–2001, Ken Dilger (TE) 2002–3.

86 Bob Moore (TE) 1976–7, Jim Obradovich (TE) 1978–83, Jay Carroll (TE) 1984, Calvin Magee (TE) 1985–8, William Harris (TE) 1989, Ed Thomas (TE) 1990–1, Tyji Armstrong (TE) 1992–5, Karl Williams (WR) 1996–2003.

87 Larry Mucker (WR) 1977–80, Gerald Carter (WR) 1981–7, Steve Carter (WR) 1987r, Willie Drewrey (WR/PR) 1989–92, George Thomas (WR) 1992, Lamar Thomas (WR) 1993–5, Nilo Silvan (WR) 1996, John Davis (TE) 1997, Bert Emanuel (WR) 1998–9, Frank Murphy (WR) 2000–1, *Keenan McCardell* (WR) 2002–3.

88 Barry Smith (WR) 1976, *Jimmie Giles* (TE)

1978–86, Jeff Spek (TE) 1986, *Mark Carrier* (WR) 1988–92, Horace Copeland (WR) 1993–7, Brice Hunter (WR) 1998, Yo Murphy (WR) 1999, Andre Hastings (WR) 2000, Milton Wynn (WR) 2001, Rickey Dudley (TE) 2002–3.

89 John McKay (WR) 1976–8, Kevin House (WR) 1980–6, Vince Heflin (WR) 1986, *Mark Carrier* (WR) 1987, Eric Streater (WR) 1987r, Greg Richardson (WR) 1988, Everett Gay (WR) 1989, Jesse Anderson (TE) 1990–2, Todd Harrison (TE) 1992, Shawn Collins (WR) 1993, Harold Bishop (TE) 1994, John Farquhar (TE) 1996, Marvin Marshall (WR) 1996, Larry Ryans (WR) 1996, Horace Copeland (WR) 1998, Mike Roberg (TE) 2001, Will Heller (TE) 2003.

90 Brad White (DT) 1981–3, Ron Holmes (DE) 1985–8, Mike Clark (DE) 1987r, Chidi Ahanotu (DE/DT) 1994–2000, Jason Maniecki (DT) 1996–8, Buck Gurley (DL) 2002, Dewayne White (DE) 2003.

91 Brian Gant (LB) 1987, Cam Jacobs (LB) 1987r, Robb White (DE/DT) 1990, Rhett Hall (DT) 1991–3, Karl Wilson (DE) 1994, Herman Smith (DE) 1995–6, Regan Upshaw (DE) 1996–9, Chartric Darby (DT) 2001–3.

92 Sean Smith (DE) 1989, Dexter Manley (DE) 1991, Shawn Price (DE) 1993–4, Anthony McFarland (DT) 1999–2003.

93 Dan Sileo (DT) 1987, Benji Roland (DE) 1990, Demetrius DuBose (LB) 1993–6, Devone Claybrooks (DL) 2002, Ron Warner (DL) 2002.

94 Mike Stensrud (DT) 1987, Charles Riggins (DE) 1987r, Robert Goff (DE) 1988–9, Toddrick McIntosh (DE) 1994–5, Steve White (DE) 1996–2001, Greg Spires (DE) 2002–3.

95 Curt Jarvis (DT) 1987–90, Mark Duckens (DE/DT) 1992, Eric Hayes (DT) 1993, Keith Powe (DE) 1994, John McLaughlin (DE) 1999–2000, Ron Warner (DE) 2003.

96 Tim Newton (DT) 1990–1, Bernard Wilson (DT) 1993–4, Bryant Mix (DE/DT) 1998, Ellis Wyms (DT) 2001–3.

97 Shawn Lee (DT) 1988–9, Darryl Grant (DT) 1991, Jeff Hunter (DE) 1994, Tyoka Jackson (DT/DE) 1996–2000, *Simeon Rice* (DE) 2001–3.

98 Tyrone Keys (DE) 1986–7, Jim Ramey (DE) 1987r, Ray Seals (DE) 1989–93, James Cannida (DT) 1998–2001, Corey Smith (DE) 2002–3.

99 Eugene Marve (LB) 1988–91, David Grant (DT) 1992, *Warren Sapp* (DT) 1995–2003.

TENNESSEE TITANS

The franchise: After being rebuffed for two years in his attempt to buy the Chicago Cardinals and move them to Houston, Bud Adams threw in with Lamar Hunt as the original two members of the "Foolish Club" of original AFL owners. 44 years later, he still owns the team although it no longer resides in Adams' home town of Houston.

The Houston Oilers were the most successful team in the earliest years of the AFL, winning titles in 1960 and 1961 and losing the 1962 championship in overtime. Each of those three teams was coached by a different man, displaying the mercurial nature and lack of patience possessed by Adams. Those early teams had a tough defense and a freewheeling passing game behind former Bear George Blanda; the running was handled by Billy Cannon, the prize draft pick for the league in 1960.

After 1962, the Oilers would have only one winning season in the next dozen years until Bum Phillips was brought in as coach in 1975. Under Phillips, Houston had a tough defense and an offense dependent on Hall of Fame runner Earl Campbell. Oiler fans filled the Astrodome with chants of "Luv Ya Blue" as the team battled heartily but could not get past the Steelers in the playoffs. More losing followed Phillips' dismissal in 1980. In 1984, Houston imported Hugh Campbell from the Canadian Football League to be their coach. Campbell flopped, but he did bring his star quarterback south with him, and Warren Moon would help turn around the franchise under coaches Jerry Glanville and Jack Pardee. The Oilers went to the Run-and-Shoot offense which established them as both perennial contenders and perennial postseason losers. Houston lost some very tough playoff games in this time. They watched John Elway and Joe Montana lead the Broncos and Chiefs back to defeat them in 1991 and 1993, but worst of all they watched Bills backup Frank Reich lead Buffalo back from 35 points down in the second half in 1992 to bounce the Oilers again.

The character of the team changed in 1994 when Jeff Fisher was hired to replace Pardee during the season. Fisher drafted quarterback Steve McNair and brought him along slowly over the next several years until he became the toughest QB in the league. He built an offense behind the steady running of Eddie George until George began to falter and McNair began to shoulder the load with his passing. Fisher held the team together as they moved to Tennessee a year before their home field was built. Their most remarkable victory came to be known as the "Music City Miracle": Buffalo came back to take the lead in the closing seconds of a 1999 playoff game, but Tennessee snatched victory back on a trick play kickoff return for a winning touchdown. They would lose that Super Bowl to the Rams by a yard at the end, but the Titans have established themselves as a team that must be reckoned with every season.

Origin of name: Oilman Bud Adams named his Houston AFL franchise the Oilers to reflect the industry of the area. When he moved the team to Tennessee 37 years later, they remained the Oilers for two years before Adams created an advisory committee to rename the team. The alliterative Titans was said to indicate "strength, leadership and other heroic qualities."

Time till first championship: Won AFL title in first year; 44 years and counting for the NFL.

Time since last championship: Never won one.

Retired numbers: The Titans have retired the numbers of three Hall of Famers—dominant runner Earl Campbell, 34, dominant guard Mike Munchak, 63 and dominant defensive lineman Elvin Bethea, 65. They also retired 43 for Jim Norton a fine defensive back and punter, but no Hall of Famer.

Other numbers worn by these players: None.

Those who wore retired numbers after the honored player: None.

Record by Decade

	Regular Season			Postseason		
	Won	Lost	Tied	Won	Lost	Championships
1960s	70	66	4	2	3	AFL — 1960, 1961
1970s	60	82	2	4	2	
1980s	62	90	0	2	4	
1990s	88	72	0	4	5	
2000s	43	21	0	2	3	
All-Time	323	331	6	14	17	(2 AFL titles)

Winning seasons: 20. Losing Seasons: 19. .500 seasons: 5.

Coaches

	Years	Record	Playoffs
Lou Rymkus	1960–1	11–7–1	1–0
Wally Lemm	1961	9–0–0	1–0
Pop Ivy	1962–3	17–11–0	0–1
Sammy Baugh	1964	4–10–0	0–0
Hugh Taylor	1965	4–10–0	0–0
Wally Lemm	1966–70	28–38–4	0–2
Ed Hughes	1971	4–9–1	0–0
Bill Peterson	1972–3	1–18–0	0–0
Sid Gillman	1973–4	8–15–0	0–0
Bum Phillips	1975–80	55–35–0	4–3
Ed Biles	1981–3	8–23–0	0–0
Chuck Studley	1983	2–8–0	0–0
Hugh Campbell	1984–5	8–22–0	0–0
Jerry Glanville	1985–9	33–32–0	2–3
Jack Pardee	1990–4	43–31–0	1–4
Jeff Fisher	1994–2003	88–62–0	5–4

Numbers that should be retired: Prolific passers George Blanda, 16, and Warren Moon, 1, could be honored. 19-year offensive lineman Bruce Matthews, 74, was a perennial Pro Bowler.

Owned numbers: No one but Jim Norton ever wore 43.

Numbers worn by Hall of Famers: Elvin Bethea 65; George Blanda 16; Earl Campbell 34; Dave Casper 87; Ken Houston 29; John Henry Johnson 35; Charlie Joiner 18/40; and Mike Munchak 63.

Star power: Wilbur Marshall took 58 from Joe Bowden; Billy Johnson took 84 from Mack Alston.

Star eclipsed: Dickie Post wore 2 because Zeke Moore wore 22. Mike Rozier wore 33 till Larry Moriarty, 30, left.

Numbers with most great players: 27 has been worn by Pro Bowl defensive backs Freddy Glick and Greg Stemrick as well as All Pro runner Eddie George. 84 has been worn star receivers Billy Johnson, Haywood Jeffries, Webster Slaughter, and Willie Davis. 89 has been worn by star receivers Bill Groman, Alvin Reed, Webster Slaughter and Frank Wychek.

Worst represented number: 39 has been worn by six runners and one linebacker, none for more than three years.

Number worn by the most players: 86 has been worn 22 times.

Player who wore the most numbers: Two players wore three numbers—center Ron Lou 51/53/58 and special teams player John Henry Mills 35/48/55.

Longest tenure wearing a number: Bruce Matthews wore 74 for 19 years from 1983 to 2001. Elvin Bethea wore 65 for 16 years from 1968 to 1983.

Number worn by first ever draft pick: Billy Cannon was the team's territorial pick in 1960 and wore 20.

Biggest draft busts: Defensive tackle John Matuszak was selected first in 1973 and washed out of Houston in one year.

Number worn by oldest player: Bruce Matthews was 40 when he wore 74 in 2001. Dave Kreig was 40 when he wore 40 in 1998.

Cameos: Hall of Famers— John Henry Johnson 35; All Pro and other notables— Chuck Cecil 26; Bill Curry 50; Tom Dempsey 23; Gary Garrison 82; Jimmy Giles 88; Jackie Harris 88; Alvin Haymond 13; Thomas Henderson 53; Terry Kinard 27; Ernie Ladd 99; Chester Marcol 5; Wilbur Marshall 58; Dave Parks 83; Bernie Parrish 30; Carl Pickens 86;

Dickie Post 2; Tim Rossovich 58; Jack Tatum 28; Vic Washington 23.

Ones who got away: Roy Gerela, 3, was the kicker for the first Steeler Super Bowl teams. Lynn Dickey, 10, was a talented quarterback for the Packers. Mark Moseley, 11, is the Redskins all-time leading scorer. Lee Johnson, 11, was still punting 15 years after leaving Houston. Charlie Joiner, 18/40, spent most of Hall of Fame career in San Diego. Runner Kenny King, 30, and punter Jeff Gossett, 8, had success with the Raiders. Norm Evans, 73, was a key member of the Dolphins Super Bowl lines. Doug Wilkerson, 63, played guard for San Diego for 14 years. Defensive end Ron McDole, 84, had a great career in Buffalo and Washington.

Least popular numbers: 00, 5 and 43 have all been worn once, while 2 and 3 have been worn twice each.

Last number to be originated: 9 was first worn by replacement kicker John Dietrich in 1987 and by regular punter Greg Montgomery in 1988. 96 was worn for the first time by defensive end Sean Jones in 1988.

Longest dormant number: 2 has not been worn since 1977.

Triskaidekaphobia notes: 13 has been worn by kick returner Alvin Haymond, receiver Derrick Mason and quarterback Kevin Daft.

Shared numbers: 29 was worn by Hall of Fame safety Ken Houston and Pro Bowl corner Darryll Lewis. 33 was worn by Pro Bowl corner W.K. Hicks and Pro Bowl runner Mike Rozier. 44 was worn by Pro Bowl runners Charley Tolar and Lorenzo White. 74 was worn by Pro Bowl linemen Leon Gray and Bruce Matthews. 79 was worn by Pro Bowl defensive ends Pat Holmes and Ray Childress. 90 has been worn by Pro Bowl linebacker George Webster and Pro Bowl defensive end Jevon Kearse.

Continuity: Returner Mel Gray was replaced in 21 by Samari Rolle; Ernest Givins was replaced in 81 by fellow receiver Chris Sanders; returner Carl Roaches was replaced in 85 by receiver Drew Hill; Charley Hennigan was replaced in 87 by fellow Pro Bowl receiver Lionel Taylor.

Discontinuity: Garland Boyette was fol-

lowed in 52 by Calvin Hunt; Don Floyd was followed in 75 by Dudley Meredith; Curley Culp was followed in 78 by Nick Eyre; White Shoes Johnson was followed in 84 by Mike Holston; Sean Jones was followed in 96 by Brett Faryniarz.

Family Connections			
Brothers			
Tody Smith	DE	1973–6	70/85
Bubba Smith	DE	1975–6	77
Kevin Dyson	WR	1998–2002	87
Andre Dyson	CB	2001–3	22
Father and Son			
Walter Highsmith	OL	1972	61
Alonzo Highsmith	RB	1987–9	32

Quarterback numbers over 19: 21 John Hadl.

Number of first black player: In 1960, safety Julian Spence 24 and tight end John White 86.

Numbers of future NFL head coaches: None.

Numbers of future NFL referees: Ron Botchan 37.

Players who played other sports: Wrestling — Wahoo McDaniel 62, Ernie Ladd 99, Ron Pritchard 58, and Carel Smith 70.

Players more famous after football: Tim Rossovich, 58, became an actor and stuntman.

First player to wear a number in the 90s: Defensive tackle Ernie Ladd wore 99 in 1966.

Number with most points scored: 3 with 1,223 points scored by Al Del Greco (1,060) and Roy Gerela (163).

Number with most yards rushing: 27 with 10.874 yards gained by Eddie George.

Number with most receptions: 81 with 1,044 passes caught by Ernest Givins (542), Chris Sanders (177), Jim Beirne (134), Bob McLeod (126), Steve Bryant (35), John Sawyer (25), and Jeff Groth (5).

Number with most touchdown passes: 1 with 196 touchdowns tossed by Warren Moon.

Number with most interceptions: 29 with 62 passes picked off by Darryll Lewis (27), Ken Houston (25), Patrick Allen (7), Willie Germany (2), and Rich Coady (1).

Oddity: The franchise has had on a number of occasions two or more players on the team at the same time with the same last name who are unrelated. In 1960 there were Bob and John White wearing 33 and 86 respectively. In 1965, there were three Fraziers— Charley 28, Wayne 56, and Willie 83. In 1972 there were Skip and John Butler wearing 2 and 87 respectively. Finally, in 1973 there were two sets— Cal and Kevin Hunt wearing 52 and 72 respectively and Billy and Dave Parks wearing 32 and 83 respectively.

Players Whose Number Is Unknown		
Ron Morrison	(T)	1960
Keith Kinderman	(RB)	1965
Eric Larkin	(T)	1987r

Team All-Time Numerical Roster

Those with an "r" following the year 1987 were replacement players during the players' strike. Pro Bowl players for each number are in *Italics*; Hall of Famers are in **Bold** type.

00 *Ken Burrough* (WR) 1971–81.

1 *Warren Moon* (QB) 1984–93, Kurt Kafentzis (S) 1987r, Gary Anderson (K) 2003.

2 Dickie Post (RB) 1971, Skip Butler (K) 1972–7.

3 Roy Gerela (K) 1969–70, Al Del Greco (K) 1991–2000.

4 David Beverly (P) 1974, Florian Kempf (K) 1982–4, Jasper Strong (WR) 1995.

5 Chester Marcol (K) 1980.

6 John James (P) 1982–4, Mike Moroski (QB) 1985, Don McPherson (QB) 1990, Ian Howfield (K) 1991, Mike Elkins (QB) 1992, Joe Nedney (K) 2001–3.

7 *Dan Pastorini* (QB) 1971–9, Tony Zendejas (K) 1985–90, Kent Sullivan (P) 1991, 1993, Bucky Richardson (QB) 1992–4, Reggie Roby (P) 1996–7, Billy Volek (QB) 2003.

8 John Reaves (QB) 1981, Archie Manning (QB) 1982–3, Joe Cooper (K) 1984, Jeff Gossett (P) 1987, Steve Superick (P) 1987r, Teddy Garcia (K) 1990.

9 John Dietrich (K) 1987r, *Greg Montgomery* (P) 1988–93, *Steve McNair* (QB) 1995–2003.

10 Don Trull (QB) 1964–9, Lynn Dickey (QB) 1971–5, Craig Bradshaw (QB) 1980, Oliver Luck (QB) 1982–6, Tony Newsom (CB) 1987, Brent Pease (QB) 1987–8, Reggie Slack (QB) 1990–1, Lee Williamson (QB) 1994.

11 Buddy Humphrey (QB) 1966, Pete Beathard (QB) 1967–9, Spike Jones (P) 1970, Mark Moseley (K) 1971–2, Dave Green (P) 1973, James Foote (QB) 1974, Tom Duniven (QB) 1977–8, Harold Bailey (WR) 1981, Lee Johnson (P) 1985–7, Billy Joe Tolliver (QB) 1994, Steve Matthews (QB) 1998.

12 Charles Milstead (QB) 1960–1, Bob Davis (QB) 1967–9, Charley Johnson (QB) 1970–1, George Amundson (RB) 1973–4, James Foote (QB) 1976, Melvin Baker (WR) 1976, Guido Merkens (DB/WR) 1978–9, Ken Stabler (QB) 1980–1, Brian Ransom (QB) 1983–4, John Witkowski (QB) 1986–7, Calvin Loveall (CB) 1988, Chris Chandler (QB) 1995–6, Billy Volek (QB) 2000–2.

13 Alvin Haymond (S) 1973, *Derrick Mason* (WR) 1997, Kevin Daft (QB) 1999.

14 Billy Anderson (QB) 1967, Bob Naponic (QB) 1970, Kent Nix (QB) 1972, Gifford Nielsen (QB) 1978–83, Cody Carlson (QB) 1987–94, Neil O'Donnell (QB) 1999–2003.

15 Jacky Lee (QB) 1960–3, 1966–7, Wayne Walker (K) 1968, Al Johnson (S) 1972–8, *Craig Hentrich* (P) 1998–2003.

16 **George Blanda** (QB) 1960–6, Kelly Cochrane (QB) 1972, *Toni Fritsch* (K) 1977–81, Frank Miotke (WR) 1990, Rich Camarillo (P) 1994–5, James Ritchey (QB) 1996.

17 Jerry Rhome (QB) 1970, Braden Beck (K) 1971, Elmo Wright (WR) 1975, Reggie Brown (WR) 1993, Will Furrer (QB) 1995, Dave Krieg (QB) 1997–8.

18 Randy Kerbow (WR) 1963–4, **Charlie Joiner** (WR) 1970–2, Paul Robinson (RB) 1972–3, Ed Baker (QB) 1972, Melvin Baker (WR) 1976, Cliff Parsley (P) 1977–82.

19 Willie Alexander (CB) 1971–9, Quintin Jones (S) 1990, Drew Bennett (WR) 2001.

20 *Billy Cannon* (RB) 1960–3, Dick Compton (WR) 1965, Sammy Weir (WR) 1965, *Miller Farr* (CB) 1967–9, Rhett Dawson (WR) 1972, Billy Parks (WR) 1975, Bill Currier (DB) 1977–9, Willie Tullis (DB) 1981–4, Allen Pinkett (RB) 1986–91, Emanuel Martin (CB) 1993, Rodney Thomas (RB) 1995–8, Mike Green (RB) 2000–2, Mike Echols (CB) 2003.

21 Ken Hall (RB) 1960–1, Bobby Brezina (RB) 1963, Pete Johns (S) 1967–8, John Douglas (CB) 1969, John Hadl (QB) 1976–7, Charles Jefferson (DB) 1979–80, Tate Randle (DB) 1982, Derrick Hatchett (CB) 1983, Bo Eason (S) 1984–7, Craig Birdsong (S) 1987r, Tracey Eaton (S) 1988–9, Leander Knight (S) 1990, Jerry Gray (CB) 1992, Mel Gray (KR/WR) 1995–7, *Samari Rolle* (CB) 1998–2003.

22 Don Brown (RB) 1960, Joe Majors (DB) 1960, Gary Wisener (CB) 1961, Bob Suci (S) 1962, Benny Nelson (S) 1964, B.W. Cheeks (RB) 1965, *Zeke Moore* (CB) 1967–77, Bill Kay (CB) 1981–3, Larry Griffin (DB) 1986, Kenny Johnson (S) 1986–9, Herbie Anderson (CB) 1991, Tony Brown (CB) 1992–3, Tomur Barnes (CB) 1994, Mike Archie (RB) 1996–8, Andre Dyson (CB) 2001–3.

23 Bobby Jancik (S) 1962–7, Bob Smith (S) 1968, *Jerry LeVias* (WR) 1969–70, Jeff Severson (S) 1973, Vic Washington (RB) 1974, Tom Dempsey (K) 1977, Greg Hill (CB) 1983, Richard Johnson (CB) 1985–92, *Blaine Bishop* (S) 1993–2001, Donnie Nickey (S) 2003.

24 Julian Spence (S) 1960–1, Mike Richardson (RB) 1969–71, Mike Montgomery (WR) 1974, Steve Brown (CB) 1983–90, Charles Clinton (CB) 1987r, Steve Jackson (CB) 1991–9, Tony Beckham (CB) 2002–3.

25 Gene Jones (CB) 1961, *Ode Burrell* (RB) 1964–9, John Charles (S) 1971–4, Kurt Knoff (DB) 1977–8, *Keith Bostic* (S) 1983–8, Bubba McDowell (S) 1989–94, Torey Hunter (CB) 1995, Denard Walker (CB) 1997–9, DeRon Jenkins (CB) 2001, Tank Williams (S) 2002–3.

26 Lawrence Elkins (WR) 1965–8, Larry Eaglin (CB) 1973, Rob Carpenter (RB) 1977–81, Darryl Meadows (DB) 1983–4, Audray McMillian (CB) 1985–7, Bo Orlando (S) 1990–4, Chuck Cecil (S) 1995, Rayna Stewart (S/CB) 1996–7, Spencer George (RB) 1998–9, Andre Woolfolk (CB) 2003.

27 *Freddy Glick* (S) 1961–6, Glenn Bass (WR) 1967–8, Joe Blahak (S) 1973, *Greg Stemrick* (CB) 1975–82, Mike Kennedy (DB) 1984, Sonny Brown (S) 1987, Donovan Small (S) 1987r, Quintin Jones (S) 1989, Terry Kinard (S) 1990, Terry Hoage (S) 1993, *Eddie George* (RB) 1996–2003.

28 *Charles Frazier* (WR) 1962–8, Andy Hopkins (RB) 1971, Bill Thomas (RB) 1973, Mike Weger (S) 1976–7, Jack Tatum (DB) 1980, Rich Thomaselli (RB) 1981–2, Allen Lyday (S) 1984–7, Emmuel Thompson (CB) 1987r, *Cris Dishman* (CB) 1988–96, George McCullough (CB) 1997–9, Aric Morris (S) 2000–2.

29 **Ken Houston** (S) 1967–72, Leonard Fairley (S) 1974, Willie Germany (S) 1975, Rich Sowells (DB) 1977, Guido Merkens (DB/WR) 1980, Patrick Allen (CB) 1985–90, Robert White (CB) 1987r, *Darryll Lewis* (CB) 1991–8, Joe Walker (S) 2001, Rich Coady (DB) 2002, Chris Brown (RB) 2003.

30 Mike Dukes (LB) 1960–3, Charles Rieves (LB) 1964, Bernie Parrish (CB) 1966, *Hoyle Granger* (RB) 1972, Don Hardeman (RB) 1975–7, Kenny King (RB) 1979, Larry Moriarty (FB) 1983–6, *Mike Rozier* (RB) 1987–90, Herman Hunter (RB) 1987r, Victor Jones (RB) 1990–1, Mike Davis (CB) 1994, Anthony Dorsett (CB) 1996–7, Donald Mitchell (CB) 1999–2002.

31 Doug Cline (LB) 1960–6, Mike Voight (RB) 1977, Brian Duncan (RB) 1978, Gary Allen (RB) 1982, Jeff Donaldson (S) 1984–9, Larry Joyner (S) 1987r, Keith McDonald (WR) 1987r, Marcus Robertson (S) 1991–2000, Gary Brown (RB) 1995, Lance Schulters (S) 2002–3.

32 Dave Smith (RB) 1960–4, Jack Spikes (RB) 1965, *Hoyle Granger* (RB) 1966–70, Ward Walsh (RB) 1971–2, Billy Parks (WR) 1973–4, Ron Lumpkin (CB) 1975, Vernon Perry (S) 1979–82, Stan Edwards (RB) 1983–6, Alonzo Highsmith (FB) 1987–9, Ricky Moore (FB) 1987r, Spencer Tillman (RB) 1992–4, Tomur Barnes (CB) 1995–7, Bobby Myers (S) 2000–1.

33 Bob White (RB) 1960, John Guzik (LB) 1961, Gene Babb (LB) 1962–3, *W.K. Hicks* (CB) 1964–9, Benny Johnson (CB) 1970–3, Mark Cotney (S) 1975, Joe Dawkins (RB) 1976, J.C. Wilson (DB) 1978–83, *Mike Rozier* (RB) 1985–6, Spencer Tillman (RB) 1987–8, Billy Bell (CB) 1989, Gary Brown (RB) 1991–5, Ronnie Harmon (RB) 1996–7, Anthony Dorsett (CB) 1998–9, Michael Booker (CB) 2000–1, Greg Comella (FB) 2002.

34 Chuck Kendall (S) 1960, Jack Laraway (LB) 1961, Dalton Hoffman (RB) 1964, Theo Viltz (CB) 1966, Joe Dawkins (RB) 1970–1, Willie Rodgers (RB) 1972–5, **Earl Campbell** (RB) 1978–84.

35 Bo Dickinson (RB) 1963, **John Henry Johnson** (RB) 1966, *Woody Campbell* (RB) 1967–71, Stan Edwards (RB) 1982, Richard Williams (RB) 1984, Ray Wallace (FB) 1986–7, Eric Cobble (RB) 1987r, *John Mills* (TE/LB) 1994, Marion Butts (RB) 1995, Spencer George (RB) 1997, Perry Phenix (S) 1998–2001, Robert Holcombe (RB) 2002–3.

36 Dalton Hoffman (RB) 1964, Donnie Stone (RB) 1966, Roy Hopkins (RB) 1967–70, Robert Holmes (RB) 1971, Bob Gresham (RB) 1973–4, Carter Hartwig (DB) 1979–84, Chuck Banks (FB) 1987, Dee Thomas (CB) 1990, Melvin Aldridge (S) 1993, Mike Echols (DB) 2002.

37 *Charles Hennigan* (WR) 1960, Ron Botchan (LB) 1961, Jess Lewis (LB) 1970, Dave Olerich (LB) 1971, Jeff Severson (S) 1974, *Mike Reinfeldt* (S) 1976–83, Rod Kush (S) 1985–6, Todd McNair (RB/FB) 1995, Rafael Robinson (S) 1996, Dainon Sidney (CB) 1998–2002, Lamont Thompson (S) 2003.

38 Rich Johnson (RB) 1969, C.L. Whittington (FS) 1974–8, Willie Joyner (RB) 1984, Mark Gehring (TE) 1987, Domingo Bryant (S) 1987–8, Mike Dumas (S) 1991–3, Dan Alexander (RB/FB) 2001, Ray Jackson (RB) 2003.

39 Tom Smiley (RB) 1970, Robert Holmes (RB) 1971–2, Art Stringer (LB) 1977, Larry Poole (RB) 1978, Adger Armstrong (RB) 1980–2, Hubert Oliver (FB) 1986, Andrew Jackson (RB) 1987, Lee Cole (CB) 1996.

40 *Tony Banfield* (CB) 1960–5, Mickey Sutton

(S) 1966, **Charlie Joiner** (WR) 1969, Lewis Jolley (RB) 1972–3, Donnie Craft (RB) 1982–3, Butch Woolfolk (RB) 1985–6, Dennis Lundy (RB) 1995, Wes Ours (FB) 2001.

41 *Mark Johnston* (CB) 1960–3, Larry Carwell (CB) 1967–8, Leroy Mitchell (CB) 1969–70, Leroy Sledge (RB) 1971, Terence Wells (RB) 1974, Sean Jackson (RB) 1994, *Frank Wycheck* (TE) 1995, Lorenzo Neal (FB) 1999–2000.

42 *Sid Blanks* (RB) 1964–8, Jim Tolbert (CB) 1972, Tommy Maxwell (S) 1974, Altie Taylor (RB) 1976, Robert Woods (WR) 1978, Boobie Clark (RB) 1979–80, Steve Avery (FB) 1989, Armon Williams (S/LB) 1997, Skip Hicks (RB) 2001, Scott McGarrahan (S) 2003.

43 *Jim Norton* (S) 1960–8.

44 *Charles Tolar* (RB) 1960–6, Johnny Peacock (S) 1969–70, Fred Willis (RB) 1972–7, *Lorenzo White* (RB) 1988–94, Steve Hendrickson (HB) 1995, James Thornton (TE) 1995, Daryl Porter (S) 2001.

45 Larry Onesti (LB) 1962–5, Tim Wilson (RB) 1977–82, Ira Valentine (RB) 1987, Tracy Johnson (FB) 1989, John Simon (RB) 2002.

46 Claude King (RB) 1961, Bob Jackson (RB) 1964, Paul Guidry (LB) 1973, Jeff Queen (TE) 1974, Oliver Nicholson (LB) 1975, Pat Carter (TE) 1994.

47 Bobby Gordon (S) 1960, Bill Tobin (RB) 1963, *Pete Jaquess* (CB) 1964–5, Allen Trammell (S) 1966, Ronnie Coleman (RB) 1974–81, Le'Shai Maston (RB) 1993–4.

48 Bob Atkins (S) 1970–5, *John Mills* (TE/LB) 1993, Todd McNair (RB/FB) 1994, Odie Harris (S/CB) 1995, Brian Natkin (TE) 2001.

49 Dick Cunningham (LB) 1973, Mike Barber (TE) 1976, Sam Williams (CB) 1976, Arrike James (TE) 1987r, Roderick Lewis (TE) 1994–7.

50 *Dennit Morris* (LB) 1960–1, *Bobby Maples* (C) 1965–70, Guy Murdock (C) 1972, Bill Curry (C) 1973, Steve Kiner (LB) 1974, Duane Benson (LB) 1975–6, Daryl Hunt (LB) 1979–84, Kirk Dodge (LB) 1986, Paul Vogel (LB) 1987r, Eddie Robinson (LB) 1992–5, Terry Killens (LB) 1996–9, Rocky Boiman (LB) 2002–3.

51 John Simerson (G) 1960, Ron Caveness (LB) 1966–8, Calvin Hunt (C) 1972, Ron Lou (C) 1973, Ted Thompson (LB) 1975–84, Eric Fairs (LB) 1986–91, Michael Barrow (LB) 1993, Lemanski Hall (LB) 1994–7, Lonnie Marts (LB) 1998, Greg Favors (LB) 1999–2001.

52 *Bob Schmidt* (C) 1961–3, Sammy Odom (LB) 1964, *Garland Boyette* (LB) 1966–72, Calvin Hunt (C) 1973, Duane Benson (LB) 1974, *Robert Brazile* (LB) 1975–84, Jay Pennison (C) 1986–90, Barron Wortham (LB) 1994–9.

53 Hugh Pitts (C) 1960, Jerry Fowler (G) 1964, John Carrell (LB) 1966, Gary Cutsinger (DE) 1967–8, Lloyd Wainscott (LB) 1969–70, Guy Mur-

dock (C) 1972, Ted Washington (LB) 1973, Fred Hoaglin (C) 1974–5, Ron Lou (C) 1976, Art Stringer (LB) 1977–81, Thomas Henderson (LB) 1980, Avon Riley (LB) 1981–6, Eugene Seale (LB) 1987–92, Thad Jefferson (LB) 1987r, *Mark Stepnoski* (C) 1995–8, *Keith Bulluck* (LB) 2000–3.

54 John Meyer (LB) 1966–7, Steve Quinn (C) 1968, Claude Harvey (LB) 1971, Gregg Bingham (LB) 1973–84, *Al Smith* (LB) 1987–96, Larry Smith (LB) 1987r, Phil Glover (LB) 1999, Rocky Calmus (LB) 2002–3.

55 John Frongillo (C) 1962–6, Marion Rushing (LB) 1968, Jess Lewis (LB) 1970, Richard Lewis (LB) 1972, Ralph Cindrich (LB) 1973–5, Carl Mauck (C) 1976–81, Jim Romano (C) 1984–6, John Flannery (G/C) 1991–4, *John Mills* (TE/LB) 1995–6, Eddie Robinson (LB) 1998–2001, Brad Kassell (LB) 2002–3.

56 Phil Perlo (G) 1960, Wayne Frazier (C) 1965, Olen Underwood (LB) 1966–70, Bob Young (G) 1971, 1980, Guy Roberts (LB) 1973–5, Dennis Havig (G) 1976, Mike Murphy (LB) 1979, Robert Abraham (LB) 1982–7, Toby Caston (LB) 1988, Scott Kozak (LB) 1989–93, Michael Barrow (LB) 1994–6, Lonnie Marts (LB) 1997, Dennis Stallings (LB) 1998, Randall Godfrey (LB) 2000–2, Ray Wells (LB) 2003.

57 George Belotti (C) 1960–1, Ed Watson (LB) 1969, Sam Gruneisen (C) 1973, Guy Roberts (LB) 1972, Steve Kiner (LB) 1975–8, John Corker (LB) 1980–2, Tim Joiner (LB) 1983–4, Walter Johnson (LB) 1987–8, Byron Johnson (LB) 1987r, Lamar Lathon (LB) 1990–4, Lenoy Jones (LB) 1996–8, Frank Chamberlin (LB) 2000–2, Jordan Kramer (LB) 2003.

58 Pete Barnes (LB) 1967–8, Ron Pritchard (LB) 1969–72, Ron Lou (C) 1973, Marvin Davis (LB) 1974, Carl Mauck (C) 1975, Tim Rossovich (LB) 1976, David Carter (C) 1977–84, Mike Kelley (C/G) 1985–7, John Brantley (LB) 1989, Joe Bowden (LB) 1992, 1996–9, Wilber Marshall (LB) 1993, James Logan (LB) 1995, Byron Thweatt (LB) 2001, Ken Amato (C) 2003.

59 Phil Croyle (LB) 1971–3, Brian McConnell (LB) 1973, Ted Washington (LB) 1974–82, *John Grimsley* (LB) 1984–90, Scott Fox (LB) 1987r, Joe Bowden (LB) 1993–5, Dennis Stallings (LB) 1997, Doug Colman (LB) 1999, Peter Sirmon (LB) 2000–3.

60 Jim McCanless (G) 1960, Buzz Guy (G) 1961, Tom Regner (G) 1967–72, Al Jenkins (G) 1973, Ed Fisher (G) 1975–82, Hicham El-Mashtoub (C) 1995–6, Kevin Long (C) 1998–2001, Aaron Graham (C) 2002.

61 *Bob Talamini* (G) 1960–7, Hank Autry (C) 1969–70, Walter Highsmith (T) 1972, Harris Jones (G) 1973–4, Larry Harris (G) 1978, Wes Phillips (T) 1979, Purvis Hunt (G/T) 1995–6, Evan Pilgrim (G) 1998, Barry Hall (OT) 2001.

62 Wahoo McDaniel (LB) 1960, Dick Frey (G) 1961, Jim Hayes (DT) 1965–6, Ed Marcontell (G) 1967, Jim LeMoine (G) 1968–9, Ken Grant (G) 1970, Jerry Sturm (C) 1971, Ralph Miller (G) 1972–3, John Schuhmacher (G) 1978–85, Jerrell Franklin (G) 1987r, Doug Kellemeyer (G) 1987r, Craig Page (C) 1999.

63 Hogan Wharton (G) 1960–3, Doug Wilkerson (G) 1970, Levert Carr (T) 1972–3, Ronnie Carroll (G/DT) 1974–5, Steve Baumgartner (DE) 1977–9, David Carter (C) 1977, **Mike Munchak** (G) 1982–93.

64 Fred Wallner (G) 1960, Willis Perkins (G) 1961, 1963, Bud McFadin (DT) 1964–5, Dick Swatland (G) 1968, Ron Saul (G) 1970–5, George Reihner (G) 1977–80, 1982, Joe Dixon (DT) 1987r, Erik Norgard (C/G) 1990–8, Gennaro DiNapoli (G) 2002.

65 Gary Greaves (DE) 1960, **Elvin Bethea** (DE) 1968–83.

66 Leo Reed (G) 1961, *Sonny Bishop* (G) 1964–9, Tom Funchess (T) 1971–3, Greg Davidson (C) 1980–2, Pat Howell (G) 1983–5, Clay Miller (T) 1987r, George Yarno (C/G) 1989, Doug Dawson (G) 1990–3, Jason Layman (T/G) 1996–9, Gennaro DiNapoli (G) 2000–1.

67 John Wittenborn (G) 1964–8, Mike Fanucci (DE) 1973, Ken Kennard (DE) 1977, Jimmy Dean (DE) 1978, Mike Stensrud (DT) 1979–85, Karl Morgan (DT) 1986, Bob Otto (DE) 1987r, Jim Reid (T/G) 1994–5, Tom Ackerman (G) 2002–3.

68 Tom Goode (C) 1962–5, Rich Stotter (LB) 1968, Brian Goodman (G) 1973–4, Al Burton (DE) 1976, Tom Randall (G) 1979, Ralph Williams (G) 1982, Les Studdard (C) 1983, Mike Golic (DT) 1986–7, Vince Stroth (G) 1987, Almon Young (G) 1987r, Tim Roberts (DT) 1992–4, Matt Martin (T) 2002.

69 Terry Stoepel (T) 1970, Solomon Freelon (G) 1972–4, Andy Dorris (DE) 1977–81, Al Steinfeld (G/T) 1983, Doug Williams (T/G) 1986–8, Brett Petersmark (C) 1987r, Jon Runyan (T) 1996–9, Zach Piller (G) 2000–3.

70 *Al Jamison* (T) 1960–2, Scott Appleton (DT) 1964–6, Carel Stith (DT) 1967–9, *Glen Ray Hines* (T) 1970, Tody Smith (DE) 1973, Ed Fisher (G) 1974, Conway Hayman (G) 1975–80, Malcolm Taylor (DE) 1982–3, Dean Steinkuhler (G/T) 1984, 1986–91, Stan Thomas (T) 1993–4, Adam Haayer (OT) 2001.

71 Pete Davidson (WR) 1960, Stanley Faulkner (T) 1964, Willie Jones (DE) 1967, Tom Domres (DT) 1968–71, Bubba McCollum (DT) 1974, Joe Owens (DE) 1976, Ken Kennard (DE) 1978–83, Richard Byrd (DT) 1985–9, Craig Veasey (DT/DE) 1992–3, 1995, Mike Teeter (DE) 1993–4, Melvin Hayes (T) 1996–7, Zach Piller (G) 1999, Fred Miller (T) 2000–3.

72 Jerry Helluin (DT) 1960, Dan Lanphear (DE) 1962, Bob Kelly (DT) 1962–4, Jack Klotz (T) 1964, George Rice (DT) 1966–70, Kevin Hunt (T) 1973–7, Mark Koncar (T) 1982, Brian Sochia (DT) 1983–5, Kent Hill (G) 1986–7, Willis Peguese (DE) 1990–2, *Brad Hopkins* (T) 1993–2003.

73 Dan Lanphear (DE) 1960, Bob Kelly (DT) 1961, Bill Herchman (DT) 1962, Norman Evans (T) 1965, George Allen (T) 1966–7, Bob Robertson (T) 1968, Leo Brooks (DT) 1970–2, Vernon Vanoy (DT) 1973, Greg Sampson (T) 1974–8, Harvey Salem (T) 1983–6, John Davis (G/C) 1987–8, David Williams (T) 1989–95, Scott Sanderson (T) 1997–2000.

74 George Shirkey (DT) 1960–1, Dudley Meredith (DT) 1963, *Willie Frazier* (TE) 1964, Arthur Strahan (DE) 1965, Willie Parker (DT) 1967–70, Gene Ferguson (T) 1971–2, *Leon Gray* (OT) 1979–81, *Bruce Matthews* (G/C/T) 1983–2001.

75 *Don Floyd* (DE) 1960–7, Dudley Meredith (DT) 1968, Elbert Drungo (T) 1969–77, Jesse Baker (DE) 1979–87, Kenny Neil (DE) 1987, Vince Stroth (G) 1988, Bill Schultz (G) 1994, Irv Eatman (T) 1995–6, Benji Olson (G) 1998–2003.

76 Dalva Allen (DE) 1960, *Walt Suggs* (T) 1962–71, Al Cowlings (LB) 1973–4, Morris Towns (T) 1977–83, Eric Moran (T) 1984–6, Doug Mikolas (NT) 1988, Jeff Alm (DT) 1990–3, Jason Mathews (T) 1998–2003.

77 *Rich Michael* (T) 1960–6, Rich Marshall (DT) 1967–8, Ben Mayes (DT) 1969, Spain Musgrove (DT) 1970, Sam Walton (T) 1971, Council Rudolph (DE) 1972, Sid Smith (C) 1974, Bubba Smith (DE) 1975–6, James Young (DE) 1977–9, Angelo Fields (T) 1980–1, Doug France (T) 1983–4, Malcolm Taylor (DE) 1986, Bruce Davis (T) 1987–9, Barry Pettyjohn (T) 1987, Scott Boucher (G) 1987r, Kevin Donnalley (T/G) 1991–7, Rod Walker (DT) 2000, Justin Hartwig (T) 2002–3.

78 Byron Beams (DT) 1961, Ed Culpepper (DT) 1962–3, Maxie Williams (G) 1965, *Glen Ray Hines* (T) 1966–9, Mike Tilleman (DT) 1971–2, John Matuszak (DT) 1973, *Curley Culp* (DT) 1974–80, Nick Eyre (T) 1981, Jerome Foster (DE) 1983–4, Don Maggs (T/G) 1986–92, Keith McCants (DE) 1993–4, Anthony Cook (DE/DT) 1995–8, John Thornton (DT) 1999–2002.

79 Orville Trask (DT) 1960–1, *Pat Holmes* (DE) 1966–72, Jim White (DE) 1974–5, Ernest Kirk (DE) 1977, Wilson Whitley (DT) 1983, Bryan Caldwell (DE) 1984, *Ray Childress* (DL) 1985–95, Saul Patu (DT) 2001.

80 James Yeats (TE) 1960, Dalva Allen (DE) 1961, Gary Cutsinger (DE) 1962–6, Andy Rice (DT) 1967, Glenn Woods (DT) 1969, Ron Mayo (TE) 1973, John Little (DT) 1975–6, Harold Bailey (WR) 1982–3, Eric Mullins (WR) 1984, Steve Tasker (WR) 1985–6, *Curtis Duncan* (WR) 1987–93, Leonard Harris (WR) 1987r, Haywood Jeffires

(WR) 1994, Michael Roan (TE) 1995–9, Chris Coleman (WR) 2000–1, Darrell Hill (WR) 2002–3.

81 *Bob McLeod* (TE) 1961–6, *Jim Beirne* (WR) 1968–73, John Sawyer (TE) 1975–6, Johnnie Dirden (WR) 1978, Jeff Groth (WR) 1979–80, Steve Bryant (WR) 1982–4, *Ernest Givins* (WR) 1986–94, Chris Sanders (WR) 1995–2002, Jake Schifino (WR) 2003.

82 John Carson (TE) 1960, *Ed Husmann* (DT) 1961–5, Ron Billingsley (DT) 1971–2, Mack Alston (TE) 1973–6, Gary Garrison (WR) 1977, Mike Renfro (WR) 1978–83, Herkie Walls (WR) 1983, Willie Drewrey (WR) 1985–8, Tony Jones (WR) 1990–1, 1993, Mario Bailey (WR) 1992, Travis Hannah (WR) 1993–5, Sheddrick Wilson (WR) 1996, Yancey Thigpen (WR) 1998–2000, Eddie Berlin (WR) 2001–3.

83 Ron Nery (DE) 1963, *Willie Frazier* (TE) 1964–5, 1971, Bruce Bergey (DT) 1971, Dave Parks (WR) 1973, Jerry Broadnax (TE) 1974, Warren Anderson (WR) 1978, Tim Smith (WR) 1980–6, Joey Walters (WR) 1987, Leonard Harris (WR) 1988–93, Malcolm Floyd (WR) 1994–6, Isaac Byrd (WR) 1997–9, Mike Leach (TE) 2000–1, Drew Bennett (WR) 2001–3.

84 Jack Atchason (TE) 1960, Ron McDole (DE) 1962, Bill Miller (DT) 1962, Ray Jacobs (DT) 1963, Johnny Baker (LB) 1963–6, Donnie Davis (TE) 1970, Mack Alston (TE) 1973, *Billy Johnson* (WR/KR) 1974–80, Mike Holston (WR) 1981–4, Haywood Jeffires (WR) 1987–93, 1995, *Webster Slaughter* (WR) 1994, Willie Davis (WR) 1997–8, Larry Brown (TE) 1999, Roell Preston (WR) 1999, Chris Jackson (WR) 2000, Bashir Yamini (WR) 2000, Shad Meier (TE) 2001–3.

85 Danny Brabham (LB) 1963–7, Floyd Rice (LB) 1971–3, Tody Smith (DE) 1974–6, Richard Ellender (WR) 1979, *Carl Roaches* (KR) 1980–4, *Drew Hill* (WR) 1985–91, Chris Darrington (WR) 1987r, Willie Drewrey (WR) 1993, Pat Carter (TE) 1994, Derek Russell (WR) 1995–7, *Derrick Mason* (WR) 1998–2003.

86 John White (TE) 1960–1, Bucky Wegener (DT) 1962–3, Stan Fanning (DE) 1964, Robert Evans (E) 1965, Monte Ledbetter (WR) 1967, Mac Haik (WR) 1968–71, Clifton McNeil (WR) 1973, Nat Hawkins (WR) 1975, Mike Barber (TE) 1976–81, Walt Arnold (TE) 1982–3, Herkie Walls (WR) 1983–4, Mike Akiu (WR) 1985–6, Oliver Williams (WR) 1987r, Kenny Jackson (WR) 1989, Alex Johnson (WR) 1991, Corey Harris (WR) 1992, Damon Mays (WR) 1992–3, Willie Davis (WR) 1996, Joey Kent (WR) 1997–9, Carl Pickens (WR) 2000, Justin McCareins (WR) 2001–3.

87 *Charles Hennigan* (WR) 1960–6, Lionel Taylor (WR) 1967–8, Paul Zaeske (WR) 1969–70, Linzy Cole (WR) 1971, Dave Smith (WR) 1972, Eddie Hinton (WR) 1973, Emmett Edwards (WR)

1975, Al Darby (WR) 1976, Conrad Rucker (TE) 1978–9, **Dave Casper** (TE) 1980–3, Jamie Williams (TE) 1984–8, Scott Eccles (TE) 1987r, Bob Mrosko (TE) 1989, Pat Coleman (WR) 1991–4, James McKeehan (TE) 1996–7, Kevin Dyson (WR) 1998–2002, Tyrone Calico (WR) 2003.

88 Albert Witcher (S) 1960, *Willard Dewveall* (TE) 1961–4, Bob Poole (TE) 1966–7, Ed Carrington (TE) 1969, Claude Harvey (LB) 1970, Allen Aldridge (DE) 1971–72, *Jim Beirne* (WR) 1975–6, Jimmie Giles (TE) 1977, Rich Caster (WR) 1978–80, Billy Brooks (WR) 1981, Chris Dressel (TE) 1983–6, Mitch Daum (TE) 1987r, Chris Verhulst (TE) 1988–9, Bernard Ford (WR) 1990, Gary Wellman (WR) 1991–4, Jackie Harris (TE) 1999, Erron Kinney (TE) 2000–3.

89 Bill Groman (WR) 1960–2, 1966, Dobie Craig (WR) 1964, George Kinney (DE) 1965, *Alvin Reed* (TE) 1967–72, Earl Thomas (WR) 1976, Eddie Foster (WR) 1977, 1979, Mike McCloskey (TE) 1983–5, Jeff Parks (TE) 1986–7, Gerald McNeil (WR) 1990, Frank Miotke (WR) 1991, *Webster Slaughter* (WR) 1992–3, Reggie Brown (WR) 1994, *Frank Wycheck* (TE) 1995–2003.

90 *George Webster* (LB) 1967–72, Daryle Skaugstad (DT) 1981–2, Bob Hamm (DE) 1983–4, Toby Caston (LB) 1987, Ezra Johnson (DE) 1990–1, Kenny Davidson (DE) 1994–5, James Roberson (DE) 1996–8, *Jevon Kearse* (DE) 1999–2003.

91 Greg Sampson (T) 1972–3, Johnny Meads (LB) 1984–92, Josh Evans (DT) 1995–9, 2001, Albert Haynesworth (DT) 2002, Anthony Dunn (DE) 2003.

92 Tom Briehl (LB) 1985–8, Anthony Spears (DE) 1989, Henry Ford (DE) 1994–2002, Albert Haynesworth (DT) 2003.

93 Sam Walton (T) 1971, Robert Lyles (LB) 1984–90, Rick Graf (LB) 1991–2, Jeremy Nunley (DE) 1994–5, Mike Halapin (DT) 1996–7, Mike Sutton (DE) 1998, Byron Frisch (DE) 2000, *Kevin Carter* (DE) 2001–3.

94 Frank Bush (LB) 1985–6, Charles Martin (DT) 1987, Glenn Montgomery (DT) 1989–95, Kendrick Burton (DE) 1996, Mike Frederick (DE) 1999, Juqua Thomas (DE) 2001, 2003.

95 *William Fuller* (DE) 1986–93, Dwain Turner (DT) 1987r, Kanavis McGhee (DE) 1995, Joe Salave'a (DT) 1998–2001.

96 *Sean Jones* (DE) 1988–93, Brett Faryniarz (LB) 1994, Gary Walker (DT) 1995–8, Natu Tuatagaloa (DT/DE) 1995, Mike Jones (DT/DE) 1999, Keith Embray (DE) 2000–1, James Atkins (DT) 2003.

97 Mike Johnson (DE) 1984–5, Robert Banks (DE) 1988, Lee Williams (DE) 1991–3, Bryant Mix (DT) 1996–7, Jason Fisk (DT) 1999–2001, Carlos Hall (DE) 2002–3.

98 Mark Studaway (DE) 1984, Lynn Madsen

(DE) 1986, Rayford Cooks (DE) 1987, Pratt Lyons (DT/DE) 1997–8, Robaire Smith (DE/DT) 2000–3.

    99 Ernie Ladd (DT) 1966, Doug Smith (DT)

1985–92, Robert Young (DE) 1996, Kenny Holmes (DE) 1997–2000, Kris Kocurek (DT) 2001, Rien Long (DT) 2003.

WASHINGTON REDSKINS

The franchise: George Preston Marshall founded the Redskins in Boston, where he owned a laundry. Marshall was a born showman who brought many innovations to the NFL — the first team marching band, the first halftime shows, and promoting the game as entertainment. Marshall also was a strong voice in league meetings, advocating separating the league into two divisions with a championship game for example. He was also egotistical and overbearing and refused to employ any black players until he was absolutely forced into it 1962.

His early Redskin teams featured Hall of Fame players Cliff Battles and Turk Edwards. When the Redskins won the Eastern Division title in 1936, Marshall had the title game moved from Boston to New York because of lack of fan support. The Redskins lost that game to the Packers and Marshall moved the team to Washington in 1937. That same year he signed Texas Christian University tailback Sammy Baugh who would lead the Redskins to nine straight winning seasons and five championship games in his 16-year tenure as Washington's signal caller. He was the best passer in the game as well as the best punter and a top-flight safety. The powerful Redskins would win the title in 1937 and 1942. That 1942 title was won 14–6 over the same Bear team that had demolished Washington 73–0 in the 1940 championship.

As Baugh slowed down, so did the team, and while the rest of the league teams were integrating with great black players, the Redskins remained lily-white losers. When Washington finally traded for star black runner/receiver Bobby Mitchell in 1962, they had not been a factor in the league in 15 years. Marshall's health began to decline and

prominent lawyer Edward Bennett Williams assumed control of the team in the late 1960s. Williams hired Vince Lombardi as coach in 1969 and Lombardi drove the Redskins to their first winning season in 14 years before he contracted cancer and died the next year.

After a season with Lombardi assistant Bill Austin as coach, Williams brought in former Ram George Allen as coach in 1971. Allen traded away draft choices in droves to create the "Over the Hill Gang," a veteran team that would reach the playoff in five of Allen's seven seasons, but would lose in its only Super Bowl appearance in 1972. Jack Kent Cooke obtained majority ownership of the team in 1974, but would not take controlling interest from Williams until 1980. Jack Pardee succeeded Allen for three years before San Diego assistant Joe Gibbs was hired as coach in 1981. In Gibbs' 12 years as coach, the Redskins would reach the Super Bowl four times and win three titles — each under a different quarterback. While the team had pummeling runner John Riggins and great receivers Art Monk and Gary Clark, they were known for their large and powerful offensive line, the "Hogs." Joe Jacoby, Russ Grimm, Mark May, Jeff Bostic and others opened holes and protected rotating quarterbacks with great skill, and the team prospered.

Since Gibbs retired in 1992, Washington has been down on its luck. Cooke died in 1997 and his estate sold the team to computer entrepreneur Daniel Snyder in 1999. Snyder has spent a great deal of money, but not particularly wisely. On the field, the Redskins have been no better than mediocre over the past dozen years. Snyder's biggest splash in 2004 was bringing back Gibbs to try to recapture the magic from the past.

Origin of name: Originally the team played in Braves Park used by the Boston Braves baseball team and used that name as well. In 1933, they moved to Fenway Park and changed their name to the Redskins which they maintained after moving to Washington four years later.

Record by Decade

	Regular Season			Postseason		
	Won	Lost	Tied	Won	Lost	Championships
1930s	46	36	8	1	1	1937
1940s	65	41	4	2	3	1942
1950s	47	70	3	0	0	
1960s	46	82	10	0	0	
1970s	91	52	1	2	5	
1980s	97	55	0	11	3	1982, 1987
1990s	79	80	1	6	3	1991
2000s	28	36	0	0	0	
All-Time	499	452	27	22	15	5

Winning seasons: 35. Losing Seasons: 27. .500 seasons: 10.

Coaches

	Years	Record	Playoffs
Lud Wray	1932	4–4–2	0–0
William Lone Star Dietz	1933–4	11–11–2	0–0
Eddie Casey	1935	2–8–1	0–0
Ray Flaherty (2)	1936–42	54–21–3	2–2
Dutch Bergman	1943	6–3–1	1–1
Dudley DeGroot	1944–5	14–5–1	0–1
Turk Edwards	1946–8	16–18–1	0–0
John Whelchel	1949	3–3–1	0–0
Herman Ball	1949–51	4–16–0	0–0
Dick Todd	1951	5–4–0	0–0
Curly Lambeau	1952–3	10–13–1	0–0
Joe Kuharich	1954–8	26–32–0	0–0
Mike Nixon	1959–60	4–18–2	0–0
Bill McPeak	1961–5	21–46–3	0–0
Otto Graham	1966–8	17–22–3	0–0
Vince Lombardi	1969	7–5–2	0–0
Bill Austin	1970	6–8	0–0
George Allen	1971–7	67–30–1	2–5
Jack Pardee	1978–80	24–24–0	0–0
Joe Gibbs (3)	1981–92	124–60–0	16–5
Ritchie Petitbon	1993	4–12–0	0–0
Norv Turner	1994–2000	49–59–1	1–1
Terry Robiskie	2000	1–2–0	0–0
Marty Schottenheimer	2001	8–8–0	0–0
Steve Spurrier	2002–3	12–20–0	0–0

(Championships in parentheses)

Time till first championship: Six years.

Time since last championship: 13 years.

Retired numbers: Only Sammy Baugh's 33 has been retired.

Other numbers worn by these players: None.

Those who wore retired numbers after the honored player: None.

Numbers that should be retired: 9 for Sonny Jurgensen, 28 for Darrell Green, 42 for Charley Taylor, and 49 for Bobby Mitchell.

Owned numbers: None, although only Jurgensen has ever worn 9.

Numbers worn by Hall of Famers: Cliff Battles 20; Sammy Baugh 33; Bill Dudley 35; Turk Edwards 17; Ken Houston 27; Sam Huff 70; Deacon Jones 75; Stan Jones 73; Sonny Jurgensen 9; Paul Krause 26; Wayne Milner 40; Bobby Mitchell 49; John Riggins 44; Charley Taylor 42.

Star power: Chris Samuels took 60 from Mark Fischer.

Star eclipsed: Richie Petitbon wore 16 because Billy Kilmer wore 17; Roosevelt Taylor wore 27 because Bil Malinchak wore 24; Maxie Baughan wore 50 because Chris Hanburger wore 55; Jim Tyrer wore 71 because Bill Brundidge wore 77; Irving Fryar wore 86 because Stephen Alexander wore 80. Coy Bacon wore 80 till Ron McDole, 79, left; Verlon Biggs wore 89 till Boyd Dowler, 86, left.

Numbers with most great players: 28 has been worn by old time All Pros George Hurley, Rick

Concannon, and Bob Masterson as well as receiver Bones Taylor, runner Scooter Scudero, and future Hall of Fame cornerback Darrell Green. 35 was worn three star backs from the early days, Riley Smith, Wilbur Moore and Bill Dudley. 72 has been worn by defensive line Pro Bowlers Joe Rutgens, Diron Talbert, and Dexter Manley. 79 has been worn by defensive line stars Volney Peters, Bob Toneff, Ron McDole, and Coy Bacon as well as Pro Bowl tackle Jim Lachey.

Worst represented numbers: 61 was worn by eight forgettable linemen and a defensive back.

Number worn by the most players: 25 has each been worn 31 times.

Player who wore the most numbers: Johnny Thomas wore three numbers — 22/41/47. Ed Khayat wore 74/87 and is listed as having worn 57/79, but those are not confirmed; Craig McEwen wore 26/32 and is listed as having worn 87/88, but those are not confirmed.

Longest tenure wearing a number: Darrell Green wore 28 for 20 years from 1983 to 2002. Sammy Baugh wore 33 for 16 years from 1937 to 1952, and Monte Coleman wore 51 for 16 years from 1979 to 1994.

Number worn by first ever draft pick: Riley Smith was picked first in 1936 and wore 35.

Biggest draft busts: Quarterback Heath Shuler 5, selected third in 1994, completed 50 percent of his passes and threw 13 tds and 19 interceptions. Heisman Trophy winner Desmond Howard 80, selected fourth in 1992, caught 66 passes in three years and returned one punt for a score.

Number worn by oldest player: Eddie Murray wore 2 as a 44 year old in 2000. Darrell Green wore 28 as a 42 year old in 2002. Jim Hart wore 17 as a 40 year old in 1984. Sonny Jurgensen wore 9 as a 40 year old in 1974.

Cameos: Hall of Famers — Deacon Jones 75; Stan Jones 73; All Pros and other notables — Flipper Anderson 83; Carl Banks 58; Steve Bartkowski 17; Michael Bates 20; Ed Beatty 56; Tom Brown 21; Mark Carrier 27; Rick Casares 35/38; Boyd Dowler 86; Jim Hart 17; Jeff Hostetler 15; Chris Jacke 13; Billy

Johnson 88; Ray Krouse 77; Dan Lewis 22; Leonard Marshall 70; Jim Martin 38; Eric Metcalf 34; Terry Metcalf 26; Matt Millen 57; Gene Mingo 21; Adrian Murrell 22; Rodney Peete 16; Floyd Peters 78; Deion Sanders 21; Roosevelt Taylor 22; Jim Tyrer 71; James Wilder 32; John Wooten 67.

Ones who got away: Kicker David Akers, 6, became the best kicker in the NFL for the Eagles while the Redskins could not find any reliable kicker. Trent Green, 10, became a star in Kansas City. Stan Humphries, 16, took the Chargers to the Super Bowl, just like Rich Gannon, 16, did for the Raiders. Frank Wychek, 22/36, is high on the Titans all time leading receiving list. Hardy Brown, 25, was a ferocious linebacker for the 49ers. Dick Lynch, 25, and Dick Modzelewski, 70, starred on the tough 1960s Giant defense. Paul Krause, 26, spent most of Hall of Fame career in Minnesota. Ben Davidson, 75, and Bob Dee, 89, were Pro Bowl defensive ends in the AFL.

Least popular numbers: 0, 00, 7 and 9 have each been worn only once.

Last number to be originated: 1 was first worn by punter Reggie Roby in 1993.

Longest dormant number: 00 has not been worn since 1946; 0 has not been worn since 1960; 9 has not been worn since 1974.

Triskaidekaphobia notes: Some decent players have worn 13 in Washington — back Ed Justice, safety Jake Scott, quarterback Frank Ryan and kicker Chris Jacke are the best. Five lesser lights also wore the number.

Shared numbers: 24 has been worn by Pro Bowl defensive backs Lemar Parrish and Champ Bailey. 30 was worn by All Pro quarterback Frank Filchock and Pro Bowl returner Brian Mitchell. 44 was worn by All Pro back Andy Farkas and Hall of Fame runner John Riggins. 56 has been worn by Pro Bowl center Len Hauss and Pro Bowl linebacker LeVar Arrington. 65 was worn by Pro Bowl guard Vince Promuto and Pro Bowl defensive tackle Dave Butz. 80 was worn by Pro Bowl defensive end Gene Brito and Pro Bowl receiver Roy Jefferson. 84 was worn by two Pro Bowl receivers, Bones Taylor and Gary Clark.

Continuity: Riley Smith was replaced in

35 by fellow All Pro back Wilbur Moore; Pro Bowl receiver Bill Anderson was replaced in 42 by Hall of Fame receiver Charley Taylor.

Discontinuity: Cliff Battles was followed in 20 by George Karamatic; Earnest Byner was followed in 21 by Todd Boykin; Terry Allen was followed in 21 by Mark McMillan; Paul Krause was followed in 26 by Bob Brunet; Gary Clark was followed in 84 by Mark Stock; Don Warren was followed in 85 by Tim McGee.

Family Connections			
Brothers			
Ray Hare	B	1940–3	42
Cecil Hare	LB	1941–5	11
Ed Khayat	DT	1957, 1962–3	74/87
Bob Khayat	G	1960, 1962–3	60
Matt Turk	P	1995–9	1
Dan Turk	C	1997–9	66
Fathers and sons			
Frank Walton	G	1934, 1944–5	21
Joe Walton	TE	1957–60	81
Joe Krakoski, Sr.	DB	1961	25
Joe Krakoski, Jr.	LB	1986	54
Terry Metcalf	RB	1981	26
Eric Metcalf	KR	2001	34

Quarterback numbers over 19: 30 Frank Filchock; 31 Larry Weldon; 33 Sammy Baugh; 34 Jimmy German; 35 Riley Smith; 42 Ray Hare; 43 Randall Bond; 45 Bob Hoffman; 52 Harry Gilmer; 77 Jack Jacobs and Tommy Mont.

Number of first black player: In 1962 the Redskins became the last NFL team to add black players with receiver Bobby Mitchell 49, guard John Nisby 62, runner Ron Hatcher 36, and halfback Leroy Jackson 22. Conversely, the Redskins were the first NFL team to draft a Hispanic player when they selected end Joe Aguirre in the ninth round of the 1941 draft. Aguirre, 19, and halfback Eddie Saenz, 99, who played for Washington from 1946 to 1951, were two of the first four Hispanic players for the 32 current NFL franchises.

Numbers of future NFL head coaches: Cliff Battles 20; Sammy Baugh 33; Algy Clark 31; Red Conkright 38; Turk Edwards 17; Frank Filchock 30; Harry Gilmer 12/52; Norb Hecker 48; Ed Khayat 74/87; Wayne Milner 40; Dick Modzelewski 70; Jack Pardee 32; Ritchie Petitbon 16; Lou Rymkus 12; Don Shula 26; Dick Stanfel 60; Hugh Taylor 28/84; Mike Tice 86; Dick Todd 41; Joe Walton 81; Willie Wilkin 36; Sam Wyche 18; Doug Wycoff 25.

Numbers of future NFL referees: Fred Wyant 11.

Players who played other sports: Baseball— Tom Brown 21; Jim Castiglia 26; Vic Janowicz 43; and Deion Sanders 21. Basketball— Hal Crisler 55; Doug Wycoff 25. Wrestling— Al Lolotai 26.

Players more famous after football: Three former Redskins paid the ultimate sacrifice for their country in World War II — guard Eddie Kahn 18/43, back Jimmy German 34, and back Keith Birlem 23.

First player to wear a number in the 70s: Quarterback Jack Jacobs wore 77 in 1946.

First player to wear a number in the 80s: End Herb Shoener wore 84 in 1948.

First player to wear a number in the 90s: Back Eddie Saenz wore 99 in 1946.

Number with most points scored: 3 with 1,381 points scored by Mark Moseley (1,207), Charlie Gogolak (168), and Ralph Guglielmi (6).

Number with most yards rushing: 44 with 10,753 yards gained by John Riggins (7,472), Andy Farkas (1,966), Moses Denson (586), Harry Dowda (405), Merle Condit (173), Steve Thurlow (143) and Vito Ananis (8).

Number with most receptions: 89 with 1.010 passes caught by Jerry Smith (421), Rod Gardner (176), Charlie Brown (128), Fred Dugan (109), James Thrash (65), Ron Middleton (34), Ed Barker (23), Terry Orr (20), Coleman Bell (13), Clyde Goodnight (12), and Ralph Thomas (9).

Number with most touchdown passes: 33 with 189 touchdowns tossed by Sammy Baugh (187), Doug Nott (1) and Bill Shepherd (1).

Numbers with most interceptions: 23 with 80 passes picked off by Brig Owens (36), Todd Bowles (13), Tony Peters (11), Claude

Crabb (9), Matt Stevens (7), and Hall Haynes (4). AND 20 with 80 passes picked off by Joe Lavender (29), Dan Sandifer (18), Bob Seymour (14), Ken Stone (5), George Rosso (4), Doyle Nix (4), Bob Freeman (3), Alvoid Mays (3).

Oddity: Although only Sammy Baugh's 33 has been retired officially, the Redskins under Jack Kent Cooke let the numbers of several stars stay unused in obvious homage: 7 has not been worn since Joe Theisman in 1985; 9 has not been worn since Sonny Jurgensen in 1974; 42 has not been worn since Charley Taylor in 1977; 43 has not been worn since Larry Brown in 1976; 44 has not been worn since John Riggins in 1985; 65 has not been worn since Dave Butz in 1988; and 81 has not been worn since Art Monk in 1993. Bobby Mitchell's 49 was not worn from 1968 until 2002.

```
┌─────────────────────────────────────┐
│        Players Whose Number          │
│            Is Unknown                │
├─────────────────────────────────────┤
│ Corrie Artman      (T)       1932    │
│ Russ Peterson      (T)       1932    │
│ Tony Plansky       (B)       1932    │
│ Milt Rehnquist     (OL)      1932    │
│ Dutch Schmidt      (E)       1932    │
│ Irv Hill           (B)       1933    │
│ John Scafide       (T)       1933    │
│ Dick Smith         (C)       1933    │
│ Mike Steponovich   (G)       1933    │
│ David Ward         (E)       1933    │
└─────────────────────────────────────┘
```

Team All-Time Numerical Roster

Those with an "r" following the year 1987 were replacement players during the players' strike. Pro Bowl and pre–1950 All Pro players for each number are in *Italics*; Hall of Famers are in **Bold** type.

00 *Steve Bagarus* (HB) 1945–6.
0 John Olszewski (RB) 1958–60.
1 *Reggie Roby* (P) 1993–4, *Matt Turk* (P) 1995–9, Scott Bentley (K) 2000.
2 Jack Weil (P) 1987r, Ralf Mojsiejenko (P) 1989–90, Kelly Goodburn (P) 1990–3, Eddie Murray (K) 1995, 2000.
3 Ralph Guglielmi (QB) 1955–60, Charlie Gogolak (K) 1966–8, *Mark Moseley* (K) 1974–86, Jeff George (QB) 2000–1.

4 Mike Bragg (P) 1968–79, Jess Atkinson (K) 1986–7, Kris Heppner (K) 2000, Michael Husted (K) 2000, Bryan Barker (P) 2001–3.
5 *Curt Knight* (K) 1969–73, Jeff Hayes (P) 1982–5, Obed Ariri (K) 1987r, Heath Shuler (QB) 1994–6, Brett Conway (K) 1998–2002.
6 Ali Haji-Sheikh (K) 1987, Bill Kenney (QB) 1989, David Akers (K) 1998–9, Tommy Barnhardt (P) 2000, Shane Matthews (QB) 2002.
7 *Joe Theismann* (QB) 1974–85.
8 Bob Holly (QB) 1982–3, Brendan Toibin (K) 1987r, *Chip Lohmiller* (K) 1988–94, Todd Husak (QB) 2000, Jose Cortez (K) 2002.
9 **Sonny Jurgensen** (QB) 1964–74.
10 Rudy Bukich (QB) 1957–8, Eagle Day (QB) 1959, Mike Connell (P) 1980–1, *Jay Schroeder* (QB) 1984–5, Jeff Rutledge (QB) 1990–2, Trent Green (QB) 1995–8, Kent Graham (QB) 2001, Craig Jarett (P) 2002, John Hall (K) 2003.
11 Ernie Pinckert (FB) 1932–40, Cecil Hare (FB) 1941–2, 1945, Al Fiorentino (G) 1943–4, Harvey Jones (DB) 1947, Fred Wyant (QB) 1956, Jim Ninowski (QB) 1967–8, Kim McQuilken (QB) 1978–80, *Mark Rypien* (QB) 1987–93, Casey Weldon (QB) 1999, Patrick Ramsey (QB) 2002–3.
12 Ed Westfall (B) 1932–3, Curly Oden (B) 1932, Ted Wright (B) 1934–5, Dick Frahm (B) 1935, Ed Britt (B) 1936–7, Boyd Morgan (B) 1939–40, John Goodyear (HB) 1942, *Lou Rymkus* (T) 1943, Larry Fuller (HB) 1944–5, Herb Shoener (E) 1948–9, Neil Ferris (DB) 1951, *Harry Gilmer* (QB) 1952, 1954, Randy Johnson (QB) 1975–6, Fred Mortensen (QB) 1979, Tom Flick (QB) 1981, Babe Laufenberg (QB) 1983–4, Steve Cox (P) 1985, Cary Conklin (QB) 1990–3, *Gus Frerotte* (QB) 1994–8, Tony Banks (QB) 2001, Gibran Hamdan (QB) 2003.
13 Gus Kenneally (E) 1932, Bob Campiglio (B) 1933, Ed Justice (HB) 1936–42, Larry Johnson (C) 1944, Ray Monaco (G) 1944, Frank Ryan (QB) 1969–70, Jake Scott (S) 1976–8, Chris Jacke (K) 1997, Derrius Thompson (WR) 2000.
14 Paul Schuette (G) 1932, Hal McPhail (FB) 1934–5, Sam Busich (E) 1936, Tillie Manton (FB) 1938, Al Kreuger (HB) 1941–2, Al Piasecky (E) 1943–5, Tom Miller (E) 1945, John Lookabaugh (E) 1946, Tom Farmer (HB) 1947–8, Billy Cox (B) 1951, *Eddie LeBaron* (QB) 1952–3, 1955–9, Dick Shiner (QB) 1964–6, Max Zendejas (K) 1986, Tommy Barnhardt (P) 1988, Cary Blanchard (K) 1998, *Brad Johnson* (QB) 1999–2000, James Tuthill (K) 2002.
15 Nip Felber (E) 1932, Benny LaPresta (B) 1933, *Jim Barber* (T) 1935–41, George Watts (T) 1942, Bob Sneddon (HB) 1944, Al Couppee (G) 1946, John Lookabaugh (E) 1947, John Hollar (RB) 1948–9, John Papit (B) 1951, George Izo (QB) 1961–4, Mike Kruczek (QB) 1980, Mike Rae (QB) 1981, Tony Robinson (QB) 1987r, Dave

Archer (QB) 1988, Greg Coleman (P) 1988, Jeff Hostetler (QB) 1997.

16 Basil Wilkerson (E) 1932, Larry Johnson (C) 1933–5, Mike Sebastian (B) 1935, Heinie Weisenbaugh (B) 1935–6, *Steve Slivinski* (G) 1939–43, Everett Sharp (T) 1944–5, John Steber (G) 1946–50, *Al Dorow* (QB) 1954–6, *Norm Snead* (QB) 1961–3, Gary Beban (QB) 1968–9, Richie Petitbon (S) 1971–2, Babe Laufenberg (QB) 1985, Ed Rubbert (QB) 1987r, Stan Humphries (QB) 1989–91, Rich Gannon (QB) 1993, Jeff Query (WR) 1995, Scott Blanton (K) 1996–8, Rodney Peete (QB) 1999.

17 **Turk Edwards** (T) 1932–9, Fred Davis (T) 1941–2, 1945, Mack Reynolds (QB) 1960, Galen Hall (QB) 1962, Harry Theofiledes (QB) 1968, *Billy Kilmer* (QB) 1971–8, Tom Owen (QB) 1982, Jim Hart (QB) 1984, Steve Bartkowski (QB) 1985, Doug Williams (QB) 1986–9, John Friesz (QB) 1994, Danny Wuerffel (QB) 2002, Rob Johnson (QB) 2003.

18 Jack Spellman (E/B) 1932, Swede Ellstrom (FB) 1934, *Ed Kahn* (G) 1935–6, Ed Michaels (G) 1937, Hank Bartos (G) 1938, Carl Erickson (C) 1938–9, Bob Titchenal (C) 1940–2, Ken Hayden (C) 1943, Pete Marcus (E) 1944, *Frank Akins* (FB) 1944–6, Joe Duckworth (E) 1947, George Cheverko (B) 1948, Art Macioszczyk (B) 1948, Ed Berrang (E) 1949–51, Jack Scarbath (QB) 1953–4, Sam Wyche (QB) 1971–3.

19 Mickey Erickson (C) 1932, Jim Kamp (T) 1933, Charley Malone (E) 1934–40, *Joe Aguirre* (E) 1941, 1943–5, Jim Pebbles (E) 1946–9, 1951, Eagle Day (QB) 1960, Dan Pierce (RB) 1970, Kenny Shedd (WR) 2000.

20 **Cliff Battles** (RB) 1932–7, George Karamatic (HB) 1938, Bob Seymour (HB) 1940–5, Dan Sandifer (HB) 1948–9, George Thomas (B) 1950–1, Jules Rykovich (B) 1952–3, George Rosso (B) 1954, Hal Norris (B) 1955–6, Doyle Nix (HB) 1958–9, Ed Vereb (RB) 1960, Bob Freeman (HB) 1962, Frank Budd (WR) 1963, Fred Mazurek (B) 1965–6, Gerry Allen (RB) 1967–9, Tommy Mason (RB) 1971–2, Ken Stone (S) 1973–5, Joe Lavender (CB) 1976–82, Michael Morton (RB) 1985, Lionel Vital (RB) 1987r, Herb Welch (DB) 1989, Alvoid Mays (CB) 1990–4, Marc Logan (FB) 1995–7, Skip Hicks (RB) 1998–2000, Michael Bates (KR) 2001, Chad Morton (RB) 2003.

21 Jack Riley (T) 1933, *Swede Olsson* (G) 1934–8, *Dick Farman* (G) 1939–43, Frank Walton (G) 1944–5, Bill Ward (C) 1946–7, Don Deeks (T) 1947, *Rob Goode* (B) 1949–51, Roy Barni (B) 1955–6, Mike Sommer (B) 1958, Gary Glick (B) 1959–60, Doyle Schick (LB) 1961, Jim Carr (LB) 1965–6, Gene Mingo (K) 1967, George Harold (B) 1968, Tom Brown (S) 1969, Larry Jones (WR) 1974–7, *Mike Nelms* (KR) 1980–4, Tim Jessie (RB) 1987, *Earnest Byner* (RB) 1989–93, Todd Boykin

(CB) 1994, *Terry Allen* (RB) 1995–8, Mark McMillian (CB) 1999, Deion Sanders (CB) 2000, Fred Smoot (CB) 2001–3.

22 Tony Siano (C) 1932, Walt Holmer (B) 1933, Gail O'Brien (T) 1934–6, Chuck Bond (T) 1937–8, Roy Zimmerman (HB) 1940–2, Doug Turley (E) 1944–8, Harry Dowda (B) 1949, Charlie Justice (B) 1950, 1952–4, Jim Crotty (B) 1960–1, Leroy Jackson (HB) 1962–3, Dan Lewis (RB) 1965, T.J. Jackson (WR) 1967, Jim Harris (DB) 1970, Roosevelt Taylor (S) 1972, *Mike Thomas* (RB) 1975–8, Buddy Hardeman (RB) 1979–80, Curtis Jordan (S) 1981–4, Danny Burmeister (DB) 1987r, Jamie Morris (RB) 1988–9, Johnny Thomas (CB) 1990, Frank Wycheck (TE) 1994, Eric Sutton (S) 1996, Jamel Williams (S) 1997–8, Adrian Murrell (RB) 2000, Kato Serwanga (DB) 2001, Sultan McCullough (RB) 2003.

23 Orien Crow (C) 1933–4, Jim Moran (G) 1935–6, Don Irwin (FB) 1936–40, Keith Birlem (HB) 1939, Elmer Madarik (DB) 1948, Hall Haynes (B) 1950–3, Claude Crabb (CB) 1962–3, Bill Hunter (DB) 1965, Brig Owens (DB) 1966–77, Tony Peters (S) 1979–82, 1984–5, Todd Bowles (S) 1986–90, 1992–3, Robert Bailey (CB) 1995, Sebastian Savage (CB) 1995, Tomur Barnes (CB) 1996, Matt Stevens (S) 1998–2000, Kijana Carter (RB) 2001, Bruce Branch (DB) 2002, Ade Jimoh (CB) 2003.

24 Joe Kresky (G) 1932, Ike Frankian (E) 1933, *Frank Bausch* (C) 1934–6, Jay Turner (HB) 1938–9, Howie Livingston (HB) 1948–50, Leon Heath (B) 1951, Blackie Kincaid (DB) 1954, *Jim Podoley* (HB) 1957–60, Johnny Sample (CB) 1963–5, Ron Rector (RB) 1966, Pete Larson (RB) 1967–8, Bob Wade (DB) 1969, Bill Malinchak (WR) 1970–4, 1976, Spencer Thomas (S) 1975, *Lemar Parrish* (CB) 1978–81, Anthony Washington (CB) 1983–4, Kelvin Bryant (RB) 1986–8, 1990, Carl Harry (WR) 1989, 1992, Pat Eilers (CB) 1993–4, Stanley Richard (S) 1995–8, *Champ Bailey* (CB) 1999–2003.

25 *Jim Musick* (FB) 1932–3, 1935–6, Doug Wycoff (FB) 1934, Mark Temple (B) 1936, Max Krause (FB) 1937–40, Ken Dow (FB) 1941, Dick Poillon (B) 1942, 1946–9, Frank Seno (HB) 1943–4, John Doolan (HB) 1945, Hardy Brown (B) 1950, John Papit (B) 1952–3, Nick Adduci (B) 1955, Tom Runnels (B) 1956–7, Dick Lynch (DB) 1958, Dick McCabe (B) 1959, Joe Krakoski (B) 1961, Pervis Atkins (HB) 1964, A.D. Whitfield (RB) 1966–8, Mike Hull (RB) 1971–4, *Eddie Brown* (S) 1975–7, Benny Malone (RB) 1978–9, Joe Washington (RB) 1981–4, Curtis Jordan (S) 1985–6, Dave Etherly (DB) 1987r, Mike Oliphant (RB) 1988, Reggie Dupard (RB) 1989–90, Pat Eilers (S) 1992, Mickey Washington (CB) 1992, Tom Carter (CB) 1993–6, Tim Denton (CB) 1998–9, Donovan Greer (DB) 2001, Rashad Bauman (CB) 2003.

26 Honolulu Hughes (B) 1932, Steve Hokuf (B) 1933–5, Vic Carroll (C/G) 1936–42, Vernon Foltz (C) 1944, Al Lolotai (T) 1945, Ralph Ruthstrom (LB) 1947, Jim Castiglia (B) 1947–8, Tom Cochran (B) 1949, Frank Spaniel (B) 1950, Ed Salem (B) 1951, Andy Davis (B) 1953, **Don Shula** (DB) 1957, Bill Stits (DB) 1959, **Paul Krause** (S) 1964–7, Bob Brunet (RB) 1968, 1970–8, Don Harris (S) 1978–9, Terry Metcalf (RB) 1981, Reggie Evans (RB) 1983, Ricky Smith (CB) 1984, Rick Badanjek (RB) 1986, Craig McEwen (TE) 1987, Wayne Wilson (RB) 1987r, Wayne Davis (CB) 1989–90, Danny Copeland (S) 1991–3, Alan Grant (CB) 1994, Muhammad Oliver (CB) 1995, *Cris Dishman* (CB) 1997–8, Curtis Buckley (CB) 1999, Tyronne Drakeford (CB) 2000, Ifeanyi Ohalete (S) 2001–3.

27 Oran Pape (B) 1932, Rabbit Weller (B) 1933, Larry Siemering (C) 1935–6, Mickey Parks (C) 1938–40, Jim Stuart (T) 1941, Joe Zeno (G) 1942–4, Earl Audet (T) 1945, Joe Bartos (B) 1950, Neil Ferris (DB) 1952, Don Monasco (DB) 1954, Art DeCarlo (B) 1956–7, Les Walters (DB) 1958, Mike Sommer (B) 1959, 1961, John Love (WR) 1967, **Ken Houston** (S) 1973–80, Brad Edwards (S) 1990–3, Keith Taylor (S) 1995–6, Marquis Walker (CB) 1996, Greg Evans (S) 1998, Tito Paul (CB) 1999, Mark Carrier (S) 2000, Central McClellion (DB) 2001, Todd Franz (DB) 2002.

28 *George Hurley* (G) 1932–3, *Rick Concannon* (G) 1934–6, Nels Peterson (E) 1937, *Bob Masterson* (E) 1938–43, Ralph Schilling (DE) 1946, *Hugh Taylor* (E) 1947–51, *Joe Scudero* (B) 1954–8, Ted Rzempoluch (DB) 1963, Ozzie Clay (HB) 1964, Dick Smith (DB) 1967–8, Jon Henderson (WR) 1970, Alvin Haymond (DB) 1972, *Herb Mul-Key* (RB) 1972–4, Trent Bryant (CB) 1981, Cris Crissy (WR) 1981, *Darrell Green* (CB) 1983–2002.

29 Jack Roberts (B) 1932, Megs Apsit (B) 1933, Frank Walton (G) 1934, Herman Gundlach (G) 1935, *Jim Karcher* (G) 1936–9, Steve Andrako (C) 1940–1, Bill DeCorrevont (HB) 1945, Oscar Britt (G) 1946, George Wilde (HB) 1947, Howard Hartley (B) 1948, Jack Dwyer (B) 1951, Paul Barry (B) 1953, Bert Zagers (B) 1955, 1957–8, Ted Vactor (CB) 1969–74, *Mark Murphy* (S) 1977–84, Reggie Branch (RB) 1986–9, David Gulledge (S) 1992, Keith Taylor (S) 1994, Scott Turner (CB) 1995–7, Sam Shade (S) 1999–2002, Todd Franz (S) 2003.

30 Lee Woodruff (FB) 1932, Flavio Tosi (E) 1934–6, Millard Howell (B) 1937, *Frank Filchock* (QB) 1938–41, 1944–5, Steve Juzwik (HB) 1942, Coye Dunn (HB) 1943, Jim Youel (QB) 1946–8, Ed Sutton (B) 1957–9, Jim Cunningham (FB) 1961–3, Bob Briggs (B) 1965, Jeff Jordan (RB) 1971–2, Bryant Salter (S) 1974–5, Jim Kiick (RB) 1977, Ike Forte (RB) 1978–80, Nick Giaquinto (RB) 1981–3, Jeff Moore (RB) 1984, Reggie Branch (RB) 1985, Dwight Garner (RB) 1986, Walter Holman (RB) 1987r, Joe Mickles (RB) 1989, *Brian Mitchell* (RB) 1990–9, Trung Canidate (RB) 2003.

31 Algy Clark (B) 1932, Roy Horstmann (FB) 1933, Pug Rentner (B) 1934, Jimmy Johnston (HB) 1939–40, Frank Clair (E) 1941, Larry Weldon (QB) 1944–5, Clyde Ehrhardt (C) 1946–9, Don Bosseler (FB) 1957–64, Joe Kantor (B) 1966, Charley Harraway (FB) 1969–73, Charlie Evans (RB) 1974, Ken Jenkins (RB) 1985, Clarence Vaughn (S) 1987–91, Allen Harvin (RB) 1987r, Gregory Clifton (WR) 1993, Darryl Pounds (CB) 1995–9, David Terrell (CB) 2000–3.

32 Rip Collins (E) 1932–5, Bob McChesney (E) 1936–42, George Cafego (HB) 1943, Sal Rosato (FB) 1945–7, Pete Stout (B) 1949–50, Leon Heath (FB) 1952–3, *Leo Elter* (B) 1955–7, Jim Wulff (B) 1960–1, Billy Ray Barnes (RB) 1962–3, Billy Clay (DB) 1966, Ray McDonald (RB) 1967–8, Henry Dyer (RB) 1969–70, Jack Pardee (LB) 1971–2, Mike Curtis (LB) 1977–8, Vernon Dean (CB) 1982–7, Craig McEwen (TE) 1988, James Wilder (RB) 1990, Ricky Ervins (RB) 1991–4, Keith Thibodeaux (CB) 1997, Toby Wright (CB) 1999, Chad Dukes (RB) 2000, Donnell Bennett (FB) 2001, Calvin Carlyle (CB) 2003.

33 Dale Waters (T) 1932–3, Ben Boswell (T) 1934, Doug Nott (B) 1935, *Bill Shepherd* (FB) 1935, **Sammy Baugh** (QB) 1937–52.

34 *Jim MacMurdo* (T) 1932–3, Steve Sinko (T) 1934–6, Bill Hartman (HB) 1938, Jimmy German (QB) 1939, Haywood Sanford (E) 1940, Mike Micka (FB) 1944, Jim Gaffney (B) 1946, Ed Quirk (FB) 1948–51, John Cloud (B) 1952–3, Jim Smith (DB) 1968, *Tony Green* (RB) 1978, Bobby Hammond (RB) 1979–80, Kevin Williams (CB) 1985, Brian Davis (CB) 1987–90, Garry Kimble (DB) 1987r, Terry Hoage (S) 1991, Martin Bayless (S) 1994, Jim Kitts (FB) 1998, Josh Symonette (S) 2000, Eric Metcalf (KR) 2001, Andre Lott (DB) 2002–3.

35 Hal Cherne (T) 1933, Phil Sarboe (B) 1934, Vic Baltzell (B) 1935, *Riley Smith* (QB) 1936–8, *Wilbur Moore* (HB) 1939–46, **Bill Dudley** (B) 1950–1, 1953, Rick Casares (FB) 1965, Joe Don Looney (RB) 1966–7, Calvin Hill (RB) 1976–7, Jack Deloplaine (RB) 1978, Lonnie Perrin (RB) 1979, Rickey Claitt (RB) 1980–1, Keith Griffin (RB) 1984–5, Martin Mayhew (CB) 1989–92, Leomont Evans (CB) 1996–9, Rashad Bauman (DB) 2002.

36 Reggie Rust (B) 1932, Ed Smith (FB) 1936, *Willie Wilkin* (T) 1939–43, Henry Harris (T) 1947–8, *Chuck Drazenovich* (LB) 1950–9, Ron Hatcher (RB) 1962, Tom Tracy (RB) 1963–4, Tom Barrington (RB) 1966, Ralph Nelson (RB) 1975, Eddie Moss (RB) 1977, Timmy Smith (RB) 1987–8, Joe Cofer (DB) 1987r, Frank Wycheck (TE) 1993, William Bell (FB) 1994–6, Le'Shai Maston (FB) 1998.

37 Marne Intrieri (G) 1933–4, Bill Young (T) 1937–42, Joe Pasqua (T) 1943, Jim Watson (C) 1945, Joe Tereshinski (E) 1947–51, Bob Sykes (B) 1952, J.W. Lockett (FB) 1964, *Pat Fischer* (CB) 1968–77, Raphel Cherry (S) 1985, Charles Jackson (S) 1987r, Travis Curtis (CB) 1988, Kevin Williams (CB) 1988, Gerald Riggs (RB) 1989–91, Darryl Morrison (S) 1993, Cedric Smith (FB) 1994–5, James Washington (S) 1996, Jesse Campbell (S) 1997–8, Larry Centers (FB) 1999–2000.

38 Ben Smith (E) 1937, Hal Bradley (E) 1938, Bob Fisher (T) 1940, *Ki Aldrich* (C) 1942, Bill Conkright (C) 1943, Jacque Jenkins (FB) 1943, 1946, Les Dye (E) 1944–5, Clyde Goodnight (DB) 1949, Jim Martin (K) 1964, Rick Casares (FB) 1965, John Seedborg (K) 1965, Larry Willis (S) 1973, Larry Smith (RB) 1974, Clarence Harmon (RB) 1977–82, George Rogers (RB) 1985–7, Willard Reaves (RB) 1989, Darryl Morrison (S) 1994–6, David Frisch (TE) 1997.

39 Ed Kawal (C) 1937, Clem Stralka (C) 1938–42, 1945–6, *Frank Akins* (FB) 1943, Zip Hanna (G) 1945, George Buksar (B) 1951–2, *Rob Goode* (RB) 1954–5, Dave Francis (B) 1963, George Hughley (B) 1965, Otis Wonsley (RB) 1981–5, Skip Lane (S) 1987r, Robert Green (RB) 1992, Tyrone Rush (RB) 1994, Ricot Joseph (DB) 2002.

40 **Wayne Milner** (E) 1936–41, 1945, John Kovatch (E) 1942, 1946, Frank Ribar (G) 1943, Billy Cox (B) 1952, 1955, Gary Lowe (DB) 1956–7, Gene Cichowski (B) 1958–9, Sam Horner (DB) 1960–1, Lonnie Sanders (DB) 1963–7, Aaron Martin (DB) 1968, Dave Kopay (RB) 1969–70, George Nock (RB) 1972, Fred Hyatt (WR) 1973, Doug Cunningham (RB) 1974, Bob Anderson (RB) 1975, Windlan Hall (S) 1977, Wilbur Jackson (RB) 1980–2, Rick Kane (RB) 1984, Jimmy Smith (RB) 1984, Alvin Walton (S) 1986–91, Reggie Brooks (RB) 1993–5, Rock Cartwright (RB) 2002–3.

41 Red Krause (C) 1938, *Dick Todd* (RB) 1939–42, 1945–8, Leo Stasica (HB) 1943, *Billy Wells* (B) 1954, 1956–7, Sid Watson (B) 1958, Bob Hudson (LB) 1959, Jim Steffen (DB) 1961–5, Mike Bass (CB) 1969–75, Brian Carpenter (CB) 1983–4, Tim Morrison (CB) 1986–7, Dennis Woodberry (DB) 1988, Chris Mandeville (CB) 1989, Johnny Thomas (CB) 1992–4, Buddy Crutchfield (CB) 1998, Lloyd Harrison (CB) 2000, Matt Bowen (S) 2003.

42 Dick Turley (FB) 1938, Ray Hare (QB) 1940–3, Jim North (T) 1944, *John Adams* (T) 1945–9, Nick Sebek (QB) 1950, *Dick Alban* (DB) 1952–5, Jerry Planutis (B) 1956, *Bill Anderson* (E) 1958–63, **Charley Taylor** (WR/RB) 1964–77.

43 *Eddie Kahn* (G) 1937, Randall Bond (QB) 1938, Bob Hoffman (QB) 1940, *Ed Cifers* (T) 1941–2, 1946, Nick Campofreda (C) 1944, Ernie Barber (C) 1945, Al Piasecky (E) 1945, Len Szafaryn (T) 1949, *John Williams* (B) 1952–3, Vic

Janowicz (B) 1954–5, Dick Haley (DB) 1959–60, Jim Kerr (DB) 1961–2, Tom Walters (DB) 1964–7, *Larry Brown* (RB) 1969–76.

44 *Andy Farkas* (FB) 1938–44, Vito Ananis (B) 1945, Merl Condit (HB) 1945, Mike Garzoni (B) 1947, Mike Roussos (T) 1948–9, Harry Dowda (B) 1950–53, Nick Adduci (B) 1954, Steve Thurlow (RB) 1966–8, Jeff Severson (DB) 1972, Moses Denson (RB) 1974–5, **John Riggins** (RB) 1976–9, 1981–5.

45 *Bo Russell* (T) 1939–40, Bob Hoffman (QB) 1941, Ed Beinor (T) 1942, Ted Lapka (E) 1943–4, 1946, Paul McKee (E) 1947–8, Dick Stovall (C) 1949, *Sam Baker* (K/P) 1953, Ralph Felton (B) 1954–60, *Leslie Duncan* (DB) 1971–3, Gerard Williams (DB) 1976–8, Jeris White (CB) 1980–2, Barry Wilburn (CB) 1985–9, Sidney Johnson (CB) 1990–2, Brian Walker (S) 1996, Mike Sellers (TE) 1998–2000, John Simon (RB) 2003.

46 Roy Young (T) 1938, John Spirida (E) 1939, Jack Banta (B) 1941, Lee Gentry (HB) 1941, Joe Gibson (E) 1943, Tom Bedore (C) 1944, Andy Natowich (HB) 1944, Joe Ungerer (T) 1944–5, Paul Stenn (T) 1946, Jack Sommers (C) 1947, Don Doll (DB) 1953, Dale Atkeson (B) 1954–6, Dale Hackbart (DB) 1961–3, Rickie Harris (DB) 1965–70, Frank Grant (WR) 1973–8, LeCharls McDaniel (CB) 1981–2, Ricky Sanders (WR) 1986, Dennis Woodberry (CB) 1987, Mike Mitchell (CB) 1987r, Ladell Betts (RB) 2002–3.

47 *George Smith* (C) 1937, 1941–3, Jack Keenan (T) 1944–5, Ernie Williamson (T) 1947, Carl Butkus (T) 1948, *Laurie Niemi* (T) 1949–51, *Dick James* (B) 1959–63, Jim Shorter (DB) 1964–7, Walter Roberts (WR) 1969–70, Duane Thomas (RB) 1973–4, Ray Waddy (CB) 1979–80, Greg Williams (S) 1982–5, Johnny Thomas (CB) 1988, A.J. Johnson (DB) 1989–94, Larry Bowie (FB) 1996–9, Bryan Thomas (FB) 2000–2, Bryan Johnson (RB) 2003.

48 Marvin Whited (G) 1942–5, Tony Leon (G) 1943, Leo Pressley (C) 1945, Weldon Edwards (T) 1948, Bob Hendren (T) 1949–51, Norb Hecker (DB) 1955–7, Ben Scotti (DB) 1959–61, Doug Elmore (B) 1962, Angelo Coia (WR) 1964–5, John Burrell (WR) 1966–7, Jon Jaqua (CB) 1970–2, Ken Coffey (S) 1983–5, Steve Gage (S) 1987–8, Marvin Williams (TE) 1987r, Ken Whisenhunt (TE) 1990, Travis Curtis (CB) 1991, *Stephen Davis* (RB) 1996–2002, Kevin Ware (TE) 2003.

49 Jim Meade (HB) 1939–40, John Koniszewski (T) 1945–6, 1948, John Sanchez (T) 1947–9, Sam Venuto (B) 1952, *Sam Baker* (K/P) 1956–9, Billy Brewer (B) 1960, **Bobby Mitchell** (WR) 1962–8, Leonard Stephens (TE) 2002.

50 Bob Nussbaumer (E) 1947–8, *Harry Ulinski* (C) 1953–6, Fred Hageman (C) 1961–4, Willie Adams (LB) 1965–6, Maxie Baughan (LB) 1974, Pete Wysocki (LB) 1975–80, Larry Kubin (LB)

1982–4, Ravin Caldwell (LB) 1987–92, Jon Kimmel (LB) 1987r, Carlton Rose (LB) 1987r, Tom Myslinski (G) 1992, Marc Raab (C) 1993, Darrick Brownlow (LB) 1995–6, Derek Smith (LB) 1997–2000, Robert Jones (LB) 2001, Larry Moore (C) 2002–3.

51 *Clyde Shugart* (G) 1939–43, Ed Merkle (G) 1944, Reid Lennan (G) 1945, Fred Boensch (G) 1947–8, Tony Momsen (C) 1952, *Jim Schrader* (C) 1954, 1956–61, Gordon Kelley (LB) 1962–3, John Reger (LB) 1964–6, Sid Williams (LB) 1967, John Didion (LB) 1969, Bob Grant (LB) 1971, Dan Ryczek (C) 1973–5, Joe Harris (LB) 1977, Monte Coleman (LB) 1979–94, Antwaune Ponds (LB) 1998, James Francis (LB) 1999, Mark Fischer (C) 2000–1, Clifton Smith (LB) 2003.

52 *Harry Gilmer* (QB) 1948–51, John Allen (C) 1955–8, Harry Butsko (LB) 1963, Heath Wingate (C) 1967, Mike Morgan (LB) 1968, Gene Hamlin (C) 1970, John Pergine (LB) 1973–5, Neal Olkewicz (LB) 1979–89, Matt Elliott (C) 1992, Cory Raymer (C) 1995–2001, Lemar Marshall (LB) 2002–3.

53 Rufus Deal (FB) 1942, Jack Smith (E) 1943, Mitch Ucovich (T) 1944, Al DeMao (C) 1945–53, *Torgy Torgeson* (LB) 1955–7, Bill Roehnelt (LB) 1960, Bob Pellegrini (LB) 1962–5, Steve Jackson (LB) 1966–7, Harold McLinton (LB) 1969–78, *Jeff Bostic* (C) 1980–93, Marvcus Patton (LB) 1995–7, Eddie Mason (LB) 1999–2002, Donny Green (LB) 2001.

54 Don Corbitt (C) 1948, Walt Cudzik (C) 1954, Bill Fulcher (LB) 1956–8, Don Croftcheck (G) 1965–6, Larry Hendershot (LB) 1967, Tom Roussel (LB) 1968–70, Bob Kuziel (C) 1975–80, Peter Cronan (LB) 1981–5, Kevin Turner (LB) 1981, Joe Krakoski (LB) 1986, Kurt Gouveia (LB) 1987–94, John Cowne (C) 1987r, Al Catanho (LB) 1996, Greg Jones (LB) 1997–2000, David Brandt (G) 2001, Jeremiah Trotter (LB) 2002–3.

55 *Ki Aldrich* (C) 1941–3, 1945–6, Harold Crisler (E) 1948–9, Jim Ricca (C) 1951–4, Allen Miller (LB) 1962–3, *Chris Hanburger* (LB) 1965–78, Mel Kaufman (LB) 1981–8, Andre Collins (LB) 1990–4, Jeff Uhlenhake (C) 1996–7, Malcolm Hamilton (LB) 1998–9, Fred Strickland (LB) 1999, Kevin Mitchell (LB) 2000–3.

56 Don Avery (T) 1946–7, *Harry Ulinski* (C) 1950–1, Dick Woodward (C) 1952, Charley Brueckman (C) 1958, Frank Kuchta (C) 1959, Ed Beatty (C) 1961, *Len Hauss* (C) 1964–77, Dan Peiffer (C) 1980, Quentin Lowry (LB) 1981–3, Trey Junkin (LB) 1984, Calvin Daniels (LB) 1986, Eric Coyle (C) 1987r, 1988, Brian Bonner (LB) 1989, Tom Myslinski (G) 1992, Rick Hamilton (LB) 1993–4, Erick Anderson (LB) 1994, Dion Foxx (LB) 1995, Chester Burnett (LB) 1998, *LeVar Arrington* (LB) 2000–3.

57 Ed Stacco (T) 1948, John Badaczewski (G)

1949–51, Dave Crossan (C) 1965–9, Stu O'Dell (LB) 1974–6, Rich Milot (LB) 1979–87, Anthony Copeland (LB) 1987, Don Graham (LB) 1989, Randy Kirk (LB) 1990, Matt Millen (LB) 1991, Guy Bingham (C) 1992–3, *Ken Harvey* (LB) 1994–8, Jay Leeuwenburg (G) 2000, Donte Curry (LB) 2001, Orantes Grant (LB) 2002–3.

58 Leo Nobile (C) 1947, Mike Katrishen (T) 1948–9, George Burman (C/G) 1971, Mike Varty (LB) 1973, Don Hover (LB) 1978–9, Dave Graf (LB) 1981, Charlie Weaver (LB) 1981, Stuart Anderson (LB) 1982–5, Shawn Burks (LB) 1986, David Jones (C) 1987, David Windham (LB) 1987r, *Wilber Marshall* (LB) 1988–92, Carl Banks (LB) 1993, Patrise Alexander (LB) 1996–8, Reggie Givens (LB) 2000, Antonio Pierce (LB) 2001–3.

59 Jim Carroll (LB) 1966, Brad Dusek (LB) 1974–81, Jim Youngblood (LB) 1984, Chris Keating (LB) 1985, Jeff Paine (LB) 1986, Angelo Snipes (LB) 1986, Ray Hitchcock (C) 1987, Eric Wilson (LB) 1987r, Dave Harbour (C) 1988–9, Mike Scully (C) 1988, John Brantley (LB) 1992–3, Chris Sedoris (C) 1996, Shawn Barber (LB) 1998–2001, Wilbert Brown (G) 2002.

60 John Jaffurs (G) 1946, Bill Gray (G) 1947–8, Joe Soboleski (G) 1949, Buddy Brown (G) 1951–2, Buddy Berschet (G) 1954–5, *Dick Stanfel* (G) 1956–8, *Bob Khayat* (G) 1960, 1962–3, Jim Carroll (LB) 1967–8, John Wilbur (G) 1971–3, Donnie Hickman (G) 1978, Gary Anderson (G) 1980, Roy Simmons (G) 1983, J.T. Turner (G) 1984, Dan McQuaid (T) 1985, Mike Wooten (C) 1987r, Fred Stokes (DE) 1989–92, Greg Huntington (T) 1993, Mark Fischer (C) 1998–9, *Chris Samuels* (T) 2000–3.

61 Bob DeFruiter (DB) 1945–7, Gene Pepper (G) 1950–3, Fran O'Brien (T) 1960–6, Jim Avery (E) 1966, Don Bandy (G) 1967–8, Dennis Johnson (DT) 1974–7, Melvin Jones (G) 1981, Ken Huff (G) 1983–5, Rick Kehr (G) 1987–8, Willard Scissum (G) 1987r, Mark Adickes (G) 1990–1, Vernice Smith (G) 1993–5, Michael Batiste (G) 1998.

62 Casimir Witucki (G) 1950–1, *Don Boll* (T) 1953–9, *John Nisby* (G) 1962–4, Darrell Dess (G) 1965–6, Ray Schoenke (G) 1966–75, Dan Nugent (G) 1976–8, 1980, Don Laster (T) 1982, Morris Towns (T) 1984, Phil Pettey (G) 1987r, Ralph Tamm (G) 1991, Darryl Moore (G) 1992–3, Ben Coleman (G) 2001.

63 Herb Siegert (G) 1949–51, Casimir Witucki (G) 1953–6, Emil Karas (LB) 1959, *Rod Breedlove* (LB) 1960–4, Ed Breding (LB) 1967–8, Steve Duich (G) 1969, Mitch Johnson (T) 1972, Fred Dean (G) 1978–80, 1982, Bruce Kimball (G) 1984, Raleigh McKenzie (C/G) 1985–94, John Gesek (C) 1995, Keith Sims (G) 1998–2000.

64 Ron Marciniak (C) 1955, Bill Fulcher (G) 1956, Mitch Johnson (T) 1966–8, Manny Sistrunk (DT) 1970–5, Ron Saul (G) 1976–81, Steve Hamilton (DE) 1985, Ralph Tamm (G) 1991, Mo Elewonibi (T) 1992–3, Trevor Matich (C) 1994–6, Andy Heck (T) 1999–2000, David Loverne (OL) 2002, Lennie Friedman (G) 2003.

65 Jim Clark (G) 1952–3, Walt Houston (G) 1955, *Vince Promuto* (G) 1960–70, Fred Sturt (G) 1974, *Dave Butz* (DT) 1975–88.

66 Jim Norman (T) 1955, Ed Voytek (G) 1957–8, Bob Whitlow (C) 1960–1, Carl Kammerer (DE) 1963–9, Myron Pottios (LB) 1971–3, Martin Imhof (DE) 1974, Jim Arneson (G) 1975, Ted Fritsch (C) 1976–9, *Joe Jacoby* (G/T) 1981–93, Dan Turk (C) 1997–9, Michael Moore (G) 2000, Matt Campbell (G) 2001, Brenden Stai (OL) 2002, Derrick Dockery (G) 2003.

67 Dave Suminski (G) 1953, Red Stephens (G) 1955–60, Bernie Darre (G) 1961, Andy Cvercko (G) 1963, Bob Reed (G) 1965, Jake Kupp (G/TE) 1966, John Wooten (G) 1968, Dan Grimm (G) 1969, Rusty Tilman (LB) 1970–7, Greg Dubinetz (G) 1979, Bruce Kimball (G) 1983, Tom Beasley (DT) 1985, Kit Lathrop (DE) 1987r, Steve Thompson (DE) 1987r, Henry Waechter (DE) 1987r, Ray Brown (G) 1989–90, 1992–5, Shar Pourdanesh (T) 1996–8, Derrick Fletcher (G) 2000, *Tre Johnson* (G) 2002, Daryl Terrell (G) 2003.

68 Ed Bagdon (G) 1952, Knox Ramsey (G) 1952–3, Dave Sparks (G) 1954, Tom Feagin (G) 1963, Willie Banks (G) 1968–9, Mike Fanucci (DE) 1972, Jim Harlan (T) 1978, Gary Anderson (G) 1980, *Russ Grimm* (G) 1981–91, Joe Patton (G/T) 1994–8, Tony Hutson (G) 2000, Ross Tucker (G) 2001, Brandon Winey (T) 2003.

69 Ron Hansen (G) 1954, Tom Goosby (G) 1966, Willie Banks (G) 1969, Perry Brooks (DT) 1978–84, R.C. Thielemann (G) 1985–8, *Mark Schlereth* (G) 1989–94, Rod Milstead (G) 1998–9, Ed Ellis (T) 2000.

70 Lou Karras (T) 1950–1, Dick Modzelewski (DT) 1953–4, Fred Miller (T) 1955, Tony Sardisco (G) 1956, *Ray Lemek* (T) 1957–61, Chuck Moore (G) 1962, **Sam Huff** (LB) 1964–7, 1969, Will Wynn (DE) 1977, Leonard Marshall (DT) 1994, Troy Drake (T) 1998, Kipp Vickers (T) 2002.

71 Jerry Houghton (T) 1950, Will Renfro (T) 1957–9, Andy Stynchula (DT) 1960–3, George Seals (DE) 1964, Spain Musgrove (DT) 1967–8, Frank Bosch (DT) 1969–70, Jim Tyrer (T) 1974, Karl Lorch (DT) 1976–81, Gary Peutz (T) 1982, *Charles Mann* (DE) 1983–93, Ron Lewis (G) 1995, Barron Tanner (DT) 1999, Ethan Albright (C) 2003.

72 Jim Staton (DT) 1951, Joe Moss (T) 1952, Erik Christensen (DE) 1956, Don Owens (DT) 1957, Jim Weatherall (DT) 1958, Don Churchwell (T) 1959, *Joe Rutgens* (DT) 1961–9, Terry Hermeling (T) 1970, *Diron Talbert* (DT) 1971–80, *Dexter Manley* (DE) 1981–9, Mike Haight (T) 1992, Al Noga (DE) 1993, Romeo Bandison (DT)

1995, Mike Flores (DE) 1995, Don Sasa (DT) 1997, Ndukwe Kalu (DE) 1998–2000, Dorian Boose (DE) 2001, Carl Powell (DL) 2002.

73 Ken Barfield (T) 1954, Mike Davlin (T) 1955, John Miller (T) 1956, 1958–9, Riley Mattson (T) 1961–4, **Stan Jones** (T) 1965, Frank Bosch (DT) 1968, Paul Laaveg (G) 1970–5, Jeff Williams (T) 1978–80, *Mark May* (G) 1981–90, Lamar Mills (DT) 1994, Mike Flores (DE) 1995, Darryl Ashmore (T) 1996–7, Paul Wiggins (T) 1998, Jamie Brown (T) 1999, Bernard Jackson (DE) 2002.

74 *Laurie Niemi* (T) 1952–3, Bob Morgan (DT) 1954, Ed Khayat (DT) 1962–3, Jim Snowden (T) 1965–72, George Starke (T) 1973–84, Marcus Koch (DE) 1986–91, Curtis McGriff (DE) 1987r, Gerald Nichols (DT) 1993, Brian Thure (T) 1995, Brad Badger (G) 1997–9, Nolan Harrison (DE) 2000, Dave Fiore (G) 2003.

75 Ed Ecker (T) 1952, Don Campora (DT) 1953, Harry Jagielski (T) 1956, Ben Davidson (DT) 1962–3, Fred Williams (T) 1964, John Kelly (T) 1966–7, Rich Marshall (DT) 1966, Fred Washington (T) 1968, Steve Wright (T) 1970, Terry Hermeling (T) 1971–3, 1975–80, **Deacon Jones** (DE) 1974, Mike Clark (DE) 1981, Pat Ogrin (DT) 1982, Darrick Brilz (G) 1987r, Mike Stensrud (DT) 1989, Eric Williams (DT) 1990–3, John Gesek (C) 1994, Bob Dahl (G) 1996–7, Anthony Cook (DE) 1999, Derrick Ham (DE) 2000.

76 *Paul Lipscomb* (DT) 1950–4, J.D. Kimmel (T) 1955–6, Don Stallings (E) 1960, Jim Prestel (T) 1966–7, Walter Rock (T) 1968–73, Tim Stokes (T) 1975–7, Bob Heinz (DT) 1978, Jerry Scanlan (T) 1980–1, Matt Mendenhall (DE) 1981–2, Rick Donnalley (C/G) 1984–5, Ron Tilton (G) 1986, Ed Simmons (T) 1987–97, Frank Frazier (G) 1987r, Jon Jansen (T) 1999–2003.

77 Jack Jacobs (QB) 1946, Tommy Mont (QB) 1947–9, Ray Krouse (DT) 1960, Steve Barnett (T) 1964, Fred Williams (T) 1965, Walter Barnes (DT) 1966–8, Bill Brundidge (DT) 1970–7, Joe Jones (DE) 1979–80, Darryl Grant (DT) 1981–90, Jim Wahler (DT) 1992–3, *Tre Johnson* (G) 1994–2000, Ethan Albright (C) 2001–2, Randy Thomas (G) 2003.

78 Ted Hazelwood (T) 1953, Don Lawrence (T) 1959–61, Ron Snidow (DE) 1963–7, Floyd Peters (DT) 1970, Mike Taylor (T) 1971, Walt Sweeney (G) 1974–5, Dallas Hickman (DE) 1976–8, Paul Smith (DE) 1979–80, Tony McGee (DE) 1982–4, Dean Hamel (DT) 1985–8, Lybrant Robinson (DE) 1989, Tim Johnson (DT) 1990–5, Ryan Kuehl (DT) 1996, Chris Zorich (DT) 1997, Doug Brown (DT) 1998–9, Bruce Smith (DE) 2000–3.

79 John Yonakor (E) 1952, Bill Hegarty (T) 1953, *Volney Peters* (T) 1954–7, *Bob Toneff* (DT) 1959–64, Dennis Crane (DT) 1968–9, Ron McDole (DE) 1971–8, Coy Bacon (DE) 1979–81, Pat

Ogrin (DT) 1981, Todd Liebenstein (DE) 1982–5, Doug Barnett (DE) 1985, Mark Carlson (T) 1987r, *Jim Lachey* (T) 1988–95, Steve Emtman (DT) 1997, Kipp Vickers (G) 1999, Dave Szott (G) 2001.

80 *Gene Brito* (DE) 1951–3, 1955–8, Steve Junker (E) 1961–2, Joe Hernandez (E) 1964, Pat Hodgson (TE) 1966, Bruce Alford (K) 1967, Bob Long (WR) 1969, *Roy Jefferson* (WR) 1971–6, Coy Bacon (DE) 1978, Kris Haines (WR) 1979, John McDaniel (WR) 1979–80, Virgil Seay (WR) 1981–4, Malcolm Barnwell (WR) 1985, Joe Phillips (WR) 1985, Eric Yarber (WR) 1986–7, Teddy Wilson (WR) 1987r, Derrick Shepard (WR) 1988, Joe Johnson (WR) 1989–91, Desmond Howard (WR) 1992–4, Olanda Truitt (WR) 1995, Bill Brooks (WR) 1996, *Stephen Alexander* (TE) 1998–2001, Jacquez Green (WR) 2002, Justin Skaggs (WR) 2002, *Laveranues Coles* (WR) 2003.

81 Dan Brown (E) 1950, Sam Morley (WR) 1954, Joe Walton (E) 1957–60, Lew Luce (B) 1961, Bob Jencks (E) 1965, Jake Kupp (TE) 1966, Ken Barefoot (E) 1968, Leo Carroll (DE) 1969, Mack Alston (TE) 1970–2, Doug Winslow (WR) 1976–7, Terry Anderson (WR) 1978, J.T. Smith (WR) 1978, Chris DeFrance (WR) 1979, *Art Monk* (WR) 1980–93.

82 Roland Dale (E) 1950, Ed Berrang (E) 1952, Fran Polsfoot (E) 1953, *John Carson* (E) 1954–9, Ken MacAfee (E) 1959, Pat Heenan (E) 1960, Dick Absher (K) 1967, Clark Miller (DE) 1969, Jimmie Jones (DE) 1971–3, Dallas Hickman (DE) 1979–81, Rich Caster (TE) 1981–2, John Sawyer (TE) 1983, Anthony Jones (TE) 1984–5, Joe Caravello (TE) 1987, John Brandes (TE) 1990–2, Ray Rowe (TE) 1992, Jim Riggs (TE) 1993, Kurt Haws (TE) 1994, Michael Westbrook (WR) 1995–2001, Byron Chamberlain (TE) 2003.

83 Al Dekker (WR) 1953, Charlie Jones (E) 1955, Ed Meadows (DB) 1959, Roy Wilkins (LB) 1960–1, Jim Norton (T) 1969, Bruce Anderson (DE) 1970, Ricky Thompson (WR) 1978–81, Dave Stief (WR) 1983, Mark McGrath (WR) 1983–5, Rich Mauti (WR) 1984, James Noble (WR) 1986, Ricky Sanders (WR) 1987–93, Richard Johnson (WR) 1987r, Tydus Winans (WR) 1994–5, Flipper Anderson (WR) 1996, Albert Connell (WR) 1997–2000, Kevin Lockett (WR) 2001–2, Willie Jackson (WR) 2002, Cliff Russell (WR) 2003.

84 Herb Shoener (E) 1948–9, *Hugh Taylor* (E) 1952–4, Tom Braatz (DE) 1957–8, Tom Osborne (E) 1960–1, Mike Hancock (TE) 1973–5, *Jean Fugett* (TE) 1976–9, Zion McKinney (WR) 1980, Greg McCrary (TE) 1981, Mike Williams (TE) 1982–4, Walt Arnold (TE) 1984, Rich Mauti (WR) 1984, *Gary Clark* (WR) 1985–92, Keiron Bigby (WR) 1987r, Joe Phillips (WR) 1987r, Mark Stock (WR) 1993, Olanda Truitt (WR) 1994, Jamie Asher (TE) 1995–8, Derrius Thompson (WR) 1999, Andre Reed (WR) 2000, Marco Battaglia

(TE) 2001, Chris Doering (WR) 2002, Patrick Johnson (WR) 2003.

85 Walt Yowarsky (E) 1951–4, *John Paluck* (DE) 1956, Tom Braatz (DE) 1959, Gene Cronin (DE) 1961–2, Bill Quinlan (DE) 1964, Marlin McKeever (LB) 1968, John Hoffman (DE) 1969–70, Clifton McNeil (WR) 1971–2, Willie Holman (DE) 1973, Brian Fryer (WR) 1976, Greg McCrary (TE) 1978, Don Warren (TE) 1979–92, Dave Truitt (TE) 1987r, Tim McGee (WR) 1993, Henry Ellard (WR) 1994–8, Mike Sellers (TE) 1998, Joe Zelenka (TE) 2000, Darnarien McCants (WR) 2002–3.

86 Steve Meilinger (E) 1956–7, *John Paluck* (DE) 1959–65, Bill Briggs (DE) 1966–7, Marlin McKeever (LB) 1969–70, Boyd Dowler (WR) 1971, Verlon Biggs (DE) 1972–5, Bill Larson (TE) 1977, John McDaniel (WR) 1978, Phil DuBois (TE) 1979–80, Clint Didier (TE) 1982–7, Mike Tice (TE) 1989, Stephen Hobbs (WR) 1990–2, Leslie Shepherd (WR) 1994–8, Irving Fryar (WR) 1999–2000, Walter Rasby (TE) 2001–2, Taylor Jacobs (WR) 2003.

87 Clyde Goodnight (E) 1950, Ed Barker (E) 1954, Ralph Thomas (E) 1955–6, Ed Khayat (DT) 1957, Fred Dugan (E) 1961–3, *Jerry Smith* (TE) 1965–77, *Charlie Brown* (WR) 1982–4, Terry Orr (TE) 1986–90, K.D. Dunn (TE) 1987r, Ron Middleton (TE) 1990–3, Coleman Bell (TE) 1994–5, James Thrash (WR) 1997–2000, Rod Gardner (WR) 2001–3.

88 Jerry Hennessey (DE) 1952–3, Chet Ostrowski (E) 1954–9, Dick Lasse (LB) 1960–1, Pat Richter (TE) 1963–70, Alvin Reed (TE) 1973–5, Danny Buggs (WR) 1976–9, Rick Walker (TE) 1980–5, Todd Frain (TE) 1986, Derek Holloway (WR) 1986, Cliff Benson (TE) 1987, Derrick Shepard (WR) 1987r, Joe Caravello (TE) 1988, Billy Johnson (WR) 1988, Ron Middleton (TE) 1988, Jimmie Johnson (TE) 1989–91, James Jenkins (TE) 1991–2000, Derrius Thompson (WR) 2001–2, Robert Royal (TE) 2003.

89 Joe Tereshinski (E) 1952–4, Bob Dee (DE) 1957–8, Art Gob (E) 1959–60, John Aveni (K) 1961, Hugh Smith (E) 1962, Jim Collier (E) 1963, Preston Carpenter (E) 1964–6, Leo Carroll (DE) 1970, Verlon Biggs (DE) 1971, Dave Robinson (LB) 1973–4, Reggie Haynes (TE) 1978, Grady Richardson (TE) 1979–80, Kenny Harrison (WR) 1980, Alvin Garrett (WR) 1981–4, Calvin Muhammad (WR) 1984–5, Clarence Verdin (WR) 1986–7, Anthony Allen (WR) 1987r, Glenn Dennison (TE) 1987r, Walter Stanley (WR) 1990, Terry Orr (TE) 1991–3, Ethan Horton (TE) 1994, Scott Galbraith (TE) 1995–6, Chris Thomas (WR) 1997–9, Zeron Flemister (TE) 2000–3.

90 Walt Arnold (TE) 1984, Bobby Curtis (LB) 1987r, Huey Richardson (LB) 1992, Rick Graf (LB) 1993, Tyronne Stowe (LB) 1994, Terry Crews (LB)

1995, Troy Barnett (DT) 1996, Kenard Lang (DE) 1997–2001, Bernard Holsey (DE) 2003.

91 Bob Raba (TE) 1981, Tony Settles (LB) 1987r, Greg Manusky (LB) 1988–90, Shane Collins (DE) 1992–4, Matt Vanderbeek (LB) 1995–6, Chris Mims (DT) 1997, David Hoelscher (DT) 1998, Delbert Cowsette (DT) 2001–2, Regan Upshaw (DE) 2003.

92 Hugh Smith (E) 1962, Derek Bunch (LB) 1987r, Dexter Nottage (DE) 1994–6, Jamal Duff (DE) 1997–8, Jerry DeLoach (DT) 2001, Daryl Gardener (DT) 2002, Martin Chase (DT) 2003.

93 Johnny Meads (LB) 1992, Jeff Faulkner (DT) 1993, Keith Willis (DT) 1993, Marc Boutte (DT) 1994–9, Otis Leverette (DE) 2001, Peppi Zellner (DE) 2003.

94 Anthony Sagnella (DT) 1987r, Bobby Wilson (DT) 1991–4, Sean Gilbert (DT) 1996, Dana Stubblefield (DT) 1998–2000, Ladairis Jackson (DL) 2002.

95 Dan Benish (DT) 1987r, William Gaines (DT) 1995–7, Dan Wilkinson (DT) 1998–2002, Lionel Dalton (DT) 2003, Ron Warner (DE) 2003.

96 Alec Gibson (DE) 1987r, Lamont Hollinquest (LB) 1993–4, Rich Owens (DE) 1995–7, Tyrone Williams (DE) 2001, Greg Scott (DE) 2002, Darrell Russell (DT) 2003.

97 Jumpy Geathers (DT) 1990–2, Sterling Palmer (DE) 1993–6, Romeo Bandison (DT) 1996, Kelvin Kinney (DE) 1997–8, Renaldo Wynn (DE) 2002–3.

98 Steve Martin (DE) 1987r, Tony Barker (LB) 1992, Tony Woods (DE) 1994–6, Twan Russell (LB) 1997–9, Jessie Armstead (LB) 2002–3.

99 Eddie Saenz (B) 1946–51, Wilbur Young (DE) 1981, Ted Karras (DT) 1987r, Tracy Rocker (DT) 1989–90, Jason Buck (DE) 1991–3, Rod Stephens (LB) 1995–6, Ryan Kuehl (DT) 1997, Keith Rucker (DT) 1997, *Marco Coleman* (DE) 1999–2001, Jermaine Haley (DT) 2003.

PART TWO.

Player by Player Listings

Team abbreviations are as follows. Three-character abbreviations are used for current teams. Four-character abbreviations beginning with x are for NFL teams that failed since 1933; four character abbreviations beginning with z are for defunct AAFC teams.

ARZ	Arizona, Phoenix, St. Louis and Chicago Cardinals
ATL	Atlanta Falcons
BAL	Baltimore Ravens
BUF	Buffalo Bills
CAR	Carolina Panthers
CHI	Chicago Bears, Chicago Staleys, Decatur Staleys
CIN	Cincinnati Bengals
CLE	Cleveland Browns
CIN	Cincinnati Bengals
DAL	Dallas Cowboys
DEN	Denver Broncos
DET	Detroit Lions, Portsmouth Spartans
GBP	Green Bay Packers
HOU	Houston Texans
IND	Indianapolis Colts, Baltimore Colts
JAX	Jacksonville Jaguars
KCC	Kansas City Chiefs, Dallas Texans
MIA	Miami Dolphins
MIN	Minnesota Vikings
NEP	New England Patriots, Boston Patriots
NOS	New Orleans Saints
NYG	New York Giants
NYJ	New York Jets, New York Titans
OAK	Oakland Raiders, Los Angeles Raiders
PHL	Philadelphia Eagles
PIT	Pittsburgh Steelers, Pittsburgh Pirates
STL	St. Louis Rams, Los Angeles Rams, Cleveland Rams
SDC	San Diego Chargers, Los Angeles Chargers
SFF	San Francisco 49ers
SEA	Seattle Seahawks
TBB	Tampa Bay Buccaneers
TEN	Tennessee Titans, Tennessee Oilers, Houston Oilers
WSH	Washington Redskins, Boston Redskins, Boston Braves
xCIN	Cincinnati Reds
xSTL	St. Louis Gunners
xBKN	Brooklyn Dodgers, Brooklyn Tigers
xBOS	Boston Yanks
xNYB	New York Bulldogs, New York Yanks
xDAL	Dallas Texans
xBAL	Baltimore Colts
zBAL	Baltimore Colts
zBRK	Brooklyn Dodgers
zBUF	Buffalo Bills, Buffalo Bisons
zCHI	Chicago Rockets, Chicago Hornets
zLAD	Los Angeles Dons
zMIA	Miami Seahawks
zNYY	New York Yankees

Abbey, Joe CHI 26, xNYB 39
Abbott, Vince SDC 10
Abbruzzi, Duke xBOS 20
Abdul-Jabbar, Karim CLE 27, MIA 33, IND 33
Abdullah, Khalid CIN 53
Abdullah, Rabih CHI 27, TBB 26/27
Abdullah, Rahim CLE 53/55
Abell, Bud KCC 52
Abercrombie, Walter PHL 32, PIT 34
Aberson, Cliff GBP 78
Abraham, Clifton CHI 48, TBB 26, CAR 24
Abraham, Donnie TBB 21, NYJ 29
Abraham, John NYJ 94
Abraham, Robert TEN 56

Abramowicz, Dan BUF 46, NOS 46, SFF 46
Abramowitz, Sid IND 69/74, NYJ 69, SEA 69
Abrams, Bobby CLE 56, DAL 50, MIN 50, NEP 50, NYG 50
Abrams, Kevin DET 24
Abramson, George GBP 12
Abruzzese, Ray BUF 46, NYJ 25
Abruzzino, Frank xBKN 30, xCIN 39
Absher, Dick ATL 57, NOS 53, PHL 53, WSH 82
Ache, Steve MIN 53
Achica, George IND 62
Acker, Bill ARZ 67, BUF 75, KCC 64/74
Ackerman, Rick OAK 58/97, SDC 91

Ackerman, Tom NOS 69, TEN 67
Acks, Ron ATL 52, GBP 57, NEP 51
Acorn, Fred TBB 27
Adamchik, Ed NYG 61, PIT ?
Adamle, Mike CHI 20, KCC 1, NYJ 1
Adamle, Tony CLE 54/74
Adams, Anthony SFF 91
Adams, Bill BUF 60
Adams, Blue JAX 26
Adams, Bob ATL 81, DEN 81, NEP 80, PIT 85
Adams, Brent ATL 62
Adams, Charlie DEN 12
Adams, Chester STL 34, CLE 42, GBP 27, xNYB 71, zBUF 42
Adams, Curtis SDC 42

Adams, David DAL 21
Adams, Doug CIN 52
Adams, Ernie DET 50
Adams, Flozell DAL 76
Adams, Gary PHL 6
Adams, George NEP 33, NYG 33
Adams, Henry ARZ 16
Adams, John CHI 39, STL 87
Adams, John WSH 42
Adams, Julius NEP 85
Adams, Keith DAL 53, PHL 57
Adams, Michael ARZ 40, NOS 40
Adams, Mike PIT 86
Adams, Neal NYG 30, zBRK 54
Adams, Pete CLE 69
Adams, Sam BLT 95, BUF 95, OAK 95, SEA 98
Adams, Sam NEP 61, NOS 61
Adams, Scott ATL 71, CHI 72, DEN 73, MIN 72, NOS 64, TBB 71
Adams, Stanley OAK 59
Adams, Stefon CLE 44, MIA 47, OAK 44
Adams, Theo PHL 61, SEA 61, TBB 73
Adams, Tom MIN 85
Adams, Tony KCC 11, MIN 7
Adams, Vashone BLT 43, CLE 43, KCC 26, NOS 27
Adams, Verlin NYG 28
Adams, Willie WSH 50
Adams, Willis CLE 80
Adamson, Ken DEN 60
Addams, Abe DET 85
Adderley, Herb GBP 26, DAL 26
Adickes, John MIN 68
Adickes, Mark KCC 61, WSH 61
Addison, Tom NEP 53
Adduci, Nick WSH 25/44
Adickes, John CHI 54
Adkins, Bob GBP 55/79
Adkins, Kevin KCC 65
Adkins, Margene DAL 23, NOS 26, NYJ 26
Adkins, Roy CHI 22
Adkins, Sam SEA 12
Affholter, Erik GBP 82
Afflis, Dick GBP 15/62/72/75
Agajanian, Ben GBP 3, KCC 3, NYG 8/41, OAK 3, PHL 89, PIT 43, SDC 3, STL 3, zLAD 3
Agase, Alex CLE 35, IND 62, zCHI 36, zLAD 36
Age, Louis CHI 79
Agee, Mel ATL 68, IND 90
Agee, Sam ARZ 11
Agee, Tommie DAL 34, KCC 32, SEA 33
Agler, Bob STL 30

Agnew, Ray NEP 92, NYG 93, STL 99
Aguiar, Louie CHI 10, KCC 5, NYJ 4, GBP 10
Aguirre, Joe WSH 19, zLAD 58/57
Ahanotu, Chidi BUF 72, SFF 72, STL 72, TBB 72/90
Ahrens, Dave ARZ 58, DET 57, IND 57, MIA 50, SEA 50
Aiello, Tony DET 17, xBKN 10
Aiken, Sam BUF 89
Aikens, Carl OAK 83
Aikman, Troy DAL 8
Aiu, Charles SDC 64, SEA 64
Akbar, Hakim NEP 25, STL 53
Akers, David PHL 2, WSH 6
Akin, Harold SDC 71
Akin, Len CHI 31
Akins, Al CLE 80, zBRK 81, zBUF 90
Akins, Chris CLE 36, DAL 29, GBP 31, NEP 34
Akins, Frank WSH 18/39
Akins, Robert ARZ 48
Akiu, Mike TEN 86
Alban, Dick WSH 42, PIT 42
Albanese, Vannie xBKN 5 4
Alberghini, Tom PIT 69
Albert, Frank SFF 13/63
Albert, Sergio ARZ 18
Alberts, Trev IND 51
Albrecht, Art ARZ 75, GBP 19, PIT 46, xBOS 17
Albrecht, Ted CHI 64
Albright, Bill NYG 75
Albright, Ethan BUF 76, MIA 71, WSH 71/77
Albright, Ira BUF 41/98
Albritton, Vince DAL 36
Alderman, Grady MIN 67, DET 67
Alderton, John PIT 83
Aldrich, Ki ARZ 48, WSH 38/55
Aldridge, Allen Jr. CLE 75, DEN 57, DET 55
Aldridge, Allen Sr. TEN 88
Aldridge, Ben GBP 40, SFF 38, xNYB 31
Aldridge, Jerry SFF 47
Aldridge, Lionel GBP 62/82, SDC 87
Aldridge, Mel ARZ 45, TEN 36
Ale, Arnold KCC 56, SDC 57
Aleaga, Ink NOS 50/54
Alex, Keith ATL 62, MIN 63
Alexakos, Steve DEN 68, NYG 60
Alexander, Brent ARZ 46, PIT 27, CAR 46
Alexander, Bruce DET 32, MIA 32
Alexander, Charles CIN 40

Alexander, Dan JAX 38, TEN 38
Alexander, Dan NYJ 60
Alexander, Dave NYJ 72, PHL 72
Alexander, Derrick BLT 82, CLE 85, KCC 82, MIN 82
Alexander, Derrick MIN 90, CLE 94
Alexander, Doc NYG 10/20/25
Alexander, Elijah DEN 58, IND 50, OAK 58, TBB 59
Alexander, Glenn BUF 45
Alexander, Harold ATL 5
Alexander, Jeff DEN 40
Alexander, John MIA 76
Alexander, John NYG 34
Alexander, Kermit SFF 39, STL 39, PHL 39
Alexander, Kevin NYG 86
Alexander, Mike BUF 86, OAK 80
Alexander, Patrise WSH 58
Alexander, Ray DAL 87, DEN 80
Alexander, Robert STL 39
Alexander, Rogers NEP 91, NYJ 51
Alexander, Shaun SEA 37
Alexander, Stephen WSH 80, SDC 80/81
Alexander, Vincent NOS 30
Alexander, Willie TEN 19
Alexis, Alton CIN 82
Alflen, Ted DEN 25
Alfonse, Julius STL 5/29
Alford, Brian NYG 80/84
Alford, Bruce Jr. BUF 46, WSH 80
Alford, Bruce Sr. xNYB 12, zNYY 51
Alford, Darnell KCC 72
Alford, Gene DET 25/37/54/59, xSTL 30
Alford, Lynwood NYJ 58
Alford, Mike ARZ 50, DET 50
Alfson, Warren xBKN 33
Alipate, Tuineau MIN 53, NYJ 41
Allard, Don NEP 12, NYJ 27
Allegre, Raul IND 2, NYG 2, NYJ 2
Allen, Anthony ATL 85, SDC 89, WSH 89
Allen, Brian CAR 52, IND 43, STL 51
Allen, Buddy DEN 22
Allen, Carl ARZ 27
Allen, Carl zBRK 70/92
Allen, Chuck SDC 50, PHL 54, PIT 58
Allen, Dalva OAK 80, TEN 76/80
Allen, David JAX 34
Allen, Derek NYG 89
Allen, Donald DEN 24
Allen, Doug BUF 59

Allen, Duane CHI 85, STL 25
Allen, Ed ARZ 30
Allen, Eddie CHI 3
Allen, Egypt CHI 47
Allen, Eric NOS 21, OAK 21, PHL 21
Allen, Ermal CLE 66
Allen, Gary DAL 31, TEN 31
Allen, George TEN 73
Allen, Gerry WSH 20, IND 44
Allen, Grady ATL 54
Allen, Greg CLE 26, TBB 28
Allen, Harvey SEA 46
Allen, Ian NYG 74
Allen, Jackie BUF 21, OAK 20, PHL 21
Allen, James CHI 20, HOU 20
Allen, James NOS 50
Allen, Jeff ARZ 37
Allen, Jeff MIA 43, SDC 27
Allen, Jimmy DET 35/40, PIT 45
Allen, John WSH 52
Allen, Kendrick NOS 99
Allen, Kevin PHL 72
Allen, Larry DAL 73
Allen, Louis PIT 65/73
Allen, Marcus KCC 32, OAK 32
Allen, Marvin NEP 39
Allen, Matt NYG 12
Allen, Nate DET 42, KCC 48, MIN 25, SFF 27
Allen, Patrick TEN 29
Allen, Taje KCC 26, STL 20
Allen, Terry WSH 21, BLT 29, MIN 21, NEP 22, NOS 20
Allen, Tremayne CHI 49
Allen, Will NYG 25
Allerman, Kurt ARZ 50/51, DET 95, GBP 60
Allert, Ty DEN 57, PHL 58, SDC 56, SEA 51
Alley, Don IND 29, PIT 83
Allison, Henry ARZ 61, DEN 73, PHL 65
Allison, Jim SDC 32
Allison, Neely NYG 11
Alliston, Buddy DEN 62
Allman, Robert CHI 28
Allotey, Victor BUF 66, KCC 69
Allred, Brian SEA 39
Allred, John CHI 84, PIT 85
Alm, Jeff TEN 76
Almodobar, Beau NYG 10
Alphin, Gerald NOS 86
Alston, Lyneal PIT 81
Alston, Mack IND 83, TEN 82/84, WSH 81
Alston, O'Brien IND 97
Alstott, Mike TBB 40
Alt, John KCC 76
Althoff, Jim CHI 70
Alton, Joe ARZ 67
Alvarez, Wilson SEA 2
Alvers, Steve BUF 87, NYJ 86

Alvord, Steve ARZ 60
Alward, Tom TBB 67
Alworth, Lance SDC 19/24, DAL 19
Alzado, Lyle DEN 77, CLE 77, OAK 77
Amato, Ken TEN 58
Amberg, John NYG 12
Ambrose, Ashley CIN 33, ATL 33, IND 33, NOS 33/43
Ambrose, Dick CLE 52
Ambrose, John xBKN 14/18
Ambrose, Walt DET ?
Ameche, Alan IND 35
Amerson, Glen PHL 46
Ames, Dave NYJ 25, DEN 22
Amey, Vince OAK 92
Amman, Richard IND 73
Amsler, Marty CHI 81, CIN 89, GBP 87
Amstutz, Joe CLE 52
Amundsen, Norm GBP 62
Amundson, George PHL 38, TEN 12
Ananis, Vito WSH 44
Andabaker, Rudy PIT 64
Anders, Kimble KCC 38
Andersen, Jason KCC 67, NEP 67
Andersen, Morten ATL 5, KCC 8, NOS 7, NYG 8
Andersen, Stanley STL 39
Anderson, Alfred MIN 46
Anderson, Anthony ATL 33, PIT 33
Anderson, Anthony SDC 24
Anderson, Antonio DAL 96
Anderson, Aric GBP 53
Anderson, Art CHI 79, PIT 63
Anderson, Bennie BLT 66
Anderson, Bill WSH 42, GBP 88
Anderson, Bill xBOS 26
Anderson, Billy TEN 14
Anderson, Bob NYG 41
Anderson, Bobby DEN 11, NEP 33, WSH 40
Anderson, Brad CHI 86
Anderson, Bruce NYG 79, STL 79, WSH 83
Anderson, Charley ARZ 87
Anderson, Chet PIT 46
Anderson, Cliff ARZ 84, NYG 82
Anderson, Curtis JAX 25
Anderson, Curtis KCC 90
Anderson, Damian ARZ 20
Anderson, Darren ATL 26, KCC 44, NEP 25, TBB 44
Anderson, Dick MIA 40
Anderson, Dick NOS 71
Anderson, Don IND 36, TBB 23
Anderson, Donny GBP 44, ARZ 44
Anderson, Dunstan ATL 73, MIA 71

Anderson, Dwayne ARZ 20
Anderson, Ed ARZ 4/16/22, CHI 18
Anderson, Eddie OAK 33, SEA 47
Anderson, Erick KCC 50, WSH 56
Anderson, Flipper DEN 83, IND 84, STL 83, WSH 83
Anderson, Fred PIT 69, SEA 63
Anderson, Gary MIN 1, PHL 1, PIT 1, SFF 1, TEN 1
Anderson, Gary SDC 40, DET 43, TBB 40
Anderson, Gary DET 60, WSH 60/68, NOS 77
Anderson, Herbie TEN 22
Anderson, Hunk CHI 18/24
Anderson, Jamal ATL 32
Anderson, Jerry CIN 31, TBB 31
Anderson, Jesse NOS 81, PIT 88, TBB 89
Anderson, John GBP 59/60
Anderson, Ken CHI 70
Anderson, Ken CIN 14
Anderson, Kim IND 26
Anderson, Larry IND 30, PIT 30
Anderson, Marcus CHI 88
Anderson, Marques GBP 20
Anderson, Max BUF 22
Anderson, Melvin PIT 83
Anderson, Mike DEN 38
Anderson, Neal CHI 35
Anderson, Ottis ARZ 32, NYG 24
Anderson, Preston CLE 40
Anderson, Ralph CHI 39/80, SDC 82
Anderson, Ralph NEP 49, PIT 49
Anderson, Rashard CAR 46
Anderson, Richie NYJ 20, DAL 20
Anderson, Rickey SDC 43
Anderson, Roger NYG 73
Anderson, Ronnie ARZ 82
Anderson, Scott MIN 56
Anderson, Scotty DET 88
Anderson, Stan DET 79
Anderson, Stevie ARZ 43/82, NYJ 88
Anderson, Stuart CLE 53, WSH 58
Anderson, Sugarfoot zLAD 56
Anderson, Taz ARZ 85, ATL 87
Anderson, Terry MIA 85, SFF 20, WSH 81
Anderson, Tim BUF 26, SFF 26
Anderson, Vickey GBP 44
Anderson, Warren ARZ 89, TEN 83
Anderson, William CHI 46
Anderson, Willie CIN 71
Anderson, Winnie NYG 24
Andolsek, Eric DET 65

Andrako, Steve WSH 29
Andrew, Troy MIA 65
Andrews, Al BUF 56
Andrews, Billy CLE 52, KCC 53, SDC 51
Andrews, George STL 52
Andrews, Jaby xSTL 66
Andrews, John IND 36/88, SDC 81
Andrews, John MIA 70
Andrews, Mitch DEN 86
Andrews, Ricky SEA 52
Andrews, Tom CHI 60, SEA 64
Andrews, William ATL 31
Andrie, George DAL 66
Andros, Plato ARZ 68
Andrus, Lou DEN 84
Andrus, Sheldon NOS 96
Andrusking, Sig xBKN 23/21
Andrusyshyn, Zenon KCC 7
Andruzzi, Joe GBP 70, NEP 63
Ane, Charley Jr. GBP 61, KCC 56
Ane, Charlie Sr. DET 50
Anelli, Mark SFF 85
Angelo, Jim PHL 69
Angsman, Elmer ARZ 7
Angulo, Richard MIN 47, STL 48
Ankrom, Scott DAL 81
Anno, Sam MIN 53, SDC 52, STL 52, TBB 56
Anthony, Charles SDC 59
Anthony, Cornelius SFF 57
Anthony, Reidel TBB 85
Anthony, Terrence ARZ 22
Anthony, Terry TBB 85
Anthony, Tyrone NOS 22
Antoine, Lionel CHI 79
Antonio Gates SDC 85
Antrum, Glenn NEP 48
Antwine, Houston NEP 65, PHL 75
Apke, Steve PIT 90
Apolskis, Charles CHI 26/38
Apolskis, Ray ARZ 26/69/75
Apple, Jim NYJ 27
Appleton, Scott SDC 70, TEN 70
Apsit, Marger GBP 44, WSH 29, xBKN 25
Apuna, Ben NYG 62
Araguz, Leo DET 2, MIN 2, OAK 2
Arapostathis, Evan ARZ 17
Arbanas, Fred KCC 84
Arbubakrr, Hasson MIN 69, TBB 69
Arbuckle, Charles IND 81
Archambeau, Lester ATL 92, DEN 92, GBP 74
Archer, Dan CIN 78, OAK 78
Archer, David ATL 16, PHL 18, WSH 15, SDC 15
Archer, Troy NYG 77
Archie, Mike TEN 22

Archuleta, Adam STL 31
Ard, Billy GBP 67, NYG 67
Ardizzone, Tony CHI 63
Arena, Tony DET ?
Arenas, Joe SFF 22/82
Ariail, Gump xCIN 20, xBKN ?
Arians, Jake BUF 9
Ariey, Mike GBP 76
Ariri, Obed TBB 2, WSH 5
Armour, JoJuan CIN 33, JAX 45
Armour, Justin BLT 88, BUF 81, DEN 83, PHL 86
Armour, Phillip IND 54
Arms, Lloyd ARZ 76
Armstead, Jessie NYG 98, WSH 98
Armstrong, Adger TBB 40/46, TEN 39
Armstrong, Antonio MIA 58
Armstrong, Bill xBKN 28
Armstrong, Bob DET 31
Armstrong, Bruce NEP 78
Armstrong, Charlie zBRK 72
Armstrong, Derick HOU 87
Armstrong, Graham STL 18/32, zBUF 43
Armstrong, Harvey IND 79, PHL 96
Armstrong, Jimmy DAL 10/35
Armstrong, John BUF 20
Armstrong, Neill PHL 80
Armstrong, Otis DEN 24
Armstrong, Ramon OAK 66
Armstrong, Trace CHI 93, MIA 93, OAK 93
Armstrong, Tyji DAL 81, STL 89, TBB 86
Arndt, Al PIT 40
Arndt, Dick PIT 71
Arneson, Jim DAL 64, WSH 66
Arneson, Mark ARZ 57
Arnett, Jon CHI 21, STL 26
Arnold, David PIT 25
Arnold, Jahine GBP 88, PIT 80
Arnold, Jay PHL 34, PIT 34
Arnold, Jim DET 6, KCC 6, MIA 6
Arnold, John DET 47
Arnold, LeFrancis DEN 65
Arnold, Walt KCC 87, TEN 86, WSH 84, WSH 90, STL 84
Aronson, Doug CIN 61
Arp, John CHI 67
Arrington, LeVar WSH 56
Arrington, Rick PHL 11
Arrobio, Chuck MIN 79
Arterburn, Elmer ARZ 7
Arthur, Gary NYJ 82
Arthur, Mike CIN 65, GBP 50, NEP 65
Artman, Corrie NYG 10, WSH ?, PIT 44
Artmore, Rodney GBP 46
Artoe, Lee CHI 1/35, zBAL 44, zLAD 44

Arvie, Herman BLT 70
Asad, Doug OAK 83
Asbury, Bill PIT 30
Aschbacher, Darrel PHL 50
Aschenbrenner, Frank zCHI 91
Ashburn, Cliff NYG 17
Ashe, Richard STL 87
Asher, Bob CHI 74, DAL 78
Asher, Jamie PHL 84, WSH 84
Ashley, Walker KCC 54, MIN 58
Ashmore, Darryl OAK 73/77, STL 75/77, WSH 73
Ashmore, Roger GBP 35/46
Ashton, Josh ARZ 31
Ashworth, Tom NEP 68
Aska, Joe OAK 35
Askea, Mike DEN 73
Askew, B.J. NYJ 35
Askin, John CLE 65
Askson, Bert GBP 88, NOS 89, PIT 76
Asmus, Jim SFF 9
Asomugha, Nnamdi OAK 21
Aspatore, Ed xCIN 26, CHI 37
Atchason, Jack NEP 85, TEN 84
Atessis, Bill NEP 73
Athas, Pete CLE 24, MIN 45, NOS 45, NYG 45
Atkeson, Dale WSH 46
Atkins, Bill BUF 20, NYJ 2, SFF 29, DEN 28
Atkins, Bob TEN 48
Atkins, Corey ATL 50
Atkins, Dave SDC 26, SFF 29
Atkins, Doug CHI 81, CLE 83, NOS 81
Atkins, Gene MIA 28, NOS 28
Atkins, George DET 62
Atkins, James BLT 74, DET 74, SEA 74, TEN,96
Atkins, Kelvin CHI 51
Atkins, Larry KCC 35/50
Atkins, Pervis OAK 39/81, STL 27, WSH 25
Atkins, Steve GBP 32, PHL 38
Atkinson, Al NYJ 62
Atkinson, Frank DEN 74, PIT 73
Atkinson, George OAK 43, DEN 47
Atkinson, Jess ARZ 10, IND 14, NYG 12, WSH 4
Atkinson, Ricky NEP 37
Atty, Alexander STL 18
Atwater, Steve DEN 27, NYJ 27
Atwood, John NYG 16
Audet, Earl WSH 27, zLAD 42
Audick, Dan ARZ 61, SDC 60, SFF 61
Auer, Howard ARZ 20, PHL 24
Auer, Jim PHL 97
Auer, Joe ATL 38, BUF 43, MIA 32
Auer, Scott KCC 68

Auer, Todd GBP 72, GBP 98
Aughtman, Dowe DAL 76
August, Steve PIT 77, SEA 76
Augustferner, Gene PIT 5
Augustyniak, Mike NYJ 35
Aupiu, David STL 90
Austin, Bill NYG 60/75
Austin, Billy IND 47
Austin, Cliff ATL 39, NOS 47, TBB 39
Austin, Darrell NYJ 67, TBB 69
Austin, Eric TBB 27
Austin, Hise GBP 27, KCC 21
Austin, Jim DET 29, xBKN 19
Austin, Kent ARZ 16
Austin, Ocie IND 37, PIT 28
Austin, Ray CHI 36, NYJ 28
Austin, Reggie CHI 39
Autrey, Billy CHI 53
Autry, Darnell CHI 21, PHL 24/26
Autry, Hank TEN 61
Auzenne, Troy CHI 70, IND 75
Avedisian, Chuck NYG 55
Avellini, Bob CHI 7, NYJ 17
Aveni, John CHI 89, WSH 89
Averno, Sisto IND 60, xBAL 32, xDAL 60, xNYB 44
Avery, Don WSH 56, zLAD ?
Avery, Jim WSH 61
Avery, John DEN 33, MIA 20, MIN 33
Avery, Ken CIN 51, KCC 53, NYG 54
Avery, Steve GBP 32, PIT 43, TEN 42
Avezzano, Joe NEP 50
Avinger, Butch NYG 34
Avrie, Herman CLE 70/73
Awalt, Rob BUF 86, DAL 89, ARZ 80
Ayanbadejo, Brendon MIA 50
Ayanbadejo, Obafemi MIA 30, MIN 49, BLT 30
Aydelette, Buddy PIT 72, GBP 62
Ayers, John DEN 67, SFF 68
Ayers, Marvin PHL 96
Ayi, Kole NEP 99, STL 54
Ayodele, Akin JAX 51
Azelby, Joe BUF 50
Azumah, Jerry CHI 23
Baab, Mike CLE 61, KCC 60, NEP 68
Baack, Steve DET 68
Babartsky, Al ARZ 18/24/46, CHI 46
Babb, Charlie MIA 49
Babb, Gene DAL 33, SFF 32, TEN 33
Babcock, Harry SFF 88
Baber, Billy KCC 45
Babers, Rod DET 26
Babich, Bob CLE 60, SDC 60
Babinecz, John CHI 52, DAL 53

Baccaglio, Martin CIN 85, SDC 84
Bachman, Jay DEN 56/65
Bachman, Ted MIA 47, SEA 46
Backes, Tom NOS 78
Backus, Jeff DET 76
Bacon , Coy STL 79, CIN 79, SDC 79, WSH 79/80
Badaczewski, John ARZ 82, CHI 68, WSH 57, xBOS 35
Badanjek, Rick ATL 47, WSH 26
Badar, Rich PIT 11
Badger, Brad MIN 74, OAK 70, WSH 74
Badgro, Red NYG 17, xBKN 32
Bagarus, Steve WSH 00, STL 00
Bagdon, Ed ARZ 55, WSH 68
Baggett, Billy xDAL 24
Baham, Curtis SEA 38
Bahnsen, Ken SFF 27
Bahr, Chris CIN 10, OAK 10, SDC 3
Bahr, Matt CLE 9, NEP 3, NYG 9, PHL 11, PIT 9, SFF 10
Bailey, Aaron IND 80
Bailey, Bill BUF 33, NEP 37
Bailey, Bill xBKN 22
Bailey, Boss DET 97
Bailey, Byron DET 45, GBP 20
Bailey, Carlton BUF 54, NYG 54, CAR 54
Bailey, Champ WSH 24
Bailey, Clarence MIA 38
Bailey, David PHL 93
Bailey, Don IND 61, TBB 61
Bailey, Edwin SEA 65
Bailey, Elmer IND 87, MIA 88
Bailey, Eric PHL 87
Bailey, Harold TEN 11/80
Bailey, Henry NYJ 85, PIT 82
Bailey, Howard PHL 20
Bailey, Jim ATL 72, NYJ 76
Bailey, Jim zCHI 33
Bailey, Johnny ARZ 20, CHI 22, STL 20/21
Bailey, Karsten GBP 85, SEA 83
Bailey, Larry ATL 68
Bailey, Mario TEN 82
Bailey, Mark KCC 39
Bailey, Monk ARZ 20
Bailey, Robert BLT 35, DAL 23, DET 35, MIA 23, STL 28, WSH 23
Bailey, Rodney PIT 94
Bailey, Stacey ATL 82
Bailey, Thomas CIN 18
Bailey, Tom PHL 31
Bailey, Victor KCC 85/88, PHL 82
Bain, Bill DEN 75, GBP 69, NEP 62, NYJ 62, STL 62
Baird, Bill NYJ 46
Baisi, Al CHI 26, PHL 63
Baker, Al DET 60, ARZ 60, CLE 60, MIN 60/77

Baker, Art BUF 33
Baker, Charles ARZ 52
Baker, Chris NYJ 81/86
Baker, Conway ARZ 22, PIT 22
Baker, Dave SFF 25
Baker, Donnell STL 83
Baker, Ed TEN 18
Baker, Eugene ATL 15/80, CAR 80
Baker, Frank GBP 12
Baker, Jason KCC 9, PHL 7, SFF 1
Baker, Jerry DEN 74
Baker, Jesse DAL 66, TEN 75
Baker, John DET 78, NYG 72, PHL 78, PIT 73/78, STL 74
Baker, John STL 4
Baker, Johnny SDC 84, TEN 84
Baker, Jon DAL 10, KCC 12
Baker, Jon NYG 60/76
Baker, Keith PHL 80
Baker, Larry NYJ 73
Baker, Mel ARZ 86, MIA 82, NEP 83, NOS 86, SDC 81, TEN 12/18
Baker, Myron CHI 91, CAR 53
Baker, Ralph NYJ 51
Baker, Robert MIA 83
Baker, Ron IND 60, PHL 63
Baker, Roy ARZ 24, GBP 5/12/17/21
Baker, Sam WSH 45/49, CLE 38, DAL 38, PHL 38
Baker, Shannon IND 84
Baker, Stephen NYG 85
Baker, Terry STL 15
Baker, Tony ARZ 44, ATL 41, CLE 43
Baker, Tony NOS 38, PHL 38, SDC 35, STL 35
Baker, Wayne SFF 78
Bakken, Jim ARZ 25
Balasz, Frank ARZ 26/44, GBP 35
Balatti, Ed SFF 57, zBUF 50, zNYY 58
Baldacci, Lou PIT 26/27
Baldassin, Mike SFF 41
Baldinger, Brian DAL 62, IND 62, PHL 62
Baldinger, Gary BUF 92, IND 94, KCC 91
Baldinger, Rich KCC 77, NEP 74, NYG 74
Baldischwiler, Karl DET 76, IND 72
Baldwin, Al GBP 19, zBUF 57
Baldwin, Bob IND 34
Baldwin, Burr zLAD 52
Baldwin, John SFF 25, zBUF 23, zNYY 21
Baldwin, Keith CLE 99, SDC 96
Baldwin, Randy BLT 23, CLE 23, MIN 37, SFF 21, CAR 23

Baldwin, Tom NYJ 95
Ball, Eric CIN 42, OAK 42
Ball, Greg STL 42
Ball, Jason SDC 60
Ball, Jerry DET 93, CLE 93, MIN 96, OAK 93
Ball, Larry DET 51, MIA 51/52, TBB 53
Ball, Michael IND 31
Ball, Sam IND 73
Ballage, Pat IND 26/40
Ballard, Clenton JAX 97
Ballard, Howard BUF 75, SEA 75
Ballard, Quinton IND 97
Ballman, Gary PIT 48/85, MIN 85, NYG 82, PHL 85
Ballou, Mike NEP 51
Balog, Bob PIT 56
Baltzell, Vic WSH 35
Banas, Stephen PHL 29, DET 6
Banaszak, John PIT 76
Banaszak, Pete OAK 40
Bandaszek, Casimir SFF 79
Bandison, Romeo WSH 72/97
Banducci, Bruno PHL 63, SFF 33/63
Bandura, John xBKN 27
Bandy, Don WSH 61
Banes, Joey IND 65
Banet, Herb GBP 21
Banfield, Tony TEN 40
Baniewicz, Mark JAX 69
Banjevic, Emil DET 11
Banker, Ted CLE 68, NYJ 63
Banks, Antonio MIN 30
Banks, Carl NYG 58, CLE 58, WSH 58
Banks, Chip CLE 56, IND 51, SDC 56
Banks, Chris ATL 76, DEN 79
Banks, Chuck IND 37, TEN 36
Banks, Estes CIN 38, OAK 38
Banks, Fred CHI 81, CLE 83, MIA 86
Banks, Gordon DAL 87, NOS 80
Banks, Mike ARZ 80/84
Banks, Robert CLE 97, TEN 97
Banks, Roy IND 86
Banks, Tavian JAX 22
Banks, Tom ARZ 54
Banks, Tony BLT 12, HOU 12, STL 12, WSH 12
Banks, Willie NEP 78, NYG 60, WSH 68/69
Bankston, Michael ARZ 63, CIN 90
Bankston, Warren OAK 46, PIT 46
Bannan, Justin BUF 97
Bannister, Alex SEA 85
Bannon, Bruce MIA 58
Banonis, Vince ARZ 11/32, DET 51
Bansavage, Al OAK 53, SDC 57

Banta, Brad DET 89, IND 83, NYJ 81
Banta, Jack PHL 33, STL 33, WSH 46
Banta-Cain, Tully NEP 48
Barbaro, Gary KCC 26
Barbay, Roland SEA 95
Barbee, Joe OAK 77
Barber, Bob GBP 70
Barber, Chris CIN 35, TBB 33
Barber, Elmer NYG 6
Barber, Ernie WSH 43
Barber, Jim WSH 15
Barber, Kantroy IND 46, MIA 48, CAR 46
Barber, Kurt NYJ 98
Barber, Marion NYJ 31
Barber, Mark STL 6
Barber, Michael IND 53, SEA 54
Barber, Mike ARZ 20
Barber, Mike CIN 86, SFF 86, TBB 84
Barber, Mike DEN 85, STL 86/89, TEN 49/86
Barber, Ronde TBB 20
Barber, Rudy MIA 72
Barber, Shawn KCC 59, PHL 56, WSH 59
Barber, Stew BUF 64/77
Barber, Tiki NYG 21
Barbolak, Pete PIT 89
Barefield, John ARZ 58
Barefoot, Ken WSH 81
Barfield, Ken WSH 73
Barisich, Carl CLE 74, MIA 78, NYG 78, SEA 74
Barker, Bryan JAX 4, KCC 4, PHL 4, WSH 4
Barker, Ed WSH 87
Barker, Hubert NYG 42
Barker, Jay CAR 11
Barker, Leo CIN 53
Barker, Richard CHI ?
Barker, Roy CLE 92, GBP 94, MIN 92, SFF 92
Barker, Tony WSH 98
Barksdale, Rod DAL 80, OAK 88
Barkum, Jerome NYJ 83
Barle, Lou DET 25, STL 8
Barlow, Corey PHL 24
Barlow, Kevan SFF 32
Barlow, Reggie JAX 84, TBB 84
Barnard, Brooks CHI 16, NEP 8
Barnard, Charles NYG 24
Barndt, Tom CIN 93, KCC 71, NYJ 96
Barnes, Al DET 86
Barnes, Benny DAL 31
Barnes, Billy Ray PHL 33, MIN 33, WSH 32
Barnes, Bruce NEP 3
Barnes, Charley KCC 82
Barnes, Darian TBB 30
Barnes, Derrick NOS 51

Barnes, Doug STL 96
Barnes, Emery GBP 85
Barnes, Erich CHI 24, CLE 40, NYG 49
Barnes, Ernie DEN 62, NYJ 73, SDC 61
Barnes, Ernie IND 95
Barnes, Gary ATL 80, CHI 86, DAL 80, GBP 80
Barnes, Jeff OAK 56
Barnes, Joe CHI 23
Barnes, Johnnie PIT 80, SDC 19, SDC 85
Barnes, Larry OAK 52, SFF 35
Barnes, Lawrence ARZ 33, PHL 38, SDC 35
Barnes, Lew ATL 85, CHI 81, KCC 80
Barnes, Lionel IND 93, JAX 94, STL 92
Barnes, Marlon CHI 32
Barnes, Mike ARZ 20
Barnes, Mike IND 63
Barnes, Pat KCC 17, OAK 4, SFF 10
Barnes, Pete ARZ 59, NEP 59, SDC 59, TEN 58
Barnes, Rashidi CLE 28
Barnes, Reggie DAL 56, PIT 50
Barnes, Rodrigo DAL 56, MIA 51, NEP 59, OAK 51
Barnes, Roosevelt DET 54
Barnes, Tomur MIN 23, TEN 22/32, WSH 23
Barnes, Walter PHL 74, DEN 73, WSH 77
Barnett, Bill MIA 70
Barnett, Buster BUF 84
Barnett, Dean DEN 86
Barnett, Doug ATL 53, WSH 79
Barnett, Fred PHL 86, MIA 80
Barnett, Harlon CLE 37, MIN 42, NEP 42
Barnett, Nick GBP 56
Barnett, Oliver ATL 72, BUF 77, SFF 72/77
Barnett, Solon GBP 27/72
Barnett, Steve CHI 73, WSH 77
Barnett, Tim KCC 82
Barnett, Tom PIT 43
Barnett, Troy NEP 98, WSH 90
Barnett, Vincent CLE 25
Barney, Eppie CLE 87
Barney, Lem DET 20
Barney, Milton ATL 84
Barnhardt, Dan PHL 26
Barnhardt, Tommy CHI 17, NOS 6/10, TBB 6, WSH 6/14, CAR 6
Barni, Roy ARZ 49, PHL 33, WSH 21
Barnum, Len NYG 10, PHL 13
Barnwell, Malcolm NOS 80, OAK 80, WSH 80
Barr, Dave STL 16

Barr, Terry DET 41
Barragar, Nate GBP 30/31/56/64
Barrett, David ARZ 36, TBB 30
Barrett, Emmett NYG 11
Barrett, Jan GBP 82, OAK 82
Barrett, Jean SFF 77
Barrett, Jeff xBKN 33/11
Barrett, Reggie DET 40
Barrett, Robert BUF 84
Barrie, Sebastian ARZ 73, GBP 67, SDC 90
Barrington, Tom NOS 32, WSH 36
Barrow, Michael NYG 58, TEN 51/56, CAR 56
Barrows, Scott DET 61
Barry, Al GBP 63/66, NYG 68, SDC 62
Barry, Fred PIT 29
Barry, Kevin GBP 71
Barry, Norm ARZ 4
Barry, Odell DEN 42
Barry, Paul ARZ 44, STL 9, WSH 29
Bartalo, Steve TBB 42
Bartee, William KCC 24
Bartholomew, Brent CHI 12, MIA 6
Bartholomew, Sam PHL 27
Bartkowski, Steve ATL 10, STL 10, WSH 17
Bartlett, Doug PHL 95
Bartlett, Earl PIT 44
Bartley, Ephesians PHL 50
Bartolo, Steve SFF 41
Barton, Don GBP 43
Barton, Eric OAK 50
Barton, Greg DET 14
Barton, Harris SFF 79
Barton, James DEN 52, KCC 50
Bartos, Hank WSH 18
Bartos, Joe WSH 27
Bartrum, Mike GBP 48, KCC 87, NEP 86, PHL 88
Barwegan, Richard CHI 26/61, IND 61, zBAL 31, zNYY 31
Barzilauskas, Carl GBP 75, NYJ 77
Barzilauskas, Fritz NYG 65, xBOS 36, xNYB 36
Basca, Nick PHL 47
Baschnagel, Brian CHI 84
Bashir, Idrees IND 28
Basing, Myrt GBP 15/27
Basinger, Mike GBP 71
Baska, Richard DEN 54
Basnight, Michael CIN 35/38
Basrak, Mike PIT 11
Bass, Anthony MIN 32
Bass, Bill zCHI 99
Bass, Dick STL 22
Bass, Don CIN 84, NOS 88
Bass, Glenn BUF 27/85/88, TEN 27

Bass, Mike DET 26, WSH 41
Bass, Norm DEN 46
Bass, Robert CHI 52
Bassett, Maurice CLE 30/38
Bassi, Dick PHL 35, CHI 35, PIT 35, SFF 35/36
Bassman, Herman PHL 19/24/29
Batch, Charlie DET 10, PIT 16
Bateman, Marv BUF 7, DAL 81
Bates, Bill DAL 40
Bates, D'Wayne CHI 87, MIN 85
Bates, Mario ARZ 24, DET 31, NOS 24
Bates, Michael CAR 24/82, CLE 83, DAL 29, NYJ 20, SEA 81, WSH 20
Bates, Patrick ATL 24, OAK 24/29
Bates, Solomon SEA 50
Bates, Ted ARZ 51/81, NYJ 56
Batinski, Stan DET 65, xBOS 84, xNYB 84
Batiste, Michael DAL 68, WSH 61
Batorski, John zBUF 54
Battaglia, Marco CAR 47, CIN 89, PIT 81, WSH 84
Battaglia, Matt PHL 52
Batteaux, Pat SDC 86
Batten, Pat DET 30
Battle, Arnaz SFF 83
Battle, Jim CLE 79
Battle, Jim MIN 63
Battle, Julian KCC 26
Battle, Mike NYJ 40
Battle, Ralph CIN 31
Battle, Ron STL 81
Battles, Ainsley JAX 26, PIT 28
Battles, Cliff WSH 20
Baty, Greg ARZ 82, MIA 84, NEP 85, STL 84
Bauer, Hank SDC 37
Bauer, John NYG 65
Baugh, Sammy WSH 33˙
Baugh, Tom CLE 64, KCC 58
Baughan, Maxie PHL 55, STL 55, WSH 50
Bauman, Alf CHI 41, PHL 73, zCHI 42
Bauman, Rashad WSH 25/35
Baumann, Charlie MIA 7
Baumgartner, Bill zBAL 29
Baumgartner, Max DET 11
Baumgartner, Steve NOS 63, TEN 63
Baumhower, Bob MIA 73
Bausch, Frank CHI 24, PHL 55, WSH 24
Bausch, Jim ARZ 47, xCIN 47
Bavaro, David ARZ 59, BUF 52, MIN,52, NEP 52
Bavaro, Mark NYG 89, CLE 48/83, PHL 84
Bawel, Ed PHL 20/81

Bax, Carl TBB 75
Baxley, Rob ARZ 70
Baxter, Brad NYJ 30
Baxter, Fred CHI 84, NEP 84, NYJ 84
Baxter, Gary BLT 28
Baxter, Jarrod HOU 47
Baxter, Lloyd GBP 33
Bayless, Martin ARZ 43, BUF 43, KCC 21/30, SDC 44, WSH 34
Bayless, Rick MIN 32
Bayless, Tom NYJ 77
Baylor, John IND 36
Baylor, Raymond SDC 75
Baylor, Tim IND 47, MIN 47
Bayne, Chris ATL 47
Baynham, Craig ARZ 48, CHI 46, DAL 46
Baze, Winford PHL 26/37
Beach, Pat ARZ 89, IND 81, PHL 83
Beach, Sanjay GBP 82, NYJ ?, SFF 83/86
Beach, Walter CLE 49, NEP 26/41
Beal, Norm ARZ 21
Beales, Bill MIA 65
Beals, Alyn SFF 53
Beals, Shawn PHL 81
Beamer, Tim BUF 46
Beamon, Autry CLE 24, MIN 27, SEA 27
Beamon, Willie NYG 21
Beams, Byron PIT 72, TEN 78
Bean, Bubba ATL 44
Bean, Robert CIN 23/49, JAX 22
Beard, Ed SFF 50
Beard, Tom BUF 54
Beasley, Aaron JAX 21, NYJ 21
Beasley, Chad CLE 68
Beasley, Fred SFF 40
Beasley, John MIN 87, NOS 85
Beasley, Terry SFF 83/88
Beasley, Tom PIT 65, WSH 67
Beathard, Pete ARZ 10, KCC 10/11, STL 12, TEN 11
Beatty, Charles PIT 37, ARZ 31
Beatty, Ed PIT 57/68, SFF 54, WSH 56
Beauchamp, Al ARZ 50, CIN 58
Beauchamp, Joe SDC 40
Beaudion, Doug SDC 45, MIA 44, NEP 27
Beautler, Tom CLE 53
Beaver, Jim PHL 65
Beavers, Aubrey MIA 53, NYJ 58
Beavers, Scott DEN 64
Beban, Gary WSH 16
Bebout, Nick ATL 63, MIN 63, SEA 63
Bech, Brett NOS 19/89
Becht, Anthony NYJ 88
Bechtol, Hub zBAL 57

Beck, Braden TEN 17
Beck, Ken GBP 73
Beck, Ray NYG 61/65
Becker, Dave CHI 49
Becker, Doug BUF 52, CHI 51
Becker, Kurt CHI 79, STL 79
Becker, Wayland CHI 21, GBP 32, PIT 30, xBKN 50/24
Beckett, Rogers CIN 45, SDC 42
Beckham, Tony TEN 24
Beckles, Ian PHL 62, TBB 62
Beckman, Brad ATL 83, NYG 88
Beckman, Ed KCC 85
Beckman, Tom ARZ 89
Bedell, Brad CLE 63
Bedford, Vance ARZ 41
Bednarik, Chuck PHL 60
Bedner, Al NYG 3/30
Bedore, Tom WSH 46
Bedosky, Mike CLE 71
Bedsole, Hal MIN 86
Beebe, Don BUF 82, GBP 82, CAR 82
Beebe, Keith NYG 44
Beecham, Earl NYG 26
Beecher, Willie MIA 1/2
Beede, Frank SEA 63
Beekley, Bruce GBP 58
Beemer, Bob DET 99
Beer, Thomas DET 48/51
Beer, Tom DEN 85, NEP 82
Beeson, Terry SEA 58, SFF 63
Behan, Chuck DET 85
Behning, Mark PIT 66
Behrman, Dave BUF 51/60, DEN 56
Beier, Tom MIA 47
Beil, Larry NYG 72
Beinor, Ed ARZ 73, WSH 45
Beirne, Jim TEN 81/88, SDC 85
Beirria, Terreal SEA 34
Beisel, Monty KCC 56/96
Beisler, Randy KCC 64, PHL 64/80, SFF 65
Belcher, Kevin DEN 73, NYG 73, OAK 76
Belden, Charles ARZ 25/39
Belichick, Steve DET 30
Belim, Chuck STL 71
Belk, Bill SFF 72
Belk, Rocky CLE 88
Belk, Veno BUF 84
Bell, Albert GBP 88
Bell, Anthony ARZ 55, DET 59, OAK 59
Bell, Bill ATL 37, NEP 8
Bell, Billy KCC 40, TEN 33
Bell, Bob ARZ 79, DET 73
Bell, Bobby Sr. KCC 78
Bell, Bobby Jr. NYJ 58, CHI 97
Bell, Carlos NOS 34
Bell, Coleman WSH 87
Bell, Ed GBP 82, zMIA 46

Bell, Ed NYJ 25, PHL 81
Bell, Eddie NYJ 7, SDC 7
Bell, Gordon ARZ 20, NYG 25
Bell, Greg BUF 28, OAK 28
Bell, Henry DEN 20
Bell, Jason DAL 33, HOU 33
Bell, Jerry TBB 82
Bell, Joe OAK 68
Bell, Kay CHI 26, NYG 50
Bell, Ken DEN 35
Bell, Kendrell PIT 97
Bell, Kerwin ATL 11, IND 12, TBB 11
Bell, Kevin NYJ 80
Bell, Leonard CIN 26
Bell, Marcus ARZ 94, SEA 55
Bell, Mark ARZ 81
Bell, Mark IND 48/90, SEA 82
Bell, Mike KCC 99
Bell, Myron CIN 40, PIT 40/42
Bell, Nick OAK 38/43
Bell, Richard PIT 21
Bell, Rick MIN 33
Bell, Ricky CHI 30/32, JAX 42
Bell, Ricky SDC 42, TBB 42
Bell, Shonn SFF 82
Bell, Terry CLE 86
Bell, Theo PIT 83, TBB 83
Bell, Todd CHI 25, PHL 49/52
Bell, Tyrone GBP 47
Bell, William WSH 36
Bellamy, Jay NOS 20, SEA 20
Bellamy, Mike PHL 81
Bellamy, Victor PHL 39
Bellinger, Bob NYG 8
Bellinger, Rodney BUF 36
Bellini, Mark IND 87
Bellino, Joe NEP 27
Bellisari, Greg TBB 52
Belotti, George SDC 57, TEN 57
Belser, Caesar SFF 50, KCC 24
Belser, Jason IND 29, KCC 29
Belton, Horace KCC 35
Belton, Willie ARZ 33, ATL 28
Belway, Brian OAK 79
Bemiller, Al BUF 50
Bender, Carey BUF 45
Bender, Wes NOS 40, OAK 49
Bendross, Jesse PHL 85, SDC 86
Benefield, David SFF 99
Benet, Ed KCC 85
Benfatti, Lou NYJ 78
Bengen, Brant SEA 13
Benhart, Eugene IND 18
Benirschke, Rolf SDC 6
Benish, Dan ATL 69, WSH 95
Benjamin, Bill IND 54
Benjamin, Guy MIA 7, NOS 7
Benjamin, Ryan CIN 21
Benjamin, Ryan TBB 66
Benjamin, Tony SEA 31
Benkert, Heinie NYG 2
Benners, Fred NYG 47

Bennett, Antoine CIN 35
Bennett, Barry MIN 78, NOS 63, NYJ 78
Bennett, Ben CHI 14, CIN 16
Bennett, Brandon CIN 36
Bennett, Charles ARZ ?
Bennett, Charles MIA 93
Bennett, Chuck DET 21
Bennett, Cornelius BUF 55/97, IND 97, ATL 97
Bennett, Darren SDC 2
Bennett, Donnell KCC 30, WSH 32
Bennett, Drew TEN 19/83
Bennett, Earl GBP 15/36
Bennett, Edgar CHI 32, GBP 34
Bennett, Lewis NYG 87
Bennett, Michael MIN 23
Bennett, Monte NOS 91, SDC 69
Bennett, Phil NEP 52
Bennett, Roy SDC 23
Bennett, Sean NYG 20/44
Bennett, Tommy ARZ 28, DET 42
Bennett, Tony GBP 90, IND 56
Bennett, Woody MIA 34, NYJ 46
Benridge, John STL 6
Benson, Brad NYG 60
Benson, Charles DET 69, MIA 78
Benson, Cliff ATL 87, NOS 83/86, WSH 88
Benson, Darren DAL 91
Benson, Duane ATL 51, OAK 50, TEN 50/52
Benson, George zBRK 73
Benson, Henry PHL 30/39
Benson, Mitchell IND 95, SDC 95
Benson, Thomas ATL 53, NEP 53, SDC 57, OAK 54
Benson, Troy NYJ 54
Bentley, Albert IND 20, PIT 28/30
Bentley, Kevin CLE 59
Bentley, LeCharles NOS 65
Bentley, Ray BUF 50, CIN 57
Bentley, Scott ATL 3, DEN 3, KCC 9, WSH 1
Benton, Jim STL 26/49, CHI 12
Bentz, Roman SFF 46, zNYY 45/33
Benyola, George NYG 3
Benz, Larry CLE 23
Bercich, Bob DAL 20
Bercich, Pete MIN 56
Berezney, Paul GBP 47, zMIA 44, zBAL 47, zLAD 40
Berger, Mitch MIN 17, NOS 17, PHL 17, STL 17
Berger, Ron NEP 88
Bergerson, Gil ARZ 48, CHI 23, xBKN 16/15

Bergeson, Eric ATL 36
Bergey, Bill CIN 66, KCC 84
Bergey, Bruce TEN 83
Bergold, Scott ARZ 74
Berlin, Eddie TEN 82
Bernard, Chuck DET 27
Bernard, David STL 22
Bernard, Karl DET 25
Bernard, Rocky SEA 99
Bernardi, Frank ARZ 49, DEN 43
Berner, Mil xCIN ?
Bernet, Ed PIT 83
Bernet, Lee DEN 74
Bernhardt, George zBRK 31, zCHI 33
Bernhardt, Roger KCC 68, NYJ 68
Bernich, Ken NYJ 53
Berns, Rick OAK 40, TBB 36
Bernstine, Rod DEN 33, SDC 84
Berquist, Jay ARZ ?
Berra, Tim IND 84
Berrang, Ed DET 85, GBP 81, WSH 18/82
Berry, Bertrand DEN 92, IND 57
Berry, Bob ATL 17, MIN 17
Berry, Connie CHI 23, DET 83, GBP 37, STL 6, zCHI 54
Berry, Dan PHL 19
Berry, Ed GBP 20, SDC 38
Berry, Gary GBP 21
Berry, Gil ARZ 28
Berry, Latin CLE 42, STL 42
Berry, Louis ATL 6
Berry, Ray MIN 50, SEA 57
Berry, Raymond IND 82
Berry, Reggie SDC 45
Berry, Rex SFF 23/83
Berry, Royce CHI 82, CIN 82
Berry, Wayne NYG 24
Berschet, Buddy WSH 60
Bertagnolli, Libero ARZ 62/66
Bertelli, Angelo zCHI 66, zLAD 65
Bertelsen, Jim STL 45
Berthusen, Bill CIN 79, NYG 79
Berti, Tony SDC 75
Berton, Sean MIN 87
Bertuca, Tony IND 51
Berzinski, Willie PHL 33
Besana, Fred BUF 11
Beson, Warren zBAL 32
Bess, Gerald BUF 21/23
Bess, Rufus BUF 21/28, MIN 21, OAK 38
Bessillieu, Don MIA 46, ARZ 46, OAK 47
Best, Art CHI 25, NYG 39
Best, Greg CLE 24, PIT 25
Best, Keith KCC 55
Bethea, Elvin TEN 65

Bethea, Larry DAL 76
Bethea, Ryan MIN 85
Bethune, Bobby SDC 43
Bethune, George STL 68
Bettencourt, Larry GBP 29/30/39
Betters, Doug MIA 75
Betterson, James PHL 34
Bettiga, Mike SFF 80
Bettis, Jerome PIT 36
Bettis, Tom CHI 65, GBP 58/65, PIT 65
Bettridge, Ed CLE 65
Bettridge, John CHI 9
Betts, Ladell WSH 46
Beuerlein, Steve CAR 7, ARZ 7, DAL 7, DEN 11, OAK 7, JAX 7
Beutler, Tom IND 53
Beverly, Dave GBP 11, TEN 4
Beverly, Dwight NOS 47
Beverly, Ed SFF 81
Beverly, Eric DET 79
Beverly, Randy NEP 27, NYJ 42
Biakabutuka, Tshimanga CAR 21
Bianchini, Frank NEP 30
Biancone, Johnny xBKN 36
Biasucci, Dean IND 4/5, STL 4
Bibla, Martin ATL 64
Bickerstaff, Eric DAL 46
Bickett, Duane IND 50, SEA 50, CAR 50
Bidwell, Josh GBP 9
Bieberstein, Adolph GBP ?
Biederman, Leo CLE 69
Biekert, Greg MIN 54, OAK 54
Bielski, Dick DAL 36, IND 31, PHL 36
Bienemann, Tom ARZ 69/82
Bieniemy, Eric CIN 21, PHL 33, SDC 32
Bigby, Keiron WSH 84
Biggs, Riley NYG 35/44
Biggs, Verlon NYJ 86, WSH 86/89
Bighead, Jack IND 80, STL 86
Bilbo, Jon ARZ 25/65/85
Bilda, Dick GBP 22
Biletnikoff, Fred OAK 14/25
Billingsley, Ron SDC 86, TEN 82
Billman, John zBRK 32, zCHI 33
Billock, Frank PIT 18
Billups, Lewis CIN 24, GBP 22
Billups, Terry DAL 29, NEP 23
Bingaman, Les DET 65
Bingham, Craig PIT 54, SDC 59
Bingham, Don CHI 46
Bingham, Dwight ATL 75
Bingham, Gregg TEN 54
Bingham, Guy ATL 65, NYJ 64, WSH 57
Binn, Dave SDC 50

Binotto, John PHL 30, PIT 5
Biodrowski, Dennis KCC 61
Biolo, John GBP 16/32
Bird, Cory IND 41
Bird, Rodger OAK 21
Bird, Steve ARZ 82, SDC 81
Birden, J.J. ATL 89, KCC 88
Birdsong, Carl ARZ 18
Birdsong, Craig TEN 21
Birdwell, Dan OAK 53
Birk, Matt MIN 75/78
Birlem, Keith ARZ 81, WSH 23
Birney, Tom GBP 16/19
Biscaha, Joe NEP 34, NYG 80
Bishop, Bill CHI 73, MIN 73
Bishop, Blaine TEN 23, PHL 24
Bishop, Don DAL 44, CHI 45, PIT 28/85
Bishop, Greg ATL 65, NYG 78
Bishop, Harold BLT 89, CLE 89, PIT 84, TBB 89
Bishop, Keith DEN 54, MIN 12
Bishop, Michael NEP 7
Bishop, Richard MIA 72, NEP 64, STL 65
Bishop, Sonny TEN 66, KCC 66, OAK 66
Bitterlich, Don SEA 4
Bivins, Charles CHI 49, BUF 35, PIT 36
Bjork, Del CHI 82
Bjorklund, Hank NYJ 40
Bjorklund, Robert PHL 50
Bjornson, Eric DAL 86, NEP 86
Black, Avion BUF 89, HOU 88
Black, Barry OAK 67
Black, Blondy zBUF 81
Black, James CLE 31
Black, James KCC 67
Black, John zBAL 85
Black, Mel NEP 94
Black, Michael PHL 77, NYG 69
Black, Mike DET 11
Black, Nathan CAR 18
Black, Stan SFF 26
Black, Tim ARZ 58
Black, Todd CHI 85
Blackburn, Bill ARZ 57
Blackledge, Todd KCC 14, PIT 14
Blacklock, Hugh CHI 21
Blackman, Ken CIN 66, TBB 66
Blackman, Robert IND 25
Blackmon, Don NEP 55
Blackmon, Harold SEA 28
Blackmon, Jon IND 71
Blackmon, Lennon CHI 11/19
Blackmon, Robert SEA 25
Blackmon, Roosevelt CIN 37, GBP 23
Blackmore, Richard PHL 27, SFF 44
Blackshear, Jeff BLT 69, GBP 69, KCC 69, SEA 69

Blackwell, Alois DAL 24
Blackwell, Hal ARZ 21
Blackwell, Kelly CHI 91, DAL 89
Blackwell, Kory NYG 26
Blackwell, Marquel NYJ 7
Blackwell, Will PIT 89
Blackwood, Glenn MIA 47
Blackwood, Lyle CIN 29, IND 44, MIA 42, SEA 28
Blade, Willie DAL 99
Blades, Al SFF 45
Blades, Bennie DET 36, SEA 36
Blades, Brian SEA 89
Blados, Brian CIN 74, IND 63, TBB 69
Blahak, Joe MIN 21, NEP 21, TBB 21, TEN 27
Blaine, Ed GBP 60, PHL 64
Blair, George SDC 39
Blair, Matt MIN 59
Blair, Michael CIN 45, GBP 27
Blair, Paul CHI 68
l MIN 68
Blair, Stanley ARZ 25
Blair, Thomas DET 81
Blaise, Kerlin DET 65/77
Blake, Jeff CIN 8, ARZ 11, BLT 18, NOS 18, NYJ 9
Blake, Ricky DAL 46
Blake, Tom xNYB 64
Blakely, Robert KCC 83
Blanchard, Cary IND 14, ARZ 15, NOS 10, NYG 19, NYJ 10, WSH 14
Blanchard, Dick NEP 49
Blanchard, Tom NOS 16, NYG 15, TBB 16
Bland, Carl DET 80, GBP 83
Bland, Tony MIN 18, MIN 84
Blanda, George CHI 16/22, OAK 16, TEN 16, xBAL 64
Blandin, Ernie CLE 48, IND 41, xBAL 41, zBAL 41
Blankenship, Brian PIT 60
Blankenship, Greg OAK 57, PIT 53
Blanks, Sid TEN 42, NEP 22
Blanton, Jerry KCC 57
Blanton, Scott WSH 16
Blaylock, Anthony CHI 47, CLE 24, SDC 37
Blaylock, Derrick KCC 23
Blazer, Phil BUF 60
Blazine, Tony ARZ 23, NYG 69
Bleaker, Mel STL 34
Bleamer, Jeff NYJ 71, PHL 67
Bledsoe, Curtis KCC 30
Bledsoe, Drew BUF 11, NEP 11
Bleeker, Mal xBKN ?
Bleeker, Mel PHL 49
Bleick, Tom ATL 48, IND 25
Bleier, Bob NEP 10
Bleier, Rocky PIT 20/26

Blessing, Paul DET 83
Blevins, Darius STL 83
Blevins, Tony IND 26, SFF 22
Bligen, Dennis NYJ 23, TBB 38
Blinka, Stan NYJ 54
Bliss, Homer ARZ ?
Bloedorn, Greg SEA 60
Blondin, Tom xCIN 34
Blood, Johnny GBP 14/20/24/26/55, PIT 15/35
Bloodgood, Al NYG 4, GBP 11
Blount, Alvin DAL 28
Blount, Ed SFF 10
Blount, Eric ARZ 25
Blount, Jeb TBB 17
Blount, Lamar zBAL 59, zBUF 72, zMIA 50
Blount, Mel PIT 47
Blount, Tony NYG 23
Blozis, Al NYG 32
Blue, Anthony SEA 22
Blue, Forest SFF 75, IND 50
Blue, Luther DET 89, PHL 80
Blumenstock, Jim NYG 42
Blumer, Herb ARZ 15/17/20
Blundin, Matt DET 12, KCC 14
Bly, Dre DET 32, STL 32
Blye, Ron PHL 33, NYG 22
Boadreaux, Frank STL 70
Boadway, Steve DET 95
Board, Dwaine NOS 76, SFF 76
Boatner, Mack TBB 34
Boatright, Bon SDC 73
Boatswain, Harry NYJ 69, PHL 69, SFF 65
Bob, Adam NYJ 52
Bober, Chris NYG 67
Bobo, Hubert NYJ 57, SDC 57
Bobo, Orlando BLT 74, CLE 74, MIN 74
Bock, Joe ARZ 64, BUF 62
Bock, John MIA 60, NYJ 68
Bock, Wayne ARZ 78
Bodden, Leigh CLE 28
Boddie, Tony DEN 24
Boden, Lynn CHI 60, DET 62
Bodenger, Maury DET 16/19/38
Boedeker, Bill GBP 31, PHL 21, CLE 99, zCHI 88
Boeke, Jim DAL 68, NOS 77, STL 78
Boensch, Fred WSH 51
Boerigter, Marc KCC 85
Boerio, Chuck GBP 65
Boggan, Rex NYG 73
Boggs, Mark IND 60
Bogue, George ARZ 26
Bohannon, Fred PIT 23
Bohling, Dewey BUF 26/41, NYJ 26
Bohlinger, Rob CAR 79
Bohlman, Frank ARZ 21
Bohm, Ron ARZ 78
Bohovich, Reed NYG 73
Boiman, Rocky TEN 50

Boireau, Michael MIN 96
Bojovic, Novo ARZ 11
Bokamper, Kim MIA 58
Bolan, George CHI 5/19
Bolcar, Ned MIA 53, SEA 55
Bolden, Gary PHL 65
Bolden, Juran ATL 21/43, GBP 46, KCC 43, CAR 43
Bolden, Leroy CLE 45
Bolden, Rickey CLE 77
Boldin, Anquan ARZ 81
Bolin, Bookie MIN 66
Bolinger, Russ DET 73
Bolkovac, Nick PIT 75
Boll, Don WSH 62, NYG 78
Boller, Kyle BLT 8
Bollinger, Brian ARZ 70, SFF 71/77
Bolton, Andrew SEA 33, DET 43
Bolton, Harry DET 46
Bolton, Ron CLE 28, NEP 27
Bolton, Scott GBP 82
Bomar, Lynn NYG 7
Bond, Chuck WSH 22
Bond, Randall PIT 55, WSH 43
Bonderrant, Bourbon CHI ?
Bone, Warren GBP 72
Bonelli, Ernie ARZ 28, PIT 74
Bonham, Shane DET 96, IND 72, SFF 78
Boniol, Chris CHI 18, DAL 18, PHL 18
Bonner, Brian WSH 56
Bonner, Glen SDC 21
Bonner, Melvin DEN 82/83
Bonner, Sherdrick ARZ 11
Bonness, Rik OAK 54, TBB 53
Bono, Steve KCC 13, GBP 13, MIN 13, PIT 15, STL 13, CAR 12, SFF 13
Booker, Marty CHI 86
Booker, Michael ATL 20, TEN 33
Booker, Vaughn CIN 96, GBP 96, KCC 99
Bookman, John KCC 22, NYJ 29, NYG 22
Bookout, Billy GBP 20
Boone, Alfonso CHI 70
Boone, David MIN 71
Boone, Greg TBB 39
Boone, J.R. CHI 55/57, GBP 22/43, SFF 24
Boone, Jack STL ?
Boose, Dorian NYJ 97, WSH 72
Booth, Clarence ARZ 45, PIT 45
Booth, Dick DET 11/84
Booth, Isaac BLT 36
Booth, Tony CAR 31
Booty, John ARZ 42, NYG 41, NYJ 42, PHL 42, TBB 44
Booty, Josh CLE 12

Boozer, Emerson NYJ 32
Borak, Fritz GBP 9
Borchardt, Jon BUF 73, SEA 76
Borcky, Dennis NYG 77
Bordano, Chris NOS 56
Bordelon, Ben SDC 69
Bordelon, Ken NOS 50
Borden, Les NYG 5
Borden, Nate BUF 75, DAL 87, GBP 87
Borders, Nate CIN 32
Borgella, Jocelyn DET 27
Borgognone, Dirk GBP 9
Borland, Kyle STL 91
Borreson, Rich DAL 84
Borton, John CLE 10
Bortz, Mark CHI 62
Borum, Jarvis ARZ 61
Boryla, Mike PHL 10, TBB 10
Bosa, John MIA 97
Bosarge, Wade MIA 48, NOS 25
Bosch, Frank WSH 71/73
Boselli, Tony JAX 71, HOU 71
Bosley, Bruce SFF 77, CLE 73
Boso, Cap ARZ 89, CHI 86
Bosseler, Don WSH 31
Bostic, James PHL 27, STL 33
Bostic, Jason BUF 29, PHL 32
Bostic, Jeff WSH 53
Bostic, Joe ARZ 71
Bostic, John DET 42
Bostic, Keith TEN 25, CLE 47
Bostic, Lewis STL 25
Boston, David ARZ 89, SDC 89
Boston, McKinley NYG 82
Boswell, Ben WSH 33, DET ?
Bosworth, Brian SEA 55
Botchan, Ron SDC 54, TEN 37
Botkin, Kirk NOS 86, PIT 84
Boucher, Scott TEN 77
Boudreaux, Jim NEP 64
Bouggess, Lee PHL 46
Bouie, Kevin ARZ 33, PHL 33/35, SDC 33
Bouie, Tony TBB 23
Bouley, Gilbert STL 42/66
Boulware, Peter BLT 58
Bouman, Todd MIN 8, NOS 4
Boures, Emil PIT 71
Boutte, Marc WSH 93, STL 96
Boutwell, Tom MIA 16
Bouwens, Shawn DET 66, JAX 66
Bouyer, Willie SEA 88
Bouza, Matt IND 85/87, SFF 81
Bova, Tony ARZ 41, PHL 85, PIT 31/41/85
Bowdell, Gordon DEN 89
Bowden, Joe DAL 58, TEN 58/59
Bowdoin, Jim DET 46, GBP 19/32/34, NYG 55, xBKN 16/5

Bowen, Ken ATL 58
Bowen, Matt GBP 28, STL 27, WSH 41
Bowens, David DEN 52, GBP 96, MIA 96
Bowens, Tim MIA 95
Bowers, Andy ARZ 71
Bowers, Bill STL 30
Bowers, R.J. CLE 34, PIT 33
Bowers, Sam CHI 84
Bowick, Tony ATL 70
Bowie, Larry MIN 61
Bowie, Larry WSH 47
Bowles, Todd SFF 22, WSH 23
Bowling, Andy ATL 51
Bowman, Barry SEA 10
Bowman, Bill DET 33
Bowman, Jim NEP 28
Bowman, Ken GBP 57
Bowman, Kevin PHL 83
Bowman, Steve NYG 27
Bowman, William PIT 43/49
Bownes, Fabien CHI 82/88, SEA 19/83
Bowser, Charles MIA 56
Bowyer, Walt DEN 65
Box, Cloyce DET 80
Boyarsky, Jerry BUF 68, CIN 61, GBP 61, NOS 77
Boyd, Bill ARZ 30
Boyd, Bob IND 40
Boyd, Bob STL 80/82
Boyd, Brent MIN 62
Boyd, Danny JAX 5
Boyd, Dennis SEA 68
Boyd, Elmo GBP 85, SFF 84
Boyd, Greg DEN 77, GBP 72, NEP 65, OAK 76, SFF 98
Boyd, Greg NEP 29, NOS 21
Boyd, James JAX 42
Boyd, Jerome SEA 60
Boyd, Lavell CIN 85
Boyd, Malik MIN 36
Boyd, Samuel PIT 42
Boyd, Sean ATL 42
Boyd, Stephen DET 57
Boyd, Tom DET 54
Boyd, Tommie DET 80
Boyda, Mike xNYB 32
Boydston, Max ARZ 83, KCC 81, OAK 84
Boyer, Brant CLE 52, JAX 52, MIA 52
Boyer, Mark IND 84, NYJ 80
Boyer, Verdi xBKN 28
Boyett, Lon SFF 82, TBB 84
Boyette, Garland TEN 52, ARZ 50
Boykin, Deral JAX 21, PHL 25, STL 21
Boykin, Greg NOS 36, SFF 33
Boykin, Todd WSH 21
Boylan, Jim MIN 80
Boyle, Jim PIT 65/77
Boyle, Knuckles NYG 33

Boynton, George OAK 27
Boynton, John MIA 71
Braase, Ordell IND 81
Braatz, Tom DAL 51, STL 83, WSH 84/85
Brabham, Cary OAK 40
Brabham, Dan CIN 85, TEN 85
Bracelin, Greg DEN 52, IND 52, OAK 54
Bracken, Don GBP 17, STL 6
Brackens, Tony JAX 90
Brackett, Gary IND 58
Brackett, M.L. CHI 63, NYG 71
Brackins, Charley GBP 15
Bradford, Corey GBP 85, HOU 85
Bradford, Paul SDC 25
Bradford, Ronnie ARZ 23, ATL 23, DEN 23, MIN 26
Bradfute, Byron DAL 77
Bradley, Bill ARZ 30, PHL 28
Bradley, Carlos PHL 59, SDC 50
Bradley, Chuck CHI 81, SDC 88
Bradley, Chuck CIN 60
Bradley, Danny DET 86
Bradley, Dave ARZ 55, GBP 61
Bradley, Ed CHI 38/67
Bradley, Ed PIT 38, SEA 38, SFF 54
Bradley, Freddie SDC 22
Bradley, Hal ARZ 30
Bradley, Hal ARZ 44, WSH 38
Bradley, Harold PHL 65, CLE 60
Bradley, Henry CLE 91
Bradley, Luther DET 27
Bradley, Melvin ARZ 56
Bradley, Steve CHI 12
Bradshaw, Charles PIT 71, DET 79, STL 79
Bradshaw, Craig TEN 10
Bradshaw, Jim PIT 21/24
Bradshaw, Morris NEP 88, OAK 81
Bradshaw, Terry PIT 12
Brady, Donny BLT 24, CLE 15
Brady, Ed CIN 55, STL 90, TBB 53
Brady, Jeff GBP 51, IND 51, MIN 50, PIT 94, SDC 95, STL 95, TBB 57, CAR 52
Brady, Kerry BUF 5, DAL 1, IND 9
Brady, Kyle JAX 80, NYJ 81/88
Brady, Pat PIT 18/28/42/82
Brady, Phil DEN 24
Brady, Rickey STL 48
Brady, Tom NEP 12
Bragg, Mike IND 4, WSH 4
Braggonier, Dennis SFF 27
Braggs, Byron GBP 73, TBB 71
Braggs, Stephen CLE 36, MIA 36

Braham, Rich ARZ 76, CIN 74
Brahaney, Tom ARZ 51
Brahm, Lawrence STL 59
Braidwood, Charles ARZ 12, DET 72, xCIN 40
Bramlett, Don MIN 61
Bramlett, John DEN 56, MIA 57, NEP 57, ATL 62
Brammer, Mark BUF 86
Branch, Bruce WSH 23
Branch, Calvin OAK 27
Branch, Cliff OAK 21
Branch, Colin CAR 28
Branch, Deion NEP 83
Branch, Mel KCC 87, MIA 86
Branch, Reggie WSH 29/30
Brandau, Art PIT 45/79
Brandenburg, Dan BUF 96
Brandes, John IND 88, NYG 82, SFF 85, WSH 82
Brandon, David ATL 51, CLE 58, SDC 58, SEA 51
Brandon, Michael IND 99, SFF 78
Brandon, Sam DEN 42
Brandt, David WSH 54
Brandt, Jim PIT 27
Brannan, Solomon NYJ 47, KCC 38
Brannon, Robert CLE 94, NOS 95
Branstetter, Kent GBP 71
Brantley, Chris BUF 82, STL 88
Brantley, John TEN 58, WSH 59
Brantley, Scot TBB 52
Branton, Gene TBB 80
Bratkowski, Zeke CHI 12, GBP 12, STL 12
Bratton, Jason BUF 29
Bratton, Melvin DEN 32
Bratzke, Chad IND 92, NYG 77
Bravo, Alex OAK 47, STL 21
Bravyak, Jack BUF 91
Braxton, David ARZ 54, CIN 58, MIN 53
Braxton, Hez SDC 35, BUF 33
Braxton, Jim BUF 34, MIA 34
Braxton, Tyrone DEN 34, MIA 34
Bray, Maurice PIT 3/11
Bray, Ray CHI 82, GBP 63
Brayton, Tyler OAK 91
Brazell, Carl STL 18
Braziel, Larry CLE 47, IND 47
Brazile, Robert TEN 52
Brazinsky, Sam zBUF 25
Brazley, Carl SDC 48
Brazzell, Chris DAL 82/85
Breaux, Don DEN 19, SDC 15
Bredde, Bill ARZ 40
Bredice, John PHL 89
Breding, Ed WSH 63
Breech, Jim CIN 3/10, OAK 5
Breeden, Louis CIN 34

Breedlove, Kevin SDC 67
Breedlove, Rod WSH 63, PIT 63
Breedon, Bill PIT 44
Breen, Adrian CIN 18
Breen, Gene GBP 61, PIT 52, STL 53
Brees, Drew SDC 9
Bregel, Jeff SFF 65
Breitenstein, Bob ATL 65, DEN 76, MIN 75
Brennan, Brian CIN 83, CLE 86, SDC 13
Brennan, Jack GBP 37
Brennan, Leo PHL 70
Brennan, Matt NYG 5
Brennan, Mike ARZ 62, BUF 64, CIN 60
Brennan, Willis ARZ 16/18/19
Brenner, Al NYG 48
Brenner, Hoby NOS 85
Brethauer, Monte IND 80/86/88
Brett, Ed ARZ ?, PIT 24
Brett, Walt ATL 67
Brettschneider, Carl ARZ 57, DET 57
Breunig, Bob DAL 53
Brew, Dorian BLT 22, SDC 22
Brewer, Billy WSH 49
Brewer, Chris CHI 32, DEN 26
Brewer, Dewell IND 26, CAR 26
Brewer, Jack MIN 42
Brewer, John PHL 36
Brewer, Johnny CLE 83, NOS 82
Brewer, Sean ATL 89, CIN 88
Brewington, Jim OAK 73
Brewster, Darrel CLE 83/88, PIT 88
Brezina, Bobby TEN 21
Brezina, Greg ATL 50
Brian, William PHL 31
Brice, Alundis DAL 21/23/29
Brice, Will CIN 10, STL 10
Briehl, Tom TEN 92
Brien, Doug IND 10, MIN 4, NOS 10, NYJ 6, SFF 4, TBB 4
Brigance, O.J. BLT 57, MIA 57/58, STL 57
Briggs, Bill WSH 86
Briggs, Bob CLE 84, KCC 84, SDC 68
Briggs, Bob WSH 30
Briggs, Greg CHI 54, DAL 43, MIN 43/54
Briggs, Lance CHI 55
Briggs, Paul DET 76
Briggs, Walter NYJ 16
Brigham, Jeremy OAK 87
Bright, Anthony CAR 81
Bright, Greg CIN 47
Bright, Leon NYG 45, TBB 29
Brightful, Lamont BLT 45
Brill, Hal DET 2

Brilz, Darrick CIN 65, SDC 73, SEA 64, WSH 75
Brim, James MIN 84
Brim, Michael ARZ 44, MIN 44, CIN 43, DET 42, NYJ 43
Brink, Larry STL 63/83, CHI 81
Brinkley, Lester DAL 63
Brinson, Dana SDC 33
Brinson, Larry DAL 36, SEA 36
Brisby, Vincent NEP 82, NYJ 82
Briscoe, Marlin BUF 86, DEN 15, DET 86, MIA 86, NEP 88, SDC 86
Brister, Bubby DEN 6, MIN 6, NYJ 6, PHL 6, PIT 6
Brister, Willie NYJ 86
Bristor, John SFF 29
Brito, Gene WSH 80, STL 80
Britt, Charley SFF 20, MIN 17, STL 17
Britt, Ed WSH 12, xBKN 6
Britt, James ATL 26
Britt, Jessie PIT 88
Britt, Maurice DET 80
Britt, Oscar WSH 29
Britt, Ralph PIT 86
Britt, Rankin PHL 18
Brittenum, Jon SDC 15
Britton, Earl ARZ 29, CHI 80
Broadnax, Jerry TEN 83
Broadstone, Marion NYG ?
Brock, Charley GBP 29
Brock, Clyde DAL 77, SFF 75
Brock, Dieter STL 5
Brock, Fred ARZ 89
Brock, Lou GBP 15/16
Brock, Lou DET 28, SDC 38, SEA 38
Brock, Matt GBP 62/94, NYJ 94
Brock, Pete NEP 58
Brock, Raheem IND 79
Brock, Stan NOS 67, SDC 67
Brock, Willie DET 53
Brockermeyer, Blake CHI 78, DEN 71, CAR 68/78
Brockhaus, Jeff SFF 5
Brockington, John GBP 42, KCC 43
Brodhead, Bob BUF 17
Brodie, John SFF 12
Brodnax, Red DEN 36
Brodnicki, Chuck xBKN 6
Brohm, Jeff DEN 11, SFF 11
Bromell, Lorenzo MIN 91, OAK 95, MIA 91
Bronson, Ben IND 18
Bronson, Zack SFF 31
Brooker, Tommy KCC 81
Brooking, Keith ATL 56
Brookins, Jason BLT 44
Brookins, Mitchell BUF 81
Brooks, Aaron NOS 2
Brooks, Ahmad BUF 47
Brooks, Barrett DET 76, GBP 77, PHL 76

Brooks, Bill BUF 80, IND 80,
    WSH 80
Brooks, Billy CIN 82, SDC 82,
    TEN 88
Brooks, Bob NYJ 35
Brooks, Bobby JAX 56, OAK 55
Brooks, Bobby NYG 37
Brooks, Bucky BUF 81, GBP 22,
    JAX 22, KCC 45, OAK 33
Brooks, Carlos ARZ 25
Brooks, Chet SFF 31
Brooks, Cliff NYJ 48, BUF 23,
    CLE 23, PHL 23
Brooks, Derrick TBB 55
Brooks, Ethan ARZ 66, ATL 73,
    BLT 77, STL 77
Brooks, Jamal DAL 50
Brooks, James CIN 21, CLE 28,
    SDC 21, TBB 20
Brooks, Jermaine DAL 92
Brooks, Jon DET 53, ATL 61,
    ARZ 65
Brooks, Kevin DAL 99, DET 97
Brooks, Larry STL 90
Brooks, Leo ARZ 70, TEN 73
Brooks, Macey CHI 83, DAL
    82
Brooks, Michael DAL 44, SDC
    32
Brooks, Michael DEN 56, DET
    50, NYG 94
Brooks, Perry WSH 69
Brooks, Reggie TBB 41, WSH
    40
Brooks, Robert DEN 85, GBP
    87
Brooks, Rodregis IND 26
Brooks, Steve DET 48
Brooks, Tony PHL 39
Brookshier, Tom PHL 40/45
Brophy, Jay MIA 53, NYJ 90
Brosky, Al ARZ 24
Bross, Mal GBP 6
Brostek, Bern STL 61
Brotzki, Bob DAL 62, IND 74
Broughton, Luther PHL
    49/84/86/88, CAR 49/84/88
Broughton, Walter BUF 81/89
Broughton, Willie DAL 84,
    IND 68, NOS 99, OAK 97
Broussard, Fred PIT 56
Broussard, Steve GBP 11
Broussard, Steve ATL 34/44,
    CIN 33, SEA 31
Brovelli, Angelo PIT 14/29
Brown, A.B. NYJ 29
Brown, Aaron ATL 91, PHL 90,
    TBB 55
Brown, Aaron GBP 74, KCC
    87
Brown, Alex CHI 96
Brown, Allen GBP 83
Brown, Andre MIA 82
Brown, Anthony CIN 75, PIT
    60

Brown, Antonio BUF 86
Brown, Arnold DET 23, SEA 20
Brown, Barry IND 36, NEP
    66/86, NYG 83
Brown, Bill MIN 30, CHI 38
Brown, Bill NEP 54
Brown, Bill xBKN 26
Brown, Bob GBP 78, CIN 78,
    SDC 78
Brown, Bob OAK 76, PHL 76,
    STL 76
Brown, Bobby CLE 89
Brown, Booker SDC 65
Brown, Boyd DEN 87, NYG 83
Brown, Bud MIA 43
Brown, Buddy GBP 62, WSH
    60
Brown, Carlos GBP 19
Brown, Cedric TBB 34
Brown, Cedrick PHL 23
Brown, Chad PIT 94, SEA 94
Brown, Chadrick ARZ 78
Brown, Charles OAK 76
Brown, Charley BUF 23, CHI 22
Brown, Charlie DET 81
Brown, Charlie NOS 22
Brown, Charlie WSH 87, ATL
    89
Brown, Chris JAX 31, PIT 23
Brown, Chris NYJ 79
Brown, Chris TEN 29
Brown, Chuck ARZ 61
Brown, Clay ATL 88, DEN 89
Brown, Cornell BLT 51/90
Brown, Corwin DET 44, NEP
    30, NYJ 44
Brown, Courtney CLE 92
Brown, Curtis BUF 47
Brown, Cyron DEN 73
Brown, Dan WSH 81
Brown, Dave ARZ 17, NYG 17
Brown, Dave NYG 5/12
Brown, Dave SEA 22, GBP 32,
    PIT 36
Brown, David PHL 56
Brown, Dean CLE 21, MIA 44
Brown, Deauntae PHL 35
Brown, Dee CAR 22, PIT 22
Brown, Delvin JAX 24
Brown, Dennis SFF 96
Brown, Derek ARZ 83, JAX 86,
    NYG 86, OAK 86
Brown, Derek NOS 20/21/24
Brown, Don NYG 47
Brown, Don SDC 61
Brown, Don TEN 22
Brown, Donald MIA 32, SDC
    32
Brown, Doug OAK 74
Brown, Doug WSH 78
Brown, Ed CHI 15, IND 14, PIT
    15
Brown, Eddie CIN 81
Brown, Eddie WSH 25, CLE 28,
    STL 25

Brown, Eric DAL 33
Brown, Eric DEN 26, HOU 24
Brown, Eric KCC 86
Brown, Ernie PIT 98
Brown, Fakhir NOS 35, SDC 24
Brown, Fred BUF 25/46
Brown, Fred PHL 55/87, STL 81
Brown, Gary GBP 68/71
Brown, Gary NYG 33, SDC 33,
    TEN 31/33
Brown, George zNYY 38, xNYB
    38
Brown, Gilbert GBP 71/93
Brown, Gordie NYJ 79
Brown, Gordon IND 42
Brown, Greg ATL 98, PHL 98
Brown, Guy DAL 59
Brown, Hardy ARZ 37, DEN
    34/46, SFF 33/73, WSH 25,
    xBAL 73, zBRK 63/60, zCHI
    60
Brown, Howie DET 64
Brown, Ivory Lee ARZ 33
Brown, J.B. ARZ 26, DET 31,
    MIA 37, PIT 27
Brown, James CLE 74, MIA 76,
    NYJ 76
Brown, Jamie DEN 70, SFF 72,
    WSH 73
Brown, Jerome PHL 99
Brown, Jim CLE 32
Brown, Joe SEA 60
Brown, John CLE 70, PIT 74
Brown, John zLAD 29
Brown, Jonathan GBP 91
Brown, Josh SEA 3
Brown, Ken CIN 86
Brown, Ken CLE 30
Brown, Ken DEN 55, GBP 74
Brown, Kevin CHI 11
Brown, Kris HOU 3, PIT 3
Brown, Lance ARZ 30, BUF 31,
    PIT 29
Brown, Laron DEN 82
Brown, Larry DAL 24/34, OAK
    24
Brown, Larry KCC 79
Brown, Larry MIN 80
Brown, Larry PIT 79/87
Brown, Larry TEN 84
Brown, Larry WSH 43
Brown, Lomas ARZ 75, CLE 75,
    DET 75, NYG 76, TBB 75
Brown, Marc BUF 86
Brown, Mark DET 52/95, MIA
    51
Brown, Mark NYJ 50
Brown, Marv DET 42
Brown, Mike CHI 30
Brown, Milford HOU 67
Brown, Monty BUF 96, NEP 93
Brown, Na PHL 85
Brown, Omar ATL 27
Brown, Orlando BLT 77/78,
    CLE 77

Brown, Otto DAL 31, NYG 21
Brown, Pete SFF 56
Brown, Preston CLE 89, NEP 81/87, NYJ 89
Brown, Ralph NYG 22
Brown, Ray ATL 34, NOS 27
Brown, Ray IND 17
Brown, Ray SFF 22
Brown, Ray SFF 65, ARZ 62, DET 61, WSH 67
Brown, Reggie ATL 46, PHL 24
Brown, Reggie DET 59
Brown, Reggie SEA 34
Brown, Reggie TEN 17/89
Brown, Richard DET 41
Brown, Richard CLE 52, MIN 52, SDC 66, STL 92
Brown, Robert ARZ 89, MIN 89, NOS 36
Brown, Robert GBP 93
Brown, Rod ARZ 31
Brown, Roger DET 76, STL 78
Brown, Roger NEP 47, NYG 26
Brown, Ron ARZ 82/83
Brown, Ron OAK 64/96
Brown, Ron STL 81/89, OAK 24
Brown, Rosey NYG 79
Brown, Ruben BUF 79
Brown, Rush ARZ 69
Brown, Selwyn TBB 28
Brown, Sheldon PHL 24/39
Brown, Sidney NEP 21
Brown, Sonny TEN 27
Brown, Stan CLE 21
Brown, Steve TEN 24
Brown, Ted MIN 23
Brown, Terry ARZ 24, CLE 24, MIN 24
Brown, Theotis ARZ 33, KCC 27, SEA 30
Brown, Thomas PHL 97, CLE 97
Brown, Tim OAK 81
Brown, Tim PHL 22, GBP 25, IND 2
Brown, Tom CIN 80
Brown, Tom MIA 36
Brown, Tom PIT 32/76
Brown, Tom GBP 40, WSH 21
Brown, Tony BUF 68/77
Brown, Tony SEA 29, TEN 22
Brown, Travis BUF 5, SEA 5
Brown, Troy NEP 80
Brown, Tyrone ATL 80
Brown, Vincent NEP 59
Brown, Wilbert NEP 60, SDC 60, WSH 59
Brown, Willie OAK 24, DEN 24
Brown, Willie PHL 23, STL 26
Browne, Jim OAK 47
Browner, Jim CIN 21
Browner, Joey MIN 47, TBB 47

Browner, Keith OAK 51, SDC 57, SFF 59, TBB 57
Browner, Ross CIN 79, GBP 79
Browning, Charlie NYJ 32
Browning, Dave NEP 74, OAK 73
Browning, Gregg NYG 80
Browning, John KCC 93
Brownlee, Claude MIA 79
Brownlow, Darrick DAL 50/59, TBB 55, WSH 50
Brubaker, Dick ARZ 87, BUF 88
Bruce, Arland SFF 19, ATL 93, OAK 56/99
Bruce, Gail SFF 54/88
Bruce, Isaac STL 80
Bruckner, Les ARZ 15
Bruckner, Nick NYJ 22/83/86
Bruder, Hank GBP 5/13/18/27/47/55, PIT 5
Brudzinski, Bob MIA 59, STL 59
Brueckman, Charley WSH 56, SDC 53
Bruener, Mark PIT 87
Bruer, Bob CHI 81, MIN 82, SFF 82
Bruggers, Bob MIA 54/56, SDC 56
Bruhin, John TBB 69
Brumbaugh, Boyd PIT 10, xBKN 8
Brumbaugh, Carl CHI 8, STL 8, xBKN 6
Brumfield, Jackson SFF 80/86
Brumfield, Jim PIT 36
Brumfield, Scott CIN 72
Brumley, Bob DET 32
Brumm, Don ARZ 86, PHL 80
Brundage, Dewey PIT 83
Brundidge, Bill WSH 77
Brune, Larry MIN 24
Brunell, Mark JAX 8, GBP 8
Brunelli, Sam DEN 64/68/72
Brunet, Bob WSH 26
Bruney, Fred NEP 33, PIT 22/41, SFF 45, STL 38
Brunner, Scott ARZ 12, NYG 12
Bruno, Dave MIN 13
Bruno, John PIT 10
Brunson, Larry DEN 82, KCC 83, OAK 82
Brunson, Mike ATL 19
Brupbacher, Ross CHI 31
Bruschi, Tedy NEP 54
Brutley, Daryon PHL 31
Brutz, Jim zCHI 42
Bryan, Billy DEN 64
Bryan, Johnny CHI 4/8/9, ARZ 6
Bryan, Rick ATL 77
Bryan, Steve DEN 95
Bryan, Walter IND 21
Bryant, Antonio DAL 88

Bryant, Beno SEA 22
Bryant, Bill NYG 21, PHL 25
Bryant, Bob KCC 89
Bryant, Bob SFF 42
Bryant, Bobby MIN 20
Bryant, Charles ATL 32, ARZ 30
Bryant, Chuck ARZ 87
Bryant, Cullen SEA 32, STL 32
Bryant, Domingo TEN 38
Bryant, Fernando JAX 25
Bryant, Hubie NEP 84, PIT 32
Bryant, Jeff SEA 77
Bryant, Junior SFF 90
Bryant, Kelvin WSH 24
Bryant, Matt NYG 8
Bryant, Steve IND 80, TEN 81
Bryant, Tim MIN 94
Bryant, Tony OAK 94
Bryant, Trent KCC 45
Bryant, Trent WSH 28
Bryant, Warren ATL 66, OAK 66
Bryant, Waymond CHI 50
Bryant, Wendell ARZ 91
Brymer, Chris DAL 60
Bryson, Shawn BUF 38
Bryson, Shawn DET 24
Brzezinski, Doug PHL 74, CAR 79
Buben, Mark CLE 75, NEP 63
Bucchianeri, Mike GBP 17/19/33
Bucek, Felix PIT 64
Buchanan, Buck KCC 86
Buchanan, Charles CLE 72
Buchanan, Ray ATL 34, IND 34
Buchanan, Richard STL 89
Buchanan, Tim CIN 52
Buchanan, Willie GBP 28, SDC 28
Buchanon, Phillip OAK 31
Buck, Art CHI 32
Buck, Cub GBP 10
Buck, Jason CIN 99, WSH 99
Buck, Mike ARZ 16, NOS 16
Buck, Vince NOS 26
Buckey, Don NYJ 91
Buckey, Jeff MIA 77, SFF 71
Buckeye, Garland ARZ 10/14
Buckhalter, Correll PHL 28
Buckler, Bill CHI 15/17
Bucklew, Philip STL 22
Buckley, Curtis NYG 28, SFF 28, TBB 28, WSH 26
Buckley, Marcus NYG 55
Buckley, Terrell DEN 27, GBP 27, MIA 27, NEP 22/27
Bucklin, Ted NYG 0
Bucklin, Tom ARZ 9
Buckman, Tom DEN 80
Buckner, Brentson CAR 99, CIN 96, PIT 96, SFF 99
Buczkowski, Bob ARZ 95, CLE 94, OAK 95

Buda, Carl PIT 55
Budd, Frank PHL 20, WSH 20
Budde, Brad KCC 66/71
Budde, Ed KCC 71
Budka, Frank STL 45
Budness, Bill OAK 48
Budrewicz, Tom NYJ 64
Buehler, George CLE 64, OAK 64
Buetow, Bart MIN 74, NYG 74
Buffington, Harry NYG 52, zBRK 33
Buffone, Doug CHI 55
Buford, Maury CHI 8, NYG 8, SDC 7
Buford, Tony ARZ 50
Bugenhagen, Gary BUF 76, NEP 67
Buggs, Danny NYG 86/88, WSH 88
Buhler, Larry GBP 52
Buie, Drew CIN 89, OAK 89
Buivid, Ray CHI 9
Bujnoch, Glenn CIN 74, TBB 77
Bukant, Joe ARZ 36, PHL 36
Bukaty, Fred DEN 33
Bukich, Rudy CHI 10/14, PIT 10, STL 10, WSH 10
Buksar, George WSH 39, xBAL 77, zCHI 70
Bulaich, Norm IND 36, MIA 31, PHL 36
Bulger, Chet ARZ 11/45/70/73, DET 71, PIT 73
Bulger, Marc STL 10
Bull, Ron CHI 29, PHL 47
Bull, Scott SFF 19
Bullard, Courtland STL 51
Bullard, Kendrick JAX 88
Bullard, Louis SEA 72
Bullocks, Amos PIT 49, DAL 22
Bullough, Chuck MIA 54
Bullough, Hank GBP 61/67
Bulluck, Brian IND 57
Bulluck, Keith TEN 53
Bultman, Art GBP 17/32/33/38/45/52, xBKN 34
Bumgardner, Joe DET 36
Bumgardner, Rex CLE 22/90, zBUF 82
Bunch, Derek WSH 92
Bunch, Jarrod NYG 33, OAK 45
Buncom, Frank SDC 55, CIN 55
Bundra, Mike CLE 72, DET 74, MIN 75, NYG 74
Bundren, Jim CLE 65
Bungarada, Ken SFF 64/72
Bunting, John PHL 95
Bunyan, John xBKN 19
Bunz, Dan DET 97, SFF 57
Buoniconti, Nick MIA 85, NEP 85
Burbage, Cornell DAL 15/82/89
Burch, Gerald OAK 86

Burch, Joe DEN 60
Burch, John ARZ 33
Burchfield, Don NOS 36
Burdick, Lloyd CHI 14, xCIN 46
Burford, Chris KCC 88
Burgeis, Glenn CHI 29
Burger, Todd CHI 63, NYJ 62
Burgess, Charlie NYG 91
Burgess, Derrick PHL 56/59
Burgess, Fernanza MIA 82, NYJ 46
Burgess, James SDC 52
Burgess, Marvell MIA 49
Burgess, Ronnie GBP 39
Burgmeier, Ted KCC 48
Burk, Adrian PHL 10, xBAL 68
Burk, Scott CIN 28
Burke, Anthony ARZ 72
Burke, Don SFF 6/32/66/68/73/38
Burke, Joe NYJ 29
Burke, John NEP 85, NYJ 85, SDC 83
Burke, Mark PHL 29
Burke, Mike STL 11
Burke, Paul CAR 84
Burke, Randy IND 84
Burke, Thomas ARZ 60/95
Burke, Vern ATL 84, NOS 83, SFF 84
Burkett, Chris BUF 85, NYJ 87
Burkett, Jack IND 55, DAL 60, NOS 55
Burkett, Jeff ARZ 35/88/89
Burks, Dialleo PHL 42/86/89, CAR 89
Burks, Randy CHI 83
Burks, Ray KCC 59
Burks, Shawn WSH 58
Burks, Steve NEP 82
Burl, Alex ARZ 22
Burleson, John DET 47, PIT 25, xCIN 33
Burleson, Nate MIN 81
Burley, Gary ATL 73, CIN 67
Burman, George CHI 68, STL 51, WSH 58
Burmeister, Danny WSH 22
Burmeister, Forrest STL 24
Burnett, Bobby BUF 21, DEN 21
Burnett, Chester CLE 54, JAX 54, WSH 56
Burnett, Dale NYG 18
Burnett, Len PIT 86
Burnett, Ray ARZ ?
Burnett, Rob CLE 90, BLT 90, MIA 90
Burnett, Victor ARZ 69/95
Burnette, Dave DAL 73
Burnette, Reggie GBP 55, TBB 50/56
Burnette, Tom PHL 19, PIT 25
Burnham, Lem PHL 67
Burnham, Tim SEA 78

Burnine, Hank NYG 82, PHL 84
Burns, Bob NYJ 33
Burns, Curry HOU 22
Burns, Ed NOS 11
Burns, Jason CIN 38
Burns, Joe BUF 35
Burns, Keith CHI 52, DEN 55/56
Burns, Lamont NYJ 63
Burns, Leon ARZ 38, SDC 38
Burns, Mike DET 29, SFF 28
Burnstein, Brent ARZ 78
Burrell, Clinton CLE 49
Burrell, George DEN 41
Burrell, John PIT 86, WSH 48
Burrell, Ode TEN 25
Burress, Plaxico PIT 80
Burris, Bo NOS 16
Burris, Buddy GBP 33
Burris, Henry CHI 10
Burris, Jeff BUF 22, CIN 21, IND 20
Burrough, John ATL 91, MIN 91, STL 95
Burrough, Jonathan BLT 85
Burrough, Ken TEN 00, NOS 00
Burroughs, Derrick BUF 29
Burroughs, Don PHL 45, STL 25
Burroughs, James IND 45
Burroughs, Sammie IND 53
Burrow, Curtis GBP 5
Burrow, Jim GBP 41
Burrow, Ken ATL 82
Burrus, Harry zBRK 54, zCHI ?, zNYY 50/83
Burruss, Lloyd KCC 34
Burse, Tony SEA 34
Burson, Jim ARZ 49, ATL 49
Burt, Jim NYG 64, SFF 64
Burton, Al NYJ 72, TEN 68
Burton, Derek MIN 71
Burton, James CHI 35
Burton, Kendrick TEN 94
Burton, Larry NOS 80, SDC 87
Burton, Leon NYJ 24
Burton, Leonard BUF 61, DET 68
Burton, Ron NEP 22
Burton, Ron ARZ 51, DAL 57, OAK 59
Burton, Shane CAR 98, CHI 94, MIA 75, NYJ 98
Busby, Sherrill xBKN 16
Busch, Mike NYG 8
Bush, Blair CIN 58, GBP 51, SEA 59, STL 51
Bush, Devin ATL 25/42, CLE 23, STL 23
Bush, Frank TEN 94
Bush, Lew KCC 51/56, SDC 58
Bush, Steve ARZ 87, CIN 88
Bushby, Thomas PHL 45, xCIN 5,39

Busich, Sam DET ?, STL 19, WSH 14
Busick, Steve DEN 58, SDC 55, STL 52
Busler, Ray ARZ 43/97
Buss, Art CHI 11, PHL 12/45
Bussell, Gerry DEN 21/22
Bussey, Barney CIN 27, TBB 27
Bussey, Dexter DET 24
Bussey, Young CHI 37
Butcher, Paul DET 96, IND 53, OAK 59, STL 59, CAR 53
Butcher, Wendell xBKN 66
Butkus, Carl NYG 62, WSH 47, zNYY 45
Butkus, Dick CHI 51
Butler, Bill DEN 51
Butler, Bill DAL 22, GBP 22/25, PIT 20, MIN 22
Butler, Bill NOS 38
Butler, Bob NYJ 63, PHL 53
Butler, Bobby ATL 23
Butler, Chuck SEA 96
Butler, Dave CLE 92
Butler, Duane MIN 31
Butler, Frank GBP 26/35/48/59/60
Butler, Gary CHI 81, KCC 82, TBB 82
Butler, Gerald KCC 86
Butler, Hillary SEA 55
Butler, Jack PIT 25/80
Butler, Jerametrius STL 23/37
Butler, Jerry BUF 80
Butler, Jim ARZ 36, ATL 33, PIT 23
Butler, John ARZ 23, PHL 27, PIT 23/27, xBKN 19
Butler, John SFF 26
Butler, Keith SEA 53
Butler, Kevin ARZ 3, CHI 6
Butler, Leroy GBP 36
Butler, Mike GBP 77
Butler, Ray IND 80, SEA 83
Butler, Skip NOS 3, NYG ?, TEN 2
Butsko, Harry WSH 52
Butterfield, Mark CHI 10
Buttle, Greg NYJ 51
Butts, Ed ARZ 3/17
Butts, Marion SDC 35, NEP 44, TEN 35
Butz, Dave WSH 65, ARZ 62
Buzin, Rich CHI 73, NYG 77, STL 77
Buzynski, Bernie BUF 55
Byars, Keith MIA 41, NEP 41, NYJ 41, PHL 41/42
Byas, Rick ATL 38
Byers, Ken MIN 66, NYG 60
Byers, Scott SDC 30
Bykowski, Frank PIT 4
Byler, Joe NYG 70
Byner, Earnest WSH 21, BLT 21, CLE 20/21/44

By'not'e, Butler DEN 28, CAR 33
Bynum, Kenny SDC 43
Bynum, Reggie BUF 88
Byrd, Boris NYG 21
Byrd, Butch BUF 42, DEN 24
Byrd, Darryl OAK 50/54
Byrd, Dennis NEP 78
Byrd, Dennis NYJ 90
Byrd, Gill SDC 22
Byrd, Isaac TEN 83, CAR 82
Byrd, Israel NOS 45
Byrd, Mac STL 23
Byrd, Richard TEN 71
Byrd, Sylvester ATL 88
Byrne, Bill PHL 66
Byrum, Carl BUF 35
Cabral, Brian ATL 51, CHI 54, GBP 65
Cabrelli, Larry PHL 84, PIT 84
Caddel, Ernie DET 1/51
Cade, Eddie NEP 41
Cade, Mossy GBP 24
Cadigan, Dave CIN 68, NYJ 66
Cadile, Jim CHI 72
Cadrez, Glenn DEN 59, KCC 51/59, NYJ 50
Cadwell, John KCC 61
Caesar, Ivan MIN 53
Cafego, George WSH 32, xBKN 23, xBOS 11
Caffey, Lee Roy GBP 60, CHI 60, DAL 60, PHL 34, SDC 50
Cagle, Chris NYG 12, xBKN 33/12
Cagle, Jim PHL 78
Cagle, John NEP 62
Cahill, Bill BUF 22
Cahill, Dave PHL 58, STL 70, ATL 73
Cahill, Ron ARZ 33
Cahoon, Tiny GBP 10/30/40
Cain, J.V. ARZ 88
Cain, Jim ARZ 53, DET 88
Cain, Joe CHI 59, SEA 59
Cain, Lynn ATL 21, STL 31
Cain, Patrick DET 65
Calcagni, Ralph PIT 47, xBOS 47
Caldwell, Alan NYG 45
Caldwell, Bruce NYG 48
Caldwell, Bryan TEN 79
Caldwell, Darryl BUF 67
Caldwell, David GBP 73
Caldwell, Mike ARZ 52, BLT 56, CAR 59, CHI 55, CLE 56, PHL 56
Caldwell, Mike SFF 13/17/81
Caldwell, Ravin WSH 50
Caldwell, Reche SDC 82
Caldwell, Scott DEN 28
Caldwell, Tony OAK 57, SEA 57

Caleb, Jamie CLE 36/37/47, MIN 23
Calhoun, Don BUF 29, NEP 44, PHL 30
Calhoun, Mike SFF 60, TBB 70
Calhoun, Rick OAK 21
Calicchio, Lonny PHL 17
Calico, Tyrone TEN 87
Caliguire, Dean PIT 61, SFF 64
Call, Jack IND 25, PIT 20
Call, Kevin IND 71/72
Callahan, Bill BUF 25
Callahan, Bob zBUF 23
Callahan, Dan NYJ 61
Callahan, Jim DET 88
Calland, Lee ATL 22, CHI 23, MIN 23, PIT 44
Callicutt, Ken DET 31
Calligaro, Len NYG 2
Callihan, Bill DET 25/34
Calloway, Chris ATL 80, NEP 82, NYG 80, PIT 88
Calloway, Ernie PHL 57/77
Calmus, Rocky TEN 54
Calvelli, Tony DET 42/65, SFF 21/31
Calvin, Tom PIT 35
Camarillo, Rich ARZ 16, NEP 3, OAK 16, STL 3, TEN 16
Cambal, Dennis NYJ 30
Cameron, Glenn CIN 50
Cameron, Jack CHI 30
Cameron, Paul PIT 34/45
Camp, Jim zBRK 80
Camp, Reggie ATL 96, CLE 96
Campana, Al ARZ 47, CHI 10/40
Campanella, Joe IND 73, xDAL 73
Campbell, Arnold BUF 90
Campbell, Bill ARZ 50/53/55, xNYB 14
Campbell, Bob PIT 23
Campbell, Carter DEN 79, NYG 79, SFF 51
Campbell, Dan DAL 86, NYG 89
Campbell, Don PIT 29
Campbell, Earl TEN 34, NOS 35
Campbell, Gary CHI 59
Campbell, Glenn NYG 9/15, PHL 29, PIT ?
Campbell, Jack SEA 71
Campbell, Jeff DEN 86, DET 87
Campbell, Jesse NYG 37, WSH 37
Campbell, Jim SDC 53
Campbell, Joe NOS 73, OAK 77, TBB 79
Campbell, John IND 55, MIN 55, PIT 53
Campbell, Joseph SDC 95
Campbell, Kelly MIN 16
Campbell, Ken NYJ 82

Campbell, Khary NYJ 53
Campbell, Lamar DET 39
Campbell, Leon CHI 32, PIT 28, xBAL 78
Campbell, Marion PHL 78, SFF 76
Campbell, Mark BUF 84, CLE 83
Campbell, Mark ARZ 90, DEN 67
Campbell, Matt WSH 66, CAR 66
Campbell, Milt CLE 48
Campbell, Ray PIT 66
Campbell, Rich GBP 19
Campbell, Russ PIT 85
Campbell, Scott ATL 10, PIT 10
Campbell, Sonny ATL 45
Campbell, Stan DET 67, OAK 67, PHL 67
Campbell, Tommy PHL 37
Campbell, Woody TEN 35
Campen, James GBP 63, NOS 59
Campfield, Billy NYG 35, PHL 37
Campiglio, Bob WSH 13
Campion, Thomas PHL 72
Campofreda, Nick WSH 43
Campora, Don WSH 75, SFF 41/76
Campos, Alan DAL 57
Canada, Larry DEN 35
Canadeo, Tony GBP 3
Canady, James CHI 8
Canady, Jim xNYB 4
Canale, Justin CIN 64, NEP 63
Canale, Rocco PHL 73, PIT 73, xBOS 45
Canale, Whit MIA 72, NEP 67
Cancik, Phil KCC 56, NYG 61
Canidate, Trung STL 24, WSH 30
Canley, Sheldon NYJ 21, SFF 20
Cannady, John NYG 52
Cannamela, Pat xDAL 35
Cannava, Al GBP 42
Cannavino, Joe BUF 27, OAK 27
Cannella, John NYG 9
Cannida, James IND 98, TBB 98
Cannon, Billy Sr. TEN 20, KCC 80, OAK 33
Cannon, Billy Jr. DAL 52
Cannon, John TBB 78
Cannon, Mark GBP 58, IND 58, KCC 70
Cantor, Leo ARZ 50/82, NYG 12
Canty, Chris NEP 26, SEA 26, NOS 35
Capece, Bill TBB 3
Capers, James CLE 59
Capers, Wayne IND 87, PIT 80

Capone, Warren DAL 59, NOS 51
Capp, Dick GBP 88, PIT 67
Cappadona, Bob NEP 33, BUF 36
Cappelletti, Gino NEP 20
Cappelletti, John SDC 25, STL 22
Cappleman, Bill DET 17, MIN 17
Capria, Carl DET 46, NYJ 29
Capuzzi, Jim GBP 23/26
Cara, Dom PIT 10
Caranci, Roland NYG 50
Carano, Glenn DAL 18
Carapella, Al SFF 45/75
Caravello, Joe SDC 46, WSH 82/88
Cardinal, Fred zNYY ?
Cardwell, Joe PIT 30
Cardwell, Lloyd DET 3/10
Carey, Bob CHI 85, STL 88/89
Carey, Brian NEP 81
Carey, Joe ARZ ?
Carey, Richard BUF 20, CIN 34
Carl, Harland CHI 41
Carlisle, Cooper DEN 65
Carlson, Cody TEN 14
Carlson, Dean KCC 9
Carlson, Hal ARZ ?
Carlson, Jeff NEP 17, TBB 7
Carlson, Mark WSH 79
Carlson, Wes GBP 11
Carlson, Zuck CHI 20
Carlton, Darryl MIA 71, TBB 70
Carlton, Wray BUF 30
Carlyle, Calvin WSH 32
Carman, Jon BUF 65
Carmazzi, Giovanni SFF 19
Carmichael, Al DEN 40, GBP 42/48
Carmichael, Harold PHL 17, DAL 17
Carmichael, Paul DEN 40
Carnelly, Ray xBKN 2
Carney, Art NYG 23/29
Carney, John SDC 3, NOS 3, STL 18, TBB 3/4
Carolan, Brett MIA 84/86, SFF 86
Carolan, Reg KCC 80, SDC 89
Caroline, J.C. CHI 25
Carollo, Joe STL 63/70, CLE 63, PHL 76
Caron, Roger IND 67/74
Carothers, Don DEN 86
Carpe, Joe PHL 24
Carpenter, Brian BUF 30, NYG 22, WSH 41
Carpenter, Chad ARZ 12
Carpenter, Dwaine SFF 35
Carpenter, John SFF 40, zBUF 45

Carpenter, Keion ATL 29, BUF 29
Carpenter, Ken CLE 20/84, DEN 89
Carpenter, Lew CLE 30, DET 32/34, GBP 33
Carpenter, Preston PIT 40, CLE 40/48, MIA 36, MIN 40, WSH 89
Carpenter, Rob NEP 81, NYJ 82, PHL 81
Carpenter, Rob NYG 26, STL 38, TEN 26
Carpenter, Ron CIN 32, MIN 36, NYJ 26
Carpenter, Ron CIN 70
Carpenter, Ron SDC 89
Carpenter, Ron STL 24
Carpenter, Steve ARZ 43, NYJ 49
Carr, Carl DET 58
Carr, Chetti OAK 20
Carr, David HOU 8
Carr, Earl PHL 32, SFF 31
Carr, Eddie SFF 85
Carr, Fred GBP 53
Carr, Gregg PIT 91
Carr, Henry NYG 28
Carr, Jim ARZ 24, PHL 21, WSH 21
Carr, Levert BUF 62/74, SDC 71, TEN 63
Carr, Lydell ARZ 45
Carr, Paul SFF 57
Carr, Reggie NYG 99
Carr, Roger IND 81, SDC 81, SEA 87
Carr, Tom NOS 65
Carraway, Stanley CLE 39
Carreker, Alphonso DEN 92, GBP 76
Carreker, Vince CLE 36
Carrell, Duane ARZ 12, DAL 10, NYJ 3, STL 17
Carrell, John TEN 53
Carrier, Mark CHI 20, DET 27, WSH 27
Carrier, Mark TBB 88/89, CLE 83, CAR 83
Carrington, Darren DEN 29, DET 27, JAX 29, OAK 21, SDC 29
Carrington, Ed TEN 88
Carroccio, Russ PHL 64, NYG 65
Carroll, Herman NOS 74
Carroll, Jay MIN 84, TBB 86
Carroll, Jim NYG 60, NYJ 55, WSH 59/60
Carroll, Leo GBP 67, WSH 81/89
Carroll, Ronnie TEN 63
Carroll, Terrence PHL 33
Carroll, Travis HOU 59, NOS 55

Carroll, Vic WSH 26, NYG 26/90

Carroll, Wesley CIN 86, NOS 80

Carruth, Rae CAR 86/89

Carson, Carlos KCC 88, PHL 87

Carson, Harry NYG 53

Carson, Howard STL 54

Carson, John WSH 82, TEN 82

Carson, Kern NYJ 45, SDC 26

Carson, Leonardo DAL 91, SDC 96

Carswell, Dwayne DEN 89

Carswell, Robert SDC 30

Carter, Alex CLE 75

Carter, Allen NEP 21

Carter, Andre SFF 96

Carter, Anthony MIN 81, DET 81

Carter, Bernard JAX 96

Carter, Blanchard TBB 66

Carter, Carl ARZ 41, CIN 45, GBP 21, TBB 44

Carter, Chris HOU 36, CIN 42, NEP 42

Carter, Cris MIN 80, MIA 88, PHL 80

Carter, Dale KCC 34, MIN 21, DEN 40, NOS 21

Carter, Daryl CHI 59

Carter, David NOS 65, TEN 58/63

Carter, Dexter NYJ 35, SFF 35

Carter, Dyshod CLE 26

Carter, Gerald TBB 87

Carter, Jim GBP 50

Carter, Jimmie ARZ 52

Carter, Joe MIA 23

Carter, Joe PHL 17/31, ARZ 29, GBP 58, xBKN 55

Carter, Jon DAL 75

Carter, Jonathan NYG 85, NYJ 84

Carter, Kent NEP 51

Carter, Kerry SEA 32

Carter, Kevin STL 93, TEN 93

Carter, Ki-jana WSH 23, CIN 32, NOS 32

Carter, Louis OAK 33, TBB 32

Carter, M.L. KCC 42

Carter, Marty ATL 25, CHI 23, DET 38, TBB 23

Carter, Michael SFF 95

Carter, Mike GBP 36, SDC 83

Carter, Pat ARZ 80, DET 87, STL 88, TEN 46/85, TEN 85

Carter, Perry KCC 22, OAK 20

Carter, Quincy DAL 17

Carter, Rodney PIT 24/44

Carter, Ross ARZ 28

Carter, Rubin DEN 68

Carter, Russell NYJ 27, OAK 29

Carter, Steve TBB 87

Carter, Tim NYG 84

Carter, Tom CHI 25, CIN 21, WSH 25

Carter, Tony CHI 30, DEN 37, GBP 39, NEP 30

Carter, Tyrone MIN 22/37, NYJ 22

Carter, Virgil CHI 11/15, CIN 11, SDC 7

Carter, Walter TBB 78

Carter, Willie ARZ 41

Carthen, Jason NEP 99

Carthens, Milt IND 68

Carthon, Maurice NYG 44, IND 44

Cartwright, Rock WSH 40

Carty, Johndale ATL 35

Carver, Dale CLE 59

Carver, Melvin IND 30, TBB 28

Carver, Shante DAL 96/98

Carwell, Larry BUF 21, NEP 41, TEN 41

Casanega, Ken SFF 83

Casanova, Tommy CIN 37

Casares, Rick CHI 35, MIA 35, WSH 35/38

Cascadden, Chad NYJ 53

Case, Ernie zBAL 67

Case, Frank KCC 95

Case, Pete NYG 65, PHL 67

Case, Scott ATL 25, DAL 25

Case, Stoney DET 15, ARZ 15, BLT 10

Casey, Bernie STL 25, SFF 30

Casey, Tim CHI 34, DEN 51

Casey, Tom zNYY 85

Cash, Chris DET 29

Cash, John DEN 66

Cash, Keith KCC 89

Cash, Kerry CHI 84, IND 88, OAK 88

Cash, Rich ATL 89, NEP 63, STL 89

Casillas, Tony ATL 75, DAL 75, NYJ 92

Casner, Ken STL 79

Cason, Aveion DAL 23, DET 5/31, STL 82

Cason, Jim SFF 43/93, STL 41

Cason, Wendell ATL 20

Caspar, Charley GBP 20/44, PIT 21/27, xSTL 99

Casper, Dave OAK 87, MIN 44, TEN 87

Cassady, Craig NOS 23

Cassady, Hopalong DET 40, CLE 40, PHL 41

Cassara, Frank SFF 32

Cassese, Tom DEN 45

Cassiano, Dick xBKN 2

Cassidy, Ron GBP 88

Caster, Richard NYJ 88, NOS 86, TEN 88, WSH 82

Castete, Jesse CHI 22, STL 23

Castiglia, Jim PHL 31, WSH 26, zBAL 29

Castille, Jeremiah DEN 28, TBB 23

Castle, Eric SDC 44

Caston, Toby DET 50, TEN 56/90

Castor, Chris SEA 83

Catanho, Al WSH 54, NEP 54

Catano, Mark BUF 68, PIT 78

Catchings, Toney CIN 56

Cater, Greg ARZ 14, BUF 7

Caterbone, Mike MIA 81

Caterbone, Tom PHL 49

Cathcart, Royal SFF 94

Cathcart, Sam SFF 28/83/86

Catlin, Tom CLE 50/54, PHL 63

Cato, Daryl zMIA 26

Cavalli, Carmen OAK 85

Cavanaugh, Matt NEP 12, NYG 6, PHL 6, SFF 6

Caveness, Ron TEN 51

Caver, James DET 41

Caver, Quinton KCC 52, PHL 55

Cavil, Ben BLT 65

Cavil, Kwame BUF 82

Cavness, Grady ATL 32, DEN 40

Cavosie, John DET 6/50

Caylor, Lowell CLE 22

Caywood, Les NYG 4/29/?, ARZ ?, xBKN 8, xCIN 27/52

Ceasar, Curtis NYJ 88

Cecil, Chuck GBP 26, ARZ 26, TEN 26

Cefalo, Jimmy MIA 81

Celeri, Bob xDAL 17, xNYB 17

Celotto, Mario BUF 58, OAK 52, STL 41

Cemore, Tony PHL 61

Cenci, John PIT 55

Centers, Larry ARZ 37, BUF 37, NEP 31, WSH 37

Cephous, Frank NYG 31

Ceppetelli, Gene PHL 54, NYG 54

Cercone, Matt MIN 48

Ceresino, Gordy SFF 58

Cerne, Joe ATL 56, SFF 56

Cerqua, Marq CHI 49, TBB 58

Cesaire, Jacques SDC 74

Cesare, Billy DET 40, MIA 33, TBB 44

Cesario, Anthony JAX 79

Cesario, Sal DAL 79

Chadwick, Jeff DET 89, SEA 88, STL 89

Chaffey, Pat ATL 28, NYJ 28

Chalenski, Mike DET 95, MIA 70, NYJ 71, PHL 71

Chalmers, George xBKN 15/19/4

Chalrton, Ike NYG 31

Chamberlain, Byron MIN 87, DEN 86, WSH 82
Chamberlain, Dan BUF 85
Chamberlain, Garth PIT 65
Chamberlin, Frank CIN 55, TEN 57
Chamberlin, Guy ARZ 13, CHI 13/23
Chambers, Bill zNYY 43/45
Chambers, Chris MIA 84
Chambers, Rusty MIA 51, NOS 51
Chambers, Wally CHI 60, TBB 60
Chamblee, Al TBB 57
Chamblin, Corey JAX 23
Champagne, Ed STL 86
Champion, Jim xNYB 35
Chancey, Robert CHI 38, DAL 35, SDC 32
Chandler, Al ARZ 87, CIN 81, NEP 82/87
Chandler, Bob BUF 81, OAK 85
Chandler, Chris ATL 12, ARZ 17, CHI 12, IND 17, STL 17, TBB 17, TEN 12
Chandler, Don GBP 34, NYG 34
Chandler, Edgar BUF 52, NEP 50
Chandler, Jeff SFF 3
Chandler, Karl DET 66, NYG 61
Chandler, Thornton DAL 85/89
Chandler, Wes NOS 89, SDC 89, SFF 81
Chandnois, Lynn PIT 14/49
Chanoine, Roger CLE 69, JAX 69
Chantiles, Tom DET 76
Chapman, Clarence CIN 24, DET 42, NOS 24
Chapman, Doug MIN 34
Chapman, Gil NOS 89
Chapman, Lamar CLE 27
Chapman, Mike ATL 70
Chapman, Ted OAK 77
Chappell, Leon ARZ 20
Chapple, Dave BUF 6, NEP 10, STL 10
Chapple, Jack SFF 58
Chappuis, Bob zBRK 99, zCHI 99
Chapura, Dick ARZ 95, CHI 94, PHL 97
Charles, John MIN 25, NEP 25, TEN 25
Charles, Mike MIA 71, OAK 95, SDC 71, STL 79
Charlton, Clifford CLE 58
Charlton, Ike JAX 23, SEA 23
Charon, Carl BUF 43
Chase, Ben DET 44
Chase, Martin BLT 92, NOS 92, WSH 92

Chatham, Matt NEP 58
Chatman, Antonio GBP 83
Chatman, Cliff NYG 31
Chatman, Jesse SDC 24
Chatman, Ricky IND 52
Chavez, Laz MIA 92
Chavis, Eddie MIA 85
Chavous, Barney DEN 79
Chavous, Corey MIN 21, ARZ 25
Cheatham, Ernie IND 66, PIT 79/82
Cheatham, Lloyd ARZ 33/66, zNYY 60
Cheek, Louis DAL 72, GBP 78, MIA 77, PHL 75
Cheek, Richard BUF 73, TEN 57
Cheeks, B.W. TEN 22
Cheever, Michael JAX 63
Chelf, Don BUF 77
Cherne, Hal WSH 35
Cheroke, George CLE 34
Cherry, Bill GBP 69
Cherry, Deron KCC 20
Cherry, Ed ARZ 14, PIT 19
Cherry, Je'Rod NEP 30, NOS 30/37, PHL 25
Cherry, Mike NYG 18
Cherry, Raphel DET 45, WSH 37
Cherry, Stan IND 59
Cherry, Tony SFF 23
Cherundolo, Charles STL 17/21, PHL 21, PIT 21
Chesley, Al CHI 57, PHL 59
Chesley, Francis GBP 53
Chesley, John MIA 86
Chesney, Chet CHI 28
Chesser, George MIA 28/31
Chesson, Wes ATL 81, PHL 21
Chester, Larry CAR 64, IND 64, MIA 64
Chester, Raymond OAK 87/88, IND 87
Chetti, Joe BUF 46
Cheubro, Red STL 35
Cheverko, George NYG 17, WSH 18
Chevrier, Randy CIN 91, DAL 95
Cheyunski, Jim BUF 50, GBP 55, IND 59, NEP 50
Chiaverini, Darrin ATL 82, CLE 84, DAL 85
Chickerneo, John NYG 39
Chickillo, Nick ARZ 68
Chickillo, Tony NYJ 75, SDC 91
Childress, Fred CLE 77, NEP 61
Childress, Joe ARZ 35
Childress, O.J. NYG 57
Childress, Ray TEN 79, DAL 72
Childs, Clarence CHI 23, NYG 48

Childs, Henry NOS 85, ATL 88, GBP 89, STL 83
Childs, Jason CAR 76
Childs, Jim ARZ 86
Childs, John SFF 76
Childs, Ron NOS 51
Chilton, Gene ARZ 51/58, KCC 62, NEP 63
Chipley, Bill xBOS 38, xNYB 38
Chirico, John NYJ 33
Chisick, Andy ARZ 30
Chlebek, Ed NYJ 2
Chmura, Mark GBP 89
Choate, Putt GBP 57
Chobian, Max DEN 15
Choma, John SFF 60/78
Chomyszak, Steve CIN 79
Chorak, Jason IND 93
Chorovich, Dick IND 78, SDC 71
Chrebet, Wayne NYJ 80
Christensen, Erik WSH 72
Christensen, Frank DET 2
Christensen, George DET 14/25/27/47/48
Christensen, Jeff CLE 11, PHL 11
Christensen, Koester DET ?
Christensen, Todd OAK 46, NYG 41
Christenson, Marty ARZ 51
Christian, Bob ATL 44, CHI 44, CAR 44
Christiansen, Bob BUF 83
Christiansen, Jack DET 19/24
Christiansen, Jeff CIN 11
Christie, Steve BUF 2, SDC 8, TBB 2
Christman, Paul ARZ 15/44, GBP 28
Christopher, Herb KCC 41
Christopher, Ryan ARZ 36
Christopherson, Jim MIN 36
Christopherson, Ryan JAX 36
Christy, Dick NYJ 45, NEP 23, PIT 20
Christy, Earl NYJ 45
Christy, Greg BUF 69
Christy, Jeff MIN 62, TBB 62
Chryplewicz, Pete DET 81
Chukwurah, Patrick MIN 50
Chung, Eugene IND 66, JAX 69, NEP 69
Churchin, Jeff CHI 70
Churchman, Ricky SFF 33
Churchwell, Don WSH 72
Churchwell, Hansen OAK 75
Chuy, Don PHL 66, STL 62
Cibulas, Joe PIT 78
Ciccolella, Mike NYG 58
Ciccone, Ben ARZ 28, PIT 16
Cichowski, Eugene PIT 20, WSH 40
Cichowski, Tom DEN 78

Cifelli, Gus DET 70, GBP 73, PHL 77, PIT 77
Cifers, Bob DET 84, GBP 16, PIT 45
Cifers, Ed CHI 14, WSH 43
Cindrich, Ralph DEN 54, NEP 55, TEN 55
Cipa, Larry NOS 13
Cisowski, Steve DAL 77
Ciurciu, Vinny CAR 50, TBB 44
Clabo, Neil MIN 12
Clack, Darryl DAL 42
Clack, Jim NYG 56/58, PIT 50
Claiborne, Chris DET 50, MIN 55
Claiborne, Robert SDC 84, TBB 81
Clair, Frank WSH 31
Claitt, Rickey WSH 35
Clancy, Jack GBP 80, MIA 24
Clancy, Kendrick PIT 96
Clancy, Sam CLE 91, IND 76, SEA 84
Clancy, Sean ARZ 52, MIA 57
Clancy, Stu NYG 4
Clanton, Chuck GBP 23
Claphan, Sam SDC 77
Claridge, Dennis ATL 10, GBP 10
Claridge, Travis ATL 71
Clark, Al DET 21, STL 44
Clark, Algy WSH 31, PHL 21/28, xBKN 4, xCIN 1,45
Clark, Allan NEP 35, BUF 35, GBP 34
Clark, Bernard CIN 57, SEA 99
Clark, Beryl ARZ 25
Clark, Bill ARZ ?
Clark, Boobie CIN 35/42, TEN 42
Clark, Bret ATL 28
Clark, Brian DEN 78, TBB 5
Clark, Bruce NOS 75, KCC 95
Clark, Bryan CIN 11, SFF 15
Clark, Charles ARZ ?
Clark, Dallas IND 44
Clark, Dan STL 94
Clark, Danny JAX 55
Clark, Darius DEN 47
Clark, Darryl CHI 37
Clark, Derrick DEN 43
Clark, Desmond CHI 88, DEN 88, MIA 85
Clark, Dexter DET 33
Clark, Don SFF 31
Clark, Dutch DET 7/12/19
Clark, Dwight SFF 87
Clark, Ernie ARZ 59, DET 59
Clark, Gary WSH 84, ARZ 84, MIA 84
Clark, Greg CHI 98, GBP 55, MIA 51/60, SDC 59, SEA 58, STL 92

Clark, Greg SFF 85
Clark, Harry CHI 4, zCHI 87, zLAD 82
Clark, Herman CHI 65/74
Clark, Howard SDC 87
Clark, Jessie GBP 33, MIN 33, ARZ 34, DET 32
Clark, Jim PIT 27
Clark, Jim WSH 65
Clark, Jon ARZ 79, CHI 72
Clark, Kelvin DEN 73, NOS 78
Clark, Ken IND 32
Clark, Ken STL 13
Clark, Kenny MIN 89
Clark, Kevin DEN 20/27
Clark, Louis SEA 84
Clark, Mario BUF 29, SFF 29
Clark, Mike PIT 83, BUF 7, DAL 17, DAL 83, PHL 84
Clark, Mike SFF 90, TBB 90, WSH 75
Clark, Monte CLE 73, DAL 73, SFF 63
Clark, Phil CHI 39, DAL 37, NEP 22
Clark, Randy ARZ 64, ATL 66, TBB 31
Clark, Reggie JAX 59, PIT 57
Clark, Rico CIN 21, IND 27, NEP 39
Clark, Robert DET 82, MIA 81, NOS 89
Clark, Ryan NYG 39
Clark, Sedric BLT 55
Clark, Spark PIT 23
Clark, Steve BUF 36
Clark, Steve MIA 76
Clark, Steve NEP 65
Clark, Torin TBB 22
Clark, Vinnie ATL 27, GBP 25, JAX 27, NOS 29
Clark, Wayne DET 61
Clark, Wayne CIN 11, KCC 13, SDC 13
Clark, Willie SDC 31
Clarke, Frank CLE 82, DAL 82
Clarke, Hagood BUF 45
Clarke, Ken MIN 71, PHL 71, SEA 67
Clarke, Leon STL 84, CLE 81, MIN 81
Clarke, Phil NOS 51
Clarks, Conrad IND 35
Clarkson, Stuart CHI 31/36
Clasby, Bob ARZ 79
Clatt, Corwin ARZ 67
Clatterbuck, Bobby NYG 12, SDC 19
Clavelle, Shannon GBP 91
Clay, Billy WSH 32
Clay, Boyd STL 21/43
Clay, Hayward DAL 83, STL 81
Clay, John OAK 78, SDC 77
Clay, Ozzie WSH 28

Clay, Randy NYG 12
Clay, Roy NYG 21
Clay, Walt zCHI 85, zLAD 80/76
Clay, Willie DET 32, NEP 32, NOS 42, PHL 25
Clayborn, Raymond NEP 26, CLE 26
Claybrooks, Devone SFF 92, CLE 79, TBB 93
Claybrooks, Felipe CLE 74/91
Claypool, Ralph ARZ 10/30
Clayton, Dan ATL 74
Clayton, Harvey NYG 21, PIT 33
Clayton, Mark MIA 83, GBP 83
Clayton, Ralph ARZ 86
Clayton, Stan NEP 76
Cleary, Paul zCHI 53, zNYY 57
Cleeland, Cam NEP 87, STL 87, NOS 85
Clemens, Bob GBP 33/35, IND 48
Clemens, Cal GBP 33
Clemens, Ray GBP 46
Clement, Anthony ARZ 65
Clement, Henry PIT 28
Clement, Johnny PIT 0, ARZ 23, zCHI 72
Clements, Chuck NYJ 7
Clements, Nate BUF 22
Clements, Tom KCC 2
Clements, Vince NYG 29
Clemons, Charlie HOU 50, NOS 56, STL 56
Clemons, Craig CHI 25/43/45
Clemons, Duane CIN 92, KCC 99, MIN 92
Clemons, Michael KCC 46
Clemons, Ray DET 55
Clemons, Topper PHL 27
Clendenen, Mike DEN 15
Cleveland, Greg MIA 61
Clifton, Chad GBP 76
Clifton, Gregory WSH 31
Clifton, Kyle NYJ 59
Cline, Doug SDC 58, TEN 31
Cline, Jackie DET 94, MIA 98, PIT 95/96
Cline, Ollie CLE 70, DET 33, zBUF 70
Cline, Tony BUF 86/88, OAK 84, PIT 48, SFF 82/84
Clinkscale, Dextor DAL 47, IND 47
Clinkscales, Joey PIT 88, TBB 83
Clinton, Charles TEN 24
Cloud, Jack GBP 82, WSH 34
Cloud, Mike KCC 34, NEP 21
Cloutier, Dave NEP 28
Clowes, John xNYB 21, zBRK 45, zCHI 46
Clune, Don NYG 88, SEA 88

Coady, Rich CHI 37/52, STL
25/38, TEN 29
Coakley, Dexter DAL 52
Coan, Bert KCC 23, SDC 26
Coates, Ben NEP 87, BLT 81
Coates, Ray NYG 49
Coates, Sherrod CLE 56
Coats, Tony CIN 61
Cobb, Bob STL 97
Cobb, Garry DAL 59, DET
53/63, PHL 50
Cobb, Marvin CIN 24, MIN 26,
PIT 25
Cobb, Mike CHI 87, CIN 89
Cobb, Reggie GBP 32, JAX 34,
NYJ 28, TBB 33/34
Cobb, Robert MIN 63, TBB 67
Cobb, Tom ARZ ?
Cobbins, Lyron ARZ 51
Cobble, Eric TEN 35
Cobbs, Duffy NEP 43
Cobourne, Avon DET 31
Cochran, Antonio SEA 78/90
Cochran, John ARZ 24
Cochran, Mark SFF 66/76
Cochran, Tom WSH 26
Cochrane, Kelly TEN 16
Cockrell, Gene NYJ 70
Cockroft, Don CLE 12
Cocozzo, Joe SDC 68
Coder, Ron ARZ 61, SEA 60
Codie, Nakia PIT 24
Cody, Bill DET 52, NOS 66,
PHL 66
Cody, Ed CHI 16, GBP 17
Cody, Mac ARZ 82
Cody, Tay SDC 27
Cofer, Joe WSH 36
Cofer, Michael DET 55/66
Cofer, Mike IND 3, NOS 4, SFF
6
Coffee, Jim ARZ 20
Coffey, Don DEN 26
Coffey, Junior ATL 34, GBP 41,
NYG 34
Coffey, Ken WSH 48
Coffey, Wayne NEP 83
Coffield, Randy NYG 59, SEA
52
Coffman, Paul GBP 82, KCC
84, MIN 89
Cofield, Tim BUF 90, KCC 54,
NYJ 50
Cogdill, Gail DET 89, ATL 15,
IND 80
Coghill, George DEN 48
Cohen, Abe NEP 62
Coia, Angelo ATL 48, CHI 46,
WSH 48
Cokely, Will BUF 92
Colavito, Steve PHL 58
Colbert, Danny SDC 46
Colbert, Darrell KCC 81

Colbert, Lewis KCC 5, SDC 5
Colbert, Rondy ARZ 26, NYG
26/35, NYG 35
Colchico, Dan NOS 86, SFF 86
Colclough, Jim NEP 81
Cole, Chris DEN 81/84
Cole, Eddie DET 50
Cole, Emerson CHI 31, CLE
30/70
Cole, Fred SDC 66
Cole, John PHL 37
Cole, Larry DAL 63
Cole, Lee TEN 39
Cole, Linzy BUF 26, CHI 25,
TEN 87
Cole, Pete NYG 36/55
Cole, Robin PIT 56, NYJ 90
Cole, Terry IND 34, MIA 31,
PIT 30
Colella, Thomas STL 34, CLE
92, DET 46, zBUF 88
Coleman, Al CIN 23, MIN 37,
PHL 8
Coleman, Andre PIT 19/83,
SDC 83, SEA 11
Coleman, Anthony DAL 41
Coleman, Ben ARZ 62, JAX 62,
SDC 62, WSH 62
Coleman, Charles NYG 83
Coleman, Chris TEN 80
Coleman, Clarence BUF 85
Coleman, Cosey TBB 60
Coleman, Dan MIN 91
Coleman, Dennis NEP 53
Coleman, Don NOS 55
Coleman, Eric NEP 22
Coleman, Fred BUF 85, NEP 84
Coleman, Greg CLE 9, MIN 8,
WSH 15
Coleman, Herb zBAL 22/29,
zCHI 25/31
Coleman, KaRon DEN 21/46
Coleman, Kenyon DAL 93,
OAK 90
Coleman, Keo GBP 54, NYJ
99
Coleman, Leonard IND 31/47,
SDC 31
Coleman, Lincoln DAL 44
Coleman, Marco WSH 99, JAX
91, MIA 90, SDC 90
Coleman, Marcus HOU 42,
NYJ 42
Coleman, Monte WSH 51
Coleman, Pat NEP 47, TEN 87
Coleman, Ralph DAL 86
Coleman, Roderick OAK 57
Coleman, Ronnie TEN 47
Coleman, Sidney ARZ 93, TBB
50/53
Coleman, Steve DEN 76
Coleman, Travis CHI 39
Coles, Laveranues WSH 80, NYJ
87
Coley, James CHI 89, IND 87

Colhouer, Jake ARZ 55, NYG
63
Colinet, Stalin CLE 93, MIN
93/99
Collett, Elmer SFF 66, IND 66
Collie, Bruce PHL 69, SFF 69
Collier, Bob STL 72
Collier, Ervin CHI 93
Collier, Floyd SFF 48
Collier, Jim NYG 89, WSH 89
Collier, Mike BUF 35, PIT 44
Collier, Reggie DAL 10, PIT 7
Collier, Steve GBP 64/70/74/92
Collier, Tim ARZ 44, KCC 37,
SFF 47
Collins, Andre CHI 52, CIN 55,
DET 53, WSH 55
Collins, Bill xBOS 65
Collins, Bobby ATL 80, BUF
84, GBP 87
Collins, Brett GBP 55, STL 54
Collins, Calvin ATL 68, MIN
65
Collins, Cecil MIA 34
Collins, Clarence ARZ 84
Collins, Dan DAL 64
Collins, Dwight MIN 84
Collins, Fabray MIN 59
Collins, Gary CLE 86
Collins, George ARZ 66
Collins, Gerald CIN 90
Collins, Glen CIN 76, SFF 79
Collins, Greg BUF 50, SEA 50,
SFF 55
Collins, Javiar DAL 70
Collins, Jerald BUF 51
Collins, Jim STL 50, SDC 55
Collins, Kerry CAR 12, NOS 13,
NYG 5
Collins, Kirk STL 42
Collins, Larry CLE 23, NOS
43
Collins, Mark GBP 26, KCC 25,
NYG 25, SEA 25
Collins, Mike BLT 63
Collins, Mo OAK 79
Collins, Patrick GBP 25
Collins, Paul ARZ 24
Collins, Ray SFF 72/43, KCC 71,
NYG 71
Collins, Rip GBP 65/88, xBAL
88, zCHI 71
Collins, Rip WSH 32
Collins, Roosevelt MIA 52
Collins, Ryan BLT 49, CLE 88
Collins, Shane WSH 91
Collins, Shawn ATL 85, CLE
80, GBP 81, TBB 89
Collins, Sonny ATL 41
Collins, Todd BUF 15, KCC 15
Collins, Todd NEP 54/59, STL
54
Collins, Tony NEP 33, MIA 34
Collins, Trent NYJ 44
Collinsworth, Cris CIN 80

Collons, Ferric NEP 92, OAK 92
Colman, Doug CLE 59, NYG 58, TEN 59
Colman, Wayne NOS 59, PHL 49
Colmer, Mickey zBRK 81/72, zNYY 73
Colo, Don CLE 70, xBAL 45, xDAL 77, xNYB 36
Colon, Harry DET 21/29, JAX 24, NEP 40
Colorito, Tony DEN 69
Colquitt, Craig IND 5, PIT 5
Colquitt, Jim SEA 5
Colston, Tim CAR 90
Colter, Jeff KCC 48, MIN 43
Colteryahn, Lloyd IND 87
Colton, George NEP 63
Colvin, Jim DAL 77, IND 67/75, NYG 72
Colvin, Rosevelt CHI 59, NEP 59
Colzie, Neal MIA 20, OAK 20, TBB 20
Combs, Chris ARZ 80
Combs, Chris JAX 96, PIT 73
Combs, Derek GBP 45, OAK 43
Combs, William PHL 82
Comeaux, Darren DEN 59, SEA 53, SFF 56/59
Comella, Greg HOU 45, NYG 34, TEN 33
Comer, Marty zBUF 52/53
Commisa, Vince xBOS 31
Commiskey, Chuck NOS 66
Comp, Irv GBP 51
Compagno, Tony PIT 44
Compton, Chuck GBP 41
Compton, Dick DET 20, PIT 45, TEN 20
Compton, Mike DET 74/77, NEP 77
Compton, Ogden ARZ 17
Comstock, Ed xBKN 6
Comstock, Rudy NYG 9, GBP 32
Conaty, Bill BUF 63
Concannon, Jack CHI 11, DET 10, GBP 10, PHL 3
Concannon, Rick WSH 28
Condit, Merl WSH 44, PIT 1, xBKN 35
Condon, Tom KCC 65, NEP 63
Condren, Glen ATL 88, NYG 70/83
Cone, Fred DAL 31, GBP 31/66
Conerly, Charlie NYG 42
Conger, Mel zBRK 56, zNYY 52
Conjar, Larry CLE 35, IND 48, PHL 25
Conklin, Cary SFF 6, WSH 12
Conkright, Bill CHI 47, STL 37, WSH 38, xBKN 37
Conlan, Shane BUF 58, STL 56

Conlee, Gerry STL 17, DET 52, SFF 22
Conley, Steve ARZ 47, CIN 38
Conley, Steven IND 59, PIT 53
Conlin, Chris IND 66, MIA 67
Conlin, Ray PHL 91
Conn, Dick NEP 22, PIT 22
Connell, Albert WSH 83, NOS 83
Connell, Mike SFF 10, WSH 10
Connelly, Mike DAL 53/54, PIT 52
Conner, Clyde SFF 86/88
Conner, Darion ATL 56, NOS 58, CAR 56, PHL 93
Conners, Dan OAK 55/60
Connolly, Harry zBRK 93
Connolly, Ted SFF 64/65, CLE 64
Connor, George CHI 71/81
Conoly, Bill ARZ 63
Conover, Frank CLE 94
Conover, Scott DET 76
Conrad, Bobby Joe ARZ 40, DAL 40
Conrad, Chris PIT 78
Conrad, J.R. NYJ 64
Conti, Enio PHL 51/67, PIT 67
Contoulis, John NYG 77
Contz, Bill CLE 75, NOS 70
Conway, Brett CLE 5, NYG 9, NYJ 1, OAK 5, WSH 5
Conway, Curtis CHI 80, NYJ 81, SDC 80
Conway, Dave GBP 35
Conwell, Ernie NOS 85, STL 45/84
Conwell, Joe PHL 79
Conzelman, Jim CHI 1/15
Cook, Anthony TEN 78, WSH 75
Cook, Charles NYG 74
Cook, Damion BLT 72
Cook, Dave ARZ 26, xBKN 22
Cook, Ed ARZ 75, ATL 75
Cook, Fred IND 72
Cook, Gene DET 88
Cook, Greg CIN 12
Cook, Jameel TBB 43
Cook, Kelly GBP 20
Cook, Kevin SEA 14
Cook, Leon PHL 72
Cook, Marv NEP 46/85, CHI 86, STL 47
Cook, Michael ARZ 62
Cook, Rashard PHL 42
Cook, Ted DET 20, GBP 48
Cook, Toi NOS 41, SFF 41, CAR 41
Cooke, Bill DET 72, GBP 78, SEA 67, SFF 76
Cooke, Ed MIA 80, CHI 80, DEN 80, IND 85, NYJ 82, PHL 86

Cooks, Johnie IND 98, NYG 98, CLE 99
Cooks, Kerry GBP 45
Cooks, Rayford TEN 98
Cooks, Terrence NEP 58
Coolbaugh, Bob OAK 43
Coombs, Larry NOS 57
Coombs, Tom NYJ 88
Coomer, Joe ARZ 50, PIT 24/56/82
Coon, Ty xBKN 8
Cooney, Mark GBP 58
Coons, Robert BUF 87
Cooper, Adrian MIN 87, PIT 87, SFF 49
Cooper, Andre DEN 81
Cooper, Bert TBB 56
Cooper, Bill SFF 34/35
Cooper, Bud STL 2
Cooper, Chris OAK 75
Cooper, Deke CAR 35, JAX 35
Cooper, Earl OAK 49, SFF 49/89
Cooper, Evan ATL 20, PHL 21
Cooper, George SFF 52
Cooper, Hal DET 18
Cooper, Jarrod CAR 40
Cooper, Jim DAL 61
Cooper, Jim zBRK 20
Cooper, Joe NYG 3, TEN 8
Cooper, Ken xBAL 33, zBAL 33
Cooper, Louis KCC 55, MIA 50, PHL 52
Cooper, Mark DEN 63, TBB 71
Cooper, Norm xBKN 25/23
Cooper, Rafael DET 23
Cooper, Reggie DAL 93
Cooper, Richard NOS 71, PHL 77
Cooper, Sam PIT 24
Cooper, Scott CLE 93
Cooper, Stephen SDC 54
Cooper, Thurlow NYJ 88
Cope, Frank NYG 1/36
Cope, Jim ATL 51
Copeland, Anthony WSH 57
Copeland, Danny KCC 25, WSH 26
Copeland, Horace OAK 80, TBB 88/89
Copeland, Jim CLE 64
Copeland, John CIN 92
Copeland, Ron CHI 36
Copeland, Russell BUF 16/85, GBP 16, PHL 86
Coppage, Al ARZ 54, CLE 53/59, zBUF 54
Coppens, Gus NYG 78
Corbett, George CHI 5
Corbett, Jim CIN 81
Corbett, Steve NEP 62
Corbitt, Don WSH 54
Corbo, Thomas STL 19
Corcoran, Jim NEP 15

Cordileone, Lou NOS 79, NYG 74, PIT 74, SFF 74, STL 51
Cordill, Oliver STL 1
Cordill, Ollie ATL 48, NOS 44, SDC 44
Corey, Walt KCC 56
Corgan, Chuck NYG 10
Corgan, Mike DET 17
Corker, John GBP 53, TEN 57
Corley, Anthony PIT 40, SDC 31
Corley, Bert zBUF 23
Corley, Chris SEA 84
Corley, Elbert zBAL 22
Cormier, Joe OAK 95
Corn, Joe STL 25
Cornelison, Jerry KCC 74
Cornelius, Charles MIA 44, SFF 28
Cornell, Bo BUF 30, CLE 33
Cornelson, Martin NYJ 64
Cornish, Frank BUF 75, CHI 73, CIN 76, DAL 68, JAX 63, MIA 71, MIN 63, PHL 68, SDC 63
Cornwell, Fred DAL 85
Coronado, Bob PIT 46
Corral, Frank STL 3
Correal, Chuck ATL 53/61
Corrington, Kip DEN 25
Corsetti, Rico NEP 93
Cortes, Julio SEA 56
Cortez, Bruce NOS 47
Cortez, Jose MIN 1, NYG 2, SFF 6, WSH 8
Corvino, Anthony NYJ 67
Coryatt, Quentin DAL 57, IND 55
Corzine, Red NYG 17/33, xCIN 3,42, xSTL 70
Cosbie, Doug DAL 84
Cosgrove, Thomas PIT 6
Coslett, Bruce CIN 88
Cosner, Don ARZ 29
Coss, Eric NYJ 62
Costa, Dave DEN 63, BUF 64/73, OAK 46, SDC 64
Costa, Paul BUF 79/82
Costello, Brad CIN 6
Costello, Joe ATL 56, OAK 94
Costello, Tom NYG 83
Costello, Vince CLE 50, NYG 57
Costict, Ray NEP 55
Coston, Zed PHL 23
Cota, Chad IND 37, NOS 37, STL 37, CAR 37
Cothran, Jeff CIN 29/46
Cothren, Paige PHL 45, STL 36
Cotney, Mark TBB 33, TEN 33
Cotton, Barney ARZ 60, CIN 70
Cotton, Craig CHI 80, DET 87, SDC 88
Cotton, Fest CLE 77

Cotton, Kenyon BLT 23
Cotton, Marcus ATL 51, CLE 58, SEA 51
Cotton, Russell PIT 10
Cottrell, Bill DEN 66, DET 52
Cottrell, Dana NEP 45
Cottrell, Ted ATL 51
Couch, Tim CLE 2
Coulter, Tex NYG 39/79
Counts, Johnny NYG 48
Couppee, Al WSH 15
Courson, Steve PIT 77, TBB 72
Courtney, Gerry xBKN 31
Courtney, Matt SFF 45
Courville, Vince DAL 44/81
Cousin, Terry ATL 24, CAR 21, CHI 21/24, MIA 21
Cousineau, Tom CLE 50, SFF 57/59
Cousino, Brad CIN 52, NYG 57, PIT 60
Cousins, Jomo ARZ 92
Coutre, Larry GBP 27, IND 24
Covert, Jim CHI 74
Covington, Damien BUF 57
Covington, Jamie NYG 29
Covington, John IND 39, NOS 39
Covington, Scott CIN 4, STL 4
Covington, Tony SEA 27, TBB 25
Cowan, Bob CLE 80, zBAL 83
Cowan, Charlie STL 73
Cowan, Larry ARZ 37, MIA 43, NEP 44
Cowan, Les CHI 89
Cowart, Sam BUF 56, NYJ 56
Cowher, Bill CLE 53, PHL 57
Cowhig, Jerry ARZ 9, PHL 36, STL 9
Cowlings, Al BUF 82, SEA 72, SFF 79, STL 70, TEN 76
Cowne, John WSH 54
Cowsette, Delbert WSH 91
Cox, Aaron IND 80, STL 84
Cox, Arthur ATL 88, CLE 83, MIA 88, SDC 88
Cox, Billy WSH 14/40
Cox, Bryan MIA 51, CHI 52, NEP 51, NOS 51, NYJ 51
Cox, Fred MIN 14
Cox, Greg NYG 38, SFF 38
Cox, James SFF 32
Cox, Jim MIA 83
Cox, Larry DEN 66/77
Cox, Norm zCHI 65
Cox, Renard JAX 36
Cox, Ron CHI 54, GBP 54
Cox, Steve CLE 15, WSH 12
Cox, Tom STL 72
Coyle, Eric WSH 56
Coyle, Ross STL 43
Crabb, Claude PHL 23, STL 49, WSH 23
Crable, Bob NYJ 50

Crabtree, Clem DET 13/72
Crabtree, Eric CIN 10, DEN 41, NEP 10
Craddock, Nate IND 32
Craft, Donnie TEN 40
Craft, Jason JAX 29
Craft, Russ PHL 33, PIT 24/40
Crafts, Jerry BUF 66, PHL 66/73
Craig, Dameyune CAR 2
Craig, Dobie OAK 42, TEN 89
Craig, Larry GBP 54
Craig, Neal BUF 42, CLE 42/49, CIN 34
Craig, Paco DET 9
Craig, Reggie BUF 86, CLE 90, KCC 80
Craig, Roger SFF 33, MIN 33, OAK 22
Craig, Steve MIN 84
Crain, Milt xBOS 23
Crakes, Joe xCIN 48
Crane, Dennis NYG 74, WSH 79
Crane, Gary DEN 68
Crane, Paul NYJ 56
Crangle, John ARZ 6
Crangle, Mike NOS 75
Crass, Bill ARZ 38
Craven, Bill CLE 23
Craver, Aaron DEN 29, MIA 32/34/44, NOS 32, SDC 34
Craver, Keyuo NOS 29/43
Crawford, Bill NYG 60
Crawford, Casey CAR 84
Crawford, Charles PHL 45
Crawford, Derrick SFF 83
Crawford, Ed NYG 21
Crawford, Elbert NEP 65
Crawford, Fred CHI 14
Crawford, Hilton BUF 45
Crawford, James CHI 27
Crawford, Jim NEP 30
Crawford, Keith GBP 45, KCC 41, NYG 15/85, STL 20
Crawford, Mike CLE 47, MIA 56
Crawford, Rufus SEA 34
Crawford, Tim CLE 55
Crawford, Vernon NEP 99
Crayne, Dick xBKN 15/3
Creech, Bob NOS 55, PHL 58
Creekmur, Lou DET 76
Cregar, Bill PIT 73
Creighton, Milan ARZ 24, ARZ 25
Cremer, Ted DET 21/85, GBP 18
Crennel, Carl PIT 31
Crenshaw, Leon GBP 70
Crenshaw, Willis ARZ 33, DEN 33
Crespino, Bob CLE 42, NYG 89
Creswell, Smiley PHL 92

Crews, Ron CLE 93
Crews, Terry PHL 54, SDC 51, STL 94, WSH 90
Cribbs, James DET 99
Cribbs, Joe BUF 20, IND 30, MIA 20, SFF 28
Crimmins, Bernie GBP 76
Crisler, Hal WSH 55, xBAL 56, xBOS 24
Crisman, Joel TBB 68
Criss, Shad JAX 27
Crissy, Cris WSH 28
Crist, Chuck NOS 44, NYG 24, SFF 24
Criswell, Jeff IND 62, KCC 69, NYJ 61/69
Criswell, Kirby ARZ 63
Criswell, Ray TBB 13
Critchfield, Larry PIT 34
Criter, Ken DEN 53/78
Crittenden, Ray NEP 81, SDC 84
Crittendon, John ARZ 86
Crocicchia, Jim NYG 9
Crocker, Chris CLE 25
Crockett, Bobby BUF 83
Crockett, Henri ATL 94, MIN 52
Crockett, Monte BUF 80
Crockett, Ray DEN 39, DET 39, KCC 39
Crockett, Willis DAL 90
Crockett, Zack IND 32, JAX 34, OAK 32
Croel, Mike BLT 51, DEN 51, NYG 51, SEA 90
Croft, Abe CHI 12
Croft, Don BUF 72, DET 79
Croft, Milburn GBP 75
Croft, Win PIT 30, xBKN 15/16
Croftcheck, Don CHI 61, WSH 54
Cromwell, Nolan STL 21
Cronan, Peter SEA 57, WSH 54
Cronin, Bill MIA 90, PHL 87
Cronin, Gene DAL 85, DET 68/85, WSH 85
Cronin, Jerry xBKN ?
Cronkhite, Doc xBKN 6
Croom, Corey NEP 26
Croom, Sylvester NOS 51
Crooms, Chris STL 25
Cropper, Marsh PIT 89
Crosby, Cleveland IND 73
Crosby, Clifton IND 31
Crosby, Phil BUF 41
Crosby, Ron NOS 51, NYJ 55
Crosby, Steve NYG 33
Cross, Bill ARZ 20
Cross, Bob ARZ 71, CHI 76, NEP 77, SFF 78, STL 57/73
Cross, Howard NYG 87
Cross, Irv PHL 27, STL 27
Cross, Jeff MIA 91

Cross, Justin BUF 63/78
Cross, Randy SFF 51/62
Crossan, Dave WSH 57
Crosswhite, Leon DET 35
Croston, Dave GBP 60
Crotty, Jim BUF 25/46, WSH 22
Crouch, Terry IND 75
Croudip, David ATL 30, SDC 28, STL 28
Crouse, Ray GBP 21
Crouthamel, Jake NEP 34
Crow, Albert NEP 72
Crow, John David ARZ 44, SFF 44
Crow, Lindon NYG 41, ARZ 40, STL 41
Crow, Orien WSH 23
Crow, Wayne BUF 22, OAK 22
Crowder, Earl ARZ 13, STL 40
Crowder, Randy MIA 74, TBB 71
Crowe, Larry ATL 25, PHL 47
Crowe, Paul SFF 92, xNYB 3
Crowell, Angelo BUF 55
Crowell, Germane DET 82
Crowell, Odis SFF 45
Crowl, Dick xBKN ?
Crowley, Jim GBP ?
Crowley, Joe xBOS 15
Croyle, Phil BUF 54, TEN 59
Crudup, Derrick OAK 23
Crum, Bob ARZ 65
Crump, Dwayne ARZ 26
Crump, Harry NEP 31
Crumpler, Alge ATL 83
Crumpler, Carlester MIN 87, SEA 48/87
Crusan, Doug MIA 77
Crutcher, Tommy Joe GBP 37/56, NYG 56
Crutchfield, Buddy NYJ 36, WSH 41
Crutchfield, Darrel PHL 29
Crutchfield, Dwayne NYJ 45, STL 45
Cryder, Bob NEP 75, SEA 78
Csonka, Larry MIA 39, NYG 39
Cuba, Paul PHL 21/23
Cudzik, Walt BUF 53, NEP 54/56, WSH 54
Cuff, Ward NYG 14, ARZ 14, GBP 21
Culbreath, Jim GBP 31, NYG 29, PHL 32
Cullars, Willie PHL 75
Cullity, Dave SFF 68
Cullom, Jim xNYB 24
Cullors, Derrick NEP 29
Culp, Curley KCC 61, TEN 78, DET 77
Culpepper, Brad CHI 76, MIN 77/77, TBB 73
Culpepper, Daunte MIN 11/12

Culpepper, Ed ARZ 73, MIN 71, TEN 78
Culpepper, Willie TBB 81
Culver, Al CHI 27/70, GBP 54
Culver, Rodney IND 35, SDC 22/35
Cumby, George BUF 58, GBP 52, PHL 91
Cumisky, Frank xBKN 13
Cummings, Ed DEN 54, NYJ 62
Cummings, Joe BUF 51, SDC 51
Cummings, Mack NYG 19
Cundiff, Billy DAL 3
Cuneo, Ernie xBKN 11
Cuningham, Harold CHI 14
Cuningham, Rick OAK 68
Cunningham, Bennie PIT 89
Cunningham, Carl DEN 50, NOS 60
Cunningham, Dick BUF 62/63, PHL 51, TEN 49
Cunningham, Doug MIN 89
Cunningham, Doug SFF 42, WSH 40
Cunningham, Ed ARZ 59/79, SEA 79
Cunningham, Eric NYJ 68
Cunningham, Jay NEP 21
Cunningham, Jim WSH 30
Cunningham, Leon DET 57
Cunningham, Pat IND 72
Cunningham, Randall PHL 12, BLT 1, DAL 7, MIN 7
Cunningham, Richie DAL 3, JAX 7, CAR 3
Cunningham, Rick ARZ 64, MIN 67
Cunningham, Sam NEP 39
Cunningham, T.J. SEA 21
Cuozzo, Gary ARZ 15, IND 15, MIN 15, NOS 15
Cupp, Keith CIN 72
Cuppoletti, Bree ARZ 47, PHL 37
Curchin, Jeff BUF 73
Curcillo, Tony ARZ 39
Curcio, Mike GBP 57, PHL 57
Cure, Armand zBAL ?
Cureton, Will CLE 16
Curly, August DET 50
Curran, Harry ARZ 15
Curran, Pat SDC 82
Curran, Willie ATL 89
Current, Mike DEN 74, MIA 71/79, TBB 74
Currie, Dan GBP 58, STL 58
Currie, Herschel ARZ 24
Currier, Bill NEP 28, NYG 29, TEN 20
Currivan, Don ARZ 18/54, PIT 63, STL 34, xBOS 29/34
Curry, Bill IND 50, GBP 50, STL 55, TEN 50
Curry, Buddy ATL 50

Curry, Craig IND 45, TBB 31
Curry, DeMarcus TBB 76
Curry, Donte WSH 57, DET 55
Curry, Eric JAX 75, TBB 75
Curry, Ivory TBB 31
Curry, Julius DET 44
Curry, Ronald OAK 1/89
Curry, Roy PIT 25
Curry, Scott GBP 61
Curry, Shane IND 91
Curtis, Bobby WSH 90
Curtis, Canute CIN 98
Curtis, Isaac CIN 85
Curtis, Kevin STL 83
Curtis, Mike IND 32, SEA 32, WSH 32
Curtis, Scott DEN 58, PHL 91
Curtis, Tom IND 25
Curtis, Travis ARZ 20, MIN 49, NYJ 49, WSH 37/48
Curzon, Harry ARZ 15
Cushing, Matt PIT 48/80
Cusick, Pete NEP 76
Cuthbert, Randy PIT 42
Cutsinger, Gary TEN 53/80
Cvercko, Andy CLE 63, DAL 62, GBP 62/67, WSH 67
Cyre, Hector GBP 3
Czarobski, Ziggy zCHI 45
Daanen, Jerry ARZ 31/41
Dabney, Carlton ATL 79
Dach, Carson NYG 57
D'Addido, Dave DET 44
Daddio, Bill ARZ 32, zBUF 55
Daffer, Ted CHI 64
Dafney, Bernard ARZ 75, BLT 72, MIN 71/75, PIT 72
Daft, Kevin SFF 17, TEN 13
D'Agostino, Frank NYJ 61, PHL 66
D'Agostino, Lou NYJ 27
Dahl, Bob CLE 72, WSH 75
Dahms, Tom ARZ 71, GBP 78, SFF 70, STL 21/71
Daigle, Anthony PIT 23
Dailey, Casey NYJ 49
Dailey, Ted PIT 22
Dalby, Dave OAK 50
Dale, Carroll GBP 84, MIN 84, STL 81
Dale, Jeffery SDC 37
Dale, Roland WSH 82
Daley, Bill zBRK 71, zCHI 71, zMIA ?, zNYY 73
Dallafior, Ken DET 67, SDC 61
Dalman, Chris SFF 50/67
D'Alonzo, Pete DET 16/39
Dalton, Antico MIN 50, NEP 93
Dalton, Lionel BLT 91, DEN 94, WSH 95
Dalton, Oakley NOS 69
Daluiso, Brad ATL 5, BUF 5, DEN 5, NYG 3

D'Amato, Mike NYJ 47
Damiani, Frank NYG 49
Damkroger, Maury NEP 51
Damore, John CHI 50
Dancewicz, Boley xBOS 22
Danelo, Joe BUF 18, GBP 18, NYG 18
Danenhauer, Eldon DEN 75
Danenhauer, William DEN 76, NEP 77
Daney, George KCC 60
Daniel, Eugene BLT 30, IND 38
Daniel, Ken IND 23, NYG 24
Daniel, Robert CAR 72
Daniel, Tim DAL 81
Daniel, Wlllie STL 46
Daniell, Av GBP 23, xBKN 14
Daniell, Jim CHI 99, CLE 40
Daniels, Bill PIT 44
Daniels, Calvin KCC 50, WSH 56
Daniels, Clem OAK 36, KCC 36, SFF 33/34
Daniels, David OAK 75
Daniels, David SEA 36/88
Daniels, Dexter BLT 53
Daniels, Dick CHI 23, DAL 21/45
Daniels, Jerome ARZ 72
Daniels, LeShun MIN 69
Daniels, Phillip CHI 93, SEA 93
Danielson, Gary CLE 18, DET 16
Danjean, Ernie GBP 64
Danmeier, Rick MIN 7
Danowski, Ed NYG 22
Dantzler, Woody ATL 30
Dar Dar, Kirby MIA 15/80/87
Darby, Al TEN 87, SEA 89, TBB 82
Darby, Byron DET 94, IND 72, PHL 94
Darby, Chartric TBB 91
Darby, Matt ARZ 43, BUF 43
Darby, Paul NYJ 84
Darche, Jean-Philippe SEA 52
Dardar, Ramsey ARZ 62
Darden, Thom CLE 27
Darden, Tony MIN 25, SDC 27
Darius, Donovan JAX 20
Darkins, Chris GBP 44
Darling, Boob GBP 17/29
Darling, James ARZ 51, NYJ 51, PHL 57
Darnell, Bill MIA 42
Darns, Phil TBB 75
Darragh, Dan BUF 10
Darre, Bernie WSH 67
Darrington, Chris TEN 85
Darrow, Barry CLE 63
Darwin, Matt PHL 78
Daugherty, Bob SFF 29
Daugherty, Dick STL 50/54/67
Daugherty, Ron MIN 82
Daukas, Lou zBRK 24

Daukas, Nick zBRK 42/40
Daum, Mitch TEN 88
Davenport, Bill GBP 16
Davenport, Charles PIT 80
Davenport, Joe Dean IND 49/80
Davenport, Najeh GBP 44
Davenport, Ron MIA 30
Davey, Don GBP 99, JAX 92
Davey, Rohan NEP 6
David, Bob STL 77, zCHI 32
David, Jim DET 25
David, Stan BUF 59
Davidds-Garrido, Norberto ARZ 64, CAR 76
Davidson, Ben OAK 83, GBP 72, WSH 75
Davidson, Bill PIT 12
Davidson, Chy NYJ 88
Davidson, Cotton KCC 19, OAK 19, IND 18/19/21
Davidson, Greg TEN 66
Davidson, Jeff DEN 62, NOS 76
Davidson, Joe ARZ 12
Davidson, Kenny CIN 96, PIT 64, TEN 90
Davidson, Pete TEN 71
Davis, Al PHL 43
Davis, Andra CLE 54
Davis, Andre CLE 87
Davis, Andre JAX 77
Davis, Andy WSH 26
Davis, Anthony BLT 56, GBP 50, KCC 50, SEA 50
Davis, Anthony STL 23, TBB 28
Davis, Antone ATL 76, PHL 77/78
Davis, Art CHI 70/78, PIT 44/45
Davis, Ben CLE 28, DET 29
Davis, Bill ARZ 57, xBKN 57, zMIA 47
Davis, Billy ARZ 55
Davis, Billy BLT 86, DAL 87
Davis, Bob NOS 15, NYJ 15, TEN 12
Davis, Bob PHL 27, STL 10, xBOS 10/59
Davis, Brad ATL 47
Davis, Brian MIN 34, SDC 31, SEA 34, SEA 36, WSH 34
Davis, Bruce CLE 85, SDC 83
Davis, Bruce OAK 79, TEN 77
Davis, Cedric ARZ 21
Davis, Charlie ARZ 76, PIT 77
Davis, Charlie CIN 26, TBB 26
Davis, Chris NYG 95
Davis, Chris SEA 35
Davis, Clarence OAK 28
Davis, Darrell NYJ 98
Davis, Dave GBP 47, NOS 86, PIT 85
Davis, Dexter ARZ 21/48, STL 29

Davis, Dick CLE 36, DEN 32, NOS 36
Davis, Dick KCC 86
Davis, Domanick HOU 37
Davis, Don NYG 76
Davis, Don NEP 51, NOS 53, STL 58, TBB 58
Davis, Donnie DAL 89, TEN 84
Davis, Dorsett DEN 96
Davis, Doug MIN 71
Davis, Elgin NEP 40
Davis, Eric SFF 24/25, CAR 25, DEN 25, DET 26
Davis, Fred CHI 24, WSH 17
Davis, Fred SEA 31
Davis, Gaines NYG 29
Davis, Gary MIA 27, TBB 28
Davis, Glenn DET 87
Davis, Glenn STL 41
Davis, Greg ARZ 5, ATL 5, MIN 5, NEP 5, SDC 7, TBB 8
Davis, Harper CHI 19, GBP 25, zLAD 88
Davis, Harrison SDC 87
Davis, Henry PIT 53, NYG 66
Davis, Isaac MIN 63, NOS 73, SDC 73
Davis, Jack DEN 62
Davis, Jack NEP 65
Davis, James DET 52
Davis, James OAK 45
Davis, Jeff TBB 58
Davis, Jerome DET 98
Davis, Jerome SFF 90
Davis, Jerry ARZ 31, xDAL 40
Davis, Jerry NYJ 23
Davis, Joe zBRK 55
Davis, John BUF 65/79, TEN 73
Davis, John CHI 47
Davis, John CHI 82, MIN 86, TBB 80/87
Davis, Johnny CLE 38, SFF 38, TBB 38
Davis, Kelvin NYG 72
Davis, Kenneth BUF 23, GBP 36
Davis, Kyle DAL 57, SFF 64
Davis, Lamar zBAL 51, zMIA 56
Davis, Lee CIN 31, IND 28
Davis, Leonard ARZ 75
Davis, Lorenzo PIT 89
Davis, Marvin DEN 78
Davis, Marvin TEN 58
Davis, Michael CLE 26, TEN 30
Davis, Mike OAK 36, SDC 36
Davis, Milt IND 20
Davis, Nathan ATL 99, DAL 77/99
Davis, Nick MIN 86
Davis, Norm PHL 64, IND 63, NOS 63
Davis, Oliver CIN 21, CLE 21
Davis, Paschall STL 55

Davis, Paul ARZ 59, ATL 59, NYG 63
Davis, Paul PIT 77
Davis, Pernell PHL 93
Davis, Preston IND 27
Davis, Ralph GBP 66
Davis, Ray DET 17
Davis, Red DET 52
Davis, Reggie SDC 84/89
Davis, Reuben ARZ 93, SDC 93, TBB 79
Davis, Richard STL 3/32
Davis, Ricky CIN 27, KCC 40, TBB 27
Davis, Rob CHI 91, GBP 60
Davis, Robert PIT 28
Davis, Roger CHI 60, NYG 66/74, STL 67
Davis, Ron ARZ 76
Davis, Ron ATL 28
Davis, Rosey NYG 77
Davis, Russell ARZ 98, CHI 95
Davis, Russell PIT 45
Davis, Sam PIT 57
Davis, Sammy SDC 22
Davis, Scott NYG 62
Davis, Scott OAK 70
Davis, Shockmain NEP 84
Davis, Sonny DAL 88
Davis, Stan PHL 81
Davis, Stephen CAR 48, WSH 48
Davis, Steve NYJ 35, PIT 35
Davis, Sylvester PHL 16
Davis, Ted IND 35, MIA 54, NOS 35
Davis, Terrell DEN 30
Davis, Thabiti NYG 82
Davis, Tommy SFF 36
Davis, Tony CIN 25/35, TBB 27
Davis, Travis IND 95, NOS 95
Davis, Travis JAX 45, NOS 47, PIT 27
Davis, Troy NOS 28
Davis, Tyree SEA 83, TBB 82
Davis, Tyrone GBP 81, NYJ 83
Davis, Tyrone NYG 39
Davis, Van zNYY 55/50
Davis, Vern PHL 16
Davis, Wayne ARZ 53
Davis, Wayne BUF 21, SDC 20, WSH 26
Davis, Wendell CHI 82
Davis, Wendell DAL 35, IND 10, SDC 89
Davis, Willie GBP 87, CLE 77/89
Davis, Willie KCC 84, TEN 84/86
Davis, Zola CLE 87
Davison, Andrew DAL 26, NYJ 39
Davison, Jerone OAK 48
Davlin, Mike WSH 73
Dawkins, Brian PHL 20

Dawkins, Dale NYJ 89
Dawkins, Joe DEN 33, NYG 26, TEN 33/34
Dawkins, Julius BUF 46/89
Dawkins, Sean IND 87, JAX 84, NOS 86, SEA 81
Dawkins, Tommy PIT 91
Dawley, Fred DET 85
Dawsey, Lawrence NOS 81, NYG 88, TBB 80
Dawsey, Stacey NOS 26, NOS 80
Dawson, Bill NEP 83
Dawson, Dale GBP 4, MIN 4, PHL 4
Dawson, Dermontti PIT 63
Dawson, Doug ARZ 66, CLE 60/69, TEN 66
Dawson, Gib GBP 26
Dawson, JaJuan CLE 88, HOU 87
Dawson, Lake IND 87, KCC 80
Dawson, Len KCC 16, CLE 18, PIT 16
Dawson, Lin NEP 87
Dawson, Mike ARZ 73, DET 73, KCC 73
Dawson, Phil CLE 4
Dawson, Rhett MIN 86, TEN 20
Day, Albert DEN 84
Day, Eagle WSH 10/19
Day, Terry NYJ 78
Day, Tom ARZ 61, BUF 60/64/78/88/89, SDC 88
Daykin, Tony ATL 55, DET 58
Dayne, Ron NYG 27
Deal, Rufus WSH 53
Dean, Floyd SFF 50/57/82
Dean, Fred CHI 63, WSH 63
Dean, Fred SDC 71, SFF 74
Dean, Hal STL 84
Dean, Jimmy TEN 67
Dean, Kevin SFF 57
Dean, Randy NYG 15
Dean, Ted PHL 35, MIN 24
Dean, Tom xBOS 44
Dean, Vernon SEA 31, WSH 32
Dean, Walter GBP 42
Dearth, James NYJ 85
DeAyala, Kiki CIN 93
DeBerg, Steve ATL 17, DEN 17, KCC 17, MIA 17, SFF 17, TBB 17
DeBernardi, Fred KCC 69
deBruijn, Case KCC 5
DeCarbo, Nick PIT 28
DeCarlo, Art IND 21/23, PIT 26, WSH 27
DeCorrevont, Bill ARZ 39, WSH 29, CHI 36, DET 76
Dee, Bob NEP 89, WSH 89
Dee, Donnie IND 48, SEA 81
Deeks, Don GBP 85, WSH 21, xBOS 41/45

Dees, Bob GBP 76
Deese, Derrick SFF 63
DeFelice, Nick NYJ 73
DeFilippo, Lou NYG 10/55
DeForest, Joe NOS 55
DeFrance, Chris WSH 81
DeFruiter, Bob DET 39, STL 50, WSH 61
Degen, Dick SDC 51
DeGraffenreid, Allen ARZ 69, CIN 85
Degrate, Tony GBP 95
DeGrenier, Jack NOS 47
DeJurnett, Charles SDC 73, STL 70
Dekdebrun, Al xBOS 66, zBUF 60, zCHI 66, zNYY 86
Dekker, Al WSH 83
Del Bello, Jack IND 19
Del Gaizo, Jim GBP 12, MIA 11, NYG 12
Del Greco, Al TEN 3, ARZ 17, GBP 10
Del Rio, Jack MIN 55, NOS 50, DAL 55, KCC 50
DeLamielleure, Joe BUF 68, CLE 64
Delaney, Jarrod MIN 89
Delaney, Jeff DET 45, IND 34, STL 41, TBB 24
Delaney, Joe KCC 37
Delauer, Robert STL 55/65
DeLeone, Tom CLE 54, CIN 50
Deleone, Tony CLE 2
Delevan, Burt ARZ 76
Delhomme, Jake CAR 17, NOS 9/12
DeLine, Steve PHL 2, SDC 6
Delisle, Jim GBP 79
Dell Isola, Johnny NYG 2
Dellenbach, Jeff GBP 67, MIA 65, NEP 66, PHL 66
Dellerba, Spiro CLE 70, zBAL 71/77
DeLoach, Jerry HOU 95, WSH 92
DeLoach, Ralph NYJ 94
DeLong, Greg BLT 85, JAX 83, MIN 85
DeLong, Keith SFF 59
DeLong, Steve SDC 56/82, CHI 87
Deloplaine, Jack CHI 33, PIT 35, WSH 35
Delpino, Robert DEN 39, STL 39
DeLuca, Sam NYJ 65, SDC 60/72
DeLuca, Tony GBP 98
Delucca, Gerry BUF 72/74, NEP 74, PHL 74
DeMao, Al WSH 53
DeMar, Enoch CLE 70
DeMarco, Bob ARZ 61, CLE 61, MIA 61, STL 55

DeMarco, Brian CIN 73, JAX 73
DeMarco, Mario DET 63
Demarie, John CLE 55/65, SEA 65
Demas, George xBKN 6
Demery, Calvin MIN 27
Demko, George PIT 74
Demory, Bill NYJ 6
DeMoss, Bob xNYB 16
Demps, Will BLT 47
Dempsey, Frank CHI 40/62
Dempsey, Jack PHL 27
Dempsey, John PIT 28
Dempsey, Tom BUF 6, NOS 19, PHL 19, STL 10, TEN 23
DeMulling, Rick IND 64
Den Herder, Vern MIA 83/86
Denman, Anthony BUF 56, CLE 55
Dennard, Mark MIA 63, PHL 65
Dennard, Preston BUF 83, GBP 88, STL 88
Dennerlein, Jerry NYG 55/66
Dennery, Mike MIA 52, OAK 54
Dennery, Vince NYG 52
Denney, Austin BUF 84, CHI 84
Denney, Ryan BUF 90/92
Dennis, Al CLE 61/62, SDC 61
Dennis, Guy CIN 63, DET 60
Dennis, Mark CIN 74, MIA 74, CAR 62/74
Dennis, Mike NYG 46, NYJ 22, SDC 45
Dennis, Mike STL 43
Dennis, Pat DAL 26, HOU 28, KCC 41
Dennison, Doug CLE 20, DAL 21
Dennison, Glenn NYJ 86, WSH 89
Dennison, Rick DEN 55
Denny, Earl MIN 28
Denson, Al DEN 88, MIN 86
Denson, Autry CHI 25, IND 40, MIA 21
Denson, Damon NEP 61
Denson, Moses WSH 44
Dent, Burnell GBP 56
Dent, Richard CHI 95, IND 96, PHL 95, SFF 95
Denton, Bob CLE 54, MIN 62
Denton, Tim SDC 22, WSH 25
Denvir, John DEN 65
DeOssie, Steve DAL 55, NEP 50/99, NYG 99, NYJ 99
DePascal, Carmine PIT 60
DePaso, Tom CIN 56
DePaul, Henry PIT 61
DePoyster, Jerry DET 15, OAK 4
DeRamus, Lee NOS 87

DeRatt, Jim NOS 32
Derby, Dean PIT 27, MIN 25
Derby, Glenn NOS 79
Derby, John DET 52
Dercher, Dan SFF 79
Deremer, Art xBKN 18
DeRiggi, Fred NEP 71
Derleth, Robert DET ?
DeRogatis, Al NYG 78
DeRoo, Brian IND 87
DeRose, Dan NYG 72
DeSantis, Dan PHL 49
Deschaine, Dick CLE 28, GBP 80
DeShane, Chuck DET 17/60
Deskin, Versil ARZ 32/45
Deskins, Don OAK 79
Dess, Darrell NYG 62, PIT 72, WSH 62
DeStefano, Fred ARZ ?
Desutter, Wayne BUF 71
Deters, Harold DAL 83
Detmer, Koy PHL 10
Detmer, Ty CLE 11, DET 14, GBP 11, PHL 14, SFF 11
Detwiler, Chuck ARZ 42, SDC 35
DeVaughn, Dennis PHL 25
Devine, Kevin JAX 26, MIN 27
DeVita, Rob SEA 58
Devliegher, Chuck BUF 74
Devlin, Chris CHI 50, CIN 51
Devlin, Joe BUF 70
Devlin, Mike ARZ 62, BUF 62
DeVries, Jared DET 95
Devrow, Billy CLE 22
Dewar, Jim CLE 94, zBRK 84
DeWeese, Ebby DET 52
Dewell, Bill ARZ 7/41
Dewveall, Willard TEN 88, CHI 88
Dexter, James ARZ 64, CAR 64
Dial, Alan PHL 24
Dial, Benjy PHL 4
Dial, Buddy PIT 83/84, DAL 26
Diamond, Charlie KCC 79
Diana, Rich MIA 33
Diaz, Jorge DAL 64, TBB 64
Diaz-Infante, David DEN 63, PHL 63, SDC 63
Dibble, Dorne DET 84/87
DiBernardo, Rick ARZ 56, STL 53
Dick, Jim MIN 52
Dickel, Dan DET 57, IND 55
Dickerson, Andy OAK 64
Dickerson, Anthony BUF 58, DAL 51
Dickerson, Bryan JAX 44
Dickerson, Eric ATL 29, IND 29, OAK 29, STL 29
Dickerson, Kori PHL 86
Dickerson, Ron KCC 23
Dickey, Charlie PIT 61

Dickey, Curtis CLE 33, IND 27/33, IND 33
Dickey, Eldridge OAK 10
Dickey, Lynn GBP 10/12, TEN 10
Dickey, Wallace DEN 71
Dickinson, Bo KCC 32, TEN 35, OAK 23/30/33
Dickinson, Parnell TBB 18
Dickinson, Richard DEN 35
Dickson, Paul ARZ 68, DAL 71, MIN 76, STL 71
Dicus, Chuck PIT 84, SDC 28
Didier, Clint GBP 80, WSH 86
Didio, Mark PIT 88
Didion, John NOS 51
Didion, John WSH 51
Diehl, Charles ARZ 27, xSTL ?
Diehl, Dave DET 32/84
Diehl, David NYG 66
Diehl, John DAL 76, IND 78, OAK 73
Dieken, Doug CLE 73
Dielman, Kris SDC 68
Diem, Ryan IND 71
Dierdorf, Dan ARZ 72
Dierking, Scott NYJ 25, TBB 25
Dieterich, Chris DET 72
Dietrich, John TEN 9
DiFilippo, Dave PHL 26/69
Diggs, Na'il GBP 59
Diggs, Shelton NYJ 80
DiGiacomo, Curt KCC 65, SDC 75
Digris, Bernie CHI 37
Dilfer, Trent TBB 12, BLT 8, SEA 4
Dilger, Ken IND 85, TBB 85
Dill, Scott ARZ 73, MIN 76, TBB 76
Dillahunt, Ellis CIN 34
Dillard, Stacey NYG 71
Dillon, Bobby GBP 44
Dillon, Corey CIN 28
Dillon, Terry MIN 25
Dils, Steve ATL 8, MIN 12, STL 8
Dilts, Bucky DEN 10, IND 10
Dilweg, Anthony GBP 8
Dilweg, Lavvie GBP 22/61
Dimancheff, Babe ARZ 87, CHI 41, xBOS 18/29
DiMidio, Tony KCC 72
Dimitroff, Tom NEP 15
Dimler, Rich CLE 92, GBP 92
Dimmick, Tom KCC 55, PHL 65
Dimry, Charles ATL 22, DEN 29, PHL 38, SDC 27, TBB 39
DiNapoli, Gennaro DAL 63, OAK 64, TEN 64/66
Dingle, Adrian SDC 90
Dingle, Antonio GBP 74, CAR 74
Dingle, Mike CIN 38

Dingle, Nate JAX 53, PHL 55, STL 53
Dinkel, Tom CIN 51/52
Dinkins, Darnell NYG 41/89
Dinkins, Howard ATL 51
Dion, Terry SEA 62
Diorio, Jerry DET 84
DiPierro, Ray GBP 21
Dirden, Johnnie TEN 81, KCC 80, PIT 87
DiRenzo, Danny PHL 82
DiRenzo, Fred NYG 41
DiRico, Robert NYG 36
Dirks, Mike PHL 62
Discenzo, Tony BUF 75, NEP 76
Disend, Leo GBP 18, xBKN 27
Dishman, Chris ARZ 67
Dishman, Cris TEN 28, KCC 26, MIN 25, WSH 26
Ditka, Mike CHI 89, DAL 89, PHL 89/98
Dittrich, John ARZ 62, BUF 60, GBP 68, OAK 68
DiVito, Joe DEN 2
Dixon, Al KCC 84, NYG 84, PHL 86, SFF 84
Dixon, Andre DET 31
Dixon, Cal MIA 63, NYJ 52
Dixon, Corey ATL 19
Dixon, David MIN 71
Dixon, Dwayne TBB 81
Dixon, Ernest KCC 56, NOS 56, OAK 58
Dixon, Floyd ATL 86, PHL 84
Dixon, Gerald CIN 51, CLE 51, SDC 51
Dixon, Hanford CLE 29
Dixon, Hewritt OAK 35, DEN 30
Dixon, James DAL 21/86
Dixon, Joe TEN 64
Dixon, Mark MIA 63
Dixon, Randy IND 69
Dixon, Rich ATL 51
Dixon, Rickey CIN 29, OAK 31
Dixon, Ron NYG 86
Dixon, Ronnie KCC 90, NOS 95, NYJ 98, PHL 90
Dixon, Titus IND 87, NYJ 89
Dixon, Tony DAL 24
Dixon, Zach PHL 25, DEN 31, IND 31, NYG 34, SEA 31
Dobbins, Herb PHL 67
Dobbins, Oliver BUF 25
Dobbs, Glenn zBRK 90, zLAD 65/95
Dobelstein, Bob NYG 67, zLAD 33
Dobler, Conrad ARZ 60/66, BUF 69, NOS 66
Dockery, Derrick WSH 66
Dockery, John NYJ 43, PIT 29
Dodd, Al CHI 23, NOS 25, ATL 41

Dodge, Dedrick DEN 33, SDC 33, SEA 33, SFF 33
Dodge, Kirk DEN 59, DET 93, TEN 50
Dodrill, Dale PIT 60/72
Dodson, Les PIT 5
Doehring, John CHI 11/27, PIT 26
Doell, Sonny xCIN ?
Doelling, Fred DAL 34
Doerger, Jerry CHI 72, SDC 65
Doering, Chris DEN 85, IND 15, PIT 83, WSH 84
Doering, Jason IND 34
Dogins, Kevin CHI 73, TBB 65
Doherty, George xBKN 38, xBOS 38, zBUF 44, zNYY 33
Dohring, Tom KCC 71
Doig, Steve DET 58, NEP 59
Dokes, Phil BUF 85
Dolbin, Jack DEN 82
Doleman, Chris ATL 56, MIN 56, SFF 56
Doll, Don DET 44, STL 48, WSH 46
Dollinger, Tony DET 44
Dolly, Dick PIT 32/71
Doman, Brandon SFF 11
Dombroski, Paul KCC 46, NEP 47, TBB 47
Dombrowski, Jim NOS 72
Dombrowski, Leon NYJ 61
Dominguez, Matt DEN 49
Domnanovich, Joe xBOS 32/34, xNYB 34
Domres, Marty IND 14, NYJ 10, SDC 14, SFF 14
Domres, Tom DEN 76, TEN 71
Don Carlos, Waldo GBP 24
Donahue, Mark CIN 66
Donahue, Mitch DEN 54, SFF 54
Donahue, Oscar MIN 84
Donaldson, Gene BUF 34, CLE 66
Donaldson, Jeff ATL 42, KCC 42, TEN 31
Donaldson, John zCHI 82
Donaldson, Ray DAL 53, IND 53, SEA 53
Donchez, Tom CHI 36
Donckers, Bill ARZ 10
Donelli, Allan PIT 16/33
Donley, Doug DAL 83
Donnahoo, Roger NYJ 35
Donnalley, Kevin CAR 65, MIA 65, NEP 23, TEN 77
Donnalley, Rick KCC 51, PIT 55, WSH 76
Donnell, Ben SDC 50
Donnelly, George SFF 20
Donnelly, Rick ATL 3, SEA 3
D'Onofrio, Mark GBP 58
Donohoe, Mike ATL 84, GBP 86

Donohue, Leon SFF 72, DAL 62
Donovan, Art IND 70, xBAL 49/70, xDAL 70, xNYB 39
Donovan, Pat DAL 67
Donovan, Tom NOS 86
Doolan, John ARZ 66, NYG 11/19, WSH 25
Dooley, Jim CHI 43
Doornink, Dan SEA 33, NYG 39
Doran, Jim DAL 83, DET 83
D'Orazio, Joe DET 60
Dorenbos, Jon BUF 54
Dorn, Torin OAK 46, STL 46
Dornbrook, Thom MIA 61, PIT 63
Dorney, Keith DET 70/71
Dorning, Dale SEA 79
Dorow, Al NYJ 12, BUF 12, PHL 10, WSH 16
Dorris, Andy ARZ 69, NOS 88, SEA 69, TEN 69
Dorris, Derek NYG 85
Dorsch, Travis CIN 10
Dorsett, Anthony OAK 33, TEN 30/33
Dorsett, Matthew GBP 23
Dorsett, Tony DAL 33, DEN 33
Dorsey, Charron HOU 66, DAL 79
Dorsey, Dean GBP 9, PHL 2
Dorsey, Dick OAK 21/81
Dorsey, Eric NYG 77
Dorsey, John GBP 99
Dorsey, Larry KCC 80, SDC 87
Dorsey, Nate NEP 66
Doss, Mike IND 20
Doss, Noble PHL 45, zNYY 83
Doss, Reggie STL 71
Dotson, Al KCC 79, MIA 79, OAK 71
Dotson, Dewayne MIA 49/59
Dotson, Earl GBP 72
Dotson, Santana GBP 71, TBB 71
Dottley, John CHI 34
Doubiago, Dan KCC 66
Douds, Jap DET 12, ARZ 47, PIT 44
Dougherty, Bob OAK 44, PIT 63/68, STL 51
Dougherty, Phil ARZ 26
Doughty, Glenn IND 35
Doughty, Mike CIN 76
Douglas, Ben xBKN 26/8
Douglas, Dameane PHL 82
Douglas, David CIN 67, NEP 67
Douglas, Derrick CLE 27, TBB 37
Douglas, Freddie TBB 84
Douglas, Hugh PHL 53, JAX 58, NYJ 99
Douglas, Jay SDC 52

Douglas, John NYG 51
Douglas, John NOS 21, TEN 21
Douglas, Leland MIA 89
Douglas, Marques BLT 94, NOS 95
Douglas, Maurice CHI 36/37
Douglas, Merrill CHI 36, DAL 34, PHL 33
Douglas, Omar NYG 82
Douglas, Otis PHL 71
Douglass, Bobby CHI 10, GBP 19, NOS 10, SDC 10
Douglass, Everett NYG 78
Douglass, Maurice NYG 24
Douglass, Mike GBP 53/65, SDC 53
Douthard, Ty CIN 45
Douthitt, Earl CHI 43
Dove, Bob ARZ 42, DET 42/78, zCHI 35/55
Dove, Eddie SFF 44, NYG 48
Dove, Jerome SDC 48
Dove, Wes SEA 64
Dow, Elwood PHL 14
Dow, Harley SFF 40
Dow, Ken WSH 25
Dowd, Gerald STL 9
Dowda, Harry PHL 44, WSH 22/44
Dowdell, Marcus ARZ 84, NOS 80/86
Dowden, Corey BLT 36, CHI 20, GBP 42
Dowden, Steve GBP 70
Dowdle, Mike DAL 30, SFF 53
Dowell, Gwyn ARZ 25
Dowler, Boyd GBP 86, WSH 86
Dowler, Tommy xBKN ?
Dowling, Brian GBP 12, NEP 14
Dowling, Pat ARZ 21
Dowling, Sean BUF 71
Downing, Eric KCC 79/92
Downing, Walt SFF 62
Downs, Bob SFF 32
Downs, Gary ATL 45, DEN 45, NYG 45
Downs, Michael ARZ 26, DAL 26
Doxzon, Todd MIA 17
Doyle, Dick PIT 41
Doyle, Skip DEN 14
Doyle, Ted ARZ 29, PHL 72, PIT 28/72
Dozier, Cornelius KCC 26
Dozier, D.J. DET 42, MIN 42
Draft, Chris ATL 54, CHI 96, SFF 57
Dragon, Oscar SDC 34
Dragos, Scott CHI 45
Drake, Bill STL 37
Drake, Jerry ARZ 76
Drake, Joe PHL 99, SFF 61
Drake, John STL 2/14
Drake, Kevin ARZ 14

Drake, Troy PHL 75, WSH 70
Drakeford, Tyronne NOS 22, SFF 22, WSH 26
Drane, Dwight BUF 45
Draper, Shawn CAR 49
Draveling, Leo xCIN 51
Drayton, Troy KCC 87, MIA 84, STL 84
Drazenovich, Chuck WSH 36
Dreher, Fred CHI 20
Dreisbach, Scott OAK 10
Dreschler, Dave GBP 61
Dressel, Chris KCC 93, NYJ 84, SFF 47/88, TEN 88
Dressen, Charley CHI 5
Dressler, Doug CIN 44, KCC 41, NEP 44
Drewrey, Willie TBB 87, TEN 82/85
Drews, Ted CHI 20/80
Dreyer, Wally CHI 3, GBP 16/42
Driscoll, Paddy ARZ 1, CHI 1/20
Driskill, Joe ARZ 45
Driver, Donald GBP 80
Driver, Stacey CLE 35
Driver, Tony BUF 25
Dronett, Shane ATL 75, DEN 99, DET 92
Drost, Jeff GBP 71
Drougas, Tom DEN 76, IND 74, KCC 76, MIA 78
Droughns, Reuben DEN 34, DET 21
Drozdov, Darren DEN 97
Druckenmiller, Jim SFF 14
Drulis, Al ARZ 39, PIT 25
Drulis, Chuck CHI 14/21, GBP 18
Drummond, Eddie DET 18
Drummond, Robert PHL 36
Drungo, Elbert BUF 79, TEN 75
Drury, Lyle CHI 23
Druschel, Rick PIT 73
Druze, Johnny xBKN 3
Dryer, Fred STL 89, NYG 89
Drzewiecki, Ron CHI 21/22
Duarte, George CHI 30
Dubenion, Elbert BUF 44
Dubinetz, Greg WSH 67
Dublinski, Tom DET 19, NYG 17
Dubofsky, Maury NYG 55
DuBois, Phil WSH 86
DuBose, Demetrius TBB 93
DuBose, Doug SFF 25
DuBose, Jimmy TBB 35
Dubzinski, Walt NYG 12, xBOS 39
Duckens, Mark DET 91, NYG 75, TBB 95
Duckett, Forey CIN 41, GBP 21, SEA 23

Duckett, Kenny DAL 86, NOS 83
Duckett, T.J. ATL 45
Duckworth, Bobby PHL 80, SDC 82, STL 82
Duckworth, Joe WSH 18
Duda, Mark ARZ 73
Dudek, Joe DEN 32
Dudek, Mitch NYJ 73
Duden, Dick NYG 87
Dudish, Andy DET 18, zBAL 88, zBUF 80
Dudley, Bill DET 35/44, PIT 3/35, WSH 35
Dudley, Brian CLE 27
Dudley, Paul NYG 23, PHL 28
Dudley, Rickey CLE 82, OAK 83, TBB 88
Duerson, Dave CHI 22, ARZ 22, NYG 26
Dufault, Paul OAK 54
Dufek, Don SEA 25
Dufek, Joe BUF 11/19
Duff, Bill CLE 62
Duff, Jamal NYG 96, WSH 92
Duff, John OAK 84
Duffy, Roger NYJ 62, PIT 62
Dufour, Dan ATL 71
Dugan, Bill MIN 56, NYG 68, SEA 66
Dugan, Fred DAL 89, SFF 87, WSH 87
Dugan, Len ARZ 27/46/48, NYG 5, PIT 39
Dugans, Ron CIN 81
Duggan, Gil ARZ 42/60/69/73, NYG 69, PIT 60, zBUF 42, zLAD 40
Dugger, Jack DET 50/74, zBUF 50, CHI 13
Duggins, George ARZ 35/43
Duhart, Paul GBP 42, PIT 42, xBOS 24
Duhe, A.J. MIA 77
Duhon, Bobby NYG 28
Duich, Steve ATL 65, WSH 63
Duke, Paul zNYY 21
Dukes, Chad JAX 42, STL 34, WSH 32
Dukes, Jamie ARZ 64, ATL 64, GBP 63
Dukes, Mike NEP 54, NYJ 55, TEN 30
DuLac, Bill NEP 68
Dulaney, Mike CHI 38, CAR 34
Duliban, Chris DAL 52
Dulin, Gary ARZ 79
Dumas, Mike BUF 38, JAX 38, SDC 20/38, TEN 38
Dumas, Tony KCC 55
Dumas, Tray STL 54
Dumbauld, Jonathan NOS 95, PHL 93
Dumler, Doug MIN 57, NEP 58
Dumont, Jim CLE 53

Dunaway, Craig PIT 88
Dunaway, Dave ATL 45, GBP 29, NYG 83
Dunaway, Jim BUF 78, MIA 78
Dunbar, Jubilee CLE 83, NOS 86
Dunbar, Karl ARZ 93, NOS 63
Dunbar, LaTarance ATL 82
Dunbar, Vaughn JAX 32, NOS 32
Duncan, Brian CLE 35, TEN 31
Duncan, Clyde ARZ 86
Duncan, Curtis TEN 80
Duncan, Frank SDC 47
Duncan, Howard DET 53
Duncan, James IND 35
Duncan, Jamie STL 59, TBB 59
Duncan, Jim NYG 86/87
Duncan, Ken GBP 18
Duncan, Maury SFF 12
Duncan, Randy KCC 15
Duncan, Rick DEN 4, DET ?, PHL 32
Duncan, Ron CLE 88
Duncan, Speedy SDC 45, WSH 45
Duncan, Tim ARZ 6
Duncum, Bobby ARZ 69
Dunek, Ken PHL 86
Dungy, Tony PIT 21, SFF 27
Duniven, Tom TEN 11
Dunlap, Bob CHI 30, NYG 12
Dunlap, Len IND 46, DET 32, SDC 39
Dunn, Anthony TEN 91
Dunn, Coye WSH 30
Dunn, Damon CLE 81/87
Dunn, David CIN 80, CLE 81, OAK 88, PIT 83
Dunn, Gary PIT 67
Dunn, Jason KCC 89, PHL 87
Dunn, K.D. NYJ 80, TBB 80/85, WSH 87
Dunn, Paul CIN 21
Dunn, Perry Lee ATL 37, DAL 37, IND 31
Dunn, Red GBP 7/11/15/16/17/32, ARZ 2
Dunn, Warrick ATL 28, TBB 28
Dunsmore, Pat CHI 91
Dunstan, Bill BUF 76, PHL 61, STL 66
Dunstan, Elwyn ARZ 38, STL 20
Dupard, Reggie NEP 21, WSH 25
Duper, Mark MIA 85
Dupre, Chuck NYJ 28
Dupre, L.G. DAL 45, IND 45
DuPree, Billy Joe DAL 89
Dupree, Marcus STL 22
Dupree, Myron DEN 21
Dupree, Terrence SFF 84

Duranko, Pete DEN 55
Durdan, Don SFF 93
Duren, Clarence ARZ 41, SDC 21
Durham, Darius SFF 84
Durham, Steve IND 72
Durishan, Jack zNYY 41
Durkee, Charlie NOS 10/15
Durko, John ARZ 45, PHL 88
Durko, Sandy CIN 29, NEP 22
Durkota, Jeff zLAD 83
Durrette, Michael SFF 64
Dusbabek, Mark MIN 59
Dusek, Brad WSH 59
Dusenberry, Bill NOS 47
Dutton, Bill PIT 16
Dutton, John IND 78, DAL 78
Dvorak, Rick MIA 75, NYG 66
Dwight, Tim ATL 83, SDC 85/87
Dworsky, Dan zLAD 65
Dwyer, Jack STL 29, WSH 29
Dwyer, Mike DAL 71
Dwyer, Nate ARZ 72
Dyal, Mike KCC 87, OAK 84, SDC 84
Dye, Ernest ARZ 65/75, STL 65
Dye, Les WSH 38
Dyer, Deon MIA 33
Dyer, Henry STL 35, WSH 32
Dyer, Ken CIN 27, SDC 49
Dykes, Donald NYJ 26, SDC 26
Dykes, Hart Lee NEP 88
Dykes, Sean NYJ 22
Dyko, Chris CHI 68
Dyson, Andre TEN 22
Dyson, Kevin CAR 85, TEN 87
Dyson, Matt OAK 59
Eaddy, James CIN 70
Eagle, Alex xBKN 12
Eaglin, Larry TEN 26
Eakin, Kay NYG 12, zMIA 96
Earhart, Ralph GBP 41
Earl, Robin CHI 39/81
Earley, Jim NYJ 47
Early, Michael BUF 64
Early, Quinn BUF 88, NOS 89, NYJ 88, SDC 87
Earon, Blaine DET 86
Earp, Jug GBP 7/9/29/38/39
Easley, Kenny SEA 45
Easley, Walt SFF 31
Easmon, Ricky DAL 42, TBB 26
Eason, Bo TEN 21
Eason, John OAK 82
Eason, Roger STL 43, GBP 40
Eason, Tony NEP 11, NYJ 11
East, Ron ATL 77, CLE 77, DAL 77/79, SDC 77, SEA 74
Eastering, Ray ATL 32
Easy, Omar KCC 43
Eatman, Irv ATL 75, KCC 75, NYJ 75, TEN 75, STL 75
Eaton, Chad NEP 90, SEA 90
Eaton, Lou NYG 0/70

Eaton, Scott NYG 20
Eaton, Tracey ATL 32, TEN 21, ARZ 21
Eaton, Vic PIT 12/14
Ebding, Harry DET 8/11/33
Eber, Rick ATL 25, SDC 49
Eberdt, Jess xBKN 22
Ebersole, John NYJ 55
Ebli, Ray ARZ 64, zBUF 53, zCHI 52
Eby, Byron DET 20
Eccles, Scott TEN 87
Echols, Donnie CLE 83
Echols, Fate ARZ 63
Echols, Mike TEN 20/36
Echols, Terry PIT 94
Eck, Keith NYG 58
Ecker, Ed CHI 22, GBP 55, WSH 75, zCHI 46
Eckhardt, Ox NYG 0
Eckl, Bob ARZ 25/46
Ecklund, Brad IND 50, xDAL 50, xNYB 22, zNYY 23
Eckwood, Jerry TBB 43
Eddings, Floyd NYG 88
Eddy, Nick DET 40
Edelman, Brad NOS 63
Edge, Shane PIT 14
Edgerson, Booker BUF 24, DEN 24
Edinger, Paul CHI 2
Edmonds, Bobby Joe SEA 30, OAK 41, TBB 41
Edmonds, Chris CIN 41/87
Edmunds, Ferrell MIA 80, SEA 82
Edmunds, Randall MIA 55, IND 52, NEP 51
Edwards, Al BUF 85
Edwards, Anthony ARZ 81/83, PHL 84
Edwards, Antonio ATL 96, NYG 95, SEA 67/94, CAR 96
Edwards, Antuan GBP 24
Edwards, Brad ATL 20/27, MIN 27, WSH 27
Edwards, Cid ARZ 39, CHI 37, SDC 37
Edwards, Dan IND 82, xDAL 82, xNYB 4, zBRK 51, zCHI 51
Edwards, Dave DAL 52
Edwards, Dave PIT 42
Edwards, Dennis STL 95
Edwards, Dixon DAL 58, MIN 59
Edwards, Donnie KCC 59, SDC 59
Edwards, Earl BUF 73, CIN 73, CLE 66, GBP 73, SFF 74
Edwards, Emmett BUF 86, TEN 87
Edwards, Glen PIT 27, SDC 27
Edwards, Herm ATL 46, PHL 46, STL 46

Edwards, Jimmy MIN 32
Edwards, Kalimba DET 98
Edwards, Kelvin DAL 81/87, NOS 83
Edwards, Lloyd OAK 36
Edwards, Marc CLE 44, JAX 44, NEP 44, SFF 44
Edwards, Mario DAL 27
Edwards, Marshall xBKN ?
Edwards, Monk NYG 60/66
Edwards, Randy SEA 68
Edwards, Robert MIA 47, NEP 47
Edwards, Ron BUF 98
Edwards, Ronald STL 67
Edwards, Stan DET 46, TEN 32/35
Edwards, Steve CHI 79
Edwards, Terrence ATL 80
Edwards, Tim NEP 98
Edwards, Troy JAX 18/86, PIT 81, STL 86
Edwards, Turk WSH 17
Edwards, Vernon SDC 95
Edwards, Weldon WSH 48
Egan, Dick ARZ 7/9
Eggers, Doug ARZ 51, IND 67
Egloff, Ron DEN 85, SDC 84
Egu, Patrick NEP 33
Ehin, Chuck SDC 78
Ehlers, Tom BUF 56, PHL 59
Ehrhardt, Clyde WSH 31
Ehrmann, Joe DET 74, IND 76
Eibner, John PHL 76/77
Eiden, Ed DET 62, PHL 71
Eidson, Jim DAL 52
Eifrid, Jim DEN 62
Eikenberg, Charles ARZ 49
Eilers, Pat CHI 25/37, MIN 24, WSH 24/25
Eischeid, Mike OAK 11, MIN 11
Eisenhauer, Larry NEP 72
Eisenhooth, John SEA 68
Eisenhooth, Stan IND 67, SEA 66
Eitzmann, Chris NEP 86
Ekern, Andy IND 79
Ekern, Carl STL 55
Ekuban, Ebenezer DAL 96
Elam, Cleveland SFF 72, DET 72
Elam, Jason DEN 1
Elam, Onzy DAL 53, NYJ 52
Elam, Shane SFF 59
Elder, Donnie DET 43, NYJ 37, PIT 37, SDC 28, TBB 40
Elena, Jack STL 60
Elewonibi, Mo WSH 64, PHL 65
Eley, Clifton MIN 86
Eley, Monroe ATL 46
Elia, Bruce MIA 50, SFF 51/55
Elias, Homer DET 61
Elias, Keith IND 23, NYG 20

Eliason, Don xBKN 15, xBOS 42
Eliopulos, Jim ARZ 57, NYJ 52
Elkins, Chief xCIN ?
Elkins, Falt ARZ 11
Elkins, Lawrence TEN 26
Elkins, Mike KCC 10, TEN 6
Elko, Bill IND 96, SDC 68/90
Ellard, Henry STL 80, NEP 17, WSH 85
Ellenbogan, Bill NYG 65
Ellender, Richard TEN 85
Ellenson, Gene zMIA 42
Eller, Carl MIN 81, SEA 71
Ellersick, Don STL 44
Ellerson, Gary DET 42, GBP 42
Elling, Aaron MIN 8
Elliot, Carlton GBP 40
Elliot, Lin DAL 2
Elliot, Tony GBP 27
Elliott, Carlton GBP 80
Elliott, Charles SFF 96, zCHI 47, zNYY 45
Elliott, Jamin CHI 87
Elliott, Jim PIT 6
Elliott, John NYJ 80
Elliott, Jumbo NYG 76, NYJ 76
Elliott, Lenvil CIN 36, SFF 35
Elliott, Lin KCC 2
Elliott, Matt CAR 52
Elliott, Ted NOS 64
Elliott, Tony NOS 99
Ellis, Allen CHI 48, SDC 48
Ellis, Clarence ATL 29
Ellis, Craig MIA 33, OAK 33
Ellis, Drew PHL 35
Ellis, Ed NEP 66, SDC 69/77, WSH 69
Ellis, Elbert CAR 89
Ellis, Gerry GBP 31
Ellis, Greg DAL 98
Ellis, Herb xNYB 55
Ellis, Jim OAK 58
Ellis, John xBKN 16
Ellis, Ken GBP 48, CLE 48, DET 20, MIA 48, STL 28
Ellis, Kwame NYJ 38
Ellis, Larry DET 28
Ellis, Ray CLE 24, PHL 24
Ellis, Roger NYJ 56
Ellis, Shaun NYJ 92
Ellis, Walt ARZ 18
Ellison, Glen OAK 27
Ellison, Jerry NEP 35, TBB 37
Ellison, Mark NYG 65
Ellison, Omar SDC 84
Ellison, Riki OAK 50, SFF 50/69
Ellison, Willie STL 33, KCC 24
Elliss, Luther DET 94
Ellitoo, Matt WSH 52
Ellstrom, Marv PHL 10, PIT 10, ARZ ?, WSH 18

Ellsworth, Percy CLE 43, NYG 43
Ellzey, Charles ARZ 55
El-Mashtoub, Hicham TEN 60
Elmendorf, Dave STL 42
Elmore, Doug WSH 48
Elnes, Leland CHI 10/11
Eloms, Joey SEA 43
Elrod, Jimbo KCC 57
Elser, Earl DET 49, xCIN 22/27, xSTL 55
Elsey, Earl zLAD 94
Elshire, Neil MIN 65/73
Elston, Art SFF 21/36, STL 55
Elter, Leo WSH 32, PIT 34/39
Elway, John DEN 7
Elwell, Jack ARZ 81
Ely, Harold CHI 11, xBKN 16/24/11/2
Ely, Larry CHI 54, CIN 59
Elzey, Paul CIN 52
Emanuel, Bert ATL 87, DET 83, MIA 87, NEP 87, TBB 87
Emanuel, Charles PHL 47
Emanuel, Frank MIA 50, NOS 52
Embray, Keith TEN 96
Embree, John DEN 89, STL 87
Embree, Mel IND 85
Emelianchik, Pete PHL 39
Emerick, Bob DET 18, STL 23
Emerson, Ox DET 7/20/45, xBKN 20
Emerson, Vernon ARZ 76
Emery, Larry ATL 24
Emmanuel, Charles MIN 47
Emmons, Carlos PHL 51, PIT 51
Emmons, Franklin PHL 44
Emtman, Steve IND 79/90, MIA 94, WSH 79
Ena, Justin PHL 59/95
Enderle, Dick ATL 63, GBP 67, NYG 62, SFF 63
Endriss, Al SFF 85
Engebretsen, Tiny GBP 34/52/69, ARZ ?, CHI 21, PIT 26, xBKN 15
Engel, Greg DET 51, SDC 60
Engel, Steve CLE 36
Engelberger, John SFF 95
England, Eric ARZ 92
Englemann, Wuert GBP 25/33
Engler, Derek NYG 69
Engles, Rick PHL 13, PIT 17, SEA 5
English, Doug DET 78
English, Keith STL 8
Englund, Harry CHI 15
Engram, Bobby CHI 81, SEA 84
Enich, Steve ARZ 66
Enis, Curtis CHI 39/44
Enis, Hunter DEN 14, KCC 14, OAK 14, SDC 17

Enke, Fred DET 24/46, IND 17, PHL 17
Enright, Rex GBP 15/20
Enyart, Bill BUF 41, OAK 46
Ephraim, Alonzo PHL 50
Epperson, Pat DEN 88
Epps, Bobby NYG 35
Epps, Jack KCC 25
Epps, Phillip GBP 85, NYJ 89
Epps, Tory ATL 74, CHI 65, NOS 79
Epstein, Hayden JAX 6, MIN 6
Erdlitz, Dick zMIA 86, PHL 11/30
Erenberg, Rich PIT 24
Erickson, Bernard CIN 50, SDC 62
Erickson, Bill NYG 76, zNYY 41
Erickson, Carl WSH 18
Erickson, Craig IND 7, MIA 7, TBB 7
Erickson, Hal ARZ 3
Erickson, Mickey ARZ 16, WSH 19
Erlandson, Tom MIA 53, BUF 53, DEN 53, SDC 58
Ernst, Mike CIN 17, DEN 16
Ervins, Ricky SFF 32, WSH 32
Erwin, Terry DEN 46
Erxleben, Russell DET 15, NOS 14
Eshmont, Len NYG 2, SFF 81
Esiason, Boomer CIN 7, ARZ 7, NYJ 7
Espinoza, Alex KCC 12
Esposito, Mike ATL 26
Esser, Clarence ARZ 67
Essink, Ron SEA 64
Estell, Richard KCC 84
Estep, Mike BUF 77, GBP 79
Estes, Don SDC 68
Estes, Larry PHL 81, KCC 74, NOS 84
Etcheverry, Sam ARZ 14, SFF 14
Etheredge, Carlos IND 81
Etherly, Dave WSH 25
Ethridge, Joe GBP 85
Ethridge, Ray BLT 85
Etienne, LeRoy SFF 50
Etter, Bob ATL 3
Ettinger, Don NYG 74
Evans, Leomont HOU 35
Evans, Byron PHL 56
Evans, Charles MIN 29, BLT 29
Evans, Charlie NYG 31, WSH 31
Evans, Chuck NOS 59
Evans, David MIN 26
Evans, Demetric DAL 92
Evans, Dick ARZ 28/35, GBP 22/53, GBP 53
Evans, Donald PHL 77, NYJ 66, PIT 66, STL 34

Evans, Doug DET 39, GBP 33, SEA 33, CAR 33
Evans, Earl ARZ 33, CHI 19/44
Evans, Fred CHI 11, CLE 99, zBUF 83, zCHI 75
Evans, Greg BUF 41, WSH 27
Evans, Heath SEA 44
Evans, Jack GBP 21
Evans, James KCC 41, TBB 38
Evans, Jay DEN 40
Evans, Jerry DEN 88
Evans, Jim NYJ 80
Evans, John ATL 87
Evans, Johnny CLE 8
Evans, Jon PIT 86
Evans, Josh NYJ 91, TEN 91
Evans, Larry DEN 56, SDC 56
Evans, Leomont WSH 35
Evans, Leon DET 66
Evans, Lon GBP 17/25/39/46/51/65
Evans, Mike KCC 94
Evans, Mike PHL 59
Evans, Murray DET 23
Evans, Norm MIA 73, SEA 73, TEN 73
Evans, Ray PIT 42
Evans, Ray SFF 38/46
Evans, Reggie WSH 26
Evans, Robert TEN 86
Evans, Russell SEA 88
Evans, Scott ARZ 74
Evans, Troy HOU 54
Evans, Vince CHI 8, OAK 11
Evansen, Paul SFF 36
Everett, Eric KCC 39, MIN 31, PHL 42, TBB 42
Everett, Jim STL 11, NOS 17
Everett, Major ATL 39, CLE 39, PHL 39
Everett, Thomas DAL 27/31, PIT 27, TBB 22
Everitt, Steve BLT 61, CLE 61, PHL 61, STL 60
Evey, Dick CHI 79, DET 77, STL 82
Eyre, Nick TEN 78
Ezerins, Vilnis STL 37
Ezor, Blake DEN 35
Faaola, Nuu MIA 34, NYJ 30
Fabini, Jason NYJ 69
Fada, Rob CHI 92, KCC 65
Fagan, Julian NOS 10, NYJ 10
Fagan, Kevin SFF 75
Faggins, DeMarcus HOU 38
Fagioli, Carl PHL 77
Fahnhorst, Jim SFF 55
Fahnhorst, Keith SFF 71/89
Failing, Fred ARZ 31
Fain, Richard ARZ 31, CHI 24, CIN 31
Faine, Jeff CLE 50
Fair, Carl CLE 42
Fair, Terry CAR 28, DET 23

Fairband, Bill OAK 86
Fairbanks, Don SEA 74
Fairchild, Greg CIN 63, CLE 61
Fairchild, Paul NEP 66
Faircloth, Art NYG 40
Fairley, Leonard TEN 29
Fairs, Eric TEN 51
Faison, Derrick STL 89
Faison, Earl SDC 86, MIA 84
Falaschi, Nello NYG 28
Falcon, Terry NEP 68, NYG 62
Falkenberg, Herb CHI 30
Falkenstein, Tony GBP 18, xBKN 32, xBOS ?
Falls, Mike DAL 63
Famiglietti, Gary CHI 2, xBOS 17
Faneca, Alan PIT 65/66
Fann, Chad ARZ 49/86, SFF 86
Fanning, Mike DET 74, SEA 74, STL 79
Fanning, Stan CHI 65, DEN 86, STL 79, TEN 86
Fantetti, Ken DET 57
Fanucci, Ledio ARZ 73
Fanucci, Mike GBP 71, TEN 67, WSH 68
Farasopoulos, Chris NOS 44, NYJ 19
Farber, Hap MIN 51, NOS 56
Fargas, Justin OAK 20
Farkas, Andy WSH 44, DET 42
Farkas, Kevin CAR 70
Farley, Dale BUF 57, MIA 58
Farley, Dick SDC 36
Farley, John CIN 33
Farman, Dick WSH 21
Farmer, Danny CIN 83
Farmer, Dave TBB 41
Farmer, George CHI 43, DET 44
Farmer, George MIA 86, STL 84
Farmer, Karl ATL 80, TBB 84
Farmer, Lonnie NEP 55
Farmer, Ray PHL 55
Farmer, Robert NYJ 25
Farmer, Roger NYJ 80
Farmer, Ted ARZ 28
Farmer, Tom STL 46, WSH 14
Farquhar, John NOS 87, PIT 86, TBB 89
Farr, D'Marco STL 75
Farr, Mel Sr. DET 24
Farr, Mel Jr. STL 34
Farr, Mike DET 81
Farr, Miller TEN 20, ARZ 20, DEN 27/44, SDC 20
Farragut, Ken PHL 53
Farrar, Vince PIT 25/40
Farrell, Ed PIT 23, xBKN 10
Farrell, Sean DEN 63, NEP 62, SEA 62, TBB 62
Farren, Paul CLE 74
Farrier, Curt KCC 70

Farrington, John CHI 84
Farrior, James NYJ 58, PIT 51
Farris, Jimmy ATL 87
Farris, John SDC 62
Farris, Kris BUF 72, PIT 77
Farris, Tom CHI 36, zCHI 65
Faryniarz, Brett SFF 57, STL 51, TEN 96, CAR 55
Fasani, Randy CAR 12
Fatafehi, Mario ARZ 79, CAR 92, DEN 68
Faucette, Chuck SDC 53
Faulk, Kevin NEP 33
Faulk, Marshall IND 28, STL 28
Faulkner, Chris SDC 84, STL 88
Faulkner, Jeff ARZ 94, IND 94, MIA 75, NOS 96, NYJ 96, WSH 93
Faulkner, Stanley TEN 71
Faumui, Taase PIT 78
Faumuina, Wilson ATL 74
Fauria, Christian NEP 88, SEA 85/86, SEA 86
Faurot, Ron NYJ 74
Faust, George ARZ 53
Faust, Paul MIN 54
Faverty, Hal GBP 51
Favors, Greg CAR 53, KCC 54, TEN 51
Favre, Brett GBP 4, ATL 4
Favron, Calvin ARZ 59
Fawcett, Jake STL 42/57, xBKN 44
Faylor, John SFF 19/47
Fazande, Jermaine SDC 35
Fazier, Cliff KCC 61
Fazier, Randy KCC 95
Fazio, Ron PHL 87
Feacher, Ricky CLE 83, NEP 83
Feagin, Tom WSH 68
Feagin, Wiley IND 61
Feagles, Jeff ARZ 10, NEP 6, NYG 10, PHL 5, SEA 10
Feamster, Tom IND 79
Fears, Tom STL 55/80
Fears, Willie CIN 96, MIN 91
Feasel, Grant IND 50, MIN 64, SEA 54
Feasel, Greg GBP 77, SDC 67
Feather, Tiny NYG 8/20/33, xCIN 29
Feathers, Beattie CHI 48, GBP 3, xBKN 44/48
Febel, Fritz CHI 28
Federico, Creig DET 34
Federspiel Joe NOS 58, IND 50
Fedora, Walt xBKN 10
Fedorovich, John CHI 34
Feehery, Gerry KCC 64, NEP 63, PHL 67
Feeley, A.J. PHL 14
Feely, Jay ATL 4
Feggins, Howard NEP 36
Feher, Nick PIT 67, SFF 37/67

Feichtinger, Andy CHI 11
Fekete, Gene CLE 70
Fekete, John zBUF 73
Felber, Fred PHL 32, WSH 15
Feldhaus, Bill DET 14/26
Feldhausen, Paul NEP 66
Feldman, Todd MIA 82
Felker, Gene xDAL 85
Feller, Happy NOS 9, PHL 1
Fellows, Mark SDC 52
Fellows, Ron DAL 27, OAK 21
Felt, Dick NEP 24, NYJ 23
Felton, Eric NOS 20, NYG 22
Felton, Joe DET 64
Felton, Ralph BUF 57, WSH 45
Felts, Bob IND 47, DET 45
Fena, Tom DET 21
Fenci, Richard PHL 29
Fencik, Gary CHI 45
Fenderson, James NOS 27/48
Fenenbock, Chuck DET 48, zCHI 86, zLAD 93
Fenerty, Gill NOS 22
Fenimore, Bob CHI 55
Fennema, Carl NYG 55
Fenner, Derrick CIN 44, OAK 34, SEA 44
Fenner, Lane SDC 42
Fenner, Lee DET ?
Fenney, Rick MIN 31
Fergerson, Duke BUF 19/84, SEA 89
Ferguson, Bill NYJ 58
Ferguson, Bob MIN 35, PIT 46
Ferguson, Charley BUF 80, CLE 85, MIN 88
Ferguson, Gene SDC 75, TEN 74
Ferguson, Howie GBP 37, SDC 37
Ferguson, Jason NYJ 72
Ferguson, Jim ATL 59, CHI 58, NOS 56
Ferguson, Joe BUF 12, DET 12, IND 12, TBB 12
Ferguson, Keith DET 77, SDC 76
Ferguson, Kevin SDC 87
Ferguson, Larry DET 46
Ferguson, Nick DEN 25, NYJ 25
Ferguson, Robert GBP 89
Ferguson, Vagas CLE 24, NEP 43
Ferko, John PHL 11/19
Fernandes, Ron IND 73
Fernandez, Manny MIA 75
Fernandez, Mervyn OAK 86
Ferragamo, Vince BUF 5, GBP 5, STL 15
Ferrante, Jack PHL 83/87
Ferrante, Orlando SDC 68
Ferrara, Frank NYG 95
Ferrari, Ron SFF 54
Ferrario, Bill GBP 63

Ferrell, Bob SFF 38
Ferrell, Earl ARZ 31
Ferris, Neil PHL 27, STL 80, WSH 12/27
Ferry, Lou ARZ 82, GBP 18, PIT 78
Fersen, Paul NOS 71
Fest, Howard CIN 72, TBB 72
Fetherston, Jim SDC 61
Fetz, Gus CHI 10
Fiala, John PIT 57
Ficca, Dan NYJ 61, OAK 69
Fichman, Leon DET 46
Fichtel, Brad STL 68
Fichtner, Ross CLE 20, NOS 28
Fiedler, Bill PHL 38
Fiedler, Jay JAX 11, MIA 9, MIN 11, PHL 11
Field, Amod ARZ 26
Field, Doak ARZ 50
Field, Harry ARZ 31
Fielder, Don TBB 65
Fieldings, Anthony DAL 54
Fields, Aaron DAL 97
Fields, Angelo GBP 79, TEN 77
Fields, Anthony DET 46
Fields, Edgar ATL 77, DET ?
Fields, Floyd SDC 26
Fields, George OAK 80
Fields, Greg IND 79
Fields, Jamie KCC 59
Fields, Jeff CAR 97
Fields, Jerry NYJ 64
Fields, Jitter IND 29, KCC 46, NOS 26
Fields, Joe NYJ 65, NYG 69
Fields, Mark CAR 58, NOS 55, STL 55
Fields, Scott ATL 56, SEA 58
Fife, Ralph ARZ 31/57, PIT 26
Fifer, Bill DET 70, NOS 69
Figaro, Cedric CLE 53, IND 58, SDC 51, STL 53
Figner, Bunny CHI 21
Figures, Deon JAX 27, PIT 21
Fike, Dan CLE 69, PIT 71
Filchock, Frank NYG 40, PIT 55, WSH 30, xBAL 64
Files, Jim NYG 58
Filipski, Gene NYG 40
Filopowicz, Steve NYG 8/23
Fina, John ARZ 74, BUF 70
Finch, Karl STL 88
Finch, Steve MIN 85
Fink, Mike NOS 44
Finkes, Matt NYJ 51
Finks, James PIT 7
Finlay, Jack STL 68
Finley, Clint KCC 38
Finn, Bernie ARZ 30
Finn, Jim IND 36, NYG 20
Finn, Mike PHL 79
Finneran, Brian ATL 86, PHL 86

Finneran, Gary OAK 76, SDC 76
Finnie, Roger ARZ 60, NOS 63, NYJ 61
Finnin, Tom GBP 71, ARZ 76, IND 77
Finzer, Dave CHI 15, SEA 15
Fiore, Dave SFF 72/74, WSH 74
Fiorentino, Al WSH 11, xBOS 35
Fiorentino, Ed xBOS ?
Fischer, Bill ARZ 72
Fischer, Clete NYG 87
Fischer, Mark WSH 51/60
Fischer, Pat ARZ 37, WSH 37
Fishback, Joe ATL 29, DAL 46, NYJ 36
Fishel, Dick xBKN 22/24/19
Fisher, Bob CHI 85
Fisher, Bob WSH 38
Fisher, Bryce BUF 95, STL 94
Fisher, Charles CIN 25
Fisher, Doug PIT 54
Fisher, Ed TEN 60/70
Fisher, Ev ARZ 10/40, PIT 8
Fisher, Jeff CHI 24
Fisher, Levar ARZ 52
Fisher, Mike ARZ 26
Fisher, Ray DAL 73, PIT 73
Fisher, Tony GBP 40
Fisher, Travis STL 22
Fisk, Bill DET 10/80/81, SFF 56, zLAD 55
Fisk, Jason MIN 72, SDC 92, TEN 97
Fiske, Max PIT 18/19/39
Fiss, Galen CLE 35
Fitzgerald, Greg CHI 96
Fitzgerald, Jamie MIN 29
Fitzgerald, John DAL 62
Fitzgerald, Kevin GBP 89
Fitzgerald, Mickey PHL 38
Fitzgerald, Mike ATL 25, MIN 37, NYG 27
Fitzgibbon, Paul ARZ 31, GBP 1418/49
Fitzhugh, Steve DEN 37
Fitzkee, Scott PHL 81, SDC 81
Fitzpatrick, James OAK 73, SDC 70
Fitzsimmons, Casey DET 82
Flagerman, Jack zLAD 20
Flagler, Terrence ARZ 32, SFF 32
Flaharty, Harry DAL 55
Flaherty, Dick GBP 6
Flaherty, Pat CHI 15
Flaherty, Ray NYG 1/6/8/44
Flaherty, Tom CIN 52
Flanagan, Dick CHI 9, DET 60/74, PIT 57
Flanagan, Ed DET 54, SDC 54
Flanagan, Latham CHI 19, ARZ ?
Flanagan, Mike GBP 58

Flanigan, Jim Jr. CHI 68/99, GBP 75, SFF 75
Flanigan, Jim Sr. GBP 55, NOS 55
Flannery, John DAL 63, STL 63, TEN 55
Flatley, Paul MIN 85, ATL 85
Fleckenstein, Bill CHI 15, DET 53, xBKN 32
Fleming, Antonio ARZ 63
Fleming, Cory DAL 82
Fleming, Don CLE 46
Fleming, George OAK 21
Fleming, Marv GBP 81, MIA 80
Flemister, Zeron WSH 89
Flemons, Ronald ATL 79
Flenniken, Mack NYG ?, ARZ 28
Fletcher, Art xBAL 53
Fletcher, Billy Ray DEN 20
Fletcher, Chris SDC 44
Fletcher, Derrick CAR 74, NEP 64, WSH 67
Fletcher, Jamar MIA 21/24
Fletcher, John CIN 71
Fletcher, London BUF 59, STL 59
Fletcher, Ollie zLAD 34
Fletcher, Simon DEN 73
Fletcher, Terrell SDC 41
Flick, Tom CLE 10, NEP 10, NYJ 8, SDC 12, WSH 12
Flint, George BUF 63/73, BUF 73
Flint, Judson BUF 28, CLE 20
Flones, Brian SEA 50
Florence, Anthony CLE 25/41
Florence, Drayton SDC 29
Florence, Paul ARZ ?
Flores, Mike PHL 95/96, WSH 72/73, WSH 73
Flores, Tom OAK 15, BUF 16/21, KCC 12
Flowers, Bernie IND 81
Flowers, Bob GBP 35
Flowers, Charlie NYJ 41, SDC 41
Flowers, Dick IND 18
Flowers, Erik BUF 96, HOU 57, STL 96
Flowers, Keith DET 50, xDAL 64/50
Flowers, Kenny ATL 48
Flowers, Larry NYG 37, NYJ 38
Flowers, Lee PIT 41
Flowers, Richmond DAL 45, NYG 44
Floyd, Anthony IND 39
Floyd, Bobby GBP 33, CHI 30
Floyd, Chris CLE 34, NEP 37
Floyd, Don TEN 75
Floyd, Eric ARZ 61/69, DEN 61, PHL 61, SDC 61
Floyd, George NYJ 38
Floyd, John ARZ 86, SDC 86

Floyd, Malcolm STL 82, TEN 83
Floyd, Victor SDC 27
Floyd, William SFF 40, CAR 40
Flutie, Darren SDC 86
Flutie, Doug BUF 7, CHI 2, NEP 2, SDC 7
Flynn, Don KCC 18, NYJ 15
Flynn, Mike BLT 62/70
Flynn, Tom GBP 41, NYG 28
Flythe, Mark NYG 95
Foggie, Fred CLE 36, PIT 36
Fogle, DeShawn PHL 52/54
Folau, Spencer BLT 71, MIA 60, NOS 71
Foldberg, Hank zBRK 52, zCHI 50
Foley, Dave BUF 78, NYJ 70
Foley, Glenn NYJ 4/14, SEA 13
Foley, Steve CIN 95, HOU 58
Foley, Steve DEN 43
Foley, Tim IND 78
Foley, Tim MIA 25
Folk, Dick xBKN 22
Folkins, Lee DAL 80/83, GBP 81, PIT 84
Folmer, Brendon DET 10
Folsom, Steve DAL 85, PHL 86
Folston, James ARZ 58, OAK 55
Foltz, Vernon PIT 59, WSH 26
Folz, Art ARZ 14/17
Fonoti, Toniu SDC 71
Fontenot, Al CHI 96, IND 99, SDC 95
Fontenot, Chris PHL 85
Fontenot, Herman CLE 28, GBP 27
Fontenot, Jerry CHI 67, NOS 62
Fontes, Wayne NYJ 26
Foote, Chris IND 66, MIN 62, NYG 66
Foote, James TEN 11/12
Foote, Larry PIT 50
Footman, Dan BLT 78, CLE 78, IND 98
Forbes, Marlon CHI 46, CLE 39
Ford, Bernard DAL 80, TEN 88
Ford, Brad DET 44
Ford, Charles PHL 32, BUF 45, CHI 32, NYG 27
Ford, Chris TBB 81
Ford, Cole BUF 5, OAK 5
Ford, Darryl ATL 48, DET 97, PIT 94
Ford, Fred BUF 26, SDC 20
Ford, Fredric PHL 46
Ford, Garrett DEN 32
Ford, Henry CLE 46, PIT 24
Ford, Henry TEN 92, NOS 92
Ford, James NOS 28
Ford, John DET 80
Ford, Len CLE 53/80, GBP 83, zLAD 50

Ford, Mike CIN 11, TBB 10
Ford, Moses PIT 87
Forde, Brian NOS 52
Fordham, Jim CHI 3
Fordham, Todd JAX 78, PIT 71
Foreman, Chuck MIN 44, NEP 22
Foreman, Jay BUF 55, HOU 56
Forester, Bill GBP 69/71
Forester, Herschel CLE 62
Forkovitch, Nick zBRK 64
Forney, Kynan ATL 65
Forney, Phil ARZ 59
Forrest, Ed SFF 24/34
Forrest, Tom CHI 62
Forsberg, Fred BUF 57, DEN 52, SDC 56
Forsey, Brock CHI 44
Forte, Aldo CHI 23, DET 25, GBP 40
Forte, Bob GBP 8/26
Forte, Ike NEP 38, NYG 35, WSH 30
Fortin, Roman ATL 65, DET 69, SDC 67
Fortmann, Dan CHI 21
Fortner, Larry ATL 9
Fortunato, Joe CHI 31
Fortune, Elliott BLT 91
Fortune, Hosea SDC 84
Foruria, John PIT 9
Foster, Barry PIT 29
Foster, Derrick NYJ 46
Foster, DeShaun CAR 20
Foster, Eddie TEN 89
Foster, Gene SDC 37
Foster, George DEN 72
Foster, Jerome MIA 78, NYJ 98, TEN 78
Foster, Larry ARZ 89
Foster, Larry DET 17/81/87
Foster, Ralph ARZ 9/60/64/77
Foster, Ron OAK 41
Foster, Roy MIA 61, SFF 67
Foster, Will NEP 55
Foules, Elbert PHL 29
Fountaine, Jamal ATL 53, SFF 52/56, CAR 50
Fourcade, John NOS 11
Fourcade, Keith NOS 53
Fournet, Sid KCC 62, NYJ 62, PIT 72, STL 68
Fouts, Dan SDC 14
Fowler, Amos DET 65
Fowler, Aubrey zBAL 80
Fowler, Bob NYJ ?
Fowler, Bobby NOS 43
Fowler, Charlie MIA 71
Fowler, Dan NYG 65
Fowler, Jerry TEN 53
Fowler, Mel CLE 67
Fowler, Todd DAL 46
Fowler, Wayne BUF 53
Fowler, Willmer BUF 23

Fowlkes, Dennis MIA 52, MIN 50
Fox, Chas ARZ 86
Fox, Mike NYG 93, CAR 93
Fox, Sam NYG 70
Fox, Scott TEN 59
Fox, Terry PHL 36, zMIA 76/52
Fox, Tim NEP 48, SDC 48, STL 48
Fox, Vernon SDC 36
Foxx, Dion MIA 57, WSH 56
Frahm, Dick WSH 12
Frahm, Herald PHL ?
Frain, Todd NEP 44, WSH 88
Fraley, Hank PHL 63
Fralic, Bill ATL 79, DET 79
France, Doug STL 77, TEN 77
Franceschi, Pete SFF 82
Franci, Jason DEN 84
Francis, Dave WSH 39
Francis, Gene ARZ 11
Francis, James CIN 50, WSH 51
Francis, Jeff CLE 13
Francis, Joe GBP 20
Francis, Jon STL 35
Francis, Phil SFF 48
Francis, Ron DAL 38
Francis, Russ NEP 81, SFF 81
Francis, Sam CHI 38, PIT 50, xBKN 10
Francis, Wallace ATL 89, BUF 89
Franck, George NYG 5/13/37
Franckhauser, Tom DAL 32, STL 81
Franckowiak, Mike DEN 31
Franco, Brian CLE 3
Franco, Ed xBOS 19
Frank, Bill DAL 76
Frank, Donald MIN 37, OAK 47, SDC 27
Frank, John SFF 86
Frank, Joseph PHL 61/70
Frank, Malcolm SEA 31
Frankhauser, Tom MIN 40
Frankian, Ike WSH 24, NYG 21
Franklin, Andra MIA 37
Franklin, Arnold NEP 87
Franklin, Aubrayo BLT 69
Franklin, Bobby CLE 22/24
Franklin, Byron BUF 85, SEA 88
Franklin, Cleveland IND 28, PHL 30
Franklin, Dennis DET 89
Franklin, George ATL 40
Franklin, Jerrell TEN 62
Franklin, Jethro SEA 90
Franklin, Keith OAK 58
Franklin, Larry TBB 80
Franklin, P.J. NOS 80
Franklin, Pat CIN 39, TBB 35
Franklin, Paul CHI 9
Franklin, Red xBKN 31/6

Franklin, Tony NEP 1, MIA 1, PHL 1
Franklin, Willie IND 30
Frankowiak, Mike BUF 36/84
Frankowski, Ray GBP 15, zLAD 37/34
Franks, Bubba GBP 88
Franks, Dennis DET 58, PHL 53
Franks, Elvis CLE 94, NYJ 74, OAK 94
Franta, Herb GBP 55
Frantz, Jack BUF 51
Franz, Nolan GBP 84
Franz, Todd CLE 22, GBP 49, WSH 27/29
Frase, Paul BLT 95, GBP 97, JAX 91, NYJ 91
Fraser, Jim DEN 51/55, KCC 51, NEP 51, NOS 51
Frazier, Al DEN 42
Frazier, Charles TEN 28, NEP 81
Frazier, Curt CIN 43
Frazier, Derrick IND 31, PHL 23
Frazier, Frank WSH 76
Frazier, Guy BUF 52, CIN 49/58
Frazier, Leslie CHI 21
Frazier, Marv DEN 86
Frazier, Paul NOS 32
Frazier, Wayne BUF 53, KCC 66, SDC 51, TEN 56
Frazier, Willie SDC 83, TEN 74/83, KCC 83
Frederick, Andy CHI 96, CLE 70, DAL 71
Frederick, Mike BLT 94, CLE 94, TEN 94
Frederickson, Tucker NYG 24
Fredrickson, Rob ARZ 59, DET 53, OAK 53
Freelon, Solomon TEN 69
Freeman, Antonio GBP 86, PHL 86
Freeman, Arturo MIA 20/27
Freeman, Bob CLE 18, PHL 41, WSH 20, GBP 41
Freeman, Eddie KCC 71
Freeman, Jack zBRK 34
Freeman, Lorenzo NYG 68, PIT 68
Freeman, Mike ATL 28/43
Freeman, Mike DEN 62, OAK 61
Freeman, Phil TBB 81
Freeman, Reggie NOS 55
Freeman, Russell DEN 68, OAK 70
Freeman, Steve BUF 22, MIN 22
Freeney, Dwight IND 93
Freitas, Jesse Jr. SDC 17
Freitas, Jesse Sr. SFF 62, zBUF 87, zCHI 60

Freitas, Makoa IND 76
Freitas, Rocky DET 76, TBB 74
French, Barry DET 67, xBAL 35, zBAL 35
French, Ernest PIT 20
Frerotte, Gus WSH 12, CIN 12, DEN 12, DET 12, MIN 12
Frerotte, Mitch BUF 59
Frey, Dick KCC 66, TEN 62
Frey, Glenn PHL 32
Frick, Ray xBKN 5
Fricke, Ben DAL 66/69
Friday, Larry BUF 39
Friede, Mike DET 86, NYG 88
Friedlund, Bob PHL 85
Friedman, Benny NYG 1, xBKN 26/17/1
Friedman, Bob PHL 72
Friedman, Lennie DEN 64, WSH 64
Friend, Benjamin STL 35
Frier, Mike CIN 97, SEA 92
Fries, Sherwood GBP 46
Friesz, John NEP 17, SDC 17, SEA 17, WSH 17
Frisch, Byron DAL 90, NYG 99, TEN 93
Frisch, David CIN 47/83, MIN 83, NEP 88, WSH 38
Fritsch, Ernest ARZ 53
Fritsch, Ted Jr. ATL 66, WSH 66
Fritsch, Ted Sr. GBP 64
Fritsch, Toni TEN 16, DAL 15, NOS 15, SDC 15
Fritts, George PHL 71
Fritts, Stan CIN 33
Fritz, Ralph PHL 63
Fritzsche, Jim PHL 72
Frizzell, William DET 26, PHL 33, TBB 33
Frketich, Len PIT 80
Frohbose, Bill DET 39
Fronczek, Andy xBKN 21
Frongillo, John TEN 55
Frost, Ken DAL 79
Frost, Scott CLE 47, NYJ 47, TBB 21
Frugone, Jim NYG 9
Frump, Milt CHI 17
Frutig, Ed DET 11, GBP 51/80
Fry, Bob DAL 75, STL 75
Fryar, Irving MIA 80, NEP 80, PHL 80, WSH 86
Frye, David ATL 58, MIA 53
Frye, Phil MIN 37
Fryer, Brian WSH 85
Fryer, Kenny xBKN 12
Fuamatu-Ma'afala, Chris JAX 45, PIT 45
Fucci, Dom DET 48
Fugett, Jean WSH 84, DAL 84
Fugler, Dick ARZ 75, PIT 75
Fujita, Scott KCC 51
Fulcher, Bill WSH 54/64

Fulcher, David CIN 33, OAK 45
Fulcher, Mondriel OAK 89
Fulhage, Scott ATL 17, CIN 17
Fuller, Charles OAK 20
Fuller, Corey BLT 26, CLE 24/25, MIN 27
Fuller, Curtis GBP 29, SEA 29
Fuller, Eddie BUF 33
Fuller, Frank ARZ 72, PHL 72, STL 71/79
Fuller, James PHL 22, SDC 40
Fuller, Jeff SFF 49
Fuller, Joe GBP 21, SDC 29
Fuller, Johnny NOS 24, SFF 23/30
Fuller, Larry ARZ 45, WSH 12
Fuller, Mike CIN 42, SDC 42
Fuller, Randy ATL 29, DEN 24, PIT 29, SEA 21
Fuller, Steve CHI 4, KCC 4, STL 4
Fuller, William PHL 95, SDC 95, TEN 95
Fullerton, Ed PIT 34
Fullington, Darrell MIN 29, NEP 29, TBB 27
Fullwood, Brent GBP 21, CLE 29
Fulton, Dan BUF 80/84, CLE 86
Fulton, Ed BUF 65, STL 68
Fulton, Ted xBKN 26/36/21/9
Fultz, Mike IND 72/92, MIA 72/76, NOS 72
Funchess, Tom MIA 70, NEP 73, TEN 66
Fuqua, John NYG 29, PIT 33
Fuqua, Ray xBKN 23
Furey, James NYJ 50
Furjanic, Tony BUF 53, MIA 58
Furman, John CLE 18
Furness, Steve DET 71, PIT 64
Furrer, Will ARZ 2, CHI 2, DEN 2, JAX 7, STL 9, TEN 17
Furrey, Mike STL 82
Furst, Tony DET 38/73
Fusina, Chuck GBP 4, TBB 14
Fussell, Tom NEP 83
Futrell, Bobby TBB 36
Gabbard, Steve GBP 72, PHL 67
Gabriel, Doug OAK 85
Gabriel, Roman PHL 5/18, STL 18
Gadbois, Dennis NEP 48
Gaddis, Bob BUF 89
Gadsden, Oronde DAL 80, MIA 86
Gaechter, Mike DAL 27
Gaffney, Derrick NYJ 81
Gaffney, Jabar HOU 86
Gaffney, Jeff SDC 4
Gaffney, Jim WSH 34

Gafford, Monk zBRK 71/80, zMIA 97
Gage, Bob PIT 77
Gage, Justin CHI 87
Gage, Steve WSH 48
Gagliano, Bob ATL 14, DET 14, IND 11, KCC 11, SDC 16, SFF 11
Gagner, Larry KCC 79, PIT 79
Gagnon, Dave CHI 21
Gagnon, Roy DET 24
Gain, Bob CLE 74/79
Gainer, Derrick DAL 39, OAK 27
Gaines, Chris MIA 58
Gaines, Clark KCC 21, NYJ 21
Gaines, Greg SEA 56
Gaines, Lawrence DET 38
Gaines, Sheldon BUF 82/86
Gaines, Wendall ARZ 89/91
Gaines, Wentford CHI 36, PIT 36
Gaines, William MIA 93, WSH 95
Gainor, Charles ARZ 18
Gaiser, George DEN 64
Gaison, Blane ATL 34
Gaiter, Tony NEP 17, SDC 85
Gaiters, Bob NYG 35, SFF 35, DEN 28
Gajan, Hokie NOS 46
Galazin, Stan NYG 34
Galbraith, Scott CLE 81, DAL 81/89, GBP 47, WSH 89
Galbreath, Harry GBP 76, MIA 62, NYJ 64
Galbreath, Tony MIN 32, NOS 34, NYG 30
Galifa, Arnold NYG 17, SFF 16
Galigher, Ed NYJ 85, SFF 75
Galimore, Willie CHI 28
Gallagher, Bernie zLAD 36
Gallagher, Dave CHI 76, DET 71, NYG 71
Gallagher, Frank ATL 68, DET 68, MIN 66
Gallaher, Allen NEP 64
Gallarneau, Hugh CHI 8
Gallegos, Chon OAK 12
Gallery, Jim ARZ 13, CIN 18, MIN 6
Gallovich, Anthony STL 1
Galloway, David ARZ 65, DEN 99
Galloway, Duane DET 40
Galloway, Joey DAL 84, SEA 84
Galloway, Mitchell BUF 82
Galvin, John MIN 90, NYJ 51/52
Galvin, John zBAL 63
Galyon, Scott MIA 58, NYG 52/58
Gamache, Vince OAK 3, SEA 2
Gambino, Lucien zBAL 77/89
Gamble, David DEN 82

Gamble, Kenny KCC 48
Gamble, R.C. NEP 13
Gamble, Trent MIA 42
Gambol, Chris DET 70, IND 74, NEP 74, SDC 74
Gambold, Bob PHL 14
Gambrell, Billy ARZ 3, DET 3
Gammon, Kendall KCC 83, NOS 46/60/62/86, PIT 60
Ganas, Rusty IND 73
Gandee, Sonny DET 85, xDAL 85
Gandy, Mike CHI 69
Gandy, Wayne NOS 72, PIT 72, STL 70
Gann, Mike ATL 76
Gannon, Chris NEP 91, SDC 84
Gannon, Rich OAK 12, KCC 12, MIN 16, WSH 16
Gant, Brian TBB 91
Gant, Earl KCC 23
Gant, Kenneth DAL 29, TBB 29
Gant, Reuben BUF 88
Gantenbein, Milt GBP 21/22/30/46/47
Gantt, Greg NYJ 8
Gantt, Jerome BUF 69
Gaona, Bob PHL 64, PIT 72
Garalczyk, Mark ARZ 76, NYJ 74
Garay, Antonio CLE 95
Garbarczyk, Tony NYJ 70
Garcia, Bubba KCC 80
Garcia, Eddie GBP 11
Garcia, Frank ARZ 63, STL 64, CAR 65
Garcia, Frank SEA 6, TBB 5
Garcia, Jeff SFF 5
Garcia, Jim ATL 76, CLE 81, NOS 80, NYG 70
Garcia, Teddy MIN 2, NEP 7, TEN 8
Gardener, Daryl DEN 99, MIA 92, WSH 92
Gardin, Ron IND 30, NEP 37
Gardner, Barry CLE 55, PHL 52
Gardner, Carwell BLT 35, BUF 35, SDC 35
Gardner, Derrick ATL 30
Gardner, Donnie MIA 79
Gardner, Ellis IND 65, KCC 75
Gardner, Moe ATL 67
Gardner, Moose GBP 14
Gardner, Rod WSH 87
Gardner, Talman NOS 88
Gardocki, Chris IND 17, CHI 17, CLE 17
Garland Jean Batiste NOS 43
Garlich, Chris ARZ 61
Garlin, Don SFF 88
Garlington, John CLE 50
Garmon, Kelvin DAL 61, SDC 63
Garnaas, Bill PIT 30

Garner, Bob NYG 9
Garner, Bob OAK 28, SDC 35
Garner, Charlie SFF 25, OAK 25, PHL 25/30
Garner, Dwight WSH 30
Garner, Hal BUF 99
Garnes, Sam NYG 20, NYJ 42
Garnett, Dave DEN 52, MIN 54
Garnett, Scott BUF 69, DEN 66, SDC 92, SFF 92
Garnett, Winfield MIN 92
Garrard, David JAX 9
Garrett, Alvin NYG 25/84, WSH 89
Garrett, Bill zBAL 30
Garrett, Bob GBP 15
Garrett, Carl NEP 30, CHI 26, NYJ 26, OAK 31
Garrett, Curtis NYG 94
Garrett, Drake DEN 23
Garrett, J.D. NEP 32
Garrett, Jason DAL 17, NYG 17
Garrett, John CIN 48
Garrett, Kevin STL 21
Garrett, Len GBP 88, NOS 83, SFF 82
Garrett, Mike IND 9
Garrett, Mike KCC 21, SDC 20/25
Garrett, Reggie PIT 86
Garrett, Shane CIN 89
Garrett, Thurman CHI 13
Garrett, W.D. CHI 44
Garrison, Gary SDC 27, TEN 82
Garrison, Walt DAL 32
Garrity, Gregg PHL 86, PIT 86
Garron, Larry NEP 40
Garror, Leon BUF 47
Garry, Ben IND 29
Gartner, Chris CLE 10
Garvey, Ed CHI 28
Garvey, Hec CHI 6, NYG 55, xBKN 28
Gary, Cleveland MIA 32, STL 43
Gary, Keith PIT 92
Gary, Olandis DEN 22, DET 33
Gary, Russell NOS 20, PHL 24/38
Gary, Willie STL 30
Garza, Dan xNYB 7, zNYY 57
Garza, Roberto ATL 63
Garza, Sammy ARZ 10
Garzoni, Mike NYG 63, WSH 44, zNYY 33
Gash, Sam BUF 33, BLT 32, NEP 33
Gash, Thane CLE 30, SFF 31
Gaskins, Percell STL 54, CAR 55
Gasparella, Joe ARZ 44, PIT 23/48
Gassert, Ron GBP 73
Gastineau, Mark NYJ 99
Gatewood, Les GBP 33/77

Gatewood, Tom NYG 83
Gatski, Frank CLE 22/52, DET 52
Gaubatz, Dennis DET 53, IND 53
Gaudio, Bob CLE 34/38
Gauer, Charles PIT 32, PHL 32/85
Gaul, Frank xNYB 20
Gault, Billy MIN 44
Gault, Don CLE 11
Gault, Willie CHI 83, OAK 83
Gaunty, Steve KCC 83
Gautt, Prentice ARZ 22, CLE 40
Gavadza, Jason CAR 49
Gavin, Charles DEN 61
Gavric, Momcilo SFF 17
Gay, Ben CLE 34
Gay, Bill ARZ 40
Gay, Bill DET 79/83, MIN 78
Gay, Blenda PHL 68, SDC 61
Gay, Everett DAL 80, TBB 89
Gay, Matt KCC 49
Gaydos, Kent GBP 86
Gayle, Rashid JAX 24
Gayle, Shaun CHI 23, SDC 23
Gaylor, Trevor ATL 81, SDC 82
Gaynor, Doug CIN 11
Gaziano, Frank xBOS 38
Gbaja-Biamila, Akbar OAK 98
Gbaja-Biamila, Kabeer GBP 94
Geason, Cory BUF 88, PIT 85
Geater, Ron DEN 92
Geathers, Jumpy ATL 97, DEN 79, NOS 97, WSH 97
Geddes, Bob DEN 57, NEP 59
Geddes, Ken SEA 36, STL 36
Gedman, Gene DET 26
Gedney, Chris ARZ 84, CHI 84
Gehring, Mark TEN 38
Gehrke, Fred STL 18, ARZ 22, SFF 18
Gehrke, Jack CIN 26, DEN 40, KCC 17
Geile, Chris DET 71
Gelatka, Chuck NYG 29
Gelbaugh, Stan ARZ 10, BUF 8, SEA 8/18
Gent, Pete DAL 35
Gentry, Byron PIT 18
Gentry, Curtiss CHI 46
Gentry, Dale zLAD 53
Gentry, Dennis CHI 29
Gentry, Lee WSH 46
George, Bill CHI 61/72, STL 61
George, Ed IND 73, PHL 64
George, Eddie TEN 27
George, Jeff ATL 1, IND 11, MIN 3, OAK 3, SEA 3, WSH 3
George, Matt PIT 2
George, Ray DET 14, PHL 23/42

George, Ron ATL 50, KCC 55, MIN 55
George, Spencer TEN 26/35
George, Steve ARZ 63, ATL 71
George, Tim CIN 89, CLE 82
George, Tony NEP 41
Gepford, Sid CHI 6
Gerak, John MIN 46/66, STL 66
Gerber, Elwood PHL 62
Geredine, Thomas ATL 84
Gerela, Roy PIT 10, SDC 9, TEN 3
Gerhard, Chris PHL 46
Gerhart, Tom PHL 25
Geri, Joe ARZ 37, PIT 35
Germaine, Joe KCC 7, STL 8
German, Jammi ATL 87, CLE 89
German, Jim ARZ 60, WSH 34
Germany, Reggie BUF 84
Germany, Willie ATL 31, DET 48, NEP 29, TEN 29
Gersbach, Carl ARZ 59, CHI 59, MIN 56, PHL 69, SDC 54
Gervais, Rick SFF 24
Gesek, John DAL 63/67, OAK 63, WSH 63/75
Getchell, Gorham zBAL 59
Getty, Charlie GBP 77, KCC 77
Getz, Fred xBKN ?
Getz, Lee KCC 71
Geyer, Bill CHI 7/11
Ghecas, Lou PHL 11
Gherke, Bruce NYG 83
Ghersanich, Vernon ARZ 41
Giacommaro, Ralph ATL 1, DEN 6
Giammona, Louie NYJ 45, PHL 33
Giancanelli, Hal PHL 27
Giannelli, Mario PHL 64
Giannetti, Frank IND 65
Gianoni, John STL 19
Giaquinto, Nick MIA 35, WSH 30
Gibbons, Jim DET 80
Gibbons, Mike NYG 76/79
Gibbs, Donnie NOS 15
Gibbs, Pat PHL 45
Gibbs, Sonny DAL 11, DET 10
Gibler, Andy CIN 48
Giblin, Robert ARZ 28, NYG 28
Gibron, Abe CLE 34/64, CHI 65, PHL 64, zBUF 40
Gibson, Aaron CHI 78, DAL 63, DET 71
Gibson, Alec WSH 96
Gibson, Antonio NOS 27
Gibson, Butch NYG 11
Gibson, Claude OAK 25, SDC 25
Gibson, Damon CIN 84, CLE 81, JAX 85

Gibson, David IND 26, TBB 34/46
Gibson, Dennis DET 98, SDC 57
Gibson, Derrick OAK 26/36
Gibson, Ernest MIA 42, NEP 43
Gibson, Joe STL 36/63, WSH 46, zBRK 22/21
Gibson, Oliver CIN 99, PIT 98
Gibson, Paul ATL 40, GBP 41
Gibson, Paul zBUF 52
Gibson, Tom CLE 71, STL 75
Giddens, Frank PHL 79
Giddens, Herschel PHL 26
Giddens, Wimpy xBOS 43
Giesler, Jon MIA 79
Gifford, Bob xBKN 22
Gifford, Frank NYG 16
Gift, Wayne STL 3
Gilbert, Ben IND 69
Gilbert, Daren NOS 77
Gilbert, Freddie ARZ 93, DEN 90
Gilbert, Gale BUF 7, SDC 13, SEA 7
Gilbert, Kline CHI 62/74
Gilbert, Lewis ATL 88, PHL 86, SFF 82, STL 89
Gilbert, Sean STL 90, OAK 90, WSH 94, CAR 94
Gilbert, Tony JAX 50
Gilburg, Tom IND 73
Gilchrist, Cookie BUF 34, DEN 2/30, MIA 2
Gilchrist, George ARZ 78
Gildea, John PIT 14/23/33, NYG 17
Gildon, Jason PIT 92
Giles, Jimmie TBB 88, DET 81, PHL 83, TEN 88
Gilius, Willie GBP 5
Gill, Owen IND 44, STL 30
Gill, Randy ARZ 59, TBB 49
Gill, Roger PHL 32
Gill, Sloko DET 51
Gillen, John ARZ 57, NEP 54
Gillespie, Scoop PIT 26
Gillespie, Willie MIN 86, TBB 83
Gillett, Fred OAK 44, SDC 33
Gillette, James STL 9/24, DET 11, GBP 16, xBOS 11
Gillette, Walker ARZ 84, NYG 84, SDC 84
Gilliam, Dondre SDC 10/86
Gilliam, Joe PIT 17
Gilliam, John MIN 42, ARZ 44, ATL 42, CHI 82, NOS 41/42
Gilliam, Jon KCC 65
Gillies, Fred ARZ 5/9/10/11/66
Gillingham, Gale GBP 68
Gillis, Don ARZ 50
Gillmore, Bryan ARZ 11/86
Gillom, Horace CLE 59/84

Gillson, Bob xBKN 21/35
Gilmer, Harry WSH 12/52, DET 12
Gilmore, Corey CLE 21
Gilmore, Jim MIA 66, PHL 75
Gilmore, John CHI 85
Ginn, Hubert IND 27/39, MIA 28/32/33, OAK 29
Ginn, Tommie DET 66
Ginney, Jerry PHL 31
Gipson, Paul DET 23, NEP 46
Gipson, Tom OAK 73
Girard, Earl PIT 41/44, DET 23, GBP 36
Gisler, Mike NEP 67, NYJ 67
Gissinger, Andrew SDC 75
Givens, David NEP 18/87
Givens, Reggie SFF 59, WSH 58
Givins, Ernest TEN 81, JAX 84
Gizzi, Chris GBP 57
Glacken, Scotty DEN 17
Gladchuk, Chet NYG 11/51
Gladden, Mack xSTL 11
Gladieux, Bob BUF 24, NEP 24
Gladman, Charles TBB 37
Gladney, Tony SFF 17/86
Glamp, Joe PIT 17
Glasglow, Brian CHI 82/98
Glasgow, Nesby IND 25, SEA 22
Glass, Bill CIN 64
Glass, Bill CLE 80, DET 53
Glass, Chip CLE 83, NYG 83
Glass, Glenn PIT 43/87, ATL 49, DEN 49, PHL 49
Glass, Leland GBP 46
Glassgow, Bill DET 22, ARZ 34
Glassic, Tom DEN 62
Glatz, Fred PIT 83
Glaze, Charles SEA 16
Glazebrook, Bob ATL 36
Gleason, Steve NOS 37
Glenn, Aaron HOU 31, NYJ 31
Glenn, Bill CHI 8
Glenn, Howard NYJ 66
Glenn, Jason NYJ 56/58
Glenn, Kerry MIA 35, NYJ 35
Glenn, Tarik IND 78
Glenn, Terry NEP 88, DAL 83, GBP 83
Glenn, Vencie MIN 25, NEP 25, NOS 29, NYG 25, SDC 25
Glick, Freddy TEN 27, ARZ 33
Glick, Gary IND 47, PIT 26/27, SDC 43, WSH 21
Gloden, Fred PHL 37, zMIA 87
Glosson, Clyde BUF 26/83
Glover, Andrew MIN 82, OAK 87
Glover, Clyde SFF 93
Glover, Kevin DET 53, SEA 53
Glover, La'Roi DAL 97, NOS 97, OAK 92
Glover, Lavar CIN 42

Glover, Phil TEN 54
Glover, Rich NYG 77, PHL 69
Glueck, Larry CHI 43
Goad, Paul SFF 36
Goad, Tim BLT 73, CLE 73, NEP 72
Goar, Guy MIA 67
Gob, Art SDC 89, WSH 89
Goble, Les ARZ 20
Goddard, Edwin STL 7/28, xBKN 7
Godfrey, Chris NYG 61, NYJ 90, SEA 60
Godfrey, Herbert STL 46
Godfrey, Randall DAL 56, SEA 53, TEN 56
Godwin, Bill xBOS 40
Goeas, Leo BLT 62, SDC 67, STL 79
Goebel, Brad CLE 8, JAX 9, PHL 8, STL 63
Goebel, Paul CHI 44
Goedeke, George DEN 67
Goff, Clark PIT 64
Goff, Mike CIN 63
Goff, Robert MIN 94, NOS 91, TBB 94
Goff, Willard ATL 70, SDC 76
Gofourth, Derrel GBP 57, SDC 69
Gogan, Kevin OAK 66, DAL 66, MIA 66, SDC 66, SFF 66
Goganious, Keith BLT 50, BUF 50/95, JAX 54
Gogolak, Charlie NEP 7, WSH 3
Gogolak, Pete BUF 3, NYG 3
Goich, Dan DET 72, NOS 77, NYG 68
Goings, Nick CAR 36/37
Goins, Robert CLE 28
Gold, Ian DEN 52
Goldberg, Bill ATL 71
Goldberg, Marshall ARZ 42/73/99
Golden, Jack NYG 51/90, TBB 58
Golden, Tim NEP 59, PHL 91
Goldenberg, Charles GBP 21/43/44/51
Golding, Joe xBOS 10
Golding, Joe xNYB 10
Goldman, Sam ARZ 70, DET 85, xBOS 42/23
Goldsberry, John ARZ 82
Goldsmith, Wen NYG 41
Goldstein, Alan OAK 81
Goldston, Ralph PHL 22
Golemgeske, John xBKN 17
Golic, Bob CLE 79, NEP 51, OAK 79
Golic, Mike MIA 96, PHL 90, TEN 68
Gollomb, Rudy PHL 14
Golsteyn, Jerry DET 17, IND

12/15, NYG 12, OAK 14, TBB 11
Goltz, Rick OAK 94
Golub, Chris KCC 47
Gompers, Bill zBUF 88
Gonda, George PIT 30
Gonsoulin, Goose DEN 23, SFF 35
Gonya, Robert PHL 27
Gonzaga, John DAL 76, DEN 79, DET 79, SFF 76
Gonzalez, Dan DAL 9
Gonzalez, Joaquin CLE 73
Gonzalez, Leon DAL 83, ATL 89
Gonzalez, Noe NEP 38
Gonzalez, Pete PIT 7
Gonzalez, Tony KCC 88
Gooch, Jeff DET 59, TBB 50
Good, Tom SDC 54
Goodburn, Kelly KCC 2, WSH 2
Goode, Chris IND 37
Goode, Conrad NYG 62, TBB 79
Goode, Don CLE 50, SDC 50
Goode, Irv ARZ 55, MIA 55
Goode, John ARZ 84, PHL 87
Goode, Kerry MIA 22, TBB 27
Goode, Rob WSH 21/39, PHL 38
Goode, Tom MIA 58, IND 54, TEN 68
Goodlow, Darryl OAK 90/98
Goodlow, Eugene NOS 88
Goodman, Andre DET 35
Goodman, Aubrey ARZ ?
Goodman, Brian DEN 62, TEN 68
Goodman, Don ARZ 37/40
Goodman, Hank DET 72
Goodman, Harvey DEN 64
Goodman, Herbert GBP 29
Goodman, John PIT 95
Goodman, Les GBP 25
Goodnight, Clyde GBP 23, WSH 38/87
Goodnight, Owen CHI 27
Goodrich, Dwayne DAL 23
Goodridge, Bob MIN 82
Goodrum, Charles MIN 68
Goodson, John PIT 17
Goodspeed, Dan SFF 72
Goodspeed, Joey SDC 45, STL 44
Goodspeed, Mark ARZ 70
Goodwin, Doug ATL 30, BUF 35
Goodwin, Hunter MIA 83, MIN 83/87
Goodwin, Jonathan NYJ 78
Goodwin, Marvin PHL 22
Goodwin, Ron PHL 31/81
Goodwin, Tod NYG 14
Goodyear, John WSH 12
Goolsby, James STL 24

Goosby, Tom CLE 64, WSH 69

Goovert, Ron DET 57

Gordon, Alex CIN 58, NYJ 55, OAK 55

Gordon, Bob ARZ 47, TEN 47

Gordon, Cornell DEN 28, NYJ 48

Gordon, Darrien ATL 21, DEN 21/23, GBP 23, OAK 23/34, SDC 21

Gordon, Dick CHI 45, GBP 7/85, SDC 88, STL 5

Gordon, Dwayne ATL 53, NYJ 54, SDC 52

Gordon, Ira SDC 69

Gordon, John DET 77

Gordon, Lamar STL 34

Gordon, Larry MIA 50

Gordon, Lennox BUF 31, IND 30

Gordon, Lou ARZ 22, CHI 19, GBP 47/53, xBKN 27

Gordon, Sonny TBB 31

Gordon, Steve SFF 59/64

Gordon, Tim ATL 41, NEP 41

Gordy, John DET 75

Gore, Gordon DET 10

Gore, Stacy MIA 3

Gorecki, Chuck PHL 51

Gorgal, Ken CHI 14, CLE 15/85, GBP 26

Gorgone, Pete NYG 25

Gorin, Brandon NEP 73/76

Gorinski, Walt PIT 20

Goss, Antonio SFF 98

Goss, Don CLE 64

Goss, Jason ARZ 25

Gossage, Gene PHL 79

Gossett, Bruce SFF 30, STL 30

Gossett, Jeff OAK 6/7, CLE 7, KCC 7, TEN 8

Gothard, Preston PIT 86

Gotshalk, Lynn ATL 65

Gottschalk, Darren NOS 82

Gouveia, Kurt PHL 54, SDC 54, WSH 54

Governali, Paul NYG 41, xBOS 4

Gowdy, Cornell DAL 44, PIT 29

Gowin, Toby DAL 4, NOS 4

Gowins, Brian CHI 11

Grabinski, Ted PIT 11/53

Grabosky, Gene BUF 78

Grabowski, Jim CHI 33, GBP 33

Grace, Clif IND 27/33, IND 33

Grace, Steve ARZ 64

Graddy, Sam DEN 83, OAK 85

Gradishar, Randy DEN 52/53

Grady, Garry MIA 29

Graf, Dave CLE 55, WSH 58

Graf, Rick MIA 58/99, TEN 93, WSH 90

Graff, Neil NEP 15, PIT 16

Gragg, Scott NYG 74, SFF 78

Graham, Aaron ARZ 54, OAK 68, TEN 60

Graham, Al DET ?, ARZ 44

Graham, Art NEP 84

Graham, Conrad CHI 37

Graham, Dan TBB 65

Graham, Daniel NEP 82

Graham, Dave PHL 78

Graham, David SEA 78

Graham, Demingo HOU 70, SDC 71

Graham, Derrick KCC 74, OAK 74, SEA 77, CAR 74

Graham, Don BUF 59, NYJ 56, TBB 53, WSH 57

Graham, Hason NEP 81

Graham, Jay BLT 34, GBP 35, SEA 35

Graham, Jeff CHI 81, NYJ 81, OAK 8, PHL 81, PIT 81, SDC 81

Graham, Kenny SDC 33, CIN 33, PIT 24

Graham, Kent ARZ 11, JAX 10, NYG 10, PIT 11, WSH 10

Graham, Les DET 23

Graham, Lyle PHL 51

Graham, Mike zLAD 85

Graham, Milt NEP 70

Graham, Otto CLE 14/60

Graham, Roger JAX 34

Graham, Scottie CIN 41, MIN 31, NYJ 33

Graham, Shayne BUF 17, CIN 17, CAR 11

Graham, Tom BUF 55, DEN 58, KCC 56, SDC 58

Graham, Tom PHL 31

Graham, William DET 33

Grain, Ed zBAL 33/45, zNYY 37

Gramatica, Bill ARZ 7

Gramatica, Martin TBB 7

Granby, John DEN 35

Grandberry, Ken CHI 47

Grandelius, Sonny NYG 24

Granderson, Rufus KCC 75

Grandinette, George xBKN 34

Grange, Garland CHI 25

Grange, Red CHI 77

Granger, Charles ARZ 23

Granger, Charlie DAL 71

Granger, Hoyle TEN 30/32, NOS 40

Granger, Norm ATL 32, DAL 28

Grannel, Dave SDC 82

Grant, Aaron DET ?

Grant, African MIA 41

Grant, Alan CIN 24, IND 26, SFF 24/26, WSH 26

Grant, Bob IND 51, WSH 51

Grant, Bud PHL 86

Grant, Charles NOS 94

Grant, Darryl TBB 97, WSH 77

Grant, David CIN 98, GBP 70, TBB 99

Grant, DeLawrence OAK 95/99

Grant, Deon CAR 27

Grant, Ernest CHI 72, MIA 97

Grant, Frank TBB 83, WSH 46

Grant, Hugh ARZ 7

Grant, John DEN 63

Grant, Ken TEN 62

Grant, Len NYG 3

Grant, Orantes DAL 56, WSH 57

Grant, Otis PHL 81, STL 82

Grant, Rosie xCIN 49

Grant, Rupert NEP 34

Grant, Stephen IND 59

Grant, Wes BUF 89, CLE 75, SDC 86

Grant, Will BUF 53, SEA 52

Grant, Willie NOS 58

Grantham, Larry NYJ 60

Granville, Billy CIN 91

Grasmanis, Paul CHI 93, DEN 95, PHL 96

Grate, Carl NYG 17

Grate, Willie BUF 85

Grau, Jeff DAL 58, MIA 47

Gravelle, Gordon NYG 71, PIT 71, STL 73

Graves, Marsharne DEN 72, IND 61

Graves, Ray PHL 51/52, PIT 52

Graves, Rory MIN 73, OAK 60

Graves, Tom PIT 50

Graves, White CIN 41, NEP 44

Gray, Bill WSH 60

Gray, Bobby CHI 25

Gray, Carlton IND 26, KCC 23, NYG 23, SEA 26

Gray, Cecil ARZ 66, GBP 71, IND 75, NOS 74, PHL 71

Gray, Chris CHI 62, MIA 62, SEA 62

Gray, Dan DET 64

Gray, David NOS 21

Gray, Derwin IND 30, CAR 44

Gray, Earnest NYG 83, ARZ 87

Gray, Hector DET 26

Gray, Jerry STL 25, TBB 20, TEN 21

Gray, Jim NYJ 28, PHL 28

Gray, Johnnie GBP 24

Gray, Ken ARZ 64

Gray, Kevin NOS 33

Gray, Leon NEP 70, NOS 72, TEN 74

Gray, Mel ARZ 85

Gray, Mel DET 23, NOS 37, PHL 28, TEN 21

Gray, Moses NYJ 73

Gray, Oscar SEA 32

Gray, Paul ATL 59

Gray, Sam PIT 23
Gray, Tim ARZ 33, KCC 46, SFF 30
Gray, Torrian MIN 23
Graybill, Mike ARZ 75, CLE 79
Grayson, Dave KCC 45, OAK 45
Grayson, David CLE 52/56, SDC 58
Graziani, Tony ATL 7/13
Grbac, Elvis KCC 11/18, BLT 18, SFF 18
Greaves, Gary TEN 65
Grecni, Dick MIN 50
Greco, Don DET 67
Greeley, Bucky CAR 60
Green, Ahman GBP 30, SEA 30
Green, Alex DAL 29/48
Green, Allen DAL 61
Green, Anthony IND 91
Green, Arthur NOS 45
Green, Barrett DET 54
Green, Bobby Joe CHI 88, PIT 89
Green, Boyce CLE 30, KCC 40, SEA 30
Green, Charley OAK 12
Green, Chris BUF 42, MIA 42
Green, Cleveland MIA 61/74
Green, Cornell DAL 34
Green, Cornell TBB 74
Green, Curtis DET 62
Green, Darrell WSH 28
Green, Dave CIN 41, TBB 4, TEN 11
Green, David CLE 34
Green, David NEP 38
Green, Donnie BUF 74, DET 67, PHL 74
Green, Donny JAX 54, WSH 53
Green, E.G. IND 84
Green, Eric PIT 86, MIA 86, NYJ 86
Green, Ernie CLE 48
Green, Gary STL 27, KCC 24
Green, Gaston DEN 28, STL 44
Green, Harold CIN 28, ATL 28, STL 30
Green, Howard BLT 95, HOU 90, NOS 95
Green, Hugh TBB 53, MIA 55
Green, Jacob SEA 79, SFF 76
Green, Jacquez DET 12, TBB 81, WSH 80
Green, Jarvis NEP 97
Green, Jerry NEP 45
Green, Jessie GBP 86, SEA 86
Green, Joe NYG 33
Green, John BUF 18, NYJ 12
Green, John PHL 89
Green, Lamont ATL 50
Green, Mark CHI 31
Green, Mike CHI 43
Green, Mike SDC 58
Green, Mike TEN 20

Green, Paul DEN 87, NOS 85, SEA 87
Green, Ray MIA 40, NYG 29, NYJ 31, CAR 29
Green, Robert CHI 22, MIN 32, WSH 39
Green, Rogerick JAX 26, TBB 26
Green, Ron CLE 43
Green, Roy ARZ 25/81, PHL 81
Green, Sammy SEA 56
Green, Tim ATL 99
Green, Tony WSH 34, NYG 34, SEA 34
Green, Trent KCC 10, STL 10, WSH 10
Green, Van BUF 21, CLE 21
Green, Victor NEP 27, NOS 23, NYJ 21
Green, William CLE 31
Green, Willie DEN 85, DET 86, TBB 82, CAR 86
Green, Woody KCC 27
Green, Yatil MIA 87
Greenberg, Ben xBKN ?
Greene, A.J. NYG 41
Greene, Andrew MIA 68, SEA 72
Greene, Danny SEA 84
Greene, Doug ARZ 40, BUF 21
Greene, Ed ARZ 21
Greene, Frank ARZ 25
Greene, Joe PIT 72/75
Greene, John DET 10/81
Greene, Ken ARZ 37, SDC 28
Greene, Kevin PIT 91, SFF 91, STL 91, CAR 91
Greene, Marcellus MIN 25
Greene, Nelson zNYY 41
Greene, Scott IND 43, CAR 43
Greene, Ted KCC 54
Greene, Tiger ATL 33, GBP 23
Greene, Tom KCC 14, NEP 14
Greene, Tony BUF 43
Greene, Tracy PIT 84, KCC 87
Greeney, Norm GBP 20, PIT 30/45
Greenfield, Tom GBP 56
Greenhalgh, Bob NYG 12
Greenlee, Fritz SFF 59
Greenshields, Don xBKN 20/3
Greenwood, Carl NYJ 22
Greenwood, David GBP 49, OAK 41, TBB 30
Greenwood, Donald STL 66, CLE 85
Greenwood, L.C. PIT 68
Greenwood, Morlon MIA 52
Greer, Al DET 82
Greer, Charles DEN 20
Greer, Curtis ARZ 75
Greer, Donovan BUF 25, DET 41, NOS 38, WSH 25
Greer, James DEN 85

Greer, Terry CLE 80, DET 89, SFF 29/82/83
Grefe, Ted DET 45
Gregg, Forrest GBP 75, DAL 79
Gregg, Kelly BLT 73/97, PHL 94
Gregor, Bob SDC 43
Gregory, Ben BUF 33
Gregory, Bill DAL 77, SEA 77
Gregory, Damian MIA 75/98
Gregory, Garlin SFF 32
Gregory, Glynn DAL 21
Gregory, Jack CLE 81, NYG 81
Gregory, Jack STL 23
Gregory, Ken IND 88, NYJ 84, PHL 80
Gregory, Ted NOS 74
Greisen, Nick NYG 54
Gremminger, Hank GBP 46, STL 46
Gresham, Bob NOS 35, NYJ 36, TEN 36
Grgich, Visco SFF 34/38/47/64
Grice, Shane TBB 68
Grier, Mario NEP 35
Grier, Rosey NYG 76, STL 76
Griese, Bob MIA 12
Griese, Brian DEN 14, MIA 14
Griesen, Chris ARZ 14
Griffen, Hal DET 26/85
Griffin, Archie CIN 45
Griffin, Bob ARZ 55, STL 58
Griffin, Bobby xNYB 61
Griffin, Chris JAX 48
Griffin, Cornelius NYG 97
Griffin, Courtney STL 42
Griffin, Damon CIN 87
Griffin, Don CLE 28, PHL 28, SFF 29
Griffin, Don zCHI 99
Griffin, Harold GBP 25
Griffin, James CIN 22, DET 34
Griffin, Jeff ARZ 35, PHL 45
Griffin, Jim CIN 76, SDC 77
Griffin, John DEN 46, STL 45
Griffin, Keith WSH 35
Griffin, Larry PIT 22, TEN 22
Griffin, Leonard KCC 98
Griffin, Quentin DEN 22
Griffin, Ray CIN 44
Griffin, Stephen KCC 39
Griffin, Steve ATL 86
Griffing, Glynn NYG 15
Griffith, Brent BUF 64
Griffith, Forrest NYG 41
Griffith, Homer ARZ 28/33
Griffith, Howard DEN 29, STL 30, CAR 30
Griffith, Justin ATL 33
Griffith, Rich JAX 85, NEP 88
Griffith, Robert MIN 24, CLE 24
Griffith, Russell SEA 6
Griffith, Wade IND 69
Grigas, John ARZ 66, PIT 66, xBOS 15/36

Grigg, Forrest CLE 48, xDAL 79/78, zBUF 40, zCHI 42

Grigg, Tex NYG 8

Griggs, Anthony CLE 53, PHL 58

Griggs, Billy NYJ 81

Griggs, David MIA 92, SDC 92

Griggs, Perry IND 28

Grigonis, Frank DET 31

Grim, Bob MIN 26/27, CHI 27, NYG 27

Grimes, Billy GBP 22, zLAD 85

Grimes, George DET 42

Grimes, Phil OAK 97

Grimes, Randy TBB 60

Grimes, Reggie NEP 97

Grimm, Dan ATL 67, GBP 67, IND 67, WSH 67

Grimm, Russ WSH 68

Grimsley, Ed IND 56

Grimsley, John TEN 59, MIA 59

Groce, Clif CIN 46

Groce, DeJuan STL 24

Groce, Ron MIN 47

Grogan, Steve NEP 14

Groman, Bill BUF 81, DEN 89, TEN 89

Groom, Jerry ARZ 57

Groomes, Mel DET 17

Grooms, Elois ARZ 78, NOS 78, PHL 98

Gros, Earl GBP 40, NOS 40, PHL 34, PIT 38

Gross, Al CLE 27

Gross, Andy NYG 64

Gross, George SDC 79

Gross, Jordan CAR 69

Gross, Lee IND 52, NOS 56

Grossart, Kyle OAK 17

Grosscup, Lee NYG 11, NYJ 17

Grossman, Burt PHL 69, SDC 92

Grossman, Jack xBKN 31/5/88/32

Grossman, Randy PIT 84

Grossman, Rex CHI 8

Grossman, Rex DET 81, xBAL 74, zBAL 74

Grosvenor, George ARZ 32, CHI 8

Groth, Jeff MIA 85, NOS 48/86, TEN 81

Grottkau, Bob DAL 64, DET 60

Grove, Roger GBP 10/11

Groves, George CLE 37, zBAL 38, zBUF 36

Grow, Monty JAX 28, KCC 22

Groza, Lou CLE 46/76

Gruber, Bob CLE 65, GBP 69, MIA 71

Gruber, Paul TBB 74

Gruneisen, Sam SDC 65, TEN 57

Grunhard, Tim KCC 61

Grupp, Bob KCC 1

Gruttadauria, Mike ARZ 60, STL 60

Grygo, Al CHI 32

Grymes, Darrell DET 80

Gucciardo, Pat NYJ 28

Gudauskas, Pete CHI 17, STL 3

Gudd, Leonard PHL 25

Gude, Henry PHL 73

Gudmundson, Scott xBOS 18

Guendling, Mike SDC 53

Gueno, Jim GBP 51

Guesman, Dick DEN 77, NYJ 72/77

Guess, Terry NOS 18

Guggemos, Neal MIN 41, NYG 41

Guglielmi, Ralph ARZ 3, NYG 3, PHL 17, WSH 3

Guidry, Kevin ARZ 37, DEN 37

Guidry, Paul BUF 59, TEN 46

Guilbeau, Rusty CLE 94, NYJ 94

Guillory, Anthony STL 88, PHL 61

Guillory, John CIN 28

Guliford, Eric MIN 84, NOS 84, CAR 84

Gulledge, David WSH 29

Gulseth, Don DEN 53

Gulyanics, George CHI 39

Guman , Mike STL 44

Gunderman, Bob PIT 82

Gundlach, Herman WSH 29

Gunn, Jimmy CHI 30, NYG 30, TBB 30

Gunn, Lance CIN 27

Gunn, Mark NOS 96, NYJ 96/98, PHL 96

Gunnels, Riley PHL 74, PIT 61/74/79

Gunner, Harry CHI 78, CIN 89

Gunter, Greg NYJ 61

Gunter, Michael KCC 38

Gurley, Buck TBB 90

Gurode, Andre DAL 65

Gursky, Al NYG 33

Gussie, Mike xBKN 3

Gustafson, Ed zBRK 22

Gustafson, Jim MIN 80

Guthrie, Grant BUF 7

Guthrie, Keith SDC 73

Gutierrez, Brock CIN 62, SFF 52

Gutknecht, Albert STL 25, xBKN 2

Gutowsky, Ace DET 5/55, xBKN 11

Guy, Benjamin SFF 7

Guy, Buzz DAL 60, DEN 63, NYG 60, TEN 60

Guy, Louie OAK 22, NYG 23

Guy, Ray OAK 8

Guynes, Thomas ARZ 70/71

Guyon, Joe NYG 11

Guyton, Myron NEP 29, NYG 29

Guzik, John NEP 97, STL 60/65, TEN 33

Gwinn, Ross NOS 62

Haak, Bob xBKN 19

Haase, Andy NYG 89

Haayer, Adam MIN 72, TEN 70

Habib, Brian DEN 75, MIN 74/91, SEA 68

Hachten, Paul NYG 66

Hackbart, Dale ARZ 49, DEN 48, GBP 40, MIN 49, WSH 46

Hackenbruck, Johnny DET 25

Hackett, Dino KCC 56, SEA 55

Hackett, Joey DEN 85, GBP 89

Hackney, Elmer DET 34, PHL 20, PIT 20

Hadd, Gary ARZ 73, DET 71

Haddad, Drew IND 84

Haddix, Michael GBP 35, PHL 26

Haddix, Wayne TBB 45, CIN 45, NYG 37

Haddon, Aldous CHI 28

Haden, Jack NYG 9

Haden, Nick PHL 62

Haden, Pat STL 11

Hadl, John SDC 21, GBP 12/21, STL 21, TEN 21

Hadley, David KCC 23

Hadley, Ron SFF 54

Hadnot, James KCC 48

Hafen, Barney DET 84

Haffner, Mike CIN 35, DEN 84

Hagberg, Roger OAK 30

Hagberg, Swede xBKN 27

Hageman, Fred WSH 50

Hagen, Halvor BUF 76/88, DAL 64, NEP 62

Hagen, Mike SEA 34

Hager, Britt DEN 54, PHL 54, STL 57

Hagerty, Horse xBKN 17

Hagerty, Jack NYG 5/13

Haggan, Mario BUF 53

Haggans, Clark PIT 53

Haggerty, Mike DET 77, NEP 75, PIT 76

Haggerty, Steve DEN 22

Haggins, Odell BUF 93

Hagins, Isaac TBB 1/81

Hagler, Scott SEA 1

Hagood, Jay NYJ 77

Hagood, Rickey SDC ?

Hagy, John BUF 22/49, KCC 22

Haight, Mike NYJ 79, WSH 72

Haik, Mac TEN 86

Haines, Byron PIT 53
Haines, Hinkey NYG 1/2
Haines, Hoot xBKN 21/31
Haines, John IND 90, MIN 90
Haines, Kris BUF 85, CHI 83, WSH 80
Hairston, Carl ARZ 98, CLE 78, PHL 78
Hairston, Russell PIT 80
Hairston, Stacey CLE 31
Hajek, Charles PHL 8
Haji-Sheikh, Ali NYG 6, ATL 6, WSH 6
Hakim, Az-Zahir DET 81, STL 81
Halapin, Mike NOS 79, TEN 93
Halas, George CHI 7
Hale, Chris BUF 26, DEN 26
Hale, Dave CHI 75
Hale, Ryan NYG 93
Haley, Charles DAL 94, SFF 94/95
Haley, Darryl CLE 68, GBP 74, NEP 68
Haley, Dick MIN 28, PIT 27, WSH 43
Haley, Jermaine MIA 94, WSH 99
Haliburton, Ronnie DEN 93
Hall, Alvin DET 35, STL 46
Hall, Barry HOU 70, TEN 61
Hall, Carlos TEN 97
Hall, Charlie CLE 59
Hall, Charlie GBP 21/44
Hall, Chris DAL 38
Hall, Corey ATL 28
Hall, Cory ATL 27, CIN 26
Hall, Courtney SDC 53
Hall, Dana CLE 25, JAX 28, SFF 28
Hall, Dante KCC 20/82
Hall, Darryl DEN 40, SFF 43
Hall, Darryl STL ?
Hall, Delton PIT 35, SDC 36
Hall, Dino CLE 26
Hall, Forrest SFF 88
Hall, Galen NYJ 17, WSH 17
Hall, Harold NYG 49
Hall, Irving PHL 32
Hall, James ATL 96, DET 63/96
Hall, Jeff STL 5
Hall, John ARZ 7/77, DET 14
Hall, John NYG ?
Hall, John NYJ 9, WSH 10
Hall, Ken ARZ 20, TEN 21
Hall, Lamont GBP 49/88, NOS 81
Hall, Lemanski CHI 53, MIN 55, TEN 51, DAL 55
Hall, Mark GBP 72
Hall, Parker STL 32, SFF 64/84

Hall, Pete NYG 12
Hall, Randy IND 33
Hall, Ray JAX 97
Hall, Rhett PHL 97, SFF 91, TBB 66/91
Hall, Ron DET 89, TBB 82
Hall, Ron NEP 23, PIT 26/49
Hall, Steven IND 35, MIN 23
Hall, Tim OAK 45
Hall, Tom DET 86, MIN 28/86, NOS 86
Hall, Travis ATL 98
Hall, Willie NOS 56, OAK 39
Hall, Windlan MIN 40, SFF 43, WSH 40
Halleck, Paul STL 16
Hallen, Bob ATL 64, SDC 62
Haller, Alan CLE 20, PIT 21, CAR 24
Halliday, Jack STL 36
Hallock, Ty CHI 49/94, DET 49, JAX 49/54/88
Halloran, Shawn ARZ 19
Hallstrom, Bernie ARZ 6
Hallstrom, Ron GBP 65, PHL 65
Halperin, Buck xBKN 23/7
Haluska, Jim CHI 11
Halverson, Bill PHL 75
Halverson, Dean ATL 59, PHL 56, STL 56
Ham, Derrick CLE 73, WSH 75
Ham, Jack PIT 59
Haman, John STL 15
Hambrick, Darren CAR 59, DAL 54
Hambrick, Troy DAL 35/42, DAL 42
Hamby, Mike BUF 75
Hamdan, Gibran WSH 12
Hamel, Dean DAL 60, WSH 78
Hamilton, Andy KCC 80, NOS 83
Hamilton, Ben DEN 50
Hamilton, Bobby NEP 91, NYJ 92
Hamilton, Conrad NYG 41
Hamilton, Darrell DEN 69
Hamilton, Harry NYJ 39, TBB 39
Hamilton, James JAX 54
Hamilton, Joe TBB 1/14
Hamilton, Keith NYG 75
Hamilton, Lawrence CIN 88, NYJ 87
Hamilton, Malcolm WSH 55
Hamilton, Michael CLE 50, MIA 50, SDC 53
Hamilton, Ray NEP 71
Hamilton, Ray DET 42, PHL 18, STL 27/44
Hamilton, Rick KCC 53, NYJ 56, WSH 56

Hamilton, Ruffin GBP 58, ATL 54
Hamilton, Skip PHL 99
Hamilton, Steve WSH 64
Hamilton, Wes MIN 61
Hamiter, Uhuru NOS 70/96, PHL 91
Hamity, Lewis CHI 3
Hamlin, Gene CHI 50, DET 58, WSH 52
Hamlin, Ken SEA 26
Hamm, Bob IND 95, KCC 90, TEN 90
Hammack, Malcom ARZ 31
Hammerstein, Mike CIN 71
Hammond, Bob NYG 33, WSH 34
Hammond, Gary ARZ 30
Hammond, Henry CHI 15
Hammond, Kim MIA 15, NEP 15
Hammond, Steve NYJ 96
Hammond, Wayne DEN 72
Hammonds, Juan JAX 97
Hammonds, Shelly MIN 23
Hamner, Thomas PHL 33
Hampton, Alonzo MIN 25, TBB 22
Hampton, Casey PIT 98
Hampton, Dan CHI 99
Hampton, Dave ATL 43, GBP 25, PHL 34
Hampton, Jermaine IND 47
Hampton, Kwante ATL 85
Hampton, Lorenzo MIA 27
Hampton, Rodney NYG 27
Hampton, William CAR 31, PHL 41
Hamrick, James KCC 4
Hanburger, Chris WSH 55
Hancock, Anthony KCC 82
Hancock, Kevin IND 51
Hancock, Mike WSH 84
Hand, Jon IND 78
Hand, Larry DET 74
Hand, Norman MIA 98, NOS 99, SDC 96, SEA 96
Hand, Omari SDC 91
Handler, Phil ARZ 7/11/32/33/46
Handley, Dick SFF 26, zBAL 24
Hanke, Carl CHI 5
Hanken, Ray NYG 37
Hanks, Ben DET 50, MIN 51
Hanks, Merton SFF 36, SEA 36
Hankton, Cortez JAX 85
Hankton, Karl PHL 82, CAR 88
Hanlon, Bob ARZ 17, PIT 45
Hanna, Jim NOS 98
Hanna, Zip WSH 39
Hannah, Charley OAK 73, TBB 73
Hannah, Herb NYG 77

Hannah, **John** NEP 73
Hannah, Shane DAL 63
Hannah, Travis TEN 82
Hannam, Ryan SEA 83
Hanneman, Chuck DET 12/88, STL 31
Hanneman, Craig NEP 74, PIT 67
Hannemann, Cliff CLE 58
Hanner, Dave GBP 77/79
Hanney, Frank GBP 19
Hannon, Tom MIN 45
Hannula, Jim CIN 66
Hanny, Frank CHI 19, DET 62
Hanousek, Matt SEA 67
Hanratty, Terry PIT 5, TBB 5
Hansen, Brian CLE 11, NEP 10, NOS 10, NYJ 11, NEP 24
Hansen, Carl NYJ 75
Hansen, Cliff ARZ 30
Hansen, Dale DET 81
Hansen, Don ATL 58, GBP 58, MIN 55, SEA 58
Hansen, Phil BUF 90
Hansen, Ron WSH 69
Hansen, Roscoe PHL 73
Hansen, Wayne CHI 14/51, DAL 52
Hanshaw, Tim SFF 77
Hanson, Chris JAX 2, GBP 7
Hanson, Dale DET 77
Hanson, Dick NYG 77
Hanson, Homer ARZ 45, xCIN 46
Hanson, Jason DET 4
Hanson, Mark MIN 63
Hanson, Swede PHL 14/42, PIT 33, xBKN 17
Hanspard, Byron ATL 24
Hantla, Bob SFF 69
Hanulak, Chet CLE 44/48
Hape, Patrick DEN 86, TBB 82
Hapes, Merle NYG 30/44
Harbaugh, Jim IND 4/12, BLT 4, CAR 5, CHI 4, SDC 4
Harbour, Dave WSH 59
Harbour, James IND 87
Hardaway, Buddy SDC 77
Hardee, Billy DEN 23, NYJ 37
Hardeman, Buddy WSH 22
Hardeman, Don IND 36, TEN 30
Harden, Bobby MIA 45
Harden, Cedric SDC 92
Harden, Derrick GBP 82
Harden, Leon GBP 28
Harden, Mike DEN 31, OAK 45
Harder, Pat ARZ 34, DET 34
Hardin, Steve IND 66
Harding, Greg NOS 28, PHL 28
Harding, Roger DET 55, GBP 31, PHL 72, STL 15, xNYB 43

Hardison, Dee BUF 74, KCC 93, NYG 79, SDC 92
Hardman, Cedrick SFF 86, OAK 86
Hardy, Adrian CIN 41/45, SFF 45
Hardy, Andre PHL 47, SEA 47, SFF 47
Hardy, Bruce MIA 84
Hardy, Carroll SFF 27
Hardy, Charles OAK 82
Hardy, Cliff CHI 17
Hardy, Darryl ARZ 54, DAL 54, SEA 58
Hardy, David OAK 4
Hardy, Edgar SFF 63
Hardy, Jim ARZ 21/22/24, DET 1, STL 21
Hardy, John CHI 38
Hardy, Kevin JAX 51, CIN 51, DAL 51
Hardy, Kevin GBP 73, SDC 80, SFF 68/86
Hardy, Larry NOS 87
Hardy, Robert SEA 75
Hardy, Robert TBB 36
Hardy, Terry ARZ 80
Hare, Cecil NYG 22, WSH 11
Hare, Eddie NEP 8
Hare, Ray WSH 42, xBKN 42, zNYY 66
Hargain, Tony KCC 81, STL 47
Hargett, Edd NOS 14
Hargrove, James GBP 20, CIN 36
Hargrove, Jim ARZ 60, MIN 50
Hargrove, Marvin PHL 80
Harkey, Lance OAK 24
Harkey, Lem PIT 34, SFF 32
Harkey, Steve NYJ 36
Harlan, Jim WSH 68
Harley, Charles CHI ?
Harlow, Pat NEP 77, OAK 75/77
Harmon, Andy PHL 91
Harmon, Clarence WSH 38
Harmon, Derrick SFF 24
Harmon, Ed CIN 57
Harmon, Ham ARZ 18
Harmon, Kevin SEA 34
Harmon, Mike NYJ 23
Harmon, Ronnie SDC 33, BUF 33, CHI 22, TEN 33
Harmon, Tom ATL 64
Harmon, Tom STL 98
Harms, Art NYG 17
Harness, Jim IND 20/41
Harold, George IND 42, WSH 21
Harper, Alan NYJ 98
Harper, Alvin DAL 80/82, TBB 80/82
Harper, Bruce NYJ 42
Harper, Charlie NYG 61

Harper, Darrell BUF 41
Harper, Dave DAL 50
Harper, Deveron NOS 28, CAR 28
Harper, Dwayne DET 40, SDC 28, SEA 29
Harper, Jack MIA 29
Harper, John ATL 52
Harper, LaSalle CHI 54, NYG 54
Harper, Mark CLE 23
Harper, Maurice PHL 10, PIT 18
Harper, Michael NYJ 46/84
Harper, Nick IND 25
Harper, Roger ATL 47
Harper, Roland CHI 35
Harper, Shawn IND 75
Harper, Willie SFF 59
Harrah, Dennis STL 60
Harraway, Charley CLE 31, WSH 31
Harrell, Gary NYG 89
Harrell, James DET 51, KCC 57
Harrell, Sam MIN 36
Harrell, Will ARZ 39, GBP 40
Harrington, Joey DET 3
Harrington, John CLE 55, zCHI 57
Harrington, LaRue SDC 34
Harrington, Perry ARZ 36, PHL 35
Harris, Al CHI 90, PHL 95
Harris, Al GBP 31, PHL 31
Harris, Amos zBRK 37
Harris, Anthony MIA 51
Harris, Antwan NEP 23
Harris, Archie DEN 78
Harris, Arlen STL 33
Harris, Atnaf HOU 81
Harris, Bernardo BLT 55, GBP 54/55
Harris, Bill ATL 35, MIN 35, NOS 30
Harris, Bill PIT ?
Harris, Bo CIN 53
Harris, Bob ARZ 50, KCC 92
Harris, Chuck CHI 75
Harris, Cliff DAL 43
Harris, Corey BLT 45, DET 25, GBP 30/81, KCC 40, MIA 25, NOS 36, SEA 30, TEN 86
Harris, Darryl MIN 32
Harris, Derrick SDC 40, STL 33/34
Harris, Dick SDC 36
Harris, Don NYG 37, WSH 26
Harris, Dud DET 60
Harris, Duriel CLE 84, DAL 86, MIA 26/82
Harris, Elmore zBRK 82
Harris, Elroy SEA 33
Harris, Eric KCC 44, STL 26
Harris, **Franco** PIT 32, SEA 34

Harris, Frank CHI 36
Harris, Henry WSH 36
Harris, Herbert NOS 80
Harris, Ike ARZ 84, NOS 82
Harris, Jack GBP 16
Harris, Jackie DAL 88, GBP 80, TBB 81, TEN 88
Harris, James STL 12, BUF 12, SDC 12
Harris, James MIN 99, STL 99
Harris, Jim CIN 26, WSH 22
Harris, Jim DAL 40, PHL 20, STL 44, KCC 44
Harris, Jim NYJ 78
Harris, Joe IND 50, MIN 52, SFF 50, STL 51, WSH 51
Harris, John OAK 29
Harris, John MIN 44, SEA 44
Harris, Johnnie NYG 37, OAK 37
Harris, Jon PHL 90
Harris, Kenny ARZ 38
Harris, Kwame SFF 77
Harris, Larry TEN 61
Harris, Leonard ATL 82, TBB 84, TEN 80/83
Harris, Leotis GBP 69
Harris, Leroy MIA 38, PHL 20
Harris, Lou PIT 49
Harris, M.L. CIN 83
Harris, Mark SFF 19/88
Harris, Marshall CLE 90, NEP 78
Harris, Marv STL 60
Harris, Michael KCC 73
Harris, Napoleon OAK 58
Harris, Nick CIN 8, DET 2
Harris, Odie ARZ 31, CLE 38, TBB 20, TEN 48
Harris, Paul TBB 52
Harris, Phil NYG 46
Harris, Quentin ARZ 29
Harris, Raymond DEN 34
Harris, Raymont CHI 29, GBP 29, NEP 29
Harris, Richard CHI 84, PHL 84, SEA 77
Harris, Rickie NEP 25, WSH 46
Harris, Robert MIN 90, NYG 97
Harris, Rod DAL 80, NOS 86, PHL 80
Harris, Ronnie ATL 82, NEP 84, SEA 81
Harris, Roy ATL 75, TBB 67
Harris, Rudy TBB 43
Harris, Sean CHI 55/57, IND 55
Harris, Steve MIN 32
Harris, Tim PIT 43
Harris, Tim GBP 97, PHL 97, SFF 92/99
Harris, Tony DEN 47, SFF 20
Harris, Walt CHI 27, IND 21
Harris, Walter SDC 46

Harris, Wendell IND 26, NYG 26
Harris, William ARZ 89, GBP 89, TBB 86
Harris, Willie CHI 86
Harrison, Anthony GBP 46
Harrison, Bob IND 20
Harrison, Bob PHL 42, PIT 30, SFF 54
Harrison, Chris DET 74
Harrison, Dennis PHL 68, ATL 68, SFF 96, STL 68
Harrison, Dick xBOS 34
Harrison, Dwight BUF 28, DEN 82, IND 28, OAK 28
Harrison, Glynn KCC 22
Harrison, Gran DET 86, PHL 80
Harrison, James PIT 93
Harrison, Jim CHI 35
Harrison, Kenny SFF 83, WSH 89
Harrison, Lloyd MIA 37, SDC 22, WSH 41
Harrison, Martin MIN 91, SEA 91, SFF 54/56
Harrison, Marvin IND 88
Harrison, Max NYG 31
Harrison, Nolan OAK 74, PIT 74, WSH 74
Harrison, Pat xBKN 19
Harrison, Reggie ARZ 32, PIT 46
Harrison, Rob OAK 25
Harrison, Rodney SDC 37, NEP 37
Harrison, Todd MIN 48, TBB 89
Harrison, Tyreo PHL 55/59
Harrison, Victor NOS 86
Harry, Carl WSH 24
Harry, Emile KCC 86, STL 22
Hart, Ben NOS 88
Hart, Clinton PHL 33
Hart, Dick BUF 62, PHL 71
Hart, Doug GBP 43
Hart, Harold NYG 30, OAK 23/34
Hart, Jeff IND 68, NOS 72
Hart, Jim ARZ 17, WSH 17
Hart, Lawrence ARZ 49
Hart, Leo ATL 10, BUF 10
Hart, Leon DET 82
Hart, Pete NYJ 33
Hart, Roy OAK 61, SEA 63
Hart, Tommy SFF 53, CHI 53, NOS 53
Hartenstine, Mike CHI 73, MIN 78
Hartings, Jeff DET 64, PIT 64
Hartle, Greg ARZ 50
Hartley, Frank BLT 48, CLE 48, SDC 89
Hartley, Howard PIT 11/20, WSH 29

Hartley, Ken NEP 7
Hartman, Bill WSH 34
Hartman, Fred CHI 35, PHL 73
Hartman, Jim xBKN 17
Hartnett, Perry CHI 71, GBP 63
Hartong, George ARZ ?
Harts, Shaunard KCC 42
Hartsell, Mark CHI 11
Hartshorn, Larry ARZ 64
Hartwell, Edgerton BLT 56
Hartwig, Carter TEN 36
Hartwig, Justin TEN 77
Hartwig, Keith GBP 82
Harty, John SFF 75
Hartzog, Bug NYG 44
Harvey, Claude TEN 54/88
Harvey, Frank ARZ 32
Harvey, George NOS 67
Harvey, James KCC 64
Harvey, James OAK 70, TEN 70
Harvey, John TBB 26
Harvey, Ken WSH 57, ARZ 56
Harvey, Marvin KCC 83
Harvey, Maurice DEN 27, DET 23, GBP 23, TBB 24
Harvey, Richard Jr. NOS 52, BUF 52, DEN 52, NEP 58, OAK 52, SDC 58
Harvey, Richard Sr. NOS 26, PHL 41
Harvey, Stacy KCC 59
Harvey, Waddey BUF 65
Harvin, Allen WSH 31
Haselrig, Carlton PIT 77, NYJ 63
Hasenohrl, George NYG 72
Haskins, Jon PHL 52, SDC 59
Haslerig, Clint BUF 41/47, MIN 87, CHI 81, NYJ 84
Haslett, Jim BUF 55, NYJ 51
Haslip, Wilbert KCC 34
Hasselbach, Harald DEN 96
Hasselbeck, Don MIN 88, NEP 80, NYG 85, OAK 87
Hasselbeck, Matt SEA 8, GBP 11
Hasselbeck, Tim CAR 7, PHL 11
Hastings, Andre NOS 88, PIT 88, TBB 88
Hastings, George DET ?
Hasty, James KCC 40, NYJ 40
Hatch, Jeff NYG 76
Hatcher, Armon SDC 29
Hatcher, Dale MIA 7, STL 3
Hatcher, Ron WSH 36
Hatchett, Derrick IND 42, TEN 21
Hatchette, Matthew JAX 81, MIN 19/89, NYJ 81
Hatfield, Mark TEN 70

Hathaway, Steve IND 58
Hathcock, Dave GBP 45, NYG 46
Hatley, John ARZ 65, CHI 65, DEN 67
Hauck, Tim DEN 37, GBP 24, IND 45, NEP 40, PHL 45, SEA 26, SFF 45
Hauser, Art ARZ 65, DEN 71, NEP 67, NYG 74, STL 65
Hauss, Len WSH 56
Haverdick, Dave DET 80
Haverdink, Kevin NOS 70/74
Havig, Dennis ATL 56, GBP 62, TEN 56
Havrilak, Sam IND 17, NOS 80
Hawkes, Michael CAR 59
Hawkins, Alex ATL 25, IND 25
Hawkins, Andy KCC 59, SDC 59, TBB 59
Hawkins, Artrell CIN 27
Hawkins, Ben CLE 18, PHL 18
Hawkins, Bill STL 70
Hawkins, Clarence OAK 26
Hawkins, Courtney PIT 88, TBB 5/85
Hawkins, Frank OAK 27
Hawkins, Garland CHI 74
Hawkins, Mike NEP 59, OAK 57
Hawkins, Nat TEN 86
Hawkins, Rip MIN 58
Hawkins, Steve NEP 80
Hawkins, Wayne OAK 65
Haworth, Steve ATL 30
Haws, Kurt WSH 82
Hawthorne, Duane DAL 38, SFF 43
Hawthorne, Ed MIA 74
Hawthorne, Greg IND 83, NEP 27, PIT 27
Hawthorne, Michael GBP 27, NOS 36
Haycraft, Ken GBP 21
Hayden, Aaron GBP 24, PHL 33, SDC 24
Hayden, Ken PHL 50, WSH 18
Hayden, Leo ARZ 32, MIN 44
Hayduk, Henry PIT 14, xBKN ?
Hayes, Billie NOS 29
Hayes, Bob DAL 22, SFF 22
Hayes, Brandon CAR 67
Hayes, Chris GBP 40, NEP 29, NYJ 30
Hayes, Donald NEP 81, CAR 81/88
Hayes, Ed PHL 47
Hayes, Eric SEA 78, STL 93, TBB 95
Hayes, Gary GBP 27
Hayes, Gerald ARZ 54

Hayes, Jarius ARZ 48/89
Hayes, Jeff CIN 5, MIA 5, WSH 5
Hayes, Jim TEN 62
Hayes, Joe PHL 80
Hayes, Jonathan PIT 85, KCC 85
Hayes, Larry NYG 37, STL 31
Hayes, Lester OAK 37
Hayes, Luther SDC 24
Hayes, Melvin NYJ 79, TEN 71
Hayes, Mercury ATL 84, NOS 89
Hayes, Ray MIN 32
Hayes, Ray NYJ 73
Hayes, Rudy PIT 35/36
Hayes, Tom ATL 27, SDC 22
Hayes, Wendell DAL 33, DEN 29/33, KCC 38
Hayes, Windrell NYJ 86
Haygood, Herb DEN 82
Hayhoe, Bill GBP 51, GBP 77
Hayman, Conway NEP 65, TEN 70
Hayman, Gary BUF 21
Haymond, Alvin IND 30, PHL 30, STL 23, TEN 13, WSH 28
Haynes, Abner KCC 28, DEN 28, MIA 28, NYJ 28
Haynes, Hall STL 20/22, WSH 23
Haynes, James NOS 92
Haynes, Joe zBUF 22
Haynes, Louis KCC 56
Haynes, Mark NYG 36, DEN 36
Haynes, Michael ATL 81/82, CHI 97
Haynes, Mike NEP 40, OAK 22
Haynes, Reggie WSH 89
Haynes, Tommy DAL 27
Haynes, Verron PIT 34
Haynesworth, Albert TEN 91/92
Hays, George GBP 88, PIT 75/80/82
Hays, Harold DAL 56, SFF 54
Hayward, Reggie DEN 98
Haywood, Alfred DEN 23
Hayworth, Tracy DET 99
Hazelhurst, Robert xBOS 65
Hazeltine, Matt SFF 55, NYG 64
Hazelton, Major CHI 49, NOS 49
Hazelwood, Ted WSH 78, zCHI 44
Headen, Andy NYG 54
Headrick, Sherrill KCC 69, CIN 69
Healey, Ed CHI 13/16
Healy, Chip ARZ 56

Healy, Don BUF 75, CHI 60, DAL 62/78
Heap, Joe NYG 48
Heap, Todd BLT 86
Heap, Walt zLAD 73/66
Heard, Herman KCC 44
Heard, Ronnie SFF 38
Hearden, Tom GBP 12, CHI 80
Hearst, Garrison SFF 20, ARZ 23, CIN 20
Heater, Don ARZ 34
Heater, Larry NYG 27
Heater, Rod xBKN 5
Heath, Clayton BUF 37, MIA 35
Heath, Jo Jo PHL 29, NYJ 37, CIN 36
Heath, Leon WSH 24/32
Heath, Rodney CIN 22
Heath, Stan GBP 39
Hebert, Bobby ATL 3, NOS 3
Hebert, Bud NYG 26
Hebert, Ken PIT 16
Hebert, Kyries HOU 36
Hebron, Vaughn DEN 22, PHL 20/45
Hecht, George zCHI 35
Heck, Andy CHI 64, SEA 66, WSH 64
Heck, Bob zCHI 56
Heck, Ralph ATL 55, NYG 55, PHL 43
Heckar, Bob STL 48
Heckard, Steve STL 20/22
Hecker, Norb STL 88, WSH 48
Hector, Johnny NYJ 34
Hector, Willie STL 62
Hedberg, Randy TBB 14
Heenan, Pat WSH 82
Heeter, Gene NYJ 85
Heffern, Shawn IND 79
Heffernan, Dave TBB 66
Heffner-Liddiard, Brody MIA 48, MIN 43
Heflin, Vic ARZ 46
Heflin, Vince MIA 88, TBB 89
Hefner, Larry GBP 51
Hegamin, George DAL 69, PHL 69, TBB 79
Hegarty, Bill PIT 76, WSH 79
Hegman, Mike DAL 58
Heidel, Jimmy ARZ 26, NOS 26
Heiden, Steve CLE 82, SDC 83
Heikkinen, Ralph xBKN 4
Heileman, Charles CHI 8
Heimburger, Craig BUF 67, GBP 75
Heimkreiter, Steve IND 58
Heimuli, Lakei CHI 38
Hein, Bob zBRK 54
Hein, Mel NYG 7

Heineman, Ken STL 7, xBKN 10

Heinrich, Don DAL 11, NYG 11, OAK 11

Heinrich, Keith CAR 80, CLE 49

Heinz, Bob MIA 72, WSH 76

Heitmann, Eric SFF 66

Hekkers, George DET 34/70, zBAL 44, zMIA 44

Held, Paul GBP 15, PIT 17

Heldt, Carl xBKN 14/15

Heller, Ron ATL 80, SEA 85, SFF 89

Heller, Ron MIA 73, PHL 73, TBB 73

Heller, Warren PIT 1/15/34

Heller, Will TBB 89

Hellestrae, Dale BLT 70, BUF 71, DAL 62/70

Helluin, Jerry CLE 79, GBP 72, TEN 72

Helton, Barry SFF 9, STL 9

Helton, Darius KCC 62

Helwig, John CHI 80

Hempel, Bill CHI 19

Hemphill, Darryl IND 27

Hempstead, Hessley DET 66

Hemsley, Nate CAR 54, DAL 58

Hendel, Andy MIA 90

Hendershot, Larry WSH 54

Henderson, E.J. MIN 56

Henderson, Jamie NYJ 23

Henderson, Jerome BUF 36, NEP 26/36, NYJ 26, PHL 26

Henderson, John JAX 98

Henderson, John DET 87, MIN 80

Henderson, Jon PIT 24, WSH 28

Henderson, Keith MIN 30, SFF 30

Henderson, Othello NOS 20

Henderson, Reuben CHI 20, SDC 20

Henderson, Thomas DAL 56, SFF 50, TEN 53

Henderson, William GBP 30/33

Henderson, Wyatt SDC 32

Henderson, Wymon DEN 24, MIN 24, STL 24

Henderson, Zac PHL 24

Hendley, David NEP 28

Hendley, Dick PIT 25

Hendley, Jim ATL 53

Hendren, Bob WSH 48

Hendren, Jerry DEN 86

Hendrian, Dutch NYG 6

Hendricks, Ted GBP 56, IND 83, OAK 83

Hendricks, Tommy MIA 51

Hendrickson, Steve DAL 50/58, PHL 48, SDC 34, SFF 56, TEN 44

Hendrix, David SDC 38

Hendrix, Manny DAL 45

Hendrix, Tim DAL 85

Hendy, John SDC 29

Henesey, Brian ARZ 39

Henke, Brad DEN 68

Henke, Ed SFF 47/75/89, ARZ 80, zLAD 44

Henke, Karl NEP 80, NYJ 70

Henley, Carey BUF 26

Henley, Darryl STL 20

Henley, June STL 26

Henley, Thomas SFF 84

Hennessey, Jerry ARZ 66, WSH 88

Hennessey, John NYJ 63

Hennessey, Tom NEP 30

Hennigan, Charles TEN 37/87

Hennigan, Mike DET 58, NYJ 52

Henning, Dan SDC 15

Hennings, Chad DAL 95

Henry, Anthony CLE 37

Henry, Bernard STL 82, IND 88

Henry, Charles MIA 87

Henry, Kevin PIT 76

Henry, Maurice PHL 53

Henry, Mike PIT 37/68, STL 53

Henry, Pete NYG 55

Henry, Steve ARZ 48, IND 44, NYG 47

Henry, Travis BUF 20

Henry, Urban GBP 83, PIT 74, STL 67

Henry, Wally PHL 89

Hensley, Dick CHI 82, NYG 85

Hensley, Dick PIT 25/44/85

Henson, Champ CIN 38

Henson, Gary DEN 89, PHL 80

Henson, Ken PIT 51

Henson, Luther NEP 70

Henton, Anthony PIT 96

Hentrich, Craig TEN 15, GBP 17

Hepburn, Lonnie DEN 43, IND 43

Heppner, Kris SEA 3, WSH 4

Herber, Arnie GBP 12/16/19/26/38/41/45/68, NYG 20

Herchman, Bill DAL 72, SFF 72, TEN 73

Hergert, Joe BUF 54

Herkenhoff, Matt KCC 60

Herline, Alan NEP 6

Herman, Chuck ATL 61

Herman, Dave NYJ 67

Hermann, Dick OAK 49

Hermann, John IND 20

Hermeling, Terry WSH 72/75

Hernandez, Adam BLT 67

Hernandez, Joe WSH 80

Hernandez, Matt MIN 60, SEA 69

Hernandez, Scott BUF 93

Herndon, Don NYJ 20

Herndon, Jimmy CHI 74, HOU 75, JAX 74

Herndon, Kelly DEN 31

Herndon, Steve DEN 79

Herock, Ken CIN 34, NEP 36, OAK 84/86

Heron, Fred ARZ 74

Herosian, Brian IND 29

Herrera, Efren BUF 1, SEA 1, DAL 1

Herring, George DEN 16

Herring, Hal CLE 20/50, zBUF 26

Herring, Kim BLT 20, STL 20

Herrmann, Don NOS 87, NYG 85

Herrmann, Mark DEN 10, IND 9, SDC 9, STL 9

Herrod, Jeff IND 54, PHL 54

Herron, Anthony DET 77

Herron, Bruce CHI 51

Herron, Mack ATL 42, NEP 42

Hershey, Kirk PHL 80, STL 22

Hertel, Rob CIN 16, PHL 16

Hertwig, Craig BUF 76, DET 71

Hervey, Edward DAL 81

Hesse, Jon DEN 50, STL 53

Hester, Jessie ATL 89, IND 84, OAK 84, STL 86

Hester, Jim CHI 86, NOS 84

Hester, Ray NOS 64

Hester, Ron MIA 53

Hetherington, Chris IND 44, OAK 44, STL 44, CAR 44

Hettema, Dave ATL 68, SFF 62/65

Hewitt, Bill CHI 56, PHL 56/82, PIT 82

Hewitt, Chris NOS 23

Hewko, Bob TBB 8

Hews, Bob BUF 72

Heyward, Craig ATL 34, CHI 45, IND 33, NOS 34/45, STL 34

Heywood, Ralph DET 31/80, xBOS 83, xNYB 83

Heywood, Ralph zCHI 57

Hibbs, Jesse CHI 54

Hibler, Mike CIN 56

Hickerson, Gene CLE 66

Hickey, Bo DEN 31

Hickey, Red PIT 39, STL 53

Hickl, Ray NYG 57

Hickman, Dallas IND 57, WSH 78/82

Hickman, Donnie DET 63, WSH 60

Hickman, Herman xBKN 22/27/28/15/1

Hickman, Kevin DET 15/81/
  82
Hickman, Larry ARZ 34, GBP
  37
Hicks, Artis PHL 77
Hicks, Brandon IND 72
Hicks, Bryan CIN 27
Hicks, Clifford BUF 27, DEN
  28, NYJ 25, NYJ 47, STL
  23/28
Hicks, Dwight SFF 22, IND 29
Hicks, Eddie NYG 29
Hicks, Eric KCC 98
Hicks, Ivan DET 43
Hicks, John NYG 74
Hicks, Kerry KCC 94
Hicks, Mark DET 94, SEA 63
Hicks, Michael CHI 44
Hicks, R.W. DET 60
Hicks, Robert BUF 77
Hicks, Skip CAR 42, TEN 42,
  WSH 20
Hicks, Sylvester KCC 75
Hicks, Tom CHI 54
Hicks, Victor STL 81
Hicks, W.K. TEN 33, NYJ 33
Hienstra, Ed NYG 29
Higdon, Alex ATL 88
Higgins, Jim ARZ 25
Higgins, Jim MIA 65
Higgins, Luke zBAL 31/32/38
Higgins, Tom ARZ 73, BUF 54,
  PHL 71
Higgs, Mark ARZ 22, DAL 21,
  MIA 21, PHL 22
High, Lennie CHI 24
Highsmith, Alonzo DAL 32,
  TBB 32, TEN 32
Highsmith, Don GBP 32, OAK
  32
Highsmith, Walter DEN 56/65,
  TEN 61
Hightower, Ben DET 86, STL
  53
Hilbert, Jon CAR 5
Hiles, Van CHI 48
Hilgenberg, Jay CHI 63, CLE
  63, NOS 62
Hilgenberg, Joel NOS 61
Hilgenberg, Wally DET 67,
  MIN 58
Hilger, Rusty DET 12, IND
  7/12, OAK 12
Hill, Barry MIA 44
Hill, Bill DAL 31
Hill, Bruce TBB 84
Hill, Calvin DAL 35, CLE 35,
  WSH 35
Hill, Charles HOU 94
Hill, Cowboy NYG 6/?
Hill, Darrell TEN 80
Hill, Dave KCC 73
Hill, David DET 81, STL 81
Hill, Derek PIT 82
Hill, Don ARZ 6, GBP 14/16

Hill, Drew TEN 85, ATL 85,
  STL 87
Hill, Eddie MIA 31, STL 24
Hill, Eric ARZ 58, SDC 54, STL
  54
Hill, Fred PHL 86
Hill, Gary MIN 43
Hill, Greg KCC 23, OAK 36,
  TEN 23
Hill, Greg DET 21, KCC 27,
  KCC 29, STL 27
Hill, Harlon CHI 87, DET 82,
  PIT 87
Hill, Harold xBKN 14
Hill, Ike BUF 28, CHI 17, MIA
  81
Hill, Irv ARZ 48, WSH ?
Hill, J.D. BUF 40, DET 41/86
Hill, Jack DEN 84
Hill, James SEA 85
Hill, Jeff CIN 19/84
Hill, Jerry IND 45
Hill, Jim CLE 49, GBP 39, SDC
  39
Hill, Jim DET 12/48, PIT 42/
  43
Hill, Jimmy ARZ 41, DET 43,
  KCC 12
Hill, John NOS 62, NYG 52,
  SFF 52
Hill, Kenny KCC 41, NYG 48,
  OAK 48
Hill, Kent STL 72, TEN 72
Hill, Kid NYG 9
Hill, King ARZ 16, MIN 10,
  PHL 10
Hill, Lonzell NOS 87
Hill, Mack Lee KCC 36
Hill, Madre CLE 34, OAK 23
Hill, Matt SEA 74
Hill, Nate GBP 90, MIA 92
Hill, Raion BUF 24/38
Hill, Ralph NYG 52
Hill, Randal ARZ 81, MIA
  81/89, NOS 81
Hill, Ray BUF 38, MIA 28
Hill, Renaldo ARZ 21/45
Hill, Rod BUF 25, DAL 25,
  DET 47, OAK 38
Hill, Sean MIA 31
Hill, Shaun MIN 12
Hill, Tony DAL 60/90
Hill, Tony DAL 80
Hill, Travis CLE 93, CAR 59
Hill, Will CLE 35
Hill, Winston NYJ 75, STL 73
Hillary, Ira CIN 89, MIN 89
Hillebrand, Bill zBAL 82
Hillebrand, Jerry ARZ 87, NYG
  87, PIT 69
Hillenbrand, Billy zCHI 66
Hillenmeyer, Hunter CHI 92
Hilliard, Dalton NOS 21/40
Hilliard, Ike NYG 88
Hilliard, John SEA 95

Hilliard, Randy CHI 47, CLE
  39, DEN 21
Hillman, Bill DET ?
Hills, Keno NOS 76
Hilpert, Hal NYG 10, xCIN ?
Hilton, Carl MIN 82
Hilton, John DET 81, GBP 86,
  MIN 85, PIT 82
Hilton, Roy ATL 78, IND 85,
  NYG 78
Hilton, Scott SFF 55
Hilton, Zachary NOS 81
Himes, Dick GBP 72
Himes, Randy BLT 81
Hinchman, Hub DET 6, ARZ
  30/32
Hindman, Stan SFF 74/80
Hines, Andre SEA 73
Hines, Glen Ray TEN 70/78,
  NOS 78, PIT 76
Hines, Jimmy KCC 81, MIA
  99
Hinkle, Bryan PIT 53
Hinkle, Clarke GBP
  27/30/33/39/41/45/48
Hinkle, George CIN 98, MIN
  98, SDC 97
Hinkle, Jack PHL 43, PIT 43,
  NYG 6
Hinnant, Mike DET 69, PIT
  67/81
Hinson, Billy ATL 66
Hinte, Hal GBP 15, PIT 50
Hinton, Chris ATL 71/75, IND
  75, MIN 75/78
Hinton, Chuck NYG 56/59
Hinton, Chuck IND 75, NYJ
  64, PIT 64
Hinton, Ed IND 33, NEP 82,
  TEN 87
Hinton, Marcus OAK 85
Hintz, Mike CHI 35
Hipp, I.M. OAK 20
Hipple, Eric DET 17
Hipps, Claude PIT 24
Hire, Doug SEA 60
Hires, Leon TBB 70
Hirsch, Buckets zBUF 73/25/
  36
Hirsch, Elroy STL 40, zCHI
  80
Hirsch, Steve DET 47
Hitchcock, Bill SEA 76
Hitchcock, Jimmy MIN 37,
  NEP 31, CAR 37
Hitchcock, Ray WSH 59
Hitt, Joel STL 7
Hix, Billy PHL 85
Hoage, Terry ARZ 34, NOS 24,
  PHL 34, SFF 41, TEN 27,
  WSH 34
Hoaglin, Fred CLE 54, IND 54,
  SEA 53, TEN 53
Hoague, Joe PIT 17, xBOS 21
Hoak, Dick PIT 42

Hoard, Leroy CLE 33, BLT 33, MIN 44, CAR 33
Hoban, Mike CHI 67
Hobbins, Jim GBP 78
Hobbs, Bill PHL 56, NOS 53
Hobbs, Daryl NOS 80, OAK 80, SEA 18
Hobbs, Homer SFF 37
Hobbs, Stephen WSH 86
Hobby, Marion NEP 60
Hobert, Billy Joe BUF 8, NOS 12, OAK 9/12, IND 14
Hobgood-Chittick, Nate SFF 76, KCC 94
Hobley, Liffort ARZ 29, MIA 29
Hobson, Victor NYJ 54
Hochstein, Russ NEP 71, TBB 65
Hock, John STL 63, ARZ 11
Hodel, Merwin NYG 35
Hodel, Nathan ARZ 48
Hodge, Damon DAL 16
Hodge, Floyd ATL 83
Hodge, Milford NEP 97, NOS 98
Hodge, Sedrick NOS 52
Hodges, Eric KCC 89
Hodges, Herman xBKN 13
Hodgins, James ARZ 42, STL 42
Hodgins, Norm CHI 34
Hodgson, Pat WSH 80
Hodson, Tom NOS 14, DAL 10, NEP 13
Hoel, Bob ARZ 48, PIT 47
Hoelscher, David WSH 91
Hoerner, Dick STL 31, xDAL 31
Hoernschemeyer, Bob DET 14, zBRK 90, zCHI 64/90
Hoey, George ARZ 45, DEN 23, NEP 23, NYJ 49, SDC 23
Hofer, Paul SFF 36/41
Hoffman, Bob STL 16, WSH 43/45, zLAD 66
Hoffman, Dalton TEN 34/36
Hoffman, Gary GBP 78, SFF 78
Hoffman, Jack CHI 82
Hoffman, John CHI 29/89
Hoffman, John ARZ 70, CHI 79, DEN 87, WSH 85
Hogan, Darrell PIT 63/73
Hogan, Marc NYJ 40
Hogan, Mike NYG 45, PHL 30/35, SFF 45
Hogan, Paul NYG 4
Hogan, Tom ARZ 7
Hoge, Merril CHI 33, PIT 33
Hogeboom, Gary ARZ 5, DAL 14, IND 7
Hoggard, D.D. CLE 48
Hogland, Doug ARZ 64, DET 64, SFF 64
Hogue, Murrell ARZ 47

Hohensee, Mike CHI 8
Hohman, John DEN 64
Hohn, Bob PIT 29
Hoisington, Al BUF 88, OAK 84
Hoke, Chris PIT 76
Hoke, Jonathan CHI 47
Hokuf, Steve WSH 26
Holcomb, Bill PIT 26
Holcomb, Kelly CLE 10, IND 13
Holcomb, Sean NEP 60
Holcomb, William PHL ?
Holcombe, Robert STL 25, TEN 35
Hold, Mike TBB 7
Holden, Curtis NOS 57
Holden, Sam NOS 70
Holden, Steve CIN 83, CLE 88
Holder, Lew zLAD 56
Holdman, Warrick CHI 53
Holecek, John ATL 59, BUF 52, SDC 52
Holifield, Jim NYG 49
Holifield, John CIN 40
Holladay, Bob SFF 27/40, STL 46
Holland, Darius CLE 73, DEN 90, DET 73, GBP 90, KCC 99, MIN 93
Holland, Jamie CLE 87, OAK 82, SDC 86
Holland, John BUF 80, MIN 85
Holland, Johnny GBP 50
Holland, Montrae NOS 61
Holland, Vern DET 72, NYG 77, CIN 76
Hollar, John DET 36, WSH 15
Hollas, Don CIN 12, OAK 12
Hollas, Hugo NOS 18, SFF 47
Holle, Eric KCC 93
Holler, Ed GBP 65, PIT 31
Holley, Ken zMIA 68
Holliday, Corey PIT 83
Holliday, Marcus STL 31
Holliday, Ron SDC 81
Holliday, Vonnie KCC 99, GBP 90
Hollie, Doug SEA 78
Hollier, Dwight IND 56, MIA 50
Hollings, Tony HOU 25
Hollingsworth, Joe PIT 37/42
Hollingsworth, Shawn DEN 73
Hollinquest, Lamont GBP 56, WSH 96
Hollis, David KCC 25, SEA 25
Hollis, Mike JAX 1, BUF 1
Holloman, Gus DEN 34, NYJ 48
Holloway, Brian NEP 76, OAK 76
Holloway, Cornell IND 25
Holloway, Derek TBB 83, WSH 88

Holloway, Glen CHI 61/62, CLE 62
Holloway, Jabari HOU 89
Holloway, Johnny ARZ 29, DAL 23
Holloway, Randy ARZ 74, MIN 75
Holloway, Stan NOS 51
Holloway, Steve TBB 80
Holloway, Tony KCC 97
Holly, Bob ATL 8, PHL 12, WSH 8
Holm, Bernard PIT 36, ARZ 18
Holm, Tony DET 23
Holman, John NYG ?
Holman, Rashad SFF 26
Holman, Rodney CIN 82, DET 82
Holman, Scott ARZ 29, NYJ 80
Holman, Walter WSH 30
Holman, Willie CHI 85, WSH 85
Holmberg, Rob CAR 58, GBP 56, IND 59, MIN 51, NEP 50, NYJ 50, OAK 57
Holmer, Walt CHI 9, ARZ 32, PIT 38, WSH 22
Holmes, Bruce KCC 57, MIN 54
Holmes, Clayton DAL 47
Holmes, Darick BUF 44, GBP 22, IND 44
Holmes, Darryl NEP 41
Holmes, Don ARZ 83
Holmes, Earl CLE 50, DET 50, PIT 50
Holmes, Ernie NEP 63, PIT 63
Holmes, Jack NOS 45
Holmes, Jaret CHI 10, JAX 3, NYG 2
Holmes, Jerry DET 43, GBP 44, NYJ 47
Holmes, John MIA 85
Holmes, Kenny NYG 90, TEN 99
Holmes, Lester ARZ 71, OAK 71, PHL 73
Holmes, Mel PIT 77
Holmes, Mike BUF 86, MIA 43, SFF 20
Holmes, Pat TEN 79, KCC 74
Holmes, Priest KCC 31, BLT 26/33
Holmes, Robert KCC 45, SDC 38, TEN 36/39
Holmes, Ron DEN 90, TBB 90
Holmes, Rudy ATL 36
Holmoe, Tom SFF 28/46
Holohan, Pete CLE 89, KCC 89, SDC 88, STL 81
Holovak, Mike CHI 15, STL 45
Holsey, Bernard IND 79, NEP 99, NYG 79, WSH 90

Holston, Mike KCC 84, TEN 84
Holt, Harry CLE 81, SDC 85
Holt, Issiac DAL 30, MIN 30
Holt, John IND 21, TBB 21
Holt, Pierce SFF 78/98, ATL 95
Holt, Robert BUF 87
Holt, Terrence DET 42
Holt, Tory STL 81/88
Holtzman, Glenn STL 79/89
Holub, E.J. KCC 55
Holz, Gordon DEN 73/74, NYJ 74
Holzer, Tom SFF 87
Homan, Dennis DAL 24, KCC 21
Homco, Thomas STL 57
Hons, Todd DET 18
Hood, Estes GBP 38
Hood, Frank PIT 45
Hood, Kerry CAR 10
Hood, Roderick PHL 29
Hood, Winford DEN 74/78
Hooker, Fair CLE 43
Hooks, Alvin PHL 80
Hooks, Bryan ARZ 97
Hooks, Jim DET 30
Hooks, Roland BUF 25
Hooper, Trell MIA 45
Hoopes, Mitch DAL 9, DET 17, SDC 10
Hoover, Brad CAR 45
Hoover, Houston ATL 69, CLE 64, MIA 64
Hoover, Mel PHL 85, DET 83
Hope, Charles GBP 70
Hope, Chris PIT 28
Hope, Neil STL 96
Hopkins, Andy TEN 28
Hopkins, Brad TEN 72
Hopkins, Jerry DEN 50, MIA 51, OAK 52
Hopkins, Roy TEN 36
Hopkins, Tam NYG 65
Hopkins, Tom CLE 70
Hopkins, Wes PHL 48
Hopp, Harry DET 31/44, zBUF 74, zLAD 95, zMIA ?
Hopper, Darrell SDC 47
Hoppock, Doug KCC 79
Hopson, Tyrone DET 64, SFF 66
Hoptowit, Al CHI 26
Horan, Mike DEN 2, CHI 2, NYG 2, PHL 2, STL 2
Hord, Roy NYJ 63, PHL 64, STL 64
Horn, Alvin CLE 38
Horn, Bob SDC 55, SFF 55
Horn, Dick IND 18
Horn, Don CLE 13, DEN 13, GBP 13, SDC 13
Horn, Joe NOS 87, KCC 84
Horn, Marty PHL 14
Horn, Rod CIN 71
Hornbeak, Jay xBKN 25

Horne, Dick NYG 49, SFF 51, zMIA 54
Horne, Greg ARZ 11, CIN 10
Horne, Tony STL 82
Horner, Sam NYG 26, WSH 40
Hornick, Bill PIT 40
Hornsby, Ron NYG 67
Hornung, Paul GBP 5
Horrell, Bill PHL 62
Horstmann, Roy ARZ 21, WSH 31
Horton, Bob SDC 30
Horton, Ethan OAK 23/88, KCC 32, WSH 89
Horton, Greg STL 63, TBB 64
Horton, Larry CHI 64
Horton, Ray CIN 20, DAL 20
Horvath, Les CLE 92, STL 12
Horween, Arnold ARZ ?
Horween, Ralph ARZ ?
Hoskins, Bob SFF 56
Hoskins, Derrick NOS 28, OAK 20
Hoss, Clark PHL 80
Hostetler, Jeff OAK 15, NYG 15, WSH 15
Hough, Jim MIN 51
Houghton, Jerry ARZ 15, WSH 71
Houghton, Mike BUF 69
House, Kevin SDC 32, STL 83, TBB 89
Houser, John ARZ 66, DAL 67, STL 62
Houser, Kevin NOS 47
Houshmandzadeh, T.J. CIN 84
Housman, Walter NOS 68
Houston, Bill DAL 86
Houston, Bobby GBP 60, KCC 57, MIN 55, NYJ 55, SDC 57
Houston, Jim CLE 82
Houston, Ken TEN 29, WSH 27
Houston, Lin CLE 32/62
Houston, Rich NYG 84
Houston, Walt WSH 65
Hovan, Chris MIN 99
Hover, Don WSH 58
Hovius, Junie NYG 43
Howard, Anthony NYG 71
Howard, Billy DET 70
Howard, Bob NEP 24, PHL 23, SDC 24
Howard, Bobbie CHI 52
Howard, Bobby TBB 25
Howard, Bryan MIN 24
Howard, Carl DAL 21, NYJ 28, TBB 25
Howard, Chris JAX 24
Howard, Dana CHI 95, STL 50
Howard, Darren NOS 93
Howard, David DAL 99, MIN 51/99, NEP 99

Howard, Desmond DET 18/80, GBP 81/82, JAX 81, OAK 80, WSH 80
Howard, Dosey NYG 5/11
Howard, Eddie SFF 2
Howard, Erik NYG 74, NYJ 74
Howard, Gene NOS 29, STL 21
Howard, Harry NYJ 39
Howard, Joey SDC 79
Howard, Paul DEN 60
Howard, Percy DAL 81
Howard, Red NYG 24
Howard, Reggie CAR 23
Howard, Ron BUF 85, DAL 87, SEA 87
Howard, Sherman CLE 30/44, xNYB 46, zNYY 76
Howard, Thomas ARZ 59, KCC 52
Howard, Todd KCC 53
Howard, Ty ARZ 27/29, CIN 20
Howard, William TBB 43
Howard, Willie MIN 91
Howe, Garry CIN 71, IND 72, PIT 78
Howe, Glen ATL 71, PIT 76
Howell, Clarence SFF 56
Howell, Delles NOS 20, NYJ 20
Howell, Earl zLAD 97
Howell, Foster xCIN ?
Howell, Jim Lee NYG 21/81
Howell, John GBP 49
Howell, John TBB 38
Howell, Lane NYG 78, PHL 79
Howell, Leroy MIN 92
Howell, Mike CLE 34, MIA 44
Howell, Millard WSH 30
Howell, Pat ATL 64, TEN 66
Howell, Steve MIA 36
Howfield, Bobby DEN 3, NYJ 3
Howfield, Ian TEN 6
Howley, Chuck DAL 54, CHI 54
Howry, Keenan MIN 82
Howton, Bill GBP 86, CLE 86, DAL 81
Hoyem, Lynn DAL 51, PHL 63
Hoyem, Steve BUF 76
Hoying, Bobby OAK 14, PHL 7
Hrabetin, Frank PHL 71, zMIA ?, zBRK 44
Hrivnak, Gary CHI 72
Huard, Brock IND 7, SEA 11
Huard, Damon MIA 11, NEP 19
Huard, John DEN 57, NOS 52
Huarte, John CHI 7, KCC 7, NEP 7, PHL 7

Hubach, Mike NEP 6
Hubbard, Bud xBKN 10
Hubbard, Cal GBP 27/38/39/40/51, NYG 41/60, PIT 35
Hubbard, Dave NOS 70
Hubbard, Marv OAK 39/44, DET 44
Hubbell, Frank STL 46
Hubbert, Brad SDC 26
Hubka, Gene PIT 35
Huckleby, Harlan GBP 25
Huddleston, Jim TBB 71
Huddleston, John OAK 57
Hudlow, Floyd ATL 24/49, BUF 49
Hudock, Mike KCC 54, MIA 52, NYJ 52
Hudson, Bill SDC 79, NEP 61
Hudson, Bob GBP 23, OAK 36
Hudson, Bob DEN 53, KCC 61, NYG 89, PHL 42/88, WSH 41
Hudson, Chris ATL 47, CHI 47, JAX 20/37
Hudson, Dick BUF 79, SDC 78
Hudson, Doug KCC 11
Hudson, Gordon SEA 85
Hudson, Jim NYJ 22/44
Hudson, John BLT 66, NYJ 65, PHL 66
Hudson, Mike SDC 28
Hudson, Nat IND 63, NOS 69
Huerta, Carlos CHI 8, STL 6
Huey, Gene SDC 38
Huff, Alan PIT 64
Huff, Ben ATL 91
Huff, Charles ATL 21
Huff, Gary CHI 19, SFF 19, TBB 19
Huff, Ken IND 62, WSH 61
Huff, Marty SFF 54
Huff, Orlando SEA 57
Huff, Sam NYG 70, WSH 70
Huffine, Ken CHI 5
Huffman, Darvell IND 85
Huffman, David MIN 56/72
Huffman, Dick STL 20
Huffman, Frank ARZ 49
Huffman, Tim GBP 74
Huffman, Vern DET 6
Hufnagel, John DEN 14/16
Hugasian, Harry CHI 48, IND 31
Huggins, Roy STL 53
Hughes, Bernie ARZ 18
Hughes, Billy CHI 24
Hughes, Bob ATL 70
Hughes, Chuck DET 85, PHL 13
Hughes, Danan KCC 83
Hughes, David PIT 36, SEA 46
Hughes, Dennis PIT 82
Hughes, Dick PIT 24/28

Hughes, Ed NYG 48, STL 49
Hughes, Ernie NYG 61, SFF 65
Hughes, George PIT 40/65
Hughes, Honolulu WSH 26
Hughes, Pat NOS 54, NYG 56
Hughes, Randy DAL 42
Hughes, Tyrone NOS 33, CHI 33, DAL 32
Hughes, Van ARZ 78, SEA 75
Hughes, William PHL 15/29
Hughley, Delvin DEN 20
Hughley, George WSH 39
Hugret, Joe xBKN 50
Hull, Bill KCC 85
Hull, Kent BUF 67
Hull, Mike CHI 33, WSH 25
Hull, Tom GBP 55, SFF 54
Hulsey, Corey BUF 71, OAK 71
Hultz, Dan CHI 67, MIN 83, PHL 83
Hultz, George ARZ 76
Humbert, Dick PHL 81
Humble, Weldon CLE 38, xDAL 66
Humiston, Mike BUF 50, IND 57, SDC 50
Humm, David BUF 10, IND 10/11, OAK 11
Hummel, Arnie ARZ 31
Humphrey, Bobby DEN 26, MIA 44
Humphrey, Bobby NYJ 48/84, STL 48
Humphrey, Buddy ARZ 11, DAL 11, STL 10, TEN 11
Humphrey, Claude ATL 87, PHL 87
Humphrey, Deon JAX 56, SDC 53, CAR 58
Humphrey, Donnie GBP 79
Humphrey, Jay MIN 67
Humphrey, Paul xBKN 16
Humphrey, Ronald IND 25
Humphrey, Tom KCC 52, NYJ 69
Humphreys, Bob DEN 2
Humphries, Leonard IND 23
Humphries, Stan SDC 12, WSH 16
Humphries, Stefan CHI 75, DEN 79
Hundon, James CIN 85
Huneke, Charlie zBRK 47, zCHI 45
Hunley, LaMonte IND 56
Hunley, Ricky ARZ 51, DEN 98, OAK 99
Hunnicutt, Jim DET 16
Hunsinger, Chuck CHI 46
Hunt, Bob CLE 31
Hunt, Bobby KCC 20, CIN 20
Hunt, Byron NYG 57
Hunt, Calvin PHL 54, TEN 51/52
Hunt, Charles TBB 55, SFF 61

Hunt, Cletidus GBP 97
Hunt, Daryl TEN 50
Hunt, Ervin GBP 45
Hunt, Gary CIN 31
Hunt, George IND 10, NYG 9
Hunt, Jackie CHI 25
Hunt, Jim NEP 79
Hunt, John DAL 79, TBB 72
Hunt, Kevin GBP 64, NEP 62, NOS 76, TEN 72
Hunt, Mike GBP 55
Hunt, Purvis TEN 61
Hunt, Robert NOS 60
Hunt, Ron CIN 72
Hunt, Sam NEP 50
Hunter, Al SEA 24
Hunter, Art CLE 56/78, GBP 70, PIT 57, STL 56
Hunter, Bill WSH 23, MIA 24
Hunter, Brice TBB 19/88
Hunter, Dameon BLT 23
Hunter, Daniel DEN 25, SDC 27
Hunter, Earnest BLT 23, CLE 23, NOS 32
Hunter, Eddie NYJ 45, TBB 37
Hunter, Herman DET 36, PHL 36, TEN 30
Hunter, Ivy Joe IND 45, NEP 45
Hunter, James DET 28
Hunter, James IND 92
Hunter, Javin BLT 84
Hunter, Jeff BUF 98, DET 97, MIA 97, TBB 97
Hunter, John ATL 68, SEA 68
Hunter, Monty ARZ 34, DAL 34
Hunter, Patrick ARZ 24, SEA 23/27
Hunter, Pete DAL 47
Hunter, Ramey DET 39
Hunter, Scott ATL 16, BUF 16, DET 10, GBP 16
Hunter, Stan NYJ 86
Hunter, Tony BUF 49/87/90, STL 87
Hunter, Tony GBP 31
Hunter, Torey TEN 25
Huntington, Greg CHI 67, JAX 66/78, WSH 60
Huntley, Richard ATL 33, CAR 34, DET 32, PIT 33
Hupke, Thomas STL 1/22, DET 22
Hurd, Jeff DAL 52/58
Hurlburt, John ARZ 5
Hurley, Bill BUF 47, NOS 28
Hurley, George WSH 28
Hurst, Maurice NEP 37
Hurston, Chuck BUF 64, KCC 85
Hurt, Eric DAL 40
Husak, Todd DEN 8, NYJ 8, WSH 8

Husmann, Ed TEN 82, DAL 66, ARZ 65/66

Hust, Al ARZ 24

Husted, Michael KCC 7, OAK 5, TBB 5, WSH 4

Hutcherson, Ken DAL 59, SDC 55

Hutchins, Paul GBP 67

Hutchinson, Bill NYG 42

Hutchinson, Chad DAL 7

Hutchinson, Ralph NYG 71

Hutchinson, Scott BUF 78/90, TBB 70

Hutchinson, Steve SEA 76

Hutchinson, Tom ATL 83, CLE 87

Hutchison, Anthony BUF 30, CHI 31

Hutchison, Chuck ARZ 65

Hutchison, Elvin DET 21

Huth, Gerry MIN 65, PHL 54/65, NYG 65

Huther, Bruce CHI 57, CLE 58, DAL 55/57

Hutson, Brian NEP 36

Hutson, Don GBP 14

Hutson, Tony DAL 66, WSH 68

Hutton, Tom MIA 4, PHL 4

Huxhold, Ken PHL 63

Huzvar, John IND 38, PHL 38

Hyatt, Fred ARZ 88, NOS 88, WSH 40

Hyche, Steve ARZ 97, CHI 58

Hyde, Glenn DEN 65/67, IND 65, KCC 52, SEA 60

Hyder, Gaylon CLE 71, STL 94

Hyland, Bob CHI 50, GBP 50/55, NEP 60, NYG 70

Hynes, Paul NYJ 33

Hynoski, Henry CLE 36

Iacavazzi, Cosmo NYJ 45

Iaquaniello, Mike MIA 48

Ieremia, Mekeli BUF 73

Ifeanyi, Israel SFF 59/95

Iglehart, Floyd STL 49

Igwebuike, Donald MIN 4, TBB 1

Ilesic, Hank SDC 8

Ilg, Ray NEP 45

Ilgenfritz, Mark CLE 77

Ilkin, Tunch PIT 62, GBP 79

Illman, Ed ARZ 6

Ilowit, Roy xBKN 18

Iman, Ken GBP 53, STL 50

Imhof, Martin ARZ 62/82, DEN 73, NEP 64, WSH 66

Imlay, Tut NYG 4

Ingalls, Bob GBP 53

Inglis, Tim CIN 92

Ingram, Brian NEP 51, SDC 52

Ingram, Byron KCC 60, TBB 61

Ingram, Darryl CLE 83, GBP 88, MIN 86

Ingram, Kevin NOS 12

Ingram, Mark GBP 82, MIA 82, NYG 82, PHL 85

Ingram, Stephen TBB 65/67, JAX 67

Ingwerson, Burt CHI 10

Inman, Jerry DEN 62

Inmon, Earl TBB 59

Innocent, Dou SEA 28

Insley, Trevor HOU 87, IND 83

Intrieri, Marne WSH 37

Inzer, Drew JAX 79

Ioane, Junior OAK 92, HOU 94

Ippolito, Anthony CHI 82

Ireland, Darwin CHI 52/60

Irons, Gerald CLE 86, OAK 86

Irons, Grant BUF 96, OAK 99

Irvin, Darrell BUF 97, SEA 70

Irvin, Ken BUF 27, MIN 22, NOS 27

Irvin, LeRoy STL 47, DET 47

Irvin, Mark MIA 46

Irvin, Michael DAL 88

Irvin, Sedrick DET 33

Irvin, Tex NYG 29

Irvin, Willie PHL 81

Irving, Terry ARZ 56

Irwin, Don WSH 23

Irwin, Heath MIA 66, NEP 63, STL 63

Irwin, Tim MIA 76, MIN 76, TBB 78

Isaacson, Ted ARZ 49

Isaia, Sale BLT 64, NEP 72

Isbell, Cecil GBP 17

Isbell, Joe Bob CLE 61, DAL 60

Isenbarger, John SFF 17

Ismail, Qadry MIN 82, NOS 82, BLT 87, IND 83, MIA 86

Ismail, Raghib DAL 81, OAK 86, CAR 81

Isom, Jason SFF 41

Isom, Ray TBB 28

Isom, Ricky MIA 20

Israel, Ron CLE 23, MIN 37

Israel, Steve NEP 21, NOS 21, SFF 31, STL 31

Issa, Jabari ARZ 72

Isselhardt, Ralph DET 15, STL 15

Itzel, John PIT 37

Iverson, Duke NYG 22, xNYB 15, zNYY 66/82

Ivery, Eddie Lee GBP 40

Ivlow, John CHI 46

Ivory, Bob DET 42

Ivory, Horace NEP 23, SEA 32

Ivy, Corey TBB 35

Ivy, Frank PIT 22, ARZ 7/42/51

Iwanowski, Mark NYJ 88

Iwuoma, Chidi DET 40, PIT 29

Izo, George ARZ 3, DET 15, PIT 15, WSH 15

Izzo, Larry MIA 53, NEP 53

Jack, Eric ATL 39

Jacke, Chris ARZ 13, GBP 13, WSH 13

Jackson, Al PHL 26

Jackson, Alcender DAL 71, GBP 64

Jackson, Alfred ATL 85

Jackson, Alfred CLE 25, MIN 25, STL 31

Jackson, Alonzo PIT 95

Jackson, Andrew TEN 39

Jackson, Arnold ARZ 84

Jackson, Bernard CIN 23, DEN 29, SDC 26

Jackson, Bernard WSH 73

Jackson, Bill CLE 36

Jackson, Billy KCC 43

Jackson, Bo OAK 34

Jackson, Bob NYG 34

Jackson, Bob PHL 28, CHI 20

Jackson, Bob TEN 46, OAK 32, SDC 40

Jackson, Bobby NYJ 40

Jackson, Brad BLT 50, CAR 50

Jackson, Calvin MIA 38

Jackson, Cedric DET 30

Jackson, Charles KCC 51, NYJ 55

Jackson, Charles WSH 37

Jackson, Charley ARZ 22, KCC 40

Jackson, Chris GBP 81/86, TEN 84

Jackson, Clarence NYJ 43

Jackson, Cleveland NYG 81

Jackson, Curtis NEP 82

Jackson, Darrell SEA 82

Jackson, David TBB 84

Jackson, Dexter ARZ 34, TBB 34

Jackson, Don PHL 10/50

Jackson, Earnest PIT 43, PHL 41, SDC 41

Jackson, Enis CLE 35

Jackson, Ernie ATL 30, DET 44, NOS 30

Jackson, Frank KCC 26, MIA 26

Jackson, Frisman CLE 88

Jackson, Gerald KCC 38

Jackson, Grady GBP 75, NOS 91, OAK 90

Jackson, Greg NOS 47, NYG 47, PHL 47, SDC 42

Jackson, Greg PHL 79

Jackson, Harold PHL 29, MIN 89, NEP 29, SEA 29, STL 29

Jackson, Honor NEP 29, NYG 20, NYG 22

Jackson, James CLE 29

Jackson, Jarious DEN 17

Jackson, Jeff ATL 51, SDC 52
Jackson, Jim SFF 38
Jackson, Joe MIN 76
Jackson, Joe NYJ 86
Jackson, Joe SEA 54
Jackson, John ARZ 18/80, CHI 82/88
Jackson, John CIN 65, PIT 65, SDC 65
Jackson, Johnnie GBP 40, SFF 40
Jackson, Johnny PHL 62
Jackson, Keith GBP 88, MIA 88, PHL 88
Jackson, Ken IND 74, xDAL 74
Jackson, Kenny PHL 81/83/84, TEN 86
Jackson, Kirby BUF 47, STL 36
Jackson, Ladairis WSH 94
Jackson, Larron ATL 68, DEN 68
Jackson, Larry DEN 78
Jackson, Lawrence ATL 68
Jackson, Lenzie CLE 81, JAX 83, PIT 83
Jackson, Leonard OAK 91
Jackson, Leroy WSH 22
Jackson, Louie NYG 21
Jackson, Marcus IND 76
Jackson, Mark ARZ 21
Jackson, Mark DEN 80, IND 84, NYG 12/89
Jackson, Mel GBP 71
Jackson, Michael BLT 81, CLE 1/81
Jackson, Michael SEA 55
Jackson, Monte STL 28, OAK 42
Jackson, Noah CHI 65, TBB 65
Jackson, Randy CHI 65
Jackson, Randy BUF 33, PHL 33, SFF 33
Jackson, Ray BUF 31, TEN 38, CLE 31
Jackson, Rich DEN 87, CLE 87, OAK 32
Jackson, Rickey NOS 57, SFF 57
Jackson, Robert CIN 37
Jackson, Robert E. CLE 68
Jackson, Robert L. CLE 56, ATL 62
Jackson, Roger DEN 25/28
Jackson, Roland ARZ 33
Jackson, Rusty BUF 4, STL 9
Jackson, Sean TEN 41
Jackson, Sheldon BUF 88
Jackson, Steve OAK 42
Jackson, Steve TEN 24
Jackson, Steve WSH 53
Jackson, Terry NYG 24, SEA 24, SFF 22

Jackson, Tim DAL 32
Jackson, Tom DEN 57
Jackson, Trent PHL 27, WSH 22
Jackson, Tyoka MIA 97, TBB 97, STL 97
Jackson, Vestee CHI 24, MIA 24
Jackson, Victor IND 39, OAK 49
Jackson, Waverly IND 74
Jackson, Wilbur SFF 40, WSH 40
Jackson, Willie ATL 80, CIN 80, DAL 83, JAX 80, NOS 88, WSH 83
Jackunas, Frank BUF 54, DEN 52
Jacobs, Allen GBP 35, NYG 30
Jacobs, Cam TBB 91
Jacobs, Dave CLE 10, NYJ 1, PHL 4
Jacobs, Harry BUF 54/56/64, NEP 83, NOS 52
Jacobs, Jack GBP 27, STL 43, WSH 77
Jacobs, Marv ARZ 82
Jacobs, Proverb NYG 73, NYJ 75, OAK 77, PHL 67
Jacobs, Ray DEN 50
Jacobs, Ray DEN 83, MIA 84, NEP 87, TEN 84
Jacobs, Taylor WSH 86
Jacobs, Tim CLE 41/47, MIA 34
Jacobson, Jack SDC 24
Jacobson, Larry NYG 75
Jacobson, Steve MIA 72
Jacoby, Joe WSH 66
Jacoby, Mitch KCC 85, STL 46/89
Jacox, Kendyl NOS 64, SDC 64
Jacquet, Nate IND 18, MIA 19/83/88, MIN 83, SDC 89
Jacunski, Harry GBP 48
Jaeger, Jeff OAK 18, CHI 1, CLE 8
Jaffurs, John WSH 60
Jagade, Harry CLE 32/72, CHI 30, zBAL 76
Jagielski, Harry ARZ 76, NEP 73, OAK 70, WSH 75
Jakes, Van GBP 24, KCC 22, NOS 22
Jakowenko, George BUF 5, OAK 6
James, Angelo PHL 42
James, Arrike TEN 49
James, Bradie DAL 56
James, Cedric MIN 89
James, Claudis GBP 16/27
James, Craig NEP 32
James, Dan CHI 74, PIT 55/77

James, Dick WSH 47, MIN 47, NYG 47
James, Edgerin IND 32
James, Garry DET 32/33
James, Jeno CAR 78
James, Jesse STL 69
James, John ATL 6, DET 6, TEN 6
James, June DET 96, IND 58
James, Lionel SDC 26
James, Lynn CIN 80, CLE 40/80
James, Nathaniel CLE 33
James, Philip NOS 50
James, Po PHL 27/33
James, Robert BUF 20
James, Roland NEP 38
James, Tommy CLE 42/82, DET ?, IND 42
James, Toran SDC 59
James, Tory CIN 26, DEN 20, OAK 20
Jameson, Larry TBB 69
Jameson, Michael CLE 22
Jamieson, Dick NYJ 15
Jamison, Al TEN 70
Jamison, George DET 58/95, KCC 57
Jammer, Quentin SDC 23
Janata, John CHI 72
Jancik, Bobby TEN 23
Janecek, Clarence PIT 16
Janerette, Charlie DEN 70, NYJ 72, STL 67, NYG 72
Janes, Ron JAX 36
Janet, Ernie CHI 64, GBP 63, PHL 64
Janiak, Len xBKN 3, STL 38
Janik, Tom BUF 27, NEP 21, DEN 26
Janikowski, Sebastian OAK 11
Jankovich, Keever ARZ 53/81, xDAL 55
Jankowski, Bruce KCC 41
Jankowski, Ed GBP 7/25
Janowicz, Vic WSH 43
Jansante, Val PIT 54/85, GBP 23
Jansen, Jon WSH 76
January, Mike CHI 94
Janus, Paul CAR 74, NYG 17/22/25
Jaqua, Jon WSH 48
Jaquess, Pete TEN 47, DEN 43, MIA 44
Jarett, Craig WSH 10
Jarmoluk, Mike PHL 78, CHI 25, xBOS 47, xNYB 47
Jarostchuk, Ilia ARZ 50, MIA 58, NEP 50
Jarvi, Toimi PHL 32, PIT 32
Jarvis, Bruce BUF 51
Jarvis, Curt TBB 95
Jarvis, Ralph IND 93
Jarvis, Ray ATL 46, BUF 80, DET 45, NEP 87

Jasper, Ed ATL 95, PHL 74
Jasper, Vince NYJ 66
Jaszewski, Floyd DET 72
Jauron, Dick DET 26, CIN 30
Jaworski, Matt IND 59
Jaworski, Ron PHL 7, KCC 7, MIA 17, STL 16
Jax, Garth ARZ 53, DAL 53
Jay, Craig GBP 26/81
Jaynes, Dave KCC 12
Jecha, Ralph CHI 69, PIT 65
Jeffcoat, Jim BUF 77, DAL 77
Jefferies, Eric CHI 24/31
Jeffers, Ed zBRK 35
Jeffers, Lemont TBB 55
Jeffers, Pat DAL 81, DEN 81/82, CAR 83
Jefferson, Billy DET 46, xBKN 30
Jefferson, Charles TEN 21
Jefferson, James SEA 20/26
Jefferson, John GBP 83, SDC 83, CLE 89
Jefferson, Joseph IND 29
Jefferson, Kevin CIN 57
Jefferson, Norm GBP 38
Jefferson, Roy PIT 87, WSH 80, IND 87
Jefferson, Shawn ATL 84, DET 87, NEP 84, SDC 80
Jefferson, Thad TEN 53
Jefferson, William PHL 43
Jeffery, Tony ARZ 28
Jeffires, Haywood NOS 80, TEN 80/84
Jeffrey, Neal SDC 19
Jeffries, Bob xBKN 24
Jeffries, Curtis CIN 87
Jeffries, Dameian NOS 96
Jeffries, Greg DET 25, MIA 25
Jelacic, Jon NYG 83, OAK 88
Jelesky, Tom PHL 77
Jelley, Tom PIT 86
Jells, Dietrich NEP 83, PHL 83
Jencks, Bob CHI 80, WSH 81
Jenison, Ray GBP 31
Jenke, Noel ATL 59, GBP 55, MIN 52
Jenkins, A.J. PIT 99
Jenkins, Al CLE 60, MIA 58, TEN 60
Jenkins, Alfred ATL 84
Jenkins, Billy STL 22, BUF 24, DEN 32, GBP 23
Jenkins, Carlos MIN 51, STL 51
Jenkins, Corey MIA 57
Jenkins, DeRon BLT 25, SDC 23, TEN 25
Jenkins, Ed BUF 24, MIA 28, NEP 30, NYG 29
Jenkins, Fletcher IND 94
Jenkins, Izel MIN 28, NYG 24, PHL 46
Jenkins, J.R. BLT 6

Jenkins, Jacque WSH 38
Jenkins, James WSH 88
Jenkins, John PIT 28
Jenkins, Jon xBAL 47, xNYB 85, zBAL 47
Jenkins, Ken DET 31, WSH 31
Jenkins, Kerry NYJ 71, TBB 71
Jenkins, Keyvan KCC 41, SDC 39
Jenkins, Kris CAR 77
Jenkins, Leon DET 31
Jenkins, MarTay ARZ 19/82
Jenkins, Melvin DET 24, SEA 24
Jenkins, Mike CIN 84
Jenkins, Robert OAK 64, STL 72
Jenkins, Ronney OAK 27, SDC 28
Jenkins, Trezelle KCC 74, NOS 72
Jenkins, Walt DET 89
Jennings, Brandon OAK 39
Jennings, Brian SFF 86
Jennings, Dave NYG 13, NYJ 4/13
Jennings, Jim GBP 85
Jennings, John ARZ 50/68/70
Jennings, Jonas BUF 75
Jennings, Keith CHI 85, DAL 84
Jennings, Ligarius CIN 25
Jennings, Lou DET 71
Jennings, Rick OAK 33, SFF 88, TBB 81
Jennings, Stanford CIN 36, NOS 36, TBB 28
Jensen, Bob xBAL 54, zCHI 57
Jensen, Derrick OAK 31
Jensen, Greg GBP 54/60
Jensen, Jerry CAR 53
Jensen, Jim DAL 37, DEN 30, GBP 33
Jensen, Jim MIA 11
Jensen, Russ OAK 18
Jensvold, Leo CHI 10
Jeralds, Luther KCC 89
Jerman, Greg MIA 60
Jerome, Jim NYJ 57
Jerue, Mark STL 59
Jervey, Travis GBP 32, ATL 36, SFF 32
Jessie, Ron STL 81, BUF 81, DET 89
Jessie, Tim WSH 21
Jessup, Bill DEN 81, SFF 55/85
Jeter, Bob GBP 21, CHI 29
Jeter, Eugene DEN 51
Jeter, Gary NEP 99, NYG 70, STL 77
Jeter, Perry CHI 21
Jeter, Tommy PHL 98, CAR 97
Jeter, Tony PIT 84
Jett, James OAK 82
Jett, John DAL 19, DET 18/19

Jett, John DET 82
Jetton, Paul CIN 68, NOS 68
Jewett, Bob CHI 86
Jiggetts, Dan CHI 62
Jilek, Dan BUF 51
Jiles, Dwayne NYG 54, PHL 53
Jimerson, A.J. OAK 58
Jimoh, Ade WSH 23
Joachim, Steve NYJ 11
Jobko, Bill ATL 57, MIN 57, STL 57
Jocher, Art xBKN 27/8
Jodat, Jim SDC 40, SEA 43, STL 43
Joe, Billy BUF 33, DEN 3, MIA 33, NYJ 35
Joe, Larry zBUF 80
Joelson, Greg SFF 93
Joesting, Herb CHI 33
Johansson, Ove PHL 10
Johns, Paul SEA 85
Johns, Pete TEN 21
Johnson, A.J. SDC 47, WSH 47
Johnson, Al ARZ 21, CHI 3, PHL 44, xBKN 4
Johnson, Al TEN 15
Johnson, Albert MIA 83, NYJ 89
Johnson, Alex TEN 86
Johnson, Alonzo NOS 19, PHL 54
Johnson, Andre DET 70
Johnson, Andre HOU 80
Johnson, Andy NEP 32
Johnson, Anthony CHI 25, IND 23, JAX 23, NYJ 32, CAR 23
Johnson, Barry DEN 86
Johnson, Benny NOS 22, TEN 33
Johnson, Bethel NEP 81
Johnson, Bill CHI 33
Johnson, Bill CIN 30
Johnson, Bill CLE 94, PHL 94, PIT 90, STL 79
Johnson, Bill GBP 50
Johnson, Bill NYG 36
Johnson, Bill SFF 23/53
Johnson, Billy ATL 81, TEN 84, WSH 88
Johnson, Billy NEP 47
Johnson, Bob CIN 54
Johnson, Bobby ARZ 42, NOS 34
Johnson, Bobby NYG 88
Johnson, Brad TBB 14, MIN 14, WSH 14
Johnson, Brent CHI 53
Johnson, Bryan WSH 47
Johnson, Bryant ARZ 83
Johnson, Butch DAL 86, DEN 86
Johnson, Byron TEN 57

Johnson, Carl NOS 77
Johnson, Cecil TBB 56, xBKN 27
Johnson, Chad CIN 85
Johnson, Charles ARZ 46, SFF 44
Johnson, Charles GBP 99
Johnson, Charles BUF 89, NEP 81, PHL 81, PIT 81
Johnson, Charley ARZ 12, TEN 12, DEN 12
Johnson, Charlie PHL 65, MIN 65
Johnson, Charlie SFF 72
Johnson, Chester PIT 6
Johnson, Chris MIN 35
Johnson, Chris PHL 30
Johnson, Chuck DEN 66
Johnson, Chuckie ARZ 72
Johnson, Clyde KCC 23
Johnson, Clyde STL 8, zLAD 49
Johnson, Cornelius IND 61
Johnson, Curley KCC 33, NYG 75, NYJ 20/33
Johnson, Curtis MIA 45
Johnson, D.J. ARZ 44, ATL 44, PIT 44
Johnson, Damian NEP 68, NYG 68
Johnson, Damone STL 86
Johnson, Dan MIA 87
Johnson, Danny GBP 58
Johnson, Darrius DEN 25
Johnson, Daryl NEP 23
Johnson, Demetrious DET 21, MIA 23
Johnson, Dennis ARZ 96
Johnson, Dennis BUF 39, NYG 89
Johnson, Dennis WSH 61, BUF 75
Johnson, Dennis MIN 52, TBB 55
Johnson, Dick KCC 85
Johnson, Dirk PHL 8
Johnson, Don PHL 40
Johnson, Donald STL ?
Johnson, Donnell CIN 68/99
Johnson, Doug ATL 11
Johnson, Dustin SEA 41
Johnson, Dwight NYG 94, PHL 62
Johnson, Earl DEN 21, NOS 21
Johnson, Eddie CLE 51
Johnson, Eddie MIN 4
Johnson, Ellis ATL 61, IND 62, NEP 38
Johnson, Eric OAK 41, PHL 49, SFF 24
Johnson, Eric SFF 82
Johnson, Essex CIN 19, TBB 19
Johnson, Ezra GBP 78/90, IND 90, TEN 90

Johnson, Farnham zCHI 54
Johnson, Filmel BUF 39
Johnson, Flip BUF 80
Johnson, Garrett NEP 60
Johnson, Gary SDC 72/79, SFF 97
Johnson, Gene MIN 41, NYG 41, PHL 27
Johnson, Gil zNYY 61
Johnson, Gilvanni DET 87
Johnson, Glenn GBP 35, zNYY 45
Johnson, Greg IND 79, MIA 73, TBB 72
Johnson, Greggory SEA 27, ARZ 27
Johnson, Harvey xNYB 62, zNYY 75/61/88
Johnson, Henry MIN 53
Johnson, Herb NYG 20
Johnson, Holbert STL 46
Johnson, Hoss TBB 73
Johnson, Howard GBP 64
Johnson, J.J. MIA 32
Johnson, Jack BUF 42, CHI 49, KCC 32
Johnson, Jack DET 16
Johnson, James DET 54, SDC 52, SFF 56
Johnson, Jarret BLT 76
Johnson, Jason DEN 87, PIT 88
Johnson, Jason IND 59/60
Johnson, Jay PHL 48
Johnson, Jeremi CIN 31
Johnson, Jerry DEN 90
Johnson, Jesse NYJ 27
Johnson, Jim CIN 29
Johnson, Jimmie DET 89, KCC 45, PHL 88, WSH 88
Johnson, Jimmy SFF 37
Johnson, Joe GBP 40, NEP 24
Johnson, Joe NOS 94, GBP 91
Johnson, Joe NYG 88
Johnson, Joe MIN 89, WSH 80
Johnson, John CHI 76, NYG 75
Johnson, John CIN 55, NOS 50, SFF 55
Johnson, John Henry DET 35, PIT 35, SFF 35, TEN 35
Johnson, Johnnie SEA 26, STL 20
Johnson, Johnny ARZ 39, NYJ 39
Johnson, Junior NOS 58
Johnson, Kelley IND 84
Johnson, Ken BUF 14
Johnson, Ken BUF 91, KCC 97
Johnson, Ken CIN 80
Johnson, Ken MIN 22, NYJ 26
Johnson, Ken NYG 48
Johnson, Kenneth GBP 39/41

Johnson, Kenny ATL 37, TEN 22
Johnson, Kermit SFF 47
Johnson, Keshon CHI 25/37, GBP 37
Johnson, Kevin CLE 85, JAX 83
Johnson, Kevin OAK 98, PHL 94
Johnson, Keyshawn NYJ 19, TBB 19
Johnson, Larry KCC 34
Johnson, Larry NYG 31, WSH 13/16
Johnson, Lawrence BUF 48, CLE 48
Johnson, Lee CIN 11, CLE 11, MIN 12, NEP 10, PHL 6, TEN 11
Johnson, Len NYG 59
Johnson, Leo CHI 8
Johnson, Leo SFF 81
Johnson, Leon CHI 32, NYJ 32, SDC 35
Johnson, LeShon ARZ 32, GBP 42, NYG 23
Johnson, Levi DET 23
Johnson, Lonnie BUF 84, KCC 83
Johnson, M.L. SEA 52
Johnson, Malcolm PIT 83
Johnson, Mario NEP 98, NYJ 78
Johnson, Mark CIN 43
Johnson, Mark BUF 50, CLE 58
Johnson, Marshall IND 29/80
Johnson, Marvin GBP 41, STL 27
Johnson, Maurice PHL 87
Johnson, Melvin KCC 35, TBB 25
Johnson, Mike CLE 59, DET 59
Johnson, Mike DAL 23
Johnson, Mike TEN 97
Johnson, Mitch CLE 74, DAL 64, STL 70, WSH 63/64
Johnson, Monte OAK 58
Johnson, Nate NOS 45
Johnson, Nate NYG 84
Johnson, Nate xNYB 36, zCHI 43, zNYY 43
Johnson, Norm ATL 9, PHL 9, PIT 9, SEA 9
Johnson, Olrick NEP 51
Johnson, Oscar CHI 1/10
Johnson, Paris ARZ 46
Johnson, Pat MIA 24
Johnson, Patrick BLT 83/85, JAX 84, WSH 84
Johnson, Pepper CLE 52/53, DET 99, NYG 52, NYJ 52
Johnson, Pete CHI 20
Johnson, Pete CIN 46, MIA 46, SDC 42

Johnson, Preston NEP 48

Johnson, Randy ATL 11, GBP 16, NYG 11, WSH 12

Johnson, Randy TBB 65

Johnson, Ray ARZ 7, STL 12

Johnson, Raylee SDC 99

Johnson, Reggie DEN 89, GBP 82/88, KCC 85, PHL 80

Johnson, Riall CIN 50

Johnson, Rich TEN 38

Johnson, Richard DET 84, WSH 83

Johnson, Richard TEN 23

Johnson, Rick DET 77

Johnson, Rob BUF 11, JAX 11, OAK 7, TBB 11, WSH 17

Johnson, Robert CHI 82

Johnson, Ron NYG 30, CLE 30

Johnson, Ron PHL 85

Johnson, Ron PIT 29

Johnson, Rudi CIN 32

Johnson, Rudy ATL 32, SFF 32

Johnson, Sammy GBP 39, MIN 48, SFF 48

Johnson, Samuel STL 89

Johnson, Sidney KCC 45, WSH 45

Johnson, Spider DET 62

Johnson, Steve NEP 85

Johnson, Ted NEP 52

Johnson, Teyo OAK 82

Johnson, Tim CIN 90, PIT 78, WSH 78

Johnson, Tim OAK 51

Johnson, Tom PHL 27

Johnson, Tom GBP 72

Johnson, Tommy JAX 21

Johnson, Tony NOS 80/86

Johnson, Tracy ATL 43, SEA 43, TBB 43, TEN 45

Johnson, Tre WSH 67/77, CLE 67

Johnson, Troy ARZ 87, DET 83, PIT 85

Johnson, Troy CHI 92, DET 95, NYJ 49/95

Johnson, Trumaine BUF 86, SDC 83

Johnson, Tyrone NOS 80

Johnson, Undra ATL 28, DAL 29, NOS 29

Johnson, Vance DEN 82

Johnson, Vaughan NOS 53, PHL 52

Johnson, Walter CLE 71, CIN 78

Johnson, Walter DAL 91

Johnson, Walter NOS 90, TEN 57

Johnson, Walter SFF 58

Johnson, Wayne IND 18

Johnson, Will CHI 89/93

Johnsos, Luke CHI 24

Johnston, Brian NYG 59

Johnston, Daryl DAL 48

Johnston, Jimmy ARZ 31, WSH 31

Johnston, Mark TEN 41, NYJ 23, OAK ?

Johnston, Pres zBUF 84, zMIA 90

Johnston, Rex PIT 28

Johnston, Swede GBP 15/37/54, xSTL 25

Johnstone, Lance MIN 51, OAK 51

Joiner, Charlie CIN 18, SDC 18, TEN 18/40

Joiner, Tim DEN 95, TEN 57

Joines, Vernon CLE 18/80

Jolitz, Evan CIN 57

Jolley, Al xBKN 10

Jolley, Doug OAK 88

Jolley, Gordon DET 64, SEA 64

Jolley, Lewis TEN 40

Jolly, Ken KCC 52

Jolly, Mike GBP 21

Jonas, Don PHL 28

Jonas, Marv xBKN ?

Jonassen, Eric ARZ 66, SDC 74

Jones, A.J. DET 34, STL 24

Jones, Aaron MIA 97, NEP 97, PIT 97

Jones, Andrew NOS 36

Jones, Anthony SDC 81, WSH 82

Jones, Arrington SFF 40

Jones, Art PIT 12/44

Jones, Ben ARZ 2

Jones, Bert IND 7, STL 17

Jones, Bill KCC 43

Jones, Billy zBRK 34

Jones, Bob ATL 40, CIN 32

Jones, Bob ATL 80, CHI 43

Jones, Bob GBP 55

Jones, Bob NYG 79

Jones, Bobby CLE 89, NYJ 89

Jones, Boyd GBP 71

Jones, Brent SFF 84/88

Jones, Brian IND 56, NOS 58

Jones, Bruce GBP 24, xBKN 23/27/18/28/71/8

Jones, Bruce PIT 47

Jones, Bryant IND 33

Jones, Calvin DEN 26, GBP 27, OAK 27/44

Jones, Cedric NEP 83, NYG 94

Jones, Charlie NOS 19, SDC 17/82, WSH 83

Jones, Chris NYG 90

Jones, Chris PHL 82

Jones, Clarence NOS 74, NYG 68, STL 72, CAR 75

Jones, Clint SDC 26, MIN 26

Jones, Cody STL 76

Jones, Curtis SDC 69

Jones, Dale DAL 51

Jones, Damon JAX 88

Jones, Dan CIN 66

Jones, Dante CHI 53, DEN 53

Jones, Daryl NYG 87

Jones, Daryll DEN 20, GBP 43

Jones, Dave CLE 41

Jones, David DEN 69, DET 51, WSH 58

Jones, David OAK 82

Jones, Deacon STL 75, SDC 75, WSH 75

Jones, Dhani NYG 55

Jones, Don NYJ 51

Jones, Don PHL 22

Jones, Donta NOS 53, PIT 54, CAR 54

Jones, Doug BUF 24, DET 46, KCC 32

Jones, Dub CLE 40/86, zBRK 73/91, zMIA 99

Jones, Dwaune HOU 18

Jones, E.J. DAL 39, KCC 48

Jones, Earl ATL 20

Jones, Ed BUF 26

Jones, Ed DAL 72

Jones, Edgar CHI 27/37, CLE 90

Jones, Ellis xBOS 27

Jones, Elmer DET 62/73, zBUF 34

Jones, Ernest DEN 72, NOS 92/95, CAR 59

Jones, Ernie ARZ 86, STL 86

Jones, Ernie NYG 31, SEA 49

Jones, Ezell NEP 74

Jones, Fred BUF 99, KCC 96

Jones, Fred KCC 53

Jones, Fred KCC 80

Jones, Freddie ARZ 85, SDC 88

Jones, Gary NYJ 25, PIT 25

Jones, Gene TEN 25

Jones, George CLE 43, JAX 43, PIT 43

Jones, Gordon TBB 84, STL 25

Jones, Greg ARZ 51

Jones, Greg BUF 36

Jones, Greg CHI 55, WSH 54

Jones, Harris SDC 58, TEN 61

Jones, Harry PHL 23

Jones, Harvey STL 12, WSH 11

Jones, Hassan KCC 81, MIN 84

Jones, Henry DEN 35

Jones, Henry BUF 20, ATL 30, MIN 21

Jones, Homer NYG 45, CLE 85

Jones, Horace OAK 82, SEA 79

Jones, Isaac IND 15

Jones, J.J. NOS 59

Jones, James BLT 97, CLE 96, DEN 93, DET 98

Jones, James DAL 23, DET 30, SEA 30

Jones, Jeff DET 70
Jones, Jermaine CHI 26
Jones, Jerry CHI 12
Jones, Jerry ATL 50, NOS 78
Jones, Jim DET 42
Jones, Jim OAK 32, STL 37
Jones, Jimmie DAL 97, PHL 98, STL 98
Jones, Jimmie DET 31
Jones, Jimmie NYJ 65, WSH 82
Jones, Jimmy CHI 80, DEN 80
Jones, Jock ARZ 55, CLE 55
Jones, Joe CLE 64/80, PHL 64, WSH 77
Jones, Joe IND 81
Jones, Joey ATL 84
Jones, John BLT 85/88
Jones, John NYJ 11
Jones, Julian PHL 27
Jones, June ATL 14
Jones, K.C. DEN 60
Jones, Keith ATL 38
Jones, Keith CLE 26
Jones, Ken BUF 69/72/73, NYJ 70
Jones, Kenyatta NEP 74
Jones, Kim NOS 32
Jones, Kirk CLE 33
Jones, LaCurtis TBB 57
Jones, Lam NYJ 80
Jones, Larry WSH 21, SFF 21/87
Jones, Lenoy CLE 51/56, TEN 57
Jones, Leonard DEN 32
Jones, Leroy SDC 68
Jones, Levi CIN 76
Jones, Lew xBKN 41
Jones, Lydell ATL 30
Jones, Marcus TBB 78
Jones, Marlon CLE 95
Jones, Marvin NYJ 54/55
Jones, Melvin WSH 61
Jones, Mike ARZ 75, NEP 96, TEN 96
Jones, Mike BUF 57
Jones, Mike NOS 86/89, MIN 89
Jones, Mike OAK 52, PIT 51/95, STL 52
Jones, Mike SEA 47, MIN 89
Jones, Mike SEA 53
Jones, Mike D. STL 90
Jones, Potsy NYG 10, GBP 37
Jones, Preston PHL 8
Jones, Quintin TEN 19/27
Jones, Ralph DET 31, zBAL 52
Jones, Ray MIA 49, PHL 21, SDC 23
Jones, Reggie CAR 81
Jones, Reggie KCC 9/11
Jones, Reggie SDC 87
Jones, Reginald NOS 27
Jones, Richard IND 39

Jones, Ricky CLE 47, IND 51
Jones, Robbie NYG 51
Jones, Robert DAL 55, MIA 52, STL 55, WSH 50
Jones, Rod KCC 81, SEA 83
Jones, Rod TBB 22, CIN 25
Jones, Rodrek CIN 60, STL 60
Jones, Roger CIN 24, TBB 24
Jones, Ron GBP 88
Jones, Rondell BLT 31, DEN 31
Jones, Rulon DEN 75
Jones, Rushen MIN 31
Jones, Scott CIN 77, GBP 71, NYJ 78
Jones, Sean TEN 96, GBP 96, OAK 99
Jones, Selwyn CLE 16, NOS 27, SEA 24
Jones, Shawn MIN 32
Jones, Spike BUF 10, BUF 11, PHL 6, TEN 11
Jones, Stan CHI 78, WSH 73
Jones, Steve ARZ 34, BUF 46
Jones, Tebucky NEP 34, NOS 34
Jones, Terry BLT 82
Jones, Terry GBP 63
Jones, Thomas ARZ 26, TBB 22
Jones, Thurman xBKN 1
Jones, Todd NEP 63
Jones, Tony ARZ 26/27
Jones, Tony ATL 83, TEN 82
Jones, Tony BLT 66, CLE 66
Jones, Tony DEN 77
Jones, Tyrone ARZ 59
Jones, Tyrone PHL 31
Jones, Victor DEN 31, KCC 46, PIT 30, TEN 30
Jones, Victor DET 57, TBB 52
Jones, Walter SEA 71
Jones, Wayne MIN 69
Jones, Willie BUF 27
Jones, Willie KCC 73
Jones, Willie OAK 90
Jones, Willie TEN 71, CIN 74/78
Jordan, Andrew MIN 83/85/89, PHL 49, TBB 48
Jordan, Antony ATL 55
Jordan, Antony IND 91
Jordan, Brian ATL 40
Jordan, Buford NOS 23
Jordan, Charles GBP 80/82, MIA 88, OAK 85, SEA 82
Jordan, Curtis TBB 25, WSH 22/25
Jordan, Darin PIT 55, SFF 90
Jordan, David NYG 69, TBB 61
Jordan, Donald CHI 49
Jordan, Henry GBP 74, CLE 72
Jordan, Homer CLE 1
Jordan, James SFF 18
Jordan, Jeff MIN 22, STL 31, WSH 30

Jordan, Jimmy NOS 45
Jordan, Kenneth GBP 55
Jordan, Kevin ARZ 86
Jordan, LaMont NYJ 34
Jordan, Larry DEN 54/85
Jordan, Leander CAR 76, JAX 76
Jordan, Lee Roy DAL 55
Jordan, Randy JAX 23, OAK 28
Jordan, Richard DET 99
Jordan, Shelby NEP 63/74, OAK 64/74
Jordan, Steve IND 6
Jordan, Steve MIN 83
Jordan, Tim NEP 93
Jordan, Tony ARZ 32
Jorden, Tim ARZ 85, PIT 84, SFF 48
Jorgensen, Wayne xBKN 18/24
Jorgenson, Carl GBP 54, PHL 42
Joseph, Dwayne CHI 32
Joseph, Elvis JAX 35
Joseph, James CIN 36, PHL 32
Joseph, Kerry CIN 12, SEA 28/40
Joseph, Red DET 70
Joseph, Ricot WSH 39
Joseph, Vance IND 43, NYJ 43
Joseph, William NYG 94
Josephson, Les STL 34
Joswick, Bob MIA 80
Jourdain, Yonel BUF 30
Joyce, Delvin NYG 33
Joyce, Don IND 76/83, ARZ 11/71, DEN 83, MIN 83
Joyce, Ericq CHI 38
Joyce, Matt ARZ 73, DET 75, SEA 77
Joyce, Terry ARZ 87
Joyner, L.C. OAK 46
Joyner, Larry TEN 31
Joyner, Seth ARZ 59, DEN 99, GBP 54, PHL 59
Joyner, Willie TEN 38
Jozwiak, Brian KCC 73
Judd, Saxon zBRK 53
Judie, Ed MIA 91, SFF 50, TBB 51
Judson, William MIA 49
Jue, Bhawoh GBP 21
Juenger, Dave CHI 38
Julian, Fred NYJ 39
Julien, Jarmar KCC 27
Juma, Kevin SEA 87
June, Cato IND 59
Jungmichel, Buddy zMIA 33
Junior, E.J. ARZ 54, MIA 54, SEA 93, TBB 50
Junker, Steve DET 88, WSH 80
Junkin, Mike CLE 54, KCC 93

Junkin, Trey ARZ 86, BUF 50, NYG 48, OAK 52/87, SEA 83, WSH 56

Jurevicius, Joe NYG 84, TBB 83

Jurgensen, Sonny PHL 9, WSH 9

Jurich, Mike xBKN 17

Jurich, Tom NOS 10

Juriga, Jim DEN 66

Jurkiewicz, Walt DET 80

Jurkovic, John CLE 67, GBP 64/92, JAX 64

Jurkovic, Mirko CHI 64

Jury, Bob SFF 26

Juster, Rube xBOS 46

Justice, Charlie WSH 22

Justice, Ed WSH 13

Justin, Kerry SEA 26

Justin, Paul CIN 10, IND 11, STL 16

Justin, Sid IND 44, STL 29

Juzwik, Steve WSH 30, zBUF 88/82, zCHI 81

Kab, Vyto DET 87, NYG 82, PHL 84

Kabealo, Michael STL 16

Kacherski, John DEN 55

Kacmarek, Jeff DET 73

Kacyvenski, Isaish SEA 58

Kaczmarek, Mike IND 52

Kadela, Dave ATL 73

Kadish, Mike BUF 71

Kadziel, Roin NEP 52

Kaesviharn, Kevin CIN 34

Kafentzis, Kurt TEN 1

Kafentzis, Mark CLE 23, IND 29

Kahl, Cy DET 23

Kahler, Bob GBP 8

Kahler, Royal GBP 72, PIT 46

Kahn, Ed WSH 18/43

Kaiser, Jason KCC 24

Kaiser, John BUF 52, SEA 60

Kakasic, George PIT 14

Kalafat, Jim STL 92

Kalimer, Karl NYJ 86

Kalina, Dave PIT 84

Kalis, Todd CIN 62, MIN 69, PIT 62

Kalmanir, Tom IND 40, STL 24

Kalsu, Bob BUF 61

Kalu, N.D. PHL 53/94, WSH 72

Kamana, John ATL 47, STL 46

Kamanu, Lew DET 85

Kaminski, Larry DEN 59

Kammerer, Carl WSH 66, SFF 66

Kamp, Jim WSH 19

Kampa, Bob BUF 70, DEN 72

Kampman, Aaron GBP 74

Kane, Carl PHL 36

Kane, Herb NYG 39

Kane, Rick DET 32, WSH 40

Kane, Tommy SEA 81

Kanell, Danny ATL 13, DEN 13, NYG 13

Kanicki, Jim CLE 69, NYG 73

Kantor, Joe WSH 31

Kapele, John PHL 77, PIT 64

Kapitansky, Bernie xBKN 3

Kaplan, Bennie PHL 77, NYG 55

Kaplan, Ken NOS 71, TBB 79

Kaplanoff, Carl xBKN 15

Kaporch, Al DET 75/76

Kapp, Joe MIN 11, NEP 11

Kapter, Alex CLE 39

Karamatic, George WSH 20

Karas, Emil SDC 56, WSH 63

Karcher, Jim WSH 29

Karcher, Ken DEN 12

Karcis, John PIT 30/64, NYG 11/50, xBKN 35/4/30/66/34

Karilivacz, Carl DET 21, NYG 21, STL 31

Karlis, Rich DEN 3, DET 1, MIN 3

Karmazin, Mike zNYY 30

Karnofsky, Abe xBOS 12

Karnofsky, Sonny PHL 40

Karpinski, Keith DET 90

Karpowich, Ed PIT 35/36

Karr, Bill CHI 22

Karras, Alex DET 71

Karras, John ARZ 44

Karras, Lou WSH 70

Karras, Ted CHI 67, DET 62, PIT 61, STL 67, WSH 99

Karrs, John STL 35

Karstens, George DET 35

Kartz, Keith DEN 72

Karwales, John ARZ 33

Kasap, Mike zBAL 46

Kasay, John CAR 4, SEA 4

Kaska, Tony DET 6, xBKN 29/9

Kasky, Ed PHL 73

Kaspar, Kevin ARZ 11/82, SEA 87, DEN 82

Kasperek, Dick ARZ 51

Kassel, Charles ARZ 12/43, CHI 24

Kassell, Brad TEN 55

Kassulke, Karl MIN 29

Katalinas, Leo GBP 11

Katcavage, Jim NYG 75

Katcik, Joe NYJ 73

Katolin, Mike CLE 62

Katrishen, Mike WSH 58

Kattus, Eric CIN 84, NYJ 49

Katzenmoyer, Andy NEP 59

Kauahi, Kani ARZ 57, GBP 62, KCC 65, SEA 62

Kaufman, Mel WSH 55

Kaufman, Napoleon OAK 26

Kaufusi, Steve PHL 94

Kaumeyer, Thom SEA 23

Kauric, Jerry CLE 2

Kavanaugh, Ken CHI 51

Kavel, George PHL 10, PIT 27

Kawal, Ed CHI 19/27, WSH 39

Kay, Bill ARZ 22, SDC 31, TEN 22

Kay, Clarence DEN 88

Kay, Rick ATL 58, STL 52

Kazadi, Muadianvita STL 59

Keahey, Duce xBKN 15

Keahey, Eulis NYG 27

Keane, Jim CHI 20, GBP 81

Keane, Tom IND 21, ARZ 21, xDAL 21

Keaner, Tom STL 10

Kearney, Jim DET 46, KCC 46, NOS 46

Kearney, Tim ARZ 56, CIN 56, KCC 50, TBB 50

Kearns, Tom ARZ 70, NYG 60

Kearse, Jevon TEN 90

Kearse, Tim IND 85

Keathley, Michael SDC 61

Keating, Bill DEN 61, MIA 72

Keating, Chris BUF 52, WSH 59

Keating, Tom OAK 74, BUF 74, KCC 74, PIT 74

Keaton, Curtis CIN 29, NOS 28

Keckin, Val SDC 16

Kecman, Dan NEP 45

Keeble, Jerry SFF 98

Keeble, Joe STL 9

Keel, Mark KCC 80, SEA 85

Keelar, Bill KCC 82

Keeling, Ray PHL 28

Keeling, Rex CIN 44

Keen, Allen PHL 24

Keenan, Jack WSH 47

Keenan, Sean ARZ 9

Keene, Bob DET 45

Keeton, Durwood NEP 29

Keever, Carl SFF 41

Kehoe, Scott MIA 71

Kehr, Rick ARZ 62, WSH 61

Keim, Mike NOS 78, SEA 78

Keisel, Brett PIT 99

Keith, Craig JAX 88, PIT 85/87

Keith, John SFF 28

Keithley, Gary ARZ 12

Kekeris, Jim GBP 72, PHL 77

Kelcher, Louie SDC 64/74, SFF 94

Kell, Paul GBP 41

Kellagher, Bill zCHI 74

Kellar, Mark MIN 39

Kellar, Scott IND 94

Kellemeyer, Doug TEN 62

Keller, Ken PHL 23

Keller, Larry NYJ 56

Keller, Mike DAL 57

Kellerman, Ernie CLE 24, BUF 24, CIN 24

Kelley, Bill GBP 26

Kelley, Bob PHL 50
Kelley, Brian NYG 55
Kelley, Chris CLE 80
Kelley, Dwight PHL 51
Kelley, Ed KCC 44
Kelley, Ed zLAD 40
Kelley, Gordon WSH 51
Kelley, Les NOS 30
Kelley, Mike SDC 10
Kelley, Mike TEN 58
Kellin, Kevin TBB 75
Kellogg, Bob ARZ 60
Kellogg, Clarence ARZ 24
Kellogg, Mike DEN 32
Kellum, Marv ARZ 59, PIT 54
Kelly, Ben MIA 20/35
Kelly, Ben NEP 31
Kelly, Bill xBKN 24
Kelly, Bob CIN 77, KCC 70,
    TEN 72/73
Kelly, Bob zBAL 89, zLAD 85
Kelly, Brian TBB 25
Kelly, Ellison NYG 71
Kelly, Elmo CHI 76
Kelly, Eric MIN 25
Kelly, Gordon SFF 83
Kelly, Jeff ATL 51
Kelly, Jim BUF 12
Kelly, Jim CHI 88
Kelly, Jim PHL 84, PIT 89
Kelly, Joe CIN 58, GBP 57, NYJ
    58, OAK 57, PHL 56, STL 52
Kelly, John WSH 75
Kelly, Leroy CLE 44
Kelly, Lewis MIN 61
Kelly, Maurice SEA 33
Kelly, Mike CIN 87, NOS 87
Kelly, Pat DEN 86/87
Kelly, Pat NYJ 19/82
Kelly, Reggie ATL 89, CIN 82
Kelly, Rob NOS 24/33/44
Kelly, Shipwreck NYG 20,
    xBKN 18/26/2/44/14
Kelly, Todd ATL 96, CIN 98,
    SFF 58
Kelm, Larry SFF 52, STL 52
Kelsay, Chad PIT 97
Kelsay, Chris BUF 90
Kelsch, Matt xBKN 25
Kelsch, Mose PIT 37
Kelso, Mark BUF 38
Kemoeatu, Ma'ake BLT 92
Kemp, Bobby CIN 26, TBB
    33
Kemp, Jack BUF 15, PIT 7/18,
    SDC 15
Kemp, Jeff PHL 16, SEA 15, SFF
    9, STL 9
Kemp, Perry CLE 22, GBP 81
Kemp, Ray PIT 45
Kempf, Florian NOS 5, TEN 4
Kempinska, Charlie SDC 67
Kendall, Chuck TEN 34
Kendall, Pete ARZ 66, SEA 66
Kendrick, Jim NYG 26

Kendrick, Vince ATL 20, TBB
    20
Kendricks, Jim CHI 6/26
Keneley, Matt SFF 75
Kenerson, John PIT 74, STL 72
Kenn, Mike ATL 78
Kennard, Derek ARZ 70/73,
    DAL 60, NOS 60
Kennard, George NYG 67
Kennard, Ken TEN 67/71
Kenneally, George ARZ 20,
    PHL 13
Kenneally, Gus WSH 13
Kennedy, Allan SFF 66
Kennedy, Bill DET 66, xBOS 31
Kennedy, Bob xNYB 85
Kennedy, Bob zLAD 82, zNYY
    70
Kennedy, Cortez SEA 96/99
Kennedy, Jimmie IND 85
Kennedy, Jimmy STL 73
Kennedy, Kenoy DEN 28
Kennedy, Lincoln OAK 72, ATL
    66/75
Kennedy, Mike BUF 21, TEN
    27
Kennedy, Sam SFF 57
Kennedy, Tom DET 68
Kennedy, Tom NYG 18
Kennerson, John NYJ 75
Kenney, Bill KCC 9, WSH 6
Kenney, Steve DET 63, PHL 73
Kennison, Eddie CHI 82, DEN
    85, KCC 87, NOS 82, STL 88
Kent, Greg DET 83, OAK 73/
    80
Kent, Joey IND 16, TEN 86
Kent, Rashod HOU 88
Kenyon, Bill NYG ?
Ker, Crawford DAL 68
Kerasiotis, Nick CHI 19
Kerbow, Randy TEN 18
Kercher, Bob GBP 18/23
Kercher, Dick DET 43
Kercheval, Ralph xBKN 22/26/1
Kerkorian, Gary IND 18, PIT
    17
Kern, Bill GBP 33
Kern, Don BUF 84, CIN 89
Kern, Rex BUF 45, IND 44
Kerner, Marlon BUF 46
Kerney, Patrick ATL 97
Kerns, John zBUF 46
Kerr, Bill zLAD 50
Kerr, Crawford DEN 68
Kerr, Jim WSH 43
Kerrigan, Mike NEP 19
Kersey, Merritt PHL 37
Kershaw, George NYG 86
Kersten, Wally STL 79, TBB
    61
Keseday, Bob ARZ 80
Ketzko, Alex DET 64
Keuper, Ken GBP 18, NYG
    20

Keur, Josh IND 83
Key, David NEP 26
Key, Sean DAL 40
Key, Wade PHL 72
Keyes, Bob OAK 24
Keyes, Jimmy MIA 52
Keyes, Leroy KCC 23
Keyes, Leroy PHL 20
Keyes, Marcus CHI 73
Keys, Brady PIT 26, ARZ 29,
    MIN 43
Keys, Howard PHL 61
Keys, Tyrone CHI 98, SDC 93,
    TBB 98
Keyworth, Jon DEN 32
Khayat, Bob WSH 60
Khayat, Ed NEP 73, PHL 73,
    WSH 74/87
Kichefski, Walt ARZ 45, PIT
    42/45
Kidd, Carl OAK 46
Kidd, John BUF 4, DET 17,
    MIA 17, NYJ 17, SDC 10
Kidd, Keith MIN 44
Kiel, Blair GBP 10, IND 5, TBB
    16
Kiel, Terrence SDC 48
Kielbasa, Max PIT 73
Kiesling, Walt ARZ 16/18/49,
    CHI 25, GBP 49/60, PIT 35
Kiewel, Jeff ATL 63
Kight, Danny BLT 12, IND 7
Kiick, George PIT 9
Kiick, Jim MIA 21, DEN 33,
    WSH 30
Kilbourn, Warren GBP 58
Kilcullen, Bob CHI 74
Kiley, Roger ARZ 18
Kilgore, Jon CHI 80, SFF 15,
    STL 13
Killens, Terry SEA 56, TEN 50,
    SFF 56
Killett, Charlie NYG 37
Killian, Gene DAL 60
Killiher, Lyons ARZ 19
Killinger, Glenn NYG 3
Killings, Cedric CAR 91, MIN
    95, SFF 71
Killorin, Pat PIT 55
Kilmer, Billy WSH 17, NOS 17,
    SFF 17
Kilroy, Bucko PHL 76, PIT 76
Kilson, Dave BUF 43
Kimball, Bobby GBP 85
Kimball, Bruce NYG 63, WSH
    63/67
Kimber, Bill NEP 86, NYG 86
Kimble, Frank PIT 60
Kimble, Garry WSH 34
Kimbrough, Elbert NOS 45,
    SFF 45, STL 83
Kimbrough, John BUF 82
Kimbrough, John zLAD 77
Kimbrough, Tony DEN 80/82
Kimmel, J.D. WSH 76, GBP 72

Knight, Sammy NOS 29, MIA 24

Knight, Shawn ARZ 75, DEN 99, NOS 78

Knight, Steve IND 63/73

Knight, Tom ARZ 22/24, BLT 22

Knoff, Kurt MIN 25, TEN 25

Knolla, John ARZ 33

Knopp, Oscar CHI 11

Knorr, Larry DET 68/88

Knorr, Micah DAL 4, DEN 4

Knowles, David NOS 66

Knox, Bill CHI 31

Knox, Charles PHL 29

Knox, Darryl PIT 50

Knox, Kevin ARZ 18/82

Knox, Mike DEN 56

Knox, Ron CHI 18

Knox, Sam DET 21

Knutson, Gene GBP 81

Knutson, Steve GBP 60, SFF 60

Koart, Matt GBP 92

Kobrosky, Mickey NYG 10

Koch, Aaron JAX 64

Koch, George STL 19, zBUF 84

Koch, Greg GBP 68, MIA 68, MIN 68

Koch, Marcus WSH 74

Koch, Pete CIN 71, KCC 74, OAK 74

Kochel, Mike ARZ 35

Kochman, Roger BUF 45

Kocourek, Dave SDC 83, MIA 83, OAK 88

Kocurek, Kris TEN 99

Kodba, Joe zBAL 28

Koegel, Vic CIN 50

Koegel, Warren ARZ 55, NYJ 53, OAK 56

Koehler, Bob ARZ 5/14/18/19, CHI 3

Koeninger, Art PHL 30

Koeper, Rich ATL 78

Koepfer, Karl DET 60

Kofler, Matt BUF 10, IND 12

Kohlbrand, Joe NOS 55

Kohn, Tim OAK 72

Kohrs, Bob PIT 90

Koken, Mike ARZ 25

Kolb, Jon PIT 55

Kolberg, Elmer PHL 16/22, PIT 8

Kolen, Mike MIA 57

Kolesar, Bob CLE 37

Kolic, Larry MIA 54/94

Kollar, Bill CIN 68, TBB 77

Kolman, Ed CHI 29, NYG 72

Kolodziej, Ross NYG 99

Kolodziejski, Chris PIT 84

Koman, Bill ARZ 34, IND 65, PHL 68

Komlo, Jeff ATL 14, DET 19, TBB 7

Kompara, John SDC 60

Koncar, Mark GBP 79, TEN 72

Kondria, John PIT 62

Konecny, Mark MIA 41, PHL 35

Konetsky, Floyd STL 38, zBAL 54

Koniszewski, John WSH 49

Konopasek, Ed GBP 68

Konovsky, Bob ARZ 67, CHI 58, DEN 73

Konrad, Rob MIA 44

Konz, Ken CLE 22

Kooistra, Scott CIN 75

Koonce, George GBP 53, SEA 53

Koons, Joe xBKN 24

Koontz, Ed NEP 54

Koontz, Joe NYG 47

Kopay, Dave DET 43, GBP 40, NOS 43, SFF 43, WSH 40

Kopcha, Joe CHI 29, DET 18

Kopenberg, Harry PHL 28

Kopp, Jeff BLT 57, JAX 57, MIA 52, NEP 91

Koppen, Dan NEP 67

Koppisch, Walt NYG 0

Korff, Mark SFF 90

Korisky, Ed xBOS 30

Kors, R.J. CIN 30, NYJ 25

Kortas, Ken ARZ 74, CHI 70, PIT 75

Korte, Steve NOS 60

Korver, Kelvin OAK 71

Kosar, Bernie CLE 19, DAL 18, MIA 19

Kosel, Stan xBKN 5

Kosens, Terry MIN 26

Koshlap, Jules PIT 29

Kosier, Kyle SFF 69/72

Kosikowski, Frank CLE 53

Kosins, Gary CHI 33

Koss, Stein KCC 80

Kostelnik, Ron GBP 77, IND 65

Kostiuk, Michael DET 71, STL 28

Kostka, Stan xBKN 30

Kotal, Ed GBP 10/13

Kotar, Doug NYG 44

Kotite, Rich PIT 88, NYG 86/87

Kottler, Martin PIT 41

Kovac, Ed IND 43, NYJ 35

Kovach, Jim NOS 52, SFF 57

Kovaleski, Mike CLE 97

Kovatch, John GBP 76, WSH 40

Kovatch, John STL 16

Kowalczyk, Walt DAL 35, OAK 35, PHL 43

Kowalkowski, Bob DET 66, GBP 67

Kowalkowski, Scott DET 52, PHL 57

Kowalski, Adolph zBRK 63

Kowalski, Andy xBKN 22, xBOS 3

Kowalski, Gary SDC 68, STL 76

Kowgios, Nick DET 30

Koy, Ernie NYG 23

Koy, Ted BUF 37/85, OAK 38

Kozak, Scott TEN 56

Kozel, Chet zBUF 41, zCHI 44

Kozerski, Bruce CIN 64

Kozlowski, Brian ATL 85, NYG 85

Kozlowski, Glen CHI 88

Kozlowski, Mike MIA 37/40

Kozlowski, Stan zMIA 73

Kraayeveld, Dave SEA 70

Kracum, George xBKN 10

Kraemer, Eldred SFF 65

Kragen, Greg DEN 71, CAR 71, KCC 71

Krahl, Jim IND 90, NYG 74, SFF 90

Krakau, Merv BUF 52, NEP 53

Krakoski, Joe OAK 27, WSH 25

Krakoski, Joe WSH 54

Krall, Gerry DET 17

Kramer, Erik ATL 14, CHI 12, DET 12, SDC 12

Kramer, Jack zBUF 43

Kramer, Jerry GBP 64

Kramer, Jordan TEN 57

Kramer, Kent MIN 89, NOS 89, PHL 87, SFF 89

Kramer, Kyle CLE 40

Kramer, Ron GBP 88, DET 83/88

Kramer, Tommy MIN 9, NOS 9

Kranz, Kenneth GBP 42

Kratch, Bob NEP 61, NYG 61

Kratzer, Dan KCC 27

Krause, Barry MIA 58

Krause, Henry xBKN 24/25

Krause, Larry GBP 30

Krause, Max NYG 25, WSH 25

Krause, Paul MIN 22, WSH 26

Krause, Red WSH 41

Krause, William STL 37

Krauss, Barry IND 55

Kraynak, Rich ATL 52, PHL 52

Kreamcheck, John CHI 58

Kreider, Dan PIT 35

Kreider, Steve CIN 86

Kreitling, Rich CHI 82, CLE 88

Krejci, Joe ARZ 25

Kremer, Ken KCC 91

Kremser, Karl MIA 15

Krenk, Mitch CHI 89

Krepfle, Keith ATL 88, PHL 84

Kresky, Joe PHL 5/26, PIT ?, WSH 24

Kresser, Eric CIN 15

Kreuger, Al WSH 14
Kreutz, Olin CHI 57
Krevis, Al CIN 75, NYJ 71
Krieg, Dave SEA 17, ARZ 17, CHI 17, DET 17, KCC 17, TEN 17
Krieg, Jim DEN 86
Krieger, Robert PHL 82/89
Kriel, Emmet PHL 25
Kriewald, Doug CHI 60
Kriewaldt, Clint DET 58, PIT 57
Krimm, John NOS 21
Kring, Frank DET 78
Krisher, Bill KCC 64, PIT 64
Kristufek, Frank xBKN 19
Krivonak, Jon zMIA 38
Krol, Joe DET 81
Kroll, Alex NYJ 55
Kroll, Bob GBP 44
Kroner, Gary DEN 12
Krouse, Ray DET 70, IND 78, NYG 70, WSH 77
Kruczek, Mike PIT 15, WSH 15
Krueger, Al zLAD 52
Krueger, Charles SFF 70
Krueger, Rolf ARZ 70, SFF 78
Krumm, Todd CHI 44
Krumrie, Tim CIN 69
Krupa, Joe PIT 75
Kruse, Bob BUF 63, OAK 62
Krutko, Larry PIT 31/39
Ksionyak, John STL 26
Kubala, Ray DEN 52
Kuberski, Bob GBP 94, NEP 93
Kubiak, Gary DEN 8
Kubin, Larry BUF 50, TBB 59, WSH 50
Kuchta, Frank DEN 52, WSH 56
Kuczynski, Bert DET 20, PHL 80
Kuechenberg, Bob MIA 67
Kuechenberg, Rudy CHI 59, ATL 59, CLE 59, GBP 59
Kuehl, Ryan CLE 97, WSH 78/99
Kuehn, Art NEP 78, SEA 54
Kuffel, Ray zBUF 55, zCHI 56
Kugler, Pete SFF 67/77
Kuharich, Joe ARZ 17/88
Kulbacki, Joe BUF 43
Kulbitski, Val zBUF 72/75
Kullman, Mike PHL 35
Kumerow, Eric MIA 90
Kunz, George ATL 75, IND 75
Kunz, Lee CHI 57
Kunz, Terry OAK 34
Kupcinet, Irv PHL 31/37
Kupp, Craig ARZ 7, DAL 9
Kupp, Jake NOS 50, ATL 65, DAL 67, WSH 67/81
Kurek, Ralph CHI 32

Kurisko, Jamie NYJ 82
Kurnick, Howie CIN 59
Kurpeikis, Justin PIT 90
Kurrasch, Roy PIT 51, zNYY 57
Kurth, Joe GBP 28/31/58
Kush, Rod BUF 42, TEN 37
Kusko, John PHL 16/21
Kusserow, Lou xNYB 56, zNYY 81
Kutner, Mal ARZ 80
Kuusisto, Bill GBP 45/52
Kuykendall, Fulton ATL 54, SFF 59
Kuziel, Bob NOS 67, WSH 54
Kuzman, John ARZ 24, SFF 46, zCHI 41
Kvaternik, Cvonimir PIT 19
Kwalick, Ted SFF 82, OAK 89
Kyle, Aaron DAL 25, DEN 22
Kyle, Jason CAR 56, CLE 57, SEA 57, SFF 57
Kyles, Trot SFF 85
Kyles, Troy NYG 21, SFF 21
Kysar, Jeff OAK 79
Laack, Galen PHL 64
Laakso, Eric MIA 68
Laaveg, Paul WSH 73
LaBeaux, Sandy TBB 29
Labounty, Matt GBP 97, SEA 67/91/99, SFF 93
Lacey, Bob MIN 88, NYG ?
Lach, Steve ARZ 37, PIT 37
LaChapelle, Sean KCC 18, STL 18/88
Lachey, Jim SDC 74, WSH 79, OAK 74
Lachman, Dick PHL 15/24
Lacina, Corbin BUF 68, CAR 64, CHI 63, MIN 63
LaCrosse, Dave PIT 54
Lacy, Ken KCC 40
Ladd, Anthony NEP 18
Ladd, Ernie SDC 77, KCC 99, TEN 99
Ladd, Jim ARZ 87
Ladygo, Pete PIT 62/66/74/76
Lafary, Dave NOS 64
LaFavor, Tron CHI 73
LaFitte, Bill xBKN 31
Lafleur, Billy SFF 4
LaFleur, David DAL 89
LaFleur, Greg ARZ 89, IND 83
Lageman, Jeff JAX 56, NYJ 56
Lagod, Chet NYG 65
LaGrand, Morris KCC 45, NOS 39
Lahar, Harold CHI 12, zBUF 31
Lahey, Pat zCHI 50
LaHood, Mike ARZ 66, STL 64/68
Lahr, Warren CLE 24/66/80
Laidlaw, Scott DAL 35, NYG 35

Laing, Aaron SDC 84, STL 45/86
Lainhart, Porter ARZ 28, PHL 18
Laird, Bruce IND 40, SDC 30
Lajousky, Bill PIT 2
Lake, Antwan DET 68
Lake, Carnell PIT 37, BLT 37, JAX 37
Lakes, Roland NYG 76, SFF 60
Lally, Bob GBP 58
LaLonde, Roger DET 65, NYG 78
Lamana, Pete zCHI 71/21/22
Lamar, Jason HOU 57
Lamar, Kevin BUF 51/62
Lamas, Joe PIT 29/33
Lamb, Brad BUF 81
Lamb, Mack MIA 45
Lamb, Rod ARZ 6
Lamb, Ron ATL 40, CIN 40, DEN 40
Lamb, Walter CHI 12
Lambeau, Curly GBP 1/14/20/42
Lambert, Dion NEP 28, SEA 34
Lambert, Frank PIT 46
Lambert, Gordon DEN 51/76
Lambert, Jack PIT 58
Lamberti, Pat DEN 50, NYJ 55
Lambrecht, Mike MIA 69
Lammons, Pete NYJ 87, GBP 86
Lamonica, Daryle OAK 3, BUF 12
LaMontagne, Noel CLE 79
Lamson, Chuck MIN 21, STL 44
Land, Dan OAK 25, TBB 24
Land, Fred SFF 45
Land, Mel MIA 52, SFF 60
Landers, Walt GBP 42
Landeta, Sean NYG 5, PHL 7, STL 5, TBB 7, GBP 7
Landolt, Kevin JAX 93
Landrigan, Jim zBAL 59
Landrum, Mike ATL 80
Landry, George CLE 48
Landry, Greg DET 11, CHI 11, IND 11
Landry, Ron MIA 38
Landry, Tom NYG 49, zNYY 85
Landsberg, Mort PHL 30, zLAD 99
Landsee, Bob PHL 65
Lane, Bobby SDC 57
Lane, Clay zNYY 46
Lane, Eric NYG 37, SEA 37
Lane, Fred CAR 32
Lane, Garcia KCC 41
Lane, Gary CLE 15, NYG 15
Lane, Les xBKN 36
Lane, MacArthur ARZ 36, GBP 36, KCC 42

Lane, Max NEP 68
Lane, Night Train ARZ 81, DET 81, STL 81
Lane, Skip KCC 26, NYJ 37, WSH 39
Lang, David DAL 38, STL 38
Lang, Gene ATL 33, DEN 33
Lang, Israel PHL 29, STL 39
Lang, Kenard WSH 90, CLE 96
Lang, Le-Lo DEN 21
Langas, Bob IND 83
Lange, Bill ARZ 68, IND 66, STL 26/65
Lange, Jim ARZ 3
Langer, Jim MIA 62, MIN 58
Langford, Jevon CIN 58/94
Langham, Antonio BLT 38, CLE 38, NEP 38, SFF 43
Langhorne, Reggie CLE 88, IND 85
Lanier, Ken DEN 67/76, OAK 79
Lanier, Willie KCC 63
Lankas, James PHL 43, GBP 23
Lankford, Paul MIA 44
Lanphear, Dan TEN 72/73
Lansdell, Grenny NYG 22
Lansford, Buck PHL 79, STL 63
Lansford, Jim xDAL 71
Lansford, Mike STL 1/4
Lantz, Montgomery PIT 32
Lanum, Jake CHI 1
Lanza, Chuck PIT 51
Lapham, Bill MIN 52, PHL 54
Lapham, Dave CIN 62
Lapka, Myron NYG 71, STL 67
Lapka, Ted WSH 45
LaPointe, Ron IND 85
LaPorta, Phil NOS 67
LaPresta, Benny WSH 15, xSTL ?
Laraba, Bob SDC 17/53
Laraway, Jack BUF 57, TEN 34
Largent, Steve SEA 80
Larkin, Eric TEN ?
Laro, Gordon JAX 40
LaRosa, Paul ARZ 5
LaRose, Dan DEN 80, DET 77, PIT 87, SFF 87
Larpenter, Carl DEN 77, KCC 67
Larrimore, Kareem DAL 41
Larsen, Gary MIN 77, STL 83
Larshied, Jack OAK 23
Larson, Bill DEN 87, DET 87, GBP 87, PHL 88, SFF 85, WSH 86
Larson, Fred ARZ 17, CHI 14/17, GBP 17
Larson, Greg NYG 53
Larson, Kurt GBP 59, IND 59
Larson, Leif BUF 97

Larson, Lou ARZ 18
Larson, Lynn IND 67
Larson, Paul ARZ 12, OAK 12
Larson, Pete WSH 24
Larson, William NEP 34
Lary, Yale DET 28
Lascari, John NYG 34
Lash, Jim MIN 82, SFF 87
Lashar, Tim CHI 16
Laskar, Greg CHI 31, ARZ 49, NYG 47
Laskey, Bill BUF 52, DEN 45, IND 51, OAK 42
Lasky, Frank NYG 71, NYG 77
Laslavic, Jim DET 52, GBP 60, SDC 54
Lassahn, Lou PIT 45
Lasse, Dick NYG 30, PIT 89/90, WSH 88
Lassic, Derrick DAL 25
Lassiter, Issac OAK 77, NEP 87, DEN 73
Lassiter, Kwamie ARZ 42, SDC 42
Laster, Art BUF 75
Laster, Don WSH 62, DET 73
Lathan, Greg OAK 81
Lathon, Lamar CAR 57, TEN 57
Lathrop, Kit DEN 75, GBP 72, KCC 70, WSH 67
Latimer, Al DET 43, PHL 29
Latimer, Don DEN 72
Latin, Jerry ARZ 32, STL 36
Latourette, Chuck ARZ 26
Latta, Greg CHI 88
Lattimore, Brian IND 21
Lattner, Johnny PIT 41
Latzke, Paul SDC 52
Lauer, Larry GBP 58
Laufenberg, Babe DAL 15, NOS 12, SDC 12, WSH 12/16
Laughlin, Jim ATL 51, GBP 62, STL 57
Laughlin, Bud SFF 36
Laughton, Jim SEA 89
Lauricella, Hank xDAL 44
Laurinaitis, Frank zBRK 36
Lauro, Lin ARZ 17
Lauter, Steve CLE 49
Laux, Ted PHL 15/27, PIT 15
Lavan, Al ATL 49
Lavelli, Dante CLE 56/86
Lavender, Joe PHL 30, WSH 20
Lavette, Robert DAL 29, PHL 22
Lavine, Paul SEA 55
Law, Dennis CIN 83
Law, Hubbard PIT 34
Law, Ty NEP 24
Lawler, Allen CHI 33
Lawless, Burton DAL 66, DET 66, MIA 71
Lawrence, Amos SFF 20
Lawrence, Ben PIT ?

Lawrence, Don WSH 78
Lawrence, Henry OAK 70
Lawrence, Jim ARZ 8/11/30, GBP 51/59
Lawrence, Kent PHL 12, ATL ?
Lawrence, Larry OAK 13, TBB 13
Lawrence, Reggie PHL 80
Lawrence, Rolland ATL 22
Laws, Joe GBP 24/29/38/41
Lawson, Jamie NEP 29, TBB 38
Lawson, Jerome BUF 21
Lawson, Odell NEP 32, NOS 39
Lawson, Roger CHI 36
Lawson, Steve CIN 68, MIN 65, SFF 65
Lay, Russ DET 23, xCIN 19, xSTL 22
Layden, Bob DET 81
Layden, Pete xNYB 17, zNYY 84/62
Layman, Jason TEN 66
Layne, Bobby DET 22, CHI 22, PIT 22, xNYB 22
Layne, George ATL 38/41
Lazetich, Milan STL 27
Lazetich, Pete PHL 73, SDC 51
Lazetich, William STL 24
Lea, Paul PIT 72
Leach, Mike DEN 48/83, TEN 83
Leach, Scott NOS 58
Leach, William NOS 74
Leaf, Ryan DAL 16, SDC 16
Leahy, Bernie CHI 6
Leahy, Bob PIT 16
Leahy, Gerald PIT 66
Leahy, Pat NYJ 5
Leahy, Ryan ARZ 61
Leaks, Roosevelt BUF 48, IND 48
Lear, Les DET 51, STL 41
Leasy, Wesley ARZ 52
Leathers, Milton PHL 27
Leavitt, Allan TBB 9
LeBaron, Eddie DAL 14
LeBeau, Dick DET 24/44
LeBel, Harper ATL 88, BLT 82, CHI 88, PHL 87, SEA 85
Leber, Ben SDC 51
Leberman, Bob IND 40
LeBlanc, Bob BUF 50
LeBlanc, Clarence NYG 35
LeBlanc, Michael NEP 27
Lechler, Shane OAK 9
Lechner, Ed NYG 31
Lechthaler, Roy PHL 34
Leckonby, Bill xBKN 34/24/4
LeClair, Jim CIN 55, DEN 10
LeClerc, Roger CHI 54/83, DEN 53
LeCount, Terry MIN 80, SFF 80

Lecture, Jim zBUF 37
Ledbetter, Homer ARZ 26
Ledbetter, Monte ATL 43, BUF 43, TEN 86
Ledbetter, Toy PHL 25
Ledford, Dwayne CAR 74, JAX 76, SFF 67/76
Ledyard, Courtney NYJ 53
Ledyard, Hal SFF 12
Lee, Amp MIN 32, PHL 28, SFF 22, STL 31
Lee, Barry CLE 68
Lee, Bernard PIT 42, PHL 11
Lee, Biff DET ?, xCIN 10,41
Lee, Bill GBP 40, xBKN 21/15
Lee, Bivian NOS 11
Lee, Bob ATL 19, MIN 19, STL 19
Lee, Bob ATL 82, ARZ 47
Lee, Buddy CHI 14
Lee, Byron PHL 58
Lee, Carl MIN 39, NOS 39
Lee, Charles GBP 82, TBB 81/82
Lee, Danzell ATL 87, PIT 84
Lee, David IND 49
Lee, Del NYJ 35
Lee, Donald MIA 85
Lee, Dwight ATL 31, SFF 49
Lee, Gary DET 83
Lee, Gene xBOS 28
Lee, Greg PIT 21
Lee, Herman CHI 70, PIT 72
Lee, Jacky TEN 15, DEN 15, KCC 15
Lee, Jeff ARZ 46
Lee, John ARZ 10
Lee, John NEP 66, SDC 69
Lee, John PIT 16
Lee, Keith IND 42, NEP 22
Lee, Ken BUF 56, DET 51
Lee, Kevin NEP 86, SFF 17
Lee, Larry DEN 68, DET 64, MIA 63/66
Lee, Lloyd SDC 36
Lee, Marcus CLE 34
Lee, Mark GBP 22, NOS 32, SFF 27
Lee, Mike SDC 58
Lee, Monte ARZ 33, DET 52, IND 67
Lee, Oudious ARZ 74
Lee, Robert NEP 60
Lee, Ron IND 34
Lee, Ron ATL 70, MIA 72, MIA 86, SEA 63
Lee, Shawn CHI 76, MIA 98, SDC 98, TBB 97
Lee, Willie KCC 78
Lee, Zeph OAK 40
Leemans, Tuffy NYG 4
Leetzow, Max DEN 81
Leeuwenberg, Rich CHI 57
Leeuwenburg, Jay CHI 58, CIN 58, IND 58, WSH 57

Lefear, Billy CLE 26
LeFebvre, Gil DET ?, xCIN 30
LeFleur, Joe CHI 2
LeForce, Clyde DET 11/22
Leftridge, Dick PIT 31
Leftwich, Byron JAX 7
Legette, Burnie NEP 35
Legette, Tyrone NOS 43, SFF 45, TBB 45
Leggett, Brad NOS 62
Leggett, Dave ARZ 7
Leggett, Earl CHI 71, NOS 72, STL 72
Leggett, Scott PHL 75
Legree, Lance NYG 70
Lehan, Michael CLE 39
Lehr, Matt DAL 68
Leicht, Jake zBAL 81
Leiding, Jeff IND 92
Leigeb, Brian IND 40
Leigh, Charles CLE 25, MIA 15/23/36, GBP 23
Leiker, Tony GBP 96
Leisk, Rube xBKN 22
Lejeune, Walt GBP 8
Lelei, Ashley DEN 85
Lemaster, Frank PHL 55
Lemek, Ray WSH 70, PIT 72
Lemmerman, Bruce ATL 18
LeMoine, Jim BUF 60, TEN 62
Lemon, Cliff CHI 9
Lemon, Mike DEN 54, NOS 52, TBB 59
Lenc, George xBKN 30
Lenkaitis, Bill NEP 67, SDC 51
Lennan, Reid WSH 51, zLAD 32
Lenon, Paris GBP 53
Lens, Greg ATL 72
Lentz, Jack DEN 28
Leo, Bobby NEP 24
Leo, Charlie NEP 63, BUF 64
Leo, Jim MIN 59, NYG 30
Leo, Rick BUF 63
Leon, Tony WSH 48, xBKN 17, xBOS 34/17
Leonard, Anthony SFF 42
Leonard, Bill zBAL 54
Leonard, Cecil NYJ 28
Leonard, Jim PHL 19
Leonard, Jim SDC 63, SFF 63, TBB 57/62
Leonard, John ARZ 12/19
Leonard, Matt JAX 96
Leonard, Tony DET 26
Leonetti, Bob zBRK 31, zBUF 30
Leopold, Bobby GBP 53, SFF 45/52
Lepsis, Matt DEN 78
Leroy, Emarlos JAX 61/93
Lesane, James CHI 49, IND 31
Leshinski, Ron PHL 89

Lester, Darrell DEN 26, GBP 29, MIN 31
Lester, Fred TBB 30
Lester, Keith IND 88
Lester, Tim DAL 34, PIT 34, STL 34
Lethridge, Zebbie MIA 37
Letlow, Russ GBP 46/62
Letsinger, Jim PIT 31
Lett, Leon DAL 78, DEN 94
Lettner, Bob BUF 59
Levanities, Stephen PHL 72
Levanti, Lou PIT 21/59
LeVeck, Jack ARZ 52, CLE 56
Levels, Dwayne CIN 52
Levenick, Dave ATL 55
Levens, Dorsey GBP 25/48, PHL 25
Levenseller, Mike BUF 87, CIN 88, TBB 84
Leverette, Otis SDC 93, WSH 93
Levey, Jim PIT 12/13
LeVias, Jerry TEN 23, SDC 25
Levingston, Bashir NYG 24
Levitt, Chad OAK 31
Levy, Chuck ARZ 4, SFF 32
Levy, Len zLAD 35
Levy, Leonard STL 76
Lewellen, Verne GBP 4/21/31/45/46
Lewis, Albert KCC 29, OAK 24/29
Lewis, Art NYG 23, STL 11/23
Lewis, Bill ARZ 51, NEP 75, OAK 51
Lewis, Bill xCIN 6
Lewis, Chad PHL 89, STL 49
Lewis, Charles ARZ 76
Lewis, Cliff CLE 62
Lewis, Cliff GBP 56
Lewis, D.D. DAL 50
Lewis, D.D. SEA 54
Lewis, Damione STL 92
Lewis, Dan DET 45, NYG 41, WSH 22
Lewis, Darren CHI 33
Lewis, Darryl CLE 88
Lewis, Darryll TEN 29, SDC 26
Lewis, Dave CIN 15
Lewis, David DET 87, MIA 87/89
Lewis, David TBB 57, STL 51, SDC 53
Lewis, Derrick NOS 89
Lewis, Eddie DET 48, SFF 22
Lewis, Ernie zCHI 73/71/64
Lewis, Frank BUF 82, PIT 43
Lewis, Garry KCC 21, OAK 21, TBB 22
Lewis, Gary GBP 81
Lewis, Gary NOS 22
Lewis, Gary NOS 93, SFF 22
Lewis, Greg DEN 20, DEN 41

Lewis, Greg PHL 83
Lewis, Harold BUF 27, IND 43, OAK 21
Lewis, Herman DEN 48
Lewis, Jamal BLT 31
Lewis, Jeff CAR 8, DEN 8
Lewis, Jermaine BLT 84, JAX 84
Lewis, Jess TEN 37, TEN 55
Lewis, Joe IND 72, PHL 71, PIT 71
Lewis, John BUF 27/35
Lewis, Jonas SFF 43
Lewis, Kenny NYJ 20/22/24
Lewis, Kevin NYG 59
Lewis, Kevin SFF 45
Lewis, Leo CLE 83, MIN 87
Lewis, Mark DET 81, GBP 89
Lewis, Marvin NOS 24
Lewis, Michael NOS 84
Lewis, Michael PHL 32
Lewis, Mike ATL 69, GBP 66
Lewis, Mo NYJ 57
Lewis, Nate CHI 82, SDC 81
Lewis, Ray BLT 52
Lewis, Reggie NOS 98
Lewis, Reggie TBB 79
Lewis, Richard BUF 56, NYJ 53/57, TEN 55
Lewis, Roderick TEN 49
Lewis, Rodney NOS 29
Lewis, Ron WSH 71
Lewis, Ronald SFF 83, GBP 85
Lewis, Scotty CHI 79
Lewis, Sherman NYJ 7
Lewis, Sid NYJ 21
Lewis, Stan CLE 75
Lewis, Tahaun OAK 20, KCC 21
Lewis, Terry SDC 32
Lewis, Thomas NYG 81
Lewis, Tim GBP 26
Lewis, Tiny DET 26
Lewis, Vernon NEP 43
Lewis, Will SEA 41
Lewis, Woodley STL 20/30, ARZ 20, DAL 23
Leyendecker, Charles PHL 35
Leypoldt, John BUF 3, NOS 3, SEA 3
Leyva, Victor CIN 77
Libson, Don SFF 42
Lick, Dennis CHI 70
Lidberg, Carl GBP 17/34/38
Liddick, Dave PIT 78
Liebel, Frank NYG 22/88, ARZ 51
Liebenstein, Todd WSH 79
Lieberum, Don NYG 28
Liggett, Bob KCC 62
Light, Matt NEP 71/72
Liles, Alva DET 63, OAK 60
Liles, Elvin STL 17
Liles, Sonny DET 20/62
Lilja, George CLE 62, DAL

64/67, NYJ 59, STL 59
Lilja, Greg NYJ 61
Lillard, Joe ARZ 19
Lilly, Bob DAL 74
Lilly, Kevin DAL 97, SFF 92
Lilly, Sammy PHL 37, SDC 26, STL 27
Lilly, Tony DEN 22
Lillywhite, Verl SFF 71/81
Limbrick, Garrett MIA 32
Lince, Dave PHL 87
Lincoln, Jeremy CHI 39, DET 25, NYG 39, SEA 39, STL 39
Lincoln, Keith SDC 22, BUF 20
Lind, Mike PIT 38, SFF 38
Lindahl, Joe NYG 34
Lindell, Rian BUF 9, SEA 9
Linden, Errol ATL 73, CLE 70, MIN 73, NOS 70
Lindon, Luke DET 77
Lindow, Al ARZ 33
Lindquist, Paul NEP 67
Lindsay, Everett BLT 61, CLE 61, MIN 61/62
Lindsey, Dale CLE 51, NOS 54
Lindsey, Hub DEN 33
Lindsey, Jim MIN 21
Lindsey, Steve DEN 2, JAX 2
Lindskog, Vic PHL 52
Lindstrom, Chris KCC 60, TBB 71/75
Lindstrom, Dave KCC 71
Line, Bill CHI 67
Lingenfelter, Bob CLE 75, MIN 76
Linger, Adam KCC 51/62
Lingmerth, Goran CLE 3
Lingner, Adam BUF 63
Linhart, Toni IND 2, NOS 7, NYJ 2
Lininger, Jack DET 55/57
Linn, Jack CIN 75, DET 72, IND 67
Linne, Aubrey IND 87
Linne, Larry NEP 80
Linnin, Chris NYG 74
Linton, Jonathan BUF 35
Lintzenich, Joseph CHI 7
Lio, Augie DET 61/73, PHL 62, xBOS 41, zBAL 37
Lipinski, Jim ARZ 64
Lipostad, Ed ARZ 66
Lippett, Ronnie NEP 42
Lipps, Louis PIT 83, NOS 86
Lipscomb, Gene IND 76, PIT 76, STL 78/85
Lipscomb, Paul WSH 76, CHI 74, GBP 47
Lipski, John PHL 20
Lisch, Rusty ARZ 16, CHI 12
Liscio, Tony DAL 64/72
Liske, Pete DEN 14, NYJ 18, PHL 14
Liter, Greg PHL 99, SFF 77

Little, Dave DET 89, KCC 84, PHL 89, ARZ 30
Little, David PIT 48/50
Little, Earl CLE 20, NOS 20/21
Little, Everett TBB 77
Little, Floyd DEN 44
Little, George MIA 99
Little, Jack IND 72
Little, Jim NYG 16
Little, John BUF 72, NYJ 57, TEN 80
Little, Larry MIA 66, SDC 73
Little, Leonard STL 57/91
Little, Steve ARZ 12
Littlefield, Carl PIT 44, STL 34
Littleton, Jody DET 57
Livers, Virgil CHI 24
Livingston, Andy NOS 48, CHI 48
Livingston, Bruce DAL 20
Livingston, Cliff MIN 55, NYG 89, STL 89
Livingston, Dale CIN 11, GBP 37
Livingston, Howie CHI 48, NYG 10/24, SFF 24/94, WSH 24
Livingston, Mike KCC 10, MIN 13
Livingston, Ted STL 13/18
Livingston, Walt NEP 24
Livingston, Warren DAL 41
Livingstone, Bob xBAL 86, zBUF ?, zCHI 82
Liwienski, Chris MIN 76
Lloyd, Dan NYG 54
Lloyd, Dave PHL 52, CLE 52, DET 52
Lloyd, Doug OAK 37
Lloyd, Greg PIT 95, CAR 95
Lloyd, Jeff BUF 75, KCC 74
Lobenstein, Bill DEN 74
Loberg, Greg NOS 61
Lockett, Charles PIT 89
Lockett, Danny DET 50
Lockett, J.W. DAL 35, IND 35, SFF 35, WSH 37
Lockett, Kevin JAX 85, KCC 81, NYJ 89, WSH 83
Lockett, Wade OAK 87
Lockhart, Carl NYG 43
Lockhart, Eugene DAL 56, NEP 51
Locklin, Billy Ray OAK 73
Locklin, Kerry DEN 89, STL 83
Lockwood, Scott NEP 40
Lodish, Mike BUF 73, DEN 97
Loepfe, Dick ARZ 64
Loewen, Chuck SDC 64
Lofton, James BUF 80/86, GBP 80, OAK 80, PHL 80, STL 22
Lofton, Oscar NEP 86
Lofton, Steve ARZ 28/42, CAR 29, NEP 38

Logan, Andy DET 76
Logan, Chuck ARZ 83, PIT 82
Logan, Dave CLE 85, DEN 89
Logan, David GBP 94, TBB 76
Logan, Dick GBP 67
Logan, Ernie ATL 73, CLE 97, JAX 93, NYJ 93
Logan, James CHI 20/37
Logan, James CIN 52, SEA 56, TEN 58
Logan, Jerry IND 20
Logan, Marc CIN 23/29, MIA 20, SFF 43, WSH 20
Logan, Mike JAX 32, PIT 31
Logan, Obert DAL 25, NOS 0
Logan, Randy PHL 41
Logel, Bob zBUF 55
Lohmeyer, John KCC 87
Lohmiller, Chip WSH 8, NOS 2, STL 8
Lokanc, Joe ARZ 27
Lollar, Slick GBP 14
Lolotai, Al WSH 26, zLAD 30
Lomack, Tony ARZ 84, STL 82
Lomakoski, John DET 64
Lomas, Mark NYJ 84
Lomax, Neil ARZ 15
London, Antonio DET 51/55, GBP 57
London, Mike SDC 57
London, Tom CLE 40
Loneker, Keith STL 64
Long, Bill PIT 82
Long, Bob DAL 56, DET 86, STL 84
Long, Bob GBP 80, ATL 80, STL 86, WSH 80
Long, Bob xBOS 11
Long, Buford NYG 22
Long, Carson BUF 5
Long, Charlie NEP 76
Long, Chuck DET 16, STL 16
Long, Darren STL 45
Long, Dave ARZ 89, NOS 89
Long, Doug SEA 88
Long, Harvey CHI 27
Long, Howie OAK 75
Long, Johnny CHI 33
Long, Ken DET 65
Long, Kevin NYJ 33
Long, Kevin TEN 60
Long, Louie DET 4
Long, Matt PHL 61
Long, Mel CLE 52/53
Long, Mike NEP 87
Long, Rien TEN 99
Long, Terry PIT 74
Long, Tim SFF 68
Longenecker, Ken PIT 71/76
Longley, Clint DAL 19, SDC 16
Longmire, Sam KCC 15
Longo, Tom ARZ 46, NYG 44
Longwell, Ryan GBP 8
Look, Dean NYJ 30

Lookabaugh, John WSH 14/15
Looker, Dane NEP 87, STL 89
Loomis, Ace CLE 46, GBP 7/43/48
Looney, Don PHL 30, PIT 30
Looney, Jim SFF 50
Looney, Joe Don DET 32, IND 32, NOS 26, WSH 35
Lopasky, Bill SFF 57
Lopienski, Tom IND 36
Lorch, Karl WSH 71
Lorenti, Chris HOU 62
Lorick, Tony IND 33, NOS 34
Losch, Jack GBP 25
Lothamer, Ed KCC 82
Lothridge, Billy ATL 26, DAL 18, MIA 7, STL 10
Lott, Andre WSH 34
Lott, Anthone CIN 30
Lott, Billy NEP 32, NYG 22, OAK 31
Lott, John PIT 51, xBKN ?
Lott, Ronnie SFF 42, NYJ 42, OAK 42
Lott, Thomas ARZ 26
Lou, Ron PHL 30/51, TEN 51/53/58
Louallen, Fletcher MIN 38
Louchiey, Corey BUF 72
Loud, Kamil BUF 89
Loudd, Rommie NEP 60, SDC 51
Louderback, Tom BUF 54, OAK 60, PHL 61
Loukas, Angelo BUF 60, NEP 66
Love, Clarence BLT 35, OAK 38, PHL 28
Love, Duval PIT 67, ARZ 67, STL 67
Love, John STL 49, WSH 27
Love, Randy ARZ 40
Love, Sean CAR 79, PHL 64, TBB 79
Love, Terry MIN 23
Love, Walt NYG 46
Loveall, Calvin ATL 27, KCC 38, TEN 12
Lovelady, Edwin NYG 88
Lovelady, Josh DET 70
Loverne, David NYJ 79, STL 61, WSH 64
LoVetere, John NYG 76, STL 76
Loville, Derek SEA 20/33, DEN 31, SFF 20
Loving, Warren BUF 30
LoVuolo, Frank NYG 89
Lowdermilk, Kirk IND 63, MIN 63
Lowe, Gary DET 43, WSH 40
Lowe, Lloyd CHI 28
Lowe, Omar MIA 24, NYJ 26
Lowe, Paul SDC 23, KCC 26

Lowe, Reggie JAX 57, PIT 90
Lowe, Woodrow SDC 51
Lowery, Michael CHI 53
Lowery, Nick KCC 8, NEP 7, NYJ 8
Lowry, Orlando IND 58/59, NEP 91
Lowry, Quentin TBB 64, WSH 56
Lowther, Jackie DET 42
Lowther, Russ PIT 33
Loyd, Alex SFF 59
Loyd, Brandon SFF 85
Loyd, Jeremy STL 56
Loyd, Mike ARZ 14
Lubischer, Steve MIA 54
Lubratovich, Lou xBKN 21/11/10/16/7/36
Lucas, Al CAR 71
Lucas, Dick PHL 87
Lucas, Jeff PIT 68
Lucas, Justin ARZ 41
Lucas, Ken SEA 21
Lucas, Ray MIA 6, NEP 15, NYJ 6/18, NYJ 18
Lucas, Richie BUF 11
Lucas, Tim DEN 58/59
Lucci, Mike DET 53, CLE 52
Luce, Derrel IND 58, MIN 57, DET 58
Luce, Lew WSH 81
Luchey [Williams], Nick CIN 30, GBP 22
Lucier, Wayne NYG 62
Luck, Oliver TEN 10
Luck, Terry CLE 7
Luckhurst, Mike ATL 18
Luckman, Sid CHI 42
Lucky, Bill GBP 71
Lucky, Mike DAL 84/86
Lueck, Bill GBP 62, PHL 62
Luft, Don PHL 89
Luhn, Nolan GBP 38
Lujack, Johnny CHI 32
Luke, Steve GBP 46
Luke, Tommy DEN 21
Luken, Tom PHL 63
Lukens, Jim zBUF 59
Lummus, Jack NYG 29
Lumpkin, Father DET 2/4/24/57, xBKN 27/0
Lumpkin, Joey BUF 59/60, BUF 60
Lumpkin, Ron NYG 47, TEN 32
Lumpkin, Sean NOS 46
Luna, Bob PIT 24, SFF 49
Lunceford, Dave ARZ 73
Lund, Bill CLE 82
Lunday, Kayo NYG 5/65
Lundy, Dennis CHI 43, TEN 40
Lundy, Lamar STL 85
Lunsford, Mel NEP 72
Lunz, Gerry ARZ 91

Lurtsema, Bob MIN 75, NYG 71, SEA 70
Lusby, Vaughn CHI 29, CIN 29
Luscinski, Lim NYJ 71
Lush, Mike ATL 34, IND 28, MIN 27
Lusk, Bo DET 57
Lusk, Hendrick MIA 83, NOS 88
Lusk, Herb PHL 32
Lusteg, Booth BUF 5/49, GBP 32, MIA 5, NYJ 5, PIT 35
Luther, Ed IND 11, SDC 11
Lutz, David DET 73, KCC 72
Luzar, Chris JAX 89
Lyday, Allen TEN 28
Lyght, Todd STL 41, DET 24
Lyle, Gary CHI 44
Lyle, Keith SDC 35, STL 35
Lyle, Rick BLT 95, CLE 95, NEP 96, NYJ 95
Lyles, Lenny IND 26/43, SFF 26
Lyles, Lester ARZ 26, NYJ 26, SDC 24
Lyles, Robert ATL 54, TEN 93
Lyman, Del GBP 15, STL 1/45
Lyman, Dustin CHI 89
Lyman, Jeff ARZ 59, BUF ?
Lyman, Link CHI 11/12/77
Lynch, Ben SFF 60
Lynch, Dick NYG 22, WSH 25
Lynch, Eric DET 26
Lynch, Fran DEN 22
Lynch, James MIN 35
Lynch, Jim KCC 51
Lynch, John TBB 47
Lynch, Lorenzo ARZ 29, CHI 43, OAK 43
Lynch, Lynn ARZ 75
Lynch, Tom BUF 61, SEA 61
Lynn, Anthony DEN 37, SFF 29
Lynn, Johnny NYJ 29
Lyon, Babe DET 63, NYG 30, xBKN 28/12, xSTL 77
Lyon, Billy GBP 98, MIN 96
Lyon, George CHI 17
Lyons, Dicky NOS 43
Lyons, John xBKN 3
Lyons, Lamar BLT 29, OAK 44
Lyons, Marty NYJ 93
Lyons, Mitch ATL 86, PIT 85
Lyons, Pratt TEN 98
Lyons, Robert CLE 49
Lyons, Tom DEN 61
Lytle, Matt CAR 9, SEA 8
Lytle, Rob DEN 41
Maack, Herb zBRK 32
Maarleveld, J.D. TBB 77
Maas, Bill KCC 63, GBP 77
Mabra, Ron ATL 29, NYJ 27
MacAfee, Ken SFF 81

MacAfee, Ken NYG 80, PHL 80, WSH 82
MacArthur, Kevin NYJ 57
Macauley, John SFF 67
MacDonald, Dan DEN 52
MacDonald, Mark MIN 71
MacDonnell, Mickey ARZ 29
MacDowell, Jay PHL 85/88
Maceau, Mel CLE 24
Macek, Don SDC 62
Macerelli, John CLE 69
Machado, J.P. NYJ 63/77
Machurek, Mike DET 14
Macioszczyk, Art PHL 31, WSH 18
Mack, Cedric ARZ 47, KCC 40, NOS 47, SDC 47
Mack, Kevin CLE 34
Mack, Kim SEA 40
Mack, Milton DET 24, NOS 24, TBB 21
Mack, Red ATL 27, GBP 27, PHL 25, PIT 23/27
Mack, Rico PIT 56
Mack, Stacey HOU 34, JAX 34
Mack, Terrence ARZ 58
Mack, Tom STL 65
Mack, Tremain CIN 34
Mackbee, Earsell MIN 46
Mackenroth, Jack DET 29
Mackey, Dee IND 85, NYJ 89, SFF 87
Mackey, John IND 88, SDC 89
Mackey, Kyle ARZ 12, MIA 15, NYJ 15, PHL 11
Mackey, Louis DAL 57
Mackie, Doug ATL 73
MacKinnon, Jacque SDC 38, OAK 37
Macklin, David IND 27
Mackorell, Johnny NYG 25
Mackovicka, Joel ARZ 34
Mackrides, Bill NYG 20, PHL 39, PIT 13
MacLeod, Robert CHI 5
MacLeod, Tom GBP 56, IND 52
MacMurdo, Jim WSH 34, PHL 6/20
Macon, Ed CHI 25, OAK 28
MacWherter, Kyle CHI 14
Maczuzak, John KCC 72
Madarik, Elmer DET 29/30/40, WSH 23, zBAL 53
Madden, Lloyd ARZ 14
Maddock, Bob ARZ 49/68
Maddox, Bob CIN 77, KCC 75
Maddox, George GBP 28
Maddox, Mark ARZ 53, BUF 55
Maddox, Tommy DEN 8, NYG 12, PIT 8, STL 8
Maderas, George SFF 40
Madise, Adrian DEN 82
Madison, Sam MIA 29

Madsen, Lynn TEN 98
Maeda, Chet ARZ 50
Maese, Joe BLT 59
Magac, Mike PIT 68, SFF 62
Magee, Calvin TBB 86
Magee, Jim xBOS 20/30
Magee, John PHL 67
Maggioli, Chick DET 19, xBAL 80, zBUF 81
Maggs, Don DEN 78, TEN 78
Magliolo, Joe zNYY 62
Magnani, Dante STL 8/24, CHI 3/4/8, DET 16
Maguire, Paul SDC 84
Magulick, George ARZ 53, PIT 53
Mahalic, Drew PHL 54, SDC 53
Mahan, Bob xBKN 2
Mahan, Sean TBB 78
Mahe, Reno PHL 34
Maher, Bruce DET 21, NYG 21
Maher, Francis PIT 76, STL 9
Mahlum, Eric IND 65
Mahoney, Ike ARZ 4
Maidlow, Scott CIN 47
Maidlow, Steve BUF 59/90
Maillard, Ralph CHI 23
Mains, Gil DET 72/84
Maitland, Jack IND 23/40, NEP 40
Majkowski, Don GBP 5/7, DET 1, IND 7
Majors, Bill BUF 25
Majors, Bobby CLE 24
Majors, Joe TEN 22
Malancon, Rydell ATL 52, GBP 54/60
Malano, Mike ATL 67
Malbrough, Anthony CLE 26
Maley, Howie xBOS 16
Malinchak, Bill DET 81, WSH 24
Malinowski, Gene xBOS 39
Malkovich, Joe PIT 33
Mallard, Josh IND 68
Mallard, Wesly NYG 51
Mallick, Fran PIT 61
Mallory, Irvin NEP 43
Mallory, John ATL 22, PHL 47
Mallory, Larry NYG 34
Mallory, Rick TBB 68
Mallouf, Ray ARZ 22/78/98, NYG 22
Malloy, Les ARZ 21
Malone, Art ATL 25, PHL 26
Malone, Benny MIA 32, WSH 25
Malone, Charley WSH 19
Malone, Darrell KCC 42, MIA 47
Malone, Mark NYJ 16, PIT 16, SDC 16
Malone, Ralph CLE 90
Malone, Van DET 39

Maloney, Norm SFF 59
Mamula, Mike PHL 59
Manca, Massimo CIN 9
Mancha, Vaughn xBOS 41
Mandarich, Tony GBP 77, IND 79
Mandarino, Mike PHL 62
Manders, Dave DAL 51
Manders, Jack CHI 10
Manders, Pug xBKN 9, xBOS 25, zBUF 74, zNYY 76
Mandeville, Chris GBP 44, WSH 41
Mandich, Jim MIA 88, PIT 87
Mandley, Pete DET 82, KCC 89
Maness, James CHI 81
Manges, Mark ARZ 18
Mangiero, Dino KCC 74, NEP 96, SEA 73
Mangum, John CHI 26
Mangum, John NEP 74
Mangum, Kris CAR 86
Mangum, Pete DEN 33, NYG 51
Maniaci, Joe CHI 11, xBKN 34/2
Maniecki, Jason TBB 90
Mankins, Jim ATL 33
Manley, Dexter WSH 72, ARZ 92, TBB 92
Manley, James MIN 75
Manley, Joe SFF 54
Manley, Leon GBP 90
Mann, Bob DET 87, GBP 31/87
Mann, Charles WSH 71, SFF 71
Mann, Dave ARZ 44
Mann, Errol DET 12, OAK 14, GBP 39
Mannelly, Pat CHI 65
Manning, Aaron CIN 44
Manning, Archie NOS 8, MIN 4, TEN 8
Manning, Brian GBP 82, MIA 83
Manning, Pete CHI 86
Manning, Peyton IND 18
Manning, Ricky CAR 24
Manning, Roosevelt PHL 65, ATL 77
Manning, Wade DAL 22, DEN 83
Manoa, Tim CLE 42, IND 44
Manor, Brison DEN 66/69, TBB 75
Manos, Sam CIN 58/60
Manoukian, Don OAK 67
Mansfield, Ray PHL 77, PIT 56/73
Mansfield, Von GBP 44, PHL 45
Manske, Ed PHL 11/36, CHI 7/18, PIT 53

Manton, Tilly WSH 14, NYG 16, PHL 33, xBKN 19
Manucci, Dan BUF 11
Manuel, Lionel NYG 86
Manuel, Marquand CIN 44
Manuel, Rod PIT 97
Manuel, Sean KCC 95, SFF 86
Manumaleuga, Frank KCC 54
Manumaleuna, Brandon STL 86
Manusky, Greg KCC 51, MIN 91, WSH 91
Manuwai, Vince JAX 67
Manzini, Bap DET 55, PHL 50/66
Manzo, Joe DET 46
Maple, Howard ARZ 35
Maples, Bobby TEN 50, PIT 51, DEN 50
Maples, Butch IND 53
Maples, Ted xCIN 25
Marangi, Gary BUF 17
Maras, Joseph PIT 14
Marchetti, Gino IND 75/89, xDAL 75/84
Marchi, Basilio PHL 55, PIT 36
Marchibroda, Ted ARZ 7, PIT 17/18
Marchiol, Ken NOS 91
Marchlewski, Frank ATL 53, BUF 57, STL 56
Marciniak, Ron WSH 64
Marcol, Chester GBP 13, TEN 5
Marcolini, Hugo zBRK 71
Marconi, Joe CHI 34, STL 34
Marcontell, Ed ARZ 65, TEN 62
Marcus, Pete WSH 18
Mare, Olindo MIA 10
Marefos, Andy NYG 70, zLAD 79
Marek, Jodie xBKN 43
Marelli, Ray ARZ 14
Margarita, Bob CHI 44
Margerum, Ken CHI 82/89, SFF 84
Margucci, Joe DET 15/81
Marinaro, Ed MIN 49, NYJ 49, SEA 49
Marino, Dan MIA 13
Marino, Vic zBAL 34
Marinovich, Marv OAK 68
Marinovich, Todd OAK 12
Marion, Brock MIA 31, DAL 31
Marion, Frank NYG 51
Marion, Fred NEP 31
Marion, Jerry PIT 85
Mark, Greg MIA 94, PHL 91
Mark, Lou xBKN 12, xBOS 30
Marker, Cliff NYG 15
Marker, Henry PIT 32
Markham, Dale ARZ 62, NYG 79

Markland, Jeff PIT 84
Marko, Steve xBKN 27
Markov, Victor STL 12
Markovich, Mark DET 68, SDC 56/65
Marks, Larry GBP 44
Marler, Seth JAX 6
Marone, Sal NYG 34
Maronic, Duke NYG 67, PHL 61
Maronic, Steve DET 44/64
Marotti, Lou ARZ 46/64/77, PIT 64
Marquardt, John ARZ 14
Marquess, Robert NYJ 55
Marrone, Doug MIA 78, NOS 75
Marrow, Mitch CAR 68
Marrow, Vince BUF 87
Marsalis, Jim KCC 40, NOS 40
Marsh, Aaron NEP 29
Marsh, Amos DAL 31, DET 31
Marsh, Curt OAK 60
Marsh, Curtis JAX 89, PIT 17
Marsh, Dick NYG 33
Marsh, Doug ARZ 80/82/87
Marsh, Frank SDC 36
Marshall, Al NEP 88
Marshall, Anthony CHI 36, PHL 35
Marshall, Arthur DEN 86, NYG 83
Marshall, Charles DEN 43
Marshall, David CLE 59, MIA 96
Marshall, Ed CIN 83, NYG 89
Marshall, Greg IND 66
Marshall, Henry KCC 89
Marshall, James NOS 23
Marshall, Jim MIN 70, CLE 80
Marshall, Larry KCC 22, MIN 48, PHL 22, STL 44
Marshall, Lemar WSH 52
Marshall, Leonard NYG 70, NYJ 70, WSH 70
Marshall, Marvin TBB 1/89
Marshall, Randy ATL 89
Marshall, Rich ATL 70, GBP 70, TEN 77, WSH 75
Marshall, Tank NYJ 68
Marshall, Torrance GBP 41/51
Marshall, Warren DEN 29
Marshall, Whit ATL 55, PHL 58
Marshall, Wilber CHI 58, NYJ 58, TEN 58, WSH 58, ARZ 55
Martha, Paul DEN 47, PIT 20
Martin, Aaron PHL 42, STL 42, WSH 40
Martin, Amos MIN 55, SEA 50
Martin, Bill CHI 22/85, ATL 85, MIN 89
Martin, Billy CHI 22

Martin, Blanche NYJ 36, SDC 33
Martin, Bob NYJ 59, SFF 54
Martin, Caleb ARZ 82
Martin, Cecil PHL 38, TBB 37
Martin, Charles ATL 94, GBP 94, TEN 94
Martin, Chris CHI 25
Martin, Chris KCC 57, MIN 56/57/94, NOS 59, STL 53
Martin, Curtis NYJ 28, NEP 28
Martin, D'Artagnan NOS 22
Martin, Dave CHI 53, KCC 58
Martin, David BUF 9/25, SDC 33
Martin, David GBP 83/87
Martin, Derrick SFF 31
Martin, Don TBB 21
Martin, Donald NEP 38, KCC 47
Martin, Doug MIN 79
Martin, Emanuel TEN 20
Martin, Emerson CAR 78
Martin, Eric NOS 84, KCC 85
Martin, Frank NYG 18, xBKN 12 10, xBOS ?
Martin, George NYG 75
Martin, Glen ARZ 27
Martin, Harvey DAL 79
Martin, Jamar DAL 34
Martin, Jamie JAX 10, STL 10/12
Martin, Jim DET 47/61/62, CLE 50, IND 47, WSH 38
Martin, John ARZ 29, PIT 29, xBOS 33
Martin, John STL 23
Martin, Kelvin DAL 83, PHL 84, SEA 84
Martin, Larry SDC 73
Martin, Manny BUF 21
Martin, Matt TEN 68
Martin, Mike CIN 88
Martin, Robbie DET 48/83, IND 31/88
Martin, Rod OAK 53
Martin, Saladin NYJ 39, SFF 29
Martin, Sammy IND 86, NEP 82
Martin, Steve HOU 99, IND 90, KCC 90, NEP 90, NYJ 91, PHL 73/91, WSH 98
Martin, Tee OAK 17, PIT 17
Martin, Terrance HOU 90
Martin, Tony SDC 81, ATL 80, MIA 80/89
Martin, Tracy NYJ 86
Martin, Vernon PIT 15
Martin, Wayne NOS 93
Martinelli, Patsy zBUF 24
Martini, Rich NOS 86, OAK 89
Martinkovic, John GBP 39/47/83, NYG 83

Martinovich, Phil CHI 19/66, DET 34, zBRK 45
Marts, Lonnie JAX 56/58, KCC 51, TBB 51/55, TEN 51/56
Marvaso, Tommy NYJ 47
Marve, Eugene BUF 54, SDC 99, TBB 99
Marvin, Mickey OAK 65
Marx, Greg ATL 78
Maryland, Russell DAL 67, GBP 67, OAK 67/97
Masini, Len zLAD 68
Masini, Leonard SFF 74
Maskas, John zBUF 34/49
Maslowski, Matt CHI 46/82, STL 48
Maslowski, Mike KCC 57
Mason, Dave GBP 43, NEP 28
Mason, Derrick TEN 13/85
Mason, Eddie JAX 53, WSH 53
Mason, Joel ARZ 17, GBP 7
Mason, Larry CLE 38, GBP 34
Mason, Lindsey SFF 78, IND 79, OAK 71
Mason, Michael JAX 75
Mason, Tommy MIN 20, STL 20, WSH 20
Mass, Wayne CHI 74, MIA 78, NEP 75, PHL 78
Massey, Carlton CLE 82, GBP 81
Massey, Chris STL 45
Massey, Jim NEP 47
Massey, Robert ARZ 40, DET 40, JAX 40, NOS 40, NYG 44
Massie, Rick DEN 83/85
Masters, Billy BUF 87, DEN 81, KCC 84
Masters, Bob CHI 37, PHL 30/31/33, PIT 31
Masters, Norm GBP 78
Masters, Walt ARZ 35/40, PHL 53, PIT 40
Masterson, Bernie CHI 33
Masterson, Bob WSH 28, xBKN 28, xBOS 28, zNYY 55
Masterson, Forest CHI 15
Mastogany, Gus CHI 29
Maston, Le'Shai JAX 35, TEN 47, WSH 36
Mastrangelo, John NYG 66, PIT 65, zNYY 32
Matalele, Stan GBP 94
Matan, Bill NYG 70
Matau, Chris STL 51
Matesic, Ed PHL 12, PIT 47
Matesic, Joe PIT ?
Matheson, Bob CLE 56, MIA 53
Matheson, Jack CHI 41, DET 82
Matheson, Riley DET 83, SFF 37, STL 11/13

Mathews, Jason IND 67/74, TEN 76
Mathews, Ned DET 12/42, SFF 73/83, xBOS 37, zCHI 97
Mathews, Ray PIT 25/44/77, DAL 25
Mathias, Ric CIN 24, IND 42
Mathis, Bill NYJ 31
Mathis, Dedric IND 23
Mathis, Kevin ATL 23, DAL 23, NOS 23
Mathis, Mark ARZ 38
Mathis, Rasheen JAX 27
Mathis, Reggie NOS 56
Mathis, Robert IND 98
Mathis, Terance ATL 81, NYJ 81, PIT 88
Mathison, Bruce BUF 7, SDC 12, SEA 13
Mathys, Charles GBP 2
Matich, Trevor DET 61, IND 64, NEP 64, NYJ 64, WSH 64
Matisi, John xBKN 15, zBUF 41
Matisi, Tony DET 27
Matlock, John ATL 53, BUF 53, CIN 52/57, NYJ 57
Matson, Ollie ARZ 33, DET 30, PHL 33, STL 33
Matson, Pat CIN 73, DEN 73, GBP 62
Matsos, Archie BUF 56, DEN 55, OAK 56, SDC 67
Matte, Tom IND 27/41
Mattes, Ron CHI 75, IND 75, SEA 70
Matthews, Al ATL 49, GBP 29, SEA 29, SFF 47
Matthews, Aubrey ATL 83, DET 83, GBP 88
Matthews, Bill NEP 53
Matthews, Bo MIA 33, NYG 41, SDC 41
Matthews, Bruce TEN 74
Matthews, Clay CLE 57, ATL 57
Matthews, Clay SFF 46/83
Matthews, Henry ATL 33, NEP 35, NOS 35
Matthews, Ira OAK 43
Matthews, Shane CAR 9, CHI 9, WSH 6
Matthews, Steve KCC 15, JAX 16, TEN 11
Matthews, Wes MIA 23
Mattiace, Frank IND 97
Mattiford, Jack DET 62
Mattingly, Frank zCHI 36
Mattioli, Fran PIT 92
Mattos, Grant SDC 86
Mattos, Harry GBP 23, STL 7
Mattox, Jack DEN 76/77
Mattson, Riley CHI 75, WSH 73

Matuszak, John KCC 79, OAK 72, TEN 78

Matuszak, Marv SFF 54, BUF 55, DEN 55, GBP 63, IND 64, PIT 56/61/64/66

Matuza, Al CHI 15

Mauck, Carl IND 65, MIA 60, SDC 55, TEN 55/58

Mauer, Andy ATL 64

Mauldin, Stan ARZ 77

Maumalanga, Chris ARZ 97, CHI 72, NYG 99, STL 98

Maumau, Viliami CAR 79

Maurer, Andy DEN 74, MIN 66, NOS 64, SFF 61

Mauti, Rich NOS 84, WSH 83/84

Maves, Earl DET 12

Mavraides, Menil PHL 64/65

Mawae, Kevin NYJ 68, SEA 52

Maxey, Curtis CIN 96

Maxie, Brett ATL 41, CAR 39, NOS 39, SFF 25

Maxson, Alvin NOS 28, NYG 36, PIT 28, TBB 28

Maxwell, Bruce DET 46

Maxwell, Tom IND 42, OAK 42, TEN 42

Maxwell, Vernon DET 57/98, IND 56, SEA 50

May, Art NEP 71

May, Bill ARZ 19

May, Chad MIN 5

May, Dean DEN 14, PHL 5

May, Deems SDC 88, SEA 88

May, Jack STL 24

May, Marc MIN 88

May, Mark WSH 73, ARZ 73, SDC 73

May, Ray DEN 56, IND 56, PIT 59

May, Sherriden NYJ 32

May, Walter CHI 19

Mayberry, Doug MIN 35, OAK 33

Mayberry, James ATL 39

Mayberry, Jermane PHL 71

Mayberry, Tony TBB 61

Mayer, Emil DET 73

Mayer, Frank GBP 19

Mayer, Shawn NEP 39

Mayes, Alonzo CHI 85

Mayes, Ben TEN 77

Mayes, Cart STL 49

Mayes, Derrick GBP 80, SEA 87

Mayes, Michael NOS 22, MIN 23, NYJ 23

Mayes, Rueben NOS 36, SEA 36

Mayes, Rufus CHI 71, CIN 71, PHL 77

Mayes, Tony ARZ 27

Mayfield, Corey JAX 98, TBB 78

Mayhew, Hayden PIT 40

Mayhew, Martin TBB 35, WSH 35

Maynard, Brad CHI 4, NYG 9

Maynard, Don NYJ 13, ARZ 13, NYG 13

Mayne, Lewis CLE 85, zBAL 88, zBRK 60

Mayo, Ron IND 83, TEN 80

Mayock, Mike NYG 39

Mays, Alvoid PIT 28, WSH 20

Mays, Damon TEN 86

Mays, Dave CLE 10, BUF 10

Mays, Jerry KCC 75

Mays, Jerry SDC 47

Mays, Kivuusama GBP 56, MIN 53

Mays, Lee PIT 89

Mays, Stafford ARZ 76, MIN 73

Maznicki, Frank CHI 4/5, xBOS 17

Mazurek, Fred WSH 20

Mazza, Vince DET 29/40, zBUF 58

Mazzanti, Gino xBAL 83

Mazzanti, Jerry DET 83, PHL 62, PIT 61

Mazzetti, Tim ATL 4

McAdams, Bob NYJ 88

McAdams, Carl NYJ 50

McAdams, Dean xBKN 60/6

McAddley, Jason ARZ 80/83

McAdoo, Derrick ARZ 33, TBB 33

McAfee, Fred NOS 25, ARZ 25, PIT 25/35, TBB 35

McAfee, George CHI 5

McAfee, Wesley PHL 40

McAleney, Ed TBB 69

McAlister, Chris BLT 21

McAlister, James NEP 37, PHL 43

McAlister, Ken KCC 94, SEA 48, SFF 48

McAllister, Deuce NOS 26

McArthur, Jack xBKN 5

McAuliffe, Jack GBP 19

McBath, Mike BUF 76

McBride, Adrian ARZ 86

McBride, Charles ARZ ?

McBride, Jack NYG 1/16/20, xBKN 26/3

McBride, Norm MIA 53

McBride, Oscar ARZ 48/87

McBride, Ron GBP 24

McBride, Tod ATL 32, GBP 27

McBurrows, Gerald ATL 22, STL 23

McCabe, Dick WSH 25

McCabe, Jerry KCC 92, NEP 52

McCabe, Richie BUF 45, PIT 22/24

McCadam, Kevin ATL 47

McCade, Mike CLE 40

McCafferty, Don NYG 87

McCaffray, Art PIT 48

McCaffrey, Bob GBP 58

McCaffrey, Ed DEN 87, NYG 81, SFF 81

McCaffrey, Mike BUF 64

McCain, Bob zBRK 51

McCall, Bob NEP 24

McCall, Don NOS 36, PIT 36

McCall, Ed CIN 82

McCall, Joe OAK 43

McCall, Reese DET 81, IND 86

McCall, Ron SDC 89

McCallister, Fred TBB 53

McCallum, Napoleon OAK 34

McCambridge, John DET 86

McCanless, Jim TEN 60

McCann, Jim KCC 5, NYG 15, SFF 15

McCann, Tim NYG 74

McCants, Darnarien WSH 85

McCants, Keith ARZ 90, TBB 52, TEN 78

McCardell, Keenan JAX 87, CLE 87, TBB 87

McCareins, Justin TEN 86

McCarren, Larry GBP 54

McCarthy, Brendan ATL 41, DEN 40

McCarthy, Jim zBRK 56/51, zCHI 52

McCarthy, John ARZ 24, PIT 24

McCarthy, Mickey KCC 81

McCarthy, Shawn NEP 11

McCartney, Pete NYJ 71

McCartney, Ron ATL 56

McCaslin, Eugene GBP 56

McCauley, Don IND 23

McCauley, Tom ATL 20

McChesney, Bob NYG 88, PHL 86, WSH 32

McClain, Cliff NYJ 42

McClain, Clint NYG 17

McClain, Dewey ATL 52

McClain, Jimmy HOU 51

McClairen, Jack PIT 87

McClanahan, Brent MIN 33

McClanahan, Randy BUF 54/58, OAK 57

McClard, Bill NOS 19, SDC 10

McCleary, Norris KCC 71/75

McClellan, Mike PHL 23

McClellion, Central WSH 27

McClendon, Skip CIN 72, IND 95, MIN 96, SDC 98

McClendon, Willie CHI 37

McCleon, Dexter KCC 22, STL 21/24

McCleskey, J.J. ARZ 44, NOS 44/86

McClinton, Curtis KCC 32

McCloskey, Mike IND 49, PHL 84, TEN 89
McCloud, Tyrus BLT 54
McCloughan, Dave GBP 23, IND 42, SEA 44
McCloughan, Kent OAK 47
McClung, Bill PIT 76, CLE 78, DET 70
McClure, Bob xBOS 43
McClure, Brian BUF 13
McClure, Todd ATL 62
McClure, Wayne CIN 65/66
McCluskey, David CIN 40
McColl, Bill CHI 83
McColl, Milt OAK 56, SFF 53
McCollum, Andy NOS 67, STL 67
McCollum, Bubba TEN 71
McCollum, Harley zCHI 46, zNYY 46
McComb, Don NEP 85
McCombs, Tony ARZ 50
McConkey, Phil ARZ 82, GBP 88, NYG 80, SDC 21
McConnell, Brian BUF 82, TEN 59
McConnell, Dewey PIT 26
McCord, Darris DET 78
McCord, Quentin ATL 88
McCormack, Hurvin CLE 99, DAL 99
McCormack, Mike CLE 74, xNYB 71
McCormick, Dave NOS 71, NOS 75, SFF 73
McCormick, John DEN 10/11, MIN 15
McCormick, Len zBAL 28
McCormick, Tom SFF 43, STL 23
McCormick, Walt SFF 38
McCorvey, Kez DET 10/83
McCown, Josh ARZ 12
McCoy, Joel DET 85
McCoy, Larry NOS 51, OAK 90
McCoy, Lloyd SDC 68
McCoy, Mike DET 63, GBP 76, NYG 79, OAK 76
McCoy, Mike C. GBP 29
McCoy, Tony ARZ 61, IND 61/94
McCrary, Fred NEP 44, NOS 44, PHL 41, SDC 44
McCrary, Greg ATL 88, SDC 88, WSH 84/85
McCrary, Hurdis GBP 19/28/29/38/43/53
McCrary, Mike BLT 99, SEA 75/92/99
McCray, Bruce CHI 31
McCray, Prentice DET 34, NEP 34
McCray, Willie SFF 76
McCreary, Bob DAL 70

McCreary, Loaird MIA 80, NYG 89
McCree, Marlon HOU 29, JAX 32
McCrumbly, John BUF 57
McCullers, Dave MIA 54
McCullough, Andy ARZ 18
McCullough, Earl DET 25, NOS 80
McCullough, George TEN 28, SFF 24
McCullough, Hal xBKN 7
McCullough, Hugh ARZ 33, PHL 25, PIT 25, xBOS 19
McCullough, Jake DEN 96
McCullough, Robert DEN 67
McCullough, Sultan WSH 22
McCullum, Sam MIN 80/84, SEA 84
McCurry, Dave NEP 40
McCurry, Mike MIN 74
McCusker, Jim ARZ 70, CLE 75, NYJ 70, PHL 75
McCutcheon, Daylon CLE 33
McCutcheon, Lawrence STL 30, BUF 30, DEN 33, SEA 30
McDade, Karl PIT 22
McDaniel, Ed MIN 58
McDaniel, Emmanuel ARZ 26, CAR 25/26, IND 39, NYG 26
McDaniel, Jeremy BUF 86
McDaniel, John CIN 86, WSH 80/86
McDaniel, LeCharls WSH 46, NYG 33
McDaniel, Orlando DEN 82
McDaniel, Randall MIN 64, TBB 64
McDaniel, Terry OAK 36, SEA 36
McDaniel, Wahoo DEN 54, MIA 54, NYJ 54, TEN 62
McDaniels, David DAL 80
McDaniels, Pellom ATL 77, KCC 77
McDermott, Gary ATL 45, BUF 32
McDermott, Lloyd ARZ 64, DET 74
McDermott, Sean HOU 80, NEP 49, TBB 84
McDole, Mardye MIN 88
McDole, Ron BUF 72, ARZ 66, TEN 84, WSH 79
McDonald, Darnell TBB 84
McDonald, Devon ARZ 55, IND 57
McDonald, Don PHL 81, xBKN 34, zNYY 58
McDonald, Don BUF 42
McDonald, Dustin GBP 42
McDonald, Dwight SDC 89
McDonald, Ed PIT 27
McDonald, James DET 83, STL 83

McDonald, Jim DET 20
McDonald, Keith DET 89
McDonald, Keith TEN 31
McDonald, Les CHI 76, DET ?, PHL 26/76
McDonald, Mark ARZ 76
McDonald, Mike ARZ 52
McDonald, Mike DET 97, STL 63
McDonald, Paul CLE 16, DAL 14
McDonald, Quintus IND 96
McDonald, Ramos MIN 34, NYG 25, SFF 35
McDonald, Ray WSH 32
McDonald, Ric CHI 54, CIN 56
McDonald, Shaun STL 84
McDonald, Tim ARZ 46, SFF 46
McDonald, Tommy PHL 25, ATL 8, CLE 29, DAL 25, STL 29
McDonald, Walt xBKN 18, zBRK 61, zCHI 61, zMIA 66
McDonough, Bob DET 21
McDonough, Coley ARZ 56, PIT 25
McDonough, Paul PIT 21, STL 19
McDonough, Robert PHL 64
McDougal, Bob GBP 19
McDougal, Kevin IND 43
McDougald, Doug NEP 70
McDougall, Gerry SDC 20
McDougle, Jerome PHL 95
McDougle, Stockar DET 73
McDowell, Anthony TBB 33/37
McDowell, Bubba CAR 25, TEN 25
McDowell, John ARZ 76, GBP 73, NYG 70
McDuffie, George DET 97
McDuffie, O.J. MIA 81
McElhenny, Hugh SFF 39, DET 39, MIN 39, NYG 39
McElmurry, Blaine JAX 38, GBP 38
McElroy, Leeland ARZ 30
McElroy, Ray CHI 47, DET 47, IND 40
McElroy, Reggie DEN 68, KCC 70, MIN 60, NYJ 68, OAK 77
McElroy, Vann OAK 26, SEA 31
McElwain, Bill ARZ ?, CHI 29
McEndoo, Jason SEA 52
McEnulty, Doug CHI 29
McEwen, Craig SDC 31, WSH 26/32
McFadden, Banks xBKN 26
McFadden, Marv PIT 61
McFadden, Paul ATL 6, NYG 6, PHL 8
McFadden, Thad BUF 89

McFadin, Bud DEN 64, STL 62, TEN 64
McFarland, Anthony TBB 92
McFarland, Jim ARZ 80/83, BUF 80, MIA 80
McFarland, Kay SFF 26
McFarlane, Nyle OAK 26
McGarity, Wane DAL 83, NOS 89
McGarrahan, Scott GBP 43, MIA 41, TEN 42
McGarry, Barney STL 30
McGarry, John GBP 61
McGaw, Walter GBP 11
McGeary, Clarence GBP 44
McGee, Ben PIT 60
McGee, Bob ARZ 4
McGee, Buford GBP 31, SDC 21, STL 24
McGee, Carl SDC 58
McGee, Dell ARZ 23/24
McGee, Ed NYG 44, xBOS 40
McGee, George NEP 75
McGee, Max GBP 85
McGee, Michael ARZ 68
McGee, Molly ATL 31
McGee, Terrence BUF 24
McGee, Tim CIN 85, WSH 85
McGee, Tony CHI 71, NEP 78, WSH 78
McGee, Tony CIN 82, DAL 80/82, NYG 44
McGee, Willie DET 86, SDC 28, SFF 81, STL 24
McGeever, John DEN 47, MIA 47
McGeoghan, Phil DEN 85
McGeorge, Rich GBP 81
McGhee, Kanavis CIN 96, NYG 96, TEN 95
McGibbony, Dub xBKN 11
McGill, Eddie ARZ 87
McGill, Karmeeleyah CIN 59
McGill, Lenny ATL 22/28, CAR 22, GBP 22
McGill, Mike ARZ 56, MIN 55
McGill, Ralph NOS 49, SFF 49
McGinest, Willie NEP 55
McGinley, Ed NYG 10
McGirl, Len xSTL 45
McGlasson, Ed NYJ 67, NYG 59, STL 54
McGlockton, Chester OAK 91, DEN 91, KCC 75, NYJ 75
McGonnigal, Bruce CLE 49
McGovern, Rob KCC 50, NEP 58, PIT 56
McGowan, Reggie NYG 18
McGrail, Joe BUF 74/91
McGrath, Mark SEA 89, WSH 83
McGraw, Jon NYJ 38
McGraw, Mike ARZ 52, DET 54

McGraw, Thurman DET 73
McGregor, Keli DEN 89, IND 83
McGrew, Dan BUF 52
McGrew, Larry NYG 57, NEP 50
McGrew, Reggie SFF 92
McGrew, Sylvester GBP 77
McGriff, Curtis NYG 76, WSH 74
McGriff, Lee TBB 83
McGriff, Travis DEN 83
McGriff, Tyrone PIT 61
McGriggs, Lamar MIN 37, NYG 38
McGruder, Michael GBP 20, MIA 28, SFF 26, TBB 21/38
McGruder, Scooter NEP 27
McGuire, Gene CHI 60, GBP 60, NOS 76
McGuire, Kaipo IND 10/11
McGuire, Monte DEN 16
McGwire, Dan SEA 10, MIA 11
McHale, Joe NEP 55
McHale, Tom MIA 72, PHL 68, TBB 73
McHan, Lamar ARZ 8, GBP 16/17, IND 14/17, SFF 15
McHugh, Pat PHL 49
McIlhenny, Don DAL 42, DET 42, GBP 42, SFF 35
McInally, Pat CIN 87
McInerney, Nick ARZ 10/11/12
McInerney, Sean CHI 68
McInnis, Hugh ARZ 86, DET 84
McIntosh, Chris SEA 75
McIntosh, Damion SDC 77
McIntosh, Joe ATL 48
McIntosh, Toddrick DAL 90, NOS 92, TBB 94
McIntyre, Guy SFF 62, GBP 62, PHL 62
McIntyre, Jeff ARZ 50, SFF 52
McIntyre, Secedrick ATL 41
McIver, Everett DAL 67, MIA 66, NYJ 67/74
McIvor, Rick ARZ 14
McJulien, Paul GBP 16, STL 16
McKalip, Bill DET 8/10
McKay, Bob CLE 78, NEP 66
McKay, John TBB 89
McKay, Roy GBP 3/22
McKee, Paul WSH 45
McKeehan, James TEN 87
McKeever, Marlin STL 86, MIN 86, PHL 85, WSH 85/86
McKeever, Vito TBB 21
McKeller, Keith BUF 84
McKenzie, Kareem NYJ 67
McKenzie, Keith BUF 91, CLE 90, GBP 73/95

McKenzie, Kevin MIA 82, PHL 88
McKenzie, Mike GBP 34
McKenzie, Raleigh GBP 63, PHL 63, SDC 63, WSH 63
McKenzie, Reggie ARZ 54, OAK 54, SFF 50
McKenzie, Reggie BUF 67, SEA 67
McKenzie, Rich CLE 99
McKibben, Mike NYJ 53
McKie, Jason CHI 37
McKinley, Alvin CAR 99, CLE 70/97
McKinley, Bill BUF 55
McKinley, Dennis ARZ 39
McKinnely, Phil ATL 73, CHI 67, STL 73
McKinney, Bill CHI 54
McKinney, Jeremy STL 68
McKinney, Odis KCC 21, NYG 23, OAK 23
McKinney, Royce BUF 41
McKinney, Seth MIA 68
McKinney, Steve HOU 76, IND 76
McKinney, Zion WSH 84
McKinnie, Bryant MIN 74
McKinnis, Hugh CLE 37, SEA 37
McKinnon, Dennis CHI 85, DAL 85, MIA 86
McKinnon, Don NEP 51
McKinnon, Ronald ARZ 57
McKissack, Dick xDAL 38
McKnight, Dennis DET 62/63, PHL 62, SDC 60
McKnight, James DAL 82, MIA 80, SEA 19/82
McKnight, Ted BUF 33, KCC 22
McKoy, Bill DEN 58, SFF 58
McKyer, Tim ATL 22, CAR 22, DEN 26, DET 33, MIA 22, PIT 24, SFF 22
McLain, Chief DET 25
McLain, Kevin STL 50
McLaughlin, Charlie xSTL ?
McLaughlin, Joe GBP 62, NYG 52
McLaughlin, John TBB 95
McLaughlin, Lee GBP 37
McLaughlin, Leon STL 50
McLaughlin, Steve STL 3
McLaughry, John NYG 17
McLean, Ray CHI 57
McLean, Ron DEN 68, KCC 62
McLean, Scott DAL 52
McLemore, Chris IND 36, OAK 20
McLemore, Dana NOS 42, SFF 43
McLemore, Thomas DET 82, IND 81, CLE 80

McLenna, Bruce DET 24
McLeod, Bob TEN 81
McLeod, Kevin TBB 43
McLeod, Mike GBP 28
McLeod, Russ xSTL 60
McLinton, Harold WSH 53
McIlhany, Dan STL 17
McMahon, Art NEP 28
McMahon, Byron ARZ 8
McMahon, Jim CHI 9, ARZ 9, GBP 9, MIN 9, PHL 9, SDC 9
McMahon, Mike DET 8
McMakin, John DET 81, PIT 89, SEA 81
McManus, Danny KCC 14
McManus, Tom JAX 55
McMath, Herb GBP 61, OAK 61
McMichael, Randy MIA 81
McMichael, Steve CHI 76, GBP 90
McMichaels, John xBKN 19
McMillan, Chuck IND 31
McMillan, Eddie BUF 41, SEA 41, STL 41
McMillan, Erik NYJ 22, CLE 28, KCC 24, PHL 43
McMillan, Ernie ARZ 73, GBP 70
McMillan, Henry SEA 92
McMillan, Randy IND 32
McMillen, Dan OAK 92, PHL 94
McMillen, Jim CHI 22
McMillian, Audray MIN 26, TEN 26
McMillian, Mark NOS 29, KCC 29, PHL 29, WSH 21, SFF 29
McMillon, Todd CHI 26
McMullan, John NYJ 68
McMullen, Billy PHL 81
McMullen, Daniel CHI 21, DET 11/22, NYG 0
McMullen, Kirk CIN 43
McMurtry, Chuck BUF 73, OAK 73
McMurtry, Greg NEP 86
McNabb, Dexter GBP 44/45, PHL 38
McNabb, Donovan PHL 5
McNair, Steve TEN 9
McNair, Todd KCC 48, TEN 37/48
McNally, Frank ARZ 45
McNamara, Bob DEN 41
McNamara, Ed PIT 68
McNanie, Sean ARZ 96, BUF 95, IND 90
McNeal, Don MIA 28
McNeal, Travis SEA 86
McNeil, Charlie SDC 27

McNeil, Clifton SFF 85, CLE 85, NYG 18, TEN 86, WSH 85
McNeil, Emanuel NYJ 92, NEP 92
McNeil, Frank xBKN 34/3
McNeil, Freeman NYJ 24
McNeil, Gerald CLE 89, TEN 89
McNeil, Pat KCC 45
McNeil, Ryan SDC 47, CLE 47, DAL 47, DEN 47, DET 47, STL 47
McNeill, Rod NOS 27, TBB 22
McNeill, Tom NOS 12, PHL 12/36, MIN 12
McNeill, Fred MIN 54
McNorton, Bruce DET 29
McNown, Cade CHI 8
McNulty, Paul ARZ ?
McPeak, Bill PIT 37/84
McPhail, Buck IND 31
McPhail, Hal WSH 14
McPhail, Jerris DET 21, MIA 32
McPhee, Frank ARZ 89
McPherson, Don PHL 9, TEN 6
McPherson, Forrest PHL 26/35, CHI 25, GBP 72
McPherson, Miles SDC 24
McQuaid, Dan MIN 60, WSH 60, IND 60
McQuarters, Ed ARZ 68
McQuarters, R.W. CHI 21, SFF 21
McQuary, Jack zLAD 95
McQuay, Leon NEP 31, NOS 25, NYG 25
McQuilken, Kim ATL 11, WSH 11
McRae, Bennie CHI 26, NYG 26
McRae, Charles OAK 73, TBB 70
McRae, Franklin CHI 58
McRae, Jerrold KCC 83, PHL 82
McRaven, William STL 22
McRoberts, Bob xBOS 17
McShane, Charles SEA 90
McSwain, Chuck DAL 35, NEP 32
McSwain, Rod NEP 23
McTyer, Tim CLE 22, PHL 24
McVea, Warren CIN 42, KCC 6
McVeigh, John SEA 53
McWatters, Bill MIN 32
McWilliams, Bill DET 6
McWilliams, Johnny ARZ 87, MIN 87
McWilliams, Tom PIT 44, zLAD 92
Mead, Jack NYG 85

Meade, Jim WSH 49
Meade, Mike DET 36, GBP 39
Meador, Ed STL 21
Meadows, Adam IND 73
Meadows, Darryl TEN 26
Meadows, Ed CHI 76/86, PHL 66, PIT 82/86, WSH 83
Meads, Johnny TEN 91, WSH 93
Mealey, Rondell GBP 32
Meamber, Tim MIN 53
Means, Dave BUF 77
Means, Natrone SDC 20, CAR 20, JAX 20
Mecham, Curt xBKN 20
Mecklenburg, Karl DEN 77/97
Medlin, Dan OAK 79, TBB 68
Medved, Ron PHL 45
Meehan, Greg CIN 45/85
Meeks, Bob DEN 61
Meeks, Bryant PIT 64
Meester, Brad JAX 63
Meggett, Dave NEP 22, NYG 30, NYJ 22
Meggysey, Dave ARZ 60
Megna, Marc CIN 58, NEP 96
Mehelich, Charles PIT 55/86
Mehl, Lance NYJ 56
Mehringer, Pete ARZ 19/23
Meier, Rob JAX 92
Meier, Shad TEN 84
Meilinger, Steve GBP 80, ARZ 81, PIT 88, WSH 86
Meinert, Dale ARZ 62
Meisenheimer, Darrel xNYB 33
Meisner, Greg KCC 69, NYG 69, STL 69
Meixler, Ed NEP 52
Melander, John CIN 62, DEN 64, NEP 64
Melinkovich, Mike ARZ 82, DET 83
Melka, James GBP 52
Mellekas, John CHI 76, PHL 65, SFF 75
Mello, Jim DET 38, STL 65, xBOS 66, zCHI 78
Mellus, John NYG 33, SFF 45, zBAL 48
Melontree, Andrew CIN 59
Melville, Dan SFF 11
Memmelaar, Dale ARZ 63/71, CLE 61/62, IND 67, DAL 70
Menasco, Don NYG 38
Mendenhall, John DET 64, NYG 64
Mendenhall, Ken IND 57
Mendenhall, Matt WSH 76
Mendenhall, Terry OAK 54
Mendez, Mario SDC 28
Mendoza, Rubin GBP 62
Menefee, Pep NYG 33
Mercein, Chuck GBP 30, NYG 29, NYJ 30

Mercer, Giradie PHL 61

Mercer, Mike BUF 7, GBP 38, KCC 15, MIN 18, OAK 10, SDC 15

Mercier, Richard CLE 65, DEN 63

Meredith, Don DAL 17

Meredith, Dudley BUF 75, TEN 74/75

Mergen, Mike ARZ 73

Mergenthal, Art STL 31

Merkel, Monte CHI 13

Merkens, Guido NOS 19, PHL 19, TEN 12/29

Merkle, Ed WSH 51

Merkovsky, Elmer ARZ 17

Merlin, Ed xBKN 29

Merlo, Jim NOS 57

Merrill, Casey GBP 78, NOS 71, NYG 71

Merrill, Mark BUF 58, CHI 50, DEN 59, GBP 62, NYJ 58, OAK 52

Merrill, Than CHI 22

Merrill, Walt xBKN 29

Merriman, Sam SEA 51

Merritt, Ahmad CHI 81

Merritt, David ARZ 50, MIA 55

Merritts, Jim IND 65

Merriweather, Mike PIT 57, GBP 97, MIN 57, NYJ 58

Merrow, Jeff ATL 75

Mertens, Jerry SFF 80

Mertens, Jim MIA 87

Mertes, Bus NYG 34, ARZ 51, zBAL 73, zLAD 90

Merz, Curt KCC 64

Mesak, Dick DET 12

Mesereau, Scott NYJ 94

Meseroll, Mark NOS 70

Mesner, Bruce BUF 74

Messer, Dale SFF 29

Messner, Mark STL 60

Messner, Max DET 54, NYG 54, PIT 54

Mestnik, Frank ARZ 36, GBP 35

Metcalf, Bo IND 28

Metcalf, Eric CLE 21, ARZ 21, ATL 21, CAR 82, GBP 22, SDC 21, WSH 34

Metcalf, Terrance CHI 60

Metcalf, Terry ARZ 21, WSH 26

Method, Russ ARZ 9

Metzelaars, Pete BUF 88, CAR 88, DET 89, SEA 88

Meuth, Kevin NYG 78

Meyer, Dennis PIT 41

Meyer, Ed BUF 62

Meyer, Ernie DET 51

Meyer, Fred PHL 80/89, PIT 80

Meyer, Gil zBAL 55

Meyer, Jim GBP 62

Meyer, John TEN 54

Meyer, Ron PIT 11

Meyers, Eddie ATL 40

Meyers, Jerry CHI 74, KCC 79

Meyers, John DAL 78, PHL 75

Meylan, Wayne CLE 59, MIN 56

Mialik, Larry ATL 83, SDC 83

Miano, Rich ATL 38, NYJ 36, PHL 38

Micech, Phil MIN 98

Michael, Bill PIT 64/85

Michael, Rich TEN 77

Michaels, Ed CHI 18, PHL 60, PIT 60, WSH 18

Michaels, Lou PIT 79, GBP 75, IND 79, STL 55

Michaels, Walt CLE 34, GBP 35, NYJ 34

Michalik, Art SFF 62, PIT 62

Michalske, Mike GBP 19/24/28/30/31/33/ 36/40/63

Michel, Mike MIA 17, PHL 2

Michel, Tom MIN 21

Michels, John GBP 77, PHL 75

Michels, John PHL 61

Micho, Bobby DEN 46/87, SDC 83

Micka, Mike WSH 34, xBOS 14/33

Mickel, Jeff STL 77

Mickell, Darren KCC 92, NOS 92/99, SDC 92

Mickens, Arnold IND 27

Mickens, Ray NYJ 24

Mickens, Terry GBP 85/88, OAK 85

Mickey, Joey DAL 83

Mickles, Joe SDC 36, WSH 30

Middendorf, Dave CIN 68

Middlebrook, Oren PHL 81

Middlebrooks, Willie DEN 23

Middleton, Dave DET 28/84, MIN 84

Middleton, Frank IND 43, SDC 30

Middleton, Frank OAK 73, TBB 73

Middleton, Kelvin PIT 37

Middleton, Rick NOS 54, SDC 57

Middleton, Ron ATL 87, CLE 87, SDC 47, STL 87, WSH 87/88

Middleton, Terdell GBP 34, TBB 39/43/44/45

Midler, Lou GBP 27, PIT 23

Mielziner, Saul NYG 6/41, xBKN 24/10/9

Mieszkowski, Ed zBRK 41

Mihajlovich, Lou GBP 41, zLAD 54

Mihal, Joe CHI 27, zCHI 43, zLAD 47

Mike, Bob SFF 47

Mikell, Quintin PHL 46

Mike-Mayer, Nick ATL 12, BUF 5, PHL 1

Mike-Mayer, Steve DET 10, IND 5, NOS 10, SFF 10

Mikeska, Russ ATL 87

Miketa, Andy DET 52

Miklich, Bill DET 63, NYG 31/65

Mikolajczyk, Ron NYG 62

Mikolajewski, Pete SDC 15

Mikolas, Doug SFF 97, TEN 76

Mikula, Tom zBRK 60

Mikulak, Mike ARZ 46/48

Milan, Don GBP 12

Milano, Arch DET 84

Milanovich, Scott TBB 13

Milburn, Darryl DET 79

Milburn, Glyn CHI 24, DEN 22, DET 33, SDC 24

Mildren, Jack IND 11, NEP 45

Milem, John CAR 98, SFF 93

Miles, Eddie PIT 46

Miles, Leo NYG 47

Miles, Ostell CIN 36

Mili, Itula SEA 49/88/89

Milinichik, Joe DET 74, SDC 71, STL 71

Milks, John SDC 61

Millard, Bryan SEA 71

Millard, Keith MIN 75, GBP 77, PHL 77, SEA 75

Millen, Hugh ATL 7, DAL 7, DEN 17, NEP 7, STL 12

Millen, Matt OAK 55, SFF 54, WSH 57

Miller, Alan OAK 37, NEP 32

Miller, Allen WSH 55

Miller, Anthony SDC 83, DAL 83, DEN 83

Miller, Arnold CLE 98

Miller, Bill BUF 81, KCC 82, OAK 89

Miller, Bill TEN 84

Miller, Billy DEN 82, HOU 82

Miller, Blake DET 62

Miller, Bob DET 74

Miller, Brandon IND 65

Miller, Brett ATL 62, NYJ 72, SDC 74

Miller, Bronzell JAX 65

Miller, Bubba NOS 67, PHL 65

Miller, Calvin NYG 76

Miller, Charles CHI 76, GBP 48, STL 25

Miller, Chris ATL 12, DEN 12, STL 12/13

Miller, Chuckie IND 28

Miller, Clark SFF 74, STL 78, WSH 82

Miller, Clay TEN 66

Miller, Cleo CLE 30/31, KCC 30
Miller, Corey MIN 55/59, NYG 57
Miller, Craig JAX 24
Miller, Dan IND 1
Miller, Darrin SEA 91
Miller, Don GBP 20, PHL 46
Miller, Don GBP 27
Miller, Don NEP 6
Miller, Donald SEA 99
Miller, Doug SDC 48
Miller, Dutch DET ?
Miller, Eddie IND 86
Miller, Eddie NYG 9
Miller, Fred IND 76
Miller, Fred STL 71
Miller, Fred TEN 71
Miller, Fred WSH 70
Miller, Hal SFF 77
Miller, Jamir ARZ 95, CLE 95
Miller, Jim ATL 55
Miller, Jim CHI 15, ATL 15, JAX 12, PIT 16
Miller, Jim DAL 3, NYG ?, SFF 3
Miller, Jim xBKN 20/23
Miller, John DET 44
Miller, John GBP 72, WSH 73
Miller, John GBP 97
Miller, Johnny SFF 66
Miller, Josh PIT 4
Miller, Junior ATL 80, NOS 84
Miller, Keith SEA 53, STL 53
Miller, Kevin MIN 87
Miller, Larry MIN 5
Miller, Les CAR 69, NOS 69, SDC 69
Miller, Mark BUF 10, CLE 15
Miller, Matt CLE 71/77
Miller, Mike NOS 80, NYG 89
Miller, Milford ARZ 26, CHI 26
Miller, Nate ATL 55
Miller, Nick CLE 52
Miller, Paul GBP 3
Miller, Paul STL 81, KCC 86, SDC 85
Miller, Ralph STL 27/38
Miller, Ralph TEN 62
Miller, Robert MIN 35
Miller, Ron STL 9
Miller, Ron STL 89
Miller, Scott MIA 82/83
Miller, Shawn STL 98
Miller, Solomon NYG 87, TBB 83
Miller, Terry ARZ 58, BUF 40, DET 57, SEA 34
Miller, Tom GBP 76, PHL 89, PIT 89, WSH 14
Miller, Willie CLE 80, STL 82
Milling, Al PHL 51
Milling, James ATL 84/87

Million, Ted MIN 64
Milloy, Lawyer NEP 36, BUF 36
Mills, Dick DET 67
Mills, Ernie CAR 89, DAL 80/85, PIT 89
Mills, Jeff DEN 52, SDC 52
Mills, Jim IND 76, SDC 66
Mills, John TEN 35/48/55, MIN 45, OAK 56
Mills, Lamar WSH 73
Mills, Pete BUF 48
Mills, Sam CAR 51, NOS 51
Mills, Shawn ATL 19
Milne, Brian CIN 44, NOS 40, SEA 44
Milner, Bill CHI 38, NYG 61
Milner, Billy MIA 79, STL 77
Milner, Wayne WSH 40
Milo, Ray KCC 27
Milon, Barnes PHL 30
Milons, Freddie PHL 85
Milot, Rich WSH 57
Milstead, Century NYG 24/25/29
Milstead, Charles TEN 12
Milstead, Rod SFF 69, WSH 69
Milton, Eldridge CHI 57
Milton, Gene MIA 28
Mimbs, Robert ARZ 35
Mims, Chris SDC 94, WSH 91
Mims, David ATL 34/85
Minarik, Henry PIT 37/82
Mincy, Charles KCC 42, MIN 21, TBB 22
Miner, Tom PIT 82/88
Mingo, Gene DEN 21, MIA 21, OAK 21, PIT 11/21, WSH 21
Minick, Paul GBP 15/23/25
Minini, Frank CHI 44, PIT 25
Minisi, Skippy NYG 39
Minniear, Randy CLE 27, NYG 27
Minniefield, Kevin ARZ 21, CHI 24
Minnifield, Frank CLE 31
Minnis, Marvin KCC 81
Minor, Claudie DEN 71
Minor, Kory CAR 52/59
Minor, Lincoln NOS 32
Minor, Travis MIA 28/34
Minor, Vic SEA 21
Minter, Barry CHI 92, CLE 50
Minter, Cedric NYJ 25
Minter, Michael PIT 92/99
Minter, Mike CAR 30
Minter, Tom BUF 20, DEN 20
Mintum, Jack CHI 20
Mioduszewski, Ed IND 26
Miotke, Frank TEN 16/89
Mira, George MIA 10, PHL 10, SFF 10
Miraldi, Dean DEN 67, OAK 64, PHL 64
Miranda, Paul IND 21, MIA 25, SEA 22

Mirer, Rick CHI 13, NYJ 3, OAK 3, SEA 3
Mirich, Rex DEN 75, NEP 76, OAK 78/87
Mischak, Bob NYJ 67, NYG 62, OAK 67/87
Misko, John DET 14, STL 6
Mistler, John BUF 29, NYG 85
Mitcham, Gene PHL 80
Mitchell, Keith HOU 59
Mitchell, Aaron DAL 34, TBB 45
Mitchell, Alvin CLE 49, DEN 49, TBB 41
Mitchell, Anthony BLT 42, JAX 42
Mitchell, Basil GBP 28
Mitchell, Bob zLAD 60
Mitchell, Bobby CLE 49, WSH 49
Mitchell, Brandon NEP 98, SEA 97
Mitchell, Brian ATL 24/36
Mitchell, Brian WSH 30, NYG 30, PHL 30
Mitchell, Buster DET 11/13/24/42, NYG 5/17, xBKN 12
Mitchell, Charles CHI 37, GBP 16
Mitchell, Charley BUF 46, DEN 27
Mitchell, Dale SFF 64
Mitchell, Derrell NOS 88
Mitchell, Devon DET 31
Mitchell, Donald TEN 30
Mitchell, Ed SDC 60
Mitchell, Fondren zMIA 84
Mitchell, Freddie PHL 84
Mitchell, Hal NYG 66
Mitchell, Jeff BLT 60, CAR 60
Mitchell, Jim ATL 86, DET 83
Mitchell, Johnny DAL 82, NYJ 83/86
Mitchell, Kawika KCC 50
Mitchell, Keith NOS 59, JAX 59
Mitchell, Ken ATL 52
Mitchell, Kevin NOS 50, SFF 55, WSH 55
Mitchell, Leonard ATL 73, PHL 74/99, PHL 99
Mitchell, Leroy NEP 41, DEN 41, TEN 41
Mitchell, Lydell IND 26, SDC 26, STL 22
Mitchell, Mack CIN 72, CLE 70
Mitchell, Martin PHL 48
Mitchell, Mel NOS 40
Mitchell, Melvin DET 64, MIN 68, MIA 60/68
Mitchell, Michael NYJ 46, WSH 46
Mitchell, Paul xNYB 59/47, zLAD 35/43, zNYY 46

Mitchell, Pete DET 83, JAX 83, NYG 83
Mitchell, Qasim CHI 72
Mitchell, Randall PHL 90
Mitchell, Roland ARZ 25, ATL 39, BUF 25, GBP 47
Mitchell, Russell NYG 74
Mitchell, Scott BLT 19, CIN 19, DET 19, MIA 19
Mitchell, Shannon SDC 89
Mitchell, Stan MIA 35
Mitchell, Stump ARZ 30
Mitchell, Tom IND 84, OAK 82, SFF 84
Mitchell, Tywan ARZ 5
Mitchell, Willie KCC 22
Mitinger, Bob SDC 82
Mitrione, Matt NYG 98
Mitz, Alonzo CIN 99, SEA 61
Mix, Bryant TBB 96, TEN 97
Mix, Ron SDC 74, OAK 77
Mixon, Bill SFF 48
Mixon, Kenny MIA 79, MIN 79
Mizell, Warner xBKN ?
Moan, Emmett STL 6
Mobley, John DEN 51
Mobley, Orson DEN 89
Mobley, Rudy zBAL 81
Mobley, Singor DAL 27
Mobley, Stacey DET 81, STL 81
Mock, Mike NYJ 50
Modesitt, Jeff TBB 82
Modzelewski, Dick CLE 74, NYG 77, PIT 79, WSH 70
Modzelewski, Ed CLE 36, PIT 39
Moe, Hal ARZ 18
Moegle, Dick SFF 47, DAL 47, PIT 47
Moffett, Tim OAK 83, SDC 86
Moffitt, Mike GBP 82
Mohardt, John ARZ 2/15, CHI 26
Mohr, Chris ATL 13, BUF 9, TBB 5
Mohring, John CLE 55, DET 62
Mohring, Mike SDC 94/98
Moje, Dick GBP 79
Mojsiejenko, Ralf SDC 2, SFF 2, WSH 2
Molden, Alex DET 40, NOS 25, SDC 25
Molden, Frank NYG 73, PHL 74, STL 78
Molden, Fred MIN 90
Molenda, Bo GBP 27/30, NYG 23
Molesworth, Keith CHI 4
Momsen, Bob DET 63, SFF 68
Momsen, Tony PIT 28/55, WSH 51
Monachino, Jim SFF 49/99
Monaco, Ray WSH 13, STL 16

Monaco, Rob ARZ 51
Monaco, Ron ARZ 91, GBP 51
Monahan, Regis DET 19, ARZ 30
Monasco, Don WSH 27
Monds, Mario CIN 93
Monds, Wonder SFF 25
Monfort, Avery ARZ 68
Monger, Matt BUF 57, NYJ 58
Monk, Art WSH 81, NYJ 81, PHL 85
Monk, Quincy NYG 93
Monnett, Bob GBP 3/5/12/18/42/50/66
Monroe, Carl SFF 32/83
Monroe, Henry GBP 43, PHL 24
Monroe, Rod ATL 84
Mont, Tommy WSH 77
Montague, Dave KCC 87
Montalbo, Mel OAK 22
Montana, Joe SFF 16, KCC 19
Montez, Alfred OAK 10
Montgomery, Alton ATL 22, DEN 22
Montgomery, Bill ARZ 43, xSTL 39
Montgomery, Blanchard SFF 38/52/60
Montgomery, Cleo CIN 28, OAK 28, CLE 24
Montgomery, Cliff xBKN 33
Montgomery, Glenn SEA 97, TEN 94
Montgomery, Greg TEN 9, BLT 9, DET 9
Montgomery, Jim DET 73
Montgomery, Joe CAR 33, NYG 33
Montgomery, Marv ATL 71, DEN 78, NOS 77
Montgomery, Mike DAL 23, SDC 23, TEN 24
Montgomery, Monty IND 34, PHL 25, SFF 24
Montgomery, Ralph ARZ 17, CHI 27
Montgomery, Randy DEN 21
Montgomery, Ross CHI 22
Montgomery, Scottie DEN 83
Montgomery, Tyrone OAK 21, STL 25
Montgomery, Wilbert PHL 31, DET 28
Montler, Mike BUF 53, DEN 52, DET 63, NEP 64
Montoute, Sanker TBB 56
Montoya, Max CIN 65, OAK 65
Montreuil, Mark SDC 40
Monty, Pete MIN 94, NYG 51
Moody, Keith BUF 46, OAK 26
Mooers, Doug NOS 74
Moog, Aaron CLE 98

Moon, Warren MIN 1, KCC 1, SEA 1, TEN 1
Mooney, Ed DET 62, IND 58
Mooney, Jim ARZ 32, xBKN 10, xCIN 15/34
Mooney, Mike SDC 73
Mooney, Tex xBKN 1
Mooney, Tim PHL 74
Mooney, Tipp CHI 4
Moor, Buddy ATL 72
Moore, Al CHI 8
Moore, Alex DEN 2
Moore, Allen GBP 55
Moore, Alvin DET 24, IND 23, SEA ?
Moore, Arthur NEP 75
Moore, Bill ARZ 25, PIT 23
Moore, Bill DET 35
Moore, Blake CIN 60, GBP 60
Moore, Bob DEN 87, OAK 88, TBB 86
Moore, Booker BUF 34
Moore, Brandon ARZ 72, NEP 70, NYJ 65, SFF 56
Moore, Brent GBP 98
Moore, Chuck WSH 70
Moore, Cliff xCIN 13
Moore, Corey BUF 54, MIA 57
Moore, Damon CHI 37, PHL 43
Moore, Dana NYG 6
Moore, Darryl WSH 62
Moore, Dave BUF 83, MIA 46, TBB 83
Moore, Dean SFF 53
Moore, Denis DET 70
Moore, Derland NOS 74, NYJ 74
Moore, Derrick ARZ 40, CAR 20, DET 31
Moore, Eric CIN 60, CLE 62, MIA 70, NYG 60
Moore, Fred SDC 71
Moore, Gene SFF 43
Moore, Gene xBKN 22
Moore, Greg NEP 54
Moore, Henry IND 27, NYG 22
Moore, Herman DET 84, NYG 82
Moore, Jason DEN 23, GBP 40, SFF 33
Moore, Jeff SEA 32, SFF 25, WSH 30
Moore, Jeff STL 86
Moore, Jerald NOS 32, STL 44
Moore, Jerry CHI 18, NOS 25
Moore, Jimmy IND 65
Moore, Joe CHI 49
Moore, Kelvin CIN 29
Moore, Ken NYG 35
Moore, Larry IND 50/72, WSH 50
Moore, Lenny IND 24
Moore, Leonard MIN 45

Moore, Leroy BUF 87, DEN 78, NEP 61
Moore, Mack MIA 91, SDC 90
Moore, Malcolm STL 84
Moore, Manfred MIN 36, OAK 36, SFF 45, TBB 44
Moore, Mark SEA 35
Moore, Marty CLE 55, NEP 58
Moore, Maulty CIN 65, MIA 65, TBB 65
Moore, McNeil CHI 29
Moore, Michael ATL 67, DEN 69, WSH 66
Moore, Nat MIA 89
Moore, Paul DET 23
Moore, Randy DEN 76
Moore, Rashad SEA 95
Moore, Red PIT 72
Moore, Reynaud NOS 21
Moore, Rich GBP 70
Moore, Ricky ARZ 37, BUF 42, TEN 32
Moore, Rob ARZ 85, NYJ 85
Moore, Robert ATL 34
Moore, Rocco CHI 71
Moore, Ron ATL 90
Moore, Ron ARZ 20/30, MIA 34, NYJ 33
Moore, Shawn DEN 12
Moore, Steve NEP 67
Moore, Stevon BLT 27, CLE 27, MIA 27
Moore, Tom GBP 25, ATL 21, STL 25
Moore, Wayne MIA 79
Moore, Wilbur WSH 35
Moore, Will JAX 81, NEP 83
Moore, Zeke TEN 22
Moorehead, Aaron IND 85
Moorehead, Emery CHI 43/87, DEN 86, NYG 80
Moorehead, Kindal CAR 94
Mooring, John NOS 73, NYJ 71
Moorman, Brian BUF 8
Moorman, Mo KCC 76
Mooty, Jim DAL 24
Morabito, Tim CAR 90, CIN 93
Morales, Gonzalo PIT 16
Moran, Eric TEN 76
Moran, Hap NYG 22/48, ARZ 21
Moran, Jim NYG 74
Moran, Jim WSH 23
Moran, Rich GBP 57
Moran, Sean BUF 98, SFF 99, STL 77
Moran, Tom NYG 8
Moreau, Doug MIA 82
Moreau, Frank JAX 22, KCC 46
Moreino, Joe NYJ 71
Moreland, Earthwind CLE 38, JAX 27
Moreland, Jake CLE 89, NYJ 37

Morelli, Francis NYJ 79
Morelli, John xBOS 16
Moreno, Moses CHI 4, SDC 13
Moreno, Zeke SDC 57
Moresco, Tim GBP 37, NYJ 37
Morey, Sean NEP 85, PHL 19/85
Morgado, Arnold KCC 21
Morgan, Anthony CHI 81, GBP 81/84
Morgan, Bill NYG 27
Morgan, Bob ARZ 76, WSH 74
Morgan, Bob PIT 37
Morgan, Boyd WSH 12
Morgan, Dan CAR 55
Morgan, Dan NYG 61
Morgan, Dennis DAL 37, PHL 42
Morgan, Don ARZ 47, MIN 31
Morgan, Dwayne ATL 73
Morgan, Joe SFF 48
Morgan, Karl TBB 67, TEN 67
Morgan, Melvin CIN 21, SFF 46
Morgan, Mike CHI 29, NOS 57, PHL 89
Morgan, Mike WSH 52
Morgan, Quincy CLE 81
Morgan, Stanley NEP 86, IND 86/88
Moriarty, Larry KCC 32, TEN 30
Moriarty, Pat CLE 25
Moriarty, Tom ATL 45, PIT 41
Morin, Milt CLE 89
Moritz, Brett TBB 67
Morley, Sam WSH 81
Morlock, Jack DET 21
Moroski, Mike ATL 15, SFF 15, TEN 6
Morrall, Earl IND 15, MIA 15, DET 14, NYG 11, PIT 10, SFF 11
Morrell, Kyle MIN 35
Morris, Aric NEP 29, TEN 28
Morris, Bam BLT 33, CHI 33, KCC 39, PIT 33
Morris, Bob NYG 11
Morris, Chris CLE 62, NOS 77
Morris, Dennit TEN 50, SFF 57
Morris, Donnie Joe KCC 22
Morris, Dwaine ATL 76, PHL 69
Morris, Frank CHI 11
Morris, George SFF 52, STL 4
Morris, Glen DET 57
Morris, Jack MIN 40, PIT 20, STL 40
Morris, Jamie NEP 24, WSH 22
Morris, Jim Bob GBP 30/47
Morris, Joe NYG 20, CLE 20
Morris, Johnny CHI 47

Morris, Jon NEP 56, CHI 63, DET 63
Morris, Larry ATL 33, CHI 33, STL 31/56
Morris, Larry GBP 43
Morris, Lee GBP 48/81/85
Morris, Maurice SEA 20
Morris, Max zBRK 56, zCHI 53
Morris, Mercury MIA 22, SDC 23
Morris, Michael KCC 68, SEA 61, ARZ 68, CLE 67, MIN 68
Morris, Randall DET 42, SEA 43
Morris, Raymond CHI 92
Morris, Riley OAK 55/92
Morris, Rob IND 94
Morris, Ron CHI 84
Morris, Sammy BUF 31/33/45
Morris, Sylvester KCC 84
Morris, Thomas TBB 24
Morris, Victor MIA 91
Morris, Wayne ARZ 24, SDC 25
Morrison, Darryl WSH 37/38
Morrison, Dennis SFF 10
Morrison, Doc xBKN 27/35/14/3
Morrison, Don DET 62, IND 79, NOS 76
Morrison, Fred CLE 32, CHI 15
Morrison, Joe NYG 40
Morrison, Pat NYG 37
Morrison, Reece CIN 26, CLE 26
Morrison, Ron TEN ?
Morrison, Steve IND 52, IND 92
Morrison, Tim WSH 41
Morriss, Guy NEP 75, PHL 50/62
Morrissey, Jim CHI 51, GBP 51
Morrow, Bob ARZ 48, NYG ?, zNYY 61
Morrow, Harold BLT 33, MIN 33
Morrow, John ARZ 30
Morrow, John CLE 56, STL 51
Morrow, Russ zBRK 21
Morrow, Tom OAK 35
Morse, Bobby NOS 35, PHL 36
Morse, Butch DET 13/27
Morse, Steve PIT 47
Mortell, Emmett PHL 31
Mortensen, Fred WSH 12
Morton, Chad NOS 30, NYJ 26, WSH 20
Morton, Craig DAL 14, DEN 7, NYG 15
Morton, Dave SFF 50
Morton, Greg BUF 79
Morton, John CHI 36, zBUF 56, zLAD 59
Morton, John SFF 36

Morton, Johnnie DET 87, KCC 80

Morton, Michael SEA 36, TBB 1/20, WSH 20

Morton, Mike GBP 53, IND 51, OAK 50, STL 53

Morze, Frank CLE 53/58, SFF 53/63

Moscrip, Monk DET 11

Mosebar, Don OAK 72

Moseley, Mark WSH 3, CLE 3, PHL 3, TEN 11

Moselle, Dom CLE 92, GBP 47/93, PHL 24

Moser, Rick MIA 31, PIT 39, TBB 35

Moser, Robert CHI 55

Moses, Don xCIN 31

Moses, Haven BUF 25, DEN 25

Moses, J.J. GBP 86, HOU 84

Moses, Kelvin NYJ 50

Mosher, Clure PIT 37

Mosier, John DEN 85, IND 88, NEP 88

Mosley, Anthony CHI 46

Mosley, Henry CHI 49/90

Mosley, Mike BUF 88

Mosley, Norm PIT 11

Mosley, Russ GBP 8

Mosley, Wayne BUF 39

Moss, Brent STL 31

Moss, Eddie ARZ 27, WSH 36

Moss, Eric MIN 79

Moss, Gary ATL 23

Moss, Joe WSH 72

Moss, Martin DET 63

Moss, Paul PIT 30, xSTL ?

Moss, Perry GBP 10

Moss, Randy MIN 84

Moss, Roland BUF 40, IND 44, NEP 86, SDC 38

Moss, Santana NYJ 83

Moss, Winston OAK 99, SEA 55, TBB 57/58

Moss, Zefross DET 71, IND 73, NEP 77

Mostardo, Rich MIN 24, CLE 22, OAK 27

Mote, Kelley DET 78/83/87, NYG 80

Moten, Bobby DEN 86

Moten, Eric SDC 77

Moten, Gary KCC 53, SFF 59/63

Moten, Mike ARZ 74

Motl, Bob zCHI 54

Motley, Marion CLE 36/76, PIT 36/37

Mott, Joe GBP 55, NYJ 51

Mott, Norm GBP 19, PIT 13, xCIN ?

Mott, Steve DET 52

Moulds, Eric BUF 80

Mowatt, Zeke NEP 81, NYG 84

Moyer, Alex MIA 54

Moyer, Ken CIN 73

Moyer, Paul SEA 21

Moynihan, Tim ARZ 11/40

Mraz, Mark ATL 67, OAK 97

Mrkonic, George PHL 72

Mrosko, Bob IND 88, NYG 80, TEN 87

Mucha, Rudolph STL 27, CHI 16

Muckensturm, Jerry CHI 58

Mucker, Larry TBB 87

Mudd, Howard SFF 68, CHI 68

Muehlheuser, Frank xBOS 23, xNYB 23

Muelhaupt, Ed BUF 70

Mueller, Jamie BUF 39/41

Mueller, Vance OAK 31/42

Muellner, Bill ARZ ?

Mugg, Garvin DET 77

Mughelli, Ovie BLT 34

Muha, Joe PHL 36

Muhammad, Calvin OAK 82, SDC 81, WSH 89

Muhammad, Muhsin CAR 87

Muhammad, Mustafah IND 21/31

Muhlmann, Horst CIN 16, PHL 16

Muirbrook, Shay OAK 52

Mularkey, Mike MIN 86, PIT 84

Mulitalo, Edwin BLT 64

Mul-Key, Herb WSH 28

Mullady, Tom NYG 81

Mullaney, Mark MIN 77

Mullen, Davlin NYJ 20

Mullen, Gary CHI 80

Mullen, Roderick CAR 28, GBP 28

Mullen, Tom ARZ 65, NYG 73

Mullen, Verne CHI 15/21, ARZ ?

Mulleneaux, Carl GBP 19

Mullenneaux, Lee ARZ 18, GBP 18, PIT 13/18, NYG 0, xCIN 9,44, xSTL 33

Mulligan, George PHL 42

Mulligan, Wayne ARZ 50, NYJ 50

Mullins, Don CHI 40

Mullins, Eric TEN 80

Mullins, Gerry PIT 72

Mullins, Noah CHI 10, NYG 20

Mulready, Jerry zCHI 51

Mumford, Tony ARZ 34

Mumley, Nick NYJ 74

Mumphord, Lloyd IND 42, MIA 26, KCC 91

Munchak, Mike TEN 63

Muncie, Chuck NOS 42, SDC 46

Munday, George NYG 9, xCIN 24/43, xSTL 35

Mundee, Fred CHI 20/36

Mundford, Marc DEN 51

Mungo, James IND 23

Munn, Lyle NYG 15

Munoz, Anthony CIN 78

Munsey, Nelson IND 31, MIN 31

Munson, Bill BUF 9, DET 19, SDC 19, SEA 19, STL 19

Murakowski, Art DET 35

Muransky, Ed OAK 76

Murchison, Ola Lee DAL 80

Murdock, Guy TEN 50/53

Murdock, Jesse OAK ?, BUF 25

Murdock, Les NYG 84

Murley, Dick PHL 68, PIT 79/94

Murphy, Bill ARZ 12/25

Murphy, Bill NEP 31

Murphy, Frank HOU 83, TBB 87

Murphy, Fred CLE 87, MIN 88

Murphy, George zLAD 60

Murphy, Ham STL 28

Murphy, James KCC 80

Murphy, Jim ARZ 19

Murphy, Kevin SDC 58, SEA 98, TBB 59

Murphy, Mark GBP 37

Murphy, Mark WSH 29

Murphy, Matt DET 49, HOU 81

Murphy, Mike TEN 56

Murphy, Phil STL 95

Murphy, Rob IND 61, SFF 68

Murphy, Tom ARZ 41

Murphy, Yo MIN 19, TBB 88, STL 83

Murray, Calvin PHL 42

Murray, Dan IND 52

Murray, Earl NYG 62, PIT 72, xBAL 30

Murray, Eddie DET 3, DAL 3, KCC 2, MIN 3, PHL 3, TBB 3, WSH 2

Murray, Francis PHL 11

Murray, Joe STL 76

Murray, Mark DEN 57

Murray, Walter IND 86

Murrell, Adrian ARZ 29, DAL 29, NYJ 29, WSH 22

Murrell, Bill ARZ 80

Murry, Don CHI 18

Murtagh, Mickey NYG 2/15/50

Murtha, Greg IND 78

Musgrave, Bill DEN 14, SFF 14

Musgrove, Spain TEN 77, WSH 71

Musick, Jim WSH 25

Musser, Neal ATL 53

Musso, George CHI 16

Musso, Johnny CHI 22

Mustafaa, Najee CLE 48, MIN 48, OAK 48
Mustard, Chad CLE 83
Muster, Brad CHI 25, NOS 22/25
Mutryn, Chet xBAL 81, zBUF 89/83
Mutscheller, Jim IND 84
Myer, Steve SEA 16
Myers, Bob IND 79
Myers, Bob SFF 27
Myers, Bobby TEN 32
Myers, Brad PHL 46, STL 28
Myers, Chip CIN 25, SFF 46
Myers, Dave xBKN 4
Myers, Denny CHI 33
Myers, Frank MIN 74
Myers, Greg CIN 31, DAL 29
Myers, Jack PHL 32, STL 31
Myers, Leonard DET 41, NEP 25, NYJ 41
Myers, Michael CLE 93, DAL 94
Myers, Tom DET 18
Myers, Tommy NOS 37
Myers, Tommy NYG 4
Myers, Wilbur DEN 29
Myhra, Steve IND 65
Myles, Deshone NOS 55, SEA 50
Myles, Godfrey DAL 98
Myles, Jesse DEN 39
Myles, Reggie CIN 37
Myles, Toby CLE 73, NYG 70, OAK 70/77
Myrtle, Chip DEN 54, SDC 53
Myslinski, Tom BUF 60, CHI 69, DAL 62, IND 67, JAX 50, PIT 61/62, WSH 50/56, WSH 56
Nabors, Roland zNYY 23
Nacelli, Andy PHL 87
Naeole, Chris JAX 65, NOS 65
Nafziger, Dana TBB 51/83
Nagel, Ray ARZ 7
Nagel, Ross ARZ 7, xNYB 45
Nagle, Browning ATL 7/13, IND 18, NYJ 8
Nagler, Gern ARZ 84/86, CLE 86, PIT 84
Nagurski, Bronko CHI 3/16
Nails, Jamie BUF 74, MIA 66
Naiota, John PIT 25
Nairne, Rob DEN 58, NOS 55
Najarian, Pete MIN 51/59, TBB 57/58
Nalen, Tom DEN 66
Nall, Craig GBP 12/16
Namath, Joe NYJ 12, STL 12
Nance, Jim NEP 35, NYJ 35
Napier, Walter KCC 76
Naponic, Bob TEN 14
Naposki, Eric IND 51, NEP 49

Nardi, Dick DET 4, PIT 10, xBKN 5
Nash, Bob NYG 18
Nash, Joe SEA 72
Nash, Kenny KCC 85
Nash, Marcus BLT 11, DEN 82
Nash, Tom GBP 19/21/26/35/37, xBKN 17/34/40
Nathan, Jo SFF 30
Nathan, Tony MIA 22
Natkin, Brian TEN 48
Natowich, Andy WSH 46
Nattiel, Michael MIN 59
Nattiel, Ricky DEN 84
Naumetz, Fred STL 22
Naumoff, Paul DET 50/58
Naumu, John zLAD 80
Nave, Steven CLE 57
Navies, Hannibal CAR 53, GBP 50
Neacy, Clem ARZ 66, CHI 80
Nead, Spencer STL 47
Neal, Dan CHI 51/52, IND 50
Neal, Ed GBP 58, CHI 58
Neal, Frankie GBP 80
Neal, Leon IND 20
Neal, Lorenzo CIN 41, NOS 22/23, SDC 41, TBB 41, TEN 41
Neal, Louis ATL 80
Neal, Randy CIN 52, SFF 52
Neal, Richard NOS 68/87, NYJ 81
Neal, Speedy BUF 41
Nealy, Ray MIA 20
Nease, Mike PHL 78
Nece, Ryan TBB 56
Neck, Tommy CHI 48
Ned, Derrick NOS 36
Ned, Larry MIN 28
Nedney, Joe ARZ 6, CAR 6, DEN 6, MIA 6, OAK 6, TEN 6
Neely, Bobby CHI 87
Neely, Ralph DAL 73
Neff, Bob MIA 43
Negus, Fred CHI 18, zCHI 27/28
Nehemiah, Renaldo SFF 83
Neidert, John CHI 63, CIN 53, NYJ 63
Neighbors, Billy NEP 73, MIA 63
Neil, Dallas ATL 49
Neil, Dan DEN 62
Neil, Jim ARZ 25
Neil, Kenny NYJ 77, TEN 75
Neill, Bill GBP 77, NYG 77
Neill, Jim NYG 12
Neils, Steve ARZ 53
Nelms, Mike WSH 21
Nelsen, Bill CLE 16, PIT 14
Nelson, Al PHL 26
Nelson, Andy IND 80

Nelson, Andy NYG 26
Nelson, Benny TEN 22
Nelson, Bill STL 67
Nelson, Bob BUF 56, OAK 51, SFF 66
Nelson, Bob GBP 79, TBB 71
Nelson, Bruce CAR 72
Nelson, Chuck BUF 13, MIN 1, STL 13
Nelson, Darrell PIT 81
Nelson, Darrin MIN 20, SDC 20
Nelson, David MIN 32
Nelson, Dennis IND 68, PHL 77
Nelson, Derrie SDC 55
Nelson, Don xBKN 20
Nelson, Edmund NEP 65, PIT 64
Nelson, Everett CHI 17
Nelson, Frank xBOS 56, xNYB 56
Nelson, Herb zBRK 52/41, zBUF 52
Nelson, Jim GBP 57, IND 57, MIN 56
Nelson, Jimmy zMIA 95
Nelson, Karl NYG 63
Nelson, Lee ARZ 38
Nelson, Mark KCC 70
Nelson, Ralph SEA 44, WSH 36
Nelson, Reggie JAX 79, SDC 66
Nelson, Rhett MIN 38
Nelson, Robert DET 22/51, xBAL 28, zLAD 22
Nelson, Shane BUF 59
Nelson, Steve NEP 57
Nelson, Teddy KCC 49
Nelson, Terry STL 83
Nemecek, Jerry xBKN 29
Nemeth, Stephen STL 10, zBAL 48, zCHI 69
Nery, Carl PIT 40
Nery, Ron DEN 80, SDC 80, TEN 83
Nesbit, Jamar CAR 63, JAX 64
Nesbitt, Dick CHI 2, ARZ 28/47, xBKN 66/99
Nesser, Al NYG 7/40
Nettles, Doug IND 30, NYG 22
Nettles, Jim PHL 9, STL 19
Neubert, Keith NYJ 86
Neufeld, Ryan DAL 39, JAX 83, BUF 88
Neuheisel, Rick SDC 7, TBB 7
Neujahr, Quentin BLT 67, JAX 65
Neuman, Bob ARZ 20
Neumann, Tom NEP 36
Nevers, Ernie ARZ 4/11/44
Nevett, Elijah NOS 24
Neville, Tom GBP 61/72, SFF 69

Neville, Tommy NEP 77, DEN 76, NYG 74

Newberry, Jeremy SFF 62

Newberry, Tom PIT 66, STL 66

Newbill, Richard MIN 53, SEA 52

Newell, Mike HOU 64

Newell, Steve SDC 25

Newhouse, Robert DAL 44

Newkirk, Robert CHI 62, NOS 64

Newland, Bob NOS 41

Newman, Anthony NOS 30, STL 26

Newman, Ed MIA 64

Newman, Harry NYG 12

Newman, Keith ATL 53, BUF 53

Newman, Pat MIN 86, CLE 86, NOS 86

Newman, Terrence DAL 41

Newman, Tim NYJ 35

Newsom, Tony TEN 10

Newsome, Billy CHI 87, IND 81, NOS 78, NYJ 87

Newsome, Craig GBP 21, SFF 27

Newsome, Harry MIN 18, PIT 18

Newsome, Ozzie CLE 82

Newsome, Richard NOS 31

Newsome, Timmy DAL 30

Newsome, Vince CLE 22, STL 22

Newson, Kendall MIA 82

Newson, Tony KCC 66

Newton, Bob CHI 78, SEA 78

Newton, Charles PHL 40

Newton, Jim IND 69

Newton, Nate DAL 61/67, CAR 73

Newton, Tim KCC 96, MIN 96, TBB 96

Newton, Tom NYJ 44

Nguyen, Dat DAL 59

Niccolai, Armand PIT 17/23/39

Nichelini, Al ARZ 43

Nicholas, Bob PIT 65

Nicholas, Calvin SFF 88

Nichols, Allen PIT 51

Nichols, Bob NEP 87

Nichols, Gerald NYJ 77, PHL 74, TBB 77, WSH 74

Nichols, Ham ARZ 73, GBP 46

Nichols, Marc SFF 58

Nichols, Mark DET 86

Nichols, Mike DEN 51

Nichols, Ricky IND 80

Nichols, Robbie IND 52

Nicholson, Calvin NOS 38

Nicholson, Frank NYG 96

Nicholson, Jim KCC 70, SFF 67

Nicholson, Oliver TEN 46

Nickel, Elbie PIT 81

Nickerson, Hardy TBB 56, GBP 56, JAX 56, PIT 54

Nickey, Donnie TEN 23

Nickla, Ed CHI 72

Nicklas, Pete OAK 70

Nicksich, George PIT 14/78/88

Nicolas, Scott CLE 58, MIA 52/57

Niedziela, Bruno zCHI 48

Niehaus, Steve MIN 71, SEA 71

Niehoff, Rob CIN 42

Nielsen, Gifford TEN 14

Nielsen, Hans CHI 6

Nielson, Walt NYG 8

Niemi, Laurie WSH 47/74

Nies, John BUF 6

Nighswander, Nick BUF 65

Niland, John DAL 76, PHL 74

Niles, Jerry NYG 39

Nilson, Reed DET 46

Ninowski, Jim CLE 11/15, DET 15, NOS 11, WSH 11

Nipp, Maurice PHL 68

Nisbet, Dave ARZ 12

Nisby, John PIT 65/67/83, WSH 62

Nitschke, Ray GBP 33/66

Nittmo, Bjorn NYG 3

Nix, Doyle GBP 41/45, KCC 25, SDC 29, WSH 20

Nix, Emery NYG 41/44

Nix, Jack SFF 58

Nix, John DAL 60

Nix, John STL 6

Nix, Kent CHI 16, PIT 10, TEN 14

Nix, Roosevelt CIN 95, MIN 79

Nixon, Fred GBP 84

Nixon, Jeff BUF 38

Nixon, Mike PIT 12, xBKN 30

Nixon, Tory SFF 20

Nkwenti, Mathias PIT 78

Noa, Kaulana STL 71

Nobile, Leo PIT 60, WSH 58

Nobis, Tommy ATL 60

Noble, Brandon DAL 75

Noble, Brian GBP 91

Noble, Don STL 86

Noble, James IND 87, WSH 83

Noble, Mike OAK 53

Nocera, John DEN 43, PHL 29

Nock, George NYJ 30/37, WSH 40

Nofsinger, Terry ARZ 14, ATL 14, PIT 12/18

Noga, Al IND 99, MIN 99, WSH 72

Noga, Niko ARZ 49/57, DET 51

Noga, Peter ARZ 57

Nolan, Dick ARZ 25, DAL 23, NYG 25

Nolan, Earl ARZ 17

Nolan, John xBOS 44, xNYB 44

Nolander, Don zBAL 33, zLAD 20

Noll, Chuck CLE 65

Nolting, Ray CHI 25/35

Nomellini, Leo SFF 42/73

Nomina, Tom DEN 68, MIA 76

Noonan, Danny DAL 73, GBP 97

Noonan, Karl MIA 89

Noppenberg, John DET 14, PIT 50

Norberg, Hank CHI 16, SFF 55

Norby, Jack PHL 26, NYG 14, xBKN 35/29, xSTL 44

Nord, Keith MIN 49

Nordquist, Mark CHI 63, PHL 68

Nordstrom, Swede NYG 10/14

Norgard, Al GBP 19/62

Norgard, Erik TEN 64

Norgren, Fred TBB 76

Nori, Mark JAX 68

Nori, Reino CHI 4, xBKN 8

Norman, Ben DEN 38

Norman, Bob ARZ 40

Norman, Chris DEN 1/4

Norman, Dennis SEA 68

Norman, Dick CHI 12

Norman, Jim WSH 66

Norman, Joe SEA 52

Norman, Josh SDC 83

Norman, Pettis DAL 84, SDC 88

Norman, Phil CHI 67

Norman, Tony MIN 97

Norris, David NYJ 17

Norris, Hal WSH 20

Norris, Jerome ATL 26

Norris, Jim OAK 72/74

Norris, Jimmy NYG 49

Norris, Jon CHI 98

Norris, Moran HOU 44, NOS 33

Norris, Trusse SDC 44

Norris, Ulysses BUF 49/89, DET 80

Norseth, Mike CIN 12, GBP 4

North, Jim WSH 42

North, John xBAL 55, zBAL 55

Northcutt, Dennis CLE 86

Northern, Gabe BUF 99, MIN 90

Norton, Don SDC 88

Norton, Jerry ARZ 25, DAL 25, GBP 23, PHL 41

Norton, Jim ATL 70, NYG 75, PHL 73, SFF 75, WSH 83

Norton, Jim TEN 43

Norton, Ken DAL 51, SFF 51

Norton, Marty GBP 13

Norton, Ray SFF 23

Norton, Rick GBP 11, MIA 11
Norvell, Jay CHI 91
Norwood, Scott BUF 11
Nosich, John PIT 29
Nott, Doug DET 26, WSH 33
Nott, Mike KCC 7
Nottage, Dexter WSH 92
Nottingham, Don IND 48, MIA 36
Novacek, Jay DAL 84, ARZ 84/85
Novak, Jack CIN 89, TBB 80
Novak, Jeff JAX 67, MIA 67
Novak, Ken IND 74
Novitsky, Craig NOS 60
Novoselsky, Brent CHI 89, MIN 85
Novotny, Ray DET 27, xBKN 22/6
Novsek, Joe OAK 71
Nowak, Gary SDC 75
Nowak, Walt PHL 81
Nowaskey, Bob CHI 20, zBAL 52, zLAD 55, xBAL 52
Nowatzke, Tom DET 35, IND 34
Noyes, Len xBKN 24
Nugent, Dan WSH 62
Nugent, David BLT 70, NEP 92
Nugent, Philip DEN 15
Nugent, Terry IND 14
Nunamaker, Julian BUF 61/88
Nunley, Frank SFF 57
Nunley, Jeremy CAR 99, TEN 93
Nunn, Freddie ARZ 50/58/78, IND 93
Nunnery, R.B. KCC 68
Nussbaumer, Bob ARZ 99, GBP 23/48, WSH 50
Nussmeier, Doug NOS 13
Nutten, Tom BUF 64, STL 61
Nutter, Buzz PIT 51, IND 50
Nutting, Ed CLE 78, DAL 76
Nuzum, Jerry PIT 22
Nuzum, Rick GBP 56, STL 51
Nuzzo, Chip BUF 40/43
Nwokorie, Chukie GBP 90, IND 91
Nye, Blaine DAL 61
Nyers, Dick IND 21/80
Nygren, Bernie zLAD 85
Nystrom, Lee GBP 70
Nyval, Vic NOS 36
Oakes, Don NEP 71, PHL 77
Oates, Bart NYG 65, SFF 66
Oates, Brad ARZ 65, DET 74, GBP 72, KCC 72
Oatis, Victor IND 84
Oats, Carleton GBP 73, OAK 85
O'Bard, Ronnie SDC 27
Obeck, Vic ARZ 75, zBRK 35
Obee, Dunc DET 52

Obee, Terry CHI 83, MIN 89
Oben, Roman CLE 72, NYG 72, TBB 72
Oberg, Tom DEN 27
O'Berry, Herman STL 42
O'Boyle, Harry GBP 41/42, PHL 16
O'Bradovich, Ed CHI 87
Obradovich, Jim NYG 89, SFF 89, TBB 86
O'Brien, Bill DET 62
O'Brien, Dave ARZ 52, MIN 74, NYG 68
O'Brien, Davey PHL 5/8
O'Brien, Fran PIT 72, WSH 61, CLE 70
O'Brien, Gail WSH 22
O'Brien, Jack PIT 89
O'Brien, Jim DET 45, IND 80
O'Brien, Ken NYJ 7/16, PHL 7
O'Brien, Mike SEA 20
Obrovac, Mike CIN 68
Obst, Henry PHL 22
O'Callaghan, John SEA 91
O'Connell, Harry CHI ?
O'Connell, Tom BUF 14, CHI 10, CLE 15
O'Connor, Bill CLE 53, xNYB 66, zBUF 54
O'Connor, Bob GBP 24
O'Connor, Dan ARZ 24
O'Connor, Paul TBB 60
O'Connor, Tom NYJ 14
Odegard, Don NYJ 21
O'Dell, Stu IND 55, WSH 57
O'Delli, Mel PIT 40
Oden, Curly WSH 12
Oden, Derrick PHL 58
Oden, McDonald CLE 84
Odle, Phil DET 23
Odom, Cliff IND 49/93, MIA 93, CLE 58
Odom, Henry PIT 44
Odom, Jason TBB 70
Odom, Joe CHI 59
Odom, Ricky KCC 38, SFF 42, STL 23
Odom, Sammy TEN 52
Odom, Steve GBP 84, NYG 84
Odomes, Nate BUF 37, ATL 38
Odoms, Riley DEN 88
O'Donahue, Pat GBP 81, SFF 83
O'Donnell, Dick GBP 5/20/30, xBKN 5
O'Donnell, Joe BUF 67
O'Donnell, Neil PIT 14, CIN 12, NYJ 14, TEN 14
O'Donoghue, Neil ARZ 11, BUF 8, TBB 6
Odson, Urban GBP 63
O'Dwyer, Matt CIN 72, NYJ 70
Oech, Verne CHI 23

Oehler, John PIT 26/33, xBKN 17
Oelerich, John CHI 7, PIT 49
Offerdahl, John MIA 56
Office, Kendrick BUF 77
Office, Tony DET 53
Offord, Willie MIN 24
Ofodile, Al BLT 89
Ogas, Dave BUF 53, OAK 61
Ogbogu, Eric DAL 90, NYJ 99, CIN 92
Ogden, Jeff BLT 87, DAL 82/85, MIA 88
Ogden, Jonathan BLT 75
Ogden, Ray ARZ 28, ATL 28, CHI 38, NOS 29
Ogle, Kendall CLE 59
Ogle, Rick ARZ 52, DET 58
Oglesby, Alfred CIN 96, GBP 98, MIA 96, NYJ 95
Oglesby, Cedrick ARZ 1
Oglesby, Paul OAK 74
Ogletree, Craig CIN 52
Ogrin, Pat WSH 75, WSH 79
Ogunleye, Adewale MIA 90/93
Ohalete, Ifeanyi WSH 26
O'Hanley, Ross NEP 25
O'Hara, Pat TBB 4
O'Hara, Shaun CLE 60
Ohlgren, Earl GBP 23
Ojo, Onome NOS 86
Okanlawon, Tony SDC 34
Okeafor, Chike SEA 56, SFF 91
Okobi, Chukky PIT 56
Okoniewski, Steve ARZ 33/36, BUF 79/88, GBP 73
Okoye, Christian KCC 35
Olander, Cliff SDC 10
Olderman, Bob KCC 64
Oldershaw, Doug NYG 39
Oldham, Chris ARZ 26/27, BUF 28, DET 42, NOS 28, PIT 24
Oldham, Ray DET 23, IND 25, NYG 25, PIT 25
Olds, Bill IND 38, PHL 38/39, SEA 39
O'Leary, Dan BUF 87, NYG 44, PIT 81
Olejniczak, Stan PIT 30
Olenchalk, John KCC 63
Olenski, Mitch DET 82, zMIA 48
Olerich, Dave ARZ 51, SFF 84, TEN 37
Oliphant, Mike CLE 33/89, WSH 25
Olive, Bobby IND 16/18
Oliver, Bob CLE 79
Oliver, Clancy ARZ 20, PIT 27
Oliver, Darryl ATL 45
Oliver, Frank BUF 42, TBB 42
Oliver, Greg PHL 48
Oliver, Hubert IND 30, TEN 39, PHL 34

Oliver, Jack CHI 71
Oliver, Jeff NYJ 70
Oliver, Louis CIN 29, MIA 25
Oliver, Maurice TBB 55
Oliver, Muhammad DEN 42, GBP 25, MIA 20, WSH 26, KCC 26
Oliver, Ralph OAK 56
Oliver, Vince ARZ 55
Oliver, Winslow ATL 26/33, CAR 20
Olivo, Brock DET 26
Olkewicz, Neal WSH 52
Olsavsky, Jerry BLT 56, PIT 55/92
Olsen, Hans IND 67
Olsen, Merlin STL 74
Olsen, Norman STL 65
Olsen, Orrin KCC 52
Olsen, Phil DEN 58, STL 72
Olsen, Ralph GBP 19
Olson, Benji TEN 75
Olson, Carl ARZ 24
Olson, Erik JAX 45
Olson, Glenn STL 25
Olson, Harold BUF 74, DEN 76
Olsonoski, Larry GBP 46/74, xNYB 26
Olssen, Lance SFF 73
Olsson, Swede WSH 21
Olszewski, Al PIT 35
Olszewski, Johnny ARZ 36, DEN 0, DET 0, WSH 0
O'Mahoney, Jim NYJ 63
O'Malley, Joe PIT 85
O'Malley, Tom GBP 76
O'Mally, Jim DEN 66
O'Neal, Andre GBP 53, KCC 52, MIN 96
O'Neal, Brian PHL 31, SFF 26
O'Neal, Deltha DEN 24
O'Neal, Jim zCHI 49/32
O'Neal, Ken NOS 82
O'Neal, Leslie KCC 91, SDC 91, STL 91
O'Neal, Robert IND 32
O'Neal, Steve NOS 10, NYJ 20
O'Neil, Bob PIT 65/86
O'Neil, Ed DET 55, GBP 56
O'Neil, Keith DAL 54
O'Neill, Bill DET ?
O'Neill, Bob NYJ 62
O'Neill, Kevin DET 59
O'Neill, Pat NEP 5
O'Neill, William STL ?
Onesti, Larry TEN 45
Onkontz, Dennis NYJ 35
Ontko, Bob IND 51
Opalewski, Ed DET 71
Opfar, David PIT 69
Opperman, Jim PHL 54
O'Quinn, John CHI 37, PHL 81

Orduna, Joe SFF 31, IND 37, NYG 49
Ori, Frank MIN 69
Oriard, Mike KCC 50
Oristaglio, Bob CLE 50, PHL 89, xBAL 57, zBUF 56
Orlando, Bo CIN 26, PIT 21, SDC 26, TEN 26
Orlich, Dan GBP 19/49
Ormsbe, Elliott PHL 40
Orns, Fred SEA 59
Orosz, Tom MIA 3, SFF 3/19
O'Rourke, Charley CHI 48, zBAL 66, zLAD 68/66
Orr, Jimmy PIT 86
Orr, Shantee HOU 53
Orr, Terry SDC 37, WSH 87/89
Ortega, Ralph ATL 55, MIA 54
Ortego, Keith CHI 89/96
Ortman, Charles PIT 18/49, xDAL ?
Orton, Greg DET 67
Orvis, Herb DET 80, IND 88
Osborn, Dave MIN 41, GBP 41
Osborn, Mike PHL 57
Osborne, Chuck OAK 98, STL 97
Osborne, Clancy MIN 31, OAK 81, SFF 33
Osborne, Eldonta ARZ 90
Osborne, Jim CHI 68
Osborne, Richard ARZ 87, NYJ 86, PHL 86/88
Osborne, Tom WSH 84
Osby, Vince SDC 56
Osgood, Kassim SDC 81
O'Shea, Terry PIT 85
Oshodin, Willie DEN 91
Osiecki, Sandy KCC 11
Osika, Craig CLE 62, SFF 71
Osley, Willie KCC 47, NEP 37
Osmanski, Bill CHI 9
Osmanski, Joe CHI 18, xNYB 80
Ossowski, Ted zNYY 46
O'Steen, Dwayne GBP 44, IND 35, OAK 35, STL 33, TBB 44
Ostendarp, Jim NYG 16
Ostroski, Jerry BUF 60
Ostrowski, Chet WSH 88
Ostrowski, Phil SFF 69
O'Sullivan, Dennis NYJ 60
Oswald, Paul ATL 67, DAL 62, PIT 51
Otis, Jim ARZ 35, KCC 35, NOS 35
Ott Carruth, Paul GBP 30, KCC 30
Ottele, Dick zLAD 65
Ottis, Brad ARZ 96, STL 95
Otto, Bob DAL 76, TEN 67
Otto, Gus OAK 34
Otto, Jim OAK 00/50
Oubre, Louis MIA 68, NOS 66

Ours, Greg MIA 63
Ours, Wes IND 44, TEN 40
Outlaw, John NEP 44, PHL 20
Overhauser, Chad HOU 79
Overmeyer, Bill PHL 56
Overstreet, David MIA 20
Overstreet, Will ATL 90
Overton, Don DET 33, NEP 29
Overton, Jerry DAL 20
Owen, Al NYG 6/8
Owen, Bill NYG 36
Owen, Steve NYG 6/12/36/44/50/55
Owen, Tom NEP 17, SFF 14, WSH 17
Owens, Artie BUF 85, NOS 49, SDC 85
Owens, Billy DAL 31
Owens, Brig WSH 23
Owens, Burgess NYJ 22, OAK 44
Owens, Dan ATL 93, DET 70/90
Owens, Darrick PIT 18
Owens, Dennis NEP 98
Owens, Don ARZ 70, PHL 70, WSH 72
Owens, James SFF 20, TBB 26, SFF 89
Owens, Jim xBAL 59
Owens, Joe NOS 72, SDC 72, TEN 71
Owens, John DET 83
Owens, Luke ARZ 78, IND 72
Owens, Marv ARZ 37, NYJ 37
Owens, Mel STL 58
Owens, Morris MIA 82, TBB 85
Owens, Pete xBKN 33
Owens, R.C. IND 27, NYG 37, SFF 27
Owens, Rich KCC 97, MIA 96, SEA 67, WSH 96
Owens, Steve DET 36
Owens, Terrell SFF 81
Owens, Terry SDC 76
Owens, Tinker NOS 83
Oxendine, Ken ATL 28/33
Ozdowski, Mike IND 51/71
Pace, Calvin ARZ 79
Pace, Jim SFF 43
Pace, Orlando STL 76
Pacella, Dave PHL 72
Pacheco, Chris STL 42
Packer, Walter SEA 40, TBB 30
Padjen, Gary IND 60/90
Padlow, Max PHL 28
Paffrath, Bob zBRK 61, zMIA 68/85
Pagac, Fred CHI 82, TBB 82
Page, Alan CHI 82, MIN 88
Page, Craig TEN 62
Page, Paul zBAL 88

Page, Solomon DAL 77, SDC 79
Pagel, Derek NYJ 25
Pagel, Mike CLE 10, IND 18, STL 14
Pagliei, Joe NYJ 40, PHL 32
Pahukoa, Jeff ATL 64, STL 69
Pahukoa, Shane NOS 35
Paige, Lee TBB 29
Paige, Stephone KCC 83
Paige, Tony DET 49, MIA 49, NYJ 49
Paine, Homer zCHI 40
Paine, Jeff KCC 95, WSH 59
Painter, Carl DET 26
Palatella, Lou SFF 68
Palazzi, Lou NYG 57
Palelei, Lonnie NYG 67, NYJ 66, PHL 77, PIT 66/68
Palepoi, Anton SEA 91
Palewicz, Al KCC 57, NYJ 53
Palm, Mike NYG 9, xCIN 53
Palmer, Carson CIN 9
Palmer, David MIN 22
Palmer, Derrell CLE 42/72, zNYY 40
Palmer, Dick ATL 51, BUF 50, MIA 50, NOS 52
Palmer, Emile NOS 75
Palmer, Gery KCC 73
Palmer, Jesse NYG 3
Palmer, Leslie PHL 40/84
Palmer, Mitch MIN 51, TBB 54
Palmer, Paul DAL 26, DET 25, KCC 26
Palmer, Randy CLE 89
Palmer, Scott ARZ 76, NYJ 72
Palmer, Sterling WSH 97
Palmer, Tom PIT 77
Paluck, John WSH 85/86
Palumbo, Sam BUF 54, CLE 50/54, GBP 53
Panciera, Don DET 28, ARZ 9, zNYY 60
Pane, Chris DEN 23
Panelli, John DET 33
Panepinto, Mike BUF 47
Panfil, Ken ARZ 74, STL 73
Pangle, Hal ARZ 21
Pankey, Irv IND 75, STL 75
Pannell, Ernie GBP 22
Panos, Joe BUF 72, PHL 63/72
Paolucci, Ben DET 77
Papach, George PIT 27
Papale, Vince PHL 83
Papas, Nick OAK 12
Pape, Oran WSH 27, GBP 56
Papit, John WSH 15/25, GBP 22
Pappio, Joe ARZ 33
Pardee, Jack STL 32, WSH 32
Pardoner, Earl ARZ 12
Pardridge, Curt SEA 82

Paremore, Bob ARZ 23
Parilli, Babe NEP 15, CLE 18, GBP 10/15/16, NYJ 15, OAK 10
Paris, Bubba SFF 77, IND 79
Parish, Don ARZ 51/57, DEN 56, STL 57
Parish, James SFF 77
Parish, Scott DEN 74
Park, Ernie CIN 74, DEN 60, MIA 61, SDC 61
Park, Kaulana NYG 39
Parker, Ace xBKN 7, xBOS 31, zNYY 88
Parker, Andy OAK 81, SDC 85
Parker, Anthony IND 43, KCC 41, MIN 27, SFF 26, STL 27, TBB 27
Parker, Artimus NYJ 24, PHL 24
Parker, Buddy ARZ 15, DET 4
Parker, Carl CIN 86
Parker, Charlie DEN 60
Parker, Chris JAX 39
Parker, Daren DEN 1
Parker, Dave xBKN 32
Parker, Demond GBP 22
Parker, Don SFF 63
Parker, Eric SDC 88
Parker, Ervin BUF 62
Parker, Frank CLE 78, NYG 72, PIT 78
Parker, Freddie GBP 39
Parker, Glenn BUF 74, KCC 62, NYG 62
Parker, Howie zNYY 66
Parker, Jeff TBB 83
Parker, Jeremiah NYG 79
Parker, Jerry CLE 54
Parker, Jim IND 77
Parker, Joe ARZ 47/81
Parker, Joel NOS 42/88
Parker, Kenny NYG 26
Parker, Kerry BUF 23, KCC 21
Parker, Larry KCC 80
Parker, Orlando NYJ 89
Parker, Rickey JAX 29
Parker, Riddick BLT 91, NEP 97, SEA 76/97
Parker, Robert KCC 43
Parker, Rodney PHL 83
Parker, Sirr CIN 24
Parker, Steve IND 78
Parker, Steve NOS 96
Parker, Vaughn SDC 70
Parker, Willie BUF 56/61, DET 61
Parker, Willie TEN 74
Parkin, Dave DET 44
Parks, Billy DAL 21, SDC 32, TEN 20/32
Parks, Dave SFF 81, NOS 83, TEN 83
Parks, Jeff TBB 85, TEN 89
Parks, Limbo SFF 66/72

Parks, Mickey WSH 27, zCHI 27
Parks, Nate KCC 72, OAK 71
Parks, Rickey MIN 81
Parlavecchio, Chet ARZ 57, GBP 57
Parmalee, Bernie MIA 30, NYJ 34
Parmer, Jim PHL 43
Parnell, Babe NYG 12/29/41
Parrella, John BUF 92, OAK 97, SDC 97
Parriott, Bill xCIN ?
Parris, Gary ARZ 89, CLE 84, SDC 80
Parrish, Bernie CLE 30, TEN 30
Parrish, Don KCC 61
Parrish, James DAL 62, PIT 79
Parrish, Lemar CIN 20, BUF 24, WSH 24
Parrish, Tony CHI 37, SFF 33
Parros, Rick DEN 24, SEA 29
Parry, Ox NYG 44
Parseghian, Ara CLE 85
Parsley, Cliff TEN 18
Parson, Ray DET 79
Parsons, Bob CHI 86
Parsons, Earle SFF 84/94
Parsons, Lloyd DET 32
Parsons, Preston ARZ 15
Partee, Dennis SDC 29
Parten, Ty CIN 93, KCC 91/97
Partridge, Rick BUF 5, NOS 17, SDC 17
Paschal, Bill NYG 8/38, xBOS 8
Paschal, Doug MIN 40
Paschka, Gordon NYG 70, PHL 61, PIT 61
Pashe, Bill NYJ 26
Paskett, Keith GBP 82
Paskvan, George GBP 68
Pasqua, Joe STL 65, WSH 37
Pasquale, Ron ARZ 67
Pasquariello, Ralph ARZ 36, STL 36
Pasquesi, Tony ARZ 75
Pass, Patrick NEP 35
Pastin, Frank PIT 38
Pastorini, Dan TEN 7, OAK 7, PHL 6, STL 10
Pastrana, Al DEN 12
Patanelli, Mike zBRK ?
Pate, Lloyd BUF 33, ARZ 74, PHL 63
Patera, Dennis SFF 14
Patera, Jack ARZ 61, DAL 56, IND 61
Paterra, Greg ATL 26
Paterra, Herb BUF 30
Pathon, Jerome IND 86, NOS 80
Patmon, DeWayne NYG 28
Patrick, Frank ARZ 24, GBP 10

Patrick, Garin IND 64
Patrick, John PIT 17/27
Patrick, Mike NEP 2
Patrick, Wayne BUF 30
Patt, Maury DET 21
Patten, David CLE 82, NEP 86, NYG 83/85
Patten, Joel CLE 69, IND 65, OAK 71, SDC 78
Patterson, Billy CHI 57
Patterson, Craig ARZ 76
Patterson, Don DET 43, NYG 21
Patterson, Elvis DAL 43, NYG 34, OAK 43, SDC 34
Patterson, Paul zCHI 83
Patterson, Reno SFF 92
Patterson, Shawn GBP 96
Patterson, William PIT 12
Pattillo, Darrell SDC 31
Pattison, Mark NOS 88, OAK 89, STL 83
Patton, Bob BUF 65
Patton, Cliff PHL 65
Patton, James BUF 99
Patton, Jerry BUF 77, MIN 79, NEP 72, PHL 77
Patton, Jimmy NYG 20
Patton, Joe WSH 68
Patton, Marvcus BUF 53, KCC 53, WSH 53
Patton, Ricky ATL 33, GBP 30, SFF 32/42
Patton, Robert NYG 71
Patu, Saul TEN 79
Patulski, Walt ARZ 74, BUF 85
Paul, Don CLE 20, ARZ 22/37
Paul, Don STL 57
Paul, Harold SDC ?
Paul, Markus CHI 36, TBB 36
Paul, Tito ARZ 27, CIN 27, DEN 28, WSH 27
Paul, Whitney KCC 53/64, NOS 51
Paulekas, Tony GBP 39
Pauley, Frank Don CHI 14
Paulk, Jeff ATL 40, NEP 46
Paulson, Dainard NYJ 40
Paup, Bryce BUF 95, GBP 95, JAX 95, MIN 95
Pavelec, Ted DET 71
Pavkov, Stan PIT 30
Pavlich, Chuck SFF 37
Pawlawski, Mike TBB 9
Paxton, Lonnie NEP 66
Paye, John SFF 15
Payne, Charlie DET ?
Payne, Ken GBP 85, PHL 82
Payne, Rod CIN 64
Payne, Russell DEN 88
Payne, Seth HOU 91, JAX 91
Payton, Eddie CLE 36, DET 34, KCC 34, MIN 31
Payton, Sean CHI 17

Payton, Walter CHI 34
Peace, Larry xBKN 2
Peacock, Elvis CIN 20, STL 34
Peacock, Johnny TEN 44
Peaks, Clarence PHL 26, PIT 36
Pear, Dave TBB 76, IND 65, OAK 74
Pearce, Pard CHI 4/10
Pearcy, Jim zCHI 30
Pearson, Aaron KCC 96
Pearson, Barry KCC 85, PIT 83
Pearson, Bert CHI 26, ARZ 46
Pearson, Dennis ATL 81
Pearson, Drew DAL 88
Pearson, Jayice KCC 24, MIN 24
Pearson, Kalvin CLE 43
Pearson, Lindell GBP 26, DET 42
Pearson, Mike JAX 72
Pearson, Preston DAL 26, IND 26, PIT 26
Pearson, Willie MIA 41
Pease, Brent TEN 10
Peat, Todd ARZ 64, OAK 64/74
Peavey, Jack DEN 71
Peay, Francis GBP 71, KCC 75, NYG 78
Pebbles, Jim WSH 19
Pedersen, Win NYG 15, NYG 66, xBOS 43
Pederson, Doug CLE 18, GBP 18, MIA 14, PHL 14
Pederson, Jim CHI 17
Peebles, Danny CLE 80, TBB 83
Peek, Antwan HOU 98
Peelle, Justin SDC 84
Peete, Rodney CAR 9, DAL 9, DET 9, OAK 16, PHL 9, WSH 16
Peets, Brian SEA 88, SFF 82
Pegg, Harold PHL 19
Pegram, Erric ATL 33/41, NYG 33, PIT 20, SDC 24
Peguese, Willis IND 96, TEN 72
Peiffer, Dan CHI 53, WSH 56
Peko, Tupe IND 56
Pelfrey, Doug CIN 9
Pelfrey, Ray ARZ 83, GBP 8/26, NYG 80, xDAL 85
Pellegrini, Bob PHL 53, WSH 53
Pellegrini, Joe ATL 64, NYJ 62/77
Pellington, Bill IND 36/65
Pelluer, Scott NOS 53
Pelluer, Steve DAL 16, KCC 11
Pelshak, Troy JAX 54, STL 91
Pelton, Mike IND 99
Pena, Bob CLE 68

Penaranda, Jairo PHL 38, STL 22
Penchion, Bob SEA 67, SFF 66, BUF 69
Penn, Chris CHI 86, KCC 81, SDC 87
Penn, Jesse DAL 59
Pennington, Chad NYJ 10
Pennington, Durwood KCC 1
Pennington, Leon TBB 59
Pennison, Jay TEN 52
Pennywell, Carlos NEP 88
Pennywell, Robert ATL 59
Penrose, Craig DEN 12, NYJ 11
Pense, Leon PIT 18
Pentecost, John MIN 66
Peoples, George DAL 22, NEP 35, TBB 38
Peoples, Woody SFF 69, PHL 69
Pepper, Gene IND 60, WSH 61
Peppers, Julius CAR 90
Perantoni, Frank zNYY 20
Percival, Mac CHI 83, DAL 33
Perdue, Bolo NYG 24, zBRK 57
Perez, Joe KCC 12
Perez, Peter CHI 19
Pergine, John STL 52, WSH 52
Perina, Bob CHI 33, xBAL 84, zBRK 70, zCHI 84, zNYY 83
Perini, Pete CHI 39, CLE 54
Perkins, Art STL 37
Perkins, Bruce IND 34, TBB 32
Perkins, Don DAL 43
Perkins, Don CHI 19, GBP 23/48/53/58
Perkins, Horace KCC 20
Perkins, Jim DEN 71
Perkins, Johnny NYG 86
Perkins, Ray DAL 92
Perkins, Ray IND 27
Perkins, Willis TEN 64, NEP ?
Perko, John ARZ 39, PIT 39, zBUF 33
Perko, Mike ATL 71
Perko, Tom GBP 56
Perlo, Phil TEN 56
Perot, Pete PHL 62, NOS 71
Perpich, George zBAL 48, zBRK 40
Perreault, Pete CIN 64, MIN 68, NYJ 64
Perretta, Ralph NYG 59, SDC 53/61
Perrie, Michael STL 6
Perriman, Brett DET 80, KCC 85, MIA 80, NOS 80
Perrin, Benny ARZ 23
Perrin, Lonnie CHI 25, DEN 33/35, WSH 35
Perrino, Mike PHL 64
Perrotti, Mike zLAD 47

Perry, Claude GBP 24/26/27/32/37/50, xBKN 31
Perry, Darren NOS 39, PIT 39
Perry, Ed MIA 89
Perry, Gerry ARZ 79, DET 79
Perry, Gerald DEN 60, OAK 71, STL 64
Perry, Jason CIN 31, MIN 31, SDC 31
Perry, Joe SFF 34/74, IND 34
Perry, Leon NYG 30
Perry, Lowell PIT 41
Perry, Mario OAK 84
Perry, Marlo BUF 58
Perry, Michael Dean CLE 92, DEN 95, KCC 95
Perry, Rod STL 49, CLE 40
Perry, Scott CIN 32, SDC 32, SFF 32
Perry, Todd CHI 75, MIA 75
Perry, Vernon NOS 32, TEN 32
Perry, Victor ARZ 70
Perry, Wiliam CHI 72, PHL 90
Perry, Wilmont NOS 33
Perryman, Dean SEA 51
Perryman, Jim BUF 23/24, IND 43
Perryman, Ray BLT 25, JAX 23, OAK 31
Perryman, Robert DAL 39, DEN 33, NEP 34
Person, Ara ARZ 30
Pesonen, Dick GBP 48, MIN 22, NYG 25
Pesuit, Wally DET 67, MIA 65
Petchel, John PIT 57, STL 17/50
Pete, Lawrence DET 96
Peter, Christian CHI 97, IND 97, NYG 99
Peter, Jason CAR 97
Peters, Anton DEN 77
Peters, Floyd PHL 72, CLE 72/73, DET 72, WSH 78
Peters, Forest ARZ ?, DET ?, xBKN 32
Peters, Frank CIN 77
Peters, Scott NYG 63, PHL 62
Peters, Tony CLE 20, WSH 23
Peters, Tyrell BLT 53
Peters, Volney WSH 79, ARZ 76, OAK 79, PHL 76, SDC 70
Petersen, Kurt DAL 65
Petersen, Ted CLE 66, IND 71, PIT 66/71
Petersmark, Brett TEN 69
Peterson, Adrian CHI 29
Peterson, Andrew CAR 60
Peterson, Anthony CHI 57, SFF 50/53
Peterson, Ben CIN 50
Peterson, Bill CIN 53/87, KCC 55

Peterson, Cal KCC 50, DAL 58, OAK 54, TBB 58
Peterson, Gerald IND 76
Peterson, Ike DET 6
Peterson, Jim STL 57, TBB 57
Peterson, Joe NEP 45
Peterson, Julian SFF 98
Peterson, Ken ARZ 30
Peterson, Ken MIN 66
Peterson, Kenny GBP 98
Peterson, Les DET 9, GBP 29/43, xBKN 18/40
Peterson, Mike IND 52, JAX 54
Peterson, Nels WSH 28, STL 11
Peterson, Phil xBKN 30
Peterson, Ray GBP 33
Peterson, Russ WSH ?
Peterson, Todd ARZ 2, KCC 2, PIT 2, SEA 2, SFF 2
Peterson, Will NYG 24
Petitbon, John CLE 44, GBP 20, xDAL 23
Petitbon, Richie CHI 17, STL 17, WSH 16
Petitgout, Luke NYG 77
Petrella, Bob MIA 48
Petrella, John PIT 11
Petrich, Bob BUF 85, SDC 85
Petrilas, Bill NYG 3/18
Petro, Steve xBKN 31
Petrovich, George ARZ 18
Petry, Stan KCC 45, NOS 45
Pettey, Phil WSH 62
Petties, Neal IND 84
Pettigrew, Gary NYG 71, PHL 88
Pettitt, Duane SDC 93
Petty, John CHI 10
Petty, Ross CHI 17
Pettyjohn, Barry TEN 77
Petway, David GBP 47
Peutz, Gary WSH 71
Peviani, Bob NYG 76
Pfohl, Bob zBAL 85
Pharr, Tommy BUF 27
Phelps, Don CLE 44/94
Phenix, Perry CAR 20, TEN 35
Phifer, Roman NEP 95, NYJ 56, STL 58
Philbin, Gerry NYJ 81, PHL 77
Philcox, Todd CIN 10, CLE 17, JAX 5, SDC 15, TBB 15
Philion, Ed BUF 71/75
Philips, Jess OAK 35
Phillips, Anthony ATL 26, MIN 28
Phillips, Bobby MIN 30
Phillips, Charles OAK 47
Phillips, Ewell NYG 19
Phillips, George STL 16
Phillips, Irvin OAK 25, SDC 23

Phillips, Jason ATL 82, DET 24
Phillips, Jermaine TBB 23/33
Phillips, Jess CIN 30, NEP 35, NOS 34
Phillips, Jim STL 82, MIN 82
Phillips, Joe KCC 75, MIN 75/91, SDC 75, STL 66
Phillips, Joe WSH 80/84
Phillips, Kim BUF 43, NOS 43
Phillips, Kirk DAL 81
Phillips, Lawrence MIA 21, SFF 33, STL 21
Phillips, Lloyd CHI 86
Phillips, Mel SFF 32
Phillips, Mike zBAL 21
Phillips, Ray ATL 48, PHL 93
Phillips, Ray CIN 59, PHL 52
Phillips, Reggie ARZ 48, CHI 48
Phillips, Rod ARZ 36, STL 39
Phillips, Ryan IND 56, NYG 91
Phillips, Wes TEN 61
Phillpott, Ed NEP 52
Philpott, Dean ARZ 37
Philyaw, Charles OAK 77
Philyaw, Dino CAR 32, NOS 37
Philyaw, Mareno ATL 82
Phipps, Mike CHI 15, CLE 15
Piasecky, Al WSH 14/43
Piatukis, George PIT 33
Picard, Bob DET 44, PHL 82
Piccolo, Bill NYG 29
Piccolo, Brian CHI 41
Piccone, Lou BUF 89, NYJ 89
Pickard, Bob DET 86
Pickel, Bill NYJ 71, OAK 71
Pickens, Bob CHI 70
Pickens, Bruce ATL 39, GBP 38, KCC 39, OAK 39
Pickens, Carl CIN 80/81, TEN 86
Pickens, Lyle DEN 26
Pickering, Clay CHI 86, CIN 42, NEP 48
Pickett, Ryan STL 79
Pidgeon, Tim MIA 94
Piel, Mike STL 95
Piepul, Milt DET 38
Pierce, Aaron BLT 81, NYG 84
Pierce, Antonio WSH 58
Pierce, Calvin CLE 42
Pierce, Dan WSH 19
Pierce, Don ARZ 54, xBKN 5
Pierce, Steve CLE 28
Pierce, Terry DEN 58
Pieri, Damon CAR 27, NYJ 26
Pierre, Joe PIT 46
Pierson, Pete IND 69, TBB 69
Pierson, Reggie DET 27, TBB 20
Pierson, Shurron OAK 55
Pietrosante, Nick DET 33, CLE 36

Pietrzak, Jim KCC 62, NOS 76, NYG 76
Pifferini, Bob CHI 58, DET 53, STL 54
Piggot, Bert zLAD 84
Pihos, Pete PHL 35
Pike, Chris CLE 75, STL 93
Pike, Mark BUF 57/94
Pilconis, Joe PHL 2/18/24/28
Pilgrim, Evan ATL 63, CHI 65, DEN 74, TEN 61
Pillath, Roger PIT 58, STL 72
Piller, Zach TEN 69/71
Pillers, Lawrence ATL 65, NYJ 76, SFF 65
Pillman, Brian CIN 58/97
Pillow, Frank TBB 80
Pinckert, Ernie WSH 11
Pincura, Stanley STL 1/15
Pinder, Cyril CHI 22, DAL 33, PHL 22
Pine, Ed PIT 58, SFF 54
Pingel, Johnny DET 37
Pinkett, Allen TEN 20
Pinkney, Cleveland TBB 61
Pinkney, Lovell STL 83
Pinkney, Reggie DET 42, IND 37
Pinkston, Todd PHL 87
Pinner, Artose DET 21
Pinney, Ray PIT 53/65/74
Pinnock, Andrew SDC 30
Pipkin, Joyce NYG 31, zLAD 62
Pippins, Woodie KCC 41
Piro, Henry PHL 89
Pirro, Rocco PIT 23, zBUF 30/35
Pisarcik, Joe NYG 9, PHL 9
Pisarkiewicz, Steve GBP 19, ARZ 15
Piskor, Ray CLE 45
Piskor, Roman zNYY 41
Pitcock, Charles TBB 55
Pittman, Bryan HOU 48
Pittman, Charlie ARZ 28, IND 42
Pittman, Danny ARZ 85, NYG 82
Pittman, Julian NOS 75
Pittman, Kavika CAR 92, DAL 97, DEN 95
Pittman, Mel PIT 4
Pittman, Michael ARZ 32, TBB 32
Pitts, Alabama PHL 50
Pitts, Chester HOU 69
Pitts, Elijah GBP 22, NOS 22, STL 22
Pitts, Frank CLE 25/85, KCC 25, OAK 85
Pitts, Hugh STL 56, TEN 53
Pitts, John BUF 48, CLE 48, DEN 48
Pitts, Mike ATL 74, NEP 93, PHL 74

Pitts, Ron BUF 27, GBP 28
Pivarnick, Joe PHL 29
Pivec, Dave DEN 82, STL 83
Planansky, Joe MIA 88
Plank, Doug CHI 46
Plank, Earl xBKN 22
Plansky, Tony NYG 7/8, WSH ?
Plantz, Ron IND 67
Planutis, Jerry WSH 42
Plasman, Dick CHI 14, ARZ 16
Platukas, George STL 70
Player, Scott ARZ 10
Pleasant, Anthony ATL 96, BLT 98, CLE 98, NEP 98, NYJ 98, SFF 94
Pleasant, Marquis CIN 81
Pleasant, Mike STL 43
Pleasant, Reggie ATL 35
Ploeger, Kurt DAL 73, GBP 71, MIN 63
Plum, Milt CLE 16, DET 16, NYG 16, STL 16
Plummer, Ahmed SFF 29
Plummer, Bruce DEN 38, IND 23, MIA 38, SFF 28
Plummer, Chad IND 16/87
Plummer, Gary SDC 50, SFF 50
Plummer, Jake ARZ 16, DEN 16
Plummer, Tony ARZ 43, ATL 35, STL 21
Plump, Dave SDC 81
Plunkett, Art ARZ 70, NEP 70
Plunkett, Jim NEP 16, OAK 16, SFF 14/16
Plunkett, Sherman NYJ 79, IND 79, SDC 70
Plunkett, Warren STL 58
Ply, Bobby BUF 23, DEN 22, KCC 14
Poage, Ray ATL 85, MIN 86, NOS 85, PHL 35
Pochman, Owen NYG 9, SFF 11
Podmajersky, Paul CHI 31
Podolak, Ed KCC 14
Podoley, Jim WSH 24
Poe, Bill CIN 61
Poe, Johnnie NOS 25
Poillon, Dick WSH 25
Poimboeuf, Lance DAL 62
Poindexter, Anthony BLT 43
Pointer, John GBP 56
Pokorny, Frank PIT 80
Polamalu, Troy PIT 43
Polanski, John DET 32, zLAD 78
Polisky, John CHI 16/27
Polk, Carlos SDC 52/93
Polk, DaShon BUF 51/52
Polk, Octus CHI 69
Pollack, Frank SFF 72/75
Pollard, Al PHL 21, xNYB 56

Pollard, Bob ARZ 82, NOS 82
Pollard, Darryl SFF 26/36, TBB 31
Pollard, Frank PIT 30/44
Pollard, Marcus IND 81
Pollard, Trent CIN 76
Polley, Tom CLE 53, PHL 57
Polley, Tommy STL 52
Pollock, Bill CHI 2
Polofsky, Gordon ARZ 60
Polowski, Larry SEA 50
Polsfoot, Fran ARZ 41, WSH 82
Polti, Randy DEN 21, MIN 29
Ponder, David DAL 97
Ponder, Willie NYG 87
Ponds, Antwaune WSH 51
Pontbriand, Ryan CLE 64
Pool, David BUF 27/29, DEN 47, MIA 27, NEP 27
Pool, Hampton CHI 76, zMIA 55
Poole, Barney IND 83, NYG 78, xDAL 62/68, xNYB 84, zNYY 58
Poole, Bob SFF 82, TEN 88
Poole, Jim NYG 23/80, ARZ 48
Poole, Keith DEN 81, NOS 83
Poole, Ken MIA 78
Poole, Larry CLE 38, TEN 39
Poole, Nathan ARZ 19/89
Poole, Nathan CIN 35, DEN 34
Poole, Ollie DET 88, zBAL 54, zNYY 52
Poole, Ray NYG 82
Poole, Shelley ATL 24
Poole, Steve NYJ 54
Poole, Tyrone CAR 38, DEN 37, IND 38, NEP 38
Popa, Eli ARZ 47
Pope, Bucky GBP 80, STL 80
Pope, Daniel CIN 13, KCC 13
Pope, Ken NEP 41
Pope, Lew xCIN 2,32
Pope, Marquez CLE 23, OAK 23/49, SDC 30, SFF 23, STL 22
Pope, Monsanto DEN 75
Popovich, John ARZ 40, PIT 40
Popovich, Milt ARZ 66/77
Popson, Ted KCC 48, SFF 85
Porcher, Robert DET 91
Porell, Tom NEP 65
Port, Chris NOS 70
Porter, Alvin BLT 24
Porter, Daryl BUF 22, DET 38, TEN 44
Porter, Jack SDC 57
Porter, Jerry OAK 84/86
Porter, Joey PIT 55
Porter, Kerry BUF 30, DEN 31, OAK 31
Porter, Kevin KCC 27, NYJ 27

Porter, Lewis KCC 26

Porter, Rick DET 46, BUF 26, IND 20

Porter, Robert NYG 28

Porter, Ron IND 55, MIN 52, PHL 50

Porter, Rufus SEA 97, NOS 59, TBB 59

Porter, Tracy DET 89, IND 87

Porter, Willie NEP 27

Porterfield, Garry DAL 86

Portilla, Jose ATL 76

Portis, Clinton DEN 26

Posey, Jeff BUF 96, CAR 90, HOU 98, JAX 58, SFF 96

Post, Bobby NYG 22

Post, Dickie SDC 22, DEN 23, TEN 2

Postus, Al PIT 10

Poteat, Hank PIT 22, TBB 21

Poth, Phil PHL 23

Poto, John xBOS 30/16

Potteiger, Earl NYG 3/4/9

Potter, Kevin CHI 20

Potter, Steve BUF 58, KCC 58, MIA 54

Pottios, Myron PIT 66, WSH 66, STL 66

Potts, Charlie DET 27

Potts, Roosevelt BLT 42, IND 35/42, MIA 42

Pough, Ernest NYG 82, PIT 22/85

Pounds, Darryl DEN 31, WSH 31

Pourdanesh, Shar PIT 67/68, WSH 67

Powe, Karl DAL 81

Powe, Keith TBB 95

Powell, Alvin MIA 78, SEA 73

Powell, Andre NYG 51

Powell, Art OAK 84, BUF 84, NYJ 84, PHL 87

Powell, Carl BLT 76, CHI 72, CIN 91, IND 92, WSH 72

Powell, Charles SFF 87, OAK 87

Powell, Craig BLT 59, CLE 59

Powell, Darnell BUF 35, NYJ 20

Powell, Dick NYG 23, xCIN 50

Powell, Jeff SDC 31

Powell, Jemeel DAL 25

Powell, Jesse MIA 56

Powell, Jim PIT 51

Powell, Marvin NOS 40

Powell, Marvin NYJ 79, TBB 74

Powell, Preston CLE 40

Powell, Ronnie CLE 80

Powell, Steve BUF 23

Powell, Tim STL 64

Powers, Clyde KCC 29, NYG 29/39

Powers, Jim SFF 15/62

Powers, John MIN 83, PIT 88

Powers, Ricky CLE 22

Powers, Warren DEN 91, STL 98

Powers, Warren OAK 20

Powlus, Ron PHL 11

Pozderac, Phil DAL 75

Prater, Dean BUF 79, KCC 79

Prather, Dale STL 30

Prather, Guy GBP 51

Pratt, Robert IND 61, SEA 61

Prchlik, John DET 75

Preas, George IND 60

Prebola, Eugene DEN 88, OAK 89

Preece, Steve DEN 23, NOS 33, PHL 33, SEA 20, STL 20

Pregulman, Merv DET 57/67, GBP 17, xNYB 61

Prentice, Travis CLE 41, MIN 30

Prescott, Harold PHL 86, GBP 31, DET ?, xNYB 46

President, Andre CHI 87, NEP 88, PHL 48

Presnell, Glenn DET 3/18/20/60

Pressley, Leo WSH 48

Prestel, Jim CLE 70, MIN 79, NYG 72, WSH 74

Preston, Dave DEN 46

Preston, John ARZ 42

Preston, Pat CHI 53

Preston, Ray SDC 52

Preston, Roell GBP 88, ATL 85, MIA 82, SFF 15, TEN 84

Prestridge, Luke DEN 11, NEP 17

Prewitt, Felto zBAL 20, zBUF 21

Priatko, Bill PIT ?

Price, Art ATL 52

Price, Cotton DET 37/42/62, zMIA 63

Price, Daryl SFF 71/91/96

Price, Dennis NYJ 20, OAK 20

Price, Derek DET 82

Price, Eddie NYG 31

Price, Elex NOS 75

Price, Ernie DET 72, SEA 62

Price, Jim DAL 89, STL 87

Price, Jim DEN 56, NYJ 67

Price, Kenny NEP 54

Price, Marcus BUF 73, NOS 70, SDC 79

Price, Mitchell STL 27, ARZ 26, CIN 32

Price, Peerless ATL 81, BUF 81

Price, Sam MIA 30

Price, Shawn BUF 91, CAR 92, SDC 91, TBB 92

Price, Stacey SDC 53

Price, Terry CHI 65

Pricer, Bill KCC 33, IND 31

Pride, Dan CHI 57

Pridemore, Tom ATL 27

Priestly, Robert PHL 81

Primus, Greg CHI 87

Primus, James ATL 49

Prince, Ryan JAX 89

Principe, Dom NYG 25/26, zBRK 94

Prindle, Mike DET 19

Pringle, Alan DET ?

Pringle, Mike ATL 24

Pringley, Mike DET 92, SDC 79

Print, Bob SDC 57

Prioleau, Pierson BUF 23, SFF 23

Prior, Anthony MIN 40, NYJ 37, OAK 25

Prior, Mike GBP 39/45, IND 39, TBB 24

Prisby, Errol DEN 25

Prisco, Nick PHL 18

Pritchard, Bosh NYG 35, PHL 30, STL 56

Pritchard, Mike ATL 35, DEN 81, SEA 85

Pritchard, Ron CIN 60, TEN 58

Pritchett, Billy CLE 39, ATL 39

Pritchett, Kelvin DET 93/94, JAX 94

Pritchett, Stanley CHI 36, MIA 36, PHL 36

Pritchett, Wes ATL 51

Pritko, Stephen STL 30, GBP 23, NYG 11, xBOS 17, xNYB 17

Proby, Bryan KCC 67

Procell, Jarrett ARZ 90

Prochaska, Raymond STL 8

Proctor, Dewey zCHI 77, zNYY 73/72

Proctor, Rex CHI 47

Proehl, Ricky ARZ 87, CAR 81, CHI 87, SEA 88, STL 87

Profit, Eugene NEP 22

Profit, Joe ATL 23, NOS 23

Prokop, Eddie zCHI 70, zNYY 72

Prokop, Joe GBP 11, MIA 7, NYG 4, NYJ 6, SDC 8, SFF 4

Promuto, Vince WSH 65

Protz, Jack SDC 50

Prout, Bob NYJ 25, OAK 29

Provence, Andrew ATL 72

Provo, Fred GBP 80

Provost, Ted ARZ 41, MIN 28

Prudhomme, Remi BUF 65/68, KCC 65, NOS 65

Pruett, Perry NEP 39

Pruitt, Greg CLE 34, OAK 34

Pruitt, James IND 49/86, MIA 81/82/87

Pruitt, Mickey CHI 46/52, DAL 52

Pruitt, Mike CLE 43, BUF 33/41, KCC 43

Pryce, Trevor DEN 93

Pryor, Barry MIA 31

Psaltis, Jim ARZ 24, GBP 48
Ptacek, Bob CLE 18
Pucci, Ben CLE 45, zBUF 40, zCHI 49
Pucillo, Mike BUF 61
Puddy, Harold SFF 46
Pudloski, Chester STL 40
Puetz, Garry NEP 77, NYJ 78, PHL 64, TBB 72
Pugh, David IND 95
Pugh, Jethro DAL 75
Pugh, Marion NYG 5/30, zMIA 67
Puki, Craig ARZ 50, SFF 54
Pumphrey, Don TBB 64
Puplis, Andy ARZ 88
Pupunu, Alfred DET 81, KCC 85, NYG 85, SDC 86/89
Purcell, Jim STL 53
Purdin, Cal ARZ 11, zBRK 73, zMIA ?
Purdy, Pid GBP 5/7/18
Pureifory, Dave CIN 68, DET 75, GBP 75
Purling, Dave STL 67
Purnell, Frank GBP 33
Purnell, James CHI 53
Purnell, Lovett BLT 80, NEP 48/85
Purvis, Andre CIN 97
Purvis, Vic NEP 31
Putman, Earl ARZ 50
Putnam, Duane STL 61, CLE 62, DAL 61
Putzier, Jeb DEN 88
Putzier, Rollin PIT 76, SFF 64/76
Puzzuoli, Dave CLE 72
Pyatt, Brad IND 84
Pyburn, Jack MIA 65/71
Pyeatt, John DEN 83
Pyle, Mike CHI 50
Pyle, Palmer IND 62, MIN 69, OAK 68
Pyles, David OAK 63
Pylman, Bob PHL 39
Pyne, George NEP 75
Pyne, Jim CLE 71, DET 61, PHL 73, TBB 60
Quaerna, Jerry DET 68
Quarles, Bernard STL 9
Quarles, Shelton TBB 53
Quatse, Jess GBP 23/36, NYG 9, PIT 48
Quayle, Frank DEN 26
Queen, Jeff OAK 47, SDC 47, TEN 46
Query, Jeff CIN 89, GBP 85, WSH 16
Quick, Greg ATL 62
Quick, Jerry PIT 76
Quick, Mike PHL 82
Quillan, Fred SFF 56
Quillen, Frank zCHI 52
Quilter, Chuck SFF 45

Quinlan, Bill CLE 84, DET 83, GBP 83, PHL 83, WSH 85
Quinlan, Skeets STL 21
Quinlan, Volney CLE 43
Quinn, Jeff TBB 15
Quinn, Jonathan JAX 12, KCC 12
Quinn, Kelly MIN 92
Quinn, Mike DAL 11, HOU 11, IND 11, PIT 11
Quinn, Steve TEN 54
Quirk, Ed WSH 34
Raab, Marc SDC 57, WSH 50
Raba, Bob IND 85, NYJ 86, WSH 91
Rabach, Casey BLT 61
Rabb, Warren BUF 17, DET 18
Rabold, Michael ARZ 65, CHI 64, DET 64, MIN 64
Raborn, Carroll PIT 13/16
Rachal, Latario SDC 85
Rackers, Neil ARZ 1, CIN 5
Rackley, David NOS 47
Rackley, Derek ATL 48
Radachowsky, George IND 21, NYJ 25
Rade, John ATL 59
Radecic, Keith ARZ 51
Radecic, Scott BUF 97, IND 52/97, KCC 97
Rademacher, Bill NEP 33, NYJ 23
Radford, Bruce ARZ 79, DEN 78, TBB 78
Radick, Ken GBP 33/35, xBKN 24
Radloff, Wayne ATL 55
Rado, Alex PIT 12
Rado, George PIT 5/13/18, PHL 27
Radosevich, George IND 52
Radosevich, George IND 72
Radovich, Bill DET 28/66/73, zLAD 33
Rae, Mike OAK 15, TBB 15, WSH 15
Raffel, Bill xBKN 26/33
Rafferty, Ian NYJ 75
Rafferty, Tom DAL 64
Rafferty, Vince GBP 50
Ragazzo, Phil PHL 31/77, NYG 39/71, STL 36
Raglin, Floyd MIA 24
Ragone, Dave HOU 4
Ragsdale, George TBB 23
Ragunas, Vince PIT 30
Ragusa, Pat NYJ 11
Raible, Steve SEA 83
Raiff, Jim IND 60
Raimey, Dave CLE 26
Raimondi, Ben zNYY 88
Raines, Mike SFF 87
Rainier, Wali CLE 58, DET 58
Rains, Dan CHI 53

Raiola, Dominic DET 51
Rajkovich, Pete PIT 19
Rakestraw, Larry CHI 12
Rakoczy, Gregg CLE 73, NEP 71
Ralph, Dan ARZ 72
Rambo, Ken-Yon DAL 87
Ramey, Jim ARZ 79, TBB 98
Ramirez, Tony DET 75
Ramsey, Chuck NYJ 15
Ramsey, Derrick DET 87, NEP 88, OAK 84
Ramsey, Frank CHI 13
Ramsey, Garrard ARZ 20
Ramsey, Greg SEA 76
Ramsey, Herschel PHL 12/88
Ramsey, Knox ARZ 70, PHL 62, WSH 68, zLAD 32
Ramsey, Nate NOS 21, PHL 24
Ramsey, Patrick WSH 11
Ramsey, Ray ARZ 87, zBRK 91, zCHI 88/81
Ramsey, Steve DEN 10, NOS 16
Ramsey, Tom IND 14, NEP 12
Ramson, Eason BUF 87, SFF 80, ARZ 80
Randall, Dennis CIN 81, NYJ 73
Randall, Greg HOU 68, NEP 64
Randall, Tom DAL 60, TEN 68
Randle El, Antwaan PIT 82
Randle, Ervin KCC 55, TBB 54
Randle, John MIN 93, SEA 93
Randle, Sonny ARZ 88, DAL 88, SFF 83
Randle, Tate IND 35, MIA 21, TEN 21
Randolph, Al BUF 24, CIN 27, DET 45, GBP 27, MIN 34, SFF 27
Randolph, Clare ARZ 17, DET 4/5/17/43
Randolph, Terry GBP 23
Randolph, Thomas CIN 20, IND 27, NYG 23
Rankin, Walt ARZ 28/40/42/63, PIT 28
Ransom, Brian TEN 12
Ransom, Derrick ARZ 95, KCC 95
Ranspot, Keith ARZ 6, DET ?, GBP 27, xBKN 14, xBOS 14
Rapacz, Johnny NYG 53, zCHI 20
Rapp, Manual STL 67, xSTL 65
Rasby, Walter CAR 88/89, DET 89, NOS 86, PIT 84, WSH 86
Rascher, Am DET 15
Rash, Lou GBP 34, PHL 28
Rashad, Ahmad MIN 28, ARZ 28, BUF 27

Rasheed, Kenyon NYG 44, NYJ
34
Rasheed, Saleem SFF 51
Raskowski, Leo PHL 45, PIT
43, xBKN 70
Rasley, Rocky DET 67, KCC 66,
NOS 66, SFF 63
Rasmussen, Kemp CAR 97
Rasmussen, Randy MIN 52,
NYJ 66, PIT 60
Rasmussen, Wayne DET 47
Rassas, Nick ATL 27
Rather, Bo CHI 80, MIA 82/85
Rathman, Tom OAK 44, SFF
44
Ratica, Joe xBKN 21
Ratigan, Brian IND 52
Ratkowski, Ray NEP 23
Ratliff, Don PHL 77
Rattay, Tim SFF 13
Ratterman, George CLE 16,
xNYB 61/25, zBUF 61
Rauch, John PHL 11, xNYB 18
Ravensburg, Bob ARZ 61
Ravotti, Eric PIT 57
Ray, Baby GBP 44/58
Ray, Darrol NYJ 28
Ray, David STL 27
Ray, Eddie ATL 44, BUF 38/42,
NEP 36, SDC 36
Ray, John IND 68
Ray, Marcus OAK 42
Ray, Ricky MIA 43, NOS 22
Ray, Terry ATL 30, NEP 23
Rayam, Tom CIN 61
Raybon, Israel CAR 92, PIT 91
Rayburn, Sam PHL 91
Rayburn, Van xBKN 3,5
Raye Jr., Jimmy STL 18
Raye, Jim PHL 30
Rayhle, Fred SEA 82
Raymer, Cory SDC 66, WSH
52
Raymond, Corey DET 31, NYG
39
Razzano, Rick CIN 51
Reach, Kevin SFF 65
Reader, Jamie PHL 34
Reader, Russ CHI 11
Readon, Ike MIA 79
Reagan, Frank NYG 4/8/44,
PHL 40
Reagor, Montae DEN 99, IND
90
Ream, Charles STL 39
Reamon, Tommy KCC 21
Reardon, Kerry KCC 15
Reasons, Gary CIN 52, NYG
55
Reaves, John CIN 11, MIN 11,
PHL 6/7, TBB 7, TEN 8
Reaves, Ken ATL 36, ARZ 36,
NOS 21
Reaves, Willard MIA 38, WSH
38

Reavis, Dave PIT 74, TBB 75
Rebowe, Rusty NOS 56
Recher, Dave PHL 50/51
Rechichar, Bert IND 44, CLE 15,
NYJ 44, PIT 44
Reckmack, Ray DET 4, xBKN
14
Rector, Ron ATL 29, WSH 24
Redd, Glen IND 58, NOS 58
Redden, Barry CLE 35, SDC 20,
STL 30
Redding, Cory DET 78
Redding, Reggie ATL 70, NEP
70
Redick, Cornelius GBP 87
Redman, Chris BLT 7
Redman, Rick SDC 66
Redmon, Anthony ARZ 60,
ATL 61, CAR 61
Redmond, J.R. NEP 21, OAK
27
Redmond, Jimmy JAX 17/87
Redmond, Rudy ATL 47, DET
46
Redmond, Thomas ARZ 65/66
Redwine, Jarvis MIN 22
Reeberg, Lucien DET 61
Reece, Beasley DAL 82, NYG
28, TBB 43
Reece, Booker STL 66
Reece, Danny TBB 46
Reece, Don zMIA 45
Reece, Geoff SEA 55, STL 54
Reece, John DAL 41, STL 21
Reece, Travis DET 36
Reed, Alvin TEN 89, WSH 88
Reed, Andre BUF 83, WSH 84
Reed, Benton NEP 71
Reed, Bob MIN 27
Reed, Bob WSH 67
Reed, Doug STL 93
Reed, Ed BLT 20
Reed, Frank ATL 28
Reed, Henry NYG 80
Reed, Jake MIN 86, NOS 86
Reed, James NYJ 93
Reed, James PHL 57
Reed, Jeff PIT 3
Reed, Joe ARZ 4/16/19
Reed, Joe DET 14, SFF 13/17/
19
Reed, Josh BUF 82
Reed, Leo DEN 76, TEN 66
Reed, Mark IND 8
Reed, Max NYG 17
Reed, Michael CAR 45, PHL
39
Reed, Oscar ATL 30, MIN 32
Reed, Robert SDC 85
Reed, Smith NYG 33
Reed, Taft PHL 17
Reed, Tony DEN 32, KCC 32
Reeder, Dan PIT 40
Reese, Albert SFF 71
Reese, Archie OAK 74, SFF 78

Reese, Booker TBB 66
Reese, Don MIA 60/76, NOS
60, SDC 60
Reese, Guy ATL 76, DAL 68,
IND 75
Reese, Hank NYG 55, PHL
20/25
Reese, Ike PHL 58
Reese, Izell BUF 43, DAL 43,
DEN 43
Reese, Jerry BUF 81
Reese, Jerry KCC 31
Reese, Jerry PIT 64
Reese, Ken DET 48
Reese, Lloyd CHI 22
Reese, Steve NYJ 52/94, TBB
52
Reeves, Bryan ARZ 80
Reeves, Carl CHI 68
Reeves, Dan DAL 30
Reeves, John SDC 52
Reeves, Ken CLE 77, PHL 66
Reeves, Marion PHL 45
Reeves, Roy BUF 28
Reeves, Walter ARZ 89, CLE
86/89, SDC 46/82
Regent, Shawn OAK 62
Reger, John PIT 50, WSH 51
Regner, Tom TEN 60
Regular, Moses NYG 86
Rehage, Steve NYG 37
Rehberg, Scott CIN 79, CLE 79,
NEP 60
Rehder, Tom NEP 76, NYG 64
Rehnquist, Milt NYG 29, WSH
?
Reich, Frank BUF 14, CAR 14,
DET 14, NYJ 7
Reichardt, Bill GBP 37
Reichenbach, Mike MIA 52,
PHL 55
Reichow, Jerry MIN 89, DET
15/80, PHL 17
Reid, Alan PHL 24
Reid, Andy BUF 33
Reid, Bill SFF 54
Reid, Floyd GBP 24/80
Reid, Gabriel CHI 48
Reid, Jim TEN 67
Reid, Joe STL 35, xDAL 52
Reid, Michael ATL 95
Reid, Mike CIN 74
Reid, Mike PHL 42
Reid, Spencer CAR 56, IND 56
Reifsnyder, Bob NYJ 79
Reihner, George TEN 64
Reilly, Dameon MIA 83
Reilly, Jim BUF 61
Reilly, Kevin NEP 55, PHL 52
Reilly, Mike CHI 62, MIN 56
Reilly, Mike STL 57
Reimers, Bruce CIN 75, TBB
66
Reinfeldt, Mike TEN 37, OAK
37

Reinhard, Bill zLAD 60/88
Reinhard, Bob STL 54, zLAD 45
Reinke, Jeff CIN 67
Reissig, Bill xBKN 0
Reisz, Albie STL 26, zBUF 63
Rembert, Johnny NEP 52
Rembert, Reggie CIN 88
Remington, Bill SFF 23
Remmert, Dennis BUF 53
Remo, Roger IND 90
Remsberg, Dan DEN 74
Renfro, Dean IND 20
Renfro, Dick SFF 73
Renfro, Leonard PHL 94
Renfro, Mel DAL 20
Renfro, Mike DAL 82, TEN 82
Renfro, Ray CLE 26
Renfro, Will PHL 66, PIT 73, WSH 71
Renfroe, Gilbert MIN 14
Rengel, Mike NOS 75
Renn, Bobby NYJ 10
Rennaker, Terry SEA 59
Renner, Bill GBP 13
Rentie, Caesar CHI 71
Rentner, Ernest CHI 7/23, WSH 31
Rentz, Larry SDC 48
Rentzel, Lance DAL 19, MIN 19, STL 13/19
Repko, Jay PHL 89
Repko, Joe PIT 38, STL 42
Reppond, Mike CHI 81
Ressler, Glenn IND 62
Restic, Joe PHL 82
Retzlaff, Pete PHL 25/44
Reutershan, Randy PIT 40
Reutt, Ray PHL 81, PIT 81
Reveiz, Fuad MIN 7, MIA 7, SDC 7
Rexer, Freeman ARZ 17/62/63, DET 52, xBOS 24
Reyes, Tutan CAR 76, NOS 76
Reynolds, Al KCC 60
Reynolds, Bill ARZ 49, xBKN 15
Reynolds, Billy CLE 46, OAK 46, PIT 46
Reynolds, Bob ARZ 71, NEP 74
Reynolds, Bob DET 24
Reynolds, Chuck CLE 55
Reynolds, Ed NEP 95, NYG 95
Reynolds, Homer xSTL 10
Reynolds, Jack STL 54/64, SFF 64
Reynolds, Jamal GBP 99
Reynolds, Jerry DAL 76, NYG 66
Reynolds, Jim PIT 74
Reynolds, Jim zMIA 73/58

Reynolds, Joffrey STL 26
Reynolds, John ARZ 24
Reynolds, M.C. BUF 14, OAK 17, ARZ 17, WSH 17
Reynolds, Owens NYG 17
Reynolds, Ricky NEP 21, TBB 29
Reynolds, Tom CHI 87, NEP 21
Rhea, Floyd ARZ 64, DET ?, xBKN 24, xBOS 42
Rhea, Hughie xBKN 25/99
Rheams, Leonta NEP 75
Rhem, Steve NOS 84
Rhett, Errict BLT 32, CLE 23, TBB 32
Rhinehart, Coby ARZ 23
Rhodemyre, Jay GBP 22/50/85
Rhodes, Bruce DET 33, SFF 23
Rhodes, Danny IND 56
Rhodes, Dominic IND 33
Rhodes, Don PIT 43
Rhodes, Ray NYG 22/82, SFF 26
Rhome, Jerry CLE 17, DAL 13, STL 17, TEN 17
Rhone, Earnie MIA 55
Rhymes, Buster MIN 88
Ribar, Frank WSH 40
Ribble, Dave DET 14
Ribble, Loran ARZ 36, PIT 18
Riblett, Paul xBKN 19/7/25/6/20/11
Ricard, Alan BLT 39
Ricardo, Benny BUF 1, DET 1, MIN 1, NOS 1, SDC 1
Ricca, Jim PHL 71, WSH 55
Rice, Allen GBP 31, MIN 36
Rice, Andy CHI 70, CIN 70, SDC 79, TEN 80, KCC 58
Rice, Dan CIN 46
Rice, Floyd NOS 55, OAK 52, SDC 57, TEN 85
Rice, George TEN 72
Rice, Harold OAK 67
Rice, Jerry SFF 80, OAK 80
Rice, Ken BUF 75, MIA 75, OAK 75
Rice, Orian NYG 2
Rice, Rodney NEP 43, TBB 31
Rice, Ron DET 28
Rice, Simeon ARZ 79/97, TBB 97
Rich, Herb NYG 27, STL 42, xBAL 87
Rich, Randy CLE 24, DEN 40, DET 31, OAK 27
Richard, Gary GBP 46
Richard, Kris SEA 42
Richard, Stanley SDC 24, WSH 24
Richards, Bobby ATL 68, PHL 68
Richards, Curvin DAL 27

Richards, Dave ATL 62, DET 67, NEP 62, SDC 65
Richards, Dick xBKN 21/11
Richards, Golden CHI 83, DAL 83
Richards, Howard DAL 70, SEA ?
Richards, Jim NYJ 26
Richards, Kink NYG 13
Richards, Paul STL 50
Richards, Perry ARZ 85, BUF 84, DET 87, NYJ 80, PIT 86/89
Richards, Ray CHI 44, DET 25
Richardson, Al ATL 56
Richardson, Al NEP 79
Richardson, Bob DEN 43
Richardson, Bucky TEN 7
Richardson, C.J. ARZ 39, SEA 29
Richardson, Damien CAR 39
Richardson, Eric BUF 82
Richardson, Gloster CLE 42, DAL 31, KCC 30
Richardson, Grady WSH 89
Richardson, Greg MIN 89, TBB 89
Richardson, Huey NYJ 95, PIT 90, WSH 90
Richardson, Jeff MIA 76, NYJ 74
Richardson, Jerry ATL 43, STL 43
Richardson, Jerry IND 87
Richardson, Jess PHL 65/72, NEP 75
Richardson, John ARZ 71, MIA 74
Richardson, Kyle BLT 5, CIN 10, MIA 5, MIN 5, SEA 5
Richardson, Mike CHI 27, SFF 27
Richardson, Mike TEN 24
Richardson, Paul PHL 81
Richardson, Pete BUF 47
Richardson, Reggie STL 37
Richardson, Terry PIT 44
Richardson, Tom NEP 49
Richardson, Tony KCC 49
Richardson, Wally ATL 14, BLT 14
Richardson, Willie IND 87, MIA 87
Richeson, Ray zCHI 32
Richey, Mike BUF 75, NOS 75
Richey, Tom CIN 68
Richey, Wade BLT 9, SDC 10, SFF 7
Richie, David DEN 99, JAX 98, SFF 93/94
Richins, Al DET 6
Richman, Harry CHI 16
Richmond, Rock PIT 38
Richter, Frank DEN 58

Richter, Les STL 48/67
Richter, Pat WSH 88
Ricketts, Tom IND 68, KCC 64, PIT 71
Ricks, Harold TBB 47
Ricks, Lawrence KCC 42
Ricks, Mikhael DET 86, KCC 85, SDC 86
Ridder, Tom IND 72
Riddick, Louis ATL 26/29, CLE 42, OAK 41
Riddick, Ray GBP 5/19/22
Riddick, Robb BUF 40
Ridge, Houston SDC 80
Ridgeway, Colin DAL 88
Ridgle, Elston ARZ 74, BUF 98, CIN 72, SEA 98, SFF 96
Ridlehuber, Preston ATL 32, BUF 31/36, OAK 37
Ridlon, Jim DAL 42, SFF 42
Riehm, Chris OAK 77
Riemersma, Jay BUF 49/85, PIT 85
Rienstra, John CLE 70, PIT 79
Riesenberg, Doug NYG 72, TBB 79
Rieth, William STL 3/6
Rieves, Charles OAK 32/48, TEN 30
Rifenberg, Dick DET 89
Riffle, Charles STL 31, zNYY 35
Riffle, Dick PHL 45, PIT 12/27
Riggins, Charles TBB 94
Riggins, John NYJ 44, WSH 44
Riggle, Bob ATL 20
Riggs, Gerald ATL 42, WSH 37
Riggs, Jim CIN 87, WSH 82
Riggs, Thron xBOS 36
Righetti, Joe CLE 70
Riley, Avon PIT 99, TEN 53
Riley, Bob CIN 66/99
Riley, Butch IND 54
Riley, Cameron PIT 47
Riley, Earl DAL 30
Riley, Eric NYJ 87
Riley, Eugene DET 89, IND 87
Riley, Jack WSH 21
Riley, Jim MIA 70
Riley, Karon ATL 51, CHI 95
Riley, Ken CIN 13
Riley, Larry DEN 26, NYJ 34
Riley, Lee DET 44, NYG 21, NYJ 22, PHL 22
Riley, Pat CHI 78/95, SEA 78
Riley, Preston NOS 84, SFF 85
Riley, Steve MIN 78
Riley, Victor KCC 66, NOS 66/68
Rimington, Dave CIN 50/52/64, PHL 50
Rindy, Stuart CHI 69
Ring, Bill SFF 30
Ringo, Jim GBP 51, PHL 54

Ringwalt, Carroll DET 53
Riordan, Tim NOS 14
Risher, Alan GBP 11, TBB 7
Risien, Cody CLE 63
Risk, Ed ARZ ?
Rison, Andre ATL 80, CLE 80, GBP 84, IND 87, JAX 81, KCC 89, OAK 80
Rissmiller, Ray BUF 74, NOS 77, PHL 77
Risvold, Ray ARZ 5
Ritcher, Jim BUF 51, ATL 51
Ritchey, James TEN 16
Ritchhart, Del DET 13
Ritchie, Jon OAK 40, PHL 48
Rivera, Gabe PIT 69
Rivera, Hank BUF 20, OAK 23/41
Rivera, Marco GBP 62
Rivera, Ron CHI 59
Rivera, Steve CHI 83, SFF 80
Rivers, Garland CHI 32
Rivers, Jamie ARZ 53, NYJ 54
Rivers, Marcellus NYG 83
Rivers, Nate NYG 34
Rivers, Reggie DEN 38
Rivers, Ron ATL 20, DET 34
Rives, Don CHI 57
Rizzo, Jack NYG 34
Rizzo, Joe DEN 59
Roach, John ARZ 12, DAL 12, GBP 10/18
Roach, Travis NYJ 63
Roaches, Carl TEN 85, NOS 83
Roaf, William KCC 77, NOS 77
Roan, Michael TEN 80
Roan, Oscar CLE 81
Robb, Joe ARZ 84, DET 84, PHL 66
Robbins, Austin GBP 99, NOS 95, OAK 95
Robbins, Barret OAK 63
Robbins, Fred MIN 98
Robbins, John ARZ 55
Robbins, Kevin STL 72
Robbins, Randy DEN 48, NEP 48
Robbins, Tootie ARZ 63, GBP 73
Roberg, Mike IND 85, TBB 89
Roberson, Bo OAK 40, BUF 46, MIA 40, SDC 26
Roberson, James JAX 92, TEN 90
Roberson, Lake DET 66
Roberson, Van SFF 49
Roberson, Vern MIA 42
Roberts, Alfredo DAL 87, KCC 87
Roberts, Archie MIA 16
Roberts, Bill GBP 22
Roberts, C.R. SFF 32
Roberts, Choo-Choo NYG 35
Roberts, Cliff OAK 71
Roberts, Fred DET 15/50

Roberts, Gary ATL 62
Roberts, George ATL 12, MIA 4, SDC 4
Roberts, Greg TBB 61
Roberts, Guy ATL 56, MIA 59, TEN 56/57
Roberts, Hal ARZ 14
Roberts, Jack WSH 29, PHL 12, PIT 19
Roberts, Larry SFF 91
Roberts, Ray DET 72, SEA 73
Roberts, Terrell CIN 30
Roberts, Tim NEP 94, TEN 68
Roberts, Tom CHI 82, NYG 39
Roberts, Walt NOS 27, CLE 27, WSH 47
Roberts, Wesley NYJ 92
Roberts, William NYG 66, NEP 76
Roberts, Willie CHI 24
Robertson, Bernard CHI 74
Robertson, Bob TEN 73
Robertson, Bob xBKN 4
Robertson, Dewayne NYJ 63
Robertson, Isiah STL 58, BUF 58
Robertson, Jamal SFF 25
Robertson, Marcus SEA 31, TEN 31
Robertson, Tom xBKN 14, zNYY 22
Robertson, Tyrone BUF 92
Robinson, Bill GBP 41, NYJ ?
Robinson, Billy CLE 30
Robinson, Bo ATL 33, DET 36, NEP 41
Robinson, Bryan CHI 98, STL 92
Robinson, Burle PHL 27
Robinson, Charles IND 66, GBP 18
Robinson, Craig NOS 70
Robinson, Damien NYJ 22, SEA 22, TBB 24
Robinson, Dave GBP 89, WSH 89
Robinson, DeJuan CLE 23
Robinson, Don ATL 74
Robinson, Ed PIT 51
Robinson, Eddie BUF 55, JAX 50, TEN 50/55
Robinson, Eugene ATL 41, CAR 41, GBP 41, SEA 41
Robinson, Frank CIN 23, DEN 36
Robinson, Fred CLE 63
Robinson, Fred MIA 91, SDC 90
Robinson, Freddie IND 47
Robinson, Gerald MIN 95, SDC 98, STL 97
Robinson, Gil PIT 25
Robinson, Glenn IND 71, TBB 64

Robinson, Greg OAK 28, STL 28

Robinson, Greg NEP 61, TBB 64

Robinson, Gregg NYJ 64

Robinson, Jack ARZ 49, PIT 29, STL 19, xBKN 22

Robinson, Jacque PHL 22

Robinson, Jeff DAL 85, DEN 94, STL 45/94

Robinson, Jeroy ARZ 50, DEN 95

Robinson, Jerry NYJ 28, SDC 29

Robinson, Jerry PHL 56, OAK 57

Robinson, Jim NYG 85, SFF 85

Robinson, Johnnie DET 49

Robinson, Johnny KCC 42

Robinson, Johnny OAK 68

Robinson, Junior DET 27, NEP 27

Robinson, Koren SEA 81

Robinson, Larry DAL 45

Robinson, Larry NYJ 49

Robinson, Lybrant WSH 78

Robinson, Marcus BLT 87, CHI 88

Robinson, Mark KCC 30, TBB 30

Robinson, Matt BUF 17, DEN 17, NYJ 17

Robinson, Michael GBP 46

Robinson, Mike CLE 92

Robinson, Patrick ARZ 82, CIN 81

Robinson, Paul CIN 18, TEN 18

Robinson, Rafael SEA 21/37, TEN 37

Robinson, Rex NEP 7

Robinson, Roderick IND 8, JAX 10

Robinson, Shelton DET 51, SEA 57

Robinson, Stacy NYG 81

Robinson, Terrence ATL 92

Robinson, Tony WSH 15

Robinson, Travaris ATL 43, TBB 28

Robinson, Virgil NOS 47

Robinson, Wayne PHL 52

Robiskie, Terry MIA 38, OAK 35

Robison, George xDAL 34

Robison, Tommy ATL 66, GBP 77

Robl, Hal ARZ 20

Robnett, Ed SFF 71

Robnett, Marshall ARZ 21/43, PIT 21

Robotti, Frank NEP 51

Robustelli, Andy NYG 81, STL 84

Roby, Reggie MIA 4, SFF 4, TBB 1, TEN 7, WSH 1

Roche, Alden DEN 77, GBP 87, SEA 75

Roche, Brian KCC 85, SDC 87

Rochester, Paul KCC 72, NYJ 72/73

Rock, Walter SFF 67, WSH 76

Rockenbach, Lyle DET 68

Rocker, David STL 92

Rocker, Tracy WSH 99

Rockford, Jim SDC 28

Rockins, Chris CLE 37

Rockwell, Henry STL 17, zLAD 29/33

Rodak, Michael STL 23

Rodak, Mike PIT 40

Rodenberger, Jeff NOS 34

Rodenhauser, Mark CAR 63, CHI 51/52, DET 63, MIN 60, PIT 60, SDC 64, SEA 61

Roder, Mirro CHI 15, TBB 5

Roderick, John MIA 87, OAK 41

Rodgers, Del GBP 35

Rodgers, Del SFF 25/35/46

Rodgers, Derrick MIA 59, NOS 59

Rodgers, Doug ATL 77

Rodgers, Hosea zLAD 73

Rodgers, John PIT 87/88

Rodgers, Johnny SDC 20

Rodgers, Tom xBOS 59

Rodgers, Tyrone SEA 91

Rodgers, Willie TEN 34

Rodriguez, Mike OAK 74

Rodriguez, Ruben DEN 4, NYG 8, SEA 5

Roe, Bill DAL 56, NOS 54

Roe, James BLT 83

Roedal, Herb OAK 61

Roehl, Jeff NYG 73

Roehlk, John CHI 64

Roehneit, Bill DEN 68, WSH 53, CHI 69

Roffler, William PHL 23

Rogalla, John PHL 32

Rogas, Dan DET 64, PHL 65

Rogel, Fran PIT 27/33/34

Rogers, Bill DET 18/62

Rogers, Charles DET 80

Rogers, Charlie BUF 31, SEA 20/31

Rogers, Chris MIN 29

Rogers, Cullen PIT 25

Rogers, Don CLE 20

Rogers, Don SDC 52

Rogers, Doug NEP 65, SFF 65

Rogers, George NOS 38, WSH 38

Rogers, Glenn TBB 21

Rogers, Glynn ARZ 35

Rogers, Jimmy NOS 41

Rogers, John xCIN 14/38

Rogers, Lamar CIN 79

Rogers, Mel CHI 51, SDC 53, STL 57

Rogers, Nick MIN 58

Rogers, Reggie BUF 77, DET 60, TBB 75

Rogers, Sam ATL 59/93, BUF 59

Rogers, Shaun DET 92

Rogers, Stan DEN 73

Rogers, Steve KCC 77

Rogers, Steve NOS 26, NYJ ?

Rogers, Tracy KCC 52

Rogers, Tyrone CLE 78

Rogge, George ARZ 41, xSTL 50

Roggeman, Tom CHI 67

Rohde, Len SFF 76

Rohrer, Jeff DAL 50

Rohrig, Herm GBP 8/80

Rokisky, John CLE 54, zCHI 56, zNYY 58

Roland, Benji TBB 93

Roland, Johnny ARZ 23, NYG 23

Rolle, Butch ARZ 82, BUF 87

Rolle, Dave DEN 35

Rolle, Samari TEN 21

Roller, Dave GBP 74, MIN 76, NYG 74

Rolling, Henry SDC 57, STL 59, TBB 55

Rollins, Baron NOS 75

Roman, George NYG 79, xBOS 31, xNYB 31

Roman, John NYJ 61

Roman, Mark CIN 20

Roman, Nick CIN 81, CLE 81

Romanik, Steve ARZ 12, CHI 12

Romaniszyn, Jim CLE 56, NEP 53

Romano, Jim OAK 52, TEN 55

Romanowski, Bill DEN 53, OAK 53, PHL 53, SFF 53

Romasko, Dave CIN 48/83

Romboli, Rudy xBOS 19

Rome, Stan KCC 87

Rome, Tag SDC 82

Romeo, Tony KCC 80, NEP 86

Romer, Rich CIN 94

Romero, Dario MIA 73/94

Romero, Ray PHL 68

Romes, Charles BUF 26, SDC 29

Romine, Al DEN 42, GBP 23/85, NEP 46

Romney, Milt CHI 10

Rone, Andre BUF 87

Ronzani, Gene CHI 6

Rooney, Bill ARZ 11, NYG 18

Rooney, Cobb ARZ 34

Roopenian, Mark BUF 99

Root, Jim ARZ 17

Roper, John CHI 55, DAL 56, PHL 53
Roque, Juan DET 73/74
Roquemore, Durwood BUF 42, KCC 38
Rorison, Jim PIT 29
Rosado, Dan SDC 66
Rosato, Sal WSH 32
Rosatti, Rosey NYG 33, GBP 12/25
Rosdahl, Harrison BUF 83
Rosdahl, Hatch KCC 76
Rose, Al GBP 34/37/47/49/52
Rose, Barry DEN 81
Rose, Bob GBP 18
Rose, Carlton WSH 50
Rose, Donovan KCC 27, MIA 26
Rose, Gene ARZ 22/37/38, NYG 26
Rose, George MIN 47, NOS 44
Rose, Joe MIA 80, STL 87
Rose, Ken CLE 52, NYJ 92, PHL 55
Rosecrans, Jim NYJ ?
Rosema, Rocky ARZ 34
Rosenbach, Timm ARZ 3
Rosenfels, Sage MIA 18
Rosenmeier, Erik BUF 75
Rosensteil, Bob OAK 89
Rosenthal, Mike MIN 75, NYG 78
Rosequist, Ted CHI 15/47, STL 17
Roskie, Ken DET 30, GBP 34/50, SFF 74
Rosnagle, Ted MIN 28
Ross, Adrian CIN 57
Ross, Alvin PHL 41
Ross, Dan CIN 84/89, GBP 81, SEA 85
Ross, Dave NYJ 80
Ross, Derek ATL 25, DAL 20/21
Ross, Dominique DAL 36
Ross, Jermaine STL 82
Ross, Kevin KCC 31, ATL 36, SDC 36
Ross, Louis BUF 87, KCC 75
Ross, Micah JAX 86, SDC 11
Ross, Oliver DEN 30, SEA 30
Ross, Oliver DAL 68, PHL 73, PIT 79
Ross, Scott NOS 55
Ross, Tim DET 93
Ross, Willie BUF 47
Rosso, George WSH 20
Rossovich, Tim PHL 82, SDC 82, TEN 58
Rossum, Allen ATL 20, GBP 20, PHL 25
Rosteck, Ernie DET 78
Rostosky, Pete PIT 63
Rote, Kyle NYG 44

Rote, Tobin GBP 18/38, DEN 11, DET 18, SDC 18
Roth, Pete MIA 32
Roth, Tom NOS 78
Rother, Tim OAK 78
Rothrock, Cliff zCHI 29
Rothschild, Doug CHI 54
Rothwell, Fred DET 61
Roton, Herbert PHL 18/36
Rouen, Tom DEN 16, NYG 10, PIT 14, SEA 16
Roundtree, Raleigh ARZ 73, SDC 74
Rourke, Jim CIN 77, KCC 70, NOS 70
Rouse, Curtis MIN 68, SDC 87
Rouse, James CHI 30
Rouse, Stillman DET 35
Rouse, Wardell TBB 52
Rouson, Lee CLE 44, NYG 22
Roussel, Tom NOS 54, PHL 54, WSH 54
Roussos, Mike DET 76, WSH 44
Roveto, John CHI 4/9
Rovinski, Tony NYG 14
Rowan, Everitt PHL 32, xBKN 17/4
Rowden, Larry CHI 53
Rowe, Bob ARZ 75
Rowe, Bob DET 8
Rowe, Dave NEP 76, NOS 76, OAK 74, SDC 74, IND 74
Rowe, Harmon NYG 22, zNYY 74/90
Rowe, Joe STL 42
Rowe, Patrick CLE 86
Rowe, Ray MIN 89, WSH 82
Rowe, Robert PHL 37
Rowell, Eugene CHI 65
Rowell, Eugene CLE 83
Rowland, Brad CHI 86
Rowland, Justin CHI 20, DEN 33, MIN 47
Rowley, Bob NYJ 63, PIT 56
Rowser, John DEN 46, GBP 28/45, PIT 48
Roy, Frank ARZ 68
Royal, Andre CAR 58, IND 56
Royal, Robert WSH 88
Royals, Mark ARZ 14, DET 3, JAX 3, MIA 3, NOS 3, PHL 5, PIT 3, TBB 3
Roye, Orpheus CLE 99, PIT 71
Royster, Mazio TBB 31/33
Royston, Ed NYG 61
Rozelle, Aubrey PIT 66
Rozier, Bob ARZ 75
Rozier, Mike TEN 30/33, ATL 30
Rozumek, Dave KCC 55
Rubbert, Ed WSH 16
Rubens, Larry CHI 52, GBP 58

Rubick, Rob DET 84
Rubino, Tony DET 66/68
Rubio, Angel ARZ 92
Rubke, Karl ATL 74, MIN 54, OAK 54, SFF 52
Rubley, T.J. DEN 11, GBP 12, STL 12
Ruby, Martin xNYB 47, zBRK 43, zNYY 40
Rucci, Todd NEP 71
Rucinski, Ed ARZ 19/23/51/75, PIT 75, xBKN 26
Rucka, Leo SFF 50
Rucker, Conrad STL 63, TBB 80, TEN 87
Rucker, Keith ARZ 79, CIN 95, KCC 96, PHL 96, WSH 99
Rucker, Mike CAR 93
Rucker, Reggie CLE 33, DAL 88, NEP 33, NYG 83
Rudd, Dwayne CLE 57, MIN 57, TBB 57
Ruddy, Tim MIA 61
Rudnay, Jack KCC 58
Rudnick, Tim IND 43
Rudolph, Ben NYJ 76
Rudolph, Coleman NYG 91, NYJ 92
Rudolph, Council ARZ 74, TBB 78, TEN 77
Rudolph, Jack MIA 55, NEP 80
Rudolph, Joe PHL 64, SFF 60
Rudolph, Martin DEN 40
Rudzinski, Paul GBP 58/66/70
Ruegamer, Grey GBP 67, NEP 67
Ruether, Mike ARZ 51, ATL 55, DEN 57, MIN 65
Ruettgers, Ken GBP 75
Ruetz, Howard GBP 75
Ruetz, Joe zCHI 33/34
Ruff, Guy PIT 36
Ruff, Orlando NOS 56, SDC 56
Ruhman, Chris CLE 68, SFF 71
Rukas, Justin xBKN 35
Rule, Gordon GBP 47
Rumph, Mike SFF 24
Runager, Max CLE 4, PHL 4, SFF 4
Runnels, Tom WSH 25
Runquist, Elmer ARZ 11
Runyan, John PHL 69, TEN 69
Ruple, Ernie PIT 73
Rush, Bob KCC 53, SDC 56
Rush, Clive GBP 81
Rush, Jerry DET 82
Rush, Tyrone WSH 39
Rushing, Marion ARZ 52, ATL 52, TEN 55
Rusinek, Mike CLE 79
Rusk, Reggie SDC 25, SEA 21, TBB 26/28

Ruskusky, Roy zNYY 50
Russ, Bernard NEP 51
Russ, Carl ATL 59, NYJ 53
Russ, Pat MIN 75
Russ, Steve DEN 58
Russas, Al DET 86
Russell, Andy PIT 34/36
Russell, Ben BUF 3/7
Russell, Bo WSH 45
Russell, Booker OAK 34, PHL 32, SDC 41
Russell, Brian MIN 27
Russell, Cliff WSH 83
Russell, Damien SFF 38
Russell, Darrell OAK 96, WSH 96
Russell, Darryl DEN 39
Russell, Derek DEN 85, TEN 85
Russell, Doug ARZ 12/32/33, STL 4
Russell, Jack xNYB 16, zNYY 53
Russell, James PHL 17, PHL 22
Russell, Ken DET 73
Russell, Leonard DEN 42, NEP 32, SDC 42, STL 42
Russell, Matt DET 54
Russell, Reb NYG 0, PHL 15
Russell, Reginald CHI 24
Russell, Rusty PHL 79
Russell, Twan ATL 55, MIA 56, WSH 98
Russell, Wade CIN 70/82
Rust, Reggie WSH 36
Rutgens, Joe WSH 72
Ruth, Mike NEP 65
Ruthstrom, Ralph STL 20, WSH 26, zBAL 84
Rutkowski, Charles BUF 85
Rutkowski, Ed BUF 40
Rutledge, Craig STL 48
Rutledge, Jeff NYG 17, STL 8, WSH 10
Rutledge, Johnny ARZ 51/58, DEN 53
Rutledge, Rod HOU 83, NEP 83
Ruud, Tom BUF 54, CIN 51
Ruzek, Roger DAL 9, PHL 7
Ruzich, Steve GBP 61
Ryan, Bill ARZ ?
Ryan, Dave DET 44, xBOS 20
Ryan, Ed PIT 46
Ryan, Frank CLE 13, STL 15, WSH 13
Ryan, Jim DEN 50
Ryan, Joe NYJ 77
Ryan, John CHI 12
Ryan, Pat NYJ 4/10, PHL 10
Ryan, Rip DET 2, DET 6
Ryan, Rocky CHI 45, PHL 45
Ryan, Sod DET 83
Ryan, Tim CHI 96/99
Ryan, Tim TBB 64

Ryans, Larry TBB 89
Rychlec, Tom BUF 81, DEN 80/81
Ryckman, Billy ATL 82
Ryczek, Dan STL 54, TBB 51, WSH 51
Ryczek, Paul ATL 53, NOS 54, PHL 73
Rydalch, Ron CHI 76
Ryder, Nick DET 34
Rydzewski, Frank ARZ 17, CHI ?
Rykovich, Jules WSH 20, CHI 11, zBUF 86, zCHI 85
Rymkus, Lou WSH 12, CLE 44
Rypien, Mark WSH 11, CLE 11, IND 16, PHL 11, STL 11
Rzempoluch, Ted WSH 28
Saalfeld, Kelly NYG 59
Saar, Brad IND 59
Sabados, Andy ARZ 38
Sabal, Ron OAK 64
Saban, Lou CLE 20/66/72
Sabasteanski, Joe xBOS 21, xNYB 21
Sabatino, Bill ATL 74, CLE 74
Sabb, Dwayne NEP 95
Sabuco, Tino SFF 24/25
Sacca, Tony ARZ 19
Sacco, Frank NEP 95
Sachs, Len ARZ 7/22
Sachse, Frank xBKN 30, xBOS 12
Sachse, Jack xBOS ?
Sacrinty, Nick CHI 4
Saddler, Rod ARZ 72, CIN 70
Sader, Stephen PIT 33, PHL 33
Sadowski, Troy ATL 88, CIN 87, JAX 89, KCC 87, NYJ 83/84, PIT 46
Saenz, Eddie WSH 99
Saffold, Saint CIN 27
Sagapolutele, Pio CLE 75, NEP 75, NOS 99
Sagely, Floyd ARZ 88, SFF 89
Sager, Ken SEA 89
Sagnella, Anthony WSH 94
Saidock, Tom BUF 75, NYJ 75, PHL 75
Saimes, George BUF 26, DEN 26
Saindon, Pat NOS 68
Salaam, Abdul NYJ 74
Salaam, Ephraim ATL 74, DEN 74
Salaam, Rashaan CHI 31, CLE 29
Salata, Paul SFF 55, xBAL 51
Salave'a, Joe SDC 95, TEN 95
Saldi, Jay CHI 81, DAL 87
Saleaumua, Dan KCC 97, DET 97, SEA 97
Saleh, Tarek CAR 92, CLE 40/54

Salem, Ed WSH 26
Salem, Harvey DEN 74, DET 73, GBP 72, TEN 73
Salisbury, Sean IND 8/13, MIN 12, SDC 8
Sally, Jerome IND 76, KCC 70, NYG 78
Salmon, Mike SFF 30
Salonen, Brian DAL 89
Salsbury, Jim DET 60, GBP 67
Salscheider, Jack NYG 40
Salter, Bryant MIA 30, SDC 30, WSH 30
Sample, Chuck GBP 38
Sample, John IND 44/47, NYJ 24, PIT 24, WSH 24
Sampleton, Lawrence MIA 80, PHL 87
Sampson, Clint DEN 84
Sampson, Greg TEN 73/91
Sampson, Howard GBP 36
Sams, Ron GBP 70, MIN 72, NYJ 77
Samson, Michael PHL 98
Samuel, Asante NEP 22
Samuel, Don PIT 66
Samuel, Khari CHI 91, DET 59
Samuels, Chris SDC 20
Samuels, Chris WSH 60
Samuels, Terry ARZ 44/89
Samuels, Tony KCC 81, TBB 80
Samuelson, Carl PIT 78/86
Sanchez, Davis SDC 33
Sanchez, Jeff DAL 26
Sanchez, John DET 77, NYG 70/76, WSH 49, zCHI 43
Sanchez, Lupe PIT 28
Sandberg, Sigurd PIT 2/28, xBKN 15, xSTL 90
Sandefur, Wayne PIT 10
Sandeman, Bill ATL 61, DAL 70, NOS 73
Sander, Mark MIA 58
Sanders, Barry DET 20
Sanders, Bob ATL 54
Sanders, Brandon NYG 34
Sanders, Charlie DET 88
Sanders, Chris TEN 81
Sanders, Chuck PIT 45
Sanders, Clarence KCC 50
Sanders, Darnell CLE 49/89
Sanders, Daryl DET 70
Sanders, Deion ATL 21, DAL 21, SFF 21, WSH 21
Sanders, Eric ATL 67, DET 64
Sanders, Frank ARZ 81, BLT 81
Sanders, Gene TBB 74
Sanders, Glenell IND 58, CHI 64, DEN 55, STL 55
Sanders, John NEP 25, PHL 26
Sanders, John PHL 67, PIT 44/55
Sanders, Ken DET 82, MIN 89

Sanders, Lewis CLE 21/25
Sanders, Lonnie ARZ 42, WSH 40
Sanders, Paul xBOS 25
Sanders, Ricky ATL 83, WSH 46/83
Sanders, Spec xNYB 81, zNYY 81
Sanders, Thomas CHI 20/31, PHL 45
Sanderson, Reggie CHI 39
Sanderson, Scott CHI 74, NOS 74, TEN 73
Sandham, Todd NEP 72
Sandifer, Bill SEA 66, SFF 60
Sandifer, Dan ARZ 21, DET 81, GBP 20/23, PHL 31, SFF 81, WSH 20
Sandig, Curtis PIT 11
Sandig, Curt zBUF 85
Sands, Terdell GBP 78, KCC 91, OAK 92
Sandusky, Alex IND 68
Sandusky, John CLE 49/78, GBP 77
Sandusky, Mike PIT 62
Sanford, Haywood WSH 34
Sanford, Leo ARZ 51/73, IND 55
Sanford, Lucius BUF 57, CLE 50
Sanford, Rick NEP 25, SEA 25
Sansen, Ollie xBKN 32/8/77/28
Santiago, O.J. ATL 88, OAK 83
Santora, Frank xBOS 27
Santos, Todd SFF 7
Sanyika, Sekou ARZ 54
Sanzotta, Mickey DET 42/62
Sape, Lauvale BUF 66
Sapienza, Americo NYJ 22
Sapolu, Jesse SFF 61
Sapp, Bob MIN 78
Sapp, Cecil DEN 37
Sapp, Gerome BLT 27
Sapp, Patrick ARZ 55, SDC 56
Sapp, Theron PHL 30, PIT 33
Sapp, Warren TBB 99
Sarafiny, Al GBP 24
Sarausky, Tony NYG 11, xBKN 69
Sarboe, Phil ARZ 41, WSH 35, xBKN 41
Sardisco, Tony NEP 64, SFF 65, WSH 70
Sargent, Broderick ARZ 39, DAL 39
Sargent, Kevin CIN 77
Sark, Harvey NYG ?, xCIN ?
Sarratt, Charley DET 40
Sarringhaus, Paul ARZ 40, DET 18
Sartin, Dan SDC 53
Sartin, Martin SDC 35
Sartori, Larry DET 45/60

Sasa, Don CAR 98, DET 98, SDC 96, WSH 72
Satcher, Doug NEP 58
Satenstein, Ollie NYG 33
Saterfield, Brian GBP 38
Satterfield, Alf SFF 48
Satterwhite, Howard IND 28, NYJ 80
Saturday, Jeff IND 63
Sauer, Craig ATL 52, MIN 59
Sauer, George Sr. GBP 17/25
Sauer, George Jr. NYJ 83
Sauerbrun, Todd CAR 10, CHI 16, KCC 5
Saul, Bill DET 58, IND 50, NOS 51, PIT 50
Saul, Rich STL 61
Saul, Ron TEN 64, WSH 64
Sauls, Mac ARZ 43
Saumer, Pete xCIN 8
Saumer, Sylvester PIT 36
Saunders, Cedric TBB 49
Saunders, John BUF 21, SFF 33
Saunders, Russ GBP 18
Sauter, Cory CHI 17, ARZ 9
Savage, Sebastian WSH 23
Savage, Tony CIN 98, SDC 79
Savatsky, Oliver STL ?
Savitsky, George PHL 64/75
Savoie, Nicky NOS 85
Savoldi, Joe CHI 54
Sawyer, Buzz DAL 8
Sawyer, Corey CIN 23
Sawyer, John DEN 83, SEA 81, TEN 81, WSH 82
Sawyer, Jon NEP 31
Sawyer, Ken CIN 22
Sawyer, Talance MIN 97
Saxon, James KCC 21/45, MIA 22, PHL 22
Saxon, Mike DAL 4, MIN 4, NEP 4
Saxton, Brian ATL 49, NYG 83
Saxton, James KCC 10
Sayers, Gale CHI 40
Sayers, Ron SDC 31
Sayler, Jace NEP 94
Sazio, Ralph zBRK 48
Sbranti, Ron DEN 54
Scafide, John WSH ?
Scales, Charley PIT 34, CLE 36, ATL 31
Scales, Dwight NYG 88, SDC 87, SEA 84, STL 87
Scales, Greg NOS 83
Scales, Hurles ARZ 38, GBP 38
Scalissi, Ted zCHI 97
Scalzi, Johnny xBKN 25
Scanlan, Jerry WSH 76
Scanlon, John ARZ 3
Scarbath, Jack PIT 12, WSH 18

Scarber, Sam SDC 30
Scardina, John MIN 78
Scardine, Carmen ARZ ?
Scarpati, Joe NOS 21, PHL 21
Scarpitto, Bob DEN 82, NEP 46, SDC 46
Scarry, Michael STL 39, CLE 20
Schaake, Elmer DET 66
Schabarum, Pete SFF 44/88
Schad, Mike PHL 79, STL 76
Schaefer, Don PHL 24
Schaffer, Joe BUF 67
Schafrath, Dick CLE 77/80
Schamel, Duke MIA 60
Schammel, Francis GBP 37
Schankweiler, Scott BUF 52
Schau, Ryan HOU 65, PHL 67
Schaukowitch, Carl DEN 67
Schaum, Greg DAL 78, NEP 76
Scheib, Skippy xBKN 5
Schenk, Ed MIN 89
Schenker, Nathan STL 38
Scherer, Bernard PIT 24, GBP 11/16/36/40
Scheuer, Babe NYG 21
Schibanoff, Alex DET 78/79
Schichtle, Henry NYG 10
Schick, Doyle WSH 21
Schiechl, John DET 52, CHI 41/66, PIT 35, SFF 24
Schifino, Jake TEN 81
Schilling, Ralph WSH 28, zBUF 54
Schillinger, Andy ARZ 25
Schindler, Steve DEN 67
Schlect, John SFF 93
Schleich, Vic zNYY 42
Schleicher, Maury ARZ 87, SDC 81
Schlereth, Mark DEN 69, WSH 69
Schlesinger, Cory DET 30
Schleusner, Vin DET 28, DET 61
Schlichter, Art IND 10
Schlinkman, Walt GBP 7
Schlopy, Todd BUF 3
Schmarr, Herm xBKN 42
Schmautz, Ray OAK 58
Schmedding, Jim SDC 64
Schmidt, Bob TEN 52, BUF 57, NEP 74, NYG 52
Schmidt, Dutch WSH ?, xCIN 36
Schmidt, George ARZ 81/91, GBP 54
Schmidt, Henry BUF 76, NYJ 74, SDC 76, SFF 74
Schmidt, Joe DET 56
Schmidt, John PIT 11
Schmidt, Roy ATL 55, MIN 68, NOS 63

Schmidt, Terry CHI 44, NOS 40

Schmiesing, Joe ARZ 82, DET 84, IND 75, NYJ 74

Schmit, Bob NYG 59

Schmitt, George ARZ 26

Schmitt, John NYJ 52/56/70, GBP 52

Schmitt, Ted PHL 41

Schmitz, Bob MIN 54, PIT 67

Schnarr, Steve BUF 23

Schneck, Mike PIT 54

Schneider, Don zBUF 89

Schneider, Leroy zBRK ?

Schneidman, Herm ARZ 17, GBP 4/51

Schnelker, Bob NYG 85, MIN 80, PHL 85, PIT 85/88

Schnellbacher, Otto NYG 83, zNYY 56

Schneller, Bill PHL 24

Schneller, John DET 12/30

Schnitker, Mike DEN 64

Schobel, Aaron BUF 94

Schobel, Matt CIN 89

Schoeman, Roy GBP 42

Schoen, Tom CLE 33

Schoenke, Ray DAL 65, WSH 62

Scholtz, Bob DET 50, NYG 55

Scholtz, Bruce SEA 58, NEP 51

Schonert, Turk ATL 14, CIN 15

Schottel, Ivan DET 55/88

Schottenheimer, Marty BUF 56/57, NEP 54

Schrader, Jim WSH 51, PHL 51

Schreiber, Adam ATL 67, MIN 60, NOS 65, NYG 67, NYJ 75, PHL 76, SEA 75

Schreiber, Larry CHI 36, SFF 35

Schroeder, Bill DET 84, GBP 19/84

Schroeder, Bill zCHI 60

Schroeder, Gene CHI 88

Schroeder, Jay WSH 10, ARZ 11, CIN 10, OAK 10/13

Schroll, Bill DET 36, zBUF 72

Schroll, Charles GBP 86

Schroy, Ken NYJ 48

Schuber, Jim xBKN ?

Schubert, Eric ARZ 11, NEP 1, NYG 3

Schubert, Steve CHI 85, NEP 87

Schuehle, Jake PHL 38

Schuelke, Karl PIT 35

Schuette, Carl GBP 17, zBUF 74/23

Schuette, Paul CHI 22, NYG 36, WSH 14

Schuh, Harry OAK 71/79, GBP 79, STL 76/79

Schuh, Jeff CIN 59, GBP 54, MIN 53

Schuhmacher, John TEN 62

Schuler, Bill NYG 75/76

Schulters, Lance SFF 30, TEN 31

Schultz, Bill CHI 67, DEN 74, IND 74, TEN 75

Schultz, Charles GBP 60

Schultz, Chris DAL 66

Schultz, Eberle PHL 48/71, ARZ 48, PIT 48/71, STL 40

Schultz, Randy CLE 33, NOS 33

Schulz, Jody PHL 53, PHL 95

Schulz, John DEN 84/86

Schulz, Kurt BUF 24, DET 45

Schumacher, Gregg STL 81

Schumacher, Kurt NOS 71, TBB 78

Schumann, Mike ARZ 84, SFF 84

Schutt, Scott CIN 59

Schwab, Ray NYG ?

Schwall, Vic ARZ 37/89

Schwammel, Ade GBP 40/50/53/57/58

Schwantz, Jim DAL 52, CHI 59/65, SFF 52

Schwartz, Bryan JAX 58

Schwartz, Don ARZ 48, NOS 48

Schwartz, Elmer ARZ 18, DET 22, PIT 39

Schwartz, Perry xBKN 99, zNYY 57

Schweda, Brian CHI 60, NOS 60

Schweder, John PIT 66/68/75/77, xBAL 37/66

Schwedes, Gerhard NYJ 30, NEP 44

Schwedes, Scott MIA 81, SDC 85

Schweidler, Dick CHI 31

Schweikert, Bob NYJ 20

Schwenk, Bud CLE 64, zBAL 40/64, zNYY 84

Schwenk, Wilson ARZ 45

Sciarra, John PHL 21

Scibelli, Joe STL 71

Scifres, Mike SDC 5

Scifres, Steve CAR 72, DAL 77, NOS 74

Scioli, Brad IND 99

Scissum, Willard WSH 61

Sciullo, Steve IND 74

Scobey, Josh ARZ 33

Scoggins, Eric SFF 63

Scoggins, Ron SEA 73

Scollard, Nick xBOS 27, xNYB 27

Scolnick, Glenn PIT 21/86

Scott, Bart BLT 57

Scott, Bill CIN 37

Scott, Bo CLE 35

Scott, Bobby NOS 12

Scott, Brian ATL 24

Scott, Carey OAK 37

Scott, Carlos ARZ 56

Scott, Cedric NYG 96, CLE 93

Scott, Chad PIT 30

Scott, Chris IND 95

Scott, Chuck DAL 47, STL 84

Scott, Clarence CLE 22, NEP 26

Scott, Clyde DET 20, PHL 27

Scott, Darnay CIN 86, DAL 85

Scott, Dave ATL 70

Scott, Dequincy SDC 78

Scott, Ed ARZ 23

Scott, Freddie Jr. ATL 84, IND 15

Scott, Freddie Sr. DET 87, IND 86

Scott, Gari PHL 16/86

Scott, George NYG 31

Scott, Greg WSH 96

Scott, Herb DAL 68

Scott, Ian CHI 95

Scott, Jake MIA 13, WSH 13

Scott, James CHI 89

Scott, Joe NYG 30

Scott, John BUF 76

Scott, Kevin DAL 35, DET 38, SDC 24

Scott, Lance ARZ 70, NYG 70

Scott, Lew DEN 45

Scott, Lindsay NOS 80

Scott, Lynn DAL 21/38

Scott, Malcolm NOS 87, NYG 80

Scott, Patrick GBP 83

Scott, Perry DET 82

Scott, Prince zMIA 57

Scott, Ralph CHI 17

Scott, Randy GBP 55, MIN 50

Scott, Ronald MIA 33

Scott, Sean DAL 52

Scott, Stanley MIA 77

Scott, Todd MIN 38, KCC 47, NYJ 38, TBB 38

Scott, Tom CIN 74

Scott, Tom PHL 82, NYG 82

Scott, Tony NYJ 27

Scott, Victor DAL 22

Scott, Vince zBUF 37

Scott, Walter NEP 94

Scott, Wilbert PIT 36

Scott, Willie KCC 81, NEP 88

Scott, Yusuf ARZ 68

Scotti, Ben PHL 48, WSH 48, SFF 28/48

Scotts, Colin ARZ 69

Scrabis, Bob NYJ 46

Scrafford, Kirk CIN 76, DEN 76, SFF 76

Scribner, Bucky GBP 13, MIN 13

Scribner, Rob STL 33

Scroggins, Tracy DET 59/97

Scruggs, Ted zBRK 50
Scudero, Joe WSH 28, PIT 26
Scully, John ATL 61
Scully, Mike WSH 59
Scurlock, Mike CAR 38, STL 22/37
Sczurek, Stan CLE 34/38, NYG 38
Seabaugh, Todd PIT 59
Seabright, Charles PIT 33, STL 25
Seabron, Thomas ARZ 58, SFF 53
Seal, Paul NOS 84, SFF 85
Sealby, Randy NEP 59
Seale, Eugene TEN 53
Seale, Sam OAK 43, SDC 30, STL 22
Seals, George CHI 67, KCC 67, WSH 71
Seals, Leon BUF 96, PHL 97
Seals, Ray CAR 99, PIT 97, TBB 98
Seams, Frank STL 50
Searcey, Bill SDC 64
Searcy, Leon JAX 72, PIT 72
Sears, Corey ARZ 94, HOU 92, STL 95
Sears, Jim ARZ 21, DEN 35, SDC 26
Sears, Vic PHL 79, PIT 79
Seau, Junior SDC 55, MIA 55
Seaverns, Justin MIA 55
Seay, Mark PHL 81, SDC 82
Seay, Virgil ATL 41, WSH 80
Sebastian, Mike PHL 34, PIT 23, STL 4, WSH 16
Sebek, Nick WSH 42
Secules, Scott DAL 10, MIA 9, NEP 10
Sedbrook, Len NYG 4/14
Seder, Tim DAL 6, JAX 3
Sedlock, Bob BUF 75
Sedoris, Chris WSH 59
Seedborg, John WSH 38
Seeman, George GBP 68
Sehorn, Jason NYG 31, STL 42
Seibering, Gerald CHI 30
Seibold, Champ ARZ 73, GBP 37/41/57/58
Seick, Red NYG 33
Seidman, Mike CAR 82
Seifert, Mike CLE 66
Seigler, Dexter SEA 23
Seiler, Paul NYJ 71/79, OAK 65
Seiple, Larry MIA 20
Seitz, Warren NYG 84, PIT 80
Selawski, Gene CLE 78, SDC 78, STL 70
Selby, Rob ARZ 74, PHL 75
Selesky, Ron MIN 60
Self, Clarence ARZ 37, DET 11, GBP 28
Selfridge, Andy BUF 64, MIA 51, NYG 57

Sellers, Donald STL 16
Sellers, Goldie DEN 21, KCC 20
Sellers, Lance CIN 55
Sellers, Mike CLE 44, WSH 45/85
Sellers, Ron NEP 34, DAL 88, MIA 34
Selmon, Dewey SDC 58, TBB 58/61
Selmon, LeeRoy TBB 63
Seltzer, Harry DET 33
Semes, Bernard PIT 33, ARZ 33
Semple, Tony DET 62
Sendlein, Robin MIA 52, MIN 57
Senn, Bill CHI 6, xBKN 33, xCIN 37, xSTL 40
Seno, Frank ARZ 46/54, WSH 25, xBOS 20/54
Sensanbaugher, Dean CLE 94, xNYB 46
Senser, Joe MIN 81
Sensibaugh, Mike ARZ 20, KCC 20
Senters, Mike CAR 47
Septien, Rafael DAL 1, STL 1
Sergienko, George xBKN 39/44, xBOS 44, zBRK 26
Serini, Washington CHI 23, GBP 73
Serwanga, Kato NEP 31, NYG 26, WSH 22
Serwanga, Wasswa MIN 29, SFF 43
Sestak, Tom BUF 70
Setcavage, Joe xBKN 16
Settle, John ATL 44
Settles, Tawambi JAX 29
Settles, Tony WSH 91
Setzer, Bobby CHI 76, SFF 90
Seubert, Rich NYG 69
Seurer, Frank KCC 10
Severs, Eric STL 82
Severson, Jeff ARZ 46, DEN 45, STL 45, TEN 23/37, WSH 44
Severson, Norris xCIN 31
Sevy, Jeff CHI 75, SEA 70
Sewell, Harley DET 66, STL 66
Sewell, Steve DEN 30
Sexton, Brent PIT 29
Sexton, Lin zLAD 89
Seymour, Bob WSH 20, zLAD 82
Seymour, Jim CHI 84
Seymour, Paul BUF 87
Seymour, Richard NEP 93
Shabazz, Siddeeq ATL 39, OAK 19
Shackelford, Don DEN 65
Shade, Sam CIN 35, WSH 29
Shaffer, Craig ARZ 53

Shaffer, George PIT 38
Shaffer, Kevin ATL 76
Shaffer, Leland NYG 4/20
Shakespeare, Stanley TBB 81
Shank, J.L. CHI 18
Shanklin, Ron PIT 25, CHI 25
Shanks, Simon ARZ 51
Shanle, Scott DAL 58, STL 54
Shanley, Jim GBP 22
Shann, Bob PHL 25
Shannon, Carver STL 47
Shannon, John CHI 75
Shannon, Larry MIA 82
Shannon, Randy DAL 53/94
Sharkey, Ed CLE 68, IND 64, PHL 66, SFF 63, xNYB 51, zNYY 30
Sharockman, Ed MIN 45
Sharp, Dan ATL 96
Sharp, Everett WSH 16
Sharp, Rick DEN 75, PIT 73
Sharpe, Luis ARZ 67
Sharpe, Montique KCC 61
Sharpe, Shannon BLT 82, DEN 81/84
Sharpe, Sterling GBP 84
Sharper, Darren GBP 42
Sharper, Jamie BLT 55, HOU 55
Shaub, Harry PHL 23
Shavers, Tyrone CLE 28
Shaw, Billy BUF 66
Shaw, Bob ARZ 60, STL 32
Shaw, Bob NOS 30
Shaw, Bobby BUF 81, JAX 81, PIT 15/82, SEA 81
Shaw, Charles SFF 31
Shaw, Dennis ARZ 11, BUF 16, KCC 12
Shaw, Eric CIN 90
Shaw, George DEN 17, IND 14, MIN 14, NYG 15
Shaw, Glenn CHI 29, OAK 32, STL 34
Shaw, Harold NEP 44
Shaw, Jesse ARZ 28
Shaw, Josh SFF 93
Shaw, Nate STL 44
Shaw, Pete NYG 44, SDC 44
Shaw, Rickie NOS 76
Shaw, Ricky NYG 51, PHL 51
Shaw, Robert DAL 52
Shaw, Scott CIN 68
Shaw, Sedrick CIN 39, CLE 25, NEP 23
Shaw, Terrance MIA 22, NEP 22, OAK 22, SDC 29
Shay, Jerry ATL 78, MIN 73, NYG 75
Shea, Aaron CLE 80
Shea, Pat SDC 64
Shearer, Brad CHI 72
Shearer, Ron DET ?
Shearin, Joe DAL 67, STL 64, TBB 64

Shears, Larry ATL 30
Shedd, Kenny OAK 84, WSH 19
Shedlosky, Ed NYG 5
Sheffield, Chris DET 28, PIT 41
Shegog, Ron NEP 42
Shehee, Rashaan KCC 22
Shelby, Willie ARZ 30, CIN 30
Sheldon, Mike MIA 68
Shell, Art OAK 78
Shell, Donnie PIT 31
Shell, Todd SFF 90
Shelley, Dex ARZ 29, DET ?, GBP 15
Shelley, Elbert ATL 37
Shelling, Chris CIN 30
Shello, Kendel IND 97
Shellogg, Alec CHI 18, xBKN 26
Shelton, Anthony SDC 23
Shelton, Daimon CHI 31, JAX 31
Shelton, L.J. ARZ 70
Shelton, Richard DEN 45, PIT 24/40
Shenefelt, Paul ARZ 41
Shepard, Charles PIT 35
Shepard, Derrick DAL 82/87, NOS 89, WSH 80/88
Shepherd, Bill DET 9, WSH 33
Shepherd, Edell TBB 3
Shepherd, Gannon JAX 67
Shepherd, Jacoby DET 38, NYJ 32, STL 22
Shepherd, Johnny BUF 24
Shepherd, Leslie CLE 86, MIA 84, WSH 86
Sheppard, Ashley JAX 96, MIN 59, STL 59
Sheppard, Henry CLE 65
Sheppard, Lito PHL 26
Sherer, Dave DAL 86, IND 86
Sheriff, Stan CLE 65, PIT 50, SFF 50
Sherk, Jerry CLE 72
Sherlag, Bob ATL 82
Sherman, Al PHL 10, PIT 10
Sherman, Bob PIT 49
Sherman, Heath PHL 23
Sherman, Rod CIN 23, DEN 84, OAK 13/23, STL 86
Sherman, Saul CHI 22
Sherman, Tom BUF 14/18, NEP 14
Sherman, Will STL 43, MIN 43, xDAL 45
Sherrard, Mike DAL 86, DEN 88, NYG 88, SFF 88
Sherrod, Bud NYG 8
Sherwin, Tim IND 83, NYG 88
Shetley, Rhoten xBKN 30, zBRK 83
Shiancoe, Vishante NYG 82

Shibest, James ATL 81
Shield, Joe GBP 18
Shields, Billy KCC 70, NYJ 66, SDC 66, SFF 67
Shields, Burrell IND 31, PIT 37
Shields, Jon DAL 63
Shields, Lebron IND 73, MIN 77
Shields, Paul IND 39
Shields, Scott PIT 47
Shields, Will KCC 68
Shiner, Dick ATL 11, CLE 18, NEP 11, NYG 17, PIT 17, WSH 14
Shinners, John CIN 64, IND 64, NOS 67
Shinnick, Don IND 66
Shipkey, Jerry PIT 33/49, CHI 23/33
Shipp, Billy NYG 74
Shipp, Jackie MIA 50, OAK 58
Shipp, Joe BUF 87
Shipp, Marcel ARZ 31
Shires, Marshall PHL 72
Shirey, Frederick STL 36
Shirk, Gary NYG 87
Shirk, John ARZ 63
Shirkey, George OAK 77, TEN 74
Shirley, Marion zNYY 42
Shiry, Bob GBP 18
Shiver, Clay CAR 60, DAL 50
Shiver, Ray STL 22
Shiver, Sanders IND 54, MIA 52
Shivers, Roy ARZ 27
Shivers, Wes ATL 67
Shlapak, Boris IND 2
Shoals, Roger CLE 75, DEN 75, DET 73
Shoate, Rod NEP 56
Shockey, Jeremy NYG 80
Shockley, Bill BUF 23, NYJ 29, PIT 14
Shoemaker, Hub CHI ?
Shoener, Hal SFF 52
Shoener, Herb WSH 12/84
Shofner, Del NYG 85, STL 29
Shofner, Jim CLE 44
Shonk, John PHL 85
Shonta, Chuck NEP 34/40
Shook, Fred ARZ 38
Short, Brandon NYG 53
Short, Laval DEN 63, TBB 64
Shorter, Jim CLE 40, PIT 21, WSH 47
Shorthose, George KCC 80
Shorts, Peter NEP 90
Shoulders, Darin IND 64
Shoults, Paul xNYB 15
Shufelt, Pete NYG 58
Shugart, Clyde WSH 51
Shugarts, Bret PIT 95
Shula, David IND 85

Shula, Don CLE 44/96, IND 25, WSH 26
Shula, Mike TBB 11
Shuler, Heath NOS 5, WSH 5
Shuler, Mickey NYJ 82, PHL 82/85
Shull, Steve MIA 52/59
Shuman, Ron SFF 50
Shumann, Mike TBB 82
Shumate, Mark GBP 71, NYJ 71
Shumon, Ron CIN 59
Shupe, Mark BUF 55
Shurnas, Marshall CLE 53
Shurtz, Hubert PIT 89
Shy, Don ARZ 31, CHI 24, NOS 28, PIT 25
Shy, Les DAL 25/46, NYG 25
Siani, Mike IND 45, OAK 49
Siano, Mike PHL 86
Siano, Tony WSH 22, xBKN 30/32
Sidle, Jimmy ATL 24
Sidney, Dainon BUF 37, TEN 37
Sidorik, Alex xBOS 61, zBAL 44
Siegal, John CHI 6/19, CHI 19
Siegert, Herb WSH 63
Siegert, Wayne xNYB ?
Siegle, Jules NYG 34
Siemering, Larry WSH 27
Sieminski, Charlie SFF 65, ATL 77, DET 61
Siemon, Jeff MIN 50
Sienkiewicz, Troy SDC 65/72
Sieradzki, Steve zNYY 77
Sierocinski, Steve xBOS ?
Sievers, Eric NEP 85, SDC 85
Sigillo, Dom DET 52, CHI 19
Siglar, Ricky CAR 75, KCC 66/72, NOS 71, SFF 63
Signaigo, Joe xNYB 24, zNYY 31
Sigurdson, Sig zBAL 56
Sikahema, Vai ARZ 36, GBP 45, PHL 22
Sikich, Mike CLE 63
Sikich, Rudolph STL 48
Sikora, Mike ARZ 64
Silas, Sam ARZ 72, NYG 72, SFF 78
Sileo, Dan TBB 93
Siler, Rich MIA 87
Silipo, Joe BUF 64
Silvan, Nilo TBB 87
Silvers, Elliot SDC 68
Silvestri, Carl ARZ 45, ATL 45
Silvestri, Don NYJ 5
Simas, Bill ARZ 30
Simensen, Don STL 65/76
Simerson, John NEP 75, PHL 53/64, PIT 72/79, TEN 51
Simeta, Mike ATL 73

Simien, Tracy KCC 54, PIT 45, SDC 57
Simington, Milt PIT 55, STL 33
Simkus, Arnie MIN 69, NYJ 76
Simmonds, Mike TBB 62
Simmons, Anthony SEA 51
Simmons, Bob KCC 73
Simmons, Brian CIN 56
Simmons, Cleo DAL 82
Simmons, Clyde PHL 96, ARZ 96, CHI 96, CIN 96, JAX 96
Simmons, Dave ARZ 53, DAL 53, NOS 53
Simmons, Dave DET 63, GBP 61, IND 60/96, CHI 57
Simmons, Ed WSH 76
Simmons, Floyd zCHI 83
Simmons, Jack DET 53/73, zBAL 32
Simmons, Jason HOU 30, PIT 23
Simmons, Jeff STL 89
Simmons, Jerry ATL 44, CHI 80, DEN 80, NOS 25, PIT 25
Simmons, John ARZ 50
Simmons, John CIN 25, GBP 32, IND 41
Simmons, Kendall PIT 73
Simmons, King SDC 41
Simmons, Leon DEN 51
Simmons, Marcello CIN 22
Simmons, Michael NOS 96
Simmons, Roy NYG 69, WSH 60
Simmons, Sam MIA 83
Simmons, Stacey IND 85
Simmons, Terrance CAR 59
Simmons, Tony CLE 18, IND 15, NEP 81, NYG 15
Simmons, Tony SDC 97
Simmons, Victor DAL 53
Simmons, Wayne BUF 55, GBP 59, KCC 56
Simms, Bob NYG 83, PIT 34
Simms, Phil NYG 11
Simon, Corey PHL 90
Simon, Jim ATL 66, DET 66/83
Simon, John TEN 45, WSH 45
Simone, Mike DEN 51
Simoneau, Mark ATL 53, PHL 53
Simonetti, Len CLE 49
Simonini, Ed IND 56, NOS 54
Simons, Keith ARZ 70, KCC 72
Simonsen, Todd TEN 71
Simonson, Dave DET 79, IND 60, NYG 67, SEA 62
Simonton, Ken BUF 30
Simpkins, Ron CIN 56, GBP 51
Simpson, Al NYG 79
Simpson, Antoine MIA 98, SDC 93

Simpson, Bill BUF 45, STL 48
Simpson, Bob MIA 70
Simpson, Carl ARZ 78, CHI 98
Simpson, Howard MIN 75
Simpson, Jack DEN 67, OAK 49/50
Simpson, Jackie PIT 47, IND 41
Simpson, Keith SEA 42/48
Simpson, Mike SFF 38
Simpson, Nate GBP 48
Simpson, O.J. BUF 32/36, SFF 32
Simpson, Tim PIT 61
Simpson, Travis GBP 67
Simpson, Willie OAK 20/39, PIT 32
Sims, Barry OAK 65
Sims, Billy DET 20
Sims, Darryl CLE 91/99, PIT 99
Sims, David SEA 35
Sims, George STL 17
Sims, Jack SEA 61
Sims, Jimmie TBB 55
Sims, Joe ATL 66, GBP 68
Sims, Keith MIA 69, WSH 63
Sims, Ken ARZ 25
Sims, Kenneth NEP 77
Sims, Marvin IND 39
Sims, Mickey CLE 78
Sims, Reggie CIN 84
Sims, Ryan KCC 90
Sims, Tom IND 92, KCC 95
Sims, Tommy IND 45
Sims, William MIN 57
Sinceno, Kaseem CHI 85, PHL 89
Sinclair, Michael SEA 70
Singer, Curt DET 72, NYJ 74, SEA 73/74
Singer, Karl NEP 68
Singer, Walt NYG 15
Singletary, Bill NYG 54
Singletary, Mike CHI 50
Singletary, Reggie GBP 68, PHL 68/97
Singleton, Al DAL 51, TBB 51
Singleton, Chris MIA 55, NEP 55
Singleton, Nate BLT 87, SFF 88
Singleton, Ron SDC 72, SFF 67
Sinko, Steve WSH 34
Sinkovitz, Frank PIT 57
Sinkwich, Frankie DET 21, zBAL 76, zNYY 77
Sinnot, John IND 79
Sinnott, Greg STL 64
Sipe, Brian CLE 17
Siragusa, Tony BLT 98, IND 98
Sirmon, Peter TEN 59

Sirochman, George DET 52, PIT 20
Sisemore, Jerry PHL 76
Sisk, John CHI 7
Sisk, John CHI 27
Sisley, Brian NYG 93
Sisson, Scott MIN 9, NEP 9
Sistrunk, Manny PHL 79, WSH 64
Sistrunk, Otis OAK 60
Sites, Vince PIT 25
Sitko, Emil ARZ 24, SFF 82
Sivell, Jim NYG 33, xBKN 28, zMIA 41/31
Siwek, Mike ARZ 68
Skaggs, Jim PHL 70
Skaggs, Justin WSH 80
Skansi, Paul PIT 81, SEA 82
Skaugstad, Daryle GBP 91, SFF 78, TEN 90
Skeate, Gil GBP 16
Skene, Doug NEP 74
Skibinski, Joe CLE 65, GBP 63
Skibinski, John CHI 30
Skinner, Gerald GBP 73
Skladany, Joe PIT 23
Skladany, Leo PHL 63, NYG 87
Skladany, Tom DET 1/15, PHL 5
Sklopan, John DEN 45
Skoglund, Bob GBP 52
Skorich, Nick PIT 12
Skoronski, Bob GBP 76
Skoronski, Ed PIT 26, STL ?, xBKN 18
Skorupan, John BUF 55, NYG 57
Skow, Jim CIN 70, SDC 98, SEA 91, STL 68, TBB 71
Skrepenak, Greg CAR 75, OAK 78
Slaby, Lou DET 51, NYG 51
Slack, Reggie TEN 10
Slade, Chris NEP 53, CAR 50
Slater, Bryant IND 46
Slater, Fred ARZ 7/14/16/47/91
Slater, Jackie STL 78
Slater, Mark PHL 61, SDC 58
Slater, Walt PIT 31
Slaton, Mark MIN 35
Slaton, Tony DAL 65, STL 61
Slaughter, Chad OAK 78
Slaughter, Chuck NOS 79
Slaughter, Mickey DEN 7/14
Slaughter, T.J. BLT 53, GBP 57, JAX 53
Slaughter, Webster CLE 5/84, KCC 85/88, NYJ 87, SDC 84, TEN 84/89
Slay, Henry PHL 95
Slechta, Jeremy HOU 79, PHL 79
Sledge, Leroy TEN 41
Sleight, Elmer GBP 34/37

Sligh, Richard OAK 73
Slivinski, Steve WSH 16
Sloan, Bonnie ARZ 79
Sloan, David DET 86, NOS 48/88
Sloan, Dwight ARZ 36, DET 36
Sloan, Steve ATL 14
Slosburg, Phil xBOS 86, xNYB 86
Slough, Greg OAK 45/58
Slovacek, Emil SDC 72
Slovak, Martin STL 5
Slutzker, Scott IND 84, NOS 81/84
Smagala, Stan DAL 42
Smail, Alex PIT 72
Small, Donovan TEN 27
Small, Eldridge NYG 18
Small, Fred PIT 54
Small, George NYG 78
Small, Gerald ATL 48, MIA 48
Small, Jessie ARZ 52, PHL 52
Small, John ATL 66, DET 84
Small, Torrance IND 87, NEP 84, NOS 83, PHL 80, STL 83
Smalls, Fred PHL 53
Smart, Rod CAR 32, PHL 24
Smedley, Eric BUF 40, IND 40
Smeenge, Joel JAX 99, NOS 99
Smeja, Rudy CHI 51, PHL 82
Smerek, Don DAL 60
Smerlas, Fred BUF 76, NEP 76, SFF 76
Smigelesky, David ATL 3
Smilanich, Bronco STL 21
Smiley, Tom CIN 45, TEN 39, DEN 39
Smith, Aaron DEN 56
Smith, Aaron PIT 91
Smith, Akili CIN 11
Smith, Al TEN 54
Smith, Allen BUF 34
Smith, Allen CHI 30/32
Smith, Allen NYJ 37
Smith, Anthony OAK 94
Smith, Antowain BUF 23, NEP 32
Smith, Art DEN 55
Smith, Artie CIN 70, DAL 93, SFF 95/99
Smith, Barry GBP 80, TBB 88
Smith, Barty GBP 33
Smith, Ben ARZ 26, DEN 26, PHL 26
Smith, Ben GBP 23, PIT 25/29, WSH 38
Smith, Bill ARZ 40
Smith, Bill zCHI 46, zLAD 48
Smith, Billy Ray IND 74/83, PIT 77, STL 80
Smith, Billy Ray SDC 54
Smith, Blaine GBP 56
Smith, Blane KCC 27
Smith, Bob CLE 43/45, PHL 43

Smith, Bob TEN 23
Smith, Bob DET 40/46, zBRK 62, zBUF 85, zCHI ?
Smith, Bob L. DET 36
Smith, Bobby BUF 20, PIT 37
Smith, Bobby DET 43, STL 23
Smith, Brad CIN 91
Smith, Brady ATL 91, NOS 91
Smith, Brent MIA 74, NYJ 74
Smith, Brian STL 96
Smith, Bruce BUF 78
Smith, Bruce GBP 42, STL 56, WSH 78
Smith, Bubba IND 78, OAK 77, TEN 77
Smith, Byron IND 91
Smith, Carl BUF 35
Smith, Cedric ARZ 45, MIN 30, NOS 30, WSH 37
Smith, Charles ARZ 19
Smith, Charles PHL 85
Smith, Charles SFF 80
Smith, Charlie OAK 23, SDC 37
Smith, Chris KCC 47
Smith, Chris NYJ 71
Smith, Chuck ATL 90, CAR 91
Smith, Clifton WSH 51
Smith, Corey TBB 98
Smith, Dallis SEA 25
Smith, Daniel DEN 20
Smith, Darrin DAL 59, NOS 54, PHL 56, SEA 59
Smith, Daryl CIN 25, MIN 25
Smith, Daryle CLE 70, DAL 75/79, PHL 63/75
Smith, Dave CIN 60
Smith, Dave KCC 70, PIT 88, TEN 87
Smith, Dave SDC 42
Smith, Dave TEN 32
Smith, Dennis ARZ 35
Smith, Dennis DEN 49
Smith, Derek SFF 50, WSH 50
Smith, Detron DEN 42, IND 42
Smith, Dick WSH 28/?
Smith, Don DEN 14
Smith, Don ATL 65, BUF 74, NYJ 74
Smith, Don BUF 30, TBB 47
Smith, Donald DAL 39
Smith, Donnell GBP 74, NEP 65
Smith, Doug NYG 38
Smith, Doug STL 56
Smith, Doug TEN 99
Smith, Dwight TBB 26
Smith, Ed ATL 86, DET 45, PHL 89
Smith, Ed DEN 75
Smith, Ed GBP 21, xNYB 11
Smith, Ed GBP 28, WSH 36
Smith, Ed IND 52
Smith, Elliot DEN 28, SDC 28

Smith, Emanuel JAX 89
Smith, Emmitt DAL 22, ARZ 22
Smith, Eric CHI 83
Smith, Ernie SFF 42
Smith, Ernie GBP 45/61
Smith, Eugene CHI 19
Smith, Fernando BLT 96, CAR 71, JAX 96, MIN 95
Smith, Fletcher CIN 31, KCC 17
Smith, Frankie CHI 29, MIA 28/29, SFF 27/29
Smith, Franky KCC 72
Smith, Gary CIN 62
Smith, Gaylon CLE 74, STL 10
Smith, Gene DET 51
Smith, George ARZ 26
Smith, George WSH 47, SFF 23/25, xBKN 57, xBOS 43
Smith, Gordon MIN 87
Smith, Greg MIN 91
Smith, Hal NEP 70, OAK 72, DEN ?
Smith, Harry DET 33
Smith, Herman TBB 91
Smith, Holden IND 84
Smith, Hugh WSH 89/92
Smith, Hunter IND 17
Smith, Irv CLE 82, NOS 82, SFF 82
Smith, J.D SFF 24, CHI 39, DAL 24
Smith, J.D. PHL 76, DET 72
Smith, J.T. ARZ 84, KCC 86, WSH 81
Smith, Jack PHL 83, WSH 53
Smith, Jackie ARZ 81, DAL 81
Smith, Jackie PHL 32
Smith, James CHI 36, OAK 38
Smith, James DEN 47
Smith, Jeff CIN 76
Smith, Jeff JAX 73, KCC 65, PIT 62
Smith, Jeff KCC 42, TBB 35
Smith, Jeff NYG 57
Smith, Jeff NYG 85
Smith, Jermaine GBP 99
Smith, Jerry GBP 61, SFF 69
Smith, Jerry WSH 87
Smith, Jim OAK 86, PIT 86
Smith, Jim WSH 34
Smith, Jim zLAD 47
Smith, Jim Ray CLE 64/84, DAL 64
Smith, Jimmy JAX 82, DAL 82
Smith, Jimmy OAK 29, MIN 43, WSH 40
Smith, Joe zBAL 56
Smith, Joey NYG 88
Smith, John CLE 88
Smith, John NEP 1
Smith, John PHL 83
Smith, Johnny Ray SDC 45, TBB 22

Smith, Justin CIN 90
Smith, Justin STL 53, TBB 59
Smith, Ken CIN 62
Smith, Ken CLE 85
Smith, Kendal CIN 83
Smith, Kenny NOS 90
Smith, Kevin DAL 26
Smith, Kevin GBP 49, OAK 39/83
Smith, Kevin PIT 41
Smith, L.J. PHL 82
Smith, Lamar CAR 26, MIA 26, NOS 26/36, SEA 25, SEA 36
Smith, Lance ARZ 61, NYG 61
Smith, Larry GBP 96, JAX 94
Smith, Larry STL 38, WSH 38
Smith, Larry TEN 54
Smith, Laverne PIT 37
Smith, Leonard ARZ 45, BUF 46
Smith, Lucious BUF 47, KCC 23, SDC 33, STL 23
Smith, Lyman MIN 79
Smith, Mark ARZ 93, CLE 74/93
Smith, Marquette CAR 22
Smith, Marquis CLE 21
Smith, Marty BUF 79
Smith, Marvel PIT 77
Smith, Matt DEN 57
Smith, Maurice ATL 43
Smith, Michael KCC 83
Smith, Mike ATL 86
Smith, Mike MIA 25
Smith, Milton PHL 30/82
Smith, Moe GBP 43
Smith, Monte DEN 65
Smith, Musa BLT 32
Smith, Myron DAL 57
Smith, Neil DEN 90, KCC 90, SDC 91
Smith, Noland KCC 1/46, SFF 1
Smith, Ollie GBP 89, IND 80
Smith, Omar NYG 68
Smith, Onterrio MIN 32
Smith, Oscar DET 25
Smith, Otis DET 23, NEP 45, NYJ 45, PHL 30
Smith, Paul DEN 70, WSH 78
Smith, Paul DET 40, SFF 27
Smith, Perry ARZ 45, DEN 45, GBP 45
Smith, Phil IND 86, PHL 83, STL 88
Smith, Quintin CHI 17
Smith, Ralph ATL 81, CLE 41, PHL 85
Smith, Raonall MIN 57
Smith, Ray PHL 29
Smith, Ray Gene CHI 20
Smith, Red GBP 7/15/19/28, NYG 5/?
Smith, Reggie ATL 16
Smith, Reggie NYJ ?
Smith, Rich PHL 35

Smith, Ricky DET 41, NEP 27, WSH 26
Smith, Rico CLE 4/84
Smith, Riley WSH 35
Smith, Robaire TEN 98
Smith, Robert MIN 20/26
Smith, Rod CAR 21/31, GBP 31, MIN 47, NEP 22
Smith, Rod DEN 80
Smith, Ron CIN 68
Smith, Ron CHI 48/84, ATL 40, OAK 27, SDC 48, STL 42
Smith, Ron PHL 81, SDC 84, STL 84
Smith, Ron PIT 10, STL 14
Smith, Royce ATL 64, NOS 66
Smith, Russ SDC 20
Smith, Russell CHI 16
Smith, Sammie DEN 32, MIA 33
Smith, Sean CHI 97, DAL 67, NEP 97, STL 97, TBB 92
Smith, Sherman SDC 47, SEA 47
Smith, Shevin STL 30, TBB 29/30
Smith, Sid KCC 70, TEN 77
Smith, Steve CAR 89
Smith, Steve JAX 21
Smith, Steve MIN 74, PHL 74/78, PIT 88
Smith, Steve OAK 35, SEA 35
Smith, Steve SFF 86
Smith, Struggy ATL 20
Smith, Stu PIT 29/44
Smith, Tarik DAL 36
Smith, Terrelle NOS 44
Smith, Thomas BUF 28, CHI 25, IND 21
Smith, Tim TEN 83
Smith, Timmy DAL 33, WSH 36
Smith, Tody BUF 85, DAL 85, TEN 70/85
Smith, Tom MIA 29
Smith, Tommie CIN 24
Smith, Tony ATL 28, CAR 28
Smith, Torin NYG 81
Smith, Travian OAK 53/56
Smith, Troy PHL 19/83
Smith, Truett PIT 30/67
Smith, Vernice ARZ 69, CHI 69, STL 62, WSH 61
Smith, Vinson ATL 52, CHI 55, DAL 57, NOS 52
Smith, Vitamin STL 77
Smith, Waddell DAL 86
Smith, Wade MIA 74
Smith, Wayne ARZ 44, DET 44, MIN 40
Smith, Wee Willie NYG 0
Smith, Wes GBP 84
Smith, Wilfred ARZ 21

Smith, Willie DEN 71, OAK 63
Smith, Willie MIA 84
Smith, Zeke IND 61, NYG 61
Smith, Zuriel DAL 87
Smolinski, Mark IND 32, NYJ 30
Smoot, Fred WSH 21
Smoot, Raymond SDC 63
Smothers, Howard PHL 77
Smukler, Dave PHL 13, xBOS 33
Smyth, Bill STL 79
Snead, Norm NYG 16, MIN 16, PHL 16, WSH 16, SFF 16
Sneddon, Bob DET 20, WSH 15, zLAD 97
Snell, Donald SEA 86
Snell, Matt NYJ 41
Snell, Ray DET 61, PIT 72, TBB 72
Snelling, Ken GBP 52
Sniadecki, Jim SFF 58
Snider, Malcolm ATL 67, GBP 67
Snider, Matt GBP 38/44, MIN 44
Snidow, Ron CLE 88, WSH 78
Snipes, Angelo KCC 52, SDC 52, WSH 59
Snorton, Matt DEN 84
Snow, Jack STL 84
Snow, Justin IND 48
Snow, Percy CHI 96, KCC 59
Snowden, Cal ARZ 87, BUF 75, SDC 71
Snowden, Jim WSH 74
Snyder, Al NEP 38
Snyder, Bill PIT 25
Snyder, Bob CHI 13/17, STL 1/4
Snyder, Loren DAL 18
Snyder, Lum PHL 73/79
Snyder, Pat IND 57
Snyder, Snitz NYG 25
Snyder, Todd ATL 80
Soar, Hank NYG 15
Sobieski, Ben BUF 64
Sobocinski, Phil ATL 53
Soboleski, Joe WSH 60, DET 60, xDAL 64, xNYB 24, zCHI 35
Sochia, Brian MIA 70, DEN 70, TEN 72
Sodaski, John PHL 96, PIT 26/49
Sohn, Ben NYG 44, xCIN ?
Sohn, Kurt NYJ 87
Sokolosky, John DET 53
Soleau, Bob PIT 34
Soliday, Jake ARZ 18
Solitis, Bob NEP 42
Solomon, Ariel MIN 69, PIT 69
Solomon, Freddie MIA 86, SFF 88

Solomon, Freddie PHL 17/84
Solomon, Jesse ATL 54, DAL 54, MIA 58, MIN 54, TBB 54/55
Solomon, Roland BUF 28/46, DAL 46, DEN 39
Solt, Ron IND 66, PHL 65
Soltau, Gordy SFF 51/82
Solvold, Mike TBB 45
Somers, George PHL 19, PIT 19
Sommer, Don BUF 72
Sommer, Mike IND 26, OAK 29, WSH 21/27
Sommers, Jack WSH 46
Songin, Butch NEP 11, NYJ 11
Songy, Treg NYJ 21
Sorce, Ross PIT 81
Sorensen, Nick JAX 41, STL 41
Sorenson, Glen GBP 33
Sorey, Jim BUF 79
Sorey, Revie CHI 69
Sorrell, Henry DEN 51
Sortet, Wilbur PIT 20
Sortun, Rick ARZ 66
Sossamon, Lou zNYY 25
Souchak, Frank PIT 19
Souders, Cecil DET 55/82
South, Ronnie NOS 11
Southard, Tommy ARZ 80
Soward, R. Jay JAX 81
Sowell, Jerald NYJ 27/33
Sowell, Robert MIA 42/45
Sowells, Rich NYJ 46, TEN 29
Spachman, Chris ARZ 97
Spadaccini, Victor STL 33
Spagnola, John GBP 89, PHL 88, SEA 88
Spangler, Gene DET 30
Spani, Gary KCC 59
Spaniel, Frank WSH 26, xBAL 85
Spann, Gary KCC 94
Sparenberg, Dave CLE 66
Sparkman, Alan STL 44
Sparks, Dave SFF 39/68, WSH 68
Sparks, Phillippi DAL 20, NYG 22
Sparlis, Al GBP 21
Spavital, Jim xBAL 76, zLAD 77
Spearman, Armegis CIN 59
Spears, Anthony TEN 92
Spears, Ernest NOS 33
Spears, Marcus CHI 76/79, KCC 70
Spears, Ron GBP 79, NEP 78
Speedie, Mac CLE 58/88
Speegle, Cliff ARZ 23
Speelman, Harry DET 43
Speer, Del CLE 43, SEA 28
Speights, Dick SDC 25
Spek, Jeff TBB 88

Spellman, Alonzo CHI 90, DAL 90, DET 90
Spellman, Jack WSH 18
Spence, Blake NYJ 82, TBB 84
Spence, Julian ARZ 49, SFF 40, TEN 24
Spencer, Darryl ATL 84
Spencer, Herb ATL 51
Spencer, Jimmy CIN 22, DEN 33, NOS 37, SDC 22
Spencer, Joe CLE 49, GBP 34/79, zBRK 40
Spencer, Maurice ARZ 46, NOS 29
Spencer, Ollie DET 73/75/76/78, GBP 77, OAK 63/67
Spencer, Tim SDC 43
Spencer, Todd PIT 36, SDC 32
Spencer, Willie MIN 31, NYG 27
Speth, George DET 73
Speyrer, Cotton IND 28, MIA 82
Spicer, Paul DET 60, JAX 95
Spicer, Rob NYJ 59
Spielman, Chris DET 54, BUF 54
Spikes, Cameron ARZ 76, HOU 78, STL 73
Spikes, Irving MIA 35/40
Spikes, Jack BUF 32, KCC 30, TEN 32
Spikes, Takeo BUF 51, CIN 51
Spilis, John GBP 85
Spiller, Phil ARZ 19, ATL 42, CIN 48
Spillers, Ray PHL 33
Spindler, Marc DET 92/93, NYJ 93
Spinks, Jack ARZ 37, GBP 61, NYG 62, PIT 37
Spinney, Art IND 63/81, xBAL 53
Spires, Greg CLE 96, NEP 94, TBB 94
Spirida, John WSH 46
Spitulski, Bob SEA 55
Spiva, Andy ATL 51
Spivey, Mike ATL 47, CHI 47, NOS 47, OAK 45
Spivey, Sebron DAL 80
Sponaugle, Bob xNYB 29
Spoon, Brandon BUF 58
Spotwood, Quinton DAL 19
Spradlin, Danny ARZ 55, DAL 55, TBB 55
Spragen, Donnie DEN 59
Spriggs, Marcus BUF 69, CLE 91, GBP 79, MIA 76
Springer, Hal NYG 27
Springs, Kirk NYJ 21/45
Springs, Ron DAL 20, TBB 20
Springs, Shawn SEA 24
Springsteen, Bill ARZ 15/18

Sprinkle, Ed CHI 7
Sprottle, Jimmy CIN 52
Spruill, Jim zBAL 46
Spurrier, Steve SFF 11, TBB 11
Squirek, Jack MIA 53, OAK 58
Squyres, Seaman xCIN 47
St. Clair, Bob SFF 79
St. Clair, John STL 70
St. Clair, Mike CIN 72, CLE 74
St. Jean, Len NEP 60
St. John, Herb zBRK 34, zCHI 34
St. Louis, Brad CIN 48
Staat, Jeremy PIT 94
Stablein, Brian DET 83, IND 86
Stabler, Ken OAK 12, NOS 16, TEN 12
Stacco, Ed DET 52, WSH 57
Stachelski, Dave NOS 89
Stachowicz, Ray CHI 19, GBP 16
Stachowski, Rich DEN 78
Stackhouse, Charles MIN 45, NYG 45
Stackpool, John PHL 36
Stacy, Bill ARZ 24
Stacy, Red DET 25
Stacy, Siran PHL 27
Stadnik, John SDC 65
Stafford, Dick PHL 86
Stafford, Harry NYG 20
Staggers, Jon DET 86, GBP 22, PIT 2
Staggs, Jeff ARZ 87, SDC 81
Stahlman, Dick GBP 34/36
Stahlman, Dick CHI 19, NYG 29/33
Stai, Brenden JAX 68, WSH 66, DET 66, PIT 68
Stalcup, Jerry DEN 62, STL 60
Staley, Bill CHI 76, CIN 83
Staley, Duce PHL 22
Stallings, Dennis TEN 56/59
Stallings, Don WSH 76
Stallings, Larry ARZ 67
Stallings, Ramondo CIN 79
Stallings, Robert ARZ 90
Stalls, Dave DAL 65, OAK 61/74, TBB 65
Stallworth, Donte NOS 83
Stallworth, John PIT 82
Stallworth, Ron NYJ 96
Stallworth, Tim DEN 85
Stambaugh, Phil JAX 17
Stamer, Josh BUF 57
Stamper, John CHI 95
Stamps, Sylvester ATL 84, TBB 24
Stams, Frank CLE 50, KCC 55
Stanback, Harry IND 93
Stanback, Haskel ATL 24
Stanciel, Jeff ATL 23

Standlee, Norm CHI 22, SFF 32/72
Stanfel, Dick DET 63, WSH 60
Stanfield, Harold CLE 88
Stanfill, Bill MIA 84
Stankavage, Scott DEN 14, MIA 14
Stanley, C.B. zBUF 46
Stanley, Chad ARZ 12, HOU 7, SFF 4
Stanley, Israel NOS 90
Stanley, Sylvester NEP 63
Stanley, Walter DET 87, GBP 87, NEP 81, SDC 8, WSH 89
Stansauk, Don GBP 63/66
Stansbury Ed HOU 40
Stanton, Bill zBUF 53
Stanton, Harry zNYY 56
Stanton, Jack PIT 20
Starch, Ken GBP 32
Stargell, Tony CHI 45, IND 45, KCC 45, NYJ 45, TBB 45
Stark, Chad SEA 37
Stark, Rohn IND 3, CAR 3, PIT 3, SEA 3
Starke, George WSH 74
Starkey, Jason ARZ 50
Starks, Duane ARZ 22, BLT 22
Starks, Marshall NYJ 25
Starks, Tim MIN 34
Starnes, John ATL 3
Staroba, Paul CLE 85, GBP 85
Starr, Bart GBP 15/16
Starret, Ben GBP 63, PIT 15
Starring, Stephen DET 81, NEP 81, TBB 81
Stasica, Leo WSH 41, xBKN 11, xBOS 28
Stasica, Stan zMIA 85
Staten, Ralph BLT 41
Staten, Randy NYG 83
Staten, Robert TBB 33
Station, Larry PIT 90
Staton, Jim WSH 72
Statuto, Art STL 21, zBUF 22
Staubach, Roger DAL 12
Stauch, Scott NOS 32
Staurovsky, Jason ARZ 17, NEP 4, NYJ 2
Stautberg, Gerald CHI 68
Stautner, Ernie PIT 70/89
Stautzenberger, Odell zBUF 32
Staysniak, Joe ARZ 78, BUF 79, IND 79, KCC 68
Steber, John WSH 16
Stecker, Aaron TBB 22/27
Stedman, Troy KCC 94
Steed, Joel PIT 93
Steele, Chuck DET 60
Steele, Ernest PIT 37, PHL 37
Steele, Glen CIN 70
Steele, Larry DEN 23
Steele, Markus DAL 55
Steele, Robert DAL 81/82, MIN 82

Steels, Anthony BUF 45, SDC 45
Steen, Frank GBP 36
Steen, Jim DET 23
Steere, Dick PHL 72
Steffen, Jim DET 20, WSH 41
Stefik, Bob zBUF ?
Stegall, Milt CIN 84
Stegent, Larry ARZ 35
Steger, Pete ARZ ?
Stehower, Ron PIT 68
Stein, Bill ARZ 1
Stein, Bob KCC 66, MIN 52, SDC 52, STL 66
Stein, Sammy NYG 23, xBKN 19
Steinbach, Eric CIN 65
Steinbach, Larry ARZ 26, CHI 28, PHL 34
Steinbrunner, Don CLE 56/74
Steiner, Rebel GBP 74
Steinfeld, Al KCC 69, NYG 63, TEN 69
Steinfort, Fred ATL 1, BUF 5, DEN 19, NEP 5, OAK 4
Steinke, Gil PHL 41
Steinke, Jim CLE 20
Steinkemper, Bill CHI 35/36
Steinkuhler, Dean TEN 70
Steinmetz, Ken xBOS 21
Stemke, Kevin OAK 10
Stemrick, Greg TEN 27, NOS 27
Stenerud, Jan GBP 10, KCC 3, MIN 3
Stenger, Brian NEP 59, PIT 61
Stenn, Paul CHI 35, NYG 69, PIT 78, WSH 46
Stennett, Stud DET 20
Stensrud, Mike KCC 67, TBB 94, TEN 67, WSH 75
Stenstrom, Steve CHI 18, SFF 18
Stepanek, Joe MIN 73
Stephanos, Bill MIN 71
Stephen, Scott GBP 54, STL 50
Stephens, Bruce NYJ 87
Stephens, Calvin NEP 68
Stephens, Darnell TBB 54
Stephens, Hal KCC 92
Stephens, Harold NYJ 12
Stephens, Jamain CIN 75, PIT 67
Stephens, John NEP 44, GBP 32, KCC 21, STL 25
Stephens, Larry CLE 68, DAL 79/79, STL 50
Stephens, Leonard WSH 49
Stephens, Mac MIN 95, NYJ 57
Stephens, Red WSH 67
Stephens, Reggie NYG 28/34
Stephens, Rich OAK 77
Stephens, Rod SEA 94, WSH 99

Stephens, Santo CIN 53, JAX 53, KCC 53
Stephens, Steve NYJ 86
Stephens, Tom NEP 45
Stephens, Travis TBB 36
Stephens, Tremayne SDC 34
Stephenson, Dave GBP 44/53/69, STL 34
Stephenson, Dwight MIA 57
Stephenson, Kay BUF 18, SDC 18
Stepnoski, Mark DAL 53/70, TEN 53
Steponovich, Mike WSH ?
Steptoe, Jack SFF 87
Sterling, John GBP 33
Sternaman, Ed CHI 2/3
Sternaman, Joe CHI 4
Stetz, Bill PHL 65
Steuber, Bob CHI 28/37, CLE 88, zBUF 80, zLAD 94
Steussie, Todd MIN 73, CAR 75
Stevens, Billy GBP 10
Stevens, Don PHL 20
Stevens, Howard IND 27, NOS 22
Stevens, Jerramy SEA 86
Stevens, Mark SFF 7
Stevens, Matt KCC 1
Stevens, Matt BUF 23, HOU 26, NEP 26, PHL 45, WSH 23
Stevens, Pete PHL 20
Stevens, Richard PHL 73
Stevenson, Art NYG 16
Stevenson, Dominique BUF 50
Stevenson, Mark DET 65
Stevenson, Ralph STL 4
Stevenson, Rickey CLE 27
Steward, Dean PHL 36, PIT 36
Stewart, Andrew CLE 96
Stewart, Curtin DAL 28
Stewart, Daleroy DAL 64
Stewart, James DET 34, JAX 33, MIN 28
Stewart, Jimmy DET 46, NOS 26
Stewart, Joe OAK 80
Stewart, Kordell PIT 10, CHI 10
Stewart, Mark MIN 95
Stewart, Matt ATL 52
Stewart, Michael MIA 35, STL 23
Stewart, Quincy NYJ 51, SFF 54
Stewart, Ralph zBAL 20, zNYY 22
Stewart, Rayna JAX 26, MIA 21, TEN 26
Stewart, Ryan DET 38/42
Stewart, Steve ATL 58, GBP 58
Stewart, Todd CAR 70
Stewart, Tony CIN 86, PHL 81

Stewart, Vaughan ARZ 37, xBKN 33

Stewart, Wayne NYJ 89, SDC 89

Stickel, Walt CHI 45, PHL 75

Stickles, Monty NOS 87, SFF 85

Stidham, Howard SFF 58

Stief, Dave ARZ 21, WSH 83

Stienke, Jim NYG 20

Stieve, Terry ARZ 68, NOS 68

Stiger, Jim DAL 40, STL 26/48

Still, Art KCC 67, BUF 72

Still, Bryan ATL 86, SDC 80

Still, Jim zBUF 63/62

Stills, Gary KCC 55/56

Stills, Ken GBP 29, MIN 27

Stillwell, Roger CHI 71

Stinchcomb, Jon NOS 78

Stinchcomb, Matt OAK 74

Stinchcomb, Pete CHI 8

Stincic, Tom DAL 56, NOS 55

Stingley, Darryl NEP 84

Stinnette, Jim DEN 36

Stinson, Lemuel ATL 30, CHI 32

Stith, Carel TEN 70

Stith, Shyrone IND 30, JAX 33

Stits, Bill DET 20, NYG 48, SFF 20, WSH 26

Stock, John PIT 88/93

Stock, Mark IND 10/15, PIT 80, WSH 84

Stockemer, Ralph KCC 21

Stockton, Herschel PHL 21

Stocz, Eric DET 49

Stoepel, Terry CHI 89, TEN 69

Stoerner, Clint DAL 5

Stofa, John CIN 15, MIA 5/15

Stofer, Ken zBUF 61

Stofko, Ed PIT 25

Stojack, Frank xBKN 19

Stokely, Brandon BLT 80, IND 83

Stokes, Barry CLE 79, GBP 79, MIA 67

Stokes, Dixie DET 17

Stokes, Eric NEP 78

Stokes, Eric SEA 37

Stokes, Fred NOS 71, STL 60/65, WSH 60

Stokes, J.J. NEP 85, SFF 83

Stokes, Jesse DEN 21

Stokes, Lee ARZ 62

Stokes, Sim DAL 31

Stokes, Tim GBP 76, NYG 74, STL 78, WSH 76

Stolfa, Anton CHI 5/12

Stolhandske, Tom SFF 86

Stoltenberg, Bryan CAR 67, NYG 67, SDC 64

Stone, Avatus IND 41

Stone, Billy CHI 5/45, xBAL 82, zBAL 82

Stone, Don DEN 34, BUF 32/34, TEN 36

Stone, Dwight CAR 80, NYJ 83, PIT 20

Stone, Jack KCC 70, OAK 75

Stone, John OAK 86

Stone, Ken ARZ 23, BUF 23/24, TBB 28, WSH 20

Stone, Michael ARZ 44

Stone, Ron NYG 65, DAL 65, SFF 65

Stonebreaker, John GBP 51

Stonebreaker, Michael CHI 58, NOS 52

Stonebreaker, Steve IND 31, MIN 82, NOS 37

Stonesifer, Don ARZ 80

Stoops, Mike CHI 44

Storm, Edward PHL 22

Storr, Greg MIA 50

Story, Bill KCC 62

Storz, Eric JAX 50

Stotsbery, Hal xBKN ?

Stotter, Rich TEN 68

Stoudt, Cliff ARZ 18, DAL 18, MIA 18, PIT 18

Stouffer, Kelly SEA 11

Stough, Glen PIT 75

Stout, Pete WSH 32

Stoutmire, Omar DAL 24, NYG 23, NYJ 26

Stovall, Dick DET 12/66, WSH 45

Stovall, Jerry ARZ 21

Stover, Jeff SFF 72

Stover, Matt BLT 3, CLE 3

Stover, Smokey KCC 35

Stowe, Otto DAL 82, DEN 82, MIA 82

Stowe, Tyronne ARZ 90/91, PIT 56/90, SEA 59, WSH 90

Stowers, Tommie KCC 48, NOS 49

Stoyanovich, Pete KCC 10, MIA 10, STL 3

Strachan, Mike NOS 33

Strachan, Steve OAK 39

Stracka, Tim CLE 87

Strada, John KCC 87, NYG 80

Strader, Red ARZ 7

Stradford, Troy DET 86, KCC 25, MIA 23, STL 21

Strahan, Art ATL 74, TEN 74

Strahan, Michael NYG 92

Stralka, Clem WSH 39

Stramiello, Mike xBKN 44/18/15/30

Strand, Eli NOS 58, PIT 61

Stransky, Bob DEN 22

Stratton, Mike BUF 58, SDC 58

Strausbaugh, Jim ARZ 48

Strauthers, Thomas DET 94, MIN 94, PHL 93

Strayhorn, Les DAL 40

Streater, Eric TBB 89

Streeter, George CHI 30, IND 46

Streets, Tai SFF 89

Strenger, Rich DET 71

Stribling, Bill NYG 81, PHL 80

Stricker, Tony NYJ 26

Strickland, Bishop SFF 35/75

Strickland, Dave DEN 63

Strickland, Donald IND 30

Strickland, Fred DAL 55, GBP 55, MIN 53, STL 53, WSH 55

Strickland, Larry CHI 55

Striegal, Bill NEP 72, OAK ?, PHL 68

Stringer, Art TEN 39/53

Stringer, Bob PHL 44

Stringer, Korey MIN 77

Stringer, Scott ARZ 28

Stringert, Hal SDC 45

Stringfellow, Joe DET 81

Strock, Don CLE 12, IND 12, MIA 10

Strode, Woody STL 39

Strofolino, Mike ARZ 57, IND 51, STL 61

Strohmeyer, George zBRK 25, zCHI 25

Strom, Frank xBKN 36

Strom, Rick PIT 11

Stromberg, Mike NYJ 68

Strong, Frank SFF 58

Strong, Jasper TEN 4

Strong, Jim NOS 42, SFF 28

Strong, Ken NYG 30/50

Strong, Mack SEA 38

Strong, Ray ATL 25

Strong, William NOS 41

Stroschein, Breck xNYB 16

Stroth, Vince SFF 60, TEN 68/75

Strother, Deon DEN 41

Stroud, Jack NYG 66

Stroud, Marcus JAX 99

Stroud, Morris KCC 83

Strozier, Art SDC 89

Strozier, Wilbur SDC 81, SEA 87

Strugar, George NYJ 73, PIT 74, STL 77

Strutt, Art PIT 44

Stryzinski, Dan ATL 4, KCC 4, NYJ 4, PIT 4, TBB 4

Strzelczyk, Justin PIT 73

Strzykalski, John SFF 45/91

Stuart, Jim WSH 27

Stuart, Roy DET 40, STL 45, zBUF 70

Stubblefield, Dana SFF 94, OAK 94, WSH 94

Stubbs, Dan PHL 93, CIN 67/96, DAL 96, MIA 96, SFF 96

Stuber, Tim CAR 62

Stuckey, Henry MIA 48, NYG 48

Stuckey, Jim NYJ 71, SFF 79
Stuckey, Shawn NEP 93
Studaway, Mark ATL 71, TBB 71, TEN 98
Studdard, Dave DEN 70
Studdard, Les KCC 64, TEN 68
Studdard, Vern NYJ 22
Studstill, Darren DAL 30, JAX 30
Studstill, Pat DET 25, NEP 2, STL 28
Studwell, Scott MIN 55
Stukes, Charlie IND 47, STL 47
Sturgeon, Cecil PHL 71
Sturgeon, Lyle GBP 26
Sturgis, Oscar DAL 90
Sturm, Jerry DEN 72, NOS 73, PHL 55, TEN 62
Sturt, Fred NEP 63, NOS 68, WSH 65
Sturtridge, Dick CHI 21
Stuvaints, Russell PIT 33
Stydahar, Joe CHI 13/18
Styles, Lorenzo ATL 59, STL 51
Stynchula, Andy DAL 87, IND 83, NYG 72, WSH 71
Sualua, Nicky DAL 45
Subis, Nick DEN 60
Suchi, Larry ATL 46
Suci, Bob NEP 21, TEN 22
Sucic, Steve DET 33, STL 46, xBOS 39
Suffridge, Bob PHL 60/75
Sugar, Leo ARZ 84, DET 84, PHL 84
Suggs, Lee CLE 44
Suggs, Shafer CIN 23, NYJ 23
Suggs, Terrell BLT 55
Suggs, Walt TEN 76
Suhey, Matt CHI 26
Suhey, Steve PIT 62
Sulaitis, Joe NYG 21/37, xBOS ?
Sulima, George PIT 88
Sullins, John DEN 50
Sullivan, Bob SFF 94, zBRK 91
Sullivan, Carl GBP 95
Sullivan, Chris NEP 74, PIT 74
Sullivan, Dan IND 71
Sullivan, Dave CLE 48, CHI 12
Sullivan, Frank PIT 18
Sullivan, George xBOS ?
Sullivan, Gerry CLE 79
Sullivan, J.T. NOS 14
Sullivan, Jim ATL 74
Sullivan, John NYJ 50
Sullivan, John GBP 38, SDC 33, SFF 43
Sullivan, Jonathan NOS 97
Sullivan, Kent KCC 10, SDC 1, TEN 7
Sullivan, Marques BUF 74
Sullivan, Mike TBB 67
Sullivan, Pat ATL 7
Sullivan, Robert PIT 27
Sullivan, Tom CLE 26, PHL 25

Sully, Ivory DET 44, STL 37, TBB 44
Suminski, Dave ARZ 61, WSH 67
Sumler, Tony DET 31
Summerall, Carl NYG 19
Summerall, Pat ARZ 81/85, DET 84, NYG 88
Summerhays, Bob GBP 77
Summers, Don DEN 85, GBP 86
Summers, Fred CLE 20
Summers, Jim DEN 46
Summers, Wilbur DET 10
Sumner, Charles CHI 26, MIN 26
Sumner, Walt CLE 29
Sumpter, Tony zCHI 34
Sunde, Milt MIN 64
Sunter, Ian CIN 19, DET 10
Superick, Steve TEN 8
Supernaw, Kywin DET 29
Supulski, Leonard PHL 80
Surtain, Patrick MIA 23
Susoeff, Nick SFF 58
Sustersic, Ed CLE 70
Sutch, George ARZ 88
Sutherin, Don NYG 26, PIT 20
Sutherland, Doug MIN 69, NOS 60, SEA 69
Sutherland, Vinnie SFF 14
Sutro, John SFF 68
Sutter, Ed BLT 54, ATL 50
Sutter, Ryan CAR 35
Suttle, Jason DEN 35
Sutton, Ed NYG 26, WSH 30
Sutton, Eric WSH 22
Sutton, Frank NYG 76
Sutton, Joe PHL 45, zBUF 86
Sutton, John NOS 20
Sutton, Mickey BUF 20, GBP 49, STL 49, TEN 40
Sutton, Mike TEN 93
Sutton, Mitch PHL 79
Sutton, Reggie NOS 29
Sutton, Ricky PIT 96
Svare, Harland NYG 84, STL 65, STL 76
Svendsen, Earl GBP 7/53/66, xBKN 18
Svendsen, George GBP 43/66
Sverchek, Paul MIN 94
Svihus, Bob NYJ 76, OAK 76
Svoboda, Bill ARZ 31/67/68, NYG 30
Swain, Bill DET 51, MIN 52, NYG 52, STL 52
Swain, John MIA 29/40, MIN 29, PIT 26
Swan, Russ DAL 51/57
Swanke, Karl GBP 67
Swann, Charles DEN 25
Swann, Eric ARZ 98, CAR 98
Swann, Lynn PIT 88

Swanson, Evar ARZ 12
Swanson, Pete KCC 73, STL 68
Swanson, Shane DEN 80
Swanson, Terry CIN 41, NEP 36
Swarn, George CLE 38
Swartwoudt, Gregg NYG 59
Swartz, Chris ARZ 17
Swatland, Dick TEN 64
Swayda, Shawn ATL 93
Swayne, Harry BLT 70, DEN 74, MIA 70, SDC 72, TBB 70
Swayne, Kevin NYJ 82
Sweeney, Calvin PIT 85
Sweeney, Jake CHI 13
Sweeney, Jim NYJ 53, PIT 66, SEA 53
Sweeney, Kevin DAL 19
Sweeney, Neal DEN 49
Sweeney, Steve OAK 89
Sweeney, Walt SDC 78, WSH 78
Sweet, Joe NEP 81, SDC 85, STL 82
Sweet, Tony NYJ 88
Sweetan, Karl DET 14, NOS 14/15, STL 10
Sweiger, Bob zCHI 80, zNYY 80
Swenson, Bob DEN 51
Swiacki, Bill NYG 81, DET 81
Swiadon, Phil xBKN 24
Swider, Larry ARZ 10, DET 12, TBB 9
Swift, Doug MIA 59
Swift, Justin PHL 89, SFF 88
Swift, Michael CAR 26, JAX 30, SDC 27
Swilley, Dennis MIN 67
Swilling, Pat DET 56, NOS 56, OAK 56
Swiney, Clovis NYJ 79
Swiney, Erwin GBP 26
Swinford, Wayne SFF 23
Swinger, Rashod ARZ 91
Swink, Jim KCC 23
Swinney, Clovis NOS 79
Swinson, Corey STL 66
Swinton, Reggie DAL 80
Swisher, Bob CHI 48
Swistowicz, Mike ARZ 44, xNYB 23
Switzer, Marvin BUF 21
Switzer, Veryl GBP 27
Swoope, Craig IND 26, TBB 41
Swoopes, Pat MIA 67, NOS 69
Swoops, Patrick KCC 67
Sword, Sam IND 98, OAK 56
Sydner, Jeff NYJ 85, PHL 85
Sydney, Harry GBP 42, SFF 24
Sydnor, Willie PIT 83
Sykes, Alfred NEP 13
Sykes, Bob WSH 37
Sykes, Gene BUF 23, DEN 23
Sykes, Jashon DEN 57

Sykes, John SDC 46
Sylvester, John zBAL 83, zNYY 75
Sylvester, Steve OAK 66
Symank, John ARZ 31, GBP 27
Symonette, Josh WSH 34
Szafaryn, Len GBP 47/51/68, PHL 74/76, WSH 43
Szakash, Paul DET 8/22/84
Szalay, Thacher CIN 66
Szaro, Rich NOS 15, NYJ ?
Szczecko, Joe ATL 71, NYG 76
Szot, Walt ARZ 36, PIT 65/89
Szott, Dave KCC 79, NYJ 79, WSH 79
Szymakowski, Dave NOS 88
Szymanski, Dick IND 52
Szymanski, Frank CHI 44, DET 83, PHL 51
Szymanski, Jim DEN 94
Tabor, Paul CHI 53
Tabor, Phil NYG 80
Tabor, Tom IND 76
Tackett, Doyle zBRK 80/62
Tackwell, Charles CHI 19, xCIN 21/50
Taffoni, Joe CLE 62, NYG 72
Tafoya, Joe CHI 99
Tagge, Jerry GBP 17
Tagliaferri, John MIA 35
Taibi, Joe NYG 82
Tait, Art xDAL 83, xNYB 51/1
Tait, John KCC 76
Talamini, Bob TEN 61, NYJ 61
Talbert, Diron WSH 72, STL 72
Talbert, Don ATL 72, DAL 71/72, NOS 72
Talcott, Don PHL 62
Taliaferro, George IND 20, PHL 24, xDAL 20, xNYB 20, zLAD 93
Taliaferro, Mike NEP 17, BUF 17, NYJ 17
Talley, Ben ATL 59, NYG 54
Talley, Darryl BUF 56, ATL 99, MIN 55
Talley, Stan OAK 5
Talton, Ken KCC 45
Talton, Tyree DET 25
Tamburello, Ben PHL 61
Tamburo, Sam xNYB 8
Tamm, Ralph CIN 71, CLE 65, KCC 64, SFF 64, WSH 62/64
Tanguay, Jim PIT 42
Tannen, Steve NYJ 21
Tanner, Barron ARZ 92, MIA 72, WSH 71
Tanner, Hamp xDAL 78/79, SFF 46/77
Tanner, John NEP 53, SDC 85
Tant, Jay ARZ 84/87
Tanuvasa, Maa DEN 98, SDC 94

Tarasovic, George DEN 65, PHL 82, PIT 50/52/53/56/63
Tarbox, Bruce STL 61
Tardits, Richard ARZ 92, NEP 53
Tarkenton, Fran MIN 10, NYG 10
Tarle, Jim JAX 5
Tarr, Jerry DEN 41
Tarrant, Bob NYG 31
Tarrant, Jim zMIA 65
Tarver, John NEP 36, PHL 49
Taseff, Carl BUF 23, CLE 98, IND 23, PHL 23
Tasker, Steve BUF 89, TEN 80
Tassos, Damon DET 6, GBP 15
Tatarek, Bob BUF 71, DET 71
Tate, David CHI 49, IND 49, NYG 49
Tate, Franklin SDC 59
Tate, John NYG 58
Tate, Lars CHI 33, TBB 34
Tate, Robert BLT 22, MIN 28/83
Tate, Rodney ATL 44, CIN 23
Tate, Willy KCC 80, TBB 82
Tatman, Pete MIN 33
Tatum, Jack OAK 31/32, TEN 28
Tatum, Jesse PIT 47
Tatum, Kinnon CAR 50
Tatupu, Mosi NEP 30, STL 30
Tausch, Terry MIN 66, SFF 66
Tauscher, Mark GBP 65
Tautalatasi, Junior DAL 25, PHL 37
Tautolo, John NYG 65, OAK 61
Tautolo, Terry DET 50, MIA 52, PHL 58, SFF 50
Tavener, John zMIA 27
Taves, Josh CAR 91, OAK 99
Taylor, Aaron GBP 73, SDC 73
Taylor, Alphonso DEN 95
Taylor, Altie DET 42, TEN 42
Taylor, Ben CLE 58
Taylor, Billy NYG 38, NYJ 38, OAK 49
Taylor, Bob NYG 65
Taylor, Bobby PHL 21
Taylor, Brian BUF 21, CHI 27
Taylor, Bruce SFF 44
Taylor, Cecil STL 48
Taylor, Charley WSH 42
Taylor, Charlie xBKN 21
Taylor, Chester BLT 29
Taylor, Chuck zMIA 37
Taylor, Cliff GBP 27, CHI 22
Taylor, Cordell JAX 23, SEA 21
Taylor, Craig CIN 20
Taylor, David IND 64
Taylor, Derrick NOS 22
Taylor, Ed MIA 45, NYJ 38
Taylor, Fred JAX 28
Taylor, Gene NEP 82, TBB 85

Taylor, Greg NEP 45
Taylor, Henry ATL 79
Taylor, Henry DET 96
Taylor, Henry MIA 98
Taylor, Hosea IND 90
Taylor, Hugh WSH 28/84
Taylor, Ike PIT 24
Taylor, James NOS 71
Taylor, Jason MIA 99
Taylor, Jay ARZ 27, KCC 27
Taylor, Jesse SDC 42
Taylor, Jim ARZ 55, PIT 57
Taylor, Jim GBP 31, NOS 31
Taylor, Jim Bob IND 12
Taylor, Joe CHI 20
Taylor, John SFF 82
Taylor, Johnnie ATL 96, MIA 54, SDC 59
Taylor, Keith IND 27, NOS 29, WSH 27/29
Taylor, Ken CHI 31, SDC 24
Taylor, Kitrick DEN 81, GBP 85, KCC 82, NEP 49, SDC 85
Taylor, Lawrence NYG 56
Taylor, Leland BLT 92
Taylor, Lionel DEN 87, CHI 32, TEN 87
Taylor, Malcolm ATL 67, OAK 96, TEN 70, TEN 77
Taylor, Michael NYJ 50
Taylor, Mike ARZ 68, NOS 77, PIT 77, WSH 78
Taylor, Otis KCC 89
Taylor, Rob TBB 72
Taylor, Roger KCC 76
Taylor, Roosevelt CHI 24, SFF 25, WSH 22
Taylor, Ryan CLE 51
Taylor, Sammie SDC 81
Taylor, Shannon BLT 54, JAX 56, SDC 94
Taylor, Steve KCC 48
Taylor, Tarzan CHI 14
Taylor, Terry ATL 24, CLE 24, DET 21, SEA 20/24
Taylor, Tom STL 62
Taylor, Travis BLT 89
Taylor, Willie GBP 89
Tays, Jim ARZ 4
Teafatiller, Guy CHI 93
Teague, George DAL 30/31, GBP 31, MIA 23
Teague, Matthew ATL 72
Teague, Pat TBB 52
Teague, Trey BUF 70, DEN 70
Teal, Jim DET 57
Teal, Jimmy BUF 86, SEA 85
Teal, Willie MIN 37, OAK 20
Tearry, Larry DET 54
Teerlinck, John SDC 77
Teeter, Mike CAR 91, MIN 67, TEN 71

Teets, Dick CLE 56

Teeuws, Len ARZ 74, STL 74

Teichelman, Lance IND 99

Teifke, Mike CLE 50

Teltschik, John PHL 10

Temp, Jim GBP 82

Temple, Mark WSH 25, xBKN 25

Ten Napel, Garth DET 57, ATL ?

Tennell, Derek CLE 81, DAL 89, DET 46, MIN 46

Tenner, Bob GBP 36

Tensi, Steve DEN 13, SDC 13

Tepe, Lou PIT 55/61

Teresa, Tony OAK 25, SFF 26

Tereshinski, Joe WSH 37/89

Terlep, George CLE 64, zBUF 62

Terrell, Daryl JAX 67, NOS 78, WSH 67

Terrell, David CHI 83

Terrell, David WSH 31

Terrell, Marvin KCC 63

Terrell, Pat CAR 40, GBP 40, NYJ 27, STL 37

Terrell, Ray CLE 84, zBAL 83

Terry, Chris CAR 70, SEA 72

Terry, Corey JAX 57, NOS 50

Terry, Doug KCC 24/25/32

Terry, Joe SEA 50

Terry, Nat DET 30, PIT 41

Terry, Rick CAR 71

Terry, Ryan ARZ 31

Terry, Tim CIN 52, SEA 59

Tesser, Rudy PIT 40

Testaverde, Vinny BLT 12, CLE 12, NYJ 16, TBB 14

Testerman, Don MIA 34, SEA 42

Teteak, Deral GBP 66

Tevis, Lee zBRK 92/82

Tew, Lowell zNYY 83

Thacker, Alvin PHL 60

Tharp, Corky NYJ 45

Tharpe, Larry ARZ 71, DET 71, PIT 71

Tharpe, Richard BUF 74/94

Thaxton, Galand ATL 53, SDC 56

Thaxton, James NOS 86, ARZ 87, CLE 84, SDC 86

Thayer, Harry DET 41

Thayer, Tom CHI 57, MIA 57

Theismann, Joe WSH 7

Thelwell, Ryan SDC 87

Theofiledes, Harry WSH 17

Thibaut, Jim zBUF 73

Thibert, Jim DEN 84

Thibodeaux, Keith ATL 26, GBP 22, MIN 27, WSH 32

Thielemann, R.C. ATL 68, WSH 69

Thierry, John CHI 91/94, CLE 53, GBP 91, ATL 55

Thigpen, Yancey PIT 82, SDC 84, TEN 82

Thomas, Aaron NYG 88, SFF 89

Thomas, Adalius BLT 96

Thomas, Andre MIN 35

Thomas, Anthony CHI 35

Thomas, Arland IND 67

Thomas, Ben ATL 72, GBP 92, NEP 99, PIT 69, STL 94

Thomas, Bill DAL 27, KCC 43, TEN 28

Thomas, Blair CAR 31, DAL 32, NEP 32, NYJ 32

Thomas, Bob CHI 16, DET 12, NYG 9, SDC 16

Thomas, Bob SDC 35, STL 35

Thomas, Broderick DAL 51, DET 51, MIN 51, TBB 51

Thomas, Bryan NYJ 99, WSH 47

Thomas, Cal DET 15/75

Thomas, Calvin CHI 33, DEN 32

Thomas, Carlton KCC 38

Thomas, Charlie KCC 49

Thomas, Charlie NOS 23

Thomas, Chris KCC 87, SFF 89, STL 89, WSH 89

Thomas, Chuck ATL 66, SFF 60

Thomas, Clendon PIT 28, STL 35, STL 46

Thomas, Corey DET 15

Thomas, Curtland NOS 85

Thomas, Damon BUF 82/86

Thomas, Dave DAL 41, JAX 41, NYG 41

Thomas, Dee TEN 36

Thomas, Derrick KCC 58

Thomas, Donnie NEP 51

Thomas, Doug SEA 85

Thomas, Duane DAL 33, WSH 47

Thomas, Earl ARZ 82, CHI 82, TEN 89

Thomas, Earlie DEN 48, NYJ 45

Thomas, Ed TBB 86

Thomas, Edward JAX 59

Thomas, Emmitt KCC 18

Thomas, Eric CIN 22, DEN 26, NYJ 22

Thomas, Fred NOS 22, SEA 22

Thomas, Garth SEA 69

Thomas, Gene KCC 45, NEP 22

Thomas, George ATL 89, TBB 87

Thomas, George NYG 20, WSH 20

Thomas, Henry MIN 97, DET 98, NEP 95, NOS 79

Thomas, Hollis PHL 78

Thomas, Ike BUF 37, DAL 37, GBP 37

Thomas, J.T. PIT 24, DEN 26

Thomas, J.T. STL 18/87

Thomas, Jason BLT 65

Thomas, Jesse IND 40, SDC 20

Thomas, Jewerl KCC 31, SDC 32, STL 33

Thomas, Jim ARZ 41

Thomas, Jimmy SFF 24

Thomas, Joe NOS 89

Thomas, John NYJ 76

Thomas, John SFF 78

Thomas, Johnny CLE 20, SDC 47, PHL 41, WSH 22/41/47

Thomas, Juqua TEN 94

Thomas, Kelly STL 73, TBB 70

Thomas, Ken KCC 35

Thomas, Kevin BUF 28

Thomas, Kevin TBB 64

Thomas, Kiwaukee JAX 24/41

Thomas, Lamar MIA 85, TBB 87

Thomas, Lavale GBP 45

Thomas, Lee CIN 78, SDC 73

Thomas, Lynn SFF 28

Thomas, Mark CAR 95, CHI 95, IND 75/90, NYG 85, SFF 72

Thomas, Markus PHL 46

Thomas, Marvin DET 98

Thomas, Mike WSH 22, SDC 22

Thomas, Norris MIA 41, TBB 41

Thomas, Orlando MIN 42/43

Thomas, Pat STL 27

Thomas, Ralph ARZ 85, WSH 87

Thomas, Randy NYJ 77, WSH 77

Thomas, Ratcliff IND 51/55

Thomas, Rex xBKN 19

Thomas, Ricky SEA 40

Thomas, Robb KCC 81, SEA 86, TBB 84

Thomas, Robert DAL 44/59, STL 55

Thomas, Rodell MIA 53/54, SEA 59

Thomas, Rodney ATL 20, MIA 24/45, STL 21, TEN 20

Thomas, Russ DET 71

Thomas, Sean ATL 22, CIN 24

Thomas, Skip OAK 26

Thomas, Speedy CIN 17, NOS 17

Thomas, Spencer IND 46, WSH 24

Thomas, Stan CHI 60, TEN 70

Thomas, Tarlos HOU 77

Thomas, Thurman BUF 34, MIA 34

Thomas, Todd KCC 62

Thomas, Tra PHL 72

Thomas, Tre NYG 29
Thomas, William PHL 51, OAK 59
Thomas, Zach DEN 82, TBB 84
Thomas, Zach MIA 54
Thomaselli, Rich TEN 28
Thomason, Bobby PHL 11, GBP 28, STL 65
Thomason, Jeff CIN 49, GBP 83, PHL 83
Thomason, Jim DET 33
Thomason, Stumpy PHL 15/29, xBKN 25/23/21/17/7/55/30
Thomasson, Leon ATL 25
Thome, Chris CLE 67
Thompson, Anthony ARZ 34, STL 32
Thompson, Anthony DEN 53
Thompson, Arland DEN 61, GBP 71, KCC 58
Thompson, Aundra GBP 43/89, IND 21, NOS 89, SDC 81
Thompson, Bennie BLT 37, CLE 37, KCC 46, NOS 37
Thompson, Billy DEN 36
Thompson, Bobby DET 33
Thompson, Bobby DET 27, NOS 27
Thompson, Broderick DAL 67, DEN 76, PHL 76, SDC 76
Thompson, Chaun CLE 51
Thompson, Clarence GBP 50, PIT 27
Thompson, Craig CIN 48
Thompson, Darrell GBP 26/39
Thompson, Dave DET 65, NOS 65
Thompson, David STL 28
Thompson, Del KCC 39
Thompson, Derrius MIA 88, WSH 13/84/88
Thompson, Don IND 83, PHL 84
Thompson, Donnell IND 54/99, PIT 90
Thompson, Emmuel TEN 28
Thompson, Ernie KCC 45, STL 32
Thompson, Gary BUF 24/38
Thompson, Hal zBRK 55
Thompson, Harry ARZ 60, STL 44/66
Thompson, Jack CIN 12, TBB 14
Thompson, James NYG 89
Thompson, Jesse DET 84
Thompson, Jim DEN 77
Thompson, John GBP 83/87
Thompson, Ken ARZ 86
Thompson, Kevin CLE 10/16
Thompson, Lamont CIN 24, TEN 37
Thompson, Leonard DET 39
Thompson, Leroy KCC 31, NEP 36, PIT 34, TBB 34

Thompson, Marty DET 81
Thompson, Michael ATL 66
Thompson, Mike CIN 93, CLE 96, JAX 95
Thompson, Norm ARZ 42/43, IND 43
Thompson, Ray ARZ 55
Thompson, Reyna NYG 21, MIA 19/24, NEP 21
Thompson, Ricky ARZ 82, IND 88, WSH 83
Thompson, Robert DEN 4
Thompson, Robert DET 90, TBB 56/59
Thompson, Rocky NYG 22
Thompson, Russ CHI 29, PHL 25
Thompson, Steve NYJ 85, NYJ 87
Thompson, Steve WSH 67
Thompson, Ted TEN 51
Thompson, Tommy CLE 24/36/54
Thompson, Tommy PHL 10/11, PIT 3
Thompson, Tommy SDC 38
Thompson, Tommy SFF 3
Thompson, Vince DET 38
Thompson, Warren NYG 97
Thompson, Weegie PIT 87
Thompson, Woody ATL 48
Thoms, Art OAK 80, PHL 80
Thornbladh, Bob KCC 50
Thornhill, Josh DET 57
Thornton, Bill ARZ 36
Thornton, Bruce ARZ 79, DAL 77
Thornton, Bubba BUF 34
Thornton, David IND 50
Thornton, George NYG 79, SDC 93
Thornton, Jack MIA 59
Thornton, James CHI 80, NYJ 80, TEN 44
Thornton, John CIN 97, TEN 78
Thornton, John CLE 91, MIN 94
Thornton, Reggie CIN 83, IND 86
Thornton, Richard PHL 28
Thornton, Rupe SFF 35/46
Thornton, Sidney PIT 38/39
Thorp, Don IND 62/78/96, KCC 71, NOS 96
Thorpe, Jim NYG 21, ARZ ?
Thorpe, Wilfred STL 26
Thrash, James PHL 80, WSH 87
Threadgill, Bruce SFF 23
Threats, Jabbar JAX 98
Thrift, Cliff CHI 52, SDC 59, STL 52
Thrower, Jim DET 21, PHL 49
Thrower, Willie CHI 14

Thuerk, Owen DET 86
Thurbon, Bob PIT 49, ARZ 49, zBUF 83, PHL 49
Thure, Brian WSH 74
Thurlow, Steve NYG 27, WSH 44
Thurman, Dennis ARZ 23, DAL 32
Thurman, Junior NOS 33
Thurston, Fuzzy GBP 63, IND 64
Thweatt, Byron TEN 58
Tice, John NOS 82
Tice, Mike MIN 83/87, SEA 86/87, WSH 86
Tidmore, Sam CLE 54
Tidwell, Bill SFF 24
Tidwell, Travis NYG 20
Tierney, Leo CLE 51, NYG 52
Tiffin, Van MIA 3, TBB 1
Tigges, Mark CIN 77
Tiggle, Calvin TBB 58
Tilleman, Mike ATL 74, MIN 74, NOS 74, TEN 78
Tiller, Jim NYJ 24
Tiller, Morgan PIT 12, xBOS 17
Tilley, Emmitt MIA 52
Tilley, Pat ARZ 83
Tillison, Ed DET 34
Tillman, Al zBAL 22
Tillman, Andre MIA 87
Tillman, Cedric DEN 87, JAX 87
Tillman, Charles CHI 33
Tillman, Faddie NOS 71
Tillman, Lawyer CAR 85, CLE 85
Tillman, Lewis CHI 27, NYG 34
Tillman, Pat ARZ 40
Tillman, Spencer SFF 23, TEN 32/33
Tillman, Travares CAR 42, BUF 28
Tillmon, Tony OAK 29
Tilman, Rusty WSH 67
Tilton, Ron WSH 76
Timberlake, Bob NYG 18
Timberlake, George GBP 53
Times, Ken ARZ 74, SFF 60
Timmer, Kirk DAL 59
Timmerman, Adam GBP 63, STL 62
Timmons, Charlie zBRK 91
Timpson, Michael CHI 83, NEP 83, PHL 83
Tindale, Tim BUF 33
Tingelhoff, Mick MIN 53
Tinker, Gerald ATL 81, GBP 82
Tinoisamoa, Pisa STL 50
Tinsley, Gaynell ARZ 11/31/43
Tinsley, Jess ARZ 21/31
Tinsley, Keith CLE 84

Tinsley, Pete GBP 21
Tinsley, Scott PHL 11
Tinsley, Sid PIT 48
Tippett, Andre NEP 56
Tippins, Ken ATL 52, DAL 98
Tipton, Dave NEP 60, NYG 71, SDC 75, SEA 75
Tipton, Gregg ARZ 12
Tipton, Howard ARZ 27/34
Tipton, Rico SEA 52
Titchenal, Bob SFF 51, WSH 18, zLAD 50
Titensor, Glen DAL 63
Tittle, Y.A. NYG 14, xBAL 63, zBAL 63, SFF 14/64
Titus, George PIT 43
Titus, Silas PIT 49, xBKN 15/2
Tiumalu, Casey STL 42
Tobeck, Robbie ATL 61, SEA 61
Tobey, Dave DEN 51, MIN 51
Tobin, Bill TEN 47
Tobin, George NYG 62
Tobin, Steve NYG 52
Toburen, Nelson GBP 61/69
Todd, Dick WSH 41
Todd, Jim DET 34
Todd, Larry OAK 22
Todd, Richard NOS 11/14, NYJ 14
Toefield, LaBrandon JAX 22
Toews, Jeff MIA 60
Toews, Loren PIT 51
Tofflemire, Joe SEA 56
Tofil, Joe xBKN 32
Toibin, Brendan WSH 8
Tolar, Charles TEN 44
Tolbert, Brandon DAL 50/53
Tolbert, Jim ARZ 45, SDC 43, TEN 42
Tolbert, Tony DAL 62/92
Toler, Ken NEP 82
Toles, Alvin NOS 54
Tolhurst, Ryan CAR 3
Tolle, Stuart DET 99
Tollefson, Chuck GBP 27/46/77
Tolleson, Tommy ATL 86
Tolliver, Billy Joe ATL 11/13, KCC 8, NOS 11, SDC 11, TEN 11
Toloumu, David ATL 24
Tom, Mel CHI 89, PHL 58/99
Tomaini, Army NYG 55
Tomaini, Johnny xBKN 26
Tomasello, Carl NYG ?
Tomasetti, Lou DET 15, PHL 15, PIT 21, zBUF 87/74
Tomasic, Andy PIT 3/4
Tomberlin, Pat IND 68, TBB 68
Tomczak, Mike CHI 18, CLE 18, GBP 18, PIT 18
Tomich, Jared GBP 75, NOS 90

Tomlin, Tommy NYG 14/32
Tomlinson, Dick PIT 62
Tomlinson, LaDainian SDC 21
Tommerson, Clarence PIT 30
Toneff, Bob SFF 62/74, WSH 79
Tonelli, Mario ARZ 58/99
Tonelli, Tony DET 15
Toner, Ed IND 28/44, NEP 75
Toner, Tom GBP 59
Toney, Anthony PHL 25
Tongue, Marco BUF 30, IND 46
Tongue, Reggie KCC 25/41, SEA 25
Tonnemaker, Clayton GBP 35/58
Toogood, Charley ARZ 70, STL 70
Toomay, Pat BUF 65, DAL 67, OAK 67, TBB 66
Toomer, Amani NYG 81/89
Toon, Al NYJ 88
Tootle, Jeff NYG 92
Topor, Ted DET 54
Topp, Bob NYG 87
Toran, Stacey OAK 30
Torczon, LaVerne BUF 87, MIA 88, NYJ 87
Torgeson, Lavern DET 53, WSH 53
Torkelson, Eric GBP 26
Torrance, Jack CHI 34
Torretta, Gino IND 2, MIN 13, SEA 13, SFF 13
Torrey, Bob MIA 38, NYG 39, PHL 39
Toscani, Frank ARZ 28, xBKN 7
Tosi, Flavio WSH 30
Tosi, John PIT 64, xBKN 26
Tosi, Mao ARZ 78
Toth, Tom MIA 76, SDC 73
Toth, Zollie IND 36, xDAL 33/36, xNYB 86
Totten, Erik PIT 39
Totten, Willie BUF 17
Toussaint, Darrell NOS 32
Tovar, Steve CAR 55, CIN 51/58, SDC 56/59, SDC 59
Towle, Steve MIA 56
Towler, Dan STL 32
Townes, Willie DAL 71, NOS 71
Towns, Bobby NEP 34
Towns, Lester CAR 57
Towns, Morris TEN 76, WSH 62
Towns, Robert ARZ 7
Townsell, JoJo NYJ 83
Townsend, Andre DEN 61
Townsend, Brian CIN 61
Townsend, Curtis ARZ 59
Townsend, Deshea PIT 26
Townsend, Greg OAK 93, PHL 93

Tracey, John BUF 51/85, PHL 80, ARZ 80, DET 30
Tracy, Tom PIT 30, WSH 36
Trafton, George CHI 13
Trahan, John KCC 83
Tramm, Ralph DEN 64
Trammell, Allen TEN 47
Trapilo, Steve NOS 65
Trapp, James BLT 38, JAX 33, OAK 27/37
Trapp, Richard BUF 28, SDC 44
Trask, Orville OAK 79, TEN 79
Travenio, Herb SDC 35
Travis, John SDC 44
Travis, Mack DET 92
Traylor, Keith CHI 94, DEN 54/94, GBP 97, KCC 94
Trayman, Wade ATL 7
Traynham, Jerry DEN 20
Traynowicz, Mark ARZ 76, BUF 62
Treadaway, John DET 76, NYG 70
Treadwell, David DEN 9, NYG 18
Trebotich, Buzz DET 64, zBAL 77
Treggs, Brian SEA 3
Trejo, Stephen DET 36
Tremble, Greg DAL 27, PHL 25
Treu, Adam OAK 62
Trigilio, Frank zMIA 72, zLAD 78
Trimble, Steve CHI 40, DEN 37
Trimble, Wayne SFF 24
Triplett, Bill ARZ 38, DET 38, NYG 38
Triplett, Larry IND 75
Triplett, Mel MIN 33, NYG 33
Triplett, Wally ARZ 40, DET 18
Tripoli, Paul TBB 24
Trippi, Charley ARZ 2/61/62
Tripson, John DET 70
Tripucka, Frank DEN 18, ARZ 8, DET 28, PHL 10, xDAL 11
Trocano, Rick CLE 12
Trocolor, Bob NYG 17, xBKN 14
Trosch, Gene KCC 74
Trost, Milt CHI 27, PHL 27
Trotter, Jeremiah PHL 54, WSH 54
Troup, Bill GBP 10, IND 12, PHL 12
Trout, Dave PIT 1/5
Truax, Billy DAL 87, STL 87
Truax, Dalton OAK 72
Trudeau, Jack CAR 10, IND 10, NYJ 10
Truelove, Tony MIN 32
Trufant, Marcus SEA 23

Truitt, Dave WSH 85
Truitt, Greg CIN 59
Truitt, Olanda MIN 89, OAK 17/88, WSH 80/84
Trull, Don NEP 19, TEN 10
Truluck, R-Kal KCC 91
Trumpy, Bob CIN 84
Truvillion, Eric DET 45
Tsoutsouvas, Lou PIT 23
Tsoutsouvas, Sam DET 8
Tuaolo, Esera GBP 98, JAX 93, ATL 95, CAR 98, MIN 95/98
Tuatagaloa, Natu CIN 96, SEA 96, TEN 96
Tubbs, Jerry DAL 50, ARZ 53, SFF 50
Tubbs, Winfred SFF 55, NOS 54
Tucker, Bill CHI 34, SFF 45
Tucker, Bob MIN 38, NYG 38
Tucker, Erroll BUF 22, NEP 21
Tucker, Gary MIA 27
Tucker, Jason DAL 87
Tucker, Mark ARZ 71
Tucker, Rex CHI 64
Tucker, Ross BUF 65, WSH 68
Tucker, Ryan CLE 72, STL 50
Tucker, Syii CAR 89
Tucker, Torrin DAL 77
Tucker, Travis CLE 87
Tucker, Wendell STL 14
Tuckett, Phil SDC 41
Tuckey, Richard STL 37
Tuggle, Anthony PIT 25
Tuggle, Jessie ATL 58
Tuggle, John NYG 38
Tuiasosopo, Manu SEA 74, SFF 78
Tuiasosopo, Marques OAK 8
Tuiasosopo, Navy STL 68
Tuinei, Mark DAL 71
Tuinei, Tom DET 71
Tuinei, Van CHI 90, IND 96, SDC 76
Tuipala, Joe NOS 58, JAX 57
Tuipulotu, Peter SDC 43
Tuitele, Maugaula NEP 58, BUF 99
Tullis, Walter GBP 20/87
Tullis, Willie IND 42, NOS 26, TEN 20
Tully, Darrell DET 4
Tuman, Jerame PIT 84
Tumulty, Tom CIN 53
Tunnell, Emlen NYG 45, GBP 45
Tupa, Tom NYJ 7, ARZ 19, CLE 7, IND 7, NEP 19, TBB 9
Tupper, Jeff DEN 91, PHL 69
Turbert, Frank xBOS 24
Turk, Dan OAK 67, PIT 51, TBB 50, WSH 66
Turk, Godwin DEN 55, NYJ 56

Turk, Matt WSH 1, MIA 1, NYJ 1
Turley, Dick WSH 42
Turley, Doug WSH 22
Turley, John PIT 24
Turley, Kyle NOS 68, STL 68
Turnbow, Guy PHL 28/33
Turnbow, Jesse CLE 71
Turnbull, Renaldo NOS 97, CAR 97
Turner, Bake IND 30, NEP 40, NYJ 29
Turner, Bill NEP 74
Turner, Bulldog CHI 66
Turner, Cecil CHI 21
Turner, Calvin TBB 70
Turner, Clem CIN 43, DEN 35
Turner, Daryl SEA 81
Turner, Deacon CIN 22
Turner, Dwain TEN 95
Turner, Eric BLT 29, CLE 29, OAK 29/42
Turner, Floyd BLT 87, IND 85/88, NOS 88
Turner, Hal DET 84
Turner, Herschel ARZ 63
Turner, J.T. NYG 68, WSH 60
Turner, James STL 13
Turner, Jay WSH 24
Turner, Jim CAR 15/80
Turner, Jim DEN 15, NYJ 11
Turner, Jimmie DAL 57
Turner, Jimmy ATL 21, CIN 35
Turner, John MIN 27, SDC 27
Turner, Keena SFF 58
Turner, Kevin CLE 59, NYG 66, SEA 60, WSH 54
Turner, Kevin NEP 34, PHL 34
Turner, Marcus ARZ 23, NYJ 23
Turner, Maurice GBP 20, MIN 24, NYJ ?
Turner, Mike MIN 61
Turner, Nate BUF 21/49, CAR 32
Turner, Nate SDC 6
Turner, Odessa NYG 83, SFF 86
Turner, Rich GBP 75
Turner, Ricky IND 12
Turner, Rocky NYJ 29
Turner, Scott DEN 21, SDC 21/29, WSH 29
Turner, T.J. MIA 95, NEP 99
Turner, Vernon BUF 86, DET 8, STL 82, TBB 30/45
Turner, Vince NYJ 2
Turner, Wylie GBP 20
Turnure, Tom DET 55/60
Turpin, Miles GBP 53, TBB 45
Turral, Willie PHL 23
Tuten, Melvin CAR 73, CIN 61, DEN 71

Tuten, Rick BUF 10, PHL 14, SEA 14, STL 11
Tuthill, James SDC 4, WSH 14
Tutson, Tom ATL 43
Tuttle, George GBP 18
Tuttle, Orville NYG 42/43/61
Tuttle, Perry ATL 86, BUF 81, TBB 81
Twedell, Francis GBP 62
Tweet, Rodney CIN 84
Twilley, Howard MIA 81
Twombly, Darren NEP 64
Twyner, Gunnard CIN 17/83, NOS 86
Tyler, Andre TBB 81
Tyler, Maurice BUF 42, DEN 23, DET 27, NYG 25, NYJ 39, SDC 25
Tyler, Pete ARZ 12
Tyler, Robert SEA 87
Tyler, Toussaint NOS 42
Tyler, Wendell SFF 26, STL 26
Tylski, Rich JAX 76, PIT 65
Tyner, Scott ATL 4
Tyree, David NYG 85
Tyree, Jim xBOS 55
Tyrell, Joe PHL 69
Tyrer, Jim KCC 77
Tyrer, Jim WSH 71
Tyrrell, Tim ATL 32, PIT 23, STL 32
Tyson, Richard DEN 72, OAK 71
Ucovich, Mitch ARZ 45, WSH 53
Uecker, Keith DEN 67, GBP 70
Uguccioni, Rocky xBKN 35
Uhlenhake, Jeff MIA 63, NOS 62, WSH 55
Ulafale, Mike DAL 93
Ulbrich, Jeff SFF 53
Ulinski, Ed CLE 36
Ulinski, Harry WSH 50/56
Ulmer, Artie ATL 50, DEN 50, MIN 53, SFF 50
Ulmer, Michael PHL 32, CHI 43
Ulrich, Chuck ARZ 72
Ulrich, Hub zMIA 51
Umenyiora, Osi NYG 72
Umont, Frank NYG 69
Umphrey, Rich NYG 59, SDC 66
Unck, Mason CLE 53
Underwood, Dimitrius DAL 91
Underwood, Forest STL 11
Underwood, John ARZ 19
Underwood, Olen DEN 50, NYG 56, TEN 56
Ungerer, Joe WSH 46
Unitas, John IND 19, SDC 19
Unrein, Terry SDC 98
Unutoa, Morris PHL 68, TBB 68

Unverzagt, Eric SEA 53
Upchurch, Rick DEN 80
Upersa, Tuufuli PHL 75
Upshaw, Gene OAK 63
Upshaw, Marvin ARZ 71, CLE 84, KCC 81
Upshaw, Regan JAX 98, OAK 91, TBB 73/91, WSH 91
Uram, Andy GBP 8/42
Urban, Alex GBP 18/23/79
Urban, Gasper zCHI 38
Urbanek, Jim MIA 79
Urch, Scott NYG 73
Uremovich, Emil DET 75/81, zCHI 44
Urenda, Herman OAK 39/83/89
Urlacher, Brian CHI 54
Usher, Darryl ARZ 82, SDC 26
Usher, Lou CHI 12
Utley, Mike DET 60/69
Utt, Ben IND 64
Uwaezuoke, Iheanyi CAR 89, DET 80, MIA 80, SFF 89
Uzdavinis, Walter STL 20
Vacanti, Sam zBAL 67/69, zCHI 69
Vactor, Ted CHI 33, WSH 29
Vairo, Dominic GBP 35
Val, Joe SFF 44
Valdez, Vernon BUF 25, OAK 25, STL 47
Valentine, Ira TEN 45
Valentine, Zack PHL 54, PIT 54
Valerie, Joe STL 64, KCC 73
Vallez, Emilo CHI 82
Van Brocklin, Norm PHL 11, STL 11/25
Van Buren, Courtney SDC 72
Van Buren, Ebert PHL 17/31
Van Buren, Steve PHL 15
Van Divier, Randy IND 79
Van Duyne, Bob IND 67
Van Dyke, Alex NYJ 86, PHL 86
Van Dyke, Bruce PIT 66, GBP 61, PHL 66
Van Dyke, Ralph CLE 71
Van Eeghen, Mark OAK 30, NEP 34
Van Every, Hal GBP 36
Van Heusen, Bill DEN 42
Van Horn, Doug DET 60, NYG 63
Van Horne, Keith CHI 78
Van Note, Jeff ATL 57
Van Pelt, Alex BUF 10, KCC 10
Van Pelt, Brad NYG 10, CLE 50, OAK 91
Van Raaphorst, Dick SDC 39, DAL 30
Van Sickle, Clyde GBP 26/31/57

Van Tone, Art DET 11, zBRK 92
Van Valkenberg, Pete GBP 40, CHI 46, BUF 36
Van Wagner Jim NOS 35
Van, Bob SFF 89
Van, Norwood STL 51
Van, Tim ARZ 16
Vance, Eric IND 37, TBB 33
Vance, Joe xBKN 11
VandenBosch, Kyle ARZ 93
Vander Kelen, Ron MIN 15
Vander Poel, Mark ARZ 69, IND 72/75
Vanderbeek, Matt IND 58, WSH 91, DAL 91
Vanderbundt, Skip NOS 52, SFF 52
Vanderjagt, Mike IND 12/13
Vandersea, Phil GBP 37/83, NOS 38
Vandeweghe, Al zBUF 53
Vanhorse, Sean DET 29, MIN 37, SDC 25
Vann, Norwood OAK 50
Vanover, Tamarick KCC 87, SDC 87
Vanoy, Vern NYG 74, GBP 73, TEN 73
Vant Hull, Fred GBP 18
Vanzo, Fred DET 22, ARZ 73
Varajon, Mike SFF 48
Vardell, Tommy CLE 44, DET 44, SFF 44
Vardian, John zBAL 87, zMIA 88
Vargo, Larry DET 85, MIN 25, NYG 25
Varrichione, Frank PIT 74, STL 70
Varty, Mike IND 51, WSH 58
Vasicek, Vic STL 35, zBUF 34
Vasys, Arunas PHL 61
Vataha, Randy GBP 18, NEP 18
Vatterott, Charles ARZ 68
Vaughan, John PIT 21
Vaughan, Pug DET 8, ARZ 12
Vaughan, Ruben OAK 99, MIN 69, SFF 72
Vaughn, Bob DEN 61
Vaughn, Clarence WSH 31
Vaughn, Darrick ATL 37, HOU 21
Vaughn, Jon KCC 21, NEP 24, SEA 22
Vaughn, Lee DAL 37
Vaughn, Tom DET 48
Vaught, Ted SFF 89
Veach, Walter CHI 15
Veal, Demetrin ATL 99
Veals, Elton PIT 38
Veasey, Craig MIA 94, PIT 91, TEN 71
Veingrad, Alan DAL 76, GBP 73
Veland, Tony CAR 36, DEN 32

Vella, John MIN 71, OAK 75
Vellone, Jim MIN 63
Venturelli, Fred CHI 55
Venuto, Jay IND 14
Venuto, Sam WSH 49
Venzke, Patrick JAX 70
Verba, Ross CLE 77, GBP 78
Verdin, Clarence IND 83, ATL 2, WSH 89
Vereb, Ed WSH 20
Vereen, Carl GBP 74
Vergara, George GBP 6
Verhulst, Chris DEN 86, TEN 88
Veris, Garin NEP 60/90, SFF 93
Verry, Norm zCHI 40
Verser, David CIN 81, CLE 85, TBB 84
Verstegen, Mike NOS 66, STL 67
Vertefeuille, Brian SDC 68
Vessels, Billy IND 21
Vesser, John ARZ 10/26/28/36
Vetrano, Joe SFF 82/92
Vetter, Jack xBKN 16
Vezmar, Walt DET 33
Viaene, David GBP 76, NEP 70
Vick, Ernie CHI 26
Vick, Michael ATL 7
Vick, Roger NYJ 43, PHL 43
Vickers, Kipp BLT 77, IND 71, WSH 70/79
Vidoni, Vic PIT 15/19
Vigorito, Tom MIA 32
Villa, Danny ARZ 74, CAR 72, KCC 72, NEP 73/75
Villanucci, Vince GBP 64
Villanueva, Danny DAL 11, STL 11
Villapiano, Phil OAK 41, BUF 41
Villarrial, Chris CHI 58
Viltz, Theo TEN 34
Vinatieri, Adam NEP 4
Vincent, Keydrick PIT 68
Vincent, Shawn PIT 43
Vincent, Ted CIN 78, SFF 66/75
Vincent, Troy PHL 23, MIA 23
Vinnola, Paul zLAD 84
Vinson, Fernandus CIN 34
Vinson, Fred GBP 31
Vinson, Tony BLT 44
Vinyard, Kenny ATL 8/70
Virkus, Scott IND 94, BUF 93, NEP 70
Visger, George SFF 90
Visnic, Larry NYG 30/31
Vital, Lionel WSH 20
Vitali, Mark KCC 6
Vitiello, Sandro CIN 11
Vlasic, Mark KCC 13, SDC 13, TBB 13

Vodicka, Joe ARZ 20, CHI 48
Vogds, Evan GBP 79, zCHI 31
Vogel, Bob IND 72
Vogel, Paul TEN 50
Vogelaar, Carroll xBOS 51, xNYB 51/83
Vogler, Tim BUF 65
Voight, Bob OAK 78
Voight, Mike TEN 31
Voigt, Stu MIN 83
Vokaty, Otto ARZ 12, NYG 5, xCIN 28
Volck, Bill ARZ 44
Volek, Billy TEN 7/12
Volk, Rick IND 21, MIA 21, NYG 23
Vollenweider, Jim SFF 33
Vollers, Kurt DAL 78
Volz, Wilbur zBUF 87
Von Oelhoffen, Kimo CIN 67, PIT 67
Von Schamann, Uwe MIA 5
Von Sonn, Andy STL 46
Vonder Ahe, Scott IND 51
Vosberg, Don NYG 49
Voss, Lloyd DEN 65, GBP 71, PIT 65
Voss, Tillie CHI 27, NYG 11
Voytek, Ed WSH 66
Vrabel, Mike NEP 50, PIT 56/96
Vucinich, Milt CHI 16
Waddle, Tom CHI 87
Waddy, Bill MIN 80, STL 80
Waddy, Jude GBP 54
Waddy, Ray WSH 47
Wade, Bill CHI 9, STL 9
Wade, Bob DEN 37, PIT 44, WSH 24
Wade, Bobby CHI 84
Wade, Charley CHI 83, GBP 89, KCC 84
Wade, Charley MIA 37
Wade, Jim xNYB 12
Wade, John JAX 66
Wade, John TBB 76
Wade, Todd MIA 71
Wade, Tommy PIT 16
Wadell, Reggie BLT 33
Wadsworth, Andre ARZ 90
Waechter, Henry WSH 67, CHI 70/75, IND 71
Waerig, John DET 46
Wafer, Carl GBP 78, NYG 72
Wager, Clifton CHI 51, ARZ 69, PIT 69
Wager, John DET 9/17/44
Wages, Harmon ATL 5
Wagner, Barry CHI 86
Wagner, Bryan CHI 15, CLE 15, GBP 9, NEP 9, SDC 9
Wagner, Lowell zNYY 87, SFF 42/92
Wagner, Mike PIT 23
Wagner, Ray CIN 63, xBKN 22

Wagner, Sid DET 15
Wagner, Steve GBP 21, PHL 42
Wagoner, Dan DET 34, MIN 31, ATL 36
Wagstaff, Jim ARZ 49, BUF 22
Wahle, Mike GBP 68
Wahler, Jim ARZ 66, WSH 77
Wainscott, Lloyd TEN 53
Wainwright, Frank BLT 82/88, MIA 82, NOS 87, PHL 87
Waiters, Van CLE 50, MIN 54
Waits, Alex SEA 5
Wakefield, Fred ARZ 97
Walbridge, Larry NYG 15
Walczak, Mark ARZ 89, BUF 87, IND 83/84, SDC 81
Waldemore, Stan NYJ 70
Walden, Bobby PIT 39, MIN 39
Waldron, Austin ARZ 17
Waldrop, Rob KCC 98
Waldroup, Kerwin DET 93
Walen, Mark DAL 95
Walendy, Craig NYG 45
Walik, Billy PHL 9
Walker, Aaron SFF 49
Walker, Adam MIN 49, PHL 29, SFF 27
Walker, Bill xBOS 44/22
Walker, Bracey CIN 27, DET 28, MIA 26, KCC 27/40
Walker, Brian DET 45, MIA 45, SEA 25, WSH 45
Walker, Bruce NEP 91
Walker, Byron SEA 89
Walker, Charles ARZ 79
Walker, Chuck ATL 79
Walker, Clarence DEN 30
Walker, Cleo ATL 79, GBP 52
Walker, Clyde KCC 54
Walker, Corey PHL 29/39
Walker, Darnell ATL 45, DET 41, SFF 38
Walker, Darwin ARZ 75, PHL 97
Walker, Denard DEN 27, MIN 26, TEN 25
Walker, Derrick KCC 82, OAK 86, SDC 89
Walker, Doak DET 37
Walker, Donnie BUF 26, NYJ 29
Walker, Dwight CLE 42, NOS 83
Walker, Elliott SFF 35
Walker, Frank NYG 41
Walker, Fulton MIA 41, OAK 41
Walker, Gary DAL 67
Walker, Gary HOU 96, JAX 96, TEN 96
Walker, Glen STL 19
Walker, Herschel DAL 34, MIN 34, NYG 34, PHL 34

Walker, Jackie TBB 56/85
Walker, James KCC 54
Walker, Javon GBP 84
Walker, Jay MIN 6
Walker, Jeff NOS 78, SDC 72
Walker, Jimmy MIN 93
Walker, Joe IND 20, TEN 29
Walker, John KCC 98
Walker, Kenny DEN 96
Walker, Kenyatta TBB 67
Walker, Kevin CIN 59
Walker, Kevin TBB 37
Walker, Langston OAK 66
Walker, Louis DAL 57
Walker, Malcolm DAL 57, GBP 54
Walker, Marquis DET 38, OAK 38, STL 38, WSH 27
Walker, Marquise TBB 82
Walker, Mickey NYG 64/65
Walker, Mike NEP 12
Walker, Mike NOS 80
Walker, Paul NYG 86
Walker, Quentin ARZ 33
Walker, Ramon HOU 41
Walker, Randy GBP 18
Walker, Rick CIN 83/88, WSH 88
Walker, Robert NYG 33
Walker, Rod GBP 95, TEN 77
Walker, Sammy GBP 23, PIT 23
Walker, Tim SEA 56
Walker, Tony IND 92
Walker, Val Joe GBP 47
Walker, Wayne DET 55
Walker, Wayne KCC 68, TEN 15
Walker, Wayne SDC 80
Walker, Wesley NYJ 85
Walker, Willie DET 40
Wallace, Aaron OAK 51/59
Wallace, Al CAR 96, PHL 96
Wallace, Anthony ATL 40
Wallace, Bev SFF 64, xNYB 53
Wallace, Bob CHI 89
Wallace, Calvin CLE 95, GBP 93
Wallace, Henry SDC 45
Wallace, Jackie IND 20, MIN 25, STL 20
Wallace, John CHI 29
Wallace, Ray PIT 43, TEN 35
Wallace, Rodney DAL 71
Wallace, Roger NYG 88
Wallace, Stan CHI 40
Wallace, Steve SFF 74, KCC 70/74
Wallace, Taco SEA 18
Waller, Bill xBKN 13
Waller, Ron STL 27, SDC 27
Wallerstedt, Brett ARZ 92, CIN 91, DEN 59, STL 53
Wallner, Fred ARZ 18/61/68, TEN 64

Walls, Craig BUF 57/96
Walls, Everson DAL 24, CLE 28, NYG 28
Walls, Henry NYJ 96
Walls, Herkie TEN 82/86
Walls, Lenny DEN 35
Walls, Raymond BLT 38, CLE 42, IND 42
Walls, Wesley CAR 85, GBP 82, NOS 85, SFF 89
Walls, Will NYG 24
Walquist, Laurie CHI 5
Walsh, Bill PIT 46/56
Walsh, Chris BUF 87, MIN 81
Walsh, Ed NYJ 64
Walsh, Jim SEA 34
Walsh, John CIN 10
Walsh, Steve CHI 4, DAL 3, IND 4, NOS 4, TBB 4
Walsh, Ward GBP 26, TEN 32
Walston, Bobby PHL 83
Walter, Dave CIN 11
Walter, Joe CIN 63
Walter, Ken CAR 13, NEP 13
Walter, Kevin CIN 83
Walter, Michael SFF 99, DAL 59
Walter, Tyson DAL 71
Walters, Danny SDC 23
Walters, Joey TEN 83
Walters, Les WSH 27
Walters, Matt NYJ 95
Walters, Pete PHL 68
Walters, Rod DET 67, KCC 76, MIA 76
Walters, Stan PHL 75, CIN 75
Walters, Tom WSH 43
Walters, Troy IND 86, MIN 82
Walterscheid, Len BUF 45, CHI 23
Walton, Alvin WSH 40
Walton, Bruce DAL 78
Walton, Chuck DET 63
Walton, Frank WSH 21/29
Walton, Joe NYG 80, WSH 81
Walton, John PHL 10/11
Walton, Larry BUF 49, DET 49
Walton, Riley KCC 88
Walton, Sam NYJ 71, TEN 77/93
Walton, Shane STL 38
Walton, Wayne KCC 72, NYG 78
Walton, Whip NYG 59
Walz, Zack ARZ 52
Wand, Seth HOU 78
Wansley, Tim TBB 31
Wantland, Hal MIA 46
Ward, Bill DET 42/67, WSH 21
Ward, Carl CLE 27, NOS 21
Ward, Chris BLT 95, MIA 67, NOS 72, NYJ 72
Ward, David CIN 51, NEP 94, WSH ?

Ward, Dedric BLT 85, NEP 17, NYJ 89, MIA 87
Ward, Elmer DET 18
Ward, Hines PIT 86
Ward, Jim IND 16, PHL 7
Ward, John CHI 78, MIN 72, TBB 73
Ward, LaShaun KCC 84
Ward, Paul DET 73/74
Ward, Phillip STL 55
Ward, Ronnie MIA 55
Warden, James STL 21
Wardlow, Duane STL 83/89
Ware, Andre DET 11
Ware, Charlie xBKN 43
Ware, David NYJ 68
Ware, Derek ARZ 85, CIN 88, DAL 89
Ware, Kevin WSH 48
Ware, Tim OAK 15, SDC 81
Warfield, Eric KCC 44
Warfield, Paul CLE 42, MIA 42
Warlick, Ernie BUF 84
Warne, Jim DET 72
Warner, Charley BUF 22, KCC 25
Warner, Curt SEA 28, STL 21
Warner, Josh CHI 67
Warner, Kurt STL 10/13
Warner, Ron NOS 98, TBB 93/95, WSH 95
Warnke, Dave TBB 2
Warren, Busit PHL 41, PIT 15
Warren, Chris SEA 42, DAL 42, PHL 35
Warren, Dewey CIN 16
Warren, Don WSH 85
Warren, Frank NOS 73
Warren, Gerard CLE 94
Warren, Jimmy MIA 49, OAK 20/22, SDC 49
Warren, John DAL 5
Warren, Lamont DET 25, IND 21, NEP 27
Warren, Morrie zBRK 73
Warren, Steve GBP 95/96
Warren, Terrance SFF 19, SEA 88
Warren, Ty NEP 94
Warren, Vince NYG 83
Warren, Xavier PIT 95/98
Warrick, Peter CIN 80
Warrington, Tex zBRK 20/30
Warwick, Lonnie ATL 59, MIN 59
Warzeka, John OAK 78
Washington, Al NYJ 52
Washington, Anthony PIT 42, WSH 24
Washington, Brian CLE 48, KCC 29/48, NYJ 48
Washington, Charles ATL 46, IND 46, KCC 46
Washington, Chris ARZ 52, TBB 51

Washington, Chuck GBP 18/38
Washington, Clarence PIT 67
Washington, Clyde NEP 31, NYJ 42
Washington, Damon NYG 29
Washington, Dave SFF 50, BUF 86, DEN 56, DET 52, NOS 55
Washington, Dewayne MIN 20, PIT 20
Washington, Dick MIA 44
Washington, Eric ARZ 40
Washington, Fred CHI 91, WSH 75
Washington, Gene MIN 84, DEN 84
Washington, Gene SFF 18, DET 18, NYG 84
Washington, Harry CHI 81, MIN 80
Washington, James DAL 37, STL 37, WSH 37
Washington, Joe ATL 30
Washington, Joe IND 20, ATL 24, SDC 24, WSH 25
Washington, John ATL 73, NEP 76, NYG 71/73
Washington, Keith BLT 93, DEN 97, DET 90, MIN 96, NYG 99
Washington, Kelly CIN 87
Washington, Ken STL 13
Washington, Lionel ARZ 48, DEN 48, OAK 23/48
Washington, Marcus IND 53
Washington, Mark DAL 46, NEP 21
Washington, Marvin DEN 95, NYJ 97, SFF 95
Washington, Mickey BUF 25, JAX 25, NEP 46, NOS 26, WSH 25
Washington, Mike TBB 40
Washington, Patrick JAX 31
Washington, Robert PIT 63
Washington, Ronnie ATL 92, IND 57, OAK 91
Washington, Russ SDC 70/85
Washington, Sam CIN 41, PIT 41
Washington, T.J. CAR 62
Washington, Ted CIN 22
Washington, Ted BUF 92, CHI 92, DEN 98, NEP 92, SFF 97
Washington, Ted TEN 53/59
Washington, Thomas KCC 64
Washington, Tim KCC 42, SFF 46
Washington, Todd HOU 77, TBB 75
Washington, Vic SFF 22, BUF 33, TEN 23
Waskiewicz, Jim ATL 59, NYJ 54
Wasserbach, Lloyd zCHI 48/37

Waterfield, Bob STL 7
Waters, Andre ARZ 20, PHL 20
Waters, Bob SFF 11
Waters, Brian KCC 54
Waters, Charlie DAL 41
Waters, Dale CLE 5, DET ?, WSH 33
Waters, Mike NOS 88, PHL 33
Watford, Gerry ARZ 64
Watkins, Bob ARZ 24, CHI 45
Watkins, Bobby DET 27
Watkins, David SFF 28
Watkins, Foster PHL 39/41
Watkins, Gordon xBKN 28
Watkins, Kendall DAL 83
Watkins, Larry BUF 38, DET 30, NYG 36, PHL 34
Watkins, Tom CLE 22, DET 23, PIT 35
Watson, Alan PIT 14
Watson, Chris BUF 21, DEN 21
Watson, Dave NEP 67
Watson, Ed TEN 57
Watson, Edwin PHL 35
Watson, Jim WSH 37
Watson, Joe DET 51
Watson, John NOS 67, SFF 67
Watson, Justin STL 33
Watson, Karlton CLE 12
Watson, Kenny CIN 33
Watson, Louis CLE 89
Watson, Mike NOS 61
Watson, Pete CIN 40
Watson, Remi CLE 6
Watson, Sid PIT 39, WSH 41
Watson, Steve DEN 81
Watson, Tim KCC 26, NYG 33, PHL 33
Watt, Joe DET 13/14, xBOS 56, xNYB 4
Watt, Walt ARZ 50
Wattelet, Frank NOS 49, STL 41
Watters, Bob NYJ 76/86
Watters, Orlando SEA 31
Watters, Ricky PHL 32, SEA 32, SFF 32
Watters, Scott BUF 60
Watts, Damon IND 36
Watts, Elbert GBP 28
Watts, George WSH 15
Watts, Randy DAL 94
Watts, Rickey CHI 80
Watts, Robert OAK 54
Watts, Ted NYG 21, OAK 20/41, SDC 28
Way, Charles NYG 30
Waymer, Dave NOS 44, OAK 44, SFF 43
Wayne, Nate DEN 54, GBP 54, PHL 54
Wayne, Reggie IND 87
Wayt, Russell DAL 33
Wear, Robert PHL 51

Weary, Fred ATL 24, HOU 61, NOS 24/42, STL 32
Weatherall, Jim PHL 77, DET 74, WSH 72
Weatherford, Jim ATL 42
Weatherington, Colston DAL 95
Weatherley, Jim ATL 58
Weatherly, Gerald CHI 45/50/84
Weathers, Andre NYG 35
Weathers, Carl OAK 49/51
Weathers, Clarence CLE 85, GBP 87, IND 85, KCC 80, NEP 82
Weathers, Curtis CLE 55/87
Weathers, Robert NEP 24
Weathersby, Dennis CIN 23
Weatherspoon, Cephus NOS 85
Weatherspoon, Chuck TBB 37
Weatherwax, Jim GBP 73
Weaver, Anthony BLT 98
Weaver, Buck DET 85
Weaver, Charles ARZ 31/32
Weaver, Charlie DET 59, WSH 58
Weaver, Emanuel CIN 70
Weaver, Gary GBP 52, OAK 52
Weaver, Herman DET 18, SEA 18
Weaver, Jed MIA 82, PHL 87, SFF 88
Weaver, John xNYB 70
Weaver, Larrye NYG 28
Webb, Allan NYG 21
Webb, Chuck GBP 30
Webb, Don NEP 42/48
Webb, George xBKN 29
Webb, Jimmy SDC 61, SFF 74
Webb, Ken CLE 34, DET 34
Webb, Richmond MIA 78, CIN 73
Webber, Dutch GBP 43, NYG 16
Weber, Chuck ARZ 89, CLE 83, PHL 51
Weber, Dick DET 20
Webster, Alex NYG 29
Webster, Cornell SEA 38
Webster, David KCC 21
Webster, Elnardo PIT 92
Webster, George TEN 90, NEP 90, PIT 90
Webster, Jason SFF 36
Webster, Kevin MIN 68
Webster, Larry BLT 79, CLE 74, MIA 79, NYJ 75
Webster, Mike PIT 52, KCC 53
Webster, Nate TBB 52
Webster, Tim GBP 38
Wedderburn, Floyd SEA 69
Weddington, Mike GBP 52
Wedel, Dick ARZ 6

Wedemeyer, Herman zBAL 87, zLAD 99
Weed, Tad PIT 27
Weedon, Don PHL 60
Weeds, Tony STL 91
Weeks, George xBKN 18
Weese, Norris DEN 14
Wegener, Bucky TEN 86
Weger, Mike DET 28, TEN 28
Wegert, Ted BUF 33, NYJ 20, PHL 46, DEN 40
Wehba, Ray GBP 57, xBKN 38
Wehrli, Roger ARZ 22
Weidner, Bert MIA 60
Weigel, Lee GBP 25
Weil, Jack DEN 13, WSH 2
Weimer, Chuck xBKN 8
Weinberg, Henry PIT 26
Weiner, Albert PHL 18
Weiner, Art xNYB 66
Weiner, Bernie xBKN 33
Weiner, Todd ATL 74, SEA 74
Weinke, Chris CAR 16
Weinmeister, Arnie NYG 73, zNYY 44
Weinstock, Isadore PHL 10
Weinstock, Izzy PIT 47
Weir, Sammy NYJ 84, TEN 20
Weisacosky, Ed MIA 51, NEP 66, NYG 51
Weisenbaugh, Heinie WSH 16, PIT 12
Weisgerber, Dick GBP 33
Weishuhn, Clayton GBP 51, NEP 53
Weiss, Howie DET 5
Weiss, John NYG 11/83
Weissenhofer, Ron NOS 56
Welborne, Tripp MIN 32
Welbourn, John PHL 76
Welch, Claxton DAL 42, NEP 43, NOS 42
Welch, Herb DET 28, NYG 27, WSH 20
Welch, Jim DET 46, IND 46
Weldin, Hal xSTL ?
Weldon, Casey PHL 11, TBB 11, WSH 11
Weldon, Larry WSH 31
Wellborn, Joe NYG 59
Weller, Rabbit WSH 27
Weller, Ray ARZ 11/17
Wellman, Gary TEN 88
Wellman, Mike GBP 65
Wells, Arthur TBB 85
Wells, Billy WSH 41, NEP 41, PHL 27, PIT 24
Wells, Bob SDC 77
Wells, Dana CIN 79
Wells, Dean CAR 95, SEA 95
Wells, Don GBP 43/84
Wells, Harold PHL 53
Wells, Joel NYG 28
Wells, Jonathan HOU 32
Wells, Kent NYG 95

Wells, Mike CIN 15, MIN 15
Wells, Mike CHI 97, DET 95, IND 95
Wells, Mike SFF 40
Wells, Norm DAL 66
Wells, Ray TEN 56
Wells, Reggie ARZ 74
Wells, Robert TEN 70
Wells, Terence TEN 41
Wells, Terry GBP 37
Wells, Warren OAK 81, DET 87
Welter, Tom ARZ 66
Wemple, Don xBKN 23
Wendell, Marty zCHI 31
Wender, Jack TBB 38
Wendlick, Joe PIT 59, PHL 59
Wendryhoski, Joe NOS 54, STL 54
Wendt, Ken ARZ ?
Wenglikowski, Al BUF 60
Wenzel, Jeff PHL 72
Wenzel, Ralph PIT 22
Wenzel, Ralph PIT 62, SDC 54/62
Werder, Dick zNYY 37
Werl, Bob NYJ 80
Werner, Greg NYJ 80
Wersching, Ray SDC 6/15, SFF 14
Wesley, Bull DET 40, NYG 17
Wesley, Dante CAR 29
Wesley, Greg KCC 25
Wesley, Joe JAX 50, SFF 56
Wesson, Ricky KCC 25
West, Bill DEN 29
West, Charlie DEN 40/42, DET 40, MIN 40
West, Dave NYJ 26
West, Derek IND 72
West, Ed ATL 83, GBP 49/86, PHL 83
West, Hodges PHL 72
West, Jeff ARZ 80, SDC 8/80, SEA 8
West, Lyle KCC 30, NYG 37
West, Mel NEP 24, NYJ 25
West, Pat GBP 25, STL 36
West, Robert KCC 26, SFF 85
West, Ronnie MIN 35
West, Stan STL 11/64, ARZ 55, NYG 62
West, Troy PHL 31
West, Walter STL 21
West, Willie BUF 47, ARZ 49, DEN 20, MIA 22, NYJ 22
Westberry, Gary DAL 65
Westbrook, Brian PHL 36
Westbrook, Bryant DET 32, GBP 32
Westbrook, Don NEP 83
Westbrook, Michael WSH 82
Westbrooks, David MIN 92
Westbrooks, Greg ARZ 52, NOS 60, OAK 52, STL 57

Wester, Cleve DET 31
Westfall, Bob DET 86
Westfall, Ed PIT 47, WSH 12
Westmoreland, Dick MIA 25, SDC 25
Westmoreland, Eric JAX 52
Weston, Jeff NYG 73
Weston, Rhondy TBB 77
Westoupal, Joe NYG 7
Wetnight, Ryan CHI 89, GBP 83
Wetoska, Bob CHI 63
Wetterlund, Chet DET 40
Wettstein, Max DEN 89
Wetz, Harlan zBRK 48
Wetzel, Damon PIT 10, CHI ?
Wetzel, Marty NYJ 58
Wetzel, Ron KCC 87
Whalen, Bill ARZ 23
Whalen, James DAL 46/81/83
Whalen, Jerry zBUF 40
Whalen, Jim DEN 83, NEP 82, PHL 81
Whaley, Ben zLAD 36
Wham, Tom ARZ 51
Wharton, Hogan TEN 63
Whatley, Jim xBKN 30/16
Wheat, Warren SEA 74
Wheatley, Tyrone NYG 28, OAK 47
Wheaton, Kenny DAL 30
Wheba, Ray GBP 17
Wheeler, Damen JAX 27
Wheeler, Dwight NEP 62, OAK 67, SDC 63
Wheeler, Ernie ARZ 41, PIT 15/44
Wheeler, Leonard CAR 37, CIN 37, MIN 37
Wheeler, Manch BUF 12
Wheeler, Mark DET 82, NEP 97, PHL 97, TBB 77
Wheeler, Ron OAK 82
Wheeler, Ted ARZ 54, CHI 69
Wheeler, Wayne CHI 85
Wheelwright, Ernie ATL 30, NOS 39, NYG 30
Whelan, Tom PIT 26
Whelihan, Craig SDC 5
Whigham, Larry NEP 25, CHI 33
Whisenhunt, Ken ATL 45, NYJ 86, WSH 48
Whitaker, Bill ARZ 55, GBP 30
Whitaker, Creston NOS 86
Whitaker, Danta CHI 88, KCC 82, MIN 82
Whitaker, Roynell TBB 29
White, Adrian GBP 38, NEP 38, NYG 36
White, Alberto OAK 96, STL 94
White, Allison PHL 21
White, Andre CIN 86, DEN 89, SDC 87

White, Arthur ARZ 35
White, Bob DAL 65/70
White, Bob CLE 46, IND 25, TEN 33, SFF 25/85
White, Brad IND 92, MIN 62, TBB 90
White, Byron "Whizzer" PIT 10, DET 24/44
White, Charles STL 33, CLE 25
White, Charlie NYJ 30, TBB 28
White, Chris JAX 74
White, Chris SEA 21
White, Clayton NYG 57
White, Craig BUF 27
White, Danny DAL 11
White, Daryl DET 67
White, David BUF 50/51, NEP 51
White, Dewayne TBB 90
White, Dez CHI 80
White, Dwayne NYJ 67, STL 67
White, Dwight PIT 78
White, Ed MIN 62, SDC 67
White, Eugene OAK 29
White, Freeman NYG 81
White, Gene GBP 88
White, Gerald DAL 37
White, Harvey NEP 10
White, Jamel CLE 30
White, James MIN 72
White, Jan BUF 80
White, Jeff NEP 2
White, Jeris TBB 45, WSH 45, MIA 41
White, Jim DEN 78, NEP 87, SEA 79, TEN 79
White, Jim NYG 77
White, John TEN 86
White, Jose JAX 93/95, MIN 97
White, Lawrence CHI 83
White, Lean STL 55
White, Lee NYJ 34, SDC 38, STL 44
White, Leon CIN 51
White, Lorenzo TEN 44, CLE 34
White, Lyman ATL 52
White, Marsh NYG 29
White, Mike CIN 63, SEA 70
White, Paul ARZ 30
White, Paul PIT 42
White, Phil NYG 0
White, Randy DAL 54
White, Ray ARZ 55
White, Ray SDC 52
White, Reggie GBP 92, CAR 92, PHL 91/92
White, Reggie JAX 22
White, Reggie NEP 90, SDC 90
White, Robb NYG 71, TBB 91

White, Robert TEN 29
White, Roy CHI 8, CHI 9
White, Russell STL 44
White, Sammy MIN 85
White, Sheldon CIN 39, DET 25, NYG 39
White, Sherman BUF 83, CIN 83
White, Stan DET 52, IND 53/54
White, Steve NYJ 95
White, Steve TBB 94
White, Tarzan NYG 12/66
White, Ted KCC 7
White, Tracy SEA 59
White, Walter KCC 81/88
White, Whizzer CHI 33
White, Wilbur DET 30, xBKN 33
White, Will IND 21
White, William ATL 35, DET 35, KCC 35
Whited, Marvin WSH 48
Whited, Mike DET 24
Whitehead, Bud SDC 47
Whitehead, Willie NOS 98
Whitehurst, David GBP 17, KCC 15
Whiteside, Keyon IND 52
Whitfield, A.D. DAL 42, WSH 25
Whitfield, Bob ATL 70
Whiting, Brandon PHL 98
Whiting, Teag ARZ 71
Whitlach, Blake NYJ 57
Whitley, Curtis CAR 64, OAK 66, SDC 64
Whitley, James GBP 25, STL 27
Whitley, Wilson CIN 75, TEN 79
Whitlow, Bob ATL 51, CLE 53, DET 51/61, WSH 66
Whitlow, Ken zMIA 22
Whitman, Josh SDC 84
Whitman, Laverne ARZ 21
Whitman, S.J. CHI 22
Whitmore, David KCC 41, NYG 41, PHL 42, SFF 41
Whitmyer, Nat SDC 41, STL 44
Whitsell, Dave NOS 23, CHI 23, DET 23
Whittaker, Scott OAK 78
Whitted, Alvis JAX 86, OAK 87
Whitten, Bobby CIN 70
Whitten, Todd NEP 15
Whittenton, Jesse GBP 47, CHI 46, STL 44
Whittingham, Cary STL 57
Whittingham, Fred DAL 53, NEP 53, NOS 59, PHL 53/56, STL 55
Whittingham, Kyle STL 52

Whittington, Arthur BUF 21, OAK 22
Whittington, Bernard CIN 97, IND 95
Whittington, C.L. TEN 38
Whittington, Mike NYG 58
Whittle, Jason NYG 66, TBB 65
Whittle, Ricky NOS 23
Whitwell, Mike CLE 21/27
Wiatrak, Johnny DET 13
Wiberg, Ossie NYG 23, xBKN 2, xCIN ?
Wichard, Murray NEP 90
Wickert, Tom KCC 66, MIA 60, NOS 66
Wickett, Lloyd DET 20
Wicks, Bob ARZ 42, GBP 49, NOS 49
Widby, Ron DAL 10/12, GBP 20
Widell, Dave ATL 79, DAL 78, DEN 79, JAX 79
Widell, Doug DEN 67, DET 67, GBP 74, IND 64
Widerquist, Chet ARZ 11
Widmer, Corey NYG 90
Widseth, Ed NYG 50
Wiegand, Eric ATL 54
Wiegert, Zach HOU 72, JAX 77, STL 73
Wiegmann, Casey CHI 60, IND 68, KCC 62
Wiehl, Joe PIT 26
Wiese, Bob DET 75
Wietecha, Ray NYG 55
Wiethe, Socko DET 48/68/78
Wiggin, Paul CLE 84/86
Wiggins, Jermaine CAR 84, IND 85, NEP 85, NYJ 85
Wiggins, Paul PIT 79, WSH 73
Wightkin, Bill CHI 53/72/86
Wikinson, Jerry SFF 60
Wilbur, John DAL 65, STL 60, WSH 60
Wilburn, Barry CLE 47, PHL 45, WSH 45
Wilburn, J.R. PIT 86
Wilburn, Steve NEP 99
Wilcher, Mike STL 94
Wilcots, Solomon CIN 41, MIN 41, PIT 41
Wilcox, Dave SFF 64
Wilcox, John PHL 71
Wilcox, Josh NOS 47
Wilde, George WSH 29
Wilder, Bert NYJ 77/82
Wilder, James TBB 32, DET 34, WSH 32
Wildung, Dick GBP 45/70
Wiley, Charles SEA 77
Wiley, Chuck ATL 99, CAR 99, MIN 94
Wiley, Jack PIT 75
Wiley, Marcellus SDC 75, BUF 75

Wiley, Michael DAL 32
Wilging, Cole xCIN 37
Wilhelm, Erik CIN 4/12
Wilhelm, Matt SDC 56
Wilhite, Gerald DEN 47
Wilhite, Kevin GBP 35
Wiliams, Brooks CHI 88
Wiliams, Derwin NEP 82
Wilkens, Elmer GBP 18
Wilkerson, Basil WSH 16, xCIN ?
Wilkerson, Bruce GBP 64, JAX 68, OAK 68
Wilkerson, Daryl IND 92
Wilkerson, Doug SDC 63, TEN 63
Wilkerson, Eric PIT 40
Wilkerson, Jimmy KCC 66
Wilkes, Reggie ATL 51, PHL 51
Wilkin, Willie WSH 36, zCHI 46
Wilkins, David SFF 66
Wilkins, Dick NYG 88, xDAL 88, zLAD 54
Wilkins, Gabe GBP 98, SFF 98
Wilkins, Gary ATL 87/96, BUF 34
Wilkins, Jeff STL 14, PHL 14, SFF 14
Wilkins, Marcus GBP 55
Wilkins, Ray STL 78, WSH 83
Wilkins, Terrence IND 10/80, STL 82
Wilkinson, Bob NYG 87
Wilkinson, Dan CIN 99, DET 72, WSH 95
Wilkinson, Jerry CLE 41, STL 70
Wilks, Jim NOS 94
Will, Erwin PHL 67
Willard, Jerrott KCC 57
Willard, Ken SFF 40, ARZ 20
Willey, Norm PHL 44/63/86
Williams, A.D. CLE 83, GBP 81, MIN 82
Williams, Aeneas ARZ 35, STL 35
Williams, Al SDC 84
Williams, Albert PIT 94
Williams, Alfred DEN 91, CIN 94, SFF 91
Williams, Allen DET 21
Williams, Alonzo STL 31
Williams, Andrew SFF 94
Williams, Armon TEN 42
Williams, Arthur CLE 26
Williams, Ben BUF 77
Williams, Ben MIN 98, PHL 90
Williams, Bernard PHL 74
Williams, Billy STL 19
Williams, Bob CHI 9
Williams, Bobbie PHL 66
Williams, Bobby ARZ 45, DET 45

Williams, Boo NOS 82
Williams, Boyd PHL 51
Williams, Brent NEP 96, NYJ 91, SEA 93
Williams, Brian DET 99, GBP 51, NOS 58
Williams, Brian MIN 29
Williams, Brian NEP 49
Williams, Brian NYG 59
Williams, Brock CHI 22
Williams, Brooks NEP 80, NOS 88
Williams, Broughton CHI 37
Williams, Byron NYG 87, PHL 80
Williams, Calvin BLT 80, PHL 89
Williams, Chad BLT 49
Williams, Charles STL 83
Williams, Charlie DAL 25/42
Williams, Charlie PHL 47
Williams, Chris ARZ 96
Williams, Chris BUF 27
Williams, Clarence ARZ 21, BUF 39
Williams, Clarence CLE 49
Williams, Clarence GBP 83
Williams, Clarence SDC 40
Williams, Clarence STL 24
Williams, Clyde ARZ 63
Williams, Clyde PHL 20
Williams, Cy xBKN ?
Williams, Dan DEN 90, KCC 92
Williams, Darryl SEA 33, CIN 31
Williams, Dave ARZ 80, PIT 82, SDC 84
Williams, Dave CHI 22
Williams, Dave SFF 30
Williams, David NYJ 73, TEN 73
Williams, David OAK 19/89, TBB 80
Williams, Del NOS 61
Williams, Delvin SFF 24, MIA 24, GBP 20
Williams, Demise OAK 33
Williams, Dokie OAK 85
Williams, Don PIT 38
Williams, Doug TBB 12, WSH 17
Williams, Doug TEN 69
Williams, Ed NEP 54
Williams, Ed CIN 43, TBB 43
Williams, Elijah ATL 21/25
Williams, Ellery NYG 85
Williams, Eric ARZ 55
Williams, Eric DET 76, SDC 92, STL 66, WSH 75
Williams, Eric PIT 21, DET ?
Williams, Erik DAL 79, BLT 76
Williams, Erwin PIT 43
Williams, Eugene SEA 54
Williams, Frank NYG 33

Williams, Frank STL 36
Williams, Fred CHI 75, WSH 75/77
Williams, Gardner DET 40
Williams, Garland zBRK 44
Williams, Gary CIN 84
Williams, Gene ATL 69, CLE 62, MIA 61
Williams, George NYG 96
Williams, Gerald CAR 98, GBP 96, PIT 98
Williams, Gerard ARZ 29, SFF 29, WSH 45
Williams, Gerome SDC 23
Williams, Grant NEP 76, SEA 69/79, STL 77
Williams, Greg WSH 47
Williams, Harvey KCC 22/44, OAK 22
Williams, Henry PHL 81
Williams, Henry OAK 45, SDC 45, STL 23
Williams, Herb ARZ 42, SFF 23
Williams, Howie GBP 29, OAK 29, SFF 28
Williams, Jake ARZ 5/19/42
Williams, Jamal SDC 76
Williams, Jamel WSH 22
Williams, James ARZ 21, BUF 29/31, SFF 27
Williams, James CHI 71
Williams, James CLE 90, JAX 90, NOS 90, SFF 53
Williams, James DET 16
Williams, James SEA 27
Williams, James SEA 88
Williams, Jamie ARZ 85, OAK 88, SFF 81, TEN 87
Williams, Jarvis MIA 26, NYG 26
Williams, Jay CAR 96, MIA 91, STL 96
Williams, Jeff CHI 74, SDC 72, STL 62, WSH 73
Williams, Jeff MIN 23
Williams, Jermaine JAX 43, KCC 43, OAK 34
Williams, Jerrol KCC 95, PIT 57/91, SDC 57, BLT 57
Williams, Jerry PHL 49, STL 22/33
Williams, Jim CIN 33
Williams, Jimmy DET 59, MIN 58, TBB 54
Williams, Jimmy SFF 23
Williams, Joe DAL 36, NOS 24
Williams, Joe NYG 25
Williams, Joe PIT 27, STL ?
Williams, Joe PIT 97
Williams, Joel ATL 54/58, PHL 59
Williams, Joel MIA 88
Williams, Joel SFF 22, xBAL 22

Williams, John BLT 36, DAL 38, IND 40, NOS 45, SEA 40
Williams, John IND 75, STL 75
Williams, John WSH 43
Williams, John L. SEA 32
. PIT 22
Williams, Johnny SFF 25
Williams, Jon NEP 44
Williams, Josh IND 96
Williams, K.D. GBP 50, OAK 59
Williams, Karl TBB 86
Williams, Keith ATL 35
Williams, Kendall IND 44
Williams, Kevin ARZ 14, BUF 82, DAL 85, SFF 82
Williams, Kevin BUF 23, WSH 34/37
Williams, Kevin GBP 20
Williams, Kevin HOU 23, MIA 38, NYJ 23
Williams, Kevin IND 21
Williams, Kevin MIN 93
Williams, Lamanzar JAX 74
Williams, Larry CLE 70, NEP 75, NOS 66
Williams, Lawrence CLE 80, KCC 40/80
Williams, Lee SDC 99, TEN 97
Williams, Leonard BUF 26
Williams, Lester NEP 72, SDC 96, SEA 72
Williams, Louis CAR 66
Williams, Marcus OAK 85
Williams, Mark GBP 51, JAX 51, STL 56, TBB 58
Williams, Marvin WSH 48
Williams, Maurice JAX 74
Williams, Maxie MIA 78, TEN 78
Williams, Melvin NOS 96
Williams, Michael ATL 42, PHL 32
Williams, Michael SFF 45
Williams, Mike BUF 68
Williams, Mike KCC 80
Williams, Mike MIA 87, DET ?
Williams, Mike SDC 29, STL 28
Williams, Mike WSH 84
Williams, Moe BLT 23, MIN 20/21
Williams, Monk CIN 6
Williams, Newton IND 39, SFF 45
Williams, Oliver CHI 93, IND 86, TEN 86
Williams, Pat BUF 93
Williams, Payton IND 28
Williams, Perry CHI 36, GBP 31
Williams, Perry NEP 38
Williams, Perry NYG 23
Williams, Pop xBKN ?

Williams, Ralph NOS 69, TEN 68

Williams, Randall DAL 89

Williams, Ray CLE 85

Williams, Ray DET 30

Williams, Ray PIT 35

Williams, Reggie CIN 57

Williams, Rex ARZ 56 \ DET 51

Williams, Richard ATL 22, TEN 35

Williams, Richard NOS 86

Williams, Ricky MIA 34, NOS 34

Williams, Ricky OAK 25

Williams, Robert DAL 23

Williams, Robert KCC 29/46, SEA 23

Williams, Robert KCC 40

Williams, Robert NOS 21

Williams, Robert PIT 28

Williams, Rodney NYG 2

Williams, Roger PHL 23, STL 46

Williams, Roland OAK 86, STL 86, TBB 81

Williams, Ronnie MIA 85, SEA 83

Williams, Roosevelt CHI 20, CLE 27

Williams, Roy DAL 31

Williams, Roy SFF 66

Williams, Sam ATL 88, DET 85/88, STL 88

Williams, Sam OAK 54

Williams, Sam SDC 47, TEN 49

Williams, Sammy BLT 72, KCC 72, SDC 79

Williams, Scott DET 38

Williams, Shaun NYG 36

Williams, Sherman DAL 20

Williams, Sid IND 64, WSH 51, CLE 67, PIT 52

Williams, Stacy CLE 43

Williams, Stan xDAL 80

Williams, Stepfret CIN 87, DAL 80

Williams, Steve IND 74

Williams, Tank TEN 25

Williams, Ted PHL 31, xBOS 22

Williams, Terry NYJ 33

Williams, Tex PHL 77, zMIA 25

Williams, Thomas ATL 69

Williams, Toby NEP 90

Williams, Tom SDC 87

Williams, Tony CIN 94, MIN 94

Williams, Tony CLE 74

Williams, Travis GBP 17/23, STL 25

Williams, Tyrone ATL 37, GBP 37

Williams, Tyrone DAL 86

Williams, Tyrone CHI 96, KCC 90/96, PHL 95, WSH 96

Williams, Van BUF 23, NYG 35

Williams, Vaughn IND 40

Williams, Vince SFF 40

Williams, Wally BLT 63, CLE 63, NOS 63

Williams, Walt CHI 43, DET 21, MIN 44

Williams, Walter xBOS 26, zCHI 82

Williams, Wandy DEN 29

Williams, Warren IND 44, PIT 42

Williams, Willie ARZ 60, NOS 65

Williams, Willie NYG 41, OAK 49

Williams, Willie PIT 27, SEA 27

Williams, Windell zBAL 53

Williamson, Carlton SFF 27

Williamson, Ernie NYG 71, WSH 47, zLAD 42

Williamson, Fred OAK 24, KCC 24, PIT 46

Williamson, Greg STL 43

Williamson, J.R. NEP 55, OAK 52

Williamson, Lee TEN 10

Willig, Matt ATL 77, CAR 71, GBP 76, NYJ 77, SFF 77

Willingham, Larry ARZ 33

Willis, Bill CLE 30/45/60

Willis, Chester OAK 38

Willis, Donald KCC 60, NOS 63

Willis, Fred CIN 33, TEN 44

Willis, Jamal SFF 24

Willis, James GBP 56, PHL 50, SEA 95

Willis, Keith BUF 93, PIT 93, WSH 93

Willis, Ken DAL 1, NYG 3, TBB 1

Willis, Larry WSH 38

Willis, Len BUF 86, NOS 89, MIN 80

Willis, Mitch ATL 73, DAL 98, OAK 98

Willis, PeterTom CHI 10

Wills, Ladell NYJ 91

Willson, Osborne PHL 15/25

Wilmer, Ray SEA 38

Wilmot, Trevor IND 96

Wilmsmeyer, Klaus MIA 8, NOS 4, SFF 10

Wilner, Jeff DEN 85, GBP 49/83

Wilson, Abu IND 37

Wilson, Adrian ARZ 22/24

Wilson, Al DEN 56

Wilson, Antonio MIN 54/59

Wilson, Ben GBP 36, STL 36

Wilson, Bernard ARZ 94, TBB 96

Wilson, Bill ARZ 42, PHL 23

Wilson, Billy SFF 52/84

Wilson, Bobby WSH 94

Wilson, Bobby xBKN 10

Wilson, Brenard ATL 22, PHL 22

Wilson, Brett MIN 27

Wilson, Butch IND 86, NYG 86

Wilson, Camp DET 16/35/66

Wilson, Cedrick SFF 84

Wilson, Charles GBP 88, NYJ 89, TBB 84

Wilson, Darrell NEP 47

Wilson, Darryal NEP 48

Wilson, Dave NOS 18

Wilson, David MIN 24, NEP 26

Wilson, Don BUF 21

Wilson, Earl SDC 93

Wilson, Ed NEP 12, KCC 12

Wilson, Eric BUF 50, WSH 59

Wilson, Eugene NEP 26

Wilson, Faye GBP 17

Wilson, Frank PIT 37

Wilson, Gene GBP 65

Wilson, George Sr. CHI 30

Wilson, George Jr. MIA 10

Wilson, Gillis CAR 92

Wilson, Gordon ARZ 31, STL 21, xBKN 23, xBOS 45

Wilson, Harry PHL 41

Wilson, J.C. TEN 33

Wilson, Jack STL 50

Wilson, Jamie CAR 73, IND 71

Wilson, Jerrel KCC 44, NEP 4

Wilson, Jerry MIA 24, SDC 20, TBB 24

Wilson, Jerry PHL 88, SFF 82

Wilson, Jim ATL 63, SFF 63, STL 77

Wilson, Joe CIN 46, NEP 23

Wilson, John STL 12

Wilson, Karl ARZ 90, BUF 73, MIA 77, NYJ 72, SDC 72, SFF 77, STL 77, TBB 91

Wilson, Larry ARZ 8

Wilson, Marc NEP 15, OAK 6

Wilson, Marcus GBP 29, OAK 40

Wilson, Michael SFF 85

Wilson, Mike ARZ 37

Wilson, Mike BUF 65, CIN 67, KCC 67

Wilson, Mike CIN 77, SEA 75

Wilson, Mule DET 8/56, NYG 6/16

Wilson, Nemiah DEN 48, CHI 21, OAK 26/48

Wilson, Otis CHI 55, OAK 50

Wilson, Ray GBP 35, NOS 42

Woodley, Richard DET 24
Woodlief, Doug STL 57
Woodring, John NYJ 57
Woodruff, Dwayne PIT 49
Woodruff, Jim ARZ ?
Woodruff, Lee PHL 11, WSH 30
Woodruff, Tony PHL 83
Woods, Carl NEP 34
Woods, Chris DEN 85, OAK 88
Woods, Don SDC 33, SFF 47
Woods, Glenn TEN 80
Woods, Icky CIN 30/31
Woods, Jerome KCC 21/31
Woods, Jerry DET 28, GBP 29
Woods, Larry DET 70, MIA 70, NYJ 70, SEA 70
Woods, LeVar ARZ 56
Woods, Mike ARZ 19
Woods, Mike IND 59
Woods, Rick PIT 22, TBB 20
Woods, Rob CLE 78
Woods, Robert DET 42, TEN 42
Woods, Robert NOS 65, NYJ 72
Woods, Tony CHI 65, SEA 57, WSH 98
Woodside, Keith GBP 33
Woodson, Abe SFF 40, ARZ 42
Woodson, Charles OAK 24
Woodson, Darren DAL 28
Woodson, Fred MIA 61
Woodson, Marv PIT 47, NOS 47
Woodson, Rod BLT 26, OAK 26, PIT 26, SFF 26
Woodson, Sean BUF 37, PHL 37
Woodson, Shawn CHI 22
Woodward, Dick WSH 56
Woody, Damien NEP 65
Woolfolk, Andre TEN 26
Woolfolk, Butch DET 21/40, NYG 25, TEN 40
Woolford, Donnell CHI 21, PIT 21
Woolford, Gary NYG 20
Woolsey, Rolly ARZ 44, CLE 25, SEA 45, DAL 45
Wooten, John CLE 60, WSH 67
Wooten, Mike WSH 60
Wooten, Ron NEP 61
Wooten, Tito IND 28, NYG 29
Word, Barry ARZ 32, KCC 23, MIN 23, NOS 34
Word, Mark CLE 90, KCC 67
Word, Roscoe BUF 47
Word, Roscoe NYG 33, NYJ 47, TBB 24
Worden, Neil PHL 32
Worden, Stu xBKN 18/30/3/23/4

Work, Jack DEN 58
Workman, Blake xCIN 35, xSTL 80
Workman, Hoge NYG 14
Workman, Vince CAR 34, GBP 46, IND 46, TBB 46
Worley, Tim CHI 38, PIT 38
Worrell, Cameron CHI 24
Wortham, Barron DAL 57, TEN 52
Worthen, Naz KCC 84
Worthen, Shawn HOU 97, MIN 95
Wortman, Keith ARZ 62, GBP 65
Woudenberg, John SFF 41, PIT 36
Woulfe, Mike PHL 63
Wozniak, John xDAL 62, xNYB 65, zBRK 35, zNYY 35
Wragge, Tony ARZ 68
Wren, Darryl NEP 27
Wren, Lowe CLE 42, NYJ 20, PIT 42
Wrighster, George JAX 87
Wright, Adrian TBB 34
Wright, Alexander DAL 81, OAK 89, STL 89
Wright, Alvin CLE 99, STL 99
Wright, Anthony BLT 2, DAL 2, PIT 1
Wright, Bo BUF 43
Wright, Brad DAL 15
Wright, Charles ARZ 46, DAL 41, TBB 21
Wright, Dana CIN 49
Wright, Elmo KCC 17, NEP 17, TEN 17
Wright, Eric CHI 83
Wright, Eric SFF 21
Wright, Ernie SDC 75/79, CIN 75
Wright, Fearon MIN 59
Wright, Felix CLE 22, MIN 22
Wright, George CLE 79, IND 60/74
Wright, Gordon NYJ 68, PHL 66
Wright, James ATL 83, DEN 87
Wright, James DEN 35
Wright, Jeff BUF 91
Wright, Jeff MIN 23
Wright, Jim xBOS 55
Wright, John ATL 45, DET 89
Wright, John zBAL 71
Wright, Johnnie IND 38
Wright, Keith CLE 89
Wright, Kenny HOU 43, MIN 20
Wright, Kenyatta BUF 57, BUF 98, NYJ 52
Wright, Lawrence CIN 42
Wright, Lonnie DEN 42
Wright, Louis DEN 20

Wright, Nate ARZ 41, ATL 24, MIN 43
Wright, Ralph xBKN 31/33/35/41
Wright, Randy GBP 16
Wright, Rayfield DAL 70/85
Wright, Steve ARZ 62, CHI 73, GBP 72, NYG 78, WSH 75
Wright, Steve DAL 73, IND 73, OAK 66
Wright, Sylvester PHL 52
Wright, Ted WSH 12, xBKN 25
Wright, Terry IND 27/40
Wright, Toby STL 32, WSH 32
Wright, Willie ARZ 52, ARZ 80
Wrightman, Tim CHI 80
Wuerffel, Danny CHI 17, GBP 7, NOS 7, WSH 17
Wukits, Al ARZ 50, PHL 50, PIT 50, zBUF 25, zMIA 25
Wulff, Jim WSH 32
Wunsch, Harry GBP 56
Wunsch, Jerry SEA 70, TBB 71
Wyant, Fred WSH 11
Wyatt, Alvin BUF 41, OAK 41
Wyatt, Antwuan PHL 85
Wyatt, Doug DET 40/46, NOS 23
Wyatt, Kervin NYG 99
Wyatt, Kevin KCC 23, SDC 30
Wyatt, Willie TBB 66
Wyche, Sam ARZ 15, BUF 13/14, CIN 14, DET 17, WSH 18
Wycheck, Frank TEN 41/89, WSH 22/36
Wycinsky, Craig CLE 67
Wycoff, Doug NYG 8, WSH 25
Wydo, Frank PHL 74/75, PIT 79
Wyhonic, John PHL 66, zBUF 33
Wyman, Dave DEN 57/92, SEA 92
Wyman, Devin NEP 72
Wyms, Ellis TBB 96
Wynn, Milton BLT 16, TBB 88
Wynn, Renaldo JAX 97, WSH 97
Wynn, Spergon CLE 13, MIN 3
Wynn, Will WSH 70, PHL 71
Wynne, Elmer CHI 17
Wynne, Harry NYG 30, xBOS 29
Wyrick, Jimmy DET 27/35, MIA 25
Wysocki, Pete WSH 50
Yablock, Izzy xBKN 1 4
Yablonski, Ventan ARZ 33
Yaccino, John BUF 25
Yackanich, Joe zNYY 32
Yagiello, Ray STL 54

Zimmerman, Leroy PIT 7, DET 6, PHL 7, WSH 22, xBOS 29
Zimny, Bob ARZ 15/63
Zirinsky, Walter STL 16
Zizak, Vince CHI 23, PHL 23
Zofko, Mickey DET 34, NYG 34
Zogg, John OAK 69
Zoia, Clyde ARZ 2/8
Zolak, Scott MIA 14, NEP 16
Zoll, Dick GBP 57
Zoll, Richard STL 20/26

Zomalt, Eric NYJ 23, PHL 27
Zombek, Joe PIT 82/85
Zontini, Lou ARZ 10, STL 23, zBUF 71
Zook, John ATL 71, ARZ 63
Zopetti, Frank PIT 76
Zordich, Mike ARZ 38, NYJ 38, PHL 36
Zorich, Chris CHI 97, WSH 78
Zorich, George CHI 14, zBAL 33, zMIA 35

Zorn, Jim GBP 18, SEA 10, TBB 10
Zucco, Vic CHI 48
Zuidmulder, Dave GBP 10/12/41
Zukauskas, Paul CLE 62/66
Zuker, Charlie xCIN 47
Zupek, Al GBP 25
Zuver, Merle GBP 14
Zuzzio, Tony DET ?
Zyntell, James PHL 9/16/21, NYG 2

APPENDIX A: THE BEST PLAYERS AT EACH NUMBER

00 Steve Bagarus (STL, WSH); John Clement (PIT); Ken Burrough (NOS, TEN); Jim Otto (OAK).

0 John Olszewski (DEN, DET, WSH).

1 Gary Anderson (PIT, SFF, TEN, MIN, PHL); Paddy Driscoll (ARZ); Benny Friedman (NYG); Curly Lambeau (GBP); Warren Moon (TEN, MIN, SEA); Garo Yepremian (MIA, NOS, TBB).

2 David Akers (PHL); Steve Christie (BUF, TBB); John Dell Isola (NYG); Charley Mathys (GBP); Charley Trippi (ARZ).

3 Tony Canadeo (GBP); Pete Gogolak (BUF, NYG); Daryle Lamonica (OAK); Mark Moseley (PHL, WSH); Eddie Murray (DAL, DET, PHL, TBB); Bronko Nagurski (CHI); Jan Stenerud (KCC).

4 Brett Favre (GBP); Tuffy Leemans (NYG); Ernie Nevers (ARZ); Adam Vinatieri.

5 Kerry Collins (NYG); Jeff Garcia (SFF); Ace Gutowsky (DET); Paul Hornung (GBP); Sean Landetta (NYG); Pat Leahy (NYJ); George McAfee (CHI); Donovan McNabb (PHL).

6 Rolf Benirschke (SDC); Kevin Butler (CHI); Steve Owens (NYG).

7 Morten Andersen (NOS); Elmer Angsman (ARZ); Dutch Clark (DET); John Elway (DEN); Boomer Esiason (CIN, NYJ, ARZ); Doug Flutie (BUF); George Halas (CHI); Mel Hein (NYG); Ron Jaworski (PHL); Bert Jones (IND); Ken O'Brien (NYJ, PHL); Dan Pastorini (TEN); Joe Theisman (WSH); Michael Vick (ATL); Bob Waterfield (STL).

8 Troy Aikman (DAL); Mark Brunell (JAX, GBP); Ray Guy (OAK); Nick Lowery (KCC, NYJ); Archie Manning (NOS, TEN); Davy O'Brien (PHL); Bill Paschal (NYG); Steve Young (SFF); Larry Wilson (ARZ).

9 Matt Bahr (CLE, PIT, NYG); Sonny Jurgensen (PHL, WSH); Jim McMahon (CHI, SDC, PHL, MIN, GBP); Steve McNair (TEN); Bill Wade (CHI, STL).

10 Steve Bartkowski (ATL); Jack Manders (CHI); Fran Tarkenton (MIN, NYG); Brad Van Pelt (NYG); Whizzer White (PIT); Jim Zorn (SEA).

11 Drew Bledsoe (NEP, BUF); Daunte Culpepper (MIN); Red Dunn (GBP); Greg Landry (DET); Link Lyman (CHI); Phil Simms (NYG); Tommy Thompson (PHL); Norm Van Brocklin (STL, PHL); Danny White (DAL).

12 Tom Brady (NEP); John Brodie (SFF); Randall Cunningham (PHL); Lynn Dickey (GBP); Bob Greise (MIA); Charley Johnson (ARZ, DEN, TEN); Jim Kelly (BUF); Joe Namath (NYJ, STL); Harry Newman (NYG); Ken Stabler (OAK, TEN); Roger Staubach (DAL); Doug Williams (TBB).

13 Frankie Albert (SFF); Guy Chamberlin (ARZ, CHI); Chris Jacke (GBP); Dave Jennings (NYG); Chester Marcol (GBP); Dan Marino (MIA); Don Maynard (NYJ, NYG, ARZ); Ken Riley (CIN); Frank Ryan (CLE); Jake Scott (MIA); Joe Stydahar (CHI); George Trafton (CHI); Kurt Warner (STL); Ken Washington (STL).

14 Ken Anderson (CIN); Fred Cox (MIN); Ward Cuff (NYG); John Drake (STL); Dan Fouts (SDC); Otto Graham (CLE); Steve Grogan (NEP); Don Hutson (GBP); Eddie Lebaron (DAL, WSH); Ed Podolak (KCC); Y.A. Tittle (NYG, SFF).

15 Dave Hostetler (NYG); Jack Kemp (BUF, SDC); Neil Lomax (ARZ); Earl Morrall (IND, MIA); Babe Parilli (NEP, GBP); Hank Soar (NYG); Bart Starr (GBP); Jim Turner (DEN); Steve Van Buren (PHL).

16 George Blanda (CHI, OAK, TEN); Len Dawson (KCC); Frank Gifford (NYG); Ed Healey (CHI); Joe Montana (SFF); George Musso (CHI); Jim Plunkett (NEP); Vinny Testaverde (NYJ).

17 Red Badgro (NYG); Harold Carmichael (PHL); Turk Edwards (WSH); Jim Hart (ARZ, WSH); Cecil Isbel (GBP); Billy Kilmer (WSH, NOS); Dave Kreig (SEA, CHI); Don Meredith (DAL); Ritchie Petitbon (CHI, STL); Brian Sipe (CLE).

18 Roman Gabriel (STL, PHL); Charlie Joiner (SDC, TEN, CIN); Peyton Manning (IND); Tobin Rote (GBP, DET, SDC); Emmitt Thomas (KCC); Gene Washington (SFF).

19 Lance Alworth (SDC, DAL); Keshawn Johnson (NYJ, TBB); Bernie Kosar (CLE, MIA); John Unitas (IND, SDC).

20 Lem Barney (DET); Ronde Barber (TBB); Cliff Battles (WSH); Bobby Bryant (MIN); Billy Cannon (TEN); Gino Cappelletti (NEP); Joe Cribbs (BUF); Deron Cherry (KCC); Brian Dawkins (PHL); Garrison Hearst (SFF); Tommy Mason (MIN); Joe Morris (NYG); Jim Patton (NYG); Mel Renfro (DAL); Barry Sanders (DET); Louis Wright (DEN).

21 Donnie Abraham (TBB); Eric Allen (PHL, NOS, OAK); Tiki Barber (NYG); Cliff Branch (OAK); James Brooks (CIN); Nolan Cromwell (STL); Dan Fortman (CHI); Mike Garrett (KCC); John Hadl (SDC, STL, GBP, TEN); Jim Lee Howell (NYG); Bob Jeter (GBP); Jim Kiick (MIA); Ed Meador (STL); Eric Metcalf (CLE); Terry Metcalf (ARZ); Deion Sanders (ATL, SFF, DAL, WSH); LaDainian Tomlinson (SDC).

22 Dick Bass (STL); Dave Brown (SEA); Timmy Brown (PHL); Ed Danowski (NYG); Lavie Dilweg (GBP); Bob Hayes (DAL); Mike Haynes (OAK); Paul Krause (MIN); Bobby Layne (DET, PIT, CHI); Keith Lincoln (SDC); Dick Lynch (NYG); Mercury Morris (MIA); Emmitt Smith (DAL); Roger Wehrli (ARZ); Buddy Young (IND).

23 Blaine Bishop (TEN, PHL); Goose Gonsoulin (DEN); Mel Gray (DET); Paul Lowe (SDC); Jim Poole (NYG); Patrick Surtain (MIA); Troy Vincent (PHL, MIA); Dave Whitsell (CHI, NOS); Travis Williams (GBP).

24 Johnny Blood (GBP); Willie Brown (OAK); Jack Christiansen (DET); Tucker Fredrickson (NYG); Gary Green (KCC); Robert Griffith (MIN); Warren Lahr (CLE); Ty Law (NEP); Freeman McNeil (NYJ); Lenny Moore (IND); J.D. Smith (SFF); Everson Walls (DAL); Del Williams (SFF, MIA); Willie Wood (GBP); Charles Woodson (OAK).

25 Jim Bakken (ARZ); Fred Biletnikoff (OAK); Scott Case (ATL); Jim David (DET); Eric Davis (SFF, CAR); Dorsey Levens (GBP); Haven Moses (DEN, BUF); Tommy McDonald (PHL, DAL); Dick Nolan (NYG); Louis Oliver (MIA).

26 Herb Adderley (GBP, DAL); Jon Arnett (STL); Gary Barbaro (KCC); Jim Benton (STL); Raymond Clayborn (NEP); Deuce McAlister (NOS); Lydell Mitchell (IND); Lloyd Mumphord (MIA); Clinton Portis (DEN); Ray Renfro (CLE); George Saimes (BUF); Robert Smith (MIN); Wendell Tyler (SFF); Rod Woodson (PIT, BLT, OAK).

27 Steve Atwater (DEN); Terrell Buckley (MIA, GBP); Irv Cross (PHL); Thom Darden (CLE); Gary Garrison (SDC); Eddie George (TEN); Bob Grim (MIN); Rodney Hampton (NYG); Ken Houston (WSH).

28 Bill Bradley (PHL); Willie Buchanan (GBP, SDC); Corey Dillon (CIN); Warrick Dunn (TBB); Marshall Faulk (STL, IND); Willie Galimore (CHI); Darrell Green (WSH); Abner Haynes (KCC); Yale Lary (DET); Curtis Martin (NEP, NYJ); Ahmad Rashad (MIN); Fred Taylor (JAX); Curt Warner (SEA); Darren Woodson (DAL).

29 Charley Brock (GBP); Eric Dickerson (STL, STL, ATL, OAK); Hanford Dixon (CLE); Harold Jackson (PHL, STL, NEP); Sammy Knight (NOS); Albert Lewis (KCC, OAK); Darryll Lewis (TEN); Sam Madison (MIA); Alex Webster (NYG).

30 Bill Brown (MIN); Terrell Davis (DEN); Ahman Green (GBP); Clarke Hinkle (GBP); Lawrence McCutcheon (STL, SEA); Dave Meggett (NYG); Brian Mitchell (WSH); Mark Van Eeghen (OAK); Bill Willis (CLE); George Wilson (CHI); Icky Woods (CIN).

31 William Andrews (ATL); Joe Fortunato (CHI); Priest Holmes (KCC); Brock Marion (MIA); Wilbert Montgomery (PHL); Eddie Price (NYG); Donnie Shell (PIT); Jim Taylor (GBP, NOS); Gaynell Tinsley (ARZ).

32 Marcus Allen (OAK, KCC); Jamal Anderson (ATL); Ottis Anderson (ARZ); Jim

Brown (CLE); Mike Curtis (IND); Franco Harris (PIT); Jack Pardee (STL, WSH); O.J. Simpson (BUF, SFF); Jack Tatum (OAK); Dan Towler (STL); Ricky Watters (SFF, PHL, SEA); John L. Williams (SEA); James Wilder (TBB).

33 Ashley Ambrose (ATL); Sammy Baugh (WSH); Roger Craig (SFF); Tony Dorsett (DAL, DEN); David Fulcher (CIN); Kenny Graham (SDC); Ollie Matson (ARZ, STL, PHL); Larry Morris (CHI); Mike Rozier (TEN).

34 Ray Buchanan (IND, ATL); Earl Campbell (TEN); Dale Carter (KCC); Don Chandler (GBP, NYG); Tony Galbreath (NOS); Cookie Gilchrist (BUF); Pat Harder (ARZ, DET); Bo Jackson (OAK); Walt Michaels (CLE); Walter Payton (CHI); Joe Perry (SFF, IND); Andy Russell (PIT); Thurman Thomas (BUF).

35 Alan Ameche (IND); Neal Anderson (CHI); Rick Casares (CHI, MIN, WSH); Marion Butts (SDC); Bill Dudley (DET, PIT, WSH); Galen Fiss (CLE); Calvin Hill (DAL); John Henry Johnson (DET, PIT, SFF, TEN); Jim Nance (NEP); Christian Okoye (KCC); Pete Pihos (PHL); Riley Smith (WSH); Aeneas Williams (ARZ, STL); Paul Younger (STL).

36 Jerome Bettis (PIT, STL); Clem Daniels (OAK); Merton Hanks (SFF); Mike Michalske (GBP), Lawyer Milloy (NEP, BUF); Marion Motley (CLE); Bill Pellington (IND); Ken Reaves (ATL); Bill Thompson (DEN); Willie Wilkin (WSH).

37 Shaun Alexander (SEA); Tommy Casanova (CIN); Larry Centers (ARZ); Pat Fischer (ARZ, WSH); Rodney Harrison (SDC); Lester Hayes (OAK); Jimmy Johnson (SFF); Carnell Lake (PIT, JAX, BLT); Tommy Myers (NOS); Doak Walker (DET).

38 Kimble Anders (KCC); Mike Anderson (DEN); Arnie Herber (GBP); Roland James (NEP); George Rogers (NOS); Bob Tucker (NYG).

39 Kermit Alexander (SFF); Ray Crockett (DET, DEN, KCC); Larry Csonka (MIA, NYG); Sam Cunningham (NEP); Carl Lee (MIN); Hugh McElhenny (SFF, NYG, MIN, DET).

40 Mike Alstott (TBB); Dick Anderson (MIA); Bob Boyd (IND); Tom Brookshier (PHL); Bobby Joe Conrad (ARZ); Frank Filchock (NYG); Mike Haynes (NEP); Elroy Hirsch (STL); Cal Hubbard (GBP); Wayne Milner (WSH); Joe Morrison (NYG); Dainard Paulsen (NYJ); Gale Sayers (CHI); Ken Willard (SFF).

41 Terry Barr (DET); Keith Byars (PHL, NEP); Todd Lyght (STL); Tom Matte (IND); Dave Osborne (MIN); Eugene Robinson (SEA, GBP); Matt Snell (NYJ); Dick Todd (WSH); Phil Villapiano (OAK, BUF); Charley Waters (DAL).

42 Ricky Bell (TBB); John Brockington (GBP); Butch Byrd (BUF); Charley Conerly (NYG); John Gilliam (MIN); Dick Hoak (PIT); Ronnie Lott (SFF); Sid Luckman (CHI); Chuck Muncie (NOS); Gerald Riggs (ATL); Johnny Robinson (KCC); Darren Sharper (GBP); Charley Taylor (WSH); Paul Warfield (CLE, MIA); Chris Warren (SEA).

43 George Atkinson (OAK); Larry Brown (WSH); Steve Foley (DEN); Buckets Goldenberg (GBP); Dave Hampton (ATL); Carl Lockhart (NYG); Lenny Lyles (IND); Jim Norton (TEN); Don Perkins (DAL); Mike Pruitt (CLE); Will Sherman (STL); Nate Wright (MIN); Roynell Young (PHL).

44 Paul Christman (ARZ); John David Crow (ARZ, SFF); Bobby Dillon (GBP); Elbert Dubenion (BUF); Chuck Foreman (MIN); Marv Hubbard (OAK), Leroy Kelly (CLE); Dick LeBeau (DET); Floyd Little (DEN); Ernie Nevers (ARZ); Pete Retzlaff (PHL); John Riggins (WSH, NYJ); Kyle Rote (NYG); Dave Waymer (NOS); Whizzer White (DET).

45 Speedy Duncan (SDC, WSH); Kenny Easley (SEA); Gary Fencik (CHI); Dave Grayson (KCC, OAK); Archie Griffin (CIN); Homer Jones (NYG; Ed Sharockman (MIN); Emlen Tunnell (NYG, GBP).

46 Dan Abramowicz (NOS); Todd Christensen (OAK); Hank Gremminger (GBP); Pete Johnson (CIN); Jim Kearney (KCC); Verne Lewellen (GBP); Tim McDonald (ARZ, SFF); Doug Plank (CHI); Bill Walsh (PTI).

47 Glenn Blackwood (MIA); Mel Blount (PIT); Joey Browner (MIN); Leroy Irvin (STL); John Lynch (TBB); Dick Moegle (SFF); Johnny Morris (CHI); John Sample (IND; Jesse Whittenton.

48 Steven Davis (WSH, Car); Ken Ellis (GBP); Beattie Feathers (CHI); Tim Fox (NEP); Ernie Green (CLE); Wes Hopkins (PHL).

49 Erich Barnes (NYG); Walt Kiesling (ARZ, GBP); Tom Landry (NYG); Ed Marinaro (MIN)Tony Richardson (KCC); Mike Siani (OAK); Dennis Smith (DEN).

50 Jim Carter (GBP); Vince Costello (CLE); Bill Curry (IND); Dave Dalby (OAK); Bobby Maples (DEN, TEN); Jeff Siemon

(MIN), Mike Singletary (CHI); Ken Strong (NYG); Jerry Tubbs (DAL); Alex Wojciechowicz (DET).

51 Dick Butkus (CHI); Monte Coleman (WSH); Randy Cross (SFF); Kevin Hardy (JAX); Pop Ivy (ARZ); Jim Lynch (KCC); Sam Mills (NOS, CAR); Jim Ringo (GBP); Jim Ritcher (BUF); Willie Thomas (PHL).

52 Robert Brazile (TEN); Garland Boyette (TEN); John Cannady (NYG); Frank Gatski (CLE, DET); Ted Johnson (NEP); Ray Lewis (BLT); Dave Lloyd (PHL); Neil Olkewicz (WSH); Dick Szymanski (IND); Mike Webster (PIT).

53 Jeff Bostic (WSH); Fred Carr (GBP); Harry Carson (NYG); Ray Donaldson (IND); Hugh Douglas (PHL); Randy Gradishar (DEN); Hugh Green (TBB); Tommy Hart (SFF); Bill Johnson (SFF); Vaughn Johnson (NOS); Mike Lucci (DET); Bob Matheson (MIA); Mick Tingelhoff (MIN); Jim Youngblood (STL).

54 Teddy Bruschi (NEP); Chuck Howley (DAL); Bob Johnson (CIN); E.J. Junior (ARZ); Larry McCarren (GBP); Fred McNeill (MIN); Chris Spielman (DET); Zack Thomas (MIA); Brian Urlacher (CHI); Randy White (DAL).

55 Maxie Baughan (PHL, STL); Derrick Brooks (TBB); Doug Buffone (CHI); Tom Fears (STL); Irv Goode (ARZ); Chris Hanburger (WSH); Matt Hazeltine (SFF); E.J. Holub (KCC); Lee Roy Jordan (DAL); Willie McGinnest (NEP); Matt Millen (OAK); Junior Seau (SDC); Scott Studwell (MIN); Wayne Walker (DET); Ray Wietecha (NYG).

56 Chris Doleman (MIN, SFF); Len Hauss (WSH); Bill Hewitt (CHI, PHL); Dante Lavelli (CLE); Ray Mansfield (PIT); Lance Mehl (NYJ); Hardy Nickerson (JAX, TBB, GBP); Jerry Robinson (PHL); Joe Schmidt (DET); Doug Smith (STL); Pat Swilling (NOS, DET); Lawrence Taylor (NYG); Andre Tippett (NEP).

57 Mark Arneson (ARZ); Ricky Jackson (NOS); Tom Jackson (DEN); Ollie Kreutz (CHI); Lamar Lathon (CAR); Mo Lewis (NYJ); Clay Matthews (CLE); Mike Merriweather (PIT, MIN); Steve Nelson (NEP); Dwight Stephenson (MIA); Jeff Van Note (ATL).

58 Carl Banks (NYG, WSH); Kim Bokamper (MIA); Peter Boulware (BLT); Dan Currie (GBp, STL); Jack Lambert (PIT); Wilber Marshall (CHI, WSH, TEN); Isiah Robert-son (STL); Jack Rudnay (KCC); Mac Speedie (CLE); Mike Stratton (BUF); Derrick Thomas (KCC); Jesse Tuggle (ATL); Keena Turner (SFF).

59 John Anderson (GBP); Matt Blair (MIN); Jack Ham (PIT); Seth Joyner (PHL).

60 Bill Austin (NYG); Chuck Bednarik (PHL); Lee Roy Caffey (GBP); Dale Dodrill (PIT); Otto Graham (CLE); Larry Grantham (NYJ); Dennis Harrah (STL); Tommy Nobis (ATL); George Preas (IND); Paul Winston (MIN).

61 Dick Barwegan (IND); Curley Culp (KCC); Bob DeMarco (ARZ); Steve Everitt (BLT, CLE); Roy Foster (MIA); Bill George (CHI, STL); Nate Newton (DAL); Jesse Sapolu (SFF); Bob Talamini (TEN).

62 Darrell Dess (NYG); Jerry Fontenot (NOS); Jim Langer (MIA); Russ Letlow (GBP); Guy McIntyre (SFF); John Nisby (WSH); Glenn Ressler (IND); Charley Trippi (ARZ); Ed White (MIN).

63 Frankie Albert (SFF); Bruno Banducci (SFF); Dermonti Dawson (PIT); Willie Lanier (KCC); Mike Munchak (TEN); Leroy Selmon (TBB); Art Spinney (IND); Dick Stanfel (DET); Fuzzy Thurston (GBP); Gene Upshaw (OAK); Doug Wilkerson (SDC).

64 Jim Burt (NYG); Ken Gray (ARZ); Jerry Kramer (GBP); Randall McDaniel (MIN); Bud McFaddin (DEN); Jack Reynolds (STL); Jim Ray Smith (CLE); Stan West (STL); Dave Wilcox (SFF).

65 Houston Antwine (NEP); Les Bingaman (DET); Elvin Bethea (TEN); Ray Brown (SFF); Dave Butz (WSH); Joe Fields (NYJ); Jon Gilliam (KCC); Wayne Hawkins (OAK); John Jackson (PIT); Tom Mack (STL); Max Montoya (CIN); Chuck Noll (CLE); Bart Oates (NYG); Vince Promuto (WSH); Gary Zimmerman (MIN).

66 George Andrie (DAL); Bill Bergey (CIN, PHL); Conrad Dobler (ARZ); Gene Hickerson (CLE); Joe Jacoby (WSH); Larry Little (MIA); Ray Nitschke (GBP); Randy Rasmussen (NYJ); Harley Sewell (DET); Billy Shaw (BUF); Don Shinnick (IND); Jack Stroud (NYG); Bulldog Turner (CHI).

67 Grady Alderman (MIN); Stan Brock (NOS); Dave Herman (NYJ); Kent Hull (BUF); Bob Kuechenberg (MIA); Reggie McKenzie (BUF); Les Richter (STL); Larry Stallings (ARZ); Art Still (KCC) Ed White (SDC).

68 Rulon Carter (DEN); Joe DeLamielleure (BUF); Gale Gillingham (GBP); L.C. Green-

wood (PIT); Russ Grimm (WSH); Dennis Harrison (PHL); Kevin Mawae (NYJ); Howard Mudd (SFF); Alex Sandusky (IND); Kyle Turley (NOS).

69 Bill Forester (GBP); Sherrill Headrick (KCC); Tim Krumrie (CIN); Woody Peoples (SFF); Doug Sutherland (MIN); Will Wolford (BUF).

70 Art Donovan (IND); Sam Huff (NYG, WSH); Charley Krueger (SFF); Henry Lawrence (OAK); Jim Marshall (MIN); Leonard Marshall (NYG, WSH); Tom Sestak (BUF); Michael Sinclair (SEA); Paul Smith (DEN); Ernie Stautner (PIT); Russ Washington (SDC); Bob Whitfield (ATL); Al Wistert (PHL, PIT); Rayfield Wright (DAL).

71 Tony Boselli (JAX); Ed Budde (KCC); George Connor (CHI); Fred Dean (SDC); Keith Fahnhorst (SFF); Walter Johnson (CLE); Walter Jones (SEA); Alex Karras (DET); Greg Kragen (DEN); Charles Mann (WSH); Joe Scibelli (STL); Mark Tuinei (DAL).

72 Dan Dierdorf (ARZ); Earl Dotson (GBP); Bob Heinz (MIA); Ed Jones (DAL); Gil Mains (DET); Dexter Manley (WSH); Joe Nash (SEA); William Perry (CHI); Joe Rutgens (WSH); Leon Searcy (JAX); Jerry Sherk (CLE); Diron Talbert (WSH); Bob Vogel (IND).

73 Larry Allen (DAL); Bob Baumhower (MIA); Charley Cowan (STL); Doug Dieken (CLE); Norm Evans (MIA); Simon Fletcher (DEN); John Hannah (NEP); Dave Hill (KCC); Joe Klecko (NYJ); Mark May (WSH); Ernie McMillan (ARZ); Ralph Neely (DAL); Leo Nomellini (SFF); Arnie Weinmeister (NYG); Ron Yary (MIN, STL).

74 Walt Barnes (PHL); Fred Dean (SFF); Henry Jordan (GBP); Tom Keating (OAK); Louie Kelcher (SDC); Bob Lilly (DAL); Mike McCormack (CLE); Ron Mix (SDC); Derland Moore (NOS); Merlin Olsen (STL); Mike Reid (CIN); Bob Toneff (SFF).

75 Lomas Brown (DET, TBB); Manny Fernandez (MIA); Joe Greene (PIT); Forrest Gregg (GBP); Winston Hill (NYJ); Deacon Jones (STL); Jim Katcavage (NYG); George Kunz (IND); Howie Long (OAK); George Martin (NYG); Jerry Mays (KCC); Keith Millard (MIN); Jonathan Ogden (BLT); Jethro Pugh (DAL); Stan Walters (PHL).

76 Bob Brown (PHL, STL, OAK); Roger Brown (DET); Lou Creekmur (DET); John Elliott (NYG, NYJ); Rosey Grier (NYG,

STL); Lou Groza (CLE); Bucko Kilroy (PHL); Gene Lipscomb (IND, PIT); Steve McMichael (CHI); Len Rohde (SFF); Bob Skoronski (GBP); Fred Smerlas (BUF); Steve Wisniewski (OAK).

77 Lyle Alzado (DEN); Stew Barber (BUF); Bruce Bosley (SFF); A.J. Duhe (MIA); Red Grange (CHI); Ernie Ladd (SDC); Stan Mauldin (ARZ); Karl Mecklenberg (DEN); Dick Modzelewski (NYG); Jim Parker (IND); Willie Roaf (NOS); Dick Schafrath (CLE); Jim Tyrer (KCC).

78 Bruce Armstrong (NEP); Bobby Bell (KCC); Marion Campbell (PHL); Al DeRogatis (NYG); Jim Dunnaway (BUF); Stan Jones (CHI); Mike Kenn (ATL); Anthony Munoz (CIN); Art Shell (OAK); Jackie Slater (STL); Bruce Smith (BUF, WSH); Bubba Smith (IND); Walt Sweeney (SDC); Richmond Webb (MIA); Dwight White (PIT).

79 Harris Barton (SFF); Rosey Brown (NYG); Ross Browner (CIN); Ray Childress (TEN); Barney Chavous (DEN); Tex Coulter (NYG); Bob Gain (CLE); Jacob Green (SEA); Dave Hanner (GBP); Jim Hunt (NEP); Gary Johnson (SDC); Jim Lachey (WSH); Ron McDole (WSH); Bob St. Clair (SFF); Vic Sears (PHL); Dave Szott (KCC).

80 Gene Brito (WSH); Troy Brown (NEP); Isaac Bruce (STL); Jack Butler (PIT); Cris Carter (MIN); Chris Collinsworth (CIN); Henry Ellard (STL); Len Ford (CLE); Irving Fryar (NEP, MIA, PHL); Jim Gibbons (DET); Steve Largent (SEA); James Lofton (GBP, BUF, OAK, PHL); Eric Moulds (BUF); Jerry Rice (SFF, OAK); Rod Smith (DEN); Kellen Winslow (SDC).

81 Doug Atkins (CHI, NOS); Tim Brown (OAK); Carl Eller (MIN); Russ Francis (NEP); Roy Green (ARZ); Desmond Howard (GBP); Billy Johnson (ATL); Night Train Lane (STL, ARZ, DET); Terrence Mathis (ATL); Art Monk (WSH); Elbie Nickel (PIT); Terrell Owens (SFF); Carl Pickens (CIN); Andy Robustelli (NYG); Jackie Smith (ARZ).

82 Raymond Berry (IND); Paul Coffman (GBP); Ozzie Newsome (CLE); Mike Quick (PHL); Jimmy Smith (JAX); John Stallworth (PIT); John Taylor (SFF).

83 Mark Clayton (MIA); Jim Doran (DET); Ted Hendricks (IND, OAK); John Jefferson (SDC); John Martinkovic (GBP); Stephone Paige (KCC); Andre Reed (BUF); George Sauer (NYJ); Pat Tilley (ARZ); Bobby Walston (PHL).

84 Gary Clark (WSH); Carroll Dale (GBP); Billy Johnson (TEN); Eric Martin (NOS); Herman Moore (DET); Randy Moss (MIN); Jay Novacek (DAL); Art Powell (NYJ, OAK); Shannon Sharpe (DEN); Sterling Sharpe (GBP); Jack Snow (STL); Bones Taylor (WSH); Bob Trumpy (CIN); Paul Wiggin (CLE); Billy Wilson (SFF).

85 Julius Adams (NEP); Nick Buoniconti (NEP, MIA); Isaac Curtis (CIN); Mark Duper (MIA); Mel Gray (ARZ); Lamar Lundy (STL); Derrick Mason (TEN); Max McGee (GBP); Del Shofner (NYG); Wesley Walker (NYJ); Jack Youngblood (STL).

86 Buck Buchanan (KCC); Gary Collins (CLE); Boyd Dowler (GBP); Earl Faison (SDC); Antonio Freeman (GBP); Cedrick Hardman (SFF); Bill Howton (GBP); Dante Lavelli (CLE); Stanley Morgan (NEP); Norm Willey (PHL); Charley Young (PHL).

87 Dave Casper (OAK); Dwight Clark (SFF); Ben Coates (NEP); Willie Davis (GBP); Jack Ferrante (PHL); Harlon Hill (CHI); Charley Hennigan (TEN); Claude Humphrey (ATL); Rich Jackson (DEN); Keenan McCardell (JAX); Jerry Smith (WSH); Lionel Taylor (DEN, TEN).

88 Terry Glenn (NEP); Jimmy Giles (TBB); Tony Gonzalez (KCC); Marvin Harrison (IND); Torry Holt (STL); Michael Irvin (DAL); Keith Jackson (PHL, MIA, GBP); Ron Kramer (GBP); John Mackey (IND); Riley Odoms (DEN); Alan Page (MIN); Drew Pearson (DAL); Sonny Randle (ARZ); Charley Sanders (DET); Lynn Swann (PIT); Al Toon (NYJ).

89 Mark Bavaro (NYG); David Boston (ARZ); Wes Chandler (SDC); Gail Cogdill (DET); Bob Dee (NEP); Mike Ditka (CHI, PHL, DAL); Gino Marchetti (IND); Nat Moore (MIA); Dave Robinson (GBP); Steve Tasker (BUF); Otis Taylor (KCC); Frank Wychek (TEN).

90 Tony Brackens (JAX); Chad Eaton (NEP); Phil Hansen (BUF); Ezra Johnson (GBP); Jevon Kearse (TEN); Chuck Smith (ATL); Neil Smith (KCC, DEN); George Webster (TEN).

91 Kevin Greene (PIT, STL, CAR); Chester McGlockton (OAK); Brian Noble (GBP); Robert Porcher (DET); John Strzykalski (SFF).

92 Shaun Ellis (NYJ); Michael Dean Perry (CLE); Michael Strahan (NYG); Ted Washington (BUF); Reggie White (PHL, GBP).

93 Trace Armstrong (MIA); Jerry Ball (DET); Gilbert Brown (GBP); Kevin Carter (STL, TEN); Marty Lyons (NYJ); Wayne Martin (NOS); Trevor Pryce (DEN); John Randle (MIN, SEA); Richard Seymour (NEP).

94 John Abraham (NYJ); Chad Brown (SEA); Luther Elliss (DET); Kabeer Gbaja-Biamila (GBP); Charles Haley (SFF, DAL); Joe Johnson (NOS); Dana Stubblefield (SFF, WSH).

95 Michael Carter (SFF); Richard Dent (CHI); William Fuller (TEN, PHL, SDC); Greg Lloyd (PIT); Bryce Paup (GBB, BUF, JAX).

96 Tom Harmon (STL); Norman Hand (SDC); Sean Jones (TEN, GBP); Cortez Kennedy (SEA); Darrell Russell (OAK); Clyde Simmons (PHL, ARZ, JAX).

97 Cornelius Bennett (BUF, IND); La'Roi Glover (NOS, DAL); Tim Harris (GBP); John Parella (SDC); Simeon Rice (ARZ); Henry Thomas (MIN); Renaldo Turnbull (NOS); Bryant Young (SFF).

98 Jessie Armstead (NYG, WSH); Julian Peterson (SFF); Tony Siragusa (IND, BLT); Eric Swann (ARZ).

99 Jerome Brown (PHL); Mark Gastineau (NYJ); Marshall Goldberg (ARZ); Dan Hampton (CHI); Levon Kirkland (PIT, SEA, PHL); Michael McCrary (SEA, BLT); Warren Sapp (TBB), Jason Taylor (MIA).

APPENDIX B:
CUMULATIVE DATA

All-Time Record by Team

	Regular Season				Postseason		
	Won	Lost	Tied	Percent	Won	Lost	Championships
Miami Dolphins	349	223	4	.609	20	19	2
Oakland Raiders	385	264	11	.592	25	18	3
Chicago Bears	641	463	42	.578	14	15	9
Dallas Cowboys	377	275	6	.578	32	22	5
San Francisco 49ers	432	333	13	.564	25	17	5
Green Bay Packers	602	472	36	.559	23	13	12
Minnesota Vikings	354	283	9	.555	17	23	0
Cleveland Browns	400	320	10	.555	11	20	4 (+ 4 AAFC titles)
New York Giants	571	477	33	.543	16	21	6
Kansas City Chiefs	349	299	12	.538	8	12	1 (+ 1 AFL title)
St. Louis Rams	476	415	20	.533	18	23	3
Washington Redskins	499	452	27	.524	22	15	5
Denver Broncos	339	311	10	.521	16	13	2
Jacksonville Jaguars	73	71	0	.507	4	4	0
Baltimore Ravens	63	64	1	.496	5	2	1
Pittsburgh Steelers	469	478	21	.495	23	17	4
Indianapolis Colts	364	371	7	.495	12	14	3
Tennessee Titans	323	331	6	.494	14	17	(2 AFL titles)
New England Patriots	314	332	9	.483	13	10	2
Buffalo Bills	313	339	8	.480	14	15	(2 AFL titles)
Detroit Lions	467	510	32	.479	7	10	4
San Diego Chargers	308	341	11	.475	7	11	(1 AFL title)
Philadelphia Eagles	412	497	25	.471	14	15	3
Seattle Seahawks	205	231	0	.470	3	6	0
New York Jets	294	358	8	.452	7	9	1
Carolina Panthers	64	80	0	.444	4	2	0
Cincinnati Bengals	234	313	1	.428	5	7	0
Arizona Cardinals	439	628	39	.416	2	5	2
New Orleans Saints	226	331	5	.407	1	5	0
Atlanta Falcons	226	344	6	.398	5	7	0
Tampa Bay Bucs	167	268	1	.384	6	7	1
Houston Texans	9	23	0	.281	0	0	0

Seasonal Records

	Winning Seasons	Losing Seasons	.500 Seasons
Chicago Bears	52	29	3
Green Bay Packers	50	26	7
New York Giants	44	28	7
Washington Redskins	35	27	10
St. Louis Rams	35	29	3
San Francisco 49ers	33	18	3
Cleveland Browns	32	16	3
Detroit Lions	32	36	6
Pittsburgh Steelers	31	34	6
Philadelphia Eagles	29	39	3
Oakland Raiders	28	11	5
Dallas Cowboys	28	14	2
Miami Dolphins	27	6	5
Minnesota Vikings	25	14	5
Kansas City Chiefs	24	16	4
Indianapolis Colts	24	23	4
New England Patriots	22	19	3
Denver Broncos	21	17	6
Arizona Cardinals	21	59	4
Tennessee Titans	20	19	5
Buffalo Bills	20	21	3
San Diego Chargers	18	20	6
New York Jets	13	21	10
Seattle Seahawks	10	13	4
Cincinnati Bengals	11	21	4
Atlanta Falcons	9	27	2
Tampa Bay Buccaneers	8	19	1
New Orleans Saints	7	25	5
Jacksonville Jaguars	4	5	0
Baltimore Ravens	3	4	1
Carolina Panthers	2	6	1
Houston Texans	0	2	0

Retired Numbers by Number

1 Ray Flaherty (NYG).
3 Tony Canadeo (GBP); Bronko Nagurski (CHI); Jan Stenerud (KCC).
4 Tuffy Leemans (NYG).
5 George McAfee (CHI).
7 Dutch Clark (DET); John Elway (DEN); George Halas (CHI); Mel Hein (NYG); Bob Waterfield (STL).
8 Archie Manning (NOS); Larry Wilson (ARZ).
10 Steve Bartkowski (ATL); Fran Tarkenton (MIN).
11 Phil Simms (NYG).
12 John Brodie (SFF); Bob Griese (MIA); Jim Kelly (BUF); Joe Namath (NYJ); the 12th Man (SEA).
13 Dan Marino (MIA); Don Maynard (NYJ).

14 Dan Fouts (SDC); Steve Grogan (NEP); Don Hutson (GBP); Otto Graham (CLE); Y.A. Tittle (NYG).
15 Bart Starr (GBP); Steve Van Buren (PHL).
16 Len Dawson (KCC); Frank Gifford (NYG); Joe Montana (SFF).
18 Frank Tripucka (DEN).
19 John Unitas (IND).
20 Barry Sanders (DET); Lem Barney (DET); Billy Sims (DET); Gino Cappelletti (NEP).
22 Bobby Layne (DET); Buddy Young (IND).
24 Lenny Moore (IND).
28 Willie Galimore (CHI)*; Abner Haynes (KCC).
31 William Anderson (ATL).
32 Al Blozis (NYG)*; Jim Brown (CLE).
33 Sammy Baugh (WSH); Stone Johnson (KCC).*
34 Earl Campbell (TEN); Walter Payton (CHI); Joe Perry (SFF).
36 Mack Lee Hill (KCC).*
37 Jimmy Johnson (SFF); Doak Walker (DET).
39 Larry Csonka (MIA); Hugh McElhenny (SFF).
40 Pat Tillman (ARZ); Tom Brooksheir (PHL); Mike Haynes (NEP); Joe Morrison (NYG); Gale Sayers (CHI).
41 Brian Piccolo (CHI).*
42 Charlie Conerly (NYG); Ronnie Lott (SFF); Sid Luckman (CHI).
43 Jim Norton (TEN).
44 Floyd Little (DEN); Pete Retzlaff (PHL).
45 Ernie Davis (CLE).*
46 Don Fleming (CLE).*
50 Ken Strong (NYG).
51 Dick Butkus (CHI).
53 Mick Tingelhoff (MIN).
54 Bob Johnson (CIN).
56 Bill Hewitt (CHI); Joe Schmidt (DET); Lawrence Taylor (NYG).
57 Steve Nelson (NEP); Jeff Van Note (ATL) .
60 Chuck Bednarik (PHL); Tommy Nobis (ATL).
61 Bill George (CHI).
63 Willie Lanier (KCC); Mike Munchak (TEN); Lee Roy Selmon (TBB).
65 Elvin Bethea (TEN).
66 Ray Nitschke (GBP); Bulldog Turner (CHI).
70 Art Donovan (IND); Charlie Krueger (SFF); Jim Marshall (MIN); Ernie Stautner (PIT); Al Wistert (PHL).

73 John Hannah (NEP); Joe Klecko (NYJ); Leo Nomellini (SFF).
74 Merlin Olsen (STL).
76 Lou Groza (CLE).
77 Red Grange (CHI); Stan Mauldin (ARZ)*; Jim Parker (IND); Korey Stringer (MIN).*
78 Bobby Bell (KCC).
79 Jim Hunt (NEP).
80 Steve Largent (SEA).
82 Raymond Berry (IND).
85 Chuck Hughes (DET).*
86 Buck Buchanan (KCC).
87 Dwight Clark (SFF).
88 J.V. Cain (ARZ)* ; Alan Page (MIN).
89 Bob Dee (NEP); Gino Marchetti (IND).
92 Reggie White (GBP).
99 Jerome Brown (PHL)*; Marshall Goldberg (ARZ).

* Number retired due to sickness, injury or death.

Owned numbers: 1 Curly Lambeau (GBP de facto); 8 Archie Manning (NOS); 12 Bob Griese (MIA); 14 Otto Graham (CLE); 16 Len Dawson (KCC); 18 Frank Tripucka (DEN); 20 Gino Cappelletti (NEP); 22 Buddy Young (IND); 28 Abner Haynes (KCC); 39 Larry Csonka (MIA); 42 Sid Luckman (CHI); 43 Jim Norton (TEN); 54 Bob Johnson (CIN); 56 Bill Hewitt (CHI); 60 Tommy Nobis (ATL); 63 Lee Roy Selmon (TBB); 70 Art Donovan (IND); 70 Jim Marshall (MIN); 80 Steve Largent (SEA); 89 Bob Dee (NEP).

Number worn by the most players for one team: 23 has been worn by 35 Green Bay Packers.

Most popular numbers according to number of index entries: 21 has been worn 487 times. The rest of the top five is 25 with 480 entries, 80 with 468, 22 with 467 and 82 and 83 with 466.

Least popular numbers according to number of index entries: Aside from 0 and 00 which have been worn only twenty-one times, 1 has the fewest entries with 115. Rounding out the top five are 2 with 125 entries, 13 with 145, 6 with 155 and 9 with 157. Looking solely at double digit numbers, the top five after 13 consists of 98 with 165, 93 with 170, 97 with 172, 69 with 207 and 19 with 219.

Player who wore five or more numbers for one team:

FIVE NUMBERS—Fred Gillies (ARZ) 5/9/10/11/66; Phil Handler (ARZ) 7/11/32/33/46; Duke Slater (ARZ) 7/14/16/47/91; Tom Day (BUF) 60/64/78/88/89; Link Lyman (CHI) 2/11/12/14/77; Frank Butler (GBP) 26/35/48/59/60; Jug Earp (GBP) 7/9/29/38/39; Milt Gantenbein (GBP) 21/22/30/46/47; Cal Hubbard (GBP) 27/38/39/40/51; Verne Lewellen (GBP) 4/21/31/45/46; Johnny Blood McNally (GBP) 14/20/24/26/55; Tom Nash (GBP) 19/21/26/35/37; Al Rose (GBP) 34/37/47/49/52; Ade Schwammel (GBP) 40/50/53/57/58.

SIX NUMBERS—Don Burke (SFF) 6/32/38/66/68/73; Hank Bruder (GBP) 5/13/18/27/47/55; Art Bultman (GBP) 17/32/33/38/45/52; Red Dunn (GBP) 7/11/15/16/17; Lon Evans (GBP) 17/25/39/46/51/65; Herdis McCrary (GBP) 19/28/29/38/43/53; Bob Monnett (GBP) 3/5/12/18/50/66; Steve Owen (NYG) 6/12/36/44/50/55; Claude Perry (GBP) 24/26/27/32/37/50; George Tarasovich (PIT) 50/52/53/56/63/82.

SEVEN NUMBERS—Clarke Hinkle (GBP) 27/30/33/39/41/45/48.

EIGHT NUMBERS—Arnie Herber (GBP) 12/16/17/26/38/41/45/68.

NINE NUMBERS—Mike Michalske (GBP) 19/24/28/30/31/33/36/40/63

Multi-team players who wore the most numbers:

NINE NUMBERS—Arnie Herber (GBP, NYG) 12/16/17/20/26/38/41/45/68 and Stumpy Thomason (PHL, XBKN) 7/15/17/21/23/25/29/30/55.

EIGHT NUMBERS—Hardy Brown (ARZ, DEN, SFF, WSH, XBAL, ZBRK, ZCHI) 25/33/34/37/46/60/63/73; Cal Hubbard (GBP, NYG, PIT) 27/35/38/39/40/41/51/60; Bull Karcis (NYG, PIT, XBKN) 4/11/30/34/35/50/64/66; Tom Nash (GBP, XBKN) 17/19/21/26/34/35/37/40.

Players who wore a number for one team for 15 or more years:

15 YEARS—Jackie Smith (ARZ) 81; Bruce Smith (BUF) 78; Ken Riley (CIN) 13; Lou Groza (CLE) 76; Too Tall Jones (DAL) 72; Bill Bates (DAL) 40; Mark Tuinei (DAL) 71; Wayne Walker (DET) 55; Jerrel Wilson (KCC) 44; Bob Kuechenberg (MIA) 67; Fred Cox (MIN) 14; Carl Eller (MIN) 81; Paul Winston (MIN) 60; Mel Hein (NYG) 7; Randy Rasmussen (NYJ) 66; Mike Webster (PIT) 52; Merlin Olsen (STL) 74; Charlie Cowan (STL) 73; Joe Scibelli (STL) 71; Dan Fouts (SDC) 14; Charlie Krueger (SFF) 70; Len Rohde (SFF) 76; Jesse Sapolu (SFF) 61.

16 YEARS—Ken Anderson (CIN) 14; Clay Matthews (CLE) 57; John Elway (DEN) 7;Bart Starr (GBP) 15; Julius Adams (NEP) 85; Jerry Rice (SFF) 80; Jimmy Johnson (SFF) 37; Elvin Bethea (TEN) 65; Sammy Baugh (WSH) 33; Monte Coleman (WSH) 51.

17 YEARS—Jim Bakken (ARZ) 25; Mike Kenn (ATL) 78; John Unitas 19 (IND); Dan Marino

(MIA) 13; Mick Tingelhoff (MIN) 53; Pat Leahy (NYJ) 5; John Brodie (SFF) 12.

18 YEARS— Jim Hart (ARZ) 17; Jeff Van Note (ATL) 57.

19 YEARS— Jim Marshall (MIN) 70; Bruce Matthews (TEN) 74.

20 YEARS— Jackie Slater (STL) 78; Darrell Green (WSH) 28.

Players who wore the same number for the most teams: Five players have worn the same number for six different teams. Ben Agajanian, 3; Steve DeBerg, 17; Ryan McNeil, 47, Joe Nedney, 6; and Mark Royals, 3.

Longest dormant number: 1 has been dormant in Green Bay for 77 years since Curly Lambeau wore it in 1926.

Number of first black players from current teams:

PRE-COLOR LINE— Duke Slater (ARZ) wore 14 in his first year 1926

POST-COLOR LINE— Bill Willis (CLE) and Marion Motley (CLE) wore 30 and 76 respectively in 1946; Ken Washington (STL) and Woody Strode (STL) wore 13 and 39 respectively in 1946.

Players who wore 0 or 00: Steve Bagarus (STL,

Quarterback Numbers Over 19

20 Joe Francis (GBP); Arnie Herber (NYG); Bill Mackrides (NYG); Travis Tidwell (NYG).

21 Jim Hardy (ARZ, STL); Tom Flores (BUF, OAK); John Hadl (GBP, SDC, STL, TEN); Cotton Davidson (IND); John Vaughn (PIT).

22 Jim Hardy (ARZ); Ray Mallouf (ARZ, NYG); Bobby Layne (CHI, DET, PIT); George Blanda (CHI); Clyde LeForce (DET); Ed Danowski (NYG).

23 Joe Barnes (CHI); Joe Gasparella (PIT); John Gildea (PIT).

24 Jim Hardy (ARZ); Fred Enke (DET); John Turley (PIT).

25 Coley McDonough (PIT); Norm Van Brocklin (STL).

27 Owen Goodnight (CHI); Jack Jacobs (GBP); Don Allard (NYJ).

28 Frank Tripucka (DET); Paul Christman (GBP); Bobby Thomason (GBP).

29 Stu Smith (PIT).

30 Bob Dunlap (CHI); Dean Look (NYJ); Truett Smith (PIT); Frank Filchock (WSH).

31 Larry Weldon (WSH).

32 Johnny Lujack (CHI).

33 Bernie Masterson (CHI); Johnny Long (CHI); Hub Lindsey (DEN); John Gildea (PIT); Sammy Baugh (WSH).

34 Jimmy German (WSH).

35 Walt Masters (PIT); John Karrs (STL); Riley Smith (WSH).

36 Tom Farris (CHI).

37 Young Bussey (CHI); Cotton Price (DET).

38 Tobin Rote (GBP).

39 Stan Heath (GBP); Bill Mackrides (PHL).

40 Walt Masters (ARZ); Ed Rutkowski (BUF); Frank Filchock (NYG); Earl Crowder (STL).

41 Paul Governali (NYG); Emery Nix (NYG).

42 Sid Luckman (CHI); Cotton Price (DET); Charlie Conerly (NYG); Ray Hare (WSH).

43 Jack Jacobs (STL); Randall Bond (WSH).

44 Paul Christman (ARZ); Emery Nix (NYG).

45 Bob Hoffman (WSH).

46 Fred Enke (DET); Bob Scrabis (NYJ).

47 Fred Benners (NYG).

48 Joe Gasparella (PIT).

49 Charles Eikenberg (ARZ); Chuck Ortman (PIT).

50 John Petchel (STL); Paul Richards (STL).

52 Harry Gilmer (WSH).

55 Vince Oliver (ARZ).

57 Billy Patterson (CHI).

58 Warren Plunkett (STL).

60 Otto Graham (CLE).

62 Cliff Lewis (CLE); Cotton Price (DET); Jesse Freitas (SFF).

63 Frankie Albert (SFF).

64 Y.A. Tittle (SFF); Parker Hall (SFF); Bev Wallace (SFF).

65 Bob Thomason (STL).

66 Lloyd Cheatham (ARZ); Ermal Allen (CLE); Gerald Leahy (PIT).

67 Truett Smith (PIT).

76 Tom O'Malley (GBP).

77 Paul Davis (PIT); Jack Jacobs (WSH); Tommy Mont (WSH).

80 Tom Heardon (CHI).

78 Ray Mallouf (ARZ).

98 Ray Mallouf (ARZ).

WSH); Ted Bucklin (NYG); Ken Burrough (TEN, NOS); Johnny Clement (PIT); Lou Eaton (NYG); Ox Eckhardt (NYG); Walt Koppisch (NYG); Obert Logan (NOS); Father Lumpkin (XBKN); Danny McMullen (NYG); Lee Mullenneaux (NYG); Johnny Olszewski (WSH, DET, DEN); Jim Otto (OAK); Bill Reissig (XBKN); Reb Russell (NYG); Wee Willie Smith (NYG); Phil White (NYG).

First player to wear a number in the 70s: Red Grange 77 (CHI) in 1925.

First player to wear a number in the 80s: Earl Britton 80 (CHI) in 1925.

First player to wear a number in the 90s: Gerry Lunz 91 (ARZ) 1925

Numbers of Future Head Coaches with Over 100 Regular Season Wins (plus two who will soon reach that total)

Coach	#	Regular Season			Postseason		
		Won	Lost	Tied	Won	Lost	Titles
Don Shula	25 (IND)	328	156	6	19	17	2
	26 (WSH)						
George Halas	7 (CHI)	318	148	31	6	3	6
Tom Landry	49 (NYG)	250	162	6	20	16	2
Curly Lambeau	1/14/20/42	226	132	22	3	2	6
	(GBP)						
Chuck Noll	65 (CLE)	193	148	1	16	8	4
Dan Reeves	30 (DAL)	190	165	2	11	9	0
Chuck Knox	DNP	186	147	1	7	11	0
Paul Brown	DNP	166	100	6	4	8	3
Marty Schottenheimer	56/57 (BUF)	165	113	1	5	11	0
	54 (NEP)						
Bud Grant	86 (PHL)	158	96	5	10	12	0
Steve Owen	6/12/36/	151	100	17	2	8	2
	44/50/55 (NYG)						
Bill Parcells	DNP	148	106	1	11	7	2
Marv Levy	DNP	143	112	0	11	8	0
Hank Stram	DNP	131	97	10	5	3	1
Weeb Ewbank	DNP	130	129	7	4	1	3
Jim Mora	DNP	125	106	0	0	6	0
Joe Gibbs	DNP	124	60	0	16	5	3
Sid Gillman	DNP	122	99	7	1	5	0
Mike Ditka	89/98	121	95	0	6	6	1
	(CHI/DAL/PHL)						
Mike Holmgren	DNP	116	76	0	9	7	1
George Allen	DNP	116	47	5	2	7	0
Bill Cowher	53 (CLE)	115	76	1	7	8	0
	57 (PHL)						
George Seifert	DNP	114	62	0	10	5	2
Don Coryell	DNP	111	83	1	3	6	0
Buddy Parker	15 (ARZ)	104	75	9	3	1	3
	4 (DET)						
John Madden	DNP	103	32	7	9	7	1
Dick Vermeil	DNP	103	94	0	6	5	1
Mike Shanahan	DNP	99	65	0	7	3	2
Dennis Green	DNP	97	62	0	4	8	0

Hall of Famer in **bold**; Active coaches in *italics*; DNP=Did Not Play NFL Football

APPENDIX C: UNIFORM NUMBERS OF NFL TEAMS THAT FAILED SINCE 1933

Cincinnati Reds (XCIN)

1933–4   3–14–1

Defaulted on player payments during the 1934 season and was suspended by the league.

39	Frank Abruzzino	C/G	1933
20	Gump Ariail	E	1934
26	Ed Aspatore	T	1934
47	Jim Bausch	B	1933
?	Mil Berner	C	1933
34	Tom Blondin	G	1933
40	Chuck Braidwood	E	1933
46	Lloyd Burdick	T	1933
33	John Burleson	T/G	1933
5, 39	Tom Bushby	B	1934
27/52	Les Caywood	C	1933–4
1, 45	Algy Clark	B	1933–4
3, 42	Red Corzine	B	1933–4
48	Joe Crakes	E	1933
?	Sonny Doell	T	1933
51	Leo Draveling	T	1933
?	Chief Elkins	B	1933
22/27	Earl Elser	T	1934
29	Tiny Feather	B	1934
49	Rosie Grant	G	1933–4
46	Homer Hanson	G	1934
?	Hal Hilpert	E	1933
?	Foster Howell	T	1934
19	Russ Lay	G	1934
10, 41	Biff Lee	G	1933–4
30	Gil LeFebvre	B	1933–4
6	Bill Lewis	B	1934
25	Ted Maples	C	1934
15/34	Jim Mooney	E	1933–4
13	Cliff Moore	B	1934
31	Don Moses	FB	1933
?	Buster Mott	B	1934
9, 44	Lee Mulleneaux	C	1933–4
24/43	George Munday	T	1933–4
53	Mike Palm	B	1933
?	Bill Parriott	FB	1934
2, 32	Lew Pope	B	1933–4
50	Dick Powell	E	1933
14/38	John Rogers	C	1933–4
?	Harvey Sark	G	1934
8	Pete Saumer	B	1934
36	Kermit Schmidt	E	1933
37	Bill Senn	HB	1933
31	Norris Severson	B	1934
?	Benny Sohn	B	1934
47	Seaman Squyres	B	1933
21/50	Cookie Tackwell	E	1933–4
28	Otto Vokaty	FB	1934
?	Ossie Wiberg	FB	1933
37	Cole Wilging	E	1934
?	Basil Wilkerson	E	1934
35	Blake Workman	B	1933
47	Charlie Zuker	T	1934

St. Louis Gunners (XSTL)

1934   1–2

Independent team purchased the suspended Cincinnati franchise on November 6, 1934, absorbed five Reds players and finished their schedule. The NFL offered a conditional reinstatement to the Gunners in 1935, but the team refused.

30	Gene Alford	B	1934
66	Jaby Andrews	B	1934

99	Cy Casper	B	1934
70	Red Corzine	B	1934
?	Charlie Diehl	G/T	1934
55	Earl Elser	T	1934
11	Mack Gladden	E	1934
25	Swede Johnston	FB	1934
?	Benny LaPresta	FB	1934
22	Russ Lay	G	1934
77	Babe Lyon	T/G	1934
45	Len McGirl	G	1934
?	Charlie McLaughlin	B	1934
60	Russ McLeod	C	1934
39	Bill Montgomery	T	1934
?	Paul Moss	E	1934
33	Lee Mulleneaux	C	1934
35	George Munday	T/G	1934
44	John Norby	B	1934
65	Manny Rapp	B	1934
10	Homer Reynolds	G	1934
50	George Rogge	E	1934
90	Sandy Sandberg	T	1934
40	Bill Senn	HB	1934
?	Hal Weldin	C	1934
80	Blake Workman	B	1934

Brooklyn Dodgers/Tigers (XBKN)

1930–44 (Known as Tigers in 1944)   60–100–9
    After merging with the Boston Yanks for the 1945 season, owner Dan Topping folded his NFL franchise and bought the New York Yankees franchise in the All American Football Conference in 1946. Six former Brooklyn players became Yankees.

30	Frank Abruzzino	C/G	1931
10	Tony Aiello	B	1944
5, 4	Vannie Albanese	B	1937
33	Warren Alfson	G	1941
14/18	John Ambrose	C	1932
23/21	Sig Andrusking	G	1937
25	Megs Apsit	B	1931
?	Gump Ariail	E	1934
28	Bill Armstrong	G	1943
19	Jim Austin	E	1937–8
32	Red Badgro	E	1936
22	Bill Bailey	E	1940–1
27	John Bandura	E	1943
33/11	Jeff Barrett	E	1936–8
50/24	Wayland Becker	E	1934–5
16/15	Gil Bergerson	G/T	1935–6
36	Johnny Biancone	B	1936
?	Mal Bleeker	G/C	1930
16/5	Jim Bowdoin	G	1932, 1934
28	Verdi Boyer	T	1936
6	Eddie Britt	B	1938
6	Chuck Brodnicki	G	1934

26	Bill Brown	QB	1943–4
8	Boyd Brumbaugh	B	1938–9
6	Carl Brumbaugh	QB	1937
34	Art Bultman	C	1931
19	John Bunyan	G/C	1932
16	Sherrill Busby	E	1940
66	Wendell Butcher	B	1938–42
19	Johnny Butler	RB	1944
23	George Cafego	QB	1940, 1943
33/12	Chris Cagle	B	1933–4
2	Ray Carnelly	B	1939
55	Joe Carter	E	1944
2	Dick Cassiano	T	1940
8	Les Caywood	G/T	1932
15/19/4	George Chalmers	C	1933
4	Algy Clark	B	1930
6	Ed Comstock	G/T	1930
35	Merl Condit	HB	1941–3
37	Bill Conkright	C	1943
22	Dave Cook	B	1936
8	Ty Coon	G	1940
25/23	Norm Cooper	C	1937–8
31	Gerry Courtney	RB	1942
15/3	Dick Crayne	B	1936–7
15/16	Win Croft	G	1935
?	Jerry Cronin	E	1932
6	Doc Cronkhite	E	1934
?	Dick Crowl	G/C	1930
13	Frank Cumisky	E	1937
11	Ernie Cuneo	G	1930
14	Ave Daniell	T	1937
57	Bill Davis	T	1943
6	George Demas	G	1934
18	Art Deremer	C	1942
27	Leo Disend	T	1938–9
38	George Doherty	G/T	1944
26/8	Ben Douglas	HB	1933
?	Tommy Dowler	B	1931
3	Johnny Druze	E	1938
12	Alex Eagle	T	1935
22	Jess Eberdt	C	1932
?	Marshall Edwards	B	1943
15	Don Eliason	E	1942
16	John Ellis	G	1944
16/24/ 11/2	Harold Ely	T	1932–4
20	Ox Emerson	G/C	1938
15	Tiny Engebretsen	G/T	1934
32	Tony Falkenstein	FB	1944
10	Scrapper Farrell	FB	1938–9
44	Jake Fawcett	T	1943
44/48	Beattie Feathers	HB	1938–9
10	Walt Fedora	FB	1942
22/24/19	Dick Fishel	FB	1933
32	Bill Fleckenstein	G	1931
22	Dick Folk	FB	1939
10	Sam Francis	FB	1939–40
31/6	Red Franklin	RB	1935–7

5	Ray Frick	C	1941
26/17/1	Benny Friedman	QB	1932–4
21	Andy Fronczek	T	1941
12	Kenny Fryer	B	1944
26/36/ 21/9	Ted Fulton	G/T	1931–2
23	Ray Fuqua	E	1935–6
28	Hec Garvey	G/T	1930
?	Fred Getz	E	1930
22	Bob Gifford	B	1942
21/35	Bob Gillson	G	1930–1
7	Ed Goddard	B	1937
17	John Golemgeske	T/G	1937–40
27	Lou Gordon	T/G	1931
34	George Grandinette	G	1943
?	Ben Greenberg	B	1930
20/3	Don Greenshields	T	1932–3
31/5/ 88/32	Jack Grossman	B	1932, 1934–5
3	Mike Gussie	G	1940
2	Al Gutnecht	G	1943
11	Ace Gutowsky	B	1939
19	Bob Haak	T/G	1939
27	Swede Hagberg	C	1930
17	Horse Hagerty	B	1930
21/31	Hoot Haines	T/G	1930–1
23/7	Buck Halperin	RB	1932
17	Swede Hanson	B	1931
42	Ray Hare	B	1944
19	Pat Harrison	T	1937
17	Jim Hartman	E	1936
?	Henry Hayduk	G	1935
5	Rod Heater	T	1940
4	Ralph Heikkinen	G	1939
10	Ken Heineman	B	1943
14/15	Carl Heldt	T	1935–6
22/27/28/ 15/1	Herman Hickman	G	1932–4
14	Harold Hill	E	1938–40
13	Herman Hodges	E	1939–42
25	Jay Hornbeak	FB	1935
10	Bud Hubbard	E	1935
50	Joe Hugret	E	1934
16	Paul Humphrey	C	1939
18	Roy Ilowit	T	1937
3	Len Janiak	B	1939
30	Billy Jefferson	B	1942
24	Bob Jeffries	G	1942
27/8	Art Jocher	G	1940, 1942
4	Bert Johnson	HB	1937
27	Cecil Johnson	B	1943–4
10	Al Jolley	T	1930
?	Marv Jonas	G	1931
23/27/18/ 28/71/8	Bruce Jones	G	1932–4
41	Lew Jones	G	1943
1	Thurman Jones	B	1941–2
18/24	Wayne Jorgensen	C	1936–7
17	Mike Jurich	T	1941–2
3	Bernie Kapitansky	G	1942
15	Carl Kaplanoff	T/G	1939
35/4/30/ 66/34	Bull Karcis	FB	1932–5
29/9	Tony Kaska	FB	1936–8
15	Duce Keahey	T/G	1942
24	Bill Kelly	B	1930
18/26/2/ 44/14	Shipwreck Kelly	B	1933–4, 1937
25	Matt Kelsch	E	1930
22/26/1	Ralph Kercheval	B	1934–40
25	**Bruiser Kinard**	T	1938–44
27	George Kinard	G	1941–2
?	Fred King	FB	1937
20	Bo Kirkland	G	1935–6
29	Frank Kirkleski	B	1931
20	Ben Kish	FB	1940–1
30/15	Harry Kloppenburg	E	1931, 1933–4
24	Joe Koons	C	1941
5	Stan Kosel	FB	1938–9
30	Stan Kostka	FB	1935
22	Andy Kowalski	E	1943–4
10	George Kracum	FB	1941
24/25	Henry Krause	C	1936–7
19	Frank Kristufek	T	1940–1
31	Bill LaFitte	E	1944
36	Les Lane	G	1939
34/24/4	Bill Leckonby	B	1939–41
21/15	Bill Lee	T	1935–7
22	Rube Leisk	G	1937
30	George Lenc	E	1939
17	Tony Leon	G	1944
?	John Lott	T	1930
21/11/10/ 16/7/36	Lou Lubratovich	T	1931–5
27/0	Father Lumpkin	FB	1935–7
28/12	Babe Lyon	T/G	1932
3	John Lyons	E	1933
2	Bob Mahan	B	1930
9	Pug Manders	FB	1939–44
34/2	Joe Maniaci	FB	1936–8
19	Tilly Manton	FB	1943
43	Jodie Marek	FB	1943
12	Lou Mark	C	1938–40
27	Steve Marko	B	1944
12, 10	Frank Martin	HB	1943–4
28	Bob Masterson	E	1944
15	John Matisi	T	1943
60/6	Dean McAdams	B	1941–3
5	Jack McArthur	C/T	1930
26/3	Jack McBride	B	1930–2
7	Hal McCullough	B	1942
34	Flip McDonald	E	1944
18	Walt McDonald	C	1935
26	Banks McFadden	HB	1940

11	Dub McGibbony	HB	1944
19	John McMichaels	B	1944
34/3	Frank McNeil	E	1932
20	Curt Mecham	B	1942
29	Ed Merlin	G	1938–9
29	Walt Merrill	T	1940–2
24/10/9	Saul Mielziner	C/T	1931–4
20/23	Jim Miller	HB	1930
12	Buster Mitchell	E	1937
?	Warner Mizell	B	1931
33	Cliff Montgomery	B	1934
10	Jim Mooney	E	1930–1
1	Tex Mooney	T	1943
22	Gene Moore	C	1938
27/35/ 14/3	Doc Morrison	C	1933–4
4	Dave Myers	G	1931
5	Dick Nardi	B	1939
17/34/40	Tom Nash	E	1933–4
20	Don Nelson	G	1937
29	Jerry Nemecek	E	1931
66/99	Dick Nesbitt	HB	1934
30	Mike Nixon	HB	1942
35/29	John Norby	B	1935
8	Reino Nori	B	1937
22/6	Ray Novotny	B	1932
24	Len Noyes	G	1938
5	Dick O'Donnell	E	1931
17	Cap Oehler	C	1935–6
33	Pete Owens	G/C	1943
7	**Ace Parker**	QB	1937–41
32	Dave Parker	E	1941
2	Larry Peace	HB	1941
31	Claude Perry	T/G	1931
32	Frosty Peters	B	1931
18/40	Les Peterson	E/T	1933
30	Phil Peterson	E	1934
31	Steve Petro	G	1940–1
5	Don Pierce	C	1942
22	Earl Plank	E	1930
24	Ken Radick	E	1931
26/33	Bill Raffel	E	1932
14	Keith Ranspot	E	1943
70	Leo Raskowski	T	1933
21	Joe Ratica	C	1939
3,5	Van Rayburn	E	1933
14	Ray Reckmack	FB	1937
0	Bill Reissig	FB	1938–9
15	Bill Reynolds	HB	1944
24	Floyd Rhea	G	1944
25/99	Hughie Rhea	G	1933
19/7/25/ 6/20/11	Paul Riblett	E	1932–6
21/11	Dick Richards	B	1933
4	Bob Robertson	HB	1942
14	Tom Robertson	C	1941–2
22	Jack Robinson	T/G	1935–6
17/4	Ev Rowan	E	1930, 1932
26	Eddie Rucinski	E	1941–2
35	Justin Rukas	G	1936
30	Frank Sachse	QB	1943–4
15	Sandy Sandberg	T	1937
32/8/ 77/28	Ollie Sansen	B	1932–5
69	Tony Sarausky	QB	1938
41	Phil Sarboe	B	1936
25	Johnny Scalzi	B	1931
5	Skippy Scheib	C	1930
42	Herm Schmarr	E	1943
?	Jim Schuber	HB	1930
99	Perry Schwartz	E	1938–42
33	Bill Senn	HB	1931
39/44	George Sergienko	T	1943–4
16	Joe Setcavage	FB	1943
26	Alec Shellogg	T	1939
30	Rhoten Shetley	FB	1940–2
30/32	Tony Siano	C	1934
28	Jim Sivell	G	1938–42, 1944
18	Ed Skoronski	E	1937
57	George Smith	C	1944
11	Leo Stasica	QB	1941
19	Sammy Stein	E/T	1932
33	Vaughn Stewart	C	1943–4
19	Frank Stojack	G	1935–6
?	Hal Stotsbery	T	1930
44/18/ 15/30	Mike Stramiello	E	1930–2, 1934
36	Frank Strom	T	1944
18	Bud Svendsen	C	1940–3
24	Phil Swiadon	G	1943
21	Charlie Taylor	FB	1944
25	Mark Temple	B	1936
7	Rex Thomas	B	1930–1
25/23/21/ 17/7/ 55/30	Stumpy Thomason	B	1930–5
15/2	Si Titus	C	1940–2
32	Joe Tofil	E	1942
26	Johnny Tomaini	E/T	1930–1
7	Bud Toscani	HB	1932
26	John Tosi	C	1939
14	Bob Trocolor	QB	1944
35	Rocky Uguccioni	E	1944
11	Joe Vance	B	1931
16	Jack Vetter	HB	1942
22	Ray Wagner	E	1931
13	Bill Waller	E	1938
43	Charlie Ware	T	1944
28	Gordon Watkins	T/G	1931
29	George Webb	E	1943
18	George Weeks	E	1944
38	Ray Wehba	E	1943
8	Chuck Weimer	B	1930
33	Bernie Weiner	T/G	1942
23	Don Wemple	E	1941

30/16	Jim Whatley	T/E	1936–8
33	Wilbur White	B	1935
2	Ossie Wiberg	FB	1932
?	Cy Williams	T	1932
?	Pop Williams	FB	1932
10	Bobby Wilson	B	1936
23	Gordon Wilson	G/T	1944
24	Bob Winslow	E	1940
18/30/ 3/23/4	Stu Worden	G/T	1930, 1932–4
31/33/ 35/41	Ralph Wright	T	1933
25	Ted Wright	B	1935
1, 4	Izzy Yablock	B	1930–1
12	John Yezerski	T	1936
6	Waddy Young	E	1939–40
21	Frank Zadworney	HB	1940
26	Gust Zarnas	G	1939

Boston Yanks (XBOS)

1944–8   14–38–3

Owner Ted Collins folded this franchise for tax purposes and bought the New York Bulldog franchise in 1949. 16 Yanks became Bulldogs.

20	Duke Abbruzzi	HB	1946
37	Art Albrecht	T/C	1944
26	Bill Anderson	E	1945
35	John Badaczewski	G	1946–8
36	Fritz Barzilauskas	G	1947–8
84	Stan Batinski	G	1948
11	George Cafego	QB	1944–5
47	Ralph Calcagni	T	1946
45	Rocco Canale	T/G	1946–7
38	Bill Chipley	E	1947–8
65	Bill Collins	G	1947
31	Vince Commisa	G	1944
23	Milt Crain	FB	1944
24	Hal Crisler	E	1946–7
15	Joe Crowley	E/DB	1944–5
29/34	Don Currivan	E	1945–8
22	Boley Dancewicz	QB	1946–8
10	Bob Davis	HB	1944–6
59	Bob Davis	T	1948
44	Tom Dean	T	1946–7
41/45	Don Deeks	T/G	1945–7
66	Al Dekdebrun	QB	1948
18/29	Babe Dimancheff	HB	1945–6
38	George Doherty	G/T	1945
32/34	Joe Domnanovich	C	1946–8
39	Walt Dubzinski	C/G	1944
24	Paul Duhart	HB	1945
42	Don Eliason	E	1946
?	Tony Falkenstein	FB	1944
17	Gary Famiglietti	FB	1946
35	Al Fiorentino	G	1945

?	Ed Fiorentino	E	1947
19	Ed Franco	T	1944
38	Frank Gaziano	G	1944
43	Wimpy Giddens	T	1944
11	Jim Gillette	HB	1946
40	Bill Godwin	C	1947–8
10	Joe Golding	HB	1947–8
42/23	Sam Goldman	E	1944, 1946–7
4	Paul Governali	QB	1946–7
15/36	John Grigas	FB	1945–7
18	Scott Gudmundson	QB	1944–5
34	Dick Harrison	E	1944
65	Robert Hazelhurst	HB	1948
83	Ralph Heywood	E	1948
21	Joe Hoague	FB	1946
47	Mike Jarmoluk	T	1948
27	Ellis Jones	G	1945
46	Rube Juster	T	1946
12	Abe Karnofsky	HB	1946
31	Bill Kennedy	G	1947
30	Ed Korisky	C	1944
3	Andy Kowalski	E	1945
28	Gene Lee	B	1946
34/17	Tony Leon	G	1945–6
41	Augie Lio	G	1944–5
11	Bob Long	HB	1947
20/30	Jim Magee	C	1944–6
16	Howie Maley	QB	1946–7
39	Gene Malinowski	B	1948
41	Vaughn Mancha	C	1948
25	Pug Manders	FB	1945
30	Lou Mark	C	1945
?	Frank Martin	HB	1945
33	Johnny Martin	B	1944–5
28	Bob Masterson	E	1945
37	Ned Mathews	HB	1945
17	Frank Maznicki	HB	1947
43	Bob McClure	G	1947–8
19	Hugh McCullough	B	1945
40	Ed McGee	T	1944–6
17	Bob McRoberts	HB	1944
66	Jim Mello	FB	1947
14/33	Mike Micka	HB	1945–8
16	John Morelli	B	1944–5
23	Frank Muehlheuser	FB	1948
56	Frank Nelson	HB	1948
44	John Nolan	T	1948
31	**Ace Parker**	QB	1945
8	Bill Paschal	FB	1947–8
43	Win Pedersen	T	1946
30/16	John Poto	HB	1947–8
17	Steve Pritko	E	1948
14	Keith Ranspot	E	1944–5
24	Freeman Rexer	E	1944
42	Floyd Rhea	G	1945
36	Thron Riggs	T	1944
59	Tom Rodgers	T	1947
31	George Roman	T	1948

19	Rudy Romboli	FB	1946–8	21	John Clowes	DT	1950–1
20	Dave Ryan	B	1948	36	Don Colo	DT	1951
21	Joe Sabasteanski	G/C	1947–8	3	Paul Crowe	DB	1951
12	Frank Sachse	QB	1945	24	Jim Cullom	G	1951
?	Jack Sachse	C	1945	16	Bob DeMoss	QB	1949
25	Paul Sanders	HB	1944	34	Joe Domnanovich	C	1949–51
27	Frank Santora	QB	1944	39	**Art Donovan**	DT	1951
27	Nick Scollard	E	1946–8	22	Brad Ecklund	C	1950–1
20/54	Frank Seno	B	1947–8	4	Dan Edwards	E	1950–1
44	George Sergienko	T	1945	55	Herb Ellis	C	1949
61	Alex Sidorik	T	1947	7	Dan Garza	E	1951
?	Steve Sierocinski	T	1946	20	Frank Gaul	T	1949
86	Phil Slosburg	B	1948	10	Joe Golding	HB	1949–51
43	George Smith	C	1945	61	Bobby Griffin	DB	1951
33	Dave Smukler	FB	1944	43	Roger Harding	C	1949
28	Leo Stasica	QB	1944	83	Ralph Heywood	E	1949
21	Ken Steinmetz	FB	1944–5	46	Sherman Howard	HB	1950–1
39	Steve Sucic	FB	1947	15	Duke Iverson	HB	1950–1
?	Joe Sulaitis	FB	1946	47	Mike Jarmoluk	DT	1949
?	George Sullivan	E	1948	85	Jon Jenkins	DT	1950
17	Morgan Tiller	E	1944	62	Harvey Johnson	G	1951
24	Frank Turbert	QB	1944	36	Nate Johnson	DT	1950
55	Jim Tyree	E	1948	85	Bob Kennedy	FB	1950
51	Carroll Vogelaar	T	1947–8	56	Lou Kusserow	FB	1950
44/22	Bill Walker	G	1944–5	17	Pete Layden	DB	1950
56	Joe Watt	HB	1947	22	**Bobby Layne**	QB	1949
22	Ted Williams	FB	1944	71	**Mike McCormack**	T	1951
26	Walter Williams	HB	1947	33	Darrel Meisenheimer	DB	1951
45	Gordon Wilson	G/T	1944	59/47	Paul Mitchell	DT	1950–1
55	Jim Wright	G	1947	23	Frank Muehlheuser	FB	1949
29	Harry Wynne	E	1944	45	Ross Nagel	DT	1951
4	Jim Youel	QB	1948	56	Frank Nelson	HB	1949
33/31	Joe Zeno	G/T	1946–7	44	John Nolan	T	1949–50
29	Roy Zimmerman	QB	1948	66	Bill O'Connor	E	1951
				26	Larry Olsonoski	G	1949
				80	Joe Osmanski	FB	1949
				56	Al Pollard	HB	1951

New York Bulldogs/Yanks (XNYB)

1949–51 (Known as the Yanks in 1950–1)
9–24–3
Absorbed 14 AAFC Yankees in 1950 while the Giants grabbed six. Collins sold the franchise back to the league after the 1951 season.

				84	Barney Poole	DE	1950–1
				61	Merv Pregulman	C	1949
				46	Hal Prescott	E	1949
				17	Steve Pritko	E	1949
39	Joe Abbey	E	1949	61/25	George Ratterman	QB	1950–1
71	Chet Adams	DT	1950	18	Johnny Rauch	QB	1949–51
31	Bennie Aldridge	DB	1950–1	31	George Roman	DT	1949
12	Bruce Alford	DB	1950–1	47	Martin Ruby	DT	1950
44	Sisto Averno	G	1951	16	Jack Russell	E	1950
36	Fritz Barzilauskas	G	1949	21	Joe Sabasteanski	G	1949
84	Stan Batinski	G	1949	81	Spec Sanders	RB/DB	1950
64	Tom Blake	T	1949	27	Nick Scollard	DE	1949
32	Mike Boyda	LB	1949	46	Dean Sensanbaugher	HB	1949
38	George Brown	G	1950	51	Ed Sharkey	G	1950
14	Bill Campbell	LB	1949	15	Paul Shoults	HB	1949
4	Jim Canady	DB	1949	?	Wayne Siegert	T	1951
17	Bob Celeri	QB	1951	24	Joe Signaigo	G	1950
35	Jim Champion	T	1950–1	86	Phil Slosburg	HB	1949
38	Bill Chipley	E	1949	11	Ed Smith	HB	1949
				24	Joe Soboleski	G/T	1951
				29	Bob Sponaugle	E	1949
				16	Breck Stroschein	DE	1951

23	Mike Swistowicz	DB	1950
51/1	Art Tait	DE	1951
20	George Taliaferro	HB/QB	1950–1
8	Sam Tamburo	DE	1949
86	Zollie Toth	FB	1950–1
51/83	Carroll Vogelaar	DT	1949–50
12	Jim Wade	HB	1949
53	Bev Wallace	QB	1951
4	Joe Watt	HB	1949
70	John Weaver	G	1949
66	Art Weiner	E	1950
65	John Wozniak	G	1950–1
50	John Yonakor	DE	1950
76	Buddy Young	HB	1950–1

Dallas Texans (XDAL)

1952   1–11–0

New franchise, but included 11 former New York Yanks. Failed by midseason and was sold back to the league. The NFL ran the team out of Hershey, PA for its last five games.

60	Sisto Averno	G	1952
24	Billy Baggett	HB	1952
73	Joe Campanella	LB	1952
35	Pat Cannamela	LB	1952
17	Bob Celeri	QB	1952
77	Don Colo	DT	1952
40	Jerry Davis	DB	1952
70	**Art Donovan**	DT	1952
50	Brad Ecklund	LB	1952
82	Dan Edwards	DE	1952
85	Gene Felker	E	1952
64/50	Keith Flowers	LB	1952
85	Sonny Gandee	DE/LB	1952
79/78	Chubby Grigg	DT	1952
31	Dick Hoerner	FB	1952
66	Weldon Humble	LB	1952
74	Ken Jackson	T/G	1952
55	Keever Jankovich	LB/DE	1952
21	Tom Keane	DB	1952
71	Jim Lansford	T	1952
44	Hank Lauricella	HB	1952
75/84	**Gino Marchetti**	DE	1952
38	Dick McKissack	DB	1952
?	Chuck Ortmann	RB	1952
85	Ray Pelfrey	E	1952
23	Johnny Petitbon	DB	1952
62/68	Barney Poole	DE	1952
52	Joe Reid	LB	1952
34	George Robison	G	1952
45	Will Sherman	DB	1952
64	Joe Soboleski	G/T	1952
83	Art Tait	DE	1952
20	George Taliaferro	HB/QB	1952

78/79	Hamp Tanner	T	1952
33/36	Zollie Toth	FB	1952
11	Frank Tripucka	QB	1952
88	Dick Wilkins	E	1952
80	Stan Williams	DB	1952
62	John Wozniak	G	1952
22	Buddy Young	HB	1952

Baltimore Colts (XBAL)

1950   1–11–0

One of three AAFC teams to fully merge into the NFL. The first Colts franchise folded after one season.

32	Sisto Averno	G	1950
64	**George Blanda**	QB	1950
41	Ernie Blandin	T	1950
73	Hardy Brown	LB	1950
77	George Buksar	B	1950
68	Adrian Burk	QB	1950
78	Leon Campbell	B	1950
88	Rip Collins	B	1950
45	Don Colo	T	1950
33	Ken Cooper	C/LB	1950
56	Hal Crisler	E	1950
49/70	**Art Donovan**	DT	1950
64	Frank Filchock	QB	1950
53	Art Fletcher	E	1950
35	Barry French	G	1950
74	Rex Grossman	B	1950
47	Jon Jenkins	T	1950
54	Bob Jensen	E	1950
34	Ed King	G	1950
72	Vito Kissell	B	1950
86	Bob Livingstone	B	1950
80	Achille Maggioli	B	1950
83	Gino Mazzanti	B	1950
30	Earl Murray	G	1950
81	Chet Mutryn	B	1950
28	Bob Nelson	C	1950
55	John North	E	1950
52	Bob Nowaskey	E	1950
57	Bob Oristaglio	E	1950
59	Jim Owens	E	1950
84	Bob Perina	B	1950
87	Herb Rich	B	1950
51	Paul Salata	E	1950
37/66	John Schweder	G	1950
85	Frank Spaniel	B	1950
76	Jim Spavital	B	1950
53	Art Spinney	E	1950
82	Bill Stone	B	1950
63	**Y.A. Tittle**	QB	1950
22	Joel Williams	C	1950
89	Ernie Zalejski	B	1950

APPENDIX D: UNIFORM NUMBERS OF DEFUNCT AAFC TEAMS

Brooklyn Dodgers (ZBRK)

1946–8   8–32–2

Unrelated to the NFL Brooklyn Dodger franchise. Merged into the New York Yankees in 1949 to form the strongest of three New York teams in 1949.

54	Neal Adams	E	1946–7
81	Al Akins	B	1947–8
70/92	Carl Allen	B	1948
72	Charlie Armstrong	B	1946
73	George Benson	B	1947
31	George Bernhardt	G	1946–8
32	John Billman	G	1946
63/60	Hardy Brown	LB	1948
33	Harry Buffington	G	1946–8
54	Harry Burrus	E	1948
80	Jim Camp	B	1948
99	Bob Chappuis	B	1948
45	John Clowes	T	1948
81/72	Mickey Colmer	B	1946–8
56	Mel Conger	E	1947
93	Harry Connolly	B	1946
20	Jim Cooper	C	1948
71	Bill Daley	B	1946
24	Lou Daukas	C	1947
42/40	Nick Daukas	T	1946–7
55	Joe Davis	E	1946
84	Jim Dewar	B	1948
90	Glenn Dobbs	B	1946–7
51	Dan Edwards	E	1948
52	Hank Foldberg	E	1948
64	Nick Forkovitch	B	1948
34	Jack Freeman	G	1946
71/80	Monk Gafford	B	1946–8
22/21	Joe Gibson	C	1946–7
22	Ed Gustafson	C	1947–8
37	Amos Harris	G	1947–8
82	Elmore Harris	B	1947
54	Bob Hein	E	1947
90	Bob Hoernschemeyer	B	1947–8
44	Frank Hrabetin	T	1946
47	Charlie Huneke	T	1947–8
35	Ed Jeffers	G	1947
34	Billy Jones	G	1947
73/91	Dub Jones	B	1946–7
53	Saxon Judd	E	1946–8
71	John Klasnic	B	1948
63	Adolph Kowalski	B	1947
36	Frank Laurinaitis	LB	1947
31	Bob Leonetti	G	1948
32	Herb Maack	G	1946
71	Hugo Marcolini	B	1948
45	Phil Martinovich	T	1946–7
60	Lew Mayne	B	1946
51	Bob McCain	E	1946
56/51	Jim McCarthy	E	1946–7
61	Walt McDonald	B	1946–8
41	Ed Mieszkowski	T	1946–7
60	Tom Mikula	B	1948
56	Max Morris	E	1948
21	Russ Morrow	C	1946–7
52/41	Herb Nelson	E/T	1947–8
35	Vic Obeck	G	1946
61	Bob Paffrath	B	1946
55	Mike Patanelli	E	1947
57	Bolo Perdue	E	1946
70	Bob Perina	B	1947
40	George Perpich	T	1946
94	Dom Principe	B	1946
73	Cal Purdin	B	1946
91	Ray Ramsey	B	1948

43	Martin Ruby	T	1946–8
48	Ralph Sazio	T	1948
42	Leroy Schneider	T	1947
50	Ted Scruggs	E	1947–8
26	George Sergienko	T	1946
83	Rhoten Shetley	B	1946
62	Bob Smith	B	1948
40	Joe Spencer	T	1948
34	Herb St. John	G	1948
25	George Strohmeyer	C	1948
91	Bob Sullivan	B	1948
80/62	Doyle Tackett	B	1946–8
92/82	Lee Tevis	B	1947–8
55	Hal Thompson	E	1947–8
91	Charlie Timmons	B	1946
92	Art Van Tone	B	1946
73	Morrie Warren	B	1948
20/30	Tex Warrington	C	1946–8
48	Harlan Wetz	T	1947
44	Garland Williams	T	1947–8
35	John Wozniak	G	1948

Buffalo Bisons/Bills (ZBUF)

1946–9   23–26–5   1–2 in the postseason
Campaigned for inclusion in NFL merger.
Team dissolved when that failed.

42	Chet Adams	T	1949
90	Al Akins	B	1948
43	Graham Armstrong	T	1947–8
50	Ed Balatti	E	1948
57	Al Baldwin	E	1947–9
23	Jack Baldwin	C	1948
54	John Batorski	E	1946
81	Blondy Black	B	1946
72	Lamar Blount	B	1947
25	Sam Brazinsky	C	1946
82	Rex Bumgardner	B	1948–9
23	Bob Callahan	C	1948
45	Jack Carpenter	T	1947–9
70	Ollie Cline	FB	1949
88	Tom Colella	B	1949
52/53	Marty Comer	E	1946–8
54	Al Coppage	E	1947
23	Bert Corley	C	1947
55	Bill Daddio	E	1946
60	Al Dekdebrun	QB	1946
44	George Doherty	T	1946–7
80	Andy Dudish	B	1946
42	Gil Duggan	T	1947
50	Jack Dugger	E	1946
53	Ray Ebli	E	1946
83	Fred Evans	B	1947
73	John Fekete	B	1946
87	Jesse Freitas	QB	1949
40	Abe Gibron	G	1949
52	Paul Gibson	E	1947–9

88	Bill Gompers	B	1948
40	Chubby Grigg	T	1946
36	George Groves	G	1947
22	Joe Haynes	C	1947
26	Hal Herring	E	1949
73/25/36	Buckets Hirsch	B/C	1947–9
74	Harry Hopp	B	1946
80	Larry Joe	B	1949
84	Pres Johnston	B	1946
34	Elmer Jones	G	1946
88/82	Steve Juzwik	B	1946–7
46	John Kerns	T	1947–9
31	Ed King	G	1948–9
51	Fay King	E	1946–7
51/52	George Kisiday	E	1948
47	John Kissell	T	1948–9
71	Vito Kissell	B	1949
47	Quentin Klenk	T	1946
36	Al Klug	G	1946
56	Nick Klutka	E	1946
84	George Koch	B	1947
41	Chet Kozel	T	1947–8
43	Jack Kramer	T	1946
55	Ray Kuffel	E	1947
72/75	Val Kulbitski	B	1946–8
31	Hal Lahar	G	1946–8
37	Jim Lecture	G	1946
30	Bob Leonetti	G	1948
81	Bob Livingstone	B	1949
55	Bob Logel	E	1949
59	Jim Lukens	E	1949
81	Chick Maggioli	B	1948
74	Pug Manders	B	1947
24	Patsy Martinelli	C	1946
34/49	John Maskas	G	1947, 1949
41	John Matisi	T	1946
58	Vince Mazza	E	1947–9
56	Jack Morton	E	1947
89/83	Chet Mutryn	B	1946–9
52	Herb Nelson	E	1946
54/55	Bill O'Connor	E	1948
56	Bob Oristaglio	E	1949
33	John Perko	G	1946
30/35	Rocco Pirro	G	1946–9
21	Felto Prewitt	C	1946–8
40	Ben Pucci	T	1946
61	George Ratterman	QB	1947–9
63	Albie Reisz	QB	1947
86	Julie Rykovich	B	1947–8
85	Curt Sandig	B	1946
54	Ralph Schilling	E	1946
89	Don Schneider	B	1948
72	Bill Schroll	LB	1949
74/23	Carl Schuette	B	1948–9
37	Vince Scott	G	1947–8
85	Bob Smith	B	1948
46	C.B. Stanley	T	1946
53	Bill Stanton	E	1949

22	Art Statuto	C	1948–9		51	Dan Edwards	E	1949
32	Odell Stautzenberger	G	1949		47	Charlie Elliott	T	1948
?	Bob Stefik	E	1948		75	Fred Evans	B	1947–8
80	Bob Steuber	B	1948		65	Tom Farris	QB	1948
63/62	Jim Still	QB	1948–9		86	Chuck Fenenbock	B	1948
61	Ken Stofer	QB	1946		50	Hank Foldberg	E	1949
70	Roy Stuart	B	1946		60	Jesse Freitas	QB	1948
86	Joe Sutton	B	1949		99	Don Griffin	B	1946
62	George Terlep	QB	1946–8		42	Chubby Grigg	T	1947
73	Jim Thibaut	B	1946		57	John Harrington	E	1947
83	Bob Thurbon	B	1946		44	Ted Hazelwood	T	1949
87/74	Lou Tomasetti	B	1946–9		35	George Hecht	G	1947
53	Al Vandeweghe	E	1946		56	Bob Heck	E	1949
34	Vic Vasicek	G	1949		57	Ralph Heywood	E	1946
87	Wilbur Volz	B	1949		66	Billy Hillenbrand	B	1946
40	Jerry Whalen	T	1948		80	**Elroy Hirsch**	B	1946–8
82/85	Alex Wizbicki	B	1947–9		64/90	Bob Hoernschemeyer	B	1946–7, 1949
25	Al Wukits	C	1946		45	Charlie Huneke	T	1946–7
33	John Wyhonic	G	1948–9		57	Bob Jensen	E	1948–9
71	Lou Zontini	B	1946		54	Farnham Johnson	E	1948

Chicago Rockets/Hornets (ZCHI)

1946–9   11–40–3
Dissolved with league.

36	Alex Agase	G	1947		43	Nate Johnson	T	1948–9
91	Frank Aschenbrenner	B	1949		81	Steve Juzwik	B	1948
33	Jim Bailey	G	1949		74	Bill Kellagher	B	1946–8
99	Bill Bass	B	1947		55	Fay King	E	1948–9
42	Alf Bauman	T	1947		47	Quentin Klenk	T	1946
33	George Bernhardt	G	1948		44	Chet Kozel	G	1948
54	Connie Berry	E	1947		56	Ray Kuffel	E	1948–9
66	Angelo Bertelli	QB	1947–8		41	John Kuzman	T	1947
33	John Billman	G	1947		50	Pat Lahey	E	1946–7
88	Bill Boedeker	B	1946		71/21/22	Pete Lamana	B/C	1946–8
60	Hardy Brown	LB	1949		73/71/64	Ernie Lewis	B	1946–9
42	Jim Brutz	T	1946, 1948		82	Bob Livingstone	B	1948
70	George Buksar	B	1949		97	Ned Mathews	B	1946
?	Harry Burrus	E	1948		36	Frank Mattingly	G	1947
99	Bob Chappuis	B	1949		52	Jim McCarthy	E	1948–9
87	Harry Clark	B	1948		46	Harley McCollum	T	1947
85	Walt Clay	B	1946–7		61	Walt McDonald	QB	1949
53	Paul Cleary	E	1949		78	Jim Mello	B	1948
72	John Clement	B	1949		43	Joe Mihal	T	1947
46	John Clowes	T	1949		53	Max Morris	E	1946–7
25/31	Herb Coleman	C	1946–8		54	Bob Motl	E	1946
71	Rip Collins	B	1949		51	Jerry Mulready	E	1947
65	Norm Cox	QB	1946–7		27/28	Fred Negus	C	1947–9
45	Ziggy Czarobski	T	1948–9		69	Steve Nemeth	QB	1946
71	Bill Daley	B	1947		48	Bruno Niedziela	T	1947
32	Bob David	G	1948		49/32	Jim O'Neal	G/T	1946–7
66	Al Dekdebrun	B	1947		40	Homer Paine	T	1949
82	John Donaldson	B	1949		27	Mickey Parks	C	1946
35/55	Bob Dove	E/G	1946–7		83	Paul Patterson	B	1949
52	Ray Ebli	E	1947		30	Jim Pearcy	G	1946–9
46	Ed Ecker	T	1948		84	Bob Perina	B	1948
					77	Dewey Proctor	B	1948
					70	Eddie Prokop	B	1948
					49	Ben Pucci	T	1947
					52	Frank Quillen	E	1946–7
					88/81	Ray Ramsey	B	1947, 1949
					20	John Rapacz	C	1948–9

32	Ray Richeson	G	1949
56	John Rokisky	E	1947
29	Cliff Rothrock	C	1947
33/34	Joe Ruetz	G	1946, 1948
85	Julie Rykovich	B	1948
43	John Sanchez	T	1947
97	Ted Scalissi	B	1947
60	Bill Schroeder	B	1946–7
83	Floyd Simmons	B	1948
46	Bill Smith	T	1948
?	Bob Smith	B	1949
35	Joe Soboleski	T	1949
34	Herb St. John	G	1949
25	George Strohmeyer	C	1949
34	Tony Sumpter	G	1946–7
80	Bob Sweiger	B	1949
38	Gasper Urban	G	1948
44	Emil Uremovich	T	1948
69	Sam Vacanti	QB	1947–8
40	Norm Verry	T	1946–7
31	Evan Vogds	G	1946–7
48/37	Lloyd Wasserbach	T	1946–7
31	Marty Wendell	G	1949
46	Willie Wilkin	T	1946
82	Walter Williams	B	1946

Los Angeles Dons (ZLAD)

1946–9   25–27–2
Dissolved with league.

3	Ben Agajanian	K	1947–8
36	Alex Agase	G	1947
58/57	Joe Aguirre	E	1946–9
56	Sugarfoot Anderson	E	1947
44	Lee Artoe	T	1946–7
42	Earl Audet	T	1946–8
?	Don Avery	T	1948
52	Burr Baldwin	E	1947–9
40	Pete Berezney	T	1947
65	Angelo Bertelli	QB	1946
29	John Brown	C	1947–9
82	Harry Clark	B	1946–8
80/76	Walt Clay	B	1947–9
88	Harper Davis	B	1949
65/95	Glenn Dobbs	B	1947–9
33	Bob Dobelstein	G	1949
40	Gil Duggan	T	1946
83	Jeff Durkota	B	1948
65	Dan Dworsky	LB	1949
94	Earl Elsey	B	1946
93	Chuck Fenenbock	B	1946–8
55	Bill Fisk	E	1948
20	Jack Flagerman	C	1948
34	Ollie Fletcher	G	1949
50	**Len Ford**	E	1948–9
37/34	Ray Frankowski	G	1946–7

36	Bernie Gallagher	G	1947
53	Dale Gentry	E	1946–8
85	Mike Graham	B	1948
85	Billy Grimes	B	1949
73/66	Walt Heap	B	1947–8
44	Ed Henke	T	1949
66	Bob Hoffman	B	1949
56	Lew Holder	E	1949
95	Harry Hopp	B	1947
97	Earl Howell	B	1949
49	Clyde Johnson	T	1948
40	Ed Kelley	T	1949
85	Bob Kelly	B	1947–8
82	Bob Kennedy	B	1949
50	Bill Kerr	E	1946
77	John Kimbrough	B	1946–8
52	Al Krueger	E	1946
99	Mort Landsberg	B	1947
32	Reid Lennan	G	1947
35	Len Levy	G	1947–8
30	Al Lolotai	G	1946–9
79	Andy Marefos	B	1946
68	Len Masini	B	1948
95	Jack McQuary	B	1946
92	Shorty McWilliams	B	1949
90	Bus Mertes	B	1946
54	Lou Mihajlovich	E	1948
47	Joe Mihal	T	1946
60	Bob Mitchell	QB	1946–8
35/43	Paul Mitchell	G/T	1946–8
59	Jack Morton	E	1946
60	George Murphy	B	1949
80	John Naumu	B	1948
22	Bob Nelson	C	1946–9
20	Don Nolander	C	1946
55	Bob Nowaskey	E	1946–8
85	Bernie Nygren	B	1946–7
68/66	Charlie O'Rourke	QB	1946–7
65	Dick Ottele	B	1948
47	Mike Perrotti	T	1948–9
84	Bert Piggot	B	1947
62	Joyce Pipkin	B	1949
78	John Polanski	B	1946
33	Bill Radovich	G	1946–7
32	Knox Ramsey	G	1948–9
60/88	Bill Reinhard	B	1947–8
45	Bob Reinhard	T	1946–9
29/33	Hank Rockwell	C/G	1946, 1948
73	Hosea Rodgers	B	1949
89	Lin Sexton	B	1948
82	Bob Seymour	B	1946
48	Bill Smith	T	1948
47	Jim Smith	T	1947
97	Bob Sneddon	B	1946
77	Jim Spavital	B	1949
94	Bob Steuber	B	1947
93	George Taliaferro	B	1949
50	Bob Titchenal	E	1947

78	Frank Trigilio	QB	1946
84	Paul Vinnola	B	1946
99	Herman Wedemeyer	B	1948
36	Ben Whaley	G	1949
54	Dick Wilkins	E	1949
42	Ernie Williamson	T	1949
55	Ab Wimberly	E	1949
41	Bernie Winkler	T	1948
27	Dick Woodard	C	1949
32	Frank Yokas	G	1946

Miami Seahawks (ZMIA)

1946   3–11–0

Failed after one season and franchise was sold back to the league.

46	Ed Bell	G	1946
44	Paul Berezney	T	1946
50	Lamar Blount	E	1946
26	Daryl Cato	C	1946
?	Bill Daley	B	1946
47	Bill Davis	T	1946
56	Lamar Davis	E	1946
96	Kay Eakin	B	1946
42	Gene Ellenson	T	1946
86	Dick Erdlitz	B	1946
76/52	Terry Fox	B	1946
97	Monk Gafford	B	1946
87	Fred Gloden	B	1946
?	Frank Hrabetin	T	1946
44	George Hekkers	T	1946
68	Ken Holley	B	1946
?	Harry Hopp	B	1946
54	Dick Horne	E	1946
72/90	Pres Johnston	B	1946
99	Dub Jones	B	1946
33	Buddy Jungmichel	G	1946
73	Stan Kozlowski	B	1946
38	Jon Krivonak	G	1946
66	Walt McDonald	B	1946
84	Fondren Mitchell	B	1946
95	Jimmy Nelson	B	1946
48	Mitch Olenski	T	1946
68/85	Bob Paffrath	B	1946
55	Hamp Pool	E	1946
63	Cotton Price	B	1946
67	Marion Pugh	B	1946
?	Cal Purdin	B	1946
45	Don Reece	T	1946
73/58	Jim Reynolds	B	1946
57	Prince Scott	E	1946
41/31	Jim Sivell	G	1946
85	Stan Stasica	B	1946
65	Jim Tarrant	B	1946
27	John Tavener	C	1946
37	Chuck Taylor	G	1946
72	Frank Trigilio	B	1946

51	Hub Ulrich	E	1946
88	John Vardian	B	1946
22	Ken Whitlow	C	1946
25	Tex Williams	C	1946
25	Al Wukits	C	1946
35	George Zorich	G	1946

New York Yankees (ZNYY)

1946–9   35–17–2   0–3 in the postseason.

Most Yankee players were absorbed by the NFL's New York Yanks and Giants.

51	Bruce Alford	E	1946–9
58	Ed Balatti	E	1948
21	Jack Baldwin	C	1946–7
31	Dick Barwegen	G	1947
45/33	Roman Bentz	T	1946–8
38	George Brown	G	1949
50/83	Harry Burrus	E	1946–7
45	Carl Butkus	T	1948
?	Fred Cardinal	B	1947
85	Tom Casey	B	1948
43/45	Bill Chambers	T	1948–9
60	Lloyd Cheatham	B	1946–8
57	Paul Cleary	E	1948
73	Mickey Colmer	B	1949
52	Mel Conger	E	1946
73	Bill Daley	B	1948
55/50	Van Davis	E	1947–9
86	Al Dekdebrun	B	1948
33	George Doherty	G	1946
83	Noble Doss	B	1949
21	Paul Duke	C	1947
41	Jack Durishan	T	1947
23	Brad Ecklund	C	1949
45	Charlie Elliott	T	1947
41	Bill Erickson	T	1949
57	Dan Garza	E	1949
33	Mike Garzoni	G	1948
37	Ed Grain	G	1947
41	Nelson Greene	T	1948
66	Ray Hare	LB	1946
76	Sherman Howard	B	1949
66/82	Duke Iverson	B	1948–9
61	Gil Johnson	B	1949
45	Glenn Johnson	T	1948
75/61/88	Harvey Johnson	B	1946–9
43	Nate Johnson	T	1946–7
30	Mike Karmazin	G	1946
70	Bob Kennedy	B	1946–9
44	**Bruiser Kinard**	T	1946–7
31	George Kinard	G	1946
57	Roy Kurrasch	E	1947
81	Lou Kusserow	B	1949
85	**Tom Landry**	B	1949
46	Clay Lane	T	1948
84/62	Pete Layden	B	1948–9
62	Joe Magliolo	B	1948

76	Pug Manders	B	1946	44	Lee Artoe	T	1948
32	John Mastrangelo	G	1949	31	Dick Barwegen	G	1948–9
55	Bob Masterson	E	1946	29	Bill Baumgartner	E	1947
46	Harley McCollum	T	1946	57	Hub Bechtol	E	1947–9
58	Flip McDonald	E	1948	47	Pete Berezney	T	1948
46	Paul Mitchell	T	1948–9	32	Warren Beson	G	1949
61	Bob Morrow	B	1946	85	John Black	B	1947
23	Roland Nabors	C	1948	41	Ernie Blandin	T	1948–9
46	Ted Ossowski	T	1947	59	Lamar Blount	E	1947
40	Derrell Palmer	T	1946–8	67	Ernie Case	B	1947
60	Don Panciera	B	1949	29	Jim Castiglia	B	1947
88	**Ace Parker**	B	1946	22/29	Herb Coleman	C	1948
66	Howie Parker	B	1948	33	Ken Cooper	C	1949
20	Frank Perantoni	C	1948–9	22	Elbert Corley	C	1948
83	Bob Perina	B	1946	83	Bob Cowan	LB	1949
41	Roman Piskor	T	1946	?	Armand Cure	B	1947
58	Barney Poole	E	1949	51	Lamar Davis	E	1947–9
52	Ollie Poole	E	1947	71/77	Spiro Dellerba	B	1948–9
73/72	Dewey Proctor	B	1946–7, 1949	88	Andy Dudish	B	1947
				80	Aubrey Fowler	B	1948
72	Eddie Prokop	B	1946–7, 1949	35	Barry French	G	1947–9
				63	John Galvin	B	1947
88	Ben Raimondi	B	1947	77/89	Lucien Gambino	B	1948–9
35	Charley Riffle	G	1946–8	30	Bill Garrett	G	1948–9
22	Tom Robertson	C	1946	59	Gorham Getchell	E	1947
58	John Rokisky	E	1948	33/45	Ed Grain	G	1947–8
74/90	Harmon Rowe	B	1947–9	74	Rex Grossman	B	1947–8
40	Martin Ruby	T	1949	38	George Groves	G	1948
50	Roy Ruskusky	E	1947	24	Dick Handley	C	1947
53	Jack Russell	E	1946–9	44	George Hekkers	T	1947
81	Spec Sanders	B	1946–8	31/32/38	Luke Higgins	G	1947
42	Vic Schleich	T	1947	82	Bill Hillebrand	B	1947–8
56	Otto Schnellbacher	B	1948–9	76	Harry Jagade	B	1949
57	Perry Schwartz	E	1946	47	Jon Jenkins	T	1949
84	Buddy Schwenk	B	1948	52	Ralph Jones	E	1947
30	Ed Sharkey	G	1947–9	46	Mike Kasap	T	1947
42	Marion Shirley	T	1948–9	89	Bob Kelly	B	1949
77	Steve Sieradzki	B	1948	80	Wayne Kinery	B	1949
31	Joe Signaigo	G	1948–9	38/41	Al Klug	T	1947–8
77	Frank Sinkwich	B	1946–7	28	Joe Kodba	C	1947
25	Lou Sossamon	C	1946–8	54	Floyd Konetsky	E	1947
56	Harry Stanton	E	1946–7	59	Jim Landrigan	E	1947
22	Ralph Stewart	C	1947–8	81	Jake Leicht	B	1948–9
80	Bob Sweiger	B	1946–8	54	Bill Leonard	E	1949
75	John Sylvester	B	1947	37	Augie Lio	G	1947
83	Lowell Tew	B	1948–9	53	Elmer Madar	E	1947
87	Lowell Wagner	B	1946–8	34	Vic Marino	G	1947
44	**Arnie Weinmeister**	T	1948–9	88	Lew Mayne	B	1948
37	Dick Werder	G	1948	28	Len McCormick	C	1948
35	John Wozniak	G	1949	48	John Mellus	T	1947–9
32	Joe Yackanich	G	1946–8	73	Bus Mertes	B	1947–8
76/80	Buddy Young	B	1947–9	55	Gil Meyer	E	1947
				81	Rudy Mobley	B	1947
				48	Steve Nemeth	B	1947
				33	Don Nolander	C	1947
				55	John North	E	1948–9
				52	Bob Nowaskey	E	1948–9
				66	Charlie O'Rourke	QB	1948–9
				88	Paul Page	B	1949

Baltimore Colts (ZBAL)

1947–9   10–29–1   0–1 in the postseason.
Included in the merger with the NFL, but folded after one year.

48	George Perpich	T	1948	82	Bill Stone	B	1949	
85	Bob Pfohl	B	1948–9	83	John Sylvester	B	1948	
21	Mike Phillips	C	1947	83	Ray Terrell	B	1947	
54	Ollie Poole	E	1948	22	Al Tillman	C	1949	
20	Felto Prewitt	C	1949	63	**Y.A. Tittle**	QB	1948–9	
84	Ralph Ruthstrom	B	1949	77	Ivan Trebotich	B	1947	
40/64	Bud Schwenk	B	1947	67/69	Sam Vacanti	B	1948–9	
44	Alex Sidorik	T	1948–9	87	John Vardian	B	1947–8	
56	Sig Sigurdson	E	1947	87	Herman Wedemeyer	B	1949	
32	Jack Simmons	G	1948	53	Windell Williams	E	1947	
76	Frank Sinkwich	B	1947	71	John Wright	B	1947	
56	Joe Smith	E	1948	30	Frank Yokas	G	1947	
46	Jim Spruill	T	1948–9	33	George Zorich	G	1947	
20	Ralph Stewart	C	1948					